T0319156

ROUTLEDGE HANDBOOK OF BOUNDED RATIONALITY

Herbert Simon's renowned theory of bounded rationality is principally interested in cognitive constraints and environmental factors and influences which prevent people from thinking or behaving according to formal rationality. Simon's theory has been expanded in numerous directions and taken up by various disciplines with an interest in how humans think and behave. This includes philosophy, psychology, neurocognitive sciences, economics, political science, sociology, management, and organization studies.

The *Routledge Handbook of Bounded Rationality* draws together an international team of leading experts to survey the recent literature and the latest developments in these related fields. The chapters feature entries on key behavioural phenomena, including reasoning, judgement, decision making, uncertainty, risk, heuristics and biases, and fast and frugal heuristics. The text also examines current ideas such as fast and slow thinking, nudge, ecological rationality, evolutionary psychology, embodied cognition, and neurophilosophy. Overall, the volume serves to provide the most complete state-of-the-art collection on bounded rationality available.

This book is essential reading for students and scholars of economics, psychology, neurocognitive sciences, political sciences, and philosophy.

Riccardo Viale is Full Professor of Cognitive Economics and Behavioural Sciences in the Department of Economics at the University of Milano-Bicocca, Italy. He is also the founder and General Secretary of the Herbert Simon Society.

ROUTLEDGE HANDBOOK OF BOUNDED RATIONALITY

Edited by Riccardo Viale

Routledge
Taylor & Francis Group

LONDON AND NEW YORK

First published 2021
by Routledge
2 Park Square, Milton Park, Abingdon, Oxon OX14 4RN

and by Routledge
52 Vanderbilt Avenue, New York, NY 10017

Routledge is an imprint of the Taylor & Francis Group, an informa business

British Library Cataloguing-in-Publication Data
A catalogue record for this book is available from the British Library

Library of Congress Cataloging-in-Publication Data
A catalog record has been requested for this book

ISBN: 978-1-138-99938-1 (hbk)
ISBN: 978-0-367-56394-3 (pbk)
ISBN: 978-1-315-65835-3 (ebk)

DOI: 10.4324/9781315658353

Typeset in Bembo
by Newgen Publishing UK

CONTENTS

Contents

Contents

CONTRIBUTORS

Maria Bagassi, University of Milano-Bicocca, Italy

Jean Baratgin, Université Paris VIII, France

Hayden Barber, Purdue University, West Lafayette, IN, USA

Samuel C. Bellini-Leite, State University of Minas Gerais, Brazil

Ian K. Belton, University of Strathclyde, Glasgow, UK

Nathan Berg, University of Otago, Dunedin, New Zealand

Cristina Bicchieri, University of Pennsylvania, Philadelphia, PA, USA

Henry Brighton, Tilburg University, the Netherlands

Christopher Cherniak, University of Maryland, College Park, MD, USA

Mandeep K. Dhami, Middlesex University, London, UK

Kirstin Dolick, Purdue University, West Lafayette, IN, USA

Giovanni Dosi, Scuola Sant'Anna, Pisa, Italy

Massimo Egidi, LUISS, Rome, Italy

Jonathan St. B. T. Evans, University of Plymouth, Plymouth, UK

Marco Faillo, University of Trento, Trento, Italy

Barbara Fasolo, London School of Economics, London, UK

Contributors

Mia Felin, University College, London, UK

Teppo Felin, Oxford University, Oxford, UK

Valentina Ferretti, London School of Economics, London, UK

Keith Frankish, University of Sheffield, Sheffield, UK

Vittorio Gallese, University of Parma, Parma, Italy

Gerd Gigerenzer, Max Planck Institute for Human Development, Berlin, Germany

Francine W. Goh, University of Nebraska, Lincoln, NE, USA

Ulrich Hoffrage, University of Lausanne, Lausanne, Switzerland

Sheena Iyengar, Columbia Business School, New York, USA

Phil N. Johnson-Laird, Princeton University, Princeton, NJ, USA

Inga Jonaityte, Università Ca' Foscari, Venice, Italy

Bryan D. Jones, University of Texas, Austin, TX, USA

Konstantinos V. Katsikopoulos, University of Southampton Business School, Southampton, UK

Kathryn Laskey, George Mason University, Washington, DC, USA

Laura Macchi, University of Milano-Bicocca, Milan, Italy

Miles MacLeod, University of Twente, the Netherlands

Luigi Marengo, LUISS, Rome, Italy

Julian N. Marewski, University of Lausanne, Lausanne, Switzerland

Laura Martignon, Ludwigsburg University, Ludwigsburg, Germany

Antonio Mastrogiorgio, Università degli Studi G. d'Annunzio Chieti e Pescara, Italy

Colin H. McCubbins, Walmart Media Group, Stanford University, CA, USA

Mathew D. McCubbins, Duke University, Durham, NC, USA

Zachary A. McGee, University of Texas, Austin, TX, USA

Hugo Mercier, Institut Jean Nicod, CNRS, Paris, France

Raffaella Misuraca, University of Palermo, Sicily

Shabnam Mousavi, Johns Hopkins University, Baltimore, MD, USA

Richard R. Nelson, Columbia University, New York, USA

Nancy J. Nersessian, Harvard University, Cambridge, MA, USA

Samuel A. Nordli, Indiana University, Bloomington, IN, USA

Adam Oliver, London School of Economics, London, UK

Thorsten Pachur, Max Planck Institute for Human Development, Berlin, Germany

Enrico Petracca, University of Bologna, Italy

Torsten Reimer, Purdue University, West Lafayette, IN, USA

Elena Reutskaja, IESE Business School, Barcelona, Spain

Ariel Rubinstein, School of Economics, Tel Aviv University, Tel Aviv, Israel

Brooke N. Shannon, University of Texas, Austin, TX, USA

Giacomo Sillari, LUISS, Rome, Italy

Özgür Şimşek, University of Bath, Bath, UK

Dan Sperber, Central European University, Vienna, Austria

Keith E. Stanovich, University of Toronto, Toronto, Canada

Keith Stenning, University of Edinburgh, Edinburgh, UK

Jeffrey R. Stevens, University of Nebraska, Lincoln, NE, USA

Jean-Louis Stilgenbauer, Facultés Libres de Philosophie et de Psychologie (IPC), Paris, France

Thomas Sturm, ICREA & Universitat Autònoma de Barcelona, Barcelona, Spain

Cass R. Sunstein, Harvard University, Cambridge, MA, USA

Paul Thagard, University of Waterloo, ON, Canada

Nicolaus Tideman, Virginia Polytechnic Institute and State University, Blacksburg, VA, USA

Clement A. Tisdell, School of Economics, the University of Queensland, Brisbane, Australia

Contributors

Peter M. Todd, Indiana University, Bloomington, IN, USA

Mark Turner, Case Western Reserve University, Cleveland, OH, USA

Riccardo Viale, University of Milano-Bicocca, Milan, Italy

Ignazio Visco, Bank of Italy, Rome, Italy

Massimo Warglien, Università Ca' Foscari, Venice, Italy

Gregory Wheeler, Frankfurt School of Finance & Management, Frankfurt, Germany

Giordano Zevi, Bank of Italy, Rome, Italy

PREFACE

The *Routledge Handbook of Bounded Rationality* takes its inspiration from the seminal work of Herbert Simon, who introduced the concept and developed it in a number of areas: from economics to administrative science; from philosophy to cognitive science; from political science to Artificial Intelligence. I started collaborating with Herbert Simon after I first met him in 1988. One product of this collaboration was the birth of the journal, *Mind & Society* in 2000. After his death in February 2001, I was one of a group of economists and cognitive scientists influenced by his work who founded the Herbert Simon Society in Turin. Its aim was to promote and update some of the many topics of Simon's research, but in particular his realist philosophy of science for an empirically based microeconomics and social science. The *Routledge Handbook of Bounded Rationality* is inspired by this work and develops a critical assessment of varied and often contradictory interpretations and applications of bounded rationality.

The project of the book stems from the meetings held at the Max Planck Institute for Human Development in Berlin and the annual workshops of the Herbert Simon Society held in New York and Turin between 2011 and 2019. I would like to thank Dan Kahneman, Joe Stiglitz, Gerd Gigerenzer, Alvin Goldman, Edward Feigenbaum, Ned Block, Dan Sperber, Colin Camerer, Peter Todd, Ralph Hertwig, Laura Martignon, Pat Langley, Denis Hilton, Barbara Fasolo, Shabnam Mousavi, Hersh Shefrin, Laura Macchi, Massimo Egidi, Giovanni Dosi and Luigi Marengo in particular, as well as the many other researchers involved in the discussions on bounded rationality that took place in these meetings.

Special thanks to Konstantinos Katsikopoulos for his precious advice and suggestions on topics and contributors.

I am indebted to Laura Gilardi and Anna Mereu for their assistance in the initial organization of the work.

I thank Sarah Cuminetti for her text editing and review of some chapters.

This Handbook would not have been possible without the support of Routledge, and in particular Andy Humphries and his collaborators, in particular, Emma Morley, and Susan Dunsmore.

Last but not least, I wish to thank the Collegio Carlo Alberto of Turin and the Herbert Simon Society for their contributions to the making of this Handbook.

Riccardo Viale
Turin,
16 April 2020

1

WHY BOUNDED RATIONALITY?

Riccardo Viale

In the philosophy of science why-questions are a way to address the foundations of scientific explanation. For Bas van Fraassen (1980), a theory of explanation is essentially a theory of why-questions. Why-questions and their answers are individuated only relative to a context.[1] The pragmatic problem of the context determines the relevance of the answer and ultimately the choice made therein.

Daniel Dennett (2017) breaks down the sense of why-questions into two options: "How come?" and "What for?". The former refers to the factual description, to the illustration of the physical or chemical process that explains a phenomenon. For example, wondering "Why did we witness a total eclipse of the moon on … July?" would refer to the earth's positioning in the orbit of the sun and the moon and the shadow projected by the earth on the moon. The latter refers instead to the reasons that explain a phenomenon. For example, asking "Why did Britons vote for Brexit?" refers to "for which reason", that is to the actual motivations – such as fear of immigration, hostility towards Brussels Eurocrats, communication errors made by the Remainers, etc. – that led the majority of Britons to vote in favour of this unexpected choice.

In some instances, a question can be answered using either of the alternatives, depending on the context of reference. Dennett asks himself the question concerning evolution by natural selection. One part of the answer may be described using the "How come?" option, that is through a description of the physico-chemical processes that led to the emergence of the first eukaryotic being. At this point, the question becomes "What for?", that is what are the reasons that led to the selection of some species over others? The question "Why bounded rationality?" can be addressed in the same way. In this case, the order of the alternatives is reversed, compared to evolutionary selection. The first question is not about why the term was introduced, that is to say, what is the reason that in 1950 led Herbert Simon to bestow this name on a series of empirical phenomena he had observed while studying administrative organization? The first question is, "For what reason?" is human rationality non-maximizing and non-optimizing, but rather bounded, heuristic, and satisficing. The answer provided in this volume indicates that it was the capacity to better adapt to the uncertainty and complexity of the environment that led to the evolutionary selection of this type of rationality over Olympic or unbounded rationality. The second question is then, "How come?", that is to say through which neurocognitive and corporal processes did bounded rationality emerge? This Handbook will try to answer

DOI: 10.4324/9781315658353-1

this question by identifying the cognitive aspects that characterize the style of human decision making and analysing the neural and motor, sensorial and visceral embodiment correlates that explain the heuristic characters of bounded of rationality.

Part I Naturalizing bounded rationality

Rationality or reason holds an important role in philosophical tradition. In brief, we can distinguish two main philosophical schools of thought on rationality (Viale, 2012): the first affirms the superiority of reason compared to intellect; the second asserts the opposite. In the former, the classical philosophical tradition, reason is the strength that liberates us from prejudices, from myth, from established but false opinions, and from appearances, and which allows a universal or common criterion to be established for all areas of human conduct. In the tradition that spans from Heraclitus, Parmenides, Plato and Aristotle to St Augustine, Descartes, Spinoza, Leibniz and the Enlightenment, reason is man's fundamental and universal guide; it is what differentiates us from animals and allows us to tell truth from falsehood, because, as Seneca states, "Reason is nothing other than a part of the divine spirit descended (or sunk) into a human body." It is universal because it is present in all persons, who, as Descartes affirms, think differently only because they apply reason differently.

In opposition to this Olympic and universal vision of reason, we find the second position. According to this minority tradition, expressed by Neoplatonism, St Thomas, medieval scholastics, Francis Bacon and, to a large extent, Kant, reason is subject to the primacy of intellect. Intellect should be regarded as superior because it is equipped with that intuitive and immediate character that allows it to gain a direct understanding of empirical reality, unlike reason which is limited by its discursive and *a priori* nature. While affirming the discursive nature of both, Kant also maintained that only that of the intellect was valid since its concepts are immediately derived from experience.

Although severely criticized by Kant, the primacy of reason and its discursive nature remains the dominant position in philosophy. This discursive and linguistic character, as summarized in Aristotle's syllogistic or in the Cartesian ideal of the chains of reasoning in geometry, leads to the formal development of the theory of rationality in the past century. The resulting logic of rationality will always maintain, as in Aristotle, the dual descriptive valence of its own procedures of reason, and normative valence in the sense of the rule for its correct use.

The philosophical tradition of rationality can be considered a subsector of the larger epistemology one. In particular, the development of the Naturalizing Epistemology programme introduced by Quine in the 1960s shaped the normative framework for the contemporary concept of bounded rationality. Let us see why (see Viale, 2013):

Among the most fundamental questions which epistemology has sought to answer are the following:

1. How ought we to arrive at our beliefs?
2. How do we arrive at our beliefs?
3. Are the processes by which we do arrive at our beliefs the ones by which we ought to arrive at our beliefs?

Traditionally, the answers to these questions were as follows: both epistemology and psychology should carry out their research independently and separately, and then, once they have answered questions 1 and 2 respectively, they will attempt to answer question 3.

For example, suppose that psychological studies were to demonstrate that people arrive at their beliefs by some kind of non-conscious mechanism that measures the coherence of new beliefs with the body of beliefs already held, and which accepts only those that cohere and rejects those that do not, this would have no bearing on the merits on the epistemological coherence theory of justification which states that one can only adopt beliefs cohering with beliefs one already has. The normative questions that epistemologists ask are completely independent of the descriptive questions psychologists ask.

However, there is another way to answer the three questions. This is the approach used by the project for naturalizing epistemology: question 1 cannot be answered independently of question 2. The question of how we actually arrive at our beliefs is therefore relevant to the question of how we ought to arrive at our beliefs.

This position is well summed up by the following passage from Quine:

> Epistemology becomes as a chapter of psychology and hence of natural science. It studies a natural phenomenon, viz. a physical human subject. This human subject is accorded a certain experimentally controlled input – certain patterns of irradiation in assorted frequencies, for instance – and with a little of time the subject delivers as output a description of the three-dimensional external world and its history. The relation between the meagre input and the torrential output is a relation that we are prompted to study for somewhat the same reasons that always prompted epistemology; namely, in order to see how evidence relates to theory, and in what ways one's theory of nature transcends any available evidence for it.
>
> *Quine, 1985, p. 24*

What prompted this reversal of approach? Largely it was the failure of the foundationalist project which tried to show that there is a class of beliefs – typically beliefs about our own sensory experience – about which it is impossible to be wrong. Moreover, these beliefs were held to be sufficient to justify the rest of our beliefs. Carnap's project was aimed at the translation, the rational reconstruction of every assertion about the world in terms of sensory data, logic and set theory.

If the project had succeeded from a "conceptual" point of view, namely, the "technical" possibility of achieving this translation, it would in any case have failed to overcome the "doctrinal" barrier, namely, the problem of preserving the content of truth within the translation. Merely by translating an assertion in terms of sensory data, logic and set theory does not mean that it can be verified by this translation. The most modest of observational generalizations will always cover more cases than those observed by the observer. Therefore, any attempt to found beliefs on immediate experience is hopeless, from a logical point of view, even if this is the simplest empirical generalization.

Also from a conceptual point of view, this translation programme produced few results. It attempted to reduce every scientific assertion to a neutral language of observational data, logic and set theory. First, an attempt was made using "direct definitions", then with "contextual definitions", by which sentences containing the term were translated into equivalent sentences lacking the term. Lastly, with the "reduction modules" of Carnap's liberalized programme, hope was given up of translating a sentence into an equivalent and it ended up by explaining a new term by specifying some sentences which are implied by the sentences containing the term, and other sentences which imply sentences containing the term.

As Quine states, this minimal objective renounces the last remaining advantage of a programme of rational reconstruction, namely, the advantage of reduction by translation.

If all we hope for is a reconstruction that links science to experience in explicit ways, short of translation, then it would seem more sensible to settle for psychology. Better to discover how science is in fact developed and learned than to fabricate a fictitious history of how our ancestors introduced those terms through a succession of Carnap's "reduction modules" (Quine, 1985, p. 21).

Does this mean that the empirical foundation of knowledge, the empirical meaning of sentences about the world, is no longer founded on solid bases? Quite the contrary. Our knowledge of the external world is based and founded precisely on the empirical meaning of language, as is actually attained in the process of each individual's learning of language. The common meaning that we attribute to words and to sentences about the external world, namely, the basis for our possibility of communicating and understanding, and also the empirical meaning of science, rest in the last instance on the common empirical basis of the common meaning we attribute to our assertions about the world, and this empirical basis can only be described and explained by empirical psychology.

A further shift towards a naturalization of epistemology occurs at the moment when the meaning of the three questions is further examined by focusing attention on the cognitive mechanisms of rationality, the various internal processes of the cognitive elaboration of beliefs, on the processes whereby from one belief we reach a different belief, namely, on the processes of deductive and inductive reasoning and inference. This is the decision-making moment of what action to take; the assessment of assumptions and hypotheses; the following of arguments and reasoning; deciding what weight and importance to give to the evidential data; the solution of problems.[2]

In the programme of naturalizing epistemology, therefore, an important chapter is occupied by a study of the natural mechanisms of reasoning, judgement, and decision making which must be immune from any kind of logicist preconception and apriorism.

To sum up, a broad concept of rationality has always been linked to normativity. The realm of *a priori* demonstrative proof, that is, the things that people were absolutely certain about, remained the goal of epistemology and science until the beginning of the twentieth century. Scientific rationality fell into a definitive crisis with the failure of the neopositivist programme and the emergence of relativism and socio-historical reductionism or, in other words, the dominance of the context of discovery over the context of justification. Likewise, in the twentieth century, the inclusive area of epistemological rationality had its radical change with the Naturalizing Epistemology programme of Willard O. Quine. There are no ways of analytically founding the truth. The only possibility is to discover the natural processes that humans follow in generating knowledge.

The realm of certainty and demonstrative proof had already experienced a strong downsizing during the seventeenth century with the acknowledgement of the irreducible uncertainty of human life and the emergence of the theory of probability. The impact of this revolution was at once directed to morality and human choice theory. Blaise Pascal and Pierre Fermat defined the border of reasonableness as the choice of the alternative that maximizes expected value. The various paradoxes from St. Petersburg to Allais and Ellsberg led to change in the theory of reasonableness, attempting to resolve the discrepancy between description and normativity. This was made by tinkering with the utility or probability function while at the same time retaining the ideal of maximization or optimization. In any case, the concept of reasonableness, after a decline of interest during the end of the nineteenth and the beginning of the twentieth century, re-emerged in the 1950s and 1960s in the form of the concept of "rationality" in economics, psychology and other social sciences. This rationality was assimilated to the calculation of probabilities, utilities and optimal decisions. The ideal of optimization entered not only the behavioural sciences but also animal biology (e.g. optimal foraging theory) and artificial intelligence (e.g. optimal artificial agents) (Gigerenzer and Selten, 2001).

As for the epistemology and also for the philosophy of science, the crisis of the *a priori* concept of rationality of choice took a major step forward in the mid-twentieth century with the introduction by Herbert Simon of Bounded Rationality theory. In Simon, the naturalistic approaches find a common interpreter: both directly in the theory of rational choice, and also in the philosophy of science where Simon, in opposition to Karl Popper, is the major supporter of the logic of discovery as the psychology of discovery; and indirectly, in epistemology where he contributed to the naturalistic theory of knowledge through his works on inductive reasoning and problem solving.

Thomas Sturm (in Chapter 3 in this volume) recognizes that naturalism has drawn a variety of connections between rationality and empirical sciences, mainly cognitive sciences. It started out as a reaction to "armchair" methods such as conceptual analysis, thought experiments or appeal to intuition. In rationality the target was to substitute the a priori standard substantive view of rationality with a procedural view that relies on the empirical behavioral models of reasoning and decision making. Sturm (Chapter 3 in this volume) writes: "One of Simon's most influential ideas was to replace the goal of maximizing expected utility by "'satisficing'" (p. 78). Understood this way, bounded rationality questions the sharp divide between the descriptive and the normative – quite different from Kahneman's understanding of the concept. However, no Is-Ought fallacy, no psychologism needs to be implied thereby. Instead, there is an underlying and legitimate principle of normativity: *Ought implies Can* (also already recognized by Kant). "The intractability of many reasoning tasks restricts the applicability of certain formal and optimizing norms, and makes it reasonable to look for different, more feasible norms" (Sturm, p. 78). Sturm emphasizes this third position between descriptive and normative, making reference to Alvin Goldman's theory of reliabilism. Goldman's approach to epistemic rationality is instrumentalist. Given certain epistemic goals, people ought to use reliable procedures to attain them. Sturm writes:

> Goldman's approach is an excellent example for this. Among other things, he shows that formal rules of the standard picture of rationality often do not map straightforwardly onto reasoning tasks. For instance, the logical law of noncontradiction, $\neg(\neg p \land p)$, states that a proposition and its negation cannot both be true. From contradictions, anything whatsoever can be derived. We should, it seems, therefore avoid inconsistencies. What do you do when you discover inconsistencies in your belief set? Are you obliged to give up the *whole* set? Certainly not; we should separate the wheat from the chaff. However, that can prove to be difficult, especially in the complex belief systems of science, when several beliefs are all tenuous but part of a systematic theory. Similar examples can be construed for other logical rules, such as deductive closure, or for rules of probability. There is, therefore, no simple derivation of norms of epistemic rationality from formal rules of the standard picture; more support for the gap mentioned earlier on.

To bridge that gap, Goldman maintains that a distinctively philosophical or "analytic" epistemology has to determine the criteria or goals of our epistemic endeavors. He defends *reliabilism*: our belief-forming mechanisms need not always guarantee truth, but to safeguard a good ratio of true and false beliefs. From psychology, we can learn what mental processes or mechanisms are reliable and which ones are not.

Sturm, p. 82

As pointed out by Rubinstein (Chapter 27 in this volume) and Gigerenzer (Chapter 2 in this volume), there are several views of bounded rationality. This is not only because bounded rationality is present in various fields such as economics, psychology and management. Even within a single field such as economics, there are clear differences. There are at least three different positions: (1) optimization under constraints; (2) failures to follow the prescriptions of the optimization model; and (3) adaptive behaviour to the environment.

Katsikopoulos (Chapter 4 in this volume) distinguishes between two cultures, which he calls "idealistic" and "pragmatic":

At a first approximation, the idealistic culture pursues a minimum departure from the neoclassical-economics framework of unbounded rationality which assumes the ideals of omniscience and optimization of a utility function and adds factors such as inequity aversion or probability weighting to the utility function. On the other hand, the pragmatic culture holds that people sometimes ignore information and use simple rules of thumb in order to achieve satisfactory outcomes.

Katsikopoulos, p. 90

Is the epistemic dimension of the two cultures an important philosophical feature? Katsikopoulos follows the tripartition proposed by Alan Musgrave in characterizing the views of the relations between facts and theory. Musgrave discusses three views of when an empirical fact lends support to a model. In the logical view, it matters only if the fact is consistent with the model's implications. In the historical view, it also matters if the model's implications were derived before or after the fact was observed. In the third view, a variant of the historical view, it is additionally relevant what the implications of the best competing model are. More support is provided for the model if its best competitor does not imply the observed fact. Thus, the logical view accepts as an epistemic aim the *explanation of known facts*. On the other hand, the historical view rejects this and aims at the *prediction of new facts*. For Katsikopoulos:

It may be argued that the idealistic culture espouses the logical view whereas the pragmatic culture is aligned with the historical view, and in particular Musgrave's variant. For example, the development of prospect theory and other risky choice models which follow the utility-times-probability mathematical form, has been following the empirical violations of the axioms of expected utility theory … On the other hand, pragmatic models such as the priority heuristic, have not been developed in order to account for these violations … but rather in order to predict new facts.

p. 95

Concerning bounded rationality, pragmatic cultures underline the importance of the environment. The importance of the environment in defining bounded rationality is expressed radically by the following quotation from Simon: "an ant [or human being], viewed as a behaving system, is quite simple. The apparent complexity of its behavior over time is largely a reflection of the complexity of the environment in which it finds itself" (1981: 63–65). This example is even more radical than the scissors metaphor: "*Human rational behaviour… is shaped by a scissors whose blades are the structure of task environments and the computational capabilities of the actor"* (Simon, 1979b; emphasis added). The environment becomes the main barycentre of rationality. This polarization is reminiscent of Karl Popper's situational logic. The environment dictates its bounds to organisms, be they ants or humans, that have species-independent and universal reactions to the structure of the environment. For example, Simon writes that we can "discover, by a careful examination of some of the fundamental structural characteristics of the environment ... the mechanisms used in decision-making" (Simon, 1956, p. 130). Simon's position tends to overlook the importance of the decision maker's biological constraints. It would appear that the embodied structure of decision making does not tell us anything interesting about the interaction between the environment and the decision maker. This is very difficult to accept because we know how fundamental the biological bounds of neural, sensorimotor and visceral systems are in driving the style of decision making. From this point of view, it would be like setting out to screw in a Phillips screw without caring if the screwdriver is a flathead or a Phillips. The topic will be analysed in depth in the following sections, and in particular in the sections on ecological rationality and embodied bounded rationality (BR). Teppo Felin and Mia Felin (Chapter 5 in this volume) focus on the BR of perception and support the importance of focusing on the biological features of the perceiver. They show how cues and stimuli coming from the environment are not species-independent but are instead specific to the organisms. They write:

> The fields of ethology and comparative biology offer the best evidence for the fact that environments are species-specific rather than general ... Each organism has its own, unique "Umwelt" (surrounding world), where awareness and perception are a function of the nature of the organism itself ...
>
> *Felin and Felin, p. 110*

A frog does not see an insect if it does not see it moving. They add:

> This highlights that what "stimulates"—or which cues become salient and naturally assessed ...—has less to do with the stimulus itself (or the objective or general 'amount' of some cue: Gigerenzer and Gaissmaier, 2011). Rather, awareness of particular stimuli has more to do with the nature of the organism ... Only those stimuli or cues that are species-specific "light up," or are processed and attended to, while many other things are ignored.
>
> *Felin and Felin, p. 110*

From this point of view, BR has to do with environments that are species-specific. Felin and Felin cite the fathers of ethology, Nikko Timbergen and Konrad Lorentz, and particularly Jacob von Uexkull, when they affirm that "every animal is surrounded with different things, the dog is surrounded by dog things and the dragonfly is surrounded by dragonfly things", that is, "each environment forms a self-enclosed unit, which is governed in all its parts by its meaning for the subject". Moreover there are pragmatic goals beyond the biological bounds which drive the selection of perception. Our perception is focused on what counts for us contingently. We are blind to things that are not part of our pragmatic attention. Therefore, BR should rely on a perception that selects cues and information from the environment according to species-specific reasons and pragmatic interests. To understand the Umwelt of frogs and men, we should focus on the embodied adaptation to the environment: a frog developed species-perception in relation to the possibility of its body and the specific affordances from the environments (see locusts and flies). Every human being X has his or her own X things environment. Pragmatic goals and special and particular embodied cognition (think of perceptual variability among individuals) select an individual X environment. This X environment is not constant, but it may also change during the life of the individual. Because pragmatic goals and embodied cognition change.

Bounded rationality played an important role in modelling scientific discovery. Discovery as the psychology of problem-solving was Herbert Simon's answer to the deductive rationality of the context of justification developed by neopositivism and post-neopositivist authors like Karl Popper and, to some extent, Imre Lakatos. Psychological feasibility and procedural rationality are the building blocks of the naturalizing philosophy of science that aims to establish a descriptive and prescriptive model of scientific discovery. Miles MacLeod and Nancy Nersessian (Chapter 6 in this volume) analyse the bounded rationality concept in a particular field of life sciences, computational systems biology. This field aims to produce large-scale models of complex biological systems. Since this field relies on computer simulation, it would be safe to assume that the computational power of automated modelling practices would overcome the limitations of the human mind. On the contrary, MacLeod and Nersessian write:

> Given the rhetoric of "big data" and automated modelling practices, one might expect that computer simulation is a resource for side-stepping human cognitive capacities and constraints. Yet even these practices still require human cognitive engagement with their products for the purposes of validation and interpretation. And, as we have discovered in our investigations of computational systems biology, much problem solving still involves researchers building their own models in situations of scarce or inadequate data, using laptop computers. Rather than freeing scientists of their cognitive limitations, using computation to extend control and understanding over ever more complex systems requires developing sophisticated problem-solving practices which push them towards these constraints.
>
> *MacLeod and Nersessian, p. 120*

They monitored two laboratories where the aim was to create high-fidelity computational models of metabolic, cell signalling, and gene-regulatory networks. These models are dynamic, tracking the changes in concentration of each metabolite, or the activity of each gene, in a network over time. This goal was never attained. The modellers should have relied on strategies to build midlevel models called "mesoscopic" that are simplified both at the system level, with only few relationships represented, and at the network level, with quite abstract non-mechanistic representations of biochemical interactions. These strategies serve to simplify running simulations, parameter fitting and mathematical analysis. The modellers tried to improve these inaccurate and unreliable models by using a sequence of increasingly complex heuristics. This was done through inferences drawn by processing information in the system comprising memory and environment through a *distributed model-based reasoning*. This coupled cognitive system reduces the cognitive load by off-loading memory to the environment and increases the bounded rational success of the models. MacLeod and Nersessian write: "The practice of mesoscopic model-building and incremental modification through building-out strategies provides an exemplar of what Simon, in a later analysis of bounded rationality, called 'procedural rationality'" (p. 126).

An important aspect of Herbert Simon's naturalistic view of rationality is linked to the psychology of problem solving. Every decision is the solution to a problem and therefore the analysis of the procedural rationality of a decision must take into account the ways in which the space of the decision making/problem solving is represented as well as the operators available, the goal, the related sub-goals, and the various steps leading to the final decision/solution. In *Human Problem Solving* (2019), Newell and Simon clearly define what is meant by problem solving according to the approach of Information Processing Psychology. This dimension of problem solving applies to everyday individual or organizational routine decisions as well as to the solution of ill-structured problems in scientific and technological research and in any creative thinking situation. The tradition that prevailed in the psychology of reasoning and decision making was based on the analysis of the conformity of the product of reasoning and decision making with the norms of deductive and inductive logic and the theory of utility. It was noted that human reasoning and decision making do not conform to those canons and this was labelled a pathology of rationality in the form of bias, error and irrational propensities. Human beings have been depicted as obtuse reasoners and decision makers predisposed to fallacies and therefore are ill-adapted to their environment. The tradition of pathological rationality focused on the formal aspect of thinking and neglected to consider the actual adaptive weight of reasoning and decision-making processes. Moreover, it remained silent and defenceless before the matters of creativity, scientific discovery, invention, and in general before the answers given to ill-structured and complex situations. The problem-solving tradition, first with Karl Duncker and then with Allen Newell and Herbert Simon, followed a remarkably different path, as clearly explained by Laura Macchi and Maria Bagassi (Chapter 7 in this volume) with reference to the Gestalt tradition. Simon writes:

> The simulation models of the 1950s were offspring of the marriage between that had emerged from symbolic logic and cybernetics, on the one side, and Wurzburg and Gestalt psychology, on the other … From Wurzburg and Gestalt psychology were inherited the ideas that long-term memory is an organization of directed associations, and that problem solving is a process of selective goal-oriented search.
>
> *Simon, 1979a, pp. 364–365*

Macchi and Bagassi write that, concerning Gestalt psychology in particular, "Duncker was not only interested in the moment when the solution was found, but also in the process of thought, the phases by which the restructuring is reached" (p. 135) and they add

> The solution process involves a *selective research in phases*, over a *delimited area*; it requires that paths explored previously that turned out to be dead ends be discarded and new paths adopted. The new path can even have been evaluated in a previous phase.
>
> *p. 135*

And, "According to Duncker, the problem solver never blunders along blindly, seeking the solution by trial and error; he proceeds by applying *heuristic strategies* and *methods*" (p. 137). This situation is particularly evident in what is defined as *insight problem solving*, that is to say the solutions that are perceived as an unexpected act of creativity. The problem is familiar to Gestaltists like Duncker for whom the sudden comprehension of the Aha! moment of the new is linked to a sudden restructuring of the thought material.

When in 1990, Simon, in collaboration with Kaplan, explored in depth the peculiarities of the search and the steps of the solution process for insight problems, he dealt with the issue of a *change in representation*, explaining that the shift to an alternative problem space occurs because a heuristic has been adopted, initiated by boundaries of salience.

Macchi and Bagassi, p. 140

Macchi and Bagassi also state:

> According to the authors, the subject who finds himself at an impasse must first of all make a conscious decision to change his way of looking at the problem, by the "Try a Switch" meta-heuristic, given that the initial representation of the problem did not provide him with the means of reaching the solution.
>
> *p. 140*

Macchi and Bagassi write that once this *decision* has been made, the subject

> must be on the lookout for the important cues that will help him select the representation that will lead to the solution, from the infinite number available. In his search for these decisive cues to switch the representation in the representation metaspace, he is assisted by adopting a heuristic that fits the problem, also called the *Notice Invariants Heuristic.*
>
> *Macchi and Bagassi, p. 140*

However, in this type of process it would appear evident that, unlike Simon's position, the dynamics of thought mainly occur at the subconscious level, with no reference to working memory or the conscious retrieval of data from long-term memory. Several psychological and neurocognitive studies (for example, on the presence of the Default Mode Network) on mind wandering and incubation show that some associative processes are unconscious and at the same time they are rule-based (Viale, 2016).

A particular perspective from which to analyse bounded rationality is the representation of mathematical reasoning tasks and the consequent educational problems. Laura Martignon, Kathryn Laskey and Keith Stenning (Chapter 8 in this volume) analyse the legacies in education left by Simon, many of which are elucidated in his *Sciences of the Artificial* (1981). Simon writes: "Solving a problem simply means representing it so as to make the solution transparent" (1996,. p. 132). Martignon, Laskey and Stenning write:

> A solution becomes transparent if it emerges from the structure in terms of which the problem has been modelled. The structure of the problem is the result of an effort of adaptation between the problem itself and the conceptual constructions of the mind. This adaptation is successful if it is ecologically rational. Ecological rationality is a fundamental characteristic of successful representations. It refers to behaviors and thought processes that are adaptive and goal-oriented in the context of the environment in which an organism is situated, thus giving survival advantage to the organism. Discovering a representation that makes a problem easily solvable gives evolutionary advantage in terms of time resources to adopters of the new representation, because they are able to solve the problem more quickly and easily than those holding to the old representation.
>
> *Martignon, Laskey and Stenning, p. 157*

Different representations are not equivalent from a cognitive point of view. Some are more adaptive and advantageous than others, because they correspond better to the cognitive features and possibilities of the agent. For example, Martignon, Laskey and Stenning write:

> An ecologically rational strategy is one our cognitive apparatus can perform naturally and easily, and that has adaptive value in a given environment. In other words, ecological rationality involves the discovery of a representation that makes an optimal or nearly optimal solution transparent. For reasoning from evidence to hypothesis, because the natural frequency representation is ecologically rational, it allows humans to perform an otherwise difficult task quickly and easily. Use of the natural frequency representation in educational settings facilitates understanding and improves performance.
>
> *p. 160*

Boundedly rational agents are limited in their computational, processing, and storage abilities. Chapter 9 in this volume by Cristina Bicchieri and Giacomo Sillari focuses on epistemic bounds, that is limits to agents' knowledge:

> Not all knowledge a boundedly rational agent possesses is explicitly stored in memory …, nor does the agent need full epistemic capacities in order to do her part in interactive situations … Indeed, there is a gulf between knowledge that is available to an agent and knowledge that is accessed by an agent …
>
> *Bicchieri and Sillari, p. 189*

In their chapter, they discuss logical models of awareness that precisely draw the distinction between unbounded (implicit) and bounded (explicit) knowledge through a formalized notion of accessibility. A specific aspect of bounded rationality is the limit to human logical abilities and in particular limits to the way real agents reason about knowledge. A useful way to understand its limits is differential accessibility

Part II Cognitive misery and mental dualism

According to many authors (Evans, Chapter 10 in this volume; Stanovich, Chapter 11 in this volume), our brains are made up of two systems: one automatic and associative (System 1) and the other reflective and analytical (System 2). The first is responsible for biases, and the other is able to correct them. They maintain that the difference between the two systems lies at the heart of bounded rationality. System 1, that prevails in numerous decisions, does not follow the normative principles of rationality. It is only System 2 that, when successfully overriding the choices of System 1, has the possibility to process normatively rational answers. The problem lies in the fact that this occurs fairly rarely. Most individuals are cognitive misers, that is, they tend to make the smallest possible effort in terms of attention and processing. Very few are able to seriously engage their analytical capabilities. However, in many everyday situations, when the time to make decisions is limited or the problems are too complex, even those few become cognitive misers. They limit their analytical capability and by so doing, they detach from the normative requirements of deductive, probabilistic and economic rationality.

There are numerous differing positions on dual-process or dual-system theories and on their relative properties. The question is, which of the 23 different theories identified by Stanovich can be deemed acceptable? An initial selection can be made by considering the neuroscientific data that seem to show that there is no single System 1, with a single set of attributes, but rather multiple cognitive and neural systems. Therefore, it is preferable to use the terminology of dual types of processing. There are at least two sets of theories: the *parallel-competitive* theories (Sloman, 1996; 2002) assume that Type 1 and 2 processing proceed in parallel, each having their say with conflicts resolved if necessary. Criterion S refers to situations where individuals are led to respond in a manner consistent with Type 1 but then come to realize an alternative responding consistent with Type 2.

In contrast, there are the *default-interventionist* theories (Evans, 2008; Evans and Stanovich, 2013). They assume that fast Type 1 processing generates intuitive default responses on which subsequent reflective Type 2 processing may or may not intervene. The list of the properties contains at least 6–10 features. Usually it is expected that these are co-occurring properties. In this case, if all of these features do not always co-occur, then the dual-process view is incorrect. In fact, Kruglanski and Gigerenzer (2011) claim that dual-process views fail because "these dimensions are unaligned rather than aligned" (p. 98). That is to say, there are no examples in which all the features co-occur.

Evans and Stanovich (2013) reply that a minimal part of the paired properties usually attributed to the two processes is defining. The majority are correlates that might or might not be present.

> In summary, our view is that the defining feature of Type 1 processing and of Type 2 processing is not the conjunction of eight different binary properties ("2 cells out of 256!"). Research has advanced since the "suggestive list of characteristics" phase of over a decade ago. Our view of the literature is that autonomous processing is the defining feature of Type 1 processing. Even more convincing is the converging evidence that the key feature of Type 2 processing is the ability to sustain the decoupling of secondary representations. The latter is a foundational cognitive requirement for hypothetical thinking.
>
> *Stanovich and Toplak, 2012, p. 7*

In conclusion, there are only two defining properties: the Type 1 processes are autonomous while the Type 2 processes are characterized by cognitive decoupling.[3] "The defining feature of Type 1 processing is its autonomy – the execution of Type 1 process is mandatory when their triggering stimuli are encountered, and they are not dependent on input from high-level control systems" (Stanovich and Toplak, 2012, p. 7). Cognitive decoupling is the defining feature of Type 2 processing. When we reason hypothetically, we create temporary models of the world and test out actions in that simulated world. In order to reason hypothetically, we must be able to prevent our primary representations of the real world from becoming confused with the secondary representations of hypothetical situations, that is, we should decouple our representations (Stanovich and Toplak, 2012). Leslie (1987) was the first to introduce the concept when she was modelling pretence by positing a secondary representation that was a copy of the primary representation but that was decoupled from the real world. Decoupling allows it to be manipulated, that is, be a mechanism for simulation. Decoupling secondary representations from the world and then maintaining the decoupling while simulations is carried out is the defining feature of Type 2 processing. Decoupling seems to be a special features of our race. Since we were becoming the first creatures to rely on cognitive simulation, it was a matter of vital importance not to become "unhooked" from the world too much of the time. Therefore, the salience of the primary representations of the worlds remained difficult and costly to overcome. Therefore, the ability to sustain mental simulations while keeping the relevant representations decoupled is likely a key aspect of the brain's computational power (Stanovich and Toplak, 2012). Decoupling is the feature of Type 2 processing to override and to reverse Type 1 processing that produces responses that are nonoptimal. To summarize, Type 1 processes are autonomous because they do not require "controlled attention and they make minimal demand on working memory and central processing resources". They are mandatory when their triggering stimuli are encountered and they are not dependent on input from high-level control systems. Type 2 processes are characterized by decoupling, that is the ability to prevent our representations of the real world from becoming confused with representations of imaginary situations. Such processing is necessary for hypothetical thinking, mental simulation, counterfactual reasoning and consequentialist decision making.

In reality, humans are cognitive misers. The tendency is to default to processing mechanisms of low computational expense (Stanovich, Chapter 11 in this volume). They engage the brain only when all else fails, and usually not even then. Cognitive misers have three rules: (1) default to Type 1 processes whenever possible; (2) when that is not possible and analytic processing is necessary, default to serial associative cognition with focal bias (as in the case of matching bias in a selection task); and (3) when the reflective mind wants to start cognitive simulation by decoupling, not complete it, that is, override failure (Stanovich, 2009, p. 69). Moreover if the analytic processes want to override the autonomous processes, it is possible that they won't succeed because the mindware is not available or it is contaminated. What is the mindware? It includes rules, procedures and strategies that can be retrieved by Type 2 analytic processes and used to transform decoupled representations to override the autonomous mind. It is mainly the product of past learning experiences. If a rule is not learned or is not well learned or is not appropriately applied, this is the cause of an override failure. For example, knowledge of the gambler fallacy for a pathological gambler (Stanovich, 2009, p. 73). But not all mindware is helpful for overriding autonomous processes. Some acquired mindware can be the direct cause of errors and biases. For example, egocentric thinking, the my-side perspective, the evaluation-disabling memes (the memes against critical thinking and for consensual dogmatic faith) or false lay psychological theories (e.g. the personal immunity to bias or the personal knowledge of the causes of own actions, etc.).

In the same direction, Evans (Chapter 10 in this volume) proposes the Default Interventionist theory as a framework for bounded rationality:

> The model assumes that Type 1 processing leads to a default intuitive answer A1 which appears in consciousness without effort or reflection. A1 is then subject to scrutiny by Type 2 processes which are effortful and require working memory. However, such scrutiny can be shallow or deep which depends on a number of factors. Motivational factors include how people are instructed, whether they have a rational thinking disposition (which inclines people to check intuitions more carefully) and the feeling or rightness (FOR) or subjective confidence that they have in A1 ... Cognitive resources included time available (speeded tasks will reduce Type 2 checking), individual differences in working memory capacity (highly correlated with IQ) and "mindware".
>
> *Evans, p. 189*

When A1 is scrutinized, it may or may not be deemed satisfactory. Whether the intuition can successfully be replaced by an answer based on explicit reasoning and knowledge, however, depends on the cognitive resources available, as Stanovich has argued. Decision making is affected by individual differences in both cognitive ability and rational thinking dispositions.

The latter measures the extent to which people will rely on intuitions or check them out by reasoning. On the basis of this work, Stanovich argues that a number of conditions must be met for someone to successfully engage in Type 2 reasoning and solve a demanding and novel experimental problem. First, people must be aware of the need for intervention by Type 2 reasoning, which is where rational thinking dispositions and feelings of rightness come into play. However, if they do intervene, then this will only be successful both if (1) they have sufficient cognitive capacity for the hypothetical reasoning involved; and (2) they have the relevant mindware, that is, formal or procedural knowledge required by the context.

An important aspect of bounded rationality is linked to the feeling of rightness (FOR) of default intuitive answers that come to mind. When the FOR is high, we are happy with our intuitions that we deem satisfactory (satisficing) for our decision making. According to Evans:

> The FOR research seems to fit a neat story of evolution and bounded rationality. Our intuitions come helpfully packaged with feelings of confidence which tell us whether we need to expend effort or not in checking them out. However, there is a snag. None of this research – on reasoning and decision-making – has provided evidence for even a partial accuracy of the FOR judgement, as observed in other fields where metacognition is studied.
>
> *p. 191*

There are two comments on these results:

> The first is that there is no clear reason to think that FOR corresponds to a stage of cognitive processing in the manner that researchers in the field assume. They could simply be conscious feelings that are by-products of the processes that determine the behaviour measures. In other words, a brain process that leads to a quick and firmly held decision, also generates conscious feelings of rightness and confidence, which in themselves have no functional significance.
>
> *Evans, p. 192*

The second is that the evolution of metacognitive feeling (like FOR) might be used simply to justify some bias in given adaptive contexts. It is well known (e.g. Stich or Sperber) that normative canons like truth and consistency are not always evolutionary adaptive. A belief bias might increase more significantly the individual's fitness before real and present dangers than a precise and correct but slow and time-consuming syllogistic reasoning. Natural selection provides the reproductive advantage of one organism over the next, not for the optimality of any one characteristic (for example, deductive reasoning).

If the mind is structured into two parts or process types,[4] Stanovich (Chapter 11) wonders which evolutionary representation can explain the emergence and the conflict between these two components of mental activity. He relies on Dawkins' discussion of replicators and vehicles:

> Replicators as entities (e.g. genes) that copy themselves and vehicles as the containers (e.g. organisms) in which replicators house themselves. It is vehicles that interact with the environment, and the differential success of the vehicles in interacting with the environment determines the success of the replicators that they house. Humans have proven to be good vehicles for genes. As have bees.
>
> *Stanovich, p. 197*

But the goal structures of bees and humans are very different (Dennett, 2017). The bee's goal structure shows a predominance of the replicator's goals over those of the vehicle. In case of conflict, the vehicle's goals are sacrificed. A given bee will sacrifice itself as a vehicle if there is greater benefit to the same genes by helping other bees (for example, causing its own death when it loses its stinger while protecting its genetically-related hive-queen). In humans, however, the replicator's goals that are mainly oriented towards reproductive fitness can be neutralized by the vehicle's goals or may not even be useful to achieve reproductive fitness. In the former case, the vehicle's goal, for example, the fulfilling of pleasure, leads us to prevent pregnancy through the adoption of contraceptives. Therefore, the reproductive goal is reduced for reasons linked to the vehicle's goals. In the latter, the goals that were effective for reproductive goals in the past are no longer useful because of the speed of environmental change. For example, the consumption of excessive fats, that was adaptively useful in the past, no longer fulfils the goals of either the vehicle or the replicator. Goals such as economic rationality and any other type of optimality are no longer among the replicator's goals, only among the vehicle's.

How does this framework relate to the dualism of the mind and bounded rationality? The mind generates, through System 1, behaviours that are mainly instinctive, linked to the hereditary component of our nervous system. These are a set of behaviours led by the replicator's long-term goals, that is to say the human genome. System 2, however, has introduced new short-term goals and new forms of reasoning and decision making aimed at fulfilling those goals. System 2 is primarily a control system focused on the interests of the whole person. It is the primary maximizer of an individual's *personal* goal satisfaction. The problem lies in the mismatch between the two systems. The goals of System 2 often correspond to interests that are common to both the vehicle and the replicator. Other times, they are in contrast with those of the replicator. In those cases, System 1 tends to prevail and rational optimality goals are therefore set aside (Viale, 2019). Stanovich (Chapter 11) is more optimistic:

> Because System 2 is more attuned to the person's needs as a coherent organism than is System 1 (which is more directly tuned to the ancient reproductive goals of the subpersonal replicators), in the minority of cases where the outputs of the two systems conflict, people will often be better off if they can accomplish an override of the System 1-triggered output. Such a system conflict could be signaling a vehicle/replicator goal mismatch and, statistically, such a mismatch is more likely to be resolved in favor of the vehicle (which all of us should want) if the System 1 output is overridden. When humans live in complex societies, basic goals and primary drives (bodily pleasure, safety, sustenance) are satisfied indirectly by maximizing secondary symbolic goals such as prestige, status, employment, and remuneration. In order to achieve many of these secondary goals, the more directly-coded System 1 responses must be suppressed—at least temporarily. Long-leashed derived goals create the conditions for a separation between the goals of evolutionary adaptation and the interests of the vehicle.
>
> *Stanovich, p. 201*

Samuel Bellini-Leite and Keith Frankish (Chapter 12 in this volume) criticize a version of the dual-process theory that seems closed to the Fodorian division of mind into encapsulated input systems and unencapsulated central system. According to Fodor, the central system is represented as an unbounded central processor, sensitive to global assessments of context and relevance. Bellini-Leite and Frankish write:

It is tempting to think of conscious thought as open-ended and unconstrained, and of nonconscious processes as inflexible and encapsulated. Cognitive psychology and computational neuroscience show that this is wrong. Conscious cognition is in fact severely limited in capacity, while nonconscious processes are tuned to the heavy demands of contextual and relevance processing. It is thus vital that modern dual-process theories do not carry over the conception of rationality implicit in Fodor's precursor theory. In thinking about the functions and capacities of the posited dual systems, the perspective of bounded rationality is essential.

p. 214

Recent models of brain functioning that undermine the rigid Fodorian distinction between strictly encapsulated systems, the modules, and free unencapsulated systems, the central processor, are the Predictive Processing (PP) theories (Clark, 2016). The brain's function is to predict proximal stimuli not only to process them. Bellini-Leite and Frankish write:

These theories see the brain as having a hierarchical structure, with lower levels being close to perceptual input mechanisms and higher levels receiving information from diverse multimodal regions. Signals flow both up and down the hierarchy, with top-down signals predicting lower-level activity and bottom-up signals flagging errors in those predictions. Predictions are based on probabilistic *generative models* distributed through the hierarchy. These models monitor statistical patterns in the layer below, generating nonconscious hypotheses in an attempt to accommodate incoming data. Within this architecture, the influence of different neural regions is modulated to reflect their success in prediction through a mechanism known as *precision weighting*.

p. 213

As outlined in the following section on embodied bounded rationality, there are no sharp boundaries between perception, judgement and action. The limited System 2 receives representations that have already been filtered and processed. Lower layers pass on only stimuli that generate high prediction errors and that may be analysed and corrected by S2.

Stanovich (Chapter 11) writes that researchers working in the heuristics and biases tradition tend to see a large gap between normative models of rational responding and descriptive models of what people actually do. These researchers have been termed *Meliorists* because they assume that human reasoning is not as good as it could be, and that thinking could be improved. However, over the last several decades, an alternative interpretation of the findings from the heuristics and biases research programme has been championed. This group of theorists have been termed the *Panglossians*. These theorists often argue either that the normative model being applied is not the appropriate one because the subject's interpretation of the task is different from what the researcher assumes it is, or that the modal response in the task makes perfect sense from an evolutionary perspective. According to Stanovich, the contrasting positions of the Panglossians and Meliorists define the differing poles in what has been termed the Great Rationality Debate in cognitive science – the debate about whether humans can be systematically irrational. The three contributions that follow outline the arguments for the Meliorist and Panglossian approaches with regard to deductive reasoning, causal reasoning and decision making. Part III on ecological rationality corresponds to what Stanovich calls the Panglossian position, as opposed to the Meliorist one that follows the tradition of Daniel Kahneman and Amos Tversky's heuristic and biases and the application to public policy by Richard Thaler and Cass Sunstein.

Phil Johnson-Laird (Chapter 13 in this volume), together with Wason, started working on mental dualism in connection with logical reasoning. Johnson-Laird's theory maintains that when dealing with a deduction, the use of mental models happens intuitively, corresponding to System 1 activity. The same deduction can also be analysed deliberately according to the rules of logic with greater difficulty and effort. This corresponds to the activation of System 2. In the case of reasoning based on mental models, the results are not logically complete, because not all the model possibilities are made explicit compared to a deliberate analysis. Johnson-Laird writes that "human reasoners are equipped with two systems for reasoning, which interact with one another. Intuitions depend on mental models, which represent only what is true" (p. 222). Bounded rationality in deduction is based on dependence on mental models. He adds:

> Our reasoning is bounded. We make deductions in domains that are undecidable or intractable in their demands on time and memory. Yet, we are rational in principle. We grasp the force of counterexamples, and spontaneously use them to refute invalid inferences. Our deductions from fully explicit models yield valid conclusions based on all the information in the premises. Alas, some inferences in life violate the desirable logical properties: their logic is incomplete, and they lack a decision procedure or a tractable one. In any case, to make a rational deduction is at least to maintain the information in the premises, to simplify, and to reach a new conclusion.
>
> *p. 217*

One of the ways in which the individual represents the environment and interacts with it is through causal attribution. When faced with any social phenomenon, for example, a fall in your stock's market value, or a natural one, like the onset of a number of physical ailments, the individual will try to understand the causes of that effect, in other words, will engage in diagnostic reasoning. Diagnostic reasoning consists in going back to the causes that triggered one or multiple effects. Formally, it means estimating the probability Pr (cause | effect). It is well known that the estimation of this probability deviates from the rational norm defined by the Bayes rule. Recent results show that people follow very varied *strategies* in order to estimate the diagnostic probability. Most often, the encountered strategies consist in combining the quantities within the Bayes rule in a sub-optimal fashion. Jean Baratgin and Jean-Louis Stilgenbauer (Chapter 14 in this volume) suggest

> the existence of additional strategies based on patterns of defeasible reasoning. In particular, two schemes appear to be psychologically plausible. The first is a form of defeasible deduction based on the *Modus Ponens* (DMP), the second is a scheme of defeasible abduction based on *Affirming the Consequent* (DAC).
>
> *p. 232*

These two reasoning patterns represent two formally different strategies for estimating the diagnostic probability Pr(cause | effect), as shown in Figure 14.3 on p. 233. They correspond respectively in the A.I. and philosophical literature to two modes of inference: abduction for DAC and deduction for DMP. First, the defeasible deduction is a weakened form of deduction that permits the production of provisionally true and/or probable conclusions. Second, abduction is a heuristic reasoning that serves to identify explanatory causes or hypotheses. Baratgin and Stilgenbauer show:

the choice of the scheme to estimate the diagnostic probability Pr(cause|effect) depends on the value of the predictive probability Pr(effect|cause). When Pr(cause|effect) < Pr(effect|cause), participants do not report any particular preference between DMP and DAC. Yet, when Pr(cause|effect) > Pr(effect|cause), participants report a clear preference for DMP to estimate the diagnostic probability.

p. 234

Decision making can be represented according to two main approaches: the alternative-based approach and the attribute-based approach. The former includes compensatory decision making. Overall values for each option in a choice set are generated before comparing options to arrive at a decision. According to the second category, attributes across options are compared and these attribute comparisons are used to make a decision. Because they compare attributes, they may not use all available information to make a choice, which categorizes many of them as heuristics. Francine Goh and Jeffery Stevens (Chapter 15 in this volume) write:

Choice data have suggested that attribute-based models can better predict choice compared to alternative-based models in some situations (e.g., when there are many options in the choice set, when calculating an overall value for an option is too cognitively taxing).

p. 243

As Part III on ecological rationality will show, the situation where attribute-based decision making is more successful is characterized by uncertainty and complexity, which are the environmental features of bounded rationality. In fact, Goh and Jeffrey write:

While the study of decision making has historically focused on alternative-based models, attribute-based models have experienced a resurgence of interest from researchers for a number of reasons. First, they follow from Simon's notion of bounded rationality because they often reflect real-world limitations faced by decision makers by using less information and simpler computations. This is especially pertinent in instances where decision makers have to make a choice from myriad options or when there is risk involved in the decision making process. Second, they capture choice data quite well, predicting multi-attribute, risky, intertemporal and strategic choices while accounting for, or bypassing, anomalies regularly encountered in the use of alternative-based models. Third, in addition to capturing choice data, attribute-based models can also capture the decision process by making predictions about eye tracking and information acquisition data.

p. 250

Part III Ockam's razor: mental monism and ecological rationality

The strong version of the dual-process account of mind is untenable. The dual list of the 6–10 properties are not co-occurring, therefore, the dual-process view is incorrect. However, even the minimal dual account of mind, based on only one defining property, autonomy for Type 1 processes and decoupling for Type 2 processes, seems untenable. Psychological and neural data seem a direct empirical falsifier (Viale, 2019). The mind or psychological processes would not be split into the first part that is prone to vices, impulsiveness and error, and the second part, wise, rational and ready to correct the errors of the first part. The mind seems to be better represented by a unified model, that is, by a single account of mental processes.

What are the features of the single account of mind and what are the implications for the bounded rationality theory? The two main anti-dualistic approaches are that of the "cognitive continuum" put forward by Hammond (1996) and Cleerman and Jimenez (2002; see also Osman, 2004) and the "rule-based processing unified theory of decision making" argued by Kruglanski and Gigerenzer (2011).

First, according to the dynamic graded continuum (DGC), different types of reasoning are dependent on the representations from which participants reason (Osman, 2004, p. 1002). The same underlying production rule can generate a variety of responses as a result of the features of the task that an individual considers relevant (Osman, 2004, p. 1003). The properties of reasoning (control, awareness, speed, etc.) vary in degree, depending on the structural features of the tasks that induce different cognitive activity (Hammond, 1996). The cognitive continuum ranges from intuition to analysis. The better-structured a task is, the more analytically induced will be the decision-making mode. Conversely, with an ill-structured task, decision making is likely to be intuition-induced (Hammond, 1996). These theories seem to fit better than dual-process theories to a set of criteria like the Criterion S,[5] the individual differences in cognitive ability, the dissociation between implicit and explicit processing, as analysed in a series of tasks as the selection task, the conjunction problem and belief bias in syllogistic reasoning (Osman, 2004, pp. 996–1005). What matters is whether in this architecture of the mind, there can be correction and reversibility after the bias has been generated. From what can be deduced from the "cognitive continuum" thesis, this type of processing appears to be triggered by the structure of the problem. If a problem is opaque and unnatural in its logical structure or if it is linguistically and pragmatically confused and deviant or if it is unfamiliar, namely, the quality of representations is poor, this will stimulate the intuitive, fast and implicit part of the mind responsible for biases. In this case, contrary to what is proposed by dual-process theories, there is no possibility of correction by the analytical component which is only stimulated by well-structured problems and the relative quality of representations (Viale, 2019).

Second, according to the "rule-based processing unified theory of decision making" argued by Kruglanski and Gigerenzer (2011), a cognitive judgement is mediated by rules that are in the individual's adaptive toolbox. How is the selection made? It follows a two-step process: first, the task and individual memory constrain the set of applicable rules, resulting in a consideration set, and, second, difficulty of instantiation, individual processing potential and (perceived) ecological rationality of the rule guide the final choice of a rule from a set (Kruglanski and Gigerenzer, 2011, p. 102).

Difficulty in instantiation means difficulty in recognizing the rule-matching cue in given circumstances. The presence of noises in the judgemental environment and weak and faint cues are responsible for this difficulty. The individual might overcome this difficulty and try to retrieve from memory rules that are difficult to access if he or she possesses sufficient processing potential. The processing potential are characterized by two features: attentional capacity and motivation. When they are low, the individual is not able to conduct an extensive memory search to retrieve the suitable rules for the structure of the task. Moreover, in such conditions, the individual may be sluggish and incapable of applying rules whose implementation requires effortful computations. The individual tends to base his or her judgement on relatively simple inferential rules and may be less able "to carefully assess the ecological rationality of a rule, that is, to properly estimate its validity in a given environment" (Kruglanski and Gigerenzer, 2011, p. 103). With limited attentional capacity and motivation, easy-to-use heuristics are used to a greater extent than more complex inferential rules. For example, it was found that the "higher the magnitude of individuals' accuracy and motivation, or their need for cognition, the greater their readiness to apply complex rules and to digest compound information" (Kruglanski and Gigerenzer, 2011, p. 102). To sum up, in situations where the suitable rules are complex, the signal to noise ratio is low, the individual has low resources, low conditions of processing potential and a low need for cognition (Petty and Cacioppo, 1986), and where there is a need for fast cognitive closure, unsuitable, easy-to-use heuristics are used. The consequence are biases and not ecologically rational decisions. This kind of decision environment is most frequent and it limits individual behaviour to choices that are not adaptive. In these cases, the reversibility of decisions taken is very difficult and it may only occasionally happen, ex post, when the individual experiences the negative consequences of his choice. But also in this case, beyond the constraints of adverse initial conditions, such as low processing potential and signal-to-noise ratio, emotional factors such as inertia, the status quo and present-day bias can also block any reversibility of choice.

To summarize, when faced with ill-structured, opaque problems and situations, there are two possible styles of decision making, according to the unified theory of mind: (1) the "need for cognition" individual may decide to invest cognitive resources and time analysing the problems; and (2) the "lack of cognition" individual is not endowed with cognitive resources and he or she takes fast decisions based on "gut feeling", and, soon afterwards, inertia, the status quo and procrastination phenomena prevent her or him from analysing the situation and improving the structure and representation. As many empirical studies show, the need for cognition people are a small minority. Generally, people lack attention, motivation and cognitive resources to analyse ill-defined and opaque problems. They rely on fast, intuitive, emotional answers and they lack the cognitive and emotional resources to analyse the problems and review the answers afterwards (Viale, 2019; forthcoming).

Hugo Mercier and Dan Sperber (Chapter 16 in this volume) hold a similar position. They write:

> In light of these results, and of the fundamental problems that affect standard dual process models, we have suggested an alternative theory that is much more in line with the ideas of bounded rationality … Instead of dividing the mind between system 1—which would mostly abide by the dictates of bounded rationality—and system 2—which wouldn't—we suggest that it is intuitions all the way up (see also Kruglanski and Gigerenze, 2011; Osman, 2004). However, some of these intuitions—which form our ability to reason—would bear on reasons, as explained presently. In this theory, reason heavily relies on its cognitive and social environment to solve problems—when to kick in, how to figure out if something is a good reason, and how to find relevant reasons.
>
> *Mercier and Sperber, p. 259*

According to Mercier and Sperber, the theory of reason concerns the central aspect of bounded rationality, that is the interactive and recursive relation between inferential activity and the environment. The theory is dubbed *the interactionist view of reason* because the reasons supporting one's theories or used to evaluate other individuals' arguments are generated at the metarepresentational level (reasons on reasons) and dialogically with ourselves (more rarely), but mostly with regard to others. The key feature of this theory is that these reasons are generated adaptively following the heuristic of satisficing:

The production of reasons, as we describe it, is a paradigmatic example of a satisficing process. The criterion to be reached is that of producing reasons good enough to convince one's interlocutor. For the interactionist account, reason evolved by being used chiefly in dialogic contexts, in which we can benefit from the back and forth of discussion to refine our arguments, instead of attempting to anticipating through extraordinary computational force what the silver bullet might be. This means, however, that people are not well prepared to produce strong reasons in the absence of feedback (except in the relatively rare circumstances where such feedback can be reliably anticipated).

Mercier and Sperber, p. 263

An important aspect of this theory concerns its implications in environment design, in the architecture of choice that promotes the generation of good reasons. The relevance of Mercier and Sperber's analysis is clear with regard to choice architecture in the theory of Nudge and Boost. As Part VII of this volume will show, one way to empower the citizens in decision making is to promote environments that boost their capacity to analyse and make conscious choices, through increasing environmental feedbacks, the heuristic simplification of information and a critical dialogue with the members of social context of reference.

What is the role of bounded rationality in the cognitive sciences? The main model explaining how information is processed and how decision are made is David Marr's (1982) model on the three levels of analysis. Originally developed with Tomaso Poggio, these three levels map onto fundamental distinctions in the study of rationality. At the highest level, termed the computational level, the aim is to identify an appropriate formal system, a calculus, used to define the problem and derive its solution. Moving down to Marr's second level, the algorithmic level, the aim is to specify the algorithms and data structures needed to compute the solution. Marr's third level of analysis is the implementation level, which considers the constraints of physically instantiating the proposed algorithms and data structures in, say, biological machinery or a conventional digital computer. Henry Brighton writes (Chapter 17 in this volume):

Marr's levels of analysis are seen as a core tenet of cognitive science … defining the de facto categories used to orientate cognitive models in relation to rationality claims … From this Marrian perspective, bounded rationality is typically seen as an attempt to inform computational-level theory development by importing constraints arising from algorithmic-level concerns. These constraints revise the problem specification, and consequently, what constitutes a rational solution.

p. 270

For example, it has been proposed that simple heuristics might be used to approximate a full Bayesian computation specified at the computational level. Ecological rationality involves a conjecture about simple heuristics, that belongs to Marr's algorithmic rather than the computational level. And given that rationality claims are traditionally made at the computational level, the assumption is that ecological rationality must therefore inherit principles of Bayesian rationality to explain the success of simple heuristics. Brighton writes:

The claim here is that ecological rationality is an adaptation to the problem of decision making in large worlds. These are environments that we can observe but our partial ignorance precludes them from being probabilistically quantifiable … and a key implication of this claim is that optimality ceases to be a meaningful characteristic of rational decisions under these conditions.

p. 277

In a large world characterized by uncertainty, problems cannot be faced through optimal computations made by a formal system, but rather through exploratory heuristics characterized by the "less-is-more" principle. Therefore, the three Marrian levels of analysis are not suitable to characterize ecological rationality, while a two-level analysis is useful to pursue a form of functionalist inquiry.

When Herbert Simon introduced the concept of BR, most economists showed little interest in Simon's question and preferred theories assuming perfect foresight and optimal computations. According to Gerd Gigerenzer (Chapter 2 in this volume), today a different phenomenon has gained momentum among economists:

> Instead of being rejected as worthless or unimportant, his concept of *bounded rationality* was hijacked and radically reframed, making his revolutionary ideas no longer recognizable. Neo-classical economists absorbed the term into the orthodoxy of perfect foresight and concluded that satisficing is quintessentially optimizing. Proponents of the heuristics-and-biases program in psychology, in contrast, appropriated the term for their own focus on human lack of rationality. This is why bounded rationality now has three faces that could hardly be more dissimilar.
>
> *Gigerenzer, p. 59*

According to Gigerenzer, there are three principles that define Simon's programme of bounded rationality:

1. *Uncertainty.* To study decision making under uncertainty, not only risk.
2. *Process.* To study the actual process of decision making, as opposed to as-if expected utility maximization.
3. *Scissors.* To study how the structure of an environment, together with the cognitive process, produces the resulting behavior.

Gigerenzer writes:

> The rationality in neoclassical economics typically refer to three pillars: consistency, maximization of expected utility, and—if learning is involved—Bayesian updating of probabilities. Leonard J. Savage (1954), known as the father of modern Bayesian decision theory, defined two conditions necessary for these three pillars of rationality:
>
> 1. *Perfect Foresight of Future States*: The agent knows the exhaustive and mutually exclusive set of future states S of the world.
> 2. *Perfect Foresight of Consequences*: The agent knows the exhaustive and mutually exclusive set C of consequences of each of his or her actions, given a state.
>
> *p. 56*

The term 'risk' may be applied to the previous situations with perfect foresight of future states and consequences. These are also called 'small worlds' by Savage (1954). What Simon noticed, however, was that the managers he observed and humans in general mostly have to deal with situations that are unlike small worlds with perfect foresight and that do not meet the assumptions for expected utility maximization and Bayesian updating (Savage, 1954, p. 16). Simon called for an empirical study of *how* humans reason when perfect foresight is not possible. The real-life problems are inside a complex environment. They are typically ill-defined problems, that is, the goals are not definite; we don't know what counts as an alternative and how many alternatives there are; it's unclear what the consequences might be and how to estimate their probabilities and utilities (Viale, 2018). This environment might be called also large world (Savage, 1954) and it is characterized by uncertainty. Small worlds instead are in principle predictable and without surprises and they are characterized by the knowledge of all relevant variables, their consequences and probabilities. The conditions of small world are the requirements of Neoclassical Rationality as Simon stressed in his Nobel Lecture (1979, p. 500). In these worlds the problems may be well defined but they can be also computationally intractable. As is well known, an example of a computational tractable problem is the dice game or the roulette game. Instead a well-defined problem such as a chess game is computationally intractable. In any case, the real world is most of the time large and these conditions of knowledge are rarely met.[6] Since they are rarely met, the normative rational requirements of neoclassical economics are unjustified and the application of their theories can easily lead to disaster (Stiglitz, 2010). Unfortunately, behavioural economics, while it criticizes the descriptive side of neoclassical economics, without really proposing an alternative realist model of decision making, retains the normative one. In fact, the heuristic and biases programme is developed to cope with what is called human irrational behaviour, characterized by biases and formal errors caused by psychological mechanisms as the heuristics. Thaler (1991, p. 138) writes very clearly about:

> A demonstration that human choices often violate the axioms of rationality does not necessarily imply any criticism of the axioms of rational choice as a normative idea. Rather, the research is implied intended to show that for descriptive purposes, alternative models are sometimes necessary.

In a large world, the axioms of rationality cannot be applied. Therefore, they cannot be considered feasible normative canons of rationality. Behavioural economists, who decades ago defined their critical contribution to the neoclassical mainstream a purely descriptive enterprise (ibid.) now advocate using behavioural concepts for prescriptive policy purposes as in the Nudge theory (Thaler and Sunstein, 2008).

When Herbert Simon began his attempt to empirically change economics, his methodological and epistemological coordinates were realist (Simon, Egidi, Viale and Marris, 1992; Simon, 2000). His main critical target was the instrumentalist *as-if* approach of Milton Friedman (1953). A descriptive enterprise in economics had to overcome the unbounded rationality assumptions of neoclassical economics as unbounded self-interest, unbounded willpower and unbounded computational capacity. The behavioural economics programme initiated by Simon had the goal of replacing these *a priori* assumptions with more realistic ones. How much psychological realism has been brought into economics by behavioural economists? Unfortunately very little because there are barriers to psychological realism that are common to neoclassical economics and that are the son of the shared reliance on Friedman's *as-if* principle (Berg and Gigerenzer, 2010). All relevant behavioural theories suffer from the same shortcomings of neoclassical economics: assuming that risky choice always emerges from a process of weighting and averaging all the relevant pieces of information; the decision maker knows the objectively feasible action set; the decision maker know the list of outcomes associates with lotteries or the probabilities of the known outcomes (Berg and Gigerenzer, 2010). The shift from neoclassical economics to behavioural economics and in particular, after the impact of Allais Paradox, from *expected utility theory* to *prospect theory*, appeared to be based on the introduction of more trans-formations with additional parameters to square the basic operation of probability-weighted averaging with observed choices over lotteries (Berg and Gigerenzer, 2010). The weighting-and-adding objective function is used *as-if* it is a model of mind. But it's not. It is a fic-tional mind, a valid instrument to make *a posteriori* inferences through the introduction of suitable parameters in order to reach a better R-squared. The same methodological model is observed in many other behavioural theories (Berg and Gigerenzer, 2010). For example, the Fehr and Schmidt *social preference model* (1999) recognizes the insight that people care about others' payoffs. Therefore, they modify the utility function through the addition of at least two additional free parameters. People are assumed not to maximize a utility function depending only on their own payoffs but a behavioural or other-gathering utility function. To do this, a decision maker assigns benefits and costs to each element of the choice space based on weighted sum of the intrinsic benefits of own payoffs together with the psychic benefits of being ahead of others and the psychic costs of falling behind others. The decision maker will select the action with the largest utility score based on the weighted summation. Another *as-if* model is Laibson's (1997) *model of impulsiveness in consumption*, a psychological bias that over-weights the present over the future. He puts more weight on the present by reducing weight on all future acts of consumption. In other words, he reduces the weight of all terms in the weighted sum of utilities except for the term representing the utility of current consumption. The unrealistic pretension is evident: the decision maker, after an exhaustive search of all possible acts of con-sumption, computes the weighted sum of utility terms for each act and chooses the one with highest weighted utility score. The deviation between the value that recovers the neoclassical version and the new parameter that reduces the weight on the future is considered the empirical confirmation of the model (Berg and Gigerenzer, 2010).

The instrumentalist methodology of behavioural economics uses the addition and man-aging of free parameters to improve the realism of the models. In so doing, it improves the within-sample fit and improves the R-squared. Most of the philosophers of science, both in the realist tradition (e.g. Hacking, 1983) and in the antirealist tradition (e.g. van Fraassen, 1980), agree on the empirical adequacy by successful prediction, particularly of novel facts, as the first principle in deciding between competing hypotheses (Viale, 2013). A large number of free parameters allow the model to fit many sets of data without proving it generates successful out-of-sample prediction. On the contrary, the most challenging test of a theory is in prediction using a single set of fixed parameters. Something that few models of behavioural economics dare to do.

In conclusion, we live in a large world where the canons of neoclassical rationality are unjus-tified both descriptively and normatively. Therefore, the reasoning errors, fallacies and biases that behavioural economists are engaged to overcome most of the time are not irrationalities. Moreover, the decision-making models that behavioural economists have introduced most of the time are an *as-if* instrumentalist tool to fit the observed choice data.

Since we live in large world characterized ontologically by complexity, recursivity, non-linearity and uncertainty, the rationality of choices should be judged by their adap-tivity and problem-solving ability. In fact, bounded rationality is not confined only to the constraints of the computational power of human mind. As in Simon's scissors metaphor (1990), rationality should be judged by the matching or mismatching of the relationship of mind-environment or in other words choice-task structure. What kind of reasoning processes are able to match the environmental tasks and solve the problems? This is an empirical question that some years ago confronted some cognitive scientists, such as Herbert Simon, Vernon Smith, Richard Selten and, in particular more directly, Gerd Gigerenzer and the ABC Research Group (Gigerenzer, Todd, and the ABC Research Group, 1999). The adaptive toolbox of formalized heuristics is the result of these empirical investigations. In a number of problems, simple heuristics were more accurate than standard statistical methods that have the same or more information. The results became known as the "less-is-more effect". There is a point where more is not better, but harmful. There is an inverse-U-shaped relation between level of accuracy and amount of information, computation, or time (Gigerenzer and Gassmaier, 2011, p. 453). For example, "starting in the late 1990s it was shown for the first time that relying on one good reason (and ignoring the rest) can lead to higher predictive accuracy than achieved by a linear multiple regression" (Gigerenzer and Gassmaier, 2011, p. 453). Herbert Simon himself spoke, in his appraisal of the volume by Gigerenzer, Todd and the ABC Research Group (1999), of a "revolution in cognitive science, striking a great blow for sanity in the approach to human rationality". The toolbox is composed of many heuristics that have been tested successfully against statistical algorithms of rationality, not in the easy task of fitting a closed sample of data but in the much harder task of prediction. They have proved to be both a better description of decision making and a better prescription on how to decide. Obviously, the adaptive success of any given heuristic depends on the particular given environment. In which environments will a given heuristic succeed, and in which will it fail? Gigerenzer, Todd et al. (2012) have identified a number of environmental structure variables:

Uncertainty: how well a criterion can be predicted.
Redundancy: the correlation between cues.
Sample size: number of observations (relative to number of cues).
Variability in weights: the distribution of the cue weights.

How do we assess the adaptive success in ecological rationality? Gigerenzer and Gassmaier (2011, p. 457) write: "The study of ecological rationality results in comparative statement of the kind 'strategy X is more accurate (frugal, fast) than Y in environment E'."

According to Julian Marewski and Ulrich Hoffrage (Chapter 18 in this volume):

The fast-and-frugal heuristics framework asks four basic questions: descriptive, ecological, applied, and methodological …

1. *Descriptive*: What heuristics do people rely on to make decisions, and when do they rely on which heuristic?
2. *Ecological*: To what environmental structure is each heuristic adapted, such that relying on that heuristic can aid people to make clever decisions; and reversely, in which environments will that heuristic fail?
3. *Applied*: How can human performance be improved so that environments match heuristics—be it by changing the environment in which people act or by changing the heuristics people rely upon?
4. *Methodological*: How can people's use of heuristics and the heuristics fits to different environments be studied?

Candidate answers to those four questions have been formulated in numerous fields and disciplines to which the fast-and-frugal heuristics program has been applied …

How can those four question aid understanding drastic environmental change—notably, the ways in which individuals think, decide, and act?

p. 284–285

They analyse how to cope with the radical environmental changes caused by the digital revolution. They proceed in six steps:

> First, we will speculate how future aversive environments might look, and second we will discuss how such environments might then influence behavior, for instance, by leading people to adopt different heuristics. Third, we will speculate how those heuristics might, in turn, shape environments, namely, the societies in which they are enacted. Subsequently, we will explore how aversive environmental change can be managed—both by an individual navigating through a changing environment (fourth) and by societies as a whole undergoing environmental change (fifth). We will close this chapter by, sixth, turning from changes in life-history to changes in evolutionary history.
>
> *Marewski and Hoffrage, p. 292*

For example, they propose three heuristic principles to create more resilient digitalized societies that avoid the growing perverse effects of interconnectedness, influenceability and traceability:

1. *Principle of disconnectedness:* Implement policies that disconnect people from each other.
2. *Principle of deceleration:* Implement policies that slow down the spread of information among people.
3. *Principle of information-loss:* Implement policies that prevent the unlimited storage of behavioral data.

Marewski and Hoffrage, p. 297

These principles aim to answer the questions leading to the sixth step, that concerns changes in evolutionary history. The digital world differs from the predigital environment. Its features make the adaptation of human beings less easy. These principles aims at shaping the digital environment in a way that increases the ecological rationality of human beings.

An important feature of ecological rationality is that it situates BR within the framework of natural selection. Ancestral environments and fitness pressure shaped the evolved capacities of human decision making. Samuel Nordli and Peter Todd (Chapter 19 in this volume) write:

> But the evolutionary perspective enables us to do more, looking at the ultimate selection pressures that operated over time in our and other species' evolutionary trajectories—that is, the study of any organism's decision making as interactions between **(A)** its evolved capacities, needs, and desires/goals, in terms of **(B)** how those aspects fit the structure of the past environmental decision-making contexts, and **(C)** how they match or mismatch the structure of the present environmental contexts.
>
> *Nordli and Todd, p. 313*

Ecological rationality expands the concept of BR by emphasizing the role of past environments to which we have adapted, the present environment in which we make decisions, and the structure of information as it is processed through decision making. In this way, "the ecological rationality approach follows in the investigative tradition of behavioral ecology as championed by Tinbergen ..., who argued that proximate (mechanistic and developmental) and ultimate (adaptive and evolutionary) analyses are each required in order to fully understand observed behaviour" (Nordli and Todd, p. 313). The weakness of current research in decision making lies in the fact that it overlooks the explanation coming from evolutionary psychology and behavioural ecology. It is focused only on the description of the mechanisms of choice. But

> this lack of evolutionary contextualization can leave unrealistic notions of rationality unchallenged, engendering a tendency to blame irrational biases or systematic inadequacies when human behavior does not match the optimal performance of normative behavioral prescriptions ... From this proximate perspective, the failure of boundedly-rational behavior to reach classically-rational levels of performance is just that: a failure.
>
> *Nordli and Todd, p. 314*

On the contrary, ecological rationality does not predefine rationality based on *a priori* analytical canons on how people should ideally behave. Instead "it seeks both to describe how people actually act in specific contexts, and to understand how decisions and actions fit together with particular environmental contexts in terms of their evolutionary provenance and adaptive significance" (Nordli and Todd, p. 314). Obviously, if past and present environments differ in important ways, this may result in a mismatch between the old mechanisms of decision making suitable for the old times and the new environment, which is responsible for non-adaptive decisions. Humans' evolved preferences for unhealthy sugary, salty and fatty foods are examples of this mismatch.

Conversely (as will be analysed also in Viale, Chapter 22 in this volume), "there are examples where ostensibly-irrational behavior (according to normative prescriptive models) may be considered perfectly reasonable when evaluated from an ecological rationality perspective" (Nordli and Todd, p. 319). There are many examples in this sense: the influence of emotions on cognition to achieve goals that are important for survival and reproduction; or the "sour grapes" effect when

> the logically unfounded belief that grapes are not any good because they cannot be reached may simply be the product of an effective proximate mechanism (i.e., emotional biases in specific contexts) that ultimately serves to discourage the pursuit of goals in situations where contextual cues indicate that goal achievement is unlikely.
>
> *Nordli and Todd, p. 319*

If we consider the matter from an evolutionary perspective, this is an adaptive behaviour that reflects "an ecologically rational strategy for balancing the risks, rewards, and probabilities that characterize the environmental structure of contexts in which motivated reasoning occurs— even in complex modern environments" (Nordli and Todd, p. 319).

Kahneman and Tversky's prospect theory and the other heuristic and biases contributions claim to be a consequence of the BR approach in decision making. In fact, Herbert Simon has inspired two directions in the modelling of decision making. According to Thorsten Pachur (Chapter 20 in this volume), "the first is *prospect theory* ... and its subsequent elaboration and formal specification in *cumulative prospect theory* ...":

> They assume that people's sensitivity to differences in the outcomes and probabilities of risky options diminishes, the further away those magnitudes are from natural reference

points (such as zero, impossibility, or certainty) and that losses carry more psychological weight than gains. These notions are described algebraically with psycho-economic functions that translate objective magnitudes of outcomes and probabilities into subjective ones. CPT is typically considered as an "as-if" model, in the sense these functions are not meant to represent the actual cognitive processes underlying choices. The second modelling tradition rooted in bounded rationality, by contrast, has developed *heuristics*, that are intended as cognitive process models.

Pachur, p. 324

Is it possible and convenient to provide some form of integration between the two kinds of modelling? Pachur explains the pros and cons of this integration.

Herbert Simon was one of the founders of Artificial Intelligence. AI was born in 1956 at the Dartmouth Conference and the dominant model was the computational model of the mind. The mind was seen as the software of the brain and AI was meant to simulate the discoveries of cognitive sciences about mental activity. According to John McCarthy, Marvin Minsky and others at the Dartmouth Conference, the goal was to "make a machine that behaves in a way that would be considered intelligent if it was a human being". However, AI developed differently than the founders intended it to. Instead of simulating the cognitive features of the human mind, AI tried to replicate a simplified model of the brain. Neural networks and multi-layered neural networks are the dominant tools of machine learning and deep learning. Deep learning programs like AlphaGo, that are so successful in the game Go, are considered the prototypes of what AI will be in the future. This is controversial. These programs are clever in games characterized by risk and computational complexity. Real life, however, is characterized mainly by uncertainty, unpredictability, and surprises. If AI wants to simulate how human beings adapt to the uncertain environment it has to change its course. The right course might be:

1. To create a map of human heuristics that are ecologically rational in given tasks and environmental settings.
2. To incorporate heuristics in evolutionary computation techniques, which are stochastic algorithms whose search methods are modelled on genetic inheritance and Darwinian strife for survival.
3. To develop robots that mirror the structure of the human body not only at the perceptual or motor level, but also at the visceral and sensorial level.[7]

Özgür Şimşek (Chapter 21 in this volume) maintains a similar position:

It is unlikely that the performance gap between people and AI can be closed by advances in computational speed only. Just like people and animals, our machines will need to learn how to be boundedly rational, in other words, how to achieve their objectives when time, computational resources, and information are limited. Models of bounded rationality ..... provide fertile ground for developing algorithmic ideas for creating such AI systems.

Şimşek, p. 339

Her chapter provides an overview of some of this research and discuss its implications for AI: "The discussion will start with one-shot comparison problems and two families of simple heuristics ... that can be used in that context: tallying and lexicographic decision rules"

(Şimşek, p. 339). She describes how these heuristics perfectly match certain characteristics of natural environments that allow them to make accurate decisions using relatively small amounts of information and computation, and how this knowledge can be applied in the context of sequential decision problems, of which the game of Go is an example, to reduce the branching factor in a simple and transparent manner.

Finally, another aspect of the ecological dimension of rationality is found in the analysis of psychopathological disorders in reasoning and decision making. According to Riccardo Viale (Chapter 22 in this volume):

> Over the years, the evaluation of what is considered reason and the equation "normality equals rationality" seems to have undergone a paradoxical change. Initially, the rationalist legacy of the eighteenth-century Enlightenment resulted in a very clear separation of reason from madness. The madman was characterized by a failure of deductive and inductive logical thinking. In the 1950s, however, this distinction disappeared when cognitive science brought to light a whole series of supposed failures of rational behaviour in the normal individual as well. What dealt a serious blow to the theories of human decision-making and judgement formation was the fact that, quite surprisingly, several reasoning flaws that had been attributed solely to the psychiatric patient were, in fact, also found in the normal individual. Over the past few years, the theory that started with the Enlightenment seems to have reversed in a circular way. If we consider rationality as based on the logical coherence adopted in economic theory, then rationality is more apparent in individuals suffering from certain neurological and psychiatric disorders than among people without a disease. Paradoxically, normality seems characterized by irrationality, and abnormality by rationality.
>
> *Viale, p. 353*

But what characterizes abnormality? Normal individuals are characterized by limitations of logical rationality, which do not make them impeccable logicians, statisticians and maximizers, but that allow them to successfully adapt to the environment to solve problems and to learn from their mistakes. From this standpoint, a behaviour can be defined as pathological. This is not because it deviates from normative standards, but because it is unable to successfully interact with the social and physical environment, in other words, to have cognitive success. The irrationality of the mental disorder is such that it differs from bounded ecological rationality because it would not allow some of the following adaptive cognitive functions (depending on the mental disorder):

1. Learning from mistakes, environmental feedbacks, in particular, advice coming from the social context.
2. Using social imitation heuristics, such as that of successful people or of the crowd that allow the individual to speed up the decision-making processes and to find solutions that are readily available to be used.
3. Realistically representing the terms of a problem in the context of a decision, without affective or emotional hyperpolarization only on some salient variables and not on others that are more relevant for the decision.
4. Having a correct non-distorted perception of spatial and temporal coordinates in the context of a decision.
5. Anticipating at the corporal level the affective effects of a future choice in a way that corresponds to the reality of the phenomenon not in a distorted or dissociated way.

According to Viale:

> Any rigidity and impermeability to the signals from the environment and the lack of a realistic representation of the variables at work do not allow adequate fitness of the structure of a decisional task to allow us to be successful in our choices. It is therefore from an ecological point of view rather than from a normative one that we can consider a behaviour irrational in the context of some mental disorders.
>
> *p. 361*

Part IV Embodied bounded rationality

Bounded rationality in human reasoning, judgement and decision making mainly results from the adaptive evolution of our central nervous system. The way in which the brain and the subcortical structures have developed provides the foundation of the features that characterize the relation between mind and environment. It is, however, not enough to refer to the brain to explain cognitive activity and decision making. As will be illustrated later, in the past few years, growing importance has been attached to other parts of the body as well, such as the peripheral nervous system, the motor apparatus, the endocrine system, the cardiovascular, respiratory and digestive systems. In interacting with the environment, decision making cannot be fully grasped without analysing the bodily parts that allow us to interact and to physically put in place our decisions. From this perspective, it is possible to talk about embodied cognition applied to decision making, or, in other words, embodied bounded rationality. The metaphor of the scissors must therefore be integrated to add one missing element. The two blades cannot function unless they are coordinated by something else: the pivot, that is the body that allows cognition to interact with the environment.

According to Vittorio Gallese, Antonio Matrogiacomo, Enrico Petracca and Riccardo Viale (Chapter 23 in this volume):

> The idea that cognition is embodied is evidenced by a number of experiments connecting body states to judgement, decision making, problem solving, attitude formation, etc. Experimental evidence shows that body variables decisively direct and affect decision making ... Further, problem solving is non-trivially dependent on body correlates such as, for instance, eye movement ... Other various experimental evidence shows that people judge steepness depending on the weight of their backpacks ... that environmental temperature affects social attitudes ... that imagined food consumption makes people satiated ... or that physical weight induces the perception of importance.
>
> *Gallese et al., p. 378–379*

Embodied cognition can help us to reconsider such a fundamental notion in bounded rationality as heuristics. Ecological rationality and the functioning of simple heuristics, in particular, would greatly benefit from inputs from neurobiological and embodied cognition studies. In fact, something is changing among ecological rationality scholars, in particular with reference to deeper analysis of the neurobiological dimension of heuristics decision making. According to Nordli and Todd (Chapter 19 in this volume), neurophysiological studies could promote a new theoretical framework for ecological rationality. For instance, those studies may contribute to understanding strategy selection in decision making, where strategy selection means the selection of a given heuristic for a particular context. The selection is successful when the selected heuristic matches the structure of a given situation. That may happen by developing a mapping between context structure and the appropriate heuristics to use. The mapping may be generated by a "strategy selection learning" procedure. According Nordli and Todd, the reinforcement learning-based mechanism of strategy selection "is consistent with accounts that tie reinforcement learning processes to the recurrent cortico-basal circuit which is the very same circuitry that is critical to the exploitation of past behavior in the form of habits and fixed action patterns" (p. 320). In particular, the basal ganglia seem to lie behind most ecologically rational behaviour. Basal ganglia seem to evaluate context and select actions based on either motor or cognitive past behaviour. This neural mechanism allows the strategy selection of adaptive heuristics based on evaluation of past behaviour.

Christopher Cherniak (Chapter 24 in this volume) analyses an interesting dimension of the boundedness of rationality in connection with brain activity. According to him. the most fundamental psychological law is that we are finite beings. The classical paradoxes of semantics and set theory "can be reexamined not as odd pathology, but instead as indications of use of 'quick and dirty heuristics'—that is, the ultimate speed-reliability tradeoffs of correctness and completeness for feasibility" (Cherniak, p. 391). Cherniak introduces an interesting parallel between psychological boundedness and neural boundedness, between rationality and brainwiring hardware. In the first case, as well as in the second, the limitation of neural resources has generated strong evolutionary pressure to employ them efficiently. He writes: "Much of higher central nervous systems operates at signal propagation velocities below the 60 mph speed limit. Since connectivity is in limited supply, network optimization is quite valuable" (p. 392). And he adds: "Connection minimization seems a first law of brain tractography, an organizing principle driving neuroanatomy ... with hitherto unreported precision" (p. 392). Thus, according to Cherniak:

> "Save wire" turns out to be a strongly predictive "best in a billion" model. Wiring minimization can be detected at multiple levels, e.g., placement of the entire brain, layout of its ganglia and/or cortex areas, subcellular architecture of dendrite arbors, etc. Much of this biological structure appears to arise for free, directly from physics.
>
> *p. 392*

A wire-saving Adjacency Heuristic may be applied to the placement of interconnected functional areas of cerebral cortex: "If components are connected, then they are placed adjacent to each other" (p. 393). Cherniak wonders how the intentional level of mind meshes with the hardware level of brain. "Prima facie, that relationship appears in tension: In some aspects, the brainwiring appears virtually perfectly optimized, yet the rationality has layers of impossibility between it and perfection ..." (p. 394). Cherniak may be right in assessing the distance of rationality from perfection if he considers environments as Savage's *small worlds* – e.g., dice games, roulette, and so on – where optimal results may be achieved. The possibility of optimal rationality is evident since the probability of the outcomes is cognizable. But in the *large worlds* – the real world of society, climate, finance, politics, and so on – the uncertainty, complexity and unpredictability of future events do not allow us to evaluate the distance of our rationality from perfection. This is because there is no possible perfection at all. In these worlds, as in the world of constrained neural resources, frugality and simplicity are the heuristic tools to pursue optimality, that is to say better adaptive fitting.

Which features of the brain can contribute to explaining bounded rationality? Paul Thagard writes (Chapter 25 in this volume):

Human brains have numerous strengths that have enabled people to spread all over the planet and increase in population to more than 7 billion. The most impressive features of human brains are not the special-purpose adaptations touted by evolutionary psychologists, but rather the general adaptability furnished by the flexible ways in which humans can learn from experience ... Nevertheless, the brain has numerous limitations that forestall optimal rationality. Our brain's assemblage of 86 billion neurons provides a lot of computing power, but elephants have three times as many. In order to have more neurons, people would need to have bigger brains that require bigger heads, but childbirth is already often a difficult procedure. Human brain size reflects a trade-off between the benefits of more processing power and ease of delivery through a pelvis that also must function for bipedal locomotion. Another constraint on human brain size concerns energy. Even though the roughly 1.4 kg of the human brain take up less than 3 percent of the average human weight, the brain uses up to 20 percent of the energy available to the body. Larger brains would require more energy, which either requires less energy available for other functions such as metabolism and reproduction, or greater sources of food. The evolution of human brains requires a trade-off between size and energy efficiency, as well as between size and birth delivery.

Thagard, p. 400–401

The size of the brain and the limited amount of information that people can store are accompanied by another weakness in its computational power. Thagard writes:

Human brains also come with limitations in speed of processing. Billions of neurons allow for massively parallel operation, but the neurons themselves are slow. A typical neuron fires up to 200 times per second, whereas current computers have operations at the rate of trillions of times per second. Why are neurons so slow? Most neural connections are chemical, requiring the movement of neurotransmitters such as glutamate and GABA from one neuron to another. This chemical transmission is slower than purely electrical signalling, which occurs rarely in brains, but it allows for flexibility in timing and the development of different kinds of pathways.

p. 401

And he adds:

If brains were faster, they would still not be able to do an infinite amount of processing, but they would be able to better approximate some of the standards required for the rational norms of deductive logic and probability and utility theory. The brain lacks the speed to be able to do all of the calculations that are acquired for absolute standards of rationality.

p. 401

Nevertheless, the brain can perform computations that are important for the survival and reproduction of organisms:

Perception, inference, and decision-making can all be modelled as processes of parallel constraint satisfaction, in which a brain or computer considers a range of possible interpretations of a conflict situation and comes up with a good but not necessarily optimal solution … For example, recognizing a moving object as an instance of prey or predator should consider alternative hypotheses about the animal, constrained by perceptual and environmental information. Parallel constraint satisfaction is efficiently computed by neural networks that implement constraints by excitatory and inhibitory links …

Thagard, p. 402

Another important feature of the brain influencing decision-making processes and lying at the heart of bounded rationality is the integration of cognition and emotion. This integration occurs between high-level areas, such as the prefrontal cortex, and the emotional systems, such as the limbic system consisting of primitive areas such as the amygdala. This interconnection interferes with the requests of decision-making rationality. For example, according to expected utility theory, probability and utility must be first calculated independently and then combined at a mathematical level. The profound integration in the brain between the cognitive and emotional centres does not allow for this separation. As Thagard maintains, utility operates on the estimation of probability and probability operates on the estimation of utility: "The brain has no firewall between cognition and emotion, so it is not surprising that people often adopt beliefs that they find emotionally appealing, in domains that range from politics to relationships" (Thagard, p. 403). A case in point concerns time discounting. People have a tendency to go for short-term small gains in neglect of long-term large gains. This is because the decision on what to do immediately stimulates areas of the ventral striatum and orbitofrontal cortex connected to the emotional sphere, while long-term evaluations occur through computations that take place in the prefrontal cortex and parietal areas that do not have strong emotional implications. Hence the integration of cognition and emotion in the brain contributes as much as size and speed limitations to the boundedness of rationality. The neural constraints of information processing prevent us from satisfying the desires of formal rationality, but appear to have an adaptive function when faced with complex and uncertain environments and scenarios. Since we have to decide mainly about an epistemic or ontological uncertain reality, no optimization based on knowledge of the options and their probability can work. Thus, some failures and biases are not really failures and biases but they are rather the only possible heuristic way to cope with uncertainty. The same limitation of attention processes connected to Miller's magic number for working memory can be viewed from an adaptive perspective. It may be an adaptive constraint to cope with uncertainty and to decide in a fast, unaware, intuitive way when faced with potential but uncertain danger rather than losing time in slow, analytic and aware thinking and decision making. Therefore, what seems to be human failures to follow normative principles (introduced only recently in the history of humankind) is, on the contrary, an adaptive and ecological rational feature and not a defect of the mind-brain.

The flexible and dynamic adaptability of the brain in various decisional contexts is highlighted also by Colin McCubbins, Mathew McCubbins and Mark Turner (Chapter 26 in this volume). They note that a number of recent discoveries provide an overview of the neural bases of decision making that differs significantly from the picture painted by neuro-computation theory in the past. The salient features of bounded rationality are explained by the way the brain functions. This is particularly true for the dynamic instability of self-expression or, in other words, constantly evolving preferences and beliefs due to experience and learning, depending on emotional and external changes. In particular,

Cognitive neuroscientists have proposed that the human brain is constantly scanning over a range of often-conflicting alternatives and collapsing that range to an action only in the moment of decision … Consider someone who wants to pick up a coffee cup. There are many ways to do so successfully. The brain may explore many of those approaches simultaneously. The neurobiological basis of action can be varied, with simultaneous but conflicting lines, each with some probability of being given, at the final instant, control over skeletal and motor programs. One of those possibilities will precipitate in the moment of action. Our enacting only one action suite does not mean that the brain was exclusively focused on that one suite; it means only that, in the moment of action, one coherent action was executed, as others were forsaken.

McCubbins et al., p. 415

Part V *Homo Oeconomicus Bundatus*

The history of economic thought shows that there was an inverse relationship between the articulated and empirical development of the economic agent's theory of mind and the attribution of rational capacity to the said agent. The greater the demand for rationality, the less the agent's psychological characterization was developed. As the previous examples show, the maximum rational capacity now required by contemporary neoclassical economics (satisfaction of the computational requisites of Bayesian decision theory) means that the agent has minimal psychological content. Instead, the opposite occurs in Hayekian subjectivism. This inverse proportionality appears to be a natural consequence of the relationship between reason and mind. Gifts of unlimited reasoning, like those ascribed to the neoclassical economic agent, are not combined with the empirical representation of a mind characterized by cognitive limits and weaknesses. The unlimited reason attributed, *a priori*, to the economic agent compresses and suffocates any space for human psychological expression. This dualism between reason and mind is not a novelty, but instead has deep, philosophical roots. It is linked to a precise tradition that can be seen as the progenitor of the model of rationality that was in vogue in economic science for two centuries (Viale, 2012). The theory of rationality inherited by the tradition that spans from Heraclitus, Parmenides, Plato and Aristotle to St Augustine, Descartes, Spinoza, Leibniz and the Enlightenment and which underlies the theory of economic action in the nineteenth century is therefore characterized by unlimited, *a priori* and linguistic-intentionalist attributes. Its supposed descriptive property is based on the *a priori* presumption of the universal rationality of the human species and not on the *a posteriori* justification of people's real rational capacities. Neoclassical economics and the model of rationality contained in von Neumann and Morgenstern's game theory are the realization of this ideal (well represented by Laplace's metaphor of the demon endowed with unlimited computational rationality).

Gerd Gigerenzer (Chapter 2 in this volume) outlines three competitive alternatives that have been using the concept of BR. Ariel Rubinstein (Chapter 27 in this volume) seems to propose a fourth one. He starts with a definition of economic theory:

Economic Theory is a collection of stories, usually expressed in formal language, about human interactions that involve joint and conflicting interests. Economic Theory is not meant to provide predictions of the future. At most, it can clarify concepts and provide non-exclusive explanations of economic phenomena. In many respects, a model in Economic Theory is no different than a story. Both a story and a model are linked to reality in an associative manner. Both the storyteller and the economic theorist have in mind a real-life situation but do not consider the story or the model to be a full description of reality. Both leave it to the reader to draw their own conclusions, if any.

Rubinstein, p. 423

There is no room for a realist methodology to establish an empirically-based microeconomics. This conceptual and analytical position[8] is reflected in the concept of BR: "Models of Bounded Rationality are for me .... models that include explicit references to procedural aspects of decision making, which are crucial for the derivation of the analytical results" (p. 423). Procedural aspects do not refer to the same phenomena here as they do for Simon and Gigerenzer. They are not derived experimentally by behavioural and cognitive studies on problem-solving and decision making. They are, on the contrary, introduced as in Millian methodology by qualitative observation, intuition and analytical deduction: "A good model of bounded rationality should include a procedure of reasoning that 'makes sense' and is somewhat related to what we observe in real life" (Rubinstein, p. 423). What Rubinstein and Gigerenzer have in common is a lack of interest in the inconsistency of the model with respect to the normative aspects of rationality (as in the heuristics and biases approach) and prefer instead to analyse the procedural aspects of behaviour: "A model in which rational agents ignore some aspect of rationality is a bad model rather than a model of bounded rationality" (Rubinstein, p. 423).

Rubinstein's is the fourth model of BR together with optimization under constraints, heuristics and biases and ecological rationality. It is the model less anchored to empirical data coming from the cognitive sciences. Are the first two models useful to develop BR? According to Clement Tisdell (Chapter 28 in this volume) and, contrary to Gigerenzer, they are:

> However, it can be argued that the first set of models are relevant to the study of bounded rationality. They highlight limits to the neoclassical vision of unrestricted rationality. While their knowledge and rationality assumptions are still too strong, they can help to identify factors that ought to influence behaviors under conditions of restricted rationality. As for the second class of models (which include behavioral ones), most (but not all) identify limits to perceptions of states of nature and common faults in reasoning, both of which can be considered to be a consequence of bounded rationality. These classes of models (mostly behavioral economic ones) do demonstrate some of the limits to unrestricted rationality.
>
> *Tisdell, p. 443*

The analytical and conceptual approach to economic theory of Rubinstein is also common to a great part of mainstream economics. Shabnam Mousavi and Nicolaus Tideman (Chapter 29 in this volume) write: "the paradigm of mainstream economics is a coherent one built logically on a *substantive* notion of rationality, with expected utility theory as its crowning achievement" (p. 448). And they quote Gary Becker (1962): "Now, everyone more or less agrees that rational behavior simply implies consistent maximization of a well-ordered function, such as utility or profit." And they add:

> In this framework, an actor seeks the best or optimal outcome, and specifying the criteria for its existence and (preferably) uniqueness occupies theorists and modellers, who rely mainly on deductive methods. Issues of how to collect data to test the theory, or building models to achieve concrete real-world goals are usually not of primary concern. The search for information is also assumed to be optimal. That is, the rational agent uses an optimal stopping rule, continuing to calculate marginal

costs and marginal benefits of further search, and stops when they are equal. This is acknowledged to be an artificial search process, with no claim to represent the actual search process. Understanding reality is thus pursued through "stylized facts" instead of through observation.

Mousavi and Tideman, p. 448

This as-if approach that pretends to transform economics in a scientific discipline is rooted in how physics was developed in the twentieth century.

In Viale (1997, pp. 18–21; 2012, pp. 179–181), I analyse the philosophy of science followed by neoclassical economics:

The model is clearly based on Newtonian mechanics but it carries two serious drawbacks. As Rosenberg pointed out (1983, reprinted in Hausman, 1994, pp. 378–380), since the nineteenth century, economists have been elaborating a theory whose form is identical to the great theoretical breakthroughs made in science from the sixteenth century onwards. The strategy is to view the behaviour economists seek to explain as reflecting forces that always move towards a stable equilibrium, which maximizes or minimizes some theoretically crucial variable. In the case of microeconomics, this crucial variable is utility (or its latter-day surrogates) and the equilibrium is provided by a level of price across all markets that maximizes this variable. This strategy is most impressively exemplified in Newtonian mechanics and in the Darwinian theory of natural selection. In Newtonian mechanics, the system's behaviour always minimizes or maximizes variables that reflect the state of the system which is mechanically possible, while in Darwinian theory, it is the environment that maximizes the fitness of individuals of a species. This strategy is crucial to the success of these theories because of the way it directs and shapes the research. If we believe that a system always acts to maximize the value of a mechanical variable – for example, total energy – and our measurement of the observable values of that variable diverges from the predictions of the theory and the initial conditions, we do not infer that the system described is failing to maximize the value of the variable in question. We do not falsify the theory, but we assume that we have incompletely described the constraints under which the system is actually operating. The axioms of these theories do not embody even implicit *ceteris paribus* clauses. With these theories, the choice is always between rejecting the auxiliary hypotheses and test conditions or rejecting the theory altogether. Hence, the only change that can be made to the theory is to deny that its subjects invariably maximize or minimize its chosen variable.

In Newtonian mechanics, attempts to describe the systems under study more completely resulted in the discovery of new planets and new laws, like those of thermodynamics. In biology, the assumption that fitness is maximized led to the discovery of forces not previously recognized to affect genetic variation within a population and led to the discovery of genetic laws that explain the persistence in a population of apparently non-adaptive traits, like sickle-cell anaemia. But what about microeconomics? The success of this strategy in other disciplines may justify the attempts made by economists to make recalcitrant facts about human behaviour and the economic systems humans have constructed fit the economic theory. Moreover, this strategy allows the use of many powerful formal tools, such as differential calculus, topology and differential geometry. But many years of work in the same direction have produced nothing comparable to the physicists' discovery of new planets or new technologies, or the biological understanding of the mechanism of adaptation and heredity. Therefore, it is time to question the merit of applying this approach to economics, since it carries all the disadvantages of empirical non-falsifiability without the advantages of the discovery of novel facts and applications.

There is also another general reason "not to ape physics" that stems from a recent philosophical debate in physics compared with the other sciences. In contemporary physics, there is a trade-off between explanatory power and factual content. As pointed out by Cartwright (1983, pp. 135–139), fundamental laws like Maxwell's equations or Schroedinger's equations have great explanatory power but do not describe the true facts about reality. The aim of these equations is to cover a wide variety of different phenomena with a small number of principles. If the fundamental laws set out to fit reality into the highly constrained structures of their mathematical formulae, they will have to distort the true picture of what happens. Quantum mechanics is a good example.[9] In fact, the explanatory power of quantum theory comes from its ability to deploy a small number of well-understood Hamiltonians to cover a wide range of cases. But this explanatory power has its price. By limiting the number of Hamiltonians (that is the mathematical representation of the kinetic and potential energies of the real system), we set constraints on our ability to represent situations realistically and we lose the true representation of the system. In physics, if we want to have a realistic representation of the phenomena, we must abandon the fundamental laws and look at the phenomenological laws like those of Galileo, Ohm or Kepler. Fundamental laws usually explain phenomenological laws not in a deductive way, as was asserted until recently – think of the Hempel-Popperian deductive nomological model – but using a model which fits the phenomenon into the theory (Cartwright, 1983, pp. 131–134). This picture of science fits Friedman's "as-if" instrumentalist methodology well: the theory is only a fictitious deductive machine to produce explanations and predictions. This model of science seems to work only for the fundamental laws of physics. If we climb up the levels of aggregation of reality, we find that already at the level of biology we are not able to find explanatory structures based on the three components – theory, model, facts – that are present in physics. Instead we find phenomenological laws with many exceptions that aim to describe complex phenomena. The same consideration applies *a fortiori* to the explanation of human behaviour. The great complexity and variability of behavioural phenomena preclude the discovery of genuine general phenomenological laws relating to particular domains of psychological reality. This absence does not allow any serious unifying mathematical abstraction, comparable to that of the fundamental laws in physics, which has the power to explain reality at the phenomenological level. The moral is that instead of "putting the cart before the horse", or in other words playing the game of the theoretical physicists and trying to elaborate fictitious, but useless, theoretical formal models of human decision-making, it would be wiser to study, patiently, the empirical phenomenology of human decision making and to try to elaborate some useful, and genuine, empirical laws that are valid, locally and contextually, for a small fragment of human reality.

Mousavi and Tideman (Chapter 29 in this volume) emphasize this point when they refer to the economists' detachment from observed behaviour as a serious flaw in their methodology. In this sense they quote an interview of Simon in *Challenge* (1986, pp. 22–23):

They [economists] don't talk about evidence at all. You read the pages where Lucas talks about why businessmen can't figure out what's happened to prices and it is just what he feels as he sits there smoking his cigarettes in his *armchair*. I don't know what Keynes smoked, but when you look at the pages where he talks about labor's money illusion, no evidence is cited. So the real differences in economics, as compared with psychology, is that almost everybody operates within the theoretical logic of utility-maximization in the neoclassical model.

When economists want to explain particular phenomena in the real world, they have to introduce new assumptions. The distinctive change in the behaviour of the economic actors comes from a change in the behavioural assumptions. No empirical evidence is given to support those changes. They emerge from the mind of the economic theorist sitting in his *armchair*.

Mousavi and Tideman, p. 449

Another contribution against armchair economics and in favour of the empirical foundation of economic theory and research on the agents' cognitive features comes from the analysis by Ignazio Visco and Giordano Zevi (Chapter 30 in this volume) on the weaknesses of rational expectations theory. They consider some of the links between concepts of bounded rationality and the approaches followed by economists in their analysis of the role played by economic agents' expectations in driving the evolution of the economy through time. Visco and Zevi write:

Indeed, the relevance of expectations has been repeatedly underlined in macroeconomic theory and policy making. However, the economists' degree of attention on how they are actually formed and on how they interact with the economic observables has followed high and low cycles. In recent years, the increasing availability of survey data and the failings of models based on purely rational representative agents have prompted renewed interest in inquiries into the direct measurement of expectations and empirical studies of their formation.

p. 465

Robert Lucas introduced analytically the theory of rational expectations without caring about the empirical dimension of decision making. Aside from the bounded rationality features of economic agents, there are also other empirical data to consider. For example, learning implies that a rational expectations equilibrium is only one of the possible outcomes when agents continuously update their expectations based on the comparison between past expectations and actual realizations. Uncertainty limits the possibility of rational expectations because it does not allow for any form of rational prediction. Visco and Zevi write:

In line with Simon's 1955 seminal contribution, later developed with March, agents use expectations based on simple heuristics as a device to willingly ignore part of the available information in order to reach local optima which, in this particular setting, beat the outcomes of fully rational choices. This strategy proves to be superior to more sophisticated ways of forming expectations, grounded for example in recursive least squares as in mainstream learning literature, due to the highly unstable and uncertain, in the Knightian sense, environment.

p. 465

What should be done in uncertain environments? Is it better to collect as much information as possible to reduce uncertainty or, on the contrary, is it preferable to end a costly and useless data collection that has no chance of increasing our knowledge of the phenomena?[10] The more-is-more principle has been a central dogma of Bayesian rationality in dealing with uncertain environments. Gregory Wheeler (Chapter 31 in this volume) writes:

> Lore has it that a fundamental principle of Bayesian rationality is for decision makers to never turn down the offer of free information. Cost-free information can only help you, never hurt you, and in the worst case will leave you at status quo ante. Purported exceptions to this principle are no exceptions at all, but instead involve a hidden cost to learning. Make those costs plain and the problem you face is one of balancing the quality of a choice against the costs to you of carrying it out, a trade-off that Bayesian methods are ideally suited to solve.
>
> *p. 471*

The implications of this principle in economic thinking are evident: a delay may occur in making the final decision if there is the opportunity to acquire some information (for example, from an experiment) relevant to the decision. According to Wheeler, in situations of Knightian uncertainty when a probability assessment does not improve after learning the outcome of an experiment, "the commonplace that 'knowledge is not disadvantageous' is false, even when the cost of obtaining the information is zero" (p. 474).

BR is recognized as an important feature by many heterodox approaches in economics. One is the new Schumpeterian programme of evolutionary economics. According to Richard Nelson (Chapter 32 in this volume), there are at least three BR factors that are fundamental for evolutionary economists: (1) it is important to distinguish between choice contexts which are familiar to the economic actor and who responds to them more or less automatically, and contexts that induce the actor to engage in serious contemplation of alternatives; (2) it is important to recognize that actors differ in the capabilities that they bring to various choice contexts; and (3) it is important to relate the perceptions of individual actors about the contexts they face, the courses of action that they understand and are competent to employ, and their judgements about which of these actions are appropriate and likely to be effective, to the beliefs and understandings and know-how of the broader community of which the actor is a part. An important feature that connects evolutionary economics to ecological rationality is the function of routines. In stable environments when actors have time to learn the kind of actions that work, they tend to perform these actions automatically. There are routines that work in an organization as well as in consumer behaviour. For example, pricing routines for household shopping and firms are mostly automatic. Nelson writes:

> Viable routines generally have a reasonable amount of flexibility built into them to enable them to adjust to the kind of variable circumstances that are to be expected in the broad context where they are operative. Household shopping routines need to be sensitive to what is and is not available at the store, and to some degree to prices. Firm pricing routines need to take costs into account. But my argument is that in established shopping routines these adjustments generally are made relatively routinely. There may be some conscious consideration of alternatives, but so long as the context remains in the normal range, wide search and intensive deliberation are highly unlikely. Similarly, the pricing routines of firms almost always are sensitive to costs,

with much of that sensitivity, if not necessarily all, built into a formula used relatively routinely.

p. 487

He proposes a decision-making model that is very close to ecological rationality. And in fact he uses the term "adaptively responsive" to denote the sensitivity of routines to broadly experienced and thus anticipated variation in the details of the context that invokes their use.

The evolutionary economics approach is very sympathetic to BR. Since its focus is on innovation, technical change, dynamics and uncertain environments, it has always criticized the normative static dimension of economic rationality. Like Richard Nelson, Giovanni Dosi, Marco Faillo and Luigi Marengo (Chapter 33 in this volume) take a step forward in criticizing the "enchanted" BR of behavioural economists like Kahneman and Tversky. They conclude:

> A multi-millennial tradition of Western thought has asked "How do people behave?" and "How do social organizations behave?", from Aristotle to St Augustin, Hume, Adam Smith, Kant, to name just a few giants. However, modern economics – and, more recently, social sciences colonized by modern economics – have taken up the answer by one of the shallowest thinkers, Bentham: people decide their courses of action by making calculations on the expected pleasures and pains associated with them. And, indeed, this *Weltanschauung* has spread all the way to the economics of marriage, of child bearing, of church going, of torture ... Our argument is that the Benthamian view is misleading or plainly wrong concerning the motivations, decision processes and nature of the actions. First, the drivers of human motivation are many more than one. As Adam Smith masterly argues in his *Theory of Moral Sentiments*, utility (what he called "prudence") is just one of them, and in a lot of social contexts, not the most important one. Second, the decision processes are very rarely explicit calculations and comparisons of outcomes. Third, the ensuing decisions very seldom look like a "rational" ("as...if") outcome of the foregoing decision processes, *even when the latter would be possible to calculate.* And in the real word, complex and evolving as it is, they rarely are. In such circumstances, we suggest, a positive theory of individual and collective behaviours has to entirely dispose of the max U(...,..., ...) apparatus, either as an actual descriptive device, and as a yardstick, whatever that means. If we are right, then also relaxations of the paradigms involving varying degrees of "bounded rationality" in the decision process and an enlargement of the arguments in the utility function (e.g. adding "intrinsic motivations", or even "altruism") are quite misleading. They are a bit like adding epicycles over epicycles in a Ptolemaic astronomy. The radical alternative we advocate is an anthropology of a *homo heuristicus* ...., socially embedded, imperfectly learning in a complex evolving environment, and with multiple drivers of his actions.

p. 501

Part VI Cognitive organization

Herbert Simon introduces the conceptual premises of BR in his PhD thesis in political science. *Administrative Behaviour* (1945) is the book based on his PhD thesis that started a new chapter in the theory of organization, management, public administration and policy. BR is a fundamental concept that explains how individual decision making gives rise to organizations and how institutions constrain individual decisions. In particular, it is evident that, in public administration and policy making, the complexity of choices and the overload of information are the determinants of the organizational and institutional changes that aim to adapt to the environment through specialization and differentiation. How does an organization adapt to the external environment? Through an internal differentiation of tasks similar to the problem-solving models that envisage breaking down problems into sub-problems. Massimo Egidi and Giacomo Sillari (Chapter 34 in this volume) write:

> Simon identified the main characteristics of *managerial decision making* by analysing the structure of the organizational process. He recognized that the core of every organization is the pattern of division of tasks and their coordination. The organization is thought of as a goal-oriented structure based on internal tasks that must be coordinated in order to achieve the organization's overall objectives. Behavior within organizations is thus goal-oriented, and goals are by and large complex and hierarchically structured, as many intermediate sub-goals need to be realized, often in a specific order, for the final goal to be achieved. The dynamics of organizational decision-making may therefore be very complex, presenting two main aspects. First, goals are often defined in very general and ambiguous terms, thus necessitating continuous revising of the sub-goals' hierarchy. Second, hidden conflicting objectives can be unearthed during various organizational decisions, and this may, again, make it necessary to revise both sub-goals and their hierarch.
>
> *p. 509–510*

How do organizational structure and problem solving relate to bounded rationality? Egidi and Sillari write:

> Indeed, in 1956, Cyert, Simon and Trow carried out an empirical analysis of managerial decision contexts that highlighted how search and learning were at the core of human rationality. The study revealed an evident "dualism" of behavior: on the one hand, there is behavior guided by a coherent choice among alternatives typical of structured and repetitive conditions; on the other, behavior characterized by highly uncertain and ill-defined conditions, where the predominant role was played by problem-solving activities. The dualism between repetitive and well-known decision contexts and ill-defined decision contexts proved to be a key distinction for our understanding of decision processes. In situations of the former kind, it highlights the process of decision-making routinization. In the latter, the necessary conditions for applying standard rational choice theory are lacking, and the most important decision process is the ability of the subjects to formulate and solve problems. This suggests that the real restrictions on rational decisions happen during the process of construction of the context of the decision. The notion of bounded rationality refers mostly to these conditions, and hence it is implicitly intertwined with the notion of problem solving.
>
> *p. 511–512*

One of the features of bounded rationality in organization is attention. From different points of view, an organization can be regarded as the answer to the limits and the constraints of human attention processes. The organization's hierarchical structure, communication channels, agenda of priorities and performance evaluation can be viewed as a recursive product of selective attention. As is known, attention is linked to the limits of executive memory and to the related computational processes that can only focus on limited information at a time. Inga Jonaitye and Massimo Warglien (Chapter 35 in this volume) write:

> The allocation of attention is commonly seen as a fundamental problem for organizations … Developing Barnard's … intuition that "narrowing choice" is a central function of executive decisions, Simon … early on identified the process of directing and channeling managers' attention as a key function of organizations … The foundations for such perspectives rely on the central role that limited attention provides in defining bounded rationality … The "limits" of decision-making rationality are to a large extent the results of the attentional bottleneck …
>
> *p. 522*

For Simon, March and Cyert, decisional constraints and the division of tasks create a close connection between attention and organizational sub-goals. Since individuals cannot pay attention to all the organizational problems in parallel, there is a need for an internal organization of attention allocating each problem or part thereof to different individuals, for the purpose, however, of ultimate coordination. Two interesting organizational models explicitly refer to attention. Jonaitye and Warglien write:

> The garbage can model … explores its coordination implications in non-routine decision making. Taking a radical departure from traditional models of organizational decision making, the garbage can model explores "organized anarchies" in which preferences are problematic, technologies are unclear, and participation is fluid … The second model was introduced by Ocasio … as the attention-based view of the firm (ABV). Ocasio describes organizations as systems of structurally distributed attention and defines attention as a cognitive process that encompasses the noticing, encoding, interpreting, and focusing of time and effort by organizational decision-makers on issues and answers.
>
> *p. 523–524*

No rational choice theory is able to explain or prescribe proper policy making and organizational development. On the contrary, bounded rationality emphasizes the adaptive modelling of successful organization and policy making that do not follow any optimal rules other than the recursive adaptation to the ever-changing and uncertain environment. Heuristic decision making seems the best way to cope with the goal of successful adaptation and ecological rationality. Torsten Reimer, Hayden Barber and Kirstin Dolick (Chapter 36 in this volume) exemplify the adaptive dimension of bounded rationality by a funny story about the Beatles:

> Like many teenage boys in Liverpool in 1960, John Lennon and Paul McCartney wanted to start a rock band. However, as their fledging band went from record company to record company with their manager Brian Epstein, it became clear: Britain was getting tired of rock and roll … On the other hand, America at that time had never seen anything like the Beatles. The Beatles received a very different reaction in the US than in Britain … It was not just the Beatles, but the pairing of the Beatles with a particular time and place that made their music so successful. The story of the Beatles points to an important aspect of the bounded rationality of groups and teams: The success or failure of a group cannot be understood without looking at the

environment in which the group is embedded. The same strategy and behavior may be successful in one environment but result in a failure in another environment.

p. 535

How can the role of adaptation be studied in group decision making? Group research that subscribes to the approach of bounded rationality focuses on the match between group strategies and characteristics of both the information and social environment. Historically, group research has often focused on group performance and productivity. The history of group research using outcome and performance measures is, by and large, a history of demonstrating group failure. This kind of result seems to be based on information environments that have been used in laboratory experiments. It may well turn out that several process losses that are described in the literature reflect group behaviors that are functional in many environments. It is the match in strategy and environment that leads to successful group outcomes. Reimer, Barber and Dolick presented research on hidden profiles that provides evidence for that claim.

The architecture of choice inside the organization is an old Simonian concept. Simon believed that organizations can place members in a psychological environment that will provide them with the information needed to make decisions correctly. Ian Belton and Mandeep Dhami (Chapter 37 in this volume) write: "organizations can establish standard working practices, train individuals, and structure the work environment so that it encourages rational thinking and consistency or regularization of practice" (p. 549). In their chapter, they evaluate the solutions that a particular kind of organization, the intelligence analysis organization, has offered to combat cognitive bias in their intelligence analysts. They identify the cognitive biases that may affect the practice of intelligence analysis and review debiasing strategies preferred by the intelligence community as opposed to those developed and tested by psychological research. However, they refer to mainstream behavioural economics and therefore do not differentiate between adaptive and non-adaptive heuristic decision making. In analysing the adaptive aspect of decision making, they have recognized that many biases are not really errors but the best possible ways to solve problems in uncertain environments such as the subject of intelligence analysis. For example, they quote fluency as a bias, whereas fluency is often an effective heuristic tool in uncertain environments such as international political situations. In any case,

> Psychologically informed and empirically tested debiasing interventions often focus on improving an individual's ability to identify tasks/situations where an intuitive response is likely to be biased, so that they can override their intuition with an appropriate deliberative strategy. Typically, interventions of this kind involve training or instruction that aim to increase understanding and awareness of cognitive biases. Other debiasing interventions aim to fill mindware gaps by teaching relevant rules (e.g., probability or logic), or specific strategies to use in a given task. Finally, some debiasing interventions involve restructuring the task environment to reduce biased behavior, either by encouraging more deliberative thinking or by inducing unbiased intuition.
>
> *Belton and Dhami, p. 553*

Part VII Behavioral public policies: nudging or boosting?

The architecture of choice is present in Herbert Simon's cognitive theory of organization. The same concept seems to inspire his political science analyses when he refers to the bounded rationality of government and citizens. In this sense, for Simon, bounded rationality and the foundation of behavioural economics may be considered the precursors of recent theories on the behavioural economics approach to public policy. In particular, Richard Thaler and Cass Sunstein (2008) have recently introduced a particular behavioural approach to public policy known as *nudge* or libertarian paternalism. A public policy intervention is classified as a nudge when it is not a coercive measure, retains freedom of choice, is based on automatic and reflex responses, does not involve methods of direct persuasion, does not significantly alter economic incentives, and revises the context of choice according to the discoveries of behavioural economics (Sunstein, Chapter 38 in this volume; Oliver, Chapter 39 in this volume). What is proposed is therefore a form of *libertarian paternalism* that has a dual valency. As *paternalism*, it aims to make up for citizens' irrational and self-harming tendencies by "gently nudging them" to decide rationally for their own good. In its *libertarian* form, it aims to give the last word to the outcome of the conscious and deliberative processes of the individual citizen who can always choose to resist the *nudge* (Sunstein, Chapter 38).

Thaler and Sunstein's thesis is that citizens are subject to many deviations of rationality that bring them to make a decision that is against their own interests. This widespread irrationality is provoked by the automatic judgement and decision-making behaviour enabled by heuristics. In this way, the individual is incapable of following a series of basic principles of rationality at a probabilistic and logical level. By doing so, he makes the wrong choice and goes against his own interests.[11] Thaler and Sunstein's theses derive in part from the programme of behavioural economics commenced in the post-war period by Herbert Simon and continued in the 1970s by Daniel Kahneman, Amos Tversky and their School. However, their approach is based on a controversial concept of *bounded rationality* focused only the study of the correspondence between judgement and decision-making performance in tests and laboratory simulations and canonical models of probabilistic and deductive rationality. It therefore highlights a constant and systematic irrational misalignment between behaviour and norm. The Behavioral Economics Nudge approach discounts a series of weaknesses in various analytical dimensions of an epistemic, epistemological, methodological and ethical nature (Viale, 2018). As is clear from the Simonian framework and from subsequent developments (Gigerenzer, Chapter 2 in this volume), there are some attributes of the concept of bounded rationality that contrast with the current approach of behavioural economics that inspired Nudge theory. This is not a rationality that is interested in questions of formal coherence, but rather in the question of ecological adaptation to the environment of choice and problem solving. It centres on the procedural and realistic attributes of rationality and not on instrumental and conventionalist ones. It recognizes that the complexity of the real environment of choice brings the player face to face with decisions in conditions of uncertainty (for example, "ill-structured problems" such as financial markets or political forecasting) rather than risk (for example, "well-structured problems", such as dice throwing or chess) (Viale, forthcoming).

The relation between bounded rationality and libertarian paternalism is controversial. For example, in Chapter 39, Adam Oliver writes:

> Underpinning libertarian paternalism is the assumption that of the many decisions that each of us make quickly and automatically each day – decisions that are guided by simple rules of thumb (i.e., the heuristics famously associated with Herbert Simon …) and influenced by various innate behavioural influences (e.g., present bias, loss aversion) – a few will lead us to act in ways that if we deliberated a little more, we would prefer not to do (e.g., present bias might lead us to eat more doughnuts than we would ideally consume if we thought about our decisions a little

more). It is noteworthy that these heuristics may have evolved because most of the time they guide us efficiently through our daily lives ... but the basic idea in libertarian paternalism is that with knowledge of the behavioural influences, the "choice architecture" (i.e., the context or environment) that people face can be redesigned such that their automatic choices are even more likely to better align with their deliberative preferences.

p. 571

Oliver's model of bounded rationality clearly emerges from the heuristics and biases tradition of Kahneman and Tversky. People are limited in their rationality and their biases may generate negative internalities. Therefore, libertarian paternalism should help to improve internalities. In his chapter, Oliver proposes to take this approach one step forward towards "a political economy of behavioural public policy that sits alongside the liberal economic tradition of John Stuart Mill, albeit being somewhat more interventionist than Mill would have allowed" (p. 570). In other words, he supports a view that focuses also on social negative externalities caused by biases, errors and free-riding behaviour. He proposes a view that aims to improve social externalities and not only internalities. The political economy of behavioural public policy proposed by Oliver "has two arms: to nurture reciprocity so as improve the stock of human flourishing, and to regulate against harm-inducing egoism to protect the capacity of people to flourish as they themselves see fit" (p. 576).

Nathan Berg (Chapter 40 in this volume) proposes a series of arguments that undermine the theoretical foundation and ethical and social consequences of nudge. For example, the important feature of diversity and heterogeneity – which is fundamental to generate knowledge, creativity, innovation, social change – is undermined by homogeneous goals of nudge policy making. Berg writes: "If populations respond to nudges as they are designed to and bring the population's profile of beliefs and behaviors into closer conformity, then multiple beneficial streams of belief and behavioral heterogeneity also risk being reduced" (p. 580). "There are risks and unintended consequences from policies that reduce heterogeneity, especially paternalistic policies motivated by the goal of 'correcting' alleged 'bias' with respect to prescribed beliefs and behaviors" (Berg, p. 580). Furthermore, why nudge people to correct their biases? The reasons behind this paternalistic policy-making programme are untenable. The propensity to violate the axioms of rationality in uncertain environments is not pathological but adaptive. The "behavioural law and economics" that justify the paternalistic aims of nudging are valid only in risky environments and not in uncertain ones. Berg writes:

> There is an alternative behavioral law and economics research program based instead on the insights of Herbert Simon. Well-performing individuals and organizations equip themselves to adapt to unstable and complex reward-generating environments by utilising decision processes that sometimes violate axiomatic logical consistency. When well-matched to the environment in which they are used, logically inconsistent decision processes—as well as beliefs and actions that deviate from economists' prescriptions—can be purposeful, in addition to providing both individual and external social benefits. Analogous to biodiversity, when heterogeneity of beliefs and decisions generates positive externalities, it should be considered a public good. The risk of encroaching on this heterogeneity (inadvertently inducing behavioral and belief monocultures) is worthwhile to consider in social-welfare analyses of nudging and other paternalistic policies.

p. 583

Decision making may be adaptive – that is, ecologically rational – if it generates a reward from the environment. Berg writes:

> One theme in the ecological rationality research program is to clearly define sets of reward-generating environments and performance metrics with respect to which a given decision process performs well. Another theme relevant to Simon-inspired behavioral law and economics is how law and regulation, in effect, can construct an environment where a heterogeneous ecology of decision rules employed by many different individuals can perform well, by an appropriately specified aggregation rule or social welfare function.
>
> *p. 581–582*

Finally, the impact of bounded rationality is found also in supporting "satisficing" policy making. Let us consider a society of "satisficers" vs. a society of "optimizers". The former requires less paternalistic and costly policies. Satisficers are free to decide without any coercive normative best choice canons. On the contrary, in the latter, behavioural economics concerns a society of optimizers who do not fall into bias errors and are nudged towards optimal rational choices. The implied paternalistic policy making is obviously much stronger and costly.[12]

Zachary McGee, Brooke Shannon and Bryan Jones (Chapter 41 in this volume) write that one of the first sets of scholars to implement bounded rationality as a microfoundation of political science were scholars studying public budgets. "Budgetary considerations are suitable subjects for exploring institutional decision making, since there is a clear budgetary process, mimicking the policy process itself" (McGee, Shannon and Jones, p. 602). Budget policy requires various decision-making phases: "In the pre-decision-making phase, even preceding agenda setting, elites identify problems and then are able to offer solutions. When problems are identified, they are placed on the agenda, and then solutions can begin to be sought and offered" (McGee, Shannon, and Jones, p. 603). Budgets are a consistent example of trade-offs and outputs characteristic of bounded rationality and the information-processing abilities of individuals and institutions.

> They inherently hold prioritization of issues and values, and reveal the capacity for attention in policy makers. The institutional constraint on policy makers in Washington for budgets is strong, as interest groups, rival parties, and a scarce amount of resources frame the debate and compromise prior to policy output, two parameters for the budgetary process.
>
> *McGee, Shannon, and Jones, p. 603*

Behavioral rationality acknowledges that individuals and institutions have similar characteristics:

> While both individuals and institutions work towards fulfilling their agendas and are goal-oriented, their goals are impeded by a limited capacity for processing information. Since attention-space is limited, agendas must be set to change policy on the most pressing issues first in case time expires before reaching the end of the agenda. These shared characteristics make policy change not incremental, but instead, in bursts.
>
> *McGee, Shannon, and Jones, p. 603*

Information processing provides easy links between individual and organizational choice:

> Information processing, in the broadest sense, examines the supply and prioritiza-
> tion of information. Usually congressional committees will receive information and
> incrementally adjust the policies they deal with. Sometimes, however, new infor-
> mation or shifts in issue definitions might cause rapid changes in the problem and
> solution definitions. These changes can result in rapid changes in the proposed policy
> solutions. Taken together, these conditions are known as the *general punctuation thesis*
> … Information is not scarce within government; in fact, information is in oversupply.
> This oversupply of information leads actors to be overwhelmed by their choice envir-
> onment. To deal with the oversupply, they must winnow out the information that is
> not useful; this winnowing process is boundedly rational. How actors search for and
> weight the information they receive (e.g. members in a committee hearing) is cru-
> cial to whether or not a policy problem is resolved or a specific solution is chosen.
> Ultimately, the decisions made about what information is important are agenda-
> setting decisions. Therefore, to think about agenda setting, attention allocation, or
> information processing is to confront bounded rationality and its influence on the
> policy process literature.
>
> *McGee, Shannon, and Jones, p. 607*

Chapter 42 by Valentina Ferretti outlines three examples of multi-methodology boosts designed
to support three key stages of the decision-making process: (1) the framing of the problem/
opportunity to be addressed; (2) the expansion of the original decision makers' mental model
about the objectives to be achieved; and, finally, (3) the elicitation of preferences about the
worthiness of the performances of the alternatives.

There are three common denominators to the behavioural decision analysis interventions
discussed in her chapter:

> First, multi-methodology boosts require time and facilitators skilled in multiple
> methods. Second, a key advantage of the proposed boosts is their applicability to
> many different domains. Third, they stretch the bounds that the uncertain and often
> constrained external environment places on human rationality, thus mitigating some
> of the associated cognitive consequences such as poor framing of decisions, insuf-
> ficient thinking about relevant objectives and scope insensitivity. In particular, the
> presence of limited information on alternatives and their consequences can be tackled
> through informed value judgments supported by the integration of sound preference
> elicitation protocols and visualization analytics, as well as through thought-provoking
> questions to expand the set of objectives and create better alternatives.
>
> *Ferretti, p. 622*

The techniques proposed in this chapter should thus be considered as "process boosts" and in
particular as "framing boosts" and as "preference elicitation boosts", which could be added to
the first taxonomy of long-term boosts proposed by Hertwig and Grune-Yanoff (2017), i.e.,
risk literacy boosts, uncertainty management boosts and motivational boosts.

One of the neoclassical economics-informed policy recommendations to protect the consumer is to supply most of the information available to allow them to choose from among
many difference options. Many governments around the world follow this recommendation

that is aimed to reduce information asymmetry and to overcome market failures. Unfortunately, though, too much information can cause information and choice overload, which have negative consequences on the accuracy of decision making and on the emotional state of the decision maker. Chapters 43 and 44 by Elena Reutskaja, Barbara Fasolo, Raffalella Misuraca and Sheena Iyengar summarize evidence collected by researchers for more than half a century on the topic of information and choice overload, exploring how people deal with large amounts of information and how they make choices from sets with multiple alternatives:

> Although economics and psychology have both traditionally emphasized the benefits of more information and more choice, a sizable body of research has demonstrated that having too much information or too many choices can lead to negative consequences. Researchers have found that too much information and choice hinders information processing and usage, motivation to act, and quality and accuracy of decisions, and that it also negatively impacts affective states of the decision makers. All in all, empirical evidence suggests that both too little and too much choice and information are "bad" and there is a "golden mean" of how much choice is enough. However, the optimal information and choice offering is not universal and depends on a vast variety of contextual and individual factors.
>
> *Reutskaja, Fasolo, Misuraca, and Iyengar, p. 633*

The results of these studies provide policy makers with some useful bounded rational advice: make the citizens' context of choice as transparent and simple as possible. Information should be limited and relevant to allow citizens to make better political, social and economic decisions. In an interview in Pittsburgh, Herbert Simon was asked whether simple decision making could be achieved by reducing the presentation of alternatives. His response was: "Partly. I think the difficulty of decision making centers very much around the degree of uncertainty and the gaps in our knowledge." Moreover, Simon (1971, p. 40) put it:

> In an information-rich world, the wealth of information means a dearth of something else: a scarcity of whatever it is that information consumes. What information consumes is rather obvious: it consumes the attention of its recipients. Hence a wealth of information creates a poverty of attention and a need to allocate that attention efficiently among the overabundance of information sources that might consume it.

Smart and ethical choice architecture should direct and preserve decision makers' attention and respect decision makers' freedom. How we manage our attention in our ever more information-rich world will ultimately dictate our future.

To conclude, a real libertarian paternalism, according bounded rationality, is aimed to supply the cognitive and educational tools to people to better process information and to improve their deliberate problem solving in the large world. In other words, to increase their ecological rationality. Therefore, the only justified libertarian paternalisms seem to be the cognitive and the educational ones (Viale, 2019; forthcoming). Both aim at empowering the citizens' decision making. *Cognitive paternalism* aims to help citizens neutralize their errors, increasing the environmental feedbacks of their choice, structuring and simplifying the complex structure of tasks and filling the gap between the contingent utility of their choice and their future utility and well-being. *Educational paternalism* aims at supplying knowledge and skills that change not only the performance but also the autonomous competence of the decision maker. This applies, for example, to financial, health and environmental education or the teaching of risk literacy and heuristic decision making.

It is important to consider how to help human reasoning. For example, the mind's statistical reasoning processes evolved to operate on natural frequencies and Bayesian computations are simpler to perform with natural frequencies than with probabilities. It is well known that if information is presented as the outcome of learning from experience, known as natural frequencies, and not as conditional probabilities, the proportion of people reasoning by Bayes rule increases a lot. Statistics expressed in terms of natural frequencies improve Bayesian inferences in finance as in many other kinds topics. Therefore, a bounded rationality-inspired architecture of choice (BRAN Bounded Rational Adaptive Nudge, in Viale, 2017; forthcoming) should change information formats in probabilistic reasoning from probabilities to natural frequencies. The importance of nudging people by the natural frequency format to reason correctly in statistical tasks is crucial in many environments. In particular, the frequency format improves the statistical and the Bayesian reasoning in many financial and medical judgements to correctly predict, for example, the probability of a disease according to prior probability and new evidence (supplied, for example, by a test with some false positives) or the probability of a fall of a Stock Exchange according to prior probability and new evidence (the bankruptcy of a big global bank). The same argument can be applied to many public policies with dramatic future implications for human life such as financial defaults, natural disasters, terrorist attacks, micro criminalities, epidemics, but also quieter social phenomena where people have prior probability and some new evidence, such as the choice of a bank in relation to various rankings or the choice of a university for their son in relation to the labour market or the choice of a hospital for a surgical operation in relation to the success rate of similar medical institutions.

This topic is related to another important component of cognitive libertarian paternalism: how to increase the *knowledge of feedback* from our choices. One of the reasons to increase the feedback is not only that we can learn from our errors and not to fall another time in the same choice. It is also that we can improve inductively our theories of the world. That is, we can improve our prediction on future states of the world, for example, our future choice of an investment or of a party or of a school. In the experiments on Bayesian learning, people learn probabilities from experience and are subsequently tested as to whether they make judgements consistent with Bayes' rule. Often the tests are successful. Therefore, many cognitive scientists conclude that people's judgements are largely consistent with this theory. This kind of test is the cognitive justification for an ecological rational role of the nudge that manages to increase the knowledge of the feedback from people's choices.

It seems possible also to design ecologically sound *mapping of choice for future welfare*. For example, when an individual has to make a choice about different mortgages or credit agreements, it is possible to simulate future simple environments with few cues in frequency formats (for example, the monthly rate) and ask him or her to imagine that situation. In this case, the attempt is to create a situational rationality dimension and to trigger embodied cognition aspects of the choice. This situation would allow him or her to better understand the future effects of his or her choice, trying to make subjective present utility converge with future utility. In other words, this architecture of choice should foster people's competence to vary their sense of psychological connectedness, that is their sense of connection with their future self. In the context of saving, this could mean that the more aware someone is of being the future recipient of today's savings, the more prepared that person will be to save for retirement. In some experiments, participants who interacted with their virtual future selves, and presumably overcame disconnectedness, were more likely to accept later monetary rewards over immediate ones.

Another proposal of cognitive paternalism is designing environments that nudge the utilization of a proper suitable heuristic. It is possible, for example, to design an environment that exploits so-called *social intelligence* by relying on heuristics designed for social information. *Imitate-the-successful heuristic*, for instance, speeds up learning of cue orders and can find orders that excel take-the-best's validity orders. Other heuristics include *imitation heuristics, tit-for-tat*, the *social-circle heuristic*, and *averaging the judgements of the others to exploit the "wisdom of crowds"* (Gigerenzer and Gassmaier, 2011).

Simplifying and structure complex choice is also a good challenge for BRAN heuristic choice. For example, trying to make choices in environment that present high redundancy and variability in weights of their structure. *High redundancy* means structure where cues are highly connected (for example, the market value of a business). *High variability* means structure where there is great difference in weight between some cues and the others (for example, the weight of APRC[13] compared to other information in the choice of a credit contract). In this structure, when there is also high uncertainty, it is likely that *one-reason decision making* as *take-the-best heuristic* is able to allow successful inferences that can be superior to those based on algorithms such as classification and regression tree or conjoint analysis. In most of the choices linked to your well-being, such as finance, education, health, food, consumption goods, housing, and so on, you have to search for more than one cue. In these cases also, you may follow a sequential heuristic that is based on one-reason decision making. An example is *elimination by aspects of lexicographic heuristics* to nudge proper choices in a large world. How? Structuring, for example, with proper software the information given to families, by *fast-and-frugal trees* in which is incorporated the lexicographic logic. This is the typical non-compensatory strategy for choosing in an ecological rational way. In this strategy, people order the cues relying on recall from the mental sample. A person does not need to learn cue orders individually but instead can learn from others, such as through teaching and imitation (Gigerenzer and Gassmaier, 2011). This is an example of BRAN nudges.

To conclude, by fostering an inspired educational libertarian paternalism, competence in risk literacy, in uncertainty management and in managing motivations and cognitive control should be boosted (Hertwig and Grune-Yanoff, 2017; 2020) with:

1. The first competence is about understanding statistical information. This competence can be achieved through (Hertwig and Grune-Yanoff, 2017): (a) graphical representations; (b) experience-based representations as opposed to description-based representations; (c) representations that avoid biasing framing effects relying, for example, on absolute instead of relative frequencies; and (d) learning how to transform opaque representation (e.g., single-event probabilities) into transparent ones (e.g. frequency-based representations).
2. When people have no access to actuarial information, they should make decisions under uncertainty, with no explicit risk information available. This is the case of most decisions in the world of finance. The competence for uncertainty management fosters procedural rules for making good financial decisions, predictions and assessments under uncertain conditions with the help of simple rules of collective intelligence: fast and frugal trees; simple heuristics; rule of thumb and procedural routines (Hertwig and Grune-Yanoff, 2017; 2020). For example, Drexler et al. (2014) found that providing microentrepreneurs with training in basic accounting heuristics and procedural routines significantly improved their financial practices and outcomes. The impact of rule-of-thumb training was significantly greater than that of standard accounting training.
3. People often lack self-control and have weak attention during financial decision making. The results are often suboptimal. An educational libertarian paternalism may foster the

competence to autonomously adjust one's motivation, and cognitive control in decision making through growth-mindset or sense-of-purpose exercises; attention state training; psychological connectedness training; reward-bundling exercises; the strategic use of automatic processes and harnessing simple implementation intentions; and training in pre-commitment strategies and self-control strategies (Hertwig and Grune-Yanoff, 2017).

Notes

1 How to identify why-questions? Consider the stock example: (⋆) Why did Adam eat the apple? The why-question asked by (⋆) is determined by:

(1)   A Topic: a proposition expressing the fact whose explanation we are asking. (e.g., in the case of (⋆), that Adam ate the apple). Neither having the same topic nor being expressed by the same sentence constitutes a criterion of identity for why-questions. In other words, the same sentence can express different why-questions. For Van Fraassen, there are various ways in which this can happen. This leads him to bring in two more contextual factors:

(2)   A Contrast Class: a set of propositions, including the topic, that determines the range of alternatives against which a why-question is asked. For example, Why did Adam eat the apple (as opposed to Eve)?, why did Adam eat the apple (as opposed to, say throwing it away because it was old)?, why did Adam eat the apple (as opposed to the oranges, the grapes, etc.)?

(3)   A Relevance Relation: "a respect-in-which a reason is requested". An example of how (3) discriminates among different why-questions: consider the question "Why was Mr. Jones killed by his wife?". On a natural understanding, it is irrelevant to answer "Because she stuck a knife in his throat, thereby causing such and such events that led to Mr. Jones's death".

2 In the past, it was believed that man was a rational animal because his reasoning was thought to comply aprioristically with the precepts of classical logic. The answer to question 2 was therefore taken as being non-problematic and established *a priori* within the terms of a positive response to question 3. What seemed to be merely a conjecture which could explain the reason for this belief in the ancients instead now seems to reveal a widespread prejudice even among the most sophisticated and modern psychologists. Even a demolisher of rationalistic certainties like Phil Johnson-Laird justifies, in a somewhat aprioristic way, human logical rationality (also if not in the sense of classical logic, but in that of the psychological theory of "mental models") by stating "that if people were intrinsically irrational, then the invention of logic, mathematics, and much else besides, would be inexplicable" (Johnson-Laird, 1983, p. 66).

3 I call this proposal *Minimal Dual Account of Mind* (Viale, 2019*)*.

4 As will be noted later, the theory of mental dualism has attracted some criticism (Kruglanski and Gigerenzer, 2011; Viale, 2019) and the unified account of the human mind appears to have become a more credible alternative.

5 Sloman's (1996) Criterion S is met when a person simultaneously holds two contradictory beliefs. The idea is that this occurs when the associative and rule-based systems arrive at conflicting responses to a situation.

6 Science aims to transform large world problems into small world problems and solutions. This is possible only when large world problems are characterized by epistemic uncertainty and not by fundamental or ontological uncertainty. The first kind of uncertainty occurs when, ideally, empirical research and the collection of data are able to supply statistical figures that characterize relevant variables, their consequences and probabilities. The second kind of uncertainty deals with events that empirical research is not able to represent probabilistically because of complexity or unpredictable surprises. The first kind of uncertainty usually applies to most biomedical research (for example, trials for a new drug) whereas the second applies to macro-political, environmental and financial phenomena (for example, the prediction of a financial crisis). For example, Covid-19, like any other infection, is typically characterized by epistemic uncertainty. In a few years biomedical research will be able to define its viral behaviour and possible treatments (*ceteris paribus* with likely mutations). On the contrary, financial markets are typically characterized by ontological uncertainty. No-one may predict their future behaviour.

7 According to authors such as Dreyfus (1992) and Winograd (1984), no computational device can imitate the human singularity of being situated in the world. Therefore, the project of Artificial Intelligence is doomed to failure.

8 It is not clear what is the difference for Rubinstein between a story and a model. In philosophy of science, stories and models are often considered similar. According to Alan Gibbard and Hal Varian (1978), a model is similar to a story. As in a caricature, it emphasizes and exaggerates some special features and neglects other features that are closer to the real phenomenon.

9 The central principle is Schroedinger's equation. This equation describes how systems subject to various forces evolve in time, but in order to know the evolution of a real system, we also need to know the mathematical representation of the kinetic and potential energies of that real system. This is called Hamiltonian representation. In principle, if we wanted to have a realistic picture of the various systems, we ought to calculate a Hamiltonian representation of each real system we wish to study. Instead, if we look at physics text-books, we discover that they contain only a limited number of Hamiltonians, which do not fit real objects, such as the hydrogen atom, but only highly fictionalized objects, such as free particle motion, the linear harmonic oscillator, piecewise constant potentials, diatomic molecules, central potential scattering, and so on.

10 I refer to ontic or structural uncertainty that is characterized by unpredictability. In situations characterized instead by epistemic uncertainty, the collection of data may increase our knowledge and predictive power. The only danger in these cases is of falling into the variance phenomenon when the data to be collected are too vast and should therefore be limited to only a small, non-representative subset.

11 The identification of biases and formal errors of judgement is not a recent phenomenon. Adam Smith highlighted both the phenomena of "loss aversion" and "hyperbolic discounting" as explanatory factors for human behaviour. Niccolò Machiavelli also drew attention to the decision-making power of both the "endowment effect" and "loss aversion". Lastly, David Hume underlined the danger of "present bias" and the myopic nature of human judgement.

12 Paradoxically, the society of satisficers might need a stronger paternalism than that of optimizers. Think of an ecological rational policy maker who wants to apply the normative side of ecological rationality. He or she will oblige people to learn all the heuristics adapted for each separate task and environment. He or she will try to nudge or oblige people to use the proper heuristics adapted for each particular environment. The result: much more paternalism, cost and complexity compared to behavioural economics nudging.

13 APRC is the Annual Percentage Rate of Charge.

References

Becker, G. (1962). "Investment in human capital: A theoretical analysis". *Journal of Political Economy*, 70(9), 9–49.

Berg, N. and Gigerenzer, G. (2010). "As-if behavioral economics: neoclassical economics in disguise?", *History of Economic Ideas*, XVIII, 1, 133–165.

Cartwright, N. (1983). *How the Laws of Physics Lie*. Oxford: Oxford University Press.

Challenge interview with Herbert A. Simon (1986). "The failure of armchair economics". Available at: http://digitalcollections.library.cmu.edu/awweb/awarchive?type=file&item=34037.

Clark, A. (2016). *Surfing Uncertainty*. Oxford: Oxford University Press.

Cleermans, A., and Jimenez, L. (2002). "Implicit learning and consciousness: A graded, dynamic perspective". In R. M. French and A. Cleermans (eds), *Implicit Learning and Consciousness: An Empirical, Philosophical and Computational Consensus in the Making* (pp. 1–40). Hove, UK: Psychology Press.

Dennett, D. (2017). *From Bacteria to Bach and Back: The Evolution of Minds*. New York: Norton.

Drexler, A., Fischer, G., and Scholar, A. (2014). "Keeping it simple: Financial literacy and rules of thumb", *American Economic Journal: Applied Economics*, 6, 1–31.

Dreyfus, H. (1992). *What computers still can't do: A critique of artificial intelligence*. Cambridge, MA: MIT Press.

Evans, St. B. T. J. (2008). "Dual-processing accounts of reasoning, judgement and social cognition". *Annual Review of Psychology*, 59, 255–278.

Evans, St. B. T. J., and Stanovich, K. E. (2013). "Dual-process theories of higher cognition: advancing the debate", *Perspectives on Psychological Science*, 8(3), 223–241.

Fehr, E. and Schmidt, K. (1999). "A theory of fairness, competition and cooperation". *Quarterly Journal of Economics*, 114, 817–868.

Friedman, M. (1953). *Essays in Positive Economics.* Chicago: University of Chicago Press.

Gibbard, A., and Varian, H. (1978). "Economic models". *Journal of Philosophy,* 75, 664–677.

Gigerenzer, G. and Gassmaier, W. (2011). "Heuristic decision making". *Annual Review of Psychology,* 62: 451–482.

Gigerenzer, G., and Selten, R. (2001). *Bounded Rationality.* Cambridge, MA: MIT Press.

Gigerenzer, G., Todd, P. M. and the ABC Research Group (eds) (1999). *Simple Heuristics that Make Us Smart.* New York: Oxford University Press.

Hacking, I. (1983). *Representing and Intervening.* Cambridge: Cambridge University Press.

Hammond, K. R. (1996). *Human Judgement and Social Policy.* Oxford: Oxford University Press.

Hertwig, R., and Grune-Yanoff, T. (2017). "Nudging and boosting: Steering or empowering good decisions". *Perspectives on Psychological Science,* 12(6), 973–986.

Hertwig, R., and Grune-Yanoff T. (2020). "Boosting and nudging: Two paths toward better financial decisions". In R. Viale, S. Mousavi, U. Filotto and B. Alemanni (eds), *Financial Education and Risk Literacy.* Aldershot: Elgar.

Kruglanski, A. W., and Gigerenzer, G. (2011). "Intuitive and deliberative judgements are based on common principles". *Psychological Review,* 118, 97–109.

Leslie, A. M. (1987). "Pretense and representation: The origins of 'theory of mind'". *Psychological Review,* 94: 412–426.

Laibson, D. (1997). "Golden eggs and hyperbolic discounting". *Quarterly Journal of Economics,* 112(2): 443–477.

Marr, D. (1982). *Vision.* San Francisco CA: Freeman.

Newell, A., and Simon, H. (2019). *Human Problem Solving.* Brattleboro, VT: EPBM.

Osman, M. (2004). "An evaluation of dual-process theories of reasoning". *Psychonomic Bulletin and Review,* 11(6), 988–1010.

Petty, R. E., and Cacioppo, J. T. (1986). "The Elaboration Likelihood Model of persuasion". In L. Berkowitz (ed.), *Advances in Experimental Social Psychology.* New York: Academic Press.

Quine, W. O. (1985). "Epistemology naturalized". In H. Kornblith (ed.), *Naturalizing Epistemology.* Cambridge: Cambridge University Press.

Rosenberg, A. (1983). "If economics is not science, what is it?" In D. M. Hausman (ed.), *The Philosophy of Economics.* Cambridge: Cambridge University Press.

Savage, L. J. (1954). *The Foundations of Statistics.* 2nd edn. New York: Dover.

Simon, H. (1956) "Rational choice and the structure of the environment". *Psychological Review,* 63(2), 129–138.

Simon, H. (1971). "Designing organizations for an information-rich world". In M. Greenberg (ed.), *Computers, Communication and the Public Interest.* Baltimore, MD: The Johns Hopkins University Press.

Simon, H. (1979a). "Information processing models of cognition". *Annual Review of Psychology,* 30: 363–396.

Simon, H. (1979b). "Rational decision making in business organizations". *American Economic Review,* 69(4), 493–513.

Simon, H. (1981). *Sciences of the Artificial.* Cambridge, MA: MIT Press.

Simon, H. (1990). "Invariants of human behaviour". *Annual Review of Psychology,* 41, 1–19.

Simon, H. (2000). "Bounded rationality in social sciences: Today and tomorrow". *Mind & Society,* 1, 25–41.

Simon, H. A., Egidi, M., Viale, R. and Marris, R. (1992). *Economics, Bounded Rationality and the Cognitive Revolution.* Aldershot: Elgar.

Sloman, S. (1996). "The empirical case for two systems of reasoning". *Psychological Bulletin,* 119, 3–22.

Sloman, S. (2002). "Two systems of reasoning". In T. Gilovich, D. Griffin and D. Kahneman (eds), *Heuristics and Biases: The Psychology of Intuitive Judgement* (pp. 379–398). Cambridge: Cambridge University Press.

Stanovich, K. E. (2009). "Distinguishing the reflective, algorithmic and autonomous minds: Is it time for a tri-process theory?" In J. Evans and K. Frankish (eds), *In Two Minds.* Oxford: Oxford University Press.

Stanovich, K. E., and Toplak, M. (2012). "Defining features versus incidental correlates of Type 1 and Type 2 processing". *Mind & Society,* 11: 3–13.

Stiglitz, G. (2010). *Freefall: America, Free Markets, and the Sinking of the World Economy.* New York: Norton.

Thaler, R. H. (1991). *Quasi Rational Economics.* New York: Russell Sage Foundation.

Thaler, R., and Sunstein, C. (2008). *Nudge.* London: Penguin.

Todd, P. M., Gigerenzer, G. and the ABC Research Group (eds) (2012). *Ecological Rationality: Intelligence in the World.* New York: Oxford University Press.

Van Fraassen, B. (1980). *The Scientific Image*. Oxford: Oxford University Press.

Viale, R. (1997). "Cognitive economics". Working Paper 1. LaSCoMES, Bocconi University.

Viale, R. (2012). *Methodological Cognitivism: Mind, Rationality and Society*. Heidelberg: Springer.

Viale, R. (2013). *Methodological Cognitivism: Cognition, Science, and Innovation*. Heidelberg: Springer.

Viale, R. (2016). "Brain driven creativity". In L. Macchi, M. Bagassi, and R. Viale (eds), *Cognitive Unconscious and Human Rationality*. Cambridge, MA: MIT Press.

Viale, R. (2017). "How to decide in the large world of finance: The Bounded Rational Adaptive Nudges (BRAN)". *Quaderni di Finanza*, 84, 99–109.

Viale, R. (2018). "The normative and descriptive weaknesses of behavioral economics-informed nudge: Depowered paternalism and unjustified libertarianism" *Mind & Society*, 1–2(17), 53–69.

Viale, R. (2019). "Architecture of the mind and libertarian paternalism: Is the reversibility of system 1 nudges likely to happen?" *Mind & Society*, 2(19).

Viale, R. (forthcoming). *Nudging*. Cambridge, MA: MIT Press.

Winograd, T. (1984). "Computer software for working with language". *Scientific American*, September.

2

WHAT IS BOUNDED RATIONALITY?

Gerd Gigerenzer

Bounded rationality has, surprisingly, three faces. The original is by Herbert A. Simon, who coined the term. The other two arrived later and bent Simon's term into meanings that could hardly be more different. Equally puzzling, the two new meanings contradict each other, each having absorbed the term into their own framework. This double take-over has been so subtle that few people notice that, when talking about bounded rationality, they are often talking about different things. The three faces of bounded rationality are not simply a matter of terminology; they reflect fundamentally dissimilar research programs and visions about the nature of human rationality. In this chapter, I will describe the three faces, explain how we got there, and outline how to develop Simon's original program.

Simon's bounded rationality

Herbert A. Simon (1916–2001) coined the term *bounded rationality*. While still a student, fresh out of a price theory class at the University of Chicago, he tried to apply the perspective of utility maximization to budget decision problems in his native Milwaukee's recreation department in the mid-1930s. To his surprise, he learned that managers did not try to compare the marginal utility of a proposed expenditure with its marginal costs, but simply added incremental changes to last year's budget and engaged in other rules of thumb. During that concrete encounter, Simon realized what managers could and could not measure, and concluded that the framework of utility maximization "was hopeless" (Simon 1988, p. 286). This discrepancy between theory and reality marked the beginning of what he later called the study of bounded rationality: "Now I had a new research problem: How do human beings reason when the conditions for rationality postulated by the model of neoclassical economics are not met?" (Simon, 1989, p. 377).

What is rationality in neoclassical economics? Although not all economists agree, they typically refer to three pillars: consistency, maximization of expected utility, and—if learning is involved—Bayesian updating of probabilities. Leonard J. Savage (1954), known as the father of modern Bayesian decision theory, defined two conditions necessary for these three pillars of rationality:

DOI: 10.4324/9781315658353-2

1. *Perfect Foresight of Future States*: The agent knows the exhaustive and mutually exclusive set *S* of future states of the world.
2. *Perfect Foresight of Consequences*: The agent knows the exhaustive and mutually exclusive set *C* of consequences of each of his or her actions, given a state.

Savage called the pair (*S, C*) a *small world*. States and consequences must necessarily be described at some limited level of detail—hence the adjective *small*. The prototype of a small world is a lottery where all possible future states (the tickets) along with all possible outcomes (the payoffs) and their probabilities are known for certain, or a game such as roulette where all states (in roulette: the 36 numbers plus zero), consequences, and probabilities are known. In a small world, nothing new or unexpected can ever happen. These conditions have been variously called unbounded rationality, full rationality, constructivist rationality, or the Bayesian rationality approach. What Simon noticed, however, was that the managers he observed and humans in general mostly have to deal with situations that are unlike small worlds with perfect foresight and that do not meet the assumptions for expected utility maximization and Bayesian updating. For instance, if the exhaustive and mutually exclusive set of future states of the world and their consequences is not known, one cannot maximize expected utility or assign prior probabilities to states that add up to one, which makes Bayesian updating unfeasible. Simon called for an empirical study of *how* humans reason when perfect foresight is not possible. In his lifetime, most economists showed little interest in Simon's question and preferred theories assuming perfect foresight.

Risk *and* uncertainty

I will use the term *risk* for situations in which agents have perfect foresight of future states and their consequences, as defined above, and also certain knowledge about the probabilities of the states. For the many situations in which this is not the case, I will use the term *uncertainty*. This distinction between risk and uncertainty goes back to Frank Knight (1921). *Uncertainty* is sometimes used to denote a small world without known probabilities (Luce & Raiffa, 1957), a situation known as *ambiguity*. Yet ambiguity contains only a minor degree of uncertainty; it still assumes perfect foresight of future states and consequences. When speaking of uncertainty, I also refer to situations that do not meet the definition of small worlds. Uncertainty is sometimes called *fundamental uncertainty* or *radical uncertainty*. It includes ambiguity and intractability (such as in chess), ill-defined problems such as budget decisions where optimal solutions cannot be known because perfect foresight is an illusion, and, in general, all future events that are not perfectly foreseeable. In short, uncertainty includes most of the interesting problems that humans face in real life.

Now we can formulate the first principle of Simon's bounded rationality program: *to study how human beings make decisions under uncertainty, not only under risk.*

Decision making under uncertainty is obviously relevant for understanding how managers, business people, or other human beings make choices. In contrast, decision making under risk is rare, mostly restricted to human-made environments such as lotteries, games, and gambling. Nevertheless, lotteries remain the stock-in-trade of decision research, defining risk aversion, regret, and loss aversion, and are the domain of modifications of expected utility theory, such as prospect theory.

Savage himself explicitly limited his theory, currently known as *Bayesian decision theory*, to small worlds only. For instance, he pointed out that his theory does not apply to planning a picnic or playing a game of chess (Savage, 1954, p. 16). When planning a picnic, one cannot know ahead all future states that might happen. And when playing chess, where a finite number of states (sequences of moves) indeed exists, the problem is intractability because no human or machine can enumerate the exhaustive set of possible moves and determine the optimal one. As a consequence, one cannot assign probabilities to these states that add up to one. To illustrate, chess has approximately 10^{120} different unique sequences of moves or games, which is a number greater than the estimated number of atoms in the universe. Savage believed it would be "utterly ridiculous" to apply rational choice theory to situations without perfect foresight (1954, p. 16). Both Simon and Savage were fully in agreement that expected utility maximization is a local but not a universal tool.

As-if *and* real decision-making processes

Simon's question is about the *process* of decision making: "How do human beings reason?" Simon criticized the fact that neo-classical economists showed surprisingly little interest in studying how people actually make decisions, but instead engaged in armchair speculation and relied mainly on their intuition. When confronted with the same kind of evidence as Simon once was, namely, that business professionals did not behave as postulated by utility theory, Milton Friedman reacted differently: He dismissed the empirical evidence as irrelevant. In his *as-if* defense, Friedman (1953) famously argued that the goal of "positive economics" is prediction, not psychological realism. The theory says that people behave *as if* they maximized their expected utility, not that they actually do. All that counts are sufficiently good predictions. I do not doubt that expected utility theory and its variants can explain behavior *after* the fact, due to its great flexibility; whether it can actually predict behavior is less clear. True predictions must be out-of-sample, not by fitting a model to known data. After reviewing 50 years of research for evidence about how well utility functions, such as utility of income functions, utility of wealth functions, and the value function in prospect theory actually predict behavior, D. Friedman, Isaac, James, and Sunder (2014) concluded: "Their power to predict out-of-sample is in the poor-to-nonexistent range, and we have seen no convincing victories over naïve alternatives" (p. 3).

Now we can formulate the second principle of Simon's bounded rationality program: *To study how human beings make decisions, as opposed to relying on as-if expected utility theories.*

In my opinion, Simon's insistence on studying the process and Friedman's goal of prediction are not incompatible opponents; they can be reconciled. My hypothesis is that by constructing realistic process models, one can, on average, make better predictions than by using as-if models. I will provide evidence for this argument below using the example of the prediction of customer purchases.

But what are the tools humans use to make good decisions under uncertainty? Knight (1921) had proposed "judgment" and "experience," but not much more. In his *General Theory*, John Maynard Keynes (1936) proposed "animal spirits," without telling us what these exactly are. In their book *Animal Spirits*, Akerlof and Shiller (2009) remedied this by moving a step forward and distinguishing five such spirits—confidence, fairness, corruption, money illusion, and stories. The authors argue that these "restless and inconsistent" elements were the principal reasons for the financial crisis of 2008 (pp. vii, 4).

Simon (1955, 1956) made a more concrete start, proposing that humans make decisions under uncertainty by relying on aspiration levels, limited search, and heuristics such as *satisficing*. In its simplest version, the satisficing rule is:

Step 1: Set an aspiration level α.
Step 2: Choose the first option that satisfies α.

To illustrate, consider a study of how real estate entrepreneurs decide in which location to invest in order to develop a new commercial high-rise or a residential area. Berg (2014) reports that of 49 professional investors, each and every one relied on a version of satisficing: *If I believe I can get at least x return within y years, then I take the option.* Here, "*x* return in *y* years" is the aspiration level. In general, an aspiration is a goal, and an aspiration level is a goal value. The psychologist Kurt Lewin (1935), who promoted the concept of aspiration, considered successful people to be those who set goals that are within their ability to reach. Using a satisficing heuristic, people can deal with uncertainty because the rule does not require perfect knowledge about all options, such as possible locations, marriage partners, or professions. How did Simon decide to study political science and economics? In his own account, he "simply picked the first profession that sounded fascinating" (1978, p. 1).

In general, satisficing can handle situations where the exhaustive and mutually exclusive set of options is not knowable, and where options need to be searched one by one. In such situations, optimizing is not an option.

Behavior = f (cognition, environment)

The third principle that defines Simon's bounded rationality is captured by his scissors analogy: behavior is a function of both cognition and environment (Simon, 1990, p. 7): "Human rational behavior (and the rational behavior of all physical symbol systems) is shaped by a scissors whose two blades are the structure of task environments and the computational capabilities of the actor."

Simon did not flesh out the scissors principle in detail; I will provide an example below in the section on ecological rationality. In general, it requires an analysis of both the heuristics people use and the structure of the environments in which they act. Economic theory analyzes the incentive structure in environments but not the actual decision strategies, assuming as-if utility maximization. Thus, it deals with only one blade. Similarly, much of psychological theorizing restricts itself to cognitive processes and is mute about environmental structure. Thus, it deals solely with the other blade. Debates in psychology tend to center around "internal" questions: whether the mind is a Bayesian or not, whether information is integrated in an additive or multiplicative way, whether the mind works by mental models or mental logic, or whether a person is risk averse or risk seeking. By analyzing only one blade of Simon's scissors, one cannot understand the ecological rationality of a heuristic, a belief, or other strategies.

To summarize, there are three principles that define Simons' program of bounded rationality:

1. *Uncertainty.* To study decision making under uncertainty, not only risk.
2. *Process.* To study the actual process of decision making, as opposed to as-if expected utility maximization.
3. *Scissors.* To study how the structure of an environment, together with the cognitive process, produces the resulting behavior.

For many of Simon's contemporaries, this program was asking too much. It clashed with the practice of reducing all uncertainties to risks by assuming perfect foresight, such as by converting real-world problems into lotteries. It also clashed with the ideal of explaining all behavior after the fact by saying that it maximizes some utility, regardless of Savage's small-world restriction. Needless to say, Simon's revolution did not happen during his lifetime.

The rejection of novel ideas is nothing new in the history of science. However, the reaction to Simon's ideas was rather unusual. Instead of being rejected as worthless or unimportant, his concept of *bounded rationality* was hijacked and radically reframed, making his revolutionary ideas no longer recognizable. Neo-classical economists absorbed the term into the orthodoxy of perfect foresight and concluded that satisficing is quintessentially optimizing. Proponents of the heuristics-and-biases program in psychology, in contrast, appropriated the term for their own focus on human lack of rationality. This is why bounded rationality now has three faces that could hardly be more dissimilar.

Bounded rationality as optimization under constraints

Satisficing involves search. Simon (1955, 1956) was one of the first to raise the topic of search in the economics literature. Note that in situations of risk, search is not an issue, given that all alternatives are already known. However, it was Stigler (1961) who popularized the topic by changing satisficing search to optimal search. In his classical example of the purchase of a second-hand car, the buyer is assumed to stop searching when the costs of further search exceed its benefits. Yet to factor costs and benefits into the equation, the buyer needs to know all alternatives and distributions in the first place, in addition to the costs of search. Stigler's approach poured search theory back into the old bottle of expected utility maximization, introducing perfect foresight once again, and reducing uncertainty to risk. With this move, satisficing is equivalent to optimizing with the constraint of search costs. In fact, Simon (1955) had ventured in the same direction earlier. There now exists a large literature in economics in which satisficing is modeled as optimization under constraints, mostly in the expected utility maximization tradition, whereas models of satisficing under uncertainty are rare. In a memorial book for the late Simon, Arrow (2004, p. 48) argued that "boundedly rational procedures are in fact fully optimal procedures when one takes account of the cost of computation in addition to the benefits and costs inherent in the problem as originally posed." Bounded rationality is thereby seen as nothing but constrained optimization in disguise.

In 1993, Thomas Sargent published his book *Bounded Rationality in Macroeconomics*, where he re-interprets "the idea of bounded rationality as a research program to build models populated by agents who behave like working economists or econometricians" (1993, p. 22). As he points out, by adding more and more constraints to optimization, models of bounded rationality become larger and mathematically more demanding, which is why there is no rush among econometricians to implement such models. Econometricians try to reduce the number of parameters, and that "is not what bounded rationality promises" (p. 5). In this view, bounded rationality makes optimization more difficult, and unbounded rationality ends up as the simpler and tractable alternative. This interpretation turned the idea of simple heuristics such as satisficing upside down. In personal conversation, Simon playfully remarked that he had considered suing authors who misused the term *bounded rationality* to mean optimization under constraints (Gigerenzer, 2004). In 1998, Ariel Rubinstein published *Modeling Bounded Rationality* and admirably included some of Simon's comments (Rubinstein, 1998). Simon criticized Rubinstein for showing no awareness of psychological research apart from that of Kahneman and Tversky. Rubinstein responded that, unlike some other economists, he was concerned neither with predicting behavior nor with giving normative advice. Rather, "by modeling bounded rationality, we try to examine the logic of a variety of principles that guide decision makers, especially within interactive systems (markets and games)" (1998, p. 191). But these logical armchair analyses were exactly what Simon was battling.

During his lifetime, Simon was highly influential in many fields, from artificial intelligence to psychology to political science. The major exception was in economics, the field in which he was awarded the Nobel Memorial Prize. In his own assessment, his program of bounded rationality was received with "something less than unbounded enthusiasm" and "largely ignored as irrelevant for economics" (Simon, 1997, p. 269). I believe that economics has missed an important call to extend its theoretical and methodological toolbox.

Bounded rationality as irrationality

Beginning in the 1970s, psychologists within the heuristics-and-biases program ventured to show that the assumptions of neo-classical economic theory are descriptively incorrect: the consistency axioms, the maximization of expected utility, and the updating of probabilities by Bayes' rule (e.g., Tversky & Kahneman, 1974). These assumptions are also known as rational choice theory. This program produced a long list of discrepancies between theory and actual behavior. A discrepancy could be due to flaws either in the theory or in behavior. Unlike Simon, the program maintained rational choice theory as normatively correct and blamed the discrepancies on people's lack of rationality. Its proponents have even defended utility theory as a universal norm against critics such as Lola Lopes (e.g., Tversky & Bar-Hillel, 1983, p. 713). Accepting rational choice theory as a universal norm and attributing deviations from this norm to people's lack of rationality is clearly not what Simon had in mind. "Bounded rationality is not irrationality" (Simon, 1985, p. 297).

Nevertheless, the heuristics-and-biases program also appropriated the term *bounded rationality* for itself. "Our research attempted to obtain a map of bounded rationality, by exploring the systematic biases that separate the beliefs that people have and the choices they make from the optimal beliefs and choices assumed in rational agent models" (Kahneman, 2003, p. 1449). Now we have a third meaning of the term: human errors, defined as whenever human judgment *deviates from rational choice theory*. That contradicts both Simon's original meaning and economists' re-interpretation of the term as economic rationality. Moreover, these alleged biases were attributed to people's use of heuristics. As a consequence, the term *heuristic* became associated with bias, contrary to a long tradition in psychology and computer science and to the definitions listed in the *Oxford English Dictionary* (n.d.).

The observation that people sometimes violate rational choice theory eventually led to *dual process theories* that "explain" this apparent flaw by assuming an error-prone "System 1" that intuitively uses heuristics and a "System 2" that operates according to rational choice theory. So far, these systems have been characterized by lists of general dichotomies (heuristic versus logical, unconscious versus conscious, and so on), without precise models of the processes, such as formal models of heuristics. Moreover, aligning "heuristic" with "unconscious" and "biases" is not even correct; every heuristic I have studied can be used both consciously and unconsciously, and can lead to better or worse decisions than what would be considered "rational" (Kruglanski & Gigerenzer, 2011).

How did bounded rationality come to be equated with people's irrationality? A key to finding an answer is found in the classical papers of Kahneman and Tversky, which are reprinted in the anthology by Kahneman, Slovic, and Tversky (1982). In these articles, neither Simon nor bounded rationality is cited. But in the Preface to the anthology, Simon is briefly mentioned, apparently more as a nod to a distinguished figure than an acknowledgment of a significant intellectual link (Lopes, 1992). Thus, the re-interpretation of bounded rationality as irrationality likely occurred as an afterthought.

Does the heuristics-and-biases research implement Simon's three principles? First, like neo-classical theory, the program does not make the distinction between risk and uncertainty. For most problems investigated, it assumes that logic or probability theory provides the correct answer. With respect to the study of the process of decision making, it has made some contributions in its work on heuristics, but these are all associated with biases. Moreover, the heuristics proposed in the 1970s have never been defined so that their predictions could be tested but instead were used to explain deviations between theory and behavior after the fact, as with the availability heuristic in the original letter-R study (Tversky & Kahneman, 1973). When availability was later more clearly defined and its predictions tested for the very same study, it was shown not to predict people's judgment (Sedlmeier, Hertwig, & Gigerenzer, 1998). Hindsight is easier than foresight. The use of labels instead of models differs from the earlier work by Tversky (1972) on elimination-by-aspect. In terms of the scissors analogy, the heuristics-and-biases program focused solely on internal explanations of behavior, without an analysis of the environmental conditions under which a heuristic is likely to succeed in reaching a goal or not. In this program, the use of heuristics is the problem and the supposed cause of errors. For decisions under uncertainty, however, heuristics are the solution, not the problem.

Homo heuristicus, *Homo economicus*, **and Homer Simpson**

The three faces of bounded rationality are not complementary, but conflicting. Let us give each of the three faces a name. *Homo heuristicus* personifies Simon's original program to study decision making under uncertainty. *Homo economicus* stands for the neo-classical program assuming situations of risk. Finally, Homer Simpson is an apt name for the program studying the deviations of people's behavior from the ideal of *Homo economicus*, attributing these to flaws in people rather in the theory (the name is from Thaler & Sunstein, 2008).

These three meanings of bounded rationality are not the only ones in circulation. Every time I enter the US to give a talk, the immigration officer asks me about the topic of my talk. Usually I respond by giving a two-sentence summary of bounded rationality. One officer nodded and remarked: "Oh, that's when you get old!" Another one got the point and said: "Oh, uncertainty, that's what I do, trying to make sense of people. Would you please write down the title of your book?" Most of the time, however, explaining bounded rationality just speeds up the process: "Oh, thanks, just go through."

I end this chapter with a short introduction to the program of ecological rationality, the modern extended version of Simon's bounded rationality.

The ecological rationality program: *Homo heuristicus*

Simon's question was descriptive: What are the tools humans use to make decisions under uncertainty? The program of ecological rationality starts from that question and extends it to three altogether, a descriptive, prescriptive, and engineering one (Gigerenzer, Hertwig, & Pachur, 2011; Gigerenzer & Selten, 2001). The descriptive question concerns the repertoire of tools that individuals and institutions rely on to make decisions under uncertainty. Simon suggested one such tool, satisficing. This repertoire is called the *adaptive toolbox*. The term *toolbox* signifies that there is more than one tool, and *adaptive* that the tools are adapted to specific classes of problems, just as a hammer is intended for nails, and a screwdriver for screws. The prescriptive questions fleshes out the scissors analogy: What environmental structures can a heuristic exploit in order to make better decisions? This question is addressed using analysis and computer simulation. The results to the first two questions provide answers to the engineering question: How can transparent, intuitive, and efficient decision systems be designed? This is the study of *intuitive design* (not covered here; see Gigerenzer et al., 2011).

The ecological rationality program is based on three methodological principles:

1. *Algorithmic models of heuristics.* Early candidates of heuristics such as availability and representativeness were largely undefined. Algorithmic models of heuristics such as satisficing replace vague labels.
2. *Competitive testing.* Models of heuristics should be tested against the best competing models, not against a null hypothesis of no effect.
3. *Test of predictions, not of data fitting.* Prediction is about the future, or about data that have not yet been observed. Fitting takes place when the data have already been observed and the parameters of a model are chosen so that they maximize the fit (such as R^2). Fitting alone is not a proper test of a model: The more free parameters are added to a model, the better it fits the data, but this does not necessarily hold for prediction, which involves uncertainty. In fact, simple heuristics can outperform more complex strategies in prediction.

The adaptive toolbox

The study of the adaptive toolbox of an individual, an organization, or a species proceeds by observation and experiment. It aims at algorithmic models of the heuristics that people actually use under uncertainty rather than aiming at as-if models of expected utility maximization. Models of bounded rationality describe not merely the outcome of a judgment or decision but also how it is reached (that is, the heuristic processes or proximal mechanisms). They also describe the building blocks of heuristics, which allow heuristics to be combined or extended. Consider once again the satisficing heuristic. In situations where one is unsure about the proper aspiration level, the basic satisficing rule can be extended to *satisficing with adaptation*:

Step 1: Set an aspiration level α.
Step 2: Choose the first option that satisfies α.
Step 3: If after time β no option has satisfied α, then change α by an amount γ and continue until an option is found.

The first two steps are identical to the basic form of satisficing, but the third allows the aspiration level to be adapted if no option is found after a certain amount of time.

To illustrate, consider the question of how car dealers should price used cars. There is no unique answer in economic theories. Building on Stigler's (1961) optimization under constraint theory, some theories assume that prices should be fine-tuned to the changes in market conditions, such as supply and demand; others assume two kinds of customers, informed shoppers who seek the lowest price and naïve customers who go for a brand name, reputation, or other surrogates for quality. To address this variability among customers, dealers should respond with mixed strategies where prices are randomized, just as some supermarkets change prices in a quasi-random way. An analysis of 628 German car dealers and over 16,000 cars showed, however, that none of these theories predicted the actual prices (Artinger & Gigerenzer, 2016). There was virtually no fine-tuning, despite drastic changes in supply, and randomizing prices was also absent.

How then do dealers set prices? In Artinger and Gigerenzer's (2016) study, almost all of the dealers (97 percent) used a satisficing heuristic. Nineteen percent of the dealers relied on the basic satisficing heuristic: They chose an initial price (the aspiration level), typically below the average price on the market, and kept it constant until the car was sold. The majority (78 percent) of dealers relied on satisficing with adaptation. Typically, they chose an initial price above the middle of the price range on the market and, if the car was not sold after about four weeks, lowered the price, and so on (Artinger & Gigerenzer, 2016). Do dealers leave money on the table by relying on satisficing? A comparison with the economic models mentioned above indicated that both versions of satisficing used by the dealers led to higher, in fact, more than double the profit. Heuristics can perform well under uncertainty.

The study of the adaptive toolbox has documented several classes of heuristics besides satisficing. One class consists of one-reason heuristics, which rely on a single powerful cue and ignore all others (see below). Another class contains lexicographic heuristics, including fast-and-frugal trees and take-the-best. Lexicographic rules also base the final decision on one reason only, but unlike one-reason heuristics, they may search through several reasons before finding the decisive one. A fourth class consists of social heuristics, designed for coordination, competition, and co-operation. An overview of these heuristics can be found in Gigerenzer and Gaissmaier (2011) and Gigerenzer et al. (2011)

Ecological rationality of heuristics

The goal of the study of ecological rationality is to determine the match between heuristics and environment, that is, the structure of environments that a given class of heuristics can exploit (Todd, Gigerenzer, & the ABC Research Group, 2012; Gigerenzer & Selten, 2001). As a first approximation, "a heuristic is ecologically rational to the degree it is adapted to the structure of the environment" (Gigerenzer & Todd, 1999, p. 13). In his Nobel lecture, Smith (2003) used this definition and generalized it from heuristics to markets. I will illustrate the study of ecological rationality with the prediction of customer behavior.

A large apparel retailer sends special offers and targeted information to customers. The retailer's goal is to target offers at "active" customers who are likely to make purchases in the future. The overall aim is to remove inactive, unprofitable customers from the customer base; identify profitable, inactive customers who should be reactivated; and determine active customers who should be targeted with regular marketing activities. But how can the marketing department predict which of their previous customers will make a purchase in the future? In the tradition of optimizing models, stochastic customer base models such as the Pareto/NBD model (NBD stands for "negative binomial distribution") have been proposed as models for repeat purchase behavior. These models try to fine-tune predictions by making complex assumptions about individual behavior and the heterogeneity across customers, assuming that customers buy at a steady albeit stochastic rate until they eventually become inactive (see Wübben & von Wangenheim, 2008). When experienced managers from a large apparel retailer were studied, however, it was found that they did not use these complex models. Instead, the managers relied on a simple rule:

> Hiatus heuristic: *If a customer has not made a purchase for nine months or longer, classify them as inactive, otherwise as active.*

The hiatus can vary, depending on the kind of business, but the decision is based on a single reason, the recency of purchase. All other cues, such as the frequency of purchase, are ignored. The hiatus heuristic is an instance of the class of *one-reason heuristics* (Gigerenzer & Gaissmaier, 2011).

Why would experienced managers rely on only a single reason? The traditional heuristics-and-biases view might conclude that relying on one reason is naïve and may be due to managers' limited cognitive capacities. From this viewpoint, managers should better use stochastic customer base models such as the Pareto/NBD model. But note that the managers are in a situation of uncertainty, not in a small world of risk. The methodology outlined above—algorithmic models of heuristics, competitive testing, and tests of predictions—explains how to perform a competitive test between the complex Pareto/NBD model and the simple hiatus heuristic. The result of such a test showed that the Pareto/NBD model did predict future purchases for 75 percent of the customers correctly, but the hiatus heuristic did so for 83 percent (Wübben & von Wangenheim, 2008). Is this apparel company an exception? Subsequent tests showed otherwise: In 60 further tests, the hiatus heuristic was, on average, better at predicting behavior than were several stochastic customer base models. Or are these stochastic customer models substandard? In the same 60 tests, the hiatus heuristic on average also better predicted behavior in comparison with logistic regression and with random forests, one of the most powerful machine learning techniques (Artinger, Kozodi, Wangenheim, & Gigerenzer, 2018). Under uncertainty, a single powerful reason can lead to more accurate, more transparent, and less costly predictions than those made by highly complex machine learning algorithms.

This existence proof of the predictive power of the heuristic does not yet tell us *when* the heuristic will succeed or not. After all, it predicted better on average, but not in every individual case. What environmental structures does the hiatus heuristic exploit when making accurate predictions with little effort? The study of the ecological rationality of heuristics provides answers to such questions (Gigerenzer et al., 2011). To illustrate, I briefly describe a condition for the ecological rationality of the hiatus heuristic, which also holds for similar one-reason heuristics.

Instead of the hiatus heuristic, consider now a linear strategy that uses and combines more cues. It uses n binary cues $x_1, ..., x_n$, with values of either +1 or –1, where the positive value indicates future purchases. The weights of the cues are $w_1, ..., w_n$, all of which are positive:

$$y = w_1 x_1 + w_2 x_2 + w_3 x_3 + ... + w_n x_n$$

The linear rule makes the inference "active" if $y > 0$, otherwise "inactive." Linear algorithms are standard approaches to prediction, which I use as reference point for a comparative analysis with one-reason heuristics. Let us give the single cue used by the heuristic the number 1, and the remaining cues the numbers 2, ..., n. Like the beta weights in a logistic regression, the weights of each of the remaining cues reflect their *additional* contribution to the higher ranked cues. If the following *dominant cue* condition holds, one can show that the linear rule cannot lead to more accurate inferences than a one-reason heuristic:

> *Dominant Cue Condition.* The weights $w_1, w_2, w_3, ... w_n$ form a dominant cue structure if they satisfy the inequality constraint:

$$w_1 > \sum_{i=2}^{n} w_i$$

In words, the condition is that the weight of the first cue is larger than the sum of the weights of all other cues. The weights 1, ½, ¼, and ⅛ are an example. If this condition holds, the linear rule will always make the same inference as the hiatus heuristic. For instance, if the dominant cue has a positive value (such as "made a purchase in the last nine months"), the hiatus heuristic leads to the inference that the customer is "active," as does the linear algorithm, whatever the values on the remaining cues are—even if all are negative. The reason is that a dominant cue cannot be overturned or compensated by the sum of all lower-ranking cues. In this situation, despite more effort, the linear strategy cannot be more accurate than the heuristic. If instead the weights were, say, 1, ¾, ½, and ¼, the dominant cue condition would not hold. For a more systematic treatment of the ecological rationality of heuristics, see Gigerenzer (2016), Martignon and Hoffrage (2002), Martignon, Katsikopoulos, and Woike (2008) and Şimşek (2013).

This analysis makes clear that the rationality of a heuristic cannot be evaluated by looking at the heuristic and concluding that it is overly simple, but only by looking at its match with the environment. Dominant cues and even noncompensatory cues (a stronger condition where dominance must hold for every cue relative to the lower-ranked ones, not only for the top cue) appear to be the rule rather than the exception in many real-world problems (Şimşek, 2013). The dominant cue condition explains when it is rational to rely on a single cue and ignore the rest. At a more general level, which I cannot cover here, the bias–variance dilemma explains in what situations simple heuristics can predict better than more complex strategies, and vice versa (Gigerenzer & Brighton, 2009).

Ecological rationality of beliefs

The study of ecological rationality is equally relevant when evaluating the rationality of beliefs. Beliefs have often been evaluated using only logic or probability theory as the gold standard, assuming situations of risk instead of uncertainty. As a result, beliefs that are correct under uncertainty have been mistaken as systematic biases and cognitive illusions (Gigerenzer, 2015; 2018; Gigerenzer, Fiedler, & Olsson, 2012). Consider intuitions about chance, where one tradition of experimental studies concludes that people in general have good intuitions (e.g., Kareev, 1992; Piaget & Inhelder, 1975) and where researchers in the heuristics-and-bias program have diagnosed systematic misconceptions. Consider a classical example.

> A fair coin is thrown four times. Which of the two strings of heads (H) and tails (T) is more likely to be encountered?
> HHH
> HHT

Most people think that HHT is more likely. This belief has been deemed a fallacy, based on the argument that each of the two strings has the same probability of occurring. The alleged fallacy was attributed to people's illusory belief in the "law of small numbers," that is, that people expect the equal probability of H and T to hold in small samples as well: HHT is more "representative" than HHH (Kahneman & Tversky, 1972).

Surprisingly, however, this popular belief is actually correct if a person observes a sequence of n coin tosses that is longer than the length k of the string (here, $k = 3$). For instance, for $n = 4$ four tosses, there are 16 possible sequences, each equally likely. Yet 4 of those contain at least one HHT, and only 3 an HHH (see Figure 2.1; Hahn & Warren, 2009). Similarly, the expected waiting time for encountering HHT is 8 tosses of a coin, compared with 14 tosses for HHH. Now we can specify the general condition under which people's belief is *ecologically rational*:

> If $k < n$, a string of Hs with a single alternation such as HHT is more likely to be encountered than a pure string such as HHH.

The belief is only a fallacy in the special case of $k = n$, or with an infinite sample, which corresponds to the population probability (Hahn & Warren, 2009). Moreover, the ecological analysis

H	H	H	H	H	H	H	H	T	T	T	T	T	T	T	T
H	H	H	H	T	T	T	T	H	H	H	H	T	T	T	T
H	H	T	T	H	H	T	T	H	H	T	T	H	H	T	T
H	T	H	T	H	T	H	T	H	T	H	T	H	T	H	T
✓	✓+	+	+	−	−	−	−	✓	+	−	−	−	−	−	−

Figure 2.1 A fair coin is flipped four times, and the result is recorded. H = heads, T = tails. Which string of flips is more likely: at least one HHH or HHT? Most people believe that HHT is more likely, whereas some researchers say that both strings are equally likely and that people's intuition are therefore biased. In fact, to encounter HHT is more likely than HHH. There are 16 possible outcomes, each equally likely; four of these have strings of HHT ("cross"), but only three strings of HHH ("check mark"). The general principle is: If the number n of tosses (here $n = 4$) is higher than the size k of the string ($k = 3$), then pure strings of heads (or tails) are less likely than those with an alteration. In this situation, people's intuition is correct (Hahn & Warren, 2009).

clarifies that the belief that HHT is more likely than HHH is not a case of the gambler's fallacy, as often assumed. The gambler's fallacy refers to the intuition that after witnessing a string of, say, two heads, one expects that the next outcome will be more likely tails than heads. This would be a true fallacy because it corresponds to the condition $k = n$. In other words, a total of three throws is considered, either HHH or HHT, and there is no sample k with the property $k < n$ (Gigerenzer, 2018).

The general point is that the statistics of a sample are not always the same as the probabilities of the population. By the same kind of ecological argument, it could be shown that the belief in the hot hand in basketball is not a fallacy, as claimed by Gilovich, Vallone, and Tversky (1985). Rather, a reanalysis of the original data showed that the belief is correct but that the researchers overlooked the difference between sample statistics and population probabilities and used the wrong gold standard (Miller & Sunjuro, 2016). Labeling a belief a bias even if no bias exists is an example of a broader phenomenon that I call the "bias bias": the tendency to see systematic biases in behavior even when there is no verifiable error at all (Gigerenzer, 2018).

The study of ecological rationality is a general approach for evaluating the rationality of heuristics and beliefs. It differs from logical rationality in that it does not compare behavior with some principle of logic or probability theory that is taken to be universally true, assuming that the situation is always one of risk. Rather, heuristics and beliefs should be evaluated against the structure of the environment, where small samples may systematically differ from a world of risk.

Guidelines for the study of decision making under uncertainty

Let me end with a summary in the form of three theoretical guidelines for studying bounded rationality:

1. *Take uncertainty seriously.* Theories of human behavior should take the distinction between risk and uncertainty seriously. What is rational under risk is not necessarily rational under uncertainty, and what is a biased belief under risk is not necessarily biased under uncertainty. In situations of risk, fine-tuned behavior is likely to be adaptive, such as continuous Bayesian probability updating. In situations of uncertainty, by contrast, simple heuristics are likely to be adaptive.

2. *Take heuristics seriously*. Under uncertainty, heuristics are not the problem but the solution. We need more studies of the adaptive toolbox of individuals and institutions and of their development over time.

3. *Take ecological rationality seriously*. Study the ecological rationality of heuristics, beliefs, and other behavior instead of their logical rationality alone.

These three insights flow from Simon's original program of bounded rationality. They open up the study of decision making to the real world in place of small-world problems where we always know the optimal solution. They also make clear that people's deviations from rationality in small worlds do not imply irrationality in the large world we live in. Under uncertainty, the bounds of rationality are both inside the mind and outside in the world. The challenge is to find out how these bounds work together. As the three insights also show, the models we build to study decision making should assume that agents are neither omniscient nor irrational. Bounded rationality is the study of rationality for mortals.

References

Akerlof, G. A., & Shiller, R. J. (2009). *Animal spirits*. Princeton, NJ: Princeton University Press.

Arrow, K. J. (2004). Is bounded rationality unbounded rational? Some ruminations. In M. Augier & J. G. March (Eds.), *Models of a man: Essays in memory of Herbert A. Simon* (pp. 47–56). Cambridge, MA: MIT Press.

Artinger, F. M., & Gigerenzer, G. (2016). The cheap twin: From the ecological rationality of heuristic pricing to the aggregate market. In J. Humphreys (Ed.), *Proceedings of the Seventy-sixth Annual Meeting of the Academy of Management*. Online ISSN: 2151–6561. doi:10.5465/ambpp.2016.206.

Artinger, F. M., Kozodi, N., Wangenheim, F., & Gigerenzer, G. (2018). Recency: Prediction with smart data. In J. Goldenberg, J. Laran, & A. Stephen (Eds.), *American Marketing Association Winter Conference Proceedings*: Vol. 29. *Integrating paradigms in a world where marketing is everywhere* (L2–L6). Chicago: American Marketing Association.

Berg, N. (2014), Success from satisficing and imitation: Entrepreneurs' location choice and implications of heuristics for local economic development, *Journal of Business Research*, 67, 1700–1709. doi:10.1016/j.jbusres.2014.02.016.

Friedman, D., Isaac, R. M., James, D., & Sunder, S. (2014). *Risky curves. On the empirical failure of expected utility*. New York: Routledge.

Friedman, M. (1953). *Essays in positive economics*. Chicago: University of Chicago Press.

Gigerenzer, G. (2004). Striking a blow for sanity in theories of rationality. In M. Augier & J. G. March (Eds.), *Models of a man: Essays in memory of Herbert A. Simon* (pp. 389–409). Cambridge, MA: MIT Press.

Gigerenzer, G. (2015). On the supposed evidence for libertarian paternalism. *Review of Philosophy and Psychology*, 6, 361–383.

Gigerenzer, G. (2016). Towards a rational theory of heuristics. In R. Frantz & L. Marsh (Eds.), *Minds, models, and milieux: Commemorating the centennial of the birth of Herbert Simon* (pp. 34–59). New York: Palgrave Macmillan.

Gigerenzer, G. (2018). The bias bias in behavioral economics. *Review of Behavioral Economics*, 5, 303–336. doi:10.1561/105.00000092.

Gigerenzer, G., & Brighton, H. (2009). Homo heuristicus: Why biased minds make better inferences. *Topics in Cognitive Science*, 1, 107–143. doi:10.1111/j.1756-8765.2008.01006.x.

Gigerenzer, G., Fiedler, K., & Olsson, H. (2012). Rethinking cognitive biases as environmental consequences. In P. M. Todd, G. Gigerenzer, & the ABC Research Group, (Eds.), *Ecological rationality: Intelligence in the world* (pp. 80–110). New York: Oxford University Press.

Gigerenzer, G., & Gaissmaier, W. (2011). Heuristic decision making. *Annual Review of Psychology*, 62, 451–482. doi:10.1146/annurev-psych-120709-145346.

Gigerenzer, G., Hertwig, R., & Pachur, T. (Eds.) (2011). *Heuristics: The foundations of adaptive behavior*. New York: Oxford University Press.

Gigerenzer, G., & Selten, R. (Eds.). (2001). *Bounded rationality: The adaptive toolbox*. Cambridge, MA: MIT Press.

Gigerenzer, G., & Todd, P. M. (1999). Fast and frugal heuristics: The adaptive toolbox. In G. Gigerenzer, P. M. Todd, & the ABC Research Group (Eds.), *Simple heuristics that make us smart* (pp. 3–34). New York: Oxford University Press.

Gilovich, T., Vallone, R. & Tversky. A. (1985). The hot hand in basketball: On the misperception of random sequences. *Cognitive Psychology*, 17, 295–314. doi:10.1016/0010-0285(85)90010-6.

Hahn, U., & Warren, P. A. (2009). Perceptions of randomness: Why three heads are better than four. *Psychological Review*, 116(2), 454–461. doi:10.1037/a0015241.

Kahneman, D. (2003). Maps of bounded rationality: Psychology for behavioral economics. *American Economic Review*, 93(5), 1449–1475.

Kahneman, D., Slovic, P., & Tversky, A. (1982). *Judgment under uncertainty: Heuristics and biases.* Cambridge: Cambridge University Press.

Kahneman, D., & Tversky, A. (1972). Subjective probability: A judgment of representativeness. *Cognitive Psychology*, 3, 430–454.

Kareev, Y. (1992). Not that bad after all: Generation of random sequences. *Journal of Experimental Psychology: Human Perception and Performance*, 18, 1189–1194. doi:10.1037/0096-1523.18.4.1189.

Keynes, J. M. (1936). *The general theory of employment, interest and money.* London: Macmillan.

Knight, F. (1921). *Risk, uncertainty and profit.* Boston, MA: Houghton Mifflin Co.

Kruglanski, A. W., & Gigerenzer, G. (2011). Intuitive and deliberative judgments are based on common principles. *Psychological Review*, 118, 97–109.

Lewin, K. A. (1935). *A dynamic theory of personality.* New York: McGraw-Hill.

Lopes, L. L. (1992). Three misleading assumptions in the customary rhetoric of the bias literature. *Theory & Psychology*, 2, 231–236. doi:10.1177/0959354392022010.

Luce, R. D., & Raiffa, H. (1957). *Games and decisions.* New York: Dover.

Martignon, L., & Hoffrage, U. (2002). Fast, frugal, and fit: Lexicographic heuristics for paired comparison. *Theory and Decision*, 52, 29–71. doi:10.1023/A:1015516217425.

Martignon, L., Katsikopoulos, K. V., & Woike, J. K. (2008). Categorization with limited resources: A family of simply heuristics. *Journal of Mathematical Psychology*, 52(6), 352–361. doi:10.1016/j.jmp.2008.04.003.

Miller, J. B., & Sanjuro, A. (2016). Surprised by the gambler's and hot hand fallacies? A truth in the law of small numbers. IGIER Working Paper No. 552. doi:10.2139/ssrn.2627354.

Oxford English Dictionary (n.d.). Heuristic. In *OED Online*. Available at: www.oed.com/view/Entry/86554?isAdvanced=false&result=1&rskey=C4NVLA& (accessed July 8, 2020).

Piaget, J., & Inhelder, B. (1975). *The origin of the idea of chance in children.* New York: Norton.

Rubinstein, A. (1998). *Modeling bounded rationality.* Cambridge, MA: MIT Press.

Sargent, T. J. (1993). *Bounded rationality in macroeconomics.* Oxford: Clarendon Press.

Savage, L. J. (1954). *The foundations of statistics.* New York: Wiley.

Sedlmeier, P., Hertwig, R., & Gigerenzer, G. (1998). Are judgments of the positional frequencies of letters systematically biased due to availability? *Journal of Experimental Psychology: Learning, Memory, and Cognition*, 24, 754–770.

Simon, H. A. (1955). A behavioral model of rational choice. *Quarterly Journal of Economics*, 69, 99–118. doi:10.2307/1884852.

Simon, H. A. (1956). Rational choice and the structure of the environment. *Psychological Review*, 63, 129–38. doi:10.1037/h0042769.

Simon, H. A. (1978). Rationality as process and as product of thought. *American Economic Review*, 68, 1–16.

Simon, H. A. (1985). Human nature in politics: The dialogue of psychology and political science. *American Political Science Review*, 79, 293–304.

Simon, H. A. (1988). Nobel laureate Simon "looks back": A low-frequency mode. *Public Administration Quarterly*, 12, 275–300.

Simon, H. A. (1989). The scientist as problem solver. In D. Klahr & K. Kotovsky (Eds.), *Complex information processing: The impact of Herbert A. Simon* (pp. 375–398). Hillsdale, NJ: Erlbaum.

Simon, H. A. (1990). Invariants of human behavior. *Annual Review of Psychology*, 41, 1–19. doi:10.1146/annurev.ps.41.020190.000245

Simon, H. A. (1997). *Models of bounded rationality*, Vol. 3: *Empirically grounded economic reason.* Cambridge, MA: MIT Press.

Şimşek, Ö. (2013). Linear decision rule as aspiration for simple decision heuristics. *Advances in Neural Information Processing Systems*, 26, 2904–2912.

Smith, V. L. (2003). Constructivist and ecological rationality in economics. *The American Economic Review,* 93(3), 465–508.

Stigler, G. J. (1961). The economics of information. *Journal of Political Economy,* 69, 213–225. doi:10.1086/ 258464.

Thaler, R. H., & Sunstein, C. R. (2008). *Nudge: Improving decisions about health, wealth, and happiness.* New Haven, CT: Yale University Press.

Todd, P. M., Gigerenzer, G., & the ABC Research Group (Eds.) (2012). *Ecological rationality: Intelligence in the world.* New York: Oxford University Press.

Tversky, A. (1972). Elimination by aspects: A theory of choice. *Psychological Review,* 79, 281–299. doi:10.1037/h0032955.

Tversky, A., & Bar-Hillel, M. (1983). Risk: The long and the short. *Journal of Experimental Psychology: Learning, Memory, and Cognition, 9*(4), 713–717. doi:10.1037/0278-7393.9.4.713.

Tversky, A., & Kahneman, D. (1973). Availability: A heuristic for judging frequency and probability. *Cognitive Psychology,* 5, 207–232.

Tversky, A., & Kahneman, D. (1974). Judgement under uncertainty: Heuristics and biases. *Science,* 185, 1124–1131. doi:10.1126/science.185.4157.1124.

Wübben M, & von Wangenheim F. (2008). Instant customer base analysis: managerial heuristics often "get it right." *Journal of Marketing,* 72, 82–93. doi:10.1509/jmkg.72.3.82.

PART I

Naturalizing bounded rationality

3

TOWARDS A CRITICAL NATURALISM ABOUT BOUNDED RATIONALITY

Thomas Sturm

Introduction

Rationality (or reason[1]) has often been declared to be a central topic of philosophy: as the source of principles either for metaphysics and ethics, or for epistemology and philosophy of science. Some authors even identify philosophy with the theory of rationality (Habermas, 1981, p. 16; Putnam, 1981, p. 113; Nozick, 1993, p. xi; Nida-Rümelin, 1996, p. 73; Grice, 2001, p. 4). However, most philosophers nowadays understand that it is not only philosophers who have developed our understanding of rationality. Beginning in the Enlightenment, and to an ever greater extent over the last century, sciences such as mathematics, statistics, economics or psychology have (partly) conquered this territory (Gigerenzer et al., 1989; Erickson et al., 2013; Sturm, forthcoming). The contributions on bounded rationality from Herbert Simon through to Gerd Gigerenzer, and their collaborators and followers, belong to this trend too.

The idea that theories of rationality obtain support from science should be grist to the mill of the philosophical doctrine of *naturalism*. While there are many versions of naturalism, they all share the view that the relation between philosophy and the sciences is (at least) one of close allies, and that the sciences contribute through their theories and methods to the solution of philosophical problems. Anti-naturalists, in turn, defend a separation of philosophy and the sciences, insisting that philosophy has *sui generis* methods for dealing with its own distinctive problems.

Both these opposing positions have been applied to rationality (Sober, 1981; Putnam, 1982; Stich, 1985, 1990, 1993; Hauptli, 1995; Pacho, 1995; Stein, 1996; Chiappe & Verwaeke, 1997; Bermúdez & Millar, 2002). Meanwhile, very few philosophers have drawn on Simon's (1956, 1957) work on *bounded* rationality (Giere, 1985, 1988; Cherniak, 1986; Gigerenzer & Sturm, 2012; deLanghe, 2013; Hahn, 2013, Chapter 8).[2] This is surprising, since bounded rationality (1) is an empirically grounded account of reasoning; and (2) does not merely have descriptive or explanatory aspirations, but normative or prescriptive ones as well. Thus, this notion of bounded rationality offers a path towards a naturalistic account of rationality—one that addresses the important issue of the normativity of rationality, which is often seen as a major challenge to any such naturalization.

No comprehensive study of the philosophical aspects of bounded rationality exists. Such a study would, at least, have to (1) explicate and scrutinize the presuppositions of the concept

DOI: 10.4324/9781315658353-4

(such as its descriptive as well as normative aspirations, or its difference to non-bounded conceptions of rationality); (2) determine areas in philosophy where models of bounded rationality might be used, and assess such uses where they exist; and (3) address the fundamental debates over its theoretical and methodological adequacy in psychology, economics, sociology, and political science, as well as the potential and limits of its interdisciplinary uses. While such a study cannot be carried out here, I shall include selected aspects of (1) and (2). I first outline three systems of reasoning that are constitutive of the "standard picture" of rationality, and highlighting two major criticisms of that picture, both associated with bounded rationality. Then, I introduce some major assumptions of naturalism and the challenges they face. Finally, I discuss the prospects and limits of bounded rationality for what I call "critical" naturalism in epistemology, with occasional considerations concerning the philosophy of science.

The "standard picture": three normative systems of rationality

We try to reason well, whether to convince others or ourselves of a point of view, to discover new knowledge that allows us to defend our pet beliefs, or to make good decisions. Our reasoning certainly can be either good or bad. However, this can only be the case if there are standards or norms of reasoning that have been agreed upon. What are they? According to Stein's (1996) useful term, the "standard picture" of rationality consists of a set of three normative systems of judgment and decision making that are dominant nowadays in numerous areas, and often opposed by defenders of bounded rationality.

One of those systems is derived from the revolution in logic that started in the nineteenth century with the work of the philosopher-mathematician Gottlob Frege (1848–1925). If we consider this, it will quickly lead us to the dominant view concerning the relation between reasoning and normativity. Frege's achievements influenced subsequent work in logic, from that of Bertrand Russell and Alfred N. Whitehead through to that of Alfred Tarski and Alan Turing. Thus, Frege's work even paved the way for modern computers—and for Simon and Newell's "Logic Theorist" program (Newell et al., 1958). Frege's main project was to show that a part of mathematics, namely, arithmetic, could be reduced to logical laws. This is the doctrine of *logicism*. Since the existing logics, as Frege found them, were insufficient for such a reduction, he radically overhauled them by creating an axiomatized predicate calculus with innovative tools for complex quantification. While his logicism was—as he himself later admitted—unsuccessful, the central achievements of his new logic are still alive and well today.

Frege was aware of views that drew no sharp distinction between logic and psychology. He rejected them by claiming that the *validity* of logical laws is independent of how people *actually* think and reason (Frege, 1966). This is his *anti-psychologism*, which has remained a forceful reason for anti-naturalism until today. Frege's main basis for this stance was that actual reasoning is subject to mistakes and fallacies, and so cannot ensure what logic guarantees. Logical rules determine whether reasoning from premises to conclusions is truth-preserving. Whether the premises of an argument are true or not cannot be decided by logic alone; but logic tells us which patterns of inference guarantee that *if* the premises are true, *then* the conclusion will also be true. The validity of logical laws has to do, among other things, with the meaning of logical connectives such as '$\rightarrow$' (interpreted as a specific version of the ordinary "if-then" conditional) and '$\neg$' (negation). Thus, *modus ponens* (1. $p \rightarrow q$; 2. p; 3. Therefore, q.) or *modus tollens* (1. $p \rightarrow q$; 2. $\neg q$; 3. Therefore, $\neg p$) are deductively valid under any interpretation of the propositional variables p and q. Of course, humans sometimes violate such rules. For instance, there is the fallacy of "denying the antecedent": 1. $p \rightarrow q$; 2. $\neg p$; 3. Therefore, $\neg q$. Consider for example:

If you are a banker, then you have a regular income. You are not a banker. Therefore, you do not have a regular income.

Clearly, you do not have to sell your soul to monetary businesses to have a regular income. In other inferences, the mistake is less easy to detect. Alan Turing considered the following argument: "If each man had a definite set of rules of conduct by which he regulated his life he would be no better than a machine. But there are no such rules, so men cannot be machines" (Turing, 1950, p. 452). Again, this is an example of the same fallacy. But maybe what those who propose such an argument really mean is:

> *Only* if each man had a definite set of rules of conduct by which he regulated his life he would be no better than a machine. But there are no such rules, so men cannot be machines.

In this case, the inference would not embody "denying the antecedent". But surely people can mix up p's and q's, neglect logical meanings, and thus end up committing a fallacy.

While logicism concerns the foundations of arithmetic, anti-psychologism concerns the basis of logic. Even psychologists such as Peter Wason (1966) and many others have accepted anti-psychologism by testing human reasoning against logical laws taken as unquestioned normative yardsticks. Neither did Simon and Newell question the validity and applicability of formal logic—the Logic Theorist was constructed to prove numerous theorems in Russell and Whitehead's *Principia Mathematica* (the so-called artificial intelligence thesis), and Simon and Newell also viewed the program as a model of human reasoning (the information-processing thesis): the Logic Theorist "provides an explanation for the processes used by humans to solve problems in symbolic logic" (Newell et al., 1958, p. 163). Thus, the logical model was projected into the mind, not the other way around (Gigerenzer & Sturm, 2007, pp. 325–327).

Anti-psychologism is often described as being based on a rejection of the Is–Ought fallacy (noted in Hume, emphasized by Kant, used and discussed further in later debates on theoretical and practical rationality; see Sturm, forthcoming): one cannot infer normative judgments from descriptive ones. For instance, from the descriptive claim that people often engage in tax evasion, it does not follow that one should engage in tax fraud. From the claim that people often do not blame others for engaging in tax fraud, it does not follow that one should not be blamed for engaging in tax fraud. Frege's anti-psychologism, however, is *not* derived from rejecting the Is–Ought fallacy. Contrary to what is sometimes asserted (e.g., Notturno, 1985), Frege did not view the laws of logic as inherently normative, but as descriptive. However, descriptive of *what*? He claimed that logical rules or patterns of inference are universally and timelessly valid. His objection to psychologism, then, addressed a specific version of this doctrine: attempts to explain logical "laws of thought" as laws of actual thinking, with the latter being understood as a chain of "subjective" mental representations. Against this version of psychologism, Frege argued that such representations are too variable to constitute a possible basis of logical laws, given their universality and timeless validity. That is why, in order to justify such laws, Frege (1966, 43) required that we accept a "third realm" (*drittes Reich*) beyond the material world and our subjective mental representations. This argument is disputed, but it cannot be discussed here (cf. e.g., Sober, 1978; Carl, 1994, Chapter 2).[3] What matters here is a straightforward point: since we can make mistakes in our reasoning, we ought to correct them, and that may involve logical laws. To deny this force of logic by claiming that our actual reasoning sometimes works in different ways is to fall prey to various kinds of psychologism.

Still, we will see that under certain conditions, the charge of psychologism can be avoided, and assumptions of bounded rationality play a role in this.

Anti-psychologism became popular beyond logic, especially through the epistemology and philosophy of science of the Vienna Circle and Popper's Falsificationism (Peckhaus, 2006). After all, not all reasoning, whether ordinary or scientific, is deductive. Many non-deductive inferences, for instance, about scientific hypotheses, use probabilities. This leads to a second normative system that is important for the standard picture: theories of probability as developed by, e.g., Rudolf Carnap or Hans Reichenbach, alongside with mathematicians and statisticians.[4] Their theories tried to do for "inductive" logic what Frege had achieved for deductive logic: an axiomatic system with clear tasks, limits, and structure, only one that normatively guides probable reasoning. While the mathematics of probability was axiomatized by the mathematician Andrej Kolmogorov (1903–1987), the meaning of probability remains disputed, and thereby so do its proper applications. There are, for instance, logical theories aimed at determining degrees of confirmation above 0 for scientific hypotheses, relative to given empirical evidence (Carnap); the so-called frequentism, which views probabilities as the limiting frequency of outcomes in long-run or potentially infinite series of similar events (Reichenbach); or the propensity theory, which takes probabilities to be properties that are inherent to sets of repeatable conditions (Karl Popper). However, none of these theories is without its problems; and none of them can claim to represent "the" meaning of 'probability': a term which is ambiguous and can serve different functions (Gigerenzer et al., 1989; Gillies, 2000). A fundamental pluralism with regard to probability is widespread today. What is more, while Carnap and others assumed that Fregean anti-psychologism concerning logic could be expanded into epistemology or philosophy of science, today it is far from clear that such a move comes without costs (Sober, 1978; Peckhaus, 2006). It would require all philosophical claims about knowledge or science to be formal or logical truths, which is highly implausible.

Third, and finally, since the mid-twentieth century, theories of rational choice have emerged, beginning with John von Neumann and Oscar Morgenstern's landmark *Theory of Games and Economic Behavior* (1944), which was itself influenced by the rise of logic. Moreover, rational choice owes much to economic theories of utility maximization that emerged in previous centuries. It seems plausible to say that if you are a rational agent, you ought to maximize your (expected) advantage, given what you believe the probability of certain outcomes to be.

So, these normative systems coalesced into the standard picture of rationality: if you are perfectly rational, you have to reason in line with logic, probability, and decision theory. Even today, these formal and optimizing theories are viewed even by many as (1) a descriptive model for human reasoning and, perhaps more importantly, (2) the normative yardsticks for such reasoning.[5] However, questions concerning the normative validity of the standard picture arise: What justifies the rules of each of these theories? And why should we reason in line with them in particular situations?

Two objections to the standard picture

I now consider two influential objections to the standard picture, both related to bounded rationality. As the term "bounded rationality" is often meant to include *all* empirical theories that try to account for informal and non-optimal reasoning using both lazy and hard constraints (Oaksford & Chater, 1991), the objections differ considerably. This, in turn, leads to different connections that one can draw between bounded rationality and naturalism.

Objection 1: Insofar as the formal theories were interpreted descriptively—not in the Fregean sense of describing a realm of logical entities and their formal relations, but as being descriptive of human thinking and decision-making—one could find *empirical* counterexamples to them. This led to the demand to build an alternative account of judgment and decision-making. Thus, Wason's (1966) four-card test aimed to refute Piaget's theory of cognitive development, according to which we master propositional calculus from age 12 onwards. Similarly, the program of "heuristics and biases" (henceforth, HB), developed by Daniel Kahneman and Amos Tversky, attempted to show that the view of "man as an intuitive statistician" (Peterson & Beach, 1967) whose behavior approximates the canons of probability was mistaken. Reasoning fallacies and mistakes that the HB program detected include conjunction errors (the "Linda problem"), neglecting the obligation to use sufficiently large statistical samples ("law of small numbers"), the base rate fallacy, and so on (Kahneman, Slovic, & Tversky, 1982; Tversky & Kahneman, 1983).

Kahneman has claimed that Simon's work is in line with the HB approach:

> [Tversky and I] explored the psychology of intuitive beliefs and choices and examined their bounded rationality. Herbert A. Simon … had proposed much earlier that decision makers should be viewed as boundedly rational, and had offered a model in which utility maximization was replaced by satisficing. Our research attempted to obtain a map of bounded rationality, by exploring the systematic biases that separate the beliefs that people have and the choices they make from the optimal beliefs and choices assumed in rational-agent models.
>
> *Kahneman, 2003, 1449; see also Kahneman, Slovic,*
> *& Tversky, 1982, pp. xi–xii*

Kahneman's view that humans are often irrational results from adopting rules of the standard picture as yardsticks. Our intuitive judgments and decisions then have to be explained in terms of so-called heuristics (e.g., "representativeness" or "availability"). Understood this way, "bounded rationality" implies that standard "rational models are psychologically unrealistic", and "maps of bounded rationality" are supposed to account for deviations from the "rational agent model" (Kahneman, 2003, p. 1449).

Objection 2: Formal and optimizing rules set substantive norms for ideal reasoners, i.e. reasoners equipped with infinite time, memory, and other resources. But, Simon said, we must distinguish between substantive and "procedural" rationality (a distinction that paved the way towards bounded rationality; see Erickson et al., 2013, Chapter 2). It is one thing to judge whether an outcome is reasonable in the light of a standard norm; it is quite another to judge whether an outcome is reasonable in the light of whether the process that leads to it is overly costly.

Importantly, there are stubborn problems of *computational intractability*. Cognitive processes which require resources that increase at an exponential rate (i.e., 2^n, or more) are regarded as creating such problems. Consider the traveling salesman problem, i.e. finding the optimal route between a number of locations when one travels to each location only once and the whole tour is as short as possible. Calculating the optimal route between e.g., 50 cities requires calculating no less than 300,000,000,000,000,000,000,000,000,000,000,000,000,000,000,000,000,000,000 possible routes. To date, no human, and no computer can do that. There is a similar situation for tasks such as finding the optimal path for winning in chess, or making investment choices, and other daily and scientific problems (Michaelewicz & Fogel, 2000). Hard computational intractability may make it impossible to use the norms of the standard picture. Even if the formalistic and optimizing approach to rationality produced rules that were valid within the axiomatic systems to which they belong, we may have to give up the close connection between the formal validity and the rationality of patterns of inference. There is, then, a gap between formal (including optimizing) rules and rationality.

Simon and others have seen this gap as a major reason for developing models of bounded rationality, in order to figure out how people actually do reason, but also how they can reason well:

> Bounded rationality dispenses with the notion of optimization and, usually, with probabilities and utilities as well. It provides an alternative to current norms, not an account that accepts current norms and studies when humans deviate from these norms. Bounded rationality means rethinking the norms as well as studying the actual behavior of minds and institutions.
>
> *Gigerenzer & Selten, 2001, p. 6*

One of Simon's most influential ideas was to replace the goal of maximizing expected utility by "satisficing". In Gigerenzer's view, reasoning (often) uses fast and frugal heuristics (henceforth, FFH) that also work with little information and computation, such as the "recognition heuristic", the "fluency heuristic", or "take the best" (for an overview of ten well-studied heuristics, see Gigerenzer & Sturm, 2012, p. 249f.). That FFH do not merely describe behavior but should, in a number of cases, also guide our judgments and decisions is justified if and insofar as reasoning processes express a certain fitness function between mind and environment (Gigerenzer, Chapter 2 in this volume). That function needs to be discovered empirically.

Understood this way, bounded rationality questions the sharp divide between the descriptive and the normative—quite different from Kahneman's understanding of the concept. However, no Is-Ought fallacy thereby needs to be implied. Instead, underlying this blurring of the boundary is a legitimate principle of normativity: *ought implies can* (also already recognized by Kant). The intractability of many reasoning tasks restricts the applicability of certain formal and optimizing norms, and thus makes it reasonable to look for different, more feasible norms.

The difference between these two objections leads to two disputes. The first, purely empirical objection has prompted discussion on the extent to which humans are rational, asked in the light of norms of the standard picture of rationality. The results range from "completely irrational" to "sometimes irrational". In contrast, the second objection has raised the question of which norms should guide good reasoning in the face of widespread intractability and uncertainty: those of the standard picture, or those of bounded rationality understood normatively (i.e., Simon's and Gigerenzer's approach)? Or maybe both? As we will see next, philosophical projects of naturalizing rationality disagree here too.

Naturalism: its aims, scope, assumptions, and problems

Although it is considerably older, naturalism has become popular since the 1960s (Quine, 1969; Kitcher, 1992; Kornblith, 1994; Rosenberg, 1996).[6] Naturalists object to "armchair" methods such as conceptual analysis, thought experiments, or appeals to intuition (DePaul & Ramsey, 1998; Kornblith, 2007), claiming that science provides better resources with its methods or theories, and viewing philosophy that isolates itself as sterile and obsolete. Some naturalists have even claimed that the traditional tasks and methods of philosophy will sooner or later be *replaced* by science (e.g., Quine, 1969).

Naturalism is a *metaphilosophical* thesis: a view about philosophy's questions, methods, and aims. To be convincing, naturalism has to prove itself by being specific as to its domains, as to what claims it makes on what grounds, and as to how it defends itself against objections. Thus, naturalism has been developed in metaphysics (Ladyman, 2007), philosophy of mind (Dennett, 1991; Dretske, 1996), ethics (Harman, 1977, Lenman, 2009), epistemology (Goldman 1986; Kornblith, 1993, 2002), philosophy of science (Giere, 1985, 1988, 1992; Laudan, 1987, 1990; Kitcher, 1993; Mi & Chen, 2007; Viale, 2013), and other domains as well (De Caro & MacArthur, 2004, 2010; Galparsoro & Cordero, 2013). Cutting across these divisions of domains, naturalists make different general claims. Two of their basic convictions are:

(ON) Reality consists only of natural objects, their properties, and relations: there are no unexplainable or irreducible supernatural entities or powers.

(MN) Philosophical questions can and should be answered by relying on the methods of the empirical sciences: there is no *a priori* philosophical knowledge and there are no special philosophical methods.

"ON" stands for "ontological naturalism", and "MN" for "methodological naturalism" (De Caro & MacArthur, 2010; Galparsoro & Cordero, 2013). Naturalists usually have additional commitments, such as to Darwinism (Rosenberg, 1996) or physicalism (Papineau, 2015). Without them, (ON) might be so uncontroversial that most non-naturalistic philosophers would accept it too. We do not know what (ON) comes down to unless we have a specific scientific theory that explains the relevant objects and their properties and relations. If one defends (ON) about the mind, one could use theories rooted in biology or neuroscience. In the area that concerns us here, rationality, naturalists usually look to psychology, but also to other sciences, such as those just mentioned. Such an expansion also helps to distinguish between psychologism and naturalism. In any case, it all depends on the quality or validity of the specific theory the naturalist offers. Naturalists acknowledge the necessity of this task of specification, and many have invested much effort in connecting scientific theories to philosophical problems.

(MN) is controversial too. To begin, can *all* philosophical questions be answered by scientific methods? Or only *some*? If so, which ones? And how can the sciences deliver? Questions concerning the nature of time, free will, knowledge, or the normative basis of morality certainly do not seem to be suited to empirical methods. With few exceptions (despite the recent development of "experimental philosophy"), philosophers do not perform observations, experiments, statistical analysis, and so on. As Nozick (1993, p. xi) has noted, what philosophers really love is not wisdom but *reasoning* as such: thinking about it as well as practicing it.

As if all that were not enough, naturalists have to face straightforward anti-naturalistic arguments, e.g., the claims that we have *a priori* knowledge that cannot be explained naturalistically (Putnam, 1982), that naturalism falls prey to naturalistic fallacies (Kim, 1988), that it leads to circularity or self-destructiveness (BonJour, 1994), triviality (Stroud, 1996), or that it lacks clarity (Sklar, 2010). We will see that similar points come up when we look at naturalism about rationality. In particular, a central challenge naturalists have to face in our case should be clear: to provide a scientific account that treats the normativity of rationality as something within the natural world, and explainable by scientific theory. This is not an easy task.

Naturalism about (bounded) rationality

Naturalists have drawn a variety of connections between rationality and the sciences. They appeal to the HB approach in order to address problems of epistemic rationality (Goldman, 1986; Stich, 1990; Kornblith, 1993; Bishop and Trout, 2005) or decision making concerning scientific theories (Solomon, 1992; Kitcher, 1993). They deal with claims of evolutionary psychology to explain the nature and foundation of rationality (Stein, 1996); and occasionally research on satisficing and FFH has been exploited as well (Giere, 1985, 1988; Cherniak, 1986; Gigerenzer & Sturm, 2012; Sturm, 2019; Hey, 2016.

Before we can move on, some clarification is needed. If naturalism about rationality merely required *some* sciences to be used in the detection, explication, and justification of the norms of rationality, then the standard picture might already count as naturalistic, since it involves results of mathematicians or economists. However, that would contradict (MN). The normative systems of the standard picture are all *a priori*, not the result of observation or experiment.[7] One might, of course, suggest dropping the reference to empirical science, thus replacing (MN) by:

> (MN*) Philosophical questions can and should be answered by relying on the methods and results of the sciences.

Stated differently, "naturalism" would just mean "scientism". This move, however, trivializes naturalism about rationality. Since the non-empirical, *a priori* character of logical rules has always been a central point of conflict between psychologism and anti-psychologism, naturalism and anti-naturalism, we should not take it for granted that a formal-rules account of rationality is naturalistic enough. The same line of reasoning works, *mutatis mutandis*, for theories of probability and decision making. The fact that Kolmogorov was a mathematician and not a philosopher does not mean that his work provided a naturalistic account of probability theory.

(MN*) might, furthermore, undermine (ON): If naturalists simply accept what comes from the formal sciences, without giving a naturalistic explanation of the relevant abstract entities and rules, then they might be asked how they deal with Frege's talk of a "third realm" of logical laws. (ON) must do better. An interesting naturalism about rationality should therefore build on genuinely *empirical* theories. No surprise, then, that many naturalists about rationality look to evolutionary and cognitive psychology, or to biology and neuroscience. For reasons of space, I cannot further discuss (ON) about rationality in this chapter (cf. Sober, 1981; Chiappe & Verwaeke, 1997).

Now, as seen above, the term "bounded rationality" has been used for both the HB program, and the Simon-Gigerenzer program of satisficing and FFH. Let us now consider each of these in turn.

Once the HB program had become popular in science, it was adopted by naturalists too. Many viewed it as the scientific version of the mundane view that humans are prone to errors and fallacies. What is more, some followed the interpretation according to which HB studies showed that humans are deeply irrational (e.g., Stich, 1985). Unfortunately, such naturalists had to recognize that results of the HB approach became increasingly contested. The criticism not only came from philosophical armchair arguments (though these could be influential: Cohen, 1981). Psychologists objected that the data of HB studies were not stable enough to claim that human beings completely violated the standard picture of rationality, that theoretical concepts such as "representativeness" or "availability" were not precise enough to permit interesting, testable predictions, or that the normative assumptions used in the experiments could be questioned as well (Gigerenzer, 1991, 1996; Lopes, 1991; Cosmides and Tooby, 1996). This psychological debate is called the "rationality wars" (Samuels, Stich, & Bishop, 2002; Sturm, 2012a).

Thus, even naturalists have to make hard choices: Do the empirical results really warrant the conclusion that humans are highly irrational? What methods, concepts, and normative assumptions should psychologists use? What do we even *mean* when we call judgments, or processes, rational or irrational? Hilary Kornblith (1993, Chapter 5), another naturalist, has discussed such questions for the "law of small numbers" (Kahneman, Slovic, & Tversky, 1982, Chapter 2). He argues that the alleged irrationality of human beings is not supported by the relevant studies, and that we can be more optimistic if we apply a background assumption from evolutionary theory:

> Just as our perceptual mechanisms are well adapted to the environment in which they typically operate and build in presuppositions about the environment which are typically true, so our inferential mechanisms may also be built around presuppositions about standard environments which allow us to gain information about those environments quickly and accurately.
>
> *Kornblith, 1993, p. 86*

He also immediately warns his reader: "There is of course, no a priori guarantee that this is the right perspective on human inference, and we should not try to force the data into such a mould" (Kornblith, 1993). Thus, naturalists do what they should abhor, given (MN): they reflect on science from a critical, normative point of view—as Kornblith says, "we *should not try* to force the data into such a mould" (emphasis added). It is, of course, the existence of conflicting approaches in cognitive psychology, or disputes over the interpretation of data that prompt Kornblith to take sides. Still, a strict and consistent naturalist should want to explain this critical, normative perspective itself again in purely naturalistic terms, by looking to e.g., a biological or psychological theory of such a critical, normative point of view. Kornblith does not do that, nor do other naturalists who engage critically with the empirical literature. Thus, while (MN★) trivializes naturalism about rationality, (MN) leads either into a regress or it implies the acceptance of an unexplained non-naturalistic perspective.

One reasonable response here is that naturalism should give up the aim of ultimately *replacing* philosophy by science, and should settle for *cooperation* between the two (cf. Feldman, 2001):

> (CMN) Philosophical questions can and should be pursued in cooperation with the sciences (e.g., by using their methods and/or results).

(CMN) does not demand that all normative claims be explained in non-normative terms. Moreover, it is compatible with a certain normative use of HB results. Consider that epistemology has different traditional tasks (Stich, 1993): the definition of the concept of knowledge (as attempted in Plato's *Theaetetus* or in much current analytic epistemology), the refutation of radical skepticism about knowledge (as pursued in Descartes' *Meditations*), or also genuinely normative tasks, such as justifying or correcting our beliefs, or providing methods for discovering new knowledge. Naturalists, when appealing to cognitive psychology, often hope to profit for the third, normative tasks.[8]

Goldman's (1986, Chapters 13, 14) approach is an excellent example of this. Among other things, he shows that formal rules in the standard picture of rationality often do not map onto reasoning tasks in a straightforward manner. For instance, the logical law of non-contradiction, $\neg(\neg p \wedge p)$, states that a proposition and its negation cannot both be true. From contradictions, anything whatsoever can be derived. We should, it seems, therefore avoid inconsistencies. But then, what do you do when you discover inconsistencies in your belief set? Are you obliged to give up the *whole* set? Certainly not: we should separate the wheat from the chaff. However, that can prove to be difficult, especially in the complex belief systems of science, where several beliefs are all tenuous but part of a systematic theory. Similar examples can be found for other logical rules, such as deductive closure, or for rules of probability. There is, therefore, no simple derivation of norms of epistemic rationality from formal rules of the standard picture. This is more support for the gap mentioned earlier on.

To bridge that gap, Goldman (1986; 2008) maintains that a distinctively philosophical or "analytic" epistemology has to determine the criteria or goals of our epistemic endeavors. He here defends *reliabilism*: our belief-forming mechanisms need not always guarantee truth, but must safeguard a good ratio of true and false beliefs. We can learn from psychology which mental processes or mechanisms are reliable, and which ones are not. Heuristics are rules of thumb that often lead to true beliefs, though they also lead to errors and fallacies; that is just an epistemic risk we have to live with. For instance, HB studies provide insight into how *not* to reason: we can, and we should, learn to control the workings of heuristics so as to avoid biases (cf. Kahneman, Slovic, & Tversky, 1982, Chapter 30; and "dual systems" theory, Evans, Chapter 10 in this volume).[9] In Goldman's cooperative naturalism, cognitive psychology will not replace philosophical epistemology, but neither will the latter thrive without the former.

What should we think of such an approach? To begin with, Goldman, like other naturalists (e.g., Giere, 1985), thinks of epistemic rationality as a means–ends notion: given certain epistemic goals, we ought to use such-and-such a method. This *instrumentalism* about epistemic rationality helps to justify certain methods over others. Since means–ends relations have to be discovered empirically, this also adds support to the idea that norms and methods can be justified empirically. However, while Goldman asserts that the goals have to be set by analytic epistemology, and while he favors a reliabilism according to which we ought to select methods that lead to a good ratio of true and false beliefs, not all naturalists agree. Some argue that we should not care whether our beliefs are true, or that the goals we should care about are primarily pragmatic ones (Giere, 1988; Stich, 1990). Furthermore, it is far from clear that instrumentalism is acceptable at all when it comes to *epistemic* rationality: whether or not epistemic reasoning is good or bad might be entirely independent of what goals we pursue. At least some of our beliefs can be found to be justified, or be rationally warranted, no matter what our specific epistemic or other goals are (Siegel, 1989; Kelly, 2003).

Another point is that Goldman (1986) does not show that naturalists have no options besides HB. We will see how the Simon–Gigerenzer conception of bounded rationality provides an alternative.[10] What is more, for HB to actually work, HB studies would have to be uncontested with respect to their claims concerning cognitive mechanisms. They simply are not. Kahneman and Tversky have long been challenged to produce process models that have real explanatory value or that allow for precise, testable predictions. The heuristics they cite, such as representativeness or availability, look more like mere redescriptions of the behavior they are supposed to explain (Gigerenzer, 1996).

However, let us assume for the sake of the argument that the HB program could do better at the explanatory and predictive tasks, and focus again on the normative issue. Goldman himself has pointed to the gap between formal rules and rationality. He, therefore, cannot—unlike Kahneman and Tversky—look back to the standard picture to provide unquestionable normative yardsticks for reasoning. For Kahneman and Tversky, but also for Goodman and many other psychologists and philosophers, heuristics are viewed as being justified by an *accuracy–effort trade-off*: we use them because looking for information and computation can be too costly; we trade a loss in accuracy for faster and more frugal cognition. The difference between the HB approach and Goldman's reliabilism is that the former views heuristics as second best, whereas the latter acquiesces in saying that there is nothing better. For the HB approach, heuristics are good as rules of thumb, but ultimately our epistemic evaluations should be made in the light of standard, formal, and optimizing rules. For Goldman, we cannot but balance the costs and benefits of reasoning mechanisms, and we should adopt an instrumentalist attitude towards the methods which we view as norms of epistemic rationality.[11]

If one turns to the Simon–Gigerenzer line of thought, then Goldman's line of argument can be disputed. Naturalists occasionally cite computational intractability (Goldman, 1986, p. 282), Simon's satisficing (Giere, 1985; Cherniak, 1986; DeLanghe, 2013), and attempts to make use of FFH in scientific theory choice (Hey, 2016; for limits concerning this area, see Nickles, 2016). However, they do so in less systematic and comprehensive ways. Actually, around the time when Gigerenzer was developing his work on FFH and "ecological rationality" (in the early 1990s, that is), Kornblith was independently taking a similar step by suggesting, as cited above, that "our inferential mechanisms may also be built around presuppositions about standard environments which allow us to gain information about those environments quickly and accurately" (Kornblith, 1993, p. 86). FFH work well when they are used in the right environments; outside them, they may lead to errors. Consider the recognition heuristic (Goldstein & Gigerenzer, 2002). The surprising result is that subjects estimate, e.g., city sizes or winners of sports tournaments better when they know less. Thus, German subjects judge the size of US cities better than US subjects, and vice versa. Recognition by name alone works very well here. So, the heuristic works if and only if the environment—here, media and other information channels—guarantee that name recognition is systematically correlated with a correct estimation of the relevant criterion. Such a simple rule works better than trying to search for much more information. Similarly so, *mutatis mutandis*, for other FFH.

There should be nothing mechanical in the normative use of heuristics: we should not rely on them blindly. Consider one of the original recognition experiments, the comparison of the sizes of San Diego and San Antonio. When the study was carried out, San Diego was larger; by 2010, San Antonio had overtaken San Diego. That change in the environment was not yet reflected in German media channels. When German subjects can judge only by name recognition, they will probably still judge San Diego to be the larger city, and thus make a mistake. While FFH can be extremely useful for many reasoning tasks, an alert reasoner will use them with caution. We have to continue to think critically for ourselves.

At the same time, FFH can offer to naturalism—specifically, to (CMN)—more than a merely instrumentalist justification of norms: not only does the connection between means and (given) ends need to be studied empirically, but the relation of fitness between a heuristic and the environment in which we can, and should, legitimately use it, is a matter of empirical investigation too. At the same time, there are limits to the usefulness of FFH:

> In some important domains, one can infer from empirical research what norms of rationality are best, as well as how human reasoning can be improved. In other domains one cannot; that is, in these the "standard" conception of rationality (Stein, 1996) as being based upon certain rules of logic or probability is not undermined by our arguments.
>
> *Gigerenzer & Sturm, 2012, p. 244*

This compatibility between the standard and the bounded conception of rationality can be deepened in two regards. First, one cannot even *formulate* FFH without basic concepts and rules of formal logic. The recognition heuristic requires a minimal grasp of the form of the "if – then" conditional: "*If* one of two objects is recognized *and* the other is not, *then* infer that the recognized object has the higher value with respect to the criterion." Other rules, such as "take the best", in addition, require the ability to master disjunction, and so on. Logical notions and rules are *built into* the very formulation of FFH. The gap between formal rules and rationality notwithstanding, a minimal dependence of bounded rationality on basic logic is unavoidable (for a similar view, cf. Cherniak, 1986).

Second, consider the claim of Gigerenzer's program that heuristics are sometimes as good as, and sometimes even beat, probabilistic norms such as regression or Bayes' theorem. In accordance with what standard is such a claim being made? Clearly, each attempt to justify a heuristic as normatively valid requires some standard against which the heuristic is tested. More specifically, when defenders of bounded rationality claim that FFH outperform classical rules of the standard picture of rationality, the only way to prove this is by comparing how FFH fare in comparison with rules of probability or statistics. Accordingly, "take the best" is checked against actual frequencies, and other heuristics against, say, the benchmarks of Bayesian rules (Martignon & Blackmond Laskey, 1999; Martignon & Hoffrage, 1999). FFH can only be normatively valid if they *compete* successfully with such rules. Both these points mean that there is, at the normative level, a compatibility and even complementarity between the standard and the bounded conceptions of rationality (for more on this, see Sturm, 2019).

Conclusion: for a critical naturalism about rationality

Time to take stock. I have tried to show how productive a careful analysis of the perplexing historical, scientific, and philosophical interactions between the standard picture of rationality, the psychology of reasoning, models of bounded rationality, and philosophical naturalism can be. The standard picture arose through the coalescence of logic, probability, and rational choice theory through the twentieth century. That picture then was criticized by both the Kahneman–Tversky HB approach, which emphasizes that humans are lazy reasoners, and by Simon and later on by Gigerenzer and his collaborators for being too mindlessly formal and optimizing in terms of what the proper norms of good reasoning are. Philosophers who defend naturalism in epistemology and philosophy of science first quickly took up the HB approach, but did so in problematic ways that threatened their own naturalism.

Simon's satisficing and Gigerenzer's FFH are better allies of philosophical naturalism. Four points can be highlighted to summarize the results concerning this claim. First, a methodological naturalism about epistemic rationality can be based on this particular version of bounded rationality, given that means–ends as well as mind–environment relations have to be studied, both of which have to be determined empirically. Second, such naturalism about rationality and, in particular FFH, can be normative, but only if heuristics are used in mindful, deliberate ways, at least in principle. Third, such naturalism is limited in its scope and potential applications, and it should be fully reflexive with regard to these limits. It should live in coexistence with the standard account of rationality by leaving, for instance, computationally tractable tasks to the latter. It even requires the standard account to some extent, since logical notions and rules are required to formulate FFH, and theories of probability in order to assess their validity. Fourth, and finally, bounded rationality cannot be expected to provide a basis for the naturalists' ontological claim (ON) concerning rationality. Research into bounded rationality is not yet mature enough to deliver a systematic theory that could be used to explain the nature of rationality in general. Maybe it never will be.

Given these four points, we can justifiably call the ensuing position, while tipping our hats to Kant, "critical naturalism". It is naturalistic because of the first point, namely, its empirical methodology, and critical in the Kantian sense due to the three other points: We should use heuristics in reflective and limited ways, and we should avoid rushing towards ontological claims that are not sufficiently warranted. But even if one does not share this refined version of naturalism, it seems to me that epistemologists and philosophers of science have, up to now, all too rarely used bounded rationality as understood by Simon and by Gigerenzer and his colleagues. More work can and should be done in this area.

Acknowledgments

For comments and discussions, the author is grateful to Riccardo Viale and Gerd Gigerenzer. Christopher Evans helped to improve the language of this chapter, and gave several highly useful recommendations concerning content too. This work was supported by the Spanish Ministry for the Economy, Industry and Competitiveness (MINECO) through the research project "Naturalism and the sciences of rationality: an integrated philosophy and history" (FFI2016–79923-P).

Notes

1 I cannot here consider the view that these terms are not synonymous, but see Sturm (2018).
2 One might think that, given its title, Stich (1993) belongs into this camp too. However, Stich only uses Simon's work in artificial intelligence (AI) to explain scientific discovery (Langley et al., 1987). AI and bounded rationality were Simon's two major research agendas; but they had no internal connection that would necessitate dealing with the former here as well. Therefore, I will leave aside Simon's research in AI, and Stich's use of it to naturalize epistemology.
3 Frege's distinction between the material realm, the realm of subjective mental representations, and the realm of objective thoughts bears similarities with Karl Popper's equally notorious division into world 1 (the physical world), world 2 (the mental world), and world 3 (the world of objective knowledge) (Popper, 1972). However, Popper's division is historically probably more influenced by his teacher, the psychologist Karl Bühler and his theory of basic functions of language (Sturm, 2012b). Moreover, while Popper's theory is clearly intended to be an ontological distinction, it is a disputed question whether Frege's claim about the "third realm" was truly intended to be an ontological claim (for a less demanding, epistemological interpretation of Frege's view, see Carl 1994, Chapters 2–4).
4 Of course, theories of probability were far longer in the making, famously starting with the Pascal–Fermat exchanges on games of chance in 1654 (Gigerenzer et al., 1989; Gillies, 2000).
5 To think that even today some experts view (a) to be true may seem false, given the heuristics-and-biases approach that is explained above. However, things are not so simple. In economics, whether (a) is taken to be true or not depends a lot on whether standard norms, e.g., for rational choices, are viewed as descriptive of individual decisions (where it seems implausible), of aggregates of decisions of many individuals, or of economic structures. On this debate, see Ross (2014).
6 There is no reliable survey showing whether or not naturalism dominates current philosophy. A preliminary attempt was made by Bourget and Chalmers (2013). When asked about their metaphilosophical position, participants (mostly professional philosophers, mostly though not exclusively from Anglo-Saxon universities) chose naturalism first (49.8 percent), followed by non-naturalism (25.9 percent) and "other" (24.3 percent). Somewhat surprisingly, the same participants overwhelmingly denied essential claims of typical naturalistic positions, such as the rejection of *a priori* knowledge (71.1 percent said such knowledge exists), or the rejection of the distinction between analytic and synthetic propositions. Perhaps this reveals that the questions were problematic, but it is also possible that many philosophers hold unusual views (to say the least).
7 This may be questioned, e.g., in the light of historical considerations. Gigerenzer et al. (1989) argue that theories of probability were sometimes revised when they clashed with what educated minds thought about probabilities. Consider the famous St. Petersburg paradox: recognizing that no reasonable person was willing to invest infinite sums of money in a coin tossing game where the expected gains were infinite did not lead to the judgment that such a person was mistaken. Instead, it led Daniel Bernoulli to substitute the concept of expectation with that of monetary values, "with the awareness that the richer you are, the more it takes to make you happy" (Gigerenzer et al., 1989, p. 15). However, it would be questionable to claim that Bernoulli had attempted to justify a normative rule by means of observation or experiment. One might see this, rather, as an instance of applying the method of *reflective equilibrium*: we develop our normative theories by considering whether instances of good reasoning fit with our best principles, and vice versa; and we adjust them when conflicts arise (see also Cohen, 1981).

8 They also try, of course, to profit from psychology for other tasks of epistemology, for instance, in providing a descriptive account of knowledge or cognition. This is what Quine's (1969) original proposal for a naturalistic epistemology comes down to, or what evolutionary epistemologists have developed. However, such *descriptive* naturalistic epistemology faces the challenge that it simply changes the game by not taking seriously enough the normative tasks of epistemology (Kim, 1988). Accordingly, in order to avoid being charged with changing the topic, a number of naturalists accepted the normative tasks too.

9 Again, this undermines excessive conclusions (e.g., Stich, 1985) on the basis of HB studies according to which humans are fundamentally irrational, a claim that is not entirely absent from Kahneman and Tversky either; see Sturm (2012a).

10 Goodman (2008) offers a more mixed assessment of the competing approaches.

11 In philosophy of science, Solomon (1992) has used the HB program to explain e.g., the geological revolution of the nineteenth century. She finds that Stich (1985) has argued convincingly against criticisms of the HB program, a judgment with which I disagree, though I cannot show this here. She also uses HB studies to explain the normative successes of choices made during the geological revolution, claiming that Alfred Wegner's choice of continental drift over contractionism was driven by aspects of representativeness (Solomon, 1992, p. 447), and that belief perseverance or availability played a role too. However, the HB program of testing how far people follow formal or optimizing rules makes sense only where such rules can be clearly stated. Only then can judgments of bias be justifiably made, and explanations in terms of heuristics be given. Suitable norms just do not exist for cases such as those Solomon discusses. Nor does Solomon explain why geologists came to agree so quickly that continental drift was the more adequate theory in the 1960s. As Solomon admits, her explanation is only tentative and perhaps not the whole story anyhow.

References

Bermúdez, J. L., & Millar, A. (Eds.) (2002). *Reason and nature*. Oxford: Oxford University Press.

Bishop, M., & Trout, J. D. (2005). *Epistemology and the psychology of human judgment*. New York: Oxford University Press.

BonJour, L. (1994). Against naturalized epistemology. *Midwest Studies in Philosophy*, 19, 283–300.

Bourget, D., & Chalmers, D. (2013). What do philosophers believe? Available at: https://philpapers.org/archive/BOUWDP

Carl, W. (1994). *Frege's theory of sense and reference*. Cambridge: Cambridge UP.

Cherniak, C. (1986). *Minimal rationality*. Cambridge, MA: MIT Press.

Chiappe, D. L., & Vervaeke, J. (1997). Fodor, Cherniak, and the naturalization of rationality. *Theory & Psychology*, 7, 799–821.

Cohen, L. J. (1981). Can human irrationality be experimentally demonstrated? *Behavioral and Brain Sciences*, 4, 317–331 (comments and responses, 331–359).

Cosmides, L., & Tooby, J. (1996). Are humans good intuitive statisticians after all? *Cognition*, 58, 1–73.

De Caro, M., & MacArthur, D. (Eds.) (2004). *Naturalism in question*. Cambridge, MA: Harvard University Press.

De Caro, M., & MacArthur, D. (Eds.) (2010). *Naturalism and normativity*. New York: Columbia University Press.

deLanghe, R. (2013). Satisficing as an account of Kuhnian rationality. *Philosophy Study*, 3, 398–411.

DePaul, M., & Ramsey, W. (Eds.) (1998). *Rethinking intuition: The psychology of intuition and its role in philosophical inquiry*. Lanham, MD: Rowman & Littlefield.

Dennett, D. (1991). *Consciousness explained*. Boston: Little, Brown & Co.

Dretske, F. (1996). *Naturalizing the mind*. Cambridge, MA: MIT Press.

Erickson, P., Klein, J., Daston, L., Lemov, R, Sturm, T., & Gordin, M. (2013). *How reason almost lost its mind*. Chicago: University of Chicago Press.

Feldman, R. (2001). Naturalized epistemology. In E. N. Zalta (Ed.), *Stanford encyclopedia of philosophy*. Available at: http://plato.stanford.edu/archives/sum2012/entries/epistemology-naturalized/

Frege, G. (1966). Der Gedanke (1918–19). In G. Frege, *Logische Untersuchungen*, ed. G. Patzig (pp. 30–53). Göttingen: Vandenhoek & Ruprecht.

Galparsoro, J. I., & Cordero, A. (Eds.) (2013). *Reflections on naturalism*. Rotterdam: Sense Publishers.

Giere, R. (1985). Philosophy of science naturalized. *Philosophy of Science*, 52, 331–356.

Giere, R. (1988). *Explaining science: A cognitive approach*. Chicago: University of Chicago Press.

Giere, R. (Ed.) (1992). *Cognitive models of science*. Minneapolis, MN: University of Minnesota Press.

Gigerenzer, G. (1991). How to make cognitive illusions disappear: Beyond heuristics and biases. *European Review of Social Psychology*, 2, 83–115.

Gigerenzer, G. (1996). On narrow norms and vague heuristics: A rebuttal to Kahneman and Tversky. *Psychological Review*, 103, 592–596.

Gigerenzer, G., & Selten, R. (2001). Rethinking rationality. In G. Gigerenzer & R. Selten (Eds.), *Bounded rationality* (pp. 1–12). Cambridge, MA: MIT Press.

Gigerenzer, G.. & Sturm, T. (2012). How (far) can rationality be naturalized? *Synthese*, 187, 243–268.

Gigerenzer, G., Swijtink, Z., Porter, T., Daston, L., Beatty, J., & Krüger, L. (1989). *The empire of chance*. Cambridge: Cambridge University Press.

Gigerenzer, G., Todd, P. M., & the ABC Research Group (Eds.) (1999). *Simple heuristics that make us smart*. New York: Oxford University Press.

Gillies, D. (2000). *Probability*. London: Routledge.

Goldman, A. (1986). *Epistemology and cognition*. Cambridge, MA: Harvard University Press.

Goldman, A. (2008). Human rationality: Epistemological and psychological perspectives. In A. Beckermann & S. Walter (Eds.), *Philosophy: Foundations and applications* (pp. 230–247). Paderborn, Germany: Mentis.

Goldstein, D. G., & Gigerenzer, G. (2002). Models of ecological rationality: The recognition heuristic. *Psychological Review*, 109, 75–90.

Grice, P. (2001). *Aspects of reason*. Oxford: Oxford University Press.

Habermas, J. (1981). *Theorie des kommunikativen Handelns*. 1. Frankfurt/M.: Suhrkamp.

Hahn, S. (2013). *Rationalität*. Paderborn: Mentis.

Harman, G. (1977). *The nature of morality*. New York: Oxford University Press.

Hauptli, B. (1995). *The reasonableness of reason: Explaining rationality naturalistically*. Chicago: Open Court.

Hey, S. (2016). Heuristics and meta-heuristics in scientific judgment. *British Journal for the Philosophy of Science*, 67, 471–495.

Kahneman, D. (2003). Maps of bounded rationality: Psychology for behavioral economics. *American Economic Review*, 93, 1449–1475.

Kahneman, D., Slovic, P., & Tversky, A. (Eds.) (1982). *Judgment under uncertainty*. New York: Cambridge University Press.

Kelly, T. (2003). Epistemic rationality as instrumental rationality: A critique. *Philosophy and Phenomenological Research*, 66, 612–640.

Kim, J. (1988). What is "naturalized epistemology"? *Philosophical Perspectives*, 2, 381–405.

Kitcher, P. (1992). The naturalists return. *Philosophical Review*, 101, 53–114.

Kitcher, P. (1993). *The advancement of science*. New York: Oxford University Press.

Kornblith, H. (1993). *Inductive inference and its natural ground*. Cambridge, MA: MIT Press.

Kornblith, H. (Ed.) (1994). *Naturalizing epistemology* (2nd ed). Cambridge, MA: MIT Press.

Kornblith, H. (2002). *Knowledge and its place in nature*. Oxford: Oxford University Press.

Kornblith, H. (2007). Naturalism and intuitions. *Grazer Philosophische Studien*, 72, 27–49.

Ladyman, J. (2007). *Everything must go: Metaphysics naturalized*. Oxford: Oxford University Press.

Langley, P., Simon, H., Bradshaw, G., & Zytkow, J. (1987). *Scientific discovery*. Cambridge, MA: MIT Press.

Laudan, L. (1987). Progress or rationality? The prospects for normative naturalism. *American Philosophical Quarterly*, 24, 19–31.

Laudan, L. (1990). Normative naturalism. *Philosophy of Science*, 57, 44–59.

Lenman, J. (2009). Naturalism without tears. *Ratio*, 12, 1–18.

Lopes, L., (1991). The rhetoric of irrationality. *Theory and Psychology*, 1, 65–82.

Martignon, L., & Blackmond Laskey, K. (1999). *Bayesian benchmarks for fast and frugal heuristics*. Oxford: Oxford University Press.

Martignon, L., & Hoffrage, U. (1999). Why does one-reason decision making work? A case study in ecological rationality. In G. Gigerenzer, P. M. Todd, & the ABC Research Group (Eds.), *Simple heuristics that make us smart* (pp. 119–140). New York: Oxford University Press.

Mele, A., & Rawlings, P. (Eds.) (2004). *The Oxford handbook of rationality*. Oxford: Oxford University Press.

Mi, C., & Chen, R. (Eds.) (2007). *Naturalized epistemology and philosophy of science*. Amsterdam: Rodopi.

Michaelewicz, Z., & Fogel, D. (2000). *How to solve it: Modern heuristics*. New York: Springer.

Newell, A., Shaw, J. C., & Simon, H. A. (1958). Elements of a theory of human problem solving. *Psychological Review*, 65, 151–166.

Nickles, T. (2016). Fast and frugal heuristics appraisal at research frontiers. In E. Ippoliti, F. Sterpetti, & T. Nickles (Eds.), *Models and inferences in science* (pp. 31–54). Heidelberg: Springer.

Nida-Rümelin, J. (1996). Zur Einheitlichkeit praktischer Rationalität. In K.-O. Apel & M. Kettner (Eds.), *Die eine Vernunft und die vielen Rationalitäten* (pp. 73–90). Frankfurt a/M: Suhrkamp.

Notturno, M. A. (1985). *Objectivity, rationality and the third realm. Justification and the grounds of psychologism: A study of Frege and Popper.* Dordrecht: Nijhoff.

Nozick, R. (1993). *The nature of rationality.* Princeton, NJ: Princeton University Press.

Oaksford, M., & Chater, N. (1991). Bounded rationality in taking risks and drawing inferences. *Theory & Psychology*, 2, 225–230.

Pacho, J. (1995). *¿Naturalizar la razón?* Madrid: Sigo XXI editores.

Papineau, D. (2015). Naturalism. In E. N. Zalta (ed.), *The Stanford encyclopedia of philosophy.* Available at: http://plato.stanford.edu/entries/naturalism/entries/naturalism/

Peckhaus, V. (2006). Psychologism and the distinction between discovery and justification. In J. Schickore & F. Steinle (Eds.), *Revisiting discovery and justification* (pp. 99–116). Berlin: Springer.

Peterson, C., & Beach, L. (1967). Man as an intuitive statistician. *Psychological Bulletin*, 68, 29–46.

Popper, K. (1972). *Objective knowledge: An evolutionary approach.* Oxford: Clarendon Press.

Putnam, H. (1981). *Reason, truth, and history.* Cambridge: Cambridge University Press.

Putnam, H. (1982). Why reason can't be naturalized. *Synthese*, 52, 3–24.

Quine, W. V. O. (1969). Epistemology naturalized. In W. V. O. Quine, *Ontological relativity and other essays* (pp. 69–90). New York: Columbia University Press.

Rosenberg, A. (1996). A field guide to recent species of naturalism. *British Journal for the Philosophy of Science*, 47, 1–29.

Ross, D. (2014). *Philosophy of economics.* London: Palgrave Macmillan.

Samuels, R., Stich, S., & Bishop, M. (2002). Ending the rationality wars: How to make disputes about human rationality disappear. In R. Elio (Ed.), *Common sense, reasoning and rationality* (pp. 236–268). New York: Oxford University Press.

Siegel, H. (1989). Philosophy of science naturalized? Some problems with Giere's naturalism. *Studies in History and Philosophy of Science*, 20, 365–375.

Simon, H. (1956). Rational choice and the structure of the environment. *Psychological Review*, 63, 129–138.

Simon, H. (1957). *Models of man.* New York: Wiley.

Sklar, L. (2010). I'd love to be a naturalist-if only I knew what naturalism was. *Philosophy of Science*, 77, 1121–1137.

Sober, E. (1978). Psychologism. *Journal for the Theory of Social Behaviour*, 8, 165–192.

Sober, E. (1981). The evolution of rationality. *Synthese*, 46, 95–120.

Solomon, M. (1992). Scientific rationality and human reasoning. *Philosophy of Science*, 59, 439–455.

Stein, E. (1996). *Without good reason.* Oxford: Clarendon.

Stich, S. (1985). Could man be an irrational animal? Some notes on the epistemology of rationality. *Synthese*, 64, 115–135.

Stich, S. (1990). *The fragmentation of reason.* Cambridge, MA: MIT Press.

Stich, S. (1993). Naturalizing epistemology: Quine, Simon, and the prospects for pragmatism. *Royal Institute for Philosophy Supplement*, 34, 1–17.

Stroud, B. (1996). The charm of naturalism. *Proceedings and Addresses of the American Philosophical Association*, 70, 43–55.

Sturm, T. (2012a). The "rationality wars" in psychology: Where they are and where they could go. *Inquiry*, 55, 66–81.

Sturm, T. (2012b). Bühler and Popper: Kantian therapies for the crisis in psychology. *Studies in History and Philosophy of Biological and Biomedical Sciences*, 43, 462–472.

Sturm, T. (2018). Rationalität versus Vernunft? Über eine Unterscheidung bei John Rawls (und anderen). In D. Sölch (Ed.), *Philosophische Sprache zwischen Tradition und Innovation* (pp. 211–233). Frankfurt a.M: Lang.

Sturm, T. (2019). Formal versus bounded norms in the psychology of rationality: Toward a multilevel analysis of their relationship. *Philosophy of the Social Sciences*, 49, 190–209.

Sturm, T. (Forthcoming). Theories of rationality and the descriptive/normative divide: A historical approach. In M. Knauff & W. Spohn (Eds.), *Handbook on rationality.* Cambridge, MA: MIT Press.

Turing, A. (1950). Computing machinery and intelligence. *Mind*, 59, 433–460.

Tversky, A., & Kahneman, D. (1983). Extensional versus intuitive reasoning: Conjunction fallacy in probability judgment. *Psychological Review*, 90, 293–315.

Viale, R. (2013). *Methodological cognitivism*, vol. 2: *Cognition, science, and innovation*. Heidelberg: Springer.

von Neumann, J., & Morgenstern, O. (1944). *Theory of games and economic behavior*. Princeton, NJ: Princeton University Press.

Wason, P. (1966). Reasoning about a rule. *Quarterly Journal of Experimental Psychology*, 20, 273–281.

4

BOUNDED RATIONALITY

The two cultures

Konstantinos V. Katsikopoulos

Introduction

Bounded rationality does not speak with one voice. This is not only because bounded rationality is researched in various fields such as economics, psychology, and management. Even within a single field such as economics, there are clear differences. For example, Selten (2001) rejects the optimization of a utility function as an expression of bounded rationality, contrary to the standard approach of behavioral economics as in bargaining games by Fehr and Schmidt (1999). There are multiple views of bounded rationality, as pointed out by Rubinstein (1998).

The first contribution of the present chapter is to analyze the formal modeling used to describe people's bounded rationality. At the risk of oversimplifying, I distinguish between two cultures, which I call "idealistic" and "pragmatic." At a first approximation, the idealistic culture pursues a minimum departure from the neoclassical-economics framework of unbounded rationality which assumes the ideals of omniscience and optimization of a utility function and adds factors such as inequity aversion or probability weighting to the utility function. On the other hand, the pragmatic culture holds that people sometimes ignore information and use simple rules of thumb in order to achieve satisfactory outcomes. Note that I do not use the label "pragmatic" as used by, among others, Friedman (1953), to emphasize some views of the practical purposes of economics, such as delivering accurate predictions. A detailed discussion of the differences in modeling between the two cultures is provided in the next section. The reality of the cultures and their differences are demonstrated by examples drawn from the literatures on risky choice and bargaining games. Note that it does not make sense to try to perfectly map specific researchers or programs of research to one or the other culture; for example, Amos Tversky worked on both cultures, with prospect theory being an idealistic model and elimination by aspects being a pragmatic model.

Although the distinction between the idealistic and pragmatic cultures of bounded rationality can be criticized, as all binary distinctions can, it provides food for thought and new insights. I aim at emulating Breiman's (2001) analysis of two cultures in statistics. Breiman argued that there exist two cultures which lead to two very different kinds of statistical theory and practice: proof-based and data-driven. Analogously, I argue in the third section that the idealistic and pragmatic cultures tell two very different stories about people's bounded rationality and how to improve it. This is the second contribution of the present chapter. Echoing

DOI: 10.4324/9781315658353-5

Morgan (2001), I conclude that these stories play a vital role in our understanding of the economic world and the policies we develop.

The two cultures: differences in modeling

Table 4.1 presents six key modeling differences between the idealistic and pragmatic cultures of research on describing people's bounded rationality. This presentation is epigrammatic. The rest of the section spells out each difference, as well as their relationships.

I first discuss the labels "idealistic" and "pragmatic," which are connected to the first difference in Table 4.1. I then discuss the second and third differences and the remaining differences.

What do the labels "idealistic" and "pragmatic" mean?

The first difference between the two cultures refers to the building blocks they use in order to generate their models. This difference is the main reason for the labels "idealistic" and "pragmatic." The idealistic culture of bounded rationality is indeed inspired by an ideal, unboundedly rational creature. This is a decision maker who possesses all information that can possibly be gathered and, based on it, makes all possible correct deductions, which she uses to make an "optimal" decision. For example, in a choice among gambles, this decision maker knows all possible outcomes of each gamble, is able to assign a numerical utility to each outcome, knows the probability with which each outcome occurs, and finally calculates the expected utility of each gamble and chooses a gamble which obtains the maximum.

The choices of an expected utility optimizer can be represented by the logical axioms jointly equivalent to expected utility theory (von Neumann and Morgenstern 1944). An example axiom is transitivity where, for all gambles x, y and z, if x is chosen over y and y is chosen over z, then x is chosen over z. According to some authors, such as Savage (1954), these axioms have normative status, meaning that a decision maker should satisfy them.

The same kinds of axioms are the building blocks of the idealistic culture of bounded rationality. A researcher can generate new models of bounded rationality by retaining some axioms of unbounded rationality, taking out others and proposing new ones. For example, Kahneman and Tversky's prospect theory (1979) always satisfies transitivity but may violate independence

Table 4.1 Six modeling differences between the idealistic and pragmatic cultures of research on describing people's bounded rationality

Bounded-rationality cultures differences in modeling	*Idealistic*	*Pragmatic*
1. Building blocks, based on which models are generated	Logical axioms (e.g. people make transitive choices)	Empirical facts (e.g. people make choices based on only one reason)
2. Assumptions about people's goal	Optimization of a utility function	Achievement of a satisfactory outcome
3. Treatment of psychological processes	No models of processes; instead, as-if optimization	Models of processes as simple rules of thumb
4. Treatment of parameters	Let parameters vary freely	Fix parameters
5. Epistemic aim	Explanation of known facts	Prediction of new facts
6. Models tested	Only from idealistic culture	From both cultures

(for all gambles x, y and z, and probabilities p, if x is chosen over y, then the compound gamble $(x, p; z, 1 - p)$ is chosen over $(y, p; z, 1 - p)$). Bounded-rationality models, such as prospect theory, have also been axiomatized by axioms that can be argued to be normative (Wakker and Tversky 1993). Thus, the prospect-theory decision maker is also ideal, just a bit less so than her expected-utility ancestor.

But not everybody is happy with this industry of transforming neoclassical models into bounded-rationality ones. Güth called it a "neoclassical repair shop" (1995, p. 342). Dissatisfaction and impatience with it run through the whole volume edited by Selten and Gigerenzer (2001), who look away from axioms to find the building blocks of bounded rationality. They have the work of Herbert Simon—the father of bounded rationality—to fall back on, who, throughout his whole career, insisted on first considering what is known about how real people actually make decisions in the real world (Katsikopoulos and Lan 2011): In the abstract of Simon's obituary, his long-standing colleague March wrote: "In particular, he persistently sought to clarify the real processes of human decision making ..." (Augier and March 2002, p. 1).

I call "pragmatic" the culture that uses empirical facts as its building blocks. As an example of a model of the pragmatic culture, take the priority heuristic for choices among risky gambles (Brandstätter, Gigerenzer, and Hertwig 2006). The heuristic is based on the fact that people often make choices by using just one reason and consider a second or third reason only if they have to (Ford et al. 1989). According to the priority heuristic, when choosing between two gambles (which lead only to gains compared to the status quo), the first reason people look at is the minimum gains of the two gambles x and y, respectively $\min(x)$ and $\min(y)$; if $|\min(x) - \min(y)| > c$ where c is a fixed threshold, then the gamble with the higher minimum gain is chosen; otherwise the second reason, which is the probabilities of the minimum gains of the two gambles, is looked up, and so on, until a reason is found which permits choosing one gamble. The existence of thresholds that allow for a choice or necessitate more search for information is an empirical fact (Tanner and Swets 1954).

It should be noted that while the models of the pragmatic culture are not primarily inspired or justified by normative axioms, they are amenable to study from a normative or axiomatic perspective. In the former case, the performance of pragmatic models, in terms of criteria such as predictive accuracy, is investigated (Katsikopoulos 2011b). In the latter case, it is tested whether or not pragmatic models satisfy axioms such as transitivity or independence (Manzini and Mariotti 2007, 2012, 2014; Katsikopoulos and Gigerenzer 2008) and pragmatic models are shown to be equivalent to a set of axioms (Drechsler, Katsikopoulos, and Gigerenzer 2014).

An analogous point can be made for the models of the idealistic culture. Idealistic models are subject to empirical study as in the experimental tests of prospect theory. But empirical facts are not the sole, or in some cases not even the primary inspiration or justification for the development of idealistic models. For example, a key assumption of cumulative prospect theory—that people weigh probabilities nonlinearly—was not only inspired by the empirical fact that people's risk attitude depends on whether outcomes are gains or losses and on if the probabilities of gains or losses are large (Tversky and Kahneman 1992). Rather, in addition to this empirical fact, there is also a crucial influence of a non-empirical factor on the development of the probability-weighting assumption. This factor is that the assumption is necessary to explain the pattern if the modeler sticks to the general mathematical form of utility-times-probability, common in idealistic models. This assumption is not necessary in other models (Katsikopoulos and Gigerenzer 2008).

Put another way, the character of the idealistic culture is logical whereas that of the pragmatic culture is ecological. Ecology here is meant in Simon's (1955, 1956) sense of the environment—physical or mental—where decision-making takes place. Simon insisted that human behavior could be well understood only if it is studied in relation to its environment. But despite the overall impact of Simon's work, in economics, his call has been heeded by the pragmatic culture but not by the much more prevalent idealistic culture.

Other authors have also discussed conceptually the different views on bounded rational. Gigerenzer (2008) proposes three views: "as-if optimization," "ecological rationality," and "irrationality" (see also Berg and Gigerenzer 2010 and Brighton and Gigerenzer 2012). As-if optimization is related to what I call idealistic culture and ecological rationality is related to what I call pragmatic culture. The irrationality view refers to empirical research which has concluded that people systematically violate axioms of logic and probability as in the heuristics-and-biases research program of Tversky and Kahneman (Kahneman, Slovic, and Tversky 1982; Tversky and Kahneman 1974). Here, I see this research as part of the idealistic culture of bounded rationality. It forms the empirical basis of this culture and gives rise to the story that people are systematically irrational and the authorities should nudge them toward better decisions, as I discuss in the third section.

Another author who has discussed different ways of conceptualizing rationality, bounded as well as unbounded, is Lee (2011). He points out that in neoclassical economics, rationality is identified with logical consistency and optimization. Here, I argue that this is also the case in the idealistic culture of bounded rationality. Intriguingly, Lee calls pragmatic the classical economic notions of rationality, such as Adam Smith's.

Finally, consider again the labels used for the two cultures. Instead of "pragmatic," one may be tempted to use another label such as "empirical." But I believe that "pragmatic" is the right choice for the kind of models represented by the entries in the right column of Table 4.1. A glance at Table 4.1 shows that these models are "more practical as opposed to idealistic" which is how the Merriam-Webster online dictionary defines the word "pragmatic." For example, in the second row, pragmatic models are defined as those in which a person's goal is to achieve a satisfactory outcome as opposed to attempt to optimize. This kind of pragmatism is successful in the real world as it has been found that, under some conditions, pragmatic models outperform optimization models in medicine, management and engineering (Katsikopoulos 2011b).

On the other hand, a difficulty with the label "idealistic" is that this word has all sorts of moral and political connotations. I do not wish to have these connotations ascribed to the bounded-rationality models and stories discussed here. In the present chapter, the idealistic culture of bounded rationality refers to work inspired by the ideal of an unbounded rational decision maker who is omniscient and optimizes a utility function.

Optimization

Simon repeatedly questioned the usual assumption of economics that people try to *optimize*. Resounding plain common sense, Simon (1947) pointed out that people rarely even think about how to optimize and instead are content to *satisfice*. As Klein (2001) argues, in the real world, satisficing may be the only choice as the optimal outcome may not be calculable or even well defined. The pragmatic culture takes this point to heart and assumes that people's goal is to achieve a satisfactory outcome. For example, Brandstätter et al.'s (2006) priority heuristic does not necessarily lead to choices that optimize expected utility or value but it does guarantee that a gamble with a much smaller minimum gain will not be chosen. On the other hand, in idealistic models, such as prospect theory, people are assumed to choose a gamble that optimizes a utility function.

Now, what exactly does it mean to say that people optimize a utility function? The typical interpretation in neoclassical economics is that people behave *as if* they optimize (Friedman 1953). The claim is not that people necessarily perform all the calculations needed in order to optimize but that their behavior agrees with the behavior that results from these calculations. That is, optimization is not meant to describe the underlying *psychological processes*, only their outcome. This neglect of process dominates the idealistic modeling of bounded rationality as well. It may seem odd to argue that, say, prospect theory does not model processes, but it indeed does not in the sense that prospect theory does not specify how exactly it can be that a person would manage to nonlinearly weight probabilities, calculate nonlinear utilities, and integrate the two (note that there are elements of a process in prospect theory, as in its initial stage of setting a reference point). I am aware that behavioral economists routinely call their models process models, but if one takes the definition of a cognitive process in the light just described, this is not so. To be fair, this is a topic of considerable dispute (Berg and Gigerenzer 2010; Gintis 2011).

In sum, the third difference in Table 4.1 is that, unlike the idealistic culture, the pragmatic culture insists on developing process models. Of course, even within the pragmatic culture, there is often disagreement about what is and what is not a process model. It seems that a large chunk of process models describe simple rules of thumb which determine how people first search for information, then stop this search and finally make a decision based on the information gathered. For example, this is the case in the priority heuristic (Brandstätter et al., 2006) as well as in an earlier tradition of models such as elimination by aspects (Tversky 1972) and satisficing (Simon 1955).

Testing models

The remaining technical differences between the idealistic and pragmatic cultures have to do with model testing. The fourth difference in Table 4.1 refers to how parameters are treated. In theory, the parameters should be estimated independently of the data used to test the model. As Luce (1999, p. 727) wrote, parameters are to be estimated "once and for all … from experiments designed to do just that." Gonzalez and Wu (1999), for example, estimated the probability weighting functions of individual decision makers. Practically, the problems start when model development in a research area is not cumulative enough in order to build on previous parameter estimates. For some researchers, these problems are formidable and they think they have a "proliferation of free parameters in many types of theories with little success in developing theories of such parameters" (Luce 1997, p. 79).

Other researchers are not so wary of parameters (the different points of view are discussed in Katsikopoulos 2011a). Overall, it is modelers within the pragmatic culture who seem to avoid the use of *free parameters*. It is advertised as a strength of the priority heuristic that it has *fixed parameters* as is also the case in many models developed by Gigerenzer and his colleagues (Gigerenzer, Hertwig, and Pachur 2011). On the other hand, it is routine in behavioral economics to develop models with multiple free parameters.

I will give an example from the literature on bargaining games. Fehr and Schmidt (1999) have developed an idealistic model where players are assumed to behave as if they optimize a utility function. This utility function includes a player's own payoff but it also includes the player's aversion to inequity, as when earning a smaller or larger payoff than other players. For example, in a two-player ultimatum game where the proposer offers a fraction $p < \frac{1}{2}$ of a unit pie to the responder and the responder accepts it, the utility of the responder equals $p - \alpha[(1 - p) - p]$ where $\alpha > 0$ measures the responder's envy due to earning less than the proposer, and the utility of the proposer equals $(1 - p) - \beta[(1 - p) - p]$ where $\beta > 0$ measures the proposer's discomfort due to earning more than the responder. These functions can be used to identify which decisions optimize the players' utilities (for the proposer, which p to offer; and for the responder, whether to accept each p or not).

Whereas in the Fehr–Schmidt model parameters α and β are allowed to vary freely, in a pragmatic model of bargaining games players are assumed to use a toolbox of rules of thumb, each with fixed parameters (Fischbacher, Hertwig, and Bruhin 2013). Examples of the rules of the proposer are that she offers $p = \frac{1}{2}$ or the largest possible p which is smaller than $\frac{1}{2}$, and examples of the rules of the responder are that she accepts all $p > 0$ or only those p such that $p > p^\star$, where $p^\star$ is what she offers when she is the proposer.

Of course, Fehr and Schmidt (1999) did attempt to estimate the parameters of their model. But this is not the point. Leaving aside the fact that there is a controversy on whether the estimation was done properly or not (Binmore and Shaked 2010; Fehr and Schmidt 2010), the point is that a model with free parameters already constituted a precisely defined model for Fehr and Schmidt (1999), while this is not the case in pragmatic models.

Now, one could argue that it is close to irrelevant, or just a matter of taste, whether a model uses free or fixed parameters; what matters is if the model can describe empirical facts well. Interestingly, it turns out that the idealistic and pragmatic cultures understand "describe" and "well" very differently. This is captured by the fifth and sixth differences in Table 4.1.

In order to understand these differences, it helps to digress and consider the work of Musgrave (1974). He discusses three views of when an empirical fact lends support to a model. In the logical view, it matters only if the fact is consistent with the model's implications. In the historical view, it also matters if the model's implications were derived before or after the fact was observed. More support is provided for the model if the derivation preceded the observation. Musgrave argues for a third view, a variant of the historical view in which it is additionally relevant what the implications of the best competing model are. More support is provided for the model if its best competitor does not imply the observed fact. Thus, the logical view accepts as an epistemic aim the *explanation of known facts* (here explanation is the consistency of a model's implications with the facts, ignoring, for example, whether or not the model proposes causal factors that lead to the facts). On the other hand, the historical view rejects this and aims at the *prediction of new facts*. A second distinction is that Musgrave's variant of the historic view considers it a plus to *competitively test models*, whereas the logical view is silent on that.

It may be argued that the idealistic culture espouses the logical view whereas the pragmatic culture is aligned with the historical view, and in particular Musgrave's variant. More specifically, models that are able to accommodate a wide range of empirical facts are highly valued in the idealistic culture even if the models were developed after the facts have been observed. For example, the development of prospect theory and other risky choice models which follow the utility-times-probability mathematical form, has been following the empirical violations of the axioms of expected utility theory (Starmer 2000). On the other hand, pragmatic models, such as the priority heuristic, have not been developed in order to account for these violations—even though later it was shown that they could do so (Katsikopoulos and Gigerenzer 2008)—but rather in order to predict new facts. This is the fifth difference in Table 4.1.

The distinction between explaining known facts and predicting new facts is sometimes acknowledged in work on idealistic models (Blanco, Engelmann, and Norman 2011; De Bruyn and Bolton 2008; Fehr and Schmidt 1999). Even in this case, one can discriminate between the idealistic and pragmatic cultures. Idealistic culture only tests models from this same culture whereas in the pragmatic culture models from both cultures are tested. For example,

Brandstätter et al. (2006) compared the predictive accuracy of the priority heuristic with that of cumulative prospect theory. On the other hand, I am not aware of studies within the idealistic culture where the performance of idealistic models is compared to that of pragmatic models. This is the sixth and final difference in Table 4.1. We next move from modeling to storytelling.

The two cultures: different stories about people's bounded rationality and how to improve it

Explanation and prediction are examples of the ultimate services that a scientific model can offer. As Morgan and Grüne-Yanoff (2013) argue, however, the intermediate services of models are just as important. Examples of intermediate services of models are to provide "insights", "platforms for further discussion" or "coherent stories" for research to continue (p. 145). In economics, where models are consumed not just by researchers but also by policy makers and the public and in fact have the potential to affect people's behavior, intermediate services such as stories are particularly important (Tuckett 2011).

According to Morgan (2001, p. 379), a *story* is "the phenomenon of grasping things together at this intervening level between complete and exhaustive detail and complete generalization." For a given bounded-rationality culture, I take this quote to mean that this culture's story lies between the empirical evidence and the formal models of the culture. In other words, I see a story as an amalgam of evidence and modeling. In my view, the function of a story is to allow the researchers who produced models, as well as the consumers of the models, including other researchers, policy makers and the public, to start a conversation about people's decision making, to keep the conversation going and to give it new twists now and then. This section analyzes the conversations of the idealistic and pragmatic cultures.

The story told by the idealistic culture

Not only is the idealistic culture inspired by an omniscient and optimizing decision maker, it never lets go of her, not really. Even though prospect theory and inequity aversion are meant as models of bounded rationality, they live in the shadow of unbounded rationality. For example, prospect theory can, when its parameters are chosen appropriately, be reduced to expected utility theory and so can inequity aversion be reduced to standard game theory. Furthermore, idealistic models of bounded rationality are meant to be descriptive (what does a real person do?) but not normative (what should an ideal person do?), so that whatever researchers have learned from these models has not changed the good old standard of ideal rationality (Bishop and Trout 2005).

I argue that the story of the idealistic culture goes like this: People are systematically behaving irrationally, but because they are in principle able to figure out how to behave rationally, they should keep trying to do so. It is clear that a person who buys this story will end up as frustrated as Tantalus ever was. This frustration is bound to lead to one of two dysfunctional behaviors: Either deny the reality of making bad decisions and hide in books about ideal rationality in order to get at least some intellectual solace or acknowledge one's dire prospects and surrender to the designs of somebody smarter (which you hope are well-meaning). The first of these behaviors is often seen in neoclassical economics and the second one in behavioral economics.

The first point above is that, according to the story of the idealistic culture, people are systematically behaving irrationally. The empirical basis of the idealistic culture is the heuristics-and-biases research program (Heukelom 2009): This program has concluded that people systematically violate axioms of logic and probability which the idealistic culture considers to be normative. The irrationality story is told in best-selling books for the public with titles such as *Predictably Irrational* (Ariely 2008) and has been integrated with startling ease in the columns and blogs of star commentators such as David Brooks of *The New York Times*.

It is important to understand why the irrationality story became such a hit. Lopes (1991) provides an insightful analysis. She points out that until the 1970s, most decision researchers believed that people were pretty good decision makers (Peterson and Beach 1967). She finds it implausible that people suddenly started making worse decisions—in fact, a bibliographic analysis showed that at that time there was similar amounts of empirical support for "good" and "bad" decision making—and attributes the change to the success of the rhetoric of irrationality. Lopes argues that it was Tversky and Kahneman, who in a series of articles that culminated in an authoritative summary in *Science* (Lopes 1974), managed to turn the beat around. This article opened up the way for the irrationality message to be spread outside psychology and notably into economics. At the point this chapter is being written, it is cited more than classic pieces in economics such as the *Theory of Games and Economic Behavior* by von Neumann and Morgenstern (1944). I single out some of the reasons Lopes provides for this rhetorical success which do not have to do with the truth of the message (a subject of intense disagreement that is beyond the scope of the present chapter, see Gigerenzer 2007 and Kahneman 2011).

To begin with, the experiments of Tversky and Kahneman are interesting puzzles, not dull drills. For example, in the Linda problem, participants are given the verbal description of a woman which suggests that she may be a feminist, and are asked to estimate if it is more probable that she is (1) a bank teller or (2) a bank teller and active in the feminist movement.

Your spontaneous answer is likely to be (2). Tversky and Kahneman argued that (1) is the correct answer because formally the probability of an event A (Linda is a bank teller) is higher than the probability of the intersection of two events A and B (Linda is a bank teller and active in the feminist movement). So, if you have some education in probability or statistics, you find yourself in the interesting position of having made a mistake, having been able to follow the reasons for it indeed being one and yet still feel somehow drawn to it. As Gould (1988) put it, "a little *homunculus* in my head continues to jump up and down, shouting at me—but she can't just be a bank teller; read the description" (emphasis added). Furthermore, as you keep on reading the article, you see that most people are like you and have made the same mistake. Fortunately, you can probably convince yourself that you are smarter than most of these people because you do understand what the mistake is. The authors themselves may have fueled your reactions by calling people's decisions "ludicrous" and "self-defeating" (Tversky and Kahneman 1971, pp. 109, 107). As Lopes summarizes, "[These] problems effectively engage interest and attention while massaging professional egos" (1991, p. 79).

As soon as it has been said that people systematically behave irrationally, the story of the idealistic culture unfolds quite smoothly. Clearly, the story continues, not all of us are irrational since some of us did come up with logic and probability and many of us have studied and mastered these tools. So, there is a job here for whoever can make us more "rational". As Lopes puts it, "The idea that people-are-irrational-and-science-has-proved-it is useful propaganda for anyone who has rationality to sell" (1991, p. 78). The questions then become: What does the idealistic culture have to sell us? And what about the pragmatic culture?

Nudge or boost?

When it comes to promoting rationality, the idealistic and pragmatic cultures could have converged to a common story. The two cultures do agree that there is a job that needs to be done: Human decision making should be supported (note, however, that the two cultures differ drastically in how they view the quality of people's decision making based on the available empirical evidence and how they go about generating empirical evidence; see Gigerenzer 1996, and Kahneman and Tversky 1996). But, as I argue below, each culture has its own story on how to get the job done and so far they are sticking to it.

As discussed earlier, the empirical part of the idealistic story is that people systematically behave irrationally. Perhaps because of that, the policy part of this story does not put much faith in people's ability to ever become "rational" on their own. So, the story goes, if we want people to behave rationally, we somehow have to steer them into doing so. In the words of Thaler and Sunstein (2008), authorities have to *nudge* people toward "better decisions about health, wealth and happiness." For example, legislators can set the default option in one's driving license so that people are organ donors and cafeteria owners can rearrange menus so that children are more likely to eat more vegetables. All the public needs to do is surrender to the well-meaning designs of those who are smarter.

The pragmatic culture tells a different story. This story is based on a different approach to gathering empirical evidence on people's rationality from that of the idealistic culture. The pragmatic culture is indifferent to testing adherence to axioms. It instead focuses on the impact of providing people with tools for boosting performance on tasks of practical importance, such as Bayesian reasoning (Fong, Krantz, and Nisbett 1986). An example of such a task is a medical doctor wanting to know the probability of a woman having breast cancer, given that she is more than 50 years old, the results of a mammography test, and the informativeness of the test. An example of a tool for doing this calculation is natural frequency formats for representing probabilities where conditional probabilities, such as the sensitivity of mammography (i.e., the probability that a mammography is positive given that a woman has breast cancer) are replaced by the corresponding joint frequencies. For example, sensitivity can be represented by the statement that out of 100 women with breast cancer, 99 have a positive mammography. This tool can improve the Bayesian reasoning of professionals (e.g., medical doctors as well as judges and lawyers) and laypeople (Hoffrage, Lindsey, Hertwig, and Gigerenzer 2000).

In other words, the story of the pragmatic culture is that people can indeed learn to behave rationally. Unlike the case of the idealistic culture, this is not a frustrating message for the public but an empowering one.

Interestingly, the story of the pragmatic culture may not appear particularly empowering when one considers the first premise of this culture which is that people do not optimize. But the story is in fact unexpectedly empowering when we also take into account that empirical studies, computer simulations and mathematical analyses show that pragmatic models can outperform optimization models (Katsikopoulos 2011b). What is required in order to reap the benefits is that people learn, or are taught, what the right pragmatic model is to use in which situation. The story of the pragmatic culture is centered on education, or as it is often more aptly called, *boost* (Hertwig and Grüne-Yanoff 2017).

Table 4.2 summarizes the above discussion by outlining three key differences of the idealistic and pragmatic cultures in story telling about people's bounded rationality and how to improve it.

In order to put the differences between the two cultures of bounded rationality into perspective, note that their stories are more similar to each other than they are to the story told by the culture of unbounded rationality. In this culture, which is prevalent in neoclassical economics, modeling is idealistic and the empirical evidence is interpreted as showing that people behave rationally in the sense of conforming to the axioms of logic and probability, except for

Table 4.2 Three key differences of the idealistic and pragmatic cultures in story telling about people's bounded rationality and how to improve it

Bounded rationality cultures differences in storytelling	Idealistic	Pragmatic
1. Gist of the story	People systematically behave irrationally; they should do better	People do well if they learn to use the right tool in the right situation
2. Psychological reactions of the public	Frustration; surrender to the designs of someone smarter	Empowerment
3. Role of the authorities	Nudge	Educate

some random violations; and the policy part of the story is to let people engage in free-market activities and reduce the role of the authorities to activities such as providing incentives.

In 2009, *Nature* published a news feature by freelance writer Michael Bond, covering both nudge and education stories. Gigerenzer comes across as a champion of education, whereas Thaler and Kahneman appear skeptical, saying that "our ability to de-bias people is quite limited" (Bond, 2009, p. 1191) and that "it takes an enormous amount of practice to change our intuition" (2009, p. 1192). There is, unfortunately, a standstill and no talk of combining the two stories.

Conclusion

Scientist and novelist C. P. Snow (1959) lamented the schism between the two cultures of the sciences and the humanities. The present chapter has the much more modest goal of analyzing the research on bounded rationality. Bounded rationality would have perhaps pleased Snow as it exhibits technical as well as story-telling aspects. On the other hand, here I showed something that could have worried Snow: There exist two distinct cultures of research on bounded rationality, the idealistic and the pragmatic, and they lead to two very different approaches to economic theory and policy. Time will tell what will come out of this tension. But if we are not aware that it exists, we cannot hope to make something good out of it.

Acknowledgments

The author wishes to thank Gerd Gigerenzer, Werner Güth, Wasilios Hariskos, Ralph Hertwig, Oliver Kirchkamp, Özgür Şimşek, Riccardo Viale, and the participants at workshops at the Warsaw School of Social Sciences and Humanities (Wroclaw campus) and the University of Paris (Villa Finaly), for their comments and suggestions.

The author acknowledges permission granted by Taylor and Francis (www.tandfonline.com) to use material from the previously published article: Katsikopoulos, K. V. (2014). Bounded rationality: the two cultures, *Journal of Economic Methodology*, 21(4), 361–374.

References

Ariely, Dan (2008). *Predictably Irrational*, New York: HarperCollins.
Augier, Mie, and James G. March (2002). A model scholar: Herbert A. Simon (1916–2001), *Journal of Economic Behavior and Organization*, 49, 1–17.

Berg, Nathan, and Gerd Gigerenzer (2010). As-if behavioral economics: Neoclassical economics in disguise, *History of Economic Ideas*, 18, 133–166.

Binmore, Ken, and Avner Shaked (2010). Experimental economics: Where next? *Journal of Economic Behavior and Organization*, 73, 87–100.

Bishop, Michael, and J. D. Trout (2005). *Epistemology and the Psychology of Human Judgment*, Oxford: Oxford University Press.

Blanco, Mariana, Dirk Engelmann, and Hans Theo Normann (2011). A within-subject analysis of other-regarding preferences, *Games and Economic Behavior*, 72, 321–338.

Bond, Michael (2009). Decision-making: Risk school, *Nature*, 461, 1189–1192.

Brandstätter, Eduard, Gerd Gigerenzer, and Ralph Hertwig, R. (2006). The priority heuristic: making choices without trade-offs. *Psychological Review*, 113, 409–432.

Breiman, Leo (2001). Statistical modeling: The two cultures, *Statistical Science*, 16, 199–231.

Brighton, Henry, and Gerd Gigerenzer (2012). Are rational actor models "rational" outside small worlds? In Samir Okasha and Ken Binmore (Eds.), *Evolution and Rationality: Decisions, Co-operation and Strategic Behavior* (pp. 84–109). Cambridge: Cambridge University Press.

De Bruin, Arnaud, and Gary E. Bolton (2008). Estimating the influence of fairness on bargaining behavior, *Management Science*, 54, 1774–1791.

Drechsler, Mareile, Konstantinos V. Katsikopoulos, and Gerd Gigerenzer (2014). Axiomatizing bounded rationality: The priority heuristic, *Theory and Decision*, 77, 183–196.

Fehr, Ernst, and Klaus Schmidt (1999). A theory of fairness, competition, and cooperation, *Quarterly Journal of Economics*, 114, 817–868.

Fehr, Ernst, and Klaus Schmidt (2010). On inequity aversion: A reply to Binmore and Shaked, *Journal of Economic Behavior and Organization*, 73, 101–108.

Fischbacher, Urs, Ralph Hertwig, and Adrian Bruhin (2013). How to model heterogeneity in costly punishment: Insights from responders' response times, *Journal of Behavioral Decision Making*, 26, 462–476.

Fong, Geoffrey T., David H. Krantz, and Richard E. Nisbett (1986). The effects of statistical training on thinking about everyday problems, *Cognitive Psychology*, 18, 253–292.

Ford, Kevin J., Neal Schmitt, Susan L. Schechtman, Brian H. Hults, and Mary L. Doherty, (1989). Process tracing methods: Contributions, problems, and neglected research questions, *Organizational Behavior and Human Decision Processes*, 43, 75–117.

Friedman, Milton (1953). *Essays in Positive Economics*, Chicago, IL: University of Chicago Press.

Gigerenzer, Gerd (1996). On narrow norms and vague heuristics: A reply to Kahneman and Tversky, *Psychological Review*, 103, 592–596.

Gigerenzer, Gerd (2007). *Gut Feelings*, London: Viking.

Gigerenzer, Gerd (2008). *Rationality for Mortals: How People Cope with Uncertainty*, New York: Oxford University Press.

Gigerenzer, Gerd, Ralph Hertwig . and Thorsten Pachur (Eds.) (2011). *Heuristics: The Foundations of Adaptive Behavior*, New York: Oxford University Press.

Gigerenzer, Gerd, and Reinhard Selten (Eds.) (2001). *Bounded Rationality: The Adaptive Toolbox*, Cambridge, MA: MIT Press.

Gintis, Herbert (2011). Lecture at the School of Economic, Political and Policy Sciences of the University of Texas at Dallas.

Gonzalez, Richard, and George Wu (1999). On the shape of the probability weighting function, *Cognitive Psychology*, 38, 129–166.

Gould, Stephen J. (1988). The streak of streaks, *The New York Review of Books*, August 18.

Güth, Werner (1995). On ultimatum bargaining experiments – A personal review, *Journal of Economic Behavior and Organization*, 27, 329–344.

Hertwig, Ralph and Till Grüne-Yanoff (2017). Nudging and boosting: Steering or empowering good decisions, *Perspectives on Psychological Science* 12, 973–986.

Heukelom, Floris (2009). *Kahneman and Tversky and the Making of Behavioral Economics*, Amsterdam: Tinbergen Institute Research Series.

Hoffrage, Ulrich, Samuel Lindsey, Ralph Hertwig, and Gerd Gigerenzer (2000). Communicating statistical information, *Science*, 290, 2261–2262.

Kahneman, Daniel (2011). *Thinking, Fast and Slow*, New York: Farrar, Strauss and Giroux.

Kahneman, Daniel, Paul Slovic, and Amos Tversky (1982). *Judgment Under Uncertainty: Heuristics and Biases*, Cambridge: Cambridge University Press.

Kahneman, Daniel, and Amos Tversky (1979). Prospect theory: An analysis of decision under risk, *Econometrica*, 47, 263–291.

Kahneman, Daniel, and Amos Tversky (1996). On the reality of cognitive illusions: A reply to Gigerenzer's critique, *Psychological Review*, 103, 582–591.

Katsikopoulos, Konstantinos V. (2011a). How to model it? Review of "Cognitive Modeling" (J. R. Busemeyer and A. Diederich), *Journal of Mathematical Psychology*, 55, 198–201.

Katsikopoulos, Konstantinos V. (2011b). Psychological heuristics for making inferences: Definition, performance, and the emerging theory and practice, *Decision Analysis*, 8, 10–29.

Katsikopoulos, Konstantinos V., and Gerd Gigerenzer (2008). One-reason decision-making: Modeling violations of expected utility theory, *Journal of Risk and Uncertainty*, 37, 35–56.

Katsikopoulos, Konstantinos V., and Dan Lan (2011). Herbert Simon's spell on judgment and decision-making, *Judgment and Decision Making*, 6, 722–732.

Klein, Gary (2001). The fiction of optimization, In Gerd Gigerenzer and Reinhard Selten (Eds.), *Bounded Rationality: The Adaptive Toolbox*, Cambridge, MA: MIT Press, pp. 103–121.

Lee, Cassey (2011). Bounded rationality and the emergence of simplicity amidst complexity, *Journal of Economic Surveys*, 25, 507–526.

Lopes, Lola L. (1991). The rhetoric of irrationality, *Theory and Psychology*, 1, 65–82.

Luce, R. Duncan (1997). Several unresolved conceptual problems of mathematical psychology, *Journal of Mathematical Psychology*, 41, 79–87.

Luce, R. Duncan (1999). Where is mathematical modeling in psychology headed? *Theory and Psychology*, 9, 723–737.

Manzini, Paola, and Marco Mariotti (2007). Sequentially rationalizable choice, *American Economic Review*, 97, 1824–1839.

Manzini, Paola, and Marco Mariotti (2012). Choice by lexicographic semiorders, *Theoretical Economics*, 7, 1–23.

Manzini, Paola, and Marco Mariotti (2014). Welfare economics and bounded rationality, *Journal of Economic Methodology*, 21, 343–360.

Merriam-Webster Online Dictionary (2013). Definition of "pragmatic". Available at: www.merriam-webster.com/dictionary/pragmatic

Morgan, Mary S. (2001). Models, stories and the economic world, *Journal of Economic Methodology*, 8, 361–384.

Morgan, Mary S., and Till Grüne-Yanoff (2013). Modeling practices in the social and human sciences. An interdisciplinary exchange, *Perspectives on Science*, 21, 143–156.

Musgrave, Alan (1974). Logical and historical theories of confirmation, *British Journal of Philosophy and Science*, 25, 1–23.

Peterson, Cameron R., and Lee Roy Beach (1967). Man as an intuitive statistician, *Psychological Bulletin*, 68, 29–46.

Rubinstein, Ariel S. (1998). *Modeling Bounded Rationality*, Cambridge, MA: MIT Press.

Savage, Leonard J. (1954). *The Foundations of Statistics*, New York: John Wiley and Sons.

Selten, Reinhard (2001). What is bounded rationality? In Gerd Gigerenzer and Reinhard Selten (Eds.), *Bounded Rationality: The Adaptive Toolbox*, Cambridge, MA: MIT Press, pp. 13–36.

Simon, Herbert A. (1947). *Administrative Behavior*, New York: The Free Press.

Simon, Herbert A. (1955). A behavioral model of rational choice. *Quarterly Journal of Economics*, 69, 99–118.

Simon, Herbert A. (1956). Rational choice and the structure of environments. *Psychological Review*, 63, 129–138.

Snow, Charles P. (1959). *The Two Cultures*, London: Cambridge University Press.

Starmer, Chris (2000). Developments in non-expected utility theory: The hunt for a descriptive theory of choice under risk, *Journal of Economic Literature*, 38, 332–382.

Tanner Jr., Wilson P., and John A. Swets (1954). A decision-making theory of signal detection, *Psychological Review*, 61, 401–409.

Thaler, Richard H., and Sunstein, Cass R. (2008). *Nudge*, London: Penguin.

Tuckett, David (2011). *Minding the Markets: An Emotional Finance View of Financial Instability*, New York: Palgrave Macmillan.

Tversky, Amos (1972). Elimination by aspects: A theory of choice, *Psychological Review*, 79, 281–299.

Tversky, Amos, and Daniel Kahneman (1971). Belief in the law of small numbers, *Psychological Bulletin*, 76, 105–110.

Tversky, Amos, and Daniel Kahneman (1974). Heuristics and biases: Judgment under uncertainty, *Science*, 185, 1124–1130.

Tversky, Amos, and Daniel Kahneman (1992). Advances in prospect theory: Cumulative representation of uncertainty, *Journal of Risk and Uncertainty*, 5, 297–323.

von Neumann, John, and Oskar Morgenstern (1944). *Theory of Games and Economic Behavior*, Princeton, NJ: Princeton University Press.

Wakker, Peter, and Amos Tversky (1993). An axiomatization of cumulative prospect-theory, *Journal of Risk and Uncertainty*, 7, 147–175.

5

SEEKING RATIONALITY

$500 bills and perceptual obviousness

Teppo Felin and Mia Felin

Introduction

The value of a hypothetical $500 bill is obvious. And because it is obvious, "there are no $500 bills on the sidewalk"—if there were, they would already be picked up (Akerlof and Yellen, 1985: 708–709; also see Frank and Bernanke, 2007).

The $500-bill "axiom" provides a useful—albeit informal—shorthand for explaining market efficiency and rational expectations. Metaphorically, everything in the economy could be seen like the proverbial $500 bill. The value of all assets is obvious: everything is correctly labeled, priced and put to its best use (Muth, 1961; cf. Arrow, 1986).[1] This is because "all agents inside the model, the econometrician, and God share the same model" (as discussed by Thomas Sargent, see Evans and Honkapohja, 2005: 566; cf. Buchanan, 1959; Frydman and Phelps, 2013). Agents are omniscient and markets are at equilibrium—put differently, objects signal their own value. This is because there is no heterogeneity in perception or expectations and therefore there are no above-normal, economic profits to be had. If there were, they would largely be a function of luck and thus be quickly competed away (Alchian, 1950; Denrell, Fang, and Winter, 2003).

Behavioral economics has stepped in to fill this vacuum and pointed out many instances where seemingly obvious value is systematically missed or left on the table, whether at the more micro level of judgment, perception, and decision making or at the more macro level of markets (Kahneman, 2003; Thaler, 2015).[2] To put this in terms of the above $500-bill axiom: economic agents may miss valuable and obvious things, like the $500 bill, because they are blind or bounded in some fashion. Bounded rationality thus provides "an alternative to classical omniscient rationality" (Simon, 1979: 357; cf. Kahneman, 2003), helping us understand why we see and attend to some things, but manage to miss and be blind to many other things. Behavioral economics further builds on these ideas (for a recent review, see Lieder and Griffiths, 2019), linking this work to empirical findings of blindness, priming, and bias from psychology and cognitive science (e.g., Bargh and Chartrand, 1999; Simons and Chabris, 1999). This research emphasizes the "prevalence of bias in human judgment" and more generally how humans "can be blind to the obvious" (Kahneman, 2011). Individuals and markets (in the aggregate) seem to routinely violate the axioms of rationality, as obvious things or sources of value are missed. Because of the pervasiveness of these biases and varied forms of boundedness, opportunities

DOI: 10.4324/9781315658353-6

for more optimal decision making and nudging abound (Stanovich et al., 2016; Sunstein and Thaler, 2008; Thaler, 2016).

In this chapter we discuss the outlines of an alternative to both neoclassical and (certain) behavioral conceptions of rationality. Just as Thaler argues "that models of rational behavior became standard because they were the easiest to solve" (2015: 1579), so we argue that behavioral models of rationality have now become standard because omniscience is easy to prove wrong.[3] In short, it is easy to show that people miss obvious things. And just as many economic models build on "bad psychology" (Clark, 1918: 4; Thaler, 2015: 1579), we argue that (some) behavioral models build on a problematic view of perception. We show how certain versions of the bounded rationality concept are built on specific perceptual assumptions: empirical findings of perceptual blindness and deviations from omniscience and full rationality. We discuss problems with the focus on perceptual blindness and value-related obviousness in behavioral economics, specifically in the context of both rational expectations and bounded rationality. We first provide a brief overview of the bounded rationality concept itself, and then discuss its foundations in the psychology of perception (see Kahneman, 2003; Simon, 1955; for a recent discussion see Chater et al., 2018). We revisit key insights from biology and the psychology of perception. We discuss two key issues: (1) perception and the organism-environment relationship; and (2) seeking or "looking for" rationality. We conclude with a discussion of the economic implications of our argument, as these relate to perception, belief heterogeneity and the origins of value in markets.

Economics, bounded rationality, and perception

Herbert Simon introduced bounded rationality as a counterweight to the full rationality presumed by many in economics. His aim was

> to replace the global rationality of economic man with a kind of rational behavior that is compatible with the *access to information* and the *computational capacities* that are *actually* possessed by organisms, including man, in the kind of environments in which such organisms exist".
>
> *1955: 99*

In short, Simon introduced a psychologically more realistic conception of rationality, behavior, and human decision making. Simon's concept of bounded rationality has become a central building block across a wide swath of disciplines, including economics, management, psychology and cognitive science (Chater et al., 2018).

What is important to our arguments in this chapter is that Simon anchored his model of rationality on certain "psychological theories of perception and cognition" (Simon, 1956: 138; cf. Felin, Koenderink, and Krueger, 2017). Simon frequently used the example of an organism searching for something of value, like food, in their environments. An organism naturally is not fully rational or aware in the sense that it knows where the most optimal sources of food might be in its environment (cf. Todd and Gigerenzer, 2003). The organism instead searches for food locally within its immediate, *visible* vicinity. Search activity is driven by the organism's "perceptual apparatus" and its "length and range of vision" (Simon, 1956: 130). The search is never complete, exhaustive, or perfectly optimal—rather, it is bounded. Organisms satisfice based on more proximate aspiration levels, foregoing full optimality and perfect rationality.

The visual and perceptual emphasis associated with Simon's concept of bounded rationality is further reinforced in the work of Daniel Kahneman (cf. Chater et al., 2018).[4] As noted by

Kahneman in his Nobel speech, behavioral economics "[relies] extensively on visual analogies" and visual perception (2003: 1450–1453; also see Kahneman, 2011). While Kahneman builds on Simon's program of research, his focus is even more strongly on the perceptual rather than computational aspects of bounded rationality. He argues that the behavior of organisms is "not guided by what [agents] are able to compute"—central to Simon's approach—"but by what they *happen to see* at a given moment" (Kahneman, 2003: 1469). The argument is that the human visual system is marred by varied forms of blindness and bias, as illustrated by visual illusions, perceptual priming and concepts like inattentional or change blindness (Simons and Chabris, 1999; also see Bargh and Chartrand, 1999). These illusions and forms of blindness also provide the central evidence of the popular press books published by scholars in the cognitive and behavioral sciences (e.g., Chabris and Simons, 2010; Chater, 2018; Kahneman, 2011). The touchstone of this program of research is the suboptimality of much decision making and pervasiveness of bias and blindness. Metaphorically, humans routinely miss (or ignore or don't see) obvious things, like proverbial $500 bills, right in front of them. This has led to a large program of research to try to nudge decision makers toward better judgments and more optimal choices (e.g., Sunstein and Thaler, 2008; Thaler, 2015; Sunstein, Chapter 38 in this volume).

Before discussing the perceptual aspects of this argument, it's worth recognizing that the behavioral program of research has recently been challenged by scholars who have failed to replicate many of the key findings that purport to provide evidence of widespread human irrationality and bias. A significant portion of the empirical studies and evidence used by Kahneman in his bestselling *Thinking, Fast and Slow* has failed to be replicated, or the work has been theoretically questioned in different ways. This includes empirical and theoretical challenges to a number of key biases and fallacies, including the hot hand fallacy (Miller and Sanjurjo, 2018), social and perceptual priming (Crandall and Sherman, 2016; Ramscar, 2016), dual process theory and the idea of System 1 and System 2 thinking (Melnikoff and Bargh, 2018), inattentional and change blindness (Chater et al., 2018; Felin et al., 2019), and so forth. Furthermore, there is also a long-standing argument about whether biases and blindness are rational heuristics, as illustrated by the rationality of the anchoring bias (Lieder et al., 2018) or the rationality of inattention (Matejka and McKay, 2015). This work on heuristics has been pioneered and further developed by Gerd Gigerenzer and his colleagues over the past decades (Gigerenzer and Todd, 1999). Furthermore, the visual illusions that are frequently referenced by behavioral scholars as metaphorical examples of blindness—extended to the context of rationality (see Kahneman, 2003)—have been shown by perception scholars not to be illusions at all (Braddick, 2018; Rogers, 2014). That said, scholars of course are actively debating these issues, and thus it is hard to point to conclusive answers (see van Buren and Scholl, 2018; Rogers, 2019). However, while these debates will undoubtedly continue, the problem is that the evidence for pervasive human bias and blindness is often couched as established, scientific facts to external audiences. For example, related to perceptual priming (a literature currently under severe empirical scrutiny), Kahneman argues that "disbelief is not an option. The results are not made up, nor are they statistical flukes. You have no choice but to accept that the major conclusions of these studies are true" (2011: 57). But in retrospect, it appears that many of these seemingly solid, empirical findings are in fact not as clear-cut and conclusive as previously thought (Felin et al., 2019; for more, see Chater et al., 2018).

In this chapter we set these issues aside and specifically discuss how assumptions about perception are essential for the rationality literature, focusing both on rational expectations and particularly the concept of bounded rationality. We argue that the underlying assumptions about perception (and what should be visually obvious) need to be carefully revisited, as these apply to varied forms of bounded rationality, judgment and decision making. Thus we make the perceptual assumptions of existing work more explicit and provide the broad outlines of an alternative.

What do we see and why? What's obvious?

Perhaps the simplest question regarding perception is, *what* do organisms (humans included) see and *why*? Or put differently, what is perceptually obvious and why? Humans and other organisms continually encounter stimuli and objects that make up or constitute their visual scene, environment or situation.[5] Some things in the visual scene (somehow) become salient and obvious, while other things remain in the background, perhaps outside awareness. And to complicate things even further, different organisms—or even two different people or organisms looking at the very same visual scene—may also differ in what they perceive. What is it, then, that we see and become aware of, and why?

A simple way to answer the question of "what do we see?" is to point to the physical objects that actually constitute any visual scene itself: the things in front of and surrounding an organism. To provide a practical illustration, you as the reader of this chapter are right now encountering a visual scene. This sentence and the book chapter you are reading are part of your visual scene. But if you lift up your gaze and look around, you will also see other things. If you are in an office, there is likely to be a desk close by, perhaps a lamp or different forms of lighting, some number of chairs, maybe a whiteboard, perhaps art or office decorations on the wall, or some number of books on the shelf. And if you direct your gaze out the window, you might see any number of other things: people walking by on the street, nearby buildings, trees and vegetation, or the sky. In short, your immediate surroundings are teeming with potential things to see, many of them obvious. But the central question here is: why—among the many things right in front of (and around) us—do we see or become aware of *certain* things, and not others?

Before addressing this question, a simple response to the "what do we see?" question is: we see what is actually there. At first glance this approach provides a very straightforward (and in fact prominent) account of perception. It suggests that there should be no mystery when it comes to perception. Perception simply records the physical things in front of (and around) us: a chair, books, computer screen, clouds, and so forth. As put by Marr in his book *Vision*, vision is a "true description of what is there" (1982: 29–30; cf. Hoffman et al., 2015). Perception then is seen as a catalogue of actual objects, things and stimuli in front of us. This in fact is the implicit assumption of wide swaths of vision science, such as ideal observer theory (Geisler, 2011), psychophysics (Kahneman, 1966; for a recent review, see Kingdom and Prins, 2016), and Bayesian approaches to vision (Kersten et al., 2004; Yuille and Kersten, 2006). More generally, this veridical approach to perception is the foundation of many (if not most) contemporary theories of vision and perception (for a review, see Hoffman et al., 2015).

One problem with this veridical, catalogue, or camera-view of perception is that it is impractical (Chater et al., 2018). Listing or capturing all of these stimuli and objects not only is not necessary or useful, but also impractical and impossible. This idea in fact metaphorically provides the visual equivalent of bounded rationality, which is that listing and accounting for all the obvious visual things in front of us would both take too much time and also defeat the very purpose of perception (or rationality) itself. Or put differently, everything is not recognizable or computable or listable, given limited resources or time. This then might yield a conception of perception as a defective camera, compared to a more omniscient ideal that somehow captures everything. But beyond this problem, a more essential issue is that the camera-view of perception doesn't tell us *which* of the many possible things in our visual scenes are salient and why. That is, why do we become aware of certain objects or stimuli and not others? Again, the problem is that visual scenes are teeming with "things:" potential objects, stimuli and cues. The fact that we miss some things, even obvious ones, might of course be the basis of calling humans blind (Simons and Chabris, 1999). Or more productively, it might be the basis of developing a theory of *why* we become aware of some things and not others.

This is where Kahneman (2003) and the behavioral program of research build on psychophysics, which focuses on salience as a function of the actual nature of particular stimuli or cues themselves. What is seen by organisms is tied to the actual, physical nature of environments confronted by organisms and agents. As put by Kahneman, "the impressions that become accessible in any particular situation are mainly determined, of course, by the *actual properties* of the object of judgment," and "physical salience [of objects and environments] *determines* accessibility" (2003: 1453, emphasis added). Importantly, some stimuli, impressions and objects are more readily accessible than others. Here Kahneman argues that these perceptual objects become salient and accessible because they have particular characteristics, such as their "size, distance, and loudness" (2003: 1453). To simplify and illustrate: a large, proximate, and "loud" stimulus or object is more readily seen, and thus obvious, compared to a small, distant, and "quiet" object. Kahneman calls these "natural assessments" (Kahneman, 2003; also see Kahneman and Frederick, 2002; Tversky and Kahneman, 1983). Visually salient objects are more readily and quickly attended to because of these stimulus characteristics. Stimulus characteristics make certain things "stand out" and become more prominent and thus visually accessible. The list of stimulus characteristics (beyond size, etc.) also includes "more abstract properties such as similarity, causal propensity, surprisingness, affective valence, and mood" (Kahneman, 2003, p. 1453). Thus this program of research offers some practical predictions arguing that certain, actual characteristics of stimuli (again, size being a particularly salient one) determine whether we see them or not.

Though the heuristics program of research disagrees with Kahneman about whether biases in fact are rational heuristics (see Gigerenzer and Goldstein, 1996; Gigerenzer and Todd, 1999), there are surprising commonalities between these two behavioral programs of research. Namely, the emphasis in the heuristics program of research is also on perception and the nature of stimuli themselves. The central construct of the heuristics program of research is an environment or perceptual "cue." Thus in their summary of the heuristics stream of research, Gigerenzer and Gaissmaier (2011) emphasize varied factors related to environmental and perceptual cues. These include "the number of cues," "cue weighting," "the correlation of cues," "cue validity," "cue addition," "the search through cues," "positive cues," "cue value," "cue ordering," "cue redundancy," "cue correlation," "cue integration," "cue combination," " cue favoring," and so forth (also see Gigerenzer and Goldstein, 1996).

Cues within the heuristics program of Gigerenzer then serve the equivalent function to Kahneman's stimulus characteristics and natural assessments. Thus in many ways, the ecological rationality sub-area of behavioral economics—pioneered by Gigerenzer and others—links with the areas of psychophysics and inverse optics which focus on perception as a function of stimulus intensity, similarity, repetition, exposure, thresholds, and signal detection (see Kingdom and Prins, 2016). This is also the basis of Bayesian views of perception (Knill and Richard, 1996), which have also had a strong influence on the bounded rationality and cognition literatures (e.g., Chater et al., 2010; Oaksford and Chater, 2007). And a similar type of emphasis on stimuli and cues can also readily be found in other areas of psychology and cognitive science, such as the situation construal and situation perception literatures (e.g., Rauthmann et al., 2014; also see Chater et al., 2018; Funder, 2016). In sum, the behavioral program in psychology and economics implicitly makes the assumption that the nature of stimuli (Kahneman, 2003) or the nature of cues (Gigerenzer and Gaissmaier, 2011) determines perception and obviousness. In the case of Kahneman, what we see is a function of (for example) how large or proximate something is. And in the case of Gigerenzer and others, cues are simply given and their varied structure (ordering, aggregation, combination, etc.) are essential for salience and perceptual awareness.

In an important sense these conceptions of rationality don't—ironically, similar to the rational expectation model of economics—meaningfully require any assumptions about the organism itself. That is, the architecture of cognition is general (Anderson, 2013). The models assume an objective conception of the environment (which has particular visual or statistical features), and organisms then have some kind of delimited, bounded, or biased view of their environment, or a view that is proximate and good enough to satisfice. This environmental focus is also captured by Simon who argued that "an ant [or human being], viewed as a behaving system, is quite simple. The apparent complexity of its behavior over time is largely a reflection of the complexity of the environment in which it finds itself" (1981: 63–65; also see Anderson, 2013). The arguments, then, are species-independent and universal (Simon, 1980), as suggested by Simon's reference to organisms in general, whether we are talking of ants or human beings. This also can be related to behavioral models in psychology that similarly encouraged scientists to move away from studying organisms but environments instead. Schwartz, for example, argued that "if you want to know why someone did something, do not ask. Analyze the person's immediate environment until you find the reward" (1978: 6). Furthermore, the universality of these arguments is reflected in how broadly these models of bounded rationality are applied, across different species and even computers. Simon argued that "since Homo Sapiens *shares some important psychological invariants* with certain nonbiological systems—the computers—I shall make frequent reference to them also" (1990: 3, emphasis added). Thus the notion of bounded rationality is more generally applied to any form of search and foraging (Abbott et al., 2015; Fawcett et al., 2014; Gershman et al., 2015).

An important wrinkle with the behavioral program of research is the fact that humans and other organisms seem to be visually blind to things that should be readily obvious—obvious given the nature of the stimuli or cues. That is, something that is large, and right in front of an organism, directly in its visual field, should be obvious (as predicted by the theory). But somehow organisms, humans included, are seemingly blind to any number of large things. Our visual scenes feature various obvious things—obvious in terms of their characteristics—but somehow we nonetheless appear to miss them. The highly-cited, classic example of this is Simons and Chabris's (1999) study of inattentional blindness, where a person dressed in a gorilla suit walks across a visual scene and many experimental subjects never see the gorilla. This is surprising, because the gorilla has many of the hallmarks of a stimulus or cue that in fact ought to make it highly salient, including the fact that it is large. Of course, in some sense these types of findings question the very idea that perception is a function of stimulus characteristics (cf. Felin et al., 2019). Next we provide an alternative way of viewing these types of findings, which we think can account for them, and also shed light on the question of bounded rationality in the context of judgment and decision making in economics.

To summarize and briefly return to the subheading of this section of our chapter—what do we see and why?—the predominant emphasis in the behavioral program has been on the nature of stimuli and cues in the immediate environment of organisms. This argument certainly is, in some ways, an improvement over rational expectations, which, in effect, presume visual omniscience. The bounded rationality literature seems to have provided a psychologically more realistic conception of perception and rationality. But next we seek to suggest some extensions and alternatives. In short, we argue that the question of "what do organisms see and why" can be answered differently and that this has important implications for how we think about human rationality and decision making in economic and social settings.

Perception and rationality

Insights from psychology and biology

In this section we consider some alternative ways to understand perception and rationality. We specifically discuss two key points: (1) perception and the organism-environment relationship; and (2) seeking or "looking for" rationality.

Before proceeding, it is worth noting that that we strongly concur with Gigerenzer and Selten's notion that "visions of rationality do not respect disciplinary boundaries" (2001: 1). This interdisciplinarity certainly was evident in the pioneering work of Herbert Simon, whose oeuvre included everything from psychology, management to computer science and beyond. And, of course, behavioral economics is strongly anchored on Kahneman's (2003) emphasis on and contributions in psychophysics (cf. Kahneman, 1966)—along with providing extensive links to psychology (Thaler, 2015)—and the attendant implications of all this for judgment and decision making. Thus we also draw insights from other literatures, specifically from the psychology of perception and biology.

Perception and the organism-environment relationship

In the literature on bounded rationality there is a strong emphasis on the nature of environments and their role in shaping or determining behavior. The argument is that we can "discover, by a careful examination of some of the fundamental structural characteristics of the environment... the mechanisms used in decision making" (Simon, 1956: 130). This focus on the environment is reflected in the aforementioned comment by Simon, namely, that the "apparent complexity of [organism] behavior over time is largely a reflection of the complexity of the environment in which it finds itself" (1969: 65–66; also see Simon, 1990). This is also evident in the analogy between visual scenes and environments, the idea that agent behavior is guided "by what they happen to see at a given moment" (Kahneman, 2003: 1469). For example, Kahneman extensively uses evidence from perceptual priming to make this point (2011: 52–68), and it is this literature that argues that "the entire environment-perception-behavior sequence is automatic, with no role played by conscious choice in producing the behavior" (Bargh and Chartrand, 1999: 466). The emphasis on the environment is equally explicit in the literature on ecological rationality, though the emphasis is somewhat different. Gigerenzer and Gaissmaier (2011) argue that environments (and their structures) are characterized by specific factors: the uncertainty, redundancy, sample size and variability of cues. The upshot is that environments are treated as objective and species-general (for a recent discussion, see Chater et al., 2018), thus leading to universal models that are said to account for rationality across species (cf. Gershman et al., 2015; Simon, 1990).

From a biological point of view, the notion that environments are general and can be objectively characterized is problematic. This is because cues and stimuli are *specific* to organisms (Koenderink, 2014). That is, what an organism attends to (or as we'll discuss, looks *for*) depends on the nature of the organism itself. This creates a confound in the organism-environment distinction. Certainly, scholars are likely to admit that organisms differ, as do their respective environments. But the problem is that these differences have not been meaningfully articulated or discussed (Chater et al., 2018).[6] And this species-specificity also fundamentally changes how we think about perception, and by extension, rationality.

The fields of ethology and comparative biology offer the best evidence for the fact that environments are species-specific rather than general (Tinbergen, 1963; for a recent review, see Burkhardt, 2018). Each organism has its own, unique "Umwelt" (surrounding world), where awareness and perception are a function of the nature of the organism itself (Uexküll, 2010). To provide a specific example, frogs may not see a juicy cricket or locust (their food) even if it is directly in front of them (Ewert, 1987). Thus an analysis of what *ought* to be salient or valuable to an organism based on any *general* stimulus characteristics will not tell us what it is actually aware of. We might of course label the frog blind or biased, but this merely creates a black box rather than meaningfully explaining what the frog sees and why. Thus the *a priori* selection of what should be obvious—in the presence of any number of other stimuli in a scene—cannot generate a scientific explanation. It turns out that frogs are visually attuned to movement and thus will snap as soon as the cricket or locust jumps. This highlights that what "stimulates"—or which cues become salient and naturally assessed (cf. Kahneman, 2003)—has less to do with the stimulus itself (or the objective or general "amount" of some cue (Gigerenzer and Gaissmaier, 2011). Rather, awareness of particular stimuli has more to do with the nature of the organism (Ewert, 1987). Only those stimuli or cues that are species-specific "light up," or are processed and attended to, while many other things are ignored.[7]

The notion that stimuli are specific to organisms changes the way we need to study the organism-environment relationship. It means that the mechanisms behind the organism-environment interaction are unique to each species, thus raising questions about species-general models (Chater et al., 2018), including extensions into the domain of bounded rationality.[8] This work was pioneered by ethologists, comparative biologists, like Niko Tinbergen and Konrad Lorenz, whose work was linked to Jakob von Uexküll. Uexküll metaphorically conceived of the species-specific environment as "a soap bubble around each creature to represent its own world, filled with the perception which it alone knows" (2010: 117). He argued that "every animal is surrounded with different things, the dog is surrounded by dog things and the dragonfly is surrounded by dragonfly things"—that is, "each environment forms a self-enclosed unit, which is governed in all its parts by its meaning for the subject" (2010: 5). These biological models didn't somehow disagree with broader evolutionary processes that might impact species at the level of populations. But this literature was highly attuned to the more proximate, immediate considerations that shape species behavior and perception (Tinbergen, 1963), and thus also provide useful insights for human settings. Thus the goal here isn't to engage in any form of "species chauvinism" (Winter, 2012)—in fact, quite the opposite—rather to merely point out species-specific factors that impact perception.

Seeking or "looking for" rationality

As we've discussed above, perceptual relevance and meaning for the behavioral program are driven by environmental characteristics, by the inherent and objective nature of objects and stimuli. Our suggested alternative focuses on the relevance and meaning that organisms themselves bring to encounters with environments. Perception, in some sense, is driven by what an organism has "in mind," what it considers relevant and meaningful for specific purposes.[9] Not only are environments specific, as discussed above, but organisms have species-specific factors that direct their perception and behavior toward certain ends and toward the selection of certain stimuli.

A powerful way to understand organism awareness and perception is by studying what the organism is searching or looking for. This "looking for"-activity is guided by a species-specific "Suchbild" (Uexküll, 2010; cf. Chater et al., 2018), a German word for search or seek image. Search images are the equivalent of what an organism has in mind, in terms of an "answer" that the organisms is looking for to satisfy its search. Frogs, for example, when hungry, are looking for certain, line-like features that move in their environment. Their behavior is motivated and directed by this search-image, and awareness is directed toward highly specific things (or what might be called answers). This "looking for"-activity comes at the expense of any number of other, obvious things that an organism might have right in front of it.

In the case of humans, the relevant search image is given by what is in the head or mind of the human actor when encountering a visual scene or situation. If you are searching for your keys, you are keenly attuned to key-like stimuli or features. Relevance and meaning are provided by the question that you have in mind, and the task that you are engaged in. This Suchbild or question might be seen as the most basic form of a heuristic. As noted by Polanyi, "the simplest heuristic effort is to search *for* an object you have mislaid" (1957: 89). Note that this "search for"-heuristic is fundamentally different from the heuristics that emphasize, say, the nature of stimuli themselves or the number of cues (Gigerenzer and Gaissmaier, 2011).[10] When scanning a room for your keys, you are ignoring vast numbers of stimuli (including obvious ones) and selectively directing awareness toward possibly relevant cues based on the "key search image" you have in mind. Note that the keys are not somehow inherently visually salient, as they are small and thus do not attract attention or awareness due to their size (as suggested by psychophysics). In searching for keys—or anything else for that matter—we ignore an indefinite number of other, perhaps obvious and large, things around us. We also do not individually "attend to" each item in our visual scene to decide whether it is the key or not. Rather, we only focus on and select key-like visual stimuli. We concentrate on the problem, question and task at hand: searching for keys. This type of motivated searching or "looking for"-activity is impossible to account for from the perspective of psychophysics or a world-to-mind oriented view of perception. In psychophysics there is no meaning or relevance (Felin, Koenderink, and Krueger, 2017; Koenderink, 2012), there are only objective stimuli and cue characteristics (Chater et al., 2018; Gigerenzer and Gaissmaier, 2011).

Any number of empirical findings from the cognitive sciences can readily be re-interpreted with this Suchbild-oriented or "looking for"-lens, especially any work that purports to provide evidence of human blindness (e.g., Simons, 1999); Simons and Rensink, 2005). That is, the *reason* that humans miss large changes or objects in their visual scene is, simply, because they have something else in mind. To put this colloquially: humans miss certain things because they are looking for other things. The problem with the empirical studies of human blindness is that they often deliberately *distract* experimental subjects (asking them to engage in some irrelevant task or answer a particular question), and then point out something that is large and blatantly obvious but missed, such as a gorilla (Felin, Felin, Krueger, and Koenderink, 2019). In other words, in these perceptual experiments, humans are effectively given a question or Suchbild of what to look for (whether counting basketball passes or engaging in other tasks), which distracts them, and therefore they miss large changes or objects. Visual scenes, of course, are teeming with many blatantly obvious things. But no progress will be made in understanding perception and rationality without focusing on the Suchbilds that direct human perception, or without a focus on the things that human actors are looking for.

What humans have "in mind" can be accounted for in many ways. Perception might be directed by a problem or question, such as the aforementioned example of looking for one's keys. Or perception might be directed by a task, such as getting to some location (or counting basketball passes (Simons and Chabris, 1999). But again, it's hard to argue that people are "blind to the obvious" (Kahneman, 2011: 23–24), as visual scenes are teeming with obvious things. And perhaps most relevant to the economic context (discussed further in the next section) is the idea that perception might be directed by a hypothesis or theory that a human has in mind. This is aptly captured by Popper who argued that "we learn only from our hypotheses what kind of observations we ought to make: whereto we ought to direct our attention: wherein to take interest" (1966: 346). This also goes for science: that is, salience is given by what we are theoretically looking for. As noted by Einstein, "whether you can observe a thing or not depends on the theory which you use. It is the theory which decides what can be observed" (Polanyi, 1971: 604). Thus whether we are talking about the labs of behavioral economics, or encounters with visual scenes in the real world, we have implicit questions or theories about what these respective situations or scenes are about, and these then direct our perception and awareness. In all, the upshot of this discussion is that organism- and theory-dependent factors structure awareness and perception, with important implications for how we think about rationality, judgment and decision making in economic and social settings as well.

Rationality and the perception of value

Opportunities and caveats

Next we discuss the economic implications of the arguments above. We also provide some important caveats. Our overall goal with this concluding section is to link the aforementioned discussion of perception and obviousness to central questions of rationality and belief heterogeneity in economic settings, as well as the idea of economic value. We make two points.

First, axiomatic assumptions about the human mind are important. As put by Simon, "nothing is more fundamental in setting our research agenda and informing our research methods than our view of the *nature* of the human beings whose behavior we are studying" (1985: 303). Thus if our theoretical "priors" about human nature are largely focused on the "prevalence of bias in human judgment" (Kahneman, 2011), then we are likely to simply focus on this, at the expense of other things. But the cost of this is that we will likely miss many other, more positive aspects of rationality and the human mind. Thus the psychology that behavioral scholars have imported into economics has been relatively one-sided—perhaps deliberately "putting in a stake" at the very opposite extreme from omniscience: rampant bias and blindness. The concern is that these bias-oriented priors—a form of scientific confirmation bias—will lead to the construction of studies that continue to show further instances of bias and blindness, deviations from omniscience. But as mentioned at the outset, providing evidence of shortfalls from omniscience is all too easy and convenient (cf. Thaler, 2015). Much of the evidence for bias may reflect a bias on the part of scholars toward fun, surprising and easy studies that prove irrationality (Krueger and Funder, 2004). This work has also led to a widespread public perception that bias and blindness are rampant problems and key features of the human mind, as suggested by popular books written by cognitive scientists (e.g., Chater, 2018; Chabris and Simons, 2010). Now, of course, humans make mistakes and errors. But the obsession with those errors has led to a rather one-sided sampling of psychology in the context of economics. Furthermore, the focus on biases and irrationality will not allow us to account for the fact that we live in the best of times, at least when it comes to any number of objective, measurable dimensions, including radical declines in poverty across the globe, exponential growth in human knowledge and staggering technological and economic progress (e.g., Pinker, 2018).

The behavioral program sees itself as an heir to Adam Smith's program of research in economics, in reintroducing a more realistic version of psychology to economics (Thaler, 2016; also see Ashraf, Camerer, and Loewenstein, 2005). But it's hard to see how the rich ways in which Smith delved "into the sentiments and mind of actors" can be squared with the strong focus on bias and irrationality. A careful re-reading of *The Theory of Moral Sentiments* or *The Wealth of Nations* shows that Smith's program of research was far more expansive and positive (Rothschild, 2013). His assumptions about human nature and the mind certainly didn't suggest any form of omniscience on the part of economic agents, as behavioral scholars rightly have pointed out. But Adam Smith certainly was not as error-oriented when discussing human nature and the human mind. In fact, he sought to endow economic actors with the same theoretical and creative capacities that we as scientists have. Adam Smith's program of research might be summarized as an effort to develop—as put by economic historian Emma Rothschild—"a theory of people with theories" (2013: 157). This suggests a radically different agenda from one that focuses on the "prevalence of bias in human judgment" (Kahneman, 2011; Thaler, 2015). This type of sentiment was also channeled by Edith Penrose in *American Economic Review* when she argued: "For the life of me I can't see why it is reasonable (on grounds other than professional pride) to endow the economist with this unreasonable degree of omniscience and prescience and not entrepreneurs" (1952: 813). Of course, no one is arguing that omniscience is psychologically or cognitively a defensible view. But allowing human agents a modicum of rationality, of a very specific type, given the uncertain and fast-paced situations they find themselves in, provides a useful way forward.

Thus an important next step is to develop models that assume that the human agents we study might in fact have some of the same theoretical capacities that we scientists do. Namely, humans have the ability to theorize, to ask questions, to pose and solve problems. There are major strands of psychology to support this view. For example, the work of William James (1912) is filled with psychological insights about rationality and how individuals navigate uncertain environments and the role that their beliefs play in doing so. More generally, there is important research in psychology and the cognitive sciences on the generative capacities of humans in the presence of impoverished stimuli and uncertain environments (Spelke et al., 1992; for a review, see Felin, Koenderink, and Krueger, 2017). All of this psychological and cognitive research deserves to be integrated into the context of judgment and decision making in economic settings. Glimmers of this approach can in fact be found in some pockets of economics and adjacent fields like management. For example, Karni and Vierø (2013) discuss the role of "growing awareness" (what they call reverse Bayesianism) in uncertain, economic environments. Eric Van den Steen (2016) discusses the role of beliefs and managerial vision in markets and in the strategy of firms. And Felin and Zenger (2017) highlight how heterogeneous managerial beliefs and theories shape markets, the emergence of firms and the origins of economic value. Firms, from this perspective, can be seen as representing a unique beliefs or "point of view" about what to do and how to structure production (Coase, 1937; King et al., 2010). Others have looked at the role of entrepreneurial judgment (Foss and Klein, 2015) or attention (Ocasio and Joseph, 2017) in the context of markets and organizations. And scholars within the domain of bounded rationality have discussed such concepts as creativity (Viale, 2016) and the wisdom of heuristics in guiding behavior in uncertain settings (Grandori, 2010).

Of course, in some sense, our arguments might be seen as creating a caricature of behavioral economics and the emphasis it places on the negative aspects of human nature and mind. There are important exceptions to our characterization. Herbert Simon's work in particular is brimming with insights that deserve more careful attention, beyond what we have discussed here. For example, throughout much of Simon's work there is an emphasis on problem-solving and goals (Simon, 1964). The specification of problems and goals indeed seems to provide a possible foundation for the type of organism-oriented conception of perception and rationality that we have discussed in this chapter. However, unfortunately the literature on problem-solving and goals has not been meaningfully incorporated into discussions of bounded rationality in cognitive science or behavioral economics (Chater, 2018; Kahneman, 2003, 2011; Thaler, 2016).

A second implication of our arguments about perception relates to the informal $500 bill-axiom we discussed at the beginning of this chapter. In some sense, the $500 provides an intriguing litmus test for explaining rational expectations and bounded rationality. The $500 bill, of course, is a rather strange example, because it hardly provides a useful proxy for discussing the vast set of possible objects and assets that might have value in economics settings. After all, the $500 bill is clearly labeled: we know what it is worth. In most economic cases of interest, value is scarcely obvious. Most things of (possible) value are rarely labeled, and there is likely to be significant disagreement about their worth. The set of possible uses for objects and assets is, quite simply, unlistable and unprestatable (Felin et al., 2016). And importantly, most of the valuable assets and activities we observe in markets require (or were the result of) some form of long-run organization and production. Thus casual references to market efficiency, using the $500 bill as an example, vastly oversimplify the economic problem. And experiments that show that humans miss obvious things, while interesting, miss the opportunity to develop theories of how truly novel value is identified, produced and organized in the first place. Thus a focus on heterogeneous perceptions, beliefs, hypotheses and theories can provide a powerful tool for explaining value in firms and markets.

When economists do in fact focus on beliefs, the focus is usually on self-fulfilling prophecies where *irrational* beliefs and delusions lead to bubbles or market collapse (e.g., Gennaioli and Shleifer, 2018; Shiller, 2015). The human psychology that is applied to study markets is about "animal spirits," wrong-headed beliefs, and illusions, which are largely used to explain negative outcomes (Akerlof and Shiller, 2010; Shiller, 2017). This type of work of course has its place. But what about the obverse? That is, what about cases where beliefs appear to be delusional (perhaps even to a large number of market constituents, including experts), or where there is significant heterogeneity and ambiguity, but these beliefs and ideas nonetheless become realities and generate value (cf. Soros, 2013; van den Steen, 2016)?[11] These types of heterogeneous beliefs and opinions ought to be at the very heart of understanding markets and value creation.[12] It seems that the fascination with delusion or bias has led us to lose track of the type of heterogeneity that animates markets and provide the underlying engine of economic growth. That is, despite biases and irrational beliefs, we nonetheless witness continued technological progress and ongoing economic growth. A central problem is that public markets and many investors have a hard time assessing uniqueness and value (Benner and Zenger, 2016; Zuckerman, 1999), thus raising questions about the obviousness of value and more general market efficiency and rationality. Again, beliefs that appear to be delusional or wrong-headed (to some, including experts and savvy market actors), somehow generate what later becomes obvious economic value. Some beliefs, ones that objectively looked impossible, become realities as new organizations are formed and certain market actors gravitate toward and invest in what (to others) appear to be excessively risky and implausible investments. Of course, there are no "rules for riches" here. But we think that our earlier discussion of heterogeneous perception and beliefs might provide some useful, scientific and empirical starting points for this type of analysis for understanding the origins and nature of economic value.

Conclusion

The aim of this chapter has been to discuss different forms of rationality—rational expectations and bounded rationality—and to make explicit the underlying assumptions that are made regarding perception, obviousness, and economic value. We discuss how insights from biology and the psychology of perception might provide the preliminary foundations of an alternative. We specifically emphasize the species-specific nature of both environments and what organisms are "searching for," suggesting central mechanisms for explaining judgment and decision making in uncertain environments. We conclude by offering some high-level remarks and possible extensions to our argument, specifically by focusing on perception, belief heterogeneity and the origins of value in markets.

Acknowledgments

An early version of this chapter was presented at the 2018 University of Oxford workshop "Science, Humanity and Meaning." The authors appreciate helpful conversations with and feedback from George Ellis, Thomas Fink, Seth Jenson, Stuart Kauffman, Aaron Reeves, Riccardo Viale, and Mark Wrathall. This chapter extends joint work published in *Psychonomic Bulletin and Review* and *Perception* with Jan Koenderink and Joachim Krueger. Any errors are our own.

Notes

1 Of course, value may not be obvious to everyone immediately, in the short run. But in the long-run—as agents search, adapt, compete, and learn (e.g., Bray and Savin, 1986; Lucas, 1986)—even semi-efficient markets will ensure that obvious value will be competed away as agents interact.

2 For more macroeconomic discussions of value and "bills left on the table," see Clemens (2011) and Olson (1996).

3 In his book on behavioral psychology and economics, Richard Thaler recounts what the psychologist Thomas Gilovich said to him: "I never cease to be amazed by the number of convenient null hypotheses economic theory has given you" (2015: 97). Of course, the notion that something is easy or convenient should not be seen as a put-down, just as Thaler argues that his comment about neoclassical economics isn't a put-down (2015: 1579). Both omniscient and behavioral approaches to rationality have certainly been useful and led to progress in our understanding of economic activity.

4 The research on bounded rationality has generated varied, proximate literatures and concepts including "computational rationality" (Gershman et al., 2015), "algorithmic rationality" (Halpern and Pass, 2015), "Bayesian rationality" (Oaksford and Chater, 2007), resource-rational analysis (Griffiths et al., 2015), and bounded awareness (Chugh and Bazerman, 2007). These literatures are closely related and roughly feature similar underlying assumptions about perception (for a recent discussion, see Chater et al., 2018; Felin, Koenderink, and Krueger, 2017).

5 Depending on one's theoretical sub-field, there are significant differences in how scholars treat situational perception versus scene statistics versus visual fields versus, and so forth (cf. Chater et al., 2018). For the purposes of this chapter, we simply utilize the language and intuition developed by Simon (1955) and Kahneman (2003), though we also build some links to existing vision research that provides an alternative (Koenderink, 2012).

6 Intriguingly, there is a brief, early recognition of this by Herbert Simon (cf. Felin, Koenderink and Krueger, 2017). Simon argues that "we are not interested in describing some physically objective world in its totality, but only those aspects of the totality that have relevance as the 'life space' of the organisms considered" (1956: 130). Our question, then, has to do with this "life space," and specifically its unique features relative to the organism in question. This organism-specific line of argument has subsequently not received attention (see Chater et al., 2018).

7 An additional bit of evidence for species-specificity comes from the idea of supernormal stimuli (Barrett, 2010; Hoffman et al., 2015). Supernormal stimuli are stimuli that are disproportionately attractive or salient to specific species. Thus certain birds may try to hatch a volleyball, because of its large size, preferring it over their own eggs. Or, a specific beetle in Australia (*Julodimorpha bakewelli*) nearly became extinct as discarded beer bottles became a supernormal stimulus for the male beetle, who tried to copulate with the bottle (the nodules or glass beads on the bottle were highly attractive to the beetle). Thus species have built-in instincts for specific perceptual aspects of their environments.

8 For related points, about embodied cognition, see Gallese et al. (Chapter 23 in this volume).

9 We are of course using "in mind" merely as informal shorthand for any number of endogenous, species-specific factors behind perception and behavior. Our discussion of "Suchbild" provides an overall way of capturing this notion. Though, as we discuss, this Suchbild (or what is "in mind," what an organization might be looking for) captures a number of disparate factors such as internal drives and motivations, as well as the questions, problems or tasks that organisms impose on environments.

10 Perhaps the closest idea to this might be the so-called "one reason"-heuristic suggested by Gigerenzer and colleagues (1999). However, the one reason heuristic is also explicitly tied to cue characteristics— such as cue order, or other ideas like stopping rules—and thus is hard to directly square with the more Suchbild-oriented approach suggested in this chapter.

11 Interestingly, some scholars have recently begun to recognize this issue under the guise of discussing the role of "narratives," which shape the attention, motivations, predictions and behavior of economic actors (see Akerlof and Snower, 2016).

12 The idea of knowledge as "justified true belief" and the social processes of belief justification (Goldman, 1999) create an interesting puzzle for value creation in the context of uncertain economic environments. That is, economic value is inherently created where there are disparate and conflicting beliefs about what the relevant possibilities and facts are (for further discussion, see Felin and Zenger, 2017). Thus the social mechanisms and "scaling" of beliefs (from some subjective state to a more objective one)—and where justification happens on the basis of working toward belief realization and mobilizing others—provide an interesting opportunity for future work.

References

Abbott, J. T., Austerweil, J. L., and Griffiths, T.L. 2015. Random walks on semantic networks can resemble optimal foraging. *Psychological Review*, 122(3), 558–569.

Akerlof, G. A., and Shiller, R. J. 2010. *Animal spirits: How human psychology drives the economy, and why it matters for global capitalism*. Princeton, NJ: Princeton University Press.

Akerlof, G. A., and Snower, D. J. 2016. Bread and bullets. *Journal of Economic Behavior & Organization*, 126, 58–71.

Akerlof, G. A., and Yellen, J. L. 1985. Can small deviations from rationality make significant differences to economic equilibria? *American Economic Review*, 75(4), 708–720.

Alchian, A. A. 1950. Uncertainty, evolution, and economic theory. *Journal of Political Economy*, 58(3), 211–221.

Anderson, J. R. 2013. *The architecture of cognition*. New York: Psychology Press.

Arrow, K. 1986. Rationality of self and others in an economic system. *Journal of Business*, 59, 385–399.

Arrow, K., and Debreu, G. 1954. Existence of an equilibrium for a competitive economy. *Econometrica*, 22, 265–290.

Ashraf, N., Camerer, C. F., and Loewenstein, G. 2005. Adam Smith, behavioral economist. *Journal of Economic Perspectives*, 19(3), 131–145.

Bargh, J. A., and Chartrand, T. L. 1999. The unbearable automaticity of being. *American Psychologist*, 54(7), 462.

Barrett, D. 2010. *Supernormal stimuli: How primal urges overran their evolutionary purpose*. New York: WW Norton & Company.

Benner, M. J., and Zenger, T. 2016. The lemons problem in markets for strategy. *Strategy Science*, 1: 71–89.

Braddick, O. 2018. Illusion research: An infantile disorder? *Perception*, 47(8), 805–806.

Bray, M. M., and Savin, N. E. 1986. Rational expectations equilibria, learning, and model specification. *Econometrica: Journal of the Econometric Society*, 54(5), 1129–1160.

Buchanan, J. M. 1959. Positive economics, welfare economics, and political economy. *The Journal of Law and Economics*, 2, 124–138.

Burkhardt, R. W. 2018. *Patterns of behavior, Konrad Lorenz, Niko Tinbergen, and the founding of ethology*. Chicago: University of Chicago Press.

Chabris, C., and Simons, D. 2010. *The invisible gorilla: And other ways our intuitions deceive us*. New York: Random House.

Chater, N., Felin, T., Funder, D. C., Gigerenzer, G., Koenderink, J. J., ... Stanovich, K. E. 2018. Mind, rationality, and cognition: An interdisciplinary debate. *Psychonomic Bulletin & Review*, 25(2), 1–34.

Chater, N., Oaksford, M., Hahn, U., and Heit, E. 2010. Bayesian models of cognition. *Wiley Interdisciplinary Reviews: Cognitive Science*, 1(6), 811–823.

Chugh, D., and Bazerman, M. H. 2007. Bounded awareness: What you fail to see can hurt you. *Mind & Society*, 6(1),1–18.

Clark, J. M. 1918. Economics and modern psychology. *Journal of Political Economy*, 26(1), 1–30.

Clemens, M. A. 2011. Economics and emigration: Trillion-dollar bills on the sidewalk? *Journal of Economic Perspectives*, 25(3), 83–106.

Coase, R. H. 1937. The nature of the firm. *Economica*, 4(16), 386–405.

Crandall, C. S., and Sherman, J. W. 2016. On the scientific superiority of conceptual replications for scientific progress. *Journal of Experimental Social Psychology*, 66, 93–99.

Denrell, J., Fang, C., and Winter, S. G. 2003. The economics of strategic opportunity. *Strategic Management Journal*, 24(10), 977–990.

Evans, G. W., and Honkapohja, S. 2005. An interview with Thomas J. Sargent. *Macroeconomic Dynamics*, 9(4), 561–583.

Ewert, J. P. 1987. Neuroethology of releasing mechanisms: Prey-catching in toads. *Behavioral and Brain Sciences*, 10(3), 337–368.

Felin, T., Felin, M., Krueger, J. I., and Koenderink, J. 2019. On surprise-hacking. *Perception*, 48(2), 109–114.

Felin, T., Kauffman, S., Mastrogiorgio, A., and Mastrogiorgio, M. 2016. Factor markets, actors and affordances. *Industrial and Corporate Change*, 25(1), 133–147.

Felin, T., Koenderink, J., and Krueger, J. I. 2017. Rationality, perception, and the all-seeing eye. *Psychonomic Bulletin & Review*, 24(4), 1040–1059.

Felin, T. , and Zenger, T. R. 2017. The theory-based view: Economic actors as theorists. *Strategy Science*, 2(4), 258–271.

Foss, N. J., and Klein, P. G. 2015. Introduction to a forum on the judgment-based approach to entrepreneurship: Accomplishments, challenges, new directions. *Journal of Institutional Economics*, 11(3), 585–599.

Frank, R. H., and Bernanke, B. 2007. *Principles of microeconomics*, 3rd ed. London: McGraw-Hill Irwin.

Frydman, R., and Phelps, E. S. (Eds.) 2013. *Rethinking expectations: The way forward for macroeconomics*. Princeton, NJ: Princeton University Press.

Funder, D. C. 2016. Taking situations seriously: The situation construal model and the Riverside Situational Q-Sort. *Current Directions in Psychological Science*, 25(3), 203–208.

Geisler, W. S. 2011. Contributions of ideal observer theory to vision research. *Vision Research*, 51(7), 771–781.

Gennaioli, N., and Shleifer, A. 2018. *A crisis of beliefs: Investor psychology and financial fragility*. Princeton, NJ: Princeton University Press.

Gershman, S. J., Horvitz, E. J., and Tenenbaum, J. B. 2015. Computational rationality: A converging paradigm for intelligence in brains, minds, and machines. *Science*, 349(6245), 273–278.

Gigerenzer, G., and Gaissmaier, W. 2011. Heuristic decision making. *Annual Review of Psychology*, 62, 451–482.

Gigerenzer, G., and Goldstein, D. G. 1996. Reasoning the fast and frugal way: Models of bounded rationality. *Psychological Review*, 103(4), 650–669.

Gigerenzer, G., and Selten, R. 2001. Rethinking rationality. In *Bounded rationality: The adaptive toolbox*. Cambridge, MA: MIT Press.

Gigerenzer, G., Todd, P. M., and the ABC Research Group (Eds.) 1999. *Simple heuristics that make us smart*. Oxford: Oxford University Press.

Goldman, A. I. 1999. *Knowledge in a social world*. Oxford: Oxford University Press.

Grandori, A. 2010. A rational heuristic model of economic decision making. *Rationality and Society*, 22(4), 477–504.

Griffiths, T. L., Lieder, F., and Goodman, N. D. 2015. Rational use of cognitive resources: Levels of analysis between the computational and the algorithmic. *Topics in Cognitive Science*, 7(2), 217–229.

Halpern, J. Y., and Pass, R. 2015. Algorithmic rationality: Game theory with costly computation. *Journal of Economic Theory*, 156, 246–268.

Hoffman, D. D., Singh, M., and Prakash, C. 2015. The interface theory of perception. *Psychonomic Bulletin & Review*, 22(6), 1480–1506.

James, W. 1912. *The sentiment of rationality and other essays*. London: Longmans, Green and Company.

Kahneman, D. 1966. Time-intensity reciprocity in acuity as a function of luminance and figure-ground contrast. *Vision Research*, 6(3–4), 207–215.

Kahneman, D. 2003. Maps of bounded rationality: Psychology for behavioral economics. *American Economic Review*, 93(5), 1449–1475.

Kahneman, D. 2011. *Thinking, fast and slow*. New York: Farrar, Straus and Giroux.

Kahneman, D., and Frederick, S. 2002. Representativeness revisited: Attribute substitution in intuitive judgment. In T. Gilovich, D. Griffin, and D. Kahneman (Eds.), *Heuristics and Biases: The Psychology of Intuitive Judgment*, Cambridge: Cambridge University Press.

Karni, E., and Vierø, M.L. 2013. "Reverse Bayesianism": A choice-based theory of growing awareness. *American Economic Review*, 103(7), 2790–2810.

Kersten, D., Mamassian, P., and Yuille, A. 2004. Object perception as Bayesian inference. *Annual Review of Psychology*, 55, 271–304.

King, B. G., Felin, T., and Whetten, D. A., 2010. Perspective—Finding the organization in organizational theory: A meta-theory of the organization as a social actor. *Organization Science*, 21(1), 290–305.

Kingdom, F. A. A., and Prins, N. 2016. *Psychophysics: A practical introduction*. New York: Academic Press.

Koenderink, J. 2012. Geometry of imaginary spaces. *Journal of Physiology*, 106, 173–182.

Koenderink, J. 2014. The all-seeing eye. *Perception*, 43, 1–6.

Knill, D. C. and Richards, W. 1996. *Perception as Bayesian inference*. Cambridge: Cambridge University Press.

Krueger, J. I., and Funder, D. C. 2004. Towards a balanced social psychology: Causes, consequences, and cures for the problem-seeking approach to social behavior and cognition. *Behavioral and Brain Sciences*, 27(3), 313–327.

Lieder, F. and Griffiths, T. L. 2019. Resource-rational analysis: Understanding human cognition as the optimal use of limited computational resources. *The Behavioral and Brain Sciences*, 43, 1–85.

Lieder, F., Griffiths, T. L., Huys, Q .J., and Goodman, N. D. 2018. The anchoring bias reflects rational use of cognitive resources. *Psychonomic Bulletin & Review*, 25(1), 322–349.

Lucas Jr, R. E. 1986. Adaptive behavior and economic theory. *Journal of Business*, 59(4), S401–S426.

Marr, D. 1982. *Vision: A computational investigation into the human representation and processing of visual information*. New York: Henry Holt and Co: Inc.

Melnikoff, D. E., and Bargh, J. A. 2018. The mythical number two. *Trends in Cognitive Sciences*, 22(4), 280–293.

Miller, J. B., and Sanjurjo, A. 2018. Surprised by the hot hand fallacy? A truth in the law of small numbers. *Econometrica*, 86(6), 2019–2047.

Muth, J. F. 1961. Rational expectations and the theory of price movements. *Econometrica: Journal of the Econometric Society*, 29(3), 315–335.

Oaksford, M., and Chater, N. 2007. *Bayesian rationality: The probabilistic approach to approach to human reasoning*. Oxford: Oxford University Press.

Ocasio, W., and Joseph, J., 2017. The attention-based view of great strategies. *Strategy Science*, 3(1), 289–294.

Olson, M. 1996. Big bills left on the sidewalk: Why some nations are rich, and others poor. *Journal of Economic Perspectives*, 10(2), 3–24.

Penrose, E. T. 1952. Biological analogies in the theory of the firm. *American Economic Review*, 42(5), 804–819.

Pinker, S. 2018. *Enlightenment now: The case for reason, science, humanism, and progress*. London: Penguin.

Polanyi, M. 1957. Problem solving. *British Journal for the Philosophy of Science*, 8, 89–103.

Polanyi, M. 1971. Genius in science. *Archives de Philosophie*, 34, 593–607.

Popper, K. 1966. *Objective knowledge: An evolutionary approach*. Oxford: Oxford University Press.

Ramscar, M. 2016. Learning and the replicability of priming effects. *Current Opinion in Psychology*, 12, 80–84.

Rauthmann, J. F., Gallardo-Pujol, D., Guillaume, E. M., Todd, E., Nave, C.S., ... Funder, D. C. 2014. The situational eight DIAMONDS: A taxonomy of major dimensions of situation characteristics. *Journal of Personality and Social Psychology*, 107(4), 677.

Rogers, B. 2014. Delusions about illusions. *Perception*, 43, 840–845.

Rogers, B. 2019. Where have all the illusions gone? *Perception*, 48(3), 193–196.

Rothschild, E. 2013. *Economic sentiments*. Cambridge, MA: Harvard University Press.

Schwartz, B. 1978. *The psychology of learning and behavior*. New York: W.W. Norton.

Shiller, R .J. 2015. *Irrational exuberance*. Princeton, NJ: Princeton University Press.

Shiller, R. J. 2017. Narrative economics. *American Economic Review*, 107(4), 967–1004.

Simon, H. A. 1955. A behavioral model of rational choice. *The Quarterly Journal of Economics*, 69(1), 99–118.

Simon, H. A. 1956. Rational choice and the structure of the environment. *Psychological Review*, 63(2), 129.

Simon, H. A. 1964. On the concept of organizational goal. *Administrative Science Quarterly*, 9(1), 1–22.

Simon, H. A. 1979. *Models of thought*. New Haven, CT: Yale University Press.

Simon, H. A. 1980. Cognitive science: The newest science of the artificial. *Cognitive Science*, 4(1), 33–46.

Simon, H. A. 1981. *Sciences of the artificial*. Cambridge, MA: MIT Press.

Simon, H. A. 1985. Human nature in politics: The dialogue of psychology with political science. *American Political Science Review*, 79, 293–304.

Simon, H. A, 1990. Invariants of human behavior. *Annual Review of Psychology*, 41(1), 1–20.

Simon, H. A. 1991. Organizations and markets. *Journal of Economic Perspectives*, 5(2), 25–44.

Simons, D. J., and Chabris, C. F., 1999. Gorillas in our midst: Sustained inattentional blindness for dynamic events. *Perception*, 28(9), 1059–1074.

Simons, D. J., and Rensink, R. A. 2005. Change blindness: Past, present, and future. *Trends in Cognitive Sciences*, 9(1), 16–20.

Soros, G. 2013. Fallibility, reflexivity, and the human uncertainty principle. *Journal of Economic Methodology*, 20(4), 309–329.

Spelke, E. S., Breinlinger, K., Macomber, J., and Jacobson, K. 1992. Origins of knowledge. *Psychological Review*, 99(4), 605–632.

Stanovich, K. E., West, R. F., and Toplak, M. E. 2016. *The rationality quotient: Toward a test of rational thinking*. Cambridge, MA: MIT Press.

Thaler, R. H. 2015. *Misbehaving: The making of behavioral economics*. New York: WW Norton.

Thaler, R. H. 2016. Behavioral economics: Past, present, and future. *American Economic Review*, 106(7), 1577–1600.

Thaler, R. H. 2017. Behavioral economics. *Journal of Political Economy*, 125(6), 1799–1805.

Thaler, R., and Sunstein, C. 2008. *Nudge: the gentle power of choice architecture*. New Haven, CT: Yale University Press.

Tinbergen, N. 1963. On aims and methods of ethology. *Zeitschrift für Tierpsychologie*, 20(4), 410–433.

Todd, P. M., and Gigerenzer, G. 2003. Bounding rationality to the world. *Journal of Economic Psychology*, 24(2), 143–165.

Tversky, A., and Kahneman, D. 1983. Extensional versus intuitive reasoning: the conjunction fallacy in probability judgment. *Psychological Review*, 90(4), 293–315.

Uexküll, J. von 2010. *A foray into the worlds of animals and humans*, trans. J. D. O'Neil. Minneapolis, MN: University of Minnesota Press.

van Buren, B., and Scholl, B. J. 2018. Visual illusions as a tool for dissociating seeing from thinking: a reply to Braddick. *Perception*, 47(10–11), 999–1001.

van den Steen, E. 2016. A formal theory of strategy. *Management Science*, 63(8), pp.2616–2636.

Viale, R. 2016. Brain-based bounded creativity. In L. Macchi, M. Bagassi, and R. Viale, (Eds.), *Cognitive unconscious and human rationality*. Cambridge, MA: MIT Press.

Winter, S. G. 2011. Problems at the foundation? Comments on Felin and Foss. *Journal of Institutional Economics*, 7(2), 257–277.

Yuille, A., and Kersten, D. 2006. Vision as Bayesian inference: Analysis by synthesis? *Trends in Cognitive Sciences*, 10(7), 301–308.

Zuckerman, E. 1999. The categorical imperative: Securities analysts and the illegitimacy discount. *American Journal of Sociology*, 104(5), 1398–1438.

6

BOUNDED RATIONALITY, DISTRIBUTED COGNITION, AND THE COMPUTATIONAL MODELING OF COMPLEX SYSTEMS

Miles MacLeod and Nancy J. Nersessian

Introduction

Computational modeling and simulation of complex systems are playing a major role in twenty-first-century scientific discovery. Given the rhetoric of "big data" and automated modeling practices, one might expect that computer simulation is a resource for side-stepping human cognitive capacities and constraints. Yet even these practices still require human cognitive engagement with their products for the purposes of validation and interpretation. And, as we have discovered in our investigations of computational systems biology, much problem-solving still involves researchers building their own models in situations of scarce or inadequate data, using laptop computers. Rather than freeing scientists from their cognitive limitations, using computation to extend control and understanding over ever more complex systems requires developing sophisticated problem-solving practices which push them toward these constraints. Several philosophers of science have had the intuition that cognitive capacities and limitations play a significant role in shaping methodological strategies and choices, especially in modeling complex systems (see, for instance, Humphreys 2009). It would seem, then, that cognitive considerations should be factored in with epistemic and practical considerations in advancing justifications for specific methodological choices in such problem-solving processes, but philosophers by and large have not examined these. Unlike most of the research in this area of philosophy, which relies on published papers concerning finished models, our research is based on the premise that it is necessary to examine the model-building practices to develop an understanding of how human cognitive capacities enable and constrain these, as well as the ways and extent to which modelers overcome cognitive limitations. Our analysis is based on a 5-year ethnographic study of model-building practices in computational systems biology. In our investigations of innovative modeling practices in systems biology, we have found the notion of bounded rationality and its mechanisms of search and satisficing particularly useful for explaining and justifying the development of modeling methods and strategies. The overarching goal of contemporary systems biology is to create high-fidelity computational models and simulations of complex biological systems. This goal largely eludes them. Instead modelers

DOI: 10.4324/9781315658353-7

rely on strategies of building mid-level models that contain modest details of system com-position and organization ("mesoscopic models") and of "building-out" rough initial models and incrementally exploring and modifying these. Thus, modelers build constrained problem spaces, and solution search operates chiefly through generating inferences about erroneous model structure, which requires both a set of search heuristics and constant feedback through computational simulation. The use of rather simplified representations, which are often far from high-fidelity, can be seen on cognitive and other grounds to be rational for the long-term goals of systems biologists, given cognitive and other constraints. This is important, since most models of biological systems currently produced in the field do not achieve the level of fidelity required for prediction and control for medical or other purposes. Nonetheless we will show that the modeling strategies currently employed provide a bounded rational solution to the problem of building such models over the long term.

However, ours is a quite different analysis of scientific problem-solving than that advanced by Simon. Specifically, we have been advancing the position that scientific problem-solving requires a distributed cognition analysis. In the case at hand, accounting for scientific discoveries through building computational representations requires a distributed cognition analysis of the *processes* of building these representations, in which the model and modeler comprise a complex distributed model-based reasoning system. Thus, we extend the notion of bounded rationality to distributed cognitive systems. Although not entertained by Simon himself, we see the analytical framework of distributed cognition as a means of further explicating his "parable of the ant," where ant and environment comprise a complex problem-solving system (Simon 1996, p. 63). In the par-able, if one simply traces the track of the ant over a two-dimensional space, its problem-solving behavior seems highly complicated. However, once the environment is factored in, each move of the ant can be recognized as a relatively simple localized response to individual obstacles. The ant's behavior is largely a reflection of constraints in the environment and basic internal representations. Simon suggested that "man" could be substituted for "ant." However, while we agree problem-solvers do make local responses based on limited information, we would add that much human problem-solving behavior is not just a *response* to an environment but a more *active use* of affordances in the environment to aid cognitive tasks. Further, humans create affordances in the environments such as external representational artifacts that "off-load" cognitive tasks to the environment, as in the case of the speed bug performing memory functions for the pilot in the process of landing a plane (Hutchins 1995a). In this brief chapter: (1) we outline the mod-eling tasks in systems biology; (2) we examine their modeling practices; (3) we present an over-view of our cognitive analysis; and (4) make a case for their bounded rationality.

Modeling tasks in systems biology

Our ethnographic study of model-building practices tracked modeling in two computational systems biology labs. In each lab the aim is to construct relatively detailed models of metabolic, cell signaling, and gene-regulatory networks. These models are dynamic, tracking the changes in concentration of each metabolite, or the activity of each gene, in a network over time. Philosophically, computational systems biology takes the stance that only high-fidelity math-ematical models can capture network behavior sufficiently to gain understanding and reliable control of these networks for medical or technological purposes. However, although the basic mathematical methods of systems biology have a long history, the potential to produce high-fidelity models has only become possible over the last 20 years with the advent of readily avail-able fast computation. It is now possible for a modeler using a laptop computer to create a model which captures 50 or more interacting biochemical elements. For the most part, modelers aim to model these biochemical networks using coupled ordinary differential equations. These networks, however, have a number of complexities which make the modeling task difficult. Structurally, the biochemical networks are highly nonlinear, exhibiting feedback effects, and having elements playing multiple roles at different points in a network (meaning that different points in the network draw on the same chemical reservoir within a cell). Cognitively, non-linearity makes it difficult for modelers to track causal relations in their model and antici-pate what modifications will achieve. Additionally, modelers never have a complete biological representation of their network ("pathway diagram") at the beginning of their project and lack sufficient data to build a highly detailed model. Indeed, since experimentalists generally do not study all interactions within a network themselves, modelers (who know little biology) need to search through the experimental literature and databases to build the pathways on their own.

With this information in hand, we can describe the modeling task. First, modelers need to assemble a pathway representation of their network, which is a line diagram connecting elem-ents in a chain according to the order in which they interact. The pathway representation allows them to map variables to a mathematical formulation and choose interaction representations to fill in that formulation. Finally, parameters to fit the model need to be estimated from the available data. Any unknown parameters can then be determined through a parameter-fitting algorithm which chooses a parameter set for the model, according to how well it can repro-duce experimental data on the network behavior. Usually some data are held over for testing the validity of the model that is produced. If all this works, then modelers can proceed to make novel predictions about system behavior, such as how to intervene optimally on the systems for medical purposes using target drug combinations.

Although this looks like a relatively straightforward set of procedures, in nearly all cases we have examined, the starting biological pathway representations modelers assemble are never adequate for the network behaviors they want to capture. Biochemical elements are missing or interactions among elements in the network are missing. At the same time, initial representations of those interactions might not be correct. The models they produce thus invariably fail to test well against the available data first time around. The task, then, of the modeler is to correct the models they have produced by deriving or inferring the location of missing elements or poor interaction descriptions in their models and hypothesizing additions or corrections to replace them. Usually a variety of corrections are required to build a model that functions adequately.

Mesoscopic modeling and the building-out strategies

Given the complexity of the systems being modeled, modelers have developed strategies that make the task cognitively tractable. In the first place, they build a lower-fidelity model that bounds the problem space. Such models are called "mesoscopic" (Voit et al. 2012), meaning they are "in between" any one level of description or biological organization in two senses. First, the systems-level is simplified such that only certain relationships or system-level behaviors are represented, rather than the full range of potential behaviors. Second, the network itself is simplified in a variety of ways, often relative to these system-level goals. Quite abstract non-mechanistic representations of biochemical interactions are applied to simplify running simulations, parameter-fitting, and mathematical analysis. Elements thought not to be rele-vant to target behaviour are left out. Subsystems are typically blackboxed and treated as linear or constant. Note that while such simplifications are typical of any modeling effort, they are problematic to the extent that systems biology aims at high-fidelity models capable of robust predictions.

The mesoscopic model delimits the problem space for searching for solutions to correct the model. Dimensions of the space represent different structural alternatives and biochemical interaction alternatives (in terms of their mathematical description). This space is also constrained by what interactions and structures are biochemically possible, although a modeler (typically from engineering) might not know all of these. The task of the modeler is to locate the alternatives which best capture the functional performance of the target network they wish to capture and also perform best in response to perturbations.[1] It is impossible for modelers to simply hypothesize the needed corrections in one hit. These more limited models still represent many interacting elements, involving many non-linearities. Although it might be possible to predict what one modification might do, understanding the implications of changing two elements is usually impossible. There is thus an imperative on modelers to develop strategies for iteratively localizing problems and fixing them. The strategy our modelers employ has been developed around a central presupposition, namely, that the initial models they formulate are within a relatively small set of changes from a good network representation. This is essential, since for the most part their strategy is constructed almost entirely around making discrete modifications to the original model and using the original model to guide their actions. We call this a "building-out" strategy. In practice, the problem space modelers confront is constructed relative to this initial model. In addition to this initial model representation, model simulation provides information as to how the dynamics of the model differ in behavior from the target. Modelers are thus, at the start, looking for modifications which bring their model into alignment with that behavior. Of course, the nature of the divergences provides clues as to where to look and what to change. With an initial model at hand, then modelers formulate their strategy around two central tasks: *explorations* and *modifications* (MacLeod 2018). Explorations are steps modelers employ to try to understand the causal relationships within the model. Explorations can be done through pen and paper representations, but usually they also require running simulations repeatedly and visualizing the results. To get the information they need, modelers will often temporarily remove elements to try to isolate particular relations. Importantly, they can use the affordances of computation to bracket nonlinear behaviors, through explorations of different parameter and input variations. These repeated processes help modelers develop what they often refer to as having a "feel for a model" (Voit et al. 2012). We have analyzed this notion in detail (Chandrasekharan and Nersessian 2015; MacLeod and Nersessian 2018) and understand it to refer to intuitions modelers build up on how particular variables and parameters in the network causally affect specific others. In more cognitive terms we characterize these intuitions as simulative mental models; internal representations which simulate causal relationships.

Explorations build up families of mental models which themselves represent at least part of the structure of the overall model. These mental models help modelers predict potentially fruitful modifications by allowing them to infer possible effects of modifications. Modifications are hypotheses modelers make which should help move the model toward a sound representation. Working from the original model, modelers can entertain a sequence of increasingly complex heuristics, including: (1) adjusting parameters; (2) adding or removing interactions between elements already in the network; (3) changing interaction formulae; (4) "de-black-boxing" a set of interactions; and (5) adding a new element to the model at different points in the network. This list of options represents discrete, localized changes to models. Each can be hypothesized and then tested according to how well the new model performs and, if heading in the right direction, new modifications can then be hypothesized. In this respect these heuristics follow a hill-climbing logic, with modelers hoping for improvements with each move but not expecting to find any fully definite solution in one hit. Hopefully within a relatively contained sequence of steps the model reaches the performance goals of the modeler. If the model fails to improve, then modelers will likely conclude that there is no cognitively accessible path from their original model to an adequate representation. The model might be incorrect in too many interrelated ways for them to untangle.

We view this building-out strategy as a means by which modelers of complex systems turn problem-solving situations with ill-defined problems, unstructured task environments, and quite general goals into a series of situations approximating those Simon envisaged. For each iteration of the model-building process, there is a relatively well-defined problem space: the modification process has a fixed representation, the goal of "fitting" that model, and a set of heuristics for facilitating what is in essence a search process. However, to understand how such computational model-building processes lead to scientific discoveries we need to embed the notions of problem space, search, and bounded rationality a different kind of cognitive analysis than that advanced by Simon.

Cognitive analysis: distributed model-based reasoning

Computational model-building provides an exemplar of what Hutchins calls creating cognitive powers (1995b; also see Chandrasekharan and Nersessian 2015). Numerous iterations of model-building (including visualizations of behavior), debugging, modifying, and simulation, build the model and modeler into a "coupled" cognitive system. The highly integrated nature of this distributed problem-solving system results in the modeler being able to manipulate and explore a much more complex set of equations that would be possible "in the head" alone—even with pen and paper resources. Scientific problem solving has always been dependent on creating and using external representations, especially various kinds of diagrams. There is a vast literature that examines the cognitive roles of these in both mundane and scientific reasoning. The roles of computational representations, which dominate contemporary science, however, have received scant attention, and what literature there is focuses on the function of model visualizations in mental modeling (Trafton, Trickett, and Mintz 2005; Trickett and Trafton 2002, 2006, 2007) and distributed problem-solving processes (Alač and Hutchins 2004; Becvar et al. 2008). The work of our research group has taken a different approach, focusing on the processes of *building* computational representations and how discoveries emerge from these processes (see, especially, Chandrasekharen and Nersessian 2015). Our analysis starts from Nersessian's account of scientific problem-solving processes in terms of "simulative model-based reasoning" where inferences are drawn in distributed cognitive processes, comprising building and manipulating mental models and external representations such as diagrams and equations (Nersessian 1992, 2002, 2008) or physical models (Nersessian et al. 2003; Nersessian 2009). Inferences are drawn through processing information in the system comprising memory ("internal") and the environment ("external")—what we call *distributed model-based reasoning*—rather than as on the traditional account where all information is abstracted from the external representations (environment) and represented and processed internally, as with Simon's ant (see Greeno 1989, for an earlier similar claim). We argue that the process of building models integrates manipulations in the mental model and in the external representation, creating a *coupled cognitive system* (Osbeck and Nersessian 2006; Nersessian 2008). Here we briefly discuss the extensions required of the framework of distributed cognition to accommodate our account of scientific problem solving, especially as it pertains to computational representations (a detailed account is provided in Chandrasekharan and Nersessian 2015). Much of the research on the function of external representations within the distributed cognition framework has focused on highly defined task environments with well-defined problems and goals, such as piloting ships and planes (Hutchins 1995b) or solving puzzles with fixed representations and rules (Zhang and

Norman 1994). These analyses focus on the way external representations change the nature of the cognitive tasks, especially by reducing cognitive load through off-loading memory to the environment. These external representations are ready-to-hand. Scant attention has been directed toward understanding the role of processes of building the external representations to alter task environments in cognitive processes during problem solving (exceptions include Kirsh 1996 and Hall et al. 2010). Scientific practices provide a prime locus for studying processes of building external representations since building problem-solving environments is a major component of scientific research (Nersessian et al. 2003; Nersessian 2012). When studying science, the focus needs to shift to the building of external structures consonant with how people actively distribute cognition (Hall et al. 2010) through creating problem-solving environments and in turn building cognitive powers (Hutchins 1995b). A research laboratory provides a good example of a problem-solving environment. It contains artifacts salient to the research, people, and socio-cultural practices. A computational model, itself, provides another example of a problem-solving environment. Through building and running the model, the researcher creates cognitive powers that extend her natural ones, such as the ability to synthesize a vast range of data, to visualize complex dynamical processes, and to run through unlimited imaginative (counterfactual) scenarios not possible in her mind alone. Indeed, we have witnessed how building computational models enables systems biology modelers with scant biological knowledge to make fundamental biological discoveries (Chandrasekharan and Nersessian 2015). Our extension of the framework to science has been based on ethnographic studies of the open, ill-formed problem solving tasks of pioneering research and of the processes by which researchers create their cognitive artifacts; in the case at hand, computational representations. The other way is which the framework of distributed cognition is in need of extension is by providing an account of the nature of the internal representations used by the human component of the system. Most research on distributed cognitive processes is silent about mental representations. Zhang and Norman (1994), which explicitly analyzes the interactions among external and internal representations in problem solving, assume the internal representations to be mental models. Nersessian (1992, 2002, 2008) has elaborated a "mental modeling framework," which she argues provides a cognitive basis for the range of model-based reasoning used in scientific practice. This framework draws from the strand of research in the mental modeling literature that examines the processes of constructing and manipulating a working memory model during reasoning and problem solving and is agnostic about the nature of the long-term memory representation. In thinking about scientific reasoning, Nersessian (2008) argues that we need to move beyond the mental models literature per se and create a synthesis of an extensive range of experimental literature spanning over 25 years on discourse and situation modeling (see, e.g., Johnson-Laird 1983; Perrrig and Kintsch 1985; Zwaan 1999), mental animation (see, e.g., Hegarty 1992; Schwartz 1995; Schwartz and Black 1996), mental spatial simulation (see, e.g., Shepard and Cooper 1982; Finke 1989; Kosslyn 1980), and embodied mental representation and perceptual simulation (see, e.g., Glenberg 1997; Bryant and Tversky 1999; Barsalou 1999; Brass, Bekkering, and Prinz 2001). She advances a "minimalist hypothesis" that "in certain problem-solving situations humans reason by constructing a mental model of the situation, events, and processes in working memory that in dynamic cases can be manipulated by simulation" (2002, p. 143). Recent psychological research on scientists and engineers as they try to solve research problems lends support to the hypothesis and further details the nature and role of mental model (or "conceptual") simulations (Trafton, Trickett, and Mintz 2005; Trickett and Trafton 2007; Christensen and Schunn 2009). For instance, Trickett and Trafton (2007) establish the importance of conceptual simulation in the data analysis phase of several different kinds of scientific fields. Most importantly, the use of such simulations increases in cases of inferential uncertainty where scientists appear to be trying to develop a general understanding of the system under investigation. They see their findings as lending support to the extension of the "minimalist hypothesis" to scientific problem-solving. Mental modeling is often carried out in the presence of real-world resources, such as diagrams and the various objects being reasoned about, as Simon has noted for design and other processes (Simon 1996). This is even more so in the case of science, where visual representations, physical models, and computational models are integral to the reasoning in problem-solving processes. Further, the representations and processing required for such sophisticated reasoning are too detailed and complex to be "in the head" alone. In cognitive psychology, the question of the interface between the mental capacity and resources in the world has largely focused on diagrams and other visual representations. Several of these analyses have proposed that the external representations are *coupled* with the mental representations in inferential processing (see, e.g., Greeno 1989; Zhang and Norman 1994; Gorman 1997; Hegarty 2005; Nersessian 2008). Our research extends internal and external representational coupling to dynamical representations: computational simulations and mental simulations. By examining the process through which external and internal representational structures are built, we can begin to understand how these are incorporated into a distributed system that performs cognitive functions such as memory and inference; in the case at hand, distributed model-based reasoning through the coupling of mental modeling and computational simulation processes. From our interview data and the pen and paper sketches the computational modelers in our study make, we have been able to discern some features of the mental representations they use in "debugging" computational models (MacLeod and Nersessian 2018). Broadly, they can be described as simulative models of causal relationships represented in their mathematical networks, which operate in a manner similar to the kinds of mental models captured in investigations of basic causal network reasoning (Hegarty 1992, 2004; Schwartz 1995). These models are qualitative (Roschelle and Greeno 1987), rather than quantitative, and the inferences drawn from them are thus qualitative in nature. Further, as with everyday causal network reasoning, these models tend to be selective and piecemeal representations of the overall systems (Hergarty 1992). In particular, nonlinear relations can be identified and bracketed with the aid of computation into different separate behaviors, allowing mental simulation of each separately. For example, the range over which a feedback structure produces stable oscillations can be separated from the range over which this structure produces more equilibrium-type behavior, and these can handled separately. Incrementally building such mental models in conjuction with processes of computational simulation and visualization creates the coupled cognitive system through which novel inferences about both the computational and real-world biological systems can be made, often leading to important discoveries (Chandrasekharan and Nersessian 2015; MacLeod and Nersessian 2018).

The bounded rationality of model-building practices in systems biology

We think it especially important to consider the rationality of modeling practices in systems biology because the field currently is failing to reach its stated epistemological goals. The practice of mesoscopic model-building and incremental modification through building-out strategies provides an exemplar of what Simon, in a later analysis of bounded rationality, called "procedural rationality" (Simon 1976), that is, the rationality of the processes through which boundedly rational decisions or problem solutions (substantive rationality) are achieved.

To show procedural rationality for a particular strategy, two claims need to be made: first, that a cognitive system is constrained (or bounded), and, second, that the strategy provides an effective pathway given these constraints, toward reaching a set of goals. Building mesoscopic models bounds the problem space of the complex biological system. This facilitates the effectiveness of the building-out strategy as there is a limit to both the complexity of the model (in terms, e.g., of the number of elements reponsible for any particular behavior) and the number of faults which explain why a model departs from the data. Any model which breaches such limits would not be tractable for mental modeling in the ways we have suggested, restricting the possibility of employing the heuristic steps fruitfully. As we have seen, the nature of the building-out strategy, to make discrete incremental modifications to a pre-existing model, suggests the extent to which modelers work to keep their operations within their cognitive limitations. Mental modeling research indicates that among other things there is a critical need to keep modeling practices within the scope of working memory. Inferences are drawn based on causal interactions among elements. As Hegarty has shown in the case of pulley systems, the ability to reason about causal networks is constrained directly by working memory (Hegarty 1992, 2004). The building-out strategy depends on being able to draw inferences as to the sources of errors and about modifications which might eliminate them, which requires starting from a more limited computational model representation. Given these constraints, one can make a good argument that the strategies of systems biology modelers provide a boundedly rational option for their model-building tasks. Producing even a mesoscopic model which captures the systems adequately at the outset is impossible due to incomplete information and the complexity of the systems. The building-out process affords error-correcting inferences. A step-wise approach takes advantage of this while keeping the modeling processes within cognitive control. Modelers resolve the model not by planning several moves ahead, but through selecting among a set of choices which, at any one time, amount to local fixes or improvements. Overall, the rationality of the building-out strategy depends on both initial models being within a relatively small number of steps from a good outcome and on the complexity of interactions within the model being constrained, such that modelers can effectively draw inferences through engagement with computational simulation. One cannot judge *a priori* how well initial models meet the conditions they need to have in order for the building-out strategy to pay-off. But, in our experience, modelers do manage to produce models through these techniques which meet their limited data-matching and prediction goals. And even though the models are not high-fidelity, some have produced significant discoveries, such as discovering unknown elements in a well-established pathway (Chandraskeharan and Nersessian 2015; MacLeod and Nersessian 2018). Such achievements are in fact a powerful endorsement of the power of this approach to modeling of complex biological systems, despite the ultimate goals of the field.

In general, we think our research shows that bounded rationality can provide not only a good description of problem-solving practices, but also a justification for methodological decision-making that, on the surface, might seem sub-optimal in fields that are attempting to understand, predict, and control complex systems by relying heavily on computational modeling and simulation. As noted, although the strategies considered enable the production of models which meet limited representational goals, such models do not achieve the scale and fidelity at which systems biology aims. A major part of the rhetoric of systems biology is that modern computation opens up the possibility of building high-fidelity models of large-scale systems, which are required for robust predictions and to advance biological theory. However, as Voit et al. (2012, p. 23) describe it, the majority of models in systems biology are not "large enough to approach the reality of cell or disease processes with high fidelity." The strategies modelers use to build these limited, mid-sized models, seem, on the face of it, to push modelers away from these goals, especially since they are rarely capable of robust predictions (MacLeod and Nersessian, 2015, 2018). This has created a challenge for the field of justifying their current practices, and systems biologists are remarkably reflective on the nature of the cogntive challenges they face and on the need to rationalize the current production of relatively small-scale models. As pioneers in the field, Voit et al. (2012) and Voit (2014) argue that the value of such models to the field is that, once built, they create tractable cognitive platforms for richer model development and provide insight into the underlying systems, by virtue of their mesoscopic nature. That is, they create potential pathways for scaling models up in detail and complexity, such that higher fidelity models can be achieved sometime in the future. Interestingly, Voit et al. locate the cognitive basis of

> [their] strategy of locally increasing granularity ... in semantic networks of learning and the way humans acquire complex knowledge ... hierarchical learning is very effective, because we are able to start simple and add information as we are capable of grasping it.
>
> *2012, p. 23*

In other words, mesoscopic models, once constructed, serve as learning platforms, facilitating a modeler's ability to build richer, more detailed models that capture more of the biological system's complexity. Hence, although current systems biology might be failing in its aim of constructing high fidelity models, the kinds of models being built are anticipated to facilitate the ability of modelers to produce more realistic models without being overwhelmed by their complexity. Detail can be added incrementally, in controlled steps using heuristics modelers have been developing. For instance, once a mesoscopic model is in place, modelers can begin to de-black-box systems which were initially black-boxed, so as to produce a model with greater precision or a wider variety of accurate behaviors. A single term operating in the model can be expanded as a sub-network. Importantly, the fact that the more expanded representation must still reproduce the original behavior it produced as a single term is an important constraint that modelers can use to help build this sub-network and pin down parameters without having to reiterate the entire model. Similarly, interactions can be modeled using more complex relations, and so on.

The analogy Voit draws with semantic learning reinforces the essential cognitive function of mesoscopic models we gave above, which is to facilitate a process of cumulative controlled cognitive development in complex contexts. This attempt by scientific practitioners to rationalize their own activities, in effect, shares the main claims of the justification we have provided of the strategy of building mesoscopic models, i.e., containing structure supports more complex model development through building-out and other heuristic strategies. Modelers operate with learning constraints, among others, and their methodological choice behavior is boundedly rational. Although some kinds of purely computational systems might be capable of modeling whole complex systems upfront, distributed human-computer problem-solving systems are not.

Conclusion

In this chapter we have described the model-building processes of system biologists, arguing that these practices should be understood as boundedly rational responses to the complexity of the modeling problems they face. The concept of bounded rationality can thus play a useful role in the field of systems biology, providing cognitive means to justify its present activities. However, as we have seen, unpacking what precisely bounds problem-solving activity and why a set of given responses might be rational in the case of systems biology, or indeed in the case of any computational science, requires addressing the nature of the human-computational system interaction. Briefly, we have tried to argue that distributed cognition and simulative mental modeling can play this role. Indeed, our case above illustrates how Simon's notions of bounded rationality and problem solving as search can be combined with a distributed cognitive framework to help better articulate and study the complex nature of modern computational science.

Note

1 Given that one of the goals of systems biology is to be able manipulate biochemical systems, it thus important that the models they build do not just capture natural equilibrium behavior, but also what will happen in response to intervention on a system.

References

Alač, M., and Hutchins, E. (2004). I see what you are saying: Action as cognition in fMRI brain mapping practice. *Journal of Cognition and Culture*, 4(3), 629–661.

Barsalou, L. W. (1999). Perceptions of perceptual symbols. *Behavioral and Brain Sciences*, 22(4), 637–660.

Becvar, A., Hollan, J., and Hutchins, E. (2008). Representing gestures as cognitive artifacts. In M. S. Ackerman, C. Halverson, T. Erickson, and W. A. Kellog (Eds.), *Resources, co-evolution, and artifacts: Theory in CSCW* (pp. 117–143). New York: Springer.

Brass, M., Bekkering, H., and Prinz, W. (2001). Movement observation affects movement execution in a simple response task. *Acta Psychologica*, 106(1–2), 3–22.

Bryant, D. J., and Tversky, B. (1999). Mental representations of perspective and spatial relations from diagrams and models. *Journal of Experimental Psychology: Learning, Memory, and Cognition*, 25(1), 137.

Chandrasekharan, S., and Nersessian, N. J. (2015). Building cognition: The construction of computational representations for scientific discovery. *Cognitive Science*, 39(8), 1727–1763.

Christensen, B. T., and Schunn, C. D. (2009). The role and impact of mental simulation in design. *Applied Cognitive Psychology*, 23(3), 327–344.

Finke, R. A. (1989). *Principles of mental imagery*. Cambridge, MA: The MIT Press.

Glenberg, A. M. (1997). Mental models, space, and embodied cognition. In T. B. Ward, S. M. Smith, and J. Vaid (Eds.), *Creative thought: An investigation of conceptual structures and processes* (pp. 495–522). Washington, DC: American Psychological Association.

Gorman, M. E. (1997). Mind in the world: Cognition and practice in the invention of the telephone. *Social Studies of Science*, 27(4), 583–624.

Greeno, J. G. (1989). Situations, mental models, and generative knowledge. In D. Klahr and K. Kotovsky (Eds.), *Complex information processing: The impact of Herbert A. Simon* (pp. 285–318). Mahwah, NJ: Lawrence Erlbaum.

Hall, R., Wieckert, K., and Wright. K. (2010). How does cognition get distributed? Case studies of making concepts general in technical and scientific work. In M. Banich and D. Caccamise (Eds.), *Generalization of knowledge: Multidisciplinary perspectives*, New York: Psychology Press.

Hegarty, M. (1992). Mental animation: Inferring motion from static displays of mechanical systems. *Journal of Experimental Psychology: Learning, Memory, and Cognition*, 18(5), 1084.

Hegarty, M. (2004). Mechanical reasoning by mental simulation. *Trends in Cognitive Sciences*, 8(6), 280–285.

Hegarty, M. (2005). Multimedia learning about physical systems. In R. E. Mayer (Ed.), *Cambridge handbook of multimedia learning* (pp. 447–465). New York: Cambridge University Press.

Humphreys, P. (2009). The philosophical novelty of computer simulation methods. *Synthese*, 169, 615–626.

Hutchins, E. (1995a). How a cockpit remembers its speed. *Cognitive Science*, 19, 265–288.

Hutchins, E. (1995b). *Cognition in the wild*. Cambridge, MA: MIT Press.

Johnson-Laird, P. N. (1983). A computational analysis of consciousness. *Cognition & Brain Theory*, 6, 499–508.

Kirsh, D. (1996). Adapting the environment instead of oneself. *Adaptive Behavior*, 4, 415–452

Kosslyn, S. M. (1980). *Image and mind*. Cambridge, MA: Harvard University Press.

MacLeod, M. (2016). Heuristic approaches to models and modeling in systems biology. *Biology & Philosophy*, 31(3), 353–372.

MacLeod, M. (2018). Model-based inferences in modeling of complex systems. *Topoi*. https://doi.org/10.1007/s11245–018–9569-x

MacLeod, M., and Nersessian, N. J. (2015). Modeling systems-level dynamics: understanding without mechanistic explanation in integrative systems biology, *Studies in History and Philosophy of Science Part C – Biological and Biomedical Science*, 49(1), 1–11.

MacLeod. M., and Nersessian, N. J. (2018). Cognitive constraints, complexity and model-building. *History and Philosophy of the Life Sciences*, 40(17).

Nersessian, N. J. (1992). How do scientists think? Capturing the dynamics of conceptual change in science. In R. Giere (Ed.), *Minnesota studies in the philosophy of science* (pp. 3–45). Minneapolis, MN: University of Minnesota Press.

Nersessian, N. J. (2002). The cognitive basis of model-based reasoning in science. In P. Carruthers, S. Stich, and M. Siegal (Eds.), *The cognitive basis of science* (pp. 133–153). Cambridge: Cambridge University Press.

Nersessian, N. J. (2008). *Creating scientific concepts*. Cambridge, MA: MIT Press.

Nersessian, N. J. (2009). How do engineering scientists think? Model-based simulation in biomedical engineering research laboratories. *Topics in Cognitive Science*, 1(4), 730–757.

Nersessian, N. J. (2012). Engineering concepts: The interplay between concept formation and modeling practices in bioengineering sciences. *Mind, Culture, and Activity*, 19(3), 222–239.

Nersessian, N. J., Kurz-Milcke, E., Newstetter, W. C., and Davies, J. (2003). Research laboratories as evolving distributed cognitive systems. In *Proceedings of the Annual Meeting of the Cognitive Science Society*. Mahwah, NJ: Lawrence Erlbaum Associates.

Osbeck, L. M., and Nersessian, N. J. (2006). The distribution of representation. *Journal for the Theory of Social Behaviour*, 36(2), 141–160.

Perrig, W., and Kintsch, W. (1985). Propositional and situational representations of text. *Journal of Memory and Language*, 24, 503–518.

Roschelle, J., and Greeno, J. G. (1987). Mental models in expert physics reasoning (Tech. Report No. GK-12). Berkeley, CA: University of California Press.

Schwartz, D. L. (1995). Reasoning about the referent of a picture versus reasoning about a picture as the referent. *Memory and Cognition*, 23, 709–722.

Schwartz, D. L., and Black, J. B. (1996). Analog imagery in mental model reasoning: Depictive models. *Cognitive Psychology*, 30(2), 154–219.

Shepard, R. N., and Cooper, L. A. (1982). *Mental images and their transformations*. Cambridge, MA: MIT Press.

Simon, H. A. (1976). From substantive to procedural rationality. In S. J. Latsis (Ed.), *Method and appraisal in economics*. Cambridge: Cambridge University Press.

Simon, H. A. (1996). *The sciences of the artificial*. Cambridge, MA; MIT Press.

Trafton, J. G., Trickett, S. B., and Mintz, F. E. (2005). Connecting internal and external representations: Spatial transformations of scientific visualizations. *Foundations of Science*, 10(1), 89–106.

Trickett, S. B., and Trafton, J. G. (2002). The instantiation and use of conceptual simulations in evaluating hypotheses: Movies-in-the-mind in scientific reasoning. In *Proceedings of the Annual Meeting of the Cognitive Science Society* 24(24).

Trickett, S. B., and Trafton, J. G. (2006). Toward a comprehensive model of graph comprehension: Making the case for spatial cognition. In *Proceedings of International Conference on Theory and Application of Diagrams* (pp. 286–300). Heidelberg: Springer.

Trickett, S. B., and Trafton, J. G. (2007). "What if…": The use of conceptual simulations in scientific reasoning. *Cognitive Science*, 31(5), 843–875.

Voit, E. O. (2014). Mesoscopic modeling as a starting point for computational analyses of cystic fibrosis as a systemic disease. *Biochimica et Biophysica Acta (BBA)-Proteins and Proteomics*, 1844(1), 258–270.

Voit, E. O., Newstetter, W. C., and Kemp, M. L. (2012). A feel for systems. *Molecular Systems Biology*, 8(1).

Voit, E. O., Qi, Z., and Kikuchi, S. (2012). Mesoscopic models of neurotransmission as intermediates between disease simulators and tools for discovering design principles. *Pharmacopsychiatry*, 45(1): 22.

Zhang, J., and Norman, D. A. (1994). Representations in distributed cognitive tasks. *Cognitive Science*, 18(1), 87–122.

Zwaan, R. A. (1999). Embodied cognition, perceptual symbols, and situation models. *Discourse Processes*, 28, 81–88.

7

BOUNDED RATIONALITY AND PROBLEM SOLVING

The interpretative function of thought

Laura Macchi and Maria Bagassi

Heuristics and insight problem solving

People whose reasoning is characterized by Wason's confirmation bias and those who use Kahneman and Tversky's heuristics would hardly seem to belong to the same species as the people Duncker and Simon write about, people who challenge with a certain degree of success the limits of their cognitive system. We believe that the diversity of the outcomes of the research on problem solving and reasoning cannot be satisfactorily explained by saying that, on the one hand, human beings are reasonable problem solvers, and, on the other, they are obtuse reasoners, predisposed to fallacies, particularly regarding principles and procedures, on which the psychology of reasoning places particular importance.

We can try to explain this paradoxical enigma of reason. At the beginning of the twentieth century, psychology was differentiating itself from philosophy and carving out a place among the sciences; to this end, to comply with requirements of "scientificity," it integrated the speculative approach adopted by philosophy with the experimental approach, basing this on logic, the discipline which constituted the foundation of the other sciences. However, it is worth noting that when psychology of thought encountered logic in the 1920s, logic was configured as mathematical, formal logic, characterized by a gradual process of "depsychologization" of logical language and of disambiguant simplification compared to natural language, intentionally pursued, and programmatically declared by modern logic. It is paradoxical that the psychology of reasoning should have taken on a depsychologized discipline as a prescriptive and descriptive model of the functioning of thought. As a consequence of logic being the normative schema in research on reasoning, experimental tasks tend to be identified as exercises in logic presented in a popularized version, dressed up as a "'real-life' situation" (Mosconi, 2016, p. 351).

We consider that the legacies of the extrapsychological disciplines, such as logic, the theory of probability, and so on have conditioned the psychology of reasoning and have had a negative impact in terms of originality and adequacy on psychological research. The psychology of reasoning, by adopting an ideological approach, superimposed on the psychological reality, burdened itself with a great limitation: the assumption of a pre-established norm, borrowed from long-standing tradition.

The development of problem solving followed a completely different path, phenomenological in nature, where the research was not affected by these legacies. Problem solving is

DOI: 10.4324/9781315658353-8

an original contribution of psychology; it is a completely new field of research and therefore unpolluted by any backdrop of speculation or theories that can affect other consolidated areas of study. There has not been the temptation, or even the possibility, to appropriate approaches or systems of knowledge created with objectives other than those of psychological research.

The most important contributions to problem solving were those of the Gestaltists in the 1920s and of Herbert Simon et al. 30 years later. Both of these contributions represent a response to the associative and behaviorist approach, recognizing the contribution of the subjective dimension in perceptual organization and, in more general terms, in thought itself.

Demonized as it had been by a materialist approach and eluding all attempts at measurement and quantification, for the Gestaltists, the mind returned, enhanced with all the dignity of an object worthy of scientific study; the essence of the activity of thought did not lie in the mere registration of an aggregate of stimuli, but rather in the ability to understand relations.

In studies on visual perception, which was the Gestaltists' original area of research, visual input was identified on the basis of our knowledge and then enhanced by inferential operations initiated by principles of relevance and coherency, or estimates of probability Cognitive integrations and interpolations are not isolated cases, they are the rule in our daily interaction with the world around us. Processes of amodal completion are those which best allow us to highlight the analogies that exist between seeing and thinking.

Frequently, these are cases of genuine perceptual problem solving in which the available cues are evaluated in the light of knowledge and context. Take, for example, the case when we recognize a person at a considerable distance. Even a scene in which many details are lacking receives a sort of interpretation (Figure 7.1).

At the time of the Gestaltists' studies on visual perception, psychology was dominated by elementaristic conceptions, inherited from philosophical associationism and the relative conviction that the study of the contents of conscience and behavior necessarily implied that they

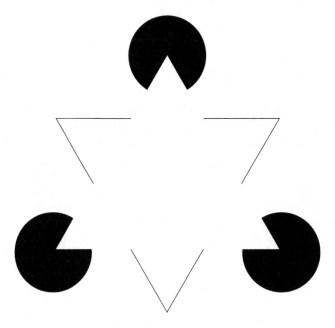

Figure 7.1 The Kanizsa Triangle

be broken down into their ultimate parts, pure sensations, acts of elementary volition, reflexes, and so on.

This approach was, however, comprehensible, as it was natural that the founders of scientific psychology would think that the procedures of the natural sciences would have endowed the investigation of issues regarding the mind with the dignity of science. Unfortunately, the analytic method adopted rendered psychological investigation sterile; it fell victim to a futile hunt for elements that did not permit the reconstruction of the real, living complexity of the psychic functions in seeing, thinking, and problem solving.

Of the critical reactions to this situation, the Gestaltists were particularly outstanding for the vivacity with which they attacked the doctrine of the elements.

For the Gestaltists, in every perception, there is a moment—the elementary and raw sensory data—and, at the same time, another moment, realized by an act of production, with which our conscience builds objects of a higher order, the structures. What determines, for example, a certain melody are the relationships between the sounds. The phenomenal "melody" fact is independent of its phenomenal constituents, sounds.[1]

> The melodic phrase is fundamentally a relational structure: the melody remains a melody even if all its sounds are substituted as long as all the temporal relations and intervals that connect the notes are maintained, from the first note on.
>
> *Kanizsa, 1980, p. 11*

Taking optical illusions as an example, Benussi showed the extent to which the productive act identifies with psychic activity. He showed in fact that it is possible to counteract the illusionary effect by forcedly focusing attention on the individual sensorial elements, thus impeding the natural tendency to organize these elements into a totality (Figure 7.2).

We are particularly aware of this "act of production" when looking at ambiguous sketches such as the candlesticks that can also be seen as two human profiles (Figure 7.3) or the face of an old woman that can also be seen as a young girl (Figure 7.4), to cite two of the best known. When we switch from one structure to the other, we have the perception of the ongoing "act of production".

When the interpretation process establishes new links between the elements in a scene (*restructuring*), or allows the imagination to see the object that is either hidden or covered and only partially visible (without anything truly perceptual being added), this is when the process of integration or mental completion, which generally is part of an interpretative process, takes over.

The Gestaltists considered that the concept of restructuring, to which they attributed a central role in visual perception, was also central in problem solving. They did not use the term

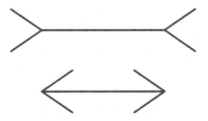

Figure 7.2   The Müller-Lyer illusion

Figure 7.3 The figure-ground organization

Figure 7.4 The young girl–old woman illusion

"problem solving," however, preferring "productive thinking," as they were convinced that thinking is not merely a *re*production of the past, a *re*emergence of ideas, images, behaviors that already existed; in addition to the *re*productive activities of thought, there are processes that create and produce that which does not yet exist.

The Gestalt psychologists focused their research on establishing the phenomenology of these productive processes and the characteristics that distinguish them from the reproductive processes; they studied the conditions that give rise to these processes or allow them to arise, and those which, on the contrary, impede them, and the decisive moments in the process when light dawns and understanding is reached. The famous "Aha!" experience of genuine insight accompanies this change in representation, the *restructuring*. This is characterized by a switch in direction that occurs together with the transformation of the problem or a change in our understanding of an essential relationship. The decisive points in thought processes, the moments of sudden comprehension, of the "Aha!," of the new, are always at the same time moments in which such a sudden restructuring of the thought-material takes place, in which something "tips over" (Duncker, 1945, pp. 29–30).

Thirty years later, the reaction of cognitivism to behaviorism had many analogies with the Gestaltists' reaction to associationism, to the point where Herbert Simon could, in a certain sense, be considered the heir of the second generation of the Gestalt theory, of which Karl Duncker was the most eminent scholar. Simon himself admitted this, sharing the key concepts of Duncker and Selz's theory, and expressing them by a Human Information Processing approach (HIP), which is characterized by the observability principle of the cognitive process. "we can see a number of quite specific connections between the formulations of Duncker and Selz, on the one hand, and our own, on the other …" (Simon 1984, p. 149).

Prior to the rise of information-processing theories, perhaps only Duncker fully shared with Selz this notion of the proper goal for problem-solving research, although some of the same flavor comes through in the writings of Koehler and the other Gestaltists. Certainly, in these two writers, the orientation to process comes through far more clearly than in other writings on this topic prior to World War II (Simon, 1984, p. 153).

> The simulation models of the 1950s were offspring of the marriage between that had emerged from symbolic logic and cybernetics, on the one side, and Würzburg and Gestalt psychology, on the other … From Würzburg and Gestalt psychology were inherited the ideas that long-term memory is an organization of directed associations, and that problem solving is a process of selective goal-oriented search.
>
> *Simon, 1979, pp. 364–365*

The legacy of Gestaltism can be considered a fruitful vantage point from which to view current research in the field of problem solving. This entails acknowledging the affinities, and, to a certain extent, the continuity between the approaches of Duncker and HIP theory, and the connections between the formulations of Duncker and Simon and colleagues, as they have exerted a decisive influence on the field of problem solving for more than half a century. Let us now consider crucial concepts of the two theories, underlining both similarities and differences.

Duncker was not only interested in the moment when the solution was found, but also in the thought process, the phases by which the restructuring is reached:

> But while, with undoubted justification, great stress was laid on the significance of restructuration or reorganization in thinking, another side of the problem was almost completely lost from view. In what way do these restructurations, and with them the solution, arise?
>
> *Duncker, 1945, pp. 29–30*

The final form of a solution is typically attained by way of mediating phases of the process, of which each one, in retrospect, possesses the character of a solution, and, in prospect, that of a problem; on the contrary, the principle, the functional value of the solution, typically arises first, and the final form of the solution in question develops only as this principle becomes successively more and more concrete. In other words, the general or "essential" properties of a solution genetically precede the specific properties (Duncker, 1945, pp. 7–8).

The solution process involves a *selective research in phases*, over a *delimited area*; previously explored paths that turned out to be dead ends must be discarded and new paths adopted. The new path can even have been evaluated in a previous phase. In fact, as Duncker stressed from the beginning of his work:

> In short, from the very first, the *deliberating* and *searching* [are] always confined to a province, which is relatively narrow as to *space* and content. Thus preparation is made for the more discrete phases of a solution by certain approximate regional demarcations, i.e., by *phases* in which necessary but not yet sufficient properties of the solution are demanded.
>
> *Duncker, 1945, p. 10*

Duncker's *genealogical tree* of the solution is made up of the aggregate of ways in which the solution can be reached, starting from the problem situation. It represents an ideal solution process similar to the HIP *typical protocol*, and, in a certain sense, anticipates the concept of "program."

> As yet we have dealt only with the progress from the superordinate to the subordinate phases (or vice versa), in other words, with progress along a given *genealogical line* ... Here the line itself is continually changed, and one way of approach gives way to another. Such a transition to phases in another line takes place typically when some tentative solution does not satisfy, or when one makes no further progress in a given direction. Another solution, more or less clearly defined, is then looked for/
>
> *Duncker, 1945, p. 12*

Duncker's description of how a problem solver deals with the search for the solution to a problem prefigures the labyrinth model of *information processing*:

> The problem solver's search for the solution, is an "odyssey" through problem space from one state of knowledge to another, until his/her knowledge state includes the solution. A person faced with a problem moves within the *problem space* just as in a labyrinth; he searches for the right path, retraces his steps when he comes up against a dead end, and sometimes even returns to the starting point; he will form and apply a strategy of sorts, making a selective search in the problem space.
>
> *Simon, Newell, & Shaw, 1979, p. 148*

Duncker and Simon used real protocols, registering attempts to solve the problem, to rebuild what is assumed to be a solution process but which will only correspond fortuitously to the succession of actual attempts made to solve the problem.

The technique used here is *thinking aloud*, which is completely different, for example, from Wundt's introspection:

> The subjects (Ss), who were mostly students of universities or of colleges, were given various thinking problems, with the request that they think aloud ... This instruction, "Think aloud", is not identical with the instruction to introspect which has been common in experiments on thought-processes. While the introspecter makes himself as thinking the object of his attention [and so differentiates himself intentionally from himself as a thinking subject],[2] the subject who is thinking aloud remains immediately directed to the problem, so to speak allowing his activity to become verbal.
>
> *Duncker, 1945, p. 2*

They both adopted a descriptive-phenomenological approach to problem solving. Just as the Gestaltists studied the principles of organization of reality in perception, which sometimes are present when a problem comes into being, so, in Simon's theory, the basic characteristics of the human cognitive system are those which generally lead to the solution of a problem. The *boundaries* are indeed characteristics, but characteristics without negative connotations. This phenomenological approach, which is in no way conditioned by an ideal functioning model borrowed from extra-psychological normative theories, allows us to think of heuristics as expressions of our intelligence.

According to Duncker, the problem solver never blunders along blindly, seeking the solution by trial and error; he proceeds by applying *heuristic strategies* and *methods*:

> the whole process, from the original setting of the problem to the final solution, appears as a series of more or less concrete proposals ... But however primitive they may be, this one thing is certain, that they cannot be discussed in terms of *meaningless, blind, trial-and-error reactions.*
>
> *Duncker, 1945, p. 3*

What is even more relevant in Duncker's concept is that the heuristic captures the intrinsic necessity of the solution itself, guiding the problem solver to incessantly analyze the conflict and to eliminate his fixation. In this sense, it constitutes the main, if not the only[3] method of thought in problem solving:

> We can therefore say that *"insistent" analyses of the situation, especially the endeavor to vary appropriate elements meaningfully sub specie of the goal, must belong to the essential nature of a solution through thinking.* We may call such relatively general procedures, *"heuristic methods of thinking."*
>
> *Duncker, 1945, pp. 20–21*

According to Simon, on the other hand, the term "heuristics" indicates any principle and expedient that contributes to reducing the time that would normally be necessary to reach a solution. Given that often an exhaustive search of all the possible ways to solve a problem is just not viable for a human being, the use of heuristics reduces the problem-solving process to manageable proportions.

But the economy of heuristics is not only an advantage, it is also an essential condition for the possibility of dealing with and solving problems, albeit at a price—the uncertainty of the outcome. Efficacious thought is only possible through the heuristic reduction of the search.

> Heuristic methods [allow us] to carry out highly selective searches, hence to cut down enormous problem spaces to sizes that a slow, serial processor could handle. *Selectivity of search*, not speed, was taken as the key organizing principle ... Heuristic methods that make this selectivity possible have turned out to be the central magic in all human problem solving that has been studied to date.
>
> *Simon & Newell, 1971, p. 147*

Simon and Newell add:

> The power of heuristics resides in their capability for examining small, promising regions of the entire space and simply ignoring the rest. We need not be concerned

with how large the haystack is, if we can identify a small part of it in which we are quite sure to find a needle.

1971, p. 151

This changes radically when considering the *psychology of reasoning*, and in particular Kahneman and Tversky's research program "Heuristics and Biases" on probability judgment. In their work, they attribute a quite different definition to heuristics, in spite of the fact that the authors explicitly state that they have taken the concept from Simon. Not only are their heuristics simplified or abbreviated procedures, but they are subject to their own criteria and mechanisms, completely foreign to the logic of the problem being dealt with and the decision to be taken. It is no longer a case of procedures that "do not guarantee finding the solution" depending on their economy, but of procedures that will lead to the correct solution of the problem purely by chance.

The uncertainty of the outcome that derives from the adoption of heuristic methods has been radicalized by the acceptance of heuristics by Kahneman and Tversky, which leads to an irrational deviation, which had nothing to do with Simon's view. According to Simon, simplification is the identification of what is salient and crucial, while Kahneman and Tversky consider it to be "neglect" of crucial information for probability judgment.

A direct consequence of this theoretical framework of the psychology of reasoning is the introduction of the theoretical construct of the *bias*, i.e., an intrinsic tendency to error of the human cognitive system. According to Kahneman and Tversky, it is the use of heuristics that produces biases.

> There are situations in which people assess the frequency of a class or the probability of an event by the ease with which instances or occurrences can be brought to mind … However, availability is affected by factors other than frequency and probability. Consequently, the reliance on availability leads to predictable biases …
>
> *Kahneman, Slovic, & Tversky, 1982, p. 11*

The challenging issue of insight problem solving

The affinities and a certain continuity between Duncker's formulation and that of the Human Information Processing Theory are quite surprising, to the extent that it is possible to consider Simon, with all due distinctions, as the heir of the Gestalt psychology. That said, the differences are crucial and given the antithetical theoretical framework of the two authors, it would not be reasonable to expect anything different. For Duncker, the theoretical framework remains that of the early Gestaltists and therefore is restructuralist. The study of the process of thought provides the means of studying "how *restructuring* comes about."

According to Duncker: "The finding of a functional value of a solution means each time a reformulation of the original problem" (1945, p. 8):

> Every solution consists in some alteration of the given situation. But not only this or that in the situation is changed …; over and beyond this the *psychological structure* of the situation as a *whole* or of certain significant parts is changed. Such alterations are called *restructurations*.
>
> *Duncker, 1945, p. 29*

This discontinuity, this alteration is not present in problem-solving process as studied by Simon (take the Crypto-arithmetic task, for example, or the Cannibals and Missionaries problem). The problem solver may make mistakes (illegal moves), following paths that turn out to be dead ends and so has to retrace his steps, and slowly but surely (step-by-step) makes his way to the solution: it is only a question of time. The difficulty lies in the calculation, the number of operations to be performed, and the quantity of data to be processed and remembered.

When the *Weltanschauung* of cognitivism informed psychology, and confidence in the possibility of making testable models for the functioning of the mind was at its highest, Simon wrote:

> The only solution to this problem is the hard solution. Psychology is now taking the road taken earlier by other sciences: it is introducing essential formalisms to describe and explain its phenomena. Natural language formulations of the phenomena of human thinking did not yield explanations of what was going on; formulations in information-processing languages appear to be yielding such explanations.
>
> *Simon & Newell, 1971, p. 148*

In that particular historical phase, to keep faith with this "hard" methodology, the aim of which is to measure—observe—every step of the problem-solving process, Simon inevitably had to exclude insight problems from his Human Information Processing research as he considered them 'ill defined' for the task environment (Hayes & Simon, 1974; Newell & Simon, 1972; Simon & Hayes, 1976). He continued to hold that "the *programmability* of the theories is the guarantor of their operationality, an *iron-clad insurance* against admitting *magical entities* into the head" (Simon, 1979).

Some years later, in response to an article Michael Wertheimer wrote in 1985, Simon expressed the same absolute faith in the possibility of translating the problem solving process for insight problems into computer programming:

> One serious difficulty in testing Gestalt theories is that the concepts that play central roles in these theories are not often defined in terms of operations or measurements, but are usually assumed to be directly understood and observable ... If we put aside our nostalgia for a rich, but largely non-operational, vocabulary, and when we focus instead on the observable processes of thought, we see that we are much further advanced in understanding these processes ... the phenomena of insight are fully visible in the behavior of today's computers when they are programmed appropriately to simulate human thinking.
>
> *Simon, 1986, pp. 242, 254*

The explanation for these very fundamental differences in the two approaches lies in the diversity of the problems they were studying. The focus on the restructuration privileged insight problems as an object of study, while interest for observability privileged the procedural, non-insight problems. The choice of the object of study was not accidental, but congenial to the different intent pursued. Futile taxonomies apart, the only distinction worthy of note is that proposed by Mosconi (2016), focusing squarely on the different kind of difficulty, i.e., between *tasks* and *problems*.

In the problems studied by Simon (the *tasks*) the difficulty lies in their *intractability*, given the basic characteristics of the *human information-processing system* (alias, the human problem solver): "serial processing, small short-term memory, infinite long-term memory with fast retrieval but slow storage – [which] impose strong constraints on the ways in which the system can seek solutions to problems in larger problem spaces" (Simon & Newell, 1971, p. 149).

In the problems studied by the Gestaltists (the *problems*), on the other hand, the difficulty does not lie in the complexity of the calculations and the burdensome process necessary to reach the solution, but in one or more critical points, that create a situation of conflict and, as a consequence, an unsurmountable impasse. None of this happens in Simon's research on problem solving.

In fact,

> If a situation is introduced in a certain perceptual structuration, and if this structure is still "real" or "alive", thinking achieves a contrary structuration only against the resistance of the former structure. The degree of this difficulty varies among individuals.
>
> *Duncker 1945, p. 108*

This, then, is the question at hand. When, in 1990, Simon, in collaboration with Kaplan, explored in depth the peculiarities of the search and the steps of the solution process for insight problems, they dealt with the issue of a *change in representation*, alias *restructuration*, in their seminal article "In search of insight." They provided

> a major extension of the standard information processing theory of problem solving to handle insight problems … the same processes that are ordinarily used to search *within* problem space can be used to search *for* a problem space (problem representation).
>
> *Kaplan & Simon, 1990, p. 376*

According to the authors, the problem solver who finds himself at an impasse must first of all make a conscious decision to change his way of looking at the problem by adopting the "Try a Switch" meta-heuristic, given that the initial representation of the problem did not provide him with the means of reaching the solution, "but the space of possible problem spaces is exceedingly *ill-defined*, in fact, *infinite*." Once this conscious decision has been made, "the subject has to have or obtain strong constraints that guide [the] search and make it highly selective," i.e., he must be on the lookout for the important cues that will help him select the representation that will lead to the solution, from the infinite number available. In his search for these decisive cues to switch the representation in the representation metaspace, he is assisted by adopting a heuristic initiated by boundaries of salience,[4] that fits the problem.

> The simulation demonstrates that once the *decision has been reached to search for a new representation*, [in the Mutilated Checkerboard insight problem] *attention to the parity cue* is sufficient to construct the new representation by modifying the initial one and to find the solution by means of a reasoning process. What leads subjects to consider the critical cues that are prerequisite to such a switch?
>
> The Notice Invariants heuristic is of great importance in permitting subjects, particularly those not given strong perceptual or verbal hints, to narrow their search for new representations.
>
> *Kaplan & Simon, 1990, p. 403*

Yet again, it is worth noticing the connection between Simon and Duncker, who defines *invariants* as the functional principles of a solution:

> To the same degree to which a solution is understood, it can be transposed, which means that under altered conditions it may be changed correspondingly in such a way as to preserve its functional value. For, one can transpose a solution only when one has grasped its functional value, its general principle, i.e., the *invariants* from which, by introduction of changed conditions, the corresponding variations of the solution follow each time.
>
> *Duncker, 1945, p. 5*

With insight problems too, the way Simon explains the difficulty revolves around a sort of "quantitative unmanageability," in this case constituted by the excessive, "infinite" number of possible representations of the problem.

This way of dealing with the switch of problem space—the change in representation—describes what happens when the person solves an insight problem, rather than actually explaining the solution process. However, what makes the problem solver focus on certain cues, rather than others, which are identified as crucial for a switch that will lead him out of the impasse, remains obscure.

Keeping the search on a level of consciousness in order to simulate the solution process, Simon conserves the key theoretical constructs of his theory such as the concepts of search and process in which the steps can always be reconstructed, and in which self-conscious and deliberative connotation is the heart.

Although he did pose the question as to what determines the switch, Simon was not able to find answers to the crucial interrogatives and so ended up with a sort of explanatory circularity. In point of fact, deciding to change the representation alone is not sufficient to solve the problem, if we do not change our understanding of an essential, new relationship.[5]

The emphasis on the observability and registrability of each step in the solution process, generating a typical protocol that can be simulated in a calculator, translates into a sort of bias, when he assumes insight problems as the object of his research, as the solution to these problems is characterized by discontinuity and the transition from the impasse to the solution remains a mystery to the problem solver himself.

Moreover, the solution can appear after a period of incubation that may vary in time, during which the problem solver withdraws into himself.[6]

The difficulty continues to be quantitative even with insight problems such as the Mutilated Checkerboard (MC) problem (see Appendix A), to the point at which, "the task would be hopeless without some source of search constraint." In the domain of the MC problem, the authors identified four potential sources of constraint: "perceptual cues in the problem, hints provided by the experimenter, prior knowledge that the subject might bring to the problem, and heuristics – in particular the Notice Invariants heuristic" (Kaplan & Simon 1990, p. 413).

There is still something magical in how problem solvers adopt the heuristic that is applicable to the solution and which is on the same level as the other constraints, only, in the light of the results, considered to be more efficient in identifying the representation or problem space that is most suited to the problem, as "focusing attention on invariant features of the problem situation allows subjects to convert a search in an enormous and unmanageable space (in which they have no relevant generators) to a search in a smaller space (with generators available)" (Kaplan & Simon 1990).

The Gestaltists would have said that the problem solvers *discover* the solution, when they "see" that in the Mutilated Checkerboard problem there is no longer reciprocal parity between the black and the white squares and so they *restructure*.

Simon himself was fully aware that the difficulty lies in the fact that "you do not know beforehand where the solution may lie" and the representation switch has still to take place.

His question: "But how is this change of representation brought about?" remains without an answer; it continues to be a mysterious event, if we do not venture beyond the conscious layer of solution processing.

The role of unconscious analytic thought in insight problem solving: the emergence of the shadow area

The difficulty in changing the representation does not appear to involve the working memory capacity, nor the conscious retrieval from memory of solutions or crucial parts of solutions to reproduce. It requires of necessity not conscious, implicit processing—incubation—and for this reason it is a challenge to the current theories of thought, regarding the central role of consciousness, given that, in these cases, restructuring (or change in representation) is not performed consciously.

Incubation, which remains the core issue in the renewed interest in insight problems is still a crucial question to be solved (Bagassi & Macchi 2016; Ball, Marsh, Litchfield, Cook, & Booth, 2015; Fleck & Weisberg, 2013; Gilhooly, Ball, & Macchi, 2018; Gilhooly, Georgiou, & Devery, 2013; Gilhooly, Georgiou, Sirota, & Paphiti-Galeano, 2015; Macchi & Bagassi, 2012, 2015; Sio & Ormerod, 2009; Threadgold, Marsh, & Ball, 2018).

A heterogeneous complex of unresolved critical issues underlies the research on this subject and still revolves around the controversy of the relationship between the conscious and unconscious layers of thought in the solution of insight problems.

However, the various mechanisms that have been proposed only describe the characteristics of the solution but do not explain the processes of reasoning that have made the solution possible (these include, for example, eliciting new information, selective forgetting, strategy switching, and relaxing self-imposed inappropriate constraints).

Moreover, a general characteristic that is common to the literature on insight problems in general, and in particular on the incubation-solution relationship, is the total absence of an analysis of the types of difficulty found in individual insight problems. In other words, what makes a difficult insight problem difficult? What kinds of difficulty are we facing? If it were possible to lay them out as a continuum in an ascending order of difficulty, we would see that, in fact, the difficulty correlates with the incubation, and this, in turn, with the possible discovery of the solution, thus allowing the restructuring process to occur. Therefore, incubation may offer a measure of the degree and type of difficulty of the problem, as it may vary in length, depending on the degree of gravity of the state of impasse (Macchi & Bagassi, 2012, 2015; Segal, 2004). We obtained experimental evidence in support of our hypothesis, using the horse-trading problem, whose answer is given here.

The horse-trading problem

A man bought a horse for £70 and sold it for £80, then he bought it back for £90, and sold it for £100. How much did he make?

In this problem the correct response (£20) is found by approximately half of those who attempt to solve it, by restructuring in two separate financial transactions[7] (see Appendix B).

We have also examined a problem that is one of the most intriguing insight problems, a genuine challenge, the study window problem, which at first sight appears impossible to solve (Macchi & Bagassi, 2014, 2015; Mosconi & D'Urso, 1974). This is an example of a problem which cannot be solved analytically, in which the impasse seems to be unsurmountable, an incubation period is necessary and the solution is the outcome of a deep restructuring (see Appendix C).

The study window problem

The study window measures 1 meter in height and 1 meter wide (Figure 7.5). The owner decides to enlarge it and calls in a workman. He instructs the man to double the area of the window without changing its shape and so that it still measures 1 meter by 1 meter. The workman carried out the commission. How did he do it?

At this point, the question is, what kind of unconscious intelligent thought operates during the incubation to solve these special problems? Through experiments in brain imaging, it is now possible to identify certain regions of the brain that contribute both to unconscious intuition and to the processing that follows. Jung-Beeman, Bowden, Haberman, Frymiare, Arambel-Liu, Greenblatt, et al. (2004) found that creative intuition is the culmination of a series of transitional cerebral states that operate in different sites and for different lengths of time. According to these authors, creative intuition is a delicate mental balancing act that requires periods of concentration from the brain but also moments in which the mind wanders and retraces its steps, in particular during the incubation period or when it comes up against a dead end.

> Incubation is actually the necessary but not sufficient condition to reach the solution. It allows the process but does not guarantee success; however, if it is inhibited, for example, by compelling participants to verbalize, the solution process will be impeded.

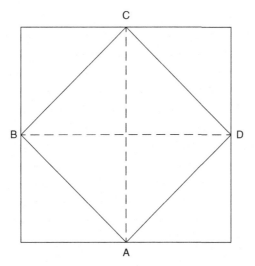

Figure 7.5 The study window problem solution

It has been observed that under these circumstances, subjects giving thinking aloud protocols often fall silent. When asked what they are thinking about, they may say "I'm not thinking about anything," an indication that they have no available strategy for the meta-level search for the new representation.

Kaplan & Simon, 1990

When the participants in these studies (Macchi & Bagassi, 2012; Schooler et al., 1993) were still exploring ways of discovering a new problem representation, they were not able to express consciously and therefore to verbalize their attempts to find the solution. Indeed, our data showed that serial "on-line" verbalization, compelling participants to "restless" verbalization, impairs reasoning in insight problem solving; this provides support for the hypothesis of the necessity of an incubation period during which the thinking processes involved are mainly unconscious. During this stage of wide-range searching, the solution still has to be found, and verbalization acts as a constraint, continuously forcing thought back to a conscious, explicit level and maintaining it in the impasse of the default representation. Conscious explicit reasoning elicited by verbalization clings to the default interpretation, thus impeding the search process, which is mainly unconscious and unreportable.

Hence, we speculate that the creative act of restructuring implies a high-level implicit thought, a sort of unconscious analytic thought; where, however, analytic thought is not to be understood in the sense of a gradual, step-by-step simplification of the difficulties in the given problem. It would rather be a gentle, unconscious analysis of the conflict between the initial problematic representation and the goal of the problem, until the same data are seen in a different light and new relations are found by exploring different interpretations, neither by exhaustive searches nor by abstractions but by involving a relationship between the data that is most pertinent to the solution of the problem. In this way, each individual stimulus takes on a different meaning with respect to the other elements and to the whole, contributing to a new representation of the problem, to the understanding of which it holistically concurs. Indeed, the original representation of the data changes when a new relation is discovered, giving rise to a gestalt, a different vision of the whole, which has a new meaning.

In other words, solving an insight problem—restructuring—means discovering a new perspective, a different sense to the existing relations. The interrelations between the elements of the default, usual interpretation have to be loosened in order to perceive new possibilities, to grasp from among many salient cues what is the most pertinent with the aim of the task, or in other words, to reach understanding. This type of process cuts across both conscious and unconscious thought.

The default representation (a preferred organization of stimulus and a generalized interpretation of the text of the problem) does not allow participants to pursue the solution.

Consider, for instance, the above-mentioned study window problem. This problem was investigated in a previous study (Macchi & Bagassi, 2014). For all the participants the problem appeared impossible to solve, and nobody actually solved it. In our view, the solution is blocked by the problem solver's mental representation of the window described in the statement, which she/he will "visualise" in the usual, orthogonal orientation (with the sides parallel to the vertical-horizontal coordinates). The information provided regarding the dimensions brings a square form to mind. The problem solver interprets the window to be a square 1 meter high by 1 meter wide, resting on one side. Furthermore, the problem states "without changing its shape," intending *geometric* shape of the two windows (square, independently of the orientation of the window), while the problem solver interprets this as meaning the *phenomenic* shape of the two windows (two squares with the same orthogonal orientation). And this is where the difficulty of the problem lies, in the mental representation of the window and the concurrent interpretation of the text of the problem (see Appendix C). Actually, spatial orientation is a decisive factor in the perception of forms (Mach, 1914). Two identical shapes seen from different orientations take on a different phenomenic identity.

The "inverted" version of the problem gave less trouble:

> The owner decides to <u>make it smaller</u> and calls in a workman. He instructs the man <u>to halve the area</u> of the window ...

With this version, 30 percent of the participants solved the problem. They started from the representation of the orthogonal square (ABCD) (see Figure 7.5) and looked for the solution within the square, trying to respect the required height and width of the window, and inevitably changing the orientation of the internal square. This time the height and width are the diagonals, rather than the side (base and height) of the square.

In another version (the "orientation" version) (Figure 7.6), it was explicit that orientation was not a mandatory attribute of the shape, and this time 66 percent of the participants found the solution immediately (see Appendix C). This confirms the hypothesis that an inappropriate representation of the relation between the orthogonal orientation of the square and its geometric shape is the origin of the *misunderstanding*.

In our view, overcoming a fixation requires elaboration and comprehension of the context that is more relevant to the aim. The interrelations between the parts of the default interpretation have to be loosened in order to perceive the new, in other words, to restructure. The impasse, the difficulty of reaching a solution, should activate an increasingly focussed and relevant search and a reconsideration of the available data in the light of the goal. It is analytical research "that recognizes the primacy of the whole, and its dynamic nature, and its decisive role in articulating its parts" (Wertheimer 1985, pp. 24, 25).

The relevance of text and the reinterpretation of perceptual stimuli, goal-oriented to the task, were worked out in unison in an interrelated interpretative "game." Over and above the macro-distinction between insight and non-insight problems, the crucial characteristic of insight problems which distinguishes them from non-insight problems is that they originate

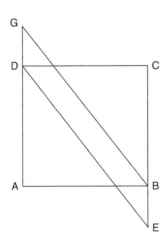

Figure 7.6 The Wertheimer's Parallelogram-Square problem

from a misunderstanding, of varying complexity and difficulty, but which always requires a restructuring process to overcome.

The Gestalt vision has been invoked, with different inflections, by the *special process* views of insight problem solving, investigating the qualitatively diverse processes that elude the control of consciousness through spreading activation of unconscious knowledge (Ohlsson, 2012; Ollinger, Jones, & Knoblich, 2008; Schooler, Ohlsson, & Brooks, 1993). This search goes beyond the boundaries of the working memory. The process that leads to the discovery of the solution through restructuring is mainly unconscious, characterized by a period of incubation, and can only be described *a posteriori* (Gilhooly, Fioratou, & Henretty, 2010). The characteristic unconsciousness with which these processes are performed has led to them being defined as automatic, spontaneous associations (Ash & Wiley, 2006; Fleck, 2008; Fleck & Weisberg, 2013; Schooler et al., 1993).

On the other hand, the cognitivist approach, known as *business as usual*, requires a greater working memory capacity for explaining insight problems: intelligence fades without the "light" of consciousness and therefore identifies with conscious reflective thought.

Both these approaches have critical aspects that reveal the complexity of the issue to hand: the former grasps the specificity of the phenomenon of discovery, which characterizes insight problems and creative thought, but is not in a position to identify the explicative processes because it does not attribute a selective quality to unconscious processes, as they continue to be merely associative, automatic, and capable of producing associations that will contribute to finding the solution almost by chance. The limit of the *business as usual* approach, on the other hand, is that it levels off the specificity of genuine insight problems, lumping them together with problems that can be solved with explicit analytic thought processes.

Recently, Weisberg (2015) has proposed an integrated theory of insight in problem solving. According to Weisberg, analytic thinking, given its dynamic nature, can produce a novel outcome; in problem solving in particular, it can generate a complex interaction between the possible solutions and the situation, such that new information constantly emerges, resulting in novelty. When we change strategy, we select a better route; this change is known as restructuration without insight and remains on the conscious, explicit plane.

Weisberg rather optimistically claims that when the restructuring does not occur and the subject is at an impasse, which

> may result in coming to mind of a new representation of the problem … That new representation may bring to mind at the very least a new way of approaching the problem and, if the problem is relatively simple, may bring with it a quick and smooth solution.
>
> *Weisberg 2015, p. 34*

However, this concept of intelligence does not explain how we suddenly see the solution to a problem after a period of fumbling in the dark (the impasse), during which our conscious analytical thought has stalled and does not extract any useful information from the failure. Thought is incapable of throwing light on the situation, and if the solution is hit upon, it has the characteristics of a "mysterious event."

Finally, also Weisberg's approach makes little progress in explaining the so-called "mysterious event" in the solution of insight problems, relegating them to situations of normal administration that can be dealt with by conscious analytical thought. However, when the solution is mainly the result of a covert and unconscious mind-wandering process, it cannot be attributed, even exclusively, to reflective, conscious thinking (Baird, Smallwood, Mrazek, Kam, Franklin, et al., 2012; Macchi & Bagassi, 2012; Smallwood & Schooler, 2006).

These problems may seem bizarre or constructed to provide an intellectual divertissement, but they are a paradigmatic case of human creativity in which intelligence is at its acme. Their study provides a privileged route to understanding the processes underlying creative thought, scientific discovery, and innovation, and all situations in which the mind has to face something in a new way.

Restructuring as reinterpreting: the interpretative heuristic

The search for meaning, in view of an objective, characterizes every activity of the human cognitive system at all levels, from perception to language and reasoning. For instance, syntax in itself does not give direct access to meaning, only on the basis of the rules that discipline it. Similarly, perceiving external reality is not just a question of registering stimuli; sensorial data have to be interpreted and organized, and relations created.

When analyzing sensory experience, it is important to realize that our conscious sensations differ *qualitatively* from the physical properties of stimuli because, as Kant and the idealists predicted, the nervous system extracts only certain pieces of information from each stimulus while ignoring others. It then *interprets* this information within the constraints of the brain's intrinsic structure and previous experience. Thus sounds, words, music, color, tones are mental creations constructed by the brain out of sensory experience. They do not exist as such outside the brain (Gardner & Johnson, 2013, p. 455).

Our view, therefore, is that this *interpretative function* is a characteristic inherent to all reasoning processes and is an adaptive characteristic of the human cognitive system in general. Rather than abstracting from contextual elements, this function exploits their potential informativeness (Levinson, 1995, 2013; Mercier & Sperber, 2011; Sperber & Wilson, 1986; Tomasello, 2009). It guarantees cognitive economy when meanings and relations are familiar, permitting recognition in a "blink of an eye."

This same process becomes much more arduous when meanings and relations are unfamiliar, obliging us to face the novel. When this happens, we have to come to terms with the fact that the usual, default interpretation will not work, and this is a necessary condition for exploring other ways of interpreting the situation. A restless, conscious, and unconscious search for other possible relations between the parts and the whole ensues until everything falls into place and nothing is left unexplained, with an interpretative heuristic-type process.

This ability always implies an analytic, multilayered reasoning, which works on a conscious and unconscious layer by processing explicit and implicit contents, presuppositions, and beliefs, but is always informed by relevance.[8]

Sometimes, however, our initial interpretation does not support understanding, and misunderstanding is inevitable; as a result, sooner or later we come up against an impasse. We are able to get out of this impasse by neglecting the default interpretation and looking for another one that is more pertinent to the situation and which helps us grasp the meaning that matches both the context and the speaker's intention; this requires continuous adjustments until all makes sense.

For instance, grasping a witty comment and understanding rhetorical figures of speech such as irony and metaphor are the result of an interpretative process adhering to or detracting from the explicit meaning as the case requires.

This analysis allows us to consider insight problems as paradigmatic examples of *misunderstanding*, in that they arise from a *quid pro quo*, a glitch in communications. When insight problems are used in research, it could be said that the researcher sets a trap, more or less intentionally, inducing an interpretation that appears to be pertinent to the data and to the text; this interpretation is adopted more or less automatically because it has been validated by use. But in point of fact, the solution presupposes a different, unusual interpretation that is only theoretically possible, just as when someone makes a witty comment, playing on an unusual interpretation of a sentence.

Indeed, the solution—*restructuring*—is a *re*-interpretation of the relationship between the data and the aim of the task, a search for the appropriate meaning carried out at a deeper level, not by automaticity. If this is true, then a disambiguant reformulation of the problem that eliminates the trap into which the subject has fallen, should produce restructuring and the way to the solution.

Our view, therefore, is that the interpretative heuristic is a characteristic inherent to all insight problem-solving processes. This in itself is not mysterious or inexplicable, it is the result of an incessant search for possible relations between the parts and the whole until everything falls into place and nothing is left unexplained, but makes sense using an interpretative heuristic-type process.

The original representation of the data changes when a new relation is discovered, giving rise to a gestalt, a different vision of the whole, something which has a new sense. The same data, seen in a different light, provide a view that is different to the default, the original starting point. As we have seen, new relations are found by exploring different interpretations, and not by exhaustive searches or abstractions.

Gestalt and Human Information Processing have really grasped the core of human thinking, describing its functioning and identifying the beauty as well as the simplicity of human intelligence, which is able to deal with both areas of tasks that are too large, reducing them to a manageable representation, but also capable of changing representation, discovering misunderstandings, restructuring. In both cases, thought always proceeds by adopting a heuristic interpretative approach, essentially aimed at identifying relationships. We think, we perceive in a context.

In the case of the insight problems, the solution requires a selective processing of the context at a deeper level than that of the default, by re-examining the relations between the data, adopting an *interpretative heuristic-type* process. In this case, our mind fluctuates between conscious and unconscious levels in a wide-ranging analytical search.

This perspective allows us to reconsider the question of *bounded rationality*. The study of how we reason highlights the principles that describe the functioning of the human thought; these are not limits, biases, which in themselves lead to error—cognitive illusions—but characteristics by which we perceive, think, and communicate. Take optical illusions, for instance. It is the same perceptive mechanism of distortion that creates three-dimensionality from the two-dimensional painting Images of art, as well as all images, do not represent reality but rather perceptions, imagination, and expectations of the viewer, and his knowledge of other images recalled from memory. Art is, in part, a creation of the mind; the sensory information, organized in accordance with Gestaltist principles, allows reality to be created by the mind.

Our claim is that the cognitive illusions as well as the perceptual illusions, are the side effect, the epiphenomenon of the functioning of the cognitive system, which is realized in the absence of context, with the occurrence of a *misunderstanding*. In the optical illusion of Mueller-Lyer, for example, the experimenter measures the objective two-dimensional length

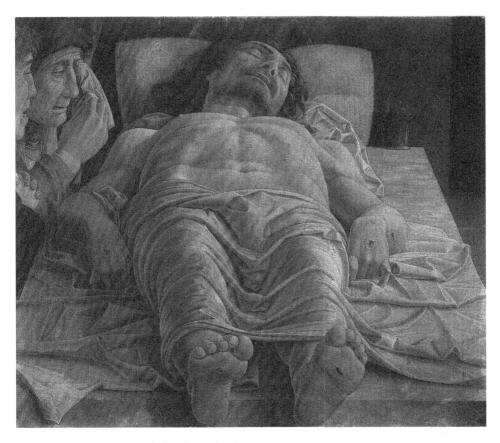

Figure 7.7   The Lamentation of Christ by Andrea Mantegna

of the two segments, neglecting the three-dimensional effects produced by extensions to the apexes (see Figure 7.2). Art, instead, *cooperatively* exploits the three-dimensional interpretation of two-dimensional data.

By dizzyingly foreshortening the perspective, Andrea Mantegna inserted the body of his dead Christ into a dilated space that has the depth of a room, in a painting of only 68 cm. by 81 cm (Figure 7.7). If the viewer moves, he preserves the perspective as in reality. In this case, the tacit cooperation between viewer and artist, on which the fruition of the artwork is based, gives life to a powerful representation of reality.

Appendix A

The classic mutilated checkerboard (MC) problem

Cover the 62 remaining squares in Figure A7.1 with 31 dominoes.

Each domino covers two adjacent squares or:

Prove logically why such a covering is impossible

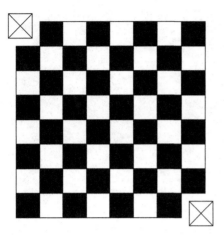

Figure A7.1

Appendix B

Horse-trading problem

A man bought a horse for £70 and sold it for 80, then he bought it back for 90, and sold it for 100. How much did he make?

The majority of problem solvers come up with one of two answers: £20 and £10 (Macchi and Bagassi, 2015).

The typical explanation for the first answer, which is the correct one, is, "the dealer makes £10 on the first transaction (70 - 80) and 10 on the second (90 - 100)," while for the second answer, the usual explanation given is "the dealer makes £10 on the first transaction, but loses this gain when he buys the horse back for 90. He then makes £10 on the last transaction, when he sells the horse again for 100."

According to Maier and Burke (1967), the difficulty of the horse-trading problem is not due to the answer being hard to find, but due to a misrepresentation of the problem. The "10 pound" answer appears to be due to the perception of the problem as being constituted of three separate financial transactions, while in fact it becomes much clearer when it is seen as two, and not three, financial operations.

Appendix C

The study window problem

The study window measures 1 meter in height and 1 meter wide. The owner decides to enlarge it and calls in a workman. He instructs the man to double the area of the window without changing its shape and so that it still measures 1 meter by 1 meter. The workman carried out the commission. How did he do it?

Solution

The solution is to be found in a square (geometric form) that "rests" on one of its angles, thus becoming a rhombus (phenomenic form). Now the dimensions given are those of the two diagonals of the represented rhombus (ABCD) (Figure A7.2).

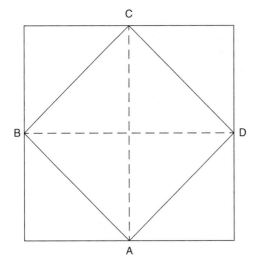

Figure A7.2

The "inverted" version

A study window measures 1 meter in height and 1 meter wide. The owner decides to make it smaller and calls in a workman. He instructs the man to halve the area of the window without changing its shape and in such a way that it still measures 1 meter by 1 meter. The workman carries out the commission. How did he do it?

Once again, 30 problem solvers attempted to solve the enigma. Nine started from the representation of the orthogonal square (ABCD) and looked for the solution within the square, trying to respect the required height and width of the window, and inevitably changing the orientation of the internal square. This time the height and width are the diagonals, rather than the sides (base and height) of the square.

We investigated this problem further by submitting a new experimental version to 30 undergraduate students from humanity faculties of the University of Milano-Bicocca, of both sexes and aged mostly between 19 and 25 years. Each participant was presented with the problem individually, with no time limit. In this version it was explicit that orientation was not a mandatory attribute of the shape.

The "orientation" version

A study window measures 1 meter in height and 1 meter wide. The owner decides to make it smaller and calls in a workman. He instructs the man to halve the area of the window: the workman can change the orientation of the window, but not its shape and in such a way that it still measures 1 meter by 1 meter. The workman carries out the commission. How did he do it?

In this version, in comparison with the control condition, 66 percent of the participants (21 out of 30; chi-square D 32.308; p < 0.001) found the solution immediately, as they were able to loosen the problem knot.

Notes

1 In this sense, in Meinong's terminology, the *superiora* are independent from the *inferiora*; on the other hand, since a melody cannot be made without notes, this independence is not absolute. It is an independence constrained by rules. The relationship systems between the pieces of the basic material constitute the mediation between the different orders. The melody remains.
2 Phrase inserted into the text by the authors of the chapter.
3 In the horse-trading problem, for instance, the correct response can be found by applying two methods, either by restructuration, or by a routine analytical process; however, only when the former method is applied can we talk of an insight problem. The study window problem, on the contrary, originates from an insurmountable fixation. This time the analytical process is not an option and the problem is solvable only by restructuration. (See Appendix B and Appendix C.)
4 "The salience, defined as strikingness or unusualness, would be responsible for the solution of insight problems" (Kaplan & Simon, 1990, p. 385).
5 This can be seen from the literature on the 9-dot problem, where the hint given to the problem solvers regarding the virtual square did not determine any change (Weisberg & Alba, 1981).
6 Even the Gestaltists didn't describe the covert work that goes on during this incubation period (and how could they, given that they were most interested in the restructuration) and this point was strongly criticized by the cognitivists and by Simon in particular.
7 However, even reasoning on the basis of three transactions in sequence, a very limited number of the participants (8 out of 37) gave the correct answer. In this case, in their mind, the loss of the £10 gained in the previous transaction translated into the reduction of the actual cost of the horse to £80. When they look at the final transaction (the sale of the horse for £100), they calculate correctly that the dealer has made £20.
8 The hypothesis that interpretation uses the conscious-unconscious level of thought is supported by the studies on selective spatial attention in the cluttered displays of Dehaene and Changeux (2011). According to Dehaene and Changeux, the gate to *the conscious access* (working memory) is always the outcome of a *nonconscious selection*, "separation of relevant versus irrelevant information, based on its saliency or relevance to current goals ... that regulates which information reaches conscious processing" (pp. 201, 202).

References

Ash, I. K., & Wiley, J. (2006). The nature of restructuring in insight: An individual-differences approach. *Psychonomic Bulletin & Review*, 13, 66–73.

Bagassi, M., & Macchi, L. (2016). The interpretative function and the emergence of unconscious analytic thought. In L. Macchi, M. Bagassi, & R. Viale (Eds.), *Cognitive unconscious and human rationality* (pp. 43–76). Cambridge, MA: MIT Press.

Baird, B., Smallwood, J., Mrazek, M. D., Kam, J. W. Y, Franklin, M. S., & Schooler, J. W. (2012). Inspired by distraction: Mind wandering facilitates creative incubation. *Psychological Science*, 23, 1117–1122.

Ball, L. J., Marsh, J. E., Litchfield, D., Cook, R. L., & Booth, N. (2015). When distraction helps: Evidence that concurrent articulation and irrelevant speech can facilitate insight problem solving, *Thinking & Reasoning*, 21, 1, 76–96.

Dehaene, S., & Changeux, J. P. (2011). Experimental and theoretical approaches to conscious processing. *Neuron*, 70, 200–227.

Duncker, K. (1945). On problem solving. *Psychological Monographs*, 58 (270), i–113. (Original in German, *Psychologie des produktiven Denkens*, Berlin: Springer, 1935).

Evans, J. S. B. T. (2010). Dual-process theories of reasoning: facts and fallacies. In K. J. Holyoak & R. G. Morrison (Eds.), *The Oxford handbook of thinking and reasoning*. Oxford: Oxford University Press.

Evans, J. St. B. T., Barston, J. L., & Pollard, P. (1983). On the conflict between logic and belief in syllogistic reasoning. *Memory & Cognition*, 11(3), 285–306.

Fleck, J. I. (2008). Working memory demands in insight versus analytic problem solving. *European Journal of Cognitive Psychology*, 20, 139–176.

Fleck, J. I., & Weisberg, R. W. (2013). Insight versus analysis: Evidence for diverse methods in problem solving. *Journal of Cognitive Psychology*, 25(4), 436–463.

Frankish, K., & Evans, J. St. B. T. (Eds.) (2009). *In two minds*. Oxford: Oxford University Press.

Gardner, E. P., & Johnson, K. O. (2013). Sensory coding. In E. R. Kandel, J. Schwartz, T. J. Jessell, S. A. St. Siegelbaum, & A. J. Hudspeth (Eds.), *Principles of neural science*. New York: McGraw-Hill.

Gilhooly, K. J., Ball, L. J., & Macchi, L. (2018). *Insight and creativity in problem soling*. London: Routledge.

Gilhooly, K. J., Fioratou, E., & Henretty, N. (2010). Verbalization and problem solving: Insight and spatial factors. *British Journal of Psychology*, 101, 81–93.

Gilhooly, K. J., Georgiou, G. J., & Devery, U. (2013). Incubation and creativity: Do something different. *Thinking and Reasoning*, 19, 137–149.

Gilhooly, K. J., Georgiou, G. J., Sirota, M., & Paphiti-Galeano, A. (2015). Incubation and suppression processes in creative problem solving. *Thinking and Reasoning*, 21, 1, 130–146.

Jung-Beeman, M., Bowden, E. M., Haberman, J., Frymiare, J. L., Arambel-Liu, S. ... Kounios, J. (2004). Neural activity when people solve verbal problems with insight. *PloS Biology*, 2(4), 1–11.

Hayes, J. R., & Simon, H. A. (1974). *Understanding written problem instructions*. In L. Gregg (Ed.), *Knowledge and cognition*. Potomac, MD: Lawrence Erlbaum Associates.

Henle, M. (1962). On the relation between logic and thinking. *Psychological Review*, 69, 366–378.

Kahneman, D., & Tversky, A. (1972). Subjective probability: A judgement of representativeness. *Cognitive Psychology*, 3, 430–454.

Kahneman, D., Slovic, P., & Tversky, A. (1982). *Judgement under uncertainty: Heuristics and biases*. Cambridge: Cambridge University Press.

Kandel, E. R. (2012). *The age of insight*. New York: Random House.

Kanizsa, G. (1980). *Grammatica del vedere*. Bologna: Il Mulino.

Kaplan, C. A., & Simon, H. A. (1990). In search of insight. *Cognitive Psychology*, 22, 374–419.

Levinson, S. C. (1995). Interactional biases in human thinking. In E. N. Goody (Ed.) *Social intelligence and interaction* (pp. 221–261). Cambridge: Cambridge University Press.

Levinson, S. C. (2000). *Presumptive meanings: The theory of generalized conversational implicature*. Cambridge, MA: MIT Press.

Levinson, S. C. (2013). Cross-cultural universals and communication structures. In M. A. Arbib (Ed.), *Language, music, and the brain: A mysterious relationship* (pp. 67–80). Cambridge, MA: MIT Press.

Macchi, L., & Bagassi, M. (2012). Intuitive and analytical processes in insight problem solving: A psycho-rhetorical approach to the study of reasoning. *Mind & Society*, 11(1), 53–67.

Macchi, L., & Bagassi, M. (2014). The interpretative heuristic in insight problem solving. *Mind & Society*, 13(1), 97–108.

Macchi, L., & Bagassi, M. (2015). When analytic thought is challenged by a misunderstanding. *Thinking & Reasoning*, 21(1), 147–164.

Macchi, L., Bagassi, M., & Viale, R. (Eds.) (2016). *Cognitive unconscious and human rationality*. Cambridge, MA: MIT Press.

Mach, E. (1914). *The analysis of sensations*. Chicago: Open Court.

Maier, N. R. F., & Burke, R. J. (1967). Response availability as a factor in the problem-solving performance of males and females. *Journal of Personality and Social Psychology*, 5(3), 304–310.

Mercier, H., & Sperber, D. (2011). Why do human reason? Arguments for an argumentative theory. *Behavioral and Brain Sciences*, 34(2), 57–74.

Mercier, H., & Sperber, D. (2017). *The enigma of reason*. Cambridge, MA: Harvard University Press).

Metcalfe, J. (1986). Feeling of knowing in memory and problem solving. *Journal of Experimental Psychology: Learning, Memory, and Cognition*, 12(2), 288–294.

Mosconi, G. (1990). *Discorso e pensiero*. Bologna: Il Mulino.

Mosconi, G. (2016). Closing thoughts. In L. Macchi, M. Bagassi, & R. Viale (Eds.), *Cognitive unconscious and human rationality* (pp. 355–363). Cambridge, MA: MIT Press.

Mosconi, G., & D'Urso, V. (1974). *Il farsi e il disfarsi del problema*. Firenze: Giunti-Barbera.

Newell, A., & Simon, H. A. (1972). *Human problem solving*. Englewood Cliffs, NJ: Prentice-Hall.

Ohlsson, S. (2012). The problems with problem solving; Reflections on the rise, current status, and possible future of a cognitive research paradigm. *Journal of Problem Solving*, 5(1), 101–128.

Ollinger, M., Jones, G., & Knoblich, G. K. (2008). Investigating the effect of mental set on insight problem solving. *Experimental Psychology*, 55(4), 270–282.

Perkins, D. (1981). *The mind's best work*. Cambridge, MA: Harvard University Press.

Rizzolatti, G., & Strick, P.L. (2013). Cognitive functions of the premotor systems. In E. R. Kandel, J. Schwartz, T. Jessell, S. A. Siegelbaum, & A. J. Hudspeth (Eds.), *Principles of neural science*. New York: McGraw-Hill..

Schooler, J. W., Ohlsson, S., & Brooks, K. (1993). Thoughts beyond words: When language overshadows insight. *Journal of Experimental Psychology: General*, 122(2), 166–183.

Schooler, J. W., Smallwood, J., Christoff, K., Handy, T. C., Reichle, E. D., & Sayette, M. A. (2011) Meta-awareness, perceptual decoupling and the wandering mind. *Trends in Cognitive Science*, 15, 319–326.

Segal, E. (2004). Incubation in insight problem solving. *Creativity Research Journal*, 16, 141–148.

Simon, H. A. (1979). Information processing models of cognition. *Annual Review of Psychology*, 30, 363–396.

Simon, H. A. (1984). Otto Selz and information processing psychology. In N. H. Frijda & A. de Groot (Eds.), *Otto Selz: His contribution to psychology*. The Hague: Mouton..

Simon, H. A. (1986). The information processing explanation of gestalt phenomena. *Computers in Human Behavior*, 2, 241–255.

Simon, H. A., & Hayes, J. R. (1976). The understanding process: Problem isomorphs. *Cognitive Psychology*, 8, 165–190.

Simon, H. A., & Newell, A. (1971). Human problem solving: The state of theory. *American Psychologist*, 21(2), 145–159.

Simon, H. A., Newell, A., & Shaw, J. C. (1979). The processes of creative thinking. In H. A. Simon (Ed.), *Models of thought* (pp. 144–174). New Haven, CT: Yale University Press. (Original work published 1962.)

Sio, U. N., & Ormerod, T. C. (2009). Does incubation enhance problem solving? A meta-analytic review. *Psychological Bulletin*, 135(1), 94–120.

Smallwood, J., & Schooler, J.W. (2006). The restless mind. *Psychological Bulletin*, 132, 946–958.

Sperber, D., & Wilson, D. (1986). *Relevance: Communication and cognition*. Oxford: Blackwell.

Sternberg, R. J., & Davidson, J. E. (Eds.) (1986). *Conceptions of giftedness*. New York: Cambridge University Press.

Stupple, E. J. N., Ball, L. J., Evans, J. S. B. T., & Kamal-Smith, E. (2011). When logic and belief collide: Individual differences in reasoning times support a selective processing model. *Journal of Cognitive Psychology*, 23(8), 931–941.

Threadgold, E., Marsh, J. E., & Ball, L. J. (2018). Normative data for 84 UK English Rebus puzzles. *Frontiers in Psychology*, 13.

Tomasello, M. (2009). *Why we cooperate*. Cambridge, MA: MIT Press.

Tversky, A., & Kahneman, D. (1983). Extension versus intuitive reasoning: The conjunction fallacy in probability judgment. *Psychological Review*, 90(4), 293–315.

Weisberg, R. W. (2015). Toward an integrated theory of insight in problem solving. *Thinking & Reasoning*, 21, 5–39.

Weisberg, R. W., & Alba, J. W. (1981). An examination of the alleged role of "fixation" in the solution of several "insight" problems. *Journal of Experimental Psychology: General*, 110(2), 169–192.

Wertheimer, M. (1925). *Drei Abhandlungen zur Gestalttheorie*. Erlangen: Verlag der Philosophischen Akademie.

Wertheimer, M. (1985). A Gestalt perspective on computer simulations of cognitive processes. *Computers on Human Behavior*, 1, 19–33.

8

SIMON'S LEGACIES FOR MATHEMATICS EDUCATORS

Laura Martignon, Kathryn Laskey, and Keith Stenning

Introduction

Herbert Simon is famous for having said: "The goal of science is to make the wonderful and the complex understandable and simple – but not less wonderful" (1996). The fundamental truth underlying Simon's words has an important parallel in mathematics education, where one might say that the goal is to devise ways to make wonderful, sometimes complex mathematical results understandable and simple—but not less wonderful. Explaining our ideas means decomposing them into understandable pieces and gluing them together with accessible arguments. In a proper "waterproof" explanation, these arguments must be backed by logical rigor. Logical rigor is sometimes an enemy of beauty and even, at times, of intuition. Mathematics, no less than the natural sciences, is in itself a collection of wonders. It has grown at the interface between the human mind/brain and nature, enabling the mind both to model natural phenomena and to tame uncertainty. In science in general and mathematics in particular, there is a certain risk in decomposing concepts into their components and explaining processes formally because fascination may fade through the exercise of formal decomposition and explanation. According to our version of Simon's statement, the good mathematics instructor should teach and explain mathematical facts while keeping both motivation and wonder alive in his/her students' minds. We cite a well-known mathematical example: It is a wonderful result of mathematics that there exist exactly five Platonic solids. Explaining this wonder requires a minimum of detailed formalism and going through this formalism demands special skills of a mathematics educator, if she wants to make the result clear and understandable without tarnishing its beauty.

This nugget of wisdom is just one of many that are found in Simon's writings. Simon's work on the sciences of the artificial yields innumerable bits of inspiration for the education of young students in mathematical thinking. For him, the artificial includes models and structures expressed in symbols developed by the mind! In other words, for Simon, mathematics and computer science are among the sciences of the artificial, as is the subject of how the human mind pursues these topics.

Many of the legacies left by Simon for the mathematics educator appear in his book, *The Sciences of the Artificial*, which first appeared in 1969 (Simon, 1996). Some of the chapters in that revolutionary book were specifically devoted to four topics of intense current interest in mathematics and computer science education: learning, representing information, bounded

DOI: 10.4324/9781315658353-9

rationality, and problem solving. Our aim in this chapter is to analyze some of these legacies and discuss their relevance to education today.

Simon's predictions

Simon and his colleague Allen Newell were among the handful of founders of the field called Artificial Intelligence. In his Preface to the second edition of *The Sciences of the Artificial* (1996), Simon explained the difference between "natural" and "artificial" intelligence, contrasting the goal-oriented essence of the artificial with the evolutionary fit of natural systems to their environments. One naturally wonders how Herbert Simon, one of the fathers of artificial intelligence, would view the accomplishments of the field, were he alive today. In a 1992 interview for UBS Nobel Perspectives,[1] Simon mentioned his four predictions on the future of computers and computer programs:

1   By the mid-1960s, computers would play chess so well that they would beat the greatest chess masters.
2   Also by the mid-1960s, computers would compose aesthetically pleasing music.
3   Computers would prove at least one new theorem.
4   Most theories of the mind's cognitive processes would be expressed as computer programs.

Simon was prescient in that all his predictions have eventually come to pass, at least to some degree. In the case of chess, his timing was off by a few decades, but he was correct that computers would eventually play at the highest levels. Computers could play quite well by the 1980s, but it was not until 1997 that a computer beat World Chess Champion Garry Kasparov.[2] Simon was also early but correct regarding musical composition. In 2017, a program from Aiva Technologies became the first musical composition program to be given official status, when the French Société des Auteurs, Compositeurs et Éditeurs de musique (SACEM) conferred upon it the official status of Composer.[3] In 1976, the Four Color Theorem, a longstanding mathematical conjecture that had frustrated mathematicians since it had been proposed in 1852, became the first major theorem to be proven by computers and human minds working together. While controversial at first, because it was too complex to be checked by hand, the proof is widely accepted today. As for the fourth prediction, Herbert Simon himself saw to it that computer theories of the mind were developed, and he became a driving force behind their acceptance by the cognitive science community. It is difficult to estimate the ratio of full computational theories to less formally expressed theories of the mind, and thus to evaluate his assessment that most theories would be computational. Nevertheless, computer modeling of cognitive processes has become a vibrant, prolific, and highly successful sub-field of psychology. Simon's insight that many cognitive processes can be explained in terms of computer models was revolutionary. The question today is rather, which are those cognitive processes, which cannot be explained in terms of computer models?

One reason Simon, along with many early AI researchers, was far too optimistic about the time frame during which critical milestones would be achieved, was the contrast between how computers and humans process information. Humans are excellent at pattern recognition and analogy, still exceeding the capabilities of computers on many tasks requiring these skills. Computers are designed to perform the kind of exacting, step-by-step, logical reasoning tasks humans find especially difficult. Because computers were so good at tasks humans find so challenging, it was easy to overestimate the difficulty of making computers perform well on tasks humans find routine and even less intelligent animals can perform well.

Simon and the early AI researchers also underestimated the difficulty of developing AI systems to tackle ill-structured problems. While acknowledging that there can be no crisp, formal boundary between well- and ill-structured problems, Simon (1973) set out the characteristics of a problem that can be regarded as well-structured, i.e., one that is amenable to solution by a computer problem solver. An ill-structured problem is then a residual category, i.e., an ill-structured problem is simply one that is not well-structured. Simon argued that whether a problem is well- or ill-structured can be a matter of context, and that "any problem with a sufficiently large base of relevant knowledge can appear to be an ill-structured problem" (Simon, 1973, p. 197). He concluded: "There appears to be no reason to suppose that concepts as yet un-invented and unknown would be needed to automate the solution of ill-structured problems." Whether Simon was correct in this conclusion is still a matter of debate among AI researchers. It is unquestionable that it has taken longer than Simon anticipated for some of the more challenging problems to succumb to automation.

In 1956, von Neumann was invited to give a set of lectures comparing the ways in which computers and brains process information. He never gave the lectures, but worked on the manuscript until his death, and it was published posthumously (von Neumann, 1958). Acknowledging that he was a mathematician and not a neuroscientist, he identified a number of ways in which computers and brains operate differently:

1   Brains are analog and computers are digital.
2   Brains process in parallel and computers process serially.
3   Unlike brains, computers have the ability to use instructions stored in memory to modify control of processing.
4   Individual brain component processes are too slow to perform the serial processes at which computers excel.

Von Neumann concluded that the language and logic used by the brain must be radically different from that of computers.

Despite these fundamental differences, the project of computational modeling of cognitive phenomena has been extremely successful, and has led to many important insights. These insights have sparked advances in decision support, automation, and also education. We are here mainly concerned with Simon's seminal insights: that cognitive processes can be described by means of computer models and that the representation of information in a given problem is a key factor for finding its solution. These insights have had far-reaching consequences for mathematics and computer science education.

Ecologically rational representations

One of Simon's most famous quotes concerns the fundamental importance of representation for solving problem: "Solving a problem simply means representing it so as to make the solution transparent" (Simon, 1996, p. 132). A solution becomes transparent if it emerges from the structure in terms of which the problem has been modeled. The structure of the problem is the result of an attempt at adaptation between the problem itself and the conceptual constructions of the mind. An adaptation is successful if it is ecologically rational (cf., Gigerener et al., 1999). Ecological rationality is a fundamental characteristic of successful representations. It refers to behaviors and thought processes that are adaptive and goal-oriented in the context of the environment in which an organism is situated, thus giving survival advantage to the organism. Discovering a representation that makes a problem easily solvable gives evolutionary advantage in terms of time resources to adopters of the new representation, because they are able to solve the problem more quickly and easily than those holding on to the old representation.

Modern mathematics education treats representations of mathematical entities as a fundamental aspect of didactics in the classroom. Special attention has been devoted, for instance, to the issue of multiple representations of numerical entities and the advantages of switching between them as a means of achieving mathematical competencies for dealing with them (Dreher & Kuntze, 2014).

For many types of problems, such as fractions and probabilities, we argue that different *mathematically* equivalent representations are far from *cognitively* equivalent. That is, some representations are more adaptive and advantageous than others, because they seem to be better aligned to the cognitive systems of human problem solvers.

We begin by describing the relevance of information formats for inference, a major component of human reasoning. Both problem solving and decision-making require inference. From old knowledge, we create and acquire new knowledge by means of chains of inferences. From partial solutions, we advance to more complete solutions by means of inferences. The introduction of so-called inference machines, that is well-described systems of rules for inference, has had immense implications for science. The inferences of these inference machines are, more often than not, produced under uncertainty. Classical logic and probability provide the two most salient, standard mechanisms invented in human history for inference machines. We will discuss the ecological rationality of representations in the context of these two inference approaches, inverting the historical order of their inception. We begin by approaching tasks of probabilistic inference.

The ecological rationality of natural frequencies for probabilistic inference

One of the problems that makes mathematics so difficult is the already mentioned tension between intuition and rigor. In a variety of areas, mathematicians have developed elegant, abstract, logically coherent theories that encompass and generalize intuitively natural concepts. Examples include numbers, probabilities, and algebraic structures. These elegant abstract theories have a pristine beauty that attracts mathematicians, and have led to powerful innovations, but can be daunting to beginning students and to the lay public. Mathematics educators therefore face the challenge of helping students to build on their natural intuition to bridge the gap between human intuition and mathematical theory.

Natural frequency and probability

An important instance of the tension between intuition and rigor is probability theory. Our intuitive, innocent, and natural understanding of probabilities fits uneasily with the formal definition as countably additive measures on sigma-algebras of sets. Formalism and rigor, especially introduced too early, may kill intuition and with it motivation. We aim at scrutinizing the *natural Bayesian* who reasons, as in Gerd Gigerenzer's recommendation, by forming simple proportions of outcomes starting from well-defined populations of cases. The natural Bayesian goes through a sequence of stages: from multiple narratives stemming from observations that are ultimately represented as a frequency tree, to expected outcomes in future phases of updating.

The natural frequency representation is adapted to our cognitive processes in a way that makes the solution to evidential reasoning problems transparent. In other words, it is ecologically rational.

Consider a physician who must reason from evidence, such as symptoms and test results, to a hypothesis, such as whether or not a patient has a disease. To approach this problem formally, as presented in textbooks, we begin with two ingredients: (1) a *prior* probability that the disease is present; and (2) likelihoods, or probabilities that the evidence would be observed if the disease was present or absent. For our example, we imagine that the evidence is a test for the disease, and it has come out positive. We use the symbols D+ and D- to denote the presence and absence of the disease, and T+ to denote a positive test result. We use our prior probability and test likelihoods to calculate the *posterior* probability that the disease is present given the positive test result:

$$\left(D+|\ T+\right) = \frac{P(T+\ |\ D+)P\left(D+\right)}{P\left(T+|D+\right)P\left(D+\right) + P\left(T+|D-\right)P\left(D-\right)} \tag{8.1}$$

The formula (8.1) is called *Bayes rule* after its inventor, the eighteenth-century philosopher and minister Thomas Bayes.

Formula (8.1) gives correct answers to the evidential reasoning problem, but it requires calculations of which only a relatively few trained individuals are capable. There is an immense literature on people's difficulties with this kind of reasoning based on conditional probabilities, and some scientists have been convinced that these difficulties point to some form of human irrationality.

There is, on the other hand, a way of representing such evidential reasoning tasks that makes the solution transparent. To use this method, called *natural frequencies* (e.g., Gigerenzer & Hoffrage, 1995), the doctor imagines a population of fictitious people, say, 1,000 of them. She divides them into those who do and do not have the disease. For example, if the disease is present in only 1 percent of the population, she would partition her imaginary 1,000 patients into 10 who have the disease and 990 who do not. Of those who have the disease, let us imagine that 80 percent will test positive. Therefore, the doctor imagines that 8 of the 10 ill patients will test positive and 2 will test negative. Now, suppose that 90 percent of those who do not have the disease will have a negative test result. In our doctor's imaginary population, this works out to 99 well patients who test positive and 891 who test negative.

This thought experiment uncovers a peculiar, and very important, characteristic of problems characterized by uncertainty: the fundamental role played by the base rate. Our doctor, like many untrained people, may be surprised to learn that, although the vast majority of ill patients have tested positive and the vast majority of well patients have tested negative, only 7 percent of the patients who test positive actually have the disease. This occurs because of the low base rate—that is, a very small proportion of our original population was ill.

Figure 8.1 compares the probability and the natural frequency representation of this evidential reasoning problem. As many an educator has discovered, students taught to apply formula (8.1) often find the result P(D|T+) = 7% surprising, sometimes even refusing to believe that the disease remains unlikely after a positive test result. By contrast, most students who work with the figure on the right immediately grasp why most patients who test positive are actually disease-free. It is readily apparent that although 107 positives is a small proportion of the 990 well patients, it is still nevertheless many more than the 8 true positives out of only 10 ill patients.

There is a wealth of literature demonstrating that people tend to neglect base rates when reasoning about this kind of problem. Even many people who have been taught Bayes rule often fall prey to this fallacy. However, performance on such tasks improves dramatically when

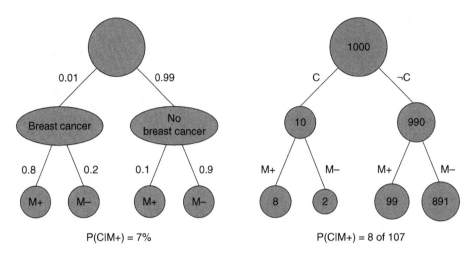

Figure 8.1 Probability and natural frequency representation of evidential reasoning

people are taught the natural frequency interpretation (Gigerenzer & Hoffrage, 1995). This improved performance has been observed in a variety of application domains (Hoffrage & Gigerenzer, 1998; Hoffrage, Lindsey, Hertwig, & Gigerenzer, 2000; Gigerenzer, 2002) and in more complex problems than reasoning with a single cue (Hoffrage, Krauss, Martignon, & Gigerenzer, 2015).

To summarize, an ecologically rational strategy is one our cognitive apparatus can perform naturally and easily, and that has adaptive value in a given environment. In other words, ecological rationality involves discovery of a representation that makes an optimal or nearly optimal solution transparent. For reasoning from evidence to hypothesis, because the natural frequency representation is ecologically rational, it allows humans to perform an otherwise difficult task quickly and easily. Because the natural frequency representation is ecologically rational, its use in educational settings facilitates understanding and improves performance.

Icon arrays and Venn diagrams

Back in the 1960s and 1970s, Venn diagrams were introduced as representations of sets in primary and secondary schools in most European countries and several other countries around the world. There were protests everywhere. In Germany, for instance, the protests both of schoolteachers and parents were so strong, that set theory was banned from primary school. This had as a consequence a reluctance to introduce probabilities earlier than in ninth grade. Also for the communication of probabilistic information in the medical and pharmaceutical domain, Venn diagrams did not enjoy acceptance.

Here again, an ecologically rational format has made its way into many sectors of communication. Otto Neurath introduced such a format during the first half of the twentieth century (he actually proposed what he called *isotypes* and arrays of such isotypes).

Icon arrays are displays of icons, which represent individuals or animals or items. The icons can exhibit special features, thus allowing for classifications. In the example in Figure 8.2a, the depicted icon array represents dogs and cats, with or without the feature "bell." One more structural way of representing the information about these house pets is

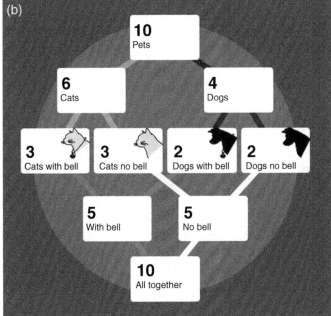

Figure 8.2 (a) An icon array representing dogs and cats, some with a bell and some without; (b) the corresponding double tree for transparent Bayesian reasoning

Source: (a) www.eeps.com/projects/wwg/ a free webpage for Risk literacy by Tim Erickson and Laura Martignon.

to organize them in a double tree: from top to bottom we first partition our house pets into cats and dogs and continue by looking in each subgroup whether the pet has a bell or not (Figure 8.2b). From bottom to top, we first look at bells, partitioning our pets into those with a bell and those without. School kids can use this representation to learn an elementary Bayesian reasoning. They learn to assess the probability—expressed in natural frequencies— that a pet with a bell is a cat, or that a dog has a bell. Thus, icon arrays combined with trees and double trees communicate information on base rates, sensitivities, specificities and predictive values in a straightforward, transparent way. They have been used in primary school with great success (Martignon & Hoffrage, 2019) coupled with corresponding natural frequencies doubletrees.

From inference based on one cue to inference based on many cues: the ecological rationality of lexicographic strategies

We commonly model situations by characterizing them in terms of a set of cues or features we can extract from them. We make inferences on these situations based on those cues. We have treated above the case of judgments or classifications based on just one cue—in that case a test—characterizing a disease. Actually, a physician usually needs more than just one test result to diagnose a disease. For instance, in the case of breast cancer, a doctor will systematically look at two cues, namely, mammography and an ultrasound test. We illustrate a possible Natural Frequency tree drawn in the *diagnostic direction*, i.e., with the end nodes corresponding to "having breast cancer" or "not having breast cancer" (Figure 8.3), in contrast with the tree of Figure 8.1, which follows *the causal direction*.

The facilitating effect of natural frequencies disappears when more cues are considered: As the number of cues grows, the size of the natural frequency tree explodes and ecological rationality is lost. The huge tree representing 6 cues, for instance, suffers from "brittleness." As it grows, the number of end nodes may become very large, while the number of cases per end node may become very small. These small numbers of cases per end node will not support reliable predictions.

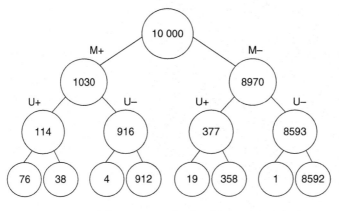

Figure 8.3 A natural frequency tree for classifying patients as having or not having breast cancer, by looking at the values of two cues, namely, a mammography and an ultrasound test

Is there an alternative ecologically rational strategy that maintains a tree structure and eliminates non-relevant information? There is, in fact, a heuristic strategy that fits the bill. Inspired by Simon, the heuristic consists of radically pruning the full tree into a minimal one based on the same set of cues. The resulting tree becomes fast-and-frugal, according to the definition of Martignon et al. (2003). The fast-and-frugal tree has a single exit at every level before the last one, where it has two. The cues are ordered by means of very simple ranking criteria. Fast-and-frugal trees are implemented step by step, reduce memory load, and can be set up and executed by the unaided mind, requiring, at most, paper and pencil.

Step-by-step procedures, that follow well-specified sequences, are a typical aspect of human behavior. We pronounce one word at a time, for instance. Time organizes our actions and thoughts in one-dimensional arrays. We are tuned for doing "first things first" and then proceeding to second and third things. This innate tendency for sequencing makes so-called lexicographic strategies for classification and decision ecologically rational. This section illustrates how sequential treatment of cues can extend and expand classifications based on one cue.

A fast-and-frugal tree does not classify optimally. Rather, to use a term coined by Simon, it *satisfices*, producing good enough solutions with reasonable cognitive effort. The predictive accuracy and the robustness of the fast-and-frugal tree have been amply demonstrated (e.g., Laskey & Martignon, 2014; Woike, Hoffrage, & Martignon, 2017; Luan, Gigerenzer, & Schooler, 2011).

Martignon et al. (2003) provided a characterization of these trees as lexicographic, supporting an ecologically rational step-by-step execution of the classification process, which can be stated as the following theorem:

> **Theorem**: For binary cues with values 0 or 1, a fast-and-frugal tree is characterized by the existence of a unique cue profile of 0's and 1's that operates as a *splitting profile* of the tree; this means that any item with a profile lexicographically lower than the splitting profile will be classified in one of the two categories, while the rest of items will be classified in the other one.

This theorem is illustrated in Figure 8.4.

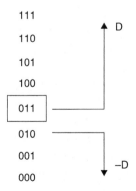

Figure 8.4 An example of a splitting profile characterizing a fast-and-frugal tree for classifying items into two complementary categories based on three cues

Source: Martignon et al. (2003).

From classification to comparison and back

The trees for classification described above belong to the class of simple heuristics inspired by Simon and analyzed for a variety of tasks by the ABC Research Group, led by Gerd Gigerenzer. Another of these heuristics tackles comparison: When two items have to be compared as to which has a higher value on a given criterion, the fast-and-frugal heuristic at hand, called Take-the-Best, proceeds as follows: It ranks the binary cues according to a simple criterion (e.g., validity) and looks at the cue profiles, comparing them lexicographically. Imagine that there were just three binary cues and the corresponding profiles were 110 and 101, as depicted in Figure 8.4. When they are compared lexicographically, 110 is larger than 101 because the first digit on the left-hand side coincides in both, but the second differs. Thus, the larger second digit corresponds to the larger number.

This simple principle is the essence of Take-the-Best. Assume, for instance, one wants to compare German cities, say, Duisburg and Ludwigsburg, as to their population. The comparison is to be based on binary cues, just as in the original example treated by Gigerenzer and Goldstein (1996). Here more than three binary cues may be necessary, if the pairs of cities to be compared can be any of all pairs in the reference of class of cities with more than 100,000 inhabitants. In fact, Gigerenzer and Goldstein considered nine binary cues, of which the first one, was simple recognition: "Do I recognize the name of the city?". If this is true for only one of the cities in the pair, then the recognized one is to be considered the larger one. If both are recognized, then one can compare the remaining "cue profiles" lexicographically. Other cues are "Is the city a state capital?," "Does the city have a soccer team playing in the National League?," or "Does it have a station where ICE trains stop?" In summary, Take-the-Best analyzes each cue, one after the other, according to the ranking by validity (i.e., its overall predictive value, or the probability of making a correct prediction if it discriminates between the two cities) and stopping the first time a cue discriminates between the items, concluding that the item with the larger value has also a larger value on the criterion.

Both the fast-and-frugal tree for classification and Take-the-Best are simple heuristics which belong in more than one of the great mathematical classes of models. On the one hand, they can be represented by trees, and, on the other hand, they are lexicographic strategies. An additional property that may be useful for computer implementation and use in applications, as well as for the comparisons in performance with models like regression (see Şimşek's Chapter 21 in this volume) is that these methods can be described in terms of linear models, which are those that "weigh and sum" cue values, in the most elementary way. In a more formal context, Martignon and Hoffrage (2002) showed that such lexicographic rules are always equivalent to weighted linear classification models with non-compensatory coefficients. A list of weights are non-compensatory if each of them is larger than the sum of all weights that follow in the list (see Figure 8.5 for an example).

On the left-hand side of Figure 8.5, we illustrate non-compensatory weights, which make a linear weighted model behave like a lexicographic strategy. On the right-hand side, we illustrate equal weights, which correspond to the tallying heuristic, which simply "counts" 1s in profiles of 1s and 0s.

In the next section, we illustrate the connection between the fast-and-frugal Take-the-Best with comparisons of natural numbers. The striking fact is that Hindu-Arabic numerals are a representation of numbers that allows the magnitude of numbers to be compared by following the Take-the-Best strategy.

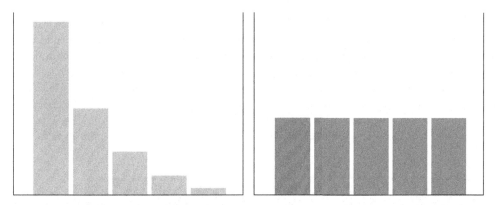

Figure 8.5   On the left side non-compensatory weights, like 2, 1, ½, ¼, 1/8. On the right side 5 weights all equal to 1.

Fast-and-frugal number comparison with the Hindu-Arabic system

Herbert Simon wrote, in Chapter 5 of *The Sciences of the Artificial*: "We all believe that arithmetic has become easier since Arabic numerals and place notation replaced Roman numerals, although I know of no theoretic treatment that explains why" (Simon, 1996).

Our aim is to use the tenets of ecological rationality to explain why arithmetic became so much easier with this new representation. We claim that "the theoretic treatment of why the decimal positional system made arithmetic calculations and comparisons so much easier than the Roman numerals" is in no small part due to the ecological rationality of the lexicographic heuristic for comparison it allows: Obviously, if a natural number has more digits than another natural number, then it is larger. What happens when they have the same number of digits? If one has to compare, say, 2056 and 2049, then one proceeds lexicographically stopping at the third place, where digits differ and declaring 2056 to be the larger one because 5 > 4. The same procedure is also valid if numbers are written in base 2, like 100000000100 and 10000000001.

Observe that these numbers written in Roman numerals are MMLVI and MMXLIX, allowing no natural, organic way for comparing them: in fact, the number with a longer representation is actually smaller, which makes little sense from the perspective of ecological rationality. More importantly, arithmetic operations become simple with place notation, being far more cumbersome with the Roman system.

For mathematics education, the connections between ecological rationality and the number system are relevant. School students learn a minimum of mathematical history. They learn about the Roman system and they learn why even Europeans finally replaced it by a system that—from the structural point of view—is far more ecologically rational. It remains a mystery why the European continent maintained the Roman numeral system for such a long time. Roman numerals were merely used to describe quantities and data, but not for comparisons nor for calculations. They mimicked, at least for numerals between 1 and 50, fingers and hands: 10 corresponded to two hands, 20 to 4 hands and 33 to 3 hands and 3 single fingers. The letter L for 50 meant "half of C," and C was the first letter of Centum, which meant 100 in Latin. The system was additive and cumulative, requiring ever more letters for representing larger numbers. Although its basic symbols may seem natural, because they depict fingers, their representation is not based on an ecologically rational structuring. Not just comparisons but also computations were cumbersome. Until the twelfth century, Italian merchants had to outsource computations on the prices of their merchandise by communicating their numbers to "abacists" who translated Roman numbers into groups of marbles and operated with these groups in a cumbersome way.

In India, and later in Persia and the Islamic countries, the positional number system had been used widely for computations since the seventh century. It was Leonardo da Pisa, also known as Fibonacci, who made the first attempts to import the Hindu-Arabic positional system to Europe, well into the twelfth century (Figure 8.6). The Church opposed this novelty and

Figure 8.6 An allegory of Arithmetic from *Margarita Philosophica*: a young woman, smiling benevolently at the young man who uses the Hindu-Arabic positional system, while his fellow at the other table uses marbles

Source: Gregor Reisch, twelfth century.

even declared the number "0," which the Arabs had called "Zifer" (from which the term "cipher" was derived), as the number of the devil. Yet Fibonacci's dream came true in the end because its ecological rationality provided such great practical utility.

The ecological rationality of defeasible logic and its role in mathematics education

In Chapter 3 of *The Sciences of the Artificial*, Simon recommends the use of multiple logics and in Chapter 5, he explains that "Multiple logics may become necessary when approaching heuristic decision making" (Simon, 1996).This is particularly true in the mathematics classroom today when instructors have to understand students' reasoning without declaring it as "wrong" simply because it does not follow the laws of classical logic. One of the responsibilities of mathematics educators today is to instruct students in identifying different forms of inferences—not just for decision making but also as tools for mathematical thinking in general. The main point we want to make here is that classical logic and probabilities are not sufficient as instruments for understanding and describing human reasoning.

Remember how, in previous sections, we treated a conditional sentence of the kind:

If she tests positive, she has the disease

We imagined a physician reasoning from evidence to hypothesis, based on knowledge of anatomical facts but also on experience. How high is the physician's confidence in this conditional? In the first part of this chapter, we have extensively discussed how the physician can treat this conditional probabilistically by estimating the probability that the patient has the disease, given that she tests positive. It is well established that physicians do not necessarily treat this implication, basing their assessment of frequencies. A fundamental treatise on physicians' decision making in inferences is David Eddy's book (Eddy, 1996), in which he presents conclusions gained from his decades of work examining his colleagues' reasoning. In fact, Eddy became known for propagating the necessity of physicians acquiring statistical literacy. One observation he made seems particularly relevant to our discussion of multiple logics: He was surprised by the fact that excellent doctors could be so bad at correctly estimating predictive values (Eddy, 1982). What they apparently had was a profound knowledge of the reasons or factors that could *enable* a positive test. Basing inferences on such "reasons" instead of frequencies is not probabilistic and it also does not follow the rules of classical logic. Nevertheless, it can be extremely successful. For example, a physician with extensive knowledge of the reasons a test could be positive without the presence of the illness in question is in a good position to order follow-up tests and to observe the patient carefully to rule out these other reasons before making a final diagnosis. Precisely here we see other logics at work, namely, defeasible logics, which take into account so-called enablers and defeaters of causal conditionals.

Psychologists have examined these different ways of reasoning and making inferences successfully. Back in 1995, Denise Cummins performed a seminal experiment. She let participants generate "defeaters" for causal conditionals, such as, "If John studies, he passes the test." She then discovered that the number of defeaters generated by a group of participants inversely predicted the confidence of another group of participants in the statements of the conditionals. In terms of heuristics, one can state that simply "tallying" defeaters inversely predicts confidence in the inference expressed by a conditional. They rely on their tallying *abnormalities* and *alternative causes*, that is "reasons" that cause conditional inferences of the *Modus Ponens* type or of the *Affirmation of the Consequent* type to be defeated on occasions. Stenning, Martignon, and Varga (2017) replicated this experiment in a within-subject design, and obtained basically the same results. They further discovered that people are ecologically rational, in that they switch from tallying defeaters or enablers to using just one of them if it is particularly strong, or sometimes two of them, if together they seem to back up their judgment strongly enough. The relevant conclusion from Cummins' experiment and our replication is that representations for inference in daily life are not just numerical or strictly logical in a classical sense but can be expressed by *narratives*, which obey defeasible logic.

In fact, strict classical logic is the instrument of adversarial communication, while defeasible logic is often the instrument of cooperative communication (Stenning, Martignon, & Varga, 2017). Adversarial communication is the mode adopted by someone who knows that peers and colleagues will be checking each step in a dialectical mode, whereas cooperative communication is the mode adopted by someone arguing to achieve progress toward a common goal. Adversarial communication can place students on the defensive and inhibit learning. Cooperative communication, on the other hand, places teachers and students in a collaboration to support learning. When a mathematics educator analyzes her students' answers, she should be aware of students' different logics before declaring that her students are committing serious mistakes. Mathematics educators are likely to be more successful if they engage their students in a cooperative pursuit of knowledge than if they act as adversaries pouncing on their students' every perceived mistake.

Conclusion

Simon devoted much of his career to promulgating the importance of what we have called ecologically rational representations and procedures. These adapt well to our cognitive apparatus and produce solutions that are good enough for the purpose. Thus, as Simon argued, solving a solution means finding a representation that makes a satisficing solution transparent. In a class attended by one of the authors, Simon argued for the necessity of satisficing with characteristic wry humor, announcing that he was insured to precisely the point that his family was indifferent as to whether he lived or died. As a brilliant pedagogical strategy, this little joke cemented in his students' mind both the impossibility of finding a genuinely optimal insurance strategy, and the necessity of *satisficing* to protect one's family.

This work has explored the role of ecologically rational representations and procedures for several common mathematical reasoning tasks: number comparison, classification, and causal inference. In each class of problems, we illustrated how ecologically rational representations and procedures make satisficing solutions transparent. As tools for education, such ecologically rational strategies support understanding, and maintain the wonder of mathematics in the minds of students.

Notes

1 The relevant excerpt can be found at this link: www.youtube.com/watch?v=ABucG05nurs.
2 See https://en.wikipedia.org/wiki/Human–computer_chess_matches.
3 See https://aibusiness.com/aiva-is-the-first-ai-to-officially-be-recognised-as-a-composer/.

References

Cummins, D. (1995) Naïve theories and causal cognition. *Memory and Cognition*, 23(5), 646–659.
Dreher, A., & Kuntze, S. (2014) Teachers' professional knowledge and noticing: The case of multiple representations in the mathematics classroom. *Educational Studies in Mathematics*, 88(1): 1–26.

Eddy, D. M. (1982) Probabilistic reasoning in clinical medicine: Problems and opportunities. In D. Kahneman, P. Slovic, & A. Tversky (Eds.), *Judgment under uncertainty: Heuristics and biases* (pp. 249–267). Cambridge: Cambridge University Press.

Eddy, D. M. (1996). *Clinical decision making: From theory to practice: a collection of essays published by the American Medical Association.* New York: Jones and Bartlett Publishers.

Gigerenzer, G., & Goldstein, D. G. (1996). Reasoning the fast and frugal way: Models of bounded rationality. *Psychological Review*, 103, 650–669.

Gigerenzer, G., & Hoffrage, U. (1995). How to improve Bayesian reasoning without instruction: Frequency formats. *Psychological Review*, 102, 684–704.

Gigerenzer, G., Todd, P. M., & the ABC Research Group (Eds.) (1999). *Simple heuristics that make us smart.* New York: Oxford University Press.

Green, L., & Mehr, D. R. (1997). What alters physicians' decisions to admit to the coronary care unit? *The Journal of Family Practice*, 45(3), 219–226.

Hoffrage, U., & Gigerenzer, G. (1998). Using natural frequencies to improve diagnostic inferences. *Academic Medicine*, 73(5), 538–540.

Hoffrage, U., Gigerenzer, G., Krauss, S., & Martignon, L. (2002). Representation facilitates reasoning: What natural frequencies are and what they are not. *Cognition*, 84, 343–352.

Hoffrage, U., Krauss, S., Martignon, L., & Gigerenzer, G. (2015). Natural frequencies improve Bayesian reasoning in simple and complex tasks. *Frontiers in Psychology*, 6(1473), 1–14.

Hoffrage, U., Lindsey, S., Hertwig, R., & Gigerenzer, G. (2000). Communicating statistical information. *Science*, 290, 2261–2262.

Laskey, K. B., & Martignon, L. (2014). Comparing fast and frugal trees and Bayesian networks for risk assessment. In K. Makar, B. de Sousa, & R. Gould (Eds.), *Sustainability in statistics education. Proceedings of the Ninth International Conference on Teaching Statistics (ICOTS9, July 2014), Flagstaff, Arizona, USA .* Voorburg, The Netherlands: International Statistical Institute.

Luan, S., Schooler, L. J., & Gigerenzer, G. (2011). A signal detection analysis of fast-and-frugal trees. *Psychological Review*, 118, 316–338.

Martignon, L., & Hoffrage, U. (2002). Fast, frugal, and fit: Simple heuristics for paired comparison. *Theory and Decision*, 52(1): 29–71.

Martignon, L., & Hoffrage, U. (2019). Wer wagt, gewinnt? Göttingen: Hogrefe.

Martignon, L., Vitouch, O., Takezawa, M., & Forster, M. (2003). Naive and yet enlightened: from natural frequencies to fast and frugal trees. In D. Hardman & L. Macchi (Eds.), *Thinking: Psychological perspectives on reasoning, judgment, and decision making*, (pp. 189–211). Chichester: Wiley.

Simon, H. (1973). The structure of ill-structured problems. *Artificial Intelligence*, 4, 181–201.

Simon, H. (1996). *The sciences of the artificial* (3rd edn). Cambridge, MA: MIT Press.

Stenning, K., Martignon, L., & Varga, A. (2017). Probability-free judgment: Integrating fast and frugal heuristics with a logic of interpretation. *Decision*, 4(3), 136–158.

Von Neumann, J. (1958). *The computer and the brain.* New Haven, CT: Yale University Press.

Woike, J. K., Hoffrage, U., & Martignon, L. (2017). Integrating and testing natural frequencies, naïve Bayes, and fast-and-frugal trees. *Decision*, 4(4), 234–260.

9

BOUNDED KNOWLEDGE

Cristina Bicchieri and Giacomo Sillari

Introduction

As is well known, there exists a chasm between the picture of perfect rationality on which modern mainstream economics is largely built, and the limited abilities in reasoning and decision making displayed by real agents. Herbert Simon's groundbreaking work (e.g., Simon, 1947; 1955; 1957) pioneered research on *bounded rationality*. At its outset, bounded rationality was a fundamental theme in the study of administrative and organizational behavior (Simon, 1947). After its inception, the study of boundedly rational agency has flourished in a variety of areas. In decision theory, the momentous conceptual shift is from focusing on a normative theory of optimal behavior to focusing on a descriptive theory of *satisficing* behavior (Simon, 1955). In satisficing, instead of maximizing her expected utility, a boundedly rational agent chooses by using a heuristic process: (1) fix *aspiration levels* for relevant variables; (2) scan possible outcomes until she identifies one that goes over her aspiration level; (3) choose accordingly.[1] Simon (1967) claims that satisficing is closer to the way in which actual human agents make their decisions, and his descriptive approach to theorizing decision making has become central to the work of behavioral economics. Instead, in neoclassical economics, the theory assumes, as Simon puts it, an "Olympian," perfect rationality of agents. Neoclassical agents are *perfect reasoners* who invariably come up with an ideal, canonical, objective representation of the decision space, and are able to perform the computationally demanding calculations leading to a choice of action that maximizes their expected utility. In order to do so, agents are required to be able to perform sophisticated logical, mathematical, and probabilistic reasoning. While common sense indicates that human agents are not able to perform such calculations, experimental evidence shows moreover that human agents (1) are persistently biased in their reasoning abilities, and (2) use, instead of probability calculus, a variety of heuristics. Heuristics may allow agents to deviate from the rationality canon and yet achieve satisficing, if suboptimal outcomes (see, e.g., Simon, 1972).

Ideal agents, however, are not only assumed to be perfect in their treatment of probabilistic reasoning. Their *logical thinking* is also supposed to be carried out flawlessly, which, of course, is descriptively untenable. Famously, the Wason Selection Task indicates that human logical abilities are highly context-dependent and their results often questionable (Wason,

DOI: 10.4324/9781315658353-10

1966). In this chapter, we look at such limitations with regards to the agents' *logical* abilities or, more generally speaking, limitations to their *epistemic rationality*.[2] There are, of course, many different ways to model such limitations, even though, with few exceptions, logicians have not been particularly interested in providing descriptively adequate representations of human logical thinking.[3] Here we will explore one possible avenue to represent *bounded epistemic rationality*. The idea, in a nutshell, is that subjects display different levels of *access* to items of knowledge and belief. Beliefs that are accessible can be explicitly held and possibly used in the agent's reasoning. Beliefs to which an agent has no access are only implicitly held and are not used in her explicit reasoning.[4]

Awareness and accessibility

In the remainder of this chapter we will look at a formal proposal to characterize differential access to information but, before we offer a formalization, it should be clear that differential accessibility is a descriptively relevant notion for behavioral economics and the characterization of bounded rationality: Bounded knowledge, as based on accessibility, is a crucial component of bounded rationality. Indeed, in his Nobel lecture, Kahneman (2003) depicts accessibility as a crucial notion for behavioral economics. The dual process theory defended by Kahneman rests on accounts of accessibility: "The core concept of the present analysis of intuitive judgments and preferences is *accessibility* – the ease with which particular mental contents come to mind" (Kahneman, 2003, p. 452). In particular, our System 1, intuitive, "fast" thinking and reasoning are characterized by accessibility. Various items affect accessibility and hence influence our intuitive reasoning: among them stimulus salience, selective attention, and response activation. The list is not exhaustive and, as Kahneman acknowledges, we do not have a full-fledged theory of accessibility. That does not mean that the notion of accessibility is not a powerful one for explanatory work. For instance, prospect theory—in which agents evaluate their possible decisions on the basis of prospects of gains and losses rather than on the expected utility associated with outcomes—is based on the observation that changes and differences are psychologically more salient, and hence more accessible, than absolute levels of stimulation. Combined with the dual process reasoning theory, the notion of accessibility explains phenomena, such as heuristics, framing effects, and risk attitudes in decision making. For example, when it comes to *framing*—the violation of rational choice theory such that decision makers tend to make different choices in non-transparently equivalent decision problems—accessibility, linked to the higher salience of differential characteristics in the description of a decision problem, influences preference, leading to different choices in equivalent settings. A cognitive effort could be made (and indeed, when it is done, it tends to succeed in reducing framing effects) to provide a canonical representation of decision problems that would transparently reveal equivalences and hence lead to same choices in equivalent decision problems. In its absence, however, decision makers are left with the vagaries of the influence exerted by contextual cues.

Even in the realm of logical reasoning, one can see accessibility at work. Take, for instance, the well-known asymmetry in providing a successful solution to the Wason's Selection Task in its abstract formulation and in a concrete formulation in which participants are asked to identify a cheater (Cox & Griggs, 1982). The latter version has a much higher rate of successful solutions, which can be readily explained by observing that formal logical rules have, in general, less accessibility than concrete "cheating-discovery module" rules (Cosmides, 1989; Cosmides & Tooby, 1989).

Representing knowledge and belief

To precisely characterize the link between accessibility and reasoning, we now confine our attention to epistemic rationality, rather than full-fledged logical deductions. The formal framework in which we propose to implement the distinction between accessible and inaccessible items of knowledge is *epistemic logic*. Epistemic logic encodes the mathematical representation of knowledge and belief. It was pioneered by Jaakko Hintikka in the 1960s, then revived by the interest of both economists and computer scientists in the 1980s and today is thriving at the intersection of disciplines like philosophy, economics, informatics, and cognitive science.

The basic idea behind formal representations of knowledge and belief is to give a semantics of such notions in terms of *possible worlds* that may or may not be *epistemically possible* for the agents. Each world validates a certain set of atomic propositions. An agent is said to *know* a given proposition at world w_1 if it holds true in all possible worlds that are epistemically possible for that agent from w_1.

Let us illustrate this key notion with a simple example (van Benthem, 2008): Ann, Bob, and Carol receive one card each from a set comprising one red, one white, and one blue card. They can see what card they have been dealt, but they cannot tell which card the other kids hold. We can represent the relevant worlds by the initials of the cards distributed to Ann, Bob, and Carol, respectively. For instance, BWR is the world in which Ann has the blue card, Bob the white card, and Carol the red card. Atoms have the form b_{Ann}, meaning that Ann holds the blue card. b_{Ann} is true in both BWR and BRW and only in those two possible worlds. Thus, for instance, Ann cannot distinguish between BWR and BRW. We can schematically represent the model M as follows, representing Ann's accessibility relation with solid lines, Bob's with dotted lines and Carol's with dashed lines (and omitting reflexive arrows) (Figure 9.1).

It is now easy to answer questions about what players know about each other. For instance: at BWR, does Ann know that Bob has the white card? She does not, since both BWR and BRW are epistemically accessible for her, and Bob has white in one state but red in the other. However, she knows that Carol does not have blue, since both in BWR and BRW, b_{Ann} holds. More complex propositions can be tested: does Bob know that Ann does not know that Bob has white? From BWR, Bob accesses BWR and RWB. At BWR Ann doesn't know b_{Bob}. From RWB, Ann accesses RBW and RWB, and she does not know that b_{Bob} either. So at all worlds accessible from BWR for Bob, Ann doesn't know b_{Bob}. Hence Bob knows that Ann doesn't know that Bob holds blue.

Knowledge and belief are distinguished in the language by imposing different axiomatic constraints. For instance, it is customary to accept the veridicality axiom[5] for knowledge (where $K\varphi$ stands for "the agent *knows* φ"):[6]

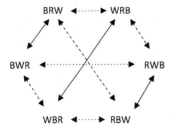

Figure 9.1 A representation of the knowledge states of three agents in terms of possible worlds and epistemic accessibility relations

$$(T) \ K\varphi \rightarrow \varphi.$$

In English, the axiom ensures that if an agent knows φ, then φ must be true. Instead of assuming veridicality, accounts of belief impose a weaker axiomatic constraint (where $B\varphi$ stands for "the agent *believes* φ"):

$$(B) \ B\varphi \rightarrow \neg B\neg\varphi.$$

Axiom (B) makes sure that beliefs are consistent, that is if an agent believes φ, then the agent does not believe its negation. These kinds of axiomatic constraints translate into structural properties of possible worlds semantics. For instance, veridicality entails that the accessibility relation be reflexive, as the agent must be able to see that φ holds at the world she is at. Veridicality is not the only property of knowledge and belief posited by epistemic logicians. Both positive and negative introspective axioms such as

$$(4) \ K\varphi \rightarrow KK\varphi$$

and

$$(5) \ \neg K\varphi \rightarrow K\neg K\varphi$$

are required. Axiom (4) says that agents know what they know, while the Socratic agent of axiom (5), if she does not know something, knows that she does not know it. These axioms, along with a few others, ensure that the accessibility relation on the set of possible worlds is an equivalence relation. This in turn entails that the accessibility relation induces a partition of the space of possible worlds, in fact, it establishes the equivalence between possible worlds models favored by philosophers and partitional models used in economics to model agents' knowledge and information. This approach to modeling knowledge and belief was proven to be extremely fruitful in economics and computer science alike, generating relevant philosophical debates as well.

While partitional models of this kind are widely used in economics or computer science applications, they present a problem, as they entail several forms of so-called *logical omniscience*: Agents are, by construction, supposed to have unrealistic logical, epistemic, and doxastic abilities.[7] In a certain sense, logical omniscience reveals that modeling epistemic agents in this formal framework is akin to endowing them with "Olympian epistemic rationality." Indeed, a structural axiom characterizing both knowledge and belief is

$$(K) \ K(\varphi \rightarrow \varphi') \rightarrow K\varphi \ \& \ K\varphi'.$$

Combining (K) and the axioms of propositional logic, epistemic systems entail that agents' knowledge is closed under logical consequence. Hence, for instance, given basic knowledge of the axioms of arithmetic, an agent is supposed to grasp all theorems logically deducible from them, and know whether an old unsolved problem such as Goldbach's conjecture[8] is true. But this particular epistemic property (closure under logical implication) represents only one facet of the so-called problem of *logical omniscience*. That is to say, epistemic logic is an adequate representation of agent's epistemic reasoning only if we accept unrealistic idealizations but not so if we are trying to model realistic agents. The problem was already apparent to Jaakko Hintikka in his seminal 1962 monograph *Knowledge and Belief* (Hintikka, 1962). His clever yet partial way out was to distinguish two senses of "knowledge": a *weak* sense, in which knowledge stands simply for *information*, and a *strong* sense, in which knowledge is information held by the agent by virtue of some kind of justification.[9] Thus, the semantic characterization of knowledge described above would in fact be a characterization of *information*, while knowledge proper would consist of items of information that are entertained (that is, *accessed*) by the agent in some relevant (epistemological or perhaps psychological) sense.[10] Thus, epistemic logic offers a powerful tool to formally and mathematically (set-theoretically) characterize the epistemic characteristics and reasoning of agents, yet the characterization is flawed in the same sense in which the characterization of rational agents in economics is flawed. The agents populating epistemic logic models, just like the agents populating microeconomic models, are perfect (logical) reasoners: They know all tautologies, they know all the consequences of what they know, and so on. In a word, their knowledge is *unbounded*. Can we nevertheless provide a characterization of *bounded knowledge* retaining the useful framework of epistemic logic?

Newell on knowledge representation

A suggestion on the direction where to look for an answer to the question above was offered by Allen Newell, one of Herbert Simon's most important co-authors in the field of Artificial Intelligence. In the "cognitive revolution" that took place in the 1950s and 1960s, the attention of psychologists moved from a basic, neural level of analysis based on stimulus-response, to a higher, symbolic level of analysis of cognitive architectures. In the first presidential address to the American Association for Artificial Intelligence, Newell (1982) points out that there is a further, higher level of analysis for cognitive systems. He calls it the *knowledge* level and in describing its characteristics points at the answer we are looking for.

An intelligent system, in the functional view of agency endorsed by Newell, is embedded in an action-oriented environment. The system's activity consists in the process from a perceptual component (that inputs task statements and information), through a representation module (that represents tasks and information as data structures), to a goal structure (the solution to the given task statement). In this picture, knowledge is perceived from the external world, and stored as it is represented in data structures.[11] Newell claims that there is a distinction between knowledge and its representation, in a way that is similar to the difference that there is between the symbolic level of a computer system and the physical implementation supporting the symbolic manipulation. More precisely, in a computer system, Newell defines a *level* as consisting of four general elements: (1) a medium (which is to be processed); (2) components together with laws of composition; (3) a system; and (4) determining the behavior of the system, laws of behavior. Different levels are determined by different elements. For instance, at the *symbolic* level, we can describe a computer system through the following elements: The medium is given by the content of computer memories, the components and their laws of composition are symbols and their syntax, while the laws of behavior are given by the semantics of the logical operators. Below the symbolic level we can describe a computer system at the *logical* level of its circuits and devices. Here the medium is bit vectors, components and composition are given by functional units (logical gates, etc.) in the processing chip, and laws of behavior are given by logical operations. We could descend to describing a system at lower level, reducing the description all the way to the physical level. Or, we could ascend, from the symbolic level, to describing the system at a higher level, what Newell calls the *knowledge level*.

At the *knowledge level*, the system is the agent; the components are goals, actions, and bodies of knowledge; the medium is knowledge, and the behavioral rule is rationality. Notice that the symbolic level constitutes the level of representation. Hence, since every level is describable in terms of the next lower level, knowledge can be represented through symbolic systems. But can we provide a description of the knowledge level without resorting to the level of representation? It turns out that we can, although we only can if we do not decouple knowledge and action. In particular, says Newell, "it is unclear in what sense [systems lacking rationality] can be said to have knowledge" (Newell, 1982, p. 100), where "rationality" stands for "principles of action." Indeed, an *agent*, at the knowledge level, is but a set of actions, bodies of knowledge, and a set of goals, rather independently of whether the agent has any physical implementation.

What, then, is *knowledge?* Knowledge, according to Newell, is whatever can be ascribed to an agent, such that the observed behavior of the agent gets to be explained (that is, computed) according to the laws of behavior encoded in the principle of rationality. The principle of rationality appears to be unqualified: "If an agent has knowledge that one of its actions will lead to one of his goals, then the agent will select that action" (Newell, 1982, p. 102). Thus, the definition of knowledge is a procedural one: an *observer* notices the action undertaken by the agent; given that the observer is familiar with the agent's goals and its rationality, the observer can therefore infer what knowledge the agent must possess. Knowledge is not defined *structurally*, for example, as physical objects, symbols standing for them and their specific properties and relations. Knowledge is rather defined *functionally* as what mediates the behavior of the agent and the principle of rationality governing the agent's actions. Can we not sever the bond between knowledge and action by providing, for example, a characterization of knowledge in terms of a physical structure corresponding to it? As Newell explains,

> The answer in a nutshell is that knowledge of the world cannot be captured in a finite structure ... Knowledge as a structure must contain at least as much variety as the set of all truths (i.e. propositions) that the agent can respond to.
>
> *Newell, 1982, p. 107*

Hence, knowledge cannot be captured in a finite physical structure, and can only be considered in its functional relation with action.

Thus, (a version of) the problem of logical omniscience presents itself when it comes to describing the epistemic aspect of an intelligent system. Ideally (at the knowledge level), the body of knowledge an agent is equipped with is unbounded, hence knowledge cannot be represented in a physical system. However, recall from above how a level of interpretation of the intelligent system *is* reducible to the next lower level. Knowledge should therefore be reducible to the level of symbols. This implies that the symbolic level necessarily encompasses only a portion of the unbounded body of knowledge that the agent possesses.

The interesting question is then: In what way does an agent extract representation from knowledge? Or, in other terms: Given the *definition* of representation above, what can its *theory* be? Building a theory of representation involves building a theory of access, to explain how agents manage to extract limited, explicit knowledge (working knowledge, representation) from their unbounded implicit knowledge. The crucial idea is that agents do so "intelligently," i.e., by judging what is relevant to the task at hand. Such a judgment, in turn, depends on the principle of rationality. Hence, knowledge and action cannot be decoupled and knowledge cannot be entirely represented at the symbolic level, since it involves both structures and *processes*. Logics, as they are "one class of representations ... uniquely fitted to the analysis of knowledge and representation" seem to be suitable for such an endeavor. In particular, epistemic logics, in which the notion of *access* can be built in, in order to achieve the distinction between (unbounded) knowledge and its (limited) representation, are natural candidates for axiomatizing theories of explicit knowledge representation. If we understand that human agents may fail to display unbounded rationality, then the bounds to an agent's knowledge depend essentially on the way accessibility displays itself in behavior, that is through phenomena like selective attention, priming, salience, and so on, resulting in biased judgments and choices.

Models of (un)awareness

In the case of Allen Newell's analysis of agency at the knowledge level, knowledge *representation* (readily available to the agent) is distinguished by knowledge *tout court* in that it consists of the latter *plus* some form of *access* to it. The slogan, by Newell, is thus:

Representation = Knowledge + Access.

How can we incorporate the issue of accessibility into the fabric of epistemic logic? An answer comes again from computer science. Fagin and Halpern (1988) proposed a *logic of awareness* in which the picture of knowledge as based on access finds a precise formalization. In their logic, there are three operators pertaining to issues epistemic: (1) an implicit knowledge operator, which behaves in the standard way illustrated above; (2) an awareness operator, which has in its scope formulas to which the agent has access to; and (3) an explicit knowledge operator, which represents the realistic notion of knowledge we are interested in and that, intuitively, is used for those items of implicit knowledge to which the agent has access or, in Fagin and Halpern's language, of which she has awareness.

The idea of introducing a function that filters an agent's unbounded knowledge to distill those items of knowledge she is in fact actively entertaining represents a first step toward the explicit introduction of context representation in logical formalisms. Technically, the intuition is that the juncture where issues of accessibility become prominent is the linguistic representation of propositions; hence the language distinguishes formulas an agent is aware of (i.e., those she has access to) and those she is not aware of. At the semantic level, each world is associated with an "awareness set," representing the propositions to which the agent has access. Implicit knowledge is defined as usual, while explicit knowledge is yielded, syntactically, by the conjunction of implicit knowledge and awareness while, semantically, the truth conditions for an agent to explicitly know φ at w hold if and only if she implicitly knows φ and φ belongs to the agent's awareness set at w.

Awareness logics are versatile, in that various properties of awareness can be axiomatically included in the system. A kind of awareness (particularly favored by economists) is the so-called awareness as generated by primitive propositions. In these systems, a subset of the set of *atoms* in the language is specified, and agents are aware of all (and only) those formulas that mention atoms from the relevant subset.[12] In the economic literature, attempts to model agent's awareness information go back to Modica and Rustichini (1994, 1999). At first, following the lead of Geanakoplos (1989, 1992), they attempted to model awareness in standard structures by dropping the negative introspection axiom and positing that $A\varphi \leftrightarrow (K\varphi \vee \neg K\neg K\varphi)$, or that an agent is aware of φ iff they know φ or, if they do not, when they ignore that they do not know φ. However, Dekel, Lipman, and Rustichini (1998) show that the standard approach trivializes awareness (either if an agent has access to one formula, she has access to all formulas or she has access to no formulas at all), and Modica and Rustichini (1999) came up with a non-standard approach introducing the notion that agents have access to a (possibly proper) subset of the set of all atoms in the language. Halpern (2001) shows that their approach, although lacking an implicit knowledge operator, is equivalent to a special case of the epistemic logic of awareness introduced by Fagin and Halpern (1988).[13]

An application to strategic reasoning

Limits to epistemic rationality are readily understood as deviations from the standards of rationality and, as such, taken to be undesirable or in violation of the normative requirements of such standards. In fact, one can question (Mercier & Sperber, 2011) the normativity of the standards, one can find (Rips, 2011) discrepancies between the standards and actual behavior, or one can find examples of theories in which limited knowledge provides a more realistic behavioral model. One such example comes from game theory and has to do with the problem of backward induction (Bicchieri & Antonelli, 1995, for a different yet related "logical" approach to the problem, see Bonanno, 1991).

Any extensive game of perfect information can be solved by backwards induction (BI). However, this solution concepts runs into difficulties were a deviation from the equilibrium path to occur. For instance, let us say that the backward-induction equilibrium involves a move by player 1 ending the game at the first node, and yet player 2 finds herself to play at the second node. That means that player 1 has deviated from the equilibrium path, and therefore that he has acted not rationally. What should player 2 do now? She cannot choose an action under the assumption that player 1 is rational, since, were player 1 in fact rational, player 2 would not have had to choose an action in the first place! Hence the assumption of rationality (and of common knowledge thereof) has to be revised, since it leads to the paradoxical conclusion that player 2 should not be called into play at all (Bicchieri, 1989). This means that when a player finds herself off the equilibrium path, she cannot assume the rationality of the other player (otherwise she would not have found herself in a deviation in the first place) and hence she lacks the ability to choose an action at an off-equilibrium node. Bicchieri and Antonelli (1995) point out that this difficulty lies at the meta-language level. The analysis of BI deviations requires: (1) the ability to reason counterfactually (since rational players do not deviate and rationality is commonly known); and (2) a theory of belief revision (since the fact that a deviation has occurred requires a reassessment of the rationality assumptions made so far). The difficulties do not appear, however, at the level of *local* decision making, as agents can be endowed with a minimal theory of the game that is sufficient to compute the BI solution starting from any node and does not come with global rationality assumptions.

Such a "modular" or "sequential" theory of the game belongs to agents whose epistemic access is limited. Epistemic access is bounded to the analysis of future nodes, while previous nodes (and possible deviations occurred thereof) remain inaccessible to players' theories. Bicchieri and Antonelli, thus, propose to adopt a dual point of view in the analysis of backward induction: the theorist's and the players'. The game theorist's view is a bird's-eye perspective on the totality of the game that does not involve sequential or modular rationality. Since the analysis of backwards induction involves paradoxical reasoning about nodes that are not reached in equilibrium (see, e.g., Bicchieri, 1989, 1997), a theory that involves global rationality has to be equipped with logical tools to cope with counterfactual reasoning and belief revision (Bicchieri, 1988). The players' theories, on the other hand, make assumptions about rationality at a node and at subsequent nodes, while history of previous play (and hence possible deviations off equilibrium, and the need for counterfactual analysis and belief revision stemming from those deviations) are not part of the theory. Bicchieri and Antonelli suggest that the logical formalisms of the two theories be distinct. A way to understand the distinction is to put to work the notion of *bounded knowledge* analyzed in this chapter and presume that players only have epistemic access, and thus full belief, to a subset of rationality ascriptions, the accessible subset being maximal at the root of the tree while shrinking as nodes get closer to the leaves of the game tree.

Conclusion

In this chapter we have looked at a specific aspect of bounded rationality: limits to human logical abilities and, in particular, limits to the way real agents reason about knowledge. In principle, infinite, human knowledge is necessarily bounded and we argued here that a useful way to understand its limits is differential accessibility. We applied the notion to the case of the backwards induction solution concept, yet once we accept the link between bounded knowledge and accessibility, many more applications become relevant. Besides the rather abstract ones mentioned above, bounded knowledge becomes relevant, for instance, when it comes to explaining the great variability of behavior observed in many experiments in response to slight situational variations (Bicchieri, 2006:46). Differential awareness elicits different behavioral norms, and hence considerations about bounded knowledge, once the static framework offered here is supplemented with suitable dynamics, can be extremely helpful in order to promote behavior change through social norm change (Bicchieri, 2016).

Notes

1 Satisficing, introduced conceptually by Simon (1947) and developed more formally in Simon (1955) has been studied subsequently, in particular, by Sauermann and Selten (1962) and more recently by Güth and collaborators (see, for a general account, Güth, 2010, or for a specific application, Güth et al., 2008).

2 For a discussion highlighting the relevance of epistemic rationality in game theory and in economics, see Bicchieri (1997), Chapter 3. In game theory, epistemic rationality deals with ways to achieve concordant beliefs leading to choosing a Nash solution (e.g., *tracing procedure*; Harsanyi & Selten, 1988, or *rational deliberation*; Skyrms, 1990). In this sense, epistemic rationality involves procedural or substantive instances of belief change, be it in terms of Bayesian upgrading, or in terms of belief revision. More generally, epistemic rationality is ascribable to an agent that entertains and believes propositions for which she has good evidence, and avoids believing those for which she does not, changing her belief in light of new evidence. For a philosophical analysis and argument in favor of the distinction between practical and epistemic rationality, see Kelly (2003).

3 The road to a deeper exploration of the psychological foundations of human thought has also been followed in the fields of logic and probability, whereas very few attempts have been made to modify the axioms of these two theories in order to predict the real behavior of individuals. For instance, Pei Wang (2001) gives an explanation of the phenomenon in terms of his non-Aristotelian NARS inference system. Another important program is based on the work of Lance Rips (1995; 2011), who developed cognitive models for deductive reasoning, such as the so-called PSYCOP, short for "Psychology of Proof" (Rips, 2008) based on assumptions about reasoners' memory, mastery of inference rules and control on specific proof processes. The model is validated empirically by comparing its "deductive abilities" with those of human, boundedly rational, laboratory experiment participants, showing that there is a significant match in the results of the deductions carried over by PSYCOP and by human reasoners. Or, for a view from the field of cognitive psychology, see Stenning and Van Lambalgen (2008). For descriptively adequate logical systems that try to account for observable behavior but are not necessarily based on psychological processes, see Balbiani et al. (2016) and Solaki et al. (2019). This contribution is intended as a step in such a direction.

4 While there is some overlap between the notion of implicit and *tacit* knowledge, it is important to stress that the two notions are quite different. For instance, explicit and implicit knowledge, in the literature we consider here, differ as a matter of an agent's accessibility (the former is accessible, the latter is not), while the definition tacit knowledge, since Polanyi's fundamental contribution (Polanyi, 1967), does not hinge on accessibility. In fact, tacit knowledge can be perfectly accessible but not readily codifiable, or transmissible, or learnable (see e.g., Howells, 1996).

5 Customarily, in epistemic logic the veridicality axiom is axiom T (for truth). Axiom B characterizes belief, while axioms 4 and 5 characterize the introspective abilities of agents.

6 We confine our argument to the single agent case. Formally, it can be generalized straightforwardly, although adding interactions and group epistemic operators need not be neutral in more substantive implications. Considering such implications rests beyond the scope of this chapter. In general, for an introduction to epistemic logic and application, the reader is referred to Fagin et al. (2004) or van Benthem (2011).

7 Notice that the problem of logical omniscience applies to both epistemic (knowledge-representing) and doxastic (belief-representing) systems. To see this, notice that some of the issues pertaining to logical omniscience depend on the fact that the semantic structures validating the axioms are partitional. But

both epistemic and doxastic semantics are based on partitional structure, one main difference being that in epistemic structures agents are never mistaken about the position of the actual world, while in doxastic structures, validating axiom (B) but not axiom (T), we allow agents to be "mistaken" about which one is the actual state of affairs. Besides the possibility of mistakes, agents are still fully omniscient, e.g., they believe in all the logical consequences of their, possibly mistaken, beliefs.

8 The claim that any integer greater than 2 is the sum of two prime numbers.

9 For a philosophical discussion of the distinction, see Sillari (2006). Artemov develops (in Artemov and Kuznets, 2009, and elsewhere) a logic of justified knowledge.

10 It is interesting to note that, though not at all based on psychological evidence, Hintikka's argument in several places appeals to intuitions recoverable among ordinary language users (e.g., validity was rethought of as "immunity from certain standards of criticism").

11 While we follow here Newell (1982), where the subject is artificial agents, this account of agency is neutral regarding its object: it can be artificial agents, as it can be human agents. As Newell (1994) points out:

> to claim that humans can be described at the knowledge level is to claim there is a way of formulating them as agents that have knowledge and goals, such that their behavior is successfully predicted by the law that says: all the person's knowledge is always used to attain the goals of the person.

Notice that this entails that knowledge is always functional. One can think of seemingly non-instrumental knowledge that, however, does play (tacitly, maybe) an instrumental role, for instance, a signaling one.

12 Clearly, these systems are still a heroic idealization of agents' deductive capabilities, since the agent is fully logical omniscient relative to the subset of the language of which the agent is aware. Thus, such models are perhaps seen as models of *un*awareness rather than awareness.

13 There are many other attempts to characterize (un)awareness. Heifetz et al. (2006) characterize it in set-theoretic terms, Sillari (2008a), in first-order logic, Halpern and Rêgo (2009) in second-order epistemic logic and several applications indicate the relevance of the notion, for instance, when it comes to Lewis's theory of convention (Sillari, 2005; 2008b), no-trade theorems (Heifetz et al., 2013), dynamic models (van Benthem and Velàzquez-Quesada, 2010; Hill, 2010; Karni and Vierø, 2013), its relation with inductive reasoning (Grant and Quiggin, 2013). A utility-based approach cognate to the idea of awareness as capturing differential access is developed by Golman and Loewenstein (2015).

References

Artemov, S., & Kuznets, R. (2009). Logical omniscience as a computational complexity problem. In *Proceedings of the 12th Conference on Theoretical Aspects of Rationality and Knowledge* (pp. 14–23). ACM.

Balbiani, P., Fernández-Duque, D., & Lorini, E. (2016). A logical theory of belief dynamics for resource-bounded agents. In *Proceedings of the 2016 International Conference on Autonomous Agents & Multiagent Systems* (pp. 644–652). International Foundation for Autonomous Agents and Multiagent Systems.

Bicchieri, C. (1988). Strategic behavior and counterfactuals. *Synthese*, 76, 135–169.

Bicchieri, C. (1989). Self-refuting theories of strategic interaction: A paradox of common knowledge. *Erkenntnis*, 30, 69–85.

Bicchieri, C. (1997). *Rationality and coordination*. Cambridge: Cambridge University Press.

Bicchieri, C. (2006). *The grammar of society: The nature and dynamics of social norms*. Cambridge: Cambridge University Press.

Bicchieri, C. (2016). *Norms in the wild: How to diagnose, measure, and change social norms*. Oxford: Oxford University Press.

Bicchieri, C., & Antonelli, G. A. (1995). Game-theoretic axioms for local rationality and bounded knowledge. *Journal of Logic, Language and Information*, 4(2), 145–167.

Bonanno, G. (1991). Extensive forms and set-theoretic forms. *Economics Letters*, 37(4), 363–370.

Cosmides, L. (1989). The logic of social exchange: Has natural selection shaped how humans reason? Studies with the Wason selection task. *Cognition*, 31(3), 187–276.

Cosmides, L., & Tooby, J. (1989). Evolutionary psychology and the generation of culture, Part II: Case study: A computational theory of social exchange. *Ethology and Sociobiology*, 10(1–3), 51–97.

Cox, J. R., & Griggs, R. A. (1982). The effects of experience on performance in Wason's selection task. *Memory & Cognition*, 10(5), 496–502.

Dekel, E., Lipman B. L., & Rustichini A. (1998). Standard state-space models preclude unawareness. *Econometrica*, 66(1), 159–173.

Fagin, R., & Halpern J. (1988). Belief, awareness and limited reasoning. *Artificial Intelligence*, 34(1), 39–76.

Fagin, R., Halpern, J. Y., Moses, Y., & Vardi, M. (2004). *Reasoning about knowledge.* Cambridge, MA: MIT Press.

Geanakoplos, J. (1989). Game theory without partitions, and applications to speculation and consensus. Cowles Foundation Discussion Paper.

Geanakoplos, J. (1992). Common knowledge, Bayesian learning and market speculation with bounded rationality. *Journal of Economic Perspectives*, 6, 58–82.

Golman, R., & Loewenstein, G. (2015). An information-gap framework for capturing preferences about uncertainty. In *Proceedings of the 15th conference on theoretical aspects of rationality and knowledge*. Available at: www.cmu.edu/dietrich/sds/docs/golman/Information-Gap Framework Golman...

Grant, S., & Quiggin, J. (2013). Inductive reasoning about unawareness. *Economic Theory*, 54(3), 717–755.

Güth, W. (2010). Satisficing and (un)bounded rationality: A formal definition and its experimental validity. *Journal of Economic Behavior & Organization*, 73(3), 308–316.

Güth, W., Levati, M. V., & Ploner, M. (2008). Is satisficing absorbable? An experimental study. *The Journal of Behavioral Finance*, 9(2), 95–105.

Halpern, J. (2001). Alternative semantics for unawareness. *Games and Economic Behavior*, 37(2), 321–339.

Halpern, J. Y., & Rêgo, L. C. (2009). Reasoning about knowledge of unawareness. *Games and Economic Behavior*, 67(2), 503–525.

Harsanyi, J. C., & Selten, R. (1988). *A general theory of equilibrium selection in games.* Cambridge, MA: MIT Press.

Heifetz, A., Meier, M., & Schipper, B. C. (2006). Interactive unawareness. *Journal of Economic Theory*, 130(1), 78–94.

Heifetz, A., Meier, M., & Schipper, B. C. (2013). Unawareness, beliefs, and speculative trade. *Games and Economic Behavior*, 77(1), 100–121.

Hill, B. (2010). Awareness dynamics. *Journal of Philosophical Logic*, 39(2), 113–137.

Hintikka, J. (1962). *Knowledge and belief.* Ithaca, NY: Cornell University Press

Howells, J. (1996). Tacit knowledge. *Technology Analysis & Strategic Management*, 8(2), 91–106.

Kahneman, D. (2003). Maps of bounded rationality: Psychology for behavioral economics. *American Economic Review*, 93(5), 1449–1475.

Karni, E., & Vierø, M. L. (2013). "Reverse Bayesianism": A choice-based theory of growing awareness. *American Economic Review*, 103(7), 2790–2810.

Kelly, T. (2003). Epistemic rationality as instrumental rationality: A critique. *Philosophy and Phenomenological Research*, 66(3), 612–640.

Mercier, H., & Sperber, D. (2011). Why do humans reason? Arguments for an argumentative theory. *Behavioral and Brain Sciences*, 34(2), 57–74.

Modica, S., & Rustichini, A. (1994). Awareness and partitional information structures. *Theory and Decision*, 37(1), 107–124.

Modica, S., & Rustichini, A. (1999). Unawareness and partitional information structures. *Games and Economic Behavior*, 27(2), 265–298.

Newell, A. (1982). The knowledge level. *Artificial Intelligence*, 18(1).

Newell, A. (1994). *Unified theories of cognition.* Cambridge, MA: Harvard University Press.

Polanyi, M. (1967/2009). *The tacit dimension.* Chicago: University of Chicago Press.

Rips, L. J. (1995). *The psychology of proof: Deductive reasoning in human thinking.* Cambridge, MA: MIT Press.

Rips, L. J. (2008). Logical approaches to human deductive reasoning. In J. E. Adler & L. J. Rips (Eds.), *Reasoning: Studies of human inference and its foundation* (pp. 187–205). Cambridge: Cambridge University Press.

Rips, L. J. (2011). *Lines of thought: Central concepts in cognitive psychology.* Oxford: Oxford University Press.

Sauermann, H., & Selten, R. (1962). Anspruchsanpassungstheorie der Unternehmung. *Zeitschrift für die gesamte Staatswissenschaft/Journal of Institutional and Theoretical Economics*, 4, 577–597.

Sillari, G. (2005). A logical framework for convention. *Synthese*, 147(2), 379–400.

Sillari, G. (2006). Models of awareness. In G. Bonanno, W. van der Hoek, & M. Wooldridge (Eds.), *Logic and the foundations of game and decision theory* (pp. 209–240). Amsterdam: Amsterdam University Press,.

Sillari, G. (2008a). Quantified logic of awareness and impossible possible worlds. *Review of Symbolic Logic*, 1(4), 1–16.

Sillari, G. (2008b). Common knowledge and convention. *Topoi*, 27(1), 29–40.

Simon, H. A. (1947). *Administrative behavior*. New York: The Macmillan Company.

Simon, H. A. (1955). A behavioral model of rational choice. *Quarterly Journal of Economics*, 69, 99–118.

Simon, H. A. (1957). *Models of man*. New York: Wiley.

Simon, H. A. (1967). Motivational and emotional controls of cognition. *Psychological Review*, 74(1), 29–39.

Simon, H. A. (1972). Theories of bounded rationality. *Decision and Organization*, 1(1), 161–176.

Skyrms, B. (1990). *The dynamics of rational deliberation*. Cambridge, MA: Harvard University Press.

Solaki, A., Berto, F., & Smets, S. (2019). The logic of fast and slow thinking. *Erkenntnis*. June.

Stenning, K., & van Lambalgen, M. (2008). *Human reasoning and cognitive science*. Cambridge, MA: MIT Press.

van Benthem, J. (2008). Logic and reasoning: Do the facts matter? *Studia Logica*, 88, 67–84, special issue, "Psychologism in Logic?," edited by H. Leitgeb.

van Benthem, J. (2011). *Logical dynamics of information and interaction*. Cambridge: Cambridge University Press.

van Benthem, J., & Velázquez-Quesada, F. R. (2010). The dynamics of awareness. *Synthese*, 177(1), 5–27.

Wang, P. (2001). Wason's cards: What is wrong. In *Proceedings of the Third International Conference on Cognitive Science* (pp. 371–375).

Wason, P. C. (1966). Reasoning. In B. M. Foss (Ed.), *New horizons in psychology*. Harmondsworth: Penguin.

PART II

Cognitive misery and mental dualism

10

BOUNDED RATIONALITY, REASONING AND DUAL PROCESSING

Jonathan St. B. T. Evans

Introduction

Traditionally, philosophers distinguish between instrumental and epistemic rationality which may be defined roughly as follows:

Instrumental rationality
Acting in such a way as to achieve one's goals.
Epistemic rationality
Attaining and maintaining true beliefs.

Both concepts are slippery. Take, for example, my goals of being an Open Golf champion and the world's most famous cognitive psychologist. As I approach 70, the chance of the former had vanished more than 50 years ago, as several years of play and practice had resulted in only a middling 15 handicap. As to the latter, any realistic hope was extinguished perhaps 40 years ago. But I am surely not *irrational* for failing to achieve these goals, even if I was wildly optimistic in even contemplating them. This, of course, is what Herb Simon's *bounded rationality* is all about. We can only achieve goals that are within our capability, either as a species or as individuals. It does make the whole idea of instrumental rationality a bit messy though. What goals should we strive to attain? Only those that are fully realistic? Or should we set our sights high to reach the limits we can?

Let us take the game of chess, whose study fascinated Simon. I also love the game and in semi-retirement play a lot online and study the game, striving to improve my standard. The game is, of course intractably difficult due to the vast search space. No human can ever master it, nor will any machine we can imagine, even though they have now overtaken the best human players. Except in simplified endgame positions, or those allowing a forced win, no human or machine can be sure that it is picking the best move. None of us can optimise; so as Simon put it, in chess as in all complex decision making, we can only *satisfice* – choose moves which appear to be good enough. Unfortunately, the heuristic search methods promoted by Simon (e.g., Newell & Simon, 1972) fell by the wayside in computer AI which came to be dominated by brute force as computers acquired ever bigger memories and faster processors. Eventually, a program of this type, Deep Blue, came to beat the world champion Gary Kasparov in 1997, even if there were deep suspicions about human intervention by the IBM team at the time. Writing recently about this, Kasparov (2017) dismisses these suspicions on the grounds that the 'human-like' moves played by Deep Blue on an IBM supercomputer were replicated within a few years by chess engines available cheaply on personal computers. He had long understood that computers would eventually prevail – it was just a matter of *speed*. What is remarkable, however, is how well the best human players can compete with the current generation of programs that can search billions of chess positions before selecting a move. Significantly, Kasparov points out that this is because computers are weak in two areas where humans are strong: pattern recognition and strategic thinking.

The striking thing about the cognitive science of chess is just how *differently* computers had to be designed to play the game in order to match human ability. This shows us that the human brain, with its massively parallel architecture, has adapted to the solution of complex problems by means that do not require brute force computation. And of course, Simon was one of the first to understand the role of perception and pattern recognition in human expertise (Chase & Simon, 1973). Like machines, human players do calculate continuations and move sequences, but only a tiny fraction of what the machines do. The recognition of *which* moves deserve attention, cued by patterns learnt by long study, is what gives humans playing strength. This, of course, is an example of *dual processing* (Evans, 2008; Evans & Stanovich, 2013). These rapid recognition processes (Type 1, autonomous) greatly reduce the load of explicit calculation (Type 2, engaging working memory). If we think of rationality as depending simply on explicit calculation and reasoning, then we do our species a great disservice. Our working memories are small and slow but our capacity for implicit learning of patterns is vast. Thus, the bounds on our rationality are a lot less severe than one might imagine. Unfortunately for the human race, however, recent developments in artificial intelligence have shown that chess programs based on machine learning and pattern recognition are even better than the best of brute force engines. Reportedly, AlphaZero, originally developed to play Go but adapted for chess, taught itself to beat the world's best brute force program in just four hours (Klein, 2017)!

If instrumental rationality is a slippery concept, then so too is epistemic rationality. In fact, the psychology of reasoning has been radically reconstructed over the past 20 years, as the model handed by philosophers proved inadequate. The traditional emphasis was on the importance of logic as the basis of rational thinking (Henle, 1962; Inhelder & Piaget, 1958), which led to the foundation of the traditional study of deductive reasoning by psychologists. If you think epistemic rationality is about *truth*, then deductive reasoning is very important because it is truth-preserving. That is to say, any deductively valid conclusion is true, provided that its premises are true. How disappointing, then, when hundreds of laboratory studies showed that human adults, typically of undergraduate student level intelligence, made numerous logical errors and showed systematic cognitive biases (Evans, Newstead, & Byrne, 1993). Moreover, they were heavily influenced by the content or meaning of logical problems, which was irrelevant to their formal structure. Such findings led to a sharp rationality debate, when the philosopher Jonathan Cohen claimed that such experimental findings could not demonstrate that people were irrational (Cohen, 1981). Eventually, psychologists working this field confronted the dilemma before them: either people are inherently irrational or else there was something wrong with the paradigm they were using to study reasoning (Evans, 2002; Oaksford & Chater, 1998).

One problem is that nothing new can be learnt by deductive reasoning, which makes it a poor standard for rationality. We can form new beliefs by induction, but we cannot be sure that they are *true*. Strangely, induction has been the poor relation, with far fewer psychological studies of inductive inference carried out (Feeney & Heit, 2007). Reasoning from the particular to the general is immensely beneficial but not logically valid. Such inductions are not truth-preserving and their conclusions can only be held provisionally, or with a degree of probability pending further evidence. But how could we cope in the world without the ability to learn? Even if one takes a modular view of the human mind, dividing it into many specialised information processing systems, one must assume that many of these have the ability to learn and modify themselves with experience (Carruthers, 2006).

Those working within the 'new paradigm' in the psychology of reasoning (Elqayam & Over, 2012; Evans, 2012; Oaksford & Chater, 2013; Over, 2009) accept that people routinely use their beliefs when reasoning and allow them to draw conclusions with degrees of probability. Some authors have suggested that Bayesian theory should replace the role once played by logic (Oaksford & Chater, 2007) although this is not a necessary constraint. It is important to recognise, however, that the new paradigm does not mean that psychologists have switched from studying deduction to induction, which is still a separate paradigm. Because the new paradigm allows people to express degrees of belief in their conclusions, it would be easy to think that it was inductive inferences that were being studied. However, the field has rather moved towards the study of *uncertain* deduction, where uncertainty in premises is reflected by uncertainty in conclusions drawn from them (Evans & Over, 2012; Evans, Thompson, & Over, 2015). At one conference, I put up a slide with one of Sherlock Holmes' famous 'deductions' (see Box 9.1) and asked the audience of reasoning researchers whether the inference he drew was actually inductive, deductive, or abductive. The great majority voted for 'inductive' but I was able to show that Holmes' argument was in fact deductively valid. Their intuition, correctly, was that Holmes' inference was uncertain. However, the uncertainty lay entirely in the *premises* from which his deduction was made. Watson may have picked the mud up somewhere else, visited the Post Office to meet a friend, and so on. But if Holmes' premises were true, then so was his conclusion.

Box 9.1 Extract from Conan-Doyle's *The Sign of Four* (1890)

(HOLMES TO WATSON) "Observation shows me that you have been to the Wigmore Street Post-Office this morning, but deduction lets me know that when there you dispatched a telegram."

"Right!" said I. "Right on both points! But I confess that I don't see how you arrived at it. It was a sudden impulse upon my part, and I have mentioned it to no one."

"It is simplicity itself," he remarked, chuckling at my surprise, – "so absurdly simple that an explanation is superfluous; and yet it may serve to define the limits of observation and of deduction. Observation tells me that you have a little reddish mould adhering to your instep. Just opposite the Wigmore Street Office they have taken up the pavement and thrown up some earth which lies in such a way that it is difficult to avoid treading in it in entering. The earth is of this peculiar reddish tint which is found, as far as I know, nowhere else in the neighbourhood. So much is observation. The rest is deduction."

"How, then, did you deduce the telegram?"

"Why, of course I knew that you had not written a letter, since I sat opposite to you all morning. I see also in your open desk there that you have a sheet of stamps and a thick bundle of post-cards. What could you go into the post-office for, then, but to send a wire? Eliminate all other factors, and the one which remains must be the truth."

The one domain in which truth is valued above all else is science. Science strives for true explanations and the avoidance of contradictions. If two theories conflict in their proposals then we take it for granted that at least one will be false, even if there is no immediate means to prove which. The history of science teaches us that false beliefs, for example, about the motion of the planets, or the evolution of life will be eventually abandoned, no matter how much prior belief is operating in their favour. Important though science is, however, it is only one domain in which (some) people need to operate. Many scientists also hold religious and political beliefs, for example, which may be directly inconsistent with their scientific beliefs, or at least not provable by the scientific method. As another example, my scientific view of psychology is inconsistent with many of the tenets of folk psychology which I resist in my scientific thinking. In everyday life, however, I apply the native folk psychology which enables all of us to function socially. Our built-in folk psychology and theory of mind are good examples of fit-for-purpose beliefs. They do not stand up to scientifically rigorous examination, but they don't need to. They are fit for the purpose for which they evolved, which is communication, social interaction and the formation of social structures.

In discussing chess earlier, I pointed out that our pattern recognition and implicit learning abilities compensate to a great extent for the limited computational capacity of executive processing, requiring working memory. So one approach to bounded rationality is the idea that we can often rely heavily on gut feelings and quick and simple heuristics for our decision making (Dijksterhuis, Bos, Nordgren, & von Baaren, 2006; Gigerenzer, 2007; Gigerenzer & Todd, 1999; Gladwell, 2005). However, there are also vast amounts of research showing the importance of general intelligence, working memory and explicit forms of reasoning in the solution of a wide variety of cognitive tasks. This supports the proposals of dual-process theory (Evans & Stanovich, 2013), in which rapid and intuitive forms of processing (Type 1) are said to combine with slower and more effortful reasoning, the latter engaging working memory (Type 2). One of the dual-process theorists who most strongly advocates the importance of Type 2 processing in rational decision making is Keith Stanovich, who together with colleagues applied the theory to individual differences in reasoning and decision-making ability (Stanovich, 1999, 2011; Stanovich, West, & Toplak, 2016). The argument here is that while people often rely on heuristics and intuitions, this can lead them into serious errors and biases. Such errors can be avoided by successful intervention with high effort reasoning, provided that the individual has the cognitive capability and the relevant knowledge. So, at this point, I need to examine the dual-process case in more detail.

Default-interventionist dual-process theory and bounded rationality

Dual-process theory is something of an intellectual minefield for several reasons. One problem is that there are many authors in cognitive and social psychology advocating various form of dual processing which appear similar but may differ in detail. All broadly identify two forms of processing: Type 1 which is intuitive and typically quick, and Type 2 which is reflective and typically slow. One important structural difference is between theories that have a *parallel-competitive* approach and those which are *default-interventionist* (terms originally introduced by Evans (2007b). Parallel-competitive theories envisage that associative (Type 1) and rule-based (Type 2) processes proceed in parallel and compete for control of our behaviour (Sloman, 1996; Smith & DeCoster, 2000). The more popular form, however, is what I termed 'default-interventionist' (DI). Theorists of this persuasion include myself, Stanovich and Kahneman (Evans, 2007a; Evans & Stanovich, 2013; Kahneman, 2011; Stanovich, 2011). The common framework is the assumption that Type 1 processes, being relatively quick and automatic, provide

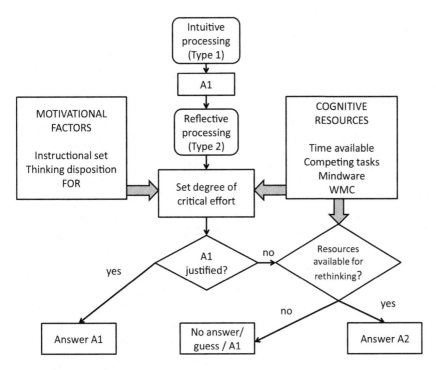

Figure 10.1   The default-interventionist process

default intuitions which are subject to scrutiny and possible intervention by Type 2 processing, which are slower and effortful. A great deal of research has been conducted by now showing that the answers people give to typical laboratory problems are affected by both experimental manipulations (e.g., time available, concurrent working memory load, instructions) and by individual differences in both cognitive ability and cognitive style. This work is reflected in the DI theory I proposed a few years ago (Evans, 2011) and shown in Figure 10.1.

The model assumes that Type 1 processing leads to a default intuitive answer A1 which appears in consciousness without effort or reflection. A1 is then subject to scrutiny by Type 2 processes which are effortful and require working memory. However, such scrutiny can be shallow or deep, which depends on a number of factors. Motivational factors include how people are instructed, whether they have a rational thinking disposition (which inclines people to check intuitions more carefully) and the feeling of rightness (FOR) or subjective confidence that they have in A1 (Thompson, Prowse Turner, & Pennycook, 2011). Cognitive resources include time available (speeded tasks will reduce Type 2 checking), individual differences in working memory capacity (highly correlated with IQ) and 'mindware', of which more shortly. When A1 is scrutinised, it may or may not be deemed satisfactory. Whether the intuition can successfully be replaced by an answer based on explicit reasoning and knowledge, however, depends on the cognitive resources available as Stanovich (2011) has argued. He has provided much empirical evidence (see also Stanovich et al., 2016) on how decision making is affected by individual differences in both cognitive ability and rational thinking dispositions. The latter measure the extent to which people will rely on intuitions or check them out by reasoning. On the basis of this work, Stanovich argues that a number of conditions must be met for someone to successfully engage in Type 2 reasoning and solve a demanding and novel experimental problem. First, people must be aware of the need for intervention by Type 2 reasoning, which is where rational thinking dispositions and feelings of rightness come into play. However, if they do intervene, then this will only be successful if both (1) they have sufficient cognitive capacity for the hypothetical reasoning involved; and (2) they have the relevant mindware – that is, formal or procedural knowledge required by the context.

The DI dual-process framework is clearly one of bounded rationality. Stanovich (2011) writes extensively about the *cognitive miser*, which is the idea that we evolved to expend as little mental effort as we can get away with. Most of our behaviour, most of the time is controlled by autonomous, Type 1 processes. This makes sense when you consider that Type 2 or executive processing engaged in working memory is a limited and essentially singular resource which can only perform one task at a time with any efficiency. Hence, this valuable resource, which corresponds with the focus of our conscious attention, must be used sparingly and for the most important tasks only. However, in laboratory tasks at least, the cognitive miser default can lead to cognitive biases and normative errors. Stanovich suggests this happens in three ways (see Stanovich, 2011, pp. 98–104). First, the system may detect no need for Type 2 intervention and default to autonomous processing. Second, a simplified and low effort form of Type 2 processing may be used to solve a problem and is equally likely to lead to a biased response. Finally, a genuine effort may be made at intervention but fail to change the default answer. As Elqayam (2012) points out, only those equipped with sufficient ability and mindware to solve the problems can fairly be accused of cognitive miserliness should they fail to do so. Stanovich (e.g., 2009) has a particular focus on the case of people with high IQs who nevertheless fail to make what he considers to be rational decisions.

There are some correspondences with Stanovich's arguments in my own writing and theoretical framework. For example, I have suggested (Evans, 2007a) that there is both a *fundamental heuristic bias* (Type 1) and a *fundamental analytic bias* (Type 2) and I apportioned approximately equal 'blame' to each in explaining the various biases in the literature. The Type 1 bias is to focus only on information which is preconsciously cued as relevant and the Type 2 bias is to focus on singular hypotheses and fail to consider alternatives. The latter corresponds to Stanovich's lazy and ineffective Type 2 processing. I also agree with Stanovich that the intervention with Type 2 reasoning does not necessarily lead to an improved response, as indicated in Figure 10.1. However, there are a couple of differences in our approach, also. First, in all my models, Type 2 processing is always involved before a decision is made, even though the default answer may well continue unchanged. Second, a major reason why people persist with A1 in Figure 10.1 is that they seek justification for an initial intuition and often end up *rationalising* this response. In fact, my very earliest papers on dual processing, in collaboration with Pete Wason, were concerned entirely with this rationalising function (Evans & Wason, 1976; Wason & Evans, 1975). On the Wason selection task, with which these papers were concerned, it was many years before I could find clear evidence that Type 2 processing might lead to a change of the intuitive response at all, although I eventually did (Evans & Ball, 2010).

This rationalisation aspect of Type 2 processing does not fit as neatly with the cognitive miser hypothesis because it does require mental effort and working memory resources to carry out, even though the default intuition is maintained. However, it is supported by evidence that we spend most time thinking about responses that are intuitively cued (Ball, Lucas, Miles, & Gale, 2003; Evans, 1996). It also fits with evolutionary accounts of explicit reasoning that link this facility to argumentation and social discourse (Mercier & Sperber, 2011). Entertaining this argument for a moment, one way in which an evolved argumentation function could become adapted to the assistance of problem solving would be precisely in the kind of model I am proposing here. Instead of simply making an intuitive response, we first seek arguments and justifications, by an internal mental process, to support them. While this may bias the system towards rationalisation and confabulation, it does at least allow the possibility that error will be detected and corrected. This is more likely to happen when more time and effort are expended on examining the intuitive response, which reflects the individual differences in *rational thinking dispositions* studied by Stanovich and others. These measures, even when based on self-report, do predict accuracy on cognitive tasks when effects of cognitive ability are statistically removed, as many studies in cognitive and social psychology have shown.

Metacognitive feelings

Metacognition is the knowledge or feeling that we have about our own cognitive processes. When we make judgements or predictions, for example, these may come with feelings of confidence which we can report upon if asked. A well-established literature in the study of judgement and decision-making reports a general phenomenon of overconfidence. When we are more confident, we are in fact more likely to be right, but not as likely as we think we are (Koehler, Brenner, & Griffin, 2002). There has been a lot of research into feeling of knowing (FOK) in memory research, which again shows imperfect correlation with actual accuracy of memories (Koriat, 1993). Of more relevance to this chapter and the bounded rationality argument is the suggestion that these metacognitive feelings have a regulatory purpose, controlling the amount of effort that is expended (Ackerman, 2014).

Valerie Thompson (2009) was the first to introduce the issue of metacognitive feelings to the psychology of reasoning. It was an attempt to solve a fundamental issue for dual process theories at the time of writing, namely, what determines whether an intervention with Type 2 processing will occur. She suggested that the default intuitive answer that comes to mind carries with it a feeling of rightness (FOR) which determines the amount of effort that will be made. When FOR is high, we will tend to accept our intuitions with little effort at reasoning and when it is low, we will intervene more. A number of empirical studies followed which supported these claims. Thompson invented a two-response paradigm, in which people are asked to give a quick intuitive answer together with the FOR rating. They are then allowed to think further for as long as they like and change the answer if they wish. On a number of different cognitive tasks, Thompson and colleagues showed that low FOR leads to greater rethinking time and more likelihood that initial answers will be changed (Thompson et al., 2011).

On the face of it, the FOR research seems to fit a neat story of evolution and bounded rationality. Our intuitions come helpfully packaged with feelings of confidence which tell us whether we need to expend effort or not in checking them out. However, there is a snag. None of this research – on reasoning and decision making – has provided evidence for even a partial accuracy of the FOR judgement, as observed in other fields where metacognition is studied. The answers which people rethink and change are as likely to be right as wrong and low FOR can lead to abandonment of an initially correct judgement. Some cues which lead to errors are particularly convincing, such as the *matching bias* which dominates choices on the abstract selection task (Thompson, Evans, & Campbell, 2013) and the compelling but wrong intuitions on the cognitive reflection task (Frederick, 2005). Belief bias is a major cause of error in syllogistic reasoning (Evans, Barston, & Pollard, 1983; Klauer, Musch, & Naumer, 2000) and yet believable conclusions inspire positive feelings of liking and confidence (Morsanyi & Handley, 2012; Shynkarkuk & Thompson, 2006). None of which evidence supports the claim that we evolved these metacognitive feelings because they are of assistance to the cognitive miser.

There are two problems with all of these metacognitive measures. First, they are introspective reports whose validity can only be established by relating them to other behavioural measures. Second, these relations are correlational rather than causal. What we know about FOR is that strong feelings are associated with answers that are given quickly and generally held on to with little effort to rethink them. Putting these two problems together, we can see that there is no clear reason to think that FOR corresponds to a stage of cognitive processing in the manner that researchers in the field assume. They could simply be conscious feelings that are by-products of the processes that determine the behaviour measures. In other words, a brain process that leads to a quick and firmly held decision, also generates conscious feelings of rightness and confidence, which in themselves are of no functional significance.

Recent studies with the Thompson two-response paradigm have suggested than on some simpler forms of syllogistic reasoning, most of the people who get it right after reflection, also got it right with their initial intuitive response (Bago & De Neys, 2017). So, it appears that no slow reflective Type 2 process was apparently involved. Connected to this is another recent finding that people of higher cognitive ability or with better mindware for the numerical problems studied have stronger intuitions leading them to the right answers, whereas those of lower ability are more likely to be influenced intuitively by prior belief (Thompson, Pennycook, Trippas, & Evans, 2018). There are actually a number of recent studies showing that people may have 'logical intuitions' (De Neys, 2012, 2017). While some authors have taken such findings as evidence against the traditional default-interventionist account, the case is not that clear-cut (Evans, 2018). First, most of these recent studies use relatively simple tasks where cues for logically correct response might well be present without need for working memory engagement. Second, those of higher cognitive ability may have acquired mindware that has become automated with practice. Although laboratory tasks that are both novel and requiring a degree of complexity for their solution typically require Type 2 processing, it is a fallacy to assume that Type 1 processes are necessarily biased or that Type 2 processing always leads to correct answers (Evans & Stanovich, 2013).

Conclusion

In the early part of this chapter, I showed that Simon's notion of bounded rationality applies both to how we can achieve our goals and to how we can organise and validate our knowledge about the world. I also argued, using the domain of chess, that while our capabilities of explicit calculation are sharply limited compared with modern computers, the brain has evolved rapid, pattern recognition systems which compensate to a large extent for this limitation. When we examine the field of dual processing in the study of reasoning and decision making, however, the dice have been loaded heavily in favour of tasks that require Type 2 processing (explicit calculation and reasoning loading on working memory) for their solution. This is because the tasks presented tend to be novel and difficult to solve on the basis of prior experience. For the same reason, this literature has given relatively bad press to intuitive or Type 1 processes which operate quickly and autonomously. In fact, the same kinds of process that enable the best human chess players to approach the standard of brute force computer programs! And yet researchers are somehow surprised when they simplify the standard laboratory tasks and find a lot of accurate Type 1 processing is involved in their solution.

I have shown that the default-interventionist dual process theories that have dominated in these fields are essentially within the bounded rationality tradition. That is to say, it is assumed that Type 1 processing will dominate by default and high effort Type 2 processing will be selectively applied. There is much accumulated evidence that this is the case (Evans, 2007a; Evans & Stanovich, 2013; Stanovich, 2011) although recent studies have somewhat muddied the waters

(De Neys, 2017). The studies by Thompson and colleagues of feelings of rightness are of much interest but produce a mixed picture. On the one hand, FOR most definitely correlates with the amount of time and effort people expend on reasoning, as opposed to reliance on initial intuitions. On the other hand, there is no evidence that these feelings are related to actual accuracy, and some major cognitive biases (e.g., matching bias, belief bias) are supported by strong and false feelings of confidence. It is at least possible that these feelings are no more than a by-product of the brain processes that lead to strongly or weakly held decisions.

While DI dual-process theory is under pressure from those inside as well as outside of the paradigm, we should not lose sight of the broader picture. First, there is no doubt that the great bulk of our behaviour is controlled by fast and automatic processing. Outside of the laboratory, such processing is often very effective and compensates for the limitations of our explicit computational capacity. There is also no doubt that we do have a central working memory system which is implicated in the successful execution of a very large range of cognitive functions (Baddeley, 2007). So the way in which our brains provide our bounded rationality simply *has* to be some kind of dual process story, whether we call these Type 1 and 2 or just autonomous and executive processes. Although some evolutionary psychologists have argued for a massively modular brain that does not depend on any general-purpose reasoning system (Cosmides & Tooby, 1992) and other prominent researchers state that we can safely rely on intuitions and gut feelings for complex decisions (Gigerenzer, 2007), these argument simply do not hold up. More than 100 years of research on general intelligence and 50 plus years of research on working memory attest to the fact that there is a central cognitive system allowing behaviour to be based on reasoning and hypothetical thought and which operates distinctly from autonomous processing. The intellectual success of our own species quite clearly depends upon it.

Acknowledgements

The author is grateful to Shira Elqayam for a critical reading of an earlier draft of this chapter.

References

Ackerman, R. (2014). The diminishing criterion role for metacognitive regulation of time investment. *Journal of Experimental Psychology General*, 143, 1349–1368.

Baddeley, A. (2007). *Working memory, thought and action*. Oxford: Oxford University Press.

Bago, B., & De Neys, W. (2017). Fast logic?: Examining the time course assumption of dual process theory. *Cognition*, 158, 90–109. doi:10.1016/j.cognition.2016.10.014

Ball, L. J., Lucas, E. J., Miles, J. N. V., & Gale, A. G. (2003). Inspection times and the selection task: What do eye-movements reveal about relevance effects? *Quarterly Journal of Experimental Psychology*, 56(6), 1053–1077.

Carruthers, P. (2006). *The architecture of the mind*. Oxford: Oxford University Press.

Chase, W. G., & Simon, H. A. (1973). Perception in chess. *Cognitive Psychology*, 4, 55–81.

Cohen, L. J. (1981). Can human irrationality be experimentally demonstrated? *Behavioral and Brain Sciences*, 4, 317–370.

Cosmides, L., & Tooby, J. (1992). Cognitive adaptations for social exchange. In J. H. Barkow, L. Cosmides & J. Tooby (Eds.), *The adapted mind: Evolutionary psychology and the generation of culture* (pp. 163–228). New York: Oxford University Press.

De Neys, W. (2012). Bias and conflict: A case for logical intuitions. *Perspectives on Psychological Science*, 7, 28–38.

De Neys, W. (Ed.) (2017). *Dual process theory 2.0*. London: Routledge.

Dijksterhuis, A., Bos, M. W., Nordgren, L. F., & von Baaren, R. B. (2006). On making the right choice: The deliberation-without-attention effect. *Science*, 311, 1005–1007.

Elqayam, S. (2012). Grounded rationality: Descriptivism in epistemic context. *Synthese*, 189, 39–49.

Elqayam, S. & Over, D. E. (2012). New paradigm in psychology of reasoning: Probabilities, beliefs and dual processing. *Mind & Society*, 11, 27–40.

Evans, J. St. B. T. (1996). Deciding before you think: Relevance and reasoning in the selection task. *British Journal of Psychology*, 87, 223–240.

Evans, J. St. B. T. (2002). Logic and human reasoning: An assessment of the deduction paradigm. *Psychological Bulletin*, 128, 978–996.

Evans, J. St. B. T. (2007a). *Hypothetical thinking: Dual processes in reasoning and judgement.* Hove: Psychology Press.

Evans, J. St. B. T. (2007b). On the resolution of conflict in dual-process theories of reasoning. *Thinking & Reasoning*, 13, 321–329.

Evans, J. St. B. T. (2008). Dual-processing accounts of reasoning, judgment and social cognition. *Annual Review of Psychology*, 59, 255–278.

Evans, J. St. B. T. (2010). *Thinking twice: Two minds in one brain.* Oxford: Oxford University Press.

Evans, J. St. B. T. (2011). Dual-process theories of reasoning: Contemporary issues and developmental applications. *Developmental Review*, 31, 86–102.

Evans, J. St. B. T. (2012). Questions and challenges for the new psychology of reasoning. *Thinking & Reasoning*, 18, 5–31.

Evans, J. St. B. T. (2018). Dual-process theory: Perspectives and problems. In W. De Neys (Ed.), *Dual process theory 2.0* (pp. 137–155). London: Routledge.

Evans, J. St. B. T., & Ball, L. J. (2010). Do people reason on the Wason selection task?: A new look at the data of Ball et al. (2003). *Quarterly Journal of Experimental Psychology*, 63(3), 434–441.

Evans, J. St. B. T., Barston, J. L., & Pollard, P. (1983). On the conflict between logic and belief in syllogistic reasoning. *Memory & Cognition*, 11, 295–306.

Evans, J. St. B. T., Newstead, S. E., & Byrne, R. M. J. (1993). *Human reasoning: The psychology of deduction.* Hove: Lawrence Erlbaum.

Evans, J. St. B. T., & Over, D. E. (2012). Reasoning to and from belief: Deduction and induction are still distinct. *Thinking & Reasoning*, 19(3–4), 267–283. doi:10.1080/13546783.2012.745450.

Evans, J. St. B. T., & Stanovich, K. E. (2013). Dual process theories of higher cognition: Advancing the debate. *Perspectives on Psychological Science*, 8, 223–241.

Evans, J. St. B. T., Thompson, V. A., & Over, D. E. (2015). Uncertain deduction and conditional reasoning. *Frontiers in Psychology*, 6. doi:10.3389/fpsyg.2015.00398.

Evans, J. St. B. T., & Wason, P.C. (1976). Rationalisation in a reasoning task. *British Journal of Psychology*, 63, 205–212.

Feeney, A., & Heit, E. (2007). *Inductive reasoning.* Cambridge: Cambridge University Press.

Frederick, S. (2005). Cognitive reflection and decision making. *Journal of Economic Perspectives*, 19(4), 25–42.

Gigerenzer, G. (2007). *Gut feelings: The intelligence of the unconscious.* London: Penguin.

Gigerenzer, G., & Todd, P. M. (1999). *Simple heuristics that make us smart.* Oxford: Oxford University Press.

Gladwell, M. (2005). *Blink.* London: Penguin.

Henle, M. (1962). On the relation between logic and thinking. *Psychological Review*, 69, 366–378.

Inhelder, B., & Piaget, J. (1958). *The growth of logical thinking.* New York: Basic Books.

Kahneman, D. (2011). *Thinking, fast and slow.* New York: Farrar, Straus and Giroux.

Kasparov, G. (2017). *Thinking deeply: Where machine intelligence ends.* London: John Murray.

Klauer, K. C., Musch, J., & Naumer, B. (2000). On belief bias in syllogistic reasoning. *Psychological Review*, 107, 852–884.

Klein, M. (2017). Google's AlphaZero destroys Stockfish in 100 game match. Available at: www.chess.com/news/view/google-s-alphazero-destroys-stockfish-in-100-game-match.

Koehler, D. J., Brenner, L., & Griffin, D. (2002). The calibration of expert judgment: heuristics and biases beyond the laboratory. In T. Gilovich, D. Griffin, & A. Kahneman (Eds.), *Heuristics and biases: The psychology of intuitive judgment.* Cambridge: Cambridge University Press.

Koriat, A. (1993). How do we know what we know? The accessibility model of the feeling of knowing. *Psychological Review*, 100, 609–639.

Mercier, H., & Sperber, D. (2011). Why do humans reason? Arguments for an argumentative theory. *Behavioral and Brain Sciences*, 34, 57–111.

Morsanyi, K., & Handley, S. (2012). Logic feels so good – I like it. Evidence for an implicit detection of logicality in syllogistic reasoning. *Journal of Experimental Psychology-Learning Memory and Cognition*, 38, 596–616.

Newell, A., & Simon, H. A. (1972). *Human problem solving.* Englewood Cliffs, NJ: Prentice-Hall.

Oaksford, M., & Chater, N. (1998). *Rationality in an uncertain world*. Hove: Psychology Press.

Oaksford, M., & Chater, N. (2007). *Bayesian rationality: The probabilistic approach to human reasoning*. Oxford: Oxford University Press.

Oaksford, M., & Chater, N. (2013). Dynamic inference and everyday conditional reasoning in the new paradigm. *Thinking & Reasoning*, 19(3–4), 346–379. doi:10.1080/13546783.2013.808163.

Over, D. E. (2009). New paradigm psychology of reasoning. *Thinking & Reasoning*, 15, 431–438.

Shynkarkuk, J. M., & Thompson, V. A. (2006). Confidence and accuracy in deductive reasoning. *Memory & Cognition*, 34, 619–632.

Sloman, S. A. (1996). The empirical case for two systems of reasoning. *Psychological Bulletin*, 119, 3–22.

Smith, E. R., & DeCoster, J. (2000). Dual-process models in social and cognitive psychology: Conceptual integration and links to underlying memory systems. *Personality and Social Psychology Review*, 4(2), 108–131.

Stanovich, K. E. (1999). *Who is rational? Studies of individual differences in reasoning*. Mahwah, NJ: Lawrence Erlbaum Associates.

Stanovich, K. E. (2009). The thinking that IQ tests miss. *Scientific American*, November/December, 33–39.

Stanovich, K. E. (2011). *Rationality and the reflective mind*. New York: Oxford University Press.

Stanovich, K. E., West, C., & Toplak, M. E. (2016). *The rationality quotient: Towards a test of rational thinking*. Cambridge, MA: MIT Press.

Thompson, V. A. (2009). Dual-process theories: A metacognitive perspective. In J. S. B. T. Evans & K. Frankish (Eds.), *In two minds: Dual processes and beyond* (pp. 171–196). Oxford: Oxford University Press.

Thompson, V. A., Evans, J. S. T., & Campbell, J. I. D. (2013). Matching bias on the selection task: It's fast and feels good. *Thinking & Reasoning*, 19(3–4), 431–452. doi:10.1080/13546783.2013.820220.

Thompson, V. A., Pennycook, G., Trippas, D., & Evans, J. St. B. T. (2018). Do smart people have better intuitions? *Journal of Experimental Psychology General*. 147(7), 945–961.

Thompson, V. A., Prowse Turner, J. A., & Pennycook, G. (2011). Intuition, reason, and metacognition. *Cognitive Psychology*, 63(3), 107–140.

Wason, P. C., & Evans, J. St. B. T. (1975). Dual processes in reasoning? *Cognition*, 3, 141–154.

11

WHY HUMANS ARE COGNITIVE MISERS AND WHAT IT MEANS FOR THE GREAT RATIONALITY DEBATE

Keith E. Stanovich

Introduction

That humans are cognitive misers has been a major theme throughout the past 50 years of research in psychology and cognitive science (see Dawes, 1976; Kahneman, 2011; Simon, 1955; 1956; Shah & Oppenheimer, 2008; Taylor, 1981; Tversky & Kahneman, 1974). Humans are cognitive misers because their basic tendency is to default to processing mechanisms of low computational expense. Humorously, Hull (2001) has said that "the rule that human beings seem to follow is to engage the brain only when all else fails—and usually not even then" (p. 37). More seriously, Richerson and Boyd (2005) have put the same point in terms of its origins in evolution: "In effect, all animals are under stringent selection pressure to be as stupid as they can get away with" (p. 135). Miserly cognitive tendencies have evolved for reasons of computational efficiency. But that same computational efficiency simultaneously guarantees that humans will be less than perfectly rational—that they will display, instead, bounded rationality.

Miserly processing and human evolution

Of course, evolution guarantees human rationality in the dictionary sense of "the quality or state of being able to reason" because evolution built the human brain. But evolution does *not* guarantee perfect rationality in a different sense—the sense used throughout cognitive science: as maximizing subjective expected utility. In contrast to maximization, natural selection works on a "better than" principle. The variation and selective retention logic of evolution "design" for the reproductive advantage of one organism over the next, not for the optimality of any one characteristic (including rationality). Natural selection is geared to immediate advantage rather than long-term strategy. Human rationality, in contrast, must incorporate the long-term interests of the individual and thus it can diverge from the short-term strategies of evolutionary adaptation.

Organisms have evolved to increase the reproductive fitness of genes, not to increase the rationality of humans, and increases in fitness do not always entail increases in rationality. For example, beliefs need not always track the world with maximum accuracy in order for fitness to increase (Mercier & Sperber, 2017; Stanovich, 2004). Evolution might fail to select out

DOI: 10.4324/9781315658353-13

epistemic mechanisms of high accuracy when they are costly in terms of organismic resources (for example, in terms of memory, energy, or attention). Unreliable, error-prone, risk-aversive strategies may well be favored by natural selection (Stich, 1990).

It is likewise in the domain of goals and desires. The purpose of evolution was not to maximize the happiness of human beings. As has become clear from research on affective forecasting (Gilbert, 2006; Kahneman, 2011), people are remarkably bad at making choices that make them happy. This should be no surprise. The reason we have pleasure circuits in our brains is to encourage us to do things (survive and reproduce, help kin) that propagate our genes. The pleasure centers were not designed to maximize the amount of time we are happy.

The instrumental rationality[1] of humans is not guaranteed by evolution for two further reasons. First, many genetic goals may no longer serve our ends because the environment has changed. The goals underlying these mechanisms have become detached from their evolutionary context (Li, van Vugt & Colarelli, 2018). Finally, the cultural evolution of rational standards is apt to occur at a pace markedly faster than that of human evolution (Richerson & Boyd, 2005; Stanovich, 2004)—thus providing ample opportunity for mental mechanisms of utility maximization to dissociate from local genetic fitness maximization.

That evolution does not guarantee perfect rationality in humans is the first fundamental concept that we need in order to resolve the Great Rationality Debate in cognitive science— the debate about how much rationality to ascribe to people (Cohen, 1981; Gigerenzer, 1996; Kahneman & Tversky, 1996; Kelman, 2011; Lee, 2006; Polonioli, 2015; Samuels & Stich, 2004; Stanovich, 1999, 2004; Stanovich & West, 2000; Stein, 1996; Tetlock & Mellers, 2002). The other two concepts that are needed are dual-process cognitive theory and an understanding of the logic of goals within the human organism. The first is well-known and has been exhaustively discussed, so I turn first to the latter (see Stanovich, 2004, for a fuller discussion).

The logic of goals in organisms of differing complexity

I will rely here on Dawkins' (1976, 1982) discussion of replicators and vehicles: replicators as entities (e.g., genes) that copy themselves and vehicles as the containers (e.g., organisms) in which replicators house themselves. It is vehicles that interact with the environment, and the differential success of the vehicles in interacting with the environment determines the success of the replicators that they house. Humans have proven to be good vehicles for genes, as have bees. But the goal structures of bees and humans are very different.

As a creature characterized primarily by a so-called Darwinian mind (see Dennett, 1996, 2017), a bee has a goal structure as indicated in Figure 11.1. The area labeled A indicates the majority of cases where the replicator and vehicle goals coincide. Not flying into a brick wall serves both the interests of the genes and of the bee itself as a coherent organism. Of course, the exact area represented by A is nothing more than a guess. The important point is that there exists a nonzero area B—a set of goals that serve only the interests of the replicators and that are antithetical to the interests of the vehicle itself.[2] A given bee will sacrifice itself as a vehicle if there is greater benefit to the same genes by helping other bees (e.g., causing its own death when it loses its stinger while protecting its genetically-related hive-Queen).

All of the goals in a bee are genetic goals pure and simple. Some of these goals overlap with the interests of the bee as a vehicle and some do not, but the bee does not know enough to care. Of course, the case of humans is radically different. The possibility of genetic interests and vehicle interests dissociating has profound implications for humans as self-contemplating vehicles.

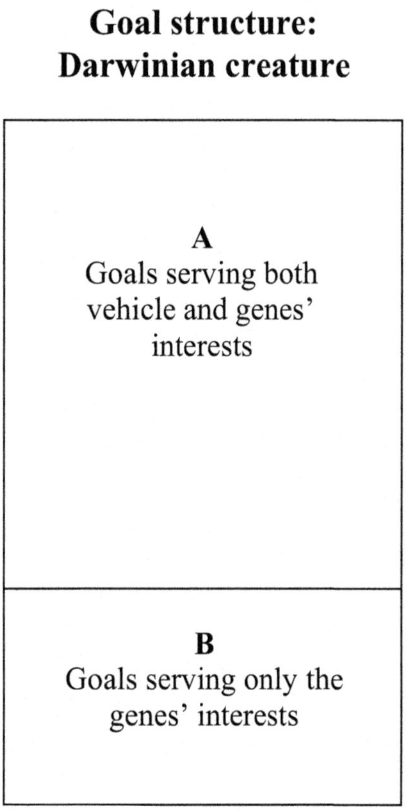

Goal structure:
Darwinian creature

A
Goals serving both
vehicle and genes'
interests

B
Goals serving only the
genes' interests

Figure 11.1 Goal structure of a Darwinian creature. The areas indicate overlap and nonoverlap of vehicle and genetic "interests."

Humans were the first organisms capable of recognizing that there may be goals embedded in their brains that serve the interests of their genes rather than their own interests *and* the first organisms capable of choosing not to pursue those goals. An organism with a flexible intelligence and long-leash goals can, unlike the situation displayed in Figure 11.1, develop goals that are completely dissociated from genetic optimization. For the first time in evolutionary history, we have the possibility of a goal structure like that displayed in Figure 11.2 (again, the sizes of these areas are pure conjecture). Here, although we have area A as before (where gene and vehicle goals coincide) and area B as before (goals serving the genes' interests but not the vehicle's), we have a new area, C, which shows that, in humans, we have the possibility of goals that serve only the vehicle's interests and not those of the genes.

Why does area C come to exist in humans? When the limits of coding the moment-by-moment responses of their vehicles were reached, the genes began adding long-leash strategies to the brain (Dennett, 1996, 2017; Stanovich, 2004). At some point in evolutionary development, these long-leash strategies increased in flexibility to the point that—to anthropomorphize—the genes said the equivalent of: "Things will be changing too fast out there, brain, for us to tell you exactly what to do—you just go ahead and do what you think is best given the general goals (survival, sexual reproduction) that we (the genes) have inserted." But once the goal has become this general, a potential gap has been created whereby behaviors that might serve the

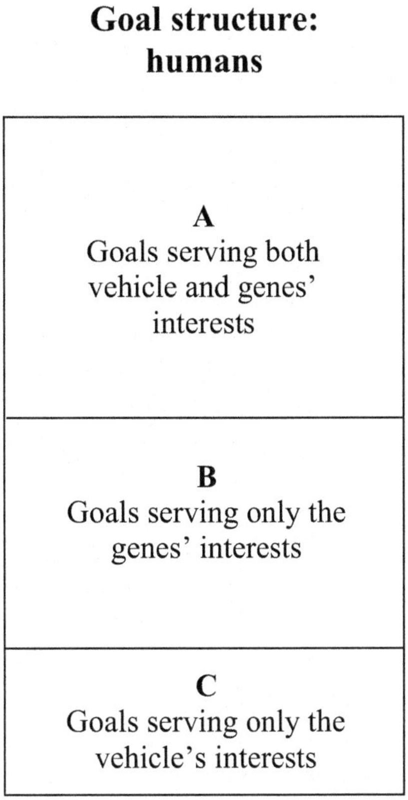

Goal structure: humans

Figure of the goal structure showing three stacked boxes:

A
Goals serving both vehicle and genes' interests

B
Goals serving only the genes' interests

C
Goals serving only the vehicle's interests

Figure 11.2   The logic of the goal structure in a human

vehicle's goal might not serve that of the genes. We need not go beyond the obvious example of sex with contraception—an act which serves the vehicle's goal of pleasure without serving the genes' goal of reproduction. The logic of the situation here is that the goals of the vehicle—being *general* instantiations of things that probabilistically tend to reproduce genes—can diverge from the specific reproductive goal itself.

Genetic and vehicle goals in a dual-process organism

The last global concept that is needed to contextualize the Great Rationality Debate is that of dual-process theory. To simplify the discussion, we need only the most basic assumptions of such a theory (Stanovich & Toplak, 2012) along with the subsequent clarifications and caveats that have been much discussed in the literature (Evans, 2008, 2014, 2018; Evans & Stanovich, 2013; Stanovich, 2011). In many such theories, the defining feature of System 1 processing is its autonomy. Execution of these processes is mandatory when their triggering stimuli are encountered, and they are not dependent on input from high-level control systems. The category of autonomous, System 1 processes would include: processes of emotional regulation; the encapsulated modules for solving specific adaptive problems that have been posited by evolutionary psychologists; processes of implicit learning; and the automatic firing of overlearned associations.

In contrast to System 1 processing, System 2 processing is nonautonomous and computationally expensive. Many System 1 processes can operate in parallel, but System 2 processing is largely serial. One of the most critical functions of System 2 processing is to override nonoptimal System 1 processing (for extensive discussion of the details of these broad generalizations, see De Neys, 2018; Evans & Stanovich, 2013; Pennycook et al., 2015; Stanovich, 2004, 2011, 2018; Thompson, 2009). There are individual differences in the System 2 tendency to override, and thus there are individual differences in how miserly people are (Stanovich, West, & Toplak, 2016).

System 1 is partially composed of older evolutionary structures (Amati & Shallice, 2007; Mithen, 1996, 2002; Reber, 1993) that more directly code the goals of the genes (reproductive success), whereas the goal structure of System 2—a more recently evolved brain capability (Evans, 2010; Mithen, 1996, 2002; Stanovich, 2004, 2011)—is more flexible and on an ongoing basis attempts to coordinate the goals of the broader social environment with the more domain-specific short-leash goals of System 1. System 2 is primarily a control system focused on the interests of the whole person. It is the primary maximizer of an individual's *personal* goal satisfaction.

Because System 2 is more attuned to the person's needs as a coherent organism than is System 1 (which is more directly tuned to the ancient reproductive goals of the subpersonal replicators), in the minority of cases where the outputs of the two systems conflict, people will often be better off if they can accomplish an override of the System 1-triggered output. Such a system conflict could be signaling a vehicle/replicator goal mismatch and, statistically, such a mismatch is more likely to be resolved in favor of the vehicle (which all of us should want) if the System 1 output is overridden.

Figure 11.3 displays a graphic representation of the logic of the situation (of course, the exact size of the areas of overlap are mere guesses; it is only the relative proportions that are necessary to sustain the argument here). It illustrates that override is a statistically good bet in cases of conflict because System 1 contains a disproportionate share of the goals serving only the genes' interests and not the vehicle's (area A) and System 2 contains a disproportionate share of the goals serving only the vehicle's interests and not the genes' (area F). An assumption reflected in Figure 11.3 is that vehicle and gene goals coincide in the vast majority of real-life situations (the areas labeled B and E). For example, accurately navigating around objects in the natural world fostered evolutionary adaptation—and it likewise serves our personal goals as we carry out our lives in the modern world. But the most important feature of Figure 11.3 is that it illustrates the asymmetries in the interests served by the goal distributions of the two systems.

Many of the goals instantiated in System 1 were acquired nonreflectively—they have not undergone an evaluation in terms of whether they served the *person's* interests (area A in Figure 11.3). They have in fact been evaluated, but by a different set of criteria entirely: whether they enhanced the longevity and fecundity of the replicators in the evolutionary past. From the standpoint of the individual person (the vehicle), these can become dangerous goals because they reflect genetic goals only.[3] They are the goals that sacrifice the vehicle to the interests of replicators—the ones that lead the bee to sacrifice itself for its genetically-related hive-Queen. These are the goals that should be strong candidates for override.

The right side of Figure 11.3 indicates the goal structure of System 2. Through its exercise of a reflective intelligence, this system derives flexible long-leash goals that often serve the overall ends of the organism but thwart the goals of the genes (area F in Figure 11.3—for example, sex with contraception; resource use after the reproductive years have ended, etc.). Of course, a reflectively acquired goal can, if habitually invoked, become part of System 1 as well (Bago & De Neys, 2017; Stanovich, 2018). This fact explains why there is a small[4] section (area

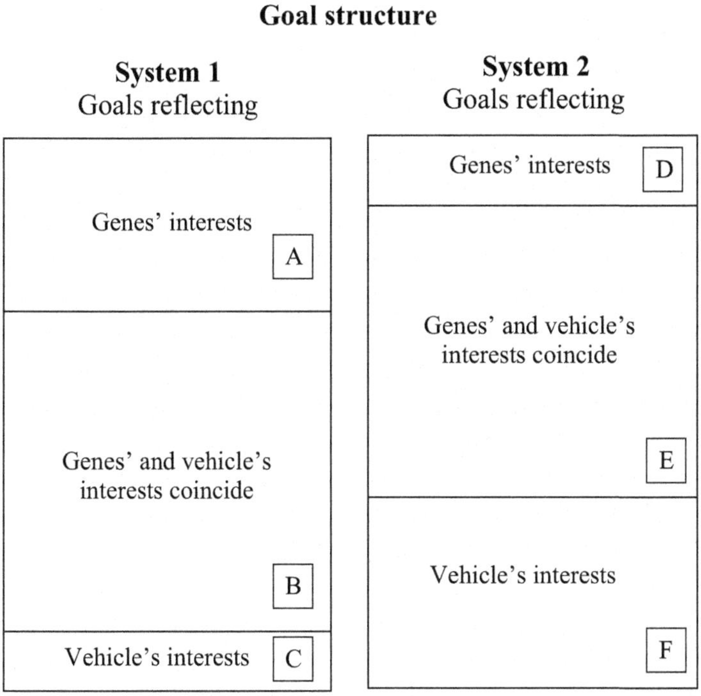

Goal structure

Figure 11.3   Genetic and vehicle goal overlap in System 1 and System 2

C) in System 1 representing goals that serve the vehicle's interests only. Reflectively acquired goal-states might be taken on for their unique advantages to the vehicle (advantages that might accrue because they trump contrary gene-installed goals—"don't flirt with your boss's wife") and then may become instantiated in System 1 through practice. We might say that in situations such as this, System 1 in humans reflects the consequences of residing in a brain along with a reflective System 2. This is why the goal-structure of System 1 in humans does not simply recapitulate the structure of a Darwinian creature depicted in Figure 11.1.

Nevertheless, with the small but important exception of area C, System 1 can be understood, roughly, as the part of the brain on a short genetic leash. In contrast, most of the goals that the System 2 is trying to coordinate are derived goals. When humans live in complex societies, basic goals and primary drives (bodily pleasure, safety, sustenance) are satisfied indirectly by maximizing secondary symbolic goals such as prestige, status, employment, and remuneration. In order to achieve many of these secondary goals, the more directly-coded System 1 responses must be suppressed—at least temporarily. Long-leashed derived goals create the conditions for a separation between the goals of evolutionary adaptation and the interests of the vehicle.

Because of its properties of autonomy, System 1 will often provide an output relevant to a problem in which System 2 is engaged. Such a system conflict could be signaling a vehicle/replicator goal mismatch and, statistically, such a mismatch is more likely to be resolved in favor of the vehicle (which all of us should want) if the System 1 output is overridden (area E + F exceeds area B + C). This is why, in cases of response conflict, override is a statistically good bet.

Reconciling the opposing positions in the Great Rationality Debate

Researchers working in the heuristics and biases tradition tend to see a large gap between normative models of rational responding and descriptive models of what people actually do. These researchers have been termed Meliorists (Stanovich, 1999, 2004, 2010) because they assume that human reasoning is not as good as it could be, and that thinking could be improved (Stanovich et al., 2016).

However, over the last several decades, an alternative interpretation of the findings from the heuristics and biases research program has been championed. Contributing to this alternative interpretation have been philosophers, evolutionary psychologists, adaptationist modelers, and ecological theorists (Cohen, 1981; Gigerenzer, 2007; Oaksford & Chater, 2007, 2012; Todd & Gigerenzer, 2000). They have reinterpreted the modal response in most of the classic heuristics and biases experiments as indicating an optimal information processing adaptation on the part of the subjects. This group of theorists—who argue that an assumption of maximal human rationality is the proper default position to take—have been termed the Panglossians.

The Panglossian theorists often argue either that the normative model being applied is not the appropriate one because the subject's interpretation of the task is different from what the researcher assumes it is, or that the modal response in the task makes perfect sense from an evolutionary perspective. The contrasting positions of the Panglossians and Meliorists define the differing poles in what has been termed the Great Rationality Debate in cognitive science—the debate about whether humans can be systematically irrational.

A reconciliation of the views of the Panglossians and Meliorists is possible, however. I argued above that the statistical distributions of the types of goals being pursued by System 1 and System 2 processing are different. Because System 2 processing is more attuned to the person's needs as a coherent organism, in the minority of cases where the outputs of the two systems conflict, people will often be better off if they can accomplish a System 1 override (the full argument[5] is contained in Stanovich, 2004). Instances where there is a conflict between the responses primed by System 1 and System 2 processing are interpreted as reflecting conflicts between two different types of optimization—fitness maximization at the subpersonal genetic level and utility maximization at the personal level.

A failure to differentiate these interests is at the heart of the disputes between researchers working in the heuristics and biases tradition and their critics in the evolutionary psychology camp. First, it certainly must be said that the evolutionary psychologists are on to something with respect to the tasks they have analyzed, because in most cases the adaptive response is the *modal* response in the task—the one most subjects give. Nevertheless, this must be reconciled with a triangulating data pattern relevant to this discussion—an analysis of patterns of covariation and individual differences across these tasks. Specifically, we have found that cognitive ability often (but not always) dissociates from the response deemed adaptive from an evolutionary analysis (Stanovich & West, 1998, 1999, 2000).

These two data patterns can be reconciled, however. The evolutionary psychologists are probably correct that most System 1 processing is evolutionarily adaptive. Nevertheless, their evolutionary interpretations do not impeach the position of the heuristics and biases researchers that the alternative response given by the minority of subjects is rational at the level of the individual. Subjects of higher analytic intelligence are simply more prone to override System 1 processing in order to produce responses that are epistemically and instrumentally rational. This rapprochement between the two camps was introduced by Stanovich (1999) and subsequent research has only reinforced it (see Kahneman and Frederick, 2002; Kelman, 2011; Samuels & Stich, 2004; Stanovich, 2004, 2011).

It is possible to continue to resist this rapprochement, of course, but only at the expense of taking rather extreme positions. A Meliorist could resist the rapprochement by continuing to deny the efficacy of much of our cognition from the standpoint of evolution—a position that denies much of evolutionary cognitive science. A Panglossian might decide to reject the rapprochement by siding with the goals of the genes over the goals of the vehicle when the two conflict. But most people find this choice unpalatable, and few of those who claim they do not have considered exactly what they are endorsing when they do. For example, Cooper (1989), in an essay describing how some nonoptimal behavioral tendencies could be genetically optimal, admits that such behaviors are indeed detrimental to the reasoner's own welfare. Nonetheless, he goes on to counter that the behaviors are still justified because: "What if the individual identifies its own welfare with that of its genotype?" (p. 477).

But who are these people with such loyalty to the random shuffle of genes that is their genotype? I really doubt that there are such people. To be precise, I am doubting whether there are people who say they value their genome *and have an accurate view of what they are valuing* when they say this. For example, in such a case, the person would have to be absolutely clear that valuing your own genome is not some proxy for valuing your children; be clear that having children does not replicate one's genome; and be clear about the fact that the genome is a *subpersonal* entity. Most people, I think, would eschew this Panglossian path if it were properly understood and adopt the view of philosopher Alan Gibbard, who offers the more reasoned view that

> a person's evolutionary *telos* explains his having the propensities in virtue of which he develops the goals he does, but his goals are distinct from this surrogate purpose. My evolutionary *telos*, the reproduction of my genes, has no straightforward bearing on what it makes sense for me to want or act to attain ... A like conclusion would hold if I knew that I was created by a deity for some purpose of his: his goal need not be mine.
>
> *1990, pp. 28–29*

Gibbard's view is shared by distinguished biologist George Williams (1988), who feels that

> There is no conceivable justification for any personal concern with the interests (long-term average proliferation) of the genes we received in the lottery of meiosis and fertilization. As Huxley was the first to recognize, there is every reason to rebel against any tendency to serve such interest.
>
> *p. 403*

Hence the title of an earlier book of mine, *The Robot's Rebellion* (Stanovich, 2004). The opportunity exists for a remarkable cultural project that involves advancing human rationality by honoring human interests over genetic interests when the two do not coincide. Its emancipatory potential is lost if we fail to see the critical divergence of interests that creates the distinction between genetic fitness and maximizing human satisfaction.

Notes

1 I define instrumental rationality standardly here as: Behaving in the world so that you get exactly what you most want, given the resources (physical and mental) available to you. More formally, economists and cognitive scientists define maximizing instrumental rationality as choosing among options based on which option has the largest expected utility.

2 Strictly speaking, there are two conceptually different subspaces within area B. There are goals that are currently serving genetic fitness that are antithetical to the vehicle's interests, and there are goals within this area that serve neither genetic nor vehicle interests. The reason there are the latter is because genetic goals arose in the ancient environment in which our brains evolved (the environment of evolutionary adaptation, EEA). Environments can change faster than evolutionary adaptations, so that some genetic goals may not always be perfectly adapted to the current environment. Whether these goals currently facilitate genetic fitness—or only facilitated reproductive fitness in the past—is irrelevant for the present argument. In either case, goals which diverge from vehicle goals reside in the brain because of the genes. For example, whether the consumption of excess fat serves current reproductive fitness or not, it is a vehicle-thwarting tendency (for most of us!), and it is there because it served reproductive fitness at some earlier point in time.

3 The caveat in note 2 is relevant here as well. When something is labeled a genetic goal, it does not necessarily mean that the goal is *currently* serving the interests of reproductive fitness—only that it did so sometime in the past in the EEA.

4 Of course, the absolute sizes of the areas in Figure 11.3 are a matter of conjecture. The argument here depends only on the assumption that area A is larger than area D.

5 The full treatment in Stanovich (2004) also discusses the case of goals serving the interests of memes (and not genes *or* vehicles).

References

Amati, D., & Shallice, T. (2007). On the emergence of modern humans. *Cognition*, 103, 358–385.

Bago, B., & De Neys, W. (2017). Fast logic? Examining the time course assumption of dual process theory. *Cognition*, 158, 90–109.

Cohen, L. J. (1981). Can human irrationality be experimentally demonstrated? *Behavioral and Brain Sciences*, 4, 317–370.

Cooper, W. S. (1989). How evolutionary biology challenges the classical theory of rational choice. *Biology and Philosophy*, 4, 457–481.

Dawes, R. M. (1976). Shallow psychology. In J. S. Carroll & J. W. Payne (Eds.), *Cognition and social behavior* (pp. 3–11). Hillsdale, NJ: Erlbaum.

Dawkins, R. (1976). *The selfish gene.* New York: Oxford University Press.

Dawkins, R. (1982). *The extended phenotype.* New York: Oxford University Press.

De Neys, W. (Ed.) (2018). *Dual process theory 2.0.* London: Routledge.

Dennett, D. C. (1996). *Kinds of minds: Toward an understanding of consciousness.* New York: Basic Books.

Dennett, D. C. (2017). *From bacteria to Bach and back.* New York: Norton.

Evans, J. St. B. T. (2008). Dual-processing accounts of reasoning, judgment and social cognition. *Annual Review of Psychology*, 59, 255–278.

Evans, J. St. B. T. (2010). *Thinking twice: Two minds in one brain.* Oxford: Oxford University Press.

Evans, J. St. B. T. (2014). *Reasoning, rationality and dual processes.* London: Psychology Press.

Evans, J. St. B. T. (2018). Dual process theory: Perspectives and problems. In W. De Neys (Ed.), *Dual process theory 2.0.* London: Routledge.

Evans, J. St. B. T., & Stanovich, K. E. (2013). Dual-process theories of higher cognition: Advancing the debate. *Perspectives on Psychological Science*, 8, 223–241.

Gibbard, A. (1990). *Wise choices, apt feelings: A theory of normative judgment.* Cambridge, MA: Harvard University Press.

Gigerenzer, G. (1996). On narrow norms and vague heuristics: A reply to Kahneman and Tversky (1996). *Psychological Review*, 103, 592–596.

Gigerenzer, G. (2007). *Gut feelings: The intelligence of the unconscious.* New York: Viking Penguin.

Gilbert, D. T. (2006). *Stumbling on happiness.* New York: Alfred A. Knopf.

Hull, D. L. (2001). *Science and selection: Essays on biological evolution and the philosophy of science.* Cambridge: Cambridge University Press.

Kahneman, D. (2011). *Thinking, fast and slow.* New York: Farrar, Straus & Giroux.

Kahneman, D., & Frederick, S. (2002). Representativeness revisited: Attribute substitution in intuitive judgment. In T. Gilovich, D. Griffin, & D. Kahneman (Eds.), *Heuristics and biases: The psychology of intuitive judgment* (pp. 49–81). New York: Cambridge University Press.

Kahneman, D., & Tversky, A. (1996). On the reality of cognitive illusions. *Psychological Review*, 103, 582–591.

Kelman, M. (2011). *The heuristics debate*. New York: Oxford University Press.

Lee, C. J. (2006). Gricean charity: The Gricean turn in psychology. *Philosophy of the Social Sciences*, 36, 193–218.

Li, N., van Vugt, M., & Colarelli, S. (2018). The evolutionary mismatch hypothesis: Implications for psychological science. *Current Directions in Psychological Science*, 27, 38–44.

Mercier, H., & Sperber, D. (2017). *The enigma of reason*. Cambridge, MA: Harvard University Press.

Mithen, S. (1996). *The prehistory of mind: The cognitive origins of art and science*. London: Thames and Hudson.

Mithen, S. (2002). Human evolution and the cognitive basis of science. In P. Carruthers, S. Stich, & M. Siegel (Eds.), *The cognitive basis of science* (pp. 23–40). Cambridge: Cambridge University Press.

Oaksford, M., & Chater, N. (2007). *Bayesian rationality: The probabilistic approach to human reasoning*. Oxford: Oxford University Press.

Oaksford, M., & Chater, N. (2012). Dual processes, probabilities, and cognitive architecture. *Mind & Society*, 11, 15–26.

Pennycook, G., Fugelsang, J. A., & Koehler, D. J. (2015). What makes us think? A three-stage dual-process model of analytic engagement. *Cognitive Psychology*, 80, 34–72.

Polonioli, A. (2015). Stanovich's arguments against the "Adaptive rationality" Project: An assessment. *Studies in History and Philosophy of Biological and Biomedical Sciences*, 40, 55–62.

Reber, A. S. (1993). *Implicit learning and tacit knowledge*. New York: Oxford University Press.

Richerson, P. J., & Boyd, R. (2005). *Not by genes alone: How culture transformed human evolution*. Chicago: University of Chicago Press.

Samuels, R., & Stich, S. P. (2004). Rationality and psychology. In A. R. Mele & P. Rawling (Eds.), *The Oxford handbook of rationality* (pp. 279–300). Oxford: Oxford University Press.

Shah, A. K., & Oppenheimer, D. M. (2008). Heuristics made easy: An effort-reduction framework. *Psychological Bulletin*, 134, 207–222.

Simon, H. A. (1955). A behavioral model of rational choice. *The Quarterly Journal of Economics*, 69, 99–118.

Simon, H. A. (1956). Rational choice and the structure of the environment. *Psychological Review*, 63, 129–138.

Stanovich, K. E. (1999). *Who is rational? Studies of individual differences in reasoning*. Mahwah, NJ: Erlbaum.

Stanovich, K. E. (2004). *The robot's rebellion: Finding meaning in the age of Darwin*. Chicago: University of Chicago Press.

Stanovich, K. E. (2010). *Decision making and rationality in the modern world*. New York: Oxford University Press.

Stanovich, K. E. (2011). *Rationality and the reflective mind*. New York: Oxford University Press.

Stanovich, K. E. (2018). Miserliness in human cognition: The interaction of detection, override, and mindware. *Thinking & Reasoning*, 24, 423–444.

Stanovich, K. E., & Toplak, M. E. (2012). Defining features versus incidental correlates of Type 1 and Type 2 processing. *Mind & Society*, 11, 3–13.

Stanovich, K. E., & West, R. F. (1998). Individual differences in rational thought. *Journal of Experimental Psychology: General*, 127, 161–188.

Stanovich, K. E., & West, R. F. (1999). Discrepancies between normative and descriptive models of decision making and the understanding/acceptance principle. *Cognitive Psychology*, 38, 349–385.

Stanovich, K. E., & West, R. F. (2000). Individual differences in reasoning: Implications for the rationality debate? *Behavioral and Brain Sciences*, 23, 645–726.

Stanovich, K. E., West, R. F., & Toplak, M. E. (2016). *The rationality quotient: Toward a test of rational thinking*. Cambridge, MA: MIT Press.

Stein, E. (1996). *Without good reason: The rationality debate in philosophy and cognitive science*. Oxford: Oxford University Press.

Stich, S. P. (1990). *The fragmentation of reason*. Cambridge, MA: MIT Press.

Taylor, S. E. (1981). The interface of cognitive and social psychology. In J. H. Harvey (Ed.), *Cognition, social behavior, and the environment* (pp. 189–211). Hillsdale, NJ: Erlbaum.

Tetlock, P. E., & Mellers, B. A. (2002). The great rationality debate. *Psychological Science*, 13, 94–99.

Thompson, V. A. (2009). Dual-process theories: A metacognitive perspective. In J. Evans & K. Frankish (Eds.), *In two minds: Dual processes and beyond* (pp. 171–195). Oxford: Oxford University Press.

Todd, P. M., & Gigerenzer, G. (2000). Precis of simple heuristics that make us smart. *Behavioral and Brain Sciences, 23,* 727–780.

Tversky, A., & Kahneman, D. (1974). Judgment under uncertainty: Heuristics and biases. *Science, 185,* 1124–1131.

Williams, G. C. (1988). Huxley's *Evolution and Ethics* in sociobiological perspective. *Zygon, 23,* 383–407.

12

BOUNDED RATIONALITY AND DUAL SYSTEMS

Samuel C. Bellini-Leite and Keith Frankish

Introduction

The notion of bounded rationality was initially developed by Herbert Simon as a corrective to the ideal models of rationality used in economics, psychology, and philosophy (Simon, 1957). Bounded rationality moderates the requirements on rational agents to reflect the limitations of human cognitive capacity and the conditions of the task environment (Simon, 1955, 1989). In a similar spirit, Christopher Cherniak has argued that traditional conceptions of rationality have no relevance for cognitive science. To adopt ideal general rationality conditions, Cherniak claims, is to deny or ignore our 'finitary predicament' – the basic fact that human reasoning is limited by constraints of time and cognitive capacity (Cherniak, 1986).

The history of the cognitive psychology of reasoning is to a large extent the story of accumulating evidence for human failure to meet standards of ideal rationality. Peter Wason started the modern study of reasoning with tasks, such as the Thog problem and the Wason selection task, which challenged the notion that human cognitive development culminates in a formal-logical stage (e.g., Wason, 1966). In the study of judgement and decision making, Daniel Kahneman and collaborators showed that humans routinely violate the axioms of probability theory and rational choice theory (Kahneman et al., 1982; Tversky, 1969). These pioneering advances led to the identification of various inherent biases in human cognition, and it is now common for researchers on reasoning and decision-making to adopt limited standards of rationality, though there is continued dispute over the precise nature of the limitations dictated (Gigerenzer, 1996; Kahneman, 2003).

A popular way to explain cognitive biases is to appeal to some form of *dual-process theory* (DP theory or DPT), developed by cognitive and social psychologists since the late 1970s (for reviews, see Frankish and Evans, 2009; Evans and Stanovich, 2013). Such theories hold that human reasoning and decision making are supported by two different processing systems: System 1, which is fast, autonomous, effortless, and nonconscious, and System 2, which is slow, controlled, effortful, and conscious.[1] It is common to ascribe biases to System 1 processing (which is seen as geared to norms of evolutionary rationality), and normative responses to System 2 processing. Individual differences in the activation and use of System 2 are often cited to explain why some individuals produce the modal, biased response in reasoning tasks, whereas others respond in line with standards of normative rationality (Stanovich, 1999).

But is the DP approach compatible with the tenets of bounded rationality? Does DPT really abandon the notion of ideal rationality, or does it merely treat it as a feature of System 2 rather than of cognition as a whole? Certainly, some writers in the bounded rationality tradition are suspicious of DPT. They deny that there is any fundamental division of mental systems and account for 'higher cognitive judgements' by positing a range of heuristics, from which a selection is made as needed (Gigerenzer and Regier, 1996; Gigerenzer and Selten, 2001; Kruglanski and Gigerenzer, 2011). In part at least, this negative attitude towards DPT may reflect a view of System 2 as some sort of ideal central system. For example, Gigerenzer writes:

> Heuristics are sometimes subsumed into a 'System 1' that is supposedly responsible for associations and making errors and is contrasted with a 'System 2' that embodies the laws of logic and probability, again without specifying models of the processes in either system.
>
> *2008, p. 21*

Now, one thing that is meant by saying that System 2 is normatively rational is that by engaging in effortful, conscious, System 2 thinking we can apply learned rules of inference, follow task instructions, and correct biased intuitive responses.[2] This has always been a central claim of DPT. It does not follow, however, that System 2 processes *must* be normatively rational in this sense. For we can also go wrong in our effortful, conscious thinking – applying unsound rules of inference, misunderstanding task instructions, and overriding intuitive responses that were in fact normatively correct. We may also consciously employ learned heuristics and rules of thumb, which give us quick and dirty solutions that may be inaccurate or biased. What System 2 gives us is a new level of *control*, which can be used to arrive at normatively correct responses but can also be misused to produce errors. It is not *definitional* of System 2 that it follows normatively correct principles. This point was perhaps not sufficiently stressed by early DP theorists, but it is now clearly acknowledged in the DP literature (see, e.g., Evans and Stanovich, 2013). To this extent, DPT contains no commitment to ideal rationality and there is no conflict with bounded rationality.

There is another worry about DPT, however, which concerns the role of System 2 in abductive inference and belief fixation. The worry has its roots in an earlier form of DPT proposed by Jerry Fodor, which divides the mind into encapsulated input systems and unencapsulated central systems (Fodor, 1983, 2001). This early form of DPT does involve a commitment to unbounded central processing, which it represents as sensitive to global assessments of context and relevance, and Fodor himself drew a bleak moral for cognitive science. Since later forms of DPT have been heavily influenced by Fodor, it is appropriate to ask whether this commitment carries over to them. If it does, then DPT not only conflicts with bounded rationality but also threatens to render part of the mind inaccessible to cognitive science.

We shall set out this worry in some detail and then go on to outline a reply to it. We shall show that there are various ways in which System 2 processing is limited and that contextual processing can be done by System 1. We shall conclude that DPT need not include a commitment to ideal rationality and can incorporate the insights of bounded rationality.

Fodor's DPT and the limits of cognitive science

The mental division proposed by Fodor is between input systems, which interpret perceptual stimuli, and central systems, which are involved in belief fixation and general problem-solving

(Fodor, 1983). Fodor argues that input systems are *modular*, and he develops a detailed account of the features of modular systems. One key property of modules is that they are *domain-specific*. They are dedicated to processing stimuli of a specific type, such as colours, faces, voices, or uttered sentences, and each is structured to deal with its own specific domain, perhaps incorporating information about it. A second core property of modular systems is that they are *informationally encapsulated* – insensitive to information stored elsewhere in the cognitive system. Thus, a module for colour perception would not draw on general knowledge about the colours of particular things. Fodor does concede that contextual information can bias perception, but he argues that this is because perception is not limited to input analysis, so the bias can be applied later by central systems (Fodor, 1983, p. 73). Similarly, he argues that priming effects in language (where experience of one word facilitates the recognition of another, semantically related one) may be due to superficial associations between lexical items *inside* the language module, rather than to the top-down influence of background knowledge about the world. Informational encapsulation of this kind is the core feature of modules, as Fodor conceives of them, and he suggests that their other features can be explained as resulting from it (Fodor, 1983, pp. 79–82).

Central systems, in Fodor's view, have contrasting features to input systems. They are domain neutral (not tailored to any specific type of task), and they are unencapsulated (and therefore nonmodular). The latter feature, Fodor argues, is a consequence of the fact that belief fixation typically involves *abductive inference* – finding the best explanation of the information available – and such inference is a global process, which is *isotropic* and *Quineian* (Fodor, 1983, 2001). To say that it is isotropic is to say that it is open-ended: any item of knowledge could in principle be relevant to the confirmation of any belief (knowledge about astronomy could be relevant to problems in subatomic physics; knowledge of economics could be relevant to evolutionary theory, and so on). To say that abductive inference is Quineian is to say that it is a holistic process: the degree of confirmation a belief receives depends on considerations such as simplicity and conservatism, which are determined globally, by the belief's relations to the rest of the belief system.

Fodor argues that because central processes have this isotropic and Quineian character, cognitive science cannot get any explanatory purchase on them. The argument (developed at length in Fodor, 2001) is at heart simple. Fodor argues that the only serious approach in contemporary cognitive science is the computational theory of mind, which identifies mental processes with formal operations upon mental representations. But such operations are sensitive only to local properties of representations, not to global properties of the belief system. Hence, the more global a process is, the less contemporary cognitive science understands it. Fodor calls this 'Fodor's First Law of the Nonexistence of Cognitive Science' (1983, p. 107).

This problem for computationalism, Fodor notes, manifests itself in the field of artificial intelligence as the notorious *frame problem* (McCarthy and Hayes, 1969; Pylyshyn, 1987). In traditional computational AI ('Good-Old-Fashioned AI' or GOFAI), a robot guides its behaviour by reference to an internal model of the world, and the programmer must provide it with a procedure for updating this model each time it acts, determining what will and will not change as a result of each action. The problem is to find a tractable way of doing this, since, given the right context, any action could change anything. What will change depends on the background state of the world, and working out what revisions to make thus involves holistic, abductive inference. Fodor concludes that cognitive science can deal only with modular, informationally encapsulated systems, the rest being inexplicable by contemporary cognitive science and resistant to artificial modelling.

Now, if we look at Simon's description of the ideally rational 'economic man' posited by traditional economic theory, we find a similarity to Fodor's conception of central processing. Like Fodorian central systems, the economic man is able to make rational choices because he has

> knowledge of the relevant aspects of his environment which, if not absolutely complete, is at least impressively clear and voluminous ... a well-organized and stable system of preferences, and a skill in computation that enables him to calculate, for the alternative courses of actions that are available to him, which will permit him to reach the highest attainable point on his preference scale.
>
> *Simon, 1955, p. 99*

By analogy, Fodorian central processing can be thought of as a 'cognitive' economic man – a powerful homunculus with a voluminous knowledge base, a coherent system of preferences, and the computational skill to determine the rational response in the light of both. Simon notes that this idealized conception provides a poor foundation for economic theory, and we think that Fodor's conception of central systems provides a poor foundation for cognitive theory.

If DPT is committed to a similarly idealized conception of System 2, then DP theorists have reason to be worried.

From Fodor to contemporary DPT

How does Fodor's division between input systems and central systems relate to the two systems posited by contemporary DPT? There are similarities. In DPT, System 1 includes input systems of the sort Fodor discusses, while System 2 processes are all central ones. However, the correspondence is not straightforward. System 1 *also* includes many processes of reasoning, problem solving, and belief fixation, which are all central ones in Fodor's scheme. In fact, in DPT, the two sorts of processing are distinguished not by their functions, but by their computational characteristics (speed, effort, seriality, consciousness, and so on).

Another similarity with Fodor's account is that many DP theorists regard System 1 processes as modular. Stanovich, for example, conceives of System 1 as a set of adaptive problem-solving sub-systems, mostly modular in character (he refers to it as The Autonomous Set of Systems, or TASS) (Stanovich, 2004). However, the notion of modularity in play here is weaker than Fodor's. Stanovich does not treat encapsulation or domain-specificity as defining features of TASS. He notes that encapsulation is a problematic feature, which may be a matter of degree, and he holds that TASS includes domain-general processes of learning and emotion-mediated behavioural regulation. In addition, he does not assume that TASS systems are innately specified with fixed neural structures, and he allows that modules can be developed through practice, as a controlled process becomes autonomous (Stanovich, 2004, pp. 38–40).

For Stanovich, the defining feature of TASS processes is that they are *autonomous* or *mandatory* – that is, they are not subject to higher-level control and, once triggered by their proprietary stimuli, they run automatically to completion. This is why they are fast and do not load on central resources, such as working memory. This does not mean that TASS/System 1 processes cannot be overridden, since higher-level processes may intervene to prevent their outputs from influencing behaviour.[3]

Despite these differences with Fodor, Stanovich's model (and modern DPT generally) still retain a sharp division between autonomous, System 1 processes and central, System 2 ones. Stanovich suggests that System 2 (he also refers to it as the *analytic system*) can be roughly characterized as exhibiting 'serial processing, central executive control, conscious awareness, capacity-demanding operations, and domain generality in the information recruited to aid computation' (Stanovich, 2004, p. 45).

Thus, though DP theorists do not treat System 2 as comprising *all* central processes, they agree with Fodor that there are *some* genuinely nonmodular, domain-general central processes, namely, the conscious, controlled ones. The challenge, then, for DP theories is to explain how System 2 can be flexible and domain-general while still being a limited, bounded system. We shall not attempt to provide an answer here. (For a detailed proposal in the spirit of DPT, see Carruthers, 2006.) Instead, we shall review some evidence relevant to a solution, showing that the division between autonomous, nonconscious, System 1 processes and controlled, conscious, System 2 processes should not be understood in Fodorian fashion as a contrast between rigidly encapsulated systems and unbounded, ideally rational ones. We shall highlight evidence that conscious, controlled cognition is computationally limited, and thus certainly not ideally rational, and then indicate how contextual processing may be done by autonomous, nonconscious processes. This points to an explanation of how the two systems together can approximate to flexible, general-purpose cognition by balancing the computational load between them.

The limitations of System 2

Cognitive psychology shows decisively that our conscious cognitive capacities are limited. This is evidenced by work on short-term and working memory (e.g., Baddeley, 1992; Miller, 1956), attention (e.g., Simon and Chabris, 1999), competing tasks with divided attention (e.g., Schneider and Shiffrin, 1977), and cognitive theories of consciousness (e.g., Baars, 1988). When anything remotely like conscious central systems are involved, what we observe is a competition for *limited* resources. Although we can perform several automatic tasks simultaneously (for example, singing while driving), when conscious, controlled cognition is required, we have a hard time multitasking. We can see, feel, hear, and move at the same time, but we cannot attend to a lecture, do maths problems, and talk about politics at the same time.

These limitations show up in various ways. Selective attention experiments reveal that people can be conscious of only a few items in a rich perceptual scene. Subjects asked to monitor the flow of certain information in a perceptual scene, such as details in a basketball game, become unconscious of other, unrelated information in the scene.[4] Other stimuli are certainly being processed, since we react to meaningful stimuli outside a monitored flow of events, such as someone calling our name. But if we switch focus to the new stimulus, we miss aspects of the scene being monitored, revealing competition for limited capacity.

In dual-task experiments, subjects are asked to complete two tasks at the same time. Initially, task interference reduces performance, but if one of the tasks becomes predictable, performance increases. This is attributed to a process of automatization – a transfer from controlled, System 2 processing to autonomous, System 1 processing, with the consequent freeing up of the limited resources available for the former (Schneider and Shiffrin, 1977).

The limits of conscious processing are closely bound up with those of working memory (see Baars and Franklin, 2003). (Indeed, some DP theorists define System 2 processes as the ones that load on working memory; Evans and Stanovich, 2013.) Working memory is believed to comprise three short-term storage capacities, or *loops*, for visuo-spatial, phonological, and episodic information, each of which is limited in the number of items it can retain and the time for which it can retain them (e.g., Baddeley, 1992). For example, in the Corsi block-tapping test, a visuo-spatial task that requires participants to track the order of cubes the experimenter points to, people can only keep up with a sequence of about five. Likewise, the phonological loop, which can be used to mentally rehearse words and numbers for a few minutes, has a limit of about seven items (Miller, 1956).

Could limited-capacity systems like these be isotropic and Quineian? We shall return to this later, but it is obvious at the outset that they could not be Quineian, since that would require that the confirmation of a single belief be influenced by many others (in principle, all of them), and certainly by many more than the seven-item limit of phonological working memory. As Carruthers notes: 'it has traditionally been assumed by philosophers that any candidate new belief should be checked for consistency with existing beliefs before being accepted. But in fact consistency-checking is demonstrably intractable, if attempted on an exhaustive basis' (2006, p. 52). Of course, a rational agent must have some sort of coherence in their belief set, but they cannot be conscious of all the important confirmation relations in their whole web of beliefs.

We suspect that the problem here stems from the fact that Fodor explicitly models the psychological processes of abductive inference and belief fixation on the processes of theory construction and confirmation in science (Fodor, 1983, pp. 104–105). There are certainly parallels between them, but there are also big differences – not least the fact that science is a social enterprise, which is carried out over an extended period of time and with large amounts of external scaffolding in the form of records and notes. At any rate, while the truth-value of a belief or the consistency of a preference may depend on its links to many other mental states, no more than a few of these links can be checked consciously. This is one thing that condemns us to bounded rationality.

If the conscious mind is so limited, why should we be tempted to assign ideal rationality to it? Perhaps the answer is that we identify our conscious processes with *us* – with the self that is supposed to be responsive to norms of rationality. From a phenomenological perspective, this is tempting, and it may lead us to think of System 2 as a powerful homunculus – an executive system or 'central meaner' (Dennett, 1991), which accesses all our knowledge and is the locus for rational decision making. This would be a serious mistake, however. Our conscious, controlled processes are *part* of our minds, just as our automatic, nonconscious ones are, and they must depend heavily on nonconscious, autonomous processing.[5]

Where does this leave us? Fodor supposed that central processes had to be highly sensitive to context and background information precisely because autonomous, peripheral systems were not (Fodor, 2001). Within the context of DPT, we can reverse this line of reasoning. Since System 2 processes are in fact severely limited, it follows that System 1 must do the work of supplying relevant, contextualized information for conscious central systems to work with (Evans, 2009). As we shall see in the next section, this conclusion accords well with new models of brain functioning, which locate contextual processing in nonconscious, probabilistic systems that are not limited by the capacity of working memory or other central resources.

The flexibility of System 1

If System 1 processing is flexible and context-sensitive, then System 2 can be freed from the burden of ideal rationality. It need not work on complex webs of content but merely on those items that have been pre-selected for relevance by System 1. And there are, in fact, good reasons for thinking that this is indeed the case.

First, as we have already noted, DP theories generally employ a weaker notion of modularity than Fodor's, placing less stress on features such as encapsulation. Carruthers, for example, notes that although modules must be *frugal*, in the sense that they draw on only a limited amount of information in their processing, it does not follow that they each have access only to a *specific* subset of information. A module might have access in principle to all the information in the system but draw on only a tiny fraction of it on each occasion, perhaps using simple search heuristics to make the selection (Carruthers, 2006, pp. 58–59).

Second, it is now widely accepted that modules needn't be persisting, innately specified structures. Rather, they may be 'soft modules' – temporary constructions, assembled from pre-existing components to deal with specific environmental problems. This point is stressed by Michael Anderson (Anderson, 2014). Although a critic of rigid modularity, Anderson does not deny that the cortex contains functionally differentiated regions, which are biased towards different response profiles (Anderson, 2014, p. 52). However, he argues that these regions can interact with each other and form coalitions to perform other tasks. When existing functionally differentiated regions are unable to solve a task as they stand, coalitions between them can be formed 'on the fly' to attempt a local resolution. Anderson dubs such constructions, composed of coalitions of different networks, 'transiently assembled local neural subsystems' or TALoNS. These coalitions generate new possibilities of interaction but are still constrained by the available abilities of the participating regions. Being formed for specific tasks, these coalitions can generate responses in a rapid, effortless manner, without engaging resource-hungry, conscious control processes.

Third, recent models of brain functioning undermine the rigid Fodorian distinction between strictly encapsulated systems and free unencapsulated systems, even within perceptual processing itself. According to currently popular *predictive processing* (PP) theories, the brain's goal is to predict proximal stimuli rather than simply to process past input (e.g., Friston, 2005; Clark, 2013, 2016). These theories see the brain as having a hierarchical structure, with lower levels being close to perceptual input mechanisms and higher levels receiving information from diverse multimodal regions. Signals flow both up and down the hierarchy, with top-down signals predicting lower-level activity and bottom-up signals flagging errors in those predictions. Predictions are based on probabilistic *generative models* distributed through the hierarchy. These models monitor statistical patterns in the layer below, generating nonconscious hypotheses in an attempt to accommodate incoming data.[6]

Within this architecture, the influence of different neural regions is modulated to reflect their success in prediction, through a mechanism known as *precision weighting*. Neural regions that do badly must accept input from other regions, whereas ones that constantly do well are granted more autonomy, allowing a form of encapsulation. Thus, the informational closure of a region reflects its success in prediction, generating a soft module, like one of Anderson's TALoNS. As Clark puts it: 'Distinctive, objectively identifiable, local processing organizations … emerge and operate within a larger, more integrative, framework in which functionally differentiated populations and sub-populations are engaged and nuanced in different ways so as to serve different tasks …' (2016, p. 150). Coalition formation and shifts in control are determined contextually, by success in accommodating new stimuli.

If this approach is on the right track, then Fodor is quite wrong to characterize input systems as strongly encapsulated. For, as Clark emphasizes, context sensitivity is pervasive in the PP account of perception, with top-down predictions guiding how stimuli are interpreted and signal distinguished from noise. For example, if someone says to you, 'Oedipus married his own nother', the currently dominant top-down prediction might constrain interpretation so that the /n/ sound is nonconsciously interpreted as /m/, and the word is consciously heard as 'mother' (Clark, 2013).

Such contextually sensitive processing can be done rapidly since stimuli that can be well accommodated by current predictions are ignored. Instead of letting all worldly informa-tion move up to higher layers, lower layers pass on only stimuli that generate high prediction error. This selectional effect is further enhanced by precision weighting. As Clark puts it, 'very low-precision prediction errors will have little or no influence upon ongoing processing and will fail to recruit or nuance higher level representations' (2016, p. 148). By these means, relevance is selected for right from the start, facilitating rapid responding.

A central feature of the PP framework is that it draws no sharp boundary between perception and cognition (or, indeed, between perception, cognition, and action). Judgement-like top-down predictions are continually modifying and being modified by perception-like bottom-up error signals. Thus, what DPT theorists would think of System 1 judgements may be more akin to perceptual processes than to explicit System 2 judgements, sharing in the context-sensitivity of perception. If one's previously calm companion starts to show signs of anger, bottom-up error signals will cause one's generative models to adapt, yielding a new prediction with a judgement-like form ('He is angry and may become violent').

Although few DP theorists have explicitly adopted PP approaches, some have stressed the perception-like character of System 1 judgements. For example, Kahneman and Frederick observe that the perception/judgement boundary 'is fuzzy and permeable: the *perception* of a stranger as menacing is inseparable from a *prediction* of future harm' (Kahneman and Frederick, 2002, p. 50). They note, moreover, that the heuristics and biases research programme (which was a major inspiration for dual-process theories) was from the start 'guided by the idea that intuitive judgments occupy a position ... between the automatic parallel operations of perception and the controlled serial operations of reasoning' (Kahneman and Frederick, 2002, p. 50). There are good reasons, then, for thinking that the dual-process conception of System 1 and PP make a natural partnership.

The moral of this is that the representations that are made available for explicit System 2 processing will have already gone through considerable prior processing and filtering. Only high error (unexpected and thus informative) stimuli reach higher levels of processing and become available for explicit System 2 reasoning. Thus, on the view we have outlined, System 2 reasoning would be neither isotropic nor Quineian. It would not be isotropic because it would not be true that any element could influence it (it receives only a small subset of the data, selected as relevant) and it would not be Quineian since it would not have access to all the information required to check for holistic consistency. In fact, it would be limited in just the ways the evidence suggests it in fact is. Thus, it could meet only bounded standards of rationality.

Conclusion

It is tempting to think of conscious thought as open-ended and unconstrained, and of nonconscious processes as inflexible and encapsulated. Cognitive psychology and computational neuroscience show that this is wrong. Conscious cognition is in fact severely limited in capacity, while nonconscious processes are tuned to the heavy demands of contextual and relevance processing. It is thus vital that modern dual-process theories do not carry over the conception of rationality implicit in Fodor's precursor theory. In thinking about the functions and capacities of the posited dual systems, the perspective of bounded rationality is essential. System 2, if it exists, is not an idealized reasoner, a cognitive analogue of Simon's 'economic man'.

Acknowledgements

The authors thank Riccardo Viale for his detailed and helpful comments on an earlier draft of this chapter.

Notes

1 More recently, there has been a tendency to speak of two *types of processing* rather than two systems (see e.g., Evans and Stanovich, 2013; Bellini-Leite, 2018). For present purposes, however, we shall use 'systems' terminology, since it better expresses the concerns we wish to address about architectural interpretations of dual-process theory.

2 Of course, the fact that System 2 *can* be used to override intuitive responses does not mean that it *will* be. System 2 thinking is effortful and demanding of cognitive resources, and people engage in it only when they have sufficient time, motivation, and cognitive capacity. And even when they do engage in it, they may still fail to override an intuitive System 1 response. For discussion, see Viale (2018).

3 Another similarity between Stanovich's DPT and Fodor's architecture is that Stanovich sees System 2 representations as decoupled from online perceptual processing, so that they can be used for offline, hypothetical thinking (e.g., Stanovich and Toplak, 2012). However, this decoupling need not bring with it the problematic features of Fodorian central processing. Decoupled representations are detached from the world, but this does not mean that they are integrated with the rest of the system's knowledge in reasoning processes that are Quinean and isotropic. Hypothetical thinking may involve only a limited number of representations held in working memory.

4 The most effective illustration is Simons and Chabris' (1999) experiment, in which participants who are required to the count passes in a video of a basketball game completely fail to notice when a person in a gorilla costume appears.

5 In fact, those who see System 2 as a personal-level system – in the sense that its processes involve intentional actions – are also those who argue against a 'central meaner' and for an illusionist view of consciousness (Dennett, 1991; Frankish 2015, 2016).

6 The claim that System 1 is supported by probabilistic calculations does not entail that the system's overt responses will respect probabilistic principles. The calculations govern the system's internal workings, and its overt responses could conform to different principles, such as those of classical logic. This is not to say that we cannot plausibly infer internal computational principles from behaviour, but we must consider a wider range of evidence, including the speed, accuracy, and range of overt responses.

References

Anderson, M. (2014). *After phrenology: Neural reuse and the interactive brain*. Cambridge, MA: MIT Press.

Baddeley, A. (1992). Working memory. *Science*, 255(5044): 556–559.

Baars, B. J. (1988). *A cognitive theory of consciousness*. Cambridge: Cambridge University Press.

Baars, B., and Franklin, S. (2003). How conscious experience and working memory interact. *Trends in Cognitive Science*, 7(4): 166–172.

Bellini-Leite, S. (2018). Dual process theory: Systems, types, minds, modes, kinds or metaphors? A critical review. *Review of Philosophy and Psychology*, 9(2): 213–225.

Carruthers, P. (2006). *The architecture of the mind*. Oxford: Oxford University Press.

Cherniak, C. (1986). *Minimal rationality*. Cambridge, MA: MIT Press.

Clark, A. (2013). Whatever next? Predictive brains, situated agents, and the future of cognitive science. *Behavioral and Brain Sciences*, 36(3): 181–204.

Clark, A. (2016). *Surfing uncertainty: Prediction, action, and the embodied mind*. Oxford: Oxford University Press.

Dennett, D. (1991). *Consciousness explained*. New York: Little, Brown.

Evans, J. (2009). How many dual-process theories do we need? One, two, or many? In J. Evans and K. Frankish (Eds.), *In two minds: Dual processes and beyond* (pp. 33–54). Oxford: Oxford University Press.

Evans, J., and Stanovich, K. (2013). Dual-process theories of higher cognition: Advancing the debate. *Perspectives on Psychological Science*, 8(3): 223–241.

Fodor, J. (1983). *The modularity of mind*. Cambridge, MA: MIT Press.

Fodor, J. (2001). *The mind doesn't work that way*. Cambridge, MA: MIT Press.

Frankish, K. (2015). Dennett's dual-process theory of reasoning. In C. Muñoz-Suárez and F. De Brigard (Eds.), *Content and consciousness revisited* (pp. 73–92). Cham: Springer.

Frankish, K. (2016). Illusionism as a theory of consciousness. *Journal of Consciousness Studies*, 23(11–12): 11–39.

Frankish, K., and Evans, J. (2009). The duality of mind: An historical perspective. In J. Evans and K. Frankish (Eds.), *In two minds: Dual processes and beyond* (pp. 1–29). Oxford: Oxford University Press.

Friston, K. (2005). A theory of cortical responses. *Philosophical Transactions of the Royal Society of London B: Biological Sciences*, 360(1456): 815–836.

Gigerenzer, G. (1996). On narrow norms and vague heuristics: A reply to Kahneman and Tversky. *Psychological Review*, 103(3): 592–596.

Gigerenzer, G. (2008). Why heuristics work. *Perspectives on Psychological Science*, 3(1): 20–29.

Gigerenzer, G., and Regier, T. (1996). How do we tell an association from a rule? Comment on Sloman (1996). *Psychological Bulletin*, 119(1): 23–26.

Gigerenzer, G., and Selten, R. (Eds.) (2001). *Bounded rationality: The adaptive toolbox*. Cambridge, MA: MIT Press.

Kahneman, D. (2003). Maps of bounded rationality: Psychology for behavioral economics. *The American Economic Review*, 93(5): 1449–1475.

Kahneman, D., and Frederick, S. (2002). Representativeness revisited: Attribute substitution in intuitive judgment. In T. Gilovich, D. Griffin, and D. Kahneman (Eds.), *Heuristics and biases: The psychology of intuitive judgment* (pp. 49–81). Cambridge: Cambridge University Press.

Kahneman, D., Slovic, P., and Tversky, A. (Eds.) (1982). *Judgment under uncertainty: Heuristics and biases*. Cambridge: Cambridge University Press.

Kruglanski, A. W., and Gigerenzer, G. (2011). Intuitive and deliberative judgments are based on common principles. *Psychological Review*, 118(1): 97–109.

Miller, G. (1956). The magical number seven, plus or minus two: Some limits on our capacity for processing information. *Psychological Review*, 63(2): 81–97.

McCarthy, J., and Hayes P. (1969). Some philosophical problems from the standpoint of artificial intelligence. In B. Meltzer and D. Michie (Eds.), *Machine intelligence* 4 (pp. 463–502). Edinburgh: Edinburgh University Press.

Pylyshyn, Z. (Ed.) (1987). *The robot's dilemma: The frame problem in artificial intelligence*. Norwood, NJ: Ablex.

Schneider, W., and Shiffrin, R. (1977). Controlled and automatic human information processing I: Detection, search and attention. *Psychological Review*, 84(1): 1–66.

Simon, H. A. (1955). A behavioral model of rational choice. *The Quarterly Journal of Economics*, 69(1): 99–118.

Simon, H. A. (1957). *Models of man: Social and rational – Mathematical essays on rational human behavior in a social setting*. New York: Wiley.

Simon, H. A. (1989). Cognitive architectures and rational analysis: Comments. Paper presented at 21st Annual Symposium on Cognition, Carnegie-Mellon University.

Simons, D., and Chabris, C. (1999). Gorillas in our midst: Sustained inattentional blindness for dynamic events. *Perception*, 28(9): 1059–1074.

Stanovich, K. (1999). *Who is rational? Studies of individual differences in reasoning*. Mahwah, NJ: Lawrence Erlbaum.

Stanovich, K. (2004). *The robot's rebellion: Finding meaning in the age of Darwin*. Chicago, IL: University of Chicago Press.

Stanovich, K. E., and Toplak, M. E. (2012). Defining features versus incidental correlates of Type 1 and Type 2 processing. *Mind & Society*, 11(1): 3–13.

Tverksy, A. (1969). Intransitivity of preferences. *Psychological Review*, 76(1): 31–48.

Viale, R. (2018). The normative and descriptive weaknesses of behavioral economics-informed nudge: Depowered paternalism and unjustified libertarianism. *Mind & Society*, 17(1–2): 53–69.

Wason, P. (1966). Reasoning, in B. Foss (Ed.), *New horizons in psychology* (pp. 135–151). Harmondsworth: Penguin.

13

MODELS AND RATIONAL DEDUCTIONS

Phil N. Johnson-Laird

Introduction

In daily life, we reason to try to reach conclusions that are true. But, since our premises are often uncertain, a sensible goal is at least to make what logicians refer to as *valid* deductions. These are inferences whose conclusions hold in every case in which their premises hold (see Jeffrey, 1981, p. 1), and so if the premises are true their conclusions are true too, e.g.:

If I'm in Britain then I drive on the left.
I'm in Britain.
Therefore, I drive on the left.

Whatever *rational* might mean – and it is open to many interpretations, rational deductions should at least be valid. They have no counterexamples, which are cases in which their premises are true but their conclusions false.

The inference above is so simple that you might think that all valid deductions in daily life can follow the formal rules of inference for a logical calculus. For instance, one such rule, appropriate for the inference above, is:

If A then B; A; Therefore, B

where A and B are variables that range over propositions. This rule is from the calculus that concerns the analogs in logic of *if, or, and,* and *not* (Jeffrey, 1981). Everyday reasoning would be straightforward if it could follow rules that were complete in that they captured all and only valid deductions, that yielded a decision about validity or invalidity in a finite number of steps, and that did so in a tractable way, that is, depending on only reasonable amounts of time and memory. Alas, some inferences in life violate these desirable properties: their logic is incomplete, and they lack a decision procedure or a tractable one. An instructive example (from Johnson-Laird, 1983, p. 140) is:

More than half the musicians were classically trained.
More than half the musicians were in rock groups.
So, at least one of the musicians was both classically trained and in a rock group.

DOI: 10.4324/9781315658353-15

The concept of "more than half" calls for a logic in which variables range over sets, and this logic is not complete, and has no decision procedure (Jeffrey, 1981, Chapter 7). Likewise, reasoning about the domain of two-dimensional spatial relations, such as "The cup is on the left of the saucer", to which we return later, is intractable for all but the simplest deductions (Johnson-Laird, 1983, p. 409; Ragni, 2003). So, even before we consider the limitations of human reasoning, deduction is bounded for any finite device (cf. Simon 2000). And yet it is to a finite device, the human brain, that we owe the proofs of incompleteness, undecidability, and intractability.

Validity is a notion that can be applied to any system of inference provided that we know the conditions in which its assertions are true. What is invalid in one logic of possibilities, for instance, is valid in another logic of possibilities, because the truth conditions for "possible" differ between the two logics (e.g., Girle, 2009). You might therefore think that, given the truth conditions for everyday assertions, rational deduction is nothing more than valid deduction. Whatever you understand *rationality* to mean, this idea is wrong. The reason why is illustrated in these three deductions, which are each valid and each silly:

1. I'm in Britain.
Therefore, it is raining or it isn't raining.

2. I'm in Britain, and if so then I drive on the left.
Therefore, if I'm in Britain, which I am, then I drive on the left.

3. I'm in Britain, and if so then I drive on the right.
Therefore, I'm in Britain or I drive on the right, or both.

In (1), the conclusion is bound to be true given the premises, because it is a tautology. But it is silly, because its conclusion has no relation to the premises. A sensible deduction needs to depend on the premises. In (2), the conclusion is bound to be true given the premises, and it does depend on them. But it is silly, because it merely repeats their contents. In (3), the conclusion is bound to be true given the premises. But it is silly, because it throws information away: the premise implies the conjunction of the two propositions. A sensible deduction is in contrast:

I'm in Britain, and if so then I drive on the right.
Therefore, I drive on the right.

Sensible deductions are accordingly inferences that maintain the information in the premises (and are thereby valid), that are parsimonious, and that yield a conclusion that was not explicit in the premises (see Johnson-Laird, 1983, p. 37; Johnson-Laird & Byrne, 1991, p. 22). If no conclusion meets these requirements then people tend to say that nothing follows from the premises – a judgement that stands in stark contrast to logic, in which infinitely many conclusions follow from any premises whatsoever. As the three examples above illustrate, most of them are silly. So, let us say: *To make a rational deduction is at least to maintain the information in the premises, to simplify, and to reach a new conclusion.*

Can naïve individuals – those who are ignorant of logic or its cognate disciplines – make rational deductions? Yes, of course. Without this ability, Aristotle and his intellectual descendants would have been unable to develop logic. You might suppose, as some theorists argue, that human beings would not have evolved or survived as a species had not at least some of them been capable of some rational deductions. This way of framing the matter recognizes two robust phenomena: people differ in deductive ability (Stanovich, 1999), and some rational deductions pertinent to daily life defeat almost everyone. Perhaps that is why logic exists.

How do individuals – naïve ones should henceforth be taken for granted – make rational deductions? The question has been under investigation for over a century, but only in recent years have cognitive scientists begun to answer it. This chapter outlines one such answer – the theory of mental models. It rests on five principles corresponding to sections in the chapter. Mental models are not uncontroversial, but the final section of the chapter shows that they explain phenomena beyond other theories of human deduction.

Possibilities underlie reasoning

The theory of mental models postulates that all inferences – even inductions, which are outside the scope of the present chapter – depend on envisaging what is possible, given premises such as assertions, diagrams, or direct observations (Johnson-Laird, 2006; Johnson-Laird & Ragni, 2019). A possibility is a simple sort of uncertainty, but a conclusion that holds in all the possibilities to which the premises refer must be valid. The major principle of human reasoning is accordingly that inferences are good only if they have no *counterexamples*, that is, possibilities in which the premises hold, but the conclusion does not.

Suppose you know about a particular electrical circuit:
If there was a short in the circuit then the fuse blew.

The salient possibility to which this assertion refers is:

Short in circuit   fuse blew

But, other cases are possible too, namely:

Not a short   fuse blew
Not a short   fuse did not blow

The first of these latter two possibilities occurs when the circuit is overloaded, and the second of them is the norm. It is hard to keep three distinct possibilities in mind, and so people tend to focus on the first one, and to make a mental note that the other cases (in which the *if*-clause of the conditional assertion does not hold) are possible. Of course, people don't use words and phrases to represent possibilities, but actual models of the world akin to those that the perceptual system constructs.

The *mental* models of the premise above are represented in the following diagram:

Short in circuit   fuse blew
        . . .

The first model is the salient one in which the *if*-clause holds. The second model (shown as an ellipsis) is an implicit one representing the other possibilities in which there wasn't a short in the circuit. Mental models underlie intuitive reasoning. You learn that there was a short in the circuit. It picks out only the first model, from which it follows at once:

The fuse blew.

Possibilities and necessities can be defined in terms of one another: if an event is possible then it is not necessarily not the case, and if an event is necessary, then it is not possibly not the case. So, what evidence shows that people model possibilities rather than necessities? If possibilities are fundamental, then reasoners should be more accurate in inferring what's possible than in inferring what's necessary. Indeed, they are faster and more accurate (Bell & Johnson-Laird, 1998). A typical experiment concerned games of one-on-one basketball, in which only two can play. So, how would you answer the question about this game:

> If Alan is in the game then Betty is in the game.
> If Cheryl is in the game then David is not in the game.
> Can Betty be in the game?

The correct answer is "yes", because both premises hold in case Alan and Betty are in the game. But, now suppose that the question is instead about a necessity:

> Must Betty be in the game?

You should grasp at once that this question is harder. In fact, if you deliberate about the matter, you will discover that there are only three possible games: Alan plays Betty, Betty plays Cheryl, or Betty plays David. So, Betty must be in any game. When the correct answer is "no", the question about whether a player must be in the game is easier to answer than the question about whether a player can be in a game. A single model that is a counterexample suffices to justify the negative answer to the first question, whereas all models of possibilities are needed to justify the negative answer to the second question. These differences in difficulty between the two "yes" answers, and the switch between the two "no" answers, show that models represent possibilities rather than necessities.

Deductions are in default of information to the contrary

An assertion, such as:

> The fault is in the software or in the cable, or both

implies three possibilities:

> It is possible that the fault is in the software.
> It is possible that the fault is in the cable.
> It is possible that the fault is in the software and in the cable.

People make these three deductions, and reject only the deduction that it is possible that the fault is in neither the software nor the cable (Hinterecker, Knauff, & Johnson-Laird, 2016). Yet, none of these inferences is valid in modal logics, which concern possibilities and necessities. To see why, consider the case in which it is impossible for the fault to be in the software but true that it is in the cable. The premise is true, but the first conclusion above is false. So, the inference is invalid. Analogous cases show that the other two inferences are also invalid. Why, then, do individuals make these inferences? The answer is that they treat the disjunction as referring to the set of possibilities in default of information to the contrary. Conversely, if they know that it is possible that the fault is in the software, possible that it is in the cable, and possible that it is in both, they can use the disjunction above to summarize their knowledge. One reason for the assumption of defaults is their ubiquity in daily life.

Facts often reveal that a valid conclusion that you drew is false. It may be a surprise, but you cope. You no longer believe your conclusion. Yet, in logic, no need exists for you to withdraw it.

Logic means never having to be sorry about any valid conclusion that you've drawn. The reason is that a self-contradiction, such as one between a conclusion and a fact, implies that any conclusion whatsoever follows validly in logic. The jargon is that logic is "monotonic", whereas everyday reasoning is "non-monotonic". The divergence is just one of many between logic and life.

When the facts contradict a valid deduction, you should change your mind, and one view of a *rational* change is that it should be minimal. As William James (1907, p. 59) wrote, "[The new fact] preserves the older stock of truths with a minimum of modification, stretching them just enough to make them admit the novelty." This parsimony seems sensible, and many cognitive scientists advocate *minimalism* of this sort (e.g., Harman, 1986; Elio & Pelletier, 1997). It implies, of course, that the rational step in dealing with a contradiction to a valid inference is to make a minimal amendment of the premises. That's not what happens in daily life. Consider this example:

> If a person is bitten by a cobra then the person dies.
> Viv was bitten by a cobra. But, Viv did not die.
> What would you infer?

Minimalism predicts that you should make a minimal change to the premises, e.g.:

> Not everyone dies if bitten by a cobra.

In fact, most individuals respond in a different way. They create an explanation that resolves the inconsistency, e.g.:

> Someone sucked the venom from the bite so it did not get into Viv's bloodstream.

Hardly a minimal change. Yet, people tend to create such causal explanations, and to judge them to be more probable than minimal amendments to the premises (Johnson-Laird, Girotto, & Legrenzi, 2004). After they have created such explanations, they even find inconsistencies harder to detect (Khemlani & Johnson-Laird, 2012). Just as individuals assume possibilities by default, so they draw conclusions by default. They give them up in the light of evidence to the contrary.

Knowledge modulates the meanings of logical terms

In logic, the analogs of such words as *if*, *or*, and *and*, have constant meanings. Earlier we saw that conditionals – assertions based on "if" – usually refer to three distinct possibilities. But, consider the conditional:

> If God exists then atheism is wrong.

It ought to refer to the possibility in which God does not exist and atheism is wrong. But it doesn't. Knowledge of the meaning of "atheism", as disbelief in God, blocks the construction of the corresponding model. So, the preceding assertion is in reality a *biconditional* equivalent to:

> If, and only if, God exists then atheism is wrong.

Our knowledge modulates our interpretations of words (e.g., Quelhas & Johnson-Laird, 2017). Yet, we are unaware for the most part of these *modulations*. In one experiment (Juhos, Quelhas, & Johnson-Laird, 2012), the participants drew their own conclusion from premises containing a biconditional:

If the client makes an order then the goods are shipped. The goods are shipped. What follows?

They tended to infer:

The client made an order.

They also drew their own conclusion from the similar premises:

If the client makes an order then the goods are shipped. The client makes the order. What follows?

They tended to infer:

The goods are shipped.

They were unaware of a subtle difference between the two sorts of conclusion: their first conclusion was in the past tense, whereas their second conclusion was in the present tense (or in the future tense in Portuguese, which was the participants' native tongue). The model theory predicts this difference. The participants use their knowledge to infer the sequence in which the two events occur, i.e., the ordering the goods comes before their shipping. The conclusion to their first inference refers to the ordering, which comes before the shipping. So, the conclusion calls for the past tense. In contrast, the conclusion to their second inference refers to the shipping, which comes after the ordering. So, the conclusion calls for the present tense, which can refer to future events in both English and Portuguese, or to the Portuguese future tense. (As its native speakers often don't realize, English has no future tense.)

The implementation of modulation in a computer program revealed that some assertions should be judged to be true *a priori*, i.e., without the need for evidence, and that other assertions should be judged to be false *a priori*. An experiment corroborated the predictions (Quelhas, Rasga, & Johnson-Laird, 2017). Individuals judged an assertion, such as:

If Mary has flu then she is ill

to be true. And they judged an assertion such as:

If Mary has flu then she is healthy

to be false. Such judgements run contrary to an influential view in philosophy that the difference between *a priori* assertions and those contingent on evidence is "an unempirical dogma of empiricism" (Quine, 1953, p. 23). Not any more.

Reasoning depends on intuitions or on deliberations, or both

Human reasoners are equipped with two systems for reasoning, which interact with one another. Intuitions depend on mental models, which represent only what is true. As we saw earlier, the assertion:

If there was a short in the circuit then the fuse blew

has these mental models:

a short in circuit   fuse blew

    . . .

Suppose you learn:

The fuse didn't blow.

It eliminates the first of the two mental models above, and so only the implicit model remains. It has no explicit content, and so it seems that nothing follows from the two premises. Many people have this intuition. If they think harder, however, their deliberations may lead them to fully explicit models of the possibilities:

a short in circuit fuse blew
not a short in circuit fuse blew
not a short in circuit fuse did not blow

The premise that the fuse did not blow rules out the first two of these models. So, only the third model remains, and it yields the conclusion:

There was not a short in the circuit.

Some people are able to make this valid deduction, but, as the theory predicts, it is harder and takes longer than the inference described earlier. It depends on deliberation and fully explicit models whereas the earlier inference depends on intuition and mental models.

 Consider the following inference, where each premise refers to two alternative possibilities:

Either the pie is on the table or else the cake is on the table.
Either the pie isn't on the table or else the cake is on the table.
Could both of these assertions be true at the same time?

Most people say, "yes". Their inference depends on mental models. Each premise refers to the possibility that the cake is on the table, and so it seems that both assertions could be true. But, let's spell out the fully explicit possibilities. The first premise refers to these two possibilities for what's on the table:

  the pie not the cake
not the pie the cake

The second premise refers to these two possibilities:

not the pie not the cake
 the pie the cake

A careful examination reveals that the two assertions have no possibility in common. So, the correct conclusion is that they cannot both be true at the same time. The intuitive inference is an illusion, just one of many different sorts (Khemlani & Johnson-Laird, 2017). What they have in common is that they follow from mental models of premises, but not from their fully explicit models. The systematic occurrence of illusory inferences is by far the most unexpected prediction of the model theory. It is a litmus test to show that reasoning is relying on mental models rather than on fully explicit models.

Simulations based on spatial, temporal, and kinematic models

So far, you may have the impression that models are just words and phrases rather than actual models of the world. In fact, models can be three-dimensional structures underlying your grasp, say, of how to get from an office on one floor of a building to its main entrance. If someone asks you to draw a path in the air of your route you can do so: the ability is a prerequisite for navigation, especially the sort that Micronesian islanders carry out without instruments, not even a compass (see, e.g., Gladwin, 1970).

When individuals make two-dimensional spatial inferences, they rely on models. Here is one such problem:

> The cup is on the right of the plate.
> The spoon is on the left of the plate.
> The knife is in front of the spoon.
> The saucer is in front of the cup.
> What is the relation between the knife and the saucer?

The premises describe a layout of the sort in this diagram of a table-top:

> spoon   plate   cup
> knife   saucer

where the items at the bottom of the diagram are in front of those at the top. It is quite easy to infer:

> The knife is on the left of the saucer.

If instead you used logical rules to derive your answer, your first step would be to deduce the relation between the spoon and cup (using the logical properties of *on the left* and *on the right*):

> The spoon is on the left of the cup.

You would then use axioms for the two-dimensional relations in the remaining premises to deduce from this intermediate conclusion that:

> The knife is on the left of the saucer.

A similar problem is most revealing:

> The plate is on the right of the cup.
> The spoon is on the left of the plate.
> The knife is in front of the spoon.
> The saucer is in front of the plate.
> What is the relation between the knife and the saucer?

The premises are consistent with two distinct layouts, because of the uncertainty of the relation between the spoon and the cup:

spoon   cup   plate   cup   spoon   plate
knife   saucer   knife   saucer

Yet, the relation between the two items in the question is the same in both layouts, and so it follows that:

The knife is on the left of the saucer.

If you used models to infer the conclusion, the deduction should be harder than the previous one, because you have to construct two models. But, if you used logical rules to infer the conclusion, then the deduction should be easier than the previous one. You no longer have to deduce the relation between the spoon and the plate, because it is stated in the second premise. Hence, the experiment is crucial in that mental models and logical rules make opposite predictions. The results of experiments corroborated the model theory, and they did so even when a later study corrected for the fact that the first premise is irrelevant in the second inference (see Byrne & Johnson-Laird, 1989; Schaeken, Girotto, & Johnson-Laird, 1998). Analogous results occur when inferences concern temporal rather than spatial relations (Schaeken, Johnson-Laird, & d'Ydewalle, 1996). And a corollary is that diagrams that make it easy to envisage alternative possibilities both speed up and enhance the accuracy of deductions (Bauer & Johnson-Laird, 1993).

The description of a sequence of events can elicit a kinematic model that itself unfolds in time. Imagine a railway track that runs from left to right. It has a siding onto which cars enter from the left, and exit to the left. Five cars are at the left end of the track: A B C D E. Figure 13.1 is a diagram of the situation. Here is a problem for you to solve:

> All but one of the cars enter the siding. The remaining car at the left end of the track moves over to the right end of the track. Now each car on the siding, one at a time, moves back to the left end of the track and immediately over to the right end. What is the resulting order of the cars at the right end of the track?

Adults, and even 10-year-old children, can deduce the final order of the cars: E D C B A. They do so by envisaging the effect of each move until the sequence ends. In other words, they simulate the sequence in a kinematic mental model (Khemlani et al., 2013). Children accompany their simulations with gestures indicating the moves they would make if they were allowed to move the cars – an outward sign of inward simulation. And they are less accurate if they are prevented from gesturing (Bucciarelli et al., 2016).

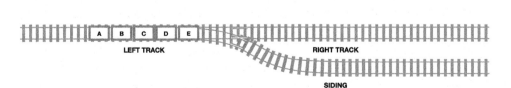

Figure 13.1   A diagram of a small railway track with five cars at the left-hand side of the track

Conclusion

Rational deductions depend on mental models. The theory is controversial in psychology, but it has led to evidence that challenges its rivals. The earliest theories of human reasoning proposed that the mind is equipped with formal rules of inference akin to those of logic (e.g., Rips, 1994). These theories cannot explain the illusory inferences described earlier, and, as we saw, when models were pitted against logic, number of models rather than number of logical steps predicted the difficulty of deductions. Because models represent possibilities, modal logic might be relevant because it deals with possibilities and necessities. But, even though there are many different modal logics (see, e.g., Girle, 2009), human reasoning diverges from all of them. One such divergence is in inferences such as:

> The fault is in the software or in the cable, or both.
> Therefore, it is possible that the fault is in the software.

It is invalid in all modal logics (for the reasons described on p. 220). Yet, as we saw, most people make such inferences (Hinterecker et al., 2016).

A radical alternative is that reasoning relies, not on logic, but on probabilities (e.g., Oaksford & Chater, 2007). This proposal has a more limited purview than the model theory. It offers no explanation of illusory or kinematic inferences. It applies to Aristotelian syllogisms, but the model theory fits the results of experiments better (Khemlani & Johnson-Laird, 2013). Possibilities with appropriate numbers are probabilities. So, the model theory offers an account of probabilistic reasoning (Johnson-Laird et al., 1999; Khemlani, Lotstein, & Johnson-Laird, 2015). In contrast, theories based on probabilities alone cannot distinguish between certainty and necessity, so they are unable to explain inferences about who *must* play in one-on-one games of basketball, as discussed above.

Our reasoning is bounded. We make deductions in domains that are undecidable or intractable in their demands on time and memory. Yet, we are rational in principle. We grasp the force of counterexamples, and spontaneously use them to refute invalid inferences. Our deductions from fully explicit models yield valid conclusions based on all the information in the premises. Indeed, models of possibilities are enough to establish principles of rationality, and the model theory itself.

References

Bauer, M. I., and Johnson-Laird, P. N. 1993. How diagrams can improve reasoning. *Psychological Science* 4, 372–378.

Bell, V., and Johnson-Laird, P. N. 1998. A model theory of modal reasoning. *Cognitive Science* 22, 25–51.

Boolos, G. S., and Jeffrey, R. C. 1980. *Computability and Logic* (3rd ed.). Cambridge: Cambridge University Press.

Bucciarelli, M., Mackiewicz, R., Khemlani, S. S., and Johnson-Laird, P. N. 2016. Children's creation of algorithms: Simulations and gestures. *Journal of Cognitive Psychology* 28, 297–318.

Byrne, R. M. J., and Johnson-Laird, P. N. 1989. Spatial reasoning. *Journal of Memory and Language* 28, 564–575.

Elio, R., and Pelletier, F.J. 1997. Belief change as prepositional update. *Cognitive Science* 21, 419–460.

Girle, R. 2009. *Modal Logics and Philosophy* (2nd ed.). London: Routledge.

Gladwin, T. 1970. *East Is a Big Bird*. Cambridge, MA: Harvard University Press.

Harman, G. 1986. *Change in View: Principles of Reasoning*. Cambridge, MA: MIT Press.

Hinterecker, T., Knauff, M., and Johnson-Laird, P. N. 2016. Modality, probability, and mental models. *Journal of Experimental Psychology: Learning, Memory, and Cognition* 42, 1606–1620.

James, W. 1907. *Pragmatism*. New York: Longmans, Green.

Jeffrey, R. 1981. *Formal Logic: Its Scope and Limits* (2nd ed.). New York: McGraw-Hill.

Johnson-Laird, P. N. 1983. *Mental Models*. Cambridge, MA: Harvard University Press.

Johnson-Laird, P. N. 2006. *How We Reason*. New York: Oxford University Press.

Johnson-Laird, P. N., and Byrne, R. M. J. 1991. *Deduction*. Hillsdale, NJ: Erlbaum.

Johnson-Laird, P. N., Girotto, V., and Legrenzi, P. 2004. Reasoning from inconsistency to consistency. *Psychological Review* 111, 640–661.

Johnson-Laird, P. N., Legrenzi, P., Girotto, V., Legrenzi, M., and Caverni, J-P. 1999. Naive probability: A mental model theory of extensional reasoning. *Psychological Review* 106, 62–88.

Johnson-Laird, P. N., and Ragni, M. 2019. Possibilities as the foundation of reasoning. *Cognition* 193, 130950.

Juhos, C. A., Quelhas, C., and Johnson-Laird, P. N. 2012. Temporal and spatial relations in sentential reasoning. *Cognition* 122, 393–404.

Khemlani, S. S., and Johnson-Laird, P. N. 2012. Hidden conflicts: Explanations make inconsistencies harder to detect. *Acta Psychologica* 139, 486–491.

Khemlani, S. S., and Johnson-Laird, P. N. 2013. The processes of inference. *Argument and Computation* 4, 4–20.

Khemlani, S. S., and Johnson-Laird, P. N. 2017. Illusions in reasoning. *Minds and Machines* 27, 11–35.

Khemlani, S. S., Lotstein, M., and Johnson-Laird, P. N. 2015. Naive probability: Model-based estimates of unique events. *Cognitive Science* 39, 1216–1258.

Khemlani, S. S., Mackiewicz, R., Bucciarelli, M., and Johnson-Laird, P. N. 2013. Kinematic mental simulations in abduction and deduction. *Proceedings of the National Academy of Sciences* 110, 16766–16771.

Oaksford, M., and Chater, N. 2007. *Bayesian Rationality: The Probabilistic Approach to Human Reasoning*. Oxford: Oxford University Press.

Quelhas, A. C., and Johnson-Laird, P. N. 2017. The modulation of disjunctive assertions. *Quarterly Journal of Experimental Psychology* 70, 703–717.

Quelhas, A. C., Rasga, C., and Johnson-Laird, P. N. 2017. A priori true and false conditionals. *Cognitive Science* 41, 1003–1030.

Quine, W. V. O. 1953. *From a Logical Point of View*. Cambridge, MA: Harvard University, Press.

Ragni, M. 2003. An arrangement calculus, its complexity and algorithmic properties. In A. Günter, R. Kruse, and B. Neumann (Eds.), *Advances in Artificial Intelligence: Proceedings of 26th Annual German Conference on AI* (pp. 580–590). Berlin: Springer.

Rips, L. 1994. *The Psychology of Proof*. Cambridge, MA: MIT Press.

Schaeken, W. S., Girotto, V., and Johnson-Laird, P. N. 1998. The effect of an irrelevant remise on temporal and spatial reasoning. *Kognitionswisschenschaft* 7, 27–32.

Schaeken, W. S., Johnson-Laird, P. N., and d'Ydewalle, G. 1996. Mental models and temporal reasoning. *Cognition* 60, 205–234.

Simon, H. A. 2000. Bounded rationality in social science: Today and tomorrow. *Mind & Society* 1, 25–39.

Stanovich, K. E. 1999. *Who Is Rational? Studies of Individual Differences in Reasoning*. Hillsdale, NJ: Erlbaum,

14

PATTERNS OF DEFEASIBLE INFERENCE IN CAUSAL DIAGNOSTIC JUDGMENT

Jean Baratgin and Jean-Louis Stilgenbauer

Introduction: what is diagnostic reasoning?

Diagnostic reasoning consists in going back to the causes that triggered one or multiple effects. For example, we reason from effect to cause when we notice the existence of certain symptoms (skin eruptions, sneezing, conjunctivitis, eczema, …) and try to identify the agent that triggered them (pollen allergy, food allergy, mite allergy, others …). The most basic form of diagnostic inference, which will be our main interest in this chapter, consists in estimating the probability of the cause from the knowledge of the effect. Formally this probability is written $\Pr(\text{cause} \mid \text{effect})$. When physicians notice that one of their patients has conjunctivitis, they might, for example, try to find out if this symptom is linked to a pollen allergy. For this, they would need to calculate the diagnostic probability associated with the cause of interest by estimating $\Pr(\text{Pollen-Allergy} \mid \text{Conjunctivitis})$.

The rational norm of causal diagnostic reasoning has evolved a lot. It went from a purely probabilistic (statistic) norm centered around the Bayes's rule to a norm centered around causal Bayesian networks. However, regardless of the rationality framework considered, people's performances systematically deviate from the predictions of these rationality norms. The *underestimation of the base rate* and the *neglect of alternative causes* are the main violations of rationality traditionally reported by psychologists. These results, which are incidentally very robust, suggest that the estimation of $\Pr(\text{cause} \mid \text{effect})$ is calculated in a limited context of rationality, or of degraded rationality, and they also suggest that this estimating process relies on the use of heuristic strategies. In this chapter, we will focus on two verbal strategies of diagnostic reasoning taking the shape of probable conditional inferences (the *defeasible Modus Ponens* and the *defeasible affirming the consequent*). Before detailing these heuristics, we will first re-contextualize the basic diagnostic activity of interest here in regard to associated reasoning. We will then clarify the level on which our work is based in comparison to research in the field of causality.

Estimating $\Pr(\text{cause} \mid \text{effect})$ reflects, as we mentioned, an *elementary* form of diagnostic reasoning (Tversky & Kahneman, 1974). It is a basic reasoning triggered when the diagnostic process starts and when we try to account for a new phenomenon (effect). Calculating the diagnostic probability helps people evaluate the intensity of the (statistical) link between the variable considered to be the potential cause (or cause of interest), and the effect to explain. However, this initial step is, insufficient to access the complete characterization of the causal role of the cause of interest and two other types of reasoning will allow the access to a deeper level of

DOI: 10.4324/9781315658353-16

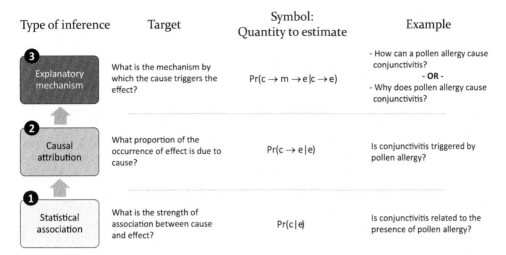

Type of inference	Target	Symbol: Quantity to estimate	Example
3 Explanatory mechanism	What is the mechanism by which the cause triggers the effect?	$Pr(c \rightarrow m \rightarrow e \mid c \rightarrow e)$	- How can a pollen allergy cause conjunctivitis? - OR - - Why does pollen allergy cause conjunctivitis?
2 Causal attribution	What proportion of the occurrence of effect is due to cause?	$Pr(c \rightarrow e \mid e)$	Is conjunctivitis triggered by pollen allergy?
1 Statistical association	What is the strength of association between cause and effect?	$Pr(c \mid e)$	Is conjunctivitis related to the presence of pollen allergy?

Figure 14.1　The three types of inferences involved in the production of a diagnosis. Reasoning is initiated by the observation of an effect (noted e), step (1) consists in detecting a potential cause (noted c) and in measuring the force of association between e and c. This first step corresponds to the elementary diagnostic reasoning with the estimation of $Pr(c \mid e)$. Step (2) consists in estimating the contribution of c in the causal influence triggering e. This inference is usually called *causal attribution* and is represented by the expression $Pr(c \rightarrow e \mid e)$. Step (3) is the most complex of all three as it is at this level that an explanatory mechanism (noted m) will be selected\conceived. This mechanism is a process (containing at least one variable) through which the influence of the cause c will be transmitted to the effect e. We can summarize this final step of the diagnostic reasoning with the expression $Pr(c \rightarrow m \rightarrow e \mid c \rightarrow e)$. This step corresponds to an *inference toward the best explanation*.

understanding (see Figure 14.1). To show the effective causal role of the cause of interest, we need to extract the statistical data by producing an inference called *causal attribution* (Cheng & Novick, 2005; Hilton & Slugoski, 1986). This reasoning consists in estimating the probability of the causal link between the cause of interest and the effect. A more elaborate form of inference will then complete the diagnostic by encouraging the selection\conception of an explanatory mechanism which will explain the mode of action of the cause. This type of reasoning is usually called inference *to the best explanation* (Douven, 2016; Lipton, 2004).

Finally, since this chapter focuses on a form of reasoning relying on causal links, it seems legitimate to put our argument in perspective in the field of research on causality. According to Williamson (2007), three great axes of research on causality exist. The first focuses on the problem of the nature of causality, the second on learning causal links, and the third on causality-based reasoning. Our work on diagnostic inference strategies is a natural extension of research in the third axis, but also in the second one since in the field of diagnosis, learning and reasoning are often quite entangled. The first axis is in contrast to the other two, completely orthogonal to the question asked in this chapter, and as a consequence we will not comment further on contemporary theories on the nature of causality.[1]

Rationality framework: from a statistical norm to causal models

Research led by the heuristics and bias program (Tversky & Kahneman, 1974) yet shows that the estimation of the diagnostic probability of individuals deviates from the diagnostic probability calculated by Bayes's rule.[2] Different tasks like the "Lawyer-Engineer problem"

(Kahneman & Tversky, 1973), the "Taxis problem" (Bar-Hillel, 1980) and the "Mammography problem" (Eddy, 1982), show the systematic neglect of the base rate of the cause of interest when estimating the diagnostic probability (for a review, see Baratgin & Politzer, 2006; Barbey & Sloman, 2007; Koehler, 1996). In the previous example of the allergy to pollens, the base rate was then defined by the prior probability (or prevalence) of this allergy within the reference population.

Yet the pure statistical information is not enough to establish an accurate diagnosis as individuals actually infer this kind of information through a causal model of the situation (or causal structure).[3] Figure 14.1 shows an elementary causal model with only one cause of interest (pollen allergy) and only one effect (conjunctivitis). This kind of object was introduced in the field of cognitive psychology in the 1990s (Waldmann & Holyoak, 1992; Waldmann, Holyoak, & Fratianne, 1995), it is a compact representation of the cause-effect relationships connecting the variables of interest to each other. Causal models have later been developed and updated to provide heuristics models to psychology allowing the testing of new hypotheses, and, on the other hand, these models provide a new framework of rational analysis of human causal inferences (Griffiths & Tenenbaum, 2005, 2009).

A causal model contains information that goes beyond the simple pattern of co-occurrences of the variables of interest, meaning the statistical data of the studied system. Individuals possessing a causal model will be able to understand the process that generated this data. This higher level of understanding implies attributing a new state to the variables of the system: each variable will be interpreted as either the *cause* or the *effect*. One other refinement consists in enriching a causal model through the introduction of mechanisms which will help accurately define the relationships between variables. Figure 14.2 represents an elementary causal model

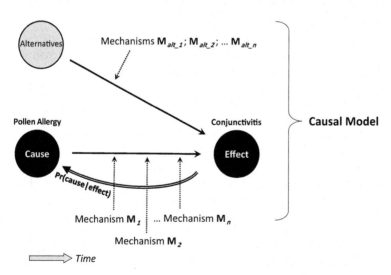

Figure 14.2 Causal model containing a single cause of interest (pollen allergy) causally linked to a single effect (conjunctivitis). The model includes a supplementary variable representing all the alternative causes potentially also triggering the effect. The elementary diagnostic reasoning shown here allows going back to the cause from the knowledge of the effect. This process consists in the estimation of the probability Pr(cause | effect) and is symbolized by the curved double arrow pointing to the cause. The causal model can also be improved through the introduction of a mechanism explaining why the cause triggers the effect (see Protzko, 2018 for a recent discussion on the concepts of cause and mechanism). In general, multiple mechanisms M_1, M_2, ... M_n (dashed arrows) compete to characterize the causal link of interest. Alternative causes also possess their own explanatory mechanisms M_{alt_1}, M_{alt_2}, ... M_{alt_n}.

based on a structure containing a single cause and a single effect. The arrow connecting those two variables implies a link of causality. The model also contains a supplementary variable representing all the different alternative causes able to trigger the same effect regrouped into one entity.

Today, representing causal knowledge of people through the use of *causal Bayes nets* (CBN) is quite common. The CBN are formal tools that were initially developed in the field of Artificial Intelligence (Pearl, 1988, 2000; Spirtes, Glymour, & Scheines, 2000). This formalism is commonly used to study causal cognition in psychology. For a detailed review of its uses in this field, see Rottman and Hastie (2014) and Rottman (2017). The great modularity of the CBN offers the possibility to represent causal structures like the one in Figure 14.2 and also allow the expression of the great variety of reasoning processes related to it. For example, Meder, Mayrhofer, and Waldmann (2009, 2014) recently suggested a model of diagnostic reasoning (structure induction model) establishing a new rational framework for elementary inferences produced from a causal structure similar to the one shown in Figure 14.2.[4] Despite being useful, not only to establish a standard of rationality but also for their heuristic qualities, we believe that this model remains insufficient in order to explain human diagnostic inferences. People have indeed limited cognitive resources (memory, attention, computational power) and of course, cannot process the complex computations required by CBN. In order to avoid this obstacle, people must build strategies to estimate the diagnostic probability. In the following section of this chapter, we will briefly describe some of these well-known strategies linked to a misuse of the Bayes's rule and will then detail a new type of strategies relying on conditional reasoning schemas.

Strategies related to the sub-optimal use of the Bayes's rule in the estimation of the diagnostic probability

The heuristics and bias program of the 1970s revealed that people's estimations of the diagnostic probability deviate from the Bayesian model. Yet, those first researchers did not take into account the influence of causal knowledge in the probabilistic reasoning. Krinski and Tenenbaum (2007) have shown that estimations of the diagnostic probability in the mammography problem were close to the Bayesian norm when the statistical information (pattern of co-occurrence of the input variables) was associated with an explicit causal model of the situation, see also Fernbach and Rehder (2012) for results of the same nature. Recent work nuances this observation (Hayes, Ngo, Hawkins, & Newell, 2018) for despite the introduction of the causal model, some people keep using non-Bayesian estimation strategies. Some participants indeed estimate the diagnostic probability $Pr(cause \mid effect)$ from the rate of false positives, by taking into account only the probability $Pr(effect \mid \neg cause)$. Other non-Bayesian estimation strategies have been described by Cohen and Staub (2015), such as those consisting in calculating a pondered sum of the probabilities mentioned in the Bayes's rule. Some participants try to calculate the diagnostic probability from the addition of the false positives rate $Pr(effect \mid \neg cause)$ to the likelihood (rate of true positives) $Pr(effect \mid cause)$.

The various strategies used by people in order to estimate the diagnostic probability suggest that the underlying cognitive processes can vary from one person to another, added to the fact that nothing prevents the observation of variations within the persons themselves depending on the time or context. The systematic study of estimation strategies appears to be crucial in order to improve the understanding of human diagnostic inferences. A limiting aspect of previous studies is the nature of the strategies identified. Indeed, these studies have specifically focused on strategies consisting in combining (in a sub-optimal fashion) quantities of the Bayes's rule (in particular the rate of false positives and true positives). Yet, other strategies of diagnostic estimation can be considered like those formed from schemas of conditional inferences.

New diagnostic estimation strategies: *defeasible Modus Ponens* and *defeasible Affirming the Consequent*

In general, diagnostic probability estimation strategies are distinguished from rational models, either purely statistical like the Bayes's rule or causal like CBN framework. If we use Marr's terminology (1982), these models are at the *computational* level of the general cognitive architecture. They are functional models that define a standard of rationality to calculate the diagnostic probability. Strategies used by people are instead at the *algorithmic* level. They represent the effective cognitive processes followed by people to estimate this probability. This level being purely descriptive, we believe the influence of language and of mechanisms related to linguistic communication in the estimation process cannot easily be ignored. It is indeed natural for people to be communicating and to be using their causal beliefs in reasoning, forming propositions and organizing them in the shape of arguments. According to Mercier and Sperber (2011), it is even the essential function of reasoning. An entire literature on causal arguments exists establishing a strong link between causal cognition and argumentation (see Hahn, Bluhm, & Zenker, 2017 for a recent review). Among the causal arguments, conditional arguments are central to the human cognition. Two patterns have been of special interest to us here because of their high psychological plausibility. The first is based on the *affirming the consequent* schema (AC), the second based on the *Modus Ponens* (MP). These two schemas will be considered in particular in defeasible forms, as a consequence, we will be using the terms *defeasible affirming the consequent* (DAC) and *defeasible Modus Ponens* (DMP). These reasonings are represented in Figure 14.3.

Initially, AC and MP were studied in their causal form by Cummins, Lubart, Alksnis, and Rist (1991), Cummins (1995) and Politzer and Bonnefon (2006). In these research studies, AC was built on a conditional in which the antecedent and the consequent respectively corresponded to a *cause* and to an *effect*. The first premise of the argument consists in declaring the *effect* (we will use here the term "effect!" to mark the initial stage of reasoning that begins with the arrival of new information), the second premise corresponds to the conditional statement and the conclusion is formed by the *cause*. AC coincides with a form of reasoning called *abduction* by the philosopher C. S. Peirce (for recent reviews, see Douven, 2011; Park, 2017). Cummins (1995) and Politzer and Bonnefon (2006) also studied a specific form of MP built on an inverted conditional in which the antecedent was an *effect* and the consequent was the *cause*. The first premise and the conclusion of this form of MP remained untouched compared to AC. They were respectively instantiated by the *effect* on one hand and the *cause* on the other. We represent below the structure of AC and of MP such as they appear in the aforementioned studies:

AC:	MP:
Effect!	Effect!
If <cause> then <effect>	If <effect> then <cause>
Cause	Cause

Those two arguments constitute, in our point of view, good candidates in order to define diagnostic probability estimation strategies, as these forms of reasoning both consist in going back to the cause (conclusion) from the observation of the effect (first premise). The conditional (the second premise) defines the type of strategy. For AC, the inference is based on the trust

---

Defeasible Affirming the Consequent (DAC):

Effect !   Conjunctivitis !

If cause, then Pr(effect)   If a patient is allergic to pollen, then he will probably have conjunctivitis
--------------------   *example*   ---
                          ⟶
Pr(cause)   Probably pollen allergy

Defeasible Modus Ponens (DMP):

Effect !   Conjunctivitis !

If effect, then Pr(cause)   If a patient has conjunctivitis, then he is probably allergic to pollen
--------------------   *example*   ---
                          ⟶
Pr(cause)   Probably pollen allergy

Figure 14.3   These two reasoning patterns represent two formally different strategies for estimating the diagnostic probability Pr(cause | effect). They correspond respectively in the A.I. and philosophical literature to two modes of inference: abduction for DAC and deduction defeasible for DMP. First, the defeasible deduction is a weakened form of deduction that permits the production of provisionally true and/or probable conclusions. Second, abduction is a heuristic reasoning that serves to identify explanatory causes or hypotheses.

put in the causality link between the antecedent and the consequent. This trust depends on the existence of alternative causes that are, just like the cause of interest, capable of triggering the effect. For MP, the mechanism which the inference relies on is, in our point of view, different, for it is rather based on the explanatory qualities of the cause of interest. Here, it's the strength of the mechanism by which the effect is produced by the cause of interest that will guide the inference.

Despite AC and MP being *a priori* interesting in order to define diagnostic reasoning strategies, those arguments are not, as they are, completely satisfying. Indeed, as we've explained above, diagnostic reasoning is an uncertain reasoning allowing the estimation of the probability of the cause of interest, given the knowledge of the effect, or formally the estimation of the probability Pr(cause | effect). AC and MP schemas must be generalized and considered in a probable form as is shown in Figure 14.3. As is shown in Figure 14.3, the probabilistic aspect is defined by the degree of probability placed, on one hand, on the consequent of the conditionals, and on the other, on the reasoning conclusions. A good diagnostic strategy should also possess the quality of being defeasible, for it is natural for people to draw a conclusion or to update its probability in the case of the arrival of new information (taking an additional premise into account for example). The defeasible aspect is shown through the dashed inference line in Figure 14.3.

In order to clearly differentiate the standard schemas AC and MP from their probable and defeasible generalization, we will from now on be talking respectively about DAC and DMP. Those two schemas, as causal diagnostic reasoning strategies, have recently been studied by Stilgenbauer and Baratgin (2018, 2019) who have shown their psychological relevance in estimating Pr(cause | effect). The authors submitted participants to an experimental paradigm of rule production, where people had to rebuild the conditional rule of DAC and DMP schemas.

Participants were only able to use two pieces of information. They received the first premise of the schema (which was certain) corresponding to the phase of the declaration of the effect. This step is symbolized in Figure 14.3 by the term "effect!." Participants then were informed of the (probable) conclusion of the reasoning, represented in Figure 14.3 by the term "Pr(cause)." The task consisted in the production of a conditional rule allowing the inference of the conclusion from the first premise. To answer, participants had at their disposal jumbled words from which they could form the rule of their choice: [1] *if cause then Pr(effect)* or the reversed rule [2] *if effect then Pr(cause)*. The kind of rule produced revealed the diagnostic estimation strategy the participants preferred. The production of a rule similar to [1] signaled a preference for the DAC estimation strategy. Similarly, the production of a rule similar to [2] revealed a preference for the DMP strategy.

The results of Stilgenbauer and Baratgin (2018, 2019) show that the participants preferred DMP, as they built rules similar to [2] to infer the conclusion "Pr(cause)" from the premise "effect!." The use of a rule like *if effect then Pr(cause)* is indeed quite natural in this situation since a direct correspondence exists between that conditional and the diagnostic probability Pr(cause | effect).[5] This is not the case with DAC inferences though, which rely on rules similar to [1] and which instead make the predictive probability Pr(effect | cause) stand out, since in this case the antecedent of the rule is made of the *cause*, and the consequent is made of the *effect*.

The results of Stilgenbauer and Baratgin (2018) also show that the participants' preferred strategy was not always DMP. Indeed, in certain situations, the DAC strategy can strongly compete with the DMP strategy. This change of preference is linked to the perceived value of the predictive probability Pr(effect | cause).[6] This result has been obtained while controlling the relative levels of the diagnostic and predictive probabilities. In a first *probabilistic context*, participants received information indicating that the diagnostic probability was higher than the predictive probability: Pr(cause | effect) > Pr(effect | cause). In a second condition, it was the opposite: the information given indicated that the diagnostic probability was lower than the predictive probability Pr(cause | effect) < Pr(effect | cause). The results show that conditional rules built by the participants depended on the probabilistic context (meaning the relative levels of the diagnostic and predictive probabilities). People, in the main, build rules similar to [2] *if effect then Pr(cause)* (DMP strategy) in the context Pr(cause | effect) > Pr(effect | cause). Yet, in the context of Pr(cause | effect) < Pr(effect | cause), the proportion of rules similar to [1] *if cause then Pr(effect)* (DAC strategy) significantly increases and does not differ from the proportion of rules similar to [2]. These results confirm the idea that people can estimate the diagnostic probability following strategies taking the form of defeasible schemas of inferences. In the following section we will report new experimental results confirming the robustness of the data we just exposed.

New experimental data: a test of diagnostic strategies through a rule evaluation paradigm

We propose here a new experiment expanding on the logic of Stilgenbauer and Baratgin (2018). The task no longer consists in *producing* a conditional rule, but to *evaluate* (and compare) the two rules that DAC and DMP are made of. The experiment procedure was the following: participants begin by receiving the first premise of the diagnostic strategy "effect!" as well as the conclusion "Pr(cause);" we then explicitly and simultaneously show them the conditional rules [1] *If cause then Pr(effect)* and [2] *If effect then Pr(cause)*. The task of the participants consists in judging if those rules are *judicious* to infer the conclusion "Pr(cause)" from the premise "effect!." Each rule is evaluated on a seven points scale (1 = not very judicious; 7 = very judicious). We assume that the rule judged to be the most judicious will indicate the preferred diagnostic estimation strategy. If the rule [1] is judged to be more judicious than rule [2], this will show that DAC is the preferred strategy to estimate the diagnostic probability. But if [2] is judged more judicious than [1], this will show a preference for DMP. In this experiment, we also recreated two probabilistic contexts identical to those in the study of Stilgenbauer and Baratgin (2018). The judgment of the participants was recorded in the context of Pr(cause|effect) > Pr(effect|cause) and also in the context Pr(cause|effect) < Pr(effect|cause).

A scenario of *fault detection* has been used to cover the situation of diagnostic reasoning. This scenario involved the operation of an industrial machine producing auto parts. The probabilistic context was introduced in a between-subject design, using pictures as shown in Figure 14.4. No matter the probabilistic context, a machine composed of multiple components was introduced to the participants. Components of this machine can malfunction, occasioning the production of faulty parts. The *components* of the machine represent the *causes* and the *defects* on the parts represent the *effects*. In Figure 14.4, the picture on the left refers to the context Pr(cause|effect) > Pr(effect|cause) and the picture on the right to the context Pr(cause|effect) < Pr(effect|cause). For example, for the picture on the left, the machine has two components that can malfunction resulting in parts produced with four defects. The malfunction of components X_1 or X_2 can cause the defects X_a, X_b, X_c, or X_d. For the two probabilistic contexts, it is impossible to have multiple components malfunctioning at the same time, neither is it possible to have multiple defects at the same time. For the left picture, the diagnostic and predictive probabilities are respectively equal to Pr(cause|effect) = ½ and Pr(effect|cause) = ¼.

Participants of the experiment were then told of the malfunction of the machine, and we used the conversation between the repairmen attempting to solve the issue to introduce simultaneously the conditional rules [1] and [2]. Before taking apart the machine, the repairmen

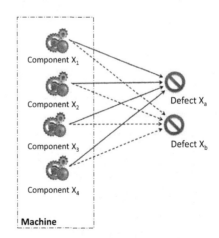

Probabilistic context:	Probabilistic context:
Pr(Component|Defect) > Pr(Defect|Component)	Pr(Component|Defect) < Pr(Defect|Component)

Figure 14.4 Experimental set-up introducing the situation of causal diagnostic reasoning. In each probabilistic context, an industrial machine is symbolized by dashed rectangles. The machines are made up of a certain number of components and their malfunction (causes) can trigger the production of faulty parts with defects (effects). The figure on the left defines the probabilistic context Pr(cause|effect) > Pr(effect|cause). For example, if we're interested in the defect X_a (*effect*) and to the component X_1 (*cause*), we have $Pr(X_1|X_a) = 1/2$ and $Pr(X_a|X_1) = 1/4$. The figure on the right defines the opposite probabilistic context Pr(cause|effect) < Pr(effect|cause) with $Pr(X_1|X_a) = 1/4$ and $Pr(X_a|X_1) = 1/2$.

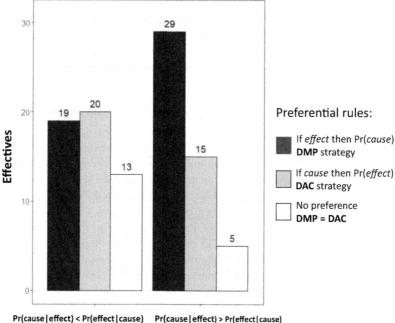

Figure 14.5 Experimental results obtained in rule evaluating. Distribution of the preferred rules of participants depending on the probabilistic context defined by the relative levels of the diagnostic and predictive probabilities.

thought out loud and one of them suggested rule [1] *If component X_1 then Pr(defect X_a)*. Another repairman then contradicted him and suggested the reversed rule [2] *If defect X_a then Pr(component X_1)*.

We recruited 101 participants for the experiment and the results are shown in Figure 14.5. We categorized participants depending on the grades they attributed to each rule. When the grade of the rule [1] was higher than the grade of the rule [2], participants were categorized in DAC. They were categorized in DMP if they graded [2] higher than [1]. In the case where participants graded the two rules the same, they were categorized in "No preference."

Calculating a χ^2 revealed a significant link between the preferred rule and the probabilistic context. In the situation Pr(cause | effect) > Pr(effect | cause), participants believe rules similar to [2] to be more judicious than rules similar to [1]. Yet, in the situation of Pr(cause | effect) < Pr(effect | cause), there was no particular preference visible between the two kinds of rules: 20 participants believed rule [1] to be more judicious than rule [2] and 19 participants believed the opposite. In the context Pr(cause | effect) > Pr(effect | cause), there are also 5 participants grading both rules as equally judicious, and 13 in the context Pr(cause | effect) < Pr(effect | cause).

These results obtained with a paradigm of rule evaluation are interesting for they corroborate those of Stilgenbauer and Baratgin (2018) who used a paradigm of rule production. This new data seems to validate the idea that it is natural for people to use defeasible strategies like DMP and DAC in order to estimate the diagnostic probability. This experiment also confirms that these two strategies are not equally preferred by individuals. Our data indicate that DMP seems to constitute the strategy by default, but in situations where the perceived value of the predictive probability increases, DAC strongly competes with this strategy.

Conclusion: the diversity of diagnostic reasoning shapes

In this chapter, we have been interested in an elementary form of diagnostic reasoning consisting in estimating the probability of a *cause* from the knowledge of its *effect*: Pr(cause | effect). We have limited ourselves to the study of inferences produced from the causal structure known *a priori* and given to participants. This structure was composed of a single cause of interest and a single effect (see Figure 14.2), we will refer to it by using the expression *cause → effect*.[7] In the literature, the majority of studies consist in the evaluation of the performance of participants compared to the rational norm that today is made up of *causal Bayesian networks*. The aim of this work was different. It intended to remain at the level of psychological processes (in other words, processes that are at the *algorithmic* level according to the terminology of D. Marr) to test the plausibility of two strategies of diagnostic inferences. The first was based on a *defeasible affirming the consequent* and the second was based on a *defeasible Modus Ponens*. Our results show that participants understand and can follow these patterns of inference to estimate the probability of a *cause* from the knowledge of its *effect*. These two strategies are important for they are natural for people, although it does not mean that they constitute the only way possible when trying to estimate Pr(cause | effect). Other ways can be imagined, for example, we can think about the use of strategies based on negated components in the shape of a *defeasible Modus Tollens* (effect!, If ¬ cause, then Pr(¬ effect) ⟹ Pr(cause))[8] or of a *defeasible denying the antecedent* (effect!, If ¬ effect, then Pr(¬ cause) ⟹ Pr(cause)). It belongs to future research to test the psychological reality of these kinds of strategies and to report their potential usage by people.

In this chapter, we studied the estimation strategies of Pr(cause | effect) for basic diagnostic inferences produced from a *cause → effect* structure known *a priori*. Yet, we believe that two other kinds of diagnostic reasoning seem to be of importance and, to our knowledge, no study exists on their estimation strategies. Figure 14.1 at the beginning of this chapter suggests an articulation between the basic diagnostic reasoning and these two complementary forms of inferences. The first is called *causal attribution* (Cheng & Novick, 2005; Hilton & Slugoski, 1986) and intervenes in the context where the causal structure is unknown. In this situation, the diagnosis relies on the *link* between the cause and the effect, and the diagnostic probability of interest will be written Pr(cause → effect | effect). The second kind of diagnostic inference that seems to us to be of importance is a bit more complex. It consists in inferring the *mechanism* explaining the nature of the causal link. A minimalistic mechanism can be reduced to a single *mediator* (in Figure 14.2, the concept of mechanism is represented by dashed arrows without actually being clarified). A mediator is a variable allowing the transmission of the influence of the cause to the effect. For example, we know today that *smoking* (cause) can trigger *lung cancer* (effect), through the *tar* (mediator) accumulating in lung alveoli (the role of tar hasn't always been clear in the past). In the context where the structure *cause → effect* is known *a priori*, we can, for example, ask ourselves if a mediator transmitting the influence of the cause to the effect exists. In this situation, the probability Pr(cause → mediator → effect | cause → effect) constitutes the diagnostic probability of interest. In statistics, a very interesting literature exists on the topic of mediation. For a reference, we can read VanderWeele (2015). Many examples of mediation can also be found in MacKinnon (2008).

Finally, we will note that the causal attribution Pr(cause → effect | effect) consists in the elaboration of a causal structure by definition unknown and that the inference of a mediator Pr(cause → mediator → effect | cause → effect) consists in the modification of the causal structure known *a priori*. In the literature dedicated to causal cognition, these processes are generally understood as learning processes allowing on the one hand the elaboration of the structure (defining the variables as *cause* and *effect*), and on the other, the estimation of its parameters (defining the probability distributions of the structure's variables). There is a third class of processes traditionally distinguished in the literature regrouping all the causal reasoning that can be done from a completely defined and parameterized structure (we can refer to Hastie, 2015; Rottman, 2017; and Rottman & Hastie, 2014 for a general review). Yet, we believe that the strategies used by people in order to estimate the diagnostic probability cannot be classified in the traditional way in effect in the field of causal cognition. The main reason for this is that in the field of diagnosis (at least) learning a causal link is often concomitant to the diagnostic reasoning itself. This is also what Meder et al. (2014) suggest with the model of *structure induction* combining learning of the causal structure with the estimation of Pr(cause | effect) (see also Meder et al., 2009). Having said that, we believe that the result or the product of the process of diagnostic inference (the potential cause, the causal link or the mediator) constitutes the central element from which a typology of diagnostic reasoning strategies can be elaborated. A future research program dedicated to the use of diagnostic estimation strategies by people will come, we hope, to bring answers to this important question.

Acknowledgments

The authors would like to thank Frank Jamet and Baptiste Jacquet for much discussion and other help in their research.

Notes

1 For readers interested in the different conceptions of causality, we recommend reading Beebee, Hitchcock, and Menzies (2009), especially Parts 2 and 3.

2 The Bayes's rule is a rule of belief updating when new convincing information is learned. It is the only possible rule of revision of beliefs in the situation of revision called focusing (the situation where the message concerns an object drawn at random from a population of objects which constitutes a certain stable universe, see Baratgin & Politzer, 2010; Walliser & Zwim, 2011). In the context of causal diagnostic, if we write c = *cause* and e = *effet*, the rule would be written in the following way: $\Pr(c|e) = \dfrac{Pr(e\,|\,c) \times Pr(c)}{Pr(e\,|\,c) \times Pr(c) + Pr(e\,|\,\neg c) \times Pr(\neg c)}$. The term $\Pr(c|e)$ corresponds to the diagnostic probability, which is the probability of the cause when the effect is present. The quantity $\Pr(e|\,c)$ is generally called *likelihood*, yet in the situation of causal diagnostic, we would rather use the rate of *true positives*, which is the probability of observing the effect when the cause is present. The quantity $\Pr(c)$ is the *prior* probability of the cause. From an objective point of view, it corresponds to the *base rate* (or prevalence) of the cause within the reference population. The term $\Pr(e|\,\neg c)$ refers to the influence of alternative causes, in other words, the probability of observing the effect without observing the cause of interest. It can also be called the rate of *false positives*. Finally, the quantity $\Pr(\neg c)$ corresponds to the *base rate* of all of the alternative causes.

3 From the historical point of view, from the very beginning of the rise of modern statistics during the nineteenth century, has started to emerge a radical separation between this discipline, on the one hand and causal concepts, on the other (such as those of strength, of mechanisms or of a causal model). Chapter 2 of Pearl and Mackenzie (2018) tells the history of this divorce which, beyond statistics, has produced considerable negative effects for all data-driven sciences. Unmistakably, this separation also had consequences for research on causal cognition. The excessive focus of the *heuristics and bias* school on statistical concepts to the detriment of the introduction of causal concepts likely stems from this divorce. Fortunately, we see today the return of causality. The "causal revolution," according to Pearl is on the way and has started planting its seeds into all sciences and in particular in cognitive psychology.

Waldmann and Hagmayer (2013) wrote an excellent review describing the evolution of causal cognition theories and in particular the shift from purely statistical models to models integrating causal concepts.

4 Meder and Mayrhofer (2017) have recently shown an interest in the more sophisticated forms of diagnostic reasoning that might be produced from causal structures containing multiple causes and effects.

5 Today, many results demonstrating that people interpret the probability of an indicative conditional such as Pr(if A, then C) as the conditional probability Pr(C|A) are available, see for example Baratgin and Politzer (2016). Yet in this work, we study strategies relying on conditionals in the shape of "if A then Pr(C)" and this type of rule constitutes the natural interpretation of Pr(if A, then C), see for this specific point Over, Douven, and Verbrugge (2013).

6 Predictive probability plays an important part in the estimation of the diagnostic probability. It influences, in particular, the accuracy of the estimations of the diagnostic probability. For example, when we ask participants to estimate from a set of data the value of the diagnostic probability, they will weight their estimations with the perceived value of the predictive probability. The lower the predictive probability, the more under-estimated the diagnostic probability is, compared to its real value contained in the data (Meder et al., 2009, 2014; see also Meder & Mayrhofer, 2017; Stilgenbauer & Baratgin, 2019; Stilgenbauer, Baratgin, & Douven, 2017).

7 Yet, in the experiment described in the previous section, we have defined different values of Pr(cause|effect) by changing the number of alternative causes (see Figure 14.4).

8 The symbol "$\Rightarrow$" represents a defeasible consequence relationship.

References

Baratgin, J., & Politzer, G. (2006). Is the mind Bayesian? The case for agnosticism. *Mind and Society*, 5(1), 1–38. http://doi.org/10.1007/s11299–006–0007–1.

Baratgin, J., & Politzer, G. (2010). Updating: A psychologically basic situation of probability revision. *Thinking & Reasoning*, 16(4), 253–287. http://doi.org/10.1080/13546783.2010.519564.

Baratgin, J., & Politzer, G. (2016). Logic, probability and inference: A methodology for a new paradigm. In L. Macchi, M. Bagassi, & R. Viale (Eds.), *Cognitive unconscious and human rationality* (pp. 119–142). Cambridge, MA: MIT Press.

Barbey, A. K., & Sloman, S. A. (2007). Base-rate respect: From ecological rationality to dual processes. *Behavioral and Brain Sciences*, 30(3), 241–254. http://doi.org/10.1017/S0140525X07001653.

Bar-Hillel, M. (1980). The base-rate fallacy in probability judgments. *Acta Psychologica*, 44(3), 211–233. http://doi.org/10.1016/0001–6918(80)90046–3.

Bechtel, W., & Abrahamsen, A. (2005). Explanation: A mechanist alternative. *Studies in History and Philosophy of Biological and Biomedical Sciences*, 36, 421–441.

Beebee, H., Hitchcock, C., & Menzies, P. (Eds.) (2009). *The Oxford handbook of causation*. Oxford: Oxford University Press. http://doi.org/10.1093/oxfordhb/9780199279739.001.0001.

Cheng, P. W., & Novick, L. R. (2005). Constraints and nonconstraints in causal learning: Reply to White (2005) and to Luhmann and Ahn (2005). *Psychological Review*, 112(3), 694–707. http://doi.org/10.1037/0033–295X.112.3.694.

Cohen, A. L., & Staub, A. (2015). Within-subject consistency and between-subject variability in Bayesian reasoning strategies. *Cognitive Psychology*, 81, 26–47. http://doi.org/10.1016/j.cogpsych.2015.08.001.

Cummins, D. (1995) Naïve theories and causal cognition. Memory and Cognition, 23(5), 646–659.

Cummins, D. D., Lubart, T., Alksnis, O., & Rist, R. (1991). Conditional reasoning and causation. *Memory & Cognition*, 19(3), 274–282.

Douven, I. (2011). Abduction. In E. N. Zalta (Ed.), *The Stanford encyclopedia of philosophy* (Spring 2011 ed.). Available at: https://stanford.library.sydney.edu.au/entries/abduction/

Douven, I. (2016). Inference to the best explanation: What is it? And why should we care? In T. Poston & K. McCain (Eds.), *Best explanations: New essays on inference to the best explanation*. Oxford: Oxford University Press.

Eddy, D. M. (1982). Probabilistic reasoning in clinical medicine: Problems and opportunities. In D. Kahneman, P. Slovic, & A. Tversky (Eds.), *Judgment under uncertainty: Heuristics and biases* (pp. 249–267). Cambridge: Cambridge University Press. http://doi.org/10.1017/CBO9780511809477.019.

Fernbach, P. M., & Rehder, B. (2012). Cognitive shortcuts in causal inference. *Argument & Computation*, 4(1), 64–88. http://doi.org/10.1080/19462166.2012.682655.

Griffiths, T. L., & Tenenbaum, J. B. (2005). Structure and strength in causal induction. *Cognitive Psychology*, 51(4), 334–384.. http://doi.org/10.1016/j.cogpsych.2005.05.004.

Griffiths, T. L., & Tenenbaum, J. B. (2009). Theory-based causal induction. *Psychological Review*, 116(4), 661–716. http://doi.org/10.1037/a0017201.

Hahn, U., Bluhm, R., & Zenker, F. (2017). Causal argument. In M. R. Waldmann (Ed.), *Oxford handbook of causal reasoning*. Oxford: Oxford University Press. http://doi.org/10.1093/oxfordhb/9780199399550.013.26.

Hastie, R. (2015). Causal thinking in judgments. In G. Keren & G. Wu (Eds.), *The Wiley Blackwell handbook of judgment and decision making* (pp. 590–628). New York: Blackwell. http://doi.org/10.1002/9781118468333.ch21.

Hayes, B. K., Ngo, J., Hawkins, G. E., & Newell, B. R. (2018). Causal explanation improves judgment under uncertainty, but rarely in a Bayesian way. *Memory and Cognition*, 46(1), 112–131. http://doi.org/10.3758/s13421–017–0750-z.

Hilton, D. J., & Slugoski, B. R. (1986). Knowledge-based causal attribution. The abnormal conditions focus model. *Psychological Review*, 93(1), 75–88. http://doi.org/10.1037/0033–295X.93.1.75.

Kahneman, D., & Tversky, A. (1973). On the psychology of prediction. *Psychological Review*, 80(4), 237–251. http://doi.org/10.1037/h0034747.

Koehler, J. J. (1996). The base rate fallacy reconsidered: Descriptive, normative, and methodological challenges. *Behavioral and Brain Sciences*, 19(1), 1–17. http://doi.org/10.1017/S0140525X00041157.

Krynski, T. R., & Tenenbaum, J. B. (2007). The role of causality in judgment under uncertainty. *Journal of Experimental Psychology General*, 136(3), 430–450. http://doi.org/10.1037/0096–3445.136.3.430.

Lipton, P. (2004). *Inference to the best explanation*. London: Routledge.

Machamer, P., Darden, L., & Carver, C. F. (2000). Thinking about mechanisms. *Philosophy of Science*, 67(1), 1–25. http://doi.org/10.1086/392759.

MacKinnon, D. (2008). *Introduction to statistical mediation analysis*. New York: Lawrence Erlbaum Associates.

Marr, D. (1982). *Vision: A computational investigation into the human representation and processing of visual information*. San Francisco: Freeman.

Meder, B., & Mayrhofer, R. (2017). Diagnostic reasoning. In M. R. Waldmann (Ed.), *Oxford handbook of causal reasoning* (pp. 433–458). Oxford: Oxford University Press. http://doi.org/10.1093/oxfordhb/9780199399550.013.23.

Meder, B., Mayrhofer, R., & Waldmann, M. R. (2009). A rational model of elemental diagnostic inference. In N. A. Taatgen & H. van Rijn (Eds.), *Proceedings of the 31st Annual Conference of the Cognitive Science Society* (pp. 2176–2181). Austin, TX: Cognitive Science Society.

Meder, B., Mayrhofer, R., & Waldmann, M. R. (2014). Structure induction in diagnostic causal reasoning. *Psychological Review*, 121(3), 277–301. http://doi.org/10.1037/a0035944.

Mercier, H., & Sperber, D. (2011). Why do humans reason? Arguments for an argumentative theory. *Behavioral and Brain Sciences*, 34(2), 57–111. http://doi.org/10.1017/S0140525X10000968.

Over, D., Douven, I., & Verbrugge, S. (2013). Scope ambiguities and conditionals. *Thinking & Reasoning*, 19(3), 284–307. http://doi.org/10.1080/13546783.2013.810172.

Park, W. (2017). *Abduction in context: The conjectural dynamics of scientific reasoning*. Berlin: Springer. http://doi.org/10.1007/978–3-319–48956–8.

Pearl, J. (1988). *Probabilistic reasoning in intelligent systems: Networks of plausible inference*. San Mateo, CA: Kaufmann. http://doi.org/10.1016/0004–3702(91)90084-W.

Pearl, J. (2000). *Causality: Models, reasoning, and inference*. New York: Cambridge University Press. http://doi.org/10.1017/CBO9780511803161.

Pearl, J., & Mackenzie, D. (2018). *The book of why: The new science of cause and effect*. New York: Basic Books.

Politzer, G., & Bonnefon, J.-F. (2006). Two varieties of conditionals and two kinds of defeaters help reveal two fundamental types of reasoning. *Mind and Language*, 21(4), 484–503.

Protzko, J. (2018). Disentangling mechanisms from causes: And the effects on science. *Foundations of Science*, 23(1), 37–50. http://doi.org/10.1007/s10699–016–9511-x.

Rottman, B. M. (2017). The acquisition and use of causal structure knowledge. In M. R. Waldmann (Ed.), *Oxford handbook of causal reasoning* (pp. 1–55). Oxford: Oxford University Press. http://doi.org/10.1093/oxfordhb/9780199399550.013.10.

Rottman, B. M., & Hastie, R. (2014). Reasoning about causal relationships: Inferences on causal networks. *Psychological Bulletin*, 140, 109–139. http://doi.org/doi.org/10.1037/a0031903.

Spirtes, P., Glymour, C., & Scheines, R. (2000). *Causation, prediction, and search*. New-York: Springer-Verlag.

Stilgenbauer, J.-L., & Baratgin, J. (2018). Étude des stratégies de raisonnement causal dans l'estimation de la probabilité diagnostique à travers un paradigme expérimental de production de règle. *Canadian Journal of Experimental Psychology/Revue Canadienne de Psychologie Expérimentale*, 72(1), 58–70. http://doi.org/doi.org/10.1037/cep0000108.

Stilgenbauer, J.-L., & Baratgin, J. (2019). Assessing the accuracy of diagnostic probability estimation: Evidence for *defeasible modus ponens*, *International Journal of Approximate Reasoning*, 105, 229–240. https://doi.org/10.1016/j.ijar.2018.11.015.

Stilgenbauer, J.-L., Baratgin, J., & Douven, I. (2017). Reasoning strategies for diagnostic probability estimates in causal contexts: Preference for defeasible deduction over abduction. In *Proceedings of the 4th International Workshop on Defeasible and Ampliative Reasoning (DARe-17) Co-located with the 14th International Conference on Logic Programming and Nonmonotonic Reasoning (LPNMR 2017)* (pp. 29–43). Espoo, Finland. Available at: http://ceur-ws.org/Vol-1872/.

Tversky, A., & Kahneman, D. (1974). Judgment under uncertainty: Heuristics and biases. *Science*, 185(4157), 1124–1131.

Van der Weele, T. (2015). *Explanation in causal inference: Methods for mediation and interaction*. New York: Oxford University Press.

Waldmann, M. R., & Hagmayer, Y. (2013). Causal reasoning. In D. Reisberg (Ed.), *Oxford handbook of cognitive psychology* (pp. 733–752). New York: Oxford University Press.

Waldmann, M. R., & Holyoak, K. J. (1992). Predictive and diagnostic learning within causal models: asymmetries in cue competition. *Journal of Experimental Psychology: General*, 121(2), 222–236. Available at: www.ncbi.nlm.nih.gov/pubmed/1534834.

Walliser, B., & Zwirn, D. (2011). Change rules for hierarchical beliefs. *International Journal of Approximate Reasoning*, 52(2), 166–183. http://doi.org/10.1016/j.ijar.2009.11.005.

Williamson, J. (2007). Causality. In D. M. Gabbay & F. Guenthner (Eds.), *Handbook of philosophical logic* (vol. 14, pp. 95–126). Dordrecht: Springer.

15

ATTRIBUTE-BASED CHOICE

Francine W. Goh and Jeffrey R. Stevens

Introduction

When sitting at your favorite café, you face the choice between a small cup of your favorite beverage for $3.50 or a large cup for $3.75. Many of us would choose the large cup. But how might we arrive at this choice? One method could generate a value for each option by combining the amount of beverage received and the cost of that beverage (Figure 15.1). After repeating this process for the second option, one could then compare the two options' values. This is an example of *alternative-based processing* because information is primarily processed within each alternative or option and options are processed in a sequential manner (Payne, Bettman, & Johnson, 1993).

Another way to make the choice is to compare within attributes and across options. *Attribute-based processing* primarily processes information within attributes or dimensions of information used in choice. In the beverage example, the amount of beverage and cost are the two relevant attributes. This method would compare the prices and may determine that they are quite similar. However, the amounts are noticeably different, and you prefer more to less beverage, so you choose the larger beverage (Figure 15.1).

These two types of processing use the same information, but they use them in different ways. Alternative-wise processing integrates within alternatives and considers options sequentially, while attribute-wise processing compares within attributes and considers options simultaneously. Though many models of choice do not explicitly define the decision-making process, they typically imply either alternative- or attribute-wise processing.

Herbert Simon (1957) proposed the notion of *bounded rationality*, which states that decision makers face constraints on information availability, time to make a decision, and computational abilities. Including all information or processing it in complicated ways may be difficult for decision makers. Instead, they may use *heuristics* that ignore information and use simpler computations to make the best possible choice given the constraints of their current situation (Payne et al., 1993; Gigerenzer, Todd, & the ABC Research Group, 1999; Selten, 2002). Models of choice include both optimization models that use all information and combine it in complex ways, as well as heuristic models. Many alternative-based models of decision making use all informational cues and combine them in a way to generate something akin to a subjective value for each option. But many heuristics are attribute-based models. Though there

DOI: 10.4324/9781315658353-17

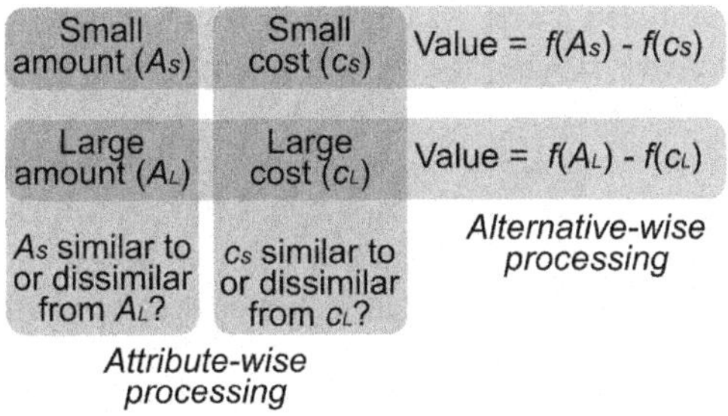

Small amount (A_s)	Small cost (c_s)	Value = $f(A_s) - f(c_s)$
Large amount (A_L)	Large cost (c_L)	Value = $f(A_L) - f(c_L)$
A_s similar to or dissimilar from A_L?	c_s similar to or dissimilar from c_L?	*Alternative-wise processing*

Attribute-wise processing

Figure 15.1 Approaches to choice. Alternative-wise processing integrates attributes (in this case, by applying some function *f* to the attributes) within alternatives to generate a composite value. Attribute-wise processing compares attributes across alternatives using a process such as similarity.

are exceptions in both directions, alternative-based approaches tend to use optimization and attribute-based approaches tend to be heuristics. Here, we briefly review alternative-based approaches to choice, then explore attribute-based approaches and what they can offer the study of decision making.

Alternative-based choice

Alternative-based models are often *compensatory* because they make tradeoffs across attributes: high values in low-weighted attributes can compensate for low values in high-weighted attributes. Though alternative-based models can sometimes involve complex calculations, these models can lead to sharper distinctions between choice options and thus facilitate optimal decision making (Russo & Dosher, 1983). Thus, most normative models of choice are alternative-based models. These models have been used to account for a range of types of decisions, including multi-attribute choice, risky choice, and intertemporal choice.

Multi-attribute choice refers to situations in which decision makers must choose between two or more options, and each option has values for a number of different attributes. For example, one might choose between apartments that differ in their price, location, security deposit, and amenities. A normative model of optimal multi-attribute choice is the weighted additive (WADD) rule (or weighted sum model) (Keeney & Raiffa, 1976). WADD is effectively a regression model that generates an overall value for each option in a choice set based on attributes that are weighted by their importance to the decision maker (Payne et al., 1993). The overall value for an option is determined by multiplying the value of each attribute by that attribute's weight and summing all of the weighted attribute values for that option. All possible options are then compared and the option with the highest overall value is selected. WADD, therefore, uses all available information, involves complex computational steps, and requires a high degree of cognitive effort (Payne et al., 1993). The equal weight rule (or Dawes' rule) is a variation of WADD in which all attributes are equally weighted (Dawes, 1979), thereby simplifying the decision-making process (Payne et al., 1993). Satisficing is another decision-making strategy that involves finding an option that satisfies a threshold or set of thresholds (Simon, 1955). Decision makers first determine minimally acceptable threshold values (or aspiration levels) for each attribute. Each option is then considered sequentially by comparing the option's attribute values to their corresponding predetermined thresholds. Options that contain any attributes that do not meet the thresholds are excluded and the first option that contains attributes which satisfy all of the attribute thresholds is selected (Payne et al., 1993).

Though satisficing is considered a type of heuristic because it does not necessarily assess all options, it uses alternative-wise processing by evaluating options in the sequence in which they occur in the choice set.

Risky choice refers to situations in which options include different outcomes occurring with different probabilities. For example, would you prefer a 100 percent chance of receiving $100 or a 50 percent chance of $200 and a 50 percent chance of $0? Researchers have proposed many models of risky choice, and most of them are alternative-based approaches using a modification of expected value. The expected value approach multiplies two attributes—the probability of an outcome and the reward amount of that outcome—and sums these over all outcomes within an option to generate an expected value (Pascal, 1654, as cited in Smith, 1984). Many other models modify the expected value approach by applying a function to the probability and/or outcome (e.g., expected utility, subjective utility, prospect theory; see Stott, 2006). The key feature of these models is that each option is summarized into a value that is compared across options.

Intertemporal choice refers to sets of options that differ in the reward amount and time delay to receiving that reward. For example, would you prefer $100 today or $150 in one year? Like risky choice models, most intertemporal choice models integrate two attributes to generate a value for each option. For intertemporal choice, the attributes are reward amount and the time delay to receiving the reward. Models of intertemporal choice apply different functions to the reward amounts and time delays and different operations to combine them (Doyle, 2013; Regenwetter et al., 2018). These operations have the effect of discounting the value of the reward amount based on the time delay. These discounting models (e.g., exponential, hyperbolic, quasi-hyperbolic, additive) generate discounted values for each option and compare them to select the least discounted option.

Attribute-based choice

Attribute-based models have also been developed to account for multi-attribute, risky, and intertemporal choice. Many attribute-based models are *non-compensatory* because they do not use all available information and therefore can avoid tradeoffs across attributes. Low-weighted attributes may be ignored and, therefore, cannot compensate for low values in high-weighted attributes. Attribute-based models can also allow for intransitive preference cycles in which option A is preferred to B, B is preferred to C, and C is preferred to A. Though alternative-based models have gained the majority of interest in the field, research on attribute-based models has grown. Here, we survey a subset of attribute-based models of multi-attribute, risky, and intertemporal choice.

Lexicographic heuristic

In the lexicographic heuristic, decision makers first decide on the attribute that is most important to them. They then compare the values of that attribute across all choice options before selecting the option with the highest value on that attribute. In instances where two options have the same value on the most important attribute, individuals will have to compare the options on the next most important attribute. This comparison process continues until one option is deemed to be better than the other option on an attribute of importance (Fishburn, 1974). Several studies have found empirical support for the usage of the lexicographic heuristic during decision making (Slovic, 1975; Tversky, Sattah, & Slovic, 1988; Kohli & Jedidi, 2007; Yee, Dahan, Hauser, & Orlin, 2007). A variation of the lexicographic heuristic is the lexicographic semi-order, where the ranking of each option's value on an attribute depends on a just noticeable difference (Tversky, 1969). Specifically, if the values of options fall within the just noticeable threshold for the target attribute, the attribute values of these options will be ranked as equal and the decision maker will have to consider the next most important attribute to break the tie.

Elimination-by-aspects heuristic

The elimination-by-aspects (EBA) heuristic combines the lexicographic heuristic with the conjunctive rule. The conjunctive rule states that decision makers make a choice by establishing minimally acceptable threshold values for attributes and then eliminating choice options that do not meet these threshold values (Dawes, 1964; Einhorn, 1970). Similar to the lexicographic heuristic, decision makers using the EBA heuristic first select the attribute (or aspect) that is most important to them. A threshold value for each attribute is then determined and the value of each option on that attribute is compared to the threshold value. Choice options that do not meet the threshold value for the attribute are eliminated and the process continues with the next most important attribute until there is only one option that meets the threshold values for all of the attributes (Tversky, 1972). Additionally, the EBA heuristic has been suggested as a heuristic used by decision makers to reduce cognitive effort when they have to make a decision from several choice options (Payne, 1976). The EBA heuristic is considered to violate the principle of rational choice because the final decision is determined by a single attribute. On the other hand, the EBA heuristic is also considered a rational heuristic because it comprises the ranking of attributes in order of their importance (Tversky, 1972; Payne et al., 1993).

Proportional difference model

The proportional difference (PD) model was initially developed to predict decision-making behavior in a risky choice setting. The PD model posits that individuals compare the values of options along the same attributes in a proportional manner (i.e., the monetary outcome and probability of receiving that outcome of one option relative to those of the other option). During this comparison process, individuals add the advantages and subtract the disadvantages for each option to obtain an adjusted difference variable. To reach a decision, individuals compare their difference variable to a decision threshold that reflects the importance of each attribute (González-Vallejo, 2002). Such decision thresholds can vary according to individual wealth status and the context of the situation (González-Vallejo, 2002; González-Vallejo, Reid, & Schiltz, 2003; González-Vallejo & Reid, 2006). The PD model has since been extended to the domain of intertemporal choice by replacing the probability dimension with the time delay to receiving the monetary outcome (Cheng & González-Vallejo, 2016). In addition, the PD model accounts for the magnitude effect (where individuals exhibit less discounting when values are larger), violations of stochastic dominance (which states that when two options are similar on one attribute, individuals will choose the option that is dominant on the differing attribute), transitivity of preferences, reflection effect (which states that individuals are risk-averse when they have to make a choice among gains and risk-seeking when they have to make a choice among losses), and additivity (which holds that preference for a delayed option should be consistent regardless of how the delay period is segmented) (González-Vallejo, 2002; González-Vallejo et al., 2003; González-Vallejo & Reid, 2006; Cheng & González-Vallejo, 2016).

Tradeoff model

The tradeoff model proposes that individuals choose from options by weighing the advantage of the monetary outcome of one option against the advantage of the time value of the other option in intertemporal choice (Scholten & Read, 2010). The tradeoff model thus also suggests that time can be converted to the same scale of measurement used for monetary outcome (Scholten, Read, & Sanborn, 2014). The tradeoff model accounts for the magnitude effect, the common difference effect (the tendency for individuals to exhibit more discounting when a delay period begins sooner compared to later), violations of transitivity of preferences, additivity, and inseparability (which states that individuals consider the value of the time delay of an option based on the value of that option's monetary outcome). In contrast to the PD model which uses the absolute monetary and time delay values of options to carry out comparisons between two options, the tradeoff model includes additional parameters that calculate value- and time-weighing functions that capture individuals' subjective perceptions of monetary values and time delays respectively (Scholten & Read, 2010; Cheng & González-Vallejo, 2016). Despite the use of a more complex formula to predict choice, the ability of the tradeoff model to predict intertemporal choice is similar to that of the PD model (Cheng & González-Vallejo, 2016).

Difference-ratio-interest-finance-time (DRIFT) model

The difference-ratio-interest-finance-time (DRIFT) model suggests that decisions in intertemporal choice are affected by how choice options are framed. Specifically, the weighted average of the absolute difference between monetary values, relative difference between monetary values, experimental interest rate offered, and extent to which individuals view the experimenter's offer as an investment rather than a consumption are balanced against the importance assigned to time (Read, Frederick, & Scholten, 2013). Read and colleagues (2013) found in their analysis of the DRIFT model that the framing of monetary outcomes as investments increased individuals' patience for small monetary values ($700) but reduced patience for large monetary values ($70,000), which suggests that the manner in which intertemporal choices are framed affects decision-making behavior. The DRIFT model can account for the magnitude effect and delay effect (which states that individuals discount less when the time delay is described in a calendar date format instead of units of delay) when the difference and ratio between monetary values and the experimental interest rates are varied (Read et al., 2013).

Intertemporal choice heuristic (ITCH) model

The intertemporal choice heuristic (ITCH) model makes use of arithmetic operations to predict choice. Individuals compare available options by first subtracting and dividing option values along their respective monetary and time dimensions to obtain absolute and relative differences. Weights that reflect the level of importance assigned to these dimensions are then added to each of the four variables and their sum calculated to arrive at a decision (Ericson, White, Laibson, & Cohen, 2015).

Although the ITCH model is similar to the DRIFT model, the two models differ in that the ITCH model calculates both absolute and relative differences in time delay whereas the DRIFT model calculates only absolute differences (Ericson et al., 2015). The ITCH model accounts for the property of additivity and the magnitude, common difference, and delay effects.

Similarity model

The similarity model was initially developed to study decision making in a risky choice setting (Rubinstein, 1988; Leland, 1994). Rubinstein (1988) suggested that individuals who have to make a decision between two lottery options will do so by comparing the similarity of monetary outcomes and similarity of probability of receiving those outcomes for both options. The similarity model has also been extended to the strategic choice domain where it suggests that individuals make a decision by comparing the similarity of payoff options (Leland, 2013) and to the intertemporal choice domain where it posits that individuals arrive at a decision by comparing the similarity of monetary outcomes and time delays of choice options (Leland, 2002; Rubinstein, 2003; Stevens, 2016).

In the domain of intertemporal choice, the version of the similarity model developed by Leland (2002) suggests that individuals compare the similarity of monetary outcomes and similarity of time delays for options. These similarity comparisons can then result in one of three decision consequences: (1) a choice is made because one option dominates the other option on one attribute but has similar values on the other attribute, (2) the choice between the two options is inconclusive because both options offer similar values on the monetary and time delay attributes, or (3) the choice between the two options is inconsequential because one option dominates the other option on one attribute but is dominated on the other attribute. When a decision is either inconclusive or inconsequential, Leland (2002) proposed that individuals will proceed to make a choice at random, whereas Rubinstein (2003) suggested that a choice must be made using another (unspecified) criterion.

Stevens (2016) added a second stage of existing discounting models if similarity analysis was inconclusive or inconsequential. The two-stage similarity models predicted individual choice better than Leland's (2002) similarity model and other discounting models alone. Finally, the similarity model accounts for the magnitude, reflection, and common difference effects, violations of stochastic dominance, and transitivity of preferences (Leland, 1994, 1998, 2002; Stevens, 2016).

Fuzzy-trace theory

Fuzzy-trace theory posits that individuals encode information presented to them in both verbatim and gist representations (Reyna & Brainerd, 1995, 2011). Verbatim representations refer to the exact remembrance of information, such as remembering a note word-for-word or the exact digits of a telephone number. On the other hand, gist representations refer to memory for the general meaning of concepts, such as one's principles or cultural norms (Reyna & Brainerd, 2011; Reyna, 2012). Several studies have shown that individuals tend to rely on gist compared to verbatim representations when they have to make decisions and that individuals prefer to make use of the simplest gist level (or categorical distinctions) whenever possible (Reyna & Farley, 2006; Reyna & Lloyd, 2006; Reyna et al., 2011; Reyna & Brainerd, 2011).

Fuzzy-trace theory suggests that decisions made in risky choice and intertemporal choice settings depend on the gist, or core, principles evoked based on the context of the situation. The evoked gist principles then make one option more salient than the other, resulting in a decision. When specifically applied to the context of intertemporal choice, the evoked gist principles will make either the smaller-sooner option or the larger-later option more salient which will in turn affect the intertemporal choice made (Reyna, 2012; Rahimi-Golkhandan, Garavito, Reyna-Brainerd, & Reyna, 2017; Reyna & Wilhelms, 2017). For example, an individual presented with a choice of either receiving $5 today or $7 in three days may think of these options in the gist representations of "receiving some money today" and "receiving some money later" respectively. According to fuzzy-trace theory, if this individual possesses a gist principle akin to "living in the moment," his gist principle would make the option to receive $5 today more attractive than the other option, resulting in him choosing the smaller-sooner option. Fuzzy-trace theory can thus be considered an attribute-based model since it compares choice options across attributes.

Process data

While many researchers have compared alternative-based and attribute-based models in terms of their ability to accurately predict choice, the two classes of models also provide an important distinction in the *process* of choice—that is, the cognitive steps required to make a choice. Therefore, it can be useful to investigate process data to explore these models, particularly data that reveal how decision makers acquire information. Researchers have used eye tracking and mouse tracking to measure information acquisition with respect to alternative- or attribute-based information processing (Schulte-Mecklenbeck, Kühberger, & Ranyard, 2010).

Eye tracking

Eye-tracking techniques monitor how individuals attend to different types of information (Duchowski, 2017). As individuals look at visual stimuli, an eye tracker records the direction and path of eye movements, thus allowing researchers insight into which information individuals consider to be important (Figure 15.2). In the first use of eye tracking to study the decision-making process, Russo and Rosen (1975) studied how individuals chose in a multi-alternative choice setting. The researchers concluded that participants compared the options presented to them in pairs and preferred to use options that were similar to one another to form these pairs whenever they could. In a similar vein, Russo and Dosher (1983) found that participants preferred to compare options along attributes in a multi-attribute choice setting. Participants also made use of attribute-wise comparisons in gambles that were expected to follow an expected value rule where the expected monetary outcome and probability of receiving that outcome are combined to calculate an overall value for each option. These eye-tracking studies thus support an attribute-based decision-making process.

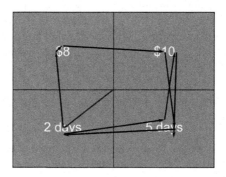

Figure 15.2 Example eye-tracking screenshot. Eye trackers record the direction and path of eye movements when individuals view information presented on a screen.

Arieli, Ben-Ami, and Rubinstein (2011) used a risky choice task to investigate whether individuals used an alternative-based or similarity-based approach to make decisions. They hypothesized that participants who used an alternative-based approach when evaluating lottery options would move their eyes within options because they were formulating an overall value for each option (see Figure 15.1). On the other hand, participants who used a similarity-based approach would move their eyes within attributes because they were comparing the options along each attribute (i.e., monetary outcome and probability).

Arieli and colleagues (2011) found that participants used attribute-based processing to make decisions in a risky choice setting when the values of the monetary outcomes and probabilities made the calculation of the overall value of each option using the alternative-based process difficult. A follow-up study conducted by Aimone, Ball, and King-Casas (2016) supported Arieli et al.'s (2011) finding and also found that attribute-based processing was associated with risk-aversive choice preferences. Further, Arieli et al. (2011) found that participants maintained attribute-based processing to make a decision when the context of the lottery options was changed from risky choice (i.e., with the dimensions being monetary outcome and probability of receiving the monetary outcome) to intertemporal choice (i.e., with the dimensions being monetary outcome and time delay of monetary outcome).

Mouse tracking

Mouselab is a computer program that allows researchers to monitor how individuals acquire information in the decision-making process by using a computer mouse as a tracking tool (Johnson, Payne, Bettman, & Schkade, 1989; Willemsen & Johnson, 2009). The information for each attribute for all options in the choice set is presented in a matrix in which the cells are covered by overlays. When individuals hover their mouse over a cell of the matrix, the overlay disappears to reveal the underlying information; when the mouse moves out of the cell, the overlay reappears and covers the information again (Figure 15.3). Mouselab also records the amount of time that individuals spend viewing each "opened" section, the order in which sections are viewed and the number of times each section is viewed, thus allowing

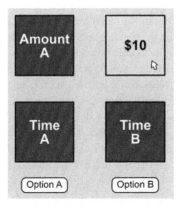

Figure 15.3 Recreated screenshot of MouselabWEB. Individuals move their mouse over each section of the matrix to display information for each option that is hidden by the overlay. The overlay reappears— and the information disappears again—when the mouse is moved out of the section.

researchers to ascertain the importance of each attribute to individuals during the decision-making process.

In a comparison of the Mouselab and eye-tracking process-tracing techniques, Lohse and Johnson (1996) found that for both techniques, participants used attribute-based processing when the *number of options* in a choice set was increased in both risky choice and multi-attribute choice settings. By contrast, participants used alternative-based processing when the *number of attributes* for each option in the choice set was increased (Lohse & Johnson, 1996). Reeck, Wall, and Johnson (2017) used Mouselab and eye tracking to study variations in search strategies in an intertemporal choice setting. They found that participants who used an attribute-based search strategy to compare options had a higher tendency to choose the larger-later option and were more susceptible to option-framing effects compared to participants who used an alternative-based search strategy. Additionally, they found that participants who spent more time looking at the amount dimension compared to time dimension of options were more patient as they chose the larger-later option more often than other participants in the study. In a study that combined risky and intertemporal choices, Konstantinidis, van Ravenzwaaij, and Newell (2017) used a computer program similar to Mouselab to study individuals' decision making in risky intertemporal choice. Participants in their study had to choose between two lottery options that differed in the dimensions of monetary outcome, probability of receiving the monetary outcome, and delay in receiving the monetary outcome. Process data demonstrated that participants preferred to use an attribute-based approach over an alternative-based approach when making their decisions.

Research using eye tracking and mouse tracking has further elucidated our understanding of how individuals acquire and process information when making decisions. Evidence from process data has shown that individuals make use of both alternative-based and attribute-based models of choice processing, and that the choice strategy that they use depends on the context of the situation at hand.

Conclusion

While the study of decision making has historically focused on alternative-based models, attribute-based models have experienced a resurgence of interest from researchers for a number of reasons. First, they follow from Simon's notion of bounded rationality because they often reflect real-world limitations faced by decision makers by using less information and simpler computations. This is especially pertinent in instances where decision makers have to make a choice from myriad options or when there is risk involved in the decision-making process. Second, they capture choice data quite well, predicting multi-attribute, risky, intertemporal, and strategic choices while accounting for, or bypassing, anomalies regularly encountered in the use of alternative-based models. Third, in addition to capturing choice data, attribute-based models can capture the decision process by making predictions about eye tracking and information acquisition data. Combined, these lines of evidence suggest that attribute-based models provide a fruitful class of decision-making models that warrant continued investigation.

Acknowledgments

This work was funded in part by the National Science Foundation (SES-1658837).

References

Aimone, J. A., Ball, S., & King-Casas, B. (2016). It's not what you see but how you see it: Using eye-tracking to study the risky decision-making process. *Journal of Neuroscience, Psychology, and Economics*, 9(3–4), 137–144. doi:10.1037/npe0000061.

Arieli, A., Ben-Ami, Y., & Rubinstein, A. (2011). Tracking decision makers under uncertainty. *American Economic Journal: Microeconomics*, 3(4), 68–76. doi:10.1257/mic.3.4.68.

Cheng, J., & González-Vallejo, C. (2016). Attribute-wise vs. alternative-wise mechanism in intertemporal choice: Testing the proportional difference, trade-off, and hyperbolic models. *Decision*, 3(3), 190–215. doi:10.1037/dec0000046.

Dawes, R. M. (1964). Social selection based on multidimensional criteria. *The Journal of Abnormal and Social Psychology*, 68(1), 104–109. doi:10.1037/h0047832.

Dawes, R. M. (1979). The robust beauty of improper linear models in decision making. *American Psychologist*, 34(7), 571–582. doi:10.1037/0003-066X.34.7.571.

Doyle, J. R. (2013). Survey of time preference, delay discounting models. *Judgment and Decision Making*, 8(2), 116–135. doi:10.2139/ssrn.1685861.

Duchowski, A. T. (2017). *Eye tracking methodology: Theory and practice* (3rd ed.). New York: Springer.

Einhorn, H. J. (1970). The use of nonlinear, noncompensatory models in decision making. *Psychological Bulletin*, 73(3), 221–230. doi:10.1037/h0028695.

Ericson, K. M. M., White, J. M., Laibson, D., & Cohen, J. D. (2015). Money earlier or later? Simple heuristics explain intertemporal choices better than delay discounting. *Psychological Science*, 26(6), 826–833. doi:10.1177/0956797615572232.

Fishburn, P. C. (1974). Lexicographic orders, utilities and decision rules: A survey. *Management Science*, 20(11), 1442–1471. doi:10.1287/mnsc.20.11.1442.

Gigerenzer, G., Todd, P. M., & the ABC Research Group (Eds.) (1999). *Simple heuristics that make us smart*. New York: Oxford University Press.

González-Vallejo, C. (2002). Making trade-offs: A probabilistic and context-sensitive model of choice behavior. *Psychological Review*, 109(1), 137–155. doi:10.1037//0033-295X.109.1.137.

González-Vallejo, C., & Reid, A. A. (2006). Quantifying persuasion effects on choice with the decision threshold of the stochastic choice model. *Organizational Behavior and Human Decision Processes*, 100(2), 250–267. doi:10.1016/j.obhdp.2006.02.001.

González-Vallejo, C., Reid, A. A., & Schiltz, J. (2003). Context effects: The proportional difference model and the reflection of preference. *Journal of Experimental Psychology, Learning, Memory & Cognition*, 29(5), 942–953. doi:10.1037/0278-7393.29.5.942.

Johnson, E. J., Payne, J. W., Bettman, J. R., & Schkade, D. A. (1989). *Monitoring information processing and decisions: The Mouselab system* (Report No. 89–4). Available at: www.dtic.mil/docs/citations/ADA205963

Keeney, R. L., & Raiffa, H. (1976). *Decisions with multiple objectives: Preferences and value tradeoffs*. New York: John Wiley & Sons.

Kohli, R., & Jedidi, K. (2007). Representation and inference of lexicographic preference models and their variants. *Marketing Science*, 26(3), 380–399. doi:10.1287/mksc.1060.0241.

Konstantinidis, E., van Ravenzwaaij, D., & Newell, B. R. (2017). Exploring the decision dynamics of risky intertemporal choice. In G. Gunzelmann, A. Howes, T. Tenbrink, & E. J. Davelaar (Eds.), *Proceedings of the 39th Annual Conference of the Cognitive Science Society* (pp. 694–699). Austin, TX: Cognitive Science Society.

Leland, J. W. (1994). Generalized similarity judgments: An alternative explanation for choice anomalies. *Journal of Risk and Uncertainty*, 9(2), 151–172. doi:10.1007/BF01064183.

Leland, J. W. (1998). Similarity judgments in choice under uncertainty: A reinterpretation of the predictions of regret theory. *Management Science*, 44(5), 659–672. doi:10.1287/mnsc.44.5.659.

Leland, J. W. (2002). Similarity judgments and anomalies in intertemporal choice. *Economic Inquiry*, 40(4), 574–581. doi:10.1093/ei/40.4.574.

Leland, J. W. (2013). Equilibrium selection, similarity judgments, and the "nothing to gain/nothing to lose" effect. *Journal of Behavioral Decision Making*, 26(5), 418–428. doi:10.1002/bdm.1772.

Lohse, G. L., & Johnson, E. J. (1996). A comparison of two process tracing methods for choice tasks. *Organizational Behavior and Human Decision Processes*, 68(1), 28–43. doi:10.1006/obhd.1996.0087.

Payne, J. W. (1976). Task complexity and contingent processing in decision making: An information search and protocol analysis. *Organizational Behavior and Human Performance*, 16(2), 366–387. doi:10.1016/0030-5073(76)90022-2.

Payne, J. W., Bettman, J. R., & Johnson, E. J. (1993). *The adaptive decision maker*. New York: Cambridge University Press.

Rahimi-Golkhandan, S., Garavito, D. M. N., Reyna-Brainerd, B. B., & Reyna, V. F. (2017). A fuzzy-trace theory of risk and time preferences in decision making: Integrating cognition and motivation. In J. R. Stevens (Ed.), *Impulsivity: How time and risk influence decision making, Nebraska Symposium on Motivation* (vol. 64, pp. 115–144). New York: Springer. doi:10.1007/978-3-319-51721-6_4.

Read, D., Frederick, S., & Scholten, M. (2013). DRIFT: An analysis of outcome framing in intertemporal choice. *Journal of Experimental Psychology, Learning, Memory & Cognition*, 39(2), 573–588. doi:10.1037/a0029177.

Reeck, C., Wall, D., & Johnson, E. J. (2017). Search predicts and changes patience in intertemporal choice. *Proceedings of the National Academy of Sciences*, 114(45), 11890–11895. doi:10.1073/pnas.1707040114.

Regenwetter, M., Cavagnaro, D. R., Popova, A., Guo, Y., Zwilling, C., Lim, S. H., & Stevens, J. R. (2018). Heterogeneity and parsimony in intertemporal choice. *Decision*, 5(2), 63–94. doi:10.1037/dec0000069.

Reyna, V. F. (2012). A new intuitionism: Meaning, memory, and development in fuzzy-trace theory. *Judgment and Decision Making*, 7(3), 332–359.

Reyna, V. F., & Brainerd, C. J. (1995). Fuzzy-trace theory: An interim synthesis. *Learning and Individual Differences*, 7(1), 1–75. doi:10.1016/1041-6080(95)90031-4.

Reyna, V. F., & Brainerd, C. J. (2011). Dual processes in decision making and developmental neuroscience: A fuzzy-trace model. *Developmental Review*, 31(2–3), 180–206. doi:10.1016/j.dr.2011.07.004.

Reyna, V. F., Estrada, S. M., DeMarinis, J. A., Myers, R. M., Stanisz, J. M., & Mills, B. A. (2011). Neurobiological and memory models of risky decision making in adolescents versus young adults. *Journal of Experimental Psychology: Learning, Memory, and Cognition*, 37(5), 1125–1142. doi:10.1037/a0023943.

Reyna, V. F., & Farley, F. (2006). Risk and rationality in adolescent decision making: Implications for theory, practice, and public policy. *Psychological Science in the Public Interest*, 7(1), 1–44. doi:10.1111/j.1529-1006.2006.00026.x.

Reyna, V. F., & Lloyd, F. J. (2006). Physician decision making and cardiac risk: Effects of knowledge, risk perception, risk tolerance, and fuzzy processing. *Journal of Experimental Psychology: Applied*, 12(3), 179–195. doi:10.1037/1076-898X.12.3.179.

Reyna, V. F., & Wilhelms, E. A. (2017). The gist of delay of gratification: Understanding and predicting problem behaviors. *Journal of Behavioral Decision Making*, 30(2), 610–625. doi:10.1002/bdm.1977.

Rubinstein, A. (1988). Similarity and decision-making under risk (is there a utility theory resolution to the Allais paradox?). *Journal of Economic Theory*, 46(1), 145–153. doi:10.1016/0022-0531(88)90154-8.

Rubinstein, A. (2003). "Economics and psychology?" The case of hyperbolic discounting. *International Economic Review*, 44(4), 1207–1216. doi:10.1111/1468-2354.t01-1-00106.

Russo, J. E., & Dosher, B. A. (1983). Strategies for multiattribute binary choice. *Journal of Experimental Psychology: Learning, Memory, and Cognition*, 9(4), 676–696. doi:10.1037/0278-7393.9.4.676.

Russo, J. E., & Rosen, L. D. (1975). An eye fixation analysis of multialternative choice. *Memory & Cognition*, 3(3), 267–276. doi10.3758/BF03212910.

Scholten, M., & Read, D. (2010). The psychology of intertemporal tradeoffs. *Psychological Review*, 117(3), 925–944. doi:10.1037/a0019619.

Scholten, M., Read, D., & Sanborn, A. (2014). Weighing outcomes by time or against time? Evaluation rules in intertemporal choice. *Cognitive Science*, 38(3), 399–438. doi:10.1111/cogs.12104.

Schulte-Mecklenbeck, M., Kühberger, A., & Ranyard, R. (2011). *A handbook of process tracing methods for decision research: A critical review and user's guide*. New York: Psychology Press.

Selten, R. (2002). What is bounded rationality? In G. Gigerenzer & R. Selten (Eds.), *Bounded rationality: The adaptive toolbox* (pp. 13–36). Cambridge, MA: MIT Press.

Simon, H. A. (1955). A behavioral model of rational choice. *The Quarterly Journal of Economics*, 69(1), 99–118. doi:10.2307/1884852.

Simon, H. A. (1957). *Models of man: Social and rational*. New York: John Wiley & Sons.

Slovic, P. (1975). Choice between equally valued alternatives. *Journal of Experimental Psychology: Human Perception and Performance*, 1(3), 280–287. doi:10.1037/0096-1523.1.3.280.

Smith, D. E. (1984). *A source book in mathematics*. Mineola, NY: Dover.

Stevens, J. R. (2016). Intertemporal similarity: Discounting as a last resort. *Journal of Behavioral Decision Making*, 29(1), 12–24. doi:10.1002/bdm.1870.

Stott, H. P. (2006). Cumulative prospect theory's functional menagerie. *Journal of Risk and Uncertainty*, 32(2), 101–130. doi:10.1007/s11166-006-8289-6.

Tversky, A. (1969). Intransitivity of preferences. *Psychological Review*, 76(1), 31–48. doi:10.1037/h0026750.

Tversky, A. (1972). Elimination by aspects: A theory of choice. *Psychological Review*, 79(4), 281–299. doi:10.1037/h0032955.

Tversky, A., Sattah, S., & Slovic, P. (1988). Contingent weighting in judgment and choice. *Psychological Review*, 95(3), 371–384. doi:10.1037/0033-295X.95.3.371.

Willemsen, M. C. & Johnson, E. J. (2009). MouselabWEB: Monitoring information acquisition processes on the web. Available at: www.mouselabweb.org/

Yee, M., Dahan, E., Hauser, J. R., & Orlin, J. (2007). Greedoid-based noncompensatory inference. *Marketing Science*, 26(4), 532–549. doi:10.1287/mksc.1060.0213.

PART III

Occam's razor

Mental monism and ecological rationality

16

BOUNDED REASON IN A SOCIAL WORLD

Hugo Mercier and Dan Sperber

Introduction

Herbert Simon (1983, pp. 34–35) distinguished three "visions of rationality": (1) the "Olympian model," which "serves, perhaps, as a model of the mind of God, but certainly not as a model of the mind of man;" (2) the "behavioral" model, which "postulates that human rationality is very limited, very much bounded by the situation and by human computational powers;" and (3) the "intuitive model," which "is in fact a component of the behavioral theory." Bounded rationality, with its intuitive component, is to be explained, Simon adds, in an evolutionary perspective. Our joint work on reasoning and in particular our book *The Enigma of Reason* (Mercier & Sperber, 2017) describes mechanisms of intuitive inference in general and the mechanism of reason in a way that is quite consistent with Simon's defense of a "bounded rationality" approach to human reason. Like other evolutionary psychologists (in particular, Leda Cosmides and John Tooby, see Tooby & Cosmides, 1992) and like Gerd Gigerenzer's 'adaptive toolbox' approach (Gigerenzer, 2007; Gigerenzer, Todd, & ABC Research Group, 1999), we don't see bounded rationality as an inferior version of Olympian rationality, nor do we think that human or other animal inferences should be measured against abstract rationality criteria. Our distinct contribution is to argue that there is an evolved mechanism that can reasonably be called "reason," the function of which is to address problems of coordination and communication by producing and evaluating reasons used as justifications or as arguments in communicative interactions.

Other approaches to human reasoning make an important but less comprehensive use of the idea of bounded rationality. Tversky and Kahneman's heuristics and biases program (Gilovich, Griffin, & Kahneman, 2002) is a case in point. The heuristics studied by Tversky and Kahneman rely on regularities in the environment to make broadly sound decisions. For instance, everything else equal, more salient information is more likely to be relevant, making the availability heuristic sensible. However, this tradition has mostly focused on the biases and errors that result from the use of heuristics (Kruger & Savitsky, 2004), suggesting that an alternative way of processing information could lead to superior results.

The heuristics and biases program has now become largely integrated into the dual process paradigm, along with other strands of research, from social psychology to reasoning—and the dual process theory has become dominant (see Melnikoff & Bargh, 2018). In this

DOI: 10.4324/9781315658353-19

paradigm, the mind is split into two types of processes. System 1 processes (intuitions) are fast, effortless, unconscious, and prone to systematic mistakes. System 2 processes (reasoning) are slow, effortful, conscious, and able to correct System 1's mistakes (e.g., Evans, 2007; Kahneman, 2003; Stanovich, 2004; for a more recent take on dual process models, see, e.g., Evans & Stanovich, 2013).

By and large, System 1 behaves as would be expected by models of bounded rationality: satisficing, relying on heuristics. System 2, by contrast, is closer to the ideal rational agent, able to correct any type of mistake made by System 1, to follow normative guidelines and yield strictly rational decisions.

However, it's far from clear how System 2 could possibly be a maximizer rather than a mere satisficer. The arguments put forward by Simon in favor of a view of rationality as bounded should apply to both System 1 and System 2. Relatedly, evolutionary psychologists have pointed out that cognitive mechanisms tend to specialize, allowing them to incorporate relevant environmental regularities and function more efficiently. System 2, by contrast, would be the ultimate generalist, able to fix the mistakes made by countless different System 1 processes, from social to statistical heuristics. Unsurprisingly, then, dual process models have been plagued by conceptual difficulties. How does System 2 know when to override System 1? How is System 2 able to find the appropriate reasons to counteract each and every System 1 heuristic? (see, e.g., De Neys, 2012; Osman, 2004).

Moreover, talking, for the sake of argument, in terms of Systems 1 and 2, it is not hard to show that System 2 fails at performing a function it couldn't fairly be expected to perform. By and large, solitary reasoning doesn't correct mistaken intuitions. The large share of participants—often the majority, sometimes the overwhelming majority—that do not provide the normatively correct answer to simple decision making or reasoning problems reflect a massive System 2 failure. After all, in most cases, the answer should be easily available to the participants.

Consider the well-known bat and ball problem (Frederick, 2005):

A bat and a ball cost $1.10 together.
The bat costs $1 more than the ball.
How much does the ball cost?

Most participants—college students well able to solve this trivial mathematical problem— give the intuitive but wrong answer of 10c, a blatant System 2 failure. Recent experiments have revealed an even more dire picture for standard dual process models, showing that of those participants who end up providing the correct answer (5c), the majority was able to do so immediately after seeing the problem, and so (from the point of view of dual process theory) through System 1 processes. Overall, only a few percent of the participants behaved as expected in standard dual process model, making an intuitive mistake and later correcting it thanks to System 2 (Bago & De Neys, 2019). The same pattern has been observed using other classic reasoning and decision-making problems and other methods (Bago, 2018; Bago & De Neys, 2017).

The reason why System 2, as a rule, fails to correct mistaken intuitions is even more of an indictment of standard dual process models. Instead of looking for reasons why our intuitions might be mistaken, or to look for reasons supporting alternative answers, System 2 suffers from a massive myside bias (or confirmation bias, see Mercier, 2016a). Once someone has an intuition about what the correct decision is, their System 2 mostly finds reasons supporting this intuition. Moreover, System 2 is lazy when it comes to evaluating our own reasons, not making sure that the reasons we find to support our intuitions are particularly foolproof (Mercier, Bonnier, & Trouche, 2016; Trouche, Johansson, Hall, & Mercier, 2016). Confirmation bias and laziness were supposed to be System 1, not System 2 features, but the evidence says otherwise.

In light of these results, and of the fundamental problems that affect standard dual process models, we have suggested an alternative theory that is much more in line with the ideas of bounded rationality (Mercier & Sperber, 2011, 2017). Instead of dividing the mind between System 1—which would mostly abide by the dictates of bounded rationality—and System 2—which wouldn't—we suggest that it is intuitions all the way up (see also Kruglanski & Gigerenzer, 2011; Osman, 2004). However, some of these intuitions bear on reasons, as explained presently. In this theory, reason heavily relies on its cognitive and social environment to solve problems—when to kick in, how to figure out if something is a good reason, and how to find relevant reasons.

An interactionist view of reason

Our account—dubbed the interactionist view of reason—differs from most existing accounts of reason—in particular, standard dual process models—on two grounds: what reason is, and what reason is for.

Following the arguments put forward by evolutionary psychologists (e.g., Sperber, 1994; Tooby & Cosmides, 1992), we suggest that the mind is a collection of cognitive mechanisms, or modules, that function each in an autonomous manner and that are related to one another by input/output relationships. Many of these modules perform inferences in which they process an input and informationally enrich or transform it in an epistemically sound way. Some of these inferential processes are completely unconscious—neither the input nor the output is consciously accessed. For others, the output is conscious and is experienced as an intuition (Thomson 2014). For example, the attribution to a speaker of an ironical intent is the conscious output of intuitive mechanisms of verbal comprehension (Wilson & Sperber, 2012). As suggested by this example, some intuitions are metarepresentational: they take as input, and/or deliver as output, representations of representations (see Sperber, 2000). The two best-studied such mechanisms deal, one, with attribution of mental states such as beliefs and desire and, the other, with comprehension, that is, with the attribution of speaker's meaning.

We suggest that reason is another of these metarepresentational mechanisms. It takes several representations as inputs—the premises and conclusion of an argument—and delivers as output an intuitive metarepresentational judgment of the quality of the support relation between premises and conclusion. Crucially, this means that reason is 'just' another cognitive mechanism among many others, which shares all the typical traits of intuitions, being fast, effortless, and involving no consciousness of the process through which the outputs are arrived at. Consider an everyday argumentative discussion—about which restaurant to go to, or which printer to buy. Reasons are generated and evaluated quickly and effortlessly, and, most of the time, with no insight as to why such and such reason was chosen, or why a given reason was found to be good or bad. Sometimes we have higher-order reasons for finding a lower reason good or bad. Such higher-order insight into the strength of lower-order reasons is, however, not to be confused with an introspective access to the inferential process itself.

When we entertain higher-order reasons for our lower-order ones, or when we use a chain of reasons, this typically involves an effort of working memory. This role of working memory has sometimes be taken to be diagnostic of reasoning proper (e.g., Evans, 2003). This kind of memory effort, however, is not really different from that of some non-reasoning tasks such as looking for one's keys left somewhere in the flat and trying to avoid both overlooking a possible place and looking twice in the same place. Unlike keeping in mind a hierarchy or a chain of reasons, the production and evaluation of each individual reason in such a hierarchy or chain are relatively effortless, as are all individual intuitive processes.

When sequences of reasons are deployed in a dialogic form, they are distributed among interlocutors, doubly diminishing the memory task: on the one hand, the individual who first invokes a given reason is motivated to bring it back into the discussion as long as it is still relevant; on the other hand, in the mind of the interlocutors, each reason is associated with its producer, providing, for remembering each individual argument, an analog of the method of loci in classical mnemonics. By contrast, in solitary reasoning these memory props are not really available. True, a solitary reasoner can imaginatively produce an internal debate of sorts. Such an ersatz is unlikely to offer the same mnemonic and dialectic benefits as a real debate. Even more relevantly here, the fact that solitary reasoning typically resorts to imagining a dialogue (just as solitary sexuality typically resorts to imagining interactive sex), underscores the second originality of our view: the claim that reason not only performs social functions (as suggested, for instance, by Billig, 1996; Gibbard, 1990; Haidt, 2001; Kuhn, 1992; Perelman & Olbrechts-Tyteca, 1958) but actually evolved to do so.

For a very long time, humans and their ancestors have evolved not only in very social environments, but more specifically in very cooperative environments, collaborating to perform a variety of tasks, from hunting to raising children. This high degree of collaboration was sustained by partner choice: people competing to be seen as reliable cooperation partners, so they would be included in more collaborations (Baumard, André, & Sperber, 2013). This means that individuals had strong incentives to maintain a good reputation as competent and diligent collaborators (Sperber & Baumard, 2012). One way of doing so is by justifying our actions. Whenever we do something that might look irrational or immoral, we can offer justifications to change the audience's mind. Figuring out whether other people's actions really are irrational or immoral involves taking into account their point of view. Hence, the audience has an incentive to listen to these justifications and, if they are found to have some merit, adapt their judgments accordingly.

Another consequence of humans' high degree of cooperation is their unprecedented ability to communicate. However, communication is a risky business, as one might be misled, manipulated, or lied to (see Maynard Smith & Harper, 2003). Humans have evolved a suite of cognitive mechanisms to limit these risks, for instance by calibrating their trust in different people as a function of their competence and diligence (Mercier, 2017, 2020; Sperber et al., 2010). However, trust calibration has limits. There are situations in which a piece of information is too important to be accepted just on trust; there are situation where communicating a piece of genuine information that could be misinterpreted may involve too much of a risk to one's reputation of trustworthiness. The best way to safeguard communication in such situations is to appeal not to authority and trust but to properties of the content of the information itself: in particular, its consistency with what is already accepted as true. Displaying this consistency is precisely what reasons do. In an exchange of arguments, speakers provide reasons to support their point of view, and their interlocutors evaluate these reasons to decide whether or not they should change their minds.

The interactionist view of reason claims that human reason is a metarepresentational cognitive mechanism, or module, used to produce reasons and to evaluate them (for a detailed account of this modularist approach, see Mercier & Sperber, 2017; for a defense against some common objections, see, Sperber & Mercier, 2018). Reason evolved because it allowed individuals to find justifications and arguments, and to evaluate the justifications and arguments offered by others, thereby overcoming the limitation of trust and allowing better coordination and communication.

When is reason triggered?

In our model, the most basic triggers of reason are social. When it comes to evaluating others' reasons, the trigger is simply being presented with a statement as a reason for some conclusion. That a statement should be understood as a reason for a given conclusion can be made explicit (for example, with connectives) but is often left implicit. When it comes to producing reasons, the basic trigger is the expression by others of criticism or doubt about our own actions or opinions (which triggers a search for justifications) or of disagreement (which triggers a search for arguments). Again, criticism or disagreement can be expressed more or less strongly and explicitly (from "that was stupid" to a frown, or even a lack of clear agreement).

While these basic triggers may be entirely external, with experience, we learn to internalize them, in particular by anticipating the need to offer reasons. For instance, adults almost always justify actions before being questioned about them (Malle, 2004). Even young children are, to some extent, able to anticipate the need for justifications. Three- and five-year-olds are more likely to offer an explicit reason supporting an unconventional choice than a conventional one (Köymen, Rosenbaum, & Tomasello, 2014). The mechanisms that allow us to anticipate the need to offer reasons are distinct from reason itself, encompassing a variety of social cognitive mechanisms.

Looking for reasons in anticipation of having to provide them can have several consequences. If we start from a strong intuition, this anticipatory search of reasons typically yields a series of poorly examined reasons supporting our initial intuition, making us more confident or driving us towards more extreme views (Koriat, Lichtenstein, & Fischhoff, 1980; Tesser, 1978). If we start from weak or conflicting intuitions, this anticipatory search of reasons is likely to drive us toward the intuition which is easiest to justify, whether it is also the best by others' standards or not (a phenomenon known as reason-based choice, see Simonson, 1989; Shafir, Simonson, & Tversky, 1993; and Mercier & Sperber, 2011 for review).

Another consequence of our tendency to anticipate the need for reasons is to make us aware that some pieces of information we encounter may become relevant as reasons. For example, if you often discuss politics with your friends, you'll find information that supports your political views relevant as reasons. This anticipation of the need for reasons is likely the main mechanism going against our general preference for information that clashes with our priors (and which is, by definition and everything else being equal, more informative). Anticipatory uses of reason would thus be driving selective exposure (our tendency, in some contexts, to look for information that supports our beliefs, see, e.g., Smith, Fabrigar, & Norris, 2008).

A substantial amount of evidence shows that anticipatory reason is triggered, and reinforced by social cues. For example, being accountable—when participants are told they will have to publicly justify their decisions—tends to reinforce reason-based choice (e.g., Simonson, 1989).

How does reason recognize good reasons?

Once reason has been triggered by the encounter with a reason—when someone provides us with an argument to change our mind, or when we read something in the newspaper that we could remember as a reason to defend our views—its task is to evaluate how good a reason it is: does the premise effectively support the conclusion? What makes this task difficult is that reasons can be about anything: whether abortion should be forbidden, which restaurant to go to, whether plate tectonics is an accurate theory, and so on and so forth. There cannot be general rules for what makes a good reason. The two most popular explicit means of evaluating arguments—logic and argumentation fallacies—are at best rough approximations, and at worst misleading tools (Boudry, Paglieri, & Pigliucci, 2015; Mercier, Boudry, Paglieri, & Trouche, 2017; Mercier & Sperber, 2017).

Instead, the evaluation of reasons has to be made on a case-by-case basis. To do this, reason relies neither on a general logic nor on a general probability calculus, but on a metacognitive capacity. Reason is both a metarepresentational and a metacognitive device (Sperber & Mercier, 2018). Whenever we encounter a piece of information presented as a reason, we check whether we would intuitively derive from what is offered as a reason the conclusion the reason purports to support. For example, if your colleague tells you: "I'm sure Bill is here, I saw his car in the car park not five minutes ago," you have intuitive access to the fact that you would draw the conclusion that Bill is here from his car having been seen in the car park five minutes ago. The more confident you would be of this conclusion, the stronger you intuit the reason given by your colleague to be.

It might seem, then, that reason doesn't add anything of value. After all, if you are disposed to infer that Bill is here from the information that your colleague saw his car in the car park, what benefit is there, over and above drawing this conclusion, in interpreting your colleague's utterance as a reason for this conclusion and moreover in evaluating this reason? Actually, there are several benefits. First, from the fact that your colleague saw Bill's car five minutes ago, you could have inferred many diverse conclusions, for instance, that Bill's car is not in the garage, that your colleague looked at the car park, that the car park is not empty, and so on indefinitely. By offering this fact as a reason for this particular conclusion, your colleague indicated the way in which this fact was relevant in the situation.

Second, reason allows you to check whether a reason would be good independently of whether you accept the premise as true or not. For example, you might not be convinced that your colleague is telling the truth in claiming to have seen Bill's car—he might be in bad faith or he might have confused someone else's car for Bill's—but still recognize that if what he says were true, it would be a good reason for the conclusion that Bill is here. Obviously, this ability to evaluate how good an argument would be if its premise were true is critical in science, as it allows us to tell how evidence not yet acquired would bear on various hypotheses. Third, evaluating the quality of reasons as reasons allows us to draw inferences about the speaker's competence. People who offer poor reasons don't just fail to change their interlocutor's mind, they might also be perceived as less competent—and conversely for people who offer particularly good reasons. Fourth, by using reasons, speakers commit, within limits, to what they deem to be good reasons. Someone who uses a given reason to support their ideas, but refuses a similar reason challenging their ideas, appears inconsistent. Fifth, understanding that a statement is presented as a reason helps guide our own search for reasons, as explained presently.

How does reason find reasons?

In the interactionist view, reason fulfills its function by making it possible to produce and to evaluate reasons. Reasons are produced to justify or to convince. Should we then expect reason to be able to find, from the get-go, very strong justifications and arguments, to be able to form long, sophisticated, well-formed pleas that anticipate most potential rebuttals? As psychologists (and others) have long noted, this is not what typically happens (see, e.g., Kuhn,

1991). Instead, when asked to justify their positions, people tend to produce relatively shallow, superficial reasons—the first thing that comes to mind, or close to it. Why aren't we better at finding good reasons? The interactionist approach provides a twofold answer (see Mercier et al., 2016).

First, it would be tremendously difficult for an individual to reliably anticipate on her own how effectively her reasons would sway her interlocutor (see Mercier, 2012). In most cases, good reasons are highly context-dependent. Imagine you're trying to convince a friend to go to a given restaurant. An ideal argument would take into account your friend's culinary preferences, the kind of restaurant they've recently been to, how much money they are willing to spend, how far they'd go, and so on and so forth. Anticipating which argument in favor of your choice of restaurant will prove convincing and which will be rebuffed is hard.

Second, fortunately, our interlocutors can help us find the most relevant arguments to convince them, obviating the need to do so on our own. In a typical informal discussion, the cost of having our first argument rejected is low (unless the argument is particularly dim). For instance, you might try to convince a friend by telling them "this restaurant makes great cocktails," but they reply that they don't feel like drinking tonight. Not only did you bear no costs for failing to convince them, but thanks to this information, you can narrow down your search for arguments, or offer a direct counter-argument—"they also make great virgin cocktails." The production of reasons, as we describe it, is a paradigmatic example of a satisficing process. The criterion to be reached is that of producing reasons good enough to convince one's interlocutor.

For the interactionist account, reason evolved by being used chiefly in dialogic contexts, in which we can benefit from the back and forth of discussion to refine our arguments, instead of attempting to anticipate through extraordinary computational force what the silver bullet might be. This means, however, that people are not well prepared to produce strong reasons in the absence of feedback (except in the relatively rare circumstances where such feedback can be reliably anticipated). In ordinary circumstances, people are likely to come up with the same kind of relatively shallow reasons that work well to open a discussion, rather than attempting to imagine a variety of potential counter-arguments and trying to pre-empt them. This explains why people tend to be lazy—as mentioned above—when evaluating their own reasons, and why, partly as a result, they often fail to correct their mistaken intuitions when reasoning on their own.

Besides providing us with direct feedback guiding our search for reasons, the social environment offers other opportunities for improving one's production of reasons. One simple opportunity consists in recycling reasons provided by others, and that we found to be good reasons. Pupils have been observed to pick up on the argument forms used by their classmates (Anderson et al., 2001). Participants who have been convinced to accept the logical answer to a reasoning problem (such as the bat and ball) are then able to reconstruct the argument in order to convince other participants (Claidière, Trouche, & Mercier, 2017).

Still, even if the social environment provides many learning opportunities, producing good reasons to justify oneself and convince others is harder than evaluating reasons provided by others. Individual variations are greater in the production than in the evaluation of reasons. The production of reasons can sometimes benefit from their evaluation "off-line" done to pretest their strength, but the converse doesn't seem to be true; to evaluate reasons, you don't have to imagine yourself producing them. In general, the study of the production of reasons presents a stronger challenge to research on reason than the evaluation of reason (Mercier, 2012).

Reason with limited resources works well in the right social setting

In the interactionist account, reason is not a mechanism or a system superior to intuition. It is a mechanism of intuition about reasons. Like all cognitive mechanisms, its benefits are weighted against its cost. It evolved under a pressure to optimize not its cognitive benefits but its cost-benefit ratio relative to that of other cognitive mechanisms with which it competes for processing resources. Outside of communicative interaction, we claim, the deployment of reason is unlikely to provide an adequate cost-benefit ratio. The social environment provides cues regarding when reason should be triggered, and how to find reasons appropriate in the situation.

Only in the right social setting can one expect reason to function well: people should help each other find progressively better reasons (see Resnick, Salmon, Zeitz, Wathen, & Holowchak, 1993), bad reasons should be shot down, and good ones carry the day. What is the right social setting? People who have time to talk with each other, ideally in small groups (Fay, Garrod, & Carletta, 2000), who share some common goals—otherwise, like poker players, they have no incentive to communicate in the first place—people, who share many inferential procedures—otherwise they can't understand each other's reasons—and who disagree on some point—otherwise reasons supporting the consensual view risk piling up unexamined, leading to group polarization or to groupthink (Janis, 1982).

A considerable amount of evidence shows that, in such social setting, reason does indeed function well. In particular, the best ideas present in a group can spread, through discussion, until everyone accepts them. Good insights can even be combined to form a better conclusion than what even the best group members would have been able to reach on their own. These positive outcomes are well-established when small groups discuss accessible logical or mathematical problems, such as the bat and ball (Moshman & Geil, 1998; Laughlin, 2011; Trouche, Sander, & Mercier, 2014; Claidière et al., 2017). They extend well to a variety of other problems: inductive problems, any sort of academic problem faced by students in schools, but also economic predictions, lie detection, medical diagnoses, and more (for reviews, see Mercier & Sperber, 2011; Mercier, 2016b). Even when ascertaining what the best answer is can be difficult, the exchange of reasons seems to point in the right direction. Juries (mock juries at least) make better-informed verdicts, more in line with the opinion of specialists (Hastie, Penrod, & Pennington, 1983). Citizens debating policies in the context of deliberative democracy experiments usually end up more enlightened, with a better grasp of the issues, and more moderate opinions (e.g., Fishkin, 2009; for reviews, see Mercier & Landemore, 2012; Gastil, 2018).

Conclusion: a bounded reason mechanism?

We share with Cosmides and Tooby and Gigerenzer the view that human rationality is bounded through and through: there is no System 2 or other superior mechanism in the human mind that aims at approximating Olympian rationality. We don't believe, however, that an evolutionary approach that recognizes the fully bounded character of human rationality is committed to seeing the faculty of reason hailed by philosopher as a wholly non-existent mechanism, a kind of psychological phlogiston. Where philosophers erred was in overestimating the power of reason and in misrepresenting its function as a prodigious enhancement of individual cognition.

There is, we have argued, a specialized mechanism that produces metarepresentational and metacognitive intuitions about reasons and that, in spite of major differences, is the best true match for reason as classically understood. Hence we call this mechanism "reason." Reasons, that is, articulated representations of facts together with the conclusion they support, are a very rare and peculiar object in the universe. This makes reason a highly domain-specific cognitive mechanism. Even so, reason indirectly provides a form of virtual domain generality. While the intuitions provided by reason are only about reasons, these reasons themselves can be about anything that humans can think about. In this respect, reason is comparable to linguistic competence: a very specialized competence that, however, makes it possible to produce and understand utterances about anything. This similarity between language and reason is not an accident: reason is mostly deployed by linguistic means and exploits the virtual domain-generality of language itself.

Reasons, we argue, are not tools for individual, solitary thinking; they are tools for social interaction aimed at justifying oneself or at convincing others and at evaluating the justifications and arguments others present to us. In performing these functions, reason is bounded not only by limited internal resources and external opportunities, but also by obstacles to the social flow of information. In situations of cooperative dialogue, reason can help overcome these obstacle and foster convergence. In the case of entrenched antagonisms, on the other hand, reason can foster polarization.

Acknowledgments

Hugo Mercier's work is supported by grants from the Agence Nationale de la Recherche (ANR-10-LABX-0087 to the IEC and ANR-10-IDEX-0001–02 to PSL). Dan Sperber's work is supported by the European Research Council under the European Union's Seventh Framework Programme (FP7/2007–2013) / ERC grant agreement n° [609819], SOMICS.

References

Anderson, R. C., Nguyen-Jahiel, K., McNurlen, B., Archodidou, A., Kim, S., Reznitskaya, A., … Gilbert, L. (2001). The snowball phenomenon: Spread of ways of talking and ways of thinking across groups of children. *Cognition and Instruction*, 19(1), 1–46.

Bago, B. (2018). *Testing the corrective assumption of dual process theory in reasoning* (PhD thesis). Paris Descartes, Paris.

Bago, B., & De Neys, W. (2017). Fast logic?: Examining the time course assumption of dual process theory. *Cognition*, 158, 90–109.

Bago, B., & De Neys, W. (2019). The smart System 1: Evidence for the intuitive nature of correct responding on the bat-and-ball problem. Thinking & Reasoning 25(3), 257–299.

Baumard, N., André, J. B., & Sperber, D. (2013). A mutualistic approach to morality: The evolution of fairness by partner choice. *Behavioral and Brain Sciences*, 36(1), 59–78.

Billig, M. (1996). *Arguing and thinking: A rhetorical approach to social psychology*. Cambridge: Cambridge University Press.

Boudry, M., Paglieri, F., & Pigliucci, M. (2015). The fake, the flimsy, and the fallacious: Demarcating arguments in real life. *Argumentation*, 29(4), 431–456.

Claidière, N., Trouche, E., & Mercier, H. (2017). Argumentation and the diffusion of counter-intuitive beliefs. *Journal of Experimental Psychology: General*, 146(7), 1052–1066.

De Neys, W. (2012). Bias and conflict: A case for logical intuitions. *Perspectives on Psychological Science*, 7(1), 28–38.

Evans, J. S. B. T. (2003). In two minds: Dual-process accounts of reasoning. *Trends in Cognitive Sciences*, 7(10), 454–459.

Evans, J. S. B. T. (2007). *Hypothetical thinking: Dual processes in reasoning and judgment*. Hove: Psychology Press.

Evans, J. S. B. T., & Stanovich, K. E. (2013). Dual-process theories of higher cognition advancing the debate. *Perspectives on Psychological Science*, 8(3), 223–241.

Fay, N., Garrod, S., & Carletta, J. (2000). Group discussion as interactive dialogue or as serial monologue: The influence of group size. *Psychological Science*, 11(6), 481–486.

Fishkin, J. S. (2009). *When the people speak: Deliberative democracy and public consultation*. Oxford: Oxford University Press.

Frederick, S. (2005). Cognitive reflection and decision making. *Journal of Economic Perspectives*, 19(4), 25–42.

Gastil, J. (2018). The lessons and limitations of experiments in democratic deliberation. *Annual Review of Law and Social Science*, 14, 271–292.

Gibbard, A. (1990). *Wise choices: Apt feelings*. Cambridge: Cambridge University Press.

Gigerenzer, G. (2007). Fast and frugal heuristics: The tools of bounded rationality. In D. Koehler & N. Harvey (Eds.), *Handbook of judgment and decision making*. Oxford: Blackwell.

Gigerenzer, G., Todd, P. M., & ABC Research Group. (1999). *Simple heuristics that make us smart*. Oxford: Oxford University Press.

Gilovich, T., Griffin, D., & Kahneman, D. (2002). *Heuristics and biases: The psychology of intuitive judgment*. Cambridge: Cambridge University Press.

Haidt, J. (2001). The emotional dog and its rational tail: A social intuitionist approach to moral judgment. *Psychological Review*, 108(4), 814–834.

Hastie, R., Penrod, S., & Pennington, N. (1983). *Inside the jury*. Cambridge, MA: Harvard University Press.

Janis, I. L. (1982). *Groupthink* (2nd rev. ed). Boston: Houghton Mifflin.

Kahneman, D. (2003). A perspective on judgment and choice: Mapping bounded rationality. *American Psychologist*, 58(9), 697–720.

Koriat, A., Lichtenstein, S., & Fischhoff, B. (1980). Reasons for confidence. *Journal of Experimental Psychology: Human Learning and Memory and Cognition*, 6, 107–118.

Köymen, B., Rosenbaum, L., & Tomasello, M. (2014). Reasoning during joint decision-making by preschool peers. *Cognitive Development*, 32, 74–85.

Kruger, J., & Savitsky, K. (2004). The "reign of error" in social psychology: On the real versus imagined consequences of problem-focused research. *Behavioral and Brain Sciences*, 27(3), 349–350.

Kruglanski, A. W., & Gigerenzer, G. (2011). Intuitive and deliberate judgments are based on common principles. *Psychological Review*, 118(1), 97.

Kuhn, D. (1991). *The skills of arguments*. Cambridge: Cambridge University Press.

Kuhn, D. (1992). Thinking as argument. *Harvard Educational Review*, 62(22), 155–178.

Laughlin, P. R. (2011). *Group problem solving*. Princeton, NJ: Princeton University Press.

Malle, B. F. (2004). *How the mind explains behavior: Folk explanations, meaning, and social interaction*. Cambridge, MA: The MIT Press.

Maynard Smith, J., & Harper, D. (2003). *Animal signals*. Oxford: Oxford University Press.

Melnikoff, D. E., & Bargh, J. A. (2018). The mythical number two. *Trends in Cognitive Sciences*, 22(4), 280–293.

Mercier, H. (2012). Looking for arguments. *Argumentation*, 26(3), 305–324.

Mercier, H. (2016a). Confirmation (or myside) bias. In R. Pohl (Ed.), *Cognitive illusions* (2nd ed., pp. 99–114). London: Psychology Press.

Mercier, H. (2016b). The argumentative theory: Predictions and empirical evidence. *Trends in Cognitive Sciences*, 20(9), 689–700.

Mercier, H. (2017). How gullible are we? A review of the evidence from psychology and social science. *Review of General Psychology*, 21(2), 103.

Mercier, H. (2020). *Not Born Yesterday: The Science of Who we Trust and What we Believe*. Princeton, NJ: Princeton University Press.

Mercier, H., Bonnier, P., & Trouche, E. (2016). Why don't people produce better arguments? In L. Macchi, M. Bagassi, & R. Viale (Eds.), *Cognitive unconscious and human rationality* (pp. 205–218). Cambridge, MA: MIT Press.

Mercier, H., Boudry, M., Paglieri, F., & Trouche, E. (2017). Natural-born arguers: Teaching how to make the best of our reasoning abilities. *Educational Psychologist*, 52(1), 1–16.

Mercier, H., & Landemore, H. (2012). Reasoning is for arguing: Understanding the successes and failures of deliberation. *Political Psychology*, 33(2), 243–258.

Mercier, H., & Sperber, D. (2011). Why do humans reason? Arguments for an argumentative theory. *Behavioral and Brain Sciences*, 34(2), 57–74.

Mercier, H., & Sperber, D. (2017). *The enigma of reason*. Cambridge, MA: Harvard University Press.

Moshman, D., & Geil, M. (1998). Collaborative reasoning: Evidence for collective rationality. *Thinking and Reasoning*, 4(3), 231–248.

Osman, M. (2004). An evaluation of dual-process theories of reasoning. *Psychonomic Bulletin and Review*, 11(6), 988–1010.

Perelman, C., & Olbrechts-Tyteca, L. (1958). *The new rhetoric: A treatise on argumentation*. Notre Dame, IN: University of Notre Dame Press.

Resnick, L. B., Salmon, M., Zeitz, C. M., Wathen, S. H., & Holowchak, M. (1993). Reasoning in conversation. *Cognition and Instruction*, 11(3/4), 347–364.

Shafir, E., Simonson, I., & Tversky, A. (1993). Reason-based choice. *Cognition*, 49(1–2), 11–36.

Simon, H. A. (1983). *Reason in human affairs*. Stanford, CA: Stanford University Press.

Simonson, I. (1989). Choice based on reasons: The case of attraction and compromise effects. *The Journal of Consumer Research*, 16(2), 158–174.

Smith, S. M., Fabrigar, L. R., & Norris, M. E. (2008). Reflecting on six decades of selective exposure research: Progress, challenges, and opportunities. *Social and Personality Psychology Compass*, 2(1), 464–493.

Sperber, D. (1994). The modularity of thought and the epidemiology of representations. In L. A. Hirschfeld & S. A. Gelman (Eds.), *Mapping the mind: Domain specificity in cognition and culture* (pp. 39–67). Cambridge: Cambridge University Press.

Sperber, D. (2000). Metarepresentations in an evolutionary perspective. In D. Sperber (Ed.), *Metarepresentations: A multidisciplinary perspective* (pp. 117–137). Oxford: Oxford University Press.

Sperber, D., & Baumard, N. (2012). Moral reputation: An evolutionary and cognitive perspective. *Mind & Language*, 27(5), 495–518.

Sperber, D., Clément, F., Heintz, C., Mascaro, O., Mercier, H., Origgi, G., & Wilson, D. (2010). Epistemic vigilance. *Mind and Language*, 25(4), 359–393.

Sperber, D., & Mercier, H. (2018). Why a modular approach to reason? *Mind & Language*, 131(4), 496–501.

Sperber, D., & Wilson, D. (1995). *Relevance: Communication and cognition*. New York: Wiley-Blackwell.

Stanovich, K. E. (2004). *The robot's rebellion*. Chicago: Chicago University Press.

Tesser, A. (1978). Self-generated attitude change. In L. Berkowitz (Ed.), *Advances in experimental social psychology* (pp. 289–338). New York: Academic Press.

Thompson, V. A. (2014). What intuitions are... And are not. In B. H. Ross (Ed.), *The psychology of learning and motivation* (vol. 60, pp. 35–75). New York: Academic Press.

Tooby, J., & Cosmides, L. (1992). The psychological foundations of culture. In J. H. Barkow, L. Cosmides, & J. Tooby (Eds.), *The adapted mind: Evolutionary psychology and the generation of culture* (p. 19). New York: Oxford University Press.

Trouche, E., Johansson, P., Hall, L., & Mercier, H. (2016). The selective laziness of reasoning. *Cognitive Science*, 40(8), 2122–2136.

Trouche, E., Sander, E., & Mercier, H. (2014). Arguments, more than confidence, explain the good performance of reasoning groups. *Journal of Experimental Psychology: General*, 143(5), 1958–1971.

Wilson, D., & Sperber, D. (2012). *Meaning and relevance*. Cambridge: Cambridge University Press.

17

RATIONALITY WITHOUT OPTIMALITY

Bounded and ecological rationality from a Marrian perspective

Henry Brighton

Does rationality imply optimality?

The idea that rationality implies optimality is so widely assumed as to seem barely worth discussing. Optimal Bayesian decision makers in the cognitive sciences, optimal foragers in biology, and Bayesian maximizers of expected utility in economics are different faces of the same interdisciplinary orthodoxy. Does bounded rationality offer something different? I will argue that ecological rationality, a development of Herbert Simon's (1957) notion of bounded rationality, provides a fully-fledged alternative to the view that rational decisions under environmental uncertainty are optimal probabilistic decisions (Gigerenzer and Selten, 2001; Gigerenzer and Brighton, 2009; Brighton, 2019). For those familiar with the concept of ecological rationality, the study of simple heuristics will likely spring to mind. The study of simple heuristics examines how minimalist decision making algorithms that ignore information can, depending on the structure of the environment, outperform familiar and more sophisticated algorithms that weigh and integrate information, or explicitly optimize a rationally justified criterion (e.g., Gigerenzer et al., 1999; Brighton, 2006; Brighton and Gigerenzer, 2007; Gigerenzer and Brighton, 2009). Rather than focus on these findings, I will scrutinize an argument often made by critics of ecological rationality: Insights arising from the study of ecological rationality are, after the fact, formally reducible to instances of optimal Bayesian inference and, furthermore, require principles of Bayesian inference to fully explain them. The claim is that ecological rationality neither undermines the use of optimality nor challenges orthodox rationality.

I will use Marr's (1982) levels of analysis to challenge this claim and argue that ecological rationality does not imply optimality. Marr's levels organize and relate functional, algorithmic, and implementational theories of information processing systems. In Marr's terms, simple heuristics studied under the rubric of ecological rationality address algorithmic level concerns, where the question is *how* organisms make decisions, not the functional question of *what* constitutes a rational decision and *why*. For some theorists, this elementary distinction between function and mechanism clarifies why ecological rationality is subservient to orthodox rationality (e.g., Chater et al., 2003; Gintis, 2012). My counterargument will be developed in three stages: (1) ecological rationality involves more than a conjecture about simple heuristics, it also rests on a statistical formulation of the problem of inductive inference under unquantifiable

DOI: 10.4324/9781315658353-20

uncertainty that neither assumes nor implies the existence of an optimal solution (Breiman, 2001; Brighton and Gigerenzer, 2007, 2012; Brighton, 2019); (2) this statistical perspective exposes the inability of optimality to characterize functional responses to ill-posed problems, and undermines the idea that function and mechanism can be studied independently; and (3) ecological rationality is incompatible with and exposes the limitations of Marr's (1982) levels of analysis, but finds support in Marr's (1977) largely overlooked views on the broader functioning of biological information processing systems.

Marr and Poggio's three levels of analysis

David Marr's book *Vision* (1982) set out an innovative approach to understanding vision as an information processing problem. As well as detailing computational models of visual processing, Marr argued that a deeper understanding of information processing systems in general, not just the visual system, requires three levels of analysis. Originally developed with Tomaso Poggio (Marr and Poggio, 1976; Poggio, 2012), these three levels map onto fundamental distinctions in the study of rationality that will recur throughout this discussion. At the highest level, termed the computational level, the goal is to identify an appropriate formal system, a calculus, used to define the problem and derive its solution. This abstract rendering of the problem details what problem the system attempts to solve and why. For example, a pocket calculator solves the problem of performing arithmetic calculations and, so the story goes, human decision makers solve the problem of maximizing expected utility when making decisions under uncertainty. Calculi used to develop computational level theories include Bayesian statistics (Griffiths and Tenenbaum, 2006), deductive logic (Baggio et al., 2014), and the mathematics of signal processing (Marr and Hildreth, 1980).

Moving down to Marr's second level, the algorithmic level, the goal is to specify the algorithms and data structures needed to compute the solution. For example, if part of the computational level theory of a pocket calculator is to calculate factorials, then at the algorithmic level this calculation, for reasons of efficiency, might be implemented using Stirling's approximation, $n! \approx \sqrt{2\pi n}\left(\dfrac{n}{e}\right)^n$, which incurs a loss in precision but requires fewer operations to compute. Similarly, it has been proposed that simple heuristics might be used to approximate a full Bayesian computation specified at the computational level (Chater et al., 2006; Oaksford and Chater, 2009).

Marr's third and final level of analysis is the implementation level, which considers the constraints of physically instantiating the proposed algorithms and data structures in, say, biological machinery or a conventional digital computer. Combined, Marr's levels consider what problem the system attempts to solve, what the solution to this problem is, how this solution is computed, and how this computation is realized in a physical device. Notice that each Marrian level corresponds to a different level of analysis rather than a different level of organization. Levels of organization in nature typically reflect part-whole relationships such as those that separate proteins from cells and individuals from groups, whereas levels of analysis separate different forms of understanding (Bechtel and Shagrir, 2015; McClamrock, 1991). For Marr, studying an information processing system without a formal understanding of the problem being addressed should be avoided, and he advocated a top-down approach to developing theories of biological information processing systems. This methodology, though, does not exclude a theorist from adopting alternative priorities when working within the Marrian framework. Constraints from implementation and algorithmic levels can, depending on the question, also drive theory development.

Why place Marr's levels at the center of this discussion? To begin with, Marr's levels of analysis are seen as "a core tenet of cognitive science" (Peebles and Cooper, 2015, p. 188), defining the de facto categories used to orientate cognitive models in relation to rationality claims. Bayesian optimality modeling in the cognitive sciences, for instance, seeks computational level theories that formulate the problems faced by the cognitive system and what constitutes a rational solution (Tenenbaum and Griffiths, 2001; Chater et al., 2006; Griffiths et al., 2012). Rarely are these models interpreted as hypotheses about *how* the cognitive system computes. Cognitive process models such as simple heuristics, on the other hand, are categorized as algorithmic level theories. Both kinds of theory can be interpreted as models of human behavior, but only the second kind involves an explicit conjecture about cognitive processing. From this Marrian perspective, bounded rationality is typically seen as an attempt to inform computational level theory development by importing constraints arising from the algorithmic and implementation levels. For example, Anderson's (1990) rational analysis of cognition and the more recent study of resource rationality (Griffiths et al., 2015) use these constraints to revise the problem specification, and consequently, what problem to which the computational level theory specifies an optimal response. Now, on the one hand, if we assume that simple heuristics are to Bayesian rationality what Stirling's approximation is to arithmetic, then as critics as have argued, studying ecological rationality without appeal to Bayesian optimality is like trying to understand how birds fly without a theory of aerodynamics (Chater and Oaksford, 1999) or understanding how people play billiards without a theory of the physics of motion (Gintis, 2012). On the other hand, both Simon (1991) and advocates of ecological rationality have rejected the proposal that the study of bounded and ecological rationality reduces to studying optimality (e.g., Gigerenzer and Selten, 2001; Brighton, 2019). What is the basis of this disagreement, and can Marr's levels be used to clarify and resolve the issue?

The statistical foundations of ecological rationality

Ecological rationality is, and always has been, more than the study of simple heuristics. The goal is to understand the adaptive fit between organisms and the structure of the environment by examining three interacting components: (1) algorithmic models of how organisms make inductive inferences, with a particular focus on simple heuristics; (2) the properties of natural environments whose probabilistic structure is either uncertain or unknown; and (3) a formulation of the problem of statistical inference that defines and quantifies the meaning of an adaptive fit. To focus this discussion, I will sidestep experimental research examining the use of simple heuristics in humans and other animals, and instead focus on the overarching hypothesis: Simple heuristics that ignore information are a vital part of how organisms successfully cope with the uncertainty of the natural world.

Results supporting this hypothesis are termed less-is-more effects, and they detail how minimalist processing strategies improve the accuracy of decisions relative to more complex and supposedly sophisticated strategies commonly assumed in the cognitive sciences and beyond. For example, when deciding which of two objects in the environment scores higher on some criterion of interest, such as which of two food items has a higher calorific content, a user of the recognition heuristic will choose the recognized object if the other object is unrecognized. A partly ignorant decision maker using this heuristic can make more accurate inferences than a more informed decision maker who weighs and integrates all available information (Goldstein and Gigerenzer, 2002). Similarly, a user of the simple heuristic take-the-best ignores correlations between cues and uses a single cue to make an inference, yet can make more accurate inferences than a decision maker who attempts to model these correlations and weighs and integrates all available cues (e.g., Gigerenzer and Goldstein, 1996; Czerlinski et al., 1999; Brighton, 2006; Brighton and Gigerenzer, 2007; Gigerenzer and Brighton, 2009; Şimşek and Buckmann, 2015). In both cases, a simple heuristic (component 1 of the interaction above) confers a function by exploiting properties of natural environments (component 2 of the interaction above). Of absolutely crucial importance to the coming discussion is component 3 of the interaction described above: The formulation of the statistical problem facing the organism. This third component also requires theoretical commitments to be made, and it is these commitments that establish, most directly, ecological rationality as a substantive alternative to orthodox rationality.

The role of statistics in constructing the rationality problem

Simple heuristics like take-the-best are supervised learning algorithms. They tackle the problem of making inductive inferences from observations of the environment where the goal is to distinguish systematic patterns that govern the observations from any noisy and accidental patterns. What is a rational solution to this problem? If we possess a complete probabilistic understanding of the environmental processes that generate the observations, then the answer is simple: The optimal Bayesian response relative to a prior and a hypothesis space expressing this probabilistic knowledge. But what if we lack what Binmore (2009) termed this "metaphysical hotline to the truth?" Or, what if the decision maker is not in what Savage (1954), the inventor of Bayesian decision theory, termed a "small world" where identifying a mutually exclusive and exhaustive set of future states of the world, consequences, and the actions that map between them is a realistic possibility? Put simply, how should an optimal response be formulated when partial or complete ignorance precludes probabilistic quantification of the uncertainties we face?

Orthodox responses to these questions cite uninformed priors, second-order probabilities, imprecise probabilities, or some other technique that assumes and proposes how we should quantify the varying degrees of uncertainty we face. Another response is to devise alternatives to Bayesian decision theory but retain the goal of optimality (e.g., Gilboa, 1987; Gilboa and Schmeidler, 1989). A third option is to accept that "it is sometimes *more* rational to admit that one does not have sufficient information for probabilistic beliefs than to pretend that one does" (Gilboa et al., 2012, p. 28). This third option represents the fork in the road where orthodox rationality and ecological rationality part ways. The orthodox view proceeds under the assumption that we can, by hook or by crook, always quantify environmental uncertainty. The study of ecological rationality sets out to examine the implications of unquantifiable uncertainty. The statistician Leo Breiman (2001) characterized two cultures of thought underlying these issues, and they map directly onto the divergent practices of orthodox rationality and ecological rationality. Figure 17.1 depicts these relationships, which are worth considering in detail because they prove critical in constructing the formal nature of the problem.

Orthodox rationality and the statistical culture of data modeling

If we start with observations, each relating a set of independent variables to a dependent variable, then the environment can be seen as a black box containing data-generating machinery that determines the joint distribution over the inputs to the black box (independent variables) and outputs (the dependent variable) shown in Figure 17.1(a). Much of traditional statistical inquiry, and this includes the practice of formulating optimal probabilistic responses to environmental uncertainty, requires that we make a conjecture about the contents of this black box, depicted in Figure 17.1(b). We might work from the assumption that dependent and independent variables are linearly related, for example. Taking a Bayesian perspective, we might

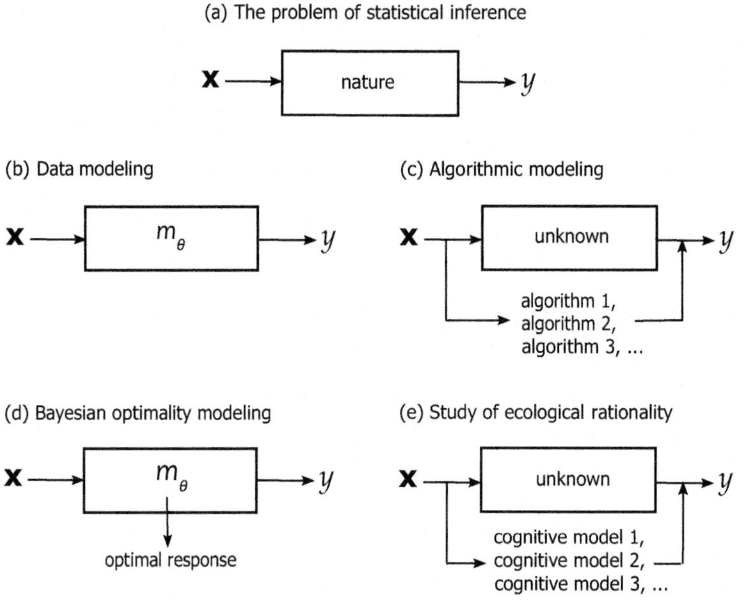

(a) The problem of statistical inference

$$x \longrightarrow \boxed{\text{nature}} \longrightarrow y$$

(b) Data modeling

$$x \longrightarrow \boxed{m_\theta} \longrightarrow y$$

(c) Algorithmic modeling

$$x \longrightarrow \boxed{\text{unknown}} \longrightarrow y$$

algorithm 1,
algorithm 2,
algorithm 3, ...

(d) Bayesian optimality modeling

$$x \longrightarrow \boxed{m_\theta} \longrightarrow y$$

optimal response

(e) Study of ecological rationality

$$x \longrightarrow \boxed{\text{unknown}} \longrightarrow y$$

cognitive model 1,
cognitive model 2,
cognitive model 3, ...

Figure 17.1 How should the problem of statistical inference be formulated? We start with observations of an unknown functional relationship between input vectors x (the independent variables) and output y (the dependent variable) determined by some aspect of nature, shown in (a). Following Breiman (2001), the statistical culture of data modeling views the conjecture of a stochastic model $y = m_\theta(x)$ of nature's black box as an essential step in statistical inference, shown in (b). Rather than attempt to model the contents of nature's black box, algorithmic modeling is an incremental search for learning algorithms that can, to varying degrees, accurately predict the input-output relationship, shown in (c). Bayesian optimality modeling conducts data modeling in order to define an optimal response (d), while the study of ecological rationality conducts algorithmic modeling and interprets predictive models as potential cognitive models, shown in (e).

Source: Diagrams (a–c) adapted from Breiman (2001).

formulate an hypothesis space, prior distribution, and various parameters that we fit using the available observations. The defining characteristic of this approach is that, at some point, a conjecture is made about the contents of the black box, and it is relative to this conjecture that subsequent claims about rationality and optimality are made. For instance, Anderson's rational analysis of cognition is a methodology for formulating the problems that the environment poses the cognitive system, and using rational solutions to these problems to derive theories of cognitive processing (Anderson, 1990, 1991; Chater and Oaksford, 1999). In both Anderson's methodology and Bayesian optimality modeling, formulating a probabilistic model of the task environment is a key step, illustrated in Figure 17.1(d) (Tenenbaum and Griffiths, 2001; Chater et al., 2006; Griffiths et al., 2012). Breiman (2001) used the term "data modeling" to describe this general approach to statistical inquiry.

Ecological rationality and the statistical culture of algorithmic modeling

An alternative approach to statistical modeling is what Breiman termed algorithmic modeling. When algorithmic modeling, we refrain from making a conjecture about the contents of the black box and instead try to predict its behavior. As shown in Figure 17.1(c), the observations are used to estimate the predictive accuracy of competing models of inductive inference, which in practice usually means comparing machine learning algorithms using a model selection criterion, such as cross-validation (Stone, 1974), where algorithms are judged on their ability to generalize to unseen cases (Hastie et al., 2001; Bishop, 2006). Crucially, learning algorithms and the probabilistic assumptions they imply tend not to be seen as models of the environment, but rather inductive biases that may explicitly introduce model infidelities in order to reduce a component of prediction error known as variance, described below (such techniques are part of the theory of regularization; see, e.g., Chen and Haykin, 2002). Among the algorithms being considered, one or more algorithm will achieve the greatest reduction in prediction error. Findings like these in no way license an optimality claim. Instead, they provide an indication of the kinds of algorithmic design decisions or statistical assumptions that improve our ability to reduce prediction error, thereby suggesting further algorithms worth evaluating.

This process is fundamentally exploratory, yields a functional understanding of the algorithms being considered, yet in no way invokes the concept of optimality to explain model performance. Specifically, one can seek to improve predictive accuracy relative to existing models without assuming that an optimal model can ever be identified, or, given the complexity and uncertainty of the natural world, meaningfully exists. How, though, is ecological rationality related to the culture of algorithmic modeling? From the outset, key results in the study of ecological rationality have rested almost exclusively on algorithmic modeling studies, where the ability of simple heuristics to reduce prediction error relative to other models has been analyzed in environments for which the optimal response is unknown and arguably unknowable (Czerlinski et al., 1999; Martignon and Laskey, 1999; Brighton, 2006; Gigerenzer and Brighton, 2009). Such studies typically proceed by investigating model performance in new environments, or new heuristics generated by combining a set of basic building blocks that include rules for information search, rules for stopping search, and rules for making decisions (Gigerenzer et al., 1999). Combining these building blocks, which are often inspired by experimental studies of decision making in humans and other animals, is one way of steering the algorithmic modeling process. In short, the study of ecological rationality, schematized in Figure 17.1(e), proceeds by studying algorithmic functioning in environments composed on observations rather than environments rendered as probabilistic models that imply optimal responses. Next I will argue that in theory too, ecological rationality is not in the business of studying optimality.

Bayesian reductionism and the limitations of optimal function

Despite the preceding points, critics have argued that when a heuristic works, one still needs a rational explanation for why it works, and so the concept of ecological rationality is ultimately subservient to Bayesian rationality. Oaksford and Chater (2009), for example, argue that Bayesian optimality modeling "cannot be replaced by, but seeks to explain, ecological rationality" (p. 110). This view extends to critics of Bayesian optimality modeling, such as Jones and Love (2011), who argue that the two approaches are "highly compatible" because "any inference algorithm implicitly embodies a prior expectation about the environment" (p. 186). Thus, even though ecological rationality does without strong probabilistic conjectures and optimality claims in practice, in theory, these concepts will be required to explain functional success. These arguments, which express a kind of Bayesian reductionism, are worth dissecting in turn.

Argument 1: Bayesian thinking is required to explain functional success

When a learning algorithm performs well in a particular environment, incurring lower prediction error than the other algorithms being considered, how can this behavior be explained? Seen through the lens of probabilistic optimality, there is a strong tendency to view this functional success as indicating a close match between the prior distributional assumptions of the algorithm and the probabilistic structure of the environment. An alternative pattern of explanation that has proven critical to understanding the success of simple heuristics is to analyze the prediction error of competing algorithms using the bias/variance decomposition (Gigerenzer and Brighton, 2009). Specifically, we can decompose prediction error into two controllable components, bias and variance, and one uncontrollable component, noise, such that they combine additively as follows (O'Sullivan, 1986; Geman et al., 1992; Hastie et al., 2001; Bishop, 2006):

$$\text{Total error} = (\text{bias})^2 + \text{variance} + \text{noise} \qquad (17.1)$$

The bias component reflects the inability of the model to capture what is systematic in the observations. The variance component, in contrast, reflects the sensitivity of the model's predictions to different observations of the same problem, such as a different sample from the same population. All algorithms face what is termed the bias/variance dilemma because methods for reducing variance tend to increase bias, whereas methods for reducing bias tend to increase variance (Geman et al., 1992). For example, a heuristic may suffer from high bias due to having a single free parameter, but this simplicity can lead to a greater reduction in variance when learning from small samples (Brighton and Gigerenzer, 2015). A competing algorithm may strike a different trade-off between bias and variance, and whether this point proves functional will depend on the sample size and the properties of the environment. Many of the algorithmic tricks used by simple heuristics and other learning algorithms to incur low prediction error are methods for reducing variance. In short, the idea that Bayesian thinking is required to explain the performance of learning algorithms is inaccurate, both in theory and in practice.

Argument 2: Bayesian explanations of functional success should be preferred

Even if the principles of Bayesian inference are not required to explain functional success, perhaps, given their elegance and foundations in probability theory, they should be preferred. A counterexample to this intuition is the naïve Bayes classifier, a simple learning algorithm that makes a strong assumption that the features (also termed cues, attributes, or independent variables) are conditionally independent of each other, given the class. Despite this assumption being highly unlikely to be met in practice, the naïve Bayes classifier has a long history of performing surprising well, particularly when learning from sparse data. Why is this? Research spanning several decades has repeatedly invoked the concepts of bias and variance to explain why the naïve Bayes classifier performs well relative to other algorithms: Despite introducing a strong bias, the conditional independence assumption is often highly effective at reducing variance (e.g., Domingos and Pazzani, 1997; Friedman, 1997; Hand and Yu, 2001; Ng and Jordan, 2002; Webb et al., 2005). Thus, even when we have a clear probabilistic formulation of a learning algorithm, it can prove more insightful to explain functional success using the bias/variance perspective than a perspective rooted in probabilistic optimality.

Argument 3: All learning algorithms imply an optimal Bayesian response

Given any supervised learning algorithm, let us assume that a probabilistic reformulation of this algorithm is always possible, such that the probabilistic conditions under which the algorithm makes Bayes optimal decisions are made explicit. Wouldn't this then prove that ecological rationality reduces to the study of optimal Bayesian inference? No. All this proves is that one aspect of algorithmic functioning is optimal functioning. When algorithmic modeling, learning algorithms can, and typically do, confer a function without being optimal. They also confer a function by virtue of their performance *relative* to other learning algorithms. Indeed, if the optimal response is indeterminable, then relative function is all we have to work with. More generally, the conditions under which an algorithm is optimal and the conditions under which it confers a function outside these optimality conditions cannot be assumed to be directly related. Reductions in prediction arise from a complex interaction between the learning algorithms being considered, the number of observations available, and properties of the environment (e.g., Perlich et al., 2003). And these complexities mean that the optimality conditions of most learning algorithms are simply not known, and attempts to identify them tend to be only partially successful (e.g., Domingos and Pazzani, 1997; Kuncheva, 2006). To summarize, optimality results are (1) of limited practical use outside the study of idealized environments for the simple reason that we tend not to know the probabilistic structure of natural environments; and (2), limited in their ability to provide a reliable indication of how well an algorithm will perform outside its optimality conditions, and relative to other algorithms.

The theory-dependence of Marrian decomposition

To recap, my argument is that Breiman's (2001) statistical cultures of data modeling and algorithmic modeling differ in how they view and respond to uncertainty, these differences have direct implications for the study of rationality, and crucially, these differences are reflected in the practices of Bayesian optimality modeling and the study of ecological rationality. The fly in the ointment is optimality. Given all this, how can the study of ecological rationality be reconciled with the Marrian perspective? Resolving this issue is of central importance because any incompatibility between ecological rationality and Marr's levels of analysis would leave us in the precarious position of advocating a view on rationality at odds with "the canonical scheme for organizing formal analyses of information processing systems" (Griffiths et al., 2015, p. 217) and "one of the most well-known theoretical constructs of twentieth century cognitive science" (Willems, 2011, p. 1). On the other hand, if ecological rationality proves to be entirely compatible with Marr's levels, then the existence of a computational-level theory would suggest, as is typically assumed, that the whole approach reduces to an optimality claim.

Ecological rationality from a Marrian perspective

Recall that the objective of a computational level theory is to identify an appropriate formal system, a calculus, used to define the problem and derive a solution. Ultimately the computational level should define the input-output mappings to be computed, perhaps approximately, by an algorithmic level theory. The problem we face now is that the statistical "goal" of algorithmic modeling, and hence ecological rationality, is both exploratory and algorithmic in nature, echoing Selten's (2001) point that "bounded rationality cannot be precisely defined. It is a problem that needs to be explored" (p. 15). In contrast to data modeling, algorithmic modeling doesn't supply a solution derived using a calculus but instead a relative understanding of the efficacy of competing algorithms. The problem facing the organism remains, only this problem is not well posed in Hadamard's (1902) sense of requiring that a solution exists, is unique, and is stable with respect to small perturbations to the problem definition. Nature doesn't always, or even often, present well-posed problems in this sense, and it is imperative that our conception of rationality should reflect this. Taken in conjunction with Marr's (1977) proposal that a computational level theory should be "expressed independently of the particular way it is computed" (pp. 37–38), the conclusion that ecological rationality is incompatible with the demands of a computational level theory is hard to avoid.

The limits of Marrian decomposition: type-1 and type-2 theories

This conclusion, that Marr's levels of analysis fall short as a canonical system and imply a limited view of algorithmic functioning, is in fact consistent with Marr's thinking when considered in light of his 1977 article published in *Artificial Intelligence* (Marr, 1977). This article addresses some of the issues discussed above, yet is largely overlooked in contemporary discussions of Marr's work. Here, Marr drew the distinction between biological information processing systems with type-1 theories (those which yield to a computational-level analysis) and those with type-2 theories (those which don't). An archetypal type-1 theory for Marr is the Fourier Transform, a mathematical operation central to edge detection that can be approximated at the algorithmic level in a number of ways (Marr and Hildreth, 1980). Marr's examples of archetypal type-2 theories include protein unfolding and the grammar of natural language. Neither of these problems, Marr speculates, are likely to have useful mathematical abstractions. He warns, for instance, that "an abstract theory of syntax may be an illusion" (p. 42), such that productive study at the computational level is likely to be questionable.

Marr's overarching point is that we should prioritize the study of problems with type-1 theories but not expect that all interesting problems will have them. This suggests three possibilities that need to be considered. First, the theorist seeks a computational level theory, finds one, and then invokes Marr's three levels of analysis to guide further theory development. Second, the theorist seek a computational level theory, fails to find one, and then pursues an alternative form of functionalist inquiry. Third, the theorist fails to adopt a functionalist perspective in the first place, overlooks a potentially insightful computational theory, and misses the opportunity to arrive at the kind of understanding that Marr advocates. Marr (1977) reserves his criticism for this third scenario, which he saw as a "waste of time" because it "amounts to studying a mechanism not a problem" (p. 46). Advocates of ecological rationality find themselves in the second scenario, and set out to examine what implications these problems have for the study of rationality. In summary, the idea that theories of cognitive processing that make functionalist claims, including claims about rationality, must be reconcilable with Marr's three levels of analysis rests on a narrow conception of the kinds of problem that the cognitive system is likely to face. This category of problem was one that Marr undoubtedly saw as a priority, but he also recognized that this category offers only a partial view of the kinds of problem tackled by biological information processing systems.

Rationality without optimality

It is commonly assumed, outside the cognitive sciences as well as within them, that "the only viable formulation of perception, thinking, and action under uncertainty is statistical inference, and the normative way of statistical inference is Bayesian" (Edelman and Shahbazi, 2011, p. 198).

Furthermore, despite the existence of alternative methods for formulating the problem of statistical inference, the corollary that "all such methods would ultimately reduce to Bayesian inference" (p. 198), if true, leaves little room for maneuver in the study of rationality. This is a form of Bayesianism, the view that the uncertainty surrounding the problems faced by the cognitive system is quantifiable, and that rational solutions to these problems are optimal probabilistic solutions. One can dispute this view without questioning Bayesian methods, probability theory, or mathematical statistics. The dispute concerns the application of these methods outside what Savage (1954), the founder of Bayesian decision theory, termed "small worlds." Savage considered it "utterly ridiculous" (p. 16) to apply his theory in large worlds where uncertainty surrounds which states, actions, and consequences are relevant, and where we suffer from varying degrees of ignorance that undermine our ability to quantify the uncertainties we face.

Deductive logics in their various guises are used to define rationality in domains that demand deductive rather than inductive reasoning, so the expectation that our conception of rationality must adapt to fit the nature of the problem should be both familiar and uncontroversial. The claim here is that ecological rationality is an adaptation to the problem of decision making in large worlds. These are environments that we can observe but our partial ignorance precludes them from being probabilistically quantifiable (Binmore, 2009; Brighton and Gigerenzer, 2012), and a key implication of this claim is that optimality ceases to be a meaningful characteristic of rational decisions under these conditions. Critics, in contrast, have argued that because ecological rationality involves a conjecture about simple heuristics, it necessarily focuses on Marr's algorithmic rather than the computational level. And given that rationality claims are traditionally made at the computational level, the assumption is that ecological rationality must therefore inherit principles of Bayesian rationality to explain the success of simple heuristics. In response, I have argued that Marr's levels of analysis are incapable of resolving this debate because the statistical commitments driving the study of ecological rationality make the problem of statistical inference exploratory, algorithmic, and ill-posed. Marr's levels of analysis, on the other hand, are tailored to well-posed problems with a precise mathematical formulation enabling the derivation of an optimal solution. As Marr (1977) himself noted, not all of the problems faced by biological systems are well-posed in this way.

In many areas of science, optimality modeling is seen as a heuristic of discovery that introduces abstractions that may or may not prove insightful when formulating problems, deriving solutions, and understanding the functioning of organisms and other complex systems (Dupré, 1987; Parker and Maynard Smith, 1990; Schoemaker, 1991). Seen in this way, it becomes imperative to consider the boundary conditions of optimality modeling, and recognize when the abstractions and assumptions needed to formulate optimality claims cease to be insightful and instead provide elegant solutions to problems of a different nature. Is the use of optimality in the study of rationality any different? I have argued that it isn't, and the basis for my argument is a statistical one rooted in the uncertainty arising from what Simon (1957) referred to as informational bounds, rather than the more commonly assumed computational, cognitive, or biological bounds that motivate the study of bounded and ecological rationality. Seen from this statistical perspective, the study of ecological rationality can cast new light on the limited ability of probabilistic optimality to capture what is functional outside idealized worlds, those where all aspects of uncertainty are probabilistically quantifiable.

References

Anderson, J. R. (1990). *The adaptive character of thought.* Lawrence Erlbaum, Hillsdale, NJ.
Anderson, J. R. (1991). Is human cognition adaptive? *Behavioral and Brain Sciences*, 14, 471–517.

Baggio, G., van Lambalgen, M., and Hagoort, P. (2014). Logic as Marr's computational level: Four case studies. *Topics in Cognitive Science*, 7(2), 287–298.

Bechtel, W. and Shagrir, O. (2015). The non-redundant contributions of Marr's three levels of analysis for explaining information-processing mechanisms. *Topics in Cognitive Science*, 7(2), 312–322.

Binmore, K. (2009). *Rational decisions*. Princeton University Press, Princeton, NJ.

Bishop, C. M. (2006). *Pattern recognition and machine learning*. Springer, New York.

Breiman, L. (2001). Statistical modeling: The two cultures. *Statistical Science*, 16, 199–231.

Brighton, H. (2006). Robust inference with simple cognitive models. In C. Lebiere, and R., Wray (Eds.), *Between a rock and a hard place: Cognitive science principles meet AI-hard problems (AAAI Technical Report SS-02–06)* (pp. 189–211). AAAI Press, Menlo Park, CA.

Brighton, H. (2019). Beyond quantified ignorance: Rebuilding rationality without the bias bias. Economics Discussion Papers No 2019–25, Kiel Institute for the World Economy.

Brighton, H. and Gigerenzer, G. (2007). Bayesian brains and cognitive mechanisms: Harmony or dissonance? In N. Chater, and M., Oaksford (Eds.), *The probabilistic mind: Prospects for Bayesian cognitive science* (pp. 189–208). Cambridge University Press, Cambridge.

Brighton, H., and Gigerenzer, G. (2012). Are rational actor models "rational" outside small worlds? In S. Okasha and K., Binmore (Eds.), *Evolution and rationality: Decisions, co-operation and strategic behaviour* (pp. 84–109). Cambridge University Press, Cambridge.

Brighton, H. and Gigerenzer, G. (2015). The bias bias. *Journal of Business Research*, 68, 1772–1784.

Chater, N. and Oaksford, M. (1999). Ten years of the rational analysis of cognition. *Trends in Cognitive Sciences*, 3(2), 57–65.

Chater, N., Oaksford, M., Nakisa, R., and Redington, M. (2003). Fast, frugal, and rational: How rational norms explain behavior. *Organizational Behavior and Human Decision Processes*, 90, 63–86.

Chater, N., Tenenbaum, J. B., and Yuille, A. (2006). Probabilistic models of cognition: Conceptual foundations. *Trends in Cognitive Sciences*, 10(7), 287–291.

Chen, Z. and Haykin, S. (2002). On different facets of regularization theory. *Neural Computation*, 14(12), 2791–2846.

Czerlinski, J., Gigerenzer, G., and Goldstein, D. G. (1999). How good are simple heuristics? In G. Gigerenzer, P. M. Todd, and the ABC Research Group (Eds.), *Simple heuristics that make us smart* (pp. 119–140). Oxford University Press, New York.

Domingos, P. and Pazzani, M. (1997). On the optimality of the simple Bayesian classifier under zero-one loss. *Machine Learning*, 29, 103–130.

Dupré, J., (Ed.) (1987). *The latest on the best: Essays on evolution and optimality*. MIT Press, Cambridge, MA.

Edelman, S. and Shahbazi, R. (2011). Survival in a world of probable objects: A fundamental reason for Bayesian enlightenment. *Behavioral and Brain Sciences*, 34(4), 197–198.

Friedman, J. H. (1997). On bias, variance, 0/1-loss, and the curse-of-dimensionality. *Data Mining and Knowledge Discovery*, 1, 55–77.

Geman, S., Bienenstock, E., and Doursat, R. (1992). Neural networks and the bias/variance dilemma. *Neural Computation*, 4, 1–58.

Gigerenzer, G. and Brighton, H. (2009). Homo heuristicus: Why biased minds make better inferences. *Topics in Cognitive Science*, 1, 107–143.

Gigerenzer, G. and Goldstein, D. G. (1996). Reasoning the fast and frugal way: Models of bounded rationality. *Psychological Review*, 103(4), 650–669.

Gigerenzer, G. and Selten, R. (2001). *Bounded rationality: The adaptive toolbox*. MIT Press, Cambridge, MA.

Gigerenzer, G., Todd, P. M., and the ABC Research Group (Eds.) (1999). *Simple heuristics that make us smart*. Oxford University Press, New York.

Gilboa, I. (1987). Expected utility with purely subjective non-additive probabilities. *Journal of Mathematical Economics*, 16, 65–88.

Gilboa, I., Postlewaite, A., and Schmeidler, D. (2012). Rationality of belief or: Why Savage's axioms are neither necessary or sufficient for rationality. *Synthese*, 187, 11–31.

Gilboa, I. and Schmeidler, D. (1989). Maxmin expected utility with a non-unique prior. *Journal of Mathematical Economics*, 18, 141–153.

Gintis, H. (2012). An evolutionary perspective on the unification of the behavioral sciences. In S. Okasha and K., Binmore (Eds.), *Evolution and rationality: Decisions, co-operation and strategic behaviour* (pp. 213–245). Cambridge University Press, Cambridge.

Goldstein, D. G., and Gigerenzer, G. (2002). Models of ecological rationality: The recognition heuristic. *Psychological Review*, 109, 75–90.

Griffiths, T. L., Lieder, F., and Goodman, N. D. (2015). Rational use of cognitive resources: Levels of analysis between the computational and the algorithmic. *Topics in Cognitive Science*, 7(2), 217– 229.

Griffiths, T. L. and Tenenbaum, J. B. (2006). Optimal predictions in everyday cognition. *Psychological Science*, 17(9), 767–773.

Griffiths, T. L., Vul, E., and Sanborn, A. N. (2012). Bridging levels of analysis for probabilistic models of cognition. *Current Directions in Psychological Science*, 21(4), 263–268.

Hadamard, J. (1902). Sur les problèmes aux dérivées partielles et leur signification physique. *Princeton University Bulletin*, 13, 49–52.

Hand, D. J. and Yu, K. (2001). Idiot's Bayes: Not so stupid after all? *International Statistical Review*, 69, 385–398.

Hastie, T., Tibshirani, R., and Friedman, J. (2001). *The elements of statistical learning: Data mining, inference, and prediction*. Springer, New York.

Jones, M. and Love, B. (2011). Bayesian fundamentalism or enlightenment? On the explanatory status and theoretical contributions of Bayesian models of cognition. *Behavioral and Brain Sciences*, 34, 169–231.

Kuncheva, L. I. (2006). On the optimality of naïve Bayes with dependent binary features. *Pattern Recognition Letters*, 27, 830–837.

Marr, D. (1977). Artificial intelligence: A personal view. *Artificial Intelligence*, 9, 37–48.

Marr, D. (1982). *Vision*. Freeman, San Francisco, CA.

Marr, D. and Hildreth, E. (1980). Theory of edge detection. *Proceedings of the Royal Society of London B*, 207, 187–217.

Marr, D. and Poggio, T. (1976). From understanding computation to understanding neural circuitry. *AI Memo* 357.

Martignon, L. and Laskey, K. B. (1999). Bayesian benchmarks for fast and frugal heuristics. In G. Gigerenzer, P. M. Todd, and the ABC Research Group (Eds), *Simple heuristics that make us smart* (pp. 169–188). Oxford University Press, New York.

McClamrock, R. (1991). Marr's three levels: A re-evaluation. *Minds and Machines*, 1(2), 185–196.

Ng, A. Y. and Jordan, M. I. (2002). On discriminative vs. generative classifiers: A comparison of logistic regression and naive Bayes. In T., Dieterich, S., Becker, and Z. Ghahramani (Eds.), *Advances in neural information processing systems (NIPS)* 14. MIT Press, Cambridge, MA.

Oaksford, M. and Chater, N. (2009). The uncertain reasoner: Bayes, logic, and rationality. *Behavioral and Brain Sciences*, 32, 105–120.

O'Sullivan, F. (1986). A statistical perspective on ill-posed inverse problems. *Statistical Science*, 1, 502–518.

Parker, G. A. and Maynard Smith, J. (1990). Optimality theory in evolutionary biology. *Nature*, 348, 27–33.

Peebles, D. and Cooper, R. P. (2015). Thirty years after Marr's vision: Levels of analysis in cognitive science. *Topics in Cognitive Science*, 7(2), 187–190.

Perlich, C., Provost, F., and Simonoff, J. S. (2003). Tree induction vs. logistic regression: A learning curve analysis. *Journal of Machine Learning Research*, 4, 211–255.

Poggio, T. (2012). The levels of understanding framework, revised. *Perception*, 41(9), 1017–1023.

Savage, L. J. (1954). *The foundations of statistics*. Wiley, New York.

Schoemaker, P. J. H. (1991). The quest for optimality: A positive heuristic of science? *Behavioral and Brain Sciences*, 14, 205–245.

Selten, R. (2001). What is bounded rationality? In G. Gigerenzer and R. Selten (Eds.), *Bounded rationality: The adaptive toolbox* (pp. 13–36). MIT Press, Cambridge, MA.

Simon, H. A. (1957). *Models of man*. John Wiley & Sons, New York.

Simon, H. A. (1991). Cognitive architectures and rational analysis: Comment. In K. Van Lehn (Ed.), *Architectures for intelligence* (pp. 25–39). Erlbaum, Hillsdale, NJ.

Şimşek, O. and Buckmann, M. (2015). Learning from small samples: An analysis of simple decision heuristics. In D. D. Lee, M. Sugiyama, and R. Garnett (Eds.), *Advances in Neural Information Processing Systems (NIPS)* 28. MIT Press, Cambridge, MA.

Stone, M. (1974). Cross-validatory choice and assessment of statistical predictions. *Journal of the Royal Statistical Society B*, 36, 111–147.

Tenenbaum, J. B. and Griffiths, T. L. (2001). Some specifics about generalization. *Behavioral and Brain Sciences*, 24, 762–778.

Webb, G. I., Boughton, J. R., and Wang, Z. (2005). Not so naive Bayes: Aggregating one dependence estimators. *Machine Learning*, 58, 5–24.

Willems, R. (2011). Re-appreciating the why of cognition: 35 years after Marr and Poggio. *Frontiers in Psychology*, 2, 244.

18

THE WINDS OF CHANGE

The Sioux, Silicon Valley, society, and simple heuristics

Julian N. Marewski and Ulrich Hoffrage

Introduction

Imagine the following: Born in 1860, Leaning-Bear, a Sioux (Lakota), grows up in the West of North America. His life unfolds amidst traditional and season-dependent tribal activities, such as hunting and gathering or moving from one camp site to another. There is regular contact with other tribes, and occasional ones with 'white' settlers. Then, suddenly, Leaning-Bear's world begins to change: More 'white' intruders enter the prairies and the Black Hills, and occasional skirmishes turn into an increasingly fierce struggle for survival (see e.g., Brown, 1971, 1974; Brown & Schmitt, 1976). In 1876, aged 16, Leaning-Bear fights in the legendary battle of the Little Big Horn; he sees George Armstrong Custer and his soldiers of the 7th U.S. Cavalry Regiment die. But shortly afterwards, the U.S. army gains control. At the age of 30, Leaning-Bear and his family live, on 'reservation land', under surveillance by government agents, no longer moving on horseback freely across the seemingly endless space of the Great Plains. Famine and government rations replace buffalo meat; and the memories of the massacre of Wounded Knee replace those of the victory of Little Big Horn. Violence, chaos, death, and misery surround him, and as time passes, alcohol enters his life. That is the end of Leaning-Bear's old world. But it is not the end of changes in his new world: Only a few years later, he finds himself surrounded by the impenetrable walls of a 'white' man's prison cell; and after release, he lives on to hear about cars and even airplanes; he sees factories and learns about a great war raging on the other side of the ocean between 1914–1918. Leaning-Bear, a man who was born in a teepee and who grew up in a world of buffalo hunting with bows and arrows, dies in 1933, at the age of 73 and in the same year Adolf Hitler seizes power in Germany.[1,2]

The story of Leaning-Bear's life is one about drastic changes in a person's environment. It is actually not only a story of change in one individual's environment, but also of change in the environment of a social collective: the Sioux nation. Changes in collective environments are common throughout human history: Genocides, wars, economic conflicts between groups, climatic catastrophes, epidemics, and technological revolutions can all lead to change.

What, then, characterizes the change in the story of Leaning-Bear more precisely? (1) The change is profoundly *disruptive*; it has terribly negative consequences for an individual's—here, Leaning-Bear's—well-being. (2) The change is *abrupt*; it is sudden, taking place within only a few years of an individual's life-time. (3) The change is *thorough;* it cuts across many, if not all, dimensions

DOI: 10.4324/9781315658353-21

of life. It affects, for instance, what Leaning-Bear and his fellow tribe members eat, which tools and artifacts they use, how they dress, who is part of their social network, and whose laws are enforced. (4) Finally, from the perspective of the individual, at the moment of such sudden, profoundly negative, and all-encompassing change, the environment becomes deeply *uncertain*: Known regularities seem to break down and the environment continues to evolve at rapid pace. In short, Leaning-Bear's story is that of a revolution breaking out upon individuals. The violent winds of change that were blowing over the prairies in the 1870s seem fundamentally different to all those storms the Sioux and other Native American tribes had encountered throughout their entire history.

Today, one might argue, we are also living through a period of rapid, extensive change. A different type of change—not produced by war, invasion, genocide, or migration, but by technology. The contemporary winds of change we are referring to are not blowing over the prairies, but across the entire planet. One of their epicenters—to the extent that is possible to locate its roots geographically—is Silicon Valley with its many technology giants (for the philosophical and historical roots of digital technologies, see Emberson, 2009; Hoffrage, 2019). Digital technology has had and will continue to have a powerful impact across many dimensions of our lives: It affects what many of us do on a daily basis to make a living, what is considered to be wrong and what is considered to be right, how we search for and how we find information, and how we organize our social lives—or, more precisely, how digital technologies affect this organization. These technologies determine, and will increasingly continue to determine, what tools we use and have access to, and it is uncertain what other aspects of our lives they will change. The digital winds of change might shape some individual's or collectives' lives later, with remnants or pockets of old, non-digital environments being at least partially conserved within and by more-or-less isolated groups. Older generations who might have scant contact with digital technology offer one example. In that pockets subsist for some time, the digital winds of change are no different from other changes in human history, including those that impacted on the Native American nations over the last centuries. A stunning historical example is the existence of the last free Apaches, bearing their own tragic history by hiding in the Sierra Madre in the North of Mexico until at least as late as the 1930s (see Goodwin & Goodwin, 2018).

Importantly, while the digital winds of change will blow into different individuals' faces sooner or later, the ongoing digital revolution has great potential to do much harm to individuals and societies as a whole. In our view, those potential negative side-effects of the digital winds of change need to be understood scientifically, such that we, to the extent that we are still in control, might be able to counteract them. That is, reflection about how sudden, profoundly negative, and all-encompassing changes affect the ways in which individuals think, decide, and act seems warranted, alongside reflection about how individuals and societies can manage such changes.

By focusing on the possible negative aspects of digitalization, this chapter considers how humans understand and manage abrupt, disruptive, and thorough changes through the theoretical lens of a psychological framework: the *fast-and-frugal heuristics approach* to decision making, developed by the ABC (Adaptive Behavior and Cognition) Research Group around Gerd Gigerenzer and colleagues (e.g., Gigerenzer, Todd, & the ABC Research Group, 1999; Gigerenzer, Hertwig, & Pachur, 2011). This theoretical lens, also known as the *simple heuristics approach*, lends itself particularly well to trying to understand how boundedly rational humans––individuals who are neither "omniscient" nor endowed with computational "omnipotence" (e.g., Gigerenzer, 2008a, p. 5 and p. 4, respectively)—behave and decide in an uncertain world. In addition to this, the framework aids reflecting about normative, prescriptive aspects of adapting to and shaping a fundamentally uncertain world.

We proceed as follows: Upon offering an overview of the fast-and-frugal heuristics research program, we sketch out what future aversive digital environments might look like, and speculate what strategies individuals and societies might rely upon in order to manage those aversive changes in their environments. We close by (1) pointing to a series of research questions about how digital environments might differ from other environments we humans have encountered both in our more recent history and over the course of our evolution as well as (2) turning to questions about children and education.

Before we start, a commentary is warranted. We acknowledge and believe that digital technologies can do, do do, and will do much good (and we are both, by no means, technology-aversive and/or change-resistant, reactionary scientists). Yet, we have decided to play devil's advocate and to focus, in this chapter, exclusively on digitalization's potential negative aspects, because we believe it is important for more people to adopt a healthily skeptical view in a time when 'going digital' has become a mantra for businessmen, politicians, administrators, and others. In so doing, we are intellectually indebted to and join others who have underlined the negative aspects of digitalization (e.g., Helbing, 2015, 2019; O'Neil, 2016; Helbing et al., 2017; SVRV, 2018).

The fast-and-frugal heuristics framework

The fast-and-frugal heuristics framework asks how the structure of environments shapes behavior and cognition. The assumption is that people can select inferential and other decision-making mechanisms from a repertoire, commonly referred to as the *adaptive toolbox* (Gigerenzer et al., 1999; for an overview, see e.g., Gigerenzer & Gaissmaier, 2011). By using different mechanisms (i.e., tools) from that toolbox as a function of the environment, people can make accurate inferences about unknown elements of their world, prevent being excluded from important social groups, find mates, or otherwise behave adaptively. Relying on tools that do not fit the environment through which people are navigating can produce maladaptive behavior and potentially catastrophic outcomes.

The idea that performance and behavior depend on an organism's environment is common to a number of research programs on human cognition. For instance, Gibson's (1986) theory of visual perception stresses that neither the perceptual system nor that system's environment can be understood in isolation; instead what matters is their interplay. According to Gibson, the environment comes with functional properties—dubbed *affordances*—that organisms can perceive and act upon. The *ACT-R theory of cognition* (e.g., Anderson et al., 2004) and the *rational analysis* (e.g., Anderson, 1991) on which parts of ACT-R are based, place emphasis on how human memory, by being adapted to the statistical structure of the environment, achieves its processing goals (see Anderson & Schooler, 1991). To give a final example, Brunswik's approach to studying human perception assumes that *achievement* (i.e., performance) depends on how individuals integrate cues available to them in the environment. According to Brunswik (e.g., 1955), it is the statistical structure of information in an environment (i) that needs to be studied in order to understand behavior and cognition, and (ii) that needs to be maintained in experiments and in observational studies aimed at assessing performance.

The fast-and-frugal heuristics research program has been influenced, to a large extent, by Brunswik's conceptual framework of *probabilistic functionalism*, and by Simon's seminal work on *bounded rationality* (e.g., Gigerenzer, Hoffrage, & Kleinbölting, 1991, and Gigerenzer & Goldstein, 1996, respectively). According to Simon (1990), "[h]uman rational behavior ... is shaped by a scissors whose two blades are the structure of task environments and the computational capabilities of the actor" (p. 7). In emerging from the interplay between mind and environment, human rationality does not correspond to that prescribed by classic, content-blind norms (e.g., Bayes rule, expected utility maximization, logic). Instead, rationality is ecological: Rational behavior is that kind of behavior that allows an individual to achieve its goals in a given task environment (for a volume on the fast-and-frugal heuristics framework that focuses on ecological rationality, see, e.g., Todd, Gigerenzer, & the ABC Research Group, 2012).

The fast-and-frugal heuristics framework's emphasis on the environment (i.e., the first blade of Simon's scissors) contrasts with the focus on traits as explanations of behavior, as it is typical for personality psychology. For instance, imagine that Leaning-Bear, at 13 had 'celebrated as victory' the slaughter of Pawnee families in Massacre Canyon, and as a 14- or 15-year old, he had joined war parties attacking 'white' intruders, and participated in raids against other tribes. Later, he had stolen horses on the reservation and then beaten up, with several other Sioux, a former army scout. Rather than attributing what some today might call 'anti-social' behavior to stable traits, deeply entrenched in Leaning-Bear's 'pathological' personality, the fast-and-frugal heuristics framework would ask how the interplay between his decision-making strategies and his environment may have led Leaning-Bear to commit those acts. Candidate mechanisms in the repertoire may be imitation strategies: Raids against others and the stealing of horses may represent behaviors that were common in Leaning-Bear's old world, so one hypothesis may read. In committing these acts, one could speculate, Leaning-Bear might have simply been imitating the behavior of respected peers. Even in our contemporary world, *not* participating in certain acts can signal distancing from social groups, with the risk of social isolation. Belongingness to a group, in turn, can be key to an individual's well-being and, ultimately, survival—especially in societies that depend on cooperative hunter-gatherer activities in harsh environments.[3]

Another assumption of the fast-and-frugal heuristics framework, adapted from Simon's work (i.e., the second blade of his scissors), is that human information-processing capacities are bounded: We do not have unlimited computational power, infinite knowledge, or endless time. In trying to achieve their goals, humans do not try to optimize or maximize, which are descriptive and/or normative building blocks in both classic and contemporary theories of human and animal behavior (e.g., Becker, 1976; Stephens & Krebs, 1986). Instead humans need to strive for solutions that are *sufficient* to achieve those goals in a given environment—they *satisfice*, as Simon (e.g., 1990) put it.

To illustrate the point, a utility-maximization approach assumes that, when deciding whether or not to steal a horse, Leaning-Bear would take into account *all* the numerous possible consequences of both stealing and not stealing (e.g., relating to the former: being arrested, getting killed; having a vision after being injured by a soldier's gunshot; gaining prestige among his tribe members, and even counting a coup; see Hassrick, 1992, on the role of coups in Sioux warfare). Moreover, he would have had to assess not only the probabilities that each of these consequences would occur, but also the utility of each one. These utilities would then have to be brought into the same currency or scale (e.g., being killed, gaining a horse, and so on would all need to be assigned a numeric value). Finally, with all that in mind, Leaning-Bear would have had to calculate which option would yield the largest expected utility and decide for that course of action. While it is certainly possible to assume that Leaning-Bear made these calculations (perhaps unconsciously), there might be a simpler way of explaining his decision which involves only one goal: to increase social prestige, thereby ignoring anything else: As far back as Leaning-Bear could remember, one way for warriors to gain recognition had been to participate in raids on other tribes, and, notably, to steal their horses (see Hassrick, 1992, on how the successful theft of horses mattered for a Sioux's social prestige and economic well-being). Indeed, prestige played and plays a role as a motor for action in other communities as well, including the Comanche of the Southern Plains (Hämäläinen, 2012), the Tiwi people of northern Australia (Hicks, Burgman, Marewski, Fidler, & Gigerenzer, 2012), or modern-day scientists, as an own particular tribe. Such a hypothesis about a driving motive could then be combined with others, focusing on the behavioral strategies relied upon to achieve a goal (e.g., imitation of others' behavior as a route to prestige; see above).

In taking up Simon's notion of bounded rationality, the fast-and-frugal heuristics framework assumes that behavioral strategies do not need to depend on massive amounts of information and complex information integration (see e.g., Marewski, Gaissmaier, & Gigerenzer, 2010). Instead, the fast-and-frugal heuristics research program stresses that people can make smart decisions by relying on particularly simple mechanisms, dubbed *heuristics*. Heuristics are strategies that ignore information (hence frugal), and that can, in so doing, enable efficient behavior, such as making decisions quickly (hence fast; see e.g., Gigerenzer & Gaissmaier, 2011). For instance, the simple *take-the-best heuristic* (Gigerenzer & Goldstein, 1996) bases inferences on just one predictor variable. In computer simulations, this heuristic has yielded, on average, more accurate inferences than multiple regression when tested, out-of-sample, in 20 different real-world environments (e.g., Czerlinski, Gigerenzer, & Goldstein, 1999; see also Brighton, 2006; Gigerenzer & Brighton, 2009; Katsikopoulos, Schooler, & Hertwig, 2010). Surprising performance has been reported for other heuristics, too—be it in marketing, criminal profiling, or forecasting of political election results, and such like (Gaissmaier & Marewski, 2011; Goldstein & Gigerenzer, 2009; Hafenbrädl, Waeger, Marewski, & Gigerenzer, 2016). Note that this is not to say that simple heuristics will always and necessarily yield smart decisions with favorable outcomes. Such a guarantee does not exist, because the relative efficacy of a heuristic depends on the environment. For example, Leaning-Bear's environment changed in many dimensions and continuing to use the same heuristics, such as imitation, despite environmental change, can lead to disaster, including punishment for horse theft, or alcoholism when imitating the alcohol consumption of others.

The research questions of the science of simple heuristics

The fast-and-frugal heuristics framework asks a series of research questions that can be grouped into four categories: descriptive, ecological, applied, and methodological (e.g., Gigerenzer, 2008b; Gigerenzer, Hoffrage, & Goldstein, 2008).

(1) *Descriptive*: What are the heuristics people have in their adaptive toolbox that they are able to rely upon—be it when it comes to making simple decisions or when navigating through a complex social world? What elements of our cognitive architecture (e.g., memory and perception) do these heuristics exploit? When and how do people choose to use which heuristic?

(2) *Ecological*: To which aspects of environmental texture is each heuristic from the toolbox adapted? How can those environments be described (e.g., in terms of statistical regularities or affordances)? Answering this question aids understanding of how selecting a heuristic in a fitting environment can aid people to make clever decisions; or, conversely, how failure can result if a heuristic is mismatched to an environment. This is a question of ecological rationality.

(3) *Applied*: How can human performance be improved by better matching heuristics to environments? Two ways of boosting performance are possible. One would be to lead people (e.g., through education) to change the heuristics they rely upon in a given environment; another would be to change (e.g., through policy-making) the environment in which people rely on given heuristics.

(4) *Methodological*: How can people's use of heuristics (the descriptive question) and the fit of the heuristics to different environments (the ecological question) be studied, and how can the effectiveness of interventions (the applied question) be tested?

Instructive answers to these four types of questions have been formulated in numerous fields and disciplines to which the fast-and-frugal heuristics program has been applied (e.g., Gigerenzer et al., 1999, 2011). How can these four questions aid our understanding of drastic environmental change, notably, the ways in which individuals think, decide, and act?

Descriptive questions would ask which heuristics people rely upon when they sense such massive changes: Are there heuristics for managing environmental change? For instance, when an individual does not know what a right or clever course of action is, relying on others and imitating their behavior are typically viable strategies: Groups can furnish resources in situations of scarcity and unpredictable access (e.g., through the pooling of food), and observing what others do can facilitate learning of what works well and what does not, thereby avoiding repetition of costly errors. But how are people's willingness, propensity, or readiness to imitate others affected by the stability of the environment?

Ecological questions would ask: Which characteristics of massively changing environments would likely increase the performance of different strategies—be they heuristics or other tools—and which characteristics of changing environments would limit those strategies' performance? For example, when it comes to making accurate inferences about unknown or future events, imitating others is likely helpful when these others can be expected to make at least minimally accurate judgments. If the future is fully unpredictable or if all individuals in a group are likely to be led astray, then relying on others will not aid making accurate inferences (but could still help inclusion in the social group; on the ecological rationality of imitating the majority of others, see Gigerenzer, 2008a). If environments differ with respect to which strategy performs best—and they may vary over time, or space, or both—then an ecological analysis becomes quite complex and its conclusions cannot be summarized in one sentence (for a review and a simulation study that compared the performance of various individual and social learning strategies depending on the stability of the environment, see McElreath, Wallin, & Fasolo, 2013).

Applied questions might prescribe asking, for instance, how imitation strategies could be turned into clever ones in a new environment; for example, by endowing at least certain individuals from a collective with training and insights (e.g., through schooling), this way creating leaders or role-models others might benefit from by imitating. Applied questions might also ask how heuristics could be used as tools (Hafenbrädl et al., 2016), and how they could be taught to foster insights and boost people's decision-making competencies (see also Grüne-Yanoff & Hertwig, 2016, on boosting; Kozyreva, Lewandowsky, & Hertwig, in press, on nudging versus boosting with a focus on internet users; and Gigerenzer, 2014, on heuristic principles for teaching).

Finally, the methodological perspective would prescribe tackling those descriptive, ecological, and applied questions by means of observational studies, laboratory experiments or, as is often done in studies of fast-and-frugal heuristics, through mathematical analysis (e.g., Martignon & Hoffrage, 2002) and computer simulation (e.g., Gigerenzer & Goldstein, 1996; Schooler & Hertwig, 2005). General guiding principles for asking methodological questions can be found in Marewski, Schooler, and Gigerenzer (2010).

The ecological focus of its research questions allows differentiating the fast-and-frugal heuristics research program further from other frameworks. Take applied questions on policy making and approaches that locate explanations for performance largely *inside* individuals, such as in psychopathic personality structures, lack of intelligence, or other traits. Corresponding to those inside-explanations, those frameworks' prescriptions might look very different than those of the fast-and-frugal heuristics program. For instance, a trait-approach to eradicate horse-stealing and other anti-social behavior might start from the basis that traits are difficult to change; hence corresponding individuals need to be 'managed,' not their environment or the changes that occurred therein. A simple way of managing individuals with undesirable traits is to eliminate them, say, by locking them away. To give another, more modern example, consider individuals involved in a scandal, such as *Dieselgate* or a case of industry bribery. Rather than seeking simplistic "one-word explanations" (Gigerenzer, 1998, p. 196) for wrong-doing (e.g., greed, recklessness, or egoism), which in the worst case can border re-description or tautology (e.g., a person behaves egoistically because she is an egoist), one could ask what behavioral strategies lead such individuals to do what they do, and what the ecological rationality of adopting those strategies is. To turn to the latter, ecological question: Could it be, for instance, that an unexpected change in their environment (e.g., how pollution should be assessed) in the past casts them and their behavior in a bad light (e.g., being reckless, behaving not particularly smart), but only today, that is, with the benefit of hindsight? This example also illustrates that, when answering the ecological question, no universal (here: time-invariant) norm for assessing rationality exists. While the fast-and-frugal heuristics framework is by no means the only program that shifts the focus from people to their interaction with their context (for an example from ethics, see e.g., Palazzo, Krings, & Hoffrage, 2012), this shift is not about sides in debates on meaningless dichotomies (e.g., inside versus outside explanations, genes versus culture and such like; on dichotomies in psychology more generally, see e.g., Newell, 1973), but rather about describing the interplay between environments and decision making mechanisms with precision.

On environments and heuristics

The functioning of heuristics cannot be assessed independently of the environment (Todd et al., 2012). Likewise, answering the four research questions set out above hinges on building adequate models of heuristics *and* environments. Environments can be characterized in multiple ways (e.g., Bullock & Todd, 1999; Czerlinski et al., 1999). For instance, they may change over time in systematic and hence predictable manners. The environment of the Plains tribes looked very different depending on the season, but the seasons were periodic. The Sioux (Lakota) of the nineteenth century were nomads and they could exploit such regularities: They knew when to be where in order to harvest ripe wild berries or to hunt (see Hassrick, 1992). More generally, environments can be described in terms of their regularities, with past research on fast-and-frugal heuristics having focused on, for instance, the statistical regularities found in modern-day informational environments (e.g., the news media, Goldstein & Gigerenzer, 2002; Schooler & Hertwig, 2005).

Moreover, environments differ between and within people. 'White' contemporaries of Leaning-Bear, living in the same area, did not live in his environment. And Leaning-Bear's biography offers an example of a difference within a person: there is a before and after the breakdown of Sioux (Lakota) military power.[4]

Furthermore, not only the objective, but also the perceived environment determines behavior and performance and such perceptions may change over time. Hence, a description of the environment in terms of its objective properties (e.g., cue inter-correlations) can be complemented by the environment's inner (e.g., mnemonic, emotional) representation (e.g., Marewski & Schooler, 2011).

Finally, an environment offers opportunities but also imposes challenges and confronts one with different tasks, such as finding a mate, maintaining friendships, or securing food and shelter. Consequently, environments can be described alongside different task-relevant dimensions. Gibson's (1986) notion of affordances, which highlights environments' functional properties (e.g., what actions does the property X afford?), offers a complement to this level of description.

Still another dimension by which an environment can be described is how much uncertainty it entails. Since the notion of uncertainty is particularly important in the context of this chapter—with its focus on uncertainty-generating changes and our digital future—let us discuss that notion in a bit more detail. In the literature on fast-and-frugal heuristics, uncertainty typically implies a world in which the full range of behavioral options is unknown, or in which the consequences of acting in a certain way are unknown, or the probabilities of these consequences occurring are inaccessible (see e.g., Mousavi & Gigerenzer, 2014, 2017, for discussions). In such a world, unforeseeable and/or surprising, fully unexpected events can ruin plans, for better or worse.[5] Savage (1972 [1954]) referred to such situations as *large(r) worlds* and contrasted them with *small(er) worlds*, a dichotomy that corresponds, roughly, to Knight's (1921) distinction between *uncertainty* and *risk* (see Binmore, 2007). Small worlds, characterized by risk, are roulette and card games: Here all options, their consequences, and probabilities of occurring are known or can be estimated with sufficient accuracy—assuming nobody cheats. From the perspective of the fast-and-frugal heuristics framework, it is only in small, risky worlds that Bayesian, subjective expected utility-maximizing, and other classic rational approaches to modeling human behavior, and performance might work well and represent adequate benchmarks for gauging human rationality (e.g., Gigerenzer, 2014; Hafenbrädl et al., 2016). In contrast, in large worlds, characterized by uncertainty, optimization is not feasible. If the decision maker does not know (1) what the consequences of behavioral options might be, or (2) what the probabilities of these consequences are (e.g., because the probabilities of relevant future events are not known, and eventually not even the events themselves are known—events that will, jointly with the chosen behavioral option, determine these consequences), or (3) eventually does not even know how any of these consequences should be evaluated, then optimization is pointless.

As a side note, optimization, as a mindset, is hence also not useful when reflecting about policies for shaping digitalization. For example, chains of unforeseen, distant future consequences, including changes in values letting current evaluations of foreseeable consequences diverge from future evaluations of the same consequences, might all be brought about by digitalization, resulting in massive uncertainty.

Importantly, the construction of models of heuristics hinges on the type and amount of uncertainty in the environment, an insight that is, actually, not always stressed in the literature on fast-and-frugal heuristics. Historically, the fast-and-frugal heuristics program started with inferential heuristics (for a brief history of this program, see Hoffrage, Hafenbrädl, & Marewski, 2018). The first heuristic formulated by members of the ABC Research Group dates back to before the group came into existence: the *PMM-algorithm* (which was a central component of a Brunswikian model on overconfidence; Gigerenzer et al., 1991). Gigerenzer and Goldstein (1996) renamed it take-the-best, referred to it as a heuristic, and determined its performance in a complete-paired comparison between all German cities with more than 100,000 inhabitants. Like other heuristics for inference, take-the-best can be described in terms of three algorithmic rules: A *search rule* and a *stopping rule*, which describe how specific cues are searched for and when information searching stops, respectively, and a *decision rule* formalizing how the cues identified are relied upon to arrive at a decision. Such heuristics are sufficiently precise in order to be implemented in computer simulations testing the accuracy of the heuristics in predicting the criterion against that of other models (e.g., other heuristics or more information-greedy statistical models, including regressions). A well-defined reference class with a finite set of objects (cities), one criterion (number of inhabitants), and nine dichotomous or dichotomized cues (e.g., a soccer team in the national league, an industrial belt)—this was, in fact, a relatively 'small' 'large world' and not a situation that would be characterized by the massive uncertainty that is typical of large (e.g., social) worlds in real life.

A first, albeit, small, step in the direction of a 'larger' world was taken by Czerlinski et al. (1999). These authors tested strategies, including heuristics, in cross-validation: Each strategy estimated its parameters in a given sample, but was then tested on another sample, taken from the same population. In this set-up, the world is still clearly defined, namely, in terms of a known criterion, and known cues, but there is noise when it comes to the assignment of objects to learning and test samples. Arguably, such variation through sampling does not entail a strong form of uncertainty.[6]

Stronger forms of uncertainty emerge, for example, when predictions have to be made out-of-population—situations where the learning sample might have little, if anything, in common with the world that one wishes to generalize. Even more uncertainty can arise when distant or quite general goals (e.g., survival, reproduction, well-being) can only be achieved if multiple intermediate goals are met and when it is far from clear how these intermediate goals should be prioritized and/or considered when deciding among options. Such complexity is likely to be found in social environments (Hertwig, Hoffrage, & the ABC Research Group, 2013).

Whereas some simple heuristics for navigating such very large, fuzzy worlds can still be cast into algorithmic search, stopping, and decision rules, others resemble guidelines, principles, or routines, tailored to specific situations or domains. An example is *"hire well and let them do their jobs,"* a simple rule that the former president of Florida International University, Modesto Maidique (2012), gleaned from CEOs whom he interviewed (cited in Gigerenzer, 2014, p. 116). Other examples, from the domain of leadership, are: *"If a person is not honest and trustworthy, the rest does not matter," "First listen, then speak," "You can't play it safe and win. Analysis will not reduce uncertainty,"* or *"When judging a plan, put as much stock in the people as in the plan"* (cited from Gigerenzer, 2014, p. 117, italics added). To return to the Sioux, Hassrick (1992) points out that a lemma of the Sioux was, *"It is better to die on the battlefield than to live to be old"* (p. 47, italics added), could this be thought of as a heuristic that would have eliminated, akin to a non-compensatory decision rule, any concerns about injury or death, such as when deciding whether to steal a horse?[7]

These heuristics for a large world characterized by massive uncertainty bear resemblance to the simple rules discussed by others (e.g., Manimala, 1992). Emphasizing their frugal nature, Sull and Eisenhardt (2015), for instance, describe such rules as "shortcut strategies that save time and effort by focusing our attention and simplifying the way we process information" (p. 5). They "allow people to act without having to stop and rethink every decision" (p. 5).

Such rules can be categorized in different ways. Sull and Eisenhardt (2015), for example, distinguish among *boundary rules* (which "define the boundaries of inclusion or exclusion, … like the 'thou shalt nots' of the Ten Commandments," p. 50), *prioritizing rules* (which "can help you rank a group of alternatives competing for scarce money, time, or attention," p. 57), *stopping rules* (e.g., "[s]top eating when I start feeling full," p. 67), *how-to rules* (that "address the basics of getting things done without prescribing every detail of what to do," p. 81), and *coordination rules* (which "guide interactions among members who intermingle in a complex system," p. 84).

Complementary ways to classify heuristics for massively uncertain worlds would be in terms of the functions they can serve (e.g., imitate-the-majority can allow for increasing accuracy of inferences, inclusion in a group, avoiding conflict, protecting oneself). Considering such functions may aid understanding of how people select between different heuristics. Conversely, the same function may be achieved by various heuristics, with such redundancies potentially enhancing the robustness of human decision-making capabilities (on Brunswik's related notion of vicarious functioning, see e.g., Wolf, 1999; on strategy selection and robustness, see e.g., Marewski & Schooler, 2011). Notwithstanding their name and classification (see also e.g., Guercini, 2019), a common feature of all such rules is that they constrain the space of possible behavioral options or decisions, and hence facilitate finding solutions to problems—and indeed, the term heuristic comes from ancient Greek and means "to discover" or "to find." This is why we conceive—and refer to—such rules or recommendations also as *heuristic principles*. In our view, when it comes to coping with the challenges offered by the winds of digitalization, these heuristic principles are more likely to be used (and be helpful) than the algorithms the fast-and-frugal heuristic program studied in its early days.

Modern-day dramatic change: from buffalo hunting on the Great Plains to the fruits of Silicon Valley

Jenny was born in 1983. When she grew up, cell phones were virtually non-existent in her world. The internet played no role in her youth and if she wanted to contact a friend she would have to call her either from home or from a public speaker phone. Calling someone in another country was expensive, the way to stay in touch with someone abroad would be to send a letter via postal mail. Twenty years later, in 2005, at the age of 22, Jenny uses the internet to find scientific articles during her university studies. She regularly looks up other information on the web, too, be it about political issues, medical conditions, or subject-matter related to her great passion: horses. She becomes excited about the prospect of a society where information is freely available to everyone, she engages in social networks, puts her CV and photos online, and writes her emails at work as if she were having a normal casual conversation with somebody, a mode of address and interaction that migrates to instant messaging services a few years later. That informal communication style is consistent with the *netiquette* of the time (a word used to refer to the rules of behavior in electronic communication). As a matter of fact, in becoming an internet actor, via email and other digital technologies, she behaves almost in the same way as she would if she were interacting with other people personally (be it face-to-face or on the phone). Jenny's life in the 2010s continues with her starting a job at a major car manufacturer, giving birth to two children, taking out the usual insurances, and buying the usual commodities. She has a customer discount card for her preferred supermarket chain, she updates the software on her computers on a regular basis, and she uses a smartphone like most of her peers. She pays for things electronically and is enthusiastic about getting paperless when it comes to managing all administrative aspects of her life, ranging from health insurance to writing a will. Cameras ensure the security of her mansion and that of most streets in the city she lives in. Jenny lives a happy life.

But then, in 2030, everything changes. Jenny's husband develops a disease, and his health insurance provider refuses to pay because the disease was allegedly present prior to him taking out the insurance policy. The insurance company 'discovered' this with the help of an algorithm which—when Jenny's husband asked for reimbursement of treatment costs—had searched through all accessible electronic records on him, pooled from multiple sources, including other companies, numerous individuals (e.g., private pictures of Jenny's husband floating around on the internet), and government databases. Jenny's husband is devastated—he does not remember having suffered from or even having been tested for that disease when he started his policy 30 years ago. Furthermore, he also has not saved any documents from that time that would allow him to prove the insurance company is wrong. But things get worse: Jenny gets arrested, charged for threatening national security. The accusation is based on emails Jenny had sent over the years, containing criticism of the government and on her having watched too many videos on the internet considered to be supportive of certain conspiracy theories. None of these activities alone would have been enough for such an accusation, but the evidence accumulated over the years such that, in 2030, the algorithms that scrutinized her electronic traces classified her as a threat. Suspicious gestures captured by cameras that filmed her when reading the email accusing her of criminal activity, as well as recordings of phone conversations with her friends (automatically saved by her phone company) provide further butter for the prosecutor's bread: She suffers from a psychopathological personality, claims the prosecution based on the available digital evidence. Once the charges become public, Jenny's friends drop her on social networks, she is fired from her job, and even her family avoids talking to her. Nobody wants to be associated with somebody like Jenny. In 2032, she commits suicide after coming to the conclusion that there is no way to escape this vicious circle. The same year, in Jenny's hometown alone, hundreds of citizens receive similar treatment, suffering public shaming and stigmatization. Some were caught watching porn, for others there were clear indications that they supported a prohibited political movement fighting against digital surveillance, some were in favor of abortion, and at least ten were caught making derogative comments about a leading political party in private (captured by their smartphones). None of those behaviors are tolerated in Jenny's world of the 2030s. And it is virtually impossible to keep behavior, preferences, or interests as a secret—the citizen of that time is entirely transparent.[8]

Helbing (2015) offers a comprehensive overview of what kind of personal data can be collected in the digital age, and in Box 18.1 we let Google's privacy policy as it stands at the time of writing, alongside a recent statement from the European Commission on creating rules for so-called "E-evidence," speak for themselves. Can both documents be seen as signposts of small but decisive steps toward Jenny's world? After all, the technology is already operational. The more interesting question, however, is who will use it, when and for what purpose, and how will such use be legitimated, enforced, and controlled?

Box 18.1 Privacy: Quo vadis?

We collect information … from figuring out … which language you speak, to … which ads you'll find most useful, the people who matter most to you online, or which YouTube videos you might like …

… We also collect the content you create, upload, or receive from others when using our services. This includes … email you write and receive, photos and videos you save, docs and spreadsheets you create, and comments you make on YouTube videos …

… We collect information about the apps, browsers, and devices you use to access Google services … The information we collect includes unique identifiers, browser type and settings, device type and settings, operating system, mobile network information including carrier name and phone number, and application version number. We also collect information about the interaction of your apps, browsers, and devices with our services, including IP address, crash reports, system activity, and the date, time, and referrer URL of your request. …

…We collect information about your activity in our services, which … may include:

- Terms you search for
- Videos you watch
- Views and interactions with content and ads
- Voice and audio information when you use audio features
- Purchase activity
- People with whom you communicate or share content
- Activity on third-party sites and apps that use our services
- Chrome browsing history you've synced with your Google Account

... we may collect telephony log information like your phone number, calling-party number, receiving-party number, forwarding numbers, time and date of calls and messages, duration of calls, routing information, and types of calls...

... We collect information about your location ...

... In some circumstances, Google also collects information about you from publicly accessible sources ...

We may also collect information about you from trusted partners, including marketing ... and security partners ....

Extracts from Google's Privacy policy[9]

★ ★ ★

To make it easier and faster for law enforcement and judicial authorities to obtain the electronic evidence they need to investigate and eventually prosecute criminals and terrorists, the Commission proposed on 17 April 2018 new rules in the form of a Regulation and a Directive, which will:

- create a European Production Order: this will allow a judicial authority in one Member State to obtain electronic evidence (such as emails, text or messages in apps, as well as information to identify a perpetrator as a first step) directly from a service provider or its legal representative in another Member State, which will be obliged to respond within 10 days, and within 6 hours in cases of emergency ...

Extract from the European Commission's online statement on "E-evidence"[10]

Why did we include two fictional characters in this chapter? What do they have in common, Leaning-Bear, the Sioux born more than 150 years ago, and Jenny, born at the end of the last millennium? First, we believe that digital technology has the potential to lead to a change in our environment that might, in a certain way, end up being almost as dramatic as the change we proposed Leaning-Bear experienced 150 years ago. Note that Jenny, born in 1983, belongs to the last generation who has a few childhood memories of a world in which computers have not yet entered the daily life of the masses. Only a few decades later, today's born-digitals find it hard to imagine a time without smartphones and internet—and no one knows how technological advances will continue. So, second, as much as Leaning-Bear's and Jenny's stories are fictional ones, the following discussion about how digitalization may change our environment is, by necessity, a speculative narrative concerning an uncertain future. We deliberately chose these fictional characters to highlight this speculative nature. However, we also believe that there is sufficient basis for our speculation and know that some of the worries we formulate are shared by others (e.g., Helbing, 2015, 2019; Helbing et al., 2017; O'Neil, 2016).

In the remainder of this chapter, we discuss what insights the fast-and-frugal heuristic framework might offer when it comes to understanding and eventually managing changes related to the digital revolution. We speculate what future aversive environments might look like. We reflect on how such environments might consequently influence behavior by leading people to adopt different heuristics. We then ask how such heuristics might, in turn, shape environments, namely, the societies in which they are enacted. Subsequently, we explore how aversive environmental changes can be managed, first, by an individual navigating through a changing environment and, second, by societies as a whole undergoing environmental change. Finally, we turn from changes in evolutionary history to the children of evolution: the digital natives.

In writing these sections, we have followed common wisdom—a meta-heuristic of sorts—for dealing with potentially aversive future environments: In order to prepare for challenges, one has to try to identify them, knowing that the future is uncertain and that surprises may occur. But even when leaving these caveats aside, it is clear that future digitalized worlds might take many forms. The goal is not to speculate about every form; rather, we focus on three aspects of digitalized worlds that we take to be particularly disruptive of individual behavior and performance (see Helbing, 2015; Helbing et al., 2017; Kozyreva et al., in press; O'Neil, 2016; SVRV, 2018).

What might future aversive digital environments look like: interconnectedness, influenceability, and traceability

First, whereas Leaning-Bear's world was one of relatively small groups, our contemporary modern world is one in which small groups intermingle with larger groups and contexts. Thanks to email, social media, and so on, we can easily reach out to people who live far away. When reflecting on how digitalization might affect our social environment, one thesis that might be formulated is that those growing social worlds make individuals more reachable by other people, including those who live on the other side of the planet. In some ways, new 'tribes,' united via digital technology over potentially thousands of miles might emerge. Such 'tribes' might share common (e.g., political) beliefs and worldviews, indeed, technology itself might contribute to creating and cementing those 'tribes' (e.g., through the selective posting of information via algorithms, resulting in echo-chambers; see Helbing et al., 2017). Needless to say, any increased ability to reach out to others can also offer more opportunities for collaboration, the sharing of knowledge and insights into warranted political and societal reforms. However, like a two-faced Janus head, the accessibility of individuals can also offer increased opportunities for attack and social destruction (e.g., Helbing, 2015). Virtual bullying and cybercrime are cases in point. Twenty years ago, a child that was bullied at one school might have moved to another school (possibly in another town) in order to be placed out of reach of his aggressors. Nowadays, the bullying can continue online through social media. Likewise, in order to steal money, robbers 20 years ago had to physically enter houses or banks. Nowadays, online theft and other types of cybercrime are possible over thousands of kilometers. The new digital world is an interconnected one. But note that not all connections are visible, at least not for John Q. Public: Individuals may have a hard time figuring out where social attacks come from—one cannot see enemies' actions on social media and unless one is part of a chat, one does not know who said what—uncertainty reigns. Indeed, it is worth asking, who, actually, is the adversary in a vastly interconnected world full of digital 'tribes'? At best, one can only sense that something is going wrong, giving rise, potentially, to paranoia and even vicious cycles. A manager's authority at a company, for instance, may be undermined by anonymous electronic messages spread widely among employees. Such messages may transform a supportive or neutral work environment into an aversive one that the manager no longer understands and, hence, cannot adequately respond to, potentially resulting in behavior that further contributes to the decline of the manager's authority.

Second, increased potential for attack comes with increased potential for influence: Be it news about shark attacks in Australia or local government corruption in some remote country, in a digitalized world, information from all parts of the globe can easily spread, and hence influence individuals' beliefs, emotions, and behaviors. How would you feel if, after watching 20 videos of shark attacks somewhere on the other side of the planet, you snorkeled over deep blue water in the Mediterranean Sea? Would you experience some kind of anxious arousal, even if you knew that any fear is completely unwarranted? Or if you hear stories, repeated over and over again, thanks to social media, about waves of violent immigrants, stealing, beating, and raping: Would you call for stricter immigration laws or even applaud the building of walls at the border of your country? Over-informed, over-aroused, and over-reactive are three words that characterize our modern, interconnected world.

A third aspect of our world that is changing is the traceability of individuals' past behavior: Individuals are likely now to leave behind far more traces of their past actions and intentions than ever before in human history. If an individual coughs on the street, laughs out loud or farts, gives a polemical speech, wears crocodile skin trousers, drives through a red traffic light, visits a brothel, does not pay her taxes, commits fraud, or hacks the bank account of his neighbor, chances are there is a trace of those actions somewhere. When we interact with a digital device, it is presumably even more likely that records of this interaction remain, and this holds true not only for our own devices but also for those beyond our own control; for instance, the devices of those to whom we sent an email, the owners of websites we visit, or the owner of a camera installed on the street or in a car. This, in turn, might create additional affordances for social destruction (see Helbing, 2015). Obviously, not all traces are visible to everyone; and, indeed, those who can access them are also those who have power—and so everything hinges on what their interests and intentions are. Moreover, the individual is not necessarily in control of the recorded traces; she does not 'own' the data and cannot destroy them. The individual might not even know what data were recorded or when. And the amount of data that can be traced back in time exceeds what the individual would be able to remember about her own actions. All of this generates uncertainty.

In short, in digitalized societies, individuals lose control of what is knowable about their own past and present behavior. At the same time, individuals can be aggressed over any distance and by any other individual on the planet, and similarly they can also be influenced over any distance (see Helbing, 2015).

What heuristics might people rely on to navigate through aversive digital environments?

Individuals who realize, ahead of time, how traceable and attackable behavior will become, might react in various ways. One might be defensive.

> Heuristic principle: *If you have to have to make a decision, act in a way that allows you to defend your decision.*

Defensive decision-making has been described in managerial and medical environments (e.g., Artinger, Artinger, & Gigerenzer, 2019; Marewski & Gigerenzer, 2012)—that is, in situations where decision makers fear punishment for their actions, such as a physician who might be afraid of being sued for a wrong diagnosis or unsuccessful treatment. Indeed, what is commonly subsumed under the label paranoia can possibly be conceived of as the end of the spectrum of cognitive and behavioral outcomes of such defensive approaches to decision making.

Increased social conformity might be another behavioral outcome displayed by individuals who think defensively about their future (see Helbing, 2015). Conformity might be produced by genuine defensive decision-making principles ("*If you act like everybody else acts, then your action can likely not be wrong*") or by mere (not necessarily intentionally defensive) imitation heuristics. Those social decision strategies can allow dealing with situations where the 'correct' or desirable course of action will never or only later reveal itself (Gigerenzer, 2008a; Hertwig et al., 2013). More generally, they may also aid an actor who has little or no knowledge about the situation at hand (Gigerenzer & Gaissmaier, 2011).

Heuristic: *"Imitate the majority"* (Gigerenzer, 2008a, p. 31)—*behave as most others do.*

It takes two to tango, but three to make a list. A third example of how individuals might adapt their behavior once they become aware of the increased traceability of actions and the potential for destruction resulting from those traces is that those individuals resort to offense as the best defense. An example of this is dash cameras, nowadays being increasingly installed in cars. The rationale is that these cameras can record the potentially hazardous behavior of other drivers, offering important legal proof in case of an accident. The downside: If an accident occurs and only one party has a dash camera, then only that party will have access to the images, allowing them to potentially control which images enter the judicial stage and which do not. Hence, those who do not have a dash camera installed might find themselves in a less advantageous situation compared to those who have, thereby eventually leading to all drivers recording each other's behavior constantly.

Heuristic principle: *If your behavior can potentially be recorded, record the behavior of everybody else who you interact with.*

What might be thought of as a digital arms race can also take place when trust among different members of an institution erodes. For instance, the prevailing communication style might gradually shift from verbal commitments and promises to the sending out of emails that summarize the contents of conversations, to eventually all details being put in writing by each party, each one trying to be the one with the best documentation—just in case. Putting others' cc on emails in work contexts—ideally higher in the hierarchy—is a notorious escalation signal, too.

Such arms races do not depend on digital media for their existence, but digital media can fuel them. Digital media facilitate the storing, copying, and sharing of content, regardless of whether it comes to individuals, companies, public administrations, governments, or secret services. Some of these agents may fear that having less information than others may be disadvantageous in a complex, competitive, or potentially threatening social world. A world that comes, moreover, with seemingly little margin for error, because behavior that represents, either in foresight or in hindsight, a 'wrong-doing,' might have a greater chance of being detected or leading to negative consequences (see also Helbing, 2015). One does not need to understand much of game theory to anticipate that corresponding fears, whether justified or not, can spiral into a desire to collect data and to store information.

What might future aversive digital societies, shaped by defensive, social, and offensive heuristics, look like?

The heuristics people might rely upon to navigate through a digital environment might, in themselves, contribute to shaping those environments. What kinds of societies could a consistent enactment of those and other defensive and offensive heuristics create? Possibly, societies governed by fear. Perhaps societies governed by mistrust in social relations. And maybe societies characterized by less individualism and less individual freedom, with the masses defining, through social media, which behaviors are acceptable for certain collectives (digital 'tribes'), and which are not. Indeed, changes in value systems might be an additional consequence (Helbing, 2015). For example, it is likely to be no coincidence that in many European countries the word "transparency" has become frequently used in public discourses: Transparency is needed, so the public outcry goes, when yet another scandal is uncovered. But calls for transparency might also transform into beliefs and the spread of heuristic principles such as *"He who has nothing to hide has no problem with sharing all information about him,"* a lack of transparency being equated with a lack of trustworthiness, or even worse, criminal intent. Still another consequence might be a lack of willingness for decision makers to take risks and potentially make mistakes (Helbing, 2015). Those decision makers might be politicians who opt for defending what they take to be 'safer' positions or entrepreneurs who opt not to promote a new technology because if things go awry, it might be easy to make a case against them thanks to the massive amounts of data collected in the brave new digital world. The lack of willingness to make mistakes, in turn, might translate into reduced opportunities for learning: after all, only those who make mistakes can learn. To avoid misunderstandings: In both analogous and digital worlds, mistakes can occur; but the difference is that they might be less likely to be detected in an analogous world and, if detected, they might be less likely to stay visible—people forget, but computers and big data do not. (For more detail, see Helbing, 2015, who discusses these and related observations, pointing, for instance, to the emergence of vicious cycles, herding effects, and the loss of independent judgment of others.)

If social relations, value systems, and the permissibility of mistakes change on a societal level, what else can happen to make things even worse? Totalitarianism, not 'just' dictated by new norms and controlled, bottom-up, by the masses through digital media, but totalitarianism put into place top-down by institutions. Institutional totalitarianism can start small, with individuals being assigned digital scores if their behavior conforms to a certain target, say, customers buying certain products in a supermarket being awarded a score that offers them a discount. This is already a reality today and might represent a slippery, habituating slope into "Super-scores" (SVRV, 2018, p. 7). Indeed, institutional totalitarianism can also start bigger, with citizen scoring systems being located, perhaps, still at the lower end of the spectrum (e.g., Helbing, 2015; Helbing et al., 2017; Hoffrage & Marewski, 2020). At the upper end of the spectrum, there might be room for total surveillance and control over all areas of life, including of life itself.

How can heuristics aid individuals to manage aversive change?

Above, we speculated about the heuristics that individuals might resort to in aversive digital environments. Are there other heuristics that could aid individuals to manage aversive change? A first move to managing aversive changes might be to recognize that they may occur—and in dramatic ways. A follow-on step may then be to reflect upon how those changes might look, much like we did above. For instance, the authors of this chapter tend to believe that some of the most dramatic changes brought about by the digital revolution might concern people's values: Behavior that is deemed acceptable or even desirable today might, within a few years, be thought of as being unacceptable (Helbing, 2015). Why? Digital technology allows actors to reach out to many individuals at once, offering tremendous potential to influence what people believe they know (Kozyreva et al., in press). Whether such inter-personal influence is steered, top-down, by individuals trying to impose their views (we firmly believe that Joseph Goebbels, Hitler's propaganda minister, would have been excited if he had had the internet at his disposal and, perhaps more importantly, under his control) or whether it emerges bottom-up through chats and social networks does not matter. If that hypothesis is correct, then it becomes potentially risky for individuals to be unable to quickly adapt their values and behavior to the new trends.

> Heuristic principle: *Avoid getting caught in a spider-web of old-world values and behavior as your world changes.*

The German expression "*Die Fahne nach dem Wind hängen*" (loosely translated: hanging the flag as the wind blows) seems to reflect this heuristic principle, or simple rule. Following this principle could have helped Leaning-Bear to realize that stealing horses is not acceptable in a reservation environment.[11] Yet, such a strategy might not always be easy to enact in a digital world in which behavior is fully traceable, offering potential for destruction even 20 years later. This is akin to stating that it might be impossible to avoid failure. If failure is unavoidable, then another set of strategies might come into play: Strategies that allow dealing with failure once it has occurred. A classic representative of this is the simple heuristic of *"not putting all your eggs into one basket"* but rather to diversify.

> Heuristic principle: *Split resources up across different, non-connected targets.*

For instance, this diversification heuristic might suggest that income should be earned not just through one job (which might be lost) but through at least two, and that those jobs should ideally come with unrelated failure modes (e.g., losing one job will not entail losing another). A simple way to decrease connectivity might be to distribute jobs, and hence income, across different individuals, that is, to pool them. Partnerships where both individuals work in largely unconnected domains (e.g., different sectors) are a case in point. If one partner loses her job, the income from the other might still offer enough resources to make for a living (e.g., until a new job is found).

Factoring in redundancy while avoiding common failure modes are simple engineering principles for creating robust systems, heuristics for resilient design. Modern passenger aircrafts are examples of this, as most important components typically exist in at least two versions that are unconnected and made in different ways. This way, a failure in one component is less likely to imply a failure in its disconnected counterpart (see e.g., Kitano, 2004).

How can heuristics aid societies to manage aversive change?

Just as there are heuristic principles for building robust machines, could there also be principles for creating societies that are potentially more robust to digital change? We believe that this might be possible (see also e.g., SVRV, 2018). For instance, Helbing et al. (2017) stress how important the encouragement of diversity might be at the societal level, the co-existence of different goals and opinions aids the creation of robust, resilient societies (see also Helbing, 2015, 2019, on robustness and digitalization). Here are four additional heuristic principles that, when implemented together, might further help to create what we would take to be more resilient digitalized societies.

> Principle of disconnectedness: *Implement policies that disconnect people from each other* (see also Helbing, 2015).

There may be different forms—weak and strong—of disconnecting people. At the upper end, there would be legal prohibitions and digital censorship. The lower end comprises much less dramatic forms. For example, users of Skype cannot receive messages or calls from others unless they explicitly approve it, technically, by having accepted a contact request. Other communication services could follow this model, leaving it to the market, that is, ultimately, to users, whether they want to have such protection against an avalanche of incoming information. Such decisions require that users are aware of the problems, potentially inviting policy makers to design corresponding educational interventions to further boost John Q. Public's digital expertise (e.g., Kozyreva et al., in press). Equally important, not only receivers but also senders should be aware of problems generated by the high degree of connectedness in modern societies. For instance, the forwarding of emails, often even without the original sender's knowledge, can cause quite a lot of harm. We, personally, think legal prohibition of such practices is neither feasible nor desirable, but we posit that more mindfulness might be healthy (e.g., with regard to a higher threshold for forwarding emails and, eventually also, for sending them in the first place).

Principle of deceleration: *Implement policies that slow down the spread of information among people.*

Rather than speeding up the flux of information via ever faster transmission speed, it might be worth slowing down the spread of information (see Helbing, 2015); for example, by setting the speed of transmission of electronically-represented information to the equivalent speed of regular long-distance travel: *Let trivial news about shark attacks in Australia travel at the same speed as it would take an individual to, physically, deliver such news!* Building time lags into a system can make the system less reactive (and e.g., foster forgetting or emotional tranquilization). Of course, there is uncertainty over what counts as trivial. For instance, information that may be trivial at t1, might turn out to be nontrivial at t2, or what is trivial for one person might not be for someone else. Another way to reduce the spread and, indirectly, the speed of information transmission may be to tax (e.g., Helbing, 2015) or otherwise charge for electronic communication, placing a burden on either the receivers or the senders of information. The challenge lies in mitigating the side-effects of such an economic approach to steering behavior, such as wealthy individuals or companies being allowed to increasingly dominate the information flux, simply because they have more resources.

While the first and second principles tackle the interconnectedness and influenceability of digital environments discussed above, the third principle tackles the traceability of individuals.

Principle of information loss: *Implement policies that prevent the unlimited storage of behavioral data.*

There are different ways to implement information loss. One might be to prohibit storing behavioral data such as browsing on the internet or messages sent out publicly via social media. Another way might be to implement systematic data loss via decay over time: *Just as human memory forgets information, digital information should systematically fade away!* What information should, over time, be lost is an extremely difficult question, with the most radical approach prescribing the forgetting, over time, of all information, and others allowing for the selective forgetting of certain (e.g., private) contents (for a legal basis in the European Union, see Article 17 GDPR).

Principle of non-sharing: *Records of individuals' behavior when interacting with digital devices cannot be shared beyond the original purpose of the recording.*

Of course, companies, non-profit organizations, governments, and other institutions do have to share data in order to function well in an interconnected, borderless world, at least that is a frequently made argument. The tricky question is to determine what kind of data ought *not* to be shareable. Why is this an issue? In digital environments, increased complexity is caused by the massive trading of information about individuals: By letting algorithms pool customer ratings with their credit score, health-related data, and other records, available in big data lakes, even minute details about an individual can become knowable and exploitable for commercial and political ends. That, in turn, can contribute to increasing traceability and influenceability. To diminish the traceability and influenceability of individuals, policies that prevent the trading and pooling of data could be put into place, including laws that prohibit such actions (see also Helbing et al., 2017, on making punishable the unauthorized use of data).

Note that this principle of non-sharing would be undermined if individuals were given the possibility to voluntarily share their data. Such voluntary authorization can be instigated by offering opt-ins and opt-outs on websites (often not very user-friendly or transparent.)[12] An example of this is to alert internet users that continuing to surf on a website constitutes cookie consent; a parallel from outside the digital realm is to inform customers that walking into a shop implies agreement with being filmed. While there are different ways to induce individuals to authorize the recording and potential sharing of their behavior, from an ethical point of view it is highly problematic that, as of today, many individuals might not understand what can be done with their data (for Germany, see SVRV, 2018). And they might never have reflected upon the possibility that their world might change. The possibility that non-sharing could be something highly desirable for them might simply not be on many people's radars and so they do not care. Moreover, understanding how data from multiple sources can be used to classify individuals, for instance, in their role as patients, customers, or citizens, into different categories requires knowledge of statistics. Corresponding statistical knowledge might simply be insufficient in the general population or in certain collectives. Those, in turn, who are aware of the risks might be averse to buying into yet other risks associated with non-sharing: Even if social exclusion or limited access to information (triggered by, for instance, shunning digital networks, messaging tools and internet search engines) do *not* spell doom for individuals who want to avoid one's behavioral data being shared, life will certainly not get easier for them if they try to prevent this data-sharing, if only because personalized digital services (e.g., web search, shopping) permit people to save time and effort. Indeed, the recording and subsequent selling of digital behavior have become a business in the digital world. Clearly, policy makers might find it hard to simply prohibit the pooling, selling, and other forms of sharing of behavioral data given that there is a market with numerous individuals consenting to such activities.

★ ★ ★

Changing tack. Above, we pointed to difficult questions arising when trying to implement each of the listed principles, such as the tricky question how to decide what information ought to be classified as trivial (or harmful), warranting its spread to be slowed down, what information to forget, or what information to share. Those questions boil down, in one way or the other, to classification problems. In any classification problem, two types of mistakes can occur: false positives (e.g., sharing information that should better not be shared) and false negatives (e.g., not sharing information that should be shared). Could such classification tasks be tackled with heuristics? An obvious candidate model for classification tasks, one might think, are *fast-and-frugal trees* (e.g., Woike, Hoffrage, & Martignon, 2017).

Yet, contrary to other (smaller-world) classification tasks where the criterion is certain and reveals itself (e.g., classifying a mushroom as poisonous or not, and then eating the mushroom), in these kind of large-world classification tasks, the criterion is fundamentally uncertain, and perhaps even unknowable. Counterfactuals, too, may be impossible to observe (e.g., what would have happened had I not sent this email to my boss or written that tweet about my neighbor?), making learning more difficult than in tasks where the counterfactual is accessible to the decider (e.g., inferring, in a TV show, which of two cities has more inhabitants, while being told after each decision what the correct answer would have been). Moreover, in those larger worlds, the criterion might be multi-dimensional and criterion values might vary over time. Hence, fast-and-frugal classification heuristics might actually not represent adequate tools to tackle those types of tasks. Instead, we believe that simple rules that foster a maximum of diversity of classification outcomes might be a better bet: If we do not know what classifications are desirable, the best option might be not to "put all your eggs into the same basket." Diversity can, too, foster robustness, to the extent, for instance, that issues arising from different classification outcomes are unconnected (see also Helbing et al., 2017).

What could these diversity-maintaining principles be? And can we entrust humans to enact them? A common belief is that we humans may suffer from systematic biases, causing not only reasoning fallacies, but also other undesirable behavioral outcomes, including discriminative behavior (e.g., against certain collectives) and/or self-serving actions. Classification algorithms are, nowadays, often seen as better alternatives to those 'biased,' 'egoistic' humans (Hoffrage & Marewski, 2015). Machines are seemingly stripped of all undesirable subjectivity; they are objective in that they can make decisions independently from humans who, in one way or the other, have to be mere objects of the decisions (e.g., what messages, written by a human, are to be deleted.)[13]

Yet, there is no bias-free classifier, whether human or algorithm-based. Any policy, explicitly or implicitly, enacts values, reflected, for instance, in how it trades off one mistake (false positives) against the other (false negatives). Moreover, human classifiers differ, not only between individuals (e.g., in values) but also over time (i.e., individuals change their views, they make mistakes in enacting their own worldviews, they forget). That is, humans do not only vary in terms of their biases, human behavior can also be conceived of as exhibiting a noise component. As a consequence, human classifiers, with all their idiosyncrasies and resulting variation in behavior, could, in principle, be their own solution to the problem they created, with the heuristic principle being, "*Put humans in full power*," that is, let humans make their own decisions about, for instance, what information to share massively, to quickly pass on, or to save on the public cloud! We write "could." Democracies can maintain diversity, but totalitarianism can synchronize human behavior. *Gleichschaltung* (i.e., making equal or uniform) is a word capturing how the Nazis reduced variation, trying to bring all elements of society in line with their ideology: a single horrific bias. The disturbing question is: Can a few digital technologies (e.g., email, social media, search engines) dramatically reduce the variation in behavior across human classifiers, a *digital Gleichschaltung*, not necessarily orchestrated top-down by authorities, but emerging bottom-up, as a vast assimilation or acculturation process, caused by the massive pooling of information?[14]

If so, a first step for policy makers may be to regulate the magnitude of those technologies' outreach. Anti-trust laws and other rules that might break up the market share of (dominating) companies might go in that direction, but such approaches fall short of solving the problem, because different companies, as well as different digital technologies that are nonetheless compatible with each other, can all support the massive spread of the same information and thereby continue reducing diversity. In short, the paradox is: Regulators should implement policies that reduce the speed, spread, and saving of information, and the resulting classification problem (e.g., what information to slow down, not share, or forget) might be best tackled by heuristic principles that foster diversity—diversity which may be destroyed by the forces unleashed (e.g., speed, spread of information) that make tackling the classification problem necessary in the first place. But that is not the end of it: a trade-off must be managed between fostering diversity and limiting it enough, such that, to put it bluntly, people can still talk to each other.

How to foster diversity? Help people construct a toolbox of heuristics for critical judgment, would be our recommendation (see Gigerenzer, 2014, who puts forward a toolbox of simple heuristics for health care, business, and other domains). This toolbox would include guiding principles such as push oneself to understand a subject matter at hand (e.g., a classification problem), even if one is not an expert in the topic (e.g., if one has no expertise in statistics) or to play devil's advocate on dominant views. Box 18.2 lists examples of heuristics for managing another important challenge, brought about by digitalization: scoring.

Box 18.2 Teaching scoring with heuristics

One of us teaches executives and other individuals, potentially affected by and/or interested in leading digitalization in companies, non-profit organizations, and other institutions. One basis of that teaching is the book, *Weapons of Math Destruction*, by O'Neil (2016), which invites us to extract, from context-rich stories, more general insights that can, in our view, be cast as heuristic principles. A few of these heuristic principles are, alongside related points (see also e.g., Helbing, 2015), listed below; they are meant to help people to reflect on scoring (e.g., of customers or citizens), such as when algorithms are used by companies (e.g., banks) or public institutions (e.g., administrations) to make decisions (e.g., which customers to offer credit to; which citizen is allowed to buy a high-speed train ticket):

1. *Convert probabilities into natural frequencies* when trying to comprehend classification problems (e.g., Gigerenzer, Gaissmaier, Kurz-Milcke, Schwartz, & Woloshin, 2007; Hoffrage, Lindsey, Hertwig, & Gigerenzer, 2000). To understand what natural frequencies are, consider the following fictional example. Imagine an algorithm is used to grade convicts; if the score is positive, the person is not let out of prison. The overall recidivism rate in that population is 5 percent, the true positive and false positive rates are 80 percent and 30 percent, respectively. What is the probability of recidivism if the score happens to turn out positive for a given criminal? Many people might find answering that question difficult and, as a result, they may blindly trust the positive score. Now, take 1,000 criminals. Of those 1,000, 50 (5 percent) will commit another crime and of these, 40 (80 percent) will score positive. Of the 950 who do not commit another crime, 285 (30 percent) get a false positive score. Since the total number of positive scores is 40 + 285 = 325, the probability of recidivism if the score is positive is only 40/325 ≈ 12 percent!

2. *Recognize that no decision—be it made by a human or a scoring algorithm—is free of values* (e.g., how to trade off false positives and false negatives, such as when building scoring algorithms like the one described in point 1's fictional example). As O'Neil (2016, p. 21) herself puts it, "models, despite their reputation for impartiality, reflect goals and ideology".

3. *Recognize that even scoring algorithms you try to program to act in line with your values* (e.g., to not discriminate on the basis of race or gender) *might end up deciding against your values*. For instance, few people would want credit-worthiness scores to include race as a variable; however, let us assume that ZIP code is predictive of income and you decide to include that variable in the score. Voilà! To the extent that people of the same race are poor and live close to each other (e.g., in ghettos), the score may end up being racist. Another way to frame this heuristic principle is that one needs to realize that there is uncertainty with respect to hidden confounds.

4. *Realize that scoring systems can create vicious circles* (e.g., criminals get poorer and even more criminal). This can happen, especially if the systems upscale (see point 8 below). Such vicious cycles can be another constitutive element of uncertainty; they can create new unknown confounds, and, without you realizing it, can lead to decisions that do not align with your values.

5. *Transparency is not the solution; at worst it helps only a bit.* Even very simple, transparent scores (e.g., produced by equal-weighting heuristics, laid open to the general public) can generate dynamic, hard-to-foresee, and non-transparent outcomes; for instance, by creating the afore-mentioned vicious circles on a societal level.

6. *Make sure that you constantly monitor the performance of your scoring algorithms.* Because environments can quickly and unexpectedly change, the performance (e.g., accuracy) of scoring algorithms can also change.

7. *Do not think of scoring in the singular. Never implement just one scoring algorithm.* Instead, approach scoring experimentally and implement several diverse algorithms. For instance, randomly assign different customers to different scoring algorithms and monitor and compare performance, such as the accuracy of the scores, across treatment groups. In so doing, if possible (e.g., ethically acceptable) also try to implement counterintuitive (out-of-the-box) algorithms (e.g., if need be, as merely hypothetical secondary scoring rules kept in the background, without consequences for people). Diversity can provide a buffer to sudden changes in environments; and diversity also aids learning about those changes (e.g., if counter-intuitive algorithms suddenly start to work well). The insight to test counter-intuitive algorithms in model comparisons (and, ideally, out-of-sample or population) reflects the development of the fast-and-frugal heuristics framework: many would not believe that less information and computation can be more (see e.g., Hertwig & Todd, 2003).

8. *Think about scale.* For example, an algorithm used to score 1,000,000 individuals which discriminates against a certain group with just a very low probability could turn out to be more devastating than another algorithm which discriminates with a high probability, but which is applied to only 1,000 individuals.

9. *Understand that you may have to make difficult decisions.* For instance, if one of your algorithms has scaled up and obtained a huge market share, then that's good for business (short term) but can be bad for society (long term). If you voluntarily give up on market share (short term), the competition may step in (and, in the worst case scenario, you may have to sacrifice your business or job).

In line with the environmental focus of the fast-and-frugal heuristics research program, perhaps law makers should also reflect in how far legal frameworks warrant adaptation, moving away from allocating agency and responsibility to individuals and more toward making the environment surrounding individuals the central unit of analysis (for other legal issues, see Helbing et al., 2017). In other words: When, why and to what extent is the individual to be held accountable (corresponding, roughly, to an inside-explanation for behavior and performance) as opposed to her/his digital environment (corresponding to an ecological explanation)?

What else could one do to aid societies to manage aversive digital change? Perhaps the best recommendation is to try to slow that change down: People need time to understand new environments in order to be able to shape them. The lemma of a "digital Enlightenment" (Helbing, 2019) might be: Let people learn about the changes (heuristic principle: *Boost John Q. Public's digital knowledge!*), and create opportunities for feedback that are forgiving of mistakes: digital error-cultures in times of uncertainty. That recommendation is in line with the notion of the adaptive toolbox of the fast-and-frugal heuristics research program. Decision makers need to be aware of the tools (i.e., decision strategies) in their repertoire; they need to be ready and able to create new ones and, equally importantly, they need to acquire expertise when it comes to selecting from among the different tools available to them. Strategy selection, calls for, at the end of the day, not a (seemingly unbiased) algorithm, but good human judgment (Hoffrage & Marewski, 2015). Of course, there may be other principles, too—principles referring to aspects of digitalized environments we did not explicitly discuss above (for more aspects, concerns and recommendations, see e.g., Gigerenzer, 2014; Helbing, 2015, 2019; Helbing et al., 2017; Kozyreva et al., in press).

Digitalization: from evolution to the children of evolution

In this chapter, we have looked at environments mainly from a life-history perspective. Another perspective might be an evolutionary one. The resilience of our make-up allowed *homo sapiens* to survive and spread over millennia. Yet, the robustness of a system is always relative to the environment in which it acts; after all, the environment forms part of the system. Without wanting to evoke catastrophic scenarios borrowed from apocalyptic science-fiction, we feel that it is paramount to consider the degree to which digital technology is able to transform human environments. Is there a possibility that, after a rapid transformation process, environments will emerge that are very different from those that our cognitive architecture evolved to be adapted to over the course of evolutionary history? Does it make sense to speculate about the extent to which design features that can make information processing systems robust might be present in the cognitive make-up of the mind *and* in the structure of pre-digital environments, but *not* in the texture of digitalized worlds?

Arguably, features of human environments that played a role in human cognitive evolution, notably, our information-processing mechanisms, were constituted by humans themselves: It is the social world with its affordances for cooperation and mating that may have shaped not only imitation and other heuristics for a social world, but more generally the mechanisms that determine how we perceive, think, feel, and act, including the ways how we *can*, potentially, perceive, think, feel, and act. According to this view, cognition is shaped and constrained by our phylogenetic history. And it is this heritage from the *environment of evolutionary adaptedness* (e.g., Tooby & Cosmides, 1992) that now stands to meet our new environments. As discussed above, digital environments may have a number of characteristics that distinguish them from pre-digital environments. All of them concern the social world:

- In digital environments, social interactions over long distances (across the globe) are possible, and they are instantaneous, that is, without a time delay. Long-distance interactions, of course, have always been possible in non-digital environments, but never throughout human evolutionary history has it been as easy, and never has it been as instantaneous.
- Humans can interact with everyone who is connected to the digital network, potentially resulting in a very large number of interaction partners. Compared to non-digital worlds, the potential number of partners has thus tremendously increased.
- In a digital world, humans do not interact with each other face-to-face, but by means of technical mediators such as social media, instant messaging services, and email. Such mediated interactions were also possible in the pre-digital world (e.g., by means of letters or messengers transmitting oral messages), but the ease of access to such indirect forms of interaction, and hence their frequency have increased in digital worlds. Equally importantly, since social information is now maintained as digital records, it is no longer forgotten.
- In contrast to the pre-digital world, in digital environments, information can be pre-processed, modified, and even fully created by non-human agents, that is, by computer programs, without either human or artificial recipients (e.g., other computer programs) of the information necessarily being aware of these manipulations. This seems to be new in human evolutionary history.

Easier, faster, longer-distance, and more frequent machine-mediated interactions might not at all represent significant changes in evolutionary terms. They might not pose, per se, any threats to the robustness of human-information processing mechanisms in social worlds. But do they create indirect potential for harm, for example, by fueling interpersonal conflict and aggression? In a digital world, there can be more connections between different elements (humans) in a social system (a group). As a consequence of this, false information (e.g., rumors about hostile agents, past or intended future aggressions) and other types of disturbance (e.g., fake news) might have a greater potential to spread (Kozyreva et al., in press). Do these disturbances also have more potential to endure, just as information is not simply sorted out by digitalized social systems over time through decay or other forms of information loss (see Helbing, 2015)? Is cooperation aided by forgiving, and is forgiving aided by forgetting, such as the forgetting of past aggressions (e.g., Stevens, Marewski, Schooler, & Gilby, 2016)? How would challenges likely to have been important to human cognitive evolution (e.g., cooperating, mating) in the past be transformed if, in the future, human information-processing systems only received information via digital technology? What are the implications for society and human interaction if all information transmitted becomes fully detached from the context in which the information was produced, including the smiles, smells, and sounds emitted by the sender (another human being) and the texture of the environment in which that sender is located (a group of anxious, angry, or happy humans)?

Rather than trying to reach back into our evolutionary history, one might adopt a more modest historical perspective; for example, by asking how different technological artifacts shaped behavior and cognition in different epochs. For instance, one might believe that digital communication comes with less trust than face-to-face communication; yet is there evidence that interpersonal trust decreased in collectives when individuals started to communicate by means of paper (e.g., writing letters)? What affordances does paper offer when it comes to deciding what and how to communicate? What affordances are special to digital media? Both allow for long-distance communication; yet only the latter allows for delivery within seconds. Paper might retain the exciting smell of the beloved one (even if it is only because perfume can be sprayed on paper); an email, in turn, affords attaching a picture and a video-conference even affords watching that lover in real time, making things like cybersex possible. Touching (or even actual sexual reproduction) is afforded by neither artifact.

To turn to another technological artifact, when the TV was invented and became available in households, these new machines afforded making many different decisions, including the decision to access information or to entertain one's children. Modern-day smartphones seem to come with these affordances, too; albeit watching a movie in front of a TV is possible for a group of up to a dozen people, watching a movie on a smartphone gets more difficult if there are more than three or four persons crowded in front of the small display. Moreover, carrying a TV around (a heavy item at the time and dependent on a mains electric power supply) was impossible, hence TVs did not pose affordances for entertaining, say, small children while waiting in line in the supermarket or in the waiting room of a doctor's practice. In contrast, smartphones afford children entertainment in any location and at any time. Moreover, TVs afforded receiving pre-selected information (e.g., a movie listed in a TV program in the analogue age) at certain points in time; smartphones, in turn, allow receiving self-selected information (e.g., any movie) at any point in time, and they also afford the sending of information. If these 'new' affordances are conceived of as decisional options that are systematically acted upon, what, then, might be the possible longer-term consequences? Could it be, for instance, that children are more likely to get used to being entertained, less used to active play, more easily bored (e.g., when there is nothing to play with), or more likely to participate in familial conflict (e.g., when boredom and impatience result in behavior that mummy and daddy are not willing to tolerate)? Will those children's upbringing and education prepare the ground for yet more environmental changes, namely when those children, as adults, shape environments themselves?

Another gift of digitalization that is entering households these days is artificial intelligence and the internet of things. Like TV and smartphones, both are entirely new from an evolutionary point of view. In contrast to adults, children do not know that these are very recent gadgets, after all, for them, everything is, at one time, new anyway. But still: What happens psychologically if a child is exposed to an electronic assistant at home, a machine one can talk to and that responds? Imagine you give a child a toy, say, a car, a doll or a teddy, that has a microphone, a motion sensor, and other built-in devices. Nowadays such toys can transmit information, ranging from the toy's position to the child's utterances (down on earth), (up) to a central server on the cloud. That information, in turn, allows inferences to be made, such as when the child sleeps or what the child likes. How do children know that a doll is more than just a doll? How should parents teach them what they can tell their doll and what not (e.g., Mum and Dad fight? We go on vacation and the house will be empty? My uncle has debts? I will be alone at the bus station tomorrow after school?). In the analogue age, children could be taught principles such as *"Do not trust strangers! Do not talk to others about X, Y, and Z (e.g., your family) at school!"* But the doll is not a stranger—it is not even an "other." Likewise, what principles can we teach children for interacting with an electronic home assistant, a device that transmits information to the cloud and that is just a box; that is, something that does not even have the shape of a being (see Box 18.3)? Manches (2019) and Manches, Duncan, Plowman, and Sabeti (2015) raise and discuss such and related issues. In particular, Manches et al. (2015) ask three questions:

> *How do IoT [Internet of Things] devices influence children's interpretation of, and interaction with, everyday things? … How is the data that is captured by IoT devices being used? … How cognisant are children and their carers of IoT devices?*
>
> p. 77, emphasis original

As they point out,

> The nature of IoT is that everyday things become interfaces for digital technology. As technology becomes more seamless, children may become less aware of how their actions are being captured and used. Without explanation, children may be unaware that hugging a teddy is providing a range of adults with intimate knowledge of their biometric data. Clearly, parents need to be informed if they are to give consent on behalf of their children, but the public's awareness of the implications of the IoT for data protection is currently quite low.
>
> *Manches et al., 2015, p. 77*

Box 18.3 Teaching children with narratives

During a presentation at the workshop of the Herbert Simon Society in November 2019, Manches pointed to the misfit of the rule *"Don't talk to strangers!"* to a world of IoT devices, including teddies with microphones. This rule is insufficient to protect children against the dangers that come with the digitalization. What rules can we teach them that are adapted to these new technologies with their new affordances for others (e.g., who have access to the cloud)? Rules for behavior are taught, across cultures, with narratives including fairy tales and holy books. Fairy tales and the bible contain mysteries and one should be careful not to destroy these with an intellectual mindset. However, one can ask what they reveal about human nature and how such an enriched understanding allows one to better understand elements of the *Zeitgeist* and technology coming with digitalization. Can the witch in *Hänsel und Gretel*, in her perfidy, reveal more about an Internet-of-Things-teddy than we think? Can we use the mirror in *Schneewittchen* to talk to our children about omniscience, self-reflection, and vanity by relating it to modern affordances such as spying, stalking, 'liking' or 'dis-liking' and cyberbullying? Who is the most beautiful, both here and at the other side of the world? What is the correspondence between a mirror, reflecting an image of oneself, and the echo in digital echo-chambers? "Smartphone, Smartphone in der Hand, wer hat die meisten 'Likes' im Land?" ["Smartphone, smartphone in my hand, who has the most 'likes' across the land?"] (Martignon & Hoffrage, 2019, p. 185).

These issues become even more disturbing when one takes into account that such devices do not need to be 'just' dolls or teddys collecting data on a toddler's movements or a young child's 'secrets'; the devices could also be digital learning games gathering inferred IQ. There could be computer games that gauge a teenager's sleeping habits or behavior in brutal virtual fights. Imagine that the collected data were indicative of (e.g., later) academic aptitude, job perform-ance, or health and consider that such data might stay on the cloud for decades, and be shared with others (e.g., insurance companies, job application portals) for an unlimited time.[15]

We want to stress that while such issues are certainly important to consider, they may actually be miniscule compared to those related to building proper representations of the physical and social world. This is already hard enough (Hirschfield & Gelman, 1994) and it is an open question how children can and will acquire concepts, such as person, agency, intelligence, intention, or responsibility if they grow up in an environment in which the winds of change have eradicated the border between man and machine. Applying a precautionary principle suggests that we should withhold digital technology from younger children for as long as possible, and this is, in fact, what many managers working for digital poster child companies in Silicon Valley do (Dwyer, 2011), but this requires some understanding, awareness, discipline, and courage (for a more in-depth discussion of the risks of digitalization for children and adolescents, see Martignon & Hoffrage, 2019). On the other hand, learning about the dangers stemming from digital devices may require exposure, or even some direct experience of them, and, if so, through vicarious learning or story-telling. Perhaps we could create tales of almighty, all-knowing beings, who can, through a spider web composed of other people, know everything about us and our lives. Will angry, almighty gods and mythological figures (e.g., the Hydra) come back into our lives, albeit in new guises? Can we even learn from millennia-old stories, religious beliefs, and other forms of wisdom, how to teach our children how to interact with these new-old 'beings'? Will there be new-old heuristics, such as "*You cannot hide anything from the gods!*" or "*Don't make the gods angry!*" Perhaps the cloud is a strikingly accurate name for gods, who, in a material sense, are new and a human creation. We find it extremely thought-provoking that Dicke and Helbing (2017) entitled their science-fiction novel, which is centered around the interaction between the protagonist Alex and a world-encompassing artificial intelligence that uses Alex's smart-home assistant as an interface, *iGod*. And interestingly enough, perhaps also some of those old stories foreshadow the cataclysmic drama of the current attempt to build a digital version of a new God. After all, the Tower of Babel, which was meant to be tall enough to reach heaven, was stopped thanks to diversity (through language), which halted the flux of information among its builders. It remains to be seen what will happen to the modern towers (shall we say, server farms accessed by artificial intelligence?).

We want to remind readers that the "Wind of Change"—a song by the Scorpions—became a kind of hymn of the fall of the Berlin Wall. This fall closed a chapter in history (Fukuyama, 2006, even declared this event marked the "end of history"), and opened a new one. What will fall and what will rise through the winds of digitalization? These and many other issues might be worth reflecting upon, not only for scientific reasons, but also when it comes to actively shaping the brave new digital world—and thereby potentially paving the way for what might follow.

Conclusion: compassion in the winds of change

Leaning-Bear and Jenny experienced drastic aversive changes in their environments; changes that they did not foresee, but had to cope with by relying on the behavioral and cognitive mechanisms available to them. They lived through them, and they suffered through them. Their life histories, despite being fictitious, can help us to think about such changes. We close this chapter with the words of a non-fictional character, a person who experienced dramatic change in his environment for real. Changes that, with Gleichschaltung and an all-dominant ideology, brought horror and devastation to large collectives. A person who decided to act against those changes, and who, in stepping out of the line dictated by that ideology, lost his life. Dietrich Bonhoeffer was executed for acting against the Nazi regime just a few days before the regime collapsed in 1945. The following lines by Bonhoeffer could be taken as a general statement on drastic aversive change:

> One has to expect that most humans will only become savvy when they themselves experience suffering. This way one can explain, *firstly*, most human's stunning inability to execute any kind of preventive action – one simply tends to believe to still be able to avoid the danger, until it is finally too late; [and this way one can explain] *secondly* the insensibility with respect to others' suffering; compassion emerges proportional to the growing fear of the threatening proximity of doom … Deedless waiting and obtuse standing on the sidelines are not Christian postures. It is not, at first, his proper sufferings, but the sufferings of his brothers, for whose sake Christ suffered, which calls the Christian to action and to co-suffering.
>
> *Bonhoeffer, 1998 [1942], pp. 33–34, translated from German, additions in brackets*

As Bonhoeffer points out, the route to wisdom may be paved by first-hand experiences. Indeed, as we have discussed in this chapter, we humans are not "omniscient," we cannot boast of computational "omnipotence" (see e.g., Gigerenzer, 2008a, p. 5 and p. 4, respectively), rather, our rationality is bounded, as is our ability to foresee the digital future. Without adequate foresight, preventive action might seem pointless. Yet, as Bonhoeffer further remarks, we are capable of something else: Compassion, as well as action and co-suffering. Compassion can be produced by environmental cues signaling growing threats to oneself. But action and co-suffering can come without threats from values. It is beholden on us to reflect whether we want to follow the heuristic "*Act once you feel compassionate!*" or its counterpart, namely, "*Act prior to feeling compassionate!*" as we encounter the winds of change.

Epilogue

In his memoirs, likely written in 1939, Bruno Stange, the great-grandfather of one of the authors, describes the following encounter with Hitler, which presumably took place in 1933: "The 'Führer' wanted to speak to the workforce in the Dynamowerk of the Siemenswerke.

What enthusiasm ... Special admission tickets were issued, multiple checks were carried out, then we were allowed to wait for three hours until the splendid Führer appeared in the presence of his paladins. For a short time, I had the opportunity to look into Hitler's eyes. A horror overcame me and back at home I said to ... my dear wife: 'I have looked into the eyes of a madman'." Today, with a benefit of hindsight and greater knowledge, we know what happened after this "madman" came to power in 1933. We wonder what our great-grandchildren will say when they read this essay after the winds of digital change have had another few decades to marry humans with machines.

Acknowledgments

We would like to thank Riccardo Viale, Benjamin Müller, and the GABE reading group at the Faculty of Business and Economics at the University of Lausanne for many helpful comments on earlier versions of this chapter. We also thank those attendees of the 2019 Workshop of the Herbert Simon Society ("The digital world, cognition and behavior") in Turin who shared their thoughts with us on digitalization. We especially owe Dirk Helbing a large debt: His warnings and notably his books *Thinking ahead: Essays on big data, digital revolution, and participatory market society* (Helbing, 2015) and *Towards digital enlightenment: Essays on the dark and light sides of the digital revolution* (Helbing, 2019) have been a major source of inspiration for us. We are also indebted to Gerd Gigerenzer, founder of the fast-and-frugal heuristics approach, and to several members of the former ABC Research Group with whom we have discussed the potential negative aspects of digitalization over the course of two working retreats. Finally, we would like to thank Barnaby Dicker and Susan Dunsmore for their careful copy-editing and Caroline Plumez and Jérémy Orsat for additional checks.

Notes

1 The character of Leaning-Bear is fully fictional; yet the story depicted here may have happened in one or the other form to individuals from Native American nations. They all experienced the dramatic breakdown of their world (see e.g., Brown, 1974 for an encompassing recent account of the history of the Lakota, see Hämäläinen, 2019; for first-hand accounts of Lakota ways of life, see Waggoner, 2013). In general, there have been numerous instances of dramatic changes during history that resulted from violence, war, or some sort of clash of civilizations. When discussing a previous version of this chapter with colleagues, some pointed to the possibility that our example of the Sioux might elicit negative emotions, in particular, among the descendants of Native Americans. However, when contemplating using another example, we realized that this concern is quite general and could be made, presumably, for all other historical examples of sudden, dramatically negative, and thorough changes in an individual's environment. These changes for the worse set the stage for the topic of this chapter. Our hope is that by looking at a grim picture of the past, we might aid reflection on new types of potentially grim future changes.

2 After having finished this chapter, we learned about Luther Standing Bear (Ota Kte, Plenty Kill), a Sioux born in the 1860s. His fascinating autobiography (Standing Bear, 2006 [1928]) tells the story of the life of a man who grew up when the world of the Sioux was changing dramatically—a man who had experienced traditional ways of life on the Great Plains, who then attended Carlisle Indian Industrial School in Pennsylvania, who later in his life traveled with Buffalo Bill to Europe where he "had the honor being introduced to King Edward the Seventh, the monarch of Great Britain" (Standing Bear, 2006 [1928], p. 256), who was injured in a train accident in 1903, and who came to write his own books. He died in 1939. The following lines, taken from his autobiography, speak for themselves about the change in his world:

> Our scouts, who had gone out to locate the buffalo, came back and reported that the plains were covered with dead bison. These had been shot by the white people. The Indians never were such wasteful, wanton killers of this noble game animal. We kept moving, fully expecting soon to run across plenty of live buffalo; but we were disappointed. I saw the bodies of hundreds of dead

buffalo lying about, just wasting, and the odor was terrible ... Now we began to see white people living in dugouts, just like wild bears, but without the long snout. These people were dirty. They had hair all over their faces, heads, arms, and hands. This was the first time many of us had ever seen white people, and they were very repulsive to us. None of us had ever seen a gorilla, else we might have thought that Darwin was right concerning these people.

Standing Bear, 2006 [1928], p. 67

3 Take the (real) story of Plenty Horses, a Lakota born in 1869, who was brought from the West to a boarding school (Carlisle Indian Industrial School) in the East (Pennsylvania), where he stayed from 1883–1888. When he went back to his tribe, a few days after the Wounded Knee Massacre (which happened on December 29, 1890), he killed an army Lieutenant by firing a bullet through the back of his head, a man with whom he had just previously "chatted" (Gitlin, 2011, p. 96). Plenty Horses was put on trial. He explained:

Five years I attended Carlisle and was educated in the ways of the white man. When I returned to my people, I was an outcast among them. I was no longer an Indian. I was not a white man. I was lonely. I shot the lieutenant so I might make a place for myself among my people. I am now one of them. I shall be hung, and the Indians will bury me as a warrior.

cited in Fear-Segal & Rose, 2016, p. 3

4 The Sioux documented events and experiences in pictorial form. These chronicles, painted on hides, are referred to as winter counts; they represent a valuable source for contemporary historians. As Hämäläinen (2019) points out, "[t]here is a tangible change in winter counts during and after the painful years between 1877 and 1890. Several counts stopped in the late 1870s, ending with Crazy Horse's death, with the U.S. Army confiscating horses, or with children sent to boarding schools. 'Big Foot killed,' reads one of the few winter counts that refers to the Wounded Knee Massacre, the silence capturing the enormity of the shock and trauma." (p. 380)

5 Also Plenty Horses' life took a surprising turn. At the end of his trial, he was not found guilty of murder and not hanged, but acquitted and released. The argument was that a state of war had existed; without a state of war also the soldiers who participated in the Wounded Knee massacre a few days beforehand could have been accused of murder, too. Assuming a state of war helped to exonerate them (Fear-Segal & Rose, 2016). Plenty Horses died in 1933, like our fictional character Leaning-Bear.

6 To the extent to which there are repeated learning opportunities (e.g., repeated model calibration and testing) *and* the compositions of the learning samples and the test samples only differ at random across repetitions *and* that average (rather than one-shot performance) matters to an organism, this kind of uncertainty might even invite attempts to 'optimize', that is, to identify the strategy in the repertoire that performs, on average, best across many test samples. While past research on fast-and-frugal heuristics has stressed assessing absolute accuracy when making inferences out-of-sample, one might, alternatively, want to identify the strategy that suffers the least when generalizing from the calibration to the test samples. Note that these two different goal functions may lead to the selection of different strategies, which, in turn, offers an interesting link to the psychology of happiness: A person's happiness, after a loss, might not depend only on the final state after the loss (e.g., health, prestige, fortune), but on comparisons with reference points in the past, that is, the magnitude of the loss. Do people make comparative evaluations when selecting their decision making strategies in environments hit by winds of change?

7 Interestingly, that lemma seems to have propelled Luther Standing Bear, as a young boy, directly into the 'white' man's world, eventually boosting his ability to navigate that new environment in later phases of his life. In his autobiography (Standing Bear, 2006 [1928]), he discusses his motivations to go East (to Pennsylvania to Carlisle Indian Industrial School) in 1879: "I was thinking of my father, and how he had many times said to me, 'Son, be brave! Die on the battle-field if necessary away from home. It is better to die young than to get old and sick and then die.' When I thought of my father, and how he had smoked the pipe of peace, and was not fighting any more, it occurred to me that this chance to go East would prove that I was brave if I were to accept it." (p. 124) He continues by pointing out: "I had come to this school merely to show my people that I was brave enough to leave the reservation and go East, not knowing what it meant and not caring." (p. 135) "It did not occur to me at that time that I was going away to learn the ways of the white man." (p. 128)

8 While our fictitious Jenny only appears in one section of this chapter, Dicke and Helbing's (2017) science fiction novel *iGod* is entirely centered around their protagonist Alex. The life of Alex is a projection of the authors' speculations, or, shall we say, informed guesses, given that both authors are scientists, and the

reader, wondering whether he has a utopia or a dystopia in his hands, is invited to imagine how a world shaped by digitalization, big data, artificial intelligence, and social scoring might soon look.

9 Available at: https://policies.google.com/privacy?hl=en#infocollect (accessed January 21, 2020).

10 Available at: https://ec.europa.eu/info/policies/justice-and-fundamental-rights/criminal-justice/e-evidence-cross-border-access-electronic-evidence_en (accessed January 21, 2020).

11 Tragically, 'horse-stealing' seemed actually acceptable to American policy-makers: In an attempt to dismount the Sioux (Lakota), their horses were taken away in the aftermath of the battle of the Little Big Horn (Waggoner, 2013).

12 Whoever has read, in detail, the long privacy statements that come with digital services knows what we are talking about: Page-long, seemingly transparent disclosure statements alerting users that their data can be pooled, sold, or otherwise shared with other parties, including other companies or government agencies.

13 Traces of this view can be found in the decision sciences, bibliometrics, and statistics, with null-hypothesis significance testing or metric-based science evaluations representing examples of seemingly automatic, objectifying decision procedures (see Marewski & Bornmann, 2020; Gigerenzer, 2018).

14 Gleichschaltung brought about by digital technologies represents just one way of reducing diversity. Another way to reduce diversity is to set *nudges* (Thaler & Sunstein, 2009) that lead a large number of people to behave in the same way, namely, in line with the behavioral options championed by the policy maker. In that sense, nudges can be thought of as potentially inducing "behavioral biases" (see also Kozyreva et al., in press, and Helbing et al., 2017, on "big nudging").

15 If such devices collected data that, furthermore, would aid in making or justifying judgments about a child's descendants, then issues related to surveillance, privacy, security, and (e.g., heath-related) discrimination would become inter-generational. Note that such inter-generational judgments would not need to be justifiable, scientifically. What would matter would be that, for instance, people in power would be able to believe or pretend that attributes (e.g., inferred IQ or psychopathic personality traits) were informative across generations. Numeric scores may be particularly susceptible to such exploitation as they may be able to lend seeming objectivity to dubious claims and/or policies, as the history of IQ and other indicators, used to score individuals, illustrates (see e.g., Gigerenzer, Swijtink, Porter, Daston, Beatty, & Krüger, 1989; Gould, 1981; Severson, 2011; Young, 1922).

References

Anderson, J. R. (1991). Is human cognition adaptive? *Behavioral and Brain Sciences*, 14, 471–517.

Anderson, J. R., Bothell, D., Byrne, M. D., Douglass, S., Lebiere, C., & Qin, Y. (2004). An integrated theory of the mind. *Psychological Review*, 111, 1036–1060.

Anderson, J. R., & Schooler, L. J. (1991). Reflections of the environment in memory. *Psychological Science*, 2, 396–408.

Artinger, F. M., Artinger, S., & Gigerenzer, G. (2019). C. Y. A.: frequency and causes of defensive decisions in public administration. *Business Research*, 12, 9–25.

Becker, G. S. (1976). *The economic approach to human behavior*. Chicago: The University of Chicago Press.

Binmore, K. (2007). Rational decisions in large worlds. *Annales d'Économie et de Statistique*, 86, 25–41.

Bonhoeffer, D. (1998 [1942]). Rechenschaft an der Wende zum Jahr 1943 [Accountability at the turn towards the year 1943]. In C. Gremmels, E. Bethge, & R. Bethge (Eds.), *Bonhoeffer: Widerstand und Ergebung. Briefe und Aufzeichnungen aus der Haft* [Bonhoeffer: Resistance and surrender. Letters and records from the time of arrest] (pp. 19–39). Gütersloh, Germany: Kaiser/Gütersloher Verlagshaus.

Brighton, H. (2006). Robust inference with simple cognitive models. In C. Lebiere & R. Wray (Eds.), *A.A.A.I. Spring Symposium: Cognitive science principles meet AI-hard problems* (pp. 17–22). Menlo Park, CA: American Association for Artificial Intelligence.

Brown, D. (1971). *The Fetterman massacre*. Lincoln, NE: University of Nebraska Press.

Brown, D. (1974). *Begrabt mein Herz an der Biegung des Flusses* [Bury my heart at the turn of the river]. München, Germany: Knaur. (Original work published in 1970 by Holt Rinehart, and Winston, New York, as "Bury My Heart at Wounded Knee".)

Brown, D., & Schmitt, M. F. (1976). *Fighting Indians of the West*. New York: Ballantine Books.

Brunswik, E. (1955). Representative design and probability theory in a functional psychology. *Psychological Review*, 62, 193–217.

Bullock, S., & Todd, P. M. (1999). Made to measure: Ecological rationality in structured environments. *Minds and Machines*, 9, 497–541.

Czerlinski, J., Gigerenzer, G., & Goldstein, D. G. (1999). How good are simple heuristics? In G. Gigerenzer, P. M. Todd, & The ABC Research Group, *Simple heuristics that make us smart* (pp. 97–118). New York: Oxford University Press.

Dicke, W., & Helbing, D. (2017). *iGod*. Wroclaw, Poland: Amazon Fullfillment.

Dwyer, L. (2011). Why are Silicon Valley executives sending their kids to a tech-free school? Available at: www.good.is/articles/why-are-silicon-valley-executives-sending-their-kids-to-a-tech-free-school (accessed January 22, 2020).

Emberson, P. (2009). *From Gondhishapur to Silicon Valley*. Tobermory, Scotland: Etheric Dimensions Press.

Fear-Segal, J. & Rose, S.D. (2016). Introduction. In J. Fear-Segal & S.D. Rose (Eds.), *Carlisle Indian Industrial School: Indigenous histories, memories, and reclamations* (pp. 1–34). Lincoln, NE: University of Nebraska Press.

Fukuyama, F. (2006). *The end of history and the last man*. New York: Simon & Schuster. (Original work published in 1992.)

Gaissmaier, W., & Marewski, J. N. (2011). Forecasting elections with mere recognition from small, lousy samples: A comparison of collective recognition, wisdom of crowds, and representative polls. *Judgment and Decision Making*, 6, 73–88.

Gibson, J. J. (1986). The ecological approach to visual perception. Hillsdale, NJ: Lawrence Erlbaum. (Original work published in 1979 by Houghton Mifflin, Boston.)

Gigerenzer, G. (1998). Surrogates for theories. *Theory & Psychology*, 8, 195–204.

Gigerenzer, G. (2008a). *Rationality for mortals: How people cope with uncertainty*. New York: Oxford University Press.

Gigerenzer, G. (2008b). Why heuristics work. *Perspectives on Psychological Science*, 3, 20–29.

Gigerenzer, G. (2014). *Risk savvy: How to make good decisions*. New York: Viking.

Gigerenzer, G. (2018). Statistical rituals: The replication delusion and how we got there. *Advances in Methods and Practices in Psychological Science*, 1, 198–218.

Gigerenzer, G., & Brighton, H. (2009). Homo heuristicus: Why biased minds make better inferences. *Topics in Cognitive Science*, 1, 107–143.

Gigerenzer, G., & Gaissmaier, W. (2011). Heuristic decision making. *Annual Review of Psychology*, 62, 451–482.

Gigerenzer, G., Gaissmaier, W., Kurz-Milcke, E., Schwartz, L. M., & Woloshin, S. (2007). Helping doctors and patients to make sense of health statistics. *Psychological Science in the Public Interest*, 8, 53–96.

Gigerenzer, G., & Goldstein, D. G. (1996). Reasoning the fast and frugal way: Models of bounded rationality. *Psychological Review*, 103, 650–669.

Gigerenzer, G., Hertwig, R., & Pachur, T. (Eds.). (2011). *Heuristics: The foundations of adaptive behavior*. New York: Oxford University Press.

Gigerenzer, G., Hoffrage, U., & Goldstein, D. G. (2008). Fast and frugal heuristics are plausible models of cognition: Reply to Dougherty, Franco-Watkins, and Thomas (2008). *Psychological Review*, 115, 230–239.

Gigerenzer, G., Hoffrage, U., & Kleinbölting, H. (1991). Probabilistic mental models: A Brunswikian theory of confidence. *Psychological Review*, 98, 506–528.

Gigerenzer, G., Swijtink, Z., Porter, T., Daston, L. J., Beatty, J., & Krueger, L. (1989). *The empire of chance: How probability changed science and everyday life*. Cambridge: Cambridge University Press.

Gigerenzer, G., Todd, P. M., & the ABC Research Group (1999). *Simple heuristics that make us smart*. New York: Oxford University Press.

Gitlin, M. (2011). *The Wounded Knee massacre*. Santa Barbara, CA: ABC-CLIO.

Goldstein, D. G., & Gigerenzer, G. (2002). Models of ecological rationality: The recognition heuristic. *Psychological Review*, 109, 75–90.

Goldstein, D. G., & Gigerenzer, G. (2009). Fast and frugal forecasting. *International Journal of Forecasting*, 25, 760–772.

Goodwin, G., & Goodwin, N. (2018). *Les guerriers silencieux: Journaux Apaches [The silent warriors: Apache diaries]*. Monaco: Groupe Elidia. (Original work published in 2000 by the University of Nebraska Press, Lincoln, as "The apaches diaries. A father-son journey".)

Gould, S. J. (1981). *The mismeasure of man*. New York: Penguin.

Grüne-Yanoff, T., & Hertwig, R. (2016). Nudge versus boost: How coherent are policy and theory? *Minds and Machines*, 26, 149–183.

Guercini, S. (2019). Heuristics as tales from the field: The problem of scope. *Mind and Society*, 18, 191–205.

Hafenbrädl, S., Waeger, D., Marewski, J. N., & Gigerenzer, G. (2016). Applied decision making with fast-and-frugal heuristics. *Journal of Applied Research in Memory and Cognition*, 5, 215–231.

Hämäläinen, P. (2012). L'Empire Comanche [The Comanche empire]. Toulouse, France: Anacharis Éditions. (Original work published in 2008 by Yale University Press, New Haven and London, as "The Comance Empire".)

Hämäläinen, P. (2019). *Lakota America: A new history of indigenous power.* New Haven, CT: Yale University Press.

Hassrick, R. B. (1992). *Das Buch der Sioux* [The book of the Sioux]. Augsburg, Germany: Weltbild Verlag. (Original work published in 1964 by the University of Oklahoma Press, Norman, as "The Sioux".)

Helbing, D. (2015). *Thinking ahead: Essays on big data, digital revolution, and participatory market society.* Cham, Switzerland: Springer Nature Switzerland.

Helbing, D. (2019). *Towards digital Enlightenment: Essays on the dark and light sides of the digital revolution.* Cham, Switzerland: Springer Nature Switzerland.

Helbing, D., Frey, B. S., Gigerenzer, G., Hafen, E., Hagner, M., Hofstetter, Y., ... Zwitter, A. (2017). Will democracy survive big data and artificial intelligence? Available at: www.scientificamerican.com/article/will-democracy-survive-big-data-and-artificial-intelligence/ (accessed January 22, 2020).

Hertwig, R., Hoffrage, U., & the ABC Research Group (2013). *Simple heuristics in a social world.* New York: Oxford University Press.

Hertwig, R., & Todd, P. M. (2003). More is not always better: The benefits of cognitive limits. In D. Hardman & L. Macchi (Eds.), *The psychology of reasoning and decision making: A handbook* (pp. 213–231). Chichester: Wiley.

Hicks, J. S., Burgman, M. A., Marewski, J. N., Fidler, F., & Gigerenzer, G. (2012). Decision making in a human population living sustainably. *Conservation Biology*, 26, 760–768.

Hirschfeld, L. A., & Gelman, S. A. (Eds.) (1994). *Mapping the mind.* Cambridge: Cambridge University Press.

Hoffrage, U. (2019). Digitalisierung: Verheissung und Verhängnis. *AGORA – in geänderter Zeitlage*, 5/6/7, 25–29.

Hoffrage, U., Hafenbrädl, S., & Marewski, J. N. (2018). The fast-and-frugal heuristics program. In L. J. Ball & V. A. Thompson (Eds.), *The Routledge international handbook of thinking & reasoning* (pp. 325–345). Abingdon: Routledge.

Hoffrage U., Lindsey S., Hertwig R., & Gigerenzer G. (2000). Communicating statistical information. *Science*, 290, 2261–2262.

Hoffrage, U., & Marewski, J. (2015). Unveiling the Lady in Black: Modeling and aiding intuition. *Journal of Applied Research in Memory and Cognition*, 4, 145–163.

Hoffrage, U., & Marewski, J. N. (2020). Social Scoring als Mensch-System-Interaktion. In O. Everling (Ed.), *Social Credit Rating: Reputation und Vertrauen beurteilen* (pp. 305–329). Springer Verlag.

Katsikopoulos, K. V., Schooler, L., & Hertwig, R. (2010). The robust beauty of ordinary information. *Psychological Review*, 117, 1259–1266.

Kitano, H. (2004). Biological robustness. *Nature Reviews Genetics*, 5, 826–837.

Knight, F. H. (1921). *Risk, uncertainty and profit.* New York: Houghton Mifflin.

Kozyreva, A., Lewandowsky, S., & Hertwig, R. (in press). Citizens versus the internet: Confronting digital challenges with cognitive tools. *Psychological Science in the Public Interest.*

Maidique, M. (2012). The leader's toolbox. Available at: https://lead.fiu.edu/resources/news/archives/the-leaders-toolbox-by-dr-modesto-maidique.html (accessed January 27, 2020).

Manches, A. (2019). The Internet of Toys for children: Risk or opportunity? Paper presented at the International Workshop of the Herbert Simon Society, The Digital World, Cognition and Behavior, Turin, Italy.

Manches, A., Duncan, P., Plowman, L., & Sabeti, S. (2015). Three questions about the Internet of things and children. *TechTrends*, 59, 76–83.

Manimala, M. (1992). Entrepreneurial heuristics: A comparison between high PI (pioneering-innovative) and low PI ventures. *Journal of Business Venturing*, 7, 477–504.

Marewski, J. N., & Bornmann, L. (2020). Opium in science and society: Numbers. Unpublished manuscript.

Marewski, J. N., Gaissmaier, W., & Gigerenzer, G. (2010). Good judgments do not require complex cognition. *Cognitive Processing*, 11, 103–121.

Marewski, J. N., & Gigerenzer, G. (2012). Heuristic decision making in medicine. *Dialogues in Clinical Neuroscience*, 14, 77–89.

Marewski, J. N., & Schooler, L. J. (2011). Cognitive niches: An ecological model of strategy selection. *Psychological Review*, 118, 393–437.

Marewski, J. N., Schooler, L. J., & Gigerenzer, G. (2010). Five principles for studying people's use of heuristics. *Acta Psychologica Sinica*, 42, 72–87.

Martignon, L., & Hoffrage, U. (2002). Fast, frugal and fit: Simple heuristics for paired comparison. *Theory and Decision*, 52, 29–71.

Martignon, L., & Hoffrage, U. (2019). *Wer wagt, gewinnt? Wie Sie die Risikokompetenz von Kindern und Jugendlichen fördern können* [He who dares wins? How you can foster the risk competence of children and adolescents]. Bern, Switzerland: Hogrefe.

McElreath, R., Wallin, A., & Fasolo, B. (2013). The evolutionary rationality of social learning. In R. Hertwig, U. Hoffrage, & the ABC Research Group, *Simple heuristics in a social world* (pp. 381–408). New York: Oxford University Press.

Mousavi, S., & Gigerenzer, G. (2014). Risk, uncertainty and heuristics. *Journal of Business Research*, 67, 1671–1678.

Mousavi, S., & Gigerenzer, G. (2017). Heuristics are tools for uncertainty. *Homo Oeconomicus*, 34, 361–379.

Newell, A. (1973). You can't play 20 questions with nature and win: Projective comments on the papers of this symposium. In W. G. Chase (Ed.), *Visual information processing* (pp. 283–310). New York: Academic Press.

O'Neil, C. (2016). *Weapons of math destruction: How Big Data increases inequality and threatens democracy.* New York: Penguin Random House.

Palazzo, G., Krings, F., & Hoffrage, U. (2012). Ethical blindness. *Journal of Business Ethics*, 109, 323–338.

Savage, L. J. (1972 [1954]). *The foundation of statistics.* New York: Dover Publications. (Original work published in 1954 by John Wiley & Sons.)

Schooler, L. J., & Hertwig, R. (2005). How forgetting aids heuristic inference. *Psychological Review*, 112, 610–628.

Severson, K. (2011). Thousands sterilized, a state weighs restitution. *New York Times*, December 9.

Simon, H. A. (1990). Invariants of human behavior. *Annual Review of Psychology*, 41, 1–19.

Standing Bear, L. (2006 [1928]). *My people the Sioux.* Lincoln, NE: University of Nebraska Press.

Stephens, D. W., & Krebs, J. R. (1986). *Foraging theory.* Princeton, NJ: Princeton University Press. (Original work published in 1928 by Houghton Mifflin Company.)

Stevens, J. R., Marewski, J. N., Schooler, L. J., & Gilby, I. C. (2016). Reflections of the social environment in chimpanzee memory: Applying rational analysis beyond humans. *Royal Society Open Science*, 3, 160293.

Sull, D. N., & Eisenhardt, K. M. (2015). *Simple rules: How to thrive in a complex world.* New York: Houghton Mifflin Harcourt.

SVRV (2018). *Verbrauchergerechtes Scoring. Gutachten des Sachverständigenrats für Verbraucherfragen* [Consumer-friendly scoring. Expert report of the Advisory Council for Consumer Affairs]. Berlin: Sachverständigenrat für Verbraucherfragen. Available at: www.svr-verbraucherfragen.de/wp-content/uploads/SVRV_Verbrauchergerechtes_Scoring.pdf (accessed December 13, 2018.)

Thaler, R. H., & Sunstein, C. R. (2009). *Nudge: Improving decisions about health, wealth, and happiness.* London: Penguin Books. (Original work published in 2008 by Yale University Press, New Haven, CT.)

Todd, P. M., Gigerenzer, G., & the ABC Research Group (2012). *Ecological rationality: Intelligence in the world.* New York: Oxford University Press.

Tooby, J., & Cosmides, L., (1992). The psychological foundations of culture. In J. H. Barkow, L. Cosmides, & J. Tooby (Eds.), *The adapted mind: Evolutionary psychology and the generation of culture* (pp. 19–136). New York: Oxford University Press.

Waggoner, J. (2013). *Witness: A Hunkpapha historian's strong-heart song of the Lakotas.* Lincoln, NE: University of Nebraska Press.

Woike, J. K., Hoffrage, U., & Martignon, L. (2017). Integrating and testing natural frequencies, Naïve Bayes, and fast-and-frugal trees. *Decision*, 4, 234–260.

Wolf, B. (1999). *Vicarious functioning as a central process-characteristic of human behavior.* Available at: http://brunswik.org/notes/essay4.html (accessed February 5, 2020).

Young, K. (1922). Intelligence tests of certain immigrant groups. *The Scientific Monthly*, 15(5), 417–434.

19

ECOLOGICAL RATIONALITY

Bounded rationality in an evolutionary light

Samuel A. Nordli and Peter M. Todd

Herbert Simon famously characterized bounded rationality as being "shaped by a scissors whose two blades are the structure of task environments and the computational capacities of the actor" (1990, p. 7). Illuminated by the "light of evolution," research on bounded rationality in humans can be seen as a proximate cross-sectional analysis of our species' current point in its evolutionary trajectory—that is, the study of human decision making and problem solving as interactions between **(A)** our present capacities, needs, and desires/goals, and **(B)** the structure of the present environmental contexts in which such decision making takes place. But the evolutionary perspective enables us to do more, looking at the ultimate selection pressures that operated over time in our and other species' evolutionary trajectories—that is, the study of any organism's decision making as interactions between **(A)** its evolved capacities, needs, and desires/goals, in terms of **(B)** how those aspects fit the structure of the past environmental decision-making contexts, and **(C)** how they match or mismatch the structure of the present environmental contexts. The study of *ecological rationality* extends the concept of bounded rationality by situating it within an evolutionary perspective: Like other Darwinian approaches to psychology (e.g., Barkow, Cosmides, & Tooby, 1992), ecological rationality emphasizes the role of the past environment to which we are adapted, the present environment in which we make decisions, and the ecology and structure of information as it is processed by decision-making mechanisms (e.g., Todd, Gigerenzer, & the ABC Research Group, 2012). Ecological rationality seeks to understand decision making in much the same way as the traditional bounded rationality approach, but posits that this understanding will necessarily be species-specific (revealing both commonalities and differences between humans and other organisms), and must be informed by each species' evolutionary history (including past environments) as well as what we know of evolutionary processes in general. In this way, the ecological rationality approach follows in the investigative tradition of behavioral ecology as championed by Tinbergen (1963), who argued that proximate (mechanistic and developmental) and ultimate (adaptive and evolutionary) analyses are each required in order to fully understand observed behavior.

DOI: 10.4324/9781315658353-22

Bounded rationality as proximate, ecological rationality as ultimate analyses

As formulated by Simon, bounded rationality is essentially concerned with mechanistic answers to proximate questions about problem solving and decision making. What decision-making mechanisms or strategies are used in a particular task environment and what are their outcomes? How do these mechanisms function? What are their practical limits? What are the relevant structures of the task environment, and how do those variables (and variation therein) affect operations and outcomes? Answers to these and other such *what* and *how* questions are integral to a well-developed understanding of human decision making and problem solving, and they often help to shape and answer the ultimate questions of *why* and *whence*. However, much of decision research tends to overlook ultimate analyses and simply settles for mechanistic descriptions as explanations. This lack of evolutionary contextualization can leave unrealistic notions of rationality unchallenged, engendering a tendency to blame irrational biases or systematic inadequacies when human behavior does not match the optimal performance of normative behavioral prescriptions (e.g., Tversky & Kahneman, 1974). From this proximate perspective, the failure of boundedly-rational behavior to reach classically rational levels of performance is just that: a failure.

Ecological rationality research charts a different course. It does not predefine rationality based on idealized expectations of how people should act in order to optimize performance (given infinite resources and unbounded capacities). Instead, it seeks both to describe how people actually act in specific contexts, and to understand how decisions and actions fit together with particular environmental contexts in terms of their evolutionary provenance and adaptive significance. Judgment and decision making are unavoidable necessities for most species, whose very existence suggests that they are adapted to be effective decision makers: Individuals who were ill-equipped to respond to basic fitness challenges—such as finding and selecting good food, a mate, and a habitat—were less likely to survive and reproduce than their more-capable contemporaries. When an organism's decision-making behavior works well in a given context, ecological rationality research explores how evolved cognitive capacities and evolved or learned decision strategies fit with environment structure to produce the adaptive behavior; conversely, when the behavior in a given context runs contrary to what might be expected (e.g., because it results in error or appears to be maladaptive), ecological rationality asks questions from an evolutionary perspective to uncover how an ultimate understanding could explain why the observed behavior occurs in that context.

Decision making: driven by goals, shaped by ecological structure and variability

For an individual decision maker (and ultimately for its species), a decision is a means to an end. In this sense, decisions and their associated goals (whether proximate or ultimate) are inseparable, as a decision represents the selection and application of behavior in service of a goal within some environment. The pursuit of a specific goal by an environmentally-situated decision maker constitutes a particular ecological context. One way that such contexts can be divided systematically is according to whether their associated goals can be achieved via the repetition or modulation of past behavior (i.e., 'past' in multiple senses, being drawn from the life history of a decision-making organism, the cultural history of its community, or the evolutionary history of its species). This can be framed in terms of exploration and exploitation: Does the structure of the present environment allow the application of some form of past behavior to achieve the goal associated with a particular context? If yes, that possibility can be exploited; if no (or if the answer is unknown), exploration may uncover new or existing means of achieving that goal, which may then be exploited for similar contexts in the future. For example, a habit is a past behavior being exploited in a current situation, while trial-and-error learning is exploration to find a new behavior for a new situation. (Furthermore, when considered as a search strategy that is applied repeatedly in various exploratory contexts, trial-and-error learning is itself a form of exploiting past behavior, in an exploratory context.) Ecological rationality can be conceptualized as the study of how individuals and species are adapted to identify and take advantage of opportunities in which past behavior can be exploited to achieve their goals in present contexts, including cases in which the exploited behavior is a strategic approach to exploration.

The use of 'past' behavior in present contexts means reusing behavior that matches particular structural features of environments that co-occur across some range of contexts over time (Todd & Brighton, 2016). For example, shifting an automobile into drive is a recurrent goal for many people; different instances of exploiting past shifting behavior will be nearly identical from day to day across slight variations in the context of driving a family car (e.g., if one's spouse has adjusted the seat), but shared features in a rented pickup truck may also permit the exploitation of past shifting behavior in a new driving context. Similarly, the anatomy, physiology, and environment of *Caenorhabditis elegans* worms share enough cross-generational features to permit an inherited mechanism to guide stereotypical patterns of locomotion during foraging (Hills, Brockie, & Maricq, 2004), which effectively allows individual worms in present environments to exploit an ancestral search strategy that was similarly successful in past environments. Indeed, as these divergent examples suggest, such exploitation is accomplished by a wide variety of mechanisms and strategies that may be learned or evolved, specific or general. Contexts (goal pursuit in different environment structures) can be organized in terms of the decision strategies that can exploit them, in a way that bridges behavioral ecology and ecological rationality (see Hutchinson & Gigerenzer, 2005), as much work in these areas (illustrated in the next section) can be characterized under this framework as studying various manifestations of the same general exploitative phenomenon.

Cue-based behavior: fast and frugal exploitation of statistical regularity

If time is not a strong pressure and/or the outcome of a decision depends on a number of important factors, it can be worthwhile collecting and integrating information regarding the specifics of those factors before making the decision. For example, as a colony prepares to relocate, ants of the species *Leptothorax albipennis* appear to collect and differentially weight information regarding a number of prospective nest site cavity characteristics—including the area, entrance size, ceiling height, and amount of ambient light for each space—before choosing the best location (Franks, Mallon, Bray, Hamilton, & Mischler, 2003). However, time is typically a significant factor for many decision contexts that animals face in the world, whether directly (e.g., a prey animal deciding in the moment how to react to a predator in pursuit) or indirectly (e.g., the more time an animal spends courting, the less time it will have for foraging), whereby animals will generally be at an advantage if they can make effective decisions faster than competitors (Todd, 2001). Thus, for contexts in which goals are achievable via some reiteration of past (i.e., recalled, inherited, or imitated) behavior, it is typically advantageous to identify those contexts and decide to implement those behaviors as quickly and efficiently as possible, assuming outcomes are equivalent. One way to achieve such efficiency is to ignore as much irrelevant information as possible, which can streamline the search for relevant information as well as minimize the time and energy spent processing it (Gigerenzer & Todd, 1999; see also the effort-reduction framework of Shah & Oppenheimer, 2008). By relying on only the subset of environmental cues that are sufficient to distinguish a given context and characterize its structure, an organism can quickly make decisions that exploit the structural regularities that are indicated by those cues. The following examples illustrate the ecologically rational use of contextual cues to exploit predictable features of environmental structure.

In behavioral ecology, *fixed action patterns*—stereotypical sequences of unlearned behavior that are triggered by certain contextual cues—are exhibited by species whose individuals have effectively inherited specific exploitative behaviors to be used in specific environmental settings that ancestral generations encountered sufficiently often for selection to occur. For instance, when greylag geese (*Anser anser*, a ground-nesting species) are brooding, the cue of visually perceiving an egg outside the nest elicits a scripted sequence of behavior whereby a goose extends its neck and uses its beak to roll the egg toward itself and into the nest (Alcock, 2005). Other exploitative strategies often studied in behavioral ecology are of *rules of thumb*, which are evolved algorithmic decision-making mechanisms used by many species to achieve particular contextualized goals. Scouts of the above-mentioned ant species, *Leptothorax albipennis*, use a rule-of-thumb algorithm to determine whether the area of potential nesting site cavities is large enough for their colonies (one of the factors in their relocation decision)—ants explore such sites twice, first laying a pheromone trail as they walk a random path of fixed length, and then walking the same distance along a new random path and assessing the rate at which it intersects its prior trail as a reliable indication of the approximate area of the cavity (Mugford, Mallon, & Franks, 2001).

Paralleling fixed action patterns, humans (and other vertebrates) form *habits* when they repeat goal-oriented behaviors in recurrent contexts: With continued and consistent repetition, a learned behavioral sequence will coalesce into a singular 'chunk' of behavior that comes to be executed automatically in its entirety upon being triggered by contextual cues (Graybiel, 2008). Habit formation is essentially a mechanism through which procedurally learned patterns of behavior come to mimic the cue-driven efficiency and efficacy of evolved behavioral sequences such as fixed action patterns (Nordli & Todd, 2017). This connection is not merely conceptual: Learned habits and inherited fixed action patterns appear to be controlled by the same recursive neural circuitry in vertebrates (Graybiel, 1995; Berridge, Aldridge, Houchard, & Zhuang, 2005), and—when observed externally—behaviors of one type can be indistinguishable from those of the other, without prior knowledge of the behaviors' ontogeny or phylogeny (Burkart, Schubiger, & van Schaik, 2017).

Likewise, rules of thumb are paralleled by the *simple heuristics* that are often studied by researchers in ecological rationality (Gigerenzer, Todd, & the ABC Research Group, 1999). A heuristic, as defined by Gigerenzer and Gaissmaier (2011), "is a strategy that ignores part of the information, with the goal of making decisions more quickly, frugally, and/or accurately than more complex methods" (p. 454). Rephrased in the framework of exploitable contexts, heuristics are cue-guided decision strategies that are used to make choices and pursue goals in particular contexts by exploiting regularities in environment structure with particular variations of past decision-making behavior. Heuristics operate in a manner that is "fast and frugal"—fast because the decision mechanism generating behavior in a given environment uses little computation, and frugal because it operates on little information. Perhaps the simplest example is the recognition heuristic, which states *if you recognize only one of two possible alternatives, choose the one you recognize.* When German students were asked which city was more populous, San Diego or San Antonio, 100 percent of them responded correctly (San Diego) compared to about 66 percent of American students answering the same question (Goldstein & Gigerenzer, 2002). Having heard of San Diego, the German students—mostly not recognizing San Antonio—were able to use the recognition heuristic to answer the question correctly in this context because larger cities are generally more famous, hence more commonly recognized (Todd, 2007). Here, recognition is information about past situations that the individual has encountered, and that crucially has a reliable structure to it: recognized options are likely to be higher on the decision criterion (here, city size). This structure paired with the simple recognition heuristic together exploit the past experience of the individual to yield good decisions in current situations.

Fixed action patterns, rules of thumb, habits, and heuristics are all examples of decision-making tools that are ecologically rational, i.e., these tools are efficient means of exploiting effective pairings of particular strategies and particular environment structures that have been discovered through past behavior to achieve goals in recurrent contexts. In the field of ecological rationality, the *adaptive toolbox* is the conceptual collection of decision-making mechanisms that an individual draws from to help them successfully navigate the world (Gigerenzer, 2001). Broadly, ecological rationality is the study of such decision-making tools, the structure of the environments in which those tools are used to make decisions, and, crucially, the specifics of how and why those tools and environments fit together to serve the ultimate interests of decision makers (Todd & Brighton, 2016). This section has stressed that ecological rationality is species-specific and pertains to the decision-making ecology of many different species, allowing work from behavioral ecology to be conceptually appreciated as ecological rationality research; however, since most of this research so far has focused on human heuristic decision making and search strategies, the remainder of this chapter will primarily focus on the ecological rationality of our own species, concluding with directions for future work.

Fitting the right tool to the right context: ecological rationality in action

Research in ecological rationality often proceeds by identifying different decision contexts, in terms of environmental information structures, that fit well with particular categories of heuristics, in terms of their information processing structures. Contextual specificity is critical: Identifying and characterizing the tools that feature in individuals' adaptive toolboxes must be done by studying their use in specific situations. This is because effective simple heuristics and other such tools are highly context-sensitive, working well in a limited set of environmental structures but possibly producing poor decisions when used in others (Gigerenzer, Todd, & the ABC Research Group, 1999).

Many heuristic strategies consist of three basic elements: a search rule, a stopping rule, and a decision rule—that is, a heuristic algorithm can often be described by how it *searches* for cues, how it *stops* that search, and how it *decides* based on the outcome of the search process (Gigerenzer, 2001). In addition to divisions by context, heuristics are often grouped according to overlap in their specific search, stopping, and decision rules. For example, *one-reason decision heuristics* are those that make decisions based on a single cue, evaluating all options (two or more) on the basis of that cue and then stopping comparisons and making a decision if one option scores higher than the others on that criterion. *Take-the-best* and the *minimalist* heuristic are examples of heuristics that base decisions on a single reason or factor, differing only in how they search through cues (Todd & Gigerenzer, 2003). Take-the-best searches through cues in a particular order, ranked according to their past successes, while the minimalist heuristic searchers through cues in a random order. Potential choices are evaluated according to their score on the first cue, only going on to consider the next cue if no option surpasses any other on the first, and so on, for instance, deciding between two entrees at a restaurant according to whichever is cheaper, or if both are the same price, according to whichever dish features the greatest number of different vegetables, etc. When used in task contexts with appropriately exploitable structure, the decisions made by take-the-best are at least as accurate as more complex processing-intensive decision strategies such as linear regression models, and typically achieve such accuracy using much less information (e.g., Gigerenzer & Goldstein, 1996; Czerlinski, Gigerenzer, & Goldstein, 1999). Figuring out which environment structures fit well with one-reason heuristics such as take-the-best is a central component of ecological rationality research.

For situations in which one-reason decision heuristics are insufficient to differentiate among available options (as in some contexts with three or more alternatives), *multiple-cue decision heuristics* can make appropriate choices based on two or more cues (Todd, 2007). The *elimination by aspects* heuristic (Tversky, 1972) is one such strategy that culls options according to selected criteria, narrowing down to a reduced set of alternatives, for instance, when deciding among multiple restaurants to visit, first eliminating all those that are more than 10 miles away, and then all those that are non-vegetarian. This process of elimination can be continued down to a single option, or a reduced set of options can be decided among by some other means of discrimination (such as switching to a one-reason heuristic, if the context allows).

In contexts in which choice alternatives have yet to be identified or encountered, or in which no known behavior can be exploited to achieve a specific goal, *sequential search heuristics* are appropriate (Todd & Gigerenzer, 2003). For example, when seeking a long-term romantic partner, how does an individual determine whether they have found a good possibility if a number of other prospective mates remain available? After being passed over, potential partners may pursue other relationships or may become uninterested in the meantime; environment structure constraints such as these are typical of some sequential search contexts, for which targets are encountered one at a time, and often cannot be retrieved after they have been passed by (e.g., job search and housing search). One solution to such sequential search problems is a *satisficing* strategy that sets an aspiration level for some criterion, and then, if an option is discovered that meets or exceeds the aspiration level, stops searching and chooses that option (Simon, 1955; Todd & Miller, 1999). Similarly, in the context of tasks with unknown behavioral solutions, a strategy of trial-and-error learning can be used to search for behaviors that successfully achieve goals.

How is a given heuristic selected for use in a particular context? This question highlights an aspect of ecological rationality research that is not well-specified: The manner in which heuristics and other decision tools in the adaptive toolbox are determined to appropriately match the structure of a given situation, otherwise known as the *strategy selection* problem (Marewski & Link, 2014). One possible solution to this problem is the development of a mapping between context structure and appropriate heuristics to use (Marewski & Schooler, 2011). This can be done in part by a "strategy selection learning" procedure as proposed by Rieskamp and Otto (2006), which suggests that strategies are applied according to predictions regarding their expected success in specific scenarios. For any given instance of strategy selection, after applying the strategy with the greatest predicted success, a process of reinforcement learning updates that expectation for future situations based on the current outcome. This process can lead to occasional errors in which the selection of a strategy results in a mismatch between behavior and environmental structure. Readers may recall examples where one of their own habits was selected inappropriately, for instance, when needing to consciously locate the gear stick in a rented car after unconsciously grasping at the air where the gear stick is found in one's own vehicle.

When behavior and beliefs diverge from expectations

Bounded and ecological rationality consider behavior as the product of actor-environment interactions, both those that are occurring now and those that have occurred in the past and shaped the current decision mechanisms and environmental structures. This means that species and their environments are subject to change. When environmental change takes place, multiple generations of selection may need to occur before a species can evolve to be adapted to new fitness challenges—thus, behavioral traits and mechanisms that are observed in present environments are typically adapted to past environmental structure, which an ecological rationality perspective prompts us to consider. If past and present environments differ in important ways, this can lead to a mismatch of old cognitive mechanisms or strategies applied to modern settings, which can result in poor decisions. An example of this is the strong evolved human preference for sugary, salty, and fatty foods, which can lead to unhealthy food choices that contribute to obesity and other chronic diseases (Cordain et al., 2005). The possibility of such mismatches—whether between past adaptations and present environments in which they are maladaptive, or between a strategy that works well in one modern setting but fails when applied to another—serves to reiterate the importance of considering particular environments and contexts when evaluating the (ecological) rationality of a particular decision strategy. Strategies are not ecologically rational in and of themselves, but only in the context of specific situations with particular environmental structure. A decision strategy such as *if there is sweet food available, eat it*, is ecologically rational in an environment where foods of high caloric density are scarce or difficult to obtain; but in wealthy modern environments where readily available foods are often specifically manufactured to satisfy this human preference for sweets, an *eat sweet food* strategy leads to bad decisions and undesirable consequences.

In addition to cases in which environments and strategies are mismatched, there are examples where ostensibly irrational behavior (according to normative prescriptive models) may be considered perfectly reasonable when evaluated from an ecological rationality perspective. Consider the "error tendencies" illustrated by Thagard (2011), in which the interaction of emotion and cognition leads to beliefs that are purportedly irrational because they are unduly influenced by motivated reasoning. Thagard suggests that the integration of cognitive and emotional information has evolved to ensure that cognitive capacities are efficiently directed toward achieving goals that are important for survival and reproduction (see also Gallese, Mastrogiorgio, Petracca, & Viale, Chapter 23 in this volume); but despite this adaptive provenance, he asserts that such integration often induces irrational beliefs when faced with the complexity of modern environments (Thagard, 2011). This suggests that errors of motivated inference may simply be further examples of environment-mechanism mismatch, but consider, for example, cases of *sour grapes* (see e.g., Elster, 1983; Kay, Jimenez, & Jost, 2002), wherein the inaccessibility of a desired result leads one to conclude that the result was not particularly desirable after all (e.g., I couldn't reach the grapes, but they were probably sour anyway). Sour grapes and other such instances of motivated reasoning do appear to lead to beliefs that are logically unsound; however, when considered from an evolutionary perspective, such processes may ultimately produce adaptive behavior that reflects an ecologically rational strategy for balancing the risks, rewards, and probabilities that characterize the environmental structure of contexts in which motivated reasoning occurs—even in complex modern environments.

To illustrate, the logically unfounded belief that grapes are not any good because they cannot be reached may simply be the product of an effective proximate mechanism (i.e., emotional biases in specific contexts) that ultimately serves to discourage the pursuit of goals in situations where contextual cues indicate that goal achievement is unlikely. Similarly, cases of fear-driven inference (e.g., I don't recognize this mole—I must have cancer!) may not be irrational "gut overreactions ... in which a feeling that something is wrong is erroneously taken as evidence that something really is wrong" (Thagard & Nussbaum, 2014, p. 43); instead, they may reflect an adaptive way to encourage cautious over-preparation when facing possible scenarios with severe fitness consequences, such as for situations in which multiple Type I errors are still less costly than a single fatal Type II error. Put another way, even if the result is a false belief, it may ultimately be ecologically rational to tend to underestimate the value of positive-but-unlikely outcomes (as in sour grapes) and to overestimate the probability of unlikely-but-costly scenarios (as in fear-driven inference) if those motivational biases respectively serve to minimize fruitless investments of time and energy and increase the chances of avoiding or mitigating the negative impact of an unlikely scenario that happens to come to pass (Haselton & Nettle, 2006). Such examples of motivated reasoning appear to be qualitatively in line with what would be expected from an adaptive system that uses emotional biases to influence behavior in response to specific contextual cues. These examples reinforce the point that prescriptive proximate-only definitions of rationality provide little explanatory insight when they classify behavior in the world as irrational because it is contrary to normative prescriptions. The biases of motivated reasoning may lead to false beliefs, but such biases should not be considered 'irrational' if they are the result of an adaptive (e.g., ecologically rational) mechanism that yields decisions that tend to appropriately balance the inherent tradeoff between risk and reward (see e.g., Pleskac & Hertwig, 2014); rather, we should understand how such mechanisms function and under what circumstances they operate, in order to combat false beliefs in cases where they may have negative practical consequences.

Future directions in research on ecological rationality

Our general understanding of behavior will continue to develop as we construct a more complete account of (1) the decision mechanisms that underlie behavior; (2) the ecological contexts in which they are applied; and (3) the structural correspondences between decision mechanisms and environments that result in successful (and unsuccessful) outcomes.

First, with respect to mechanisms, a full theoretical framework of ecological rationality will be promoted by an understanding of the neurophysiological mechanisms that support and produce decision behavior and cognition. For example, integrating work across cognitive neuroscience and neurophysiology with research on ecological rationality will help solve the problem of strategy selection. In this regard, one promising avenue to explore involves the potential role played by neural circuitry involving the basal ganglia, a set of subcortical nuclei in vertebrates. The reinforcement learning-based mechanism of strategy selection, as proposed by Otto and Rieskamp (2006), is consistent with accounts that tie reinforcement learning processes to recurrent cortico-basal circuitry (e.g., Yin & Knowlton, 2006), which is the very same circuitry that is critical to the exploitation of past behavior in the form of habits and fixed action patterns. Indeed, this circuitry may be critical to most ecologically rational behavior. Graybiel (2008) explains how "repetitive behaviors, whether motor or cognitive, are built up in part through the action of basal ganglia-based neural circuits that can iteratively evaluate contexts and select actions and can then form chunked representations of action sequences" (p. 361), which aptly characterizes the general process of exploiting past behavior in present contexts, and offers a solution to strategy selection that is grounded in neurophysiology. Under this neurological framework, an evaluative process determines the structure of the present context, whereby a connection is made to past behavior, which is selected by the system, allowing a specific behavioral sequence to attempt to exploit the contextual structure and achieve an associated goal.

Second, more work is needed on systematic approaches to uncovering characteristics of environment structure that are important in decision making. As mentioned above, behavioral ecology (and other ecological perspectives) can supply useful theoretical frameworks (see e.g., Wilke et al., 2018). The study of situations in social psychology may also provide a different unified approach (Todd & Gigerenzer, 2020). This perspective builds on Lewin's (1936) proposal of field theory, which describes behavior (*B*) as the product of some function (*f*) operating on a person (*P*) and their environment (*E*), formulated by the simple equation

$$B = f(P, E)$$

A person's perceptions of their current environment then goes into defining a given situation. One of the challenges ahead is to determine whether different types of situations, as studied by social psychology, can be described as different patterns of information that particular decision heuristics can exploit, as studied in ecological rationality.

Finally, although ecological rationality seeks to understand behavior from appropriate proximate and ultimate perspectives—to provide accurate *descriptions* of how and why behavior occurs in specific contexts—the field also aims to facilitate accurate *predictions* of what behaviors will occur under specific conditions and, ultimately, to use such a comprehensive understanding to help people and institutions make better decisions (Gigerenzer & Todd, 2012).

References

Alcock, J. (2005). *Animal behavior: An evolutionary approach* (8th ed.). Sinauer Associates, Inc.

Barkow, J. H., Cosmides, L., & Tooby, J. (Eds.) (1992). *The adapted mind: Evolutionary psychology and the generation of culture*. Oxford: Oxford University Press.

Berridge, K. C., Aldridge, J. W., Houchard, K. R., & Zhuang, X. (2005). Sequential super-stereotypy of an instinctive fixed action pattern in hyper-dopaminergic mutant mice: A model of obsessive compulsive disorder and Tourette's. *BMC Biology*, 3(4).

Burkart, J. M., Schubiger, M. N., & van Schaik, C. P. (2017). The evolution of general intelligence. *Behavioral and Brain Sciences*, 40.

Cordain, L., Eaton, S. B., Sebastian, A., Mann, N., Lindberg, S., Watkins, B. A., ... & Brand-Miller, J. (2005). Origins and evolution of the Western diet: Health implications for the 21st century. *The American Journal of Clinical Nutrition*, 81(2), 341–354.

Czerlinski, J., Gigerenzer, G., & Goldstein, D. G. (1999). How good are simple heuristics? In G. Gigerenzer, P. M. Todd, & the ABC Research Group (Eds.), *Simple heuristics that make us smart* (pp. 97–118). New York: Oxford University Press.

Dobzhansky, T. (1964). Biology, molecular and organismic. *Integrative and Comparative Biology*, 4(4), 443–452.

Elster, J. (1983). *Sour grapes*. Cambridge: Cambridge University Press.

Franks, N. R., Mallon, E. B., Bray, H. E., Hamilton, M. J., & Mischler, T. C. (2003). Strategies for choosing between alternatives with different attributes: Exemplified by house-hunting ants. *Animal Behaviour*, 65, 215–223.

Gigerenzer, G. (2001). The adaptive toolbox. In G. Gigerenzer & R. Selten (Eds.), *Bounded rationality: The adaptive toolbox* (pp. 37–50). Cambridge, MA: MIT Press.

Gigerenzer, G., & Gaissmaier, W. (2011). Heuristic decision making. *The Annual Review of Psychology*, 62, 451–482.

Gigerener, G., & Goldstein, D. G. (1996). Reasoning the fast and frugal way: Models of bounded rationality. *Psychological Review*, 103(4), 650–669.

Gigerenzer, G., & Todd, P. M. (1999). Fast and frugal heuristics: The adaptive toolbox. In G. Gigerenzer, P. M. Todd, & the ABC Research Group (Eds.), *Simple heuristics that make us smart* (pp. 3–36). New York: Oxford University Press.

Gigerenzer, G., Todd, P. M., & the ABC Research Group (Eds.). (1999). *Simple heuristics that make us smart.* New York: Oxford University Press.

Goldstein, D. G., & Gigerenzer, G. (2002). Models of ecological rationality: The recognition heuristic. *Psychological Review*, 109(1), 75–90.

Graybiel, A. M. (1995). Building action repertoires: Memory and learning functions of the basal ganglia. *Current Opinion in Neurobiology*, 5, 733–741.

Graybiel, A. M. (2008). Habits, rituals, and the evaluative brain. *The Annual Review of Neuroscience*, 31, 359–387.

Haselton, M. G., & Nettle, D. (2006). The paranoid optimist: An integrative evolutionary model of cognitive biases. *Personality and Social Psychology Review*, 10(1), 47–66.

Hills, T., Brockie, P. J., & Maricq, A. V. (2004). Dopamine and glutamate control area-restricted search behavior in *Caenorhabditis elegans*. *The Journal of Neuroscience*, 24(5), 1217–1225.

Hutchinson, J. M. C., & Gigerenzer, G. (2005). Simple heuristics and rules of thumb: Where psychologists and behavioural biologists might meet. *Behavioural Processes*, 69, 97–124.

Kay, A. C., Jimenez, M. C., & Jost, J. T. (2002). Sour grapes, sweet lemons, and the anticipatory rationalization of the status quo. *Personality and Social Psychology Bulletin*, 28(9), 1300–1312.

Lewin, K. (1936). *Principles of topological psychology.* New York: McGraw-Hill.

Marewski, J. N., & Link, D. (2014). Strategy selection: An introduction to the modeling challenge. *Wiley Interdisciplinary Reviews: Cognitive Science*, 5, 39–59.

Marewski, J. N., & Schooler, L. J. (2011). Cognitive niches: An ecological model of strategy selection. *Psychological Review*, 118, 393–437.

Mugford, S. T., Mallon, E. B., & Franks, N. R. (2001). The accuracy of Buffon's needle: A rule of thumb used by ants to estimate area. *Behavioral Ecology*, 12(6), 655–658.

Nordli, S. A., & Todd, P. M. (2017). Habit formation generates secondary modules that emulate the efficiency of evolved behavior. *Behavioral and Brain Sciences*, 40, 41.

Pleskac, T. J., & Hertwig, R. (2014). Ecologically rational choice and the structure of the environment. *Journal of Experimental Psychology General*, 143(5), 2000–2019.

Rieskamp, J., & Otto, P. E. (2006). SSL: A theory of how people learn to select strategies. *Journal of Experimental Psychology General*, 135(2), 207–236.

Simon, H. A. (1955). A behavioral model of rational choice. *The Quarterly Journal of Economics*, 69(1), 99–118.

Simon, H. A. (1990). Invariants of human behavior. *Annual Review of Psychology*, 41, 1–20.

Shah, A. K., & Oppenheimer, D. M. (2008). Heuristics made easy: An effort-reduction framework. *Psychological Bulletin*, 134(2), 207–222.

Thagard, P. (2011). Critical thinking and informal logic: Neuropsychological perspectives. *Informal Logic*, 31(3), 152–170.

Thagard, P., & Nussbaum, A. D. (2014). Fear-driven inference: Mechanisms of gut overreaction. In L. Magnani (Ed.), *Model-based reasoning in science and technology* (pp. 43–53). Berlin: Springer-Verlag.

Tinbergen, N. (1963). On aims and methods of ethology. *Zeitschrift für Tierpsychologie*, 20, 410–433.

Todd, P. M. (2001). Fast and frugal heuristics for environmentally bounded minds. In G. Gigerenzer & R. Selten (Eds.), *Bounded rationality: The adaptive toolbox* (pp. 51–70). Cambridge, MA: MIT Press.

Todd, P. M. (2007). How much information do we need? *European Journal of Operational Research*, 177, 1317–1332.

Todd, P. M., & Brighton, H. (2016). Building the theory of ecological rationality. *Minds & Machines*, 26, 9–30.

Todd, P. M., & Gigerenzer, G. (2003). Bounding rationality to the world. *Journal of Economic Psychology*, 24, 143–165.

Todd, P. M., and Gigerenzer, G. (2020). The ecological rationality of situations: Behavior = *f*(Adaptive Toolbox, Environment). In J. F. Rauthmann, R. A. Sherman, & D. C. Funder (Eds.), *The Oxford handbook of psychological situations* (pp. 143–158). New York: Oxford University Press.

Todd, P. M., Gigerenzer, G., & the ABC Research Group (Eds.) (2012). *Ecological rationality: Intelligence in the world.* Oxford: Oxford University Press.

Todd, P. M., & Miller, G. F. (1999). From pride and prejudice to persuasion: Satisficing in mate search. In G. Gigerenzer, P. M. Todd, & the ABC Research Group (Eds.), *Simple heuristics that make us smart* (pp. 287–308). Oxford: Oxford University Press.

Tversky, A. (1972). Elimination by aspects: A theory of choice. *Psychological Review*, 79(4), 281–299.

Tversky, A., & Kahneman, D. (1974). Judgment under uncertainty: Heuristics and biases. *Science*, 185(4157), 1124–1131.

Wilke, A., Lydick, J., Bedell, V., Dawley, T., Treat, J., ... Langen, T. A. (2018). Spatial dependency in local resource distributions. *Evolutionary Behavioral Sciences*, 12(3), 163–172.

Yin, H. H., & Knowlton, B. J. (2006). The role of the basal ganglia in habit formation. *Nature Reviews: Neuroscience*, 7, 464–476.

20

MAPPING HEURISTICS AND PROSPECT THEORY

A study of theory integration

Thorsten Pachur

One of the most valuable methodological tools in the behavioral science repertoire is to build models of behavior. The predictions of the models can then be contrasted with data, either to refute a model or to refine it. Formal models often have adjustable parameters representing behaviorally relevant constructs, and variability on these constructs can be measured by fitting the models to empirical data.

Herbert Simon's (1956, 1990) idea of bounded rationality—according to which successful and adaptive behavior is shaped by the mind's natural limits with respect to information processing and computational power—has inspired two directions in the modeling of decision making. First, *prospect theory* (Kahneman & Tversky, 1979) and its subsequent elaboration and formal specification in *cumulative prospect theory* (CPT; Tversky & Kahneman, 1992) assume that people's sensitivity to differences in the outcomes and probabilities of risky options diminishes the further away those magnitudes are from natural reference points (such as zero, impossibility, or certainty) and that losses carry more psychological weight than gains. These notions are described algebraically with psycho-economic functions that translate objective magnitudes of outcomes and probabilities into subjective ones. CPT is typically considered an "as-if" model, in the sense these functions are not meant to represent the actual cognitive processes underlying choices. The second modeling tradition rooted in bounded rationality, by contrast, has developed *heuristics*, that are intended as cognitive process models. Heuristics implement bounded rationality by describing choices as being based on simplifying information processing operations, such as lexicographic search, difference thresholds, stopping rules, and limited search (e.g., Brandstätter, Gigerenzer, & Hertwig, 2006; Payne, Bettman, & Johnson, 1993; Thorngate, 1980; Venkatraman, Payne, & Huettel, 2014).

Despite their common theoretical roots, CPT and heuristics thus rely on very different conceptual languages—algebraic functions vs. simple information processing operations—to model boundedly rational decision making. Potentially due to these differences, there have been only few attempts to systematically connect the two approaches.[1] As a consequence, theoretical concepts for characterizing risky choice—such as probability weighting, risk aversion, and loss aversion—exist side-by-side with theoretical concepts characterizing heuristic cognitive processes—such as lexicographic search, difference thresholds, stopping rules, and one-reason

DOI: 10.4324/9781315658353-23

decision making (see below for details), with only little understanding of how these concepts relate to each other (but see Willemsen, Böckenholt, & Johnson, 2011). Moreover, it is little understood how heuristics might relate to empirical choice phenomena that have critically shaped the development of CPT. Take, as an example, the fourfold pattern of risk attitudes (other phenomena include the common ratio effect, the certainty effect, and reflection effect). The fourfold pattern refers to the finding that whether people appear risk averse or risk seeking shifts depending on whether the options offer positive or negative outcomes and whether the probability of the risky outcome is high or low. CPT accounts for the fourfold pattern by assuming distorted probability weighting, where rare events are overweighted and common events are underweighted (relative to their objective probabilities). But there might be other, more process-oriented accounts (e.g., heuristics) that can explain the fourfold pattern—a possibility that has hardly been pursued.

In this chapter I will illustrate how CPT and heuristics can be brought together to their mutual benefit. The analyses presented contribute to theory integration (e.g., Gigerenzer, 2017) by clarifying the relationship between the different theoretical concepts of CPT and heuristic decision making. For instance, I show that the typical assumption in CPT of distorted probability weighting can arise from a hallmark of heuristic processing: limited search. Conversely, CPT's conceptual language can be used to isolate and measure how properties of the choices produced by heuristics change across choice ecologies.

It should be emphasized that the primary goal of this theory integration is not to eventually merge the approaches in a unified theory. Instead, it aims to overcome the disintegration between alternative theoretical accounts of decisions under risk by contributing to a better understanding of how the frameworks overlap and how they complement each other in describing behavior. The field of risky choice is teeming with theories that together provide a rich conceptual repertoire to account for decisions under risk: in addition to heuristics and prospect theory, there are, for instance, the transfer-of-attention exchange model (e.g., Birnbaum, 2008), the security-potential aspiration model (Lopes & Oden, 1993), the proportional difference model (González-Vallejo, 2002), and decision field theory (Busemeyer & Townsend, 1993). Work on these theories, however, has mostly either focused on the performance of a single theory, or pitted some of these theories against each other. As a consequence, we know little of the extent to which the conceptual languages of these theories cover separate parts of the terrain or whether they overlap in their explanatory contribution. Importantly, the theory integration pursued here can also lead to new predictions. For instance, if heuristic choices can be reflected in nonlinear probability weighting, which in turn accounts for a particular choice phenomenon, insights into the boundary conditions of the use of the heuristics can used to predict moderating conditions for the emergence of the choice phenomenon. Eventually, a better understanding of the network between the theories might contribute to a unification of existing approaches, but this is not necessary for theory integration to be useful.

In the following, I first describe CPT and heuristics in more detail before presenting an analysis that shows how CPT accommodates the choices produced by various heuristics in the shapes of its weighting and value functions. I then illustrate how prominent choice phenomena that have shaped critical assumptions in CPT could arise from heuristic information processing. Finally, I highlight an important added value from this theory integration, namely, that insights about the contingent nature of heuristic information processing (e.g., Payne, 1976) can be used to derive novel predictions regarding moderating conditions for the occurrence of the choice phenomena.

Two modeling approaches for boundedly rational risky choice
Cumulative prospect theory

CPT was developed as an attempt to account for empirical violations of expected value (EV) and expected utility (EU) theory, such as the common ratio effect (also known as the Allais paradox; Allais, 1953), the fourfold pattern of risk attitudes, and the certainty effect. In EV theory, the valuation of a risky option A with outcomes

$$x_m > \dots > x_1 \geq 0 > y_1 > \dots > y_n$$

and corresponding probabilities

$$p_m \dots p_1 \text{ and } q_1 \dots q_n$$

follows from summing the outcomes, each weighted by its probability, i.e.,

$$EV = \sum_{i=1}^{N} x_i p_i.$$

In CPT, by contrast, it is assumed that outcomes and probabilities are subject to a nonlinear transformation. The transformation of outcomes is described by a value function that is defined as shown in Equation (20.1):

$$v(x) = x^\alpha$$
$$v(y) = -\lambda(-y)^\alpha$$

The parameter α governs how strongly differences in objective outcomes are reflected in differences in subjective value and thus indicates outcome sensitivity (with lower values indicating less sensitivity). Parameter λ reflects the relative weighting of losses and gains; with values of λ larger than 1, a higher weight is given to losses, indicating loss aversion. The left panel of Figure 20.1 depicts value functions for different values of α and λ.

The transformation of the outcomes' probabilities (more precisely, the rank-dependent, cumulative probability distribution) is described with a probability weighting function. A commonly used parameterization of the weighting function (see Goldstein & Einhorn, 1987) separates the curvature of the probability weighting function from its elevation and is defined as shown in Equation (20.2):

$$w^+ = \frac{\delta^+ p^{\gamma^+}}{\delta^+ p^{\gamma^+} + (1-p)^{\gamma^+}} \quad \text{for} \quad x$$

$$w^- = \frac{\delta^- p^{\gamma^-}}{\delta^- p^{\gamma^-} + (1-p)^{\gamma^-}} \quad \text{for} \quad y,$$

with γ^+ and γ^- governing the curvature of the weighting function in the gain and loss domains, respectively (in the following analyses, a common γ for both domains is estimated). Lower values on γ^+ and γ^- indicate greater curvature and thus lower sensitivity to probabilities. The parameters δ^+ and δ^- govern the elevation of the weighting function for gains and losses, respectively, and are often interpreted as indicating the degree of optimism thus risk seeking (e.g., Gonzalez & Wu, 1999). Higher values on δ^+ indicate higher risk seeking in the gain domain, higher values on δ^- indicate higher risk aversion in the loss domain. The right

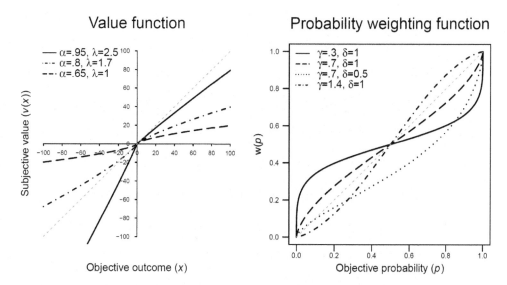

Figure 20.1 CPT's value function for different values of the outcome sensitivity (α) and loss aversion (λ) parameters (left); and the probability weighting function for different values of the probability-sensitivity (γ) and elevation (δ) parameters (right)

panel of Figure 20.1 depicts probability weighting functions for different values of the γ and δ parameters. Assuming these transformations of the objective outcomes and probabilities of risky options, as formalized in the value function and the weighting function, CPT can account for the violations of people's choices of EV and EU theory mentioned above (for a more extensive discussion of CPT, see Wakker, 2010).

Heuristics

Whereas CPT's value and weighting function are not meant to describe the cognitive processes leading to a choice, researchers following the heuristics approach use conceptual building blocks that acknowledge which mental operations actual decision makers are able to perform. These include lexicographic search (i.e., the sequential consideration of attributes, which in risky choice are the possible outcomes and their probabilities), within-attribute comparison of options, difference thresholds (i.e., boundaries indicating when two attribute values are to be treated as different), stopping rules (i.e., conditions under which information search is truncated), and one-reason decision making (i.e., basing a choice on a single attribute).

Table 20.1 gives an overview of five heuristics of risky choice. Some involve extremely simple processing and consider only a single attribute. Take, for instance, the minimax heuristic (e.g., Savage, 1954). In order to choose between options—each described by possible outcomes and their probabilities—minimax focuses exclusively on each option's worst possible outcome and chooses the option whose worst outcome is more attractive. All other attributes—that is, the other outcomes and all probabilities—are ignored. The least-likely heuristic (Thorngate, 1980) is somewhat more complex. Having likewise identified the worst possible outcome of each option in a first step, it bases its decision on the probability of that outcome, choosing the option whose worst possible outcome is least probable. The most-likely heuristic (Thorngate, 1980) also has a two-step structure: It first identifies each option's most likely outcome and then

Table 20.1 Five heuristics of risky choice

Heuristic	Description
Minimax	Choose the option with the highest minimum outcome.[1]
Maximax	Choose the option with the highest outcome.[1]
Least-likely	Identify each option's worst outcome. Then choose the option with the lowest probability of the worst outcome.[1]
Most-likely	Identify each option's most likely outcome. Then choose the option with the highest most likely outcome.[1]
Priority heuristic	Go through attributes in the following order: minimum gain, probability of minimum gain, and maximum gain. Stop examination if the minimum gains differ by 1/10 (or more) of the maximum gain; otherwise, stop examination if the probabilities differ by 1/10 (or more) of the probability scale. Choose the option with the more attractive gain (probability). For options with more than two outcomes, the search rule is identical, apart from the addition of a fourth reason: probability of maximum gain. For loss lotteries, "gains" are replaced by "losses." For mixed lotteries, "gains" are replaced by "outcomes."

Note: [1]If the decisive reason does not discriminate, the heuristic choses randomly. Heuristics are taken from Thorngate (1980) and Brandstätter et al. (2006).

chooses the option whose most likely outcome is more attractive. Finally, some heuristics implement difference thresholds (also known as aspiration levels) and involve conditional processing of attributes. The priority heuristic (Brandstätter et al., 2006), for example, first considers the options' minimum gain or loss, depending on the domain. If the two options differ sufficiently on that attribute (formalized by a difference threshold, defined as 10 percent of the maximum gain or loss), it chooses the option with the more attractive minimum outcome. If the difference between the options does not exceed the difference threshold, the priority heuristic moves on to the next attribute, the probabilities of the outcomes. If the probabilities differ by at least 10 percent (the difference threshold for the probability attribute), the heuristic chooses the option with the lower probability of the minimum outcome; otherwise, it moves on to the next attribute, the maximum outcome, and chooses the option that is most attractive on that attribute.

Mapping heuristics onto CPT

How could CPT and heuristics—despite using very different modeling frameworks to describe people's decisions under risk—be related to each other? Gigerenzer (2017) has sketched out an approach to theory integration. Rather than submitting theories to critical tests (e.g., Popper, [1934] 1959) or pitting them against each other, the goal is to build networks between theories, integrating and connecting empirical phenomena and theoretical concepts, in order to achieve greater coherence in a field, identifying alternative routes to explain the same behavior or to see how they complement each other.

So how can heuristics and CPT be meaningfully integrated? Different heuristics make different assumptions about which attributes are considered, the order in which attributes are considered, and which attribute determines a choice. As a consequence, they also differ in the priority they give to probability information and to the minimum and maximum outcomes. The crucial idea is now to use CPT to measure theoretical properties of the heuristics' choices, such as the degree of probability sensitivity, risk aversion, and loss aversion. Differences between the heuristics on these theoretical properties can then be linked to differences in the heuristics' information processing architectures. Elaborating these connections therefore helps to illuminate how CPT's theoretical constructs, and key empirical phenomena (e.g., fourfold pattern) that have shaped CPT, might be related to information processing principles. I next describe such a theory-integration analysis of CPT and heuristics.

What shapes of CPT's weighting and value function do heuristics produce?

In order to understand how heuristics map onto the conceptual framework of CPT, Pachur, Suter, and Hertwig (2017) investigated how the choices produced by the heuristics described in Table 20.1 would be reflected in CPT's weighting and value functions. To that end, they estimated the shapes of functions that reproduce, as best as possible, the heuristics' choices. The results, shown in Figure 20.2, indicate that the five heuristics gave rise to very distinct value and weighting functions.[2] For instance, the choices of the minimax and the maximax heuristics were accommodated in CPT by assuming very strongly curved weighting functions (upper row of Figure 20.2), indicating very low probability sensitivity. Importantly, this result is consistent with the heuristics' information processing architecture, which completely ignores probability information. For minimax, moreover, the elevation of the resulting weighting function was very low for gains and very high for losses, indicating generally high risk aversion. For maximax, the pattern was reversed, indicating generally high risk seeking. For the priority heuristic, the curvature of the weighting function was not quite as pronounced as for minimax and maximax, indicating higher probability sensitivity—again consistent with the fact that the heuristic considers probability information when the first-ranked attribute does not discriminate between the options (this was the case in around 20 percent of the choice problems used in the analysis). The weighting functions estimated for the choices of the least-likely and most-likely heuristics, finally, showed the least pronounced curvature, indicating high probability sensitivity and therefore accurately reflecting that these heuristics always consider probability information (though in different ways).

The lower row of Figure 20.2 shows CPT's value functions that best describe the choices produced by the heuristics. Here as well there were considerable differences between the heuristics, and these differences were consistent with the differences between the heuristics in terms of how their information processing architectures treat outcome information: the least-likely heuristic, which never bases its choices on outcomes, yields a very strongly curved value function, indicating very low outcome sensitivity. The minimax, maximax, and most-likely heuristics, for all of which outcomes are the decisive attribute, have a less curved value function, indicating high outcome sensitivity.

These results highlight two things. First, they demonstrate that CPT's weighting and value functions, though not meant to represent cognitive mechanisms, can meaningfully measure characteristics of the cognitive mechanism underlying choices: Choices produced by heuristics whose information processing architecture implement different degrees of attention to probabilities and outcomes are accommodated in CPT by systematic differences in the curvature of the weighting and value functions, respectively, with lower attention giving rise to stronger curvatures. Pachur et al. (2017) showed the CPT profiles produced by different heuristics are sufficiently distinct from each other to allow differentiating which heuristic produced a set of choices. Second, it is not necessary to assume differential distributions of attention at the high and low ends of the probability scale to produce overweighting of rare and underweighting of common events (e.g., Bordalo, Gennaioli, & Shleifer, 2012; Hogarth & Einhorn, 1990).

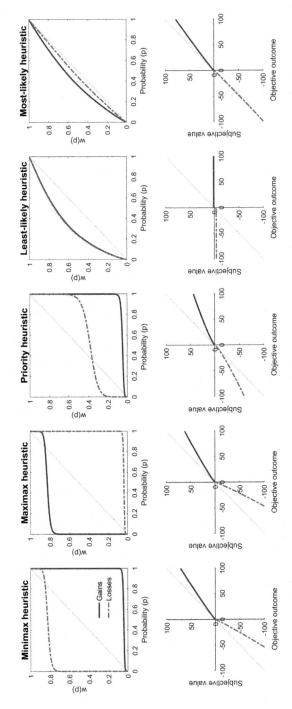

Figure 20.2 CPT's weighting function (upper row) and value functions (lower row) estimated for the choices of the five heuristics described in Table 20.1

Instead, this pattern can arise from a single cognitive mechanism, namely, reduced attention to *any* probability information (for other proposals, see Bhatia, 2014; Johnson & Busemeyer, 2016). This means that the apparent overweighting of low-probability events can, ironically, result from underattending to low probabilities.

Characterizing changes in the behavior of heuristics across environments

In some heuristics, the character of the choices they produce depends on the structure of the environment. For instance, in the priority heuristic, whether a choice is made based on a probability attribute depends on whether the minimum outcomes in a decision problem differ sufficiently. In the most-likely heuristic, whether the option it chooses has a very attractive or a rather unattractive outcome depends on which of the two outcomes is more likely—and thus whether and how outcomes and probabilities are correlated. In the following, I show how the CPT framework can make visible and measure these interdependencies between environmental structures and the properties of heuristic choices.

One fundamental property of choice behavior is the strength of the tendency to pick or to avoid the more risky option—that is, how risk-seeking or risk-averse choices are. A common measure of an option's risk is the *coefficient of variation* (CV; e.g., Weber, Shafir, & Blais, 2004), with a higher CV indicating higher risk.[3] In CPT, the tendency to choose the riskier option is reflected in the elevation of the weighting function. To see how the apparent risk attitude—defined as the willingness to choose the option with a higher CV—produced by heuristics might differ across environments, let us first consider the minimax heuristic. As mentioned above, minimax produces strongly risk-averse (risk-seeking) choices in the gain (loss) domain; the opposite holds for maximax. The high level of risk aversion and risk seeking, respectively, generated by these heuristics is due to their focus on extreme outcomes (either the minimum or the maximum outcome). The option with the more attractive minimum outcome (which minimax chooses) is usually the less risky one, because (unless it is a dominating option) its maximum outcome is usually rather unattractive (and the range of outcomes of that option is usually smaller, yielding a lower CV). The option with the more attractive maximum outcome (which maximax chooses) is usually the more risky one, because its minimum outcome is usually rather unattractive (and the range of outcomes thus rather large, yielding a higher CV).

Minimax and maximax give rise to risk aversion and risk seeking, respectively, irrespective of the degree to which outcomes and probabilities are correlated, a key property of decision environments (e.g., Pleskac & Hertwig, 2014). But consider the most-likely heuristic. Recall that it first identifies each option's most likely outcome and then picks the option where that outcome is more attractive. In environments in which the magnitudes of outcomes and their probabilities are negatively correlated, the most likely outcome of the option chosen by the most-likely heuristic is usually also the minimum one in the gain domain and the maximum one in the loss domain. As a consequence, the heuristic should produce risk-averse choices in the gain domain and risk-seeking choices in the loss domain in such environments. Importantly, the regularity that the most likely outcome is also the minimum gain (or the maximum loss) does not hold in an uncorrelated environment, where the magnitude of the outcomes and their probabilities are not correlated; here, the heuristic should thus produce neither systematically risk-averse or risk-seeking, but risk-neutral choices. In other words, the risk attitude produced by the most-likely heuristic is contingent on the structure of the environment.

CPT can make visible such contingent risk attitudes of heuristics through the elevation of the probability weighting function, governed by the parameter δ (see Equation 20.2). In Pachur et al. (2017), we measured the dependency of the most-likely heuristic's degree of risk

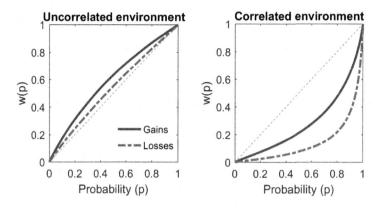

Figure 20.3 Probability weighting functions estimated for choices produced by the most-likely heuristic, separately for an environment in which the magnitudes of outcomes and probabilities were uncorrelated (left panel) and an environment in which the magnitudes of outcomes and probabilities were negatively correlated (right panel).

aversion on the structure of the environment by estimating CPT's weighting and value function for choices produced by the heuristic, separately for an environment in which outcomes and probabilities were negatively correlated (within a decision problem) and an environment in which outcomes and probabilities were uncorrelated. Figure 20.3 shows the resulting weighting functions (the elevation parameter δ was estimated separately for the probabilities of gain and loss outcomes). As can be seen, the most-likely heuristic produced distinct shapes in the two environments, mainly driven by differences in the elevation parameter. In the uncorrelated environment, the weighting function was approximately linear (and δ close to 1), indicating that the heuristic produced risk-neutral choices. In the correlated environment, by contrast, the elevation was very low (and δ rather small), indicating strong risk aversion in the gain domain and strong risk seeking in the loss domain. The other heuristics in Table 20.1 did not show such contingency in the risk attitudes (see Pachur et al., 2017, for details).

To summarize, the parametric measurement framework of CPT makes it possible to track how the behavior of heuristics is affected (or not) by the structure of the environment. Although the qualitative shift in the risk attitude of the most-likely heuristic across environments that we observed in the present analysis could, in principle, also be derived without invoking CPT, CPT has the advantage that it also captures more gradual changes in behavior in response to more gradual changes in the structure of the environment (e.g., correlations between outcomes and probabilities of different strengths).

Connecting phenomena

The previous section has shown how theory integration between CPT and heuristics can be achieved by mapping the two theoretical frameworks onto each other. Another route to theory integration is to connect empirical phenomena that are rooted in different theoretical traditions (Gigerenzer, 2017). In this section, I apply this approach for CPT and heuristics, considering the aforementioned fourfold pattern of risk attitudes (Tversky & Kahneman, 1992; Tversky & Fox, 1995). The fourfold pattern has played an important role in the development of CPT and is illustrated in Table 20.2. When the risky option offers a gain with a relatively high probability, people display risk aversion, with the majority choosing a safe option over a risky option.

Table 20.2 The fourfold pattern of risk attitudes

Probability level	Domain	
	Gains	Losses
Low	$32, .1; $0, .9 vs. $3, 1 Risk seeking (48%)[a]	−$32, .1; $0, .9 vs. −$3, 1 Risk aversion (36%)
High	$4, .8; $0, .2 vs. $3, 1 Risk aversion (36%)	−$4, .8; $0, .2 vs. −$3, 1 Risk seeking (72%)

Notes:
Typical risk attitude observed for the lottery problems, containing a safe option and a risky option with the specific combination of probability level and domain. the percentages in brackets indicate the proportions of choices of the risky option in Hertwig, Barron, Weber, and Erev (2004).

a Although this particular choice proportion observed in Hertwig et al. (2004) does not represent risk seeking, risk seeking is often observed for other choice problems of the same type—in particular, when risk attitudes are estimated with certainty equivalents (e.g., Tversky & Fox, 1995; Tversky & Kahneman, 1992; for a discussion, see Harbaugh, Krause, & Vesterlund, 2010).

When the risky gain has a low probability, choices are more risk seeking, in that the willingness to choose the risky option is increased. In the loss domain, the opposite holds (i.e., people are risk seeking for low-probability losses and risk averse for high-probability losses).

CPT accounts for the fourfold pattern with its assumption of an inverse S-shaped weighting function, where low-probability events are overweighted and high-probability events are underweighted relative to their objective probabilities. As Brandstätter et al. (2006) showed, however, the fourfold pattern is also consistent with heuristic information processing. Specifically, it can follow from the heuristic principles of lexicographic processing, difference thresholds, stopping rules, and one-reason decision making implemented by the priority heuristic. Here is how, starting with the choice problem with a low-probability gain. Comparing a safe gain of $3 with a 1 percent chance of winning $32, the priority heuristic starts by comparing the options' minimum gains: $3 for the safe option and $0 for the risky option. Because the difference between these two outcomes does not exceed the difference threshold of 10 percent of the maximum gain ($3 < $32 ⋆ .1 = $3.2), the priority heuristic next compares the probabilities of the minimum gains. Because for the risky option this probability is lower than for the safe option (.9 < 1), the risky option is chosen, giving rise to risk-seeking behavior. For the choice problem with a high-probability gain, the choice is made on the first attribute, the minimum gain, because the difference between the options on that attribute exceeds the difference threshold ($3 > $4 ⋆ .1 = $0.4), and the safe option is chosen, giving rise to risk-averse behavior. In the problem with a low-probability loss, the priority heuristic first compares the minimum losses. Because this attribute does not discriminate between the options ($3 < $32 ⋆.1 = $3.2), the heuristic next considers the probabilities of the minimum losses. The safe option has a higher probability (1 > .9) and is thus picked, leading to risk aversion. In the problem with a high-probability loss, the heuristic makes a decision on the first attribute, the minimum loss, because the difference between the options on that attribute exceeds the difference threshold ($3 > $4 ⋆ .1 = $0.4); the risky option is chosen because its minimum loss is smaller ($0 < −$3), leading to risk seeking.

This example illustrates how empirical phenomena that have shaped key assumptions in CPT—such as an inverse S-shaped weighting function—could also arise from heuristic information processing. It thereby also points to the cognitive mechanisms behind these hallmark features in CPT. Specifically, the apparent overweighting of low-probability events and underweighting of high-probability events can result from key principles of heuristic information processing: lexicographic search, difference thresholds, stopping rules, and one-reason decision making. Brandstätter et al. (2006) illustrate how also the possibility effect, the common ratio effect, the reflection effect, and the certainty effect are consistent with the information-processing architecture of the priority heuristic.

One interesting implication of building bridges between heuristics and these empirical choice phenomena is that insights about the boundary conditions of heuristic information processing can also cast light on potential moderators of the choice phenomena, allowing respective hypotheses to be formulated. For instance, Pachur, Hertwig, and Wolkewitz (2014; see also Suter, Pachur, & Hertwig, 2016) showed that the neglect of probability information in risky choice is more pronounced when outcomes are affect-rich (e.g., averse medical side-effects) than when they are affect-poor (e.g., moderate amounts of monetary losses). Higher probability neglect is associated with a more pronounced curvature of CPT's weighting function, which is in turn related to the strength of the fourfold pattern. It follows that the fourfold pattern could be more pronounced when outcomes are affect-rich than when they are affect-poor—a prediction that only emerges once CPT and heuristics have been connected.

Conclusion

This chapter has illustrated the potential of bringing together CPT and heuristics—two models of boundedly rational decision making formulated in very different conceptual languages and with very different modeling goals. In addition to building a network between CPT and heuristics, a further benefit of this theory integration is that it forges connections between the influential parametric framework of CPT and process-tracing methods that originated in work on heuristics (see Pachur, Schulte-Mecklenbeck, Murphy, & Hertwig, 2018). But theory integration can also accentuate aspects in which the two approaches diverge. For instance, whereas the algebraic framework of CPT, based on continuous functions, enforces transitive choice patterns, the conditional nature of the information search of lexicographic heuristics, such as the priority heuristic, can lead to intransitive choices (see also Tversky, 1969).

It is important to emphasize again that theory integration does not seek to replace one approach with the other—even if one approach may in some respects be descriptively superior to the other. Rather, theory-integration analyses are complementary, taking into account that each approach has its relative strengths and limitations. CPT has been shown to be often more versatile than heuristics in predicting choices across a large range of choice problems (e.g., Glöckner & Pachur, 2012; but see Mohnert, Pachur, & Lieder, 2019). Conversely, process analyses have obtained clear evidence for heuristic processes (e.g., Mann & Ball, 1994; Pachur et al., 2013; Payne & Braunstein, 1978; Su et al., 2013; Venkatraman et al., 2014). Thus, based on the respective merits of each approach, insights from integrating CPT and heuristics will eventually contribute to making both approaches more complete and guide further theory development.

In conclusion, although the development of new models is without doubt important, it is also crucial to take stock of existing models and to elaborate the conceptual network that connects them; as argued in this chapter, this can even lead to novel predictions, highlighting how different models can enrich each other. Such theory integration can target qualitatively different modeling frameworks, as presented in this chapter (see also Bhatia, 2017, for analyses relating heuristics with connectionist models), but is equally applicable and informative for relating models with similar roots (e.g., different types of diffusion models; Khodadadi & Townsend, 2015). It is time to dissolve the boundaries that have separated accounts of bounded rationality and to progress toward a more comprehensive perspective of how the mind, and models of it, work.

Acknowledgments

The author thanks Veronika Zilker and Julia Groß for constructive comments on a previous draft of this chapter, and Susannah Goss for editing the manuscript.

Notes

1 Kahneman and Tversky (1979) proposed heuristic editing operations (e.g., cancellation, segregation, combination) that people might apply before evaluating lotteries, but these operations were barely investigated further. Moreover, whenever CPT and heuristics of risky choice have been considered within the same analysis, they have been treated as rival accounts (e.g., Brandstätter et al., 2006; Fiedler, 2010; Glöckner & Herbold, 2011; Glöckner & Pachur, 2012; Pachur, Hertwig, Gigerenzer, & Brandstätter, 2013; Su et al., 2013).
2 Unsurprisingly, CPT cannot mimic the heuristics' choices perfectly. Moreover, there are differences between the heuristics in how well CPT can capture their choices. For instance, CPT accommodated the choices by minimax and maximax heuristics better than those of the least-likely heuristic. See Pachur et al. (2017) for more details.
3 The CV is a standardized measure of risk and expresses the amount of risk per unit of return. It is a function of the outcomes and probabilities of an option, and is larger, the larger the range and the more skewed the distribution of possible outcomes. In addition, *ceteris paribus*, the CV is larger, the more the distribution of probabilities is similarly skewed as the distribution of outcomes, but in the opposite direction.

Specifically, the CV is defined as the standard deviation of an option, $\sigma = \sqrt{\sum_{i=1}^{N} x_i^2 \times p_i - \left(\sum_{i=1}^{N} x_i \times p_i\right)^2}$,

with N outcomes x and probabilities p, divided by the absolute value of the option's expected value.

References

Allais, M. (1953). Le comportement de l'homme rationel devant le risque: Critique des postulats et axioms de l'école americaine [Rational man's behavior in face of risk: Critique of the American School's postulates and axioms]. *Econometrica*, 21, 503–546.

Bhatia, S. (2014). Sequential sampling and paradoxes of risky choice. *Psychonomic Bulletin & Review*, 21, 1095–1111.

Bhatia, S. (2017). Choice rules and accumulator networks. *Decision*, 4, 146–170.

Birnbaum, M. H., & Chavez, A. (1997). Tests of theories of decision making: Violations of branch independence and distribution independence. *Organizational Behavior and Human Decision Processes*, 71, 161–194.

Busemeyer, J. R., & Townsend, J. T. (1993). Decision field-theory: A dynamic cognitive approach to decision making in an uncertain environment. *Psychological Review*, 100, 432–459.

Bordalo, P., Gennaioli, N., & Shleifer, A. (2012). Salience theory of choice under risk. *Quarterly Journal of Economics*, 127, 1243–1285.

Brandstätter, E., Gigerenzer, G., & Hertwig, R. (2006). The priority heuristic: Making choices without trade-offs. *Psychological Review*, 113, 409–432.

Fiedler, K. (2010). How to study cognitive decision algorithms: The case of the priority heuristic. *Judgment and Decision Making*, 5, 21–32.

Gigerenzer, G. (2017). A theory integration program. *Decision*, 4, 133–145.

Glöckner, A., & Herbold, A.-K. (2011). An eye-tracking study on information processing in risky decisions: Evidence for compensatory strategies based on automatic processes. *Journal of Behavioral Decision Making*, 24, 71–98.

Glöckner, A., & Pachur, T. (2012). Cognitive models of risky choice: Parameter stability and predictive accuracy of prospect theory. *Cognition*, 123, 21–32.

Goldstein, W. M., & Einhorn, H. J. (1987). Expression theory and the preference reversal phenomenon. *Psychological Review*, 94, 236–254.

Gonzalez, R., & Wu, G. (1999). On the shape of the probability weighting function. *Cognitive Psychology*, 38, 129–166.

González-Vallejo, C. (2002). Making trade-offs: A probabilistic and context-sensitive model of choice behavior. *Psychological Review*, 109, 137–154.

Harbaugh, W. T., Krause, K., & Vesterlund, L. (2010). The fourfold pattern of risk attitudes in choice and pricing tasks. *The Economic Journal*, 120, 595–611.

Hertwig, R., Barron, G., Weber, E. U., & Erev, I. (2004). Decisions from experience and the effect of rare events in risky choice. *Psychological Science*, 15, 534–539.

Hogarth, R. M., & Einhorn, H. J. (1990). Venture theory: A model of decision weights. *Management Science*, 36, 780–803.

Johnson, J. J., & Busemeyer, J. R. (2016). A computational model of the attention process in risky choice. *Decision*, 3, 254–280.

Kahneman, D., & Tversky, A. (1979). Prospect theory: An analysis of decision under risk. *Econometrica*, 47, 263–291.

Kahneman, D., & Tversky, A. (Eds.). (2000). *Choices, values, and frames*. Cambridge: Cambridge University Press.

Khodadadi, A., & Townsend, J. T. (2015). On mimicry among sequential sampling models. *Journal of Mathematical Psychology*, 68–69, 37–48.

Mann, L., & Ball, C. (1994). The relationship between search strategy and risky choice. *Australian Journal of Psychology*, 46, 131–136.

Mohnert, F., Pachur, T., & Lieder, F. (2019). What's in the adaptive toolbox and how do people choose from it? Rational models of strategy selection in risky choice. In A., Goel, C. Seifert, & C. Freksa, (Eds.), *Proceedings of the 41st Annual Meeting of the Cognitive Science Society* (pp. 2378–2384). London: Cognitive Science Society.

Pachur, T., Hertwig, R., Gigerenzer, G., & Brandstätter, E. (2013). Testing process predictions of models of risky choice: A quantitative model comparison approach. *Frontiers in Psychology*, 4, 646.

Pachur, T., Hertwig, R., & Wolkewitz, R. (2014). The affect gap in risky choice: Affect-rich outcomes attenuate attention to probability information. *Decision*, 1, 64–78.

Pachur, T., Schulte-Mecklenbeck, M., Murphy, R. O., & Hertwig, R. (2018). Prospect theory reflects selective allocation of attention. *Journal of Experimental Psychology: General*, 147, 147–169.

Pachur, T., Suter, R. S., & Hertwig, R. (2017). How the twain can meet: Prospect theory and models of heuristics in risky choice. *Cognitive Psychology*, 93, 44–73.

Payne, J. W. (1976). Task complexity and contingent processing in decision making: An information search and protocol analysis. *Organizational Behavior and Human Performance*, 16, 366–387.

Payne, J. W., & Braunstein, M. L. (1978). Risky choice: An examination of information acquisition behavior. *Memory and Cognition*, 6, 554–561.

Payne, J. W., Bettman, J. R., & Johnson, E. J. (1993). *The adaptive decision maker*. Cambridge: Cambridge University Press.

Pleskac, T. J., & Hertwig, R. (2014). Ecologically rational choice and the structure of the environment. *Journal of Experimental Psychology General*, 143, 2000–2019.

Popper, K. R. ([1934)] 1959). *The logic of scientific discovery*. London Hutchinson.

Savage, L. J. (1954). *The foundations of statistics*. New York: Wiley.

Simon, H. A. (1956). Rational choice and the structure of the environment. *Psychological Review*, 63, 129–138.

Simon, H. A. (1990). Invariants of human behavior. *Annual Review of Psychology*, 41, 1–19.

Su, Y., Rao, L., Sun, H., Du, X., Li, X., & Li, S. (2013). Is making a risky choice based on a weighting and adding process? An eye-tracking investigation. *Journal of Experimental Psychology: Learning, Memory and Cognition*, 39, 1765–1780.

Suter, R. S., Pachur, T., & Hertwig, R. (2016). How affect shapes risky choice: Distorted probability weighting versus probability neglect. *Journal of Behavioral Decision Making*, 29, 437–449.

Thorngate, W. (1980). Efficient decision heuristics. *Behavioral Science*, 25, 219–225.

Tversky, A. (1969). Intransitivity of preference. *Psychological Review*, 76, 31–48.

Tversky, A., & Fox, C. R. (1995). Weighing risk and uncertainty. *Psychological Review*, 102, 269–283.

Tversky, A., & Kahneman, D. (1992). Advances in prospect theory: Cumulative representation of uncertainty. *Journal of Risk and Uncertainty*, 5, 297–323.

Venkatraman, V., Payne, J. W., & Huettel, S. A. (2014). An overall probability of winning heuristic for complex risky decisions: Choice and eye fixation evidence. *Organizational Behavior and Human Decision Processes*, 125, 73–87.

Wakker, P. P. (2010). *Prospect theory for risk and ambiguity*. Cambridge: Cambridge University Press.

Weber, E. U., Shafir, S., & Blais, A. R. (2004). Predicting risk sensitivity in humans and lower animals: Risk as variance or coefficient of variation. *Psychological Review*, 111, 430–445.

Willemsen, M. C., Böckenholt, U., & Johnson, E. J. (2011). Choice by value encoding and value construction: Processes of loss aversion. *Journal of Experimental Psychology: General*, 140, 303–324.

21

BOUNDED RATIONALITY FOR ARTIFICIAL INTELLIGENCE

Özgür Şimşek

The capabilities of Artificial Intelligence (AI) systems have grown tremendously in recent years. For instance, in the ancient board game of Go, which was long seen as a grand challenge for AI, the best player in the world is now a computer program (Silver et al., 2018). What is impressive is not only the level of performance attained in the game but also the fact that the program learned how to play on its own, starting with only rudimentary knowledge about the rules of the game. In fact, the same program learned to master other board games, including chess and shogi, using the same learning algorithm. Reinforcement learning, the AI approach employed to train the system, holds great promise for the future. It allows artificial agents to learn from their own experience, through trial and error, without relying on advice from human experts. Not only does this require minimal effort from system designers but it also makes it possible for the resulting system to surpass human experts in performance.

Reinforcement learning is not a new approach to AI. It has had many notable successes in the past. For example, more than 20 years ago, reinforcement learning was used to develop a program that learned how to play backgammon, another ancient board game beloved in many regions of the world (Tesauro, 1995). This program was arguably the best backgammon player in the world at the time.

While the successes of AI are truly exciting, it must be noted that the intelligence developed by current systems is effective in very narrow environments. For example, the game of Go is a highly confined environment with a very small number of well-defined rules that never change. In contrast, people and animals function effectively in a world that is complex, dynamic, and deeply uncertain. Furthermore, existing AI systems require very large amounts of experience in order to achieve high levels of performance. In contrast, people and animals can learn from much smaller amounts of experience, sometimes even from a single piece of experience. In board games such as Go, a program can easily play millions of games with itself to improve its performance. But, in many real-world problems, obtaining such huge amounts of experience is simply not possible.

Why have the capabilities of AI systems grown so tremendously in recent years? The most fundamental reason is the vast increase in the speed of computation. Going forward, further technological advances will enable even faster computation, continuing to extend the

DOI: 10.4324/9781315658353-24

capabilities of our AI systems. But it is unlikely that the performance gap between people and AI can be closed by advances in computational speed only. Just like people and animals, our machines will need to learn how to be boundedly rational, in other words, how to achieve their objectives when time, computational resources, and information are limited.

Models of bounded rationality (Simon, 1956; Rubinstein, 1998; Gigerenzer & Selten, 2002) provide fertile ground for developing algorithmic ideas for creating such AI systems. Early work in AI was in fact rooted in this view of bounded rationality. In their work on problem solving, Newell, Shaw and Simon (1958) modelled reasoning as search and suggested that the search space could be made tractable and navigated by using heuristics. The same approach was also used in modelling the processes of scientific discovery (Langley, Shaw, & Simon, 1987). Since these early years, the theory of bounded rationality has advanced considerably, with contributions from diverse fields, including cognitive psychology, economics, and operations research. During this time, machine intelligence grew in leaps and bounds in many areas, including probabilistic reasoning and statistical learning, but it had limited contact with new advances in bounded rationality.

This chapter will provide an overview of some the more recent research in bounded rationality and discuss its implications for AI. The discussion will start with one-shot comparison problems and two families of simple heuristics (Gigerenzer, Todd, & the ABC Research Group, 1999; Gigerenzer, Hertwig, & Pachur, 2011) that can be used in that context: tallying and lexicographic decision rules. I will describe how these heuristics perfectly match certain characteristics of natural environments that allow them to make accurate decisions using relatively small amounts of information and computation. The discussion will then progress to how this knowledge can be applied in the context of sequential decision problems, of which the game of Go is an example, to reduce the branching factor in a simple and transparent manner. I will describe how, using ideas from the literature on bounded rationality, it was possible to reduce the average branching factor in the game of Tetris from 17 to 1 (Şimşek et al., 2016).[1] The branching factor shows the number of alternative actions at a decision point. It is one of the fundamental reasons why AI remains a challenge. This drastic reduction is therefore significant, especially because the approach is not specific to Tetris but is applicable to sequential decision problems broadly. Furthermore, the reasons for eliminating the vast majority of branches are easy to explain, making the approach transparent, a property that is becoming increasingly more desirable, even critical, in AI systems.

The comparison problem

People and animals spend much of their time comparing alternatives available to them. For example, a tiger may compare various prey in its vicinity to determine which one to attack, a venture capitalist may compare various companies to determine which one to invest in, and an ant colony may compare various nest areas to determine where to settle. In all of these cases, the true criterion for selection is unavailable—for example, the venture capitalist does not know the future return on investment—but a decision must still be made using the available information.

We will first examine a one-shot version of this decision problem. Specifically, we will define the comparison problem as follows: Determine which of a given number of objects has the highest value on a specified (but unobserved) criterion, given the values of a number of attributes on the objects. For example, which of two stocks will bring a larger return on investment five years from now, given known attributes of the stocks such as type of industry, current value, and return on investment in the last three months?

One common approach to the comparison problem is to estimate the criterion as a function of the attributes of the object, for example, as a linear function:

$$\hat{y} = w_0 + w_1 x_1 + \ldots + w_k x_k, \tag{21.1}$$

where $\hat{y}$ is the estimate of the criterion, $x_1, \ldots, x_k$ are the attribute values, w_0 is a constant, and $w_1, \ldots, w_k$ are attribute weights. This estimate leads to the following decision rule in choosing between objects A and B:

$$\text{Choose object } A \text{ if } w_0 + w_1 \left(x_1^A - x_1^B \right) + \ldots + w_k \left(x_k^A - x_k^B \right) > 0,$$

$$\text{choose object } B \text{ if } w_0 + w_1 \left(x_1^A - x_1^B \right) + \ldots + w_k \left(x_k^A - x_k^B \right) < 0,$$

$$\text{choose randomly if } w_0 + w_1 \left(x_1^A - x_1^B \right) + \ldots + w_k \left(x_k^A - x_k^B \right) = 0.$$

Comparison using simple decision heuristics

Alternatively, one can compare objects using decision heuristics. These are simple methods that use few pieces of information and combine the pieces in simple ways. We will focus on two well-known and widely used families of heuristics: lexicographic decision rules and tallying.

Lexicographic decision rules examine attributes one at a time, in a specific order, until an attribute is found that discriminates between the two objects. An attribute is said to *discriminate* between two objects if its value differs on the two objects. The first discriminating attribute, and that attribute alone, is used to make the decision. In other words, a lexicographic decision rule orders the attributes in importance and decides based on only the most important attribute on which the alternatives differ.

Lexicographic decision rules are *noncompensatory*. That is, differences in the value of one attribute, no matter how large, cannot compensate for any difference in the value of an attribute ranked higher in importance. For example, if quality is ranked more important than price, a lower price cannot compensate for a difference in quality: the selected item will be the one with the highest quality, regardless of the cost.

While lexicographic decision rules use the attributes one at a time, starting with the most important attribute, tallying uses all attributes simultaneously, giving them equal weight. If attributes are binary, taking on values of 0 or 1, tallying is equivalent to a majority vote, where each attribute either votes for one alternative over the other (if one alternative is higher in attribute value) or abstains from voting (if alternatives are identical in attribute value).

Tallying has a long history of use and has been known to perform well in many contexts, especially when generalizing to previously unseen decision problems (Dawes & Corrigan, 1974; Dawes, 1979; Einhorn & Hogarth, 1975). Competitive testing of lexicographic decision rules is more recent and has shown similar results (e.g., Czerlinski, Gigerenzer, & Goldstein, 1999).

Over the years, both families of heuristics have been compared to various statistical learning methods, including linear regression, naïve Bayes, Bayesian networks, support vector machines, nearest-neighbor methods, decision trees, and neural networks. The result that emerges from these studies is that decision heuristics can compete remarkably well with more complex statistical methods, outperforming them on many occasions, especially when there is a small number of training examples (Brighton, 2006; Katsikopoulos, 2011; Şimşek & Buckmann, 2015; Buckmann & Şimşek, 2017). These results have stimulated a rich scientific literature on how, and under what conditions, simple heuristics can yield accurate decisions.

When are decision heuristics accurate?

This question has been explored from various viewpoints in the scientific literature. One productive viewpoint has been to examine decision heuristics as approximations to the linear decision rule, asking the following question: If the environment is linear, in other words, if the relationship between the criterion and the attributes is linear as reflected by Equation (21.1), do various heuristics yield accurate decisions? Research has shown that they do, under at least three conditions: simple dominance (Hogarth and Karelaia, 2006), cumulative dominance (Kirkwood and Sarin, 1985; Baucells et al., 2008), and noncompensatoriness (Martignon and Hoffrage, 2002; Katsikopoulos and Martignon, 2006; Şimşek, 2013). Furthermore, evidence suggests that these conditions are prevalent in natural environments (Şimşek, 2013). What follows is a description of these conditions in some detail, followed by a simple illustrative example.

Assume that the relationship between the criterion and the attributes is linear as shown in Equation (21.1). Let x_i^A denote the value of attribute i for object A. Let the direction of attribute i, denoted by d_i, equal -1, 0, or $+1$, respectively, if the corresponding attribute weight is negative, zero, or positive. Let attribute order refer to the order in which $|w_i|$ decrease. Finally, recall that an attribute is said to discriminate between two objects if its value differs on the two objects.

We will assume that the values of attribute weights are not known, so the linear decision rule cannot be applied directly. The question we will explore is whether it is still possible to make decisions that are identical to those of the linear decision rule. In particular, we will explore whether it is possible to do so using simple decision heuristics such as tallying or lexicographic decision rules. These heuristics do not need or use attribute weights but they do require some knowledge about the environment. Specifically, tallying requires that attribute directions are known while the lexicographic decision rule requires that both attribute directions and attribute order are known.

To simplify exposition, and without loss of generality, discussion of the three conditions below assumes that the attributes are ordered such that the sequence $|w_1|,\ldots,|w_k|$ is non-increasing.

1 Simple dominance. Object A simply dominates object B if $\forall i \left(d_i x_i^A \geq d_i x_i^B \right)$ and $\exists i \left(d_i x_i^A > d_i x_i^B \right)$. Objects A and B are dominance equivalent if $\forall i \left(d_i x_i^A = d_i x_i^B \right)$. If object A simply dominates object B, it follows that object A has the higher criterion value. If two objects are dominance equivalent, they have identical criterion values. To check for simple dominance, it suffices to know attribute directions; the exact values of the attribute weights or their order are not needed. Simple dominance is a very useful condition. When it is present, most decision heuristics choose accurately if their attribute directions are accurate. These include tallying and the lexicographic decision rule with any ordering of the attributes.

2 Cumulative dominance. Let $z_i = \sum_{j=1}^{i} d_j x_j$, $i = 1,\ldots,k$, denote the cumulative profile of an object.

Object A cumulatively dominates object B if $\forall i \left(z_i^A \geq z_i^B \right)$ and $\exists i \left(z_i^A > z_i^B \right)$. If object A cumulatively dominates object B, it follows that object A has the higher criterion value. To check for cumulative dominance, it suffices to know the attribute directions and order;

the exact values of attribute weights are not needed. When cumulative dominance is present, the lexicographic decision rule decides accurately if its attribute directions and order are set accurately, and tallying decides accurately if its attribute directions are set accurately, with one exception: tallying may find a tie even though one of the decision alternatives actually has a higher criterion value than the other one.

3   Noncompensatoriness. Consider the following lexicographic decision rule: examine the attributes in non-increasing absolute value of their weights; identify the first attribute that discriminates between the objects; choose the object whose value on this attribute is more favorable (that is, higher if attribute direction is positive, and lower if negative). If this lexicographic decision rule decides correctly, the decision problem is said to exhibit noncompensation (Şimşek, 2013). Noncompensation holds with probability 1 if the attributes are binary, taking on values of 0 or 1, and the weights satisfy the set of constraints

$$|w_i| > \sum_{j=i+1}^{k} |w_j|, \quad i = 1,\ldots,k-1, \quad \text{(Martignon and Hoffrage, 2002). Such weights are called}$$

noncompensatory. One example is the sequence 1, 0.5, 0.25, 0.125. If attributes are not binary or weights are not noncompensatory, noncompensation may or may not hold, depending on the attribute weights and the attribute values of the objects being compared.

Both simple and cumulative dominance are transitive: if object A dominates object B, and object B dominates object C, it follows that object A dominates object C. Simple dominance implies cumulative dominance. Both types of dominance imply noncompensation.

When one or more of these three conditions hold, the decision problem can be considered to be easy in the following sense: the correct decision can be made without knowledge of the exact linear relationship between the criterion and the attributes. It suffices to know only the attribute directions, and, in two of the conditions, also the attribute order. Furthermore, decision heuristics such as lexicographic rules and tallying make accurate decisions.

An illustrative example

As an illustrative example, consider a set of coins of the United States. Let the sequence $\langle x_{\$1}, x_{50¢}, x_{25¢}, x_{10¢}, x_{5¢}, x_{1¢} \rangle$ denote the number of each coin type in the set. Let V denote the total dollar value of the coins in the set, which is given by the following linear equation, Equation (21.2):

$$V = x_{\$1} + 0.5x_{50¢} + 0.25x_{25¢} + 0.10x_{10¢} + 0.05x_{5¢} + 0.01x_{1¢}. \tag{21.2}$$

Assume you are given two sets of coins and asked to determine which set has the higher value. Using the linear equation above, the correct answer can be computed easily. However, this approach would require knowing the exact value of each coin type. If this information is not available, it is still possible to make the correct decision under the three conditions described earlier. Below are examples from each condition.

Coin set ⟨4, 4, 4, 0, 0, 0⟩ simply dominates coin set ⟨4, 3, 2, 0, 0, 0⟩. With no knowledge of the dollar value of the various coin types, we can correctly, and with certainty, identify the first set as the set with the higher value. If deciding using the tallying heuristic, we would compute the total number of coins in each set, obtaining 12 for the first set and 9 for the second set, and pick the first set because of its higher count. We would therefore decide correctly. Similarly, by using the lexicographic decision rule with any ordering of the coins, we would decide correctly. For instance, consider the accurate ordering of the coins from the most to the least valuable. We would first compare the sets with respect to the counts of the $1 coin, the highest-valued coin type. Because both sets have four $1 coins, we would then compare the sets with respect to the counts of the 50¢ coin. The first set has four 50¢ coins while the second set has only three such coins. We would then terminate the decision process, picking the first set, without examining the remaining coin types.

Coin set ⟨4, 4, 4, 0, 0, 0⟩ cumulatively (but not simply) dominates the coin set ⟨2, 5, 1, 0, 0, 0⟩. Tallying would pick the first set because it has more coins than the second set. The lexicographic decision rule with the correct coin order would also pick the first set because the first set has more $1 coins than the second set. Both heuristics would be accurate.

Coin set ⟨1, 0, 0, 0, 0, 0⟩ neither simply nor cumulatively dominates the coin set ⟨0, 1, 1, 1, 1, 1⟩. Note, however, that the weights of the linear equation (Equation 21.2) are noncompensatory and the attribute values are binary (there is either 0 or 1 of each coin type in each coin set). Consequently, noncompensation holds with probability 1. Using the lexicographic decision rule with the correct coin order, we are guaranteed to decide accurately. Specifically, the lexicographic decision rule would pick the first coin set because it contains more of the highest-valued coin type than the second set, correctly reasoning that the coins of lower value will not be able to compensate for this difference.

How prevalent are "easy" problems?

These three conditions are theoretically interesting but are they empirically relevant? In other words, are they encountered frequently when making decisions? Evidence from a large, diverse collection of data sets suggests that they are (Şimşek, 2013).

This evidence comes from 51 natural data sets obtained from a wide variety of sources, including online data repositories, textbooks, research publications, and individual scientists collecting field data. The subjects were diverse, including biology, business, computer science, ecology, economics, education, engineering, environmental science, medicine, political science, psychology, sociology, sports, and transportation. The datasets varied in size, ranging from 12 to 601 objects, corresponding to 66–180,300 distinct paired comparisons. The data sets also varied in the amount of information available for making decisions, with number of attributes ranging from 3 to 21.

Table 21.1 shows the prevalence of various conditions in two columns. Prevalence is measured as the proportion of paired comparisons encountered in a data set where the reported condition was observed, for example, where one of the objects dominated the other object or the objects were dominance-equivalent, which also allows simple heuristics to decide accurately. The first column shows the results from the original datasets. In this case, numerical attributes were used as given. The second column shows the results when numerical attributes were dichotomized around the median, assigning the median value to the category with fewer objects. For instance, with height as a numerical attribute, the first column shows the results when height was used as given (for example, 182 cm) while the second column shows the results with height taking on a value of 0 or 1, indicating only whether the height of the given object was above or below the median height in the data set.

In addition to the prevalence of exact simple and cumulative dominance, Table 21.1 also reports the prevalence of close approximations to these two conditions. Exact dominance allows one to compare accurately *with certainty*, without knowing the exact values of the weights. Approximate dominance allows one to compare accurately *with very high probability*. For instance, consider a problem where 9 out of 10 attributes favor object *A* against object

Table 21.1 Prevalence of simple dominance, cumulative dominance, and noncompensation in 51 natural data sets

Condition	Median prevalence (data used as given)	Median prevalence (data dichotomized)
Simple dominance	0.16	0.54
Approximate simple dominance	0.31	0.59
Cumulative dominance	0.62	0.89
Approximate cumulative dominance	0.77	0.92
Noncompensation	0.85	0.96

Source: Şimşek (2013).

B. Although we cannot be certain that the correct decision is object A, that would be a very good bet. The approximate dominance results reported in Table 21.1 were computed with an expected accuracy rate of 0.99.

Table 21.1 shows that, on average, simple dominance held in 16 percent, cumulative dominance in 62 percent, and noncompensation in 85 percent of the pairwise comparisons in a data set. When approximations were allowed, prevalence of both simple and cumulative dominance increased by 15 percent. Furthermore, when attributes were available only in dichotomized form, the prevalence of all conditions increased substantially.

These results are useful in understanding why simple decision heuristics perform remarkably well when tested on natural data sets. They are also useful in understanding the source of error when heuristics decide incorrectly. Specifically, when error rates are examined through the lens of bias-variance decomposition (Geman et al., 1992; Brighton & Gigerenzer, 2008; Gigerenzer & Brighton, 2009), the three conditions discussed here are particularly relevant for the bias component of the error. Although simple decision heuristics have very little flexibility in model selection, they may not be introducing much additional bias compared to a linear model.

Sequential decision problems

Many real-world problems are sequential in nature, where a successful outcome depends not on a single decision but a series of related decisions. For example, driving safely to a destination to arrive on time for an appointment requires a long sequence of interrelated decisions. These types of problems can be viewed as a series of comparison problems, albeit ones that have complex dependencies. Consequently, the three conditions that make single-shot comparison problems easy can also make sequential decision problems easy, if decision algorithms are tailored to exploit them.

Here, I will discuss one particular sequential decision environment in depth: the game of Tetris,[2] one of the most popular video games of all time. Artificial players can learn to play Tetris very well, removing on average hundreds of thousands of rows. One of the best artificial players is BCTS (Thiery & Scherrer, 2009), which uses a linear evaluation function with eight attributes. These attributes and their weights are shown in Table 21.2. For each new piece (called a *tetrimino*) to be placed on the board, BCTS evaluates all possible placements using this linear evaluation function and selects the placement with the highest value.

Table 21.2 The attributes and weights of a linear evaluation function for playing Tetris, developed by Thiery and Scherrer (2009)

Attribute	Weight
Rows with holes	−24.04
Column transitions	−19.77
Holes	−13.08
Landing height	−12.63
Cumulative wells	−10.49
Row transitions	−9.22
Eroded piece cells	+6.60
Hole depth	−1.61

Note:
Three key concepts used in attribute definitions are holes, wells, and transitions. A *hole* is an empty cell that has one or more full cells placed higher than itself in the same column. A *well* is a succession of empty cells in a column such that the immediate cells on the left and on the right are full. A *transition* is a switch from a full cell to an empty cell, or vice versa, when moving along a row or a column. When computing wells and transitions, it is assumed that the outside of the grid is full.

The number of possible legal placements of a tetrimino ranges from 0–34, with a median value of 17. For example, the square tetrimino can be placed in 9 different ways on an empty board. Because the evaluation function is linear, the three conditions discussed earlier can be used to reduce the number of placements under consideration without losing the placement that BCTS considers to be the best. For example, any placement that is simply or cumulatively dominated by one or more other placements can safely be eliminated.

The question of interest, once again, is how often the three conditions are observed when playing Tetris. In other words, when considering various placements of the new tetrimino, how often does one placement simply or cumulatively dominate another placement, thus allowing the player to eliminate the dominated placement from further consideration? And, how often do the lower-ranked attributes fail to compensate for the difference in the highest-ranked attribute that discriminates between the alternatives? In other words, if we were to place the tetriminos using the lexicographic decision rule rather than the linear evaluation function of BCTS, how often would we choose the placement chosen by BCTS?

The answers to these questions depend on the states encountered while playing the game, which depends on how one plays the game, in other words, how the placements are chosen as the game progresses. Below is a summary of the results reported by Şimşek et al. (2016) when the game was played by BCTS. Results were similar when the games were played by people or by a controller that selected placements randomly.

The lexicographic decision rule selected the same placement as BCTS 68 percent of the time. The lexicographic rule was applied as follows. The attributes were used sequentially, one at a time, in the order listed in Table 21.2, to reduce the number of placements further and further, until there was only one placement left. With each feature, only those placements with the best (highest or lowest, depending on the sign of the feature weight) value for this feature were kept, while the remaining placements were eliminated.

Filtering by simple dominance reduced the median number of decision alternatives (placements of the tetrimino) from 17 to 3, while filtering by cumulative dominance further reduced it to 1. This result can be stated as follows. Ordinarily, a player has 17 placements to consider (on average). By simply knowing the sign of the attribute weights (or guessing correctly, which is easy to do in this domain), the player can reduce this number to 3 (on average). If the attribute order is also known, this number further reduces to 1 (on average). This is remarkable. With only one placement left, there is no decision left to make! And there is certainty that the remaining placement is the one that would have been chosen by BCTS.

This substantial reduction in the branching factor, however, is not enough to play the game well. Consider an artificial player that first filters the available actions by cumulative dominance, then chooses randomly among the remaining actions. If the game score is increased by one point with each eliminated row, this player reaches a median score of 510 in the game, which corresponds to emptying the Tetris board more than 25 times. This is a considerable achievement given that it is very difficult to eliminate rows by chance—a player who chooses actions randomly generally finishes the game with a score of zero—but it is far below the median score of 709,636 achieved by BCTS.

In summary, simple dominance, cumulative dominance, and noncompensation are all prevalent in Tetris. Şimşek et al. (2016) report substantial improvements in the learning rates and in the game score reached when dominance filters are inserted into existing reinforcement algorithms. An important question for AI is how these structures in the environment can be exploited fully, for faster and more effective learning.

Concluding remarks

In the history of AI, algorithmic ideas inspired by natural intelligence have been among the most fruitful. They include neural networks (inspired by the brain) and reinforcement learning (inspired by animal learning), both of which were central to the development of the artificial Go player that defeated one of the best human players in the history of this board game. The theory of bounded rationality is a similar inspirational resource, untapped by current AI systems. It seeks to explain, algorithmically and mathematically, how people are able to make good decisions even though they are almost always constrained by limited time, information, and computational resources. For fundamental shifts in the capabilities of our AI systems, we need fundamentally new ideas in our learning algorithms. The theory of bounded rationality is a useful foundation for developing such ideas in service of creating AI systems that can function effectively and transparently in large, complex, uncertain decision environments.

Notes

1 The branching factor is the number of alternative actions that need to be evaluated at a decision point and is one of the fundamental reasons why Artificial Intelligence is intractable.
2 Tetris is played on a two-dimensional grid, which is initially empty. The grid gradually fills up as pieces of different shapes, called *tetriminos*, fall from the top of the grid, one at a time, piling up on each other. The player can control how each tetrimino lands by rotating it and moving it horizontally, to the left or to the right, any number of times, as the tetrimino falls one row at a time. The tetrimino continues to fall until one of its cells sits directly on top of a full cell or on the grid floor. When an entire row of the grid becomes full, the row is deleted, creating additional space on the grid. The game ends when there is no space at the top of the grid for the next tetrimino. The standard grid is 20 cells high and 10 cells wide. Tetriminos each occupy four cells and have seven different shapes.

References

Baucells, M., Carrasco, J. A., & Hogarth, R. M. (2008). Cumulative dominance and heuristic performance in binary multiattribute choice. *Operations Research*, 56(5), 1289–1304.

Brighton, H. (2006). Robust inference with simple cognitive models. In C. Lebiere & B. Wray (Eds.), AAAI spring symposium: Cognitive science principles meet AI-hard problems (pp. 17–22). Menlo Park, CA: American Association for Artificial Intelligence.

Brighton, H., & Gigerenzer, G. (2008). Bayesian brains and cognitive mechanisms: Harmony or dissonance? In N. Chater & M., Oaksford (Eds.), *The probabilistic mind: Prospects for Bayesian cognitive science* (pp. 189–208). New York: Oxford University Press.

Buckmann, M., & Şimşek, Ö. (2017). Decision heuristics for comparison: How good are they? In T. V. Guy, M. Kárný, D. Rios-Insua, & D. H. Wolpert (Eds.), Proceedings of the NIPS 2016 Workshop on Imperfect Decision Makers, vol. 58 of Proceedings of Machine Learning Research, pp. 1–11.

Czerlinski, J., Gigerenzer, G., & Goldstein, D. G. (1999). How good are simple heuristics? In G. Gigerenzer, P. M. Todd, & the ABC Research Group (Eds.), *Simple heuristics that make us smart* (pp. 97–118). New York: Oxford University Press.

Dawes, R. M. (1979). The robust beauty of improper linear models in decision making. *American Psychologist*, 34(7), 571–582.

Dawes, R. M., & Corrigan, B. (1974). Linear models in decision making. *Psychological Bulletin*, 81(2), 95–106.

Einhorn, H. J., & Hogarth, R. M. (1975). Unit weighting schemes for decision making. *Organizational Behavior and Human Performance*, 13(2), 171–192.

Geman, S., Bienenstock, E., & Doursat, R. (1992). Neural networks and the bias/variance dilemma. *Neural Computation*, 4(1), 1–58.

Gigerenzer, G., & Brighton, H. (2009). Homo heuristicus: Why biased minds make better inferences. *Topics in Cognitive Science*, 1(1), 107–143.

Gigerenzer, G., Hertwig, R., & Pachur, T. (Eds.) (2011). *Heuristics: The foundations of adaptive behavior*. New York: Oxford University Press.

Gigerenzer, G., & Selten, R. (2002). *Bounded rationality: The adaptive toolbox*. Cambridge, MA: MIT Press.

Gigerenzer, G., Todd, P. M., & the ABC Research Group (Eds.) (1999). *Simple heuristics that make us smart*. New York: Oxford University Press.

Hogarth, R. M., & Karelaia, N. (2006). "Take-the-best" and other simple strategies: Why and when they work "well" with binary cues. *Theory and Decision*, 61(3), 205–249.

Katsikopoulos, K. V. (2011). Psychological heuristics for making inferences: Definition, performance, and the emerging theory and practice. *Decision Analysis*, 8(1), 10–29.

Katsikopoulos, K. V., & Martignon, L. (2006). Naive heuristics for paired comparisons: Some results on their relative accuracy. *Journal of Mathematical Psychology*, 50(5), 488–494.

Kirkwood, C. W., & Sarin, R. K. (1985). Ranking with partial information: A method and an application. *Operations Research*, 33(1), 38–48.

Langley, P., Simon, H. A., Bradshaw, G. L., & Zytkow, J. M. (1987). *Scientific discovery: Computational explorations of the creative processes*. Cambridge, MA: MIT Press.

Martignon, L., & Hoffrage, U. (2002). Fast, frugal, and fit: Simple heuristics for paired comparison. *Theory and Decision*, 52(1), 29–71.

Newell, A., Shaw, J. C., & Simon, H. A. (1958). Elements of a theory of human problem solving. *Psychological Review*, 65(3), 151–166.

Rubinstein, A. (1998). *Modeling bounded rationality*. Cambridge, MA: MIT Press,

Silver, D., Hubert, T., Schrittwieser, J., Antonoglou, I., Lai, M., ... Hassabis, D. (2018). A general reinforcement learning algorithm that masters chess, shogi, and go through self-play. *Science*, 362(6419), 1140–1144.

Simon, H. A. (1956). Rational choice and the structure of the environment. *Psychological Review*, 63(2), 129–138.

Şimşek, Ö. (2013). Linear decision rule as aspiration for simple decision heuristics. In C., Burges, L. Bottou, M. Welling, Z. Ghahramani, & K. Weinberger (Eds.), *Advances in Neural Information Processing Systems* 26, 2904–2912.

Şimşek, Ö., Algorta, S., & Kothiyal, A. (2016). Why most decisions are easy in Tetris—And perhaps in other sequential decision problems, as well. In *Proceedings of the 33rd International Conference on Machine Learning*, pp. 1757–1765.

Şimşek, Ö., & Buckmann, M. (2015). Learning from small samples: An analysis of simple decision heuristics. In C. Cortes, N. D. Lawrence, D. D. Lee, M. Sugiyama, & R. Garnett (Eds.), *Advances in Neural Information Processing Systems* 28, 3159–3167.

Tesauro, G. (1995). Temporal difference learning and TD-Gammon. *Communications of the ACM*, 38(3), 58–69.

Thiery, C., & Scherrer, B. (2009). Building controllers for Tetris. *International Computer Games Association Journal*, 32, 3–11.

22

PSYCHOPATHOLOGICAL IRRATIONALITY AND BOUNDED RATIONALITY

Why is autism economically rational?

Riccardo Viale

Deductive irrationality in madness?

As noted by Michel Foucault in his *History of Madness* (1961), during the age of the Enlightenment in the sixteenth and seventeenth centuries, the theme of rationality and irrationality became one of the main intellectual and political issues of the time. Reason was defined according to normative canons and it was the center of gravity of political and social action. Any behavior that did not adhere to those canons was considered irrational, "unreasonable," a sign of madness. In the Middle Ages, madness was treated as a disease of the spirit and a moral disorder to be contained and punished. The madman was considered to be possessed in his body and soul by the devil and for this reason he was subjected to corporal and moral punishments. During the Enlightenment, madness came to be regarded instead as a reversible deviation of reason, a condition that should not be punished but rather treated by segregating the madman in the appropriate medical facility. The Enlightenment was therefore tolerant toward madness, even though it relegated mentally disturbed individuals to the margins of society. The thread between the Enlightenment and the psychopathology of the twentieth century is evident. The madman deviated from the normative principles of reasons established by the canons of logical thinking, and possibly from the main social norms and habits. In this sense, normal thinking was expressed through correct inferences from a deductive point of view, consistent beliefs that are not mutually contradictory, and a pursuit of the truth as correspondence to reality.

As Viale has emphasized (2013), the presence of rooted prejudices of a logicist type in the study of human inferential performances is well illustrated by a number of traditional theories on schizophrenic thinking. In many of the theories on abnormal and, in particular, schizophrenic thinking present in treatises of psychopathology and psychiatry, we find the thesis on conformity of normal human deductive reasoning set out along the lines of classical logic.

For years, psychopathology, in order to characterize schizophrenic psychotic reasoning, used a normal model of reasoning which considered it aprioristically compliant with the precepts of classical logic. According to some theories prevalent in psychiatry, the schizophrenic displays a clear deviation from classical canons of logical reasoning. This different logical behavior was thought to be characteristic not only of the psychotic but also of cognitive behaviors in men who lived in archaic cultures, and it was therefore termed, by Arieti, for example, "paleologic"

DOI: 10.4324/9781315658353-25

(Arieti 1963). The paleologic individual does not reason using Aristotelian logic, but uses a *sui generis* logic. This type of thinking is fundamentally based on a principle described by Von Domarus (1925, 1944). After his studies on schizophrenia, this author formulated a theory which in a slightly modified form can be stated as follows: "Whereas the normal person accepts identity only on the basis of identical subjects, the schizophrenic accepts identity based on identical predicates." For example, if the following information is given to a normal individual, "All men are mortal; Socrates is a man," the normal person will be able to conclude, "Socrates is mortal." This conclusion is valid because the subject of the major premise (all men) contains the subject of the minor premise (Socrates).

If, on the other hand, a schizophrenic thinks, "a has the property x," and "b has the property x," in some cases, he may conclude that "a is b." This conclusion, which would seem insane to a normal person, is reached, according to some authors, because the identity of the predicate of the two premises, "x," makes the schizophrenic accept the identity of the two subjects, "a" and "b."

Moreover, the schizophrenic attributes a much broader meaning to the predicate. There is a tendency to identify a part with the whole (for example, a room with the house to which the room belongs). Therefore, it can be said that a = a + b + c because the two terms of the equation have a in common (a term that assumes the function of an "identifying link").

In the schizophrenic, these forms of paleologic reasoning are usually automatic, in the same way that the application of some laws of Aristotelian logic is automatic for normal individuals. According to Von Domarus, the first three laws of traditional Aristotelian logic are annulled (the principle of identity, non-contradiction, the excluded middle). Furthermore, paleologic thinking seeks the origin and cause of an event in a different way to logical thinking: by confusing the real world and the psychological world, it looks for the causes of an event in personal and subjective reasons rather than in reasons of an external nature. In other words, the causality present in objective explanations concerning the physical world is replaced by the causality based on psychological and subjective causal factors. Here, too, the authors identify a clear link with the thinking of young children and in particular with primitive thinking.

Another theory linked to the traditional model of rationality and normality of reason in the sense of conformity to the principles of classical logic is that of Matte Blanco (1981). He identifies a number of fundamental laws in schizophrenic thinking and uses them in an attempt to explain the symptoms found.

1. *Principle of generalisation*: an individual thing is treated as if it were an element of a class. This class is treated as a subclass of a more general class, and so on, to form a chain of generalizations. This differs from normal behavior in that often higher classes are chosen for shared characteristics of an accessory not for their fundamental nature.
2. *Principle of symmetry*: the schizophrenic treats the converse of a relation as being identical to the relation itself. From this follows several important corollaries: mainly the disappearance of time and any part being identical to the whole. According to Matte Blanco, these principles can explain a number of characteristics of schizophrenic thinking, such as literal interpretation of metaphor, displacement, condensation, concrete thinking. The principle of symmetry has the property of eliminating any possibility of logical organization in the sector of thinking where it is applied. The typical reasoning of schizophrenic thinking may be defined as "bi-logical" in that in part it respects traditional bivalent logic and in part symmetrical logic.

These theories are conceptual edifices whose foundations rest on an *a priori* definition of the deductive performance of normal humans, nowadays empirically proved by cognitive psychology (Viale, 2012). We need only take two examples highlighted by Wason and Johnson-Laird (1972, pp. 236–238).

The thesis whereby paleologic logic is characterized in relation to normal logic, on the grounds of being governed by the principle that two classes are identical if they have some attribute in common, is not adequate because this particular inferential fallacy is just an example of what Chapman and Chapman (1959) call "probabilistic inference," an error which normal subjects often make when an argument lacks thematic content. To give an example, if the syllogism is of the kind:

Some A are B
Some C are B
Then both A and C show the property of being Bs and hence they will be assumed to be linked in some way. This will produce the conclusion "Some A are C" which is a common error in this problem.[1]

Similarly, the thesis put forward by Matte Blanco whereby the root of the schizophrenic thought process is that all relational terms are treated as if they were symmetrical is weakened by the finding of a similar phenomenon called "illicit conversion" (Chapman & Chapman 1959), which frequently occurs among normal individuals when the tasks are abstract. Illicit conversion is the fallacy caused by the inversion of the subject and predicate in a proposition:

No P are Q
Therefore no Q are P.[2]

From this and other experimental observations, it can therefore be demonstrated that normal subjects too, at times, show forms of reasoning, traditionally seen as aberrant and considered peculiar to the cognitive symptomatology of schizophrenia. It is no longer convincing, therefore, to characterize schizophrenic reasoning based on the infraction of the laws of the classical logicist ideal of deductive rationality.

Is normality irrational and abnormality rational? It is also normal subjects, and not only schizophrenics, who show deviations in their deductive reasoning. Over the past 50 years, many empirical studies have been presented stigmatizing the irrationality of human thought. The most famous study in the field of the psychology of deductive reasoning was the one presented by Wason (1966) on selection tasks. In this study, and in numerous subsequent ones, it was demonstrated that when performing abstract tasks, individuals do not apply some fundamental rules of logic like *modus tollens* and are also often exposed to confirmation bias (also known as the "fallacy of affirming the consequent"). In the field of the psychology of probabilistic judgment and decision making, the heuristics and biases program led by Daniel Kahneman and Amos Tversky (for an overview, see Kahneman, 2011) has produced a vast quantity of data—obtained mainly through abstract tests and characterized by situations involving risk (betting, lotteries, and games)—which has outlined an alarming inclination toward bias, systematic errors, and cognitive distortions in normal subjects. Conversely, recent studies paint a picture that it is the exact opposite of the one outlined above concerning the deductive irrationality of the psychotic subject. These studies examine the rationality of judgment and decision making in patients suffering from neurological and psychiatric impairments. Paradoxically, unlike the so-called *normal* individuals, these patients seem not to be subject to a series of biases of rationality. In their paper, Hertwig and Volz (2013) examined a series of studies analyzing the behavior of neurological and psychiatric patients in various decision-making contexts. Hertwig and Volz summarize the results of these studies as follows (2013, p. 547):

> (i) Patients with damage to the ventromedial prefrontal cortex (VMPFC) were more coherent in their preferences in a consumer choice context (i.e., the Pepsi paradox)[3] (Koenigs & Tranel, 2008). Likewise, they did not fall prey to the correspondence bias and, thus, made more advantageous decisions in an investment context (Koscik & Tranel, 2013). (ii) In moral dilemmas in which the utilitarian choice (a weaker benchmark of rationality) implies emotionally aversive behavior, patients with VMPFC damage, frontotemporal dementia, or frontal traumatic brain injury showed a greater propensity to make utilitarian judgments (Young & Koenigs, 2007; Mendez, 2009). (iii) Patients with OFC lesions made choices between gambles that were guided more by the expected value of the gambles than by reported or anticipated regret (Camille et al., 2004). (iv) Patients with any of various focal lesions (including damage to the OFC) were less subject to myopic loss aversion and, thus, made more advantageous decisions (resulting in higher income) in an investment task (Shiv et al. 2005). (v) Participants with a virtual lesion to the right dorsolateral PFC (induced through transcranial magnetic stimulation) exhibited higher acceptance of unfair offers in the ultimatum game (Knock et al., 2006). (vi) Patients with autism were less responsive to the framing of monetary outcomes as either losses or gains and, thus, exhibited more internally consistent behavior (De Martino et al., 2008).
>
> *Hertwig & Volz, 2013 p. 547*

Can abnormality be conducive to rationality? In some cases, the answer is yes, if we consider the type of rationality that is under examination and that has been made the basis for judgment based on the rationality and irrationality of human behavior. What is it that characterizes this type of rationality in the examples of neurological and mental disorders mentioned above, where behavior appears to be more rational in mentally disturbed individuals compared to normal individuals? It is substantially the lack of influence of emotion, which translates as awareness of the consequences of one's choices on one's utility and, on a prosocial level, on that of others. Hertwig and Volz (2013, p. 549) underline this point by analyzing previous cases. Humans with damage to the dorsolateral PFC (Knock et al., 2006), which weakens "the emotional impulses associated with fairness goals," are free to follow their selfish impulses without restraint, thereby maximizing material income. A lack of the "emotional associations" that are the "driving force behind commercial advertisements" enables patients with damage to the VMPFC to show coherent taste-based brand preferences in the Pepsi paradox (Koenigs & Travel, 2006). Attenuated "prosocial sentiments" (Mendez, 2009, p. 614) and weaker emotional reactions to the possibility of causing direct harm to others enable patients with damage to the VMPFC or OFC to overcome emotional revulsion at the "means" of an action (e.g., smothering a baby to quieten it) and focus on its "ends" (saving the lives of several others) (Young & Koenigs, 2007). Similarly, dampened "emotional responses" to the possibility of losses liberate patients with "deficient emotional circuitry" from myopic loss aversion (Shiv et al., 2005, p. 435, p. 436) and the experience of regret (Camille et al., 2004). The case concerning the reduction of ambiguity aversion and the Ellsberg paradox in patients with damage to the orbitofrontal cortex (OFC) versus normal subjects (Hsu et al., 2005) contains yet another reference to the reduction of the affection component.[4] In point of fact, when ambiguity and uncertainty are compared to certainty and certain probabilities, they generate anxiety and insecurity that lead one to avoid them. In case of damage to the OFC, weaker emotional reactions to ambiguity prevented the subject from falling into the Ellsberg paradox.

Autism is a psychiatric disorder in which the lack of an emotional dimension seems to result in the debiasing of the framing effect. A failure to "integrate emotional contextual cues into the decision making process" enables patients with autism to choose in an internally consistent way, that is, independently of option framing (i.e. loss versus gain (De Martino et al., 2008, p. 10746). Loss aversion caused by heavier emotional content of loss vs. gain is not active in autism and, as demonstrated by De Martino et al. (2008), behavior is less subject to the framing effect. In short, an autistic individual does not show any greater propensity to risk in loss frames, nor a greater aversion to risk in gain frames. The rational behavior of the autistic subject that has been highlighted by research is emblematic of irrationality corresponding solely to a cold calculating capacity without any external influences of an affective type and without the capacity to grasp, understand, and predict empathically any altruistic and social behavior in other people.

From coherence to correspondence: the goal of cognitive success

Over the years, the evaluation of what is considered reason and the equation "normality equals rationality" seem to have undergone a paradoxical change. Initially, the rationalist legacy of the eighteenth-century Enlightenment resulted in a very clear separation of reason from madness. The madman was characterized by a failure of deductive and inductive logical thinking. In the 1950s, however, this distinction disappeared when cognitive science brought to light a whole series of supposed failures of rational behavior in the normal individual as well. What dealt a serious blow to the theories of human decision-making and judgment formation was the fact that, quite surprisingly, several reasoning flaws that had been attributed solely to the psychiatric patient were, in fact, also found in the normal individual. Over the past few years, the theory that started with the Enlightenment seems to have reversed in a circular way. If we consider rationality as based on the logical coherence adopted in economic theory, then rationality is more apparent in individuals suffering from certain neurological and psychiatric disorders than among people without these diseases. Paradoxically, normality seems characterized by irrationality, and abnormality by rationality. Why this paradox? In my view, the reason is that adherence to a formal concept of rationality as consistent with the norms of deductive logic, the theory of probability, and the theory of utility, is incorrect. Moreover, the analysis of conformity of human behavior to those norms is mostly performed in abstract tests, with little relation to real life, and generally under conditions of risk. There is, therefore, a triple anti-ecological bias at work here: behavioral irrationality is not assessed in its capacity to adapt to the real environment and to solve environmental problems. Instead, it is tested in abstract and artificial situations rather than the real world. The world to which the tests pertain is characterized by risk (in gaming, betting, and lotteries, the possibilities and probabilities are fixed), but not uncertainty (in reality, we often don't know all the possibilities and therefore cannot correctly estimate all probabilities). The paradox lies in the fact that we do not consider the lesson from the theory of bounded rationality, aptly expressed by the Herbert Simon's metaphor (1990) of a pair of scissors to emphasize how cognition and environment work in tandem: "Human rational behaviour … is shaped by a scissors whose blades are the structure of task environments and the computational capabilities of the actor" (p. 7). Often the real environments have an unlimited space of possibilities because they are characterized by uncertainty or they have a limited space but they are computationally intractable. Therefore, the classical model of rationality, characterized by coherence with formal norms of logic, probability, and utility cannot be applied (Simon, 1978).

This section will analyze what it means to apply the concept of bounded rationality in the evaluation of human rationality or irrationality. As highlighted by the metaphor of the scissors, judgment of the rationality of human behavior does not depend on its conformity to some formal norm, but only on its cognitive success in given specific environmental tasks.

What is cognitive success?

The judgment of rationality of human behavior depends on its ability to adapt to specific environmental tasks. This ecological adaptability happens if the decision maker is successful in coping with the cognitive requirements of a specific environmental task. The requirements may be different. When one has to solve an abstract task like Tower of Hanoi or Missionaries and Cannibals, the requirement is to find a solution. The same problem solving requirements may be found in many tasks of everyday life, from replacing a tire to dealing with the failures of our computer software. When one has to make a financial investment, the requirement seems different, that is to say making good predictions about the future value of one's investments. The same requirement seems to apply also when one is engaged in a negotiation, or needs to find a reliable partner or has to decide which approach may be better suited to pursue one's research. According to some authors (Schurz & Hertwig, 2019), cognitive success should be analyzed only in term of predictive power of the cognitive method used to deal with a task. In other words, according to Schurz and Hertwig (2019, p. 16):

> the predictive success of a cognitive system or (more generally) a cognitive method depends on two components that are commonly in competition and whose optimization thus involves a trade-off. In the psychological literature, this trade-off is reflected in the distinction between the ecological validity of a prediction method (Brunswik, 1952; Gigerenzer et al., 1999) and its applicability.

The ecological validity refers to the validity of the system in condition in which it is applicable. The applicability is the scope of conditions under which it can be applied. Or in other words it "is the percentage of targets for which the method renders a prediction, among all intended targets of prediction" (Schurz & Hertwig, 2019, p. 17). Does the reduction of cognitive success to successful predictions include most successful adaptive answers to environmental tasks? According to Schurz and Hertwig (2019, p. 16), the answer is yes:

> The core meaning of the cognitive success of a system (including algorithms, heuristics, rules) is defined in terms of successful predictions, assuming a comprehensive meaning of prediction that includes, besides the predictions of events or effects, predictions of possible causes (explanatory abductions) and in particular predictions of the utilities of actions (decision problems).

In fact, this reduction of cognitive success to successful prediction excludes a number of cognitive human abilities to adapt to complex environments. In 1986, Herbert Simon wrote:

> The work of managers, of scientists, of engineers, of lawyers—the work that steers the course of society and its economic and governmental organizations—is largely work of making decisions and solving problems. It is work of choosing issues that require attention, setting goals, finding or designing suitable courses of action, and evaluating and choosing among alternative actions. The first three of these activities–fixing

agendas, setting goals, and designing actions—are usually called *problem solving;* the last, evaluating and choosing, is usually called *decision making.*

Simon, 1986, p. 1

In dealing with a task, humans have to frame problems, set goals, and develop alternatives. Evaluations and judgments about the future effects of the choice are the final stages of the cognitive activity. This is particularly true when the task is an ill-structured problem. When a problem is complex, it has ambiguous goals and shifting problem formulations, cognitive success is characterized mainly by setting goals and designing actions. Herbert Simon offers the example of design-related problems:

> The work of architects offers a good example of what is involved in solving ill-structured problems. An architect begins with some very general specifications of what is wanted by a client. The initial goals are modified and substantially elaborated as the architect proceeds with the task. Initial design ideas, recorded in drawings and diagrams, themselves suggest new criteria, new possibilities, and new requirements. Throughout the whole process of design, the emerging conception provides continual feedback that reminds the architect of additional considerations that need to be taken into account.
>
> *Simon, 1986, p. 15*

Most of the problems of corporate strategy or government policy are as ill-structured as problems of architectural and engineering design or of scientific activity. Reducing cognitive success to predictive ability is the product of the decision-making tradition and in particular of the theory of subjective expected utility (SEU). The theory of subjective expected utility combines two subjective concepts: first, a personal utility function, and, second, a personal probability distribution (usually based on Bayesian probability theory) that corresponds to the predictive component. Which decision the person prefers depends on which subjective expected utility is higher. Different people may make different decisions because they may have different utility functions or different beliefs about the probabilities of different outcomes. The decision-making tradition follows the syntactic structure of SEU theory. It deals solely with analytic judgments and choices and it is not interested in how to frame problems, set goals, and develop a suitable course of action (Viale, Macchi, & Bagassi, in preparation). On the contrary, cognitive success in most human activities is based precisely on the successful completion of those problem-solving phases. In reality, decision-making, including the predictive success of judgements, may be considered a subordinate stage of problem solving (Viale, Macchi, & Bagassi, in preparation).

Are syntactical rules adaptive?

Rationality has always been defined in terms of coherence, assuming that a single syntactical rule suffices to evaluate behavior. We have seen earlier how the very evaluation of irrationality and rationality in mental disorders itself was carried out against syntactical rules. As noted by Arkes et al. (2016, Table 1), there are many examples of coherence rules interpreted as normative for rational behavior. All the norms are solely defined in term of a syntactical rule whereas pragmatic or functional goals do not enter the normative analysis (Arkes et al., 2016). Thus, the question is: "How useful and feasible are these rules in individual choices?" One of the reasons why attention turned to the coherence of economists and scholars in decision making was the theory that violation resulted in material costs for the violator. Arkes, Gigerenzer, and Hertwig (2016) analyzed the validity of this theory and found no empirical evidence in this regard. To answer this question, they conducted several systematic *Web of Knowledge* searches for the major coherence rules reported in the literature, and in addition they conducted a survey among 1,000 researchers of the Society for Judgement and Decision Making. Their systematic literature searches suggest that there is little empirical evidence that violations of coherence norms are costly, or if they are, that they survive arbitrage and learning. The survey further confirmed this result. Among the phenomena of violation of coherence that were studied were the violation of transitivity and the related "money-pump," the violation of procedural invariance and the related preference reversal, the framing effect, and the independence of irrelevant alternatives condition (Arkes et al., 2016). In some cases, rather than generating material damage, the violation of coherence seems to generate an adaptive effect. This adaptive incoherence (Arkes et al., 2016) stems from the content-blind syntactic characteristics of formal norms. These fail to account for the pragmatic adaptive objectives of the decision-maker that may conflict with the requirements of formal coherence. Sometimes violating the norms based on transitivity, non-contradiction, consistency, and propositional logic may be adaptive. A case in point is illustrated by Amartya Sen (1993) and shows that sometimes violating the consistency of the norm of "independence of irrelevant alternatives" (or *Property Alpha*)[5] may be necessary. The following two choices are inconsistent because they violate Property Alpha.

A is chosen over B given the options [A, B], and
B is chosen over A given the options [A, B, C].

Can Property Alpha guide the rationality of our choices without considering the background knowledge of values, social norms, external environmental and contextual conditions in which we are called to choose? According to Sen (2002), the idea of internal consistency of choice "is essentially confused, and there is no way of determining whether a choice function is consistent or not without referring to something external to choice behaviour (such as objectives, values, or norms)." Let's consider this example: John is asked to go to a club with Jane, the fiancée of his friend Carl. Out of respect for his friend, John decides not to go out with Jane (A) instead of going out with her (B). One hour later, he receives a phone call in which he is informed that he can meet Carl that night at the club (C). At this point, John decides to go out with Jane (B) in a way that will not violate the principle of respect toward his friend.

What appears to be an internal inconsistency is not, in fact, if we consider the values, social norms, and environmental constraints in the equation. In this example the heuristic norm was "It is not socially correct to go to a club alone with the girlfriend of a friend." Moreover, what often appears to be an incoherent behavior corresponds instead to a coherent strategy that generated it. In this example the heuristic rule is coherent and generates a behavior that is at first sight incoherent. Judgment on rationality cannot therefore be limited only to the observable behavior (as is implicit in the economic theory of the revealed preference approach by Paul Samuelson, 1938), but has to open the black box of rules and heuristics that generated it. And it must also question the adaptive success of the behavior as compared to the context. Lastly, the poor adaptivity of coherence norms is also rooted in their cognitive unfeasibility. Herbert Simon's theory of bounded rationality is part of the naturalizing programs of decisional norms that, starting with Willard Orman Quine and continuing with Christopher Cherniak, Steven Stich, Alvin Goldman, Steven Kornblith, and others, have addressed the issue of the visibility of the norms for the acquisition of knowledge and for decision making in economic, social, and moral areas. If a procedure is unfeasible at the cognitive or perceptive level, it cannot be adopted as a normative reference. Coherence as a behavioral norm is unfeasible because it is computationally intractable (Arkes et al., 2016). For example, applying the principle of non-contradiction to 20 beliefs in social interaction between two people would require testing 1,770 copies of beliefs. Considering at least a few seconds (say, 5) per pair, it would take up to two and a half hours to do it. If we consider that people generally have many more beliefs than 20, and more to the point, we apply them to many more people than two, we realize how unfeasible the application of this principle is. A second difficulty must be added to the feasibility of the application of the rules of coherence in reality: the rules of coherence—such as transitivity, consistency, and non-contradiction—can be applied when there are no conflicting goals or preferences (Arkes et al., 2016). In reality, though there are many conflicting goals. In this case, if you try to have a behavior that is consistent with a goal (for example, living long), you are forced not to be consistent with another goal (enjoying unhealthy food). This is another case in which coherence becomes an objective that is impossible at the adaptive level.

Heuristics and ecological rationality

Cognitive biases characterizing normal or abnormal thinking are identified according to a principle of coherence. This principle represents the basis of the program "Heuristics and Biases" by Tversky and Kahneman (1974) and lies at the heart of *libertarian paternalism* in public policy by Thaler and Sunstein (2008; for a critical overview of libertarian paternalism, see Viale, forthcoming). But there is an alternative approach that is based on the principle of correspondence as a benchmark for judging rationality. The principle of correspondence deals with the relationship between behavior and the environment, according to what was illustrated above when discussing bounded rationality. The measure of the success of this relationship can be assessed not formally but pragmatically. In general, the evaluation concerns the capacity to reach the goals of some kind of task, be it the prediction of an event, solving a practical problem, or other objectives aimed at our happiness and environmental survival. Thus, instead of being syntactical, behavioral rules become functional or ecological. Instead of being *logical*, rationality becomes *ecological*. Without dwelling on the characteristics of ecological rationality that are discussed in detail in this volume (for a summary, see also Gigerenzer & Gaissmaier, 2011), the main passages of an evaluation according to ecological rationality can be broken down as follows (Arkes, Gigerenzer, & Hertwig, 2016):

1. Identify the goal of an individual or a group.
2. Identify the set of strategies an individual or group has available to reach that goal ("the adaptive toolbox").
3. Identify the structural properties of the environment in which the strategies should operate.
4. Determine the "ecological rationality" of the strategies in the environment, that is, a set of environmental conditions that specify when a given strategy is likely to reach the goal better than a competing strategy (Arkes et al., 2016).

The "adaptive toolbox" is constituted by a series of rules of thumb, heuristics,[6] and algorithms used, according to the structural properties of the environment. The most important environmental condition is uncertainty, that is to say, the situation characterized by the unpredictability of future states of the world and, consequently, the impossibility of estimating the probability of the consequences of one's options (and what happens in conditions of risk). Faced with the descriptive and normative failure of the optimizing algorithms in decision making under conditions of uncertainties, in the 1990s, an articulated research program was developed around heuristics, which attempted to formalize and test them empirically in situations of uncertain choice (Gigerenzer, Todd, & the ABC Research Group, 1999). The basic principle was simplicity. The greater accuracy of the results obtained in comparison with decision-making methods of a statistical type can also be summarized by the standard of "less is more." It was observed that there is an inverse U relationship between the level of accuracy of the results and the quantity of information, computation or time. Beyond a certain threshold, "more is harmful," that is to say, a greater quantity hinders the result (Gigerenzer & Gassmaier, 2011). The methods tested were those of linear and nonlinear multiple regression, Bayesian analysis, etc. Simon, in his commentary to Gigerenzer, Todd, and the ABC Research Group (1999), refers to a "revolution in cognitive science that represents an extraordinary impulse in favour of good sense in the approach to human rationality." How can we explain the positive role of simplicity in decisional contexts characterized by uncertainty? Let us consider an example of heuristic decision. For reasons of economic and marketing planning, large commercial chains are often called to deal with the problem of distinguishing between active customers, that is to say those who might return to buy again, from those who are inactive. In general, these companies can rely on a database of customer purchases. Based on this data, an inferential statistical algorithm is traditionally applied to predict which clients will be active in the future. A recent study (Wübben & Wangenheim, 2008) highlighted how expert managers use a simple rule of "time since last purchase," which can be described as a "hiatus heuristic" (Gigerenzer & Gassmaier, 2011, p. 455): "If a client has not made a purchase for a number of months (the hiatus), the customer is classified as inactive. Otherwise, he/she is simply classified as active."

Depending on the commercial sector, the hiatus may be different. Technological products or those with a higher turnover (e.g., electronics) have shorter hiatuses as compared to more traditional products with a lower turnover (e.g., furniture). This heuristic disregards basic statistical information, while the Pareto/NBD model generally analyzes at least 40 weeks' worth of data to calculate its parameters. Wübben and Wangenheim (2008) tested the predictive success of the two decisional models in the sectors of clothing, airlines, and online sales of CDs. On average, the hiatus heuristic was successful in predicting the type of customers, in the next 40 weeks, in 80 percent of cases as compared to 76 percent of the Pareto/NBD model. This type of heuristic is based solely on one indicator that is deemed valid. It is part of a category known as "single-reason heuristics" whereby the individual, when faced with two alternatives, chooses the one with the strongest reason ("take-the-best heuristic").[7]

Another example introduces another category of heuristics based on simplicity and frugality, "recognition-based" heuristics (Goldstein & Gigerenzer, 2009). An experiment carried out in 2006 by Serwe and Frings compared amateur tennis players (with only episodical knowledge of tennis matches) against members of the Association of Tennis Professionals and other expert associations (who were intimately familiar with all the international players) in their capacity to predict the results of the 2004 Wimbledon tournament. It turned out that the amateurs correctly predicted 72 percent of the tournament's outcomes compared to an average of 68 percent among the experts. The same study was repeated for the 2006 tournament and yielded the same results. Similar evidence emerged with regard to other predictions, for example, the performance of shares on the stock market. Ortmann et al. (2008) verified that on average, the returns of stock portfolios picked solely by recognition surpass the returns of managed assets and those managed by stock exchange experts. Unlike heuristics that are based on a reason, in this case it is the sense of recognition, of familiarity toward a certain name, event, or object that dictates our choice. This can happen not only when we see that name, but also when that name comes to mind first ("take-the-first heuristic"). And if we recognize more than one name, we attach the greatest value to the one that we recognize fastest ("fluency heuristic") (Schooler & Hertwig, 2005). An example of this heuristic successfully applied to predict stock exchange performances can be found in Alter and Oppenheimer (2006). The structure of heuristics has also been studied for the purpose of formalization by simulation objectives. Following on from Herbert Simon's work, three fundamental elements have been identified as general components making up many, but not all, heuristics (Gigerenzer et al., 1999):

1. Rules of research that specify the directions in which to search for information (e.g., the hiatus heuristic looks for information concerning the recency of the last purchase made). "Stopping rules" that specify when the search ends (the search ends when the information on recency is found).
2. The rules of decision-making that specify how the final decision is made (use the threshold of *n* months for the decision of whether the customer is regular or not).

The study of heuristics based on the principle of "less is more" was, in the past, mainly descriptive. As the examples above indicate, though, there is an interesting prescriptive aspect to heuristics that tries to answer the question of when their use is preferable compared to the use of more complex strategies in uncertain environments. In other words, it is a matter of understanding which characteristics of the decision-making environment make the use of heuristics preferable over optimization algorithms. The question is one of understanding when heuristics allow us to make better predictive inferences, particularly in situations of uncertainty where we have little time and little computing power. The answer to this question allows us to understand when a heuristic is adaptive, that is to say, improves our ecological rationality. The structural variables of a task that seem to favour the success of a heuristic in a decision-making environment characterized by uncertainty are the following[8] (Todd et al., 2011):

1   *Redundancy*: This is the level of interconnection of signals in the environment. The more interconnected they are, the more we can rely on a single signal or reason. For example, when dealing with people with psychiatric issues or who exhibit violent behavior, it is generally sufficient to consider one signal to reliably infer the associated behavioral profile. The profiles of deviant personalities often possess a coherent structure of interconnected psychological characteristics. This is what taxi drivers working late at night do, for example, when they have to assess the reliability of a potential customer quickly and intuitively.
2   *Variability*: This has to do with the weight and the importance of signals. When there are some signals that are more important and representative than others, it is enough to intercept one of the signals to generate accurate inferences. For example, when choosing among different credit contract alternatives or mortgage loans, in Italy, the EAPR[9] is the most important variable that can enable one to decide quickly and accurately.
3   *Size of the sample*: When faced with situations of uncertainty, most samples of available data are never enough to allow complex algorithms to estimate ex-ante the value of their parameters for predictive purposes. For example, predicting the performance of ten stocks traded on Wall Street would require historical information on those stocks, along with similar ones, to generate any inference, as algorithms, such as Markowitz's "mean-variance portfolio" algorithm tell us. A limited data sample would be flawed by virtue of their having a high variance. In these cases, therefore, basing one's decision on data can be misleading.[10] It is better to use the heuristic approach, and this is what Markowitz did when he had to invest his severance package using the heuristic 1/N.

In uncertain situations, the use of decisional heuristics can occur either automatically and intuitively or in a deliberate and reasoned way. How do you select which heuristic or heuristics? Some of these, as animal ethology teaches us, are inbred and selected through evolution. The spatial localization capacity of insects and birds is one such example. In humans, most heuristics are, however, learned by individual learning and social imitation. Once these heuristics are memorized, they become part of our knowledge and are retrieved implicitly and intuitively or explicitly and deliberately depending on the task at hand. What are the fundamental building blocks of heuristics? These are the expression of some cognitive characteristics even when the psychological mechanisms at the basis of the heuristic decision-making are still unclear. Some central inbred capacities certainly include recognition memory and frequency monitoring. Additionally, there are more sensory properties like the visual tracking of an object (present in the "gaze heuristic") and social ones like social imitation and social rules (Gigerenzer & Gaissmaier, 2011). To these acquired functions, others like aspiration levels, ordered search, and the one-reason stopping rule (Hertwig & Herzog, 2009, p. 678) are added. An important role is performed by emotion, especially in social-type heuristics. As we will see later, emotion plays a key role in the ecological irrationality of psychiatric disorders.

Social rationality

The social dimension of human beings entails that most of their decisions are made in contexts where others social actors are involved. This may happen in various ways and for each of these ways, we can refer to social ecological rationality. Hertwig and Herzog (2009) identify four such ways, of which I will discuss the two most relevant ones for the analysis of mental disease:

1. Social information in games against nature: Each one of us, when making a prediction about a natural event (such as the risk of contracting malaria while traveling to India) or solving a practical problem (buying a house) tends to use the knowledge accumulated through personal experience, but primarily the knowledge handed down in society. It is a knowledge of behaviors, preferences, decision-making modes, and problem solving of others that guides our behavior. Depending on our trust in other people, our information social circle may be small or large. Others may be a direct source of information through direct questions, or simulated by putting oneself in the shoes of others when dealing with a problem or a prediction to be made.
2. Social learning in games against nature: When dealing with the problems of everyday life, we cannot count on our personal experience, but we need to base our decision on what others are doing. Social learning leads to a reduction in the costs (time and errors) that individual learning would require, and allows us to use behaviors that have been selected because they are successful (Richerson & Boyd, 2005). This is also been explained at the evolutionary level (Boyd & Richerson, 2005). What are the rules that allow us to use social learning best? First of all, imitation or related advice-giving. That allows individuals to learn about their environments without engaging in potentially hazardous learning trials or wasting time and energy on exploration (Henrich & McElreath, 2003). According to the "Imitate the successful" heuristic (Boyd & Richerson, 2005), the individual looks for the most successful person in her reference group and imitates her behavior. This heuristic is particularly effective for learning the cue orders for lexicographic strategies (Garcia-Retamero, Takezawa, & Gigerenzer, 2006, 2007). In this type of heuristics (as in satisficing and elimination by aspects), the critical point is the choice of the cue orders through which to sequentially make the final selection of the option in a process of comparing

several alternatives in stages. Counting on the experience of the most successful can entail a considerable decisional advantage. Depending on situational cues and task structures, the imitation heuristics may be by majority[11] or by the nearest individual. Another route through which social learning can occur is by actively seeking the advice of others or by interpreting institutional arrangements as implicit recommendations (Hertwig & Herzog, 2009).[12] Social heuristics present the same building blocks as non-social ones with the addition of social rules, social imitation, and emotion.

Ecological irrationality of psychiatric disorders

The articulation of psychiatric disorders is varied and subject to periodic changes in classification. The *Diagnostic and Statistical Manual of Mental Disorders* (DSM) is now in its fifth edition since 1952. In that time several changes have taken place. One significant example: in the DSM V (American Psychiatric Association, 2013), all the paranoid and catatonic subcategories have been removed from schizophrenia after having been the basis of all psychiatry manuals. Even the expression "psychiatric condition" has been abandoned and replaced by "psychiatric disorder." When dealing with the rational aspect of these disorders, I will mostly refer to the classification of the DSM IV (American Psychiatric Association, 2000) and particularly to personality disorders and bipolar, phobic, or obsessive-compulsive disorders.

As previously noted, most individuals are characterized by limitations of logical rationality, which do not make them impeccable logicians, statisticians, and maximizers, but that allow them to successfully adapt to the environment to solve problems and to learn from their mistakes.[13] From this standpoint, a behavior can be defined as pathological. This is not because it deviates from normative standards, but because it is unable to successfully interact with the social and physical environment, in other words, to have cognitive success. The irrationality of the mental disorder is such that it differs from bounded ecological rationality because it would not allow some of the following adaptive cognitive functions (depending on the mental disorder): (1) learning from mistakes or environmental feedback, in particular, advice from the social context; (2) using social imitation heuristics, like that of successful people or of the crowd, that allow the individual to speed up the decision-making processes and to find solutions that are readily available; (3) realistically representing the terms of a problem in the context of a decision, without affective or emotional hyperpolarization, based only on some salient variables and not on others that are more relevant to the decision; (4) having a correct non-distorted perception of spatial and temporal coordinates in the context of a decision; and (5) anticipating at the corporal level (e.g., somatic marker, Damasio, 1994) the affective effects of a future choice in a way that corresponds to the reality of the phenomenon not in a distorted or dissociated way (Viale, 2019). Any rigidity and impermeability to the signals from the environment and the lack of a realistic representation of the variables at work do not allow adequate fitness of the structure of a decisional task to allow us to be successful in our choices. It is therefore from an ecological point of view rather than from a normative one that we can consider a behavior irrational in the context of some mental disorders. We will now analyze some of these points in more detail. This analysis will be entirely hypothetical, given the absence of empirical data from the study of ecological rationality in individuals affected by mental disorder.

Impermeability to environmental feedbacks

One of the peculiar characteristics of ecological rationality is the possibility of learning specific decision-making options for a set of environmental tasks through decisional learning.

This means remaining open and permeable to the reinforcement mechanisms coming from the environment as responses to previous decisions, and adjusting the subsequent decision to be more adaptive. In these conditions, it is possible, for example, to develop forms of judgment and decisions that tend to converge toward the requirements of the Bayes theorem. For example, it is well known that if information is presented as the outcome of learning from experience, known as natural frequencies, and not as conditional probabilities, the proportion of people reasoning by Bayes' rule increases greatly (Gigerenzer & Hoffrage, 1995). Nudge theory, too (Thaler & Sunstein, 2008), deals with the problem of helping citizens through System 2 nudges that reinforce their decisional learning capacity (Viale, forthcoming). Among them one of the most important is the creation of environments that are rich in feedback that allows the citizen to adapt his decision-making process to previous experience.[14] This prerequisite of ecological rationality is almost never fulfilled in the case of mental disorders. Patients with borderline personality disorder (BPD) tend to make risky choice and are unable to improve their performance by experience (Schuermann et al., 2011). A reduced feedback related negatively predicted an inability to learn from negative feedbacks (Mak & Lam, 2013). As the following clinical examples will show, various emotional and cognitive disorders tend to be impermeable to environmental responses. Delirium and hallucinations are experienced as real and do not allow corrections. The schizophrenic really sees images and hears voices that do not exist. If you suffer from paranoid delirium, you believe that threats to your life are genuine and not falsifiable possibilities. Depression, phobias, and impulsive compulsive disorders are cognitively correctable, but the emotional dimension is too strong to lead to a real correction. The patient may acknowledge that the causes of the disorder are excessive or not existent, but the affective and emotional state of polarization is predominant over this judgment. Reinforcement learning through feedbacks, describing how the brain can choose and value courses of actions according to their long-term future value, may account for how depressive symptoms may result from aberrant valuations and prior beliefs about the loss of agency ("helplessness") (Adams et al., 2016). Lastly, personality disorders present a framework of rigidity and impermeability, on an emotional basis, to forms of learning and improvement of reasoning and decision-making procedures (Gangemi et al., 2013; Johnson-Laird et al., 2006).

Disabled social learning

First of all, the structure of social environmental tasks is characterized by uncertainty more strictly than non-social ones. The complexity and unpredictability of human decisions and interaction between different social actors make social tasks primarily characterized by ambiguity and uncertainty. This characteristic of the task structure makes the use of heuristic rules a necessity for adaptive success. In the case of mental disorders, there may be a distorted opposite tendency to underestimate or overdramatize the uncertainty of the tasks, and accordingly to approach the decision-making process in a non-adaptive way. Mental disorders like narcissistic or bipolar personality disorder in the hypomaniac phase tend to represent the external environment as characterized by predictable and limited options of which the individuals are aware and which are under their control. The illusion of control (Langer, 1975) and overconfidence (Moore & Schatz, 2017) are phenomena in cognitive psychology that have been studied in the normal adult and which are accentuated in the case of certain mental disorders. On the contrary, patients suffering from hysterical or phobic personality have the tendency to accentuate the possibility of danger and adversity. That makes the patient constantly insecure with respect to future events and leads him to attach greater uncertainty to tasks, even when the contexts present few variables and they are relatively closed to external events. As noted above, social heuristics differ from non-social heuristics in their respective building blocks: social rules, social imitation, and emotion. When talking about interaction with the environment, the most relevant component in the evaluation of ecological rationality in mental disorder is the social one. Mental disorders are above all disorders concerning social relations, because it is at the social level that its consequences become most disabling. Let us consider, according to the list of components of social rationality (Hertwig & Herzog, 2009), the various forms of ecological irrationality. First of all, there is a misguided use of social information in the prediction of events and problem solving. This is particularly evident in schizophrenic patients, and autistic ones as well, but also in individuals suffering from less crippling mental disorders like paranoid personality, phobic personality, or obsessive personality. In all these disorders it is difficult for the individual to refer to other people as sources of knowledge. This occurs both at the direct level and the simulated level. It is very difficult for them to ask other people for information, including close relatives. In the case of autism, even the simulation of what other people would do or think becomes impossible. The informative social circle cannot be created and the individual can only rely on his/her own idiosyncratic and limited knowledge. It is, however, primarily mostly in social learning that the ecological rationality gap in mental disorder emerges. The competitive advantage of resorting to imitation heuristics and social rules is absent in psychotic patients, but is also lacking in many pathological and borderline personalities. An obsessive personality finds it difficult to delegate to others due to lack of trust. A paranoid personality believes that others are out to harm him/her and therefore is averse to any reference to social examples. The antisocial personality is in conflict with social norms and rules. The narcissistic personality tends to overestimate his or her individual capacities and to underestimate those of others. Schizoid personality presents an absence of desire for close relationships with other human beings and an emotional detachment from people around them and reality in general. In all these cases, the individual is not inclined to rely on social intelligence to deal with everyday decisions and finds himself experimenting instead and making decisions without relying on other people's experience. These decisions are uniquely personal, complex, and difficult because of the variables at play and the difficulty in calculating the results of his decisions. In particular, the identification of cue orders for a compared choice between alternatives is suboptimal, because it relies entirely on individual learning instead of being based on social imitation. The opposite situation can also be observed, however, in patients with a borderline personality disorder (BPD) characterized by a strong emotional component. For example, in the case of a hysterical personality, the greater emotional response increases mentalization, defined as a form of interpretation of human behavior in terms of intentional mental states (Sharp et al., 2011). A "hypermentalizing" tendency increases the cooperative answer in the trust game. BPD patients were better at adjusting their investment to the fairness of their virtual partner and assessing relevant emotional cues from unfair trustees, and at using objective fairness of their counterparts to guide responses (Sharp et al., 2011). The "hypermentalizing" tendency generates social reactions that may not always be appropriate and poorer social perspective coordination, that is, the capacity to both differentiate from and integrate the perspectives of self with those of others (Jennings et al., 2012). BPD patients had a biased perception of participation. They more easily felt excluded even when included, in turn having an increase in other-focused negative emotions (Staebler et al., 2011). This tendency reflects on the use of social heuristics by exaggeratedly accentuating an acritical identification with one's choices and with other people's cue orders, with no real selection of the source based on merit and reliability.

Distorted emotions as building blocks

Emotion is one of the two central specific building blocks of social heuristics (Hertwig & Herzog, 2009). Its importance in guiding heuristic decision making is evident. Also evident is the fact that its distortion, either in terms of hyperstimulation or hypostimulation, has negative effects on the ecological rationality of individuals. According to some authors (Johnson-Laird et al., 2006; Gangemi et al., 2013), psychological illnesses are disorders in emotion, not intellect. In particular, hyper-basic emotions tend to occur at the onset of psychological illnesses. Using the Multifaceted Empathy test, BPD patients were found to have significant impairments in emotional empathy that could contribute to dysfunctional emotional and social responses (Diziobek et al., 2011). They exhibit more overall errors in recognizing facial expressions[15] on facial morph tasks, in particular, those with negative valence with fearful and surprised expressions (Domes et al., 2008). This indicates an attentional bias for fearful faces characterized by difficulty in disengaging attention from threatening stimuli. As noted, patients with BPD tend to make riskier choices because they are unable to learn to adjust them based on negative feedback (Schuermann et al., 2011). According to the distorted emotional salience of events, the tendency toward risk will change. For example, the phobic patient will tend to attach greater weight to events that are not risky and, based on them, his behavior will become risk-averse and very prudential. Conversely, the narcissistic or bipolar patient in their hypomanic phase will underestimate risk, will lean toward illusion control and will show a marked propensity for risk. Lastly, emotion in psychotics reflects on their analysis of data relevant to choices. People with psychosis make decisions on the basis of less evidence. They jump to the conclusion (JTC). In a systematic review and meta-analysis to investigate the magnitude and specificity of the JTC, they found that JTC is linked to emotional content as greater probability of having delusions, and it generates a more extreme reasoning style than people with other mental health conditions (Dudley et al., 2015). How does emotion reflect on the individual's ecological rationality? Emotion reflects on the salience of memorized information. When we have an experience that has a strong emotional component, this information will become easier to retrieve later. For example, if we have an emotional experience that is extremely positive concerning the teaching of philosophy, when deciding about your children's education, in the cue order generated, good philosophy teaching will be at the top of the ranking when comparing lexicographically a number of schools. Another example concerns the fact that if we admire a pair of parents for how they have educated their children and for their children's school performance, we will be inclined to imitate their choices in a selection of school or in the selection of extracurricular activities, like the type of summer school. Emotion shapes the dynamic or social heuristics and the associated social ecological rationality. The emotional label makes salient who we consider to be a success in which social group to take as a reference for the imitation of social rules. Under point 2 we noted the emotional component in some BPDs, such as hysterical personality, generates an excessive mentalization that can have negative effects on social heuristics and social coordination. A similar distortion in the role of emotion in heuristic decision making can also be observed in other mental disorders, such as bipolar syndrome, where the emotional sphere is altered, for example, in hypomanic phases when overconfidence and egocentrism prevail, with salient information concerning mostly groups or leaders, who are in favor of one's theories or designs or visions of the world. The hypomaniac will tend to base his choices on his overestimated capacity to learn and evaluate instead of relying on the people who are close to him, who, under different conditions, he would admire for the success they have achieved. By contrast, in depressive phases, this individual has limited confidence in himself, but at the same time is not very open to social learning. Unlike the hypomaniac, the mildly depressed person is extremely critical and skeptical about other people's capacities. His emotional sphere, characterized by pessimism and negativity, leads him not to remain enthusiastic about external events, and consequently to attribute scarce salience to information that he has memorized. Only very few events manage to overcome the threshold of positive attention and salience. When this happens, the selection threshold is extremely high and leads to a good ecological rationality in decision making. The situation is different with seriously depressed individuals. In these cases, depression pervades all cognitive activity and every bit of information tends to confirm pessimism and affective suffering. Social learning becomes impossible because every bit of external information is distorted through the depressive filter. In other mental disorders, like obsessive-compulsive personality or paranoid personality, hyperemotional stimuli generate polarization in distortion of the emotional salience of information, leading to a recall of distorted information that is not ecologically rational. The paranoid is focused on information confirming the hostile attitude of other people. The obsessive concentrates on information that confirms his fears. The role of information salience is central in the ecological functioning of many heuristics and it has acquired growing importance in explaining some psychiatric disorders. For example, Jim van Os and Shitij Kapur (2009) propose replacing the term schizophrenia with "salience disorder." Hallucinations are described as the expression of aberrant salience of visual and auditory information. In hallucinations, some sensorial input acquires salience when the relative neural signal is amplified at the expense of others. This attracts our attention in an aberrant way. According to Shitij Kapur (2003), hallucinations reflect a direct experience of the aberrant salience of internal representations. Thus, a person like Mr B—as described by Michael Gazzaniga (2018)—believes that the FBI is constantly spying on him and any visual and auditory information becomes salient to prove his delirium. He cuts social relations because he believes that the people around him are paid by the FBI to inform on his actions. At home, he does not shower naked, because he thinks he is being observed. What is interesting here is that Mr B's delirium appears rational according to specific hallucinations. Paradoxically these delusional, delirious beliefs are a rational cognitive effort to give meaning to salient aberrant sensorial experiences. Consequently, Mr B is formally rational in connection with the salient aberrant experiences, but he is not ecologically rational because his hallucinations distort the salience of external information and decrease his cognitive success in coping with the environment.

Some paradoxes of psychopathological irrationality

If the negative role of mental disorders on the individual's ecological rationality appears evident, a few last reflections can be made on some paradoxes. The following are examples thereof.

Greater logical rationality in psychiatric patients

Consider this clinical description of an impulsive-compulsive behavior (from Gangemi, Mancini, & Johnson-Laird, 2013, p. 48):

> The photographer must have been close to Rock Hudson because the photograph was a "close up." So, the photographer himself might have been contaminated. So, when he developed the negative, he could have contaminated it. The negative was in contact with the print of the photograph and so could have contaminated it. The man in charge of printing the newspaper used the photograph, and so, he could have passed its contamination on to the newspaper's printer. The printing press could have

passed the contamination on to the picture in every newspaper. So, when I touched the newspaper, I may have been contaminated with the HIV virus.

The patient's reasoning is impeccable. She constructs a long chain of logical inferences that aim to demonstrate that she has contracted HIV. According to Gangemi et al. (2013), she realizes that the conclusion is unlikely, yet typically for such patients, she cannot reject it. The chain of logical inferences is based on a distorted knowledge of reality that she accepts arbitrarily and in an ad hoc manner.

Logical rationality in several mental disorders can also be found in this simulation of consistency of choice. As noted above, the norm of "independence of irrelevant alternatives" presupposes this in the case of John and his choice to go to the club, when faced with two alternatives A and B, he cannot prefer A to B. Subsequently, when a third alternative C is added, a preference reversal occurs and John opts for B over A. John makes this inversion because his reference is not only internal to preferences, but also external, that is to say, relating to social norms. In this case, according to the norm, it would be correct not to go to a club with the girlfriend of a friend. A different situation can be observed in the case of several mental disorders, where the reference to social norms tends to dissolve. If John had an antisocial or narcissistic personality, he would not have taken into account the social norm of correctness. He would have chosen B, going to the club with Jane, in both the first and second cases (with and without the alternative of meeting Carl at the club). By so doing, John would not have broken the norm of "independence of irrelevant alternatives" and his behavior would have been correct from the point of view of logical rationality. Paradoxically, this, like other mental disorders, generates behaviors that are more coherent with the dictates of logical rationality, unlike what was believed to be case in the past. This confirms that the criterion of logical rationality is not adequate to account for the adaptive success and ecological rationality of human behavior. Is the hypoemotion of mental disorders linked to economic rationality? Above, we have seen that patients with autism were less responsive to the framing of monetary outcomes as either losses or gains and, thus, exhibited more internally consistent behavior. Loss aversion caused by heavier emotional content of loss vs. gain does not apply to autism and, as shown by De Martino et al. (2008), the behavior is less subject to the framing effect. In short, given the presence of fewer emotional states, the autistic individual has no greater propensity to risk in frames of loss and no greater aversion to risk in frames of gain. Neurological or mental disorders, reducing the activation of emotional mechanisms, generate behaviors that are more coherent in the choice of a product, satisfy the criteria of maximizing social utility, neutralize myopic loss aversion and the regret effect, are more rational in the ultimatum game, and are less subject to fear in situations characterized by ambiguity and uncertainty (Hertwig & Volz, 2013). In short, hypoemotionality makes behaviors more economically rational. These phenomena confirm the gap between economic rationality and adaptive success in real social environmental contexts. Human reason is characterized by the role of emotions and intuitions in guiding decision-making of a heuristic type. The gut feeling (Gigerenzer, 2007) is often the best option when making a decision in situations characterized by ambiguity, uncertainty, and stringent time constraints. Cold rationality devoid of any emotional content would make the subject unable to swiftly adapt to situations and would lead to adaptive failure.

Ecological rationality of the paranoid mind?

In the previous example concerning John's behavior toward the decision of whether or not to go to the club with Jane, it was concluded that, while it violated the rational norm of "independence of irrelevant alternatives," his behavior was certainly coherent with his strategy and adaptive to the social context, and therefore ecologically rational. The coherence between strategies and behavior is not only a characteristic of a normal subject. It could happen that in cases of mental disorders, one's behavior derives from a strategy that is coherent to one's heuristic rules, but the result does not appear to be (at least at first glance) ecological compared to the social context in which the decision is made. For example, a paranoid personality in a company may behave according to his own heuristics (for example, the rule whereby "If you see two colleagues who are talking and looking at you, then they are plotting something against you"), his behavior may be coherent (for example, by trying to boycott their work in the office), but presumably not adaptive to his work interests (by forcing his colleagues to marginalize him and demean him and generating an organizational malaise that would frame him as the person responsible for the situation). The word "presumably" is used here because we might wonder if these are the only adaptive criteria to be considered when judging his ecological rationality. If our judgment results from an analysis of all external constraints and the objectives of a paranoid personality on which to evaluate the success of his behavior, then those that appear to us to be negative results (like work marginalization and hostility on the part of his colleagues) may appear to the paranoid as unintentional objectives pursued in order to confirm his hypothesis of persecution through a self-evident "hindsight bias" and "confirmation bias." The classic self-fulfilling prophecy would thus be: "I was right to suspect my colleagues. They took their masks off and they are unfairly persecuting me." This is particularly true if we consider not only borderline patients, but paranoid schizophrenia, where hypotheses of persecution take on proportions of true delirium. Depending on the objective and the external environmental context, it could be ecologically rational for a paranoid patient to behave in a way that allows him to achieve results that from our perspective are extremely negative. This could be labeled irrational only if we assume a normative, benchmark for well-being and adaptive success that is external in nature by which to evaluate the paranoid individual's behavior. That is, we would be forced to judge ecological rationality, not only based on the individual's success in achieving internal, endogenous objectives, but also in relation to external, exogenous, conventional norms regarding social well-being or individual wellness. In other words, we would have to take on a paternalistic evaluation approach. If the behavior was to be judged only on the basis of subjective objectives and environmental constraints, then, paradoxically, the judgment would be that the behavior is coherent and ecologically rational.

Conclusion: what role for the brain?

Unlike neurological diseases where the biological foundation of the alterations was never in question, in psychiatry, this has happened in alternate phases. The main reason was empirical evidence at the cellular level of many neurological diseases, especially those of the degenerative and traumatic type, and the lack of psychiatric ones. Moreover, there was a strong cultural resistance against considering psychiatric disorders of a cognitive, perceptive and emotional type as diseases of the body and not of the mind. This is also because at the time there were no instruments capable of detecting relevant cellular changes. In any case, the study of neurological diseases in the past has led to great advances in knowledge of both the central and peripheral nervous system. Today, the situation has changed dramatically. As noted by Ferrer (2018), innovation in the fields of imaging, CAT scans, and electroencephalography allows us today to highlight even minimal changes in neuronal metabolism and electrical potential for actions, something that was unthinkable only a short time ago. This has allowed us to study, in completely new ways, the cognitive, perceptive, and emotional alterations in the fields of psychiatric diseases. This type of analysis has allowed us to define in a brand-new way the relationship between the environment, inheritance, and neuronal alteration, and thus to better calibrate the possible therapies. Eric Kandel, in his book *The Disordered Mind* (2018), starts from this relationship and asks the question: in light of the current knowledge of genetics in neuroscience, is it possible to find a synthesis integrating the influence of the social environment, the role of psychological therapies, and the biological dimension of mental alteration? To this end, he offers autism as an example. Human beings are genetically social animals. Human mental development and decision-making processes are constantly influenced by what other people are doing. The use of social heuristics, that is to say decision-based rules of imitation of other people's behavior, gives us the advantage of the ability to solve many problems without having to find a solution by ourselves. The capacity to imitate and interact socially is based on the capacity to read and simulate the mind and the behavior of others (Viale, 2019). Leslie Brothers (2002) identified a series of interconnected cerebral regions that elaborate social information and which are relevant to autism. This "social brain" is made up of various parts that are responsible for emotion (amygdala), the interpretation of biological motion (the upper temporal lobe), the simulation of other people's behavior (mirror neurons), the theory of the mind (the frontal-temporal system), and facial recognition (inferior temporal cortex). Through fMRI (Functional Magnetic Resonance Imaging), Stephen Gotts and colleagues (2012) recently discovered that in autistic individuals, the neural circuit of this social brain is altered. In particular, this alteration explains two important characteristics of the autistic mind: the difficulty in understanding the meaning of biological movements like stretching out a hand or walking toward another person, and the inability to understand our relationship between gaze and intention, and anticipating and simulating other people's behavior based on that input. Scholars like Bruno Bettelheim argued that autism does not have a biological basis, but that it was the result of inadequate maternal care (the regrettable and imputable theory of the "refrigerator mother"). Today research has not only identified the neural mechanisms that are at the root of autism, but is also discovering the related genetic mutations. This begins with one key observation: in homozygous twins (twins with the same genetic code), if one is autistic, the probability that both are autistic is 90 percent.

Looking at the origins of autism, the environmental influence does not appear to be relevant, and this makes it difficult to identify potential treatment based on psychological therapy. However, in other forms of mental disorders, the biological role of the social environment and psychological therapy appears much more significant. By "biological role," we refer to the capacity to modify the synaptic connections responsible for mental alterations. This is a qualifying point for Kandel, that allows him to discuss the synergy between pharmacology and psychotherapy. In pharmacological therapy, one can consider a biological-type treatment that acts on the mediators and synaptic receptors, and the same is true also for cognitive behavioural psychotherapy. This has been demonstrated through fMRI, which highlights the effects of psychotherapy on the activation of cerebral areas. One relevant example concerns depression. Today it is possible with an fMRI to identify the patients who require psychotherapy and those who also need pharmacological treatment. Some time ago, Helen Mayberg (2009) identified the neural circuit of depression and discovered that when the basal activity of one of its components, the right anterior insula (responsible for self-conscience and social experience) is below average, people respond well to psychotherapy and not to anti-depressants, while when basal activity is above average, the opposite is true. A relevant contribution to addressing the neurobiological basis of mental illness and the rational characteristics of thought can come from the studies of the emerging field of neurocomputational psychiatry.[16] It might describe how computational models of cognition can infer the current state of the environment and weigh up future actions. It might allow us to understand how the abnormal perceptions, thoughts, and behaviors that are currently used to define psychiatric disorders relate to normal functions and neural processes. For example, reinforcement learning, describing how the brain can choose and value courses of actions according to their long-term future value, may account for how depressive symptoms may result from aberrant valuations and prior belief about the loss of agency (Adams et al., 2016). Or the notion of the brain as a Bayesian inference machine may account for how several cortical abnormalities in schizophrenia might reduce precision in predictive coding, biasing Bayesian inference toward sensory data and away from prior beliefs (Adams et al., 2013). It would be interesting to analyse from a neurocomputational standpoint the failure to satisfy the ecological rationality in some mental disorders.

In conclusion, the ecological irrationality of mental disorders was discussed using a conceptual hypothetical approach. The theme, however, deserves greater attention and empirical study, which could favor the cognitive foundation of psychopathology based on ecological rationality. This chapter aimed to provide ideas concerning a future research program using, alongside the instruments of cognitive psychology, those of neurobiology and, in particular, neurocomputational psychiatry, to provide tools to identify the causes of the limited ecological adaptability of the psychiatric subject.

Acknowledgments

The author wishes to thank Ralph Hertwig and Gerd Gigerenzer for their invaluable and useful suggestions.

Notes

1 Stated simply, probabilistic inference claims that whenever the two end-terms share the middle term in common, they will be assumed to be related to each other. In other words, if the end-terms are related positively, then a positive conclusion will be drawn, while if they are related negatively, then a negative conclusion will be drawn (Evans et al. 1993, p. 239).

2 Conversion is a validating form of immediate inference for E (Negative Universal Proposition)—and I (Affirmative Particular Proposition)-type categorical propositions. To convert such a proposition is to switch the subject and predicate terms of the proposition, which is non-validating for the A (Affirmative Universal Proposition)—and O (Negative Particular Proposition) type propositions. Hence, the fallacy of illicit conversion is converting an A- or O-type proposition. For example, "We like the beautiful and don't like the ugly; therefore, what we like is beautiful, and what we don't like is ugly..."

3 The Pepsi paradox refers to the observation that Pepsi is preferred to Coke in blind taste tests, despite Coke being regarded as the more successful brand.

4 Suppose two urns each contain 100 balls. The risky urn contains 50 red and 50 black balls. The ambiguous urn contains red and black balls in unknown proportions. When individuals who stand to receive a prize for drawing a red ball are invited to choose between the two urns, they generally prefer the risky to the ambiguous urn. When they are subsequently promised a prize for drawing a black ball, their aversion to the ambiguous urn remains. This persistent preference, which leads humans to stray from the axioms of standard decision theory, has been interpreted as ambiguity aversion. If individuals prefer to draw a red ball from the risky rather than the ambiguous urn, then their subjective probability of drawing a red ball from the ambiguous urn must be 0.5. Therefore, they should prefer to draw a black ball from the ambiguous rather than the risky urn, but most do not. However, the "right" kind of brain damage seems to cure humans of ambiguity aversion.

5 It is not only humans who violate this type of norms; animals do too. For example, honeybees violate transitivity in their preferences, preferring flower A to B, B to C, and C to D, and yet preferring D to A (Shafir, 1994). The violation of syntactical norms appears to be essential for survival.

6 Heuristic refers here to a strategy ignoring part of the information for the purpose of making decisions faster, more frugally and/or more accurately than when using more complex methods (Gigerenzer & Gassmaier, 2011).

7 With a sequential study on several reasons, there are heuristics of the lexicographical and satisficing type. In this case, too, the decision is made based on one reason without any compensatory analysis of the trade-off between the weights of the various reasons. It is on the basis of these models that the "fast-and-frugal trees" were conceived; these are decisional trees the branches of which present a binary choice to which heuristics based on one reason are applied.

8 Decisions in conditions of uncertainty do not include risk situations with a high number of alternatives in which heuristics can still be successfully applied. For example, when playing chess, the alternatives are theoretically knowable, but in fact are so numerous as to produce a computational explosion of the decisional problem. As Simon correctly points out, the only solution is the heuristic decision.

9 The Effective Annual Percentage Rate (EAPR) is the effective annual interest rate, including all contract expenses.

10 In these cases, we are faced with the "bias-variance" dilemma. On one hand, statistical samples carry the danger of variance. On the other, heuristics that ignore basic statistical information risk generating bias. Consider, for example, the "base-rate fallacy" in the ex post evaluation of the phenomenon based on new information. When the amount of data to be collected is enormous, the error derived from small samples is higher than that derived from the information bias of the heuristics (Gigerenzer & Gassmaier, 2011).

11 Nudge theory (Thaler & Sunstein, 2008) applies the imitation of social rules as an instrument to direct the citizens toward behaviors related to their well-being, or the social or environmental good. In fact, the imitative behavior that is encouraged refers to social imitation heuristics (Viale, forthcoming).

12 This last heuristic is also at the heart of the interpretation of the efficacy of policy defaults as implicit recommendations in Nudge theory (Thaler & Sunstein, 2008; Viale, forthcoming).

13 This type of limited and ecological rationality is such because it builds on the "embodied" dimension of cognition. Without this embodiment, limited individual rationality would not be ecological, in that it would not possess the terminals to interact successfully with the environment (for an in-depth analysis of this theme, see Chapter 23 by Gallese, Mastrogiorgio, Petracca, & Viale in this volume).

14 Feedbacks are an important concept also in the theory of complexity and in particular in Complex Adaptive Systems (CAS). When the interactions are not independent, feedback can enter the system and alter its dynamics. When feedback is negative, changes get absorbed and the system tends toward stability. When it is positive, changes get amplified, leading to instability (Miller and Page, 2007, p. 50). Systems that settle into equilibrium tend to include negative feedback. On the contrary, systems that generate complexity tend to include positive feedback. An example is the phenomenon of network externality.

15 This test is relevant because facial emotion recognition may contribute to social cognitive responses.

16 Neurocomputational psychiatry aims to describe the relationship between the brain's neurobiology, its environment, and mental symptoms in computational mathematical terms (Adams et al., 2016).

References

Adams, A. R., Huys, Q., & Roiser, J. P. (2016). Computational psychiatry: towards a mathematically informed understanding of mental illness. *Journal of Neurological and Neurosurgical Psychiatry*, 87(1), 53–63.

Adams, A. R., Stephan, K. E., Brown, H. R., Frith, C. D., & Friston, K. J. (2013). The computational anatomy of psychosis. *Frontiers in Psychiatry*, 4, 1–26.

Alos-Ferrer, C. (2018). Analisi critica di "Social Neuroscience": la ricerca sul cervello sociale e l'economia si influenzano a vicenda? *Sistemi Intelligenti*, XXX, 2, 229–274.

Alter, A.L., & Oppenheimer, D.M. (2006). Predicting short-term stock fluctuations by using processing fluency., *Proceedings of the National Academy of Sciences U.S.A.*, 103, 9369–9372.

American Psychiatric Association (2000). *Diagnostic and statistical manual of mental disorders* (DSM-IV-TR). Washington, DC: APA.

American Psychiatric Association (2013). *Diagnostic and statistical manual of mental disorders* (DSM-V-TR). Washington, DC: APA.

Arieti, S. (1963). *Interpretazione della schizofrenia*. Milan: Feltrinelli.

Arkes, H.R., Gigerenzer, G., & Hertwig, R. (2016). How bad is incoherence? *Decision*, 3(1), 20–39.

Bara, B. G. (Ed.) (2005). *Nuovo manuale di psicoterapia cognitiva*. Turin: Bollati Boringhieri.

Boyd, R., & Richerson, P. J. (2005). *The origin and evolution of cultures*. New York: Oxford University Press.

Brothers, L. (2002). The social brain: A project for integrate primate behaviour and neurophysiology in anew domain. *Concepts in Neuroscience*, 1, 27–51.

Brunswik, E. (1952). The conceptual framework of psychology. In *International encyclopedia of unified science* (Vol. 1, no. 10, pp. 4–102). Chicago: University of Chicago Press.

Camille N. et al. (2004). The involvement of the orbitofrontal cortex in the experience of regret. *Science*, 304, 1167–1170.

Chapman, L. J., & Chapman, J. P. (1959). Atmosphere effect re-examined. *Journal of Experimental Psychology*, 58, 220–226.

Clark, A. (2016). *Surfing uncertainty: Prediction, action, and the embodied mind*. Oxford: Oxford University Press.

Damasio, A. (1994). *Descartes' error*. New York: Avon.

De Martino, B., Harrison, N. A., Knafo, S., Bird, G., & Dolan, R. J. (2008). Explaining enhanced logical consistency during decision making in autism. *Journal of Neuroscience*, 28, 10746–10750.

Domes, G., Czieschnek, D., Weidler, F., et al. (2008). Recognition of facial affect in borderline personality disorder. *Journal of Personality Disorders*, 22, 135–147.

Dudley, R., Taylor, P., Wickman, S., & Hutton, P. (2015). Psychosis, delusions, and the 'jumping to conclusions' reasoning bias: A systematic review and meta-analysis. *Schizophrenia Bulletin*, 42(3), 652–665.

Dziobek, I., Preissler, S., Grozdanovic, Z., et al. (2011) Neuronal correlates of altered empathy and social cognition in borderline personality disorder. *Neuroimage*, 57, 539–548.

Evans, J. St. B., Over, D. E., & Manktelow, K. I. (1993). Reasoning, decision making and rationality, *Cognition*, 49(1–2), 165–187.

Foucault, M. (1961). *History of madness*. London: Routledge.

Gangemi, A., Mancini, F., & Johnson-Laird, P. (2013). Emotion, reasoning, and psychopathology. In I. Blanchette (Ed.), *Emotion and reasoning*. London: Psychology Press.

Garcia-Retamero, R., Takezawa, M., & Gigerenzer, G. (2006). How to learn good cue orders: When social learning benefits simple heuristics. In R. Sun & N. Miyake (Eds.), *Proceedings of the 28th annual conference of the Cognitive Science Society* (pp. 1352–1358). Mahwah, NJ: Erlbaum.

Gazzaniga, M. S. (2018). *The consciousness instinct: Unraveling the mystery of the brain makes the mind*. New York: Farrar, Straus, and Giroux

Gigerenzer, G. (2007). *Gut feeling*. London: Penguin.

Gigerenzer, G., & Gaissmaier, (2011). Heuristic decision making. *The Annual Review of Psychology*, 62, 451–482.

Gigerenzer, G., & Hoffrage, U., (1995). How to improve Bayesian reasoning without instructions: Frequency formats. *Psychological Review*, 102, 684–704.

Gigerenzer, G., Todd, P. M. & the ABC Research Group (Eds.) (1999). *Simple heuristics that make us smart*. New York: Oxford University Press.

Goldstein, D. G., & Gigerenzer G. (2009). Fast and frugal forecasting. *International Journal of Forecasting*, 24, 760–77 2.

Gotts, S.J., Simmons, W. K., Milbury, L. A., Wallace, G. L., Cox, R. W., & Mertin, A. (2012). Fractional of social brain circuits in autism spectrum disorders. *Brain*, 135, 9, 2711–2725.

Henrich, J., & McElreath, P. (2003). The evolution of cultural evolution. *Evolutionary Anthropology: Issues, News, and Reviews*, 12(3), 123–135.

Hertwig, R., & Herzog, M. S. (2009). Fast and frugal heuristics: Tools of social rationality. 27(5), 661–698.

Hertwig, R., & Volz, K. G. (2013). Abnormality, rationality, and sanity. *Trends in Cognitive Sciences*, 17(1), 547–549.

Hsu, M., Bhatt, M., Adolphs, R., Tranel, D., & Camerer, C. F. (2005). Neural systems responding to degrees of uncertainty in human decision-making. *Science*, 310, 1680–1683.

Jennings, T. C., Hulbert, C. A., Jackson, H. J., et al. (2012). Social perspective coordination in youth with borderline personality pathology. *Journal of Personality Disorders*, 26, 126–140.

Johnson-Laird, P. N., Mancini, F., & Gangemi, A. (2006). A hyper-emotion theory of psychological illnesses. *Psychological Review*, 113, 822–842.

Kahneman, D. (2011). *Thinking, fast and slow*. New York: Farrar, Strauss & Giroux

Kandell, E. (2018). *La mente alterata*. Milan: Cortina.

Kapur, S. (2003). Psychosis as a state of aberrant salience: A framework linking biology, phenomenology, and pharmacology in schizophrenia. *American Journal of Psychiatry*, 160, 13–23.

Knoch D. et al. (2006). Diminishing reciprocal fairness by disrupting the right prefrontal cortex. *Science*, 314, 829–832.

Koenigs, M., & Tranel, D. (2008) Prefrontal cortex damage abolishes brand-cued changes in cola preference. *Social Cognitive and Affective Neuroscience*, 3, 1–6.

Koscik T.R., & Tranel D. (2013). Abnormal causal attribution leads to advantageous economic decision-making: a neuropsychological approach. *Journal of Cognitive Neuroscience*, 25, 1372–1382.

Langer, E. J. (1975). The illusion of control. *Journal of Personality and Social Psychology*, 32(2), 311–328.

Mark, A., & Lam, L. (2013). Neurocognitive profiles of people with borderline personality disorder. *Current Opinion in Psychiatry*, 26, 90–96.

Matte Blanco, I. (1981). *L'inconscio come insiemi infiniti*. Turin: Einaudi.

Mayberg, H. S. (2009). Targeted electrode-based modulation of neural circuits for depression. *Journal of Clinical Investigation*, 119(4), 717–725.

Mendez, M. F. (2009). The neurobiology of moral behavior: Review and neuropsychiatric implications. *CNS Spectrums*, 14, 608–620.

Miller, J.H., & Page, S.E. (2007). *Complex adaptive systems*. Princeton NJ: Princeton University Press.

Moore, D. A., & Schatz, D. (2017). The three faces of overconfidence. *Social and Personality Psychology Compass*, 11(8).

Ortmann, A., Gigerenzer, G., Borges, B., & Goldstein, D.G. (2008). The recognition heuristic: A fast and frugal way to investment choice? In C. R. Plott & V. L. Smith (Eds.), *Handbook of experimental economics results*, vol. 1. Amsterdam: North Holland.

Richerson, P. J., & Boyd, R. (2005). *Not by gene alone: How culture transformed human evolution*. Chicago: University of Chicago Press.

Samuelson, P. (1938). A note on the pure theory of consumers. *Economica*, 6, 61–71.

Schooler, L. J., & Hertwig, R. (2005). How forgetting aids heuristic inference. *Psychological Review*, 112, 610–628.

Schuermann, B., Kathmann, N., Stiglmayr, C., & Endrass, T. (2011) Impaired decision making and feedback evaluation in borderline personality disorder. *Psychological Medicine*, 41(9), 1917–1927.

Schurtz, G., & Hetwig, G. (2019). Cognitive success: A consequentialist account of rationality in cognition. *Topics in Cognitive Science*, 11, 7–36.

Sen, A. (1993). Internal consistency of choice. *Econometrica*, 61, 495–521.

Sen, A. (2002). *Rationality and freedom*. Cambridge, MA: Harvard University Press.

Serwe S., & Frings C. (2006). Who will win Wimbledon? The recognition heuristic in predicting sport events. *Journal of Behavioral Decision Making*, 19, 321–332.

Shafir, E. (1994). Uncertainty and the difficulty of thinking through disjunctions. *Cognition*, 50(1–3), 403–430.

Shafir, S., & Smith, W. (2002) Context-dependent violations of rational choice in honeybees (*Apis mellifera*) and gray jays (*Perisoreus canadensis*). *Behavioral Ecology and Sociobiology*, 51, 180–187.

Sharp, C., Pane, H., Ha, C., et al. (2011). Theory of mind and emotion regulation difficulties in adolescents with borderline traits. *Journal of the American Academy of Child and Adolescent Psychiatry*, 50, 563–573.e1.

Shiv, B., Lowenstein, G., Bechara, A., Damasio, H., & Damasio, A. (2005). Investment behavior and the negative side of emotion. *Psychological Science* 16, 435–439.

Simon, H. (1978). Rational decision making in business organizations. In A. Lindbeck (Ed.), *From Nobel lectures, economics 1969–1980*. Singapore: World Scientific Publishing Co.

Simon, H. (1986). *Decision making and problem solving*. Washington, DC: National Academy Press.

Simon, H. (1990). Invariants of human behaviour. *Annual Review of Psychology*, 41, 1–19.

Staebler, K., Renneberg, B., Stopsack, M., et al. (2011). Facial emotional expression in reaction to social exclusion in borderline personality disorder. *Psychological Medicine*, 41, 1929–1938.

Thaler, R., & Sunstein, C. (2008). *Nudge*. London: Penguin.

Todd, P. M., Gigerenzer, G., & the ABC Research Group (2012). *Ecological rationality: Intelligence in the world*. New York: Oxford University Press.

Tversky, A., & Kahneman, D. (1974). Judgement under uncertainty: Heuristics and biases. *Science*, 185, 1124–1131.

Van Os, J., & Kapur, S. (2009). Schizophrenia. *The Lancet*, 374, 635–645.

Viale, R. (2012). *Methodological cognitivism*. Vol. I. *Mind, rationality and society*. Heidelberg: Springer.

Viale, R. (2013). *Methodological cognitivism*. Vol. II. *Cognition, science and innovation*. Heidelberg: Springer.

Viale, R. (2019). La razionalità limitata "embodied" alla base del cervello sociale ed economico. *Sistemi Intelligenti*, 1.

Viale, R. (forthcoming). *Nudging*. Cambridge, MA: MIT Press.

Viale, R., Macchi, L., & Bagassi, M. (in preparation). Decision making as problem solving.

von Domarus, E. (1925). Ueber die Beziehung des normalen zum schizophrenen Denken. *Archives of Psychiatry*, 74, 641–646.

von Domarus, E. (1944). *The specific laws of logic in schizophrenia*. Berkeley, CA: University of California Press.

Wason, P.C. (1966). Reasoning about a rule. *Quarterly Journal of Experimental Psychology*, 20(3), 273–281.

Wason, P. C., & Johnson-Laird, P. N. (1972). *The psychology of reasoning*. Cambridge, MA: Harvard University Press.

Wübben, M. & Wangenheim F. (2008). Instant customer base analysis: managerial heuristics often "get it right". *Journal of Marketing*, 72, 82–93.

Young L., & Koenigs M. (2007). Investigating emotion in moral cognition: a review of evidence from functional neuroimaging and neuropsychology. *British Medical Bulletin*, 84, 69–79.

PART IV

Embodied bounded rationality

23

EMBODIED BOUNDED RATIONALITY

Vittorio Gallese, Antonio Mastrogiorgio, Enrico Petracca,
and Riccardo Viale

The root of bounded rationality in cognitive psychology and the bounds of embodied cognition

There is little doubt that one of Simon's key contributions throughout his scientific career—if not the main one—was rooting the notion of bounded rationality in cognitive psychology (Simon, 1976). He called his notion of bounded rationality in the cognitive psychology realm "cognitivism" (Haugeland, 1978), an approach, also known as the "information-processing" approach, which he contributed to affirming together with his colleague Allen Newell, starting in the mid-1950s. According to cognitivism, cognition works through the internal (i.e. mental) manipulation of representations of the external environment accomplished through referential "symbols" (e.g., Newell & Simon, 1972). Connecting Simon's theory of cognition to his theory of rationality is the notion that cognition works in a way that is *necessary and sufficient* for intelligent behavior (what is known as the "physical symbol system hypothesis," see Newell & Simon, 1976). The idea that results from integrating Simon's view of cognition with his view of bounded rationality is that rationality is a "process and product of thought" (Simon, 1978), in which the internal bounds of reason (Simon, 1955) adapt to the external bounds of the environment (Simon, 1956) in a disembodied fashion.

In this picture, in fact, there is no place for flesh and blood. Patokorpi (2008) has emphasized that there is an inner tension in Simon's thought, as, on the one hand, he was a strong advocate for a realistic approach to the bounds of rationality, while, on the other, he represented them through the "unbounded" power of digital computation and the metaphor of computers. This inner tension, which did not simply concern Simon's thought but an entire generation of cognitive scientists, would have huge consequences in the history of cognitive psychology. In the early 1990s, Newell and Simon's physical symbol system hypothesis was questioned when the "embodied robots" designed by Rodney Brooks proved able to simulate simple forms of intelligent behavior by externalizing most of cognition onto the physical properties of environments, thus dispensing with abstract symbolic processing (Brooks, 1991). This is just one instance from the recent history of cognitive science pointing to the fact that while bounded rationality remains a pivotal notion in behavioral economics and economic psychology, new theoretical views and massive experimental evidence in cognitive science have superseded

DOI: 10.4324/9781315658353-27

cognitivism and its abstract representation of cognition (Wallace et al., 2007). Contemporary cognitive psychology emphasizes that cognition is "embodied," as it constitutively depends on body states, on the morphological traits of the human body, and on the sensory-motor system (see, e.g., Wilson, 2002). As such, it can be said to introduce another "bound" to human cognition, able to integrate the internal bounds represented by cognitive limitations and the external bounds of task environments: the human body. In this chapter, we argue that, in so far as the human body represents a new bound for human cognition, it can also have an important role in the re-conceptualization of bounded rationality. Since the new approach of embodied cognition is so recent, it is still rather plural and variegated, and as such far from a stable synthesis (for reviews on the issue of conceptual pluralism in embodied cognition, see the classic Wilson, 2002; for more recent reviews, see Gallese & Lakoff, 2005; Clark, 2008; Kiverstein & Clark, 2009). Without the claim of being exhaustive, here is a list of classic books on the idea that the body is a constitutive part of cognition: Varela, Thompson, & Rosch (1991); Clancey (1997); Clark (1997); Lakoff & Johnson (1999); Rowlands (1999); Shapiro (2004); Gallagher (2005); and Pfeifer & Bongard (2006). As a matter of terminology, although different labels have been used to identify and distinguish different views of embodiment, we will refer to them all by means of the common synthetic label "embodied cognition" (Calvo & Gomila, 2008; Shapiro, 2014).

The morphology of the human body and the sensory-motor system in cognition

Different arguments have been provided to support the idea that cognition is embodied. We will consider here two main categories of arguments: the evolutionary arguments on the one hand, and the developmental arguments on the other (Meier et al. 2012). An evolutionary argument for embodied cognition consists in emphasizing that the brain is structured by evolutionary layers, so that the new layers exploit and build upon the resources of older ones, which were mostly devoted to 'lower' cognitive activities like sensory-motor control (this has been called the "principle of neural exploitation," see Gallese 2008, or "principle of neural reuse," see Anderson, 2010). Another evolutionary argument concerns the emergence of cognitive artifacts from the morphological traits of the human body as is the case, for example, with numeric systems. It is well known that numeric systems depend on the underlying morphological traits used for counting (e.g., the 10-based numeral system uses the 10 fingers of the hands, while other numeric systems stem from the use of other bodily resources; see Gibbs, 2006). Numeric processing, as such, is not an abstract process (Cohen Kados & Walsh, 2009). In this regard, even the disembodied cognitive artifact *par excellence*, the entire apparatus of mathematics, is rooted in the human body (Lakoff & Nuñez, 2000). On the other hand, the developmental arguments for embodiment focus on childhood learning, emphasizing the role of the child's exploration of the surrounding space (and the related physical sensations) in the development of cognitive faculties and structures in adulthood (e.g., Williams, Huang, & Bargh, 2009). Further, developmental processes of imitation, based on "embodied simulation" (Gallese 2003, 2007), lie at the root of intersubjectivity (e.g., Gallese & Goldman, 1998; Iacoboni, 2009; Gallese 2014). Far from being just an alternative hypothesis on the foundations of cognition, the idea that cognition is embodied is evidenced by a number of experiments connecting body states to judgment, decision-making, problem-solving, attitude formation, etc. Experimental evidence shows that body variables decisively direct and affect decision-making (see the classic study by Damasio, 1994; for a review of related neuroeconomics evidence, see Reimann & Bechara, 2010). Further, problem-solving is non-trivially dependent on body correlates like, for instance, eye movement (e.g., Werner & Raab, 2014). Other various experimental evidence shows that people judge steepness depending on the weight of their backpacks (Bhalla & Proffitt, 1999), that environmental temperature affects social attitudes (e.g., Zhong & Leonardelli, 2008), that imagined food consumption makes people satiated (Morewedge, Huh, & Vosgerau, 2010), or that physical weight induces the perception of importance (Jostmann, Lakens & Schubert, 2009).

A more complex view of Simon's scissors

Most of the experimental findings introduced above simply do not make sense in the cognitivist paradigm. This is mainly because an entire conceptual locus, the human body, was missing in the cognitivist picture of cognition. This is mostly visible if we consider the famous metaphor that Simon used to introduce bounded rationality: the scissors metaphor. As Newell and Simon said:

> Just as a scissors cannot cut paper without two blades, a theory of thinking and problem solving cannot predict behavior unless it encompasses both an analysis of the structure of task environments and an analysis of the limits of rational adaptation to task requirements.
>
> *1972, p. 55*

The existence of two "blades," cognition and environment, is not able by itself, however, to express the richness of human cognitive activity. In other words, human cognition is underdetermined by the two *loci* of the scissors metaphor.

Before exploring the reasons and consequences of this underdetermination, it is important to say something on the connection between Simon's "bounded rationality" and Gerd Gigerenzer's "ecological rationality." As is well known, Gigerenzer was deeply inspired by Simon's scissors metaphor (e.g., Gigerenzer & Goldstein, 1996). In line with Simon, Gigerenzer's notion of ecological rationality for heuristic judgment maintains that "A heuristic is ecologically rational to the degree that it is adapted to the structure of the environment" (Gigerenzer et al., 1999, p. 13). Furthermore, although much less committed than Simon to the cognitivist approach to cognition, Gigerenzer admits that ecological rationality's program is inspired by "Simon and Newell's emphasis on creating precise computational models" (Gigerenzer et al., 1999, p. 26; see Petracca, 2017, for further points of contact between the two views). Undoubtedly, ecological rationality moves a step forward with respect to Simon's bounded rationality by emphasizing the crucial requirements of ecology for rational adaptation, but the 'cognitive' dimension of ecology remains either Simonian (e.g., when emphasizing the modularity of human intelligence, Gigerenzer, 1997) or not fully explored.

In a true ecological model of cognition, the role of the human body is pivotal (Hirose, 2002). Although one may still maintain that adaptation is between "cognition" and "environments," this is not a good reason to rule out the role of the human body as a mediating evolutionary or developmental interface. This is why we propose to enrich the traditional scissors metaphor by identifying another conceptual locus, the human body, which would metaphorically take the place of the 'pivot' of the scissors. In the next two sections, we will explore how heuristics and representations, two notions that are central in Simon's traditional view of bounded rationality, can be reconceptualized in the light of embodied cognition.

Rules of thumb: embodied heuristics

Embodied cognition can help to reconsider such a fundamental notion in bounded rationality as heuristics. This may be accomplished, at a first level of approximation, by emphasizing that a common name for heuristic is the "rule of thumb": an expression emphasizing that heuristics originate from body resources used for inferential purposes. The thumb can be considered as a true cognitive resource, either when it is institutionally established as a measuring device or when it is used on the fly as a tool to estimate approximate distance, length, etc. Less speculatively, the heuristic that better represents the *trait d'union* between ecological rationality and the embodied cognition approach is the "gaze heuristic," which is worth examining in some detail. It is important to note, incidentally, that Gigerenzer discussed this well-known heuristic in his more 'embodied' book, when he explicitly emphasized the notion of "gut feelings" (Gigerenzer, 2007). The gaze heuristic is a heuristic that is used to correct motion, on the fly, to achieve a spatial goal (see Hamlin, 2017); as such, it is used in many real-world activities like, for instance, catching a ball flying through the air, chasing prey, or landing an airplane. Contrary to the idea that individuals unconsciously perform complicate computations in this kind of task (Dawkins, 1976), the gaze heuristic shows that humans simply exploit the coupling between the visual perceptual apparatus and the invariant (because of the laws of physics, the relative invariance of human environments, etc.) properties of motor tasks. The gaze heuristic specifically reads: "Fix the gaze on the objective and adapt movement and running speed so that the angle of gaze remains constant." A wide array of motor tasks are possible through this heuristic without the need to rely on complex computations, simply by focusing on one variable: the object's angle. The gaze heuristics shows that adaptation occurs not only between cognition and environments, but it also crucially involves the structure of the perceptual and motor apparatuses.

Affordances and heuristics

The gaze heuristic is based on a fundamental principle: perceptive estimations are driven by pragmatic reasons, as perception aims to facilitate individuals' adaption to different situations (Mastrogiorgio & Petracca, 2018). The gaze mechanism is therefore a form of *ecological rationality* based on perceptual processing (Viale, 2017). However, the perception of environmental information (used by individuals to make decisions) is not a static and passive activity like taking a photograph. It involves instead the active research and manipulation of the inputs coming from eyes, head, and trunk movements. Moreover, an external object is perceived through the signals that it sends to the individual, so as to trigger neuro-motor patterns functional to this interaction. Objects 'speak' to the individual and 'tell' her/him what to do to allow interaction. This is the 'affordance' offered by the object, which the individual is invited to 'follow.' The concept of affordance, introduced by the psychologist of perception James Gibson (1950, 1979), concerns the dynamic relations that are established between an agent and a perceived object. Any perceptual stimulus coming from objects not only represents a collection of properties, but also triggers a possibility for action coupled with the sensory and motor characteristics of the perceiver. Our motor system is activated every time we observe an object that can be grasped, and get ready to perform an action congruent with the physical features of the object (Caruana & Borghi, 2016). For instance, a ball thrown in the air induces the action of picking up the ball, and this is true for any other stimulus (the irregular slope of a mountain triggers the affordance of climbing it, etc.). Evidence of this *embodied* mark of perception comes from neuroscience. By observing the effect of damage to the inferotemporal and parietal regions, it was noted that during the observation of an object the information is sorted along two different cerebral channels: a *ventral pathway*, which connects the visual to the temporal cortex and oversees semantic recognition processes, and a *dorsal pathway* in the cortex, which reaches the parietal lobe and processes the pragmatic aspects connected to visual-motor transformation and to action (Caruana & Borghi, 2016). The parietal lobe, however, presents features that are particularly interesting to explain the motor aspects involved in perception. In this region, a *dorso-dorsal pathway* can be observed, as well as a *ventro-dorsal* one, and the *intraparietal sulcus* (dividing the inferior parietal lobule from the superior one). The first pathway of visuomotor transformation is aimed to enable the action of reaching and grabbing objects. The second pathway concerns instead the storage of motor programs. The *intraparietal sulcus* is, however, the element that presents the most significant characteristics in terms of visuomotor coordination. The neuronal composition of its anterior part (AIP, *Anterior Intraparietal Area*) presents visual, visuomotor, and motor neurons that are activated, selectively, every time we observe objects that can be grasped. During the mere observation of graspable objects, this area automatically instantiates a grasping action, regardless of the actual will to grasp them. The same happens also in the area of F5 mirror neurons, to which the AIP is connected. According to Rob Ellis and Mike Tucker (2000), the affordances concerning the automatic grasping of objects occur because of the repeated co-occurrence of visual and action patterns. For example, the repeated past association that has occurred between the ball falling and the action to pick it up results in an affordance consisting in the automatic behavior to reach it, typical of the gaze heuristic. Moreover, it would not seem possible for affordances to be triggered indiscriminately, without any 'top-down' adjustment stemming from the context of outcomes and goals to be achieved. Since we are surrounded by many objects and each of them has multiple affordances (e.g., a cup may be grasped by the handle, the base, the lip, etc.), it is unlikely that our brain engages in responding to this proliferation of affordances indiscriminately (Caruana & Borghi, 2016, p. 48). Tipper and his team (2006) performed a clever experiment that seems to demonstrate that the effect of affordances is task-driven and not automatic. For example, when facing a book on a table, if the goal is grasping the book to put it on a shelf, a power grasp affordance will be triggered. If, instead, the goal is to flip through the pages, a precision grasp one will be triggered. Thus, when the ball is falling down, the grabbing affordance is activated when we find ourselves in the context of playing and the goal is to grab the ball. This may be not the case if we are taking our dog for a walk in a park and people are playing with a ball in the distance. Almost all objects have conflicting and competing affordances, and it is the context and our goals that make us select the coherent one. The context may be physical or social. For example, when the grasping distance of an object makes it too far away in an extra-personal space (physical context effect), no affordance is triggered. If instead it is within the peri-personal space of the individual (social context effect), the affordance is triggered. Our capacity to understand other people's intentions, through what is called *embodied simulation* (see below), leads us to treat them as avatars with regard to the perception of objects and their affordances, as if we want to act in their place. This effect seems to be generated by embodied simulation working as a "mind-reading" activity (Viale, 2012).

These remarks on sensory-motor aspects of perception may provide the basis for a variety of decision-making heuristics. As noted earlier, gaze heuristics can be explained according to a sensory-motor model. Other heuristics, such as the ones based on recognition like the "take-the-first" heuristic, can be explained within the same framework (Viale, 2017). If we think of recognition as the first option coming to mind when playing a team game and having to pass the ball to a teammate, it is clear that this process relies on sensory-motor memory. The repeated co-occurrence of similar situations in previous games with the same teammates (or different players occupying similar positions) in the game dynamics leads to the creation of mnemonic patterns (e.g., through the ventro-dorsal pathway for the storage of motor programs) of a sensory-motor type that trigger automatic decisions about passing the ball. The player passes the ball to the first player corresponding to the sensory-motor memory patterns. In other words, it is the affordance of the teammate in a certain position on the field that triggers the player's sensory-motor memory and that makes him/her pass the ball in a certain way.

Heuristics and embodied emotions

People often talk about decisions based on a "gut feeling." Particularly when a decision is taken under time pressure, with limited information, and when the effect of this decision has implications on one's well-being, one does not rely on complex computations but on gut feelings. Consider the required speed in financial trading decisions: there is no time for in-depth reasoning, as decisions have to be made in just a few seconds. Only intuition and gut feeling can work as decision makers. Gigerenzer (2007) presents numerous examples of decisions taken in this way. What characterizes gut-based decisions? These are decisions where the emotional component contained in choosing one option over another is expressed positively or negatively at the bodily level (Damasio, 1994). When the taxi driver takes one glance at the customer and feels a "knot in the stomach," he or she suddenly decides the customer cannot be trusted and it is not safe to take him on board.

The role of emotions is evident in many other aspects of decision making. When using the recognition heuristic, it is the emotional element of familiarity that often leads us to pick one option over another (Viale, 2017). Emotion plays an important role also in the case of "one reason-based" heuristics (Gigerenzer & Gaissmaier, 2011). Let us consider the "take-the-best" heuristic, according to which, when making a choice, an individual retrieves from memory situations, facts, and reasons, and uses the first cue in order to evaluate alternatives. The emotion related to specific episodes is important to strengthen memorization and the subsequent retrieval. Heuristics based on recognition and on "one reason" have the capacity to generate decisions that are more adaptive if compared to the algorithms of (neo)classical rationality. They allow us to deal with an environment characterized by uncertainty and complexity through rapid decisions that are simple, frugal, and effective in terms of prediction. They are therefore the center of gravity of the *ecological* dimension of *bounded rationality* (Viale, 2017). This adaptive capacity can be explained precisely by the role that emotion plays in the interaction between the individual and the environment. The mechanisms of emotion seem to refer to the functions of the *ventromedial prefrontal cortex*, which includes the *orbitofrontal cortex*. By virtue of its multiple incoming connections with sensory and enteroceptive areas and of its outgoing connections with the autonomous nervous system, the ventromedial cortex serves to read physical expressions and to assess the physiological state of the body. In this way, it reads physical sensations connected to decision-making options and automatically leads the individual toward those that are characterized by well-being and pleasure, avoiding negative ones. Another important cortical structure involved in the emotional experience is the *insula* or *Island of Reil*. Its *posterior part* functions as a primary enteroceptive cortex in its own right. It receives a variety of stimuli from gustative representation to pain, tactile sensations, disgust, visceromotor control, thermoception, etc. According to the neuroscientist Bud Craig (2011), the posterior insula processes this information and constitutes a sort of cerebral map of corporal states. The *ventral* part of the *insula* instead works for the subsequent processing of this map to generate a sort of re-interpretation of the emotional experience. In short, the insula functions as an 'emotional eye' of corporal states, interpreting them, and generating, together with the ventromedial prefrontal cortex, choices and decisions. (Neural imaging tests could verify the hypothesis that recognition and one-reason-based heuristics rely on ventromedial prefrontal cortex and insula activation, and are therefore driven by emotional salience-based retrieval.)

Embodied representations and simulations

Central notions in Simon's approach to cognitive psychology and bounded rationality are those of mental representation and simulation. Characteristically, in Simon's framework, mental representations and simulations would be constituted of abstract and amodal 'symbols' (Newell & Simon, 1972, 1976). Embodied cognition does not completely rule out the role of representations and simulations in cognition (even if this is not true for all approaches to embodied cognition, see Petracca, 2017), but definitely rejects the idea that they are abstract and amodal.

One of the most exciting contributions of neuroscience to the debate about the nature of the human mind and its functional mechanisms is the discovery of the cognitive role of the cortical motor system. Empirical research has demonstrated, first in non-human primates and then in humans, that the cortical motor system is functionally organized in terms of motor goals. Many cortical motor neurons, both in the frontal and parietal lobes, do not discharge during the execution of elementary movements, but are only active before and during purposive motor acts, i.e., movements executed to accomplish specific motor outcomes, like grasping, tearing, holding, or manipulating objects. The teleological dimension of behavior thus entirely belongs to the functional properties of the motor system. A further element of novelty about the cognitive role of the motor system is provided by the robust evidence of its involvement in perception: premotor and parietal areas contain motor neurons that also perceptually respond to visual, auditory, and somatosensory inputs (see Gallese & Cuccio, 2015).

The discovery—first in macaque monkeys, then in humans—of "mirror neurons" revealed the cognitive role of the motor system in social cognition. Mirror neurons are motor neurons that respond both when a given movement or action is performed and when it is observed being performed by someone else. Mirror neurons reveal a new empirically founded notion of intersubjectivity connoted first and foremost as intercorporeality: the mutual resonance of intentionally meaningful sensorimotor behaviors. The ability to understand others as intentional agents does not exclusively depend on propositional competence, but it is in the first place dependent on the relational nature of action. According to this hypothesis, it is possible to directly understand others' basic actions by means of the motor equivalence between what others do and what the observer can do. Thus, intercorporeality becomes the primordial source of knowledge that we have of others.

These findings led to the "Motor Cognition" hypothesis (see Gallese et al., 2009): cognitive abilities like the mapping of space and its perception, the perception of objects occupying our visual landscape, the hierarchical representation of action with respect to a distal goal, the detection of others' motor goals, and the anticipation of their actions are possible because of the peculiar functional architecture of the motor system, organized in terms of goal-directed motor acts. The same motor circuits that control individuals' behavior within their environment also map distances, locations, and objects in that very same environment, thus defining and shaping in motor terms their representational content. The way the visual world is represented by the motor system incorporates agents' idiosyncratic way to interact with it.

Empirical research demonstrated that the human brain is also endowed with mirror mechanisms in the domain of emotions and sensations: the very same nervous structures involved in the subjective experience of emotions and sensations are also active when such emotions and sensations are recognized in others. For example, witnessing someone expressing a given emotion (e.g., disgust, pain, etc.) or undergoing a given sensation (e.g., touch) recruits some of the viscero-motor (e.g., *anterior insula*) and sensori-motor (e.g., SII, *ventral premotor cortex*) brain areas activated when one experiences the same emotion or sensation, respectively. Other cortical regions, though, are exclusively recruited for one's own and not for others' emotions, or are activated for one's own tactile sensation, but are actually deactivated when observing someone else being touched (for review, see Gallese, 2014; Gallese & Cuccio, 2015).

Embodied simulation theory makes use of a notion of embodiment according to which mental states or processes are embodied because of their bodily format. The bodily format of a mental representation constrains what such mental representation can represent, because of the bodily constraints posed by the specific nature of the human body. Similar constraints apply both to the representations of one's own actions, emotions, or sensations involved in actually acting and experiencing, and also to the corresponding representations involved when observing someone else performing a given action or experiencing a given emotion or sensation. These constraints are similar because the representations have a common bodily format. Hence, embodied simulation is the reuse of mental states and processes involving representations that have a bodily format. The nature and the range of what can be achieved with embodied simulation are constrained by the bodily format of the representations involved.

To put it simply, the producer and repository of representational content are not the brain per se, but the brain-body system, by means of its interactions with the world of which it is part. The proper development of this functional architecture likely scaffolds more cognitively sophisticated social cognitive abilities. As recently argued, embodied simulation as a component of cognitive models, when recruited by the situated and contextualized process of meaning construction, is an integral part of linguistic meaning, including conceptual knowledge (Cuccio & Gallese, 2018).

The disembodied approach of current social neurosciences

What is the position of social neuroscience research today with respect to embodied cognition? Carlos Alós-Ferrer (2018), in line with Cacioppo et al. (2006) and Schutt et al. (2015), attempts to survey the contribution of neuroscience to social sciences and economics. As recently noted (Viale, 2019), he correctly emphasizes that social sciences can no longer function without the empirical data provided by the research at the intersection between social cognitive psychology and neuroscience. This need not only results from an epistemological change in economics, but it is rooted in a deeper evolutionary argument: the bidirectionality between brain and the social world. The brain and the early forms of social organization co-evolved over time. While the role of the neurocognitive apparatus in the genesis of social phenomena is now widely accepted, the importance of understanding social evolution for brain studies is not. As Alós-Ferrer writes:

> Understanding which characteristics this coevolution selected for and why they provided an evolutionary advantage provides a far better understanding of the nature and functioning of the brain than statistical studies on the relative proportion of neurons and glial cells in each brain region.
>
> *2018, p. 235*

And this integration between hereditary dimension, social environment, and biological component explains, among other things, also the development and the treatment of mental illness (as highlighted in Eric Kandell's recent book, Kandell, 2018). The representation made by Alós-Ferrer of the relation between neuroscience and society suffers, however, from a neuro-cognitivist bias, which is typical of neuroeconomics: forgetting the body as a fundamental bridge between the brain and the environment. Accordingly, this bias also regards bounded rationality as lacking conformity to the standards of economic rationality (thus making it a synonym for irrationality) and not as a way to adapt to an uncertain and complex social world.

Alós-Ferrer's approach adopts the epistemological stance of cognitivism with the sole diffe-rence that behavior and decision-making processes are analyzed on the basis of neurocognitive models, which are centered on the brain (Legrenzi & Umiltà, 2011; Gallagher, 2018a, 2018b). What is lacking in this analysis is the 'embodied' dimension of cognition, that is, the integra-tion of central nervous system with all the other visceral, sensory, and motor body parts. The neurocognitivist bias of contemporary social neurosciences results in the polarization of the analysis of the social brain mostly in terms of theory of the mind (Theory Theory of the Mind, or TT). This focus on the theory of the mind as the central element of the social brain stems from a distance from ecological and embodied arguments. Accordingly, this leads to overlooking a fundamental component of that function altogether, namely, mind reading, originating in "embodied simulation" produced by the mirror neurons system (Rizzolatti et al., 2001; Goldman, 2006; Iacoboni, 2008; see above). According to the TT, the attribution of mental states to others is possible only through the construction and the development of a theory on these states (Premack & Woodruff, 1978). Understanding or predicting others' actions means engaging in a theoretical inference on propositional attitudes like beliefs, desires, and intentions of others, through conscious and intentional representations of the other person's mental states. In this perspective, there is no room for automatic, unconscious forms of "mind reading" or an empathetic interpretation of emotional states or "mind feeling" (Viale, 2011, 2012). TT is typically the expression of the "disembodied cognition" of the cognitivist approach, and finds its natural collocation in behavioral economics and neuroeconomics. According to Alós-Ferrer, the theory of the mind is the cognitive equivalent of the game theory, which is fundamental to understanding social interaction. As he writes: "Social neuroscience is to decision neuroscience as game theory is to decision theory" (Alós-Ferrer, 2018, p. 259).[1]

As noted, the mutual understanding of social behaviors seems to occur mostly through an embodied simulation mediated by the mirror neurons system. This type of study shows that the social brain cannot be reduced to the fronto-temporal network of the theory of the mind. On the contrary, it seems to point to the fact that conscious and intentional neurocognitive activity is the tip of the iceberg of our social interaction. Most of our social life takes place through processes of automatic, unconscious simulation that is often empathetic with other people's behavior, and, hence, embodied. The development and recognition of the self occur through the imitation of others, and one's personal identity seems shaped by a reflection onto others. The newborn child seems to develop mirror neurons through the repeated imitation of the expressions of the adults he or she interacts with. His/her brain, for example, associates the image of his/her mother's smiling face with the motor level intended to replicate it. Mirror neurons would therefore serve as the basis of the reflection of our behavior in others. Through mirror neurons, we see ourselves in others. Pfeiffer et al. (2008), for example, found a correl-ation in children between emotional empathy, measured according to the *Interpersonal Reactivity Index*, and the increase in mirror neurons' activity while observing facial expressions with an emotional component. The same increase was found in children who were more sociable, more open, and with more relations than others. Other data seem to indicate that mirror neurons are activated every time a social identification process occurs. This activation was observed, for example, with advertisements and the identification with political figures (Iacoboni, 2008). In this way, they seem to provide the basis for understanding social identity, one of the fundamental mechanisms at the origin of social interaction and the related decision-making processes.

In the emotional and empathetic dimension, mirror neurons also explain a series of emotional social contagions. A case in point is contagious laughter, as mirror neurons explain why we laugh more when we are in the company of others and why we laugh when others do. The "audience effect" of empathic resonance also occurs for negative expressions, like pain, disgust, anger, etc. While, on the one hand, we suffer more when we are in the presence of others, on the other hand, we identify ourselves, empathically, with the suffering of others (Chartrand & Bargh, 1999; Longo et al., 2008; Heyes, 2011). Lastly, the embodied simulation of mirror neurons is clearly a useful decision-making tool in social contexts. When we are making rapid and intuitive decisions, the capacity to simulate other people's emotions and actions provides important contextual elements to make adaptive choices. This type of simulation therefore plays a heuristic role that fits into the toolkit of bounded and ecological rationality.

Conclusion

The re-conceptualization of human rationality in light of the embodied perspective is gradually emerging in literature under the name of "embodied rationality" (see Spellman & Schnall, 2009; Mastrogiorgio & Petracca, 2015, 2016; Viale, 2017; Gallagher, 2018a, 2018b; see also Oullier & Basso, 2010). This chapter aims to show that the adaptive and ecological dimension of bounded rationality should be better analyzed by assuming an embodied cognition perspective. Ecological rationality and the functioning of simple heuristics, in particular, would greatly benefit from inputs from neurobiological and embodied cognition studies. Until now, few reflections about these opportunities have been made in the framework of the ecological rationality approach. It remains mainly characterized by reference to information processing psychology (see Petracca, 2017) and by a Marrian algorithmic level of analysis (Marr, 1982; Brighton, Chapter 17 in this volume). In fact, something is changing among ecological rationality scholars, in particular with reference to deeper analysis of the neurobiological dimension of heuristics decision making. According to Nordli and Todd (Chapter 19 in this volume), neurophysiological studies would promote a new theoretical framework for ecological rationality. For instance, those studies may contribute to understanding strategy selection in decision making, where strategy selection means the selection of a given heuristic for a particular context. The selection is successful when the selected heuristic matches the structure of a given situation. That may happen by developing a mapping between context structure and appropriate heuristics to use (Marewsky & Schooler, 2011). The mapping may be generated by a "strategy selection learning" procedure as proposed by Rieskamp and Otto (2006), as strategies are selected according to predictions regarding their expected results in particular tasks and contexts. According Nordli and Todd (Chapter 19 in this volume), the reinforcement learning-based mechanism of strategy selection

> is consistent with accounts that tie reinforcement learning processes to recurrent cortico-basal circuitry (e.g., Yin & Knowlton, 2006), which is the very same circuitry that is critical to the exploitation of past behavior in the form of habits and fixed action patterns.
>
> *Nordli & Todd, p. 320*

In particular, the basal ganglia seem to lie behind most ecologically rational behavior. Basal ganglia seem to evaluate context and select actions based on either motor or cognitive past behavior

(Graybel, 2008, quoted in Nordli & Todd, Chapter 19 in this volume). This neural mechanism allows the strategy selection of adaptive heuristics based on evaluation of past behavior.[2]

In conclusion, as the arguments in this chapter and previous references to strategy selection aim to show, embodied bounded rationality is the new framework to study adaptive decision-making processes.

Notes

1 This means that game theory overrides the theory of decision making and finds its equivalent in the whole of social neuroscience, which should rely on its formal rigor to prevent the fragmentation of neuroscientific research on the theory of the mind. This desire extends to the point of wishing that neuroscience, while thinking about thought, turns to game theory as a means to formalize the "thinking of the thought thinking the thought thinking ..." This seems to be a wish of neoclassical and cognitivist inspiration—which is actually untenable, given the limited computation capacities of the human brain and particularly of its operative memory.

2 There are other examples of neural modeling of adaptive behavior. One is proposed by Bhui (in press). It is well known that the way we feel about an outcome depends on how we compare it to our past and present experiences. However, it is not so clear what kind of comparisons we make, or even why we make comparisons at all. Bhui refers to theoretical neuroscience to explain why this context dependence is adaptive. Our sense of value may adapt to our experiences for the same computational reason that our eyes adapt to light and dark: our neurons have a limited capacity to process information, which is best spent distinguishing among the stimulus values we expect to encounter in our local environment. Bhui shows that influential psychological theories of context-sensitive judgment can be derived from the neurocomputational principle of efficient coding. This unites conflicting cognitive, behavioral, and neural findings spanning both perceptual and value-based judgment across multiple species into a single neurobiologically-grounded framework.

References

Alós-Ferrer, C. (2018). A review essay on social neuroscience: Can research on the social brain and economics inform each other? *Journal of Economic Literature*, 56(1), 234–64.

Anderson, M. L. (2010). Neural reuse: A fundamental organizational principle of the brain. *Behavioral and Brain Sciences*, 33(4), 245–266.

Bhalla, M., & Proffitt, D. R. (1999). Visual–motor recalibration in geographical slant perception. *Journal of Experimental Psychology: Human Perception and Performance*, 25(4), 1076–1096.

Bhui, R. (in press). Testing optimal timing in value-linked decision making. *Computational Brain & Behavior*.

Brooks, R. A. (1991). Intelligence without representation. *Artificial Intelligence*, 47(1–3), 139–159.

Cacioppo, J. T., Visser, P. S., & Pickett, C. L. (Eds.) (2006). *Social neuroscience: people thinking about thinking people*. Cambridge, MA: MIT Press.

Calvo P., & Gomila T. (Eds.) (2008). *Handbook of cognitive science: An embodied approach*, San Diego, CA: Elsevier.

Caruana, F., & Borghi, A. M. (2016). *Il cervello in azione: Introduzione alle nuove scienze della mente*. Bologne: Il Mulino.

Chartrand, T. L., & Bargh, J. A. (1999). The chameleon effect: The perception-behavior link and social interaction. *Journal of Personality and Social Psychology*, 76(6), 893–910.

Clancey, W. (1997). *Situated cognition: On human knowledge and computer representations*. Cambridge: Cambridge University Press.

Clark, A. (1997). *Being there: Putting brain, body, and world together again*. Cambridge, MA: MIT Press.

Clark, A. (2008). Pressing the flesh: A tension in the study of the embodied, embedded mind?. *Philosophical and Phenomenological Research*, 76(1), 37–59.

Cohen Kadosh, R. C., & Walsh, V. (2009). Numerical representation in the parietal lobes: Abstract or not abstract? *Behavioral and Brain Sciences*, 32(3–4), 313–328.

Craig, A. D. (2011) Interoceptive cortex in the posterior insula: Comment on Garcia-Larrea *et al.* 2010 Brain 133, 2528. *Brain*, 134(4).

Cuccio, V., & Gallese, V. (2018). A Peircean account of concepts: Grounding abstraction in phylogeny through a comparative neuroscientific perspective. *Philosophical Transactions of the Royal Society of London B*, 373, 20170128.

Damasio A. (1994). *Descartes' error: Emotion, reason, and the human brain*. New York: Putnam Publishing.

Dawkins, R. (1976). *The selfish gene*. New York: Oxford University Press.

Dorfman, H. M., Bhui, R., Hughes, B. L., & Gershman, S. J. (in press). Causal inference about good and bad outcomes. *Psychological Science*.

Ellis, R., & Tucker, M. (2000). Micro-affordance: The potentiation of components of action by seen objects. *British Journal of Psychology*, 91(4), 451–471.

Gallagher, S. (2005). *How the body shapes the mind*. New York: Oxford University Press.

Gallagher, S. (2018a). Embodied rationality. In G. Bronner & F. Di Iorio (Eds.), *The mystery of rationality: Mind, beliefs and social science* (pp. 83–94). Berlin: Springer.

Gallagher, S. (2018b). Decentering the brain: Embodied cognition and the critique of neurocentrism and narrow-minded philosophy of mind. *Constructionist Foundations*, 14(1), 101–134.

Gallese, V. (2003). The manifold nature of interpersonal relations: The quest for a common mechanism. *Philosophical Transactions of the Royal Society of London B*, 358, 517–528.

Gallese V. (2007). Before and below 'theory of mind': Embodied simulation and the neural correlates of social cognition. *Philosophical Transactions of the Royal Society of London B*, 362, 659–669.

Gallese V. (2008). Mirror neurons and the social nature of language: The neural exploitation hypothesis. *Social Neuroscience*, 3, 317–333.

Gallese V. (2014). Bodily selves in relation: Embodied simulation as second-person perspective on intersubjectivity. *Philosophical Transactions of the Royal Society of London B*, 369, 20130177.

Gallese V., & Cuccio, V. (2015) The paradigmatic body: Embodied simulation, intersubjectivity and the bodily self. In T. Metzinger & J. M. Windt (Eds.), *Open MIND* (pp. 1–23). Frankfurt: MIND Group.

Gallese, V., Fadiga, L., Fogassi, L., & Rizzolatti, G. (1996). Action recognition in the premotor cortex. *Brain*, 119, 593–609.

Gallese, V., & Goldman, A. (1998). Mirror neurons and the simulation theory of mind-reading. *Trends in Cognitive Sciences*, 2(12), 493–501.

Gallese, V., & Lakoff, G. (2005). The brain's concepts: The role of the sensory-motor system in reason and language. *Cognitive Neuropsychology*, 22, 455–479.

Gallese, V., Rochat, M., Cossu, G., & Sinigaglia, C. (2009). Motor cognition and its role in the phylogeny and ontogeny of intentional understanding. *Developmental Psychology*, 45, 103–113.

Gibbs, R. W. Jr. (2006). *Embodiment and cognitive science*. New York: Cambridge University Press

Gibson, J. J. (1950). *The perception of the visual world*. Boston: Houghton Mifflin.

Gibson, J. J. (1979). *The ecological approach to visual perception*. Boston: Houghton Mifflin.

Gigerenzer, G. (1997). The modularity of social intelligence. In A. Whiten & R. W. Byrne, (Eds.), *Machiavellian intelligence II: Extensions and evaluations* (pp. 264–288). Cambridge: Cambridge University Press.

Gigerenzer, G. (2007). *Gut feelings: The intelligence of the unconscious*. London: Penguin.

Gigerenzer, G., & Gaissmaier, W. (2011). Heuristic decision making. *Annual Review of Psychology*, 62, 451–482.

Gigerenzer, G., & Goldstein, D. G. (1996). Reasoning the fast and frugal way: models of bounded rationality. *Psychological Review*, 103(4), 650–669.

Gigerenzer, G., Todd, P. M., & the ABC Research Group (Eds.) (1999). *Simple heuristics that make us smart*. New York: Oxford University Press.

Goldman, A. (2006). *Simulating mind*. New York: Oxford University Press.

Graybiel, A. M. (2008). Habits, rituals, and the evaluative brain. *The Annual Review of Neuroscience*, 31, 359–387.

Hamlin, R. P. (2017). "The gaze heuristic": Biography of an adaptively rational decision process. *Topics in Cognitive Science*, 9(2), 264–288.

Haugeland, J. (1978). The nature and plausibility of cognitivism. *Behavioral and Brain Sciences*, 1(2), 215–226.

Heyes, C. (2011). Automatic imitation. *Psychological Bulletin*, 137(3), 463–483.

Hirose, N. (2002). An ecological approach to embodiment and cognition. *Cognitive Systems Research*, 3(3), 289–299.

Iacoboni, M. (2008). *Mirroring people: The new science of how we connect with others*. New York: Farrar, Strauss and Giroux.

Iacoboni, M. (2009). Imitation, empathy, and mirror neurons. *Annual Review of Psychology*, 60, 653–670.

Jostmann, N. B., Lakens, D., & Schubert, T. W. (2009). Weight as an embodiment of importance. *Psychological Science*, 20(9), 1169–1174.

Kandell, E. (2018). *The disordered mind*. New York: Farrar, Strauss and Giroux

Kiverstein, J., & Clark, A. (2009). Introduction: Mind embodied, embedded, enacted: One church or many? *Topoi*, 28(1), 1–7.

Lakoff, G., & Johnson, M. (1999). *Philosophy in the flesh: The embodied mind and its challenge to Western thought*. New York: Basic Books.

Lakoff, G., & Nuñez, R. (2000). *Where mathematics comes from: How the embodied mind brings mathematics into being*. New York: Basic Books.

Legrenzi, P., & Umiltà, C. (2011). *Neuromania: On the limits of brain science*. New York: Oxford University Press.

Longo, M. R., Kosobud, A., & Bertenthal, B. I. (2008). Automatic imitation of biomechanically possible and impossible actions: Effects of priming movements versus goals. *Journal of Experimental Psychology: Human Perception and Performance*, 34(2), 489–501.

Marewski, J. N., & Schooler, L. J. (2011). Cognitive niches: An ecological model of strategy selection. *Psychological Review*, 118, 393–437.

Marr, D. (1982). *Vision*. San Francisco, CA: Freeman.

Mastrogiorgio, A., & Petracca, E. (2015). Razionalità incarnata. *Sistemi Intelligenti*, 27(3), 481–504.

Mastrogiorgio, A., & Petracca, E. (2016). Embodying rationality. In L. Magnani & C. Casadio (Eds.), *Model-based reasoning in science and technology* (pp. 219–237), Berlin: Springer.

Mastrogiorgio, A., & Petracca, E. (2018). Satisficing as an alternative to optimality and suboptimality in perceptual decision-making. *Behavioral and Brain Sciences*, 41, e235.

Meier, B. P., Schnall, S., Schwarz, N., & Bargh, J. A. (2012). Embodiment in social psychology. *Topics in Cognitive Science*, 4(4), 705–716.

Morewedge, C. K., Huh, Y. E., & Vosgerau, J. (2010). Thought for food: Imagined consumption reduces actual consumption. *Science*, 330(6010), 1530–1533.

Newell, A., & Simon, H. A. (1972). *Human problem solving*. Englewood Cliffs, NJ: Prentice-Hall.

Newell, A., & Simon, H.A. (1976). Computer science as empirical inquiry: Symbols and search. *Communications of the ACM*, 19(3), 113–126.

Oullier, O., & Basso, F. (2010). Embodied economics: How bodily information shapes the social coordination dynamics of decision-making. *Philosophical Transactions of the Royal Society B*, 365(1538), 291–301.

Patokorpi, E. (2008). Simon's paradox: Bounded rationality and the computer metaphor of the mind. *Human Systems Management*, 27(4), 285–294.

Petracca, E. (2017). A cognition paradigm clash: Simon, situated cognition and the interpretation of bounded rationality. *Journal of Economic Methodology*, 24(1), 20–40.

Pfeifer, R., & Bongard, J. (2006). *How the body shapes the way we think: A new view of intelligence*. Cambridge, MA: MIT Press.

Pfeiffer, J., Iacoboni, M., Mazziotta, J. C., & Dapretto, M. (2008). Mirroring other emotions relates to empathy and interpersonal competence in children, *Neuroimage*, 39, 2076–2085.

Premack, D., & Woodruff, G. (1978). Does the chimpanzee have a theory of mind? *The Behavioural and Brain Sciences*, 1, 515–526.

Reimann, M., & Bechara, A. (2010). The somatic marker framework as a neurological theory of decision-making: Review, conceptual comparisons, and future neuroeconomics research. *Journal of Economic Psychology*, 31(5), 767–776.

Rieskamp, J., & Otto, P. E. (2006). SSL: A theory of how people learn to select strategies. *Journal of Experimental Psychology General*, 135(2), 207–236.

Rizzolatti, G., Fogassi, L., & Gallese, V. (2001). Neurophysiological mechanisms underlying the understanding and imitation in action. *Nature Review Neuroscience*, 2, 661–670.

Rowlands, M. (1999). *The body in mind: Understanding cognitive processes*. Cambridge: Cambridge University Press.

Schutt, R. K., Seidman, L. J., & Keshavan, M. S. (Eds.) (2015). *Social neuroscience: Brain, mind, and society*. Cambridge, MA: Harvard University Press.

Shapiro, L. (2004). *The mind incarnate*. Cambridge, MA: MIT Press.

Shapiro, L. (Ed.) (2014). *The Routledge handbook of embodied cognition*. Abingdon: Routledge.

Simon, H. A. (1955). A behavioral model of rational choice. *The Quarterly Journal of Economics*, 69(1), 99–118.

Simon, H. A. (1956). Rational choice and the structure of the environment. *Psychological Review*, 63(2), 129–138.

Simon, H. A. (1976). From substantive to procedural rationality. In S. J. Latsis (Ed.), *Method and appraisal in economics*. Cambridge: Cambridge University Press.

Simon, H. A. (1978). Rationality as process and product of thought. *American Economic Review*, 68(2), 1–15.

Spellman, B., and Schnall, S. (2009). Embodied rationality. *Queen's Law Journal*, 35(1), 117–164.

Tipper, S. P., Paul, M. A., & Hayes, A. E. (2006). Vision-for-action: The effects of object property discrimination and action state on affordance compatibility. *Psychonomic Bulletin & Review*, 13, 493–498.

Varela, F., Thompson, E., & Rosch, E. (1991). *The embodied mind: Cognitive science and human experience*. Cambridge, MA: MIT Press.

Viale R. (2011). Brain reading social action. *International Journal of Economics*, 58(4), 337–58.

Viale, R. (2012). *Methodological cognitivism*. Vol. 1: *Mind, rationality and society*. Heidelberg: Springer.

Viale, R. (2017). Corpo e razionalità. In A. Coricelli & D. Martelli (Eds.), *Neurofinanza. Le basi neuronali delle scelte finanziarie*. Milan: Egea.

Viale, R. (2019) La razionalita limitata 'embodied' alla base del cervello sociale ed economic. *Sistemi Intelligenti*, XXXI, 1.

Wallace, B., Ross, A., Davies, J. B., & Anderson T. (Eds.) (2007) *The mind, the body and the world: Psychology after cognitivism*. London: Imprint Academic.

Werner K., & Raab M. (2014). Moving your eyes to solution: Effects of movements on the perception of a problem-solving task, *Quarterly Journal of Experimental Psychology*, 67(8), 1571–1578.

Williams, L. E., Huang, J. Y., & Bargh, J. A. (2009). The scaffolded mind: Higher mental processes are grounded in early experience of the physical world. *European Journal of Social Psychology*, 39(7), 1257–1267.

Wilson, M. (2002). Six views of embodied cognition. *Psychonomic Bulletin and Review*, 9, 625–636.

Yin, H. H., & Knowlton, B. J. (2006). The role of the basal ganglia in habit formation. *Nature Reviews Neuroscience*, 7(6), 464–476.

Zhong, C. B., & Leonardelli, G. J. (2008). Cold and lonely: Does social exclusion literally feel cold? *Psychological Science*, 19(9), 838–842.

24

EXTENDING THE BOUNDED RATIONALITY FRAMEWORK

Bounded-resource models in biology

Christopher Cherniak

Perhaps the most fundamental psychological law is that we are finite organisms (Cherniak, 1986). Bounded-resource models of the agent characterize our rationality as falling in the "Goldilocks" range, between nothing and perfection. This is not a mere quirk: The apercu motivating the rationality critiques is conveyed by the recognition that standard idealizations entail some deductive omniscience, for instance, triviality of portions of the deductive sciences. Such ideal agent/logicians, if computational, would violate Church's Theorem on undecidability of first-order logic (Church, 1936) (see Figure 24.1). This insight in turn indicates that NP-completeness (Garey & Johnson, 1979) is of corresponding interest: core computational intractability of a cosmos-consuming scale is a practical counterpart to traditional absolute uncomputability—another layer of impossibility between the idealizations and reality (Cherniak, 1984). This is some of the philosophical significance of computational complexity (Aaronson, 2013; Dean: 2016). The formalism of scarcity of interconnections is combinatorial network optimization theory, which emerged from the field of microcircuit design, and itself includes many important intractable problems.

The research program here stems from a holistic rather than compartmentalized perspective: Philosophy and science are distinct but inextricably interconnected. For instance, the classical paradoxes of semantics (e.g., the Liar Paradox (Tarski, [1935] 1983) and set theory (e.g., Russell's Paradox (Russell, 1903)) can be reexamined not as mere odd pathology, but instead as deep indications of the use of "quick and dirty heuristics"—that is, the ultimate speed-reliability tradeoffs of correctness and completeness for feasibility. Three disparate fields thereby converge: (1) computational complexity theory; (2) empirical psychology of quick and dirty heuristics; and (3) philosophical theory of bounded-resource rationality. In this way, the bounded rationality models provide a foundation of current "behavioral economics" (Nobel Prize Committee, 2017).

Brainwiring optimization

In addition, it is natural to explore extending the bounded-resource approach in this way down from rationality to the brainwiring hardware level. Specifically, long-range connectivity is a critically constrained neural resource, with great evolutionary pressure to employ efficiently.

DOI: 10.4324/9781315658353-28

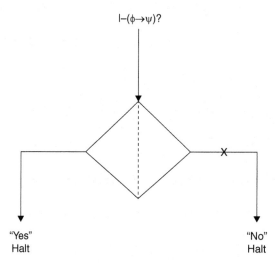

Figure 24.1 Standard rationality idealizations of the agent require a deeply non-possible object: an Ideal Logician. If its logical competence is represented in a finite algorithm, then it must violate Church's Theorem (1936): There is no "Yes/No" decision procedure for first-order predicate calculus. A proof procedure exists—the left-hand half ("Yes" semi-algorithm) of the full algorithm—but that cannot suffice for perfect rationality. Nor can any quick and dirty heuristic procedure.

Hence, "brain as microchip": Connection minimization appears to be a first law of brain tractography, an organizing principle driving neuroanatomy (Cherniak: 1994a), with hitherto unreported precision.

Our laboratory has therefore been assessing how well wiring-optimization concepts from computer microcircuit engineering apply to brain structure. "Save wire" turns out to be a strongly predictive "best in a billion" model. Wiring minimization can be perceived at multiple levels, e.g., placement of the entire brain, layout of its ganglia and/or cortex areas, subcellular architecture of dendrite arbors, etc. Much of this biological structure appears to arise "for free," directly from physics.

Of course, if connectivity in a nervous system were unbounded or cost-free, there would be no pressure for its economical deployment. However, much of higher central nervous systems operates at signal propagation velocities not at light speed, but below the 60 mph speed limit. Since connectivity is in limited supply, network optimization is quite valuable. As a result, this scarce wiring is highly optimized, a prima facie paradoxical consequence.

For instance, a key specific wiring problem is component placement optimization: For a set of interconnected components, what are the positionings of the components that min-imize total interconnection costs (e.g., wire length)? Surprisingly, this idea seems to account very precisely for aspects of neuroanatomy at multiple hierarchical levels. For example, the nervous system of the nematode worm *Caenorhabditis elegans* (Wood, 1988) includes 11 gangli-onic components, which have 11! (~40,000,000) alternative possible anteroposterior orderings. In fact, "the actual is the ideal" here, in that the actual layout happens to require the min-imum total possible wire length, a predictive success story (Cherniak, 1994b). However, such problems are NP-complete: exact solutions generally appear to entail brute-force searches, with exponentially exploding costs. Despite local minima traps, such neuroanatomy optimization is approximated well by "mesh of springs" energy-minimization mechanisms (Cherniak et al., 2002). (See discussion below of the "genomic bottleneck".)

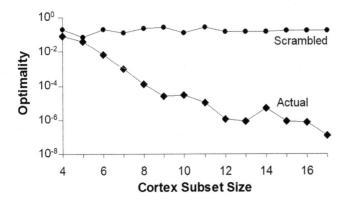

Figure 24.2 "Size Law" trend for macaque visual cortex areas—increasing optimality with increased subsystem size. The system of components is 17 contiguous central visual areas of macaque cortex. A layout is scored in terms of its violations of the Adjacency Rule. A series of nested compact subsets of the set of visual areas is generated; each subset is compared with all possible alternative layouts of that subset for adjacency-rule optimality. As subset size increases, optimality-ranking of the actual layout consistently improves. Layout optimality rank for the complete visual system analyzed is in top 0.000000119 of all possible alternative layouts of the full 17 area set. For comparison, the corresponding analysis for a layout of the 17 visual areas with their adjacencies randomly shuffled shows no trend toward improving optimality. This analysis includes only 17 of the total 73 areas of macaque cortex (Cherniak et al., 2004).

A corresponding approach can be explored for the placement of the interconnected functional areas of the cerebral cortex. (For an overview of the anatomy of the human cortex white-matter connections, see Carpenter and Sutin, 1983.) A first strategy is to use a simpler connection cost measure, conformance of a cortex layout to a wire-saving Adjacency Heuristic: "If components are connected, then they are placed adjacent to each other." Extensive sampling of all possible layouts is still required to verify the best ones. For example, for 17 core visual areas of macaque cortex, the actual layout of this subsystem ranks in the top 10^{-6} layouts best minimizing their adjacency costing (Cherniak et al., 2004). Similar high optimality rankings also hold for the core set of visual areas of cat cortex, and also for rat olfactory cortex and amygdala (see Figure 24.2).

Furthermore, a "Size Law" appears to apply to systems with such local-global tradeoffs: "If a complete system is in fact perfectly optimized, then the smaller the subset of it evaluated in isolation, the poorer the optimization tends to appear." (This seems to be a generalization of a related perspective-dependent idea in theology, to account for the problem of evil (Tooley, 2015)—of apparent local imperfections in the universe with an omnipotent, benevolent deity.) The Size Law applies well to each of the above brain systems, as well as elsewhere (e.g., for microchip design).

We have also reported similar Size Law optimization results for *C. elegans* ganglia, rat amygdala and olfactory cortex, cat visual cortex, and combined cat visual auditory and somatosensory cortex. The human brain appears to be the most complex physical structure presently known in the universe, an ultimate big dataset. With such a network optimization framework, these "Save wire" results have been extended and replicated for the (1) complete (2) living and (3) human cerebrum via fMRI, another predictive success (Lewis et al., 2012)—a "Mount Everest" of neural optimization.

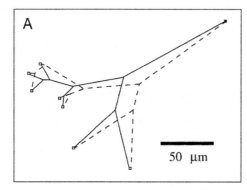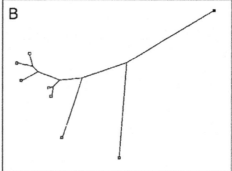

Figure 24.3   Actual versus optimal arbors: mouse thalamus extrinsic axon, ascending reticular formation. The arbor best fits a volume-minimizing model. (A) Wireframe representation of 8-terminal subtree of observed arbor. The actual tree, with actual topology in its actual embedding, appears in broken lines. Optimal embedding of the actual topology with respect to volume minimization is superimposed in solid lines. The cost in volume of the actual arbor exceeds that of the optimized embedding of its topology by 2.20 percent. (B) "Best of all possible topologies" connecting the given terminal loci: the optimal topology with respect to volume, optimally embedded. The volume cost of the actual arbor exceeds that of the optimal topology by 2.47 percent. Only 10 of the 10,395 possible alternative topologies here have lower total volume costs, when optimally embedded, than the actual topology (Cherniak et al., 1999).

In addition, neuron dendrite and axon arbors also appear significantly to approximate a generalization of minimum-cost Steiner trees (Cherniak et al., 1999). These optimal structures are derivable via simple fluid dynamics. ("Instant arbors, just add water.") Evolution gets a free ride from the physics. This seems to constitute some of the most complex biostructure presently derivable from simple (non-DNA) physical processes (see Figure 24.3). Such a "Physics suffices" account of biological morphogenesis constitutes "Nongenomic Nativism"—innateness without DNA: The *tabula rasa* is pre-formatted. One rationale for the pre-biotic pervading the biotic in this way is to cope with the "genomic bottleneck": Like other organism systems, the genome has limited capacities. The more neuroanatomy for free, directly from physics, the less the genome information-carrying load.

A basic question arises: Neural wiring minimization is of course of value, but why should it seem to have such a high priority—sometimes apparently near-maximal? The significance of ultra-fine neural optimization remains an open question.

An additional methodological issue concerns how the intentional level of mind meshes with the hardware level of the brain. Prima facie, that relationship appears in tension: In some aspects, the brainwiring appears virtually perfectly optimized, yet the rationality has layers of impossibility between it and perfection (Cherniak, 2009). Perhaps this is another manifestation of irreducibility of the mental—the familiar loose fit of each domain with the other.

Genome as nanobrain

A next section of this research program: Similar computation theory concepts can be used for understanding the structure and function of organism DNA. The Crick-Watson double-helix model (Alberts et al., 2015) emerged at the same place and time as Alan Turing's final work, on morphogenesis, namely, Cambridge around 1950. So an idea of DNA-as-Turing-machine-tape has circulated for decades.

In particular, the genome itself can be treated like a "nano-brain" or pico-computer to see whether similar connection minimization strategies also appear in gene networks. As outlined above, for decades we have reported wiring optimization in the brain that begins to approach some of the most precisely confirmed predictions in neuroscience.

Two meta-models of the genome compete today: One is a "genome as hairball" idea, of the very vehicle of innateness itself effectively possessing minimal structure. (For example, our genome is a mess. It is "in an alarming state of disarray" (Alberts et al., 2015).) The other picture, examined here, is structuralist—that the genome itself has large-scale global patterns.

We are now exploring a connection-minimization model for the human genome. Information transmission may not be cost-free even within a cell, nucleus, or genome. For instance, genes strongly expressed in particular tissues are not just randomly distributed in the genome. Rather, the arrangement of such tissue-specific gene positions in the complete chromosome set mirrors the antero-posterior, and dorso-ventral, configuration of the tissue-locations in the body. A statistically significant supra-chromosomal "genome homunculus"—a global, multi-dimensional, somatotopic mapping of the human body—appears to extend across chromosome territories in the entire sperm cell nucleus (Cherniak & Rodriguez-Esteban, 2013) (see Figure 24.4). Such a mapping is a strategy for connection cost-minimization (e.g., cf. body maps reported in sensory and motor cortex since the nineteenth century). Also, corresponding finer-scale somatotopic mappings seem to occur on each individual autosomal chromosome (Cherniak & Rodriguez-Esteban, 2015).

Furthermore, the organelle sub-structure of the typical individual eukaryotic animal cell also turns out to map similarly as a "cellunculus" onto the total genome, via organelle-specific genes that express more strongly in particular organelle types (Cherniak & Rodriguez-Esteban, 2018) (see Figure 24.5). So, genome as palimpsest: multiple maps, at different scales, seem superimposed upon the genome.

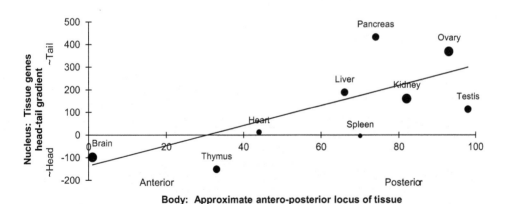

Figure 24.4 Antero-posterior "gradient of gradients" in nucleus. Tissue location in human body correlates significantly with pattern of tissue genes' positions in cell nucleus. (For 9 datapoints each weighted by their own significance, $r^2 = 0.62$; $p < 0.01$, two-tailed.) That is, tissue location-in-body relates to its genes' distribution-gradient in the complete genome. The more forward-placed a tissue in the body, the more forward-placed its genes on chromosomes in nucleus. The head of the genome homunculus is at the head of the sperm cell nucleus. A corresponding body-genome mapping also holds for the dorso-ventral body axis (Cherniak & Rodriguez-Esteban, 2013). In addition, the body similarly maps onto individual chromosomes (Cherniak and Rodriguez-Esteban, 2015).

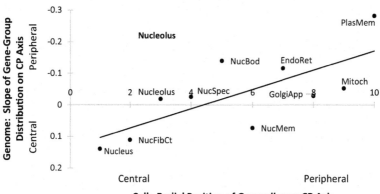

Figure 24.5 Isomorphism of cell microanatomy and large-scale human genome structure: Components positioned more centrally in a cell tend to have their genes correspondingly concentrated on chromosomes sited more toward the center of genome. In a plot of 10 organelles, this cell–genome correlation is significant ($r^2 = 0.540$; $p < 0.015$, two-tailed). Each of the datapoints is labeled with its organelle-name (Cherniak & Rodriguez-Esteban, 2018).

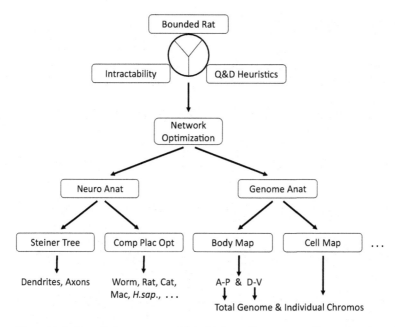

Figure 24.6 Bounded-resource models in biology: Concept map. For explanation of terms, refer to preceding text.

Conclusion: The argument of this chapter starts with a synoptic view, from a "knowledge without borders" perspective. The chapter aimed to extend the bounded rationality framework, sketching some of the terrain of more realistic limited-resource models in the life sciences. —Limits for growth: of mind, brain, genome, and other biological systems. Figure 24.6 summarizes the derivation of the research program. Further "Bounded Biology" results of this type now also have support.

References

Aaronson, S. 2013. Why philosophers should care about computational complexity. In J. Copeland, C., Posy, & O. Shagrir (Eds.), *Computability: Turing, Gödel, Church, & Beyond* (pp. 261–327). Cambridge, MA: MIT Press.

Alberts, B., Johnson, A., Lewis J., Raff, M., Roberts, K., & Walter, P. 2015. *Molecular biology of the cell* (6th ed.). New York: Garland Science, Chapter 4.

Carpenter M., & Sutin, J. 1983. *Human neuroanatomy* (8th ed.). Baltimore, MD: Williams & Wilkins, Chapters 2, 19.

Cherniak, C. 1984. Computational complexity and the universal acceptance of logic. *Journal of Philosophy*, 81, 739–758.

Cherniak, C. 1986. *Minimal rationality*. Cambridge, MA: MIT Press.

Cherniak, C. 1994a. Philosophy and computational neuroanatomy. *Philosophical Studies*, 73, 89–107.

Cherniak, C. 1994b. Component placement optimization in the brain, *Journal of Neuroscience*, 14, 2418–2427.

Cherniak, C. 2009. Minimal rationality and optimal brain wiring. In C. Glymour, W. Wei, & D. Westerstahl (Eds.), Logic, methodology and philosophy of science: Proceedings of 13th International Congress (pp. 443–454). London: College Publications.

Cherniak, C., Changizi, M., & Kang, D. 1999. Large-scale optimization of neuron arbors. *Physical Review E*, 59, 6001–6009.

Cherniak, C., Mokhtarzada Z., & Nodelman, U. 2002. Optimal-wiring models of neuroanatomy. In G. Ascoli (Ed.), *Computational neuroanatomy: Principles and methods* (pp. 71–82). Berlin: Springer.

Cherniak, C., Mokhtarzada, Z., Rodriguez-Esteban, R., & Changizi, B. 2004. Global optimization of cerebral cortex layout. *Proceedings of the National Academy of Sciences of the U.S.A.*, 101, 1081–1086.

Cherniak C., & Rodriguez-Esteban, R. 2013. Body maps on the human genome. *Molecular Cytogenetics*, 6(1), 61.

Cherniak C., & Rodriguez-Esteban, R. 2015. Body maps on human chromosomes. Tech Report, UMIACS-TR-2015–04. College Park, MD: University of Maryland Institute for Advanced Computer Studies.

Cherniak C., & Rodriguez-Esteban, R. 2018. Cell maps on the human genome. Tech Report, 2018 UMIACS-TR-2018–01. College Park, MD: University of Maryland Institute for Advanced Computer Studies,

Church, A. 1936. An unsolvable problem of elementary number theory. *American Journal of Mathematics*, 58 (2), 345–363.

Dean, S. 2016. Computational complexity theory. In E. Zalta (Ed.), *Stanford encyclopedia of philosophy* (pp. 261–327). Available at: http://plato.stanford.edu

Garey, M., & Johnson, D. 1979. *Computers and intractability: A guide to the theory of NP-Completeness*. San Francisco: W. H. Freeman.

Lewis, S., Christova, P., Jerde, T., & Georgopoulos, A. 2012. A compact and realistic cerebral cortical layout derived from prewhitened resting-state fMRI time series: Cherniak's adjacency rule, size law, and metamodule grouping upheld. *Frontiers in Neuroanatomy*, 36.

Nobel Prize Committee 2017. The Prize in Economic Sciences 2017: Scientific background: Richard H. Thaler: integrating economics with psychology. Stockholm. Available at: Nobelprize.org.

Russell, B. 1903. *Principles of mathematics*. Cambridge: Cambridge University Press.

Tarski, A. [1935] 1983. The concept of truth in formalized languages,. In J. Corcoran (Ed.), *Logic, semantics, metamathematics* (2nd ed.), Indianapolis: Hackett.

Tooley, M. 2015. The problem of evil. In E. Zalta (Ed.), *Stanford encyclopedia of philosophy*. Available at: https://plato.stanford.edu/archives/fall2015/entries/evil/

Wood, W. (Ed.) 1988. The Nematode *Caenorhabditis elegans*. Plainview, NY: Cold Spring Harbor Laboratory.

25

HOW RATIONALITY IS BOUNDED BY THE BRAIN

Paul Thagard

When Richard Thaler was asked how he planned to spend the million dollars from his 2017 Nobel Prize in economics, he replied: "I will try to spend it as irrationally as possible" (Politi, 2017). Thaler's prize was awarded for decades of research showing that people are not nearly as rational as economists have assumed.

Why are people frequently irrational? There are still many economists and philosophers who believe that people are fundamentally rational, but a large accumulation of evidence from psychology and behavioral economics shows that people often fall short of rational standards. The evidence is descriptive, showing that people make thinking errors in systematic ways. But these descriptions leave open the question of *why* people do not think in ways that support their long-term interests.

Cognitive science usually explains thinking in terms of mental representations and processes, but advances in neuroscience make it increasingly feasible to explain many mental processes as brain mechanisms. So the question becomes: What are the brain mechanisms that lead people to be irrational?

The term "bounded rationality" originated in the 1950s in the writings of Herbert Simon (e.g., Simon, 1972), but appreciation that people are often limited in their rationality goes back to Aristotle and Francis Bacon. The human brain is marvelous in many of its accomplishments, but I will describe its inherent limitations in size, speed, and cognitive-emotional functioning.

Herbert Simon (2000, p. 25) characterized bounded rationality as follows:

> Bounded rationality is simply the idea that the choices people make are determined not only by some consistent overall goal and the properties of the external world, but also by the knowledge that decision makers do and don't have of the world, their ability or inability to evoke that knowledge when it is relevant, to work out the consequences of their actions, to conjure up possible courses of action, to cope with uncertainty (including uncertainty deriving from the possible responses of other actors), and to adjudicate among their many competing wants. Rationality is bounded because these abilities are severely limited.

I show how these mental limitations derive in part from brain limitations.

DOI: 10.4324/9781315658353-29

Table 25.1 3-analysis of *rational*

Exemplars	Logical deduction, probabilistic reasoning and statistical inference, making decisions based on maximizing expected utility.
Typical features	Following rules of reason, careful, conscious.
Explanations	Explains: why people get true beliefs; why people make good decisions. Explained by: ability of humans to follow appropriate rules of reasoning.

Table 25.2 3-analysis of *irrational*

Exemplars	Fallacious deductive inferences such as affirming the consequent; defective probabilistic inferences such as judging a conjunction to be more probable than either of its conjuncts; making bad decisions such as emphasizing sunk costs rather than future expectations.
Typical features	Violation of normative rules, careless succumbing to fallacies and biases.
Explanations	Explains: why people arrive at dumb beliefs and make bad decisions. Explained by: susceptibility to psychological processes that interfere with the application of good rules.

What is rationality?

The question "what is rationality?" sounds like a request for a definition, but decades of work on the psychology of concepts show that concepts outside of mathematics are rarely susceptible to clear definitions in terms of necessary and sufficient conditions. Rather, concepts are better characterized in terms of the exemplars that provide standard examples of them, typical conditions for the concept, and explanations that the concepts can be used to provide (Murphy, 2002). A new neural theory of concepts shows how to combine all three of these aspects of concepts in a unified neural model (Blouw, Solodkin, Thagard, & Eliasmith, 2016).

Accordingly, we can characterize concepts by identifying these three dimensions of exemplars, typical features, and explanations, a method of conceptual analysis that Thagard (2019a) calls "3-analysis." Table 25.1 provides a 3-analysis of the concept *rational*.

According to currently dominant traditions, standard examples of rationality include using formal logic to deduce truths from truths, using probability theory to perform inductive reasoning, and using maximization of expected utility to decide what to do by combining probabilities and utilities to choose actions. The typical features of being rational include carefully and consciously applying such normative rules. Such applications explain why people sometimes succeed in acquiring true beliefs and making good decisions. That people are rational is explained by their ability to follow rules. This concept of rationality is complemented by the prevalent concept of irrationality, which can also be captured by a 3-analysis, as shown in Table 25.2.

The recognition of irrationality

Formal logic begin with Aristotle's doctrine of the syllogism, but Aristotle also recognized that people often fall short of good syllogistic reasoning. His *Sophistical Refutations* describes numerous fallacies that people are prone to commit, such as equivocating on the meanings of ambiguous words (Aristotle, 1984). The study of fallacious reasoning has a long history in philosophy and survives today in the discipline of informal logic (Hanson, 2015).

In the seventeenth century, Francis Bacon (1960) provided a sophisticated discussion of inductive reasoning in *Novum Organon*. In addition to giving good advice about how to go from observations to generalizations, Bacon generated a list of mistakes that people often make in inductive reasoning. He called them "idols," which he colorfully described as idols of the tribe (due to human nature), idols of the cave (due to what a particular human cares about), idols of the marketplace (due to communication), and idols of the theater (due to philosophical prejudices). Bacon's idols capture some of the errors recognized by twentieth-century psychologists, such as the availability heuristic and motivated inference.

In the 1950s, Herbert Simon recognized the limited extent of human rationality, but he did not systematically investigate the ways in which people fall short of good decision making and inductive inference. Beginning in the 1970s, psychologists such as Daniel Kahneman and Amos Tversky and economists, such as Richard Thaler, conducted experiments that identify many ways in which human thinking falls short of good reasoning (Kahneman & Tversky, 2000; Thaler, 2015).

I use the term "error tendencies" to cover all the fallacies, idols, heuristics, biases, and typical mistakes that have been identified by philosophers, psychologists, and economists, and have compiled more than 50 of them (Thagard, 2011). Why are there so many? Why did evolution by natural selection fail to optimize people's ability to reason well about what to believe and what to do?

The biological answer is that brains have evolved to be only somewhat effective at performing deductive, inductive, and practical inferences. Optimization is constrained by biological mechanisms and the difficulties of survival and reproduction in changing environments. I will describe how these constraints have produced brain mechanisms that often work well but are limited by size, speed, cognitive-emotional functions, and limitations of attention and consciousness.

Brain size and speed

The argument that people must be rational because of optimization through natural selection has two flaws. First, it gets evolution wrong, because natural selection does not optimize (Gould & Lewontin, 1979). Rather, nature selects for organisms that are somewhat better at surviving and reproducing than organisms with different genes.

Second, the optimization argument forgets that the current standards of rationality are relatively recent cultural innovations. Humans have been around for at least 100,000 years, but formal logic only began with Aristotle around 2,500 years ago, and sophisticated understanding of deduction only began with the work of Gottlob Frege and Charles Peirce in the late nineteenth century. Probability and utility theories are products of mathematical thinking that began in the seventeenth and eighteenth centuries, and the elegant version now used by economists was only developed in the 1940s. For some purposes, these tools are useful, but there is no reason to suppose that they are built into the human brain by evolution.

Human brains have numerous strengths that have enabled people to spread all over the planet and increase in population to more than 7 billion. The most impressive features of human brains are not the special-purpose adaptations touted by evolutionary psychologists, but rather the general adaptability furnished by the flexible ways in which humans can learn from experience (Quartz & Sejnowski, 1997).

Nevertheless, the brain has numerous limitations that forestall optimal rationality. Our brain's assemblage of 86 billion neurons provides a lot of computing power, but elephants have three times as many. In order to have more neurons, people would need to have bigger brains that require bigger heads, but childbirth is already often a difficult procedure. Human brain size reflects a trade-off between the benefits of more processing power and ease of delivery through a pelvis that also must function for bipedal locomotion.

Another constraint on human brain size concerns energy. Even though the roughly 1.4 kg of the human brain take up less than 3 percent of the average human weight, the brain uses up to 20 percent of the energy available to the body. Larger brains would require more energy, which either requires less energy available for other functions such as metabolism and reproduction, or greater sources of food. The evolution of human brains requires a trade-off between size and energy efficiency, as well as between size and birth delivery.

These limitations on the size of human brains place important constraints on rationality because there is a limited amount of information that people can store. Some philosophers have maintained that it is rational to believe all the logical consequences of one's beliefs. An infinite set cannot be stored in any human brain or even in all the computers run by Amazon and Google.

Moreover, even for a finite number of beliefs, the size limitation of the brain places sharp constraints on the combinations of beliefs that can be considered. Educated people have a vocabulary of around 30,000 words, so with 10 beliefs for each word they would have 300,000 beliefs. Understanding is growing of how such beliefs can be stored in the human brain through distributed representations (Eliasmith, 2013). But brains cannot accommodate belief revisions that require consideration of combinations of $2^{300,000}$ subsets of these beliefs. Such subsets are required for considering whether human belief systems are consistent. So it is unreasonable to expect that people should be consistent in their beliefs.

Human brains also come with limitations in speed of processing. Billions of neurons allow for massively parallel operation, but the neurons themselves are slow. A typical neuron fires up to 200 times per second, whereas current computers have operations at the rate of trillions of times per second.

Why are neurons so slow? Most neural connections are chemical, requiring the movement of neurotransmitters such as glutamate and gamma aminobutyric acid (GABA) from one neuron to another. This chemical transmission is slower than purely electrical signaling, which occurs rarely in brains, but it allows for flexibility in timing and the development of different kinds of pathways.

In principle, the brain could operate with only two neurotransmitters, one for enabling one neuron to excite another (increasing its rate of firing), and another for enabling one neuron to inhibit another (decreasing its rate of firing). Glutamate and GABA play these excitatory and inhibitory roles, respectively. But there also dozens of neurotransmitters that operate in human brains, carrying out diverse functions at different time scales. For example, circuitry involving the neurotransmitter dopamine is important for motor control and learning about rewards, while circuitry involving serotonin influences perception and emotion.

If brains were faster, they still would not be able to do an infinite amount of processing, but they would be able to better approximate some of the standards required for the rational norms of deductive logic and probability and utility theory. The brain lacks the speed to be able to do all of the calculations that are required for absolute standards of rationality. I estimate that speed and size limitations contribute to more than 30 of the 53 error tendencies listed in Thagard (2011). For example, people would be less prone to representativeness (the tendency to use assessments of similarity in causal reasoning) if they had the cognitive capacity to do fuller statistical calculations.

On the other hand, brains are appropriately efficient at carrying out computations that are important for the survival and reproduction of organisms. Perception, inference, and decision-making can all be modeled as processes of parallel constraint satisfaction, in which a brain or computer considers a range of possible interpretations of a conflict situation and comes up with a good but not necessarily optimal solution (Rumelhart & McClelland, 1986; Thagard, 2019a). For example, recognizing a moving object as an instance of prey or predator should consider alternative hypotheses about the animal, constrained by perceptual and environmental information. Parallel constraint satisfaction is efficiently computed by neural networks that implement constraints by excitatory and inhibitory links (Thagard, 2000).

Therefore, the brain can be understood as an engine of coherence rather than deduction or calculation. Coherence requires satisfying multiple constraints in parallel, not making zillions of calculations. In general, coherence is computationally intractable (Thagard and Verbeurgt, 1998), but in practice is efficient as long as the number of inhibitory connections is small compared to the number of excitatory ones, as is true of the brain (van Rooij, Blokpoel, Kwishout, & Wareham, 2018).

In sum, human rationality is bounded by the limited size and speed of the brain, but it can often function well by making coherence judgments rather than overextending itself by making too many deductions and calculations. In exciting work in progress, Dan Simon and Stephen Read show that a large number of cognitive biases can be explained by thinking of the mind as a coherence process. My aim is less specific, to show why the alternative methods of rational calculation are at odds with the size and speed of the brain.

Brain integration of cognition and emotion

Rationality is also bounded by more specific aspects of how brains function, including the integration of cognition and emotion and the limited role of consciousness. An obsolete view of the brain takes it as combining a recent cognitive system consisting of areas such as the prefrontal cortex built on top of an ancient limbic system consisting of primitive areas such as the amygdala. This view was exploded by findings that the most high-level areas are intensely interconnected with the emotional systems (Damasio, 1994; Pessoa, 2013).

The integration of cognition and emotion in the brain is generally a feature rather than a bug. Accounts of deduction and probability assume that the brain is largely a syntactic engine, with semantics (meaning) and pragmatics (context and purpose) only playing peripheral roles. But syntax alone cannot explain numerous aspects of human thinking, such as performance in the selection task of Wason (1966) and the complexity of analogical inference (Holyoak & Thagard, 1995). Standard computer programs are fabulous at rapid syntactic manipulations, but are much less successful in the semantics of connections to the world and the pragmatics of accomplishing important goals in particular contexts.

In contrast, neural representations mingle syntax and semantics by means of representations that can simultaneously handle relational structure and connections to the world. The best current account of this mingling is Chris Eliasmith's (2013) Semantic Pointer Architecture, which shows how populations of neurons can retain information gained from the world by sensory and motor operations, but also build up syntactically-rich structures. It thereby provides a biologically plausible synthesis of syntax and semantics.

This architecture extends to explain emotions as brain representations that integrate information drawn from (1) physiological changes in the body; (2) cognitive appraisals in the brain; and (3) contextual information including the use of language in humans (Thagard & Schröder, 2014; Thagard 2019a, 2019b; Kajić, Schröder, Stewart, & Thagard, 2019). Emotions that pervade cognition show how goals and purposes can fundamentally influence the operation of the neural system, making it a pragmatic as well as a syntactic and semantic addition. Hence adding emotions to the Semantic Pointer Architecture shows how brains accomplish a synthesis of syntax, semantics, and pragmatics. This integration helps to ensure that human thinking is not just idle deduction or calculation, but operates effectively in the world and accomplishes human goals and purposes.

Nevertheless, the evolutionary feature of integration of cognition and emotion comes with bugs. In the brain, cognitions and emotions are not independent of each other, unlike the calculations in expected utility theory where probabilities and utilities are distinct before being mathematically combined. Under different circumstances, the brain might have evolved with separate modules for probability calculations, utility calculations, and their integration in calculations of expected utility. But these are cultural developments that came late in the history of our species.

Some of the error tendencies (bugs) that arise from illicit mingling of cognitions and emotions are shown in Table 25.3. Normatively, calculations of probabilities and utilities should be independent of each other, but independence fails in the brain. Motivated inference is the well-known tendency of people to base their beliefs not just on relevant evidence, but on what they want to believe (Kunda, 1990). This thinking is more complicated than wishful thinking, because it requires interactions of goals, memory, and inference making. The brain has no firewall between cognition and emotion, so it is not surprising that people often adopt beliefs that they find emotionally appealing, in domains that range from politics to relationships. For example, people who like particular politicians find it hard to believe that they have misbehaved.

Surprisingly, however, people do not always believe what makes them happy, but instead believe things because they scare them, which is fear-driven inference. The classic example is Shakespeare's Othello, who has only scanty evidence that his wife is unfaithful, but cannot block the inference of infidelity because fear keeps him thinking about it. The emotional significance of the hypothesis of unfaithfulness is so strong that it hijacks attention while Othello ignores contrary evidence and alternative hypotheses. High disutility prompts an estimation of high probability.

Another illicit interaction of probability and utility is sour grapes, where the fox concludes that the grapes are sour because he cannot reach them. Logically, low utility should be

Table 25.3 Error tendencies resulting from confusions of probability and utility caused by cognition-emotion interactions

Error tendency	Example	Illicit interaction
Motivated inference	I really want that job, so I'm sure to get it.	high utility → high probability
Fear-driven inference	I'm terrified that this mole is cancerous, so it must be.	high disutility → high probability
Sour grapes	I can't afford a BMW, but they're too unreliable anyway.	low probability → low utility
Rationalization	I have to go to Moose Jaw, so it should be a fun city.	high probability → high utility

Source: Based on Thagard (2019c).

independent of low probability, but the brain again mixes cognition and emotion to yield the dubious conclusion.

Another mixture that people succumb to is rationalization, where the high probability of an occurrence makes us think that it is at least okay, with more utility than we would otherwise judge it to have. After Donald Trump was elected president, many pundits erroneously argued that it could not really be as bad as initially feared because of political constraints on the presidency. For emotional rather than cognitive reasons, people have a tendency to accept their current situations.

Other familiar error tendencies in decision making result from inappropriate interconnections of cognition and emotion. People are prone to the fallacy of sunk costs, making their decisions based on past results rather than on future expectations. For example, people sometimes stay in careers and romantic relationships too long, because of past investments rather than considerations of future prospects. Instead of calculating the expected utility of continuing the career or the relationship, people are driven to avoid the emotion of regret that they would feel if they bailed out, along with the possibility of other negative social emotions such as embarrassment, guilt, and shame. Such emotions get in the way of rational calculations about what to do in the future rather than focusing on the unchangeable past.

Similarly, emotional effects on cognition explain the well-known tendency of people to be unduly influenced by immediate context rather than by long-term effects. People have a tendency to go for short-term small gains in neglect of long-term large gains that they prefer on reflection. For example, people tend to buy things immediately rather than save for retirement. A famous example of this time discounting is the psychological study in which most children choose to eat a marshmallow immediately rather than wait a short time to get two marshmallows.

The neural explanation of time discounting is that different brain areas are involved (McClure et al., 2007). Decisions about what to do immediately engage emotion-related areas such as the ventral striatum and orbitofrontal cortex, whereas decisions about what to do in the long run are not so emotionally engaging and therefore can be done by calculations in prefrontal and parietal areas. Faced with immediate rewards, people do not perform calculations of long-term expected utilities, with emotion overwhelming cognition.

Other well-known incursions of emotion into decision making include risk aversion and the tendency to frame losses as more salient than gains. Neurobiological investigations find that loss aversion correlates with activity in the amygdala, suggesting that dealing with losses has greater emotional effect than dealing with gains (De Martino, Kumaran, Seymour, & Dolan, 2006). I estimate that more than half of the 53 error tendencies listed in Thagard (2011) have a substantial emotional component. Hence the integration of cognition and emotion in the brain contributes as much as size and speed limitations to the boundedness of rationality.

Brain limitations on attention and consciousness

In his best-selling book, *Thinking, Fast and Slow*, Daniel Kahneman (2011) uses dual processes theories of mind to explain why people are so prone to the many thinking biases that he and Amos Tversky identified. Like many other psychologists, he distinguishes between System 1, which is fast, automatic, involuntary, and unconscious, and System 2 which is slow, deliberate, voluntary, and conscious. The distinction explains numerous thinking biases as resulting from the unreflective operations of System 1, whereas System 2 allows people to apply appropriate formal rules such as theories of probability and utility.

The problem with this explanation is that there is no specification of how the two systems actually operate. Suggestions have been made about how the two systems might map onto different areas of the brain, but these proposals have not stood up to empirical scrutiny (Spunt, 2015). Dual process theory is a useful, descriptive, way of classifying different kinds of thinking, but provides no explanation of them, because it does not specify the mechanisms that underlie either of the processes.

Thagard (2019a, Chapter 8) uses the Semantic Pointer Architecture to describe mechanisms that produce the differences between thinking fast and slow. In the slow mode, inferences and actions take place because of interactions among brain areas that interpret sensory inputs, evaluate sensory inputs, and generate new neural representations. The slow mode is much rarer and occurs when competition among brain representations generates conscious awareness via a small subset of them.

Since George Miller's (1956) landmark paper on the magical number seven, psychologists have been aware that conscious, working memory is severely limited. The reasons for this limitation are not clear: it may be an adaptive feature designed to focus mental resources on potential actions, which have to be serial rather than parallel; or it may just be a side effect of the large amount of neural resources required to produce bindings of representations accessible to consciousness.

Either way, consciousness is limited in ways that block people's awareness of their failures to follow normative principles rather than committing the errors so far. For example, when people persist in relationships or businesses because of the sunk cost error tendency, they may not be aware that they are failing to do a good calculation of the expected consequences of their actions because of emotions such as regret and embarrassment. On the other hand, the emotional importance of personal relationships and careers should encourage people to consider what past events reveal about the satisfaction of their basic goals, and thereby discourage them from tossing away what worked in the past based on a superficial calculation of future gains. For example, if you have spent years in a romantic relationship, it is worthwhile reflecting on why there were some good times before making inferences about future consequences.

Most inferences in decision-making occur unconsciously, without people being aware of what they were doing. The limits of conscious attention exacerbate the limits of size and speed discussed earlier. Even if the brain has the resources to carry out complex inferences, it often does not have the capacity to become aware of how it is performing. Hence, people cannot consciously check whether they are following appropriating normative rules or just sliding into error tendencies.

Without completely reengineering the brain in a way that is not evolutionarily available, there is no way to enable people to make more of their thinking consciously evaluable by normative principles. People can use external memory such as paper and spreadsheets to write down relevant considerations, overcoming the limitations of working memory and attention.

Conclusion: helping brains to be more rational

Faced with the perplexing plethora of error tendencies, we can ask how people can be helped to think more rationally. The standard pedagogical method is to teach critical thinking courses in which students are made aware of fallacies, biases, and other error tendencies, in the hope that this awareness will reduce mistakes. That is the practice that I followed when I taught critical thinking, and students said they thought that the class helped. But careful studies of the effectiveness of critical thinking instruction are rare (Cotter & Tally, 2009).

A deeper strategy would be to look critically at what counts as rationality. My 3-analysis of rationality in Table 25.1 assumes that people should aim to meet the standards of deductive logic, probability theory, and utility theory, but these have psychological and philosophical limitations. Outside mathematics, logical deduction is rare, so it does not provide much of a standard for rational inference. Far more common is abductive inference, where hypotheses are accepted because they provide the best explanation of the available evidence. Such inference is better understood as based on coherence rather than on formal principles (Thagard, 1989, 2000).

Probability theory is immensely useful when frequencies are known, for example, in games of chance and statistically rich sciences. But the applicability of probabilities understood as subjective degrees of belief is much more contentious, because their potential objectivity and psychological reality are suspect (Thagard, 2019c). When we know statistical probabilities, we should use them, but wildly guessing about them does not further the aims of making good inferences.

Similarly, the theory of expected utility theory assumed by economists rests on psychologically dubious foundations. Whereas nineteenth-century theorists such as Bentham viewed utility as a psychological quantity, twentieth-century economists tried to reconstruct utility from preferences. The result was mathematically elegant, but got the causal explanation backward. People have the preferences that they do because of estimations of value, not utilities because of preferences. Hence it is not clear that the theory of expected utility provides the desired normative standard for decision-making. An alternative is to view decisions as inferences to the best plan, where assessment of actions is based on coherence with emotion-laden goals (Thagard, 2006, 2019c).

Accordingly, we should consider replacing the exemplars of rationality in Table 25.1 with some of the following: coherence-based abductive inference, probabilistic inference in appropriate domains, and decisions based on inference to the best plan (Thagard, 2000). The other dimensions of the 3-analysis survive, but take on a less formal and more realistic aim to help people improve their acquisition of beliefs and their choices of actions. People still qualify as frequently irrational, for example, in motivated inference, but at least we have a better sense of why they succumb because of close ties between normative practices and irrational deviations.

It is an open question whether understanding the roots of bounded rationality in the brain can help people to avoid error tendencies. There need to be controlled experiments that evaluate the effectiveness in improving inferences about beliefs and actions under these conditions:

1. Make people aware of error tendencies with vivid examples, as is currently done in critical thinking courses.
2. Make people aware of error tendencies along with psychological explanations of why people are prone to them, such as dual process theories of cognition and social influences (Nisbett, 2015).
3. Make people aware of error tendencies along with neural explanations of why people are prone to them, including the brain limitations with respect to size, speed, cognition-emotion interactions, and limitations of consciousness.

My conjecture is that understanding why people are so prone to irrational inferences might help students of critical thinking to be more rational.

Regardless of pedagogic effectiveness, understanding how rationality is bounded by the brain should allow psychologists, economists, and philosophers to have a better theoretical understanding of why people are so frequently irrational.

Acknowledgments

The author thanks Riccardo Viale for helpful comments.

References

Aristotle. (1984). *The complete works of Aristotle*. Princeton,, NJ: Princeton University Press.

Bacon, F. (1960). *The New Organon and related writings*. Indianapolis: Bobbs-Merrill.

Blouw, P., Solodkin, E., Thagard, P., & Eliasmith, C. (2016). Concepts as semantic pointers: A framework and computational model. *Cognitive Science*, 40, 1128–1162.

Cotter, E. M., & Tally, C. S. (2009). Do critical thinking exercises improve critical thinking skills? *Educational Research Quarterly*, 33(2), 3.

Damasio, A. R. (1994). *Descartes' error: Emotion, reason, and the human brain*. New York: G. P. Putnam's Sons.

De Martino, B., Kumaran, D., Seymour, B., & Dolan, R. J. (2006). Frames, biases, and rational decision-making in the human brain. *Science*, 313(5787), 684–687.

Eliasmith, C. (2013). *How to build a brain: A neural architecture for biological cognition*. Oxford: Oxford University Press.

Gould, S. J., & Lewontin, R. C. (1979). The spandrels of San Marco and the Panglossian paradigm: A critique of the adaptationist programme. *Proceedings of the Royal Society of London B*, 205(1161), 581–598.

Hanson, H. (2015). Fallacies. *Stanford encyclopedia of philosophy*. Available at: https://plato.stanford.edu/entries/fallacies/

Holyoak, K. J., & Thagard, P. (1995). *Mental leaps: Analogy in creative thought*. Cambridge, MA: MIT Press/Bradford Books.

Kahnemann, D. (2011). *Thinking, fast and slow*. Toronto: Doubleday.

Kahneman, D., & Tversky, A. (Eds.) (2000). *Choices, values, and frames*. Cambridge: Cambridge University Press.

Kajić, I., Schröder, T., Stewart, T. C., & Thagard, P. (2019). The semantic pointer theory of emotions. Cognitive Systems Research, 58: 35–53.

Kunda, Z. (1990). The case for motivated reasoning. *Psychological Bulletin*, 108, 480–498.

McClure, S. M., Ericson, K. M., Laibson, D. I., Loewenstein, G., & Cohen, J. D. (2007). Time discounting for primary rewards. *Journal of Neuroscience*, 27(21), 5796–5804.

Miller, G. A. (1956). The magical number seven, plus or minus two: Some limits on our capacity for processing information. *Psychological Review*, 63, 81–97.

Murphy, G. L. (2002). *The big book of concepts*. Cambridge, MA: MIT Press.

Nisbett, R. E. (2015). *Mindware: Tools for smart thinking*. New York: Farrar, Straus, and Giroux.

Pessoa, L. (2013). *The cognitive-emotional brain: From interactions to integration*. Cambridge, MA: MIT Press.

Politi, D. (2017). Richard Thaler wins economics Nobel for recognizing people are irrational. *Slate*. Available at: www.slate.com/blogs/the_slatest/2017/10/09/richard_thaler_wins_economics_nobel_for_recognizing_that_people_are_irrational.html.

Quartz, S. R., & Sejnowski, T. J. (1997). The neural basis of cognitive development: A constructivist manifesto. *Behavioral and Brain Sciences*, 20, 537–556.

Rumelhart, D. E., & McClelland, J. L. (Eds.) (1986). *Parallel distributed processing: Explorations in the microstructure of cognition*. Cambridge, MA: MIT Press/Bradford Books.

Simon, H. A. (1972). Theories of bounded rationality. *Decision and Organization*, 1(1), 161–176.

Simon, H. A. (2000). Bounded rationality in social science: Today and tomorrow. *Mind & Society*, 1(1), 25–39.

Spunt, R. P. (2015). Dual-process theories in social cognitive neuroscience. In A. Toga & M. D. Lieberman (Eds.), *Brain mapping: An encyclopedic reference* (pp. 211–215). Amsterdam: Elsevier.

Thagard, P. (1989). Explanatory coherence. *Behavioral and Brain Sciences*, 12, 435–467.

Thagard, P. (2000). *Coherence in thought and action*. Cambridge, MA: MIT Press.

Thagard, P. (2006). *Hot thought: Mechanisms and applications of emotional cognition*. Cambridge, MA: MIT Press.

Thagard, P. (2011). Critical thinking and informal logic: Neuropsychological perspectives. *Informal Logic*, 31, 152–170.

Thagard, P. (2019a). *Brain-mind: From neurons to consciousness and creativity*. Oxford: Oxford University Press.

Thagard, P. (2019b). *Mind-society: From brains to social sciences and professions*. Oxford: Oxford University Press.

Thagard, P. (2019c). *Natural philosophy: From social brains to knowledge, reality, morality, and beauty.* Oxford: Oxford University Press.

Thagard, P., & Schröder, T. (2014). Emotions as semantic pointers: Constructive neural mechanisms. In L. F. Barrett & J. A. Russell (Eds.), *The psychological construction of emotions* (pp. 144–167). New York: Guilford.

Thagard, P., & Verbeurgt, K. (1998). Coherence as constraint satisfaction. *Cognitive Science*, 22, 1–24.

Thaler, R. H. (2015). *Misbehaving: How economics became behavioural.* New York: Norton.

van Rooij, I., Blokpoel, M., Kwisthout, J., & Wareham, T. (2018). *Cognition and intractability: A guide to classical and parameterized complexity analysis.* Cambridge: Cambridge University Press.

Wason, P. C. (1966). Reasoning. In B. M. Foss (Ed.), *New horizons in psychology* (pp. 1–43). Harmondsworth: Penguin.

26

BUILDING A NEW RATIONALITY FROM THE NEW COGNITIVE NEUROSCIENCE

Colin H. McCubbins, Mathew D. McCubbins, and Mark Turner

The theory of mind within the theory of games

Game-theoretic models are used to explain human interactions across a wide range of activities, such as allocation of security forces, allocation of health care services, and the design of political, legal, social, and market institutions (Roth, 1990; Fudenberg and Tirole, 1991; Kagel and Roth, 1997). Despite the widespread use of game-theoretic models to explain human behavior, we often observe behavior, from voting to the divergence of political parties' platforms to market bubbles and crashes that do not easily accord with game-theoretic predictions (Camerer, 2003, 2008). Further, it is a common finding that experimental subjects, in tightly controlled settings, do not make choices that comport with Nash equilibrium strategies, or indeed, von Neumann-Morgenstern utility maximization (Plott, 1967; Smith, 2010).

To begin, we need to define our terms and identify game theory's flaws. A game is defined by identifying the items in PAISPOE:

- *Players*;
- *Actions* available to players;
- *Information* they have about the game; the timing of access to such information; including the knowledge the players have about what other players know or will know and when those other players will know it;
- *Strategies* define the action rules that specify what actions to take under every circumstance;
- *Payoffs* associated with each outcome;
- *Outcomes* which define the consequences of the game;
- and, finally, *Equilibria*. A Nash Equilibrium (NE) results when, given their strategies, no player can do better by changing her strategy while all others remain unchanged. An equilibrium concept defines which strategies are allowed and which are precluded.

Noncooperative games, at least in their classical format, assume that subjects share common knowledge. Classical game theory requires players to have correct and consistent beliefs. That is, individuals are perfectly able to predict the actions of others and those others are, likewise, perfectly able to predict that individual's actions. Thus, the equilibrium path in any game is *predictable by assumption*. To have "correct beliefs" is to regard other players as following

DOI: 10.4324/9781315658353-30

NE strategies and to predict that they follow classical equilibrium strategies. Indeed, it is also required that players know that other players know that all players, including themselves, are following NE strategies, and so on, ad infinitum. As Lupia, Levine, and Zharinova (2010) note, the condition is even stronger, in that a Nash Equilibrium "requires shared conjectures. … Common Nash refinements … continue to require that actors share identical conjectures of other players' strategies" (p. 106). This is part of what economists assume when they accept that the players in a game share 'common knowledge.' As Smith (2000, p. 9) writes, "The common knowledge assumption underlies all of game theory and much of economic theory … Without such common knowledge, people would fail to reason their way to the solution arrived at cognitively by the theorist."

Unfortunately, the natural, biological, or cognitive means of achieving such knowledge are not specified in game theory; rather, it is merely assumed that, given enough time and effort, players can all learn what behaviors to adopt and when to adopt them, or, barring this possibility, that societies will adopt rules, laws, or norms to restrict and channel behavior to more efficient forms. Prior work on subjects' beliefs in experimental settings suggest that subjects possess non-equilibrium beliefs (Croson, 2007) and that, in at least some settings, their behavior can be reasonable, given such beliefs, although this is not always true (Camerer, Ho, and Chong, 2004).

The laboratory and market mispredictions of game theory have led to the establishment of behavioral game theory. The main approach of behavioral game theory has been to propose systematic deviations from the predictions of rationality in classical game theory, deviations that arise from, for example, character type, cognitive overloads or other reasoning, constraints and conditions of memory, or informational limitations. The fundamental idea of behavioral game theory is that, if we know the deviations, then we can correct our predictions accordingly, and so get it right. Indeed, if we know these deviations, we can anticipate them and we can nudge people to act more in accord with the equilibrium predictions of classical game theory, as modified by behavioral game theory (Sunstein, 2014).

There are two problems with this approach, however, and each is fatal. (1) For the chooser to contemplate the range of possible deviations actually makes it exponentially harder for the chooser to figure out a path to an equilibrium, since there are many dozens of possible deviations. This array of possible deviations makes the theoretical models useless for modeling human thought or human behavior in general (Roth, 1990). Modeling deviations is helpful only if the deviations are *consistent*, so that scientists (and indeed decision-makers) can make predictions about future choices on the basis of past choices. They must be able to generalize from the particular deviation. But as we have shown (Lucas, McCubbins, and Turner 2015; McCubbins, Turner, and Weller 2012), the deviations are not consistent. In general, deviations from classical models are not consistent for any individual from one task to the next or between individuals for the same task. In addition, people's beliefs are in general not consistent with their choices. Accordingly, all hope is hollow that we can construct a general behavioral game theory.

Building a new rationality from the new cognitive neuroscience

To address the discrepancy between predicted and actual behavior, we must build a better theory of human behavior. To do this, we must start with an appreciation of how we actually reason. As cognitive science has shown, intuitive notions of how the mind works (vision, language, memory, etc.) may be very useful for humans to hold as scaffolding for consciousness, but they are comprehensively wrong and simplistic. Intuitive notions of how we reason are not a basis for science. How we reason must be discovered, not assumed, and certainly not borrowed from intuition.

The first step in designing a new model of human choice is to determine why game theory failed. We propose that the failure of game theory derives from its mistaken theory of mind. In this theory of mind,

- People have unitary selves and fixed preferences about outcomes.
- People think about hypothetical paths that lead to outcomes.
- People have cognitive models about other people, including
  - those other people have unitary selves and consistent preferences about outcomes;
  - those other people think about hypothetical paths that lead to outcomes;
  - those other people have cognitive models about other people.
- An actor considers everyone's fixed preferences (to the extent that they are known), the choices available to each actor at each moment in the rest of the decision tree, the information known to each actor at each moment, and the ultimate payoffs to the actors of ending up at each of the specific possible final outcomes.
- An actor chooses, at a moment of decision, the available choice that can lead rationally to the expected best outcome available for the actor. "Rationally" in this picture means not only that the actor will choose in this way but also that the actor understands that the other actors will choose in this way.
- Accordingly, actors make choices by backward induction, looking ahead to the final outcomes, and making choices at each node along the way so as to create a path to the expected best outcome for the actor at the end. In this picture, an actor's self is fixed throughout the course of complicated action, however many moments of choice are required, and indeed fixed across all games.

Flexibility and blending

In contrast, the world's cultures have unhesitatingly recognized human flexibility. Even conditioned and trained humans in utterly confining conditions do not comply reliably to expectations of fixity. To succeed at all, game theory must control the activity of actors by imposing extreme, artificial constraints—as in chess, tic-tac-toe, or common-value auctions. A thorough theory of human decision-making will subsume game theory as a limiting case. The reverse subsumption is impossible, because modeling the vast majority of human choosing requires eliminating the constraints on flexibility imposed by game theory.

Many researchers outside game theory have proposed theories, according to which any human being contains multiple selves (Angyal, 1965; Baumeister, 1998; Berne, 1961; Elster, 1985; Lester, 2010; Mischel, 1968; Rowan, 1990). We acknowledge this tradition and take the view that an individual assembles, on the fly, very many versions of self, one in each moment of choosing. Indeed, a self assembled in such a brief moment might never be assembled by that individual human being again.

If the self is not fixed, how do we model choice by a self? Turner (2014, Chapter 4), reviews how selves are assembled via *conceptual blending*. A conceptual blend can have many inputs, including inputs that conflict strongly with each other. Structure can be projected selectively from each of these inputs to create a coherent blend with emergent structure of its own. Consider Bill and Peter, brothers-in-law, each happy. Bill is a mathematically-talented professor in the Eastern time zone who likes investing and San Francisco. Peter is a stockbroker in San Francisco. Bill wonders, analogically, should he move to San Francisco and be a stockbroker and get a huge raise? No: Bill is a night owl but Peter must arise at 5:30am Pacific Time to deal with the stock market's opening at 9:30am Eastern Time. Mentally, Bill has created a new, blended person—Bill-as-Peter, who is miserable arising at 5:30am every morning to do his stockbroker job, even though misery is not in any of the inputs. This kind of blending, depending on what is active in the mind as an input, what is selectively projected to the blend, and what new structure arises in the blend, is standard for human beings despite its utter incompatibility with the conception of selves in game theory.

Possible inputs to a conceptual blend are very many, including memories of previous selves, ideas of other people's selves, ideas of selves which we encountered through reports, news, books, fiction, songs, movies, fairytales, or generic conceptions of character. Activation of ideas is highly variable in the brain; the potential inputs vary moment-to-moment. Projection to the blend is highly selective. Quite variable ranges of emergent meaning can develop in the blend.

There are analogies and disanalogies across all the different selves one has been, in reality or imagination. In constructing a self by blending, one may select some inputs and compress the analogies connecting them to an *identity* in the blend, and compress the disanalogies into *change* for that identity. For example, there are astonishing disanalogies between a person before marrying and the "identical" person after marrying. The analogies are compressed to an *identity*—the person—and the disanalogies are compressed to change for that identity: Mary *got married*, or Mary *became* a wife. This common compression pattern—analogies to identity, disanalogies to change—is extremely common in mental blending. It is the same pattern we use for "dinosaurs turned into birds," "the fences get taller as you drive west across the United States," and "his girlfriend gets younger every year." The resulting blend of a stable self is a useful illusion. Fauconnier and Turner (2008) explore constraints on blending and argue that nearly all attempts at blending take place outside of consciousness and fail almost immediately. Very few survive to be embraced by a community.

Adam Smith masterfully analyzed the creation of variable selves through blending (Turner, 2014). However, classical economics now pays no attention to the role of the dynamic and highly variable construction of a self over time. This failing is at the root of game theory's mistaken view of mind.

Selves and choices in wayfinding

A person in a moment needs a self that serves for collective action but not the straitjacket internal consistency assumed by game theory. Person A encountering person B needs to be a self in the moment of encounter, but there might be many serviceable selves, and the brain may be running many of those incompatible alternatives in parallel. One will precipitate in the moment of action, but that does not indicate that the brain was bent exclusively on that approach. It means only that one self precipitates to serve the moment of action. A different precipitation might occur in the same circumstances next time. A human being about to act needs a sense of a stable self, one that will make a choice leading to the next choice point, where the self will be different but not randomly so. Stability is important; uniqueness, stasis, rigidity are not.

Or, a small group of colleagues, ignorant of the town, meet and decide to go out. Each participant needs to know how to choose at any given choice point. The chooser needs a wayfinding marker: You Are Here Now. Or perhaps several such markers, only one to precipitate at the moment of choice. The chooser needs to be a wayfinder in this scene. The chooser does not need to try to model this as a game.

Choosers are wayfinders. At each choice point, the self may differ, in a different story. The possibility space of these alternative selves in stories is large. All that is needed is for one self to precipitate for each choice.

Collective action in the wild

The design of actual choice situations in the wild supports our view of choosing as wayfinding. Consider a restaurant. The owner does not seek equilibria by saying to customers, "Tell us what you want, and we will see whether we can make it." Instead, the restaurant imposes constraints on the customer by its name, style, design, menu, suggestions ("for those who prefer something light"), presentations (dessert cart, case of grilled vegetables), safety valves (corkage), delegates (the bartender or mother who chooses for you).

Selves and choices in cognitive neuroscience

The view of people as wayfinders, inventors of multiple selves in multiple stories, accords with suggestions in recent cognitive neuroscience.

What is the brain doing? Older views of the brain as driven by tasks prompted by external stimuli have been cast into doubt by evidence suggesting that most of the brain's work is intrinsic. When human beings are unengaged in tasks, many brain networks are highly active, but what they might be doing is hotly debated in cognitive neuroscience. One of the main proposals is that the brain is largely engaged in composing matrices of stories and selves. We clarify that the engagement imagined is of course *not* during moments of focused decision making, which are task-oriented, but instead in the temporal background to such moments, preparing resources for such brief moments of choosing when they arise. Michael Anderson (2014, p. 113) writes:

> Over the past few years there has been growing interest in something called "resting state functional MRI," a technique for seeing what your brain is doing when you aren't doing much of anything at all. It turns out that brains at rest are pretty restless, consuming far more energy than they do when doing. More interesting, "resting" activity is not random but highly coherent, consistent, and predictable. The discovery of the brain's characteristic resting behavior led some years ago to the postulation of a "default network" for the brain—a set of regions that consistently cooperate to do ... well, what, exactly, we don't know. But surely it must be something interesting. Your brain would hardly waste all of that energy dancing to the beat of its inner drummer if it didn't serve some function, right?
>
> Our ignorance regarding the function of all that fluctuation isn't for lack of trying. The discovery of the brain's default network has led to hundreds of studies relating the default network to the brain's anatomical structure as well as to mood disorders, such as depression, developmental problems, such as autism, and degenerative diseases, such as Alzheimer's. It has even been suggested that resting-state activity holds the key (cue deep voice and echo effect) to understanding consciousness itself (e.g., Raichle, 2010). Now, when neuroscientists start brandishing the "c" word, there are two predictable reactions: increased public interest and attention and increased scientific scrutiny and criticism. Both have happened here, generating a cadre of enthusiastic adherents and an equally committed group of critics who question whether we should continue wasting

our energy figuring out why the brain appears to be wasting its energy. Or, as one prominent neuroscientist put it to me recently, "It's just such a fad. I kind of hate it."

Hyperbolic allusions to cracking the mystery of consciousness excepted, I don't think anybody should hate it. But to see why we should, if not love, then at least care about the brain's intrinsic activity requires us to think about brain function in a new and unfamiliar way.

In earlier notions of the computational brain, it was easy to view brains as having programming that remained fixed and that responded to external stimuli by taking inputs and computing actions in response. The fit between the theory of the computational brain and theory of games was pat: the chooser has preferences and rationality and, given knowledge of external circumstances, computes a choice and enacts it. But, today's cognitive neuroscience is more compatible with the view that action is driven largely by intrinsic and imaginative construction of selves and stories in a process of wayfinding through life.

The brain as an imagination engine for selves and stories

The Neuron Doctrine was compatible with a computational view of the brain as producing 1s and 0s in response to input much the way a theoretical Turing machine operates by receiving input—one symbol on a tape at a time—and changing the static state of the machine according to algorithms for responding to the symbol. Instead, recent work paints a picture of a brain engaged in largely intrinsic work, often connected to constructing selves and narratives. As Kaplan et al. (2017, p. 5) write:

> In attempting to characterize the kind of psychological operations that appear to engage this (i.e. the default) network, researchers have described them as related to social cognition (Mars et al. 2012), internally directed processing (Immordino-Yang et al. 2012), mental time travel (Ostby et al. 2012), or self-related processing (Northoff and Qin 2011). Interestingly, all of these operations are either involved in the processing of narratives or rely on a narrative organization of information. For example, the majority of studies that have shown cortical midline activations for self-related processing have focused on aspects of the autobiographical self, such as personality trait judgment, rather than transient present-moment aspects of the self (Northoff et al. 2006). The autobiographical self is, in essence, a process of generating fragmentary narratives of our personal lives built from a multitude of recorded experiences (Damasio 1998). These same midline structures are activated just as much or more when we think about the biographies of other people (Araujo et al. 2013, 2014), suggesting that the processing of narratives may be more important for activating these structures than self-relatedness.

The search for neuroscientifically relevant human psychological factors (NRPs)

Contemporary cognitive neuroscience is reconsidering what might be the "neuroscientifically relevant human psychological factors." Back-of-the-envelope notions of the mind as a system of passive perception, active response, fear, greed, desire, executive function, inference, memory, etc., were an unfortunate place for psychology and economics to begin (see Anderson, 2014, for a review). A view of higher-order human cognition as largely intrinsic and constantly blending even strongly incompatible inputs in imaginative ways to produce innovations—in selves, stories, and possibilities—was largely unavailable in these previous folk psychological notions. Even less available was an idea of mental activity as generating simultaneously very many of these blending networks, in parallel, often with strong conflicts between them, and of action—including enacted choice—as the momentary precipitation of just one of these parallel imaginative lines into an attractor basin in the behavioral landscape. Such ideas of mental activity are being actively explored in the new cognitive neuroscience.

Dynamical cognition

Cognitive neuroscientists have proposed that the human brain is constantly scanning over a range of often-conflicting alternatives and collapsing that range to an action only in the moment of decision (Spivey, 2008). Consider someone who wants to pick up a coffee cup. There are many ways to do so successfully. The brain may explore many of those approaches simultaneously. The neurobiological basis of action can be varied, with simultaneous but conflicting lines, each with some probability of being given, at the final instant, control over skeletal and motor programs. One of those possibilities will precipitate in the moment of action. Our enacting only one action suite does not mean that the brain was exclusively focused on that one suite; it means only that, in the moment of action, one coherent action was executed, as others were forsaken.

The analysis for picking up the coffee cup applies to any moment of choice. The human being requires great flexibility. Stability of self is not repetition or fixity but instead a coherent migration path. Perhaps the next moment of picking up the coffee cup will have a self who is inviting, or dismissive, or finalizing the communicative turn, or trying to elongate the moment, or oblivious to the coffee because she is paying attention to other things, or styled as uncaring, or attentive, or sensitive, or concerned with the warmth of the coffee, or turning from that sip of coffee to more important or less important things, or simply bored with the usual ways of picking up a coffee cup.

Action appears to be unitary and specific: we must pick up the cup just one way, not lots of incompatible ways. Misled by the cause-effect isomorphism fallacy, we think the cause must have the attributes of the effect. Given that performed actions in the world are unitary and specific and form a nice chain, it is easy to imagine that the mind works something like that. Instead, as Spivey (2008) explains, it is better to think of multiple pathways of thinking happening in parallel and of one of them precipitating into an attractor basin for the purpose of performing a specific action. But the neural activity could drop into a different attractor basin.

Towards a new model of rationality

From the observations of the brain's intrinsic work, we can develop a new model of rationality. The main assumption of this model is what we call the *Principle of Least Cognitive Effort*—that is to say, people will most likely choose the path of action that requires the least cognitive effort. Often they will not, but most often they will.

It is noteworthy that this is not a simple reformulation of the Cognitive Miser Hypothesis, which states that the brain actively and unconsciously avoids spending computational effort on tasks if it can be avoided. It would seem that the model of the brain as a limited memory computer is being slowly proven flawed, as neuroscience research has demonstrated that brains have much larger computational ability than we had previously hypothesized or observed. Instead, we argue here that the Principle of Least Cognitive Effort is a *conscious* choice that individuals are making: that is, this is *not* the result of the brain somehow trying to save itself from its own limitations but rather the individual trying to save what limited time they have in the day. As

415

such, the limiting factor here is not brain computational ability but rather individual time and energy.

This model of rationality requires that we make assumptions similar to those in PAISPOE. We will, however, depart in significant ways. Instead of modeling individual actions as binary, consistent responses derived from external stimuli, we can develop a probabilistic model of choice that is more compatible with observations in cognitive neuroscience and game theoretic experimentation. Individual behavior in the moment is unique and it is conditional on experience. Given a game, an individual will respond by choosing one of many potential selves to act with in this setting. The choice of self determines the payoffs for any particular outcome and it affects the information conditions. A person's *type* will determine how the game is played.

To this model of decision, we add that behavior is also conditional on *context*: the who, what, where, when, and why. Context is a parameter that changes the probability space over which an individual is making a decision; it forces that individual to reconsider the construction of the theory of self and the theory of mind that they are using in a specific game. Context is a multidimensional construct that is also dependent on time. Consider the scenario in which an individual is visiting a restaurant for the second time in two days. The who, what, where, and why are the same, but the *when* is different. Thus, we may expect that individual to order something completely different even though the choice situation is the same as it was the day before except that it is now the following day. Thus, context, itself, is conditional on previous context, which creates path dependence in action as well as the strategies and equilibria that follow.

Suppose that each individual has a set of types. For any specific context and game combination, there is a subset of types that have a non-zero probability of being chosen by that individual for use in that situation. Thus, in considering the choice of strategy, in other words an action plan, the choice space over types and the type chosen greatly affect the equilibria.

These subsets of types for individuals define the probability space of actions that an individual can choose from, given a particular context and game. This probability space of actions is narrowed to a single action at time t when a decision is necessary. We can define the probability function of actions Θ as a function of an individual's type T, context C, and the game Γ. This probability function has a density corresponding to the probability of a specific action being taken. We assume that the highest peak of this density function corresponds to an individual's most commonly completed action.

This probability space of actions defines the cognitive *sum over actions* much in the same way that quantum path integral formulation defines the *sum over histories* of a particle: there is a continuum of *possible* actions that an individual can take but a much narrower band of *likely* actions. The most likely of these, given the assumption above, is the action that requires the least cognitive effort. Because expertise reduces the cognitive effort of taking an action, we would thus infer that the probability density would become unimodal and narrower, such that the potential range of actions for the expert would be much less varied and more structured. Thus, expertise would conduce to action path *consistency*: we would expect an individual to have a similar response to the same game and context over repeated trials. However, the exact opposite would occur in the absence of expertise: the probability density would become much wider and possibly have multiple modes, which would lead an individual's responses to be *inconsistent*. This model, then, has the potential to corroborate laboratory experimental results.

Simon long ago studied the decision-making speed and accuracy of experienced chess players as an example of the impact that expertise has on cognition:

We have seen that a major component of expertise is the ability to recognize a very large number of specific relevant cues when they are present in any situation and then to retrieve from memory information about what to do when those particular cues are noticed. Because of this knowledge and recognition capability, experts can respond to new situations very rapidly – and usually with considerable accuracy.

Simon, 1957

Chase and Simon's (1973) experimental studies on chess expertise exemplify the type of cognitive action this model supposes. While it has historically been the case that laboratory experiments that expose subjects to game theoretic situations tend to produce results far afield from what would be expected, given the mathematical models they purport to study, it is also likely that the subjects being studied are just not experts in participating in these types of situations in a laboratory setting. Thus, we would expect responses to these situations to be inconsistent and slow, just like the chess novice's responses to chess scenarios in Chase and Simon (1973). Having an understanding of how expertise shapes the cognitive space that individuals are working in seems key to moving forward with a broader theory of cognition and can help to design better laboratory experiments that have greater levels of external validity.

Conclusion

As Engel (2005) argues, human beings are by nature flexible and variable, so much so that cultures must invent institutions to generate enough predictability in human performance to make interactions even possible.[1] Cultures exploit the great flexibility of the human imagination to invent institutions for the purpose of generating sufficient regularity and predictability in the face of otherwise uncontrollably wild behavior. In the last 50,000 years or so—a blink of the eye in evolutionary time—cultures have invented contracts, classrooms, courts, constitutions, retail counters, certified public accountants, conjugal arrangements, ... One of their central purposes is to enforce patterns that constrain possibilities and generate predictability. It is impossible to model human collective action unconstrained by cultural institutions, because the possibilities for human collective action are too many and too variable. As Wittgenstein writes and Geertz quotes (Geertz, 1973, p. 13):

> We ... say of some people that they are transparent to us. It is, however, important as regards this observation that one human being can be a complete enigma to another. We learn this when we come into a strange country with entirely strange traditions; and, what is more, even given a mastery of the country's language. We do not understand the people. (And not because of not knowing what they are saying to themselves.) We cannot find our feet with them. —Ludgwig Wittgenstein.

Geertz himself comments:

> [C]ulture is best seen not as complexes of concrete behavior patterns—customs, usages, traditions, habit clusters—as has, by and large, been the case up to now, but as a set of control mechanisms—plans, recipes, rules, instructions (what computer engineers call "programs")—for the governing of behavior.

Geertz 1973, p. 44

and "One of the most significant facts about us may finally be that we all begin with the natural equipment to live a thousand kinds of life but end in the end having lived only one" (Geertz, 1973, p. 45).

Game theory represents the utter extreme of eliminating personal flexibility, by creating draconian governing conditions under which we might have expected to be able to predict both behavior and an understanding of that behavior. However, as has been demonstrated in decades of experimentation, people retain impressive flexibility even under these conditions.

We have proposed that, in the wild, people use flexible but orderly mental processes, such as conceptual blending and narrative imagination, to operate as wayfinders, constructing selves as they go along to make choices. We have argued that this is consistent with modern cognitive neuroscience. Our prescription for finding our way forward in creating a new rationality is to explore a fruitful alliance between institutionalist views of collective action and cognitive neuroscientific views of multiple, variable selves in multiple, various stories and their precipitation in some moments into individual coherent actions.

Note

1 This kind of unpredictability (and the resulting lack of equilibrium) was discussed by Quine (2013) in terms of the indeterminacy of translation. Quine argues that we do not have an identity criterion for most of our utterances and thus there is no way for people to be sure that their translation of a sentence is the correct one.

References

Anderson, M. 2014. *After phrenology: Neural reuse and the interactive brain*. Cambridge, MA: MIT Press.

Angyal, A. 1965. *Neurosis and treatment*. New York: Wiley.

Baumeister, R. F. 1998. The self. In D. T. Gilbert, S. T. Fiske, and G. Lindzey (Eds.), *The handbook of social psychology*. Vol. 1. (pp. 680–740). Boston: McGraw-Hill.

Berne, E. 1961. *Transactional analysis in psychotherapy*. New York: Grove Press.

Camerer, C. F. 2003. *Behavioral game theory*. New York: Russell Sage Foundation/ Princeton, NJ: Princeton University Press.

Camerer, C. 2008. The Potential of Neuroeconomics. *Economics and Philosophy*, 24(3), 369–379. doi:10.1017/S0266267108002022.

Camerer, C. F., Ho T. H., and Chong. K. 2004. A cognitive hierarchy model of games. *Quarterly Journal of Economics*, 119(3), 861–898.

Chase, W. G., and Simon, H. A. 1973. Perception in chess. *Cognitive Psychology*, 4, 55–81.

Croson, R. 2007. Theories of commitment, altruism and reciprocity: Evidence from linear public goods games. *Economic Inquiry*, 45, 199–216.

Denzau, A., and North, D. C. 2000. Shared mental models: Ideologies and institutions. In A., Lupia, M., McCubbins, and S. Popkin (Eds.), *Elements of reason: Cognition, choice and the bounds of rationality*. Cambridge: Cambridge University Press.

Elster, J. (Ed.) 1985. *The multiple self*. Cambridge: Cambridge University Press.

Engel, C. 2005. *Generating predictability: Institutional analysis and institutional design*. Cambridge: Cambridge University Press.

Fauconnier, G., and Turner, M. 2008. *The way we think: Conceptual blending and the mind's hidden complexities*. New York: Basic Books.

Fudenberg, D., and Tirole, J. 1991. *Game theory*. Cambridge, MA: MIT Press.

Geertz, C. 1973. *The interpretation of cultures*. New York: Basic Books.

Gigerenzer, G. 2000. *Adaptive thinking: Rationality in the real world*. New York: Oxford University Press.

Kagel, J. H., and Roth, A. E. (Eds.) 1997. *The handbook of experimental economics*. Princeton, NJ: Princeton University Press.

Kaplan, J. T., Gimbel, S. I., Dehghani, M., Immordino-Yang, M. H., Sagae, K., ... Damasio, A. 2017. Processing narratives concerning protected values: A cross-cultural investigation of neural correlates. *Cerebral Cortex*, 27(2), 1428–1438.

Lester, D. 2010. *A multiple self theory of personality*. Hauppauge, NY: Nova Science.

Lucas, G. M., McCubbins M. D., and Turner M. 2015. Against game theory. In R. A. Scott and S. M. Kosslyn (Eds.), *Emerging trends in the social and behavioral sciences: An interdisciplinary, searchable, and linkable resource*. Hoboken, NJ: Wiley.

Lupia, A., Levine, A. S., and Zharinova, N. 2010. Should political scientists use the self confirming equilibrium concept? Benefits, costs and an application to the jury theorem. *Political Analysis*, 18, 103–123.

McCubbins, M. D., and Turner, M., 2012. Going cognitive: Tools for rebuilding the social sciences. In R. Sun, P. Thagard, N. Ross, B. Shore, and S. Feldman (Eds.), *Grounding Social Sciences in Cognitive Sciences*, Cambridge, MA: MIT Press.

McCubbins, M. D., Turner, M., and Weller, N. 2012. The mythology of game theory. In *International Conference on Social Computing, Behavioral-Cultural Modeling, and Prediction* (pp. 27–34). Berlin: Springer.

McKelvey, R., and Page, R. T. 1990. Public and private information: An experimental study of information pooling. *Econometrica*, 58, 1321–1339.

Mischel, W. 1968 *Personality and assessment*. New York: Wiley.

Plott, C. R. 1967. A notion of equilibrium and its possibility under majority rule. *The American Economic Review*, 57(4), 787–806.

Quine, W. O. 2013. Translation and meaning. In W. O. Quine, *Word and object* (new ed.), (pp. 23–72). Cambridge, MA: MIT Press.

Raichle,, M. 2010. The brain's dark energy. *Scientific American*, 302(3), 44–49.

Rasmusen, E. 2006. *Games and information* (4th ed.). Oxford: Blackwell Publishers.

Roth, A. E. 1990. New physicians: A natural experiment in market organization. *Science*, 250, 1524–1528.

Rowan, J. 1990. *Subpersonalities*. London: Routledge.

Simon, H. 1957. A behavioral model of rational choice. In H. Simon, *Models of man, social and rational: Mathematical essays on rational human behavior in a social setting*. New York: Wiley.

Smith, A. 2010. *The theory of moral sentiments*. London: Penguin.

Smith, V. 2000. Rational choice: The contrast between economics and psychology. In *Bargaining and Market Behavior: Essays in Experimental Economics* (pp. 7–24). New York: Cambridge University Press.

Spivey, M. 2008. *The continuity of mind*. Oxford: Oxford University Press.

Sunstein, C. R. 2014. *Why nudge? The politics of libertarian paternalism*. New Haven, CT: Yale University Press.

Turner, M. 2009. The scope of human thought. Available at: http://onthehuman.org/humannature/.

Turner, M. 2014. *The origin of ideas: Blending, creativity, and the human spark*. New York: Oxford University Press.

PART V

Homo Oeconomicus Bundatus

27

MODELING BOUNDED RATIONALITY IN ECONOMIC THEORY

Four examples

Ariel Rubinstein

Introduction

The terms bounded rationality and economic theory mean different things to different people. For me (see Rubinstein (2012)), economic theory is a collection of stories, usually expressed in formal language, about human interactions that involve joint and conflicting interests. Economic theory is not meant to provide predictions of the future. At most, it can clarify concepts and provide non-exclusive explanations of economic phenomena. In many respects, a model in economic theory is no different than a story. Both a story and a model are linked to reality in an associative manner. Both the storyteller and the economic theorist have in mind a real-life situation but do not consider the story or the model to be a full description of reality. Both leave it to the reader to draw their own conclusions, if any.

For me, models of bounded rationality are (see Rubinstein (1998)) models that include explicit references to procedural aspects of decision making. A common critique of bounded rationality models is that they are more specific, less general, and more arbitrary than models in the mainstream areas of economic theory, such as general equilibrium or game theory in which full rationality is assumed. In response, I would claim that every model makes very (very) special assumptions. Without strong assumptions, there would be no conclusions. It is true that rationality is a special assumption since it is viewed by many as being normative, whereas models of bounded rationality are viewed as dealing with deviations from normative behavior. Returning to the analogy of a story: What story is more interesting—one about normative people who behave "according to the book" or one about people who deviate from normative behavior?

Not every model that is inconsistent with some aspect of rationality is a model of bounded rationality. A model in which rational agents ignore some aspect of rationality is a bad model rather than a model of bounded rationality. A good model of bounded rationality should include a procedure of reasoning that "makes sense" and is somewhat related to what we observe in real life.

DOI: 10.4324/9781315658353-32

I am not a big fan of abstract methodological discussions. I prefer to demonstrate an approach by discussing examples. Accordingly, the chapter discusses four models, in which economic agents are assumed to reason in systematic ways using a well-defined procedure that is outside the standard scope of rational behavior. My choice of models is totally subjective. I am partial to these models because I was involved in constructing and analyzing them over the last 35 years. Rubinstein (1998) surveyed the field at the time, while Spiegler (2011) surveys more recent models in which aspects of bounded rationality have been inserted into classic models of industrial economics.

Bounded rationality and mechanism design

Story

The director of a prestigious MBA program has been persuaded by Choi, Kariv, Muller, and Silverman (2014) that transitivity is strongly correlated with success in life (as measured by wealth). Thus, he decides to accept only those candidates who hold transitive preferences.

Accordingly, the director designs a simple test. He presents three alternatives a, b and c to each candidate and asks them to respond to a questionnaire consisting of three questions $Q(a, b)$, $Q(b, c)$ and $Q(a, c)$ where $Q(x, y)$ is the quiz question:

Do you prefer x to y or y to x?
○ I prefer x to y.
○ I prefer y to x.

For each of the three questions a candidate must respond by clicking on one and only one of the two possible answers. Thus, the questionnaire has eight possible sets of responses.

The director is obligated by law to inform candidates about the conditions that will gain them admission to the program. The director has specified the following two conditions:

R1: If you prefer a to b and b to c then you must prefer a to c.
R2: If you prefer c to b and b to a then you must prefer c to a.

The candidates are reminded that an "if" proposition is violated only if its antecedent (the "if" part) is satisfied and its consequent (the "then" part) is not.

The director was hoping that the candidates would feel obliged to report the truth and thus the simple questionnaire should separate perfectly between "good" candidates who hold transitive preferences and "bad" candidates who do not. In order to encourage instinctive responses, the director also sets a short time limit for completing the questionnaire.

A disappointment: the director learns that all the candidates have been admitted and concludes that the candidates with cyclical preferences had gamed the system. The frustrated director opens an investigation. Researchers are rushed to the scene. They interview candidates to reveal how they answered the questionnaire so "successfully". Apparently, candidates treated the questionnaire as a puzzle to be solved in order to be admitted to the program. The time limit made solving the "puzzle" a challenging task. The following procedure was identified:

Step 1: Examine whether your honest set of answers satisfies all the conditions. If it does, then happily submit those answers. If not, go to step 2.

Step 2: Find a condition that is violated by your honest answers (that is, your true answers satisfy the antecedent but not the consequent of the condition). Try modifying your answers with respect only to the consequent. If the modified set of answers satisfies all conditions, then submit them. If not, iterate step 2 (starting with your honest set of answers) until it is exhausted. Then, proceed to Step 3.

Step 3: Give up. Submit the honest answers (and be rejected).

Faced with the questionnaire and the admission conditions, a "good" candidate (who has transitive preferences) reports the truth and is admitted. What about a "bad" candidate with cyclical preferences $a \succ b \succ c \succ a$ (or $c \succ b \succ a \succ c$)? An honest response satisfies R2 (the antecedent is false) but violates R1. The candidate remains with the true answers to $Q(a, b)$ and $Q(b, c)$ and modifies his answer to $Q(a, c)$. Thus, he responds as if he holds the preferences $a \succ b \succ c$ and is admitted. In this way, all the candidates are admitted.

Realizing that people are prepared to cheat (when they have to) by using the procedure to find a persuasive set of responses, the director tries to come up with a modified set of admission conditions so that all the good candidates will pass the test while the bad candidates will not. He adds two new admission conditions, so that the new set of admission conditions is as follows:

R1: If you prefer a to b and b to c, then you must prefer a to c.
R2: If you prefer c to b and b to a, then you must prefer c to a.
R3: If you prefer a to b and a to c, then you must prefer c to b.
R4: If you prefer c to a and c to b, then you must prefer a to b.

This set of conditions seems a bit odd. How would the candidates respond to it?

First, consider a "good" candidate who holds the transitive relation $b \succ a \succ c$ (or one of the following three other preferences : $b \succ c \succ a$, $a \succ c \succ b$ or $c \succ a \succ b$). None of the antecedents of the four conditions are satisfied and responding truthfully leads to acceptance, as desired by both the candidates and the manager.

What about a "good" candidate who holds the preferences $a \succ b \succ c$ (or $c \succ b \succ a$)? If he responds truthfully, then he violates R3 and is rejected. However, he is induced by the violation of R3 to modify his answer to $Q(b, c)$; this leads him to respond as if he holds the preferences $a \succ c \succ b$ and thus he cheats successfully.

On the other hand, a "bad" candidate with cyclical preferences $a \succ b \succ c \succ a$, (or their counterpart) violates only R1 and is led to try only the set of answers corresponding to the preferences $a \succ b \succ c$ which do not satisfy the set of conditions. Thus, such a candidate fails the test, as desired by the program director.

A happy ending, at least for the program director. Interestingly, he does not mind that some candidates cheat. The questionnaire "works" in the sense that it separates between the good and bad candidates. Actually, the director also finds that there is no alternative set of conditions which will separate between the two types of candidates without some good candidates having to cheat. He concludes that "white lies" are sometimes necessary.

Discussion

This section is based on Glazer and Rubinstein (2012). The model comes under the rubric of Bounded Rationality since it explicitly specifies a process of reasoning used by the individuals. The paper characterizes the circumstances under which the designer of the mechanism is able to implement his target given that the individuals use the discussed procedure. Conditions under which implementation does not require that some "good" candidates need to cheat are established as well.

No one claims that most people use this exact procedure. Nonetheless, Glazer and Rubinstein (2012) provide experimental evidence that the two central ingredients of the procedure are present in many people's minds: (1) The truth is the anchor for cheating. When one invents a false set of answers, he starts from the truth and modifies it to look better. (2) Given that an "if" sentence is violated, an individual who wishes to cheat successfully will modify his true set of answers by reversing his answer to fit in the *consequent* of the condition. Note that without (1) separation between the candidates would be impossible.

In the current story, the bounded rationality of the candidates is an advantage for the designer. If all candidates were fully rational, as is commonly assumed in the mechanism design literature, all of them would be able to game the system if necessary. It is the cognitive imperfection of the individuals which *opens a door* to obtaining a desirable outcome.

Bibliographic notes

1 Glazer and Rubinstein (2014) study a related model in which a candidate responds to a questionnaire without being notified of the acceptance conditions though he has access to the data about the set of responses that achieve admission and tries to make sense of things. There is a bound on the complexity of the regularities that the candidates can detect in the data. It is shown that whatever this bound is, the director can construct a sufficiently complex questionnaire such that agents who respond honestly to the questionnaire will be treated optimally and the probability that a dishonest agent will cheat successfully is "very small".

2 de Clippel (2014) investigates Maskin's classical implementation question in environments in which individuals follow systematic procedures of choice that are not consistent with rational behavior.

3 Li (2017) is motivated by an observation that bidders in an ascending bid auction tend to wait until the bid reaches their reservation value whereas a majority of bidders don't report the true value in the "equivalent" second-bid auction. An *obviously dominant strategy* is one in which the decision at each decision node is "obvious" in the sense that it does not depend on conjecture about the other players' actions. Li identifies several targets that are implementable using an extensive game in which the desirable outcome is obtained through obviously dominant strategies. Glazer and Rubinstein (1996) is an earlier paper that suggests a different criterion for simple implementation.

Elections and sampling equilibrium

Story

Three candidates are running for office. A large number of voters will participate in the elections and each will cast one vote in favor of one of the candidates. The issues on the agenda are "hot" and all of the voters are expected to cast their ballots. The winner will be the candidate with the largest number of votes (even if he does not achieve an absolute majority).

The candidates are labeled as Left, Center, and Right. The population of voters is split into three classes *Leftist, Centrist,* and *Rightist* with the proportions A, x and p:

Leftist: Individuals with the preferences $L \succ C \succ R$.
Centrist: Individuals with the preferences $C \succ L \sim R$.
Rightist: Individuals with the preferences $R \succ C \succ L$.

It is known that the Leftist and Rightist groups are more or less of equal size and that the Centrist group is smaller but not negligible ($1/3 < \lambda = \rho < 3/7$). Some observers predict that C will win since some of the leftists and rightists will vote for C in order to prevent the election of the candidate on the other extreme. Some view such a result as a desirable compromise. Others find it unacceptable that the least popular candidate might win the election.

Voters by nature tend to vote sincerely, but they will nonetheless vote for another candidate if they think that their candidate will certainly lose and the race between the other two candidates is close. In such an event, they vote for their second choice.

Surveys are forbidden and voters base their prediction of the election results on occasional discussions with casual acquaintances who express their voting intentions (without specifying their first choice). As is often the case, people say that they "talked with several people" but actually mean that they talked with just two. Thus, based on a sample of size two, people decide who to vote for. Therefore, they may change their mind during the campaign according to the sample results.

Some game theorists and political scientists analyze complicated models in which voters think strategically, in the sense that they put themselves in the shoes of other voters, calculate correctly the distribution over states conditional on the infinitesimal probability event that their personal vote will be pivotal, and vote optimally given that event. No traces of such behavior can be found in our story (nor in real life). No standard game-theoretical considerations are used. At each moment in the campaign, each voter constructs his prediction and decides who to vote for based on the small sample he has drawn.

Accordingly, if a voter samples two people who intend to vote for the same candidate, the voter treats the election as already decided, concludes that his vote will not make any difference and votes sincerely. If the two sampled individuals intend to vote for two different candidates, he views himself as pivotal and votes for the candidate he prefers out of these two (who is not necessarily his favorite). Thus, a C supporter intends to vote sincerely, regardless of the sample findings. An L supporter will vote sincerely unless he draws a sample of "C and R" and then votes for C. An R supporter will vote for C if his sample is "C and L" and sincerely otherwise.

Thus, although voters are stubborn in their political views and never change their basic position, they may change their intention during the campaign on the basis of the sample. The proportions of voters voting for each candidate will fluctuate until eventually stabilizing around a distribution of votes which we call *equilibrium.*

Given that all C followers vote C, L supporters will never vote R and R supporters will never vote L, a distribution of votes is characterized by two numbers: a, the proportion of the L camp that votes C, and b, the proportion of the R camp that votes C. In equilibrium, those proportions are stable. Notice that even when equilibrium is reached, members of the L and R camps may still change their intentions; however, in equilibrium, the changes are "balanced" and the distribution of votes remains constant.

Election day arrives. The ballots are closed. Will C win? Let's examine the equilibrium. Recall that the distribution of the L,C,R groups is (λ, $1 - 2\lambda$, λ). If at some point in time the proportions of manipulative voters are a and b, then the proportions of voters' intentions (following the above procedure) is ($\lambda(1-a)$, $\lambda a + (1 - 2\lambda) + \lambda b$, $\rho(1-b)$). The proportion of L supporters who will sample "C and R" is $2[\lambda a + (1 - 2\lambda) + \lambda b][\lambda(1-b)]$. The distribution is stable if this proportion is equal to a (and analogously for R). Thus, equilibrium is characterized by two equations:

$$a = 2[\lambda a + (1 - 2\lambda) + \lambda b][\lambda(1 - b)]$$

and

$$b = 2[\lambda a + (1 - 2\lambda) + \rho b][\lambda(1 - a))].$$

This set of two equations has a unique solution which can easily be calculated and accordingly the minority candidate C will win! Incidentally, when the size of C's base drops below 1/7, candidate C would lose, at least according to the story we have told.

Discussion

This section is based on Osborne and Rubinstein (2003). The bounded rationality component of the model is the procedure used by each voter to estimate the results. The paper analyses some variants of the model. An example of a result: R will not be elected whenever his base is smaller than that of L, regardless of C's base.

As mentioned before, the procedure of choice assumed here is in sharp contrast to what is assumed in standard game-theoretical voting models, in which a voter is assumed to fully calculate the conditions under which his vote will be pivotal given the correct expectations about the votes of all other voters.

Bibliographic notes

1   The model was inspired by Osborne and Rubinstein (1998) who proposed the concept of S-1 equilibrium and applied it to symmetric two-player games. A population of players is pair-wise randomly matched to play a game. A newcomer to the population samples each of the potential actions once by interviewing one person whose experience depends on the behavior of the randomly matched player he played against. Then, the newcomer chooses the action which, according to the sample, yields the best outcome. An equilibrium is a stable distribution of choices in a population, in the sense that the probability that a player chooses a particular strategy is equal to the frequency of the strategy in the distribution. This equilibrium concept differs fundamentally from the standard game-theoretical analysis and has special properties. For example, a dominated strategy (which is never the best response against any belief about the other player's behavior) might appear with positive probability in support of the equilibrium when the symmetric game has at least three strategies.

2   Rani Spiegler constructed several economic models in which individuals follow an S-1 type of procedure (see Spiegler 2011, Chapters 6 and 7). Spiegler (2006a) presents and analyses a model of a market for quacks. The market consists of several healers whose success rates are identical to that of "non-treatment." The healers compete on price. Patients rely on "anecdotal" evidence regarding the healers' success and also sample the free non-treatment. Spiegler (2006b) presents a model of competition between providers of a service in which each chooses a distribution of "price" in the range (-∞, 1). Consumers sample each of the providers and choose the one with the lowest price (which might be negative). The uniqueness of the symmetric Nash equilibrium with expected price of 1/2 is proven. Increasing the number of competitors leads to a mean-preserving spread in the equilibrium price distribution.

Long interactions and finite automata

Story

Two players are involved in a repeated Prisoner's Dilemma interaction. Each of the players chooses one of two modes of behavior each day: *C* (cooperative) or *D* (noncooperative). A player's daily payoff if he chooses the action corresponding to a row while his partner chooses the action associated with a column is given by the corresponding entry in the following matrix:

	C	D
C	3	1
D	4	0

Each period ends with one of four outcomes *(C, C)*, *(C, D)*, *(D, C)*, or *(D, D)* and the four pairs of payoffs that can be obtained each day are (3,3), (1,4), (4,1), or (1,1). The infinitely long interaction yields an infinite sequence of outcomes and two streams of payoffs, one for each player. A player cares only about his long-term average payoff.

In the long-term interaction (i.e., a repeated game), each player chooses a strategy, i.e. a plan that specifies whether to play *C* or *D* after every possible sequence of his opponent's actions. A strategy can be complex since it specifies an action for an infinite number of contingencies. A player's "language" in formulating a strategy is a *finite automaton* (machine). This is not an actual machine used to play the strategy but rather an abstract description of the mental process used by players to determine an action at each point in time after any history he might encounter.

A finite automaton consists of:

1 a finite set of states (of mind);
2 an initial state from which the machine starts operating;
3 an output function that indicates, for each state, one action (C or D) which the player will play whenever his machine reaches that state.
4 a transition function which determines the next state of the machine for each state and each possible observation (C or D) of the action taken by the other player.

The two machines are operated in the expected way: The two initial states and the two output functions determine the first-period pair of actions. Each player observes the other player's action and his transition function determines the next state of his machine. The process continues recursively as if each pair of states is the initial one.

Any weighted average of the four one-shot payoff pairs that equal at least 1 (a payoff each player can guarantee by playing *D*) is a long-term average payoff vector of some stable pair of strategies (stable in the Nash equilibrium sense). In other words, no player can increase his average payoff by using a different strategy. To obtain such a pair of average payoffs (π_1, π_2), players can play in a cycle of length $n_{D,D}+n_{D,C}+n_{C,D}+n_{C,C}$ so that the outcome (i, j) will appear ni_j times in the cycle such that

$$\frac{n_{1,1}(1,1)+n_{4,0}(4,0)+n_{0,4}(0,4)+n_{3,3}(3,3)}{n_{1,1}+n_{4,0}+n_{0,4}+n_{3,3}}=(\pi_1, \pi_2)$$

Players will support this path of play by threatening that any deviation will trigger moving to the non-cooperative behavior forever.

However, in our story and unlike the standard repeated game model, a player cares not only about his stream of payoffs but also about the complexity of the machine he employs, which is measured by the number of states in the machine (without taking into account the complexity of the transition function). Players view the complexity as a secondary consideration after the desire to increase the average payoff. Thus, a pair of machines will not be stable if one of the players can replace his machine with another that either yields a higher average payoff or the same payoff but less complexity. In other words, each player has lexicographic preferences with the first priority being to increase average payoff and the second to reduce complexity.

Initially, the two players use a naïve strategy—the one-state machine *MC* (see Figure 27.1) which plays *C* independently of what is observed. This situation is not stable. One of the players modifies his machine to M_D, which plays *D* independently of what it observes. Such a deviation improves his payoff each period without increasing complexity.

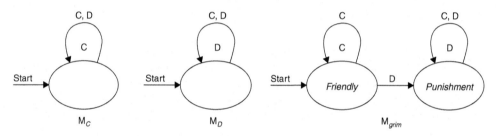

Figure 27.1

The two players then adopt the machine M_{grim}. This machine has two states: *friendly* and *punishment*. The initial state is *friendly*. The output function assigns *C* to *friendly* and *D* to *punishment*. In the case that *D* is observed when the machine is at *friendly*, it moves to *punishment*, which is a terminal state. A player who plays against *Mgrim* cannot increase his long-term average payoff whatever machine he chooses. However, eventually one of the players notices that he can reduce the complexity of his machine without losing payoff by dropping the state *punishment* which does not lead to any loss in terms of payoff.

The situation has some happier endings. Following are two examples:

Give and Take

Player 1 chooses the two-state machine M_1 (see Figure 27.2) with initial state *Take*, in which he plays *D* and moves to the second state *Give* after the other player plays *C*. If M_1 reaches *Give* it plays *C* and moves to *Take* independently of what it observes. Note that "giving" means playing *C* and tolerating the other player playing *D*. "Taking" means playing *D* and expecting the other player to play *C*. Player 2 adopts the machine M_2 which is identical to *M1* except that its initial state is *Take*.

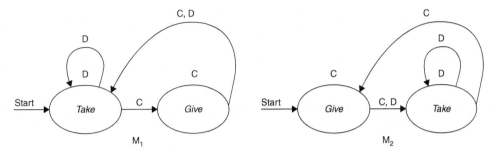

Figure 27.2

Adopting this pair of machines results in stability. Players expect to alternate between giving and taking. A player's threat against the other player "not giving" is to avoid moving to *Give*, a state in which he is supposed to give until the other player gives. As long as player 1 follows *M1* and player 2 follows *M2*, the players will alternate turns between giving and taking and each player obtains an average payoff of 2.5. No player can save on states without losing on payoff and no player can increase his average payoff no matter what he does.

The cooperative equilibrium

Each player uses the machine *M★* (see Figure 27.3) which has two states: *Showoff* and *Cooperative*. In *Showoff*, a player plays *D* and moves to *Cooperative* only if the other player plays *D*. In *Cooperative*, the machine plays *C* and moves to Showoff only if the other player played *D*. The machine's initial state is *Showoff*. Thus, players start by proving their ability to punish one another and then and only then move to the cooperative mode.

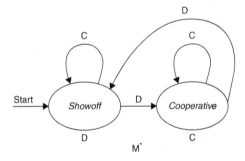

Figure 27.3

Each player obtains an average payoff of 3. A player cannot increase his payoff whatever he does. Reducing the number of states would cause a payoff loss (the one-state machines *MD* and *MC* achieve an average of only 1 or 0 against *M★*).

Discussion

This section is based on Rubinstein (1986) and Abreu and Rubinstein (1988). The bounded rationality component of the model is the complexity of the strategy and the desire of players to minimize it as long as the repeated game payoff is not reduced.

The two equilibria described above demonstrate the logic of two different types of social arrangements. In the first, players alternate between giving and taking; the threat not to give tomorrow deters the other player from not giving today. The second arrangement achieves ideal cooperation but on the way players must demonstrate their ability to punish if necessary.

Abreu and Rubinstein (1988) characterize the Nash equilibria of the infinitely repeated game with finite automata for (1) general one-shot two-player games; (2) discounting evaluation criterion; and (3) any preferences that are increasing in the payoffs and decreasing in complexity. The payoff vectors that can be obtained are those on the "cross" in Figure 27.4:

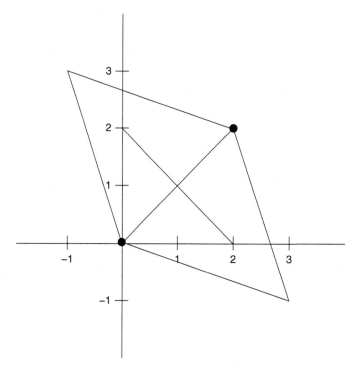

Figure 27.4

A few structural results were proven, such as that the two machines must have the same number of states in equilibrium and that there is a one-to-one correspondence between the occurrence of states in the two machines (namely, in equilibrium a machine "knows" the state of the other player's machine). An improved presentation of the results, following Piccione (1992), appears in Rubinstein (1998, Chapter 8).

In a previous paper, Rubinstein (1986) showed that the only equilibria of the machine game with the additional constraint that all states are revisited infinitely often (otherwise they would eventually be dropped) yield either the non-cooperative outcome or cyclical combinations of (C, D) and (D, C) only. Cooperation cannot be obtained in such an equilibrium.

Bibliographic notes

1 Neyman (1985) and Ben Porath (1993) investigate a repeated game with finite automata in which the number of states a player can use in his machine is exogenously bounded. Neyman

(1985) shows that in the finite-horizon Prisoner's Dilemma, cooperation can be achieved in equilibrium by applying the idea that the machines waste their limited resources by following an initial string of actions ("a password to heaven") that prevents them from identifying the point in time—toward the end of the game—at which it is profitable for them to deviate to the non-cooperative mode of behavior without being punished in the future. Ben Porath (1993) shows that in an infinitely repeated zero-sum game, if players use the "limit of the means" criterion and are limited in the size of the automaton they can use, then as long as the number of states of one machine is not much larger (in a well-defined sense explained there), the equilibrium payoff vector will be close to the equilibrium payoff of the basic game.

2   Examples of other models of repeated games with bounds on the strategies: Lehrer (1988) studies the model of repeated games with bounded recall and Megiddo and Wigderson (1986) and Chen, Tang and Wang (2017) study the model of repeated games in which players use Turing machines instead of finite automata.

3   Eliaz (2003) and Spiegler (2004) study models of repeated games and bargaining where the simplicity considerations were applied to the player's belief regarding the opponent's strategy, rather than his own.

Agents with different models in mind

Story

Each of two agents, 1 and 2, wishes to purchase a particular service each day. The service is provided by *P* (a provider) but can also be obtained from a local source at a price of 6 by agent 1 and at the price of 4 by agent 2.

All involved parties interact daily for a "very long period of time." Every morning, without knowing the price charged by *P*, each agent decides whether to purchase the service from the local source or to go to *P*. A cost of 3 is associated with each daily trip to *P*.

While the agents are making their daily decisions, *P* posts a price at which he commits to sell the service to whoever asks for it. The provider *P* can supply the service at no cost to one or both agents. An agent who comes to *P* is informed of the price offer and decides whether to buy the service from *P* or return to the local price. At the end of the period, the price becomes common knowledge to all individuals.

The provider cares only about his average long-run profits. He commits to a sequence of prices. An agent behaves myopically in every period. He makes the trip to *P* only if his expected costs (given his beliefs) do not exceed the local charge. He bases his belief on the regularities he detects in this sequence. The ability to detect a regularity is given by a non-negative integer *k* (referred to as the *order*) which expresses a player's "cognitive depth": an agent of order *k* detects all regularities of the type "after a particular string of *k* prices the price will be ..." but cannot detect more complicated regularities. Thus, an agent of order 0, for example, only learns the frequency at which different prices appear in the price sequence. An agent of order 1 learns the frequency of each price given the last price. If the real sequence is (0,0,1,1,0,0,1,1...) an agent of order 0 or 1 will always believe that the next element in the sequence is 0 or 1 with equal probability. An agent of order 2 (or higher) will accurately predict the next element in the sequence since the last two periods fully "encode" the next element.

Our two agents differ in their ability to recognize patterns. While agent 1 can detect a pattern that determines the next price based on the last three periods *(k₁ = 3)*, agent 2 is more sophisticated (which aligns with the assumption that his outside option is better than agent 1's) and can detect patterns on the basis of the last 4 periods *(k₂ = 4)*. Nothing essential would change in the story if we replace these bounds with any other non-negative integers k_1 and k_2, as long as $k_1 < k_2$.

The provider understands that if he always charges a price higher than 3, then he will not attract any customers; if he constantly charges a price between 1 and 3, then only agent 1 will make the trip; and if he always charges a price of 1 or below, then both agents will buy his service but his profits will be at most 2. Thus, by charging any constant price P his daily profits cannot exceed 3.

Furthermore, the provider realizes that if both agents have the same cognitive limit, then using random price sequences will not help him since both agents will eventually compare their local price to the expected price plus 3 and he would not make more than what he would have with a constant price.

Finally, it comes to the provider's attention that he can obtain higher profits if he wisely exploits the differences in the agents' cognitive ability and the correlation between an agent's order and the agent's outside option, namely, that the more sophisticated agent has a better outside option.

He learns about the existence of "DeBruijn sequences of order k" (for every k). To understand this concept, consider the following infinite sequence of prices which has a cycle of length 16 and is an example of a a DeBruijn sequence of order 4:

$$(5,5,5,5,1,5,5,1,1,5,1,5,1,1,1,1,....).$$

An agent with $k = 16$ would, of course, be able to detect a rule that creates this sequence and to correctly predict the next period's price. In fact, any agent with $k \geq 4$ would also be able to do so. The sequence is built so that all 16 combinations of 4 prices (1 and 5) appear in the cycle exactly once and thus the last four prices predict the next element in the sequence. On the other hand, the last three values in the sequence predict that it is equally likely that the next price will be 1 or 5. Thus, an agent with $k = 4$ would be able to predict that a low price follows four high prices, that after a sequence of three high prices and one low price always comes a high price, etc. An agent with $k = 3$ will always maintain the belief that the next price will be either 1 or 5.

Thus, agent 2 will know when the low price will be posted and will approach the provider only on mornings when he expects the price to be 1. Agent 1 is not able to find any useful regularity. After the appearance of any 3 numbers, he will believe that there is an equal chance of observing a high or a low price. His expected price is 3, so he every morning he approaches the provider and buys the service.

Thus, the provider has found a non-constant sequence, which is complicated enough that agent 1 is left confused and regular enough so that agent 2 is able to predict fairly well. The provider's expected profit is $7/2$ per period, which is more than he could obtain using any constant price sequence.

Discussion

This section is based on Piccione and Rubinstein (2003). The bounded rationality element in this model is the limited ability of agents to recognize patterns. Once there is a correlation between this ability and other economic factors, sophisticated manipulators can try to use the correlation as a way to sort out agents to their benefit. Conditions for this manipulation are analyzed in the paper.

From an economic perspective, this line of research is related to Spence (1973). However, whereas in Spence (1973), the correlation is between two materialistic factors (productivity and ease of performing a worthless task), here the separation between agents is based on the correlation between a materialistic factor (the willingness to pay) and cognitive ability (to recognize patterns in a time series). Note that the separation can also emerge in market equilibrium without the explicit interference of an interested party.

Bibiliographic notes

1 Rubinstein (1993) is an earlier paper demonstrating the ability of a monopolist to use the correlation between cognitive differences and willingness to pay in order to increase his profits. The modeling of agents' limits in understanding a multi-part price offer makes use of the formal concept of a perceptron.

2 Eyster and Piccione (2013) is a model of competitive markets, in which riskneutral traders trade a one-period bond against an infinitely lived asset in each period. Traders lack structural knowledge of the situation and use various incomplete theories of the type discussed in this section in order to form statistically correct beliefs about the long-term asset price in the next period. One of the results is that the price of the long-term asset is affected by the diversity in the agents' cognitive levels.

3 In a series of papers starting with Jehiel (2005), Philippe Jehiel developed the concept of *analogy-based equilibrium*. The basic idea is related to the way we play games like chess. When planning a move, we evaluate the board positions that it can lead to. In analogy-based equilibrium, those evaluations are "correct on average." Players differ in their partition of the set of situations they bundle together, where finer partitions reflect a better understanding of the situation.

4 Spiegler (2011, Chapter 8.) includes a pedagogical exposition of the model and links it to other concepts like Jehiel's.

5 Rani Spiegler suggests a general framework for studying economic agents who have imperfect understanding of correlation structures and causal relations (Spiegler, 2016). Spiegler (2018) identifies a condition under which the wrong model does not allow an outsider to systematically fool the agent.

Acknowledgments

I would like to thank Jacob Glazer, Martin Osborne, Michele Piccione and Rani Spiegler for their comments.

References

Abreu, Dilip and Ariel Rubinstein. 1988. "The structure of Nash equilibrium in repeated games with finite automata." *Econometrica*, 56, 1259–1282.

Ben-Porath, Elhanan. 1993. "Repeated games with finite automata." *Journal of Economic Theory*, 59, 17–32.

Chen, Lijie, Pingzhong, Tang, and Ruosong, Wang. 2017. "Bounded rationality of restricted Turing machines." In Proceedings of Thirty-First AAAI Conference on Artificial Intelligence, AAAI, pp. 444–450.

Choi, Syngjoo, Shachar Kariv, Wieland Muller, and Dan Silverman. 2014. "Who is (more) rational?" *American Economic Review*, 104, 1518–1550.

de Clippel, Geoffroy. 2014. "Behavioral implementation." *The American Economic Review*, 104, 2975–3002.

Eliaz, Kfir. 2003. "Nash equilibrium when players account for the complexity of their forecasts?." *Games Economic Behavior*, 44, 286–310.

Eyster, Erik and Michele Piccione. 2013. An approach to asset-pricing under incomplete and diverse perceptions," *Econometrica, 81,* 1483–1506.

Glazer, Jacob and Ariel Rubinstein. 1996. "An extensive game as a guide for solving a normal game, with Jacob Glazer." *Journal of Economic Theory,* 70, 32–42.

Glazer, Jacob and Ariel Rubinstein. 2012. "A model of persuasion with a boundedly rational agent." *Journal of Political Economy, 120,* 1057–1082.

Glazer, Jacob and Ariel Rubinstein. 2014. "Complex questionnaires." *Econometrica, 82,* 1529–1541.

Jehiel, Philippe. 2005. "Analogy-based expectation equilibrium." *Journal of Economic Theory, 123,* 81–104.

Lehrer, Ehud. 1988. "Repeated games with stationary bounded recall strategies." *Journal of Economic Theory, 46,* 130–144.

Li, Shengwu. 2017. "Obviously strategy-proof mechanisms." *American Economic Review, 107,* 3257–3287.

Megiddo, Nimrod and Avi Wigderson. 1986. "On play by means of computing machines." in *Theoretical Aspects of Reasoning About Knowledge Proceedings of the 1986 Conference,* 259–274.

Osborne, Martin and Ariel Rubinstein. 1998. "Games with procedurally rational players." *American Economic Review, 88,* 834–847.

Osborne, Martin and Ariel Rubinstein. 2003. "Sampling equilibrium with an application to strategic voting." *Games and Economic Behavior, 45,* 434–441.

Piccione, Michele 1992. "Finite automata equilibria with discounting." *Journal of Economic Theory, 56,* 180–193.

Piccione, Michele and Ariel Rubinstein. 2003. "Modeling the economic interaction of agents with diverse abilities to recognize equilibrium patterns." *Journal of European Economic Association, 1,* 212–223.

Rubinstein, Ariel. 1986. "Finite automata play the repeated Prisoner's Dilemma." *Journal of Economic Theory, 39,* 83–96.

Rubinstein, Ariel. 1993. "On price recognition and computational complexity in a monopolistic model." *Journal of Political Economy, 101,* 473–484.

Rubinstein, Ariel. 1998. *Modeling Bounded Rationality.* Cambridge, MA: MIT Press.

Rubinstein, Ariel. 2012. *Economic Fables.* Cambridge: Open Book Publishers.

Spence, Michael. 1973. "Job market signaling." *Quarterly Journal of Economics, 87,* 355–374.

Spiegler, Ran. 2004. "Simplicity of beliefs and delay tactics in a concession game." *Games and Economic Behavior, 47,* 200–220.

Spiegler, Ran. 2006a. "The market for quacks." *Review of Economic Studies, 73,* 11131131.

Spiegler, Ran. 2006b. "Competition over agents with boundedly rational expectations." *Theoretical Economics, 1,* 207–231.

Spiegler, Ran. 2011. *Bounded Rationality and Industrial Organization.* Oxford: Oxford University Press.

Spiegler, Ran. 2016. "Bayesian networks and boundedly rational expectations." *Quarterly Journal of Economics, 131,* 1243–1290.

Spiegler, Ran. 2018. "Can agents with causal misperceptions be systematically fooled?" mimeo. Available at: papers.ssrn.com/sol3/papers.cfm?abstract_id=2807830.

28

BOUNDED RATIONALITY, SATISFICING AND THE EVOLUTION OF ECONOMIC THOUGHT

Diverse concepts

Clement A. Tisdell

Introduction

Neoclassical economic models are based on the absence of any constraints on the exercise of rationality and most rely heavily on optimization goals in order to predict economic outcomes. This is particularly evident in traditional microeconomic theory. Most theories presume that both consumers and producers are omniscient and not hindered in any way in making decisions needed to achieve their optimization goals. As is well known, these assumptions are too stringent to reflect reality and have probably become more so as the economic world has evolved to become more complex.

This does not mean that neoclassical economic theories have no value for understanding the operation of economic systems, especially market systems. Many do have predictive value, even if it is sometimes only of a qualitative nature, e.g., prediction of price changes as a result of alterations in the market supply or demand conditions for commodities. Furthermore, the assumption of unrestricted rationality optimization is stronger than is required for perfect decision making of the type assumed in neoclassical economics (Tisdell, 1975). Nevertheless, there are many economic situations in which the presence of bounded rationality is a significant influence on economic behaviour, and is consequential for the evaluation of this behaviour and economic valuation.

In this chapter, an initial sketch will first be provided of the influence of the concept of bounded rationality on the evolution of economic thought. It is then argued that it is imperative to clarify the various meanings of the concepts of rationality and bounded rationality. Attention is paid to the evolution of economic thought taking into account the diversity of these concepts. Subsequently, the analysis considers satisficing behaviour as a reaction to bounded rationality. Simon (1957, 1961) stressed the importance of this type of behaviour. His emphasis on satisficing behaviour contrasts strongly with the central assumption of unbounded optimizing behaviour in neoclassical economic theories. Before concluding, an overall assessment of the place of bounded rationality in economics is provided. Note that the coverage of this chapter is very selective because of limited space.

DOI: 10.4324/9781315658353-33

An initial sketch of bounded rationality in economic thought

Some questioning of the applicability of the neoclassical model of economic behaviour had begun already in the 1930s. For example, in relation to macroeconomic theory, Keynes (1936) emphasized the importance of "animal spirits" as an influence on the behaviour of investors and the effect of this on the level of economic activity. Hall and Hitch (1939) came to the conclusion that cost-plus pricing was prevalent in several sectors of the economy. This was attributed to two different possible causes: it could be a result of oligopolistic market behaviour. Alternatively, it might be employed as a rule of thumb because many firms lack the capacity to determine their profit-maximizing level of pricing. Hall and Hitch (1939) found the latter to be very important. This publication subsequently sparked debate about whether this cost-plus procedure might, in fact, maximize a firm's profit and whether all firms are profit-maximizers.

Another important development in the evolution of economic thought about bounded rationality was the publication of the theory of *Games and Economic Behavior* (von Neumann and Morgenstern, 1944). It highlighted limits to the exercise of unrestricted individual rationality as a means for providing solutions to group behaviour involving conflict. In addition, it helped to explain failures to achieve socially optimal group outcomes, such as Pareto optimality (Tisdell, 1996). For example, it indicated that under omniscient conditions for decision making, economic behaviour cannot be precisely determined, as in the case of zero-sum games where the solution relies on mixed strategies and in empty-core games involving the possibility of transactionless coalition formation. This development of the theory of games prompted Simon (1955) to doubt the applicability of the unrestricted neoclassical rationality assumption as a determinant of economic behaviour, and he further developed his concept of bounded rationality as being more relevant. It is, however, pertinent to note that Morgenstern was aware of limits to the applicability to economics of the neoclassical concept of unlimited rationality (Morgenstern, 1964).

As an alternative approach to economic behaviour, Herbert Simon proposed a satisficing theory of decision making and economic behaviour. The cost of obtaining information, of retaining it, and of reasoning, was seen as an important restriction on the ability of individuals to make absolutely optimal (perfect) decisions of the type assumed in neoclassical economics. The assumption of satisficing behaviour was subsequently applied to consumer behaviour and to the theory of the firm, particularly to the latter.

Another significant but embryonic development was the publication of an article by Baumol and Quandt (1964) outlining a theory of optimally imperfect decisions. This provided insights into how much information gathering, the amount of its retention, and the extent of reasoning in decision making are likely to be economically optimal. They pointed out that the use of some rules of thumb (such as those employed by some firms in adopting cost-plus pricing) could be rational from an economic optimization perspective.

The type of modelling of Baumol and Quandt (1964) belongs to the class of modelling of bounded rationality sometimes described as optimization under constraint, that is, optimization which takes into account the cost of decision-making. An earlier example of this was the stopping rule of Stigler (1961) for searching for the purchase of a used car, namely, stop searching when the extra cost of searching equals the extra expected benefits. Similar sorts of stopping rules have been adopted for quality control involving serial sampling by producers and are relevant to other types of sampling. However, Gigerenzer and Selten (2002, pp. 4–5) question whether this type of optimization modelling captures the essence of the occurrence of bounded rationality. This issue will be considered in the discussion section.

Tisdell (1963; 1968; 1996; 2013) emphasized that, as a result of bounded rationality (and other factors), economic behaviours can be expected to be diverse and that this diversity had been neglected in neoclassical theory. Nevertheless, diverse behaviours have predictable economic consequences. Empirical investigations are needed to determine the extent of that diversity and its other attributes such as its variation with the passage of time. Studies in behavioural economics, experimental economics and psychological economics are all relevant to exploring this aspect of economics.

Another area of economic thought (which has advanced as a result of giving attention to the occurrence of bounded rationality) is whether it is more desirable to follow rules rather than discretion in decision making, that is, the benefits of engaging in flexible or less flexible types of decision making. The more flexible type of decision making may, for example, involve adjusting controlled variables based on short-term predictions of uncontrolled variables in an attempt to achieve a particular objective. The size and nature of the divergence between the predicted and actual values of controlled variables may be such that greater benefit can be obtained by ignoring short-term predictions and acting on long-term central tendency predictions, for example, predicted central values of the uncontrolled variables (or approximations to these) (Tisdell, 1971).

Friedman (1968) pointed out that following rules rather than engaging in discretionary zig-zag or fine-tuning behaviour could result in a more desirable type of monetary policy. Tisdell (1971, 1974), in criticizing Muth's theory of rational expectations (Muth, 1961), came to a similar conclusion and pointed out that this also applied to other areas of economics as well.

Rapid development of other areas of economics associated with the concept of bounded rationality occurred in the 1970s. Considerable attention was paid to how the transaction costs involved in economic organization resulted in participants in economic activity having incomplete knowledge (see, for example, Williamson, 1975). Issues such as the following were highlighted: principal-agent problems, the incompleteness of contracts and the importance of trust in exchange (Williamson, 1975, 1979) and the possibility of market collapse or the impeded operations of markets due to the asymmetry of information of market participants (Akerlof, 1970). These phenomena were shown to be a source of potential economic loss.

Neoclassical economic theories of behaviour were mostly based on introspection but also obtained empirical support from observations of the operations of markets. This was partly because the assumption of unrestricted rationality is stronger than necessary for qualitative predictions about how many markets work (Tisdell, 1975). Nevertheless, it became increasingly clear that not all economic phenomena could be understood or predicted by relying on the assumption of unrestricted (unbounded) rationality. This led to an upsurge in the development of behavioural economics and psychological economics and to increasing attention being paid to experimental economics. However, questions have been raised about whether many of the advances made in these fields of inquiry are consistent with the theory of bounded rationality. For example, Gigerenzer and Selten (2002, p. 4) claim they are not, and they also argue that optimizing theories based on decision making under constraints do not reflect the essence of bounded rationality. In order to help clarify this problem, it is helpful to consider the different meanings of the word "rational" as specified in English dictionaries. This will provide scope for some discussion of additional theories of economic behaviour which have been associated with bounded rationality as well as consideration of the concept of ecological rationality.

Different meanings of rationality and the further development of economic thought, including the concept of ecological rationality

The word "rationality" can have several different meanings in English, according to English dictionaries. Two relevant different meanings, as stated in the Australian *Macquarie Dictionary* (Delbridge, 1981) are:

A decision or behaviour is rational if it involves reasoning (Type 1 rationality).[1]
A decision or behaviour can be judged to be rational if it is reasonable or sensible (Type 2 rationality).[2]

The *New English Dictionary and Thesaurus* (Anon, 1994) gives the same interpretations of the word "rationality". Given the first interpretation, a behaviour that does not involve reasoning would not be a rational form of behaviour. Nevertheless, it could be effective for particular purposes, such as instinctive behaviour is in particular circumstances and is judged to be rational in the second sense of the word. The second meaning involves judgement about whether a behaviour is reasonable. Whether or not a behaviour is judged to be reasonable or sensible can depend upon the circumstances surrounding the behaviour (that is, the environment). Given the second meaning, behaviour that does not involve forethought or reasoning can be rational. Moreover, given this meaning, "excessive" forethought or reasoning in decision-making is not reasonable and therefore is irrational.

Not all decisions and behaviours which are effective in achieving a desired outcome are based on reasoning. For example, some instinctive and emotional behaviours are effective in particular circumstances for achieving desired ends. They are not a result of type 1 rationality, but may satisfy type 2 rationality.

Given the two meanings of rationality outlined above, it is clear that the extent to which rationality is present in decision making and behaviour can vary in degrees. Moreover, the presence of rationality in the second sense outlined above is subject to personal judgement. For example, much of the study of ecological rationality is focused on non-optimizing behaviours which are sensible (given bounded rationality) and behaviours that are effective for some particular purpose given the surrounds in which they occur. Gerd Gigerenzer is a prominent advocate of this approach which concentrates on type 2 rationality.

Gigerenzer and Selten (2002, p. 38) describe ecological rationality as "the match between heuristics and environmental structures" and indicate that this requires paying particular attention to satisficing behaviours as part of search and decision making and the adoption of fast and frugal heuristics, for example, involving the use of cues in making decisions. However, this ecological approach is even wider than this because it judges some behaviours to be rational which do not involve heuristics or rules of thumb. These can include some forms of intuitive and emotional behaviour as well as various social norms. These behaviours are considered to be rational if they are effective in achieving a desired end or purpose.[3] Also, the Gigerenzer group of ecological rationalists is aware that the amount of thought it is rational to give to a decision depends on the time constraint faced by decision makers. However, this group rejects the relevance of economic models of optimization based on constrained decision making and even more strongly rejects the neoclassical model of unbounded rationality (Selten, 2002). They also cast doubts on the relevance to bounded rationality of behavioural psychological studies, such as those associated with Kahneman (2003) (Gigerenzer and Selten, 2002, p. 4).

An overlapping but narrower view of ecological rationality is adopted by Vernon Smith (2003). He describes ecological rationality as "an emergent order based on trial-and-error cultural and biological evolutionary processes" (Smith, 2003, pp. 499–500). His primary concern is with group rationality in economics. He rejects the relevance of constructivist rationality, namely, that social mechanisms are as a rule thoughtfully created to serve a perceived intended purpose (Smith, 2003, p. 470). In general, he believes that evolutionary processes and trial-and-error processes are effective in developing optimal social rules of behaviour and social norms that are beneficial in promoting desirable social ends. However, his view is too sweeping. In the past, some societies developed social norms and religious beliefs which did not promote desirable social ends. Examples of this have been proposed by Diamond (2011). These include the deforestation of Easter Island (Rapa Nui in the Pacific Ocean) by its original inhabitants and the Mayan collapse. Several other societies have engaged in persistent irrational behaviours – some as a result of their religious beliefs or their adoption of forms of unsustainable economic development – which eventually proved to be catastrophic from their point of view, for example, early producers of copper and bronze in central Europe (Tisdell and Svizzero, 2018). Today there are concerns that we may not be able to establish effective norms and behaviours to restrict global warming "adequately". Theoretically, there is no guarantee that selective evolutionary processes will result in the prevalence of "optimal" decisions or even socially satisfactory ones (Tisdell, 2013).[4]

Another approach to considering the consequences of bounded rationality in economics is based on the unearthing biases in economic behaviour. This type of approach to bounded rationality was initially developed by Amos Tversky and Daniel Kahneman. Kahneman (2003, p. 1449) explains that this type of research about bounded rationality explores "the systematic biases that separate the beliefs that people have and the choices they make from optimal beliefs and choices assumed in rational-agent choice models". These biases are mainly identified by relying on experiments but may also be discovered by considering observations from non-experimental situations (Camerer et al., 2003).

One of the significant results from this line of enquiry, which has extended the findings of Thaler (1980) demonstrates the importance of loss aversion, endowment or status quo effect as an influence on several types of economic decision-making. Kahneman (2003, p. 1457) explains that this effect is present when "the value of a good to an individual appears to be higher when the good is viewed as something that could be lost or given up when the same good is evaluated as a potential gain". Examples are given by Kahneman (1990), Tversky and Kahneman (1991) and Kahneman et al. (1991). Bandara and Tisdell (2005) found evidence of the importance of this effect in relation to willingness to pay for the conservation of elephants in Sri Lanka. The status quo effect is not allowed for in traditional economic theory. There can be several reasons for the occurrence of this effect, for example, a psychological desire to keep valued items which one already has (possessiveness), transaction cost considerations, and the possibility that the consumption or enjoyment of the commodity alters the taste of the possessor. These aspects require further investigation.

Another aspect of bounded rationality which has been paid much attention by contributors to behavioural economics is the importance of frames in shaping decisions (Kahneman, 2003). The emphasis, in this case, is on how individuals perceive alternative possible states of nature, or more generally, possibilities. Both the selective nature of perceptions and their distortions are studied. These aspects of perception are relevant for predicting economic behaviours and also for assessing the worth and limitations of economic valuation studies, particularly those valuing alterations in the supply of public and quasi-public goods, especially environmental goods. Results from these investigations (and other types of studies) demonstrate that economic valuation (reliant on the assumptions of neoclassical economics) of the demand for changes in the supply of public goods, particularly environmental goods, can be problematic.

Satisficing and bounded rationality

Simon (1957; 1961) stressed that, because of the presence of bounded rationality, individuals and organizations often adopt satisficing behaviours or rules rather than optimizing. In principle, satisficing behaviours which occur because of bounded rationality can take several different forms. Some such behaviours may be based on aspiration levels or targets for performance. These are usually not optimal in the neoclassical sense. The degree to which these targets are adaptive is liable to vary. Other behaviours of a satisficing type may rely on rules of thumb or heuristics and limited cues about states of nature. If they give satisfactory benefits, their use may persist. However, this is not always so. Searches may continue for more effective rules of thumb, heuristics and cues, especially if the environments in which decisions are to be made alter. The adaptive rationality of heuristic decision making is important.

Not all satisficing behaviour is a result of bounded rationality, even though some forms are at odds with the underlying assumptions of neoclassical economic theory. (Bendor, 2015, p. 774) states, for example:

> Bounded rationality should not be confused with a theory (e. g., of satisficing), much less with a specific formal model (e.g., Simon, 1957). It is best considered a research program: a sequence of theories with overlapping sets of assumptions, aimed at solving similar problems ... In principle, the program's empirical domain is vast—it is as imperialistic as the rational choice program—and so its set of possible theories is also very large.[5]

Baumol's theory of behaviour of an imperfectly competitive corporation assumes that the company tries to maximize the value of its sales subject to ensuring that its shareholders receive a satisfactory level of return on their capital (Baumol, 1959).[6] In this instance, bounded rationality is not involved in this constrained optimization theory. Sahlins' theory of the affluence of some ancient societies supposes that members of these societies were completely satisfied with their low level of consumption of material goods (Sahlins, 1972). It does not rely, per se, on any assumptions about bounded rationality (Tisdell, 2018). Some theories also exist which suppose that the utility obtained by individuals is a function of the difference between the level of the income to which they aspire (or some other economic variables) and the levels achieved. This is, for example, a component of Weckstein's model (Weckstein, 1962). Such constructs may but need not involve bounded rationality.[7] These types of models are of particular interest because they raise questions about how aspiration levels are determined and adjusted.

Another relevant rationality aspect of satisficing goals is the extent to which possible failure to achieve these goals should be foreshadowed and when and in what depth plans ought to be drawn up to address this possibility? To what extent is delay in decision making a result of bounded rationality or due to other factors such as social embedding? These two types of behaviours are, for example, highlighted by Tisdell and Svizzero (2017) in their discussion of the transition of ancient societies from hunting and gathering to agriculture.

Discussion

Gigerenzer and Selten (2002) suggest that two sets of models that are often discussed under the banner of bounded rationality have not been appropriately classified. They state:

> Bounded rationality is neither optimization nor irrationality. Nevertheless, a class of models *known as optimization under constraints* is referred to in the literature as 'bounded rationality', and the class of empirical demonstrations of 'so-called' errors and fallacies in judgment and decision-making has been labeled 'bounded rationality'. The fact that these two classes have little if anything in common reveals the distortion that the concept of bounded rationality has suffered.
>
> *Gigerenzer and Selten, 2002, p. 4*

However, the first set of models is relevant to the study of bounded rationality because they highlight limits to the neoclassical vision of unrestricted rationality. While their knowledge and rationality assumptions are still too strong, they can help to identify factors that ought to influence behaviours under conditions of restricted rationality. As for the second class of models (which include behavioural ones), most (but not all) identify limits to perceptions of states of nature and common faults in reasoning, both of which can be considered to be a consequence of bounded rationality. These classes of models (mostly behavioural economic ones) do demonstrate some of the limits to unrestricted rationality and can have predictive value.

One of the important consequences of bounded rationality is that it gives rise to variations or differences in the behaviours of individuals and groups. Individuals differ in the perception of states of nature, in the estimates of probabilities and risk, and in their willingness to take risks. This aspect has been stressed by Tisdell (1963, 1968) and in some of his later publications. These variations have predictable economic consequences but they have not been given enough attention in the economic literature. Bendor (2015, p. 774) mentions that behavioural (economic) theories do not pay enough attention to differences in human behaviour. Differences and changes in behaviours all have important economic consequences.

The time available for decision making limits the scope for the gathering of information and reasoning, as stressed by Selten (2002). Sometimes, there is a definite end-point by which a decision must be made and action taken. In extreme cases, there may be little or no time available for rational decision making involving data collection and thought. In these cases, action may be dictated by instinct or learned reactions. In other cases, a final decision may be delayed, resulting in both benefits and costs. Some of the factors that influence the optimality of delayed decisions have been examined by Tisdell (1970; 1996, Chapter 5). Where decisions may have to be made at short notice, it can be rational to prepare for these in advance of their possible occurrence. However, the amount of rational preparation can be expected to vary.

The value of the strategy of delaying decisions to gain extra information depends on the environmental scope for responding to this information, as does the ability of decision makers to take advantage of changes in economic information (Tisdell, 1970, 1996, Chapter 5). Therefore, apart from collecting more information, a rational response to bounded rationality can be to alter the environment in which decisions can have effect, for example, it may be possible to change existing environments to allow greater flexibility for responding to decisions. Examples of this include the adoption of production processes (techniques) that exhibit greater adaptability than otherwise in the production of different commodities (Tisdell, 1963, 1968) and an increasing liquidity of assets to take advantage of varying investment opportunities which are subject to uncertainty. However, changing economic environments in this way usually comes at a cost. Therefore, analysis and judgement are necessary to decide whether acting in this way is worthwhile.

A related concept in environmental economics is the precautionary principle (Tisdell, 2010, 2015). If unrestricted rationality occurred, this principle would be irrelevant. Because the environmental future is uncertain, it becomes relevant. One of the manifestations of the principle is that in view of uncertainty, it is often desirable to keep options open, for example, conserve biodiversity. This permits advantage to be taken of new information which may become available in the future. Once again, environmental variation may be made in order to provide greater flexibility in available decision-making strategies. This may come at a cost, and how sensible it is depends on attitudes to the bearing of risk or uncertainty and the anticipated net benefits from increased flexibility.

Gigerenzer and others have emphasized the importance of fast and frugal heuristics and the use of selective cues as a guide to behaviour. Presumably, the usefulness of these as reasonable guides to behaviour depends on the economic situation that is being responded to. Considerable use of these types of heuristics appears to be made in trading in financial markets, for example, trading on the stock exchange. Identifying the types of cues that traders use for exchange in these markets (and other markets) is also important for predicting and evaluating their consequences. This opens up a large area for empirical economic research. This is particularly so because different individuals and groups may employ different rules of thumb and cues. Mixed behaviours of market participants as well as alterations in the diversity of these behaviours can be important for the operation of markets (Lasselle et al., 2005; Tisdell, 2013).

Conclusion

Neoclassical economic theory pays no attention to the costs and other restrictions on rational decision making and has therefore developed optimizing models of economic behaviour which assume unrestricted rationality. These models are, in fact, special cases. Nevertheless, they do have some predictive value because their assumptions are stronger than is necessary for forecasting or explaining some types of economic behaviour and for providing a guide to how some markets work. On the other hand, it is a mistake to assume that all economic behaviour reasonably accords with that assumed in neoclassical economic theory. The realization of this has resulted in substantial progress in economic thought in recent decades and has created a new academic environment in which further progress is being facilitated, for example, as a result of joint contributions by psychologists, economists and others.

In this short chapter, it has not been possible to consider all the advances in economic thought which have stemmed from research on bounded rationality. Much of this research is based on examining particular situations. We are now challenged to determine whether general principles can be distilled from these studies. It is also important that greater attention be paid analytically to determine how reasonable or sensible decisions made and behaviours observed under conditions of bounded rationality are, that is to go beyond the empirical determination of the impact of bounded rationality on behaviours and decision-making. For example, to what extent can the rules of thumb used for economic decision-making be improved or replaced by ones that are more effective in achieving desired goals? To what extent are decision-makers cognisant of the factors which ought to guide their decisions when they are acting under bounded rationality and is there scope for them to improve their decisions by paying greater attention to such factors?

The presence of bounded rationality has also created complications for methods derived from neoclassical economics of valuing public goods and experiential goods, especially environmental commodities. Results from the application of these methods (both revealed and elicited preference methods) need to be treated with caution given the presence of bounded rationality and the occurrence of biases in observed behaviours and in responses to elicitation of values (see, for example, Tisdell, 2017, Chapter 4, especially Table 4.1; as well as Tisdell, 2014). The challenge now is to determine what use can sensibly be made of these results for the purpose of social economic valuation.

Notes

1 A problem with this meaning is that not all decision making and behaviour involving reasoning would normally be regarded as rational. For example, illogical reasoning, failure to assess the environment appropriately, excessive or insufficient reasoning may be sources of irrationality. Also, this meaning seems to imply conscience deduction but, as mentioned in the text, some behaviours that do not involve reasoning could (in particular circumstances) be rational.
2 This meaning enables a wider range of behaviours to be regarded as rational than the previous one. It leaves open the question of who is to judge whether a decision or behaviour is sensible or reasonable. A reviewer of the draft of this chapter suggested that this should be mainly judged by the decision maker. However, in most societies, others are mainly called on to judge the rationality of decisions or behaviours of individuals or groups. For instance, a clinically insane person may believe that he/she is asking rationally but others may judge otherwise.
3 A problem here is that some of these behaviours may only be effective for a limited period of time and they trap individuals in a long-term situation which is unsatisfactory. Furthermore, some behaviours could be effective by chance for a limited period of time, e.g., forms of gambling or risk-taking. Even though they may be effective for a while, they are not rational from a long-term point of view.
4 Social embedding of various kinds can result in societies being unable to take advantage of the mistakes or errors of earlier societies or groups. See, for example, Tisdell (2017, Chapter 5). Also, as societies evolve and become larger, their proneness to prisoner dilemma-type problems may increase, as is illustrated by a number of sustainability issues including those associated with human-induced climate change.
5 While satisficing behaviours are only one of the many ways of responding to bounded rationality, not all satisficing behaviours are a consequence of bounded rationality. Satisficing behaviour, for example, occurs if there are thresholds in preference functions and uncertainties are absent.
6 The level of this satisfactory return from the point of view of shareholders is the prevailing rate of return on capital in the capital market.
7 Weckstein does not include uncertainty and bounded rationality in his modelling of decision-making. For further discussion of Weckstein's model, see Tisdell (1983) or Chapter 14 in Tisdell (1996). Although Weckstein does not incorporate bounded rationality into his type of modelling, it can be allowed for in these types of models. For instance, the difference between what is aspired to and what can be achieved is often uncertain. Consequently, a dynamic interplay is frequently observed between these two behavioural components with adjustment being made to aspirations in the light of learning about what it is possible to achieve.

References

Akerlof, G. (1970). 'The market for lemons: quality and the market mechanism', *The Quarterly Journal of Economics*, 84(3), 488–500. doi:https://doi.org/10.2307/1879431.

Anon (1994). *New English dictionary and thesaurus*, New Lanark: Geddes and Grosset.

Bandara, R., and Tisdell, C. (2005). 'Changing abundance of elephants and willingness to pay for their conservation', *Journal of Environmental Management*, 76(1), 47–59. doi:10.1016/j.jenvman. 2005.01.007.

Baumol, W. J. (1959). *Business behavior, value and growth*, New York: Macmillan.

Baumol, W. J., and Quandt, R. E. (1964). 'Rules of thumb and optimally imperfect decisions', *American Economic Review*, 54, 23–46.

Bendor, J. (2015). 'Bounded rationality', in *International encyclopedia of the social & behavioral sciences* (pp. 773–776). Oxford: Elsevier.

Camerer, C., Loewenstein, G., and Rabin, M. (eds) (2003). *Advances in behavioral economics.* New York: Russell Sage Foundation/Princeton, NJ: Princeton University Press.

Delbridge, A. (1981). *The Macquarie dictionary*, St Leonards, NSW, Australia: Macquarie Library.

Diamond, J. (2011). *Collapse: How societies choose to fail or succeed*, Revised ed. New York: Penguin.

Friedman, M. (1968). 'The role of monetary policy', *The American Economic Review*, 58(1), 1–17.

Gigerenzer, G., and Selten, R. (eds) (2002). *Bounded rationality: The adaptive toolbox*, Cambridge, MA: MIT Press.

Hall, R., and Hitch, C. (1939). 'Price theory and business behaviour', *Oxford Economic Papers*, 2, 12–45.

Kahneman, D. (1990). 'Experimental tests of the endowment effect and the Coase theorem', *Journal of Political Economy*, 98(6). 1325–1348. doi:10.1086/261737.

Kahneman, D. (2003). 'Maps of bounded rationality: Psychology for behavioral economics', *American Economic Review*, 93(5). 1449–1475. doi:10.1257/000282803322655392.

Kahneman, D., Knetsch, J. L., and Thaler, R. H. (1991). 'The endowment effect, loss aversion and status quo bias', *Journal of Economic Perspectives*, 5, 193–206.

Keynes, J. M. (1936). *The general theory of employment, interest and money*, London: Macmillan.

Lasselle, L., Svizzero, S., and Tisdell, C. (2005). 'Stability and cycles in a cobweb model with heterogeneous expectations', *Macroeconomic Dynamics*, 9(5), 630–650. doi:10.1017/s1365100505050017.

Morgenstern, O. (1964). 'Pareto optimum and economic organization', in W. Krelle and H. Müller (eds), *Systeme und Methoden in den Wirtschafts- und Sozialwissenschaften*, Tübingen: J.C.B. Mohn.

Muth, J. F. (1961). 'Rational expectations and the theory of price movements', *Econometrica*, 29, 315–335.

Sahlins, M. (1972). *Stone Age economics*, Chicago: Aldine de Gruyter.

Selten, R. (2002). 'What is bounded rationality?', in G. Gigerenzer and R. Selten (eds), *Bounded rationality: The adaptive toolbox* (pp. 13–36). Cambridge, MA: MIT Press.

Simon, H. (1955). 'A behavioral model of rational choice', *The Quarterly Journal of Economics*, 5, 99–118.

Simon, H. (1957). *Models of man*, New York: John Wiley & Sons, Ltd.

Simon, H. (1961). *Administrative behavior*, New York: The Macmillan Company,

Smith, V. L. (2003). 'Constructivist and ecological rationality in economics', *American Economic Review*, 93(3), 465–508. doi:10.1257/000282803322156954.

Stigler, G. J. (1961). 'The economics of information', *Journal of Political Economy*, 69(3), 213–225. doi:10.1086/258464.

Thaler, R. (1980). 'Toward a positive theory of consumer choice', *Journal of Economic Behavior and Organization*, 1(1), 39–60. doi:10.1016/0167-2681(80)90051-7.

Tisdell, C. A. (1963). 'Price uncertainty, production and profit', PhD thesis, Australian National University, Canberra.

Tisdell, C. A. (1968). *The theory of price uncertainty, production and profit*, Princeton, NJ: Princeton University Press,

Tisdell, C. A. (1970). 'Implications of learning for economic planning', *Economic Planning*, 10(3), 177–192.

Tisdell, C. A. (1971). 'Economic policy, forecasting and flexibility', *Weltwirtschaftliches Archiv-Review of World Economics*, 106(1), 34–54.

Tisdell, C. A. (1974). 'Comments on Muth's note on economic policy, forecasting and flexibility', *Review of World Economics*, 110(1), 176–177.

Tisdell, C. A. (1975). 'Concepts of rationality in economics', *Philosophy of the Social Sciences*, 5(3), 259–272.

Tisdell, C. A. (1983). 'Dissent from value, preference and choice theory in economics', *International Journal of Social Economics*, 10(2), 32–43.

Tisdell, C. A. (1996). *Bounded rationality and economic evolution*, Cheltenham: Edward Elgar.

Tisdell, C. A. (2010). 'The precautionary principle revisited: Its interpretations and their conservation consequences', *Singapore Economic Review*, 55, 335–352.

Tisdell, C. A. (2013). *Competition, diversity and economic performance: Processes, complexities, and ecological similarities*, Cheltenham: Edward Elgar.

Tisdell, C. A. (2014). *Human values and biodiversity conservation*, Cheltenham: Edward Elgar.

Tisdell, C. A. (2015). *Sustaining biodiversity and ecosystem functions: Economic issues*, Cheltenham: Edward Elgar.

Tisdell, C. A. (2017). *Economics and environmental change: The challenges we face*, Cheltenham: Edward Elgar.

Tisdell, C. A. (2018). 'The sustainability and desirability of the traditional economies of Australian Aborigines: Controversial issues', *Economic Analysis and Policy*, 57, 1–8. doi:org/10.1016/j.eap.2017.11.001.

Tisdell, C. A. and Svizzero, S. (2017). 'Optimization theories of the transition from foraging to agriculture: A critical assessment and proposed alternatives', Social Evolution and History: Studies in the Evolution of Human Societies, 16(1), 3–30.

Tisdell, C. A., and Svizzero, S. (2018). 'The economic rise and fall of the Silesian Únětice cultural populations: A case of ecologically unsustainable development?', *Anthropologie*, 56(1), 21–38.

Tversky, A., and Kahneman, D. (1991). 'Loss aversion in riskless choice: A reference-dependent model', *The Quarterly Journal of Economics*, 106(4), 1039–1061.

von Neumann, J., and Morgenstern, O. (1944). *Theory of games and economic behavior*, Princeton, NJ: Princeton University Press.

Weckstein, R. S. (1962). 'Welfare criteria and changing tastes', *The American Economic Review*, 52(1), 133–153.

Williamson, O. E. (1975). *Markets and hierarchies: Analysis and anti-trust implications*, New York: Free Press.

Williamson, O. E. (1979). 'Transaction-cost economics: The governance of contractual relations', *The Journal of Law and Economics*, 12(2), 233–262.

29

BEYOND ECONOMISTS' ARMCHAIRS

The rise of procedural economics

Shabnam Mousavi and Nicolaus Tideman

Outcome vs. process in modeling choice

The paradigm of mainstream economics is a coherent one built logically on a *substantive* notion of rationality, with expected utility theory as its crowning achievement. As Gary Becker (1962) neatly summarized, "now, everyone more or less agrees that rational behavior simply implies consistent maximization of a well-ordered function, such as utility or profit." In this framework, an actor seeks the best or optimal outcome, and specifying the criteria for its existence and (preferably) uniqueness occupies theorists and modelers, who rely mainly on deductive methods. Issues of how to collect data for testing the theory, or building models to achieve concrete real-world goals are usually not of primary concern. The search for information is also assumed to be optimal. That is, the rational agent uses an optimal stopping rule, continuing to calculate marginal costs and marginal benefits of further search, and stops when they are equal. This is acknowledged to be an artificial search process, with no claim to represent the actual search process. Understanding reality is thus pursued through "stylized facts"[1] (Abad & Khalifa, 2015) instead of through observation. Clever stylized facts, "as-if" locutions (Lehtinen, 2013), and coherent axioms are the bread and butter of the smooth operationalization of concepts in the realm of general equilibrium economic models and subjective expected utility, wherein polished artefacts are used to account for the behavior of utility-maximizing individuals and profit-maximizing firms. Game theory from mathematics (von Neumann & Morgenstern, 1944), equilibrium analysis akin to physics (Arrow & Debreu, 1954), and the axioms of statistical decision theory (Savage, 1954) allowed economics to claim the status of being a science.[2] The social legitimacy of this claim was sealed when, in 1968, Riksbank, the Swedish Central Bank, established an endowment in perpetuity with the Nobel Foundation, to award a prestigious prize in Economic Sciences. Interestingly, the prize was awarded not only to economists and mathematicians, constructors of the rational core of the economics discipline, e.g., Arrow in 1972, Debreu in 1983, Becker in 1992, Nash in 1994, but also to scientists who took alternative views on the topic, the most famous of them arguably being Herbert Alexander Simon in 1978 (after receiving the Turing Award in 1975, together with Newell).

In his Nobel Prize lecture, Simon, (1978b) propounded: "There are no direct observations that individuals or firms do actually equate marginal costs and revenues." That is, real-world individuals (firms) do not show indications of utility (profit) maximization with unbounded

DOI: 10.4324/9781315658353-34

rationality. The actual form of observed rationality exerted by individuals and firms has a bounded nature.

The initial thrust of bounded rationality was to question the relevance of (subjective) expected utility calculations for observed human behavior. The general features of a boundedly rational agent, sans the term itself, are described as administrative behavior in Simon (1955). The term "principle of bounded rationality" first appeared in the *Models of Man* (Simon, 1957, p. 200), and later in a chapter (Simon, 1972) entitled "Theories of bounded rationality." Simon viewed economists' detachment from observed behavior as a serious flaw in their methodology. He advocated the tradition in psychology, of starting from evidence for studying, modeling, and theorizing about human choice behavior (Barros, 2010). In an interview with *Challenge* in 1986, he elaborated:

> They [economists] don't talk about evidence at all. You read the pages where Lucas talks about why businessmen can't figure out what's happened to prices and it is just what he feels as he sits there smoking his cigarettes in his *armchair*. I don't know what Keynes smoked, but when you look at the pages where he talks about labor's money illusion, no evidence is cited. So the real differences in economics, as compared with psychology, is that almost everybody operates within the theoretical logic of utility-maximization in the neoclassical model.
>
> When economists want to explain particular phenomena in the real world, they have to introduce new assumptions. The distinctive change in the behavior of the economic actors comes from a change in the behavioral assumptions. No empirical evidence is given to support those changes. They emerge from the mind of the economic theorist sitting in his *armchair*.
>
> The Swedish economist Assar Lindbeck recently did a survey of some 30 business-cycle theories. When I read it, I saw a pattern emerging as one theorist after another attempted to explain how unemployment developed. Each introduced into his model some particular *behavioral departure from perfect economic rationality*. I'm sure each departure led to a journal article on business cycles, and in response, other economists soon joined the debate. All of this theory and debate was over assumptions, but not one was bolstered by evidence from empirical observation. Economists treat behavior as if it were in fact the right behavior for the actual circumstances: that the world is out there, people see that world accurately, understand that world, and adapt perfectly to it. That is what I call "substantively rational behavior."
>
> *Challenge, 1986, pp. 22–23*

Background and focus

This chapter discusses the trend of the integration of bounded rationality concepts into the economists' toolkit. In the early 2000s, entertaining the possibility of axiomatizing bounded rationality as a primary framework—as opposed to formalizing it as partial deviations from full rationality—produced a doctoral dissertation (Mousavi, 2002) for one author of this chapter under the supervision of the other author. The core argument of that dissertation was that parts of the initial idea of bounded rationality do not lend themselves to the tools that populate the paradigm of full or substantive rationality, namely, optimization techniques and the focus on existence (and uniqueness) of answers. Alternatively, in an imaginative new paradigm where goals not only can be multiple and incommensurable, but also do not need to be predetermined, bounded rationality can be formalized. One suggested means of doing so entails turning the focus from cognitive limitations to the nature and structure of goals pursued by real-world boundedly rational agents.

Another central argument arose from the observation that fundamental uncertainties of situations, the ones that cannot be reduced to risk calculation, do not paralyze decision makers. This fact seems to be lost on economic modelers, who focus intently on reducing uncertainty in formal representations of choice behavior. But people make simple and hard choices every day without reducing all aspects of their situations to ones with probabilities assigned to them. In other words, decisions are made all the time under persisting, irreducible uncertainty. Mousavi (2002) argued that this characteristic of actual choice behavior calls for moving away from quantifiable uncertainty and systematic processes for reducing it. A first step in this direction is to allow goals to remain less than fully specified during the process of inquiry, in order to permit an ontic notion of uncertainty (see also Mousavi & Garrison, 2003; Mousavi, 2018). Technical requirements for such formalization were scarcely developed at the time, and notable attempts in this direction, e.g., Bewley (1986, 1987) on individual choice behavior under Knightian uncertainty, and March and Simon (1958) on goal generation (as opposed to goal orientation) in firms, did not get into the mainstream of economic modeling. Much has been achieved since.

In what follows, we draw on two themes from Mousavi (2002). The first is to position bounded rationality in the larger framework of social sciences by employing Simon's view[3] on the satisficing nature of search and stopping rules. The second is to juxtapose the substantive rationality of neoclassical economics with procedural bounded rationality, going on to point out less discussed commonalities between these two views of rationality, which we find to be rooted in a Humian notion of uncertainty (Hume, 1739 [1985]). Hume's empiricism and epistemic conception of uncertainty father modern economic modeling methodologically (Binmore, 2011). Finally, we recount the basics of the cognitive revolution, which sets the context for the Simonian approach to the study of human behavior. The arguments from 2002 are brought up to date through additions, modifications, and afterthoughts. The main message is that over the decades since Simon called on economists to stroll away from their armchairs, they have kept central notions of full rationality near and dear, while branching out into other fields in a series of ongoing methodical efforts to tie down bounded rationality. Experimental economists play a pronounced role in this movement. This rising procedural metropolis of economics has now successfully acquired and built many behavioral and cognitive science suburbs.

The satisficer: the poster child of bounded rationality

Satisficing is a theory of search (Bendor, 2010). The term is a combination of "satisfying" and "sufficing," which can be juxtaposed, respectively, to "necessary" and "sufficient" as requirements for mathematical completeness. Thus, replacing "necessary" with "satisfying" sums up what bounded rationality changes in rational choice theory, and "sufficiency"—not having been replaced by an alternative—is the part that remains intact and is thus the common component of modeling both fully and boundedly rational behavior. To elaborate further on this parallel connection, note that instead of requiring all criteria for a substantively rational optimum of an objective function of many variables, a problem can be solved in a boundedly rational way by satisfying target variables, say, through a sequential scheme. The magnitude of available computational resources and attainable information provides a satisfactory solution of a boundedly rational problem, when the potential limitlessness of search and calculation necessitated by substantive rationality can defy solvability. (Think of solvability in familiar terms of uniqueness and existence.)

The most famous of all boundedly rational agents is the satisficer, who divides the known options into two categories, satisficing and non-satisficing, then chooses an available satisficing option (Newell & Simon, 1972)—a process also known as achieving a "good-enough" choice. The satisficer needs only one criterion, a threshold of acceptability called an aspiration level. If a choice cannot be made in a unique way or does not exist, then the agent will attempt to adjust the aspiration level (up or down) or to expand/contract the set of alternatives, or both (Simon, 1955, 1957). If finding satisficing options are easy and low cost, the agent will raise the aspiration level and can simultaneously look for more options, and vice versa. Notice, however, that these two activities, adjusting the level of aspiration versus the set of choice options, are not the same and can be triggered by different underlying conditions. For instance, a higher level of persistence is associated with finding more options rather than adjusting the aspiration level. Also, persistence corresponds to the effort of information gathering.

The satisficer is best understood in contrast to the rational representative agent (Kirman, 1992) or the "economic man." A major operational property of rational formalization is its independence of the situation. That is, the rational agent acts the same way across situations, and thus the maximization of utility remains a process that yields the optimal outcome from a full exploration of information, configuration of relevant distributions, and a comprehensive cost-benefit calculation (Güth & Kliemt, 2000). Simon's "administrative men," in contrast, are sensitive to the structure of the environment, e.g., the organization, within which they search for, obtain, and analyze information to make their choices and solve the problems they face. Their process of problem solving cannot be configured independently of their situation. Whereas the cross-situation mobility of the rational economic man brings about an elegant, tractable, coherent formalism, the "muddling through" of the administrative man defies clean formalization. The representative agent configuration allows for seamless scaling, whereas the complication of formalizing boundedly rational processes escalates quickly as the situation of choice acquires more dimensions, becomes more than pairwise comparisons, or does not lend itself to a binary structure that can generate thresholds for setting aspiration levels. At a more fundamental level, this complication is verbalized by Viale (2012, pp. 161–162):

> Insofar as Simon's bounded and procedural rationality seeks to be a realistic representation of human cognitive activity, it finds its *raison d'être* in the hypothesis and knowledge of psychology. The first question we have to ask is: "what type of psychology?". There are almost as many types of psychology as there are psychologists! ... [even] the sea of cognitive psychology too has grown increasingly stormy.

An important challenge facing modelers from both camps, substantive and procedural rationality, is to account for the observed data collected on choice processes. Competition in this domain becomes a matter of fluency with techniques. Rational choice theory can expand and extend preference structures to account for "deviations" from full rationality. Artful executions of this method have generated marvels, such as Gary Becker's seminal work that analyzed, in the framework of rational choice theory, problems from other disciplines, such as discrimination (Becker, 1971) and marriage (Becker, 1973, 1974a) from sociology and criminology (Becker, 1974b), and from law. In Simon's words:

> Becker follows Milton Friedman's advice that economists should focus on testing the conclusions of a theory, not testing the factual assumptions that underlie it. In his *Treatise on the Family*, Becker [1981] looks at the steady rise in the labor force participation of married women since World War II. The major cause for this change,

he believes, is the growth in the productivity of women as the American economy developed. ... He could also have asked if the increase in women's weekly earnings might have resulted from an increase in average hours worked; that is a form rather than a consequence of greater labor force participation. But he explains it all in terms of an unexplained shift in the demand curve for women's labor. He doesn't say why this event should have taken place at this particular moment in American history. Was it an unexpected shock, or a continuing development?

Challenge, 1986, p. 20

In another place, Simon (1978a) makes the connection between his idea and Becker's clear, "What Becker [1962: Irrational behavior and economic theory] calls *irrationality* in his article would be called *bounded rationality* here" (p. 3). Interestingly, the formally "weaker" and functionally "broader" definition of rationality allowed economics to expand its domain from the early days of being "the science which treats of those social phenomena that are due to wealth-getting and wealth-using activities of man" (Ely, 1930, p. 4) to the Samuelsonian "the study of the allocation of scarce resources among unlimited and competing uses" (*Encyclopedia of the Social Sciences*, vol. 4, p. 472, cited by Simon, 1978a). While the consequences of the bounded conception of rationality range all over social sciences (Simon, 2000), our attention in the current chapter is limited to its implications for economics, on which we elaborate further next.

Economics: thesis, antithesis, synthesis

Interestingly, in the 1930s, Ely described economics as "a branch of sociology. Next to language it is the best developed of them all, and is by far the best introduction to the larger group." He urged broadening the definition of economics to

the science (1) which treats of those social phenomena due to the wealth-getting and wealth-using activity of man, and (2) which deals with all other branches of his life in so far as they affect his social activity in this respect.

All the while, Ely keeps economics at the center of social sciences.[4]

Whereas Simon seems to view economics as expanding its domain from Ely to Samuelson, it seems to us that the Samuelsonian definition is merely more technical, context-free, and is thus actually narrower in scope. That is, economics went from a broad verbal social science (following Ely) to a mathematically oriented technique-centered quest (following Samuelson), then returned to apply those refined tools to a wider scope of problems (such as bounded rationality). Along this path, economics exceeded other branches of social sciences in formalization and is now an apparatus for turning observations from experiments and field studies into discrete models, all with respect to one central theory of rational choice. Triumphantly, the economists' toolkit has generated reliable mechanisms for capturing observations in elaborate descriptive accounts—observations that were originally suggestive of a paradigm change, as they appeared to violate rationality's characteristic assumptions.

Gary Becker, trained in sociology (recall that Ely viewed economics as a branch of sociology), spent his professional career developing rigorous accounts of social topics by expanding rational choice theory. As he put it, "The purpose ... is to show how the important theorems of modern economics result from a general principle which not only includes rational behavior and survivor arguments as special cases, but also much irrational behavior" (Becker, 1962, p. 2).

It is tempting to imagine that accounting for the context equates to realistic modeling. That does not follow, however, since modelers are only as good as their tools and the formalization of observed phenomena has to be channeled through abstraction. For instance, a skillful modeler in the framework of bounded rationality can extend the definition and scope of the target to accommodate deviations from a pre-specified form of bounded rationality such as satisficing behavior—technically, in the same way that rational choice theory users extend preferences to account for deviations from full rationality. Linking empirical data to formal statements remains a matter of fluency in mathematical techniques, whereas the claim to capture the actual process at play is at best speculative. Besides psychological conditions, neurological and physiological markers have been studied and documented in association with certain behavior patterns, shedding light on even more aspects involved in the generation of humans' observed choice behaviors. As more aspects of the problem unravel, so emerge more and deeper puzzles to grapple with. One of the most plausible data-driven perspectives we have encountered so far is that of accepting the multiplicity of processes that people employ in face of the same problem (Harrison 2018).[5] Added to this is the possibility that the same process of choice can be employed in different situations by the same person or by different people. In other words, a fundamental flaw in the neoclassical methodology is the tireless search for one-to-one and even onto mappings that can generate functional forms for formalizing choice behavior (Mousavi & Gigerenzer, 2017). On the other hand, a main guiding insight from taking the bounded rationality stance lies in liberation from the constraint of looking for a one-size-fits-all structure to make scientific sense of human choice behavior. The admission of the bounded rationality approach into the methodology of modeling choice behavior implies multiplicity of the ways in which the same problem can be tackled by different agents, say, a group of satisficers, each holding a different aspiration level, or giving their individual limited attention to different choice sets.

There is more to Simon's method. He criticizes armchair economists who "don't seem to hesitate to extrapolate from themselves to the population. But they shouldn't" (*Challenge*, 1986, p. 25). At the same time, he warns against seeking the answer in extensive data collection (a criterion for enhancing the accuracy of statistical inference). Simon shares a very important insight that multiplicity is not extensive:

> Take a mechanical puzzle, like this one on my desk, and give it to ten people. You will get quite a range of individual behavior in trying to solve it. But you won't learn very much more from the next ten people you give it to. So the idea that we must have huge samples in order to know how a system works is not necessarily so. Human beings aren't that variable.
>
> *Challenge, 1986, p. 25*

This vision calls for rethinking the value of big data in exploring beliefs and decision making tools, notwithstanding its value for profiling individual preferences. This passage also provides a Simonian valuation of the limits on the knowledge and insight that can result from the study of multiplicity determinants such as analytic vs. intuitive as distinctive modes of cognition.

The satisficer as the poster child for bounded rationality, both in its static version of fixed aspiration level and the two dynamic dimensions of adjusting the choice set or the aspiration level, is a gate to investigating human choice behavior in many ways that depart from rational choice theory. In practice, however, the elegance and convenience of the tools and techniques from rational choice theory have largely resulted in the transfer of them to the realm of bounded rationality—so much so that the many emerging forms of theorizing about bounded rationality are still presented with respect to the rational choice benchmarks, and not as primarily self-containing structures. Bounded rationality was born from revisiting human choice behavior through the lens of cognitive psychology. A closer look at cognitive science can shed light on why some old ways are actively lingering in the new frameworks developed since the rise of the concept of bounded rationality.

What substantive and procedural rationality (don't) share

To appreciate the form of bounded rationality that Simon upholds as the alternative to the rationality of the economic man, take a step back to the origin of the idea. Howard Gardner's (1985) acclaimed history of the cognitive revolution, *The Mind's New Science*, acknowledges Herbert Simon as one of the founders of the field, for which Gardner identifies the five following tenets:

[1] the belief that, in talking about human cognitive activities, it is necessary to speak about mental representations and to point to a level of analysis wholly separate from the biological or neurological, on the one hand, and the sociological or cultural, on the other.

[2] the computer as the most viable model of how the human mind functions.

[3] the deliberate decision to de-emphasize certain factors which may be important for cognitive functioning but whose inclusion at this point would unnecessarily complicate the cognitive-scientific enterprise. These factors include the influence of affective factors or emotions, the contribution of historical and cultural factors, and the role of the background context in which particular actions or thoughts occur.

[4] cognitive scientists harbor the faith that much is to be gained from interdisciplinary studies.

[5] a key ingredient in contemporary cognitive science is the agenda of issues, and set of concerns, which have long exercised epistemologists in the Western philosophical tradition.

Gardner, 1985, pp. 6–7

Simon's cognitive psychology, in adherence to these five tenets, depicts the path from substantive to procedural (bounded) rationality (Simon, 1979), whereby he lays out the following four defining aspects of the psychology of choice (or deliberation), and declares the fourth one outside his domain of study. (By and large, the biological and neurological conditions of risky choice do not specifically interest Simon.)

1 *The study of cognitive processes* involves the elements of action in problem situations and consists of three strands: learning, problem solving, and concept attainment. Learning refers to extraction of information from one situation and the consequent storing and use of this information in similar problem situations. Problem solving involves gathering information from various sources in different manners and combining the components to arrive at a course of action for solving the problem at hand. In problem solving research, trial-and-error procedures are complemented by insights. Concept attainment refers to generalization and extraction of rules from existing problem situations to predict patterns and attain solutions to future problems.

2 *Computational efficiency* refers to the time and effort required to solve a problem, for which Simon retains the normative status of mathematical computation: "computational efficiency is a search for procedural rationality, and computational mathematics is a normative theory of such rationality" (Simon, 1979, p. 69).

3 *Computation: risky decisions.* Viewing the human mind as a computer that deals with risky decisions by computations that are constrained by the limits of cognitive functioning, stemming from and affected by biological, neurological, cultural, and sociological conditions. This is a systems view of the human organism, which is a pillar of cognitive science.

4 *Man's computational efficiency* is only of interest to Simon in association with thinking, not acting. He clarifies, "In my comparison of computer and Man, I am leaving out of account the greater sophistication of Man's input and output system, and the parallel processing capabilities of his senses and his limbs. I will be primarily concerned here with thinking, secondarily with perceiving, and not at all with sensing or acting" (Simon, 1979, p. 72, fn).

On this ground, the difference between Simon and neoclassical economics in the study of human choice behavior can be understood as interest in and focus on different aspects of the phenomenon. Simon is focusing on the cognitive processes involved in gathering, storing, and interpreting information for solving present or future problems. Rational choice theory in economics, on the other hand, has largely left the middle processing stage in a black box and focused on reconstructing reasoning schemas (Smith, 2007) that map a given situation to the final action, grounded in the fundamental assumption that best actions deliver optimal payoff as defined with respect to a specifiable preference ordering. Simon's focus on the process opens an exciting gate into exploration of the economists' black box, while leaving biological and emotional mechanisms for other fields.

Conclusion

The visionary polymath Simon foresaw that for economics to survive and thrive, substantive rationality must be augmented with procedural components and that this requires acquiring tools from other disciplines (Simon, 1978a, pp. 2–3):

> Economics has largely been preoccupied with *results* of rational choice rather than the *process* of choice. Yet as economic analysis acquires a broader concern with dynamics of choice under uncertainty, it will become more and more essential to consider choice processes. In the past twenty years [1960s–1970s], there have been important advances in our understanding of procedural rationality, particularly as a result of research in artificial intelligence and cognitive psychology. The importation of these theories of the processes of choice into economics could provide immense help in deepening our understanding of the dynamics of rationality, and of the influences upon choice of the institutional structure within which it takes place.

Today, economics have absorbed the knowledge and techniques from operations research for achieving targets. Also, the behavioralization of economics has resulted in the absorption of psychology to a great extent. This trend of enriching economics with tools from other disciplines is an ongoing one: In the footsteps of cognitive psychology, evolutionary theory, bioeconomics, and neuroeconomics have gradually joined the family of economic science—with more yet to join the club. All the while, the supremacy of rational choice theory, both as the normative benchmark and as the central primary formalization with respect to which the many versions of boundedness of rationality are being operationalized, remain strongly intact. Today, economics—as a whole, including its behavioral branch—has successfully acquired the alternative rival of process modeling by systematically following a simple technical recipe: Add procedural to substantive as needed to incorporate bounded rationality.

Simon presented bounded rationality in contrast to substantive rationality that is fixated on outcomes and oblivious to procedures. He invited economists to leave their armchairs and observe the many ways in which actual human behavior defies the calculus of costs and benefits. This chapter recounted some early Simonian cognitive-based notions that initiated departure from the deductive economics methodology of rational choice theory. Today, the adoption of procedural rationality notions from other fields has effectively customized bounded rationality in the economists' arsenal. This is a development that we propose to call *procedural economics* in reference to the decades-long efforts of formalizing observed (boundedly rational) choice behavior processes with respect to and as a result of extensions of rational choice theory.

Notes

1 For a brief overview, see the helpful slides available at the link below, starting with this definition: "*Stylized facts* refer to generalizations that hold approximately, but not exactly." /www.albany.edu/~bd445/Economics_301_Intermediate_Macroeconomics_Slides_Spring_2014/Stylized_Facts_of_Economic_Growth.pdf.
2 The use of the term "Economic Science(s)" is not rare nowadays. Economics' status as a science, however, has been continuously debated for over a century: from Thorstein Veblen's (1898) *Why is economics not an evolutionary science?* to Alfred Eichner's (1983) *Why economics is not yet a science.* The longing to be a science among economists has been also dubbed "physics envy." (Do an online search of "physics envy + economics" for a flow of opinions on all sides of the matter.)
3 For a critical review of the Simonian view of expectations and beliefs, valuation, cognitive abilities, and Turing machines, see Mousavi and Garrison (2003).
4 Ely concludes his suggestion for a broader definition of economics as follows: "Of course the other social sciences require a similar extension, and so they all are dependent upon economics."
5 Glenn Harrison (1990) has worked with several collaborators (e.g., Harrison, List & Towe, 2007) on the development of a field that he calls behavioral econometrics, where he applies rigorous econometric methods to the data while keeping an open mind about the human behavioral phenomena at work and trying to account for them by allowing different strategies to surface in solving one problem by several subjects, say, by clustering them into groups that can be modeled as users of satisficing, maximization, minimax, etc.

References

Abad, L. A., & Khalifa, K. (2015). What are stylized facts? *Journal of Economic Methodology* 22(2): 143–156. doi:10.1080/1350178X.2015.1024878.

Arrow, K. J., & Debreu, G. (1954). Existence of an equilibrium for a competitive economy. *Econometrica* 22(3): 265–290. doi:10.2307/1907353.

Barros, G. (2010). Herbert A. Simon and the concept of rationality: Boundaries and procedures. *Brazilian Journal of Political Economy* 30(3): 455–472.

Becker, G. S. (1962). Irrational behavior and economic theory. *Journal of Political Economy* 70: 1–13.

Becker, G. S. (1971). *The economics of discrimination.* Chicago: University of Chicago Press.

Becker, G. S. (1973). A theory of marriage: part I. *Journal of Political Economy* 81(4): 813–46. doi:10.1086/260084.

Becker, G. S. (1974a). A theory of marriage: part II. *Journal of Political Economy, Special Issue: Marriage, Family Human Capital, and Fertility (part 2)* 82 (2): s11–s26. doi:10.1086/260287.

Becker, G. S. (1974b). *Essays in the economics of crime and punishment.* New York: National Bureau of Economic Research, distributed by Columbia University Press.

Becker, G. S. (1981). *A treatise on the family.* Cambridge, MA: Harvard University Press.

Bendor, J. (2010). *Bounded rationality and politics.* Oakland, CA: University of California Press.

Bewley, T. F. (1986). Knightian decision theory: Part I. *Cowles Foundation Discussion Papers* 807. Cowles Foundation for Research in Economics, Yale University.

Bewley, T. F. (1987). Knightian decision theory: Part II. Intertemporal problems. *Cowles Foundation Discussion Papers* 835. Cowles Foundation for Research in Economics, Yale University.

Binmore, K. (2011). David Hume: Grandfather of modern economics? Working Paper.

Challenge (1986). Interview with Herbert A. Simon: The failure of armchair economics. Available at: http://digitalcollections.library.cmu.edu/awweb/awarchive?type=file&item=34037.

Eichner, A. S. (1983). Why economics is not yet a science. *Journal of Economic Issues* 17(2): 507–520. doi:10.1080/00213624.1983.11504135.

Ely, R. T. (1930). *Outlines of economics* (rev. ed.). New York: Macmillan.

Harrison, G. W. (1990). Risk attitudes in first price auction experiments: A Bayesian analysis. *Review of Economics and Statistics* 72, 541–546.

Harrison, G. W., List, J. A., & Towe, C. (2007). Naturally occurring preferences and exogenous laboratory experiments: A case study of risk aversion. *Econometrica* 75, 433–458.

Hume, D. (1739 [1985]). *A treatise of human nature.* London: Penguin.

Gardner, H. (1985) *The mind's new science: A history of the cognitive revolution.* New York: Basic Books.

Güth, W., & Kliemt, H. (2000). From full to bounded rationality: The limits of unlimited rationality. *ZiF – Mitteilungen special 2000*, Zentrum für interdisziplinäre Forschung der Universität Bielefeld. 1–15.

Harrison, G. W. (2018). The methodologies of behavioral econometrics. In M. Nagatsu & A. Ruzzene (Eds.), *Philosophy and social science: An interdisciplinary dialogue.* London: Bloomsbury. Available at: https://cear.gsu.edu/files/2017/03/WP_2017_04_The-Methodologies-of-Behavioral-Econometrics_2018_0409.pdf

Kirman, A. P. (1992). Whom or what does the representative individual represent? *Journal of Economic Perspectives* 6(2): 117–136.

Lehtinen, A. (2013). Three kinds of 'as-if' claims. *Journal of Economic Methodology* 20(2): 184–205. doi:10.1080/1350178X.2013.801560.

March, J. G. & Simon, H. A. (1958) *Organizations.* New York: John Wiley & Sons.

Mousavi, S. (2002) Methodological foundations for bounded rationality as a primary framework. Doctoral dissertation. Available at: http://theses.lib.vt.edu/theses/available/etd-12222002–183717/

Mousavi, S. (2018). Behavioral policymaking with bounded rationality. In R. Viale, S. Mousavi, B. Alemanni, & U. Filotto (Eds.), *The behavioral finance revolution: A new approach to financial policies and regulations.* Cheltenham: Edward Elgar.

Mousavi, S., & Garrison, J. (2003). Toward a transactional theory of decision making: Creative rationality as functional coordination in context. *Journal of Economic Methodology* 10(2): 131–156.

Mousavi, S., & Gigerenzer, G. (2017). Heuristics are tools for uncertainty. *Journal of Homo Oeconomicus* 34: 361–379.

Newell, A., & Simon, H. A. (1972). *Human problem solving.* Englewood Cliffs, NJ: Prentice-Hall.

Savage, L. J. (1954). *The foundations of statistics.* New York: John Wiley and Sons.

Simon, H. A. (1955). A behavioral model of rational choice. *Quarterly Journal of Economics* 69(1): 99–118.

Simon, H. A. (1957). *Models of man: Social and rational. Mathematical essays on rational human behavior in a social setting.* New York: John Wiley & Sons, Inc.

Simon, H. A. (1972). Theories of bounded rationality. In C. B. McGuire & R. Radner (Eds.), *Decision and organization* (pp. 161–176). Amsterdam: North-Holland.

Simon, H. A. (1978a). Rationality as process and as product of thought. *American Economics Review* 68(2): 1–16.

Simon, H. A. (1978b) Nobel Prize Lecture: Rational decision-making in business organizations. Available at: www.nobelprize.org/nobel_prizes/economic-sciences/laureates/1978/simon-lecture.html

Simon, H. A. (1979). From substantive to procedural rationality. In F. Hahn & M. Hollis (Eds.), *Philosophy and economic theory*, Essay 5. Oxford: Oxford University Press.

Simon, H. A. (2000). Bounded rationality in social science: Today and tomorrow. *Mind and Society* 1(1): 25–39. https://doi.org/10.1007/BF02512227

Smith, V. X. (2007). *Rationality in economics: Constructivist and ecological forms.* New York: Cambridge University Press.

Veblen, T. (1898). Why is economics not an evolutionary science? *The Quarterly Journal of Economics* 12(4): 373–397.

Viale, R. (2012). *Methodological cognitivism*. vol. 1: Mind, rationality, and society. Berlin: Springer.

Von Neumann, J. & Morgenstern O. (1944), *Theory of games and economic behavior*, Princeton, NJ: Princeton University Press.

30

BOUNDED RATIONALITY AND EXPECTATIONS IN ECONOMICS

Ignazio Visco and Giordano Zevi

Introduction

In his contribution to the *Scandinavian Journal of Economics* on the occasion of Herbert Simon's Nobel Prize award in 1979, Albert Ando identified a consistent theme running through Simon's vast contribution to economics: his attempt "to construct a comprehensive framework for modelling and analysing the behaviour of man", acknowledging the implicit "limitations of his ability to comprehend, describe and analyse" the complex environment he inhabits.[1] In essence, this is a rich and, to a large extent, exhaustive description of Simon's work, and it provides the foundations for an operational definition of "bounded rationality", resulting, with the benefit of hindsight, even more far-reaching than was Ando's original intention.

At the time, bounded rationality in economics was generally meant to indicate the subject of Ando's companion paper in the same journal, in which William Baumol compared the "satisficing" criterion followed by Simon's economic agents in their attempts to reach the best decisions with the traditional microeconomic optimisation problem, which essentially consists in the constrained maximisation of a utility function of some sort. The crucial difference, Baumol noted, was that maximisation required a process of comparison of all the available alternatives, while Simon's satisficing criterion was aimed at pinning down "the first decision encountered which passes the acceptability test",[2] among those decisions which are subjectively considered to be feasible.[3]

In Simon's view, this satisficing criterion was not intended to contrast with rationality. On the contrary, this kind of behaviour was plausibly motivated at the very least by some significant informational deficiency and, more in general, by the natural constraints on the economic agents' ability to gain, store and process the information they receive. In a nutshell, Simon pointed out that since in most cases identifying and comparing all the possible alternatives is, in fact, a very costly option computationally, if at all feasible, it should generally be excluded by agents who are rational. Therefore, they will simplify the choice problem they face by only concentrating their efforts on a subset of all the possible choices,[4] and on devising the best strategies to delimit such a subset.

With the passing of time, however, bounded rationality in economics came to be defined not only as the procedural rationality implicit in the satisficing criterion, but also as the broader "consistent theme" Ando had identified in Simon's work, the studying of the behaviour of man

DOI: 10.4324/9781315658353-35

459

when faced with economic choices. Moreover, the renewed attention that scholars and policy makers have progressively accorded to the limits of economic agents' knowledge, and to the recognition of their more common salient psychological traits, has even led some researchers to consider it as being the study of the deep consequences of including the actors' cognitive restrictions within a standard maximisation framework. The unifying theme of these two originally separate streams in Simon's thinking, as it was progressively received by the economics profession, is the recognition that economic agents have to devise behavioural strategies in a space where rationality (in the neo-classical utility-maximising sense) is itself a scarce resource, subject to the law of diminishing returns. Exercising rationality requires effort. This holds true for both the procedurally rational economic agents of theoretical models and those whose real-life decisions are the subject of empirical work. Consequences are pervasive, especially when studying organisations and institutions.[5]

When rationality is costly, then, there is scope to cut these costs along a number of dimensions (time, computational power, etc.). In his survey on the advances of behavioural economics, DellaVigna frames Simon's original contribution as one that was made to the "non-standard decision making" stream, as opposed to other lines of research dedicated to non-standard preferences and non-standard beliefs.[6] Somewhat in line with, or stemming from, Simon's contribution are other works investigating the "limited attention" (or rational inattention, in macroeconomics parlance[7]) paid by agents to aspects of the choice problems they face that are not deemed salient, with salience (a thoroughly subjective criterion) being, therefore, the constraint that determines the previously quoted "acceptability" region. The deviation from the choices that would be made under the same circumstances by neoclassical agents, measured by the welfare losses that they would incur if they had to identify all the alternatives that are possible in principle, could then be meaningfully used to measure the savings made thanks to the procedural rationality implemented by Simon's agents.

In this environment, heuristics (i.e. simple decision-making rules based on repeated experience, observation, intuition or common wisdom) are rational strategies and can be a very efficient tool for making choices when the cost for acquiring and processing information is high. According to some views,[8] other perturbations of the choice process, such as framing (i.e., the impact of changes in the external context on the final outcome of a problem of choice), endowment effects (i.e., the influence of any given initial condition on preferences, even when these conditions could, in principle, be swapped at no cost) and sunk-cost fallacies (i.e., in a choice problem, non-zero weights given to sunk costs that, theoretically, should be deemed irrelevant) are disturbances of little or no importance, as they are scarcely able to modify the terms of the choice problem for procedurally rational agents.[9]

Bounded rationality and expectations

We will briefly consider the possible links between Simon's bounded rationality ideas and the different approaches adopted by economists in dealing with household and business expectations on the evolution of economic variables. By connecting the choices made in the present to possible future scenarios, expectations drive the evolution of the economy over time. How expectations are formed also changes through time, as economic systems evolve and adjust continuously. Fittingly with some procedural notions of rationality, households and businesses need to learn how best to make decisions in an environment of continuous change and adaptation.[10]

Adapting to new circumstances is indeed a common experience. It requires the selection of implicit or deliberate strategies, based both on free as well as on costly information and on the more or less sophisticated methods and tools needed to process this information. Lessons learned in the past, for example, on how best to collect and treat the available information, may provide skills that could be applied valuably to decrypting the present and plan for the future. However, change is often itself a non-stationary process, in a statistical sense. Deep recessions, technological revolutions, institutional transformations and sudden changes in social habits can all make the set of abilities possessed by the economic subjects abruptly obsolete, including those related to the comprehension of the neighbouring environment. Crucially, they can also induce a rapid decay in the usefulness of routines followed by economic agents in the formation of their expectations, something that necessarily leaves them in need of re-learning and defining new routines.

Such a description does not appear to be controversial. Indeed, in the history of economics, the relevance of expectations for any intertemporal decisions (i.e., almost all relevant economic decisions, except for the simplest ones in static environments) has been repeatedly underlined.[11] However, the economists' degree of attention to how expectations are actually formed and to how they interact with the economic "observables" has followed high and low cycles.[12]

One "high" part of the cycle coincided with the prevalence of Keynesian theories, deeply informed by the recognition of the radical difference between risky and uncertain events[13] and of the wide-ranging consequences that the latter could exert – mediated by their impact on expectations – on the functioning of the economy.[14] On the contrary, a "low" cycle began when Bob Lucas famously criticised the way expectations were treated by macroeconomists at the time, rightly pointing out that they should not, in general, be invariant to changes in "the structure of series relevant to the decision maker", and in particular to changes in economic policy.[15]

In a few years, his critique had been fully taken on board by the discipline. However, Lucas did not suggest improving either the use of expectations in macroeconomic models, or the tools used to measure them, in order to identify the revision processes that businesses and individuals implement when the underlying reality changes. Rather, he ignored the early attempts of empirical research on expectations and instead introduced the powerful construct of the rational expectations hypothesis, based on Jack Muth's earlier work.[16] Muth, who had previously shared ground-breaking empirical work on expectations with Simon,[17] described the hypothesis of rational expectations as a situation in which the agents' average subjective probabilities on the distribution of the relevant variables coincide with the conditional probabilities in the "true" model of the economy, making "optimal" use of all the information available in the economy and deviating from perfect foresight only by some random noise.

Although Muth's contribution was originally intended for some specific and somewhat narrow circumstances, Lucas extended it by assuming it to be a necessary consistency condition in macroeconomic models, and the sheer theoretical power of the Muth-Lucas construct came to be seen as a revolution. In a few years the "rational" expectations hypothesis spread through the practice of the profession of macroeconomics, most of the time in conjunction with the notion of a "natural" level of unemployment, in a fundamentally stable environment.[18] It is perhaps somewhat ironic that in the (general) equilibrium representation of the economy associated with the rational expectations hypothesis, there is no role for the state of (subjective) expectations.

Three complementary conditions coincided to make the success complete: (1) rational expectations allowed leading macroeconomic models to be closed in a straightforward way, spurring great waves of new research in macroeconomics; (2) rational expectations were seen as a natural benchmark for the comparison of the deviations posed by other formulations of expectations;[19] and (3) the findings of models that included rational expectations did not appear to be obviously contradicted by the empirics of the economy, at least in advanced economies (to which most of those models were applied) and chiefly in the US, in particular during the period of the so-called "Great Moderation".

Indeed, in the relatively stable economic environment that prevailed during this period, it could also be argued that, in forming their expectations about the future paths of aggregate variables, the agents who populate the macroeconomic models did not have to be entirely rational in the fullest neo-classical sense of the word (i.e., able to consider all available possibilities, compare them at no cost and subsequently select the best one). The hypothesis of rational expectations could be unobtrusively introduced by assuming that economic agents lived in an environment that they had come to know sufficiently well over time, following a readily available learning procedure.[20]

It should also be mentioned that a number of critiques were raised early on. Davidson pointed to the fact that if the economic processes move in time, so that the data-generating processes are non-time invariant and the economic world these processes describe is not ergodic, Muth's rational expectations hypothesis cannot hold, as "calculable probability statements may have no relation to future events".[21] Pesaran observed that rational expectations could be plausible only in contexts where all uncertainty was exogenous to the subjects formulating the expectations, meaning that, subjectively, the actions of those agents were not relevant in shaping the aggregate economic outcomes.[22] Outside the realm of rational expectations, there were both non-stationary economic environments and also circumstances like the "beauty contest" famously described by Keynes (i.e. states of the world where the collective outcomes came from a general second-guessing of other agents' behaviour).[23] The latter is a good description of the conditions of endogenous uncertainty.

A more nuanced view on expectations has started to prevail again only in the last decade or so. Dynamic stochastic general equilibrium (DSGE) models, which have been the workhorse of the new classical (and neo-Keynesian) macroeconomics originating from the rational expectations revolution, began increasingly to allow for the presence of rigidities and free parameters directly linked to intuitions on the actual workings of the economies that predated the rational expectation revolution.[24] Models retained their tendency to gravitate towards a long-run equilibrium, but they became much slower to converge, aiming to allow in their theoretical framework for the complexities of the economies that have challenged policy makers and academics alike in the wake of the so-called Great Recession.[25] In such more complex theoretic environments, expectations are re-gaining the central position that was attributed to them by the original Keynes' contribution.

The cycle thus appears to have now turned towards the "high" region again, with new characteristics, in particular, a stronger focus on micro-data. Recent work has promoted a renewed interest in empirical inquiries on how expectations are actually formed. The larger and ever increasing availability of survey-based data on subjective expectations, collected from businesses and individuals, represents a crucial motivation of this current research.[26] The fact that the empirical expectations recovered in the surveys repeatedly deviate from implied rational expectations reinforces this motivation (and is not surprising at a time of great disruptions in the global economy).[27] It has also been suggested that the progressive marginalisation of empirical studies on expectations formation from the mainstream economic research has come to the great detriment of the discipline.[28] In monetary policy making, while ample use of survey data, especially on savings and income, has been made for a long time by central banks,[29] it is mostly in the last decade that special attention has been paid to measures of inflation expectations. In this respect, the risks of de-anchoring have been thoroughly assessed, making extensive reference to household, business and professional forecasters' survey data.[30]

The extent to which expectations collected directly from households and firms help to better forecast their future behaviour remains, of course, an open empirical question. However, careful extraction of the information they contain is undoubtedly useful in order to empirically discriminate among alternative hypotheses. Over time, both before as well as after Muth's proposal of the rational expectations hypothesis and its exponential adoption in macroeconomic literature following works by Lucas, Thomas Sargent, Edward Prescott and many other prominent economists not limited to the neoclassical camp, various suggestions on how economic agents may form their expectations have been advanced, following extrapolative, adaptive, regressive, error-learning or return-to-normality specifications.[31] In a recent review by Manski about the increasingly relevant field of probabilistic expectations collection in micro data sets, the evolution of thinking about the formation of expectations in policy analysis is discussed in depth.[32] Manski's conclusion is that the ongoing progressive demise in policy analyses of the rational expectation assumptions (a welcome development) should not be accompanied by a proliferation of alternative ad hoc models of expectations formation (a confusing consequence). Careful empirical work would be needed in order to discriminate among these alternative models. In addition, while up to now most of the work on eliciting expectations from individual agents has been pursued by microeconomists, Manski advocates a more direct involvement of macroeconomists even at this early stage, given the crucial impact of expectations on the macroeconomic aggregates. Surveys can shed light not only on the state of expectations, but also on the main drivers of their revisions, when the economic reality changes.

These arguments had long been made by Herbert Simon himself, when he discussed objections to behavioural criticism of the rational expectation hypothesis, in particular those calling attention to its overall lack of coherence. He acknowledged these objections, accepting that simply highlighting the general shortcomings of a theory does not guarantee its demise, unless a newly formed alternative theory has been developed, which is also Mark Blaug's familiar argument that "you cannot beat something with nothing".[33] However, in Simon's words, Behaviouralism could be built only through extensive empirical research, and this had to be done even in times when it did not yet provide a fully-fledged alternative to mainstream theory. Consequently, the dispute around expectations could be settled only by "painstaking microeconomic empirical study of human decision making and problem solving".[34]

Interestingly, this analysis had also to be done in order to pin down and estimate the particular deviation from full rationality that was needed to complement Lucas's rational expectations-based models in order to generate a meaningful business cycle theory: the inability of Lucas's agents to fully discriminate between shocks to own prices and shocks on the general level of prices. The failure of the Lucas islands model to confirm its results when the stochastic environment in which the agents act is not stationary was also pointed out by Albert Ando, Simon's former student and co-author, even if with a different focus.[35] Ando suggested that there was a lack of coherence between the professed general value of agents' expectations in Lucas's model and the strict (but not explicit) hypotheses under which they acted. As the fortune of Lucas's contribution was partly linked to his critique of previous models' ad hoc assumptions, rather than to new empirical findings disproving such models, Ando's assessment was particularly sharp. Equilibrium cycle models, in the Lucas and Sargent formulations, were unable, in his view, to say anything significant about the origins of business cycles.[36] Adding to Ando's and Benjamin Friedman's view, Simon pointed out that Muth's expectations were more a special case than "a paradigm for rational behaviour under uncertainty"[37] and that their implied decision rule, rather than rational, should be labelled a "consistent expectations" rule.[38]

Simon also addressed the fundamental non-stationarity of economic systems and the existence of states of the world where endogenous uncertainty is pervasive. For Simon's rationally-satisficing agents, the "acceptability region", in which the first satisficing choice must lie, is historically and institutionally determined. Inherently unstable economies will tend to gravitate towards the path set by institutions that have been devised to contrast such perceived instabilities.[39] This will produce conventions and habits as well as simple decision rules which individual agents will then be able to use in their choice-making, helping them to solve their particular beauty contest-like problems while saving on costly rationality. History is of the essence, and this renders any attempt to approximate the mechanisms of expectation formation without specific knowledge of the local circumstances driving the economy relatively useless.[40] Welcome discipline on theorising about expectations must therefore come from the empirical analysis and its detection of regularities.

Cognitive limitations and learning

The comparison between the economic agents' theoretical cognitive abilities and the outcomes derived from empirically observed data is particularly relevant in policy making. A rich research agenda is associated with the need to understand how agents learn from past mistakes and from the availability of new information on the state of the world they are in. "Learning" as identified in the influential contribution by George Evans and Seppo Honkapohja, implies that a rational expectations equilibrium is only one of the possible outcomes when agents continuously update their expectations based on the comparison between past expectations and actual realisations.[41]

The roots of this stream of literature can be found in simpler models, such as the cobweb described by Nerlove, that showed how the extrapolation of specific adaptive expectations functions could lead either to equilibria (not necessarily unique) or to explosive outcomes.[42] Error-learning mechanisms are, in fact, very general, and can rationalise sophisticated optimal forecasting rules.[43] Muth himself advanced his own rational expectations hypothesis in order to estimate the parameters of a model of adaptive expectations (where the change in the expected price level depends only on the forecast error just observed). Learning by boundedly rational agents is central also to Sargent's successive research on expectations in macroeconomics,[44] where the limitations of the straightforward rational expectation hypotheses are contrasted with a more nuanced view of rationality, one that weakens the strong informational assumptions implicit in Lucas's and Sargent's original contributions.[45]

The application of these tools in monetary policy has far-reaching policy implications. For example, Ferrero describes an environment where boundedly rational agents face the issue of formulating expectations on the future rate of inflation.[46] In this environment, economic agents learn from their past mistaken predictions by combining old and new information to form new beliefs; the policy maker (specifically in this case the monetary policy authority) can exert some influence on the agents' learning process. The model is able to explain why policies that would be optimal under rational expectations could instead perform poorly when knowledge is imperfect. It also highlights that, under some conditions, converging to a rational expectations equilibrium could take an extremely long time, making it ill-suited to represent an anchor for rational agents. Welfare consequences are pervasive, especially when the policy maker is willing to influence the public learning rules.[47] In recent work, Busetti et al. investigate the effects of a sequence of deflationary shocks on expected and actual inflation and output in the context of a New Keynesian model where agents have incomplete information about the workings of the economy and form expectations through adaptive learning processes.[48] They show that the learning process could imply a de-anchoring of inflation expectations from the central bank's target that is entirely data-driven, through the workings and feedback of the learning process.

More complex agent-based models have also been employed to explore the impact of het-erogeneous expectations in environments where there could not exist any rational expectations equilibrium towards which agents can coordinate.[49] In line with Simon's (1955) seminal con-tribution, later developed with March, agents use expectations based on simple heuristics as a device to willingly ignore part of the available information in order to reach local optima which, in this particular setting, beat the outcomes of fully rational choices.[50] This strategy proves to be superior to more sophisticated ways of forming expectations, grounded, for example, in recur-sive least squares as in mainstream learning literature, due to the highly unstable and uncertain, in the Knightian sense, environment. Rather than making the case for a general superiority of simple versus sophisticated rules, this stream of works provides a counterexample to the opposite claim, even in the event that information is not costly *per se*. There are conditions under which less is clearly more.

Again, rules of thumb, traditions and common received wisdom can be somewhat effective tools in helping economic agents to efficiently reach their goals. It should be noted that also the results that come from the learning behaviour of boundedly rational (though not neces-sarily *à la* Simon) agents could and should be confronted with the "direct observation of human behaviour in the market and in the firm" available from survey-based data on expectations.[51] Indeed, the strategy that Simon recommended to economists in the early 1980s was that of securing "new kinds of data at the micro level, data that will provide direct evidence about the behaviour of economic agents and the ways in which they go about making their decisions".[52] The massive amount of empirical work at the level of individual decision makers, that was only envisioned more than 30 years ago when Simon was advancing his criticism of rational expectations, has now been made possible by the availability of data and computational power.

Conclusion

Individual agents' expectations on the state and evolution of the economy have a great influ-ence on macroeconomic variables. Macroeconomists have oscillated between giving prominent importance to survey-based expectations data (as in the first analyses of business cycles in the immediate aftermath of the Second World War) and ignoring empirical data on expectations altogether, relying instead on model-consistent rational expectations. In recent years, the increasing availability of individual survey data and the failings of models based on purely rational (representative) agents have prompted renewed interest in inquiries into the direct measurement of individual expectations and empirical studies of their formation. Herbert Simon's legacy provides a useful guide for both these activities.

Over the past decades, the success by policy makers in stabilising expectations could have generated the falsely reassuring conclusion that expectations are of limited consequence and can be assumed away. In fact, the unbiasedness that stems from Muth's original rational expectations hypothesis could hold both when agents behave as neo-classically rational agents as well as when they inhabit a sufficiently stable economic environment and follow a boundedly-rational learning procedure. Conclusions, however, differ when the economy is hit by sudden changes such as deep recessions, technological revolutions, institutional transformations, and rapid modifications in social habits. In such cases, which are by far the most common, possibly excluding only the 1960s and the couple of decades of the so-called Great Moderation around the turn of the last century, in a world populated by neoclassical agents, economies would be stabilised only by a quick, widespread agreement on the new general economic equilibrium (or its deep parameters), or if agents are closer to boundedly-rational ones, with the help of the actions of institutions and other focal actors. In the latter case, stories and narratives, as pointed out by Akerlof and Shiller, as well as norms and conventions (in the spirit of Keynes and Simon) may become prominent macroeconomic forces.[53]

Sound new research on expectations is warranted. It should be both empirical and theoretical. On the empirical side, better and larger data collecting is already ongoing. Big data techniques could possibly complement more traditional survey-based methods. With regard to theory, research on learning and information has been a promising avenue and should regain importance. Discipline in relation to a model internal consistency provided by the rational expectation hypothesis could be meaningfully substituted by strong, repeated empirical verification in order to avoid the proliferation of model-specific settings of expectations.

Finally, institutions should pay particular attention to current research on agents' cognitive limits. The reason is twofold. It would help, on the one hand, to perfect their policy tools, by relying on models better apt to gauge the reactions of businesses and households to policy interventions, and it would improve, on the other hand, their ability to drive the economy in times of great disruption, by better focusing on salient communication to the general public. In following Simon, economists and social scientists in general, not only those of strict behaviourist observance, could also benefit from this heightened institutional attention, as policy actions could provide the replicability they need in order to discriminate between model-specific local behavioural hypotheses and more general behavioural traits to be possibly included in macroeconomic models.

Notes

1 Ando (1979, p. 83).
2 Baumol (1979, p. 76).
3 That is, decisions that lie in a region of the space defined by a set of acceptability constraints.
4 Simon (1955).
5 Simon (1978).
6 DellaVigna (2009, p. 348).
7 Sims (2003).
8 See, among others, Gigerenzer (1996).
9 For an alternative view, that deems these perturbations as fundamental for modeling human choices, see Tversky and Kahneman (1974, 1981) and Kahneman, Knetsch and Thaler (1991).
10 See also Visco (2013).
11 The seminal works of Keynes (1936) and Hicks (1939) are well known examples.
12 The heterogeneous relevance of expectations in economic models that have been progressively considered mainstream has also made it difficult to develop a "theory of expectations", one that would form a basis for a well-defined field in the economic discipline dedicated to expectations. For an extensive analysis of this issue, see the Introduction to Visco (1985) and Visco (2009a).
13 Keynes (1921), Knight (1921).
14 Keynes (1936).
15 Lucas (1976, p. 41).
16 Muth (1961).
17 Holt, Modigliani, Muth and Simon (1960). In their contribution the authors derived a decision rule for firms that found the optimal level of production, given the state of inventories and the expectations on future sales. The cooperation, in Simon's words, of two Keynesian economists, one rational expectationist and a behaviouralist, gave origins to contributions that came to be prominent but opposing: the rational expectation hypothesis and the bounded rationality streams of research. An analysis is given in Egidi (2017).
18 As Simon (1984, p. 49) fittingly observed, the special virtue of these terms was largely due to their ability to "win instantly by taking the breath away from would-be disputants, whose very skepticism now accuses them of 'unnaturalness' or 'irrationality', as the case may be."
19 Woodford (2013, p. 304).

20 See Evans and Honkapohja (2001). In a stable environment a learning procedure based on a set comprising only the past realisations of the variable to be expected may lead to an unbiased though possibly inefficient expectation of its future path.
21 Davidson (1982, p. 190).
22 Pesaran (1988, Chapter 2).
23 Keynes (1936, p. 156).
24 Visco (2009a).
25 Visco (2009b).
26 For a survey on recent contributions see Coibion, Gorodnichenko and Kamdar (2018). See also Visco (1984) for an extensive discussion of results from early surveys of price expectations, as well as an empirical analysis of the formation of expectations in Italy from the early 1950s through the late 1970s.
27 Similar results hold for the years following the 1973–74 oil crisis, see Visco (1984, Chapters 4 and 5). See also Cukierman (1986).
28 Gennaioli, Ma and Shleifer (2016, p. 380).
29 For example, Banca d'Italia has carried out a Survey on Household Income and Wealth (SHIW) since the mid-1960s, complemented over the years by a number of surveys on firms' intentions and expectations. Similar information is gauged for instance by the Survey of Consumer Finances (SCF) and by several business surveys produced by the Federal Reserve System (e.g. the Empire State Manufacturing Survey by the New York Fed). In addition, both the Philadelphia Federal Reserve Bank (since 1968) and the European Central Bank (since 2002) release quarterly surveys on professional forecasters' expectations about real and nominal macroeconomic variables (SPF).
30 Recent work by Aruoba (2016) and Doh and Oksol (2018) use direct observations on agents' expectations to estimate the term structure of inflation expectations in the United States and evaluate the degree to which inflation expectations have been anchored over time. Buono and Formai (2018) use expectations recovered from the Consensus Economics survey to compare inflation anchoring in the euro area versus other major economies. Łyziak and Paloviita (2017) show some signs of de-anchoring in the euro area inflation expectations in one analysis based on the ECB Survey of Professional Forecasters and on the European Commission Consumer survey.
31 See, for a succinct overview of some of the proposals advanced in the literature, Visco (1984, Chapter 6).
32 Manski (2018) reviews and extend a previous contribution on the same issue (Manski, 2004) where the use of survey-based expectations data in macroeconomic modelling was strongly suggested. Based on new empirical evidence, directly eliciting probabilistic expectations from households and businesses in surveys is found to be particularly effective.
33 Simon (1984, p. 52) summarising Blaug (1980, p. 186).
34 Simon (1984, p. 35).
35 Ando (1983).
36 See Lucas (1972, 1980) and Sargent (1976).
37 Simon (1979, p. 505).
38 Simon (1978, p. 10); see also Friedman (1979) and Ando (1981).
39 On this, see Simon (1958) and for similar arguments Keynes (1936, Chapter 12), even if it should be acknowledged that, according to Simon, "Keynes' modes of reasoning in the *General Theory* are only locally heretical. His general form of argumentation is the one that is standard in economics: what might be called 'what would I do if I were a rational man' argumentation" (Simon, 1984, p. 36).
40 A more radical approach addressing the interaction between historical evolutions, market and non-market behaviour and economic theorizing is found in Polanyi (1944).
41 Evans and Honkapohja (2001).
42 Nerlove (1958).
43 See, for a perceptive analysis, Rose (1972).
44 Sargent (1993).
45 According to Sent (1997), the link between Sargent's and Simon's bounded rationalities is still, after all, rather weak. This does not reduce the influence exerted by Simon, but while Sargent advanced in a world of adaptively learning (based on parallel computing) standard utility-maximising agents, Simon kept a clear distance from neoclassical theory, maintaining the prominence of "satisficing" behaviour and dismissing the adoption of parallel adaptive computing systems while continuing to prefer the recourse to more traditional serial symbol processing procedures.
46 Ferrero (2007).

47 "A policy-maker who considers his role in determining the dynamics of the agents' learning process could choose a policy rule that induces agents to learn at a given speed, affecting the welfare of society along the transition." (Ferrero 2007, p. 3034).

48 Busetti, Ferrero, Gerali and Locarno (2014) and Busetti, Delle Monache, Gerali and Locarno (2017).

49 See, for a recent contribution, Dosi, Napoletano, Roventini, Stiglitz and Treibich (2017).

50 See Simon (1955) and March and Simon (1993).

51 Simon (1984, p. 52).

52 Simon (1984, p. 40), where he also observes, somewhat surprised, that a similar suggestion had also been advanced by Lucas in his book on the business cycle (Lucas, 1980, pp. 288–289).

53 Akerlof and Shiller (2009).

References

Akerlof, G. A. and R. J. Shiller, 2009. *Animal spirits*, Princeton, NJ: Princeton University Press.

Ando, A., 1979. "On the contributions of Herbert A. Simon to economics", *The Scandinavian Journal of Economics*, 81(1), 83–93.

Ando, A., 1981. "On a theoretical and empirical basis of macroeconomic models", in J. Kmenta and J. B. Ramsey (eds), *Large-scale macro-econometric models: Theory and practice*, (pp. 329–367), Amsterdam: North-Holland.

Ando, A., 1983. "Equilibrium business-cycle models: an appraisal", in F. G. Adams and B. G. Hickman (eds), *Global econometrics: Essays in honor of Lawrence R. Klein* (pp. 39–67), Cambridge, MA: MIT Press.

Aruoba, S. B, 2016. "Term structures of inflation expectations and real interest rates", Federal Reserve Bank of Philadelphia, Working Paper 16–09, December.

Baumol, W. J., 1979. "On the contributions of Herbert A. Simon to economics", *The Scandinavian Journal of Economics*, 81(1), 74–82.

Blaug, M., 1980. *The methodology of economics*, Cambridge: Cambridge University Press.

Busetti, F., G. Ferrero, A. Gerali and A. Locarno, 2014. "Deflationary shocks and de-anchoring of inflation expectations", Banca d'Italia, Occasional Papers 252.

Busetti, F., D. Delle Monache, A. Gerali and A. Locarno, 2017. "Trust, but verify. de-anchoring of inflation expectations under learning and heterogeneity", European Central Bank, Working Paper 1994.

Buono, I. and S. Formai, 2018. "New evidence on the evolution of the anchoring of inflation expectations", *Journal of Macroeconomics*, 57, 39–54.

Coibion, O., Y. Gorodnichenko and R. Kamdar, 2018. "The formation of expectations, inflation and the Phillips curve", *Journal of Economic Literature*, 56(4).

Cukierman, A. 1986. "Measuring inflationary expectations. A review essay", *Journal of Monetary Economics*, 17, 315–324.

Davidson, P., 1982. "Rational expectations: A fallacious foundation for studying crucial decision-making processes", *Journal of Post-Keynesian Economics*, 5(2), 182–198.

DellaVigna, S., 2009. "Psychology and economics: Evidence from the field", *Journal of Economic Literature*, 47(2), 315–372.

Doh, T. and A. Oksol, 2018. "Has the anchoring of inflation expectations changed in the United States during the past decade? Federal Reserve Bank of Kansas City", *Economic Review*, 103(1), 31–58.

Dosi G., M. Napoletano, A. Roventini, J. E. Stiglitz, and T. Treibich, 2017. "Rational heuristics? Expectations and behaviors in evolving economies with heterogeneous interacting agents", Scuola Superiore Sant'Anna, Pisa, LEM Working Paper 31.

Egidi M., 2017. "Paths in contemporary economics and sciences of artificial intelligence that originate from Simon's bounded rationality approach", *PSL Quarterly Review*, 70(279), 7–33.

Evans, G. W. and S. Honkapohja, 2001. *Learning and expectations in macroeconomics*, Princeton, NJ: Princeton University Press.

Ferrero, G., 2007. "Monetary policy, learning and the speed of convergence", *Journal of Economic Dynamics & Control*, 31(9), 3006–3041.

Friedman, B. M., 1979. "Optimal expectations and the extreme information assumptions of 'rational expectations' macromodels", *Journal of Monetary Economics*, 5(1), 23–41.

Gennaioli, N., Y. Ma and A. Shleifer, 2016. "Expectations and investment", NBER Macroeconomics Annual, 30, 379–442.

Gigerenzer, G., 1996. "On narrow norms and vague heuristics: A reply to Kahneman and Tversky", *Psychological Review*, 103(3), 592–596.

Hicks, J. R., 1939. *Value and capital*, Oxford: Clarendon Press.

Holt, C. C., F. Modigliani, J. F. Muth and H. A. Simon, 1960. *Planning production, inventories and work force*, Englewood Cliffs, NJ: Prentice-Hall.

Kahneman, D., J. L. Knetsch and R. H. Thaler, 1991. "Anomalies: The endowment effect, loss aversion, and status quo bias", *Journal of Economic Perspectives*, 5(1), 193–206.

Keynes, J. M., 1921. *A treatise on probability*, London: Macmillan.

Keynes, J. M., 1936. *The general theory of employment, interest and money*, London: Macmillan.

Knight, F. H., 1921. *Risk, uncertainty and profit*, New York: Houghton Mifflin.

Łyziak, T. and Paloviita, M., 2017. "Anchoring of inflation expectations in the euro area: Recent evidence based on survey data", *European Journal of Political Economy*, 46, 52–73.

Lucas, R. E., 1972. "Expectations and the neutrality of money", *Journal of Economic Theory*, 4(2), 103–124.

Lucas, R. E., 1976. "Econometric policy evaluation: a critique", Carnegie-Rochester Conference Series on Public Policy, 1(1), 19–46.

Lucas, R. E., 1980. *Methods and problems in business cycle theory*, Cambridge, MA: The MIT Press.

Manski, C. F., 2004. "Measuring expectations", *Econometrica*, 72(5), 1329–1376.

Manski, C .F., 2018. "Survey measurement of probabilistic macroeconomic expectations: Progress and promise", *NBER Macroeconomics Annual*, 32(1), 411–471.

March, J. G. and H. A. Simon, 1993. "Organizations revised", *Industrial and Corporate Change*, 2(3), 299–316.

Muth, J. F., 1961. "Rational expectations and the theory of price movements", *Econometrica*, 29(3), 315–335.

Nerlove, M., 1958. "Adaptive expectations and cobweb phenomena", *Quarterly Journal of Economics*, 72(2), 227–240.

Pesaran, H., 1988. *The limits to rational expectations*, Oxford: Basil Blackwell.

Polanyi, K., 1944. *The great transformation*, New York: Farrar & Rinehart.

Rose, D. E., 1972. "A general error-learning model of expectations formation", University of Manchester, Inflation Workshop Discussion Paper.

Sargent, T. J., 1976. "A classical macroeconomic model for the United States", *Journal of Political Economy*, 84(2), 207–237.

Sargent, T. J., 1993. *Bounded rationality in macroeconomics*, Oxford: Oxford University Press.

Sent, E. M., 1997. "Sargent versus Simon: Bounded rationality unbound", *Cambridge Journal of Economics*, 21, 323–338.

Simon, H. A., 1955. "A behavioral model of rational choice", *Quarterly Journal of Economics*, 69(1), 99–118.

Simon, H. A., 1958. "The role of expectations in an adaptive or behavioristic model", in M. J Bowman, (ed.), *Expectations, uncertainty and business behavior* (pp. 49–58), New York: Social Science Research Council,

Simon, H. A., 1978. "Rationality as process and as product of thought", *American Economic Review*, 68(2), 1–16.

Simon, H. A., 1979. "Rational decision making in business organizations", *American Economic Review*, 69(4), 493–513.

Simon, H. A., 1984. "On the behavioral and rational foundations of economic dynamics", *Journal of Economic Behavior and Organization*, 5(1), 35–55.

Sims, C. A., 2003. "Implications of rational inattention", *Journal of Monetary Economics*, 50(3), 665–690.

Tversky, A. and D. Kahneman, 1974. "Judgement under uncertainty: Heuristics and biases", *Science*, 185.

Tversky, A. and D. Kahneman, 1981. "The framing of decisions and the psychology of choice", *Science*, 211 (4481).

Visco, I., 1984. *Price expectations in rising inflation*, Amsterdam: North Holland.

Visco, I., 1985. Le aspettative nell'analisi economica, Bologna: il Mulino.

Visco, I., 2009a. "On the role of expectations in Keynesian and today's economics (and economies)", paper presented at Accademia Nazionale dei Lincei, Rome, 11–12 March (available at the Banca d'Italia's website)

Visco, I., 2009b. "The financial crisis and economists' forecasts", *BIS Review*, 49.

Visco, I., 2013. "The aftermath of the crisis: Regulation, supervision and the role of central banks", *CEPR Policy Insight*, 68.

Woodford, M., 2013. "Macroeconomic analysis without the rational expectations hypothesis", *Annual Review of Economics*, 5, 303–346.

31

LESS IS MORE
FOR BAYESIANS, TOO

Gregory Wheeler

Lore has it that a fundamental principle of Bayesian rationality is for decision makers to never turn down the offer of free information. Cost-free information can only help you, never hurt you, and in the worst case will leave you at status quo ante. Purported exceptions to this principle are no exceptions at all, but instead involve a hidden cost to learning. Make those costs plain and the problem you face is one of balancing the quality of a choice against the costs to you of carrying it out, a trade-off that Bayesian methods are ideally suited to solve.

This piece of Bayesian lore, that rationality compels you to never turn down free information, is sometimes called *Good's Principle*, after I. J. Good's concise formalization of the reasoning behind it (Good, 1967). But the argument goes back to the beginning of modern Bayesian probability theory, with remarks by Ramsey (1931), an argument by Savage (1972), the formalization of a key piece of it by Raiffa and Schlaiffer (1961), followed thereafter by assertions in textbooks, starting with Lindley (1965). Put a bit more carefully, Good's principle recommends to delay making a terminal decision between alternative courses of action if there is an opportunity to learn, at zero cost, the outcome of an experiment relevant to the decision (Pedersen and Wheeler, 2015). This will be put more carefully still later in this chapter.

Objections to Good's principle have surfaced in the last half-century, some of which are well known by now but others less so, forming part of a rich discussion of the value of information to rational decision making (Wakker, 1988; Machina, 1989; Seidenfeld, 1994; Grünwald and Halpern, 2004; Gigerenzer and Brighton, 2009; Siniscalchi, 2011; Hill, 2013; Pedersen and Wheeler, 2015). Since then, a picture has emerged about the value of information that is more restricted and more nuanced than Good's principle states, suggesting a revision to Bayesian lore. For even in highly idealized settings, ignorance can be a virtue. Sometimes less is more for Bayesians, too.

Asymmetric information in strategic games

The first dent to this folklore comes from the theory of games, where some strategic interactions can result in a player being better off having less information. George Akerlof's study of market failures created by asymmetric information is a classic example (Akerlof, 1970). *Adverse selection*

DOI: 10.4324/9781315658353-36

occurs when one side of a trade has less information than the other side and withdraws from trading from fear of being unfairly taken advantage of by the more informed party. Akerlof offered the used car market as an example where adverse selection occurs, a particularly apt example in 1970. A used car salesman will know which cars on the lot are bad and which are good, knowledge an ordinary consumer will not have. But the consumer will know that the dealer knows which car is of which quality type and recognize the upper hand the dealer has in any trade. Afraid of paying a good-car price and driving home in a bad one, the customer may choose not to buy any car at all. The reasoning for this idealized single transaction generalizes, resulting in a market failure for used cars where nobody is willing to pay more than the going rate for a bad car.

Used car dealers have overcome their adverse selection problem by certifying the quality of used cars, and backing those claims with a warranty, thereby leveling the information playing field between dealers and customers by letting customers in on what dealers know about the quality of the cars they sell. (Making better cars has helped, too.) Yet, since the problem here is asymmetrical information, this isn't the only way to restore the market. Rather than making consumers as informed as dealers, another option is to make dealers as ignorant as consumers.

The following example, due to Martin Osborne, illustrates the ignorance option (Osborne 2003, 9.3). Imagine there are two states of the world, ω_1 and ω_2—which could be understood to correspond to the state in which a car is more likely to be good than bad and vice versa, for instance. Suppose there are two Bayesians, Player 1 and Player 2, but neither player knows which state of the world they are in. Both are ignorant, so they both assign a probability of one-half to ω_1 and one-half to ω_2. Figure 31.1 gives the payoff tables for Player 1 and Player 2, where the material difference to each player from their uncertainty over which state they are in, ω_1 or ω_2, is reflected in the last two columns of the respective payoff tables. Given this setup, with both players ignorant of the state, the strategy L is Player 2's unique best response to every strategy of Player 1, which yields Player 2 the expected payoff of $2-2(1-\varepsilon)p$, whereas M and R both yield $\frac{3}{2} - \frac{3}{2}(1-\varepsilon)p$ where p is the probability Player 1 assigns to T. Player 1's unique best response to L is B. Therefore, (B,L) is the unique Nash equilibrium of the game, yielding each player a payoff of 2.

Now imagine that instead of both players being ignorant of which state they are in, exactly one of the players is informed of the state. Specifically, suppose Player 2 is informed of the state

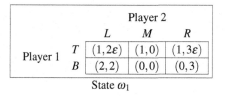

Figure 31.1   Payoffs to Players 1 and 2 in states ω_1 and ω_2 with $0 \le \epsilon \le \frac{1}{2}$

Source: Osborne (2003).

whereas Player 1 remains ignorant but nevertheless knows that Player 2 is informed. In this game (T, (R, M)) is the unique Nash equilibrium yielding to her at most a payoff of 1.5. Why? Choosing R is Player 2's best response in state ω_1 and her worst response in ω_2. Similarly, M is Player 2's best response in ω_2 and worst in ω_1. Player 1 knows this too, knows that Player 2 is informed of the state, thus knows that Player 2 will never choose L. With column L removed from consideration, Player 1's best response to (M,R) is T.

Despite her information advantage over Player 1, Player 2's payoff in this second game is 3ϵ in each state, which is at most 1.5. Thus, Player 2 is worse off learning the state than remaining ignorant. Given the choice between the original game, where both players are ignorant, and the second game in which Player 1 remains ignorant but Player 2 is informed, it is rational for Player 2 to choose to remain ignorant, even if the information about the state is offered to her for free.

Akerlof's and Osborne's examples are part of a broader collection of counter-intuitive results that can arise when the rational choice of one player changes the probability assessments of another about which state will occur. In this case, the negative value of information stems from *act-state dependence* of Player 1's strategic response to Player 2's informed choice. Osborne seems to think that the prospect of information having negative value appears only in games, not in decision problems:

> A decision-maker in a single-person decision problem cannot be worse off if she has more information: if she wishes, she can ignore the information. In a game the same is not true: if a player has more information and the other players know that she has more information, then she may be worse off.
>
> *Osborne, 2003, p. 281*

This position that Osborne expresses, that Good's principle governs single-person decision making but not strategic decision making (i.e., games), remains something of a received view on the possibility of negative-valued information. Over the last half-century, decision and game theorists have become keenly aware of the crucial role that act-state independence plays in standard decision theory, aided by a slew of puzzles and aberrant behavior in examples that are found upon close inspection to depend on violations of this independence condition (Kadane, Seidenfeld, and Schervish, 2008). Act-state independence is the first thing to go in the theory of games, however, as the whole point of strategic decision making is to factor in the consequences to you from the rational acts of others. So, one might conclude, to avoid the specter of negative-valued information, restrict the scope of Good's principle to single-person decision problems. That, in a nutshell, is the received view on Good's principle. The received view is wrong, however.

Good by Savage

To see why single-person decision-making is not immune to negative-valued information, let us consider more carefully Savage's argument that it is immune. To be clear at the outset, our analysis will not uncover a mathematical mistake or faulty theorem. Rather, our aim is to draw attention to another important type of qualification to Good's principle.

Good's principle appears in Savage's discussion in *Foundations of Statistics* of the differences between a basic decision problem and a derived decision problem. A *basic* decision problem is one in which an agent is to choose a basic action from among a collection he judges to be available for choice. A *derived* decision problem is one in which the agent is to choose from the same collection of basic actions but only after considering the associated conditional expected utilities for a basic action given each possible outcome of some experiment. Given the assumption that you wish to maximize your expected utility, why should you prefer a derived decision problem over a basic decision problem? Because you cannot be made worse off in expectation and may well come out better. "It is almost obvious," Savage remarks,

> that the value of a derived problem cannot be less, and typically is greater, than the value of the basic problem from which it is derived. After all, any basic act is among the derived acts, so that any expected utility that can be attained by deciding on a basic act can be attained by deciding on the same basic act considered as a derived act. In short, the person is free to ignore the observation. That obvious fact is the theory's expression of the commonplace that knowledge is not disadvantageous.
>
> *Savage, 1972, p. 107*

Good later showed that Carnap's principle of total evidence (Carnap, 1947) follows as a consequence of the principle to maximize expected utility, so long as the costs of acquiring information are negligible.

> [I]n expectation, it pays to take into account further evidence, provided that the cost of collecting and using this evidence, although positive, can be ignored. In particular, we should use all the evidence *already* available, provided that the cost of doing so is negligible. With this proviso then, the principle of total evidence follows from the principle of rationality.
>
> *Good, 1967, p. 319*

Our discussion in the next two sections will be helped along by introducing a bit of formalism now to set up Savage's version of Good's principle.

Following (Pedersen and Wheeler, 2015), consider an illustration of Good's principle in Figure 31.2. Suppose that at some time t_1 you are to face a choice, A, among two courses of action, a_1 or a_2. Prior to this choice you face a decision, O, at some time t_0 prior to t_1, between o_1, the *basic decision* of choosing a_1 or a_2 at time t_1, and o_2, the *derived decision* of choosing a_1 or a_2 at some later time t_2 after you have observed, at no cost, the outcome of an experiment ε, with outcomes e_1 or e_2.[1]

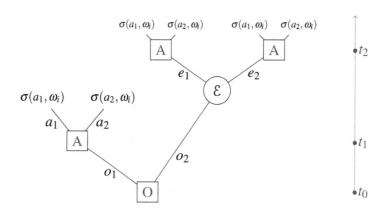

Figure 31.2 Illustration of Good's principle

Choice, being governed here by dominance reasoning, comes after ruling out those options for choice that are worse than all others. Those acts that survive the cull are *admissible* for choice. Suppose that your judgments of admissibility can be represented in terms of subjective expected utility maximization with respect to a real-valued expectation $\mathbb{E}_p[\cdot]$ agreeing with a real-valued probability function p defined on a Boolean algebra $\mathscr{A}$ over the set of states Ω and a real-valued utility function u defined over the set of consequences.[2] Then, at time t_0 you confront a decision problem $O = \{o_1, o_2\}$. If you implement option o_1 at time t_0, then at time t_1 you will face a decision problem $A = \{a_1, a_2\}$ without observing the outcome of experiment $\mathcal{E}$. If you implement option o_2 at time t_0, then at time t_2 you will face the same decision problem A after observing the outcome of experiment $\mathcal{E}$.

Abusing notation, let 'o_1' also stand for the event of facing the decision problem A after implementing option o_1 at t_0. (Context should make clear which use of 'o_1' we intend.) In a similar manner, let '$o_2, \mathcal{E} = e_i$' stand for the event of facing the decision problem A after implementing o_2 and observing the outcome e_i of experiment $\mathcal{E}$. The *choice set* $\mathbf{c}$ of admissible options from A for choice given each alternative, written $\mathbf{c}(A \mid o_1)$ and $\mathbf{c}(A \mid o_2, \mathcal{E} = e_i)$ for options o_1 and o_2, respectively, may be defined by Equations (31.1) and (31.2):

$$\mathbf{c}(A \mid o_1) = \arg\max_{a \in A} \mathbb{E}_{p(\cdot \mid o_1)}\left[(u \circ \sigma)(a, p(d\omega \mid o_1))\right] \tag{31.1}$$

$$\mathbf{c}(A \mid o_2, \mathcal{E} = e_i) = \arg\max_{a \in A} \mathbb{E}_p(\cdot \mid o_2, \mathcal{E} = e_i)\left[(u \circ \sigma)(a, p(d\omega \mid o_2, \mathcal{E} = e_i))\right] \tag{31.2}$$

where $\circ$ denotes functional composition.

Good's principle assumes that at t_0 you are certain, regardless of whether or not you choose to observe the outcome of experiment $\mathcal{E}$, that you will choose an option $a \in A$ that maximizes your expected utility. This assumption is codified in how admissible choices are determined for each option o_1 and o_2 in Equations (31.1) and (31.2), respectively. A second assumption is that your preferences over consequences remain unchanged. A third assumption is that your beliefs given hypotheses accord with Bayesian conditionalization. With all of this in place, Good's principle states that your expectation of (1) *your maximum conditional expected utility of choosing from A under option o_1* is less than or equal to (2) *your maximum conditional expected utility under o_2 of choosing from A given experiment $\mathcal{E}$*. Your expectation of (2) is strictly greater than (1) unless there is an action from A that maximizes conditional expected utility from A regardless of the experimental outcome of $\mathcal{E}$. In other words, unless the experiment is irrelevant (i.e., probabilistically independent), then $\mathbf{c}(O) = \{o_2\}$.

Uncertainty and imprecision

According to the canonical theory of synchronic decision making under risk, a perfectly rational person is one whose comparative assessments of a set of consequences satisfies the recommendation to maximize expected utility. What underpins this claim is the assumption that a person's qualitative comparative judgments of those consequences (aka, *preferences*) are structured in a particular way (*satisfy specific axioms*) to admit a mathematical representation in terms of inequalities of mathematical *expectations*, ordered from worst to best on the real number line. This structuring of preference through qualitative axioms to admit a numerical representation is the subject of expected utility theory (Wheeler, 2018, §1.1).

Savage's theory tells us how to represent preference in terms of some pair of numerical probability and numerical utility functions, an ingenious extension of prior work that showed how to quantify each piece separately, principally von Neumann and Morgenstern's numerical representation of utility, which presupposes a numerical probability function (von Neumann and Morgenstern, 1944); and de Finetti's numerical representation of probability, which presupposes a cardinal utility function (de Finetti, 1974). Let's focus here on probability assessments, which for Bayesians are understood as a person's partial beliefs.

Consider what it means for a person to have a partial belief in the proposition, L, expressing that a particular car is a lemon. What does it mean for a person to have a partial of belief of 0.40 that L is true? According to the Ramsey-de Finetti conception of partial belief, this means the person is *indifferent* between two sorts of hypothetical transactions. The first hypothetical transaction calls on him to *buy* a contract for €0.40 that pays him €1 if the car is a lemon, whereas the second hypothetical transaction calls on him to *sell* such a contract for the same price. Put differently, the first type requires the person to surrender a sure 40 cents for the promise of 1 Euro on the event of A occurring and risk receiving 0 if L does not occur. The second type of transaction requires the person to accept payment of the sure reward of 40 cents in exchange for agreeing to risk paying back 1 Euro on the event of L occurring and paying out nothing—in terms of this contract—otherwise. The choice of price is up to the person, the utility of Euros is assumed to be linear, and the stakes are presumed to be small enough to not bankrupt the person yet large enough for him to care. (De Finetti was a thoroughly pragmatic fellow, a point sometimes lost on his critics.) The price of 40 cents is fair to this person just in case he is indifferent between buying and selling contracts on L at 40 cents. A person is rational just in case there is no possible way to put together a finite set of buy and sell positions on that person's announced fair prices to cause him a sure loss, a return to that person of a value less than zero no matter how the uncertain events in those contracts are resolved.

We rehearse this canonical account in order to introduce a slight generalization. Airport currency exchange counters post different prices for buying and selling trades between a pair of currencies. While they do so primarily to turn a profit, the same idea can be used to express your uncertainty about the event, or events, controlling the payoffs in the contract. So, rather than require decision makers to post the *same* number for buying as for selling a contract, we wish to allow for the possibility that they post different numbers. Put differently, rather than oblige an agent to give a single two-sided price for betting on and against the event L, written $P(L)$, we instead oblige the agent to give two one-sided numbers: (1) a one-sided *lower probability* denoting the maximum buying price for a bet on L, written $\underline{P}(L)$; and (2) a one-sided *upper probability* denoting the minimum selling price for a bet on L, written $\overline{P}(L)$.

Notice that for someone whose fair price is $P(L)$, he will judge any price $\alpha < P(L)$ to buy a bet on L (to bet on L) as desirable. Similarly, prices to sell a bet on L (to bet against L) that are strictly greater than $P(L)$ will likewise be judged desirable. It is only the fair price, the single numerical value of $P(L)$, that marks the agent's indifference. Similar reasoning applies to the one-sided lower probability $\underline{P}(L)$. Any price $\alpha < \underline{P}(L)$ will be judged a desirable price to bet on L, and any $\alpha > \overline{P}(L)$ will be judged a desirable price to bet against L. The difference is that there are (possibly) two price points where the agent expresses indifference between a sure award and risky reward in the same currency, namely, when the buying price for a bet on L is $\underline{P}(L)$ and when the selling price for bets on L is $\overline{P}(L)$. Only when they are the same value is the agent committed to a fair price. Since $0 \le \underline{P}(L) \le \overline{P}(L) \le 1$, one consequence is that any price

$\underline{p}$ offered between the agent's lower and upper probabilities for L, any α such that $\underline{P}(L) < \alpha < \overline{P}(L)$, the agent is neither obligated to sell nor to buy contracts on L.

It is a commonplace to distinguish between risk and uncertainty, an idea that both Knight and Keynes put forward a century ago (Keynes, 1921; Knight, 1921). The notion that it is sometimes sensible to permit a bounded range of probability values rather than to insist on numerically determinate probability values is an even older idea, dating back at least to (Bernoulli, 1713) and (Boole, 1854). But the rich mathematical and philosophical consequences from working out these ideas have only begun to come into focus more recently (Walley, 1991; Augustin, Coolen, de Cooman, and Troffaes, 2014; Troffaes and de Cooman, 2014).

The lower probability model presented above is very basic and supplied with a behavioral interpretation that is very close to the original, canonical model: instead of one number to describe two attitudes, we allow each attitude to have its own number. This slight change, however, from a fair-price model to a buying and selling price model of belief, is enough to put another dent in Good's principle. We turn to see how, next.

Dilating probabilities

What does Knightian uncertainty look like in our bare-bones lower probability model? The short answer is that we have the means to distinguish between indifference and incomparability, and to do so behaviorally in the same simple terms of the canonical Bayesian model. For a longer answer and a consequence, an example.

Suppose there is a ticket that pays to its owner 100 euros on the event of G, *Germany wins the next World Cup*. If you owned such a ticket, how much would you demand to part with it? 100 euros would make you whole, so you should at least be indifferent between receiving a sure 100 for the promise of 100 on the event of G being true.[3] Similarly, if you are sure they would lose, the ticket would be worthless to you, so you would find any (positive) price a desirable selling price. Conversely, how much would you pay to buy such a ticket? Here again if you were maximally uncertain (but otherwise abided by the setup for the model), you might not be willing to pay anything for such a ticket. In such a case, your lower probability would be 0. If instead you were certain they will win, you would find any price less than 100 euros desirable and be indifferent to owning the ticket and having a 100 euro note in your pocket: for you, being certain of the outcome G, those two rewards are equivalent.

For my part, I would not know how to give a fair price for G. This does not rule out being bullied by a Bayesian into announcing one, but then again that would be a different decision problem. Hypothetically, I would pay up to 10 euros for a chance to win 100 if Germany won the next World Cup. They've done it before, I reckon, so there is some chance they could do it next time. On the other hand, if I had such a ticket, what price would I accept to relinquish my chance at 100 euros if they win? Here I might accept nothing less than 90 euros. So, any price between 10 and 90 euros I would neither buy nor sell a 100 euro contract on G. These prices don't have to be symmetric, nor need they be calibrated to a statistical model. This is still a subjective probability model and these are my attitudes toward buying and selling hypothetical 100 euro contracts on G.

Let us introduce some notation to reason with attitudes like the one I have toward G. A *lower probability space* is a quadruple $(\Omega, \mathscr{A}, \mathbb{P}, \underline{P})$ such that Ω is a set of states, $\mathscr{A}$ is an algebra over Ω, $\mathbb{P}$ is a nonempty set of probability functions on $\mathscr{A}$, and $\underline{P}$ is a *lower probability function* on $\mathscr{A}$ with respect to $\mathbb{P}$—that is, $\underline{P}(F) = \inf \{p(F) : p \in \mathbb{P}\}$ for each $F \in \mathscr{A}$. The value $\underline{P}(F)$ is called the *lower probability* of F. The *upper probability function* $\overline{P}$ is then defined by stipulating that $\overline{P}(F) =$

1– $\underline{P}(F)$ for each $F \in \mathscr{A}$; the value $\overline{P}(F)$ is called the *upper probability* of F. If $\underline{P}(H) > 0$, then conditional lower and upper probabilities are defined as $\underline{P}(E|H) = \inf \{p(F|H) : p \in \mathbb{P}\}$ and $\overline{P}$ $(F|H) = \sup\{p(F|H) : p \in \mathbb{P}\}$, respectively.

Now return to the highly uncertain event, G, that Germany wins the next World Cup. The upper probability of G is close to 1, $\overline{P}(G) = .9$, and its lower probability is close to 0, $\underline{P}(G) = .1$, such that

$$\overline{P}(G) - \underline{P}(G) = 0.8. \tag{31.3}$$

Next, imagine a fair coin toss, whose outcomes are heads (H) and tails (H^c). The outcomes of this normal coin flip form a partition, $\varepsilon = \{H, H^c\}$, and the same is true of this future championship title, $\mathscr{G} = \{G, G^c\}$. With these preliminaries in place, we rehearse an example from (Seidenfeld, 1994) in which a probability estimate of an event becomes less precise upon receiving information about how the tossed coin lands, regardless of whether it lands heads or lands tails.

Since we judge the coin flip to be fair, our expectation of the coin landing heads is the same as our expectation of it landing tails.

$$\underline{P}(H) = \overline{P}(H) = \frac{1}{2} = \underline{P}(H^c) = \overline{P}(H^c). \tag{31.4}$$

Equation (31.4) is what a fair price looks like in a lower probability model. We also assume that the outcome of this coin toss landing heads is *independent* of Germany winning this future championship. If any pair of events are probabilistically independent, surely the events *heads* and *Germany wins!* are. So, for each $p \in \mathbb{P}$, we have

$$p(G \cap H) = p(G)p(H) = \frac{p(G)}{2}. \tag{31.5}$$

Lastly, let F be the event of either G and H both occurring or both failing to occur, namely, $F := (G \cap H) \cup (G^c \cap H^c)$. Given our setup, it follows that the probability of F is determinate: that is, $p(F) = \frac{1}{2}$, for all $p \in \mathbb{P}$.

Proof. For each $p \in \mathbb{P}$, observe that

$$\begin{aligned}
p(F) &= p(G, H) + p(G^c, H^c) \\
&= \frac{p(G)}{2} + \frac{1 - p(G)}{2} \quad \text{[by (31.5)]} \\
&= \frac{p(G) + 1 - p(G)}{2} \\
&= \frac{1}{2}.
\end{aligned} \tag{31.6}$$

Figure 31.3 may help to fix intuitions as to why $p(F) = \frac{1}{2}$, for all $p \in \mathbb{P}$, is so by visualizing three probability mass functions that differ with respect to the probability that G. Note that the counter-diagonal is the complement of F, F^c, which is the event that Germany wins if and only if the coin lands tails. Put differently, if Germany winning and the coin landing heads are each coded as "success" and Germany losing and tails are coded as "failure," the event F says that the coin and Germany both succeed or both fail, whereas the complement event F^c that exactly one of the two succeeds.

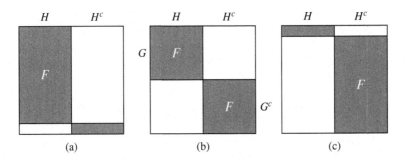

Figure 31.3 Tables for an uncertain event (row) $\mathcal{G} = \{G, G^c\}$, a fair coin randomizer (column) $\varepsilon = \{H, H^c\}$, and the pivotal event (diagonal) F denoting G if and only if H. (a) illustrates when $p(G) = \frac{9}{10}$ and $p(G^c) = \frac{1}{10}$, (b) when $p(G) = p(G^c) = \frac{1}{2}$, and (c) when $p(G) = \frac{1}{10}$ and $p(G^c) = \frac{9}{10}$, for $p \in \mathbb{P}$. For each (a), (b), and (c), $p(F) = \frac{1}{2}$.

Let ε be a positive measurable partition of Ω. We say that ε *dilates* F just in case for each $e \in \varepsilon$:

$$\underline{P}(F \mid \varepsilon = e) < \underline{P}(F) \le \overline{P}(F) < \overline{P}(F \mid \varepsilon = e).$$

In other words, ε dilates F just in case the closed interval $\left[\underline{P}(F), \overline{P}(F)\right]$ is contained in the open interval $\left(\underline{P}(E \mid \varepsilon = e), \overline{P}(E \mid \varepsilon = 3)\right)$ for each $e \in \varepsilon$ (Walley, 1991, Seidenfeld and Wasserman, 1993, Pedersen and Wheeler, 2014). What is remarkable about dilation is the specter of turning a more precise estimate of F into a less precise estimate, no matter what event from the partition occurs.

Observe that in our World Cup example, F is dilated by the coin toss $\varepsilon = \{H, H^c\}$: although the initial estimate of F is precisely one-half, learning the outcome of the coin toss, whether heads or tails, dilates the probability estimate of F from one-half to [.1,.9].

Proof. We show that $0.1 = \underline{P}(F|H) < \underline{P}(F) = \frac{1}{2}$.

$$\underline{P}(F \mid H) = \inf\left\{p(F \mid H) : p \in \mathbb{P}\right\}$$

$$= \inf\left\{\frac{p([(G \cap H) \cup (G^c \cap H^c)] \cap H)}{p(H)} : p \in \mathbb{P}\right\}$$

$$= \inf\left\{\frac{p(G \cap H)}{p(H)} : p \in \mathbb{P}\right\}$$

$$= \inf\left\{\frac{p(G)p(H)}{p(H)} : p \in \mathbb{P}\right\}$$

$$= 0.1$$

A similar argument establishes $\frac{9}{10} = \overline{P}(F|H) > \frac{1}{2}$, and the same argument holds if instead the coin lands tails, i.e., $\underline{P}(F|H^c) = \frac{1}{10}$ and $\overline{P}(F|H^c) = \frac{9}{10}$. Thus, F is dilated by the coin toss, $\varepsilon = \{H, H^c\}$.

Here again Figure 31.3 may help fix intuitions about this result. Notice that the observation of the coin landing heads (H) effectively restricts attention to the first column. Since we learn that H has occurred, the possibilities in the second column associated with tails (H^c) are ruled out. But, the probability mass assigned to the event F in the first column varies widely in Figures 31.3(a), 31.3(b), and 31.3(c). Only in Figure 31.3(b) does the F have the value $\frac{1}{2}$; Figures 31.3(a) and 31.3(c) reveal that the range of uncertainty for F given H is precisely the uncertainty for G displayed in Equation (31.3). The same argument applies if the coin instead landed tails. As these two outcomes exhaust the possible outcomes of the coin toss, being told that the coin was tossed is enough for a Bayesian to dilate his probability assessment of F. For a discussion of the philosophical and mathematical features of dilation, see (Pedersen and Wheeler 2014, 2015).

Good's principle and dilation

Recall the illustration of Good's principle in Figure 31.2. Following the presentation in (Pedersen and Wheeler, 2015) of an example due to (Seidenfeld 1994), suppose that at t_0 you face a decision problem $O = \{o_1, o_2\}$ where, as before, option o_1 is a basic decision problem A in which you are to choose at t_1 between two acts: a_1, which pays you €1 if E occurs and 'pays' you -€1 if E^c, i.e., $\sigma(a_1, F) = €1$ and $\sigma(a_1, F^c) = -€1$;[4] or the act a_2 which 'pays' you a constant -€0.50. Assume that your utility is linear in euro amounts with $u(€x) = x$. Figure 31.4 fills in these details.

In this basic decision problem A, which is the result of implementing option o_1, the subjective expected utility of a_1 is €0 and the subjective expected utility of a_2 is -€0.50. So, a_1 is uniquely admissible from A: receiving nothing is better than paying 50 cents.

Turn now to option o_2, whereby at t_2 you face a derived decision problem conditional on the outcome of experiment ε. Here you are confronted with the same decision problem A at t_2 after learning (only) that H obtains or H^c obtains at t_1. In the derived decision problem act a_1 is inadmissible against a_2. Why? Because in the basic decision problem $p(F) = \frac{1}{2}$, but in the derived decision problem F is dilated by ε to 0.1 and 0.9: whether the outcome of the fair coin toss is heads or tails, F conditional on that outcome is highly uncertain. Thus, in the derived decision problem, there are probability mass functions $p \in \mathbb{P}$ whereby $p(F^c)$ is .9, in which case the minimum expected utility of a_1 is -€0.80. So, in the derived decision problem, by Savage's maxmin decision rule, a_2 has a *higher minimum expected value* (-€0.50) *than* a_1 (-€0.80) regardless of the outcome of the experiment, ε.

Assume that a decision maker is certain that she will not change her preferences, will update her belief state by Generalized Bayesian conditionalization (Walley 1991), and that she will choose to maximize her minimal expected utility. Then, in a pairwise choice between a_1 of

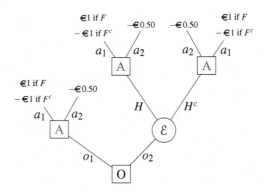

Figure 31.4 A sequential decision example

the basic decision problem determined by option o_1, which has an expected value of zero, and a_2 of the derived decision problem determined by option o_2, which has an expected value of -$0.50, observing cost-free information at t_1, i.e., learning the outcome of the fair coin toss €, is devalued. Here, under the conditions for Good's principle slightly adapted to a lower probability model, we have a case where the decision maker would strictly prefer *not* to receive cost-free information!

Conclusion

Let's review. The informal version of Bayesian lore has it that it is irrational to turn down cost-free information, since the worst case—when the information is irrelevant to your decision at hand—will leave you at status quo ante. The first restriction to Good's principle is that it does not apply to strategic decision problems, where strategic considerations may disadvantage a player with more information than her opponent. The problem of adverse selection is the classic example, and we discussed Akerlof's market for lemons example and Osborne's formalization. This limitation is fairly well known, however, which is why Good's principle is usually formulated to govern single-person decisions. We then formalized Savage's version of Good's principle in terms of his distinction between a basic and derived decision problem, and where the role maxmin reasoning plays is clear. But, in what may be less widely known, we appealed to the phenomenon of dilation to argue that there are exceptions to Good's principle even for single-person decision problems. Specifically, if one introduces an upper and lower probability model to accommodate a modest form of "Knightian uncertainty," then a probability assessment can become less precise after learning the outcome of an experiment, no matter how that experiment turns out. Finally, we returned to our discussion of basic and derived decision problems in Savage's framework to show that this dilation example can be plugged into Savage's original formulation of Good's principle to show that, by applying Savage's maxmin principle, the decision maker would rationally choose to forgo the offer to receive cost-free information about the coin flip experiment ε. Thus, for imprecise probabilities, the "commonplace that knowledge is not disadvantageous" is false, even when the costs of obtaining the information is zero. The upshot is that the scope of Good's principle is far narrower than originally conceived and narrower still than many current decision theorists maintain.

The role that Bayesian methods ought to play in models of bounded rationality remains controversial, and there are some good reasons. Models of bounded rationality typically focus on procedures, algorithms, or psychological processes involved in reaching a decision, securing a goal, or making a judgment, yet these details are ignored in the canonical model. Another branch of bounded rationality focuses on adaptive behavior, and coherent comparative judgments are not, directly at least, the most obvious way to frame this problem.

But it would be incautious to dismiss all of the tools of statistical decision theory, and unwise to ignore the developments in the field over the last half-century. It is hoped that a wider awareness of *better outcomes with less information* results in decision theory—even under the strict adherence to the highly idealized conditions of those mathematical models—will plant a seed of future progress in psychology, where concrete examples are well known. From studying axiomatic departures from the canonical Bayesian theory, it is hoped that the grip of Bayesian dogma will loosen to expand the range of new, creative possibilities for applying a set of practical and powerful mathematical methods to the study of bounded rationality (Wheeler, 2018).

Coda: blinded by omniscience

We end with a short remark on logical omniscience. Most formal models of judgment and decision making entail logical omniscience, the presumption that agents have complete knowledge of all that logically follows from their commitments combined together with any and all set of options that are admissible to them for choice. This is as psychologically unrealistic as it is difficult, technically, to remove from formal models. The problem is especially troublesome to Bayesian decision theory, making it difficult to apply the theory to uncertainty about matters of logic and mathematics. Savage, ever prescient, saw the problem that logical omniscience poses to the subjective theory of probability:

> The analysis should be careful not to prove too much; for some departures from theory are inevitable, and some even laudable. For example, a person required to risk money on a remote digit of π would, in order to comply fully with the theory, have to compute the digit, though this would really be wasteful if the cost of computation were more than the prize involved. For the postulates of the theory imply that you should behave in accordance with the logical implications of all that you know. Is it possible to improve the theory in this respect, making allowances within it for the cost of thinking, or would that entail paradox, as I am inclined to believe but unable to demonstrate?
>
> *Savage, 1967, excerpted from Savage's prepublished draft.*
> *See notes in Seidenfeld et al., 2012*

Notes

1 Good's principle is a synchronic rationality principle, governing here the synchronic choice at t_0 between options o_1 and o_2. Our informal discussion of choices taken at future times ought to be viewed as all hypothetical choices entertained at t_0. Put differently, in choosing between o_1 and o_2, we are comparing at $t0$ the consequences from engaging in two lines of suppositional reasoning.
2 Often a uniqueness result for probabilities and utilities accompanies the representation result (asserting, for example, that the probability function is unique and that the utility function is unique up to a positive affine transformation).
3 Assume a euro today is worth the same euro in the future, or that values are so-adjusted.
4 Here we abuse our notation by writing σ(a,F) = €1, for instance, to express that σ(a,·) is a constant €1 on F.

References

Akerlof, G. A. (1970). The market for "lemons": Quality uncertainty and the market mechanism. *The Quarterly Journal of Economics* 84(3), 488–500.

Augustin, T., F. P. A., Coolen, G., de Cooman, and Troffaes, M. C. M. (2014). *Introduction to Imprecise Probabilities*. Chichester: Wiley.

Bernoulli, J. (1713). *Ars Conjectandi*. Basel: Thurnisius.

Boole, G. (1854). *An Investigation of the Laws of Thought*. New York: Dover.

Carnap, R. (1947). On the application of inductive logic. *Philosophy and Phenomenological Research* 8, 133–148.

de Finetti, B. (1974). *Theory of Probability: A Critical Introductory Treatment*, Vols 1 and 2. Chichester: John Wiley & Sons, Ltd.

Gigerenzer, G., and Brighton, H. (2009). *Homo heuristicus*: Why biased minds make better inferences. *Topics in Cognitive Science* 1(1), 107–143.

Good, I. J. (1967). On the principle of total evidence. *The British Journal for the Philosophy of Science* 17(4), 319–321.

Grünwald, P., and Halpern, J. Y. (2004). When ignorance is bliss. In J. Y. Halpern (Ed.), *Proceedings of the 20th Conference on Uncertainty in Artificial Intelligence (UAI '04)* (pp. 226–234). Arlington, VA: AUAI Press.

Hill, B. (2013). Dynamic consistency and ambiguity: A reappraisal. Technical Report ECO/SCD-2013–983. Paris: HEC Paris,

Kadane, J. B., Seidenfeld, T., and Schervish M. J. (2008). Is ignorance bliss? *Journal of Philosophy* 105(1), 5–36.

Keynes, J. M. (1921). *A Treatise on Probability*. London: Macmillan.

Knight, F. H. (1921). *Risk, Uncertainty and Profit*. Boston: Houghton Mifflin.

Lindley, D. V. (1965). *Introduction to Probability and Statistics*. Cambridge: Cambridge University Press.

Machina, M. J. (1989). Dynamic consistency and non-expected utility models of choice under uncertainty. *Journal of Economic Literature* 27(4), 1622–1668.

Osborne, M. J. (2003). *An Introduction to Game Theory*. Oxford: Oxford University Press.

Pedersen, A. P., and Wheeler, G. (2014). Demystifying dilation. *Erkenntnis* 79(6), 1305–1342.

Pedersen, A. P., and Wheeler, G. (2015). Dilation, disintegrations, and delayed decisions. In *Proceedings of the 9th Symposium on Imprecise Probabilities and Their Applications (ISIPTA)*, Pescara, Italy, pp. 227–236.

Raiffa, H., and Schlaiffer, R. (1961). *Applied Statistical Decision Theory*, Vol. 1 of *Studies in Managerial Economics*. Boston: Harvard Business School Publications.

Ramsey, F. P. (1931). *The Foundations of Mathematics and Other Essays*, vol. 1. New York: Humanities Press.

Savage, L. J. (1967). Difficulties in the theory of personal probability. *Philosophy of Science* 34(4), 311–325.

Savage, L. J. (1972). *Foundations of Statistics* (2nd ed.). New York: Dover.

Seidenfeld, T. (1994). When normal and extensive form decisions differ. In D. Prawitz, B. Skyrms, and D. Westerstahl (Eds.), *Logic, Methodology and Philosophy of Science*. Oxford: Elsevier Science B. V.

Seidenfeld, T., Schervish, M. J., and Kadane, J. B. (2012). What kind of uncertainty is that? Using personal probability for expressing one's thinking about logical and mathematical propositions. *Journal of Philosophy* 109(8–9), 516–533.

Seidenfeld, T., and Wasserman, L. (1993). Dilation for sets of probabilities. *The Annals of Statistics* 21(9), 1139–1154.

Siniscalchi, M. (2011). Dynamic choice under ambiguity. *Theoretical Economics* 6, 379–421.

Troffaes, M. C. M., and de Cooman, G. (2014). *Lower Previsions*. Chichester: Wiley.

von Neumann, J., and Morgenstern, O. (1944). *Theory of Games and Economic Behavior*. Princeton, NJ: Princeton University Press.

Wakker, P. (1988). Nonexpected utility as aversion of information. *Journal of Behavioral Decision Making* 1, 169–175.

Walley, P. (1991). *Statistical Reasoning with Imprecise Probabilities*. London: Chapman and Hall.

Wheeler, G. (2018). Bounded rationality. In E. N. Zalta (Ed.), *The Stanford Encyclopedia of Philosophy* (Winter 2018 ed.). Stanford, CA: Metaphysics Research Lab, Stanford University.

32

BOUNDED RATIONALITY AS THE COGNITIVE BASIS FOR EVOLUTIONARY ECONOMICS

Richard R. Nelson

A foundational feature of modern evolutionary economics[1] is its commitment both to a Schumpeterian perspective on modern capitalist economies as dynamic systems,[2] always evolving, with change being driven largely by innovation, and to the proposition developed by Herbert Simon and his colleagues that the behaviors of human and organizational actors should be understood as boundedly rational.[3] The way the presumption that economic actors are boundedly rational is employed in evolutionary economics is consistent in a broad sense with the way that concept has been used in other arenas of research and writing, but the contexts and modes of behavior treated go significantly beyond the more conventional orientation. The objective of this chapter is to explain why and how the presumption of individual and organizational bounded rationality has been used in evolutionary economics.

Innovation, continuing unpredictable change, and bounded rationality

The evolutionary economics described in this chapter is based on a perspective regarding what is going on in the economy that is very different from that presented in today's standard textbooks. The overarching difference is that evolutionary economists see continuing change, largely driven by innovation, as a central characteristic of modern capitalist economies. Evolutionary economists are Schumpeterian in that basic sense. This means that innovation, and operation in contexts where innovation-driven change is going on, are fundamental aspects of what economic actors do and the contexts in which they operate. Of course, economic sectors and activities differ in the pace and character of change. In many parts of the economy, innovation is rapid and continuing and the context for economic action taking is almost always shifting and providing new challenges and opportunities. And while in some activities and sectors, the rate of innovation is more limited, attempts at doing something new are going on almost everywhere in the economy, and so too change that can make obsolete old ways of doing things. This is a very different perspective on the nature and context for economic action taking than that described in the standard economics textbooks.

Proponents of the neoclassical economic theory that provides the intellectual scaffolding for the conventional view of what economic activity is all about never explain or rationalize how

DOI: 10.4324/9781315658353-37

economic actors come to be able to choose courses of action that are optimum for them, given their objectives and the context in which they are operating. It is highly relevant to our discussion here, however, that almost no formulation of that theory of behavior mentions attempts by economic actors to do something that has not been done before, or the difficulties they face when they are operating in contexts that they have not previously experienced. While in evolutionary economics not all situations are of these sorts, many of the most important are. And this has led us to develop a version of Simon's bounded rationality as our basic assumption about the cognitive strengths and limits of economic actors, and our theory of how they behave.

The perspective on economic behavior as mostly "boundedly rational" has the particular attractiveness for economists of being consonant with the traditional economic theory of behavior, going back to the days of Adam Smith, that sees economic actors doing what they do with purposes in mind and in many contexts at least a rough understanding of the consequences of following various courses of action. I believe that, treated with care, and recognizing human fallibility, this broad theoretical perspective has shown considerable explanatory and predictive power. The problem with the full-blown rational behavior theory of neoclassical economics is that it does not recognize these caveats, and they are particularly germane in contexts important to evolutionary economics.

The proposition that human rationality is bounded highlights that there are limits to the reasoning power of the human mind as well as of the knowledge and information actors can master and work with. As Simon has stressed, the contexts for human action very often are too complicated or subtle for actors to understand and take into account adequately the wide range of factors bearing on what they should be doing. I would like to add that this general argument is quite open to recognition of significant differences across contexts in the strength of human understanding.

However, I would propose that, to address the range of phenomena of particular interest to Schumpeterian economists, several distinctions and factors need to be highlighted much more than they have been to date in the literature on bounded rationality.

First, it is important to distinguish between choice contexts which are familiar to the economic actor and who responds to them more or less automatically by taking actions that have sufficed before in this kind of context, and contexts that induce the actor to engage in serious contemplation of alternatives. And where action taking is preceded by conscious deliberation, it is important to distinguish between contexts where the actor's attention is focused on courses of action the actor has followed before, perhaps in another context, and perhaps others well known in his community, and those that involve trying to do something new. Schumpeterian and evolutionary economists of course have a special interest in the latter – that is what innovation is all about – but innovation only can be understood in juxtaposition to more routine behavior, and more generally action taking that involves doing the familiar.

Second, particularly for understanding the kinds of phenomena that most interest Schumpeterian economists, it is important to recognize that actors differ in the capabilities that they bring to various choice contexts. They differ in their knowledge and experience, and in the skills they possess. For these reasons they may differ significantly in what they do in contexts that, to an outside observer, may look basically the same. And some will do better than others will. I note that this aspect of behavior – differences in capabilities – has received little attention from either main line economists, or scholars working with the theory that economic actors are boundedly rational. Yet differences in capabilities obviously are of central interest to Schumpeterian and evolutionary economists.

A third important limitation of most of the writings on economic behavior, including those oriented by the assumption of bounded rationality, that needs to be remedied is the failure to relate the perceptions of individual actors about the contexts they face, the courses of action that they understand and are competent to employ, and their judgments about which of these actions are appropriate and likely to be effective, to the beliefs and understandings and know-how of the broader community of which the actor is a part. This can and has been raised as a criticism of modern psychology in general. And it is hardly recognized in behavioral economics.

I want to argue that it is especially important that Schumpeterian economists clearly recognize the social and cultural context of action taking. We are centrally interested in how modern capitalist economies have become so productive, and the sources and mechanisms of future progress. When one observes powerful and complex methods being used by individuals and organizations to achieve their ends, it is almost a sure thing that the heart of the knowledge base of what they are doing is shared by their professional peers, and is acquired by individuals only as they are part of this broader community. And almost always powerful knowledge, common to professionals in a field of activity, has been achieved through a lengthy cultural learning process.

To return to the general theme, under the perspective on economic behavior and cognition I am describing here, economic actors are assumed to be boundedly rational. When in contexts that call for them to do something, they proceed with some notions about the outcomes they would like to see happen, a perception of at least some actions they might take that seem plausible, and some thoughts on which of these might be most appropriate. But the contexts they face differ widely, and they go about generating the actions they actually take in different ways in different kinds of contexts.

In contexts where change is relatively slow, actors are likely to respond to the requirement to do something by following patterns of behavior that they have used successfully before. In other situations, the context is different from what the actor has faced before, or while the context may be familiar, for various reasons the actor may want to consider a range of options before doing anything. Simon himself made this distinction in a number of his analyses, and this also is a distinction made by Daniel Kahneman (2011).[4] Sidney Winter has reminded me that John Dewey ([1922] 2002) presented a similar view of behavior, with perhaps more emphasis on the role played by emotion and anxiety in some contexts.

I note that Kahneman puts less weight than do I on the argument that routine behavior often is highly effective. Also, he seems to presume to a greater extent than do I that active deliberation is highly likely to come up with an effective course of action. It may or may not. I would propose that the chances are better that it will when the actor's own experience or the knowledge the actor has of what others have done effectively includes actions that will be effective in this context. Where dealing with the problem induces or requires a quite new attack on it, the chances of speedy success are slim. With continued effort and cogitation, success may be achieved thought trial and error learning. But it may not.

Innovating is a rational activity, in that those who try have particular objectives in mind and draw as best they can on the knowledge they have. But that rationality surely is bounded.

Routines

The range of actions that need to be taken even over a short period of time by an economic actor often is far too great for that actor to be able to think carefully before taking each required action. However, where the environment for action has been relatively tranquil, actors generally have had time to learn the kinds of action that works in that context and what doesn't. The argument above is that most of the actions one observes in such contexts should be understood as actors following routines that have in the past yielded satisfactory outcomes, and are triggered relatively automatically by circumstances under which action along these lines seems appropriate.

I suggest that individual or household shopping for the kinds of items bought relatively regularly largely involves following routines. In my recent paper with Davide Consoli (Nelson and Consoli, 2010) we propose that much of household behavior can be understood in terms of the routines they use. And of course a quite extensive empirical and theoretical literature exists, arguing that firm behavior largely involves the following of established routines.[5] In our earlier work, Sidney Winter and I used the term "routine" to characterize these aspects of firm behavior. Here I am using it to denote the relatively automatic behavior patterns of any economic actor.

The fact that little conscious thought is involved in the invoking and execution of a routine does not imply that routines are crude ways of doing things. The routines a store has for reordering stock and for setting prices may be quite elaborate, even though once in place they are carried out routinely. The operation of highly sophisticated technologies largely involves the use of routines. Many of the routines used by economic actors are very powerful and highly effective in meeting their objectives.

Also, routines need not be rigid. Indeed, viable routines generally have a reasonable amount of flexibility built into them to enable them to adjust to the kind of variable circumstances that are to be expected in the broad context where they are operative. Household shopping routines need to be sensitive to what is and is not available at the store, and to some degree to prices. Firm pricing routines need to take costs into account. But my argument is that in established shopping routines, these adjustments generally are made relatively routinely. There may be some conscious consideration of alternatives, but so long as the context remains in the normal range, wide search and intensive deliberation are highly unlikely. Similarly, the pricing routines of firms almost always are sensitive to costs, with much of that sensitivity, if not necessarily all, built into a formula used relatively routinely.

Elsewhere (Nelson, 2013), I have used the term "adaptively responsive" to denote the sensitivity of routines to broadly experienced and thus anticipated variation in the details of the context that invokes their use. My proposal is that most routines that are used for a significant time are adaptively responsive.

Economists of a neoclassical persuasion would be inclined to argue that routines persistently employed by an economic actor must be, in some sense, optimal. Proponents of the view that the rationality of economic actors is bounded would point out that the fact that behavior is reasonably effective, given the actors goals, and adaptively responsive to common variations in context for action taking, do not imply optimality. However, that an actor continues to use a particular routine indicates that the results are "satisfactory" in the sense that doing things in a significantly different way is not being actively considered.[6] On the other hand, of course, some of the actions that are carried out routinely by some actors are clearly clumsy, and some likely even counterproductive, given the objectives they aim to reach. An important challenge for evolutionary economics is to illuminate the conditions under which routines are effective, and those where they often are not.

From one point of view, to explain or predict what an economic actor does in a domain of activity marked by the use of routines, it is sufficient to identify and analyze the routines that are in use. And this is exactly what is done in studies like those reported in the classic book by Cyert and March (1963), *A Behavioral Theory of the Firm*.

But for the theory of behavior to have depth, it is important to understand why the routines in use are what they are. I have argued that the neoclassical mode of answering that question – to propose that they are optimal – is not convincing if one holds to a theory of bounded rationality, and wants an explanation, not simply a purported characterization, of observed behavior. Under evolutionary theory such an explanation needs to be posed in terms of learning and selection processes.

Deliberating, problem solving, choosing

The proposition that much of the economic behavior one observes at any time should be understood as actors following routines is not meant to play down the role of deliberation, problem solving, and often creativity in the generation of economic activity. These more active cognitive processes are brought into play when economic actors face contexts with which they are not familiar and for this or other reasons no established response seems appropriate, or more generally where the actor for whatever reason wants to do something new. And, of course, in many cases they are involved in the genesis of prevailing routines in the first place.

This perspective is, of course, very Schumpeterian. Chapter 1 of his *Theory of Economic Development* (Schumpeter, 1934) is all about routine activity in an economic steady state. In the actual economic world as we know it, no context is as constant as the context for economic action Schumpeter depicts in Chapter 1, or is laid out in general equilibrium theory. However, evolutionary economists would argue that at any time a good portion of economic activity proceeds in contexts that are regular enough so that behavior that follows an established routine can suffice to meet the actor's objectives, at least if the routine used has a certain amount of built in flexibility.

In Chapter 2, Schumpeter describes a very different kind of economic behavior: innovation. Innovation is creative by desire or necessity, uncertain as to success, often failing, sometimes winning big. But involving thinking and problem solving in an essential way.

In recent years cognitive scientists have significantly improved our understanding of how the cognitive capabilities and practices of human beings differ from those of other higher animals; the most interesting comparisons have been with other primates.[7] There would appear to be two basic capabilities that humans have that other primates do not. One is built in biologically. The other, while based on this, is essentially cultural.

Other animals share with humans the ability to solve problems by doing different things until they find something that works, and then carrying over what has been learned to subsequent experiences with situations like that. But humans have the ability, that even other primates have to a far lesser degree, to in effect reflect on a context or a way of doing something (perhaps something they have observed others doing) even when that context is not present or that action not being actually implemented, in effect, anticipating future situations and actions.[8] Thus, the kind of deliberation we are considering here would seem to be a capability that is largely unique to humans.

And humans are unique in having the capacity for cumulative collective learning. While the cutting edge of progress generally has been discovery or trying out of a new method by an individual actor, major advances over time have depended on the spread across the community of what has been learned, and the further building on that by others.[9] The development of shared language has been essential for this to happen to any major extent. There is no question that the ability of humans to reflect and gather and process relevant knowledge prior to action is an important capability in its own right. However, I would argue that, in the absence of strong cultural know-how that has been developed over time through collective learning on which that capability can draw, what human reflection can achieve on its own is modest.

In my view, Schumpeter draws too sharp a line between innovating, and the imitative responses by followers to the innovations of others. The latter also requires ability to conceptualize a way of doing something that is new for the particular actor, and often involves considerable uncertainty.

However, what is a new situation or new activity for a particular actor will tend to be conceived very differently if that actor knows about and can draw on the experience of other actors, than if the actor is all alone, as it were. Much of what actors do that is new to them is invoked by their knowledge of the experience of others. The abandonment by an actor of an old routine and the adoption of a new one may be induced simply by knowledge that others are doing something different and doing well, as contrasted with any compelling evidence that the old routine is not yielding satisfactory results. While direct imitation often is not easy, and the efforts of one economic actor to do what another is doing may achieve something somewhat or widely different, at any time a shared body of know-how provides the basis for the range of activities used in a field, and is the reason why one generally observes a certain amount of similarity in what the various actors are doing.

Innovation and the advance of know-how

While I believe the lines are blurred not sharp, the term "innovation" as contrasted with "imitation" connotes an endeavor by an actor to do something new not only to that actor, but to the community of actors doing roughly similar things. Empirical research shows clearly that innovators, like imitators, almost always draw heavily on know-how, and more general knowledge, possessed by their peer community. And a large share of innovation is based on and aims to improve artifacts and processes that are in use, often used by the innovator. But innovators are reaching beyond what has been done before. And if they are successful, what they have achieved sooner or later becomes part of the knowledge base shared by that community. That is, know-how in an area of economic activity advances over time through an evolutionary process driven largely by the innovation going on.

The principal difference between the orientation of evolutionary and Schumpeterian economists, and that of today's more orthodox orientation to the study of economics, is our focus on innovation. Our argument is that what makes economic activity today so effective in meeting a wide variety of human wants is that the means we have available to achieve our ends have become so powerful as the result of cumulative innovation. It is not because economic decision makers are so effective. Human economic decision making remains, as it always has been, often mechanical, sometimes creative, but in these cases often mistake-ridden. Human rationality is bounded.

While there has been considerable research over the years by scholars of management on what makes firms successful, there is little evidence that firm managers today are more effective than firm managers were a half century or a century ago. The failure rates of new firms, and of new ventures by established firms, remains high. Business management remains an art, in which luck is an important factor determining success.

The situation is similar regarding household purchases and other decisions regarding how they spend their money. It is not for naught that we have in place a number of regulatory agencies justified explicitly by the proposition that households often have limited understanding of what they are buying. Wesley Clair Mitchell's *The Backward Art of Spending Money*, published in 1912, rings as true today as it was then.

However, boundedly rational human actors can achieve remarkably good outcomes, if the know-how they have to work with, the means they know how to use, are good enough.

And where powerful know-how is available, and one observes highly effective human action going on, the principal reason is not so much that someone or some organization has effectively thought through the background problem and surmised, or calculated, a good way of doing things in that context, but rather that there has been a lot of collective learning going on generally over a considerable period of time that, cumulatively, has led to the development of ways of doing things that work reasonably, or even extraordinarily, well. Thus, a key part of the theory of behavior and cognition that we need is a theory of how collective learning occurs.

Attempts at innovation clearly are the key driving force. However, a key premise of evolutionary economics, amply supported by empirical evidence, is that the efforts of economic actors to venture beyond established practice almost always are associated with uncertain outcomes (see Dosi and Nelson, 2010, for a broad review). While in areas where knowledge is reasonably strong, innovative efforts are far from blind, nonetheless all areas of innovative activity are marked by failures as well as successes, and even the most knowledgeable experts sometimes turn out to be wrong. A fundamental consequence is that, while economic progress certainly depends on the creative efforts of individual inventors and innovators, it depends at least as much on the existence of a number of potential innovators holding somewhat different perceptions of the most promising routes to advance, with competition in ex-post practice being a large part of the selection process determining the winners. And continuing progress depends on the essence of what has been achieved in one round of innovative effort becoming part of the collective knowledge base for the next round.

Put more generally, the remarkable increases in human knowhow that have been achieved over the years have been the result of the work of boundedly rational human actors, operating in a dynamic evolutionary context in which at any time effective new ways of doing things are separated from the not-so-good, and brought into wider practice. And in turn this sets the stage for the next round of efforts to advance the state of the art, which in turn are subject to selection mechanisms.

A brief summing up

Earlier I noted that, since the times of Adam Smith, economists observing the behavior of economic actors in the contexts in which they had a central interest have assessed these behaviors as largely reasonably rational, given the actors' apparent objectives, and the range of options they faced.

But over the past half-century, modern neoclassical economics has transformed what had been a quite flexible view of what "rationality" means into the much narrower notion that economic actors "optimized." Evolutionary economists have not been alone in arguing that this has been a very unfortunate development. Our position is that the presumption that economic actors mostly behave rationally is a powerful and useful theoretical position to take so long as that rationality is understood as bounded. The conception of rational behavior must have room for both creativity and habit, for both insightful understanding of the situation, and biased or simply ignorant views of what is going on.

I believe that the kind of perspective on economic behavior and cognition that I have sketched here, based on the presumption that economic behavior is "boundedly rational" and recognizing important differences associated with different kinds of contexts and conditions, has the promise of doing this. It provides a much better and richer characterization of economic behavior that is for the most part purposeful and functional than the theory of full-blown optimization that neoclassical theory is stuck with. It is applicable across a much wider spectrum of conditions. And for those who care about such matters, it provides an explanation for much of economic behavior that one actually can believe.

Notes

1 Key references here are Nelson and Winter (1982), and Nelson and colleagues (2018).
2 This perspective is first laid out in Schumpeter (1934).
3 The most relevant references for our discussion here are Simon (1957) and Cyert and March (1963).
4 These two different modes of action taking were built into most of the models developed in Nelson and Winter (1982).
5 For a fine review of the literature on organizational routines, see Becker (2004).
6 This is Herbert Simon's concept of "satisficing."
7 Donald (1991) provides a splendid discussion of these and related matters.
8 There is some evidence that certain other animals have this capability, but to a very limited degree.
9 Other species have the capability of spreading the effective behaviors learned by one individual to others in the community, but not of building further and cumulatively from that.

References

Becker, M. (2004). Organizational routines: A review of the literature, *Industrial and Corporate Change*, 13(4), 643–678.
Cyert, R., and March, J. (1963). *A Behavioral Theory of the Firm*, Englewood Cliffs, NJ: Prentice Hall.
Dewey, J. (2002 [1922]). *Human Nature and Conduct*, Minola, NY: Henry Holt.
Donald, M. (1991). *Origins of the Modern Mind*, Cambridge, MA: Harvard University Press.
Dosi, G., and Nelson, R. (2010). Technical change and industrial dynamics as evolutionary processes, in B. Hall and N. Rosenberg (Eds.), *Economics of Innovation*, Amsterdam Elsevier.
Kahneman, D. (2011). *Thinking, Fast and Slow*, New York Macmillan.
Mitchell, W. C. (1912). The backward art of spending money, *American Economic Review*, June, 269–281.
Nelson, R. (2013). Demand, supply, and their interaction on markets as seen from the perspective of evolutionary economic theory, *Journal of Evolutionary Economics*, 23(1), 17–38.
Nelson, R., and Consoli, D. (2010). An evolutionary theory of household behavior, *Journal of Evolutionary Economics*, 20(5), 665–687.
Nelson, R., Dosi, G., Helfat, C., Pyka, A., Saviotti, P., ... Dopfer, K. (2018) *An Overview of Modern Evolutionary Economics*, Cambridge: Cambridge University Press.
Nelson, R., and Winter, S. (1982). *An Evolutionary Theory of Economic Change*, Cambridge, MA: Harvard University Press.
Schumpeter, J. (1934), *The Theory of Economic Development*, Cambridge, MA: Harvard University Press,
Simon, H. (1957), *Models of Man*, New York: John Wiley & Sons, Inc.

33

BEYOND "BOUNDED RATIONALITY"

Behaviours and learning in complex evolving worlds

Giovanni Dosi, Marco Faillo, and Luigi Marengo

Introduction

Let us begin by the very notion of bounded rationality. Should we assume that there is an "unbounded" rationality as a benchmark? Should one start, in order to describe and interpret human behaviour from a model which assumes that we, human beings, have complete and well-defined knowledge of our preferences, all possible states of the world, all possible actions (our "technologies"), and the mappings among them?[1]

Savage was extremely careful in limiting his choice-theoretic exercise to the normative domain and to "small worlds", i.e., stationary and isolated portions of the world wherein decision makers know the full set of possible events and can attribute probabilities to them (Savage, 1954).

Jumping from this normative small world domain to the descriptive framework where one builds theory of human behaviour in a complex world, characterized by radical uncertainty, a multiplicity of interactive agents, and persistent endogenous innovation – we suggest – is deeply misleading. Having "Olympic rationality" as a benchmark is like starting from the thermo-dynamic equilibrium death with full entropy in order to interpret the biological world!

Rather, the question should be: how do human agents and organizations thereof behave in complex and changing environments? Answering this question, we suggest, entails also a significant departure from what is now accepted as behavioural economics, often meant as the analysis of more or less significant deviations – called "biases" – from the "Olympic rationality". On the contrary, we suggest, human beings and human organizations behave quite distinctively from the prescriptive model derived from the axioms of rationality.

As is well known, the standard decision-theoretic model depicts agency (and, *in primis*, economic agency) as a problem of choice where rational actors select, among a set of alternative courses of action, the one which will produce (in expectation) the maximum outcome as measured against some utility yardstick. In that, agents are postulated to know the entire set of possible events of "nature", all possible actions which are open to them, and all notional outcomes of the mapping between actions and events (or at least come to know them after some learning process). Clearly, these are quite demanding assumptions on knowledge embodied into or accessible to the agents – which hardly apply to complex and changing environments. In

DOI: 10.4324/9781315658353-38

fact, they *cannot* apply almost by definition in all environments where innovations of some kind are allowed to occur – irrespective of whether they relate to technologies, behavioural repertoires or organizational arrangements. If an innovation is truly an innovation, it could not have been in the set of events that all agents were able to contemplate before the innovation actually occurred.

Moreover, equally demanding are the implicit assumptions concerning the *procedural rationality* involved in the decision process.

As a paradigmatic illustration, take the usual decision-theoretic sequence leading from (1) representation/"understanding" of the environment (conditional on whatever available "information"), to (2) evaluation/judgement; (3) choice; (4) actions, and, ultimately, (5) consequences – determined, e.g., by the stochastic pairing of actions and "events of nature" and/or actions by other agents.

In order for this "rationalist" view to hold, at least two assumptions are crucial. First, the linearity of that sequence must strictly hold. That is, one must rule out the possibility of reversing, so to speak, the procedural sequence. For example, one cannot have preferences and representations which adapt to an action that has already been undertaken. and, likewise, one must assume that consequences do not influence preferences (i.e. preferences are not endogenous).

Second, at each step of the process agents must be endowed with, or able to build, the appropriate algorithm in order to tackle the task at hand – whether it is representing the environment, evaluating alternatives or choosing courses of action, etc.

There are, indeed, a few rather compelling reasons why these assumptions might be a misleading starting point for any *positive* theory of learning and choice.

Human agents tackle every day, with varying degrees of success, highly complex and "hard" (in the sense of computability theory) problems with their highly limited computational capabilities. Cognitive sciences have made impressive progress in the recent decades in understanding how we do that. We are bad in processing information, we cannot handle more than a very limited number of the overwhelming number of interdependencies the characterize our world, but nevertheless we go along, sometimes decently well, with simple but useful representations and simple but effective heuristics. As suggested by Gigerenzer and his group, such heuristics are not the outcome of our biases, although they may sometimes produce them (Gigerenzer et al., 1999). On the contrary it is their very simplicity which makes them "smart", and generally well adapted to the complex and fast-changing world in which we live. They require simple representations and neglect part of the available information, that is, they radically depart from that model of rationality which assumes correct representation and unlimited information processing capabilities, but, on the contrary, excel in simplicity, frugality, adaptability, i.e., features with are not even considered in the rational choice framework. "Olympic rationality", in fact, implies the availability of some inferential machinery able to extract the "correct" information from environmental signals, Bayes rule being one of them, and possibly also the most demanding in terms of what the agents must know from the start about alternative hypotheses on what the world "really is". But, again, such an inferential machinery cannot be innocently postulated. Indeed, outside the rather special domain of "small worlds" whose structure is known *ex ante* to the agents, a few impossibility theorems from computation theory tell us that a generic inferential procedure does not and cannot exist (more on this point in Binmore, 1990; Dosi and Egidi, 1991; Dosi et al., 1994). This applies even more to so-called "Rational Expectations". It has repeatedly been shown that agents cannot generically learn even in simple stationary environment, and less so in complex evolving ones. More than that: under the latter circumstances trying sophisticated forms of learning is bad for the agents – in terms of prediction and performance – and is bad for the system – in terms of its growth and stability (on both points, see the discussion and the results from Dosi, Napoletano, Roventini, Stiglitz, and Trebich, 2017).[2]

Complexity arguments also imply a radical critique to the idea that "rationality" – however defined – rather than being an approximation to the empirical behaviours of purposeful, cognitively quite sophisticated, agents, could be, so to speak, an "objective" property of behaviours in equilibrium. Add the presumption that (most) observed behaviours are indeed *equilibrium* ones. And finally postulate some dynamics of individual adaptation or intra-population selection leading there. What one gets is some version of the famous "as...if" hypothesis, suggested by Milton Friedman (1953) and rejuvenated in different fashions by more recent efforts to formalize learning/adaptation processes whose outcome is precisely the "rationality" assumed from the start (archetypical examples of this faith can be found in Sargent, 1993, and McGrattan and Marimon, 1995).

A thorough, critical, discussion of the "as...if" epistemology has been put forward by Sidney Winter, in various essays (e.g., Winter, 1971) to which we refer the interested reader (and see also Silverberg, 1988; Andersen, 1994 and Hodgson, 1988).

For our purposes here, let us just note the following:

1 Any "as...if" hypothesis on rationality, taken seriously, is bound to involve quite a few restrictions similar to those briefly overviewed earlier with reference to more "constructive" notions of rational behaviours, simply transposed into a more "ecological" dimension – whether it is the "ecology" of minds, ideas, organisations, populations, etc. That is, canonical rationality, *stricto sensu*, postulates that one decides and acts by purposefully using the appropriate procedures (or by learning them in purposeful, procedurally coherent, ways). "As...if"'s of any kind apparently relax the demands on what agents must consciously know about the environment, their goals, the process of achieving them, but at the same time must assume some background mechanism that generates the available alternatives – *which must include the "correct" ones*. However, without any further knowledge of the specific mechanisms, such a possibility remains a very dubious shortcut. And it is utterly unlikely when there are infinite alternatives which ought to be scanned.

2 While "realistic" interpretations of rationality put most of the burden of explanation upon the power of inbuilt cognition, "as...if" accounts shift it to selection dynamics – no matter whether driven by behavioural reinforcements alike salivating Pavlovian dogs, or by differential reproduction of traits within populations.[3] But, then, supporters of the view ought to show, at the very least, robust convergence properties of some *empirically justifiable* selection dynamics. As it stands, in our view, nothing like that is in sight. On the contrary, except for very special set-ups, negative results are abundant in e.g., evolutionary games or other forms of decentralized interactions – no matter whether applied to biology or economics – path-dependency cannot easily be disposed of; cyclical limit behaviours might occur (cf. Posch, 1997, Marengo and Pasquali (2011), and Kaniovski et al., 1997), etc. And all this appears even before accounting for environments which are genuinely evolutionary in the sense that novelties can emerge over time.

But, even more importantly, we can add that, in complex worlds, selection is almost powerless as an optimization mechanism. If the entities under selection have some internal structure made up of many interdependent components, such structural properties pose huge constraints on the evolution, and selection alone cannot break such a constraint (Kauffman, 1993). For instance, in biological evolution, the question whether an organism is optimal is nonsensical.

No doubt that standing on two legs has given us some useful evolutionary advantage, but is also a cause of many "inefficiencies" (back and knee weakness, difficulties in giving birth, etc.). Again, Gigerenzer and colleagues suggest an idea of "ecological rationality" rather than Olympic rationality, i.e., a system of heuristics that have co-evolved (Todd and Gigerenzer, 2012) and may all be suboptimal (whatever this may mean) if taken separately, but together produce a decently working system.

Another major perspective maintains that cognitive and behavioural assumptions must keep some empirical foundations and, thus, when needed, account for constraints on memory, on the maximum levels of complexity of problem-solving algorithms, and on computational time. It is, in a broad sense, the *bounded rationality* approach, pioneered by the works of Simon (1986) and developed in quite different fashions in e.g., organizational studies (starting from March and Simon, 1958 and Cyert and March, 1963); evolutionary theories (building on Nelson and Winter, 1982; see also Dosi et al., 1988; Hodgson, 1993; Andersen, 1994); "evolutionary games" (for a rather technical overview, cf. Weibull, 1995; for insightful remarks on bounded rationality and games in general, Kreps, 1996, and also in otherwise quite orthodox macroeconomics, see e.g., Sargent, 1993). Again, this is not the place to undertake any review of this vast literature. However, few comments are required.

Of course, the very idea of "bounds" on rationality implies that, at least in finite time, agents so represented fall short of full *substantively rational* behaviours, the latter involving among other things, (1) a full knowledge of all possible contingencies; (2) an exhaustive exploration of the entire decision tree; and (3) a correct appreciation of the utility evaluations of all mappings between actions, events and outcomes (Simon, 1986).

Given that, a first issue concerns the characterization of the origins and nature of the "boundedness" itself. It is not at all irrelevant whether it relates mainly to limitations on the memory that agents carry over from the past, or to algorithmic complexity of the decision problem to be addresses, or to limited ability of defining preferences over (expected) outcomes.

Or, more radically, couldn't it be due to the fact that agents get it basically wrong (in terms of representation of the environment, etc.)?

Here the theory faces a subtle but crucial crossroads. One alternative – unfortunately found too often in economic models, and especially but not only, in game theory – is to select the bounded-rationality assumptions with extreme casualness, suspiciously well-fitted to the mathematics the authors know and to the results one wants to obtain. We have no problem in associating ourselves to those who denounce the ad hocry of the procedure. The other alternative entails the acknowledgement of an *empirical discipline* upon the restrictions one puts upon the purported rationality of the agents. No doubt, we want to advocate here the scientific soundness of this procedure, notwithstanding the inevitable "phenomenological" diversity of cognitive and behavioural representations one is likely to get. That is, whether and how "rationality is bound" is likely to depend on the nature of the decision problem at hand, the context in which the decision-maker is placed, the pre-existing learning skills of the agents, etc. Taxonomical exercises are inevitable, with their seemingly clumsy reputation. But, in a metaphor inspired by Keith Pavitt, this is a bit like the comparison of Greek to modern chemistry. The former, based on the symmetry of just four elements, was very elegant, grounded in underlying philosophical principles, utterly irrelevant, and, from what we know nowadays, essentially wrong. The latter is clumsy, taxonomic, and for a long time (until quantum mechanics) lacking underlying foundations, but is certainly descriptively and operationally more robust.

A second major issue, regards *procedural* rationality. Granted the bounds on "substantive" rational agency, as defined above, when and to what extent should one maintain any assumption of coherent purposefulness and logical algorithmic consistency of the agents?[4] In a first approximation, Simon's approach suggests such a theoretical commitment (associated indeed to major contributions to the identification of *constructive* procedures for learning and problem-solving in this vein (Newell and Simon, 1972; Simon, 1976). However, even procedural consistency might not be at all a generic property of empirical agents, and a lot of evidence from most social disciplines seems to point in this direction.

Third, and relatedly, the very notion of "bounded rationality" (of, we repeat, the vast majority of contemporary economists, though not of Herbert Simon) commits from the start to an implicit idea that "full rationality" is the underlying yardstick for comparison. In turn, this implies the possibility of identifying some metrics upon which "boundedness" and, dynamically, learning efforts could be measured and assessed. In quite a few circumstances this can be fruitfully done[5] but in others it might not be possible either in practice or even in principle. In particular, this applies to search and learning in complex functional spaces (as many problems within and outside the economic arena commonly do).[6] And, of course, this is also the case of most problems involving discovery and/or adaptation to novelty.

Since indeed these features are typical of evolutionary environments, an implication is that one might need to go well beyond a restricted notion of "bounded rationality", simply characterized as an imperfect approximation to a supposedly "full" one – which, in these circumstances, one is even unable to define what it should precisely be.

But then, again, how does one represent learning agents in these circumstances? Our somewhat radical suggestion is that evolutionary theories ought to make a much greater and systematic use of the evidence from other cognitive and social sciences as sort of "building blocks" for the hypotheses on cognition, learning and behaviours that one adopts. We fully realize that such a perspective almost inevitably entails the abandonment of any invariant axiomatics of decision and choice. But, to paraphrase Thaler (1992), this boils down again to the alternative between being "vaguely right" or "precisely wrong": we certainly advocate the former (however, compare McGrattan and Marimon (1995) for a sophisticated contrary view).

In this respect, the discussion of *routines* as foundational behavioural assumptions of evolutionary models in Nelson and Winter (1982) is an excellent example of the methodology we have in mind, unfortunately not pursued enough in subsequent evolutionary studies (see Cohen et al., 1996; Becker 2004; Becker et al., 2005).

There are, however, many other fields where a positive theory of learning in economics can draw, ranging from cognitive and social psychology all the way to anthropology and sociology of knowledge.

Cognitive categories and problem solving

A crucial aspect of learning regards most often *cognition*, that is the process by which decision makers form and modify representations in order to make some sense of a reality which is generally too complex and uncertain to be fully understood. Hence, the necessity to acknowledge the existence (and persistence) of a systematic gap between the agents' cognitive abilities and "reality" (were there an omniscient observer able to fully grasp it). Such a gap can take at least two often interrelated forms,[7] namely, first, the *knowledge gap*, involving incomplete, fuzzy or simply wrong representations of the environment and, second, a *problem-solving* gap between the complexity of the tasks agents face and their capabilities in accomplishing them.

Regarding both, evolutionary theories of learning might significantly benefit from that branch of cognitive studies concerned with the nature and changes of *categories and mental models* (in different perspectives, cf. Johnson-Laird, 1983; Holland et al., 1986; Lakoff, 1987; Margolis, 1987; and the presentation of a few alternative theories in Mayer, 1992). It is crucial to notice that, if one accepts any "mental model" view, learning cannot be reduced to information-acquisition (possibly *cum* Bayesian processing of it), but rather is centred around the construction of new cognitive categories and "models of the world".

In turn, a robust evidence shows that cognitive categories are not clear-cut constructions with sharp boundaries and put together in fully consistent interpretative models. Rather, they seem to display (in all our minds!) blurred contours, shaded by an intrinsic fuzziness, held around some cognitively guiding "prototypes", and organized together in ill-structured systems kept operational also via a lot of default hierarchies (cf. on all those points, see Tversky and Kahneman, 1982; Holland et al., 1986; Kahneman and Tversky, 1986; Lakoff, 1987; Hahn and Ramscar, 2001; Gärdenfors, 2004; Fehr, 2005).[8] In this domain, note, however, a subtle but fundamental difference: is "prototypization" a "bias" or an inherent property of cognitive categorization? That is, is it similar to e.g., anchoring biases, *à la* Tversky and Kahneman, in principle still linkable to Olympic rationality with variable doses of "boundedness"? Or, on the contrary, is it intimately related to the very nature of mental categories? The answer we suggest is indeed in favour of the latter interpretation.[9]

Framing and social embeddedness

Cognitive categories, it has repeatedly been shown, go together with various mechanisms of *framing* by which information is interpreted and also rendered operationally meaningful to the decision makers (cf. Kahneman et al., 1982; Borcherding et al., 1990; March, 1994).

Frames appear to be indeed a ubiquitous feature of both decision making and learning. What one understands is filtered by the cognitive categories that one holds and the repertoires of elicited problem-solving skills depend on the ways the problem itself is framed. That is, framing effects occurs along all stages of the decision process – affecting representations, judgements and the selection of behaviours (cf. Kahneman et al., 1982), and, concerning the patterns of activation of experts' skills (Ericsson and Smith, 1991).

As James March put it:

> Decisions are framed by beliefs that define the problem to be addressed, the information that must be collected, and the dimensions that must be evaluated. Decision makers adopt paradigms to tell themselves what perspective to take on a problem, what questions should be asked, and what technologies should be used to ask the questions. Such frames focus attention and simplify analysis. They direct attention to different options and different preferences. A decision will be made in one way if it is framed as a problem of maintaining profits and in a different way if it is framed as a problem of maintaining market share. A situation will lead to different decisions if it is seen as being about "the value of innovation" rather than "the importance of not losing face".
>
> *1994, p. 14*

Note that in this view, "frames" include a set of (non-necessarily consistent) beliefs over "what the problem is" and the goals that should be achieved in that case; cognitive categories deemed to be appropriate to the problem; and a related menu of behavioural repertoires.

Moreover, framing mechanisms appear at different levels of cognitive and behavioural observation: they do so in rather elementary acts of judgement and choice, but are also a general organizing principle of social experience and collective interactions (Bateson, 1972; Goffman, 1974).

One can intuitively appreciate also the links between framing processes and *social embeddedness* of both cognition and action.[10]

Frames, in the broad definition given above, have long been recognized in the sociological, psychological and anthropological literature (whatever name is used to refer to them) as being grounded in the collective experience of the actors and in the history of the institutions in which agency is nested.[11]

Indeed, embeddedness seems to go a striking long way and affect even the understanding and use of cognitively basic categories, such as that of causality and the very processes by which humans undertake basic operations, such as inferences, generalisations, deductions, etc. (Luria, 1976; Lakoff, 1987; D'Andrade, 2001; Kitayama, 2002; Oyserman and Lee, 2008).

Far away from standard rationality, a long and unjustly forgotten broadly defined Austrian tradition has tried to capture cognition and decision outside the straitjacket of the "max-something" framework. Hayek's "Sensory Order" (Hayek, 1952) is probably the most sophisticated synthesis of that view which

> not only emphasizes that the only ways open to people for making sense of their environment are the ways they already possess (the environment does not dictate how they see it), and whose probabilistic analysis of how the 'ways' at a person's disposal get called upon (the probabilities being a function of recent use and cumulative use) to see if there is a match with incoming stimuli provides a 'plastic' view of the mind.[12]

Related to Hayek's Sensory Order, are the ideas of Personal Construct Psychology (Kelly, 1955), in which the organizational structure that an individual creates to make sense of the world limits her permeability to new ways of thinking. This line of thinking was first applied in economics in Loasby (1983), where it is argued that organizational change is problematic if "core" constructs are involved, even if what is going on in the firm's environment may require the development of a new construct in order to adapt and survive.

A somewhat parallel and almost entirely distinct literature focuses upon the crucial role of tacit knowledge (Polanyi, 1966). Building on that notion, behavioural and evolutionary economists have made a fruitful use of habits and, collectively, routines (see below) in order to characterize behavioural patterns.

By "genuinely behavioural" we mean that interpretative tradition which tries to characterize behavioural regularities in their own right (archetypical examples are Cyert and March, 1992, and March and Simon, 1958) as distinct from the somewhat more restrained approach to the description of actual behaviours in terms of deviations from some normative notion of prefect rationality as discussed above.

First, even in the simplest setups including stationary environments, satisficing behaviour may yield a probability of surviving for ever, while maximizing ones are sure to yield death to inferior options in finite time (Dutta and Radner, 1999). That is the exact opposite to the "as if" hypothesis.

Second, heuristics tend to be "fast and frugal", meaning that they are rules of thumb for decision making that are ecologically sound, simple enough to operate when time, information and computation are limited and grounded in human psychological capabilities, such as memory and perception (Gigerenzer and Goldstein, 1996).

Third, in largely unknown environments, even if stationary in their fundamentals, higher "competence gaps" may hinder the agent's capacity to assess which behaviour is the most appropriate in which environmental conditions. Behavioural inertia is the outcome, other things being equal, of higher environmental dynamics: "uncertainty is the basic source of predictable behaviour ... [T]he flexibility of behaviour to react to information is constrained to the smaller behavioural repertoires that can be reliably administered" (Heiner, 1983, p. 585). Indeed, this insightful conjecture from a strikingly neglected path-breaking demonstration is explored in Dosi, Napoletano, Roventini, Stiglitz, and Trebich, 2017), together with its applicability to non-stationary environment.

Fourth, and closer to our concern here, memory does not involve primarily information on past events (say, the memory of an econometrician going back in her time series), but rather memory of heuristics – both in their pattern recognition side and behavioural one.

From individuals to organizations

As already mentioned, one side of the story is, in a broad sense, cognitive. The view of organizations as fragmented and multidimensional interpretation systems is grounded on the importance of collective information processing mechanisms that yield shared understandings (Daft and Weick, 1984), or "cognitive theories" (Argyris and Schön, 1978), of the environment in which they operate, and that assist organizations to bear uncertainty, besides, as we shall see, manage environmental and problem-solving complexity. If one subscribes to the notion that organizational learning is a process of refinement of shared cognitive frames involving action-outcome relationships (Duncan and Weiss, 1979), and that this knowledge is retained – at least for some time – and can be recalled upon necessity, this is like saying that organizational learning is in fact the process of building an organizational memory. This cognitive part of the memory is made up of "mental artefacts" embodying shared beliefs, interpretative frameworks, codes and cultures by which the organization interprets the state of the environment and its own "internal states" (Levitt and March, 1988).

Together, there is an operational side to the organizational memory involving the coupling between stimuli (events and signals, both external and internal ones) with responses (actions), making up a set of rules that remain available to guide the orientation of the organization and execute its operations. In this domain, memory largely relates to the ensemble of organizational routines – patterned actions that are employed as responses to environmental or internal stimuli, possibly filtered and elaborated via the elements of cognitive memory (much more on routines in Nelson and Winter, 1982; Cohen et al., 1996; Becker, 2004; Becker et al., 2005, and the literature reviewed here). As Cohen and Bacdayan (1994) put it, this procedural side is the "memory of how things are done", bearing a close resemblance to individual skills and habits, often with relatively automatic and unarticulated features (p. 554).

Cognitive and operational memories entail an "if...then" structure. Signals from the environment, as well as from other parts of the organization, elicit particular cognitive responses, conditional upon the "collective mental models" that the organization holds, which are in turn conditional upon the structure of its cognitive memory. Cognitive memory maps signals from an otherwise unknown world into "cognitive states" (e.g., "... this year the conditions of the market are such that demand for X is high ..."). Conversely, the operational memory elicits operating routines in response to cognitive states ("... produce X ..."), internal states of the organization ("...prepare the machine M to start producing piece P..."") and also environmental feedbacks ("... after all X is not selling too well ..."). In turn, the organizational memory embodies the specific features of what an organization "thinks" and does, and what it is "good at", that is, its distinct capabilities.[13]

Modelling routines, memory and learning

For a long time all the way to the present, organizational models have run far behind the qualitative interpretations briefly discussed above. Some catching-up has occurred, however, especially in the field of modelling learning processes in high dimensional spaces with relatively limited adaptation mechanisms. A promising candidate to model routines and memory finds its roots into the formalism of Classifier Systems (CSs) (Holland, 1975; Holland et al., 1986). In a nutshell, a CS is a system of interlinked condition/action rules that partly evolves according to the revealed environmental payoffs.

Dosi, Marengo, Paraskevopoulou and Valente (2017) present a model which links Classifiers Systems and NK fitness landscape models (Kauffman, 1993). The former provides a model of a memory system that accounts for both cognitive and operational memory, while they use the latter to represent an environment in which exogenous environmental traits and organizational actions or policies interact in a complex way to determine the organization fitness or payoff. While in standard NK models (e.g., Levinthal, 1997), cognition, actions and resulting payoffs are folded together in a mapping between "traits" and their "fitness", they unfold such a map, explicitly defining the cognition/action/environmental feedbacks and modelling their (evolving) coupling. This is, we believe, a first major advance with respect to the existing literature. The organization explores a complex and possibly changing landscape in which some dimensions are outside its control (the environmental traits) and some are within (the action traits). Since the former contribute to determine the payoff of the latter, the organization must base its search over the action landscape on an internal representation (its cognition) of the environmental landscape. When the landscape is complex enough and the organization has cognitive and memory bounds, such an internal representation can only be partial, imperfect and possibly wrong. However, in practice, through the accumulation of experience, organizations can develop better representations that enable them to act successfully in such a complex environment. This is a way of saying that organizations painstakingly and imperfectly learn and develop models of their environment. However, there is an exogenous world "out there" which is indeed the object of learning, and which of course is not controlled by the organization. Rather the organization has to learn what to do – the know-how – conditional on (what it believes to be) the characteristics of the landscape mapping the combinations of state-of-the-world and actions into payoffs. This is also another major difference vis-à-vis the NK modelling style wherein the "blackboxing" renders all the landscape notionally under the control of the agent. Moreover, the CS formalism allows a straightforward study of learning via non-local search, which, if undertaken at all in NK frameworks, turns out to be quite arbitrary.

In fact, the characteristics and evolution of organizational memory mirror the characteristics and evolution of organizational routines. In the case of routines, the memory elicits a "relatively complex pattern of behaviour triggered by a relatively small number of initiating signals or choices" (Cohen et al., 1996). How small or big is the initiating set of signals in itself is an important interpretative question, which has to do with the ways the organization categorizes environmental and intra-organizational information. And, likewise, the behavioural patterns are likely to display different degrees of conditionality upon particular sets of signals. So, at one extreme, the action pattern might be totally unconditional and "robust": "perform a given sequence of actions irrespectively of the perceived state of the world". At the opposite extreme actions might be very contingent on the fine structure of the "if" part, detailing very precisely the environmental conditions triggering the action part.

Conclusion

A multi-millennial tradition of Western thought has asked "how do people behave?" and "how do social organization behave?", from Aristotle to St Augustin, Hume, Adam Smith, Kant, to name only a few giants. However, modern economics – and more recently social sciences colonized by modern economics – have taken up the answer by one of the shallowest thinkers, Bentham: people decide their courses of action by making calculations on the expected pleasures and pains associated with them. And, indeed, this *Weltanschauung* has spread all the way to the economics of marriage, of child bearing, of church going, of torture… (some more comments in Dosi and Roventini, 2016).

Our argument is that the Benthamian view is misleading or plainly wrong concerning the motivations, decision processes and nature of the actions.

First, the drivers of human motivation are many more than one. As Adam Smith masterly argues in its *Theory of Moral Sentiments*, utility (what he called "prudence") is just one of them, and in a lot of social contexts, not the most important one.

Second, the decision processes are very rarely explicit calculations and comparisons of outcomes.

Third, the ensuing decisions very seldom look like a "rational" ("as…if") outcome of the foregoing decision processes, *even when the latter would be possible to calculate*. And in the real word, complex and evolving as it is, they rarely are.

In such circumstances, we suggest, a positive theory of individual and collective behaviours has to entirely dispose of the max U(…,…, …) apparatus, either as an actual descriptive device, and as a yardstick, whatever that means. If we are right, then also relaxations of the paradigms involving varying degrees of "bounded rationality" in the decision process and an enlargement of the arguments in the utility function (e.g., adding "intrinsic motivations", or even "altruism") are quite misleading. They are a bit like adding epicycles over epicycles in a Ptolemaic astronomy.

The radical alternative we advocate is an anthropology of a *homo heuristicus* (Gigerenzer and Brighton, 2009), socially embedded, imperfectly learning in a complex evolving environment, and with multiple drivers of his actions.

A tall task, but it is time to break away from a paradigm that trivializes the analysis of human behaviour, reducing it to sterile exercises of maximization over some arbitrary and ad hoc functions.

Acknowledgements

We thank Riccardo Viale for his insightful comments and suggestions. GD acknowledges the earlier support of the ISIGrowth project under grant agreement No. 649186 ISIGrowth, GD and LM the current support of the GROWINPRO project grant n. 822781, both from the European Union Horizon 2020 Programme.

This work draws heavily on previous publications, in particular, Dosi, Marengo and Fagiolo (2004) and Dosi et al. (2017).

Notes

1 Note that here and throughout we address the notion of bounded rationality used by most contemporary economists as a "full rationality" minus some frictions, memory limitations, biases, noise, etc. and not the much richer notion conceived by Herbert Simon which stood from the very cognitive and perceptual boundaries in the interactions between humans and their environments.

2 Admittedly, the point is not uncontroversial as some scholars suggest that perceptual processes and categorizations are consistent with Bayes rule (e.g. Griffith, Kemp and Tenenbaum, 2008). We are not cognitive scientists, but frankly we find it hard to believe that people learn in Bayesian manners how to swim in the Heraclitean river where you can never bathe twice. More generally, for a thorough discussion of descriptive (as opposed to normative) theories of cognition and action, see Viale (2018).

3 Incidentally, note that the outcomes of pure "Pavlovian" – i.e., reinforcement-driven, consciously blind – and "Bayesian" – apparently sophisticated rational – dynamics can be shown to be sometimes asymptotically equivalent (see the review in Suppes 1995a, 1995b, who develops much older intuitions from behaviourist psychology, e.g. Bush and Mosteller, 1955). However, in order for that equivalence to hold, reinforcements must operate in the same direction as the Bayesian inferential machinery, which is, indeed, a hard demand to make. The so-called condition of "weak monotonicity" in the dynamics of adjustment that one generally finds in evolutionary games is a necessary, albeit not sufficient, condition to this effect. Moreover, a subtle question regards the interpretative value that one should attribute to asymptotic results: what do they tell us about finite time properties of empirical observations? (We shall briefly come back to the issue below.)

4 Note that procedural rationality requires all the "linearity assumptions" mentioned above (ruling out, for example, state-dependent preferences) and also consistent search heuristics (allowing, for example, assessment rules along any decision tree which at least in probability lead in the "right" direction).

5 Promising results stem from a better understanding of the formal structure of problem-solving heuristics (cf. e.g. Pearl, 1984; Vassilakis, 1997; and, in a suggestive experimentally-based instance, Cohen and Bacdayan, 1994, and Egidi, 1996). See also below.

6 For example, in Dosi et al. (1999) consider quantity- and price-setting as cases to the point.

7 Heiner (1983) introduces a similar concept which he calls the "C-D (competence-difficulty) gap". In his definition, such a gap reflects the agent's imperfect capabilities to correctly process the available information and act reliably. Heiner's C-D gap does not properly belong to the realm of cognitive gaps, but it rather captures their behavioural consequences.

8 "Prototypization" is easy to intuitively understand: you would give a sparrow rather than a penguin as an example of what a bird is. But with that it is also easier to understand the basic ambiguity of borderliners, fuzziness and categorical attributions by default (how should one treat a duck-billed platypus?, as a mammal? or should one create a separate category, that of ovoviviparous?). A discussion of these issues bearing on economic judgements and behaviours is found in Tordjman (1998).

9 For a thorough discussion of algorithmic processes, see Lakoff (1987) and Bonini et al. (1999).

10 On the notion of "social embeddedness" as from contemporary economic sociology, see Granovetter (1985) and several contributions in Smelser and Swedberg (2006). A discussion quite germane to the argument developed here is found in Tordjman (1998).

11 Within an enormous literature, just think of a good deal of the sociological tradition influenced by the works of Talcott Parson or of the classic Bourdieu (1977); in anthropology, among others, cf. the discussions of "embeddedness" by Karl Polanyi (1944, 1957); and Geertz (1963); see also Edgerton (1985).

12 See also Frantz and Leeson (2013) for a recent reappraisal of the Hayekian view in relation to behavioural economics.

13 Within a very large literature, cf. for instance Helfat et al. (2006) and the critical survey in Dosi et al. (2008).

References

Andersen, E. S (1994). *Evolutionary Economics: Post-Schumpeterian Contributions*, London: Pinter.

Argyris, C., and Schön, D. (1978). *Organisational learning: A Theory of Action Perspective*. Reading, MA: Addison-Wesley.

Bateson, G. (1972). *Steps to an Ecology of Mind*, New York: Ballantine Books.

Becker, M. C. (2004). "Organizational routines: A review of the literature". *Industrial and Corporate Change* 13(4): 643–678.

Becker, M. C., Lazaric, N., Nelson, R. R., and Winter, S. G. (2005). "Applying organizational routines in understanding organizational change", *Industrial and Corporate Change* 14 (5): 775–791.

Binmore, K. (1990). *Essays on the Foundations of Game Theory*, Oxford: Blackwell.

Bonini, N., Osherson, D., Viale, R., and Williamson, T. (1999). On the psychology of vague predicatives, Mind and Language 14: 377–393.

Borcherding, K., Larichev, D. L., and Messick, D. M. (Eds.) (1990). *Contemporary Issues in Decision Making*, New York: North-Holland.

Bourdieu, P. (1977). *Outline of a Theory of Practice*, Cambridge: Cambridge University Press.

Bush, R. R., and Mosteller, F. (1955). *Stochastic Models for Learning*, New York: Wiley

Cohen, M. D., and Bacdayan, P. (1994). "Organizational routines are stored as procedural memory: Evidence from a laboratory study", *Organizational Science* 5: 554–568.

Cohen, M. D., Burkhart, R., Dosi, G., Egidi, M., Marengo, L., ... Coriat, B. (1996). "Routines and other recurring action patterns of organisations: Contemporary research issues", *Industrial and Corporate Change* 5: 653–698.

Cyert, R. M., and March, J. G. (1992). *A Behavioral Theory of the Firm* (2nd ed.), Oxford: Basil Blackwell.

D'Andrade, R. (2001). "A cognitivist's view of the units debate in cultural anthropology", *Cross-Cultural Research*, 35, 242–257.

Daft, R., and Weick, K. (1984). "Toward a model of organizations as interpretation systems", *Academy of Management Review*, 9(2), 284–295.

Dosi, G., and Egidi, M. (1991). "Substantive and procedural uncertainty: An exploration of economic behaviours in changing environments", *Journal of Evolutionary Economics*, 1(2): 145–168.

Dosi, G., Fabiani, S., Aversi, R., and Meacci, M. (1994). "The dynamics of international differentiation: A multi-country evolutionary model", *Industrial and Corporate Change*, 3: 225–241.

Dosi, G., Faillo, M., and Marengo, L. (2008), "Organizational capabilities, patterns of knowledge accumulation and governance structure in business firms: An introduction", *Organization Studies*, 29(August): 1165–1185.

Dosi, G., Freeman, C., Nelson, R. R., Silverberg, G., and Soete, L. (Eds.) (1988). *Technical Change and Economic Theory*, London: Pinter.

Dosi, G., Marengo, L., Bassanini, A., and Valente, M. (1999). "Norms as emergent properties of adaptive learning: The case of economic routines", *Journal of Evolutionary Economics*, 9(1): 5–26.

Dosi G., Marengo, L., and Fagiolo, G. (2004). "Learning in evolutionary environments", in K. Dopfer (Ed.), *The Evolutionary Foundations of Economics* (pp. 255–328). Cambridge: Cambridge University Press.

Dosi, G., Marengo, L., Paraskevopoulou, E., and Valente, M. (2017). "A model of cognitive and operational memory of organizations in changing worlds", *Cambridge Journal of Economics*, 41(1): 775–806.

Dosi, G., Napoletano, M., Roventini, A., Stiglitz, J., and Trebich, T. (2017). "Rational heuristics? Expectations and behaviors in evolving economies with heterogeneous interacting agents", S. Anna School of Advanced Studies, LEM Working Paper, 2017/31.

Dosi, G., and Roventini, A. (2016). "The irresistible fetish of utility theory: From 'pleasure and pain' to rationalising torture", *Intereconomics*, 51(1): 286–287.

Duncan, R. B., and Weiss, A. (1979). "Organizational learning: Implications for organizational design", in B. Staw (Ed.), *Research in Organizational Behavior*. Oxford: Elsevier.

Dutta, P. K., and Radner, R. (1999). "Profit maximization and the market selection hypothesis", *Review of Economic Studies*, 66(4): 769–798.

Edgerton, R. B. (1985). *Rules, Exceptions and Social Order*, Berkeley, CA: University of California Press.

Egidi, M. (1996) "Routines, hierarchies of problems, procedural behaviour: Some evidence from experiments", in K. J. Arrow, E. Colombatto, M. Perlman, and C. Schmidt (Eds), *The Rational Foundations of Economic Behaviour* (pp. 303–333). London: Macmillan.

Ericsson, K. A., and Smith, J. (Eds) (1991). *Toward a General Theory of Expertise*, Cambridge: Cambridge University Press.

Fehr, B. (2005). "The role of prototypes in interpersonal cognition", in M. Baldwin (Ed.), *Interpersonal Cognition* (pp. 180–205), New York: Guilford Press.

Frantz, R., and Leeson, R. (Eds) (2013). *Hayek and Behavioral Economics*, Basingstoke: Palgrave Macmillan.

Friedman, M. (1953). *Essays in Positive Economics*, Chicago: University of Chicago Press.

Gärdenfors, P. (2004). *Conceptual Spaces: The Geometry of Thought*, Cambridge, MA: MIT Press.

Geertz, C. (1963). *Peddlers and Princes*, Chicago: University of Chicago Press.

Gigerenzer, G., and Brighton, H. (2009). *Homo heuristicus*: Why biased minds make better inference, *Topics in Cognitive Science*, 1: 107–143.

Gigerenzer, G., and Goldstein, D. G. (1996). "Reasoning the fast and frugal way: Models of bounded rationality", *Psychological Review*, 103, 650–669.

Gigerenzer, G., Todd, P. M., and the ABC Research Group (Eds) (1999). *Simple Heuristics That Make Us Smart*. New York: Oxford University Press.

Gigerenzer, G., Todd, P. M., and the ABC Research Group (Eds) (2012). *Ecological Rationality: Intelligence in the World*. New York: Oxford University Press.

Goffman, E. (1974). *Frame Analysis: An Essay on the Organisation of Experience*, Harmondsworth: Penguin.

Granovetter, M. (1985). "Economic action and social structure: The problem of embeddedness." *American Journal of Sociology*, 91(3): 481–510.

Griffiths, T. L., Kemp, C., and Tenenbaum, J. B. (2008). "Bayesian models of cognition", in R. Sun (Ed.), *The Cambridge Handbook of Computational Psychology* (pp. 59–100). New York: Cambridge University Press,

Hahn, U., and Ramscar, M. (2001). *Similarity and Categorization*, Oxford: Oxford University Press.

Hayek, F. A. (1952). *The Sensory Order*, Chicago: University of Chicago Press.

Heiner, R. A. (1983). "The origin of predictable behaviour", *American Economic Review*, 73(4): 560–595.

Helfat, C., Peteraf, E., Singh, M., Mitchell, W., Teece, D. ... Winter, S.G. (2006). *Dynamic Capabilities: Understanding Strategic Change in Organizations*. Oxford: Blackwell.

Hodgson, G. M. (1988). *Economics and Institutions: A Manifesto for a Modern Institutional Economics*, Cambridge: Polity Press.

Hodgson, G. M. (1993). *The Economics of Institutions*. Aldershot: Edward Elgar.

Holland, J. H. (1975). *Adaptation in Natural and Artificial Systems*. Ann Arbor, MI: University of Michigan Press.

Holland, J. H., Holyoak, K. J., Nisbett, R. E., and Thagard, P. R. (Eds) (1986). *Induction: Processes of Inference, Learning and Discovery*, Cambridge, MA: MIT Press.

Johnson-Laird, P. N. (1983). *Mental Models*, Cambridge, MA: Harvard University Press.

Kaniovski, Y. M., Kryazhimskiy, A. V., and Young, H. P. (1997). Learning equilibria in games played by heterogeneous populations. IIASA Interim Report. IIASA, Laxenburg, Austria.

Kahneman, D., Slovic, P., and Tversky, A. (Eds) (1982). *Judgment under Uncertainty: Heuristics and Biases*, Cambridge: Cambridge University Press.

Kahneman, D., and Tversky, A. (1986). "Rational choice and the framing of decision", *Journal of Business* 59: 251–278.

Kauffman, S. A. (1993). *The Origins of Order*, Oxford: Oxford University Press.

Kelly, G. A. (1955). *The Psychology of Personal Constructs*, vol. 1: Clinical Diagnosis and Psychotherapy, New York: Norton.

Kitayama, S. (2002). "Culture and basic psychological processes: Toward a system view of culture: Comment on Oyserman et al. (2002)". *Psychological Bulletin*, 128: 89–96.

Kreps, D. M. (1996). "Market, hierarchies and mathematical economic theory", *Industrial and Corporate Change* 5: 561–595.

Lakoff G. (1987). *Women, Fire and Dangerous Things: What Categories Reveal About the Mind*, Chicago: University of Chicago Press.

Levinthal, D. (1997). "Adaptation on rugged landscapes." *Management Science*, 43(7): 934–950.

Levitt, B., and March J. G. (1988). "Organizational learning", *Annual Review of Sociology*, 14(1), 319–338.

Loasby, B. J. (1983). "Knowledge, learning and the enterprise", in P. Wiseman (Ed.), *Beyond Positive Economics?* London: Macmillan.

Luria, A. R. (1976). *Cognitive Development: Its Cultural and Social Foundations*, Cambridge, MA: Harvard University Press.

March, J. G. (1994). *A Primer on Decision Making: How Decisions Happen*, New York: Free Press.

March, J. G., and Simon, H. A. (1958). *Organizations*, New York: Basil Blackwell.

Marengo, L. (1992). "Coordination and organizational learning in the firm", *Journal of Evolutionary Economics*, 2(4): 313–326.

Marengo, L., and Pasquali, C. (2011). "The construction of choice: A computational voting model", *Journal of Economic Interaction and Coordination*, 6: 139–156.

Margolis, H. (1987). *Patterns, Thinking and Cognition*, Chicago: University of Chicago Press.

Mayer, R. E. (1992). *Thinking, Problem Solving and Cognition*, New York: W. H. Freeman.

McGrattan, E. R., and Marimon, R. (1995). "On adaptive learning in strategic games". In A. Kirman, and M. Salmon (Eds), *Learning and Rationality in Economics*, Oxford: Basil Blackwell Publishers.

Nelson, R. R., and Winter, S. G. (1982). *An Evolutionary Theory of Economic Change*, Cambridge, MA: Harvard University Press.

Newell, A., and Simon, H. A. (1972). *Human Problem Solving*, Englewood Cliffs, NJ: Prentice Hall.

Oyserman, D., and Lee, S. W. S. (2008). "Does culture influence what and how we think? Effects of priming individualism and collectivism", *Psychological Bulletin*, 134: 311–342.

Pearl, J. (1984). *Heuristics: Intelligent Search Strategies for Computer Problem Solving*, Reading, MA: Addison-Wesley.

Posch, M. (1997). "Cycling in a stochastic learning algorithm for normal form games", *Journal of Evolutionary Economics*, 7: 193–207.

Polanyi, K. (1944). *The Great Transformation*, Boston: Beacon Press.

Polanyi, K. (Ed.) (1957). *Trade and Market in the Early Empires*, Glencoe, MN: Free Press.

Polanyi, M. (1966). *The Tacit Dimension*, London: Routledge & Kegan Paul.

Sargent, T. J. (1993). *Bounded Rationality in Economics*, Oxford: Clarendon Press.

Savage, L. (1954). *The Foundations of Statistics*, New York: Wiley.

Silverberg, G. (1988) "Modelling economic dynamics and technical change: mathematical approaches to self-organisation and evolution", in G. Dosi, C. Freeman, R. Nelson, G. Silverberg, and L. Soete (Eds.), *Technical Change and Economic Theory*, London: Pinter.

Silverberg, G., and Verspagen, B. (1994). "Learning, innovation and economic growth: A long-run model of industrial dynamics", *Industrial and Corporate Change*, 3: 199–223.

Simon, H. A. (1976). "From substantive to procedural rationality", in S. J. Latsis (Ed.), *Method and Appraisal in Economics* (pp. 129–148). Cambridge: Cambridge University Press.

Simon, H. A. (1986). "Rationality in psychology and economics", *The Journal of Business*, 59(4).

Smelser, N. J., and Swedberg, R. (Eds) (2006). *The Handbook of Economic Sociology*, 2nd ed., Princeton, NJ: Princeton University Press.

Suppes, P. (1995a). "A survey of mathematical learning theory 1950–1995", mimeo, Stanford University.

Suppes, P. (1995b). "Learning by doing, or practice makes perfect", mimeo, Stanford University.

Thaler, R. H. (1992). *The Winner's Curse: Paradoxes and Anomalies of Economic Life*, New York: Free Press.

Tordjman, H. (1998). "The formation of beliefs on financial markets: Representativeness and prototypes", in N. Lazaric and E. Lorenz (Eds), *Trust and Economic Learning*, London: Edward Elgar.

Tversky, A., and Kahneman, D. (1982). "Judgments of and by representativeness", in D. Kahneman, P. Slovic, and A. Tversky (Eds), *Judgment under Uncertainty: Heuristics and Biases* (pp. 84–98). Cambridge: Cambridge University Press.

Vassilakis, S. (1997). "Accelerating new product development by overcoming complexity constraints", *Journal of Mathematical Economics*, 28(3): 341–373.

Viale. R. (2018). "The normative and descriptive weaknesses of behavioral economics-informed nudge: Depowered paternalism and unjustified libertarianism", *Mind and Society*, 17: 53–69.

Weibull, J. (1995). *Evolutionary Game Theory*, Cambridge, MA: MIT Press.

Winter, S. G. (1971). "Satisficing, selection and the innovative remnant", *Quarterly Journal of Economics*, 85: 237–61.

PART VI

Cognitive organization

34
BOUNDED RATIONALITY AND ORGANIZATIONAL DECISION MAKING

Massimo Egidi and Giacomo Sillari

Introduction

Rational choice and human decision making are two different processes. The distinction between the two became more and more apparent as the notion of bounded rationality was proposed and developed. By the 1950s, rational choice was fully formalized, thanks to the foundational work on Expected Utility Theory carried out by Von Neumann and Morgenstern (1947), as well as that of Jimmy Savage (1954). Rational choice assumes that all conditions surrounding a risky choice are given and known by the decision maker, who links means and ends in a coherent choice among the acts at her disposal. Human decision-making, on the other hand, investigates whether and how these conditions can be established, and how individuals make decisions when they are not established, i.e., when data are not fully available, or not fully processed, or preferences are ill-defined. In these cases, processes widely different from rational choice are active: Decision framing, decision setting, search, categorization, representation are all notions developed to try and capture the subtleties and intricacies of human decision making. Such notions allow the understanding of the processes behind choice, and reveal the limits and bounds of human decision-making abilities. Thus, the endpoints of both human and organizational decision making are not rational, but rather boundedly rational choices.

Are managers rational?

Simon developed the idea of *bounded rationality* in his PhD dissertation,[1] later published in the book, *Administrative Behavior* (Simon, 1947). The book opened up the "black box" of the internal mechanisms of organizations. Simon identified the main characteristics of *managerial decision making* by analyzing the structure of the organizational process. He recognized that the core of every organization is the pattern of the division of tasks and their coordination. The organization is thought of as a goal-oriented structure based on internal tasks that must be coordinated in order to achieve the organization's overall objectives. Behavior within organizations is thus goal-oriented, and goals are by and large complex and hierarchically structured, as many intermediate sub-goals need to be realized, often in a specific order, for the final goal to be achieved. The dynamics of organizational decision-making may therefore be very complex, presenting two main aspects. First, goals are often defined in very general and ambiguous terms, thus necessitating continuous revising of the sub-goals' hierarchy. Second, hidden conflicting objectives can be unearthed during various organizational decisions, and this may, again, make it necessary to revise both sub-goals and their hierarchy.

Rationality in organizations

The complexity of the organizational environment is a perfect arena for evaluating the complexity of decision making and the feasibility of the standard model of rational decision making. Indeed, in this context the rich variety of elements characterizing our decision processes becomes more apparent, illuminating the fact that standard "rationality," conceived as means-ends consistency, is only the final element of a more intricate decision process. Decisions, in a nutshell, are the result of several operations, such as searching and selecting relevant information, framing the context of decision, providing an appropriate categorization of its elements, attempting to reduce uncertainty, and so on. Such operations are prerequisites of choice requiring the activation of complex mental activities, well beyond mere means-end consistency.

In particular, according to Simon, the search for relevant information, knowledge acquisition, and learning are the most important processes for achieving a good or rational decision in complex conditions. In the organizational context, the classic processes of division of labor and subsequent coordination are pervasive, and decision-making conditions present themselves highly unstructured or ill-defined. This, as we shall see, makes standard Expected Utility Theory (EUT) inadequate as a model of choice. Indeed, during the 1950s, when EUT was the standard tool for the market theory of both consumer and production (and hence of economic equilibrium), we see that no attempts were made to extend this approach to the internal mechanisms of organizations. By describing the entrepreneur's production decision as an optimal, utility-maximizing choice, the model was assuming as a matter of fact all internal organizational processes as fixed, since the production function was supposed to fully represent a given technology and organizational form.

Besides Simon, the only approach to the problem of rationality in organizational and evolutionary settings that suggested the need for new analytical tools (other than EUT-based approaches), was due to Schumpeter. His analysis presupposes limits of individuals' rationality both in economics and politics. These limits are clarified and explored under the label "conscious rationality," that is, rationality characterized by individual volition leading to purposeful action. In his view, individuals may have different degrees of conscious rationality, depending on how familiar they are with the domain of a given decision, and on how deliberate is the decision they make.[2] Schumpeter's views are strikingly close to Herbert Simon's models of bounded rationality. Despite a successful acceptance of many of his analytic positions,[3] the attempts to formalize Schumpeter's ideas have been relatively limited, due to the difficulties in applying the standard theory of rational decision to conditions of innovation. Later in this chapter, we will argue also through an example that Simon's bounded rationality approach, sharing several crucial elements with Schumpeter's approach to rationality, is key to a deeper understanding of decision making in contexts of *organizational* innovation.

Rationality, psychology, economics

To fully appreciate the relevance of the idea of bounded rationality in the context of organization, it is useful to consider it in the light of the intellectual endeavors to produce a "pure" theory of human reasoning carried over in various contexts (probability theory, logic, decision theory) during the nineteenth and twentieth centuries. In the words of Reinhardt Selten:

Modern mainstream economic theory is largely based on an unrealistic picture of human decision making. Economic agents are portrayed as fully rational Bayesian maximizers of subjective utility. This view of economics is not based on empirical evidence, but rather on the simultaneous axiomatization of utility and subjective probability. In the fundamental book of Savage the axioms are consistency requirements on actions with actions defined as mappings from states of the world to consequences (Savage 1954). One can only admire the imposing structure built by Savage. It has a strong intellectual appeal as a concept of ideal rationality. However, it is wrong to assume that human beings conform to this ideal.[4]

Selten's quote highlights two main issues. The first issue is that ideal rationality, as defined by the axioms of rational choice in their more widely accepted version—EUT—requires both logical consistency and coherence with probability theory. Moreover, ideal rationality also requires unlimited computing capacity, as the procedure to discover the optimal choice may necessitate an astronomically vast number of calculations while ideal agents would be able to perform them subject to no limitations.

The second issue raised by Selten pertains to the nature and available evidence of the discrepancy between real and ideal behavior. Such discrepancies had been spotted and discussed during the creation and development of logic, of probability theory, and of rational choice, independently from one another. For instance, probability theory was first developed by and large in order to answer normative questions about gambling, and it was soon apparent that gamblers' behavior deviated significantly from the rules of probability calculus. Laplace maintains[5] that probability theory may help individuals to rationally correct the misleading illusions generated by the "sensorium" (what today we would call the cognitive system).[5] In logic, too, during the nineteenth century and in particular with the work of Gottlob Frege, it was apparent that there is a great distance between the psychology of human reasoning, on the one hand, and the laws on which logic was based, on the other.[6] In economics, the formalization of rational choice culminating in EUT followed the same anti-psychologistic stance, and when the theory was found descriptively wanting by the experimental work of Maurice Allais (1953) showing that human decision-makers violate the axioms of rational choice, a natural response to his results was to create more sophisticated versions of EUT by weakening or dropping some of its axioms.

During the same years in which Allais performed his experiments, Herbert Simon began pioneering his bounded rationality approach, shedding light on the limits of rationality and exploring decision mechanisms from the vantage point of the cognitive processes involved in them. Simon's approach is orthogonal to attempts of mending EUT by tinkering with its axioms. Simon, along with many other scholars, chose to follow a different route altogether, one in which human decision making was modeled on the basis of the complexity of the underlying psychological mechanisms.

Bounded rationality and problem solving

If rational choice theory is removed from the reality of human reasoning, a theory originating from empirical observations might offer better insights to identify the main mechanisms undergirding human decision making. Indeed, in 1956, Cyert, Simon, and Trow carried out an empirical analysis of managerial decision contexts that highlighted how search and learning were at the core of human rationality.[7] The study revealed an evident "dualism" of behavior: On the one hand, there is behavior guided by a coherent choice among alternatives typical of structured and repetitive conditions; on the other, behavior characterized by highly uncertain and ill-defined conditions, where the predominant role was played by problem-solving activities.

The dualism between repetitive and well-known decision contexts and ill-defined decision contexts proved to be a key distinction for our understanding of decision processes. In situations of the former kind, it highlights the process of decision-making routinization. In the latter, the necessary conditions for applying standard rational choice theory are lacking, and the most important decision process is the ability of the subjects to formulate and solve problems.[8] This suggests that the real restrictions on rational decisions happen during the process of construction of the context of the decision, leading to the working representation of the decision problem. The notion of bounded rationality refers mostly to these conditions, and hence it is implicitly intertwined with the notion of problem solving.

The dual process account of reasoning

The 1960s were the years of the greatest challenge against the axiomatic foundations of rational choice. On the one hand, Allais's critique aroused renewed interest in psychology; on the other, Simon made clear that if human intelligence was to be thoroughly understood, it had to be "decomposed" into its many complex processes and elements. Induction, reasoning, and problem solving were, in Simon's view, the true protagonists for comprehending human bounded rationality, and hence producing more realistic models of economic and organizational phenomena.

One of the components of the discovery of the cognitive limits of rationality was originated by Luchins (1942), and Luchins and Luchins (1950), who performed experiments on "mechanization of thought." They conducted experiments with subjects exposed to mathematical problems that had solutions at different levels of efficiency. The authors showed that subjects, having identified a simple solution to a task in a given (repetitive) context, may automatically and systematically apply the solution to other contexts, even if it proves to be suboptimal. The experiments demonstrate that once a mental computation, deliberately performed to solve a given problem, has been repeatedly applied to solve analogous problems, it may become mechanized. Mechanization enables individuals to pass from deliberate effortful mental activity to partially automatic, unconscious, and effortless mental operations.

This phenomenon has been further explored by psychologists, and our understanding deepened through a great deal of experiments. Among these, the experiments on chess by Simon and colleagues provided important new findings. Simon maintains that, in the course of acquiring their skill, chess players store chunks in long-term memory corresponding to patterns of pieces. Their recalling such patterns from long-term memory, during the match, is fast and automatic, and forms the basis for the conscious process of symbolic manipulation of the recalled mental items.

> One key to understanding chess mastery ... seems to lie in the immediate perceptual processing, for it is here that the game is structured, and it is here in the static analysis that the good moves are generated for subsequent processing. Behind this perceptual analysis, as with all skills ... lies an extensive cognitive apparatus amassed through years of constant practice. What was once accomplished by slow, conscious deductive reasoning is now arrived at by fast, unconscious perceptual processing. It is no mistake of language for the chess master to say that he 'sees' the right move.[9]

The experiments made by Simon and colleagues then led to the discovery that the architecture of thinking is characterized by a complex interaction between the automatic and fast recall of the elements stored in the long-term memory and the conscious process of symbolic manipulation over the mental items. This dualism between unconscious and deliberate aspects of the process of thinking has been further explored over the past years, also outside of the context of chess, by many authors, for instance, in Schneider and Shiffrin (1977), Hogarth (2001), Evans (2003), Evans and Frankish (2009), Stanovich (1999), Stanovich and West (2000) and many others. While in Simon and in the subsequent literature the use of chunks was to show how to construct a decision strategy, Kahneman adopts the dual system theory functionally to introduce accessibility as the main theoretical concept at work in the explanation of rational choice relative to the problem at hand.[10]

Organizations and routines
Routinized and not routinized behavior

As we have seen, the observation of managerial decisions within large organizations made clear the dualism between repetitive decisions in stationary conditions and innovative decisions in ill-defined and evolving environment. The latter (which Simon and March analyze preponderantly) is the extreme case of decisions (much more likely to happen) made in complex situations in which it is too costly or unfeasible to compute a strategy to achieve an optimal solution. In *Organizations*, March and Simon expand on this observation, and provide a definition of "routinized behaviors":

> We will regard a set of activities as routinized, [then,] to the degree that choice has been simplified by the development of a fixed response to defined stimuli. If search has been eliminated, but a choice remains in the form of clearly defined and systematic computing routine, we will say that the activities are routinized.[11]

A part of this definition should be highlighted: Routinized behaviors take place when "search has been eliminated," i.e., when the individual learning and problem-solving process stops.[12] The reference to the process of mechanization of thought previously studied in chess players is evident in the quote above, where it is considered in the context of a multiplicity of individuals. When *individual* behaviors are routinized, as suggested in the literature, the mental load required to decide is reduced and choice becomes an automatic and familiar process. March and Simon suggest that this process happens also in the minds of individuals while they are cooperating to achieve a shared, common goal. Cooperation, reciprocal adaptability, and the shared belief in common goals are the most important requirements for individuals participating in the same *program* within an organization. Moreover, they assume the differentiation among members according to their roles and to the knowledge required to perform tasks, as well as their interdependence.[13] By extending to group (or team) behavior the properties of Simon's chunking theory, we can tackle the question of how prior knowledge automatically recalled from the long-term memory of different individuals must be re-composed, as if it were a puzzle, and how the collective decision process must be simplified and reduced to automatic and habitual process.[14] March and Simon suggest that this kind of process occurs. They do so by claiming that if all participants in a program become familiar and expert in their specific role and do not search for new solutions any further, then a routine is established as a collection of repetitive *organizational procedures*. At the same time, they offer a "micro-individual" definition of *routinized behaviors* of the individuals involved into the same organizational procedure:[15]

> Problem-solving activities can generally be identified by the extent to which they involve *search;* search aimed at discovering alternatives of action or consequences of action. "Discovering" alternatives may involve inventing and elaborating whole *performance programs* where these are not already available in the problem solver's repertory.[16]

Problem-solving activity is then the core process within organizations, searching for better results and higher efficiency. This search is performed in every area in which more efficient goals might be achieved (aspiration levels). A process ends up when the search leads to a satisficing result, i.e., a new "performance program, or simply a program, has been discovered." A "performance program" is intended as an *organizational procedure*, i.e., it consists of a *repository of rules*, that, in response to organizational conditions, prescribe the appropriate behavior for each of the individuals collaborating to achieve a shared goal.[17] The main characteristics of these rules, is that they are *prescriptions* that originate during problem solving and that come to be used again when the same conditions apply. Such procedures have basic analogies with computer programs as both consist in prescriptions about what is to be done (*action*) when a given *condition* applies. However, unlike computer programs in which prescriptions must be explicitly and specifically given in an artificial language, in human procedures, prescriptions can be largely implicit. In general, not all contents of a procedure involving humans need to be conceptually and verbally specified. A large part of the verbal prescriptions may be very general and synthetic,[18] assuming that individuals will have sufficient competence to activate it correctly. This aspect has a fundamental importance because humans, while putting into effect a procedure, are supposed to retain large discretionary power, enabling them to specify and realize prescriptions even when they are generic or unclear, or even pushing them to discover new alternatives:

> A program may specify only general goals, and leave unspecified the exact activities to be used in reaching them. Moreover, knowledge of the means-ends connections may be sufficiently incomplete and inexact that these cannot be very well specified in advance. Then "discretion" refers to the development and modification of the *performance program* through problem-solving and learning processes.[19]

A procedure then can be *not fully specified*, and in this case the individuals who put it in effect must have competences *to autonomously construct the parts which are not specified*. This shows that individual micro-creativity is a necessary component of the process of realizing a procedure.

The "discretionary" character of large parts of a program presupposes the "creative" ability of individuals to fill the gaps of imperfectly specified programs.[20]

Further evolutions of the notion of organizational routine

The notion of routine was revisited 30 years after *Organization* by Nelson and Winter's *Evolutionary Theory of Economic Change*.[21] In their approach to organizations, they consider routines as the basic elements of an organization's life, and innovation as the engine of routine creation. One relevant element on which they focus attention is the role and transmission of tacit knowledge.[22] Routines may consist of actions that are often not verbalized, and need not be transmitted in the form of messages. Routines, or better *organizational* routines, are not formally defined and are implicitly treated as behavioral patterns. Expanding March and Simon's notion, Nelson and Winter attribute to organizational routines the role of basic units in the evolutionary process of organizational change. This perspective slightly changes the original meaning of "routinized programs" in March and Simon's approach, as the evolutionary approach ends up attributing to the "organizational routine" more properties than March and Simon do in their problem-solving context.[23] Many definitions of organizational routines have been proposed in these years, with slight differences intended to capture different properties. The attempt to unify and operationalize these requirements is still ongoing after many decades.[24]

Besides there being a repository of a stored collective knowledge (as we have seen above, an idea already present *in nuce* in March and Simon), an issue often debated in the literature pertains to how to understand routines both as stable entities (especially in relation to internal conflicts) and simultaneously as a source of change. We suggest that going back to the original Simon and March approach solves this apparent contradiction. In fact, as we have previously remarked a (human) routine is never *fully specified*, presupposing therefore that the individuals effecting it need to possess the competences necessary to autonomously supply the underspecified parts of the routines, hence expressing micro-creativity. This implies that micro search processes are still active also when an organization has produced a certain set of stable routines. Thus, micro-innovations (mutations) can still emerge.[25] This way, the apparent contradictory property of being stable while also potentially a source of change can be categorized and modeled.

Of course, more radical innovations can happen within organizations through the introduction of new top-down programs. The distinction between micro-innovations (mutations) and radical innovations can be treated by using the properties of complex systems, and in particular the decomposability features of the rules system. In fact, according to the original meaning of "routinized programs" in March and Simon, routines can be modeled as systems of if-then rules (Holland et al., 1986) that evolve through learning and adaptation. A system of condition-action rules embeds a representation of the problem(s) the organization faces. The condition part of the rules refers to the set of states (both of the world and internal) that are considered as equivalent or indistinguishable and therefore activate the same course of action. The action parts instead prescribe what ought to be done for each of these perceived situations.[26]

Marengo (2015) presents a simple model of organizational problem-solving where the generation of solutions is constrained by the representation of the problem and, in particular, by the conjectural decomposition of the problem it embeds. Routines are temporary solutions and may undergo small local changes which are reinforced as long as the routine keeps being functional or even improves. By adding up a number of these small local changes, the initial routine may finally evolve into a considerably different one. Two elements play a key role in this evolutionary dynamics of routines: The decomposition of the problem and the selection mechanism. The former sets the constraints to the generation of variations, in the sense that small local changes can only take place within the given decomposition (or division of labor). The latter defines the set of routines which are considered at least equally functional to the current one and therefore the set of variants which are acceptable. When such a set is small, i.e., small changes in a functional routine tend to damage its functionality, most variations will not be viable and routines will tend to be rigid and persistent. When, on the contrary, the set is relatively large, a routine will more easily evolve into a new one.[27]

Empirical evidence: switching from routinization to exploration

We select, among many others, three examples of experimental evidence related to routines and bounded rationality. Two are laboratory experiments, and the third is a field experiment.

The experiments illustrate some of the crucial issues in organizational bounded rationality described above: Routinization of behavior, switching from routinized to exploratory behavior, and whether routinization hinders creativity.

Target the Two (TTT) is a card game introduced by Cohen and Bacdayan (1994). Pairs of participants to the experiment need to cooperate in order to achieve a common goal. They are rewarded according to the success of the cooperative strategy they apply, rather than according to individual performances. Thus, participants must discover a good strategy *jointly*, and then follow it cooperatively in order to achieve their goal. Cohen and Bacdayan observe a laboratory tournament of pairs of players to study the emergence of routinized behavior involving coordination and cooperation. They make the first relevant attempt to explore in laboratory the emergence of rules of coordination, or *organizational routines*.

Egidi and Narduzzo (1997) find that *Target the Two* admits of two different strategies, whose efficiency depends upon the card distribution. In the lab, players who are trained to play one strategy continue to use it more frequently also in contexts in which the alternative strategy would be more efficient. This phenomenon shows that the *Einstellung* effect may happen also in a cooperative context.[28] Most players' performances become automatic, their prior knowledge triggering automatic reactions that direct attention toward the cards relevant to the more familiar strategy. In this way, they do not search for cards relevant to the strategy that would be more efficient given the current card distribution on the board, and automatically select familiar cards instead.[29] In terms of Simon's definitions, each of the two groups of players discovers a different organizational routine and persists in using it even when it becomes not efficient. Indeed, in this game only a limited subset of players explore more deeply the space of possible actions and use the routine performing best in the current conditions. They are fully rational, in the sense that their behavior is not routinized and they rationally select the more efficient between the two available routines. In TTT the attention of routinized players is strictly driven by the familiar strategy (analogously to situations of confirmation bias). Here the question arises, whether routinization of behavior may prevent the discovery of a new strategy. An answer comes from a field study by Ohly, Sonnentag, and Pluntke (2006). The authors examine the relationship between routinization and creativity in a randomly selected sample of 278 employees of a German high-tech company. They look at four characteristics (job control, job complexity, time pressure, and supervisor support) and a range of other creative and proactive behaviors. Regression analyses reveal that in addition to work characteristics, routinization is generally positively related to creative and proactive behaviors due to available resources that can be used to develop new ideas while working.

The problem of the switch from routinized to exploratory behavior has been studied also at the level of neural activity. Schuck et al. (2015) show through multivariate neuroimaging analyses that, in the classification task described below, before subjects spontaneously change to an alternative strategy, the medial prefrontal cortex (MPFC) encodes information irrelevant for the current strategy but necessary for the new one. Thus, they indicate that behavioral changes, the realization of the existence of a "better" strategy, and the decision to implement the new strategy, all lag significantly behind changes in cerebral activity that indicate brain sensitivity to the new strategy. Preceding the shift to a new strategy there is therefore a largely unconscious process. For this reason, the shift from exploitation to exploration strategies does not seem to be the outcome of a conscious, optimal response to a problem-solving procedure, as neural changes correlated with the (reported) change in the decision method (hence in representation) happen *before* the actual behavior change. The medial prefrontal cortex functions in this situation as a "planning and evaluation" unit for exploration of new strategies. Furthermore, Schuck et al. (2015) also establish that the categorization strategy yielding the current representation linked to the problem-solving method becomes entrenched at the physiological level, as it is accompanied by inhibition of alternative categorizations of the problem at hand. In other words, once a given strategy has become established, the MPFC tends to inhibit those elements that could bring about an alternative categorization of the problem, making it more difficult for the agent to adopt an innovative strategy. Exploration is hindered by our own devices, yet when we adopt exploratory behavior, we do so before we become conscious of its adoption.

Creativity and innovation

The cognitive limits of human reasoning were fundamental pillars in the Schumpeterian analysis scheme, both for the theory of innovation and the theory of democracy.[30] Schumpeter considers the innovative activity as a "*creative response*" to external changes. He claims that this activity can be understood *ex post*, but cannot be predicted "*ex ante*." It is illuminating to interpret Schumpeter's description of the capacity for innovative activity (or "seeing things in a way which afterwards proves to be true, even though it cannot be established at the moment") through the theory of bounded rationality.

As we have seen, according to Simon, solving a problem requires a selective search that presupposes automatic recollection from long-term memory prior to conscious deliberation. In this context, the interaction between automatic and deliberate thinking explains, as we know, the chess master's superiority over a novice. The master has the advantage of automatically using heuristics accumulated through years of constant practice.[31] In the same vein, the more a novice learns and memorizes new strategies, the less mental effort he needs to play.[32] Now imagine a chess club where members organize a tournament with a grand master as opponent. Suppose all of the participants have an average level of competence: During the tournament, players will be mostly unable to predict the grand master's moves because he draws upon a vastly wider repertoire of strategies and can explore in much greater depth than his opponent the possible sequences of moves and countermoves at her disposal. To the eyes of the club players, the master's strategy is *unpredictable*, and exhibits precisely the characteristics that Schumpeter attributes to an innovator:

> From the standpoint of the observer who is in full possession of all relevant facts, it can always be understood *ex post*; but it can practically never be understood *ex ante*; that is to say, it cannot be predicted by applying the ordinary rules of inference from the pre-existing facts.[33]

Then, we could explain innovation purely on the basis of the *competence gap*[34] between the innovator and other individuals. This shows that there are possible analytical tools that can help to decodify innovative behaviors, while a direct application of standard expected utility theory to this context does not seem to be appropriate.

Conclusion

We conclude by highlighting the momentous impulse that bounded rationality has given to organizational science. The discovery of the dual nature of decisions within organizations (routine and search) led March and Simon to completely redefine the definition and analysis of the notion of "planning." Planning ceases to be a static and mechanical activity based on rational decisions immersed in a world of complete information, and becomes instead based on "organizational learning." Search, therefore, becomes a key activity in organizations, and as such becomes possible to differential improvement, giving rise to differentiation in organizational performances. Adaptation is now the crucial element generating differentiation and sub-optimalities. A relevant conceptual improvement is that not only organizations learn, but they also make errors during the learning process, and – as March's behavioral description shows – because adaptation may easily lead to sub-optimal organizational configurations, errors may be systematic and stable in the long run. Both of these developments have spawned a vast literature.

We have argued that bounded rationality is a component of the theory of problem solving, assuming that individuals are natural problem solvers and that their *central ability is thinking*. This implies that behind the bounds of rationality there lie the same cognitive processes generating creativity: problem framing, problem solving, searching, categorizing, memorizing, etc. Simon's theory incorporates problem solving into the process of rational decision. In the bounded rationality approach, requisites of consistency were relaxed, but at the same time new elements (knowledge acquisition and creativity) became of the essence. Moreover, while empirically based, the theory of problem solving has developed into a highly abstract setting foundational of Artificial Intelligence. In their seminal *Human Problem Solving*, Newell and Simon (1972) establish a formal theory of problem solving: The goal was to uncover the secrets of human cognition and transfer it into formal representation. They took up one of Turing's central statements – if a problem can be clearly described with appropriate language, then it can be transferred into a form computable by a machine – and began to build artifacts mimicking human cognitive skills. The artificial reproduction of certain aspects of human problem solving was a new strategy with which to understand the human mind. Simon worked in parallel on giving strong impetus to the empirical analysis of cognitive processes. As we have remarked, the starting point was analysis of the game of chess, from which he moved beyond the notion of calculation by first introducing the idea of "symbolic manipulation" and then directly considering the determinants of cognitive processes in order to transfer to formal artificial tools.

The nineteenth-century view considered logic and probability as theories representing the "laws" of human thought.[35] To some extent the development of Artificial Intelligence started with Simon's theory of problem solving, under the assumption of bounded rationality, representing a modern version of the same idea that Turing was explicitly supporting. This opened up a deep unsolved question of the limits of constructing formal models of intelligence (or, in the words of Turing, building a mechanical intelligence). A question tackled by Turing himself and later by Gödel, with the discovery of the limits of computability. Whatever the opinion we can express on the "great perspective" of discovery of the "laws" of human thought, the approach of bounded rationality has opened the doors for the study of the mental processes involved in search and reasoning and started with the formal representation of these processes, both in the individual and organizational context.

Notes

1 "The dissertation contains the foundation and much of the superstructure of the theory of bounded rationality that has been my lodestar for nearly fifty years" (Simon 1996, p. 86).
2 Schumpeter (1942, p. 363).
3 The contemporary theory of representative democracy is founded on Schumpeter's theory of democracy (see, for example, Held, 2006). Contemporary theories of innovation also draw widely on Schumpeter's ideas.
4 Cf. Selten (2001 p. 13).
5 Laplace ([1825] 1995).
6 See, for instance, Frege ([1884] 1934).
7 Cyert et al. (1956, p. 238).

8 Of course, much exists in between the two extremes (e.g., well-structured analytical problems such as logical or mathematical problems, or opaque problems tackled intuitively).

9 Chase and Simon (1973, p. 56).

10 See Kahneman's Nobel Prize Lecture, delivered on December 8, 2002, revised in Kahneman (2003). Dual process theory has been criticized (notably by Gigerenzer and the ABC Research Group), see, for instance, Viale (2018, 2019), where it is argued that there is a continuum rather than a dichotomy.

11 March and Simon (1958, p. 142).

12 It is not the case that individual learning always fully resolves and stops problem-solving processes, rather, the problem at hand is transformed as new problem-solving processes may arise.

13 See e.g., Orasanu and Salas (1993).

14 See e.g., Orasanu (1990), Glickman et al. (1987).

15 A relatively restricted literature has been dedicated to the development of this point (see Orasanu and Salas 1993).

16 March and Simon (1958, pp. 160–161).

17 Hereinafter. we will use the word *procedure* instead of *program*, to distinguish computer programs from human programs.

18 A possibly relevant part of the search can be entirely unconscious; see, for instance, Macchi et al. (2016).

19 March and Simon (1958, p. 170).

20 The discretionary processes emerging in routines are well illustrated in a field experiment by Narduzzo, Rocco, and Warglien (2002).

21 Nelson and Winter (1982).

22 See Polanyi (1958).

23 Among the most relevant, the role of tacit knowledge, memory, distributed authority structure, and conflict are deepened.

24 As well described in Becker (2002) and further developed in Becker (2008). See also Feldman (2000).

25 See Ohly, Sonnentag, and Pluntke (2006).

26 Actions can operate on the environment or simply generate new "internal" states which in turn activate other rules. Therefore, a system of condition-action rule can be interpreted as a kind of organizational mental model (Johnson-Laird, 1983) and a memory of the organization (Dosi et al., 2017).

27 In both cases simple heuristics may serve the decision maker well, in the former case, by rigidly designing a specific routinized solution to a stable problem, in the latter, or when the environment is in flux, by suggesting different possible solutions.

28 See Luchins (1942).

29 This suggests that the automatic recall depends on the accessibility that the different strategies have in the player's mind. See Egidi (2016, pp. 199–201).

30 See Egidi (2017b).

31 Chase and Simon (1973, p. 56).

32 See Egidi (2017a).

33 Schumpeter (1947, p. 150).

34 See Heiner (1983, p. 562), in which a competence gap arises through the differential abilities of agents relative to mapping informational signals to true events.

35 The expression "laws of thought" gained prominence after the publication of *An Investigation of the Laws of Thought on Which are Founded the Mathematical Theories of Logic and Probabilities* by George Boole (1854). Today the distinction between psychology (as a study of mental phenomena) and logic (as a study of valid inference) is widely accepted even though the links between the two areas are debated by many authors.

References

Allais, M. (1953). Le comportement de l'homme rationnel devant le risque: critique des postulats et axiomes de l'Ecole Americaine. *Econometrica*, 21(4), 503–546.

Becker, M. C. (2004). Organizational routines: A review of the literature. Industrial and corporate change, 13(4), 643–678.

Becker, M. C (Ed.) (2008). *Handbook of organizational routines*, Cheltenham: Edward Elgar

Boole G. (1854). *An investigation of the laws of thought: on which are founded the mathematical theories of logic and probabilities*. New York: Dover Publications

Chase, W. G., and Simon, H. A. (1973). Perception in chess. *Cognitive Psychology*, 4(1), 55–81.

Cohen, M. D., and Bacdayan, P. (1994). Organizational routines are stored as procedural memory. *Organization Science*, 5, 554–568.

Cyert, R. M., Simon, H. A., and Trow, D. B. (1956). Observation of a business decision. *The Journal of Business*, 29(4), 237–248.

Dosi, G., Marengo, L., Paraskevopoulou, E., and Valente M. (2017). A model of cognitive and operational memory of organizations in changing worlds. *Cambridge Journal of Economics*, 41, 775–806.

Dosi, G., Nelson, R. R., and Winter, S. G. (Eds.) (2002). The nature and dynamics of organizational capabilities. Oxford: Oxford University Press.

Egidi, M. (2016). Organizational decisions in the lab. In R. Frantz and L. March (Eds.), *Minds, models and milieux* (pp. 106–206). Basingstoke: Palgrave Macmillan.

Egidi, M. (2017a). Paths in contemporary economics and sciences of artificial intelligence that originate from Simon's bounded rationality approach. *PSL Quarterly Review*, 70(280), 7–33.

Egidi, M. (2017b). Schumpeter's picture of economic and political institutions in the light of a cognitive approach to human behavior. *Journal of Evolutionary Economics*, 27, 139–159.

Egidi, M., and Narduzzo, A. (1997). The emergence of path dependent behaviors in cooperative contexts. *International Journal of Industrial Organization*, 15(6), 677–709.

Evans, J. (2003). In two minds: Dual-process accounts of reasoning. *Trends in Cognitive Sciences* 7(1010), 454–459.

Evans, J. S. B. T., and Frankish, K. (Eds.) (2009). *In two minds: Dual processes and beyond.* New York: Oxford University Press.

Feldman, M. S. (2000). Organizational routines as a source of continuous change. *Organization Science*, 11(6), 611–629.

Frege, G. ([1884] 1934). *Grundlagen der Arithmetik.* Breslau: Marcus.

Gigerenzer, G., and Selten, R. (2001). *Bounded rationality: The adaptive toolbox.* Cambridge, MA: MIT Press.

Glickman, A. S., Zimmer, S., Montero, R. C., Guerette, P. J., Campbell, W. J., ... Salas, E. (1987). The evolution of teamwork skills: An empirical assessment with implications for training (Tech. Rep. No. 87–016). Orlando, FL: Naval Training Systems Center.

Heiner, R. A. (1983). The origin of predictable behavior. *The American Economic Review*, 7(4), 560–595.

Held, D. (2006). *Models of democracy.* Cambridge: Polity.

Hogarth, R. M. (2001). *Educating intuition.* Chicago: University of Chicago Press.

Holland, J. H., Holyoak, K. J., Nisbett, R. E., and Thagard. P. R. (1986). *Induction: Processes of inference, learning and discovery.* Cambridge, MA: MIT Press.

Johnson-Laird, P. N. (1983). *Mental models.* Cambridge, MA: Harvard University Press.

Kahneman, D. (2003). Maps of bounded rationality: Psychology for behavioral economics. *American Economic Review*, 93(5), 1449–1475.

Laplace, P. S. de (1995). *Philosophical essay on probabilities.* Berlin: Springer Verlag.

Luchins, A. S. (1942). Mechanization in problem solving: The effect of Einstellung. *Psychological Monographs*, 54(6).

Luchins, A. S., and Luchins, E. H. (1950). New experimental attempts at preventing mechanization in problem solving. *The Journal of General Psychology*, 42(2), 279–297.

Macchi, L., Bagassi, M., and Viale, R. (Eds.) (2016). *Cognitive unconscious and human rationality.* Cambridge, MA: MIT Press.

March, J. G. (1991). Exploration and exploitation in organizational learning. *Organization Science*, 2(1), 71–87.

March, J. G., and Simon, H. A. (1958). *Organizations*, New York: Wiley.

Marengo, L. (2015). Representation, search and the evolution of routines in problem solving, *Industrial and Corporate Change*, 24, 951–980.

Narduzzo, A., Rocco, E., and Warglien, M. (2002) Talking about routines in the field. In G. Dosi, R. R, Nelson, and S. G. Winter (Eds.), The nature and dynamics of organizational capabilities (pp. 27–50). Oxford: Oxford University Press.

Nelson, R. R., and Winter, S. G. (1982). *An evolutionary theory of economic change.* Cambridge, MA: Harvard University Press.

Newell, A., and Simon, H. A. (1972). *Human problem solving.* Englewood Cliffs, NJ: Prentice-Hall.

Ohly, S., Sonnentag, S., and Pluntke, F. (2006). Routinization, work characteristics and their relationships with creative and proactive behaviors. *Journal of Organizational Behavior: The International Journal of Industrial, Occupational and Organizational Psychology and Behavior*, 27(3), 257–279.

Orasanu, J., and Salas, E. (1993). Team decision making in complex environments. In G. Klein, J., Orasanu, R. Calderwood, and C. Zsambok (Eds.), Decision-making in action: Models and methods. Norwood, NJ: Ablex.

Orasanu, J. (1990). Shared mental models and crew decision making (Tech. Rep. No. 46). Princeton, NJ: Princeton University, Cognitive Sciences Laboratory.

Polanyi, M. (1958). *Personal knowledge*. London: Routledge.

Savage, L. J. (1954). *The foundations of statistics*. New York: Wiley.

Schneider, W., and Shiffrin, R. (1977). Controlled and automatic human information processing: I. Detection, search, and attention. *Psychological Review* 84(2), 127–190.

Schuck, N. W., Gaschler, R., Wenke, D., Heinzle, J., Frensch, P. A., ... Reverberi, C. (2015). Medial prefrontal cortex predicts internally driven strategy shifts. *Neuron*, 86(1), 331–340.

Schumpeter, J. A. (1942). *Capitalism, socialism and democracy*. New York: Harper and Brothers.

Schumpeter, J. A. (1947). The creative response in economic history. *The Journal of Economic History*, 7(2), 149–159.

Selten, R. (2001). What is bounded rationality? In G. Gigerenzer and R. Selten (Eds.), *Bounded rationality: The adaptive toolbox* (pp. 13–37). Cambridge, MA: MIT Press.

Simon, H. A. (1947). *Administrative behavior: A study of decision-making processes in administrative organization*. New York: Free Press.

Simon, H. A. (1996). *The sciences of the artificial*. Cambridge, MA: MIT Press.

Shiffrin, R. M., and Schneider, W. E. (1977). Controlled and automatic human information processing: II. Perceptual learning, automatic attending, and a general theory. *Psychological Review*, 84, 128–190.

Stanovich, K. E. (1999). *Who is rational? Studies of individual differences in reasoning*. Hillsdale, NJ: Erlbaum.

Stanovich, K. E., and West, R. F. (2000). Individual differences in reasoning: Implications for the rationality debate. *Behavioral and Brain Sciences* 23, 645–726.

Viale, R. (2018). The normative and descriptive weaknesses of behavioral economics-informed nudge: Depowered paternalism and unjustified libertarianism. *Mind & Society*, 17(1–2), 53–69.

Viale, R. (2019). Architecture of the mind and libertarian paternalism: Is the reversibility of Type 1 nudges likely to happen? *Minds & Machines* (submitted).

von Neumann, J. and Morgenstern, O. (1947). *The theory of games and economic behavior*. Princeton, NJ: Princeton University Press.

35

ATTENTION AND ORGANIZATIONS

Inga Jonaityte and Massimo Warglien

Bounded rationality, attention, and organizations: the Carnegie perspective

[I]n an information-rich world, the wealth of information ... creates a poverty of attention and a need to allocate that attention efficiently among the overabundance of information sources that might consume it.

Simon, 1971, p. 40

The allocation of attention is commonly seen as a fundamental problem for organizations (Bouquet and Birkinshaw, 2008; Ocasio, 2011; Joseph and Wilson, 2018). Developing Barnard's (1938) intuition that "narrowing choice" is a central function of executive decisions, Simon (1947) early on identified the process of directing and channeling managers' attention as a key function of organizations, and also provided the almost iconic description of attention management featured in the epigraph. The foundations for such perspectives rely on the central role that limited attention provides in defining bounded rationality (Simon, 1983). The "limits" of decision-making rationality are to a large extent the results of the attentional bottleneck (Simon, 1947).

The notion that attention is a scarce resource and that its allocation is central to intelligent behavior has, of course, a longer history and deep roots in psychology. *Administrative Behavior* resorts to classical sources, such as James (1890) and Tolman (1932), to provide the conceptual background and basic definitions of attention.

> Everyone knows what attention is. It is the taking possession by the mind, in clear and vivid form, of one out of what seem several simultaneously possible objects or trains of thought. Focalization, concentration, of consciousness are of its essence. It implies withdrawal from some things in order to deal effectively with others, and is a condition which has a real opposite in the confused, dazed, scatterbrained state which in French is called distraction, and Zerstreutheit in German.
>
> *James, 1890, pp. 403–404*

DOI: 10.4324/9781315658353-41

However, what characterizes organizational views of attention is "a dual emphasis on cognition (limited attention capacity) and structure (how organization shapes individual's attention)" (Festré and Garouste, 2015). Just as the cognitive limitations of individuals help explain how organizations are structured, organizations in turn help understand how individual attention is distributed and coordinated in collective systems.

Early work from the Carnegie School (Simon, 1947; March and Simon, 1958) emphasized some fundamental ways in which organizations provide "attention-directors" as a response to human cognitive limits. To that end, two general, hierarchical systems were proposed to design the architecture of attention in organizations.

1 *Decision hierarchies.* "Prior controlling decisions" create a narrow frame of action for individual decision makers. Organizations provide a stratification of decisions levels that allow decisions on the spot to be guided by broader rationality considerations. Thus, organizational hierarchies can be seen as nested systems of decision premises, ensuring that lower-level decisions are constrained and coordinated by higher-level ones.
2 *Division of labor.* Organizations design and assign tasks to single members, and thus direct their attention to those tasks. By reducing interdependences between different tasks, organizations reduce the number of features that each agent has to pay attention to. Tasks have to be designed in ways that are compatible with individual attention capacity (the "span of attention," March and Simon, 1958). Division of labor determines selective perception by agents specialized in a task. For example, Dearborne, DeWitt, and Simon (1958) have shown how industrial executives see the aspects of a situation that relate to the tasks and goals of their department.

In Simon's original framework, decision premises and division of labor create a close connection between attention and (sub)goals. Both processes define a hierarchy of subgoals attached to tasks that selectively orient individual actions. The conceptual frame here is one of collective problem solving. Cyert and March (1963) introduce a more genuine political perspective on goals and attention. It is a natural implication of the notion of limited attention that individuals cannot simultaneously attend to all dimensions of a decision, and thus attention to different features can only be allocated sequentially (Simon, 1947). If attention to goals is limited, shifts in attention will affect preference orderings. Cyert and March (1963) focus on how the logic of organizational coalition making can affect sequential attentional dynamics. They suggest that stakeholders in organizations generally have conflicting goals that make it impossible to find stable and consistent set of organizational objectives. Instead, organizations can resolve conflicting demands on their decisions by paying attention to different goals in a sequential rather than simultaneous way. For example, when there are conflicting pressures to "smooth production" and "satisfy consumers" the problem could be resolved by first satisfying the former and then the latter. "Quasi-resolution of conflict" becomes an alternative to the standard view of organizational coalition making, opposing shifting attention to side-payments, and dynamic inconsistency of goals to coherent solutions. Phenomena like the present bias (O'Donoghue and Rabin, 1999) and related forms of temporal myopia further facilitate quasi-resolution of conflict and may be complementary to attentional shifts.

Two important further contributions stemmed from the original Carnegie approach, providing new insights and a different perspective on attention in organizations: *the garbage can model* and *the attention-based theory of the firm.*

While Cyert and March emphasize the political implications of the sequential allocation of attention, the garbage can model (Cohen, March, and Olsen, 1972) explores its coordination implications in non-routine decision making. In a radical departure from traditional models of organizational decision making, the garbage can model explores "organized anarchies" in which preferences are problematic, technologies are unclear, and participation is fluid. Despite its quite radical language, the garbage can model combines important elements of the Carnegie tradition: the "ambiguity of goals" further develops Cyert-March's sequential attention to goals. Attention is a scarce resource, participants to decision processes can pay attention to only one choice at a time, and they have a preference for focusing on choices being close to be made. The main novelty of the model comes from the way these ingredients are combined into a flow of independent streams of decision makers, choice opportunities, and problems. As has been noted (Ocasio, 2012), this introduces an ecological view of how attention is allocated in organizations. Patterns of coordinated organizational decision making arise from the competing demands on the participants' attention and the way they are streaming over time. The result is a subversion of the classical problem-solving structure. Most choices are made by flight (as problems move to other choice opportunities) or by oversight (as most problems still have to be attached to a choice arena), rather than by resolution. Again, some similarity with Cyert and March's quasi-resolution of conflict can be noticed. In organized anarchies, choices are made because the attention of decision makers is focused on issues from which conflicting demands have been temporarily removed. Distraction has an adaptive value.

Building on the dual emphasis on structure and cognition by Simon (1947) and other earlier works (March and Simon, 1958; Cyert and March, 1963; Cohen et al., 1972; Weick, 1979), Ocasio (1997) developed the attention-based view of the firm (ABV). Ocasio describes organizations as systems of structurally distributed attention and defines attention as a cognitive process that encompasses the "noticing, encoding, interpreting, and focusing of time and effort by organizational decision-makers" on issues and answers (Ocasio, 1997, p. 189). Ocasio, whose definition echoes the one provided by James (1890), emphasizes the relevance of attention in decision making, as already underscored by Simon (1947, p. 110). This theory highlights the relationship between individual and organizational information processing: (1) actions of decision makers and subsequent organizational moves depend on the issues and answers the former focus their attention on; (2) in turn, decision makers' focus of attention depends on specific situation and the organizational and environmental context they are in. Later, Ocasio (2011) stresses that attention can be classified into three interacting varieties: (1) *attentional perspective*, which refers to the focus of attention across space and time; (2) *attentional engagement*, that is, the extent by which a firm attends to organizational agendas and sustains vigilance in problem solving over time; and (3) *attentional selection*, and thus the decision as to which stimuli to address at any given time. Subsequent ABV studies focused mostly on topics such as the effect of attention structures on decision-making (e.g., Maula, Keil, and Zahra, 2013; Wilson and Joseph, 2015) and top-down and bottom-up attentional processes (e.g., Shepherd, McMullen, and Jennings, 2007; Zbaracki and Bergen, 2015). Joseph and Wilson (2018) amalgamate these two topics: Whereas previous ABV studies mostly focused on the consequences of the distribution of attention, these authors also stress the role played by organizational tensions and architectural complexity in influencing the distribution of attention.

Attention at work: organizational mechanisms

While the Carnegie classics deal with attention in broad terms, they also provide a way to look at familiar organizational phenomena in a new perspective. Different organizational mechanisms have been analyzed in terms of attentional processes, allowing a reinterpretation of their functions and ways of operating. Here we will focus on some examples.

Control systems (and more generally accounting systems) provide an interesting case, and they were among the first to be analyzed in an attention framework. Control systems are usually described as information feedback systems. Goals and targets are set, current results are regularly compared with the targets, and feedback is used to correct deviations and keep the organization focused on implementing its original strategies (Anthony and Govindarajan, 2007). However, a focus on attention may suggest a different interpretation. In their study of the controller's department in seven organizations, Simon et al. (1954) had already made a distinction between score-card and attention-directing use of information. The score-card question is "Am I doing well or badly?" The attention-directing one is "what problems should I look into?" (Simon et al., 1954, p. 3). It was observed that the attention-directing use of control systems is always paired with the score-card one. Attentional uses of control systems are tightly related to the exertion of the "principle of exception": accounting data direct the attention of managers toward "out of line" situations and trigger direct hierarchical intervention to address them. In a subsequent study encompassing 19 major companies, Simons (1991) found that top managers selectively use control systems to focus attention on strategic uncertainties. As a result, control systems favor the generation of new strategic initiatives in response to emergent uncertainties, rather than just supporting the implementation of current strategies. In a similar vein, Vanderbosch (1999) finds that executive support systems have the fundamental function of concentrating management attention and helping managers to have a focusing influence on the organization.

March and Simon (1958) suggested that the structure of *communication channels* in organizations will affect attention-allocation phenomena by determining which type of stimuli will reach which type of organizational members, and the awareness agents have of the consequences of their actions. In turn, ease of access, saliency, and channel affordances may feed back on organizational flows of communication and the use of different channels (Treem and Leonardi, 2012). Recent research, mostly in the light of Ocasio's ABV theory, has stressed the role of communication channels in the process of attentional engagement. Ocasio and Joseph (2005) extended the ABV theory by explaining the structure and role of communication channels in the distribution of organizational attention, and formulation and implementation of the strategic plan. Distribution and integration of attention occur through the organization's communication channels (Joseph and Ocasio, 2012). Recent studies demonstrate how distribution of attention is affected by specific communication channels. For example, Bouquet and Birkinshaw (2008) explain how subsidiary firms may actively gain or lose the positive attention and efforts of their parent corporate headquarters managers, and how they can have more control over the attention their parent companies dedicate to them. Dutton, Ashford, O'Neill, and Lawrence (2001) explore issue selling and describe how managers' initiatives may shape the attention of top management, and thereby, influence the organizational moves and performance.

Most attention research primarily focuses on structures of communication channels to measure the response to the environmental stimuli (Joseph and Ocasio, 2012). Ocasio, Laamanen, and Vaara (2018) propose communication as a process by which actors can attend to and engage with organizational and environmental issues and initiatives. Comparing the examples of Apple and Motorola companies, Ocasio and Joseph (2018) demonstrate that integrating attention through communication channels with the communications within those channels can be useful in reaching coherence in strategy formulation and implementation. Apple's focus on sustaining organizational attention over the implementation of its strategy, as opposed to the lack of it by Motorola, contribute to the explanation of why Apple succeeded in making smartphones the digital hub, integrating different technologies, while Motorola experienced strategic failure despite moving with similar intents.

Corporate *governance* mechanisms also affect patterns of attention at the top of organizations, sometimes in subtle ways. In particular, the board composition matters, as it affects the diversity of cognitive lenses through which board members look at issues. Tuggle, Simmon, Reutzel, and Bierman (2010) and Tuggle, Schnatterly, and Johnson (2010) argue that heterogeneity on a board of directors influences their patterns of attention by affecting how boards allocate their attention between monitoring functions and discussing new entrepreneurial issues. Tuggle et al. (2010) analyzed a sample of 210 firms by collecting data on board compositions and the text of their board minutes. They suggest that tenure variance, firm/industry background heterogeneity, and the proportion of directors with output-oriented backgrounds are positively associated with the discussion of entrepreneurial issues. Some recent studies examine how governance may affect the attention given to issues and the responses that are formulated. Galbreath's findings (2018) highlight that certain attention structures link boards, inasmuch boards engage in environmental scanning and stakeholder debate. Galbreath also finds interaction between environmental scanning and women on boards, and between stakeholder debate and women on boards. Gender diversity is likely to shift attention through a change in the nature of the attention-directing structures (e.g., environmental scanning, stakeholder debate), rather than through a direct effect.

Surprisingly, little heed has been paid to the role of incentives in directing attention in organizations, despite Simon's (1947) early remark that motivation (together with emotion) is the mechanism responsible for the allocation of attention to competing tasks. It is somehow ironic that inquiry into the role of incentive mechanisms as attention allocation systems has been mostly left to "rational" theories of organizations, in particular to agency models. In their seminal paper on multitasking, Holmstrom and Milgrom (1991) have pointed out that "when there are multiple tasks, incentive pay not only serves to allocate risks and motivate hard work, but also direct the allocation of the agents' attention among their various duties" (p. 25). In their view, attention is a scarce resource that agents have to allocate among tasks that exert competing pressure. Incentives will affect which dimensions of his/her job an agent will pay attention to. As a result, "an increase in an agent's compensation in any specific task will cause some reallocation of attention away from other tasks."

Despite its original rationalistic flavor, the problem of multitasking offers an important window on mechanisms directing attention in organizations and invites closer empirical analysis. There is ample psychological evidence supporting the claim that incentives have an important role in directing human attention among competing stimuli. Stimuli associated with rewards gain prominence in individual attention and are recognized more promptly (O'Brien and Raymond, 2012). If this can generally help to maintain attention focused on relevant items, it can also generate peculiar distortions. For example, stimuli that are associated with rewards but are irrelevant to the current task can capture attention and distract from task-relevant attention (Anderson, Laurent, and Yantis, 2011).

Similar phenomena seem to emerge at the collective level of organized activity. In her excellent review on the provision of incentives on firms, Prendergast (1999) provides ample documentation on the potentially distortive effects of incentives on the allocation of attention (and consequently, selective effort), especially in multitasking situations. For example, when agents are subject to piece-rate incentives, they are less likely to help other workers (Drago and Garvey, 1998). This applies also to temporal allocation: when incentives are provided in rather distant moments of time, a distorted temporal allocation of effort is often observed, with much effort concentrated before the evaluation date, and then falling again after evaluation (Asch, 1990). While these effects can be attributed to rational calculation (e.g., distorted temporal allocation of effort may result from intertemporal discounting; Prendergast 1999), an interpretation in terms of limited attention seems equally plausible. More research is needed to disentangle these two explanations.

An especially interesting example of how attention relates to incentives is provided by the so-called crowding-out problem (Frey and Oberholzer-Gee, 1997; Fehr and List, 2004; Gneezy, Meier, and Rey-Biel, 2011). It has repeatedly been observed that explicit incentives addressed at inducing behaviors, such as cooperation, trust, or education may actually produce a contrary effect. For example, pro-social behavior may actually be discouraged rather than favored by the introduction of monetary incentives meant to support it. A well-known case is that of blood donation: the introduction of a monetary reward for blood donors actually causes a drop in blood donation, unless an option is left to leave money to a charity (Mellström and Johannesson, 2008). In the employment relationship, the introduction of incentives that rely on monitoring and fining agents who underperform may significantly decrease the agents' effort (Fehr and Gächter, 2002). A basic explanation of the crowding-out effect relies on the fact that incentives direct attention toward certain features of social interaction (Heyman and Ariely, 2004) and thus induce different frames of the decision situation, e.g., from social to monetary (Gneezy et al., 2011). On the contrary, positive affect factors may activate prosocial frames and direct attention toward non-job-specific behaviors and tasks, triggering Organizational Citizenship behavior (Organ, 1988).

The adaptive value of (in)attention

Organizations can be conceived as adaptive responses to the cognitive limits of individuals. "Organizations will have structure ... insofar as there are boundaries of rationality ... If there were not boundaries to rationality ... there could be no stable organizational structure" (March and Simon, 1958, p. 192). A fundamental function of organizations is to manage the gap between the overabundance of information in the world and the limited attention of individual minds. Many features of organizational structures and mechanisms are responses to such limitation (Simon, 1971).

However, attention is not just a problem that organizations have to solve. Attentional processes significantly contribute to how organizations adapt to their environments, and, as such, they have their own, relevant adaptive value. First of all, attentional processes are a fundamental trigger of organizational adaptive responses (Simon, 1947; Nigam and Ocasio, 2010). Sequential shifts in attention are especially relevant to understanding adaptive change, also because they connect cognitive components to the reshaping of organizational coalitions. In his analysis of corporate environmentalism from 1960 to 1993, Hoffman (1999) shows how changes in the chemical industry were triggered by attention shifts related to specific events. These changes were accompanied by transformations in the patterns of interactions among stakeholders.

Attentional processes have adaptive relevance also because they affect which features of the environment organizations pay attention to as they change. Individuals and organizations do not consider all stimuli from their environment but pay attention selectively to only a few of them (Ocasio, 1997). This leads to selective responses that end up determining to which environmental subsystems organizations will adapt to. Weick (1979) has aptly defined such a process as enactment: through focused attention and response, an organization selects (and to some extent "creates") the environment to which it is adapting. This means that the fitness criteria that determine successful adaptation are to some extent endogenous, and that attention actively contributes to generating them.

The adaptive value of attention is enhanced by the shifting nature of organization goals. The very notion of adaptive success depends upon the criteria with which organizational performance emerge, often as a result of quasi-resolution of conflict. As Cyert and March (1963) have suggested, a fundamental way in which organizations adapt is by learning which performance criteria to attend for. This also means that organizational learning defines its own criteria of success. Attentional shifts triggering change and the subsequent organizational adaptation may often result from the dynamics of aspiration levels connected to different goals. By analyzing growth patterns in the insurance industry, Greve (2008) has shown how firm's growth may be the result of a shift of attention to size when profitability goals are satisfied.

Whereas attentional constraints may be seen as a cognitive limitation, they also bring some advantages as far as adaptive processes are concerned. The "less is more" argument (Gigerenzer and Todd, 1999) seems to apply also in the context of attention allocation. In this context, it is worth noticing that scholars of language acquisition have suggested that processing limits of children increase their ability to learn a language (Newport, 1990; Entman, 1993) because processing limits favor focusing on the crucial components of language. In a related essay, Kareev (1995) has shown that processing limitations can produce positive bias in detecting correlations in the environment, which in turn may enhance early detection of potentially informative relationships among variables. A first important implication of attentional limit is that only a few features of experience are indeed considered feed learning. In a dimensionally rich environment, limiting attention to a few features can certainly limit in the long term the accuracy of learning processes. However, it can considerably improve the speed of learning and adaptive performance in the short run. "Speed of learning favors selective attention" (Kruschke and Hullinger, 2010). In turn, selective attention affects the speed of learning (Knudsen and Warglien, 2018). If organizations have limited time to learn, in some environments this advantage may turn out to be important. Knudsen and Warglien (2018) show that in skewed environments where different cues have different informative value, agents with limited attention will learn from a subset of features only and adapt faster than "broad-minded" agents who consider all features presented by experience. Moreover, if short-term learning-speed advantage leads organizations to have access to more information (e.g., because they acquire more customers), the adaptive advantage might become a permanent one, even in the long run. Finally, attention limits may reduce the negative effects of overfitting that may be caused by considering a too-large asset of variables in learning (Goldstein and Gigerenzer, 2009; see also Artinger, Petersen, Gigerenzer, and Weibler, 2015); in fact, they act as a sort of "model selection" constraint that improves the robustness of inferences. Whether these advantages of limited processing apply to organizational learning, especially in non-stationary environments and facing changes, is still an open and under-investigated issue (Bingham and Eisenhardt, 2011) that certainly deserves more attention.

Inattention: from the economist's point of view

Limited attention (often: inattention) has become a hot topic in economics. Many economists have no problem in assuming that attention is a scarce resource, and as such an excellent subject for economic inquiry. Gabaix (2017) offers an excellent introduction to this rapidly growing field of inquiry and suggests that the concept of limited attention has the potential to explain and unify many behavioral anomalies.

The basic paradigm of inattention is that when agents receive a signal with n dimensions, agents "pay attention" only to $m < n$ dimensions, substituting the signal value with a default one in the remaining $n-m$ dimensions. In more graded version, they can pay "partial" attention to each dimension, adjusting the default value in direction of the signal value. Regardless, inattention generates an "anchoring and adjustment" process in which the set of defaults is partially adjusted toward the signal values. Gabaix (2017) shows how a large set of familiar decision-making biases can be modeled as special cases of the inattention paradigm. For example, quasi-hyperbolic discounting (Laibson, 1997) can be modeled as inattention to the future, providing a simple interpretation of intertemporal-choice anomalies. This interpretation is also normatively manageable, as exponential discounting can be preserved, in this case, the normative reference.

Organizational economics has provided some interesting applications of the inattention paradigm to classical organizational issues. Consider, for example, the tradeoffs between the two most general forms of organizational coordination (March and Simon, 1958): decentralized communication and standardized behavior. Decentralized communication relies on continuous, multilateral feedback among agents. Standardized behavior resorts to predefined rules that established *ex ante* which behavior is appropriate in which context, e.g., through standard operating procedures. It is possible to frame such tradeoffs in attentional terms. Decentralized communication taxes agents' attention, while standard operating procedures save attention resources by making use of a default. Dessein and Santos (2006) build a simple model in which the quality of communication between two organizational agents is a function of the cost of attention. Agents have aligned interests (a team model), must perform multiple tasks, and their payoff depends on (1) how accurately their action matches the current state of the environment and (2) on how well they coordinate their actions. The "standard operating procedure" captures the optimal response to the average state of the environment. There are n tasks to coordinate, and each agent is allocated a task – and only he/she can observe the current state of the environment in such dimension and transmit it to the other agents – but successful transmission is a function of attention. Dessein and Santos show that attentional factors determine the adaptability of an organization: under low-attention conditions, standard operating procedures minimize the cost of miscoordination but make the organization unresponsive, as the agent who observes the true state of the environment will prefer to act according to standard operating procedures rather than respond to the current state, thereby incurring the risk of miscoordination with other agents. Moreover, they show that attention limits the division of labor: as tasks are more fractioned, organizations become more rigid as the cost of miscoordination by feedback will increase with the number of tasks to coordinate.

In a subsequent development of the model, Dessein, Galeotti, and Santos (2016) show that organizations can structure in asymmetric ways the distribution of attention, by focusing all coordination by feedback on a few focal tasks while leaving other tasks to standardized behavior. This example shows the remarkable potential for a dialogue between the economics of inattention and the models of bounded rationality. The role of standard-operating procedures as economizers of attention, the interactions of attention and division of labor, and hybrid models of coordination in which standardization of some tasks frees attention for non-routine coordination, are classical themes of the Carnegie tradition, and these recent models offer new insights and qualifications that enrich our understanding of these issues. An interesting aspect is that such models are typically equilibrium ones, and require that attentional limits are common knowledge, which is a problem leading to the well-known problems of "super-rational" awareness of bounded rationality.

Open questions

The numbers of studies on "attention to attention" have been steadily increasing in recent years, but there are important theoretical areas and empirical issues that still need to be addressed and offer relevant opportunities for new research (e.g., van Knippenberg, Dahlander, Haas, and George, 2015). Here we suggest a few of them that we find of special priority.

1. *Better integrating organizational attention and organizational learning models.* Models of organizational learning do not usually consider the effect of attentional factors on adaptive performance. Particularly important issues concern the potential benefits of attention limits: Does bounded attention improve learning performance? In which type of environments? What attention mechanisms favor learning? A second major *terra incognita* is how attentional mechanisms help cope with changes in the structure of the environment. Most organizational learning models consider only stationary environments. On the other hand, empirical studies suggest that attention plays a major role in how organizations perceive disruptive events and trigger response to changing environments. The study of adaptation to non-stationary environments opens a set of new questions for students of organizational learning. Some of them are exquisitely attentional. How is non-stationarity recognized? And, if it is recognized, what forces may determine under-reaction (or maybe over-reaction)? How does responding to novelty imply redistributing attentional across organizational members?

2. *Organizational politics and attention.* Organizational cognition and the study of political processes in organization have remained substantially separate domains of inquiry. As originally suggested by Cyert and March (1963), the allocation of attention is a crucial connecting link between these two domains. One area where this is especially evident is organizational communication. Communication affects selective attention (Entman 1993) and helps determine the frames through which organizational actors perceive and interpret decision-making issues and their own interest. This offers opportunities to model "cognitive coalitions" in organizations in which the patterns of alignment of organizational actors in coalitions depend on which dimensions of the coalitional problem are activated by selective attention. Interestingly enough, this seems also an issue that lends itself naturally to experimental treatment. A model of quasi-resolution of conflict might be mature.

3. *Attention failures.* The negative side of the attention limits is the failure of individuals and organizations to detect relevant events and understand changes in their environment (Bansal, Kim, and Wood, 2018), reinforcing the structural (Hannan and Freeman, 1984) and cognitive (Tripsas and Gavetti, 2000) forces leading to organizational inertia. Bounded awareness is the other face of focusing, as it prevents people from considering relevant, available, and perceivable information for informed decision-making (Chugh and Bazerman, 2007). This focusing failure is closely related to well-documented psychology research, such as "inattentional blindness" (Neisser, 1979), "focalism" (Wilson, Wheatley, Meyers, Gilbert, and Axsom, 2000), and "information avoidance" (Golman, Hagmann, and Loewenstein, 2017). This a general problem: for example, Zegart (2006) pointed out that despite the many signals collected about the possibility of a severe terroristic threat, the counter-terrorism agencies did not adjust rapidly enough to prevent the 11 September 2001 attacks. This adaptation failure, which originated in politics, had the consequence that the agencies involved failed to achieve the changes they believed were needed very urgently. Identifying the organizational mechanisms responsible for collective attention failures may require going beyond analogies with individual processes and, instead, articulating how the distribution of attention and the communication channels integrating it work or do not work in detecting threats (e.g., Rerup, 2009; Vuori and Huy, 2016) and opportunities (Shepherd, Mcmullen, and Ocasio, 2017) outside the attentional focus of an organization. This topic may require looking more carefully into the processes through which organizations update

or fail to update their attention rules (Cyert and March, 1963) by responding to weak signals from the environment.

4. *Developing experimental paradigms.* Ocasio (2011) has lamented a lack of cumulativity in research on organizational attention. One natural research strategy to increase cumulativity would be to put both theoretical propositions and inspirations from field observations into hypotheses that can be tested through careful, reproducible laboratory experimentation. Despite the burgeoning development of experimental paradigms to study attention in psychology (e.g., Fawcett, Risko, and Kingstone, 2015), very little has been done in the field of organization research. Experiments on organizational attention should address aspects that are usually absent in psychological research but would be key parameters in the design of an organizational lab setting. Three of them are especially relevant. (a) *The distribution of attention.* A fundamental feature of organizations is that attention is structurally distributed. Experiments should enable to specify the distribution of attention of agents. (b) *Mechanisms of attention integration.* Organizations provide a multiplicity of mechanisms integrating individual attention processes (hierarchies, decision premises, communication, etc.). An organizational experiment should enable evaluation of how these mechanisms interact with attention distribution in affecting organizational performance. (c) *Strategic aspects of attention.* Experiments should enable control of the effect of how different interests affect attention allocation. Examples include the effect of incentives, attention capture, and strategic manipulation of agendas.

References

Anderson, Brian A., Laurent, Patryk A., and Yantis, Steven. 2011. Value-driven attentional capture. *Proceedings of the National Academy of Sciences of the U.S.A.*, 108(25): 10367–10371.

Anthony, Robert N., and Govindarajan, Vijay, 2007. *Management Control Systems.* 12th ed. Boston: McGraw-Hill/Irwin.

Artinger, Florian, Petersen, Malte, Gigerenzer, Gerd, and Weibler, Jürgen. 2015. Heuristics as adaptive decision strategies in management. *Journal of Organizational Behavior*, 36(S1): S33–S52.

Asch, Beth J. 1990. Do incentives matter? The case of navy recruiters. *Industrial and Labor Relations Review*, 43(3): 89S–106S.

Bansal, Pratima, Kim, Anna, and Wood, Michael O. 2018. Hidden in plain sight: The importance of scale in organizations' attention to issues. *The Academy of Management Review*, 43(2): 217–241.

Barnard, Chester I. 1938. *The Functions of the Executive.* Cambridge, MA: Harvard University Press.

Bingham, Christopher B., and Eisenhardt, Kathleen M. 2011. Rational heuristics: The 'simple rules' that strategists learn from process experience. *Strategic Management Journal*, 32(13): 1437–1464.

Bouquet, Cyril and Birkinshaw, Julian. 2008. Weight versus voice: How foreign subsidiaries gain attention from corporate headquarters. *Academy of Management Journal*, 51(3): 577–601, doi:10.5465/amj.2008.32626039.

Chugh, Dolly, and Bazerman, Max H. 2007. Bounded awareness: What you fail to see can hurt you. *Mind & Society*, 6(1): 1–18.

Cohen, Michael D., March, James G., and Olsen, Johan P. 1972. A garbage can model of organizational choice. *Administrative Science Quarterly*, 17(1): 1–25.

Cyert, Richard M., and March, James G. 1963. *A Behavioral Theory of the Firm.* Englewood Cliffs, NJ: Prentice-Hall.

Dearborn, DeWitt C., and Simon, Herbert A. 1958. Selective perception: A note on the departmental identifications of executives. *Sociometry*, 21(2): 140–144.

Dessein, Wouter, Galeotti, Andrea, and Santos, Tano. 2016. Rational inattention and organizational focus. *American Economic Review*, 106(6): 1522–1536, doi:10.1257/aer.20140741.

Dessein, Wouter, and Santos, Tano. 2006. Adaptive organizations. *Journal of Political Economy*, 114(5): 956–995, doi:10.1086/508031.

Drago, Robert, and Garvey, Gerald T. 1998. Incentives for helping on the job: Theory and evidence. *Journal of Labor Economics*, 16(1): 1–25.

Dutton, J. E., Ashford, S. J., O'Neill, R. M., and Lawrence, K. A. 2001. Moves that matter: Issue selling and organizational change. *Academy of Management Journal*, 44(4): 716–736, doi:10.2307/3069412.

Entman, Robert M. 1993. Framing: Toward clarification of a fractured paradigm. *Journal of Communication*, 43(4): 51–58.

Fawcett, Jonathan, Risko, Evan, and Kingstone, Alan. 2015. *The Handbook of Attention*. Cambridge, MA: MIT Press.

Fehr, Ernst, and Gächter, Simon. 2002. Do incentive contracts crowd out voluntary cooperation? IEW Working Papers 034, Institute for Empirical Research in Economics, University of Zurich.

Fehr, Ernst, and List, John A. 2004. The hidden costs and returns of incentives: Trust and trustworthiness among CEOs. *Journal of the European Economic Association*, 2(5): 743–771.

Festre´, Agnes, and Garrouste, Pierre. 2015. The 'Economics of Attention': A history of economic thought perspective. *Oeconomia: History, Methodology, Philosophy*, 5(1): 3–36.

Frey, Bruno S., and Oberholzer-Gee, Felix. 1997. The cost of price incentives: An empirical analysis of motivation crowding-out. *The American Economic Review*, 87(4): 746–755.

Gabaix, Xavier. 2017. Behavioral inattention. NBER Working Paper No. w24096, National Bureau of Economic Research, Cambridge, MA.

Galbreath, Jeremy. 2018. Do boards of directors influence corporate sustainable development? An attention-based analysis: Board influence on corporate sustainable development. *Business Strategy and the Environment*, doi:10.1002/bse.2028.

Gigerenzer, Gerd, and Todd, Peter M. 1999. *Simple heuristics that make us smart*. New York: Oxford University Press.

Gneezy, Uri, Meier, Stephan, and Rey-Biel, Pedro. 2011. When and why incentives (don't) work to modify behavior. *Journal of Economic Perspectives*, 25(4): 191–210, doi:10.1257/ jep.25.4.191.

Goldstein, Daniel G., and Gigerenzer, Gerd. 2009. Fast and frugal forecasting. *International Journal of Forecasting*, 25(4): 760–772.

Golman, Russell, Hagmann, David, and Loewenstein, George. 2017. Information avoidance. *Journal of Economic Literature*, 55(1): 96–135, doi:10.1257/jel.20151245.

Greve, Henrich R. 2008. A behavioral theory of firm growth: Sequential attention to size and performance goals. *Academy of Management Journal*, 51(3): 476–494, doi:10.5465/amj.2008.32625975.

Hannan, M. T., and Freeman, J. 1984. Structural inertia and organizational change. *American Sociological Review*, 49: 149–164.

Heyman, James, and Ariely, Dan. 2004. Effort for payment: A tale of two markets. *Psychological Science*, 15(11): 787–793.

Hoffman, Andrew J. 1999. Institutional evolution and change: Environmentalism and the us chemical industry. *Academy of Management Journal*, 42(4): 351–371.

Holmstrom, Bengt, and Milgrom, Paul. 1991. Multitask principal-agent analyses: Incentive contracts, asset ownership, and job design. *Journal of Law, Economics, & Organization*, 7: 24–25.

James, William. 1890. *The Principles of Psychology*. New York: Henry Holt and Company.

Joseph, John, and Ocasio, William. 2012. Architecture, attention, and adaptation in the multibusiness firm: General Electric from 1951 to 2001. *Strategic Management Journal*, 33(6): 633–660, doi:10.1002/ smj.1971.

Joseph, John, and Wilson, Alex J. 2018. The growth of the firm: An attention-based view. *Strategic Management Journal*, 39(6): 1779–1800, doi:10.1002/smj.2715.

Kaplan, Sarah. 2008. Framing contests: Strategy making under uncertainty. *Organization Science*, 19(5): 729–752, doi:10.1287/orsc.1070.0340.

Kareev, Yaakov. 1995. Through a narrow window: Working memory capacity and the detection of covariation. *Cognition*, 56(3): 263–269.

Knudsen, Thorbjørn, and Warglien, Massimo. 2018. Why less is more: The power of simple cognitive representations in organizational search and learning. SOD-SDU Working Paper, Strategic Organization Design, University of Southern Denmark.

Kruschke, John K., and Hullinger, Richard A. 2010. Evolution of attention in learning. In Nestor A. Schmajuk (Ed.), *Computational Models of Conditioning* (pp. 10–52). Cambridge: Cambridge University Press.

Laibson, David. 1997. Golden eggs and hyperbolic discounting. *The Quarterly Journal of Economics*, 112(2): 443–478, doi:10.1162/003355397555253.

March, J. G., and Simon, H. 1958. *Organizations*. New York: John Wiley & Sons.

Maula, Markku V. J., Keil, Thomas, and Zahra, Shaker A. 2013. Top management's attention to discontinuous technological change: Corporate venture capital as an alert mechanism. *Organization Science*, 24(3): 926–947.

Mellström, Carl, and Johannesson, Magnus. 2008. Crowding out in blood donation: Was Titmuss right? *Journal of the European Economic Association*, 6(4): 845–863.

Neisser, Ulric. 1979. The concept of intelligence. *Intelligence*, 3(3): 217–227.

Newport, Elissa L. 1990.Maturational constraints on language learning. *Cognitive Science*, 14(1): 11–28.

Nigam, Amit, and Ocasio, William. 2010. Event attention, environmental sensemaking, and change in institutional logics: An inductive analysis of the effects of public attention to Clinton's health care reform initiative. *Organization Science*, 21(4): 823–841.

O'Brien, Jennifer L., and Raymond, Jane E. 2012. Learned predictiveness speeds visual processing. *Psychological Science*, 23(4): 359–363.

Ocasio, William. 1997. Towards an attention-based view of the firm. *Strategic Management Journal*, 18(S1): 187–206.

Ocasio, William. 2011. Attention to attention. *Organization Science*, 22(5): 1286–1296.

Ocasio, William. 2012. Situated attention, loose and tight coupling, and the garbage can model. In Alessandro Lomi, and J. Richard Harrison (Eds.), *The Garbage Can Model of Organizational Choice: Looking Forward at Forty*, volume 36 of *Research in the Sociology of Organizations* (pp. 293–317). Bingley, UK: Emerald Group Publishing Limited.

Ocasio, William, and Joseph, John. 2008. Rise and fall – or transformation? the evolution of strategic planning at the General Electric Company, 1940–2006. *Long Range Planning*, 41(3): 248–272.

Ocasio, William, and Joseph, John. 2018. The attention-based view of great strategies. *Strategy Science*, 3(1): 289–294.

Ocasio, William, Laamanen, Tomi, and Vaara, Eero. 2018. Communication and attention dynamics: An attention-based view of strategic change. *Strategic Management Journal*, 39(1): 155–167.

O'Donoghue, T., and Rabin, M. 1999. Doing it now or later. *American Economic Review*, 89(1): 103–124.

Organ, Dennis W. 1988. *Organizational Citizenship Behavior: The Good Soldier Syndrome*. Washington, DC: Lexington Books/DC Heath and Com.

Prendergast, Canice. 1999. The provision of incentives in firms. *Journal of Economic Literature*, 37(1): 7–63.

Rerup, Claus. 2009. Attentional triangulation: Learning from unexpected rare crises. *Organizational Science*, 5(20): 876893.

Shepherd, D. A.. McMullen, J. S., and Jennings, P. D. 2007. The formation of opportunity beliefs: Overcoming ignorance and reducing doubt. *Strategic Entrepreneurship Journal*, 1(1–2): 75–95.

Shepherd, Dean A., McMullen, Jeffery S., and Ocasio, William. 2017. Is that an opportunity? An attention model of top managers' opportunity beliefs for strategic action. *Strategic Management Journal*, 38(3): 626–644.

Simon, Herbert A. 1947. *Administrative Behavior: A Study of the Decision-Making Process in Administrative Organization*. New York: Macmillan.

Simon, Herbert A. 1954. Centralization vs. decentralization in organizing the controller's department: A research study and report. Number 4 in A1. Controllership Foundation.

Simon, Herbert A. 1971. Designing organizations for an information-rich world. *Computers, Communications, and the Public Interest*, 72: 37.

Simon, Herbert A. 1982. *Reason in Human Affairs*, vol. 1982. Stanford, CA: Stanford University Press.

Simons, Robert. 1991. Strategic orientation and top management attention to control systems. *Strategic Management Journal*, 12(1): 49–62.

Tolman, Edward C. 1932. *Purposive Behavior in Animals and Men*. New York: The Century Co.

Treem, J. W., and Leonardi, P. 2012. Social media use in organizations: Exploring the affordances of visibility, editability, persistence and association. *Communication Yearbook*, 36: 143–189.

Tripsas, Mary, and Giovanni Gavetti. 2000. Capabilities, cognition, and inertia: Evidence from digital imaging. *Strategic Management Journal*, 21(10–11): 1147–1161.

Tuggle, Chris S., Simmon, David G., Reutzel, Chris R., and Bierman, Leonard. 2010. Commanding board of director attention: Investigating how organizational performance and CEO duality affect board members attention to monitoring. *Strategic Management Journal*, 31(9): 946–968.

Tuggle, Christopher S., Schnatterly, Karen, and Johnson, Richard A. 2010. Attention patterns in the boardroom: How board composition and processes affect discussion of entrepreneurial issues. *The Academy of Management Journal*, 53(3): 550–571.

Vandenbosch, Betty. 1999. An empirical analysis of the association between the use of executive support systems and perceived organizational competitiveness. *Accounting, Organizations and Society*, 24(1): 77–92.

van Knippenberg, Daan, Dahlander, Linus, Haas, Martine R., and George, Gerard. 2015. Information, attention, and decision making. *Academy of Management Journal*, 58(3): 649–657, doi:10.5465/amj.2015.4003.

Vuori, Timo O., and Huy, Quy N. 2016. Distributed attention and shared emotions in the innovation process: How Nokia lost the smartphone battle. *Administrative Science Quarterly*, 61(1): 9–51. doi:10.1177/0001839215606951.

Weick, Karl E. 1979. *The social psychology of organizing* (2nd ed.). New York: Random House.

Wilson, Alex James, and Joseph, John. 2015. Organizational attention and technological search in the multibusiness firm: Motorola from 1974 to 1997. In Giovanni Gavetti, and William Ocasio (Eds.), *Cognition and Strategy*, vol. 32 of *Advances in Strategic Management: A Research Annual* (pp. 407–435). Bingley: Emerald Group Publishing Limited.

Wilson, Timothy D., Wheatley, Thalia, Meyers, Jonathan M., Gilbert, Daniel T., and Axsom, Danny. 2000. Focalism: A source of durability bias in affective forecasting. *Journal of Personality and Social Psychology*, 78(5): 821–836.

Zbaracki, Mark J., and Bergen, Mark. 2015. Managing market attention. In Giovanni Gavetti and William Ocasio (Eds.), *Cognition and Strategy*, volume 32 of *Advances in Strategic Management: A Research Annual* (pp. 371–405). Bingley: Emerald Group Publishing Limited.

Zegart, Amy B. 2006. An empirical analysis of failed intelligence reforms before September 11. *Political Science Quarterly*, 121(1): 33–60.

36

THE BOUNDED RATIONALITY OF GROUPS AND TEAMS

Torsten Reimer, Hayden Barber, and Kirstin Dolick

Like many teenage boys in Liverpool in 1960, John Lennon and Paul McCartney wanted to start a rock band. However, as their fledgling band went from record company to record company with their manager Brian Epstein, it became clear: Britain was getting tired of rock and roll. According to Dick Rowe, who famously turned them down from Decca Records, "Not to mince words, Mr. Epstein, we don't like your boys' sound. Groups of guitarists are on their way out" (Lewisohn, 2013, p. 557). On the other hand, America at that time had never seen anything like The Beatles. The Beatles received a very different reaction in the US than in Britain. Seventy-three million Americans—the largest audience to view a show at that time—tuned in to the *Ed Sullivan Show* on February 9, 1964, to watch the optimism and joviality of four young Brits. The Beatles had enjoyed only moderate success in Britain, but their success skyrocketed in the US. It was not just The Beatles, but the pairing of The Beatles with a particular time and place that made their music so successful. The story of The Beatles points to an important aspect of the bounded rationality of groups and teams: The success or failure of a group cannot be understood without looking at the environment in which the group is embedded. The same strategy and behavior may be successful in one environment but result in a failure in another environment. Thus, it can be adaptive to change strategies such that they match the characteristics of environments; and, at times, it can also be adaptive to change or switch environments. Different from classic standards of rationality such as logical consistency, bounded rationality focuses on the match between a decision strategy or problem procedure and characteristics of the environment (Gigerenzer & Selten, 2001). Common characteristics of environments that have been studied in individual decision-making research include characteristics of the structure of the information environment, such as the similarity of choice alternatives and the similarity of the attributes that describe the choice alternatives (Gigerenzer & Gaissmaier, 2011). In the context of groups and teams, the environment also includes social characteristics of the group members such as the distribution of knowledge about the choice alternatives and the distribution of preferences among the involved members for specific attributes (see Reimer, Roland, & Russell, 2017).

The concept of bounded rationality offers a new perspective on the study of groups and teams. *Bounded rationality* can be seen as a guiding principle to conduct research that focuses

DOI: 10.4324/9781315658353-42

on three inter-related questions: (1) *The strategy*: Which strategies *should* groups use to form decisions and solve problems (prescriptive question) and which strategies *do* groups use to form decisions (descriptive question)?; (2) *The environment*: What are the characteristics of the social and non-social environments in which groups form decisions?; and (3) *Group adaptivity*: Are groups able to form ecologically rational decisions by selecting strategies that match the structure of their social and non-social environments?

The descriptive strategy question is the only question out of the three questions that has repeatedly received attention in the literature on groups and teams (e.g., see Davis, 1982; Kerr, MacCoun, & Kramer, 1996). Hardly any studies have looked at the second or third questions regarding the information environments that are encountered by groups and the match between group decision strategies and those environments. Likewise, only few studies have addressed the question of how groups *should* form their decisions (e.g., see Hastie & Kameda, 2005). The history of group research, though, is filled with studies that have evaluated group performance, including the quality of group decisions and problem solutions. This history is—by and large—a history of failure, documenting the irrationality and poor performance of groups. Accordingly, there is an abundance of studies on process losses in groups, whereas only few studies on groups and teams identified process gains (for an example of a process gain, see research on the Koehler effect, Kerr & Seok, 2011).

The notion of bounded rationality offers new conceptual and methodological perspectives on the study of groups that hold the promise of providing alternative interpretations of at least some of the process losses that have been described in the literature. In the remainder of our chapter, we will first introduce a prominent task in group research, the hidden-profile task, that is often cited as an example demonstrating that groups fail to form good decisions. Extensive research on this task has suggested that groups are not able to connect the dots and integrate relevant knowledge and, as a consequence, form poor decisions (for overviews, see Lu, Yuan, & McLeod, 2012; Sohrab, Waller, & Kaplan, 2015). We demonstrate that approaching this task from the perspective of bounded rationality can alter the interpretation of those findings. Guided by the bounded rationality perspective, we illustrate in which situations groups can solve hidden-profile tasks. The study of the bounded rationality of groups and teams is in its infancy but has much to offer to the field of group communication and decision making. We conclude by highlighting key insights from group research that has explored the bounded rationality of groups and offer questions for future research.

Bounded rationality as an eye-opener: the case of hidden profiles

Research on groups and teams has often taken an information-processing perspective by describing how task-related knowledge is distributed in groups and which pieces of information groups discuss when forming decisions (e.g., Hinsz, Tindale, & Vollrath, 1997; Reimer et al., 2017). A prominent task in this research tradition is the hidden-profile task (Stasser & Titus, 1985; Stasser & Abele, 2020). Hidden-profile tasks are choice tasks in which groups are asked to choose among a number of choice alternatives. The tasks are typically constructed such that one choice alternative has more positive and fewer negative attributes than the other alternatives in the choice set and is therefore assumed to be the best alternative (Stasser & Titus, 1985, Note 1). However, it is unknown to the individual group members at the outset that this "best choice" has the most positive attributes as each member receives only a partial and biased set of the information on the choice alternatives prior to group deliberation: Information items on the choice alternatives are distributed such that each member has more positive and fewer negative information items on a choice alternative that is different from the best choice.

As an example, consider the following simplified scenario (see Committee 1 in Table 36.1). A three-member personnel committee has to decide which of two candidates, *Steven* or *Peter*, is better suited for an open position for a sales manager. Each of the two candidates is described in terms of several attributes including specific skills and personality traits. The columns in Table 36.1 list the attributes for each candidate, and the first three rows depict the particular set of information items that each group member is given prior to the group deliberation. The last row (*Group knowledge*) describes the information that is known to the group as a whole. For the sake of simplicity, only positive and fewer attributes as in experiments with hidden profiles are used in the example (see Reimer, Kuendig, Hoffrage, Park, & Hinsz, 2007, for the description of a more complex problem).

As illustrated in Table 36.1, each group member of Committee 1 knows that *Steven* has a business degree and that he is a reliable and kind person. Regarding *Peter*, the group knows that Peter has an engineering degree and that he can be described by a number of positive attributes—he is organized, punctual, well respected, open-minded, and hard working. Overall, there are six positive attributes in favor of Peter compared to three attributes that speak in favor of Steven. Based on the mere number of positive attributes, *one would expect that the group would pick Peter* (see the *Group knowledge* row in Table 36.1). However, note that the three committee members all have the same information about Steven (this information is shared), whereas their knowledge about Peter is unshared. As a consequence, *each individual group member is likely to prefer Steven at the outset* as each group member knows more positive attributes about Steven than they do about Peter. Thus, the question arises: Are groups able to connect the dots in their group discussions and discover that, overall, Peter is described by more positive attributes than Steven?

The literature on hidden profiles suggests that groups are unable to connect the dots in this situation: A vast majority of groups fail to detect hidden profiles by choosing the alternative that is preferred by most members at the outset (Steven in our example; for overviews, see Sohrab et al., 2015; Luan et al., 2012). Empirical studies included various types of groups (e.g., professional teams in organizations; teams of doctors and nurses) as well as a variety of tasks (e.g., medical choice tasks, murder mysteries, and personnel selection tasks).

Why are groups not able to detect hidden profiles? The most prominent explanations for the hidden-profile effect focus on why those pieces of information that are shared by all group members have more impact on group decisions than unshared pieces of information. One explanation is based on the sampling advantage of shared information, that is, the observation that groups tend to exchange more of their shared than unshared information items and also pay more attention to shared information when it is brought up during group discussions (Stasser & Titus, 1985; Reimer, Reimer, & Hinsz, 2010; Wittenbaum & Park, 2001). If the group members of Committee 1 primarily exchange their shared information on Steven, they will fail to become aware that Peter's profile has more positive attributes than Steven's profile.

A second prominent explanation is based on the observation that shared compared to unshared information also has a greater impact on the preferences of the individual group members at the outset because shared information is known to more group members (the common-knowledge effect; see Gigone & Hastie, 1993). Hidden-profile tasks are set up such that shared information favors the preferences that group members form before they enter group discussions. If the group integrates members' initial preferences on the basis of a social combination rule like the majority rule, groups will fail to choose the hidden-profile alternative. Groups only rarely choose an alternative that is not proposed by at least one member at the outset (e.g., Brodbeck, Kerschreiter, Mojzisch, Frey, & Schulz-Hardt, 2002; Reimer, 1999). In short, according to these two explanations, groups fail to connect the dots in hidden-profile

Table 36.1 Two hidden profiles in information environments with two alternatives (Candidate A and B), three group members (Members 1 to 3), and unique (Committee 1) or common attributes (Committee 2)

Committee 1: unique attributes

Member/group	Knowledge about Steven	Knowledge about Peter	Decision based on a count of positive attributes
Member 1	Reliable, kind, business degree	Organized, open-minded	Steven
Member 2	Reliable, kind, business degree	Hard working, respected	Steven
Member 3	Reliable, kind, business degree	Punctual, engineering degree	Steven
Group knowledge	Reliable, kind, business degree	Organized, open-minded, punctual, respected, hardworking, engineering degree	Peter

Committee 2: common attributes

Member/group	Knowledge about Steven	Knowledge about Peter	Decision based on a count of positive attributes
Member 1	*Reliable*, kind, business degree	*Reliable*, organized	Steven
Member 2	Reliable, *kind*, business degree	*Kind*, open-minded	Steven
Member 3	Reliable, kind, *business degree*	*Business degree*, hardworking	Steven
Group knowledge	*Reliable, kind, business degree*	*Reliable, kind, business degree*, organized, open-minded, hard working	Peter

Notes: In the examples, attributes are assumed to be positive throughout. Thus, each attribute speaks, if present, in favor of the particular candidate. Attributes that do not discriminate between alternatives are written in italics. The numbers of information items that are known to the group and to the individual group members as well as the two candidates' sum scores are held constant across the two committees. The profile on Peter is hidden to the individual group members. *Group knowledge* displays the information items that are known to the group as a whole.

tasks because their shared information has more impact on the group members' individual preferences (common-knowledge effect) and is also more likely to be mentioned during discussion than unshared information (sampling advantage of shared information).

The starting point of our journey was the conviction that the notion of bounded rationality can help us better understand the failure of groups in experiments using hidden-profile tasks. Approaching hidden profiles from a bounded-rationality perspective suggests we apply the three questions introduced at the beginning of the chapter: (1) Which strategies should groups use when facing hidden-profile tasks (prescriptive question), and which strategies do they use when solving these tasks (descriptive question)? (2) What are the characteristics of the information environments that are used in hidden-profile research? and (3) How would ecologically rational groups behave when facing hidden-profile tasks? To answer these questions, we conducted a number of simulation studies, a meta-analysis, and experiments with interacting groups. This journey enabled us to identify a condition in which all groups were able to connect the dots and choose the hidden-profile alternative. The following sections summarize the lessons learned by addressing the three questions and provide open questions for future research.

Which strategy should groups use to solve hidden-profile tasks?

Whereas most research on hidden profiles has focused on factors that affect the amount of pooled information, the question of how the available information should be processed and integrated into a decision has been addressed by only a few studies (e.g., see Stasser, 1988; Chernyshenko, Miner, Baumann, & Sniezek, 2003).

One strategy would be to discuss *all* the available information, particularly the unshared information, and to choose the alternative that has the highest sum score. Such a communication-based unit weight linear model (Reimer & Hoffrage, 2005) would always detect hidden profiles. It is intuitive that group decisions would not be affected by the distribution of information if members exchanged and integrated all of their knowledge. However, because this would be a very inefficient and laborious endeavor, we conducted several simulation studies, in which we aimed to identify plausible decision strategies that detect hidden profiles and limit information processing at the same time (Reimer & Hoffrage, 2005; Reimer et al., 2007).

In one set of simulations, we first generated random information distributions by distributing information on a choice task randomly among the simulated members of a group. In these simulations, four-member committees selected one of three candidates in an information environment that had an outside criterion. Introducing an outside criterion allowed us to determine the strategies' accuracies under various conditions. In addition, we constructed four environments in which we systematically varied the distributions of cue validities. The validity of a cue refers to the percentage of cases in which a cue makes a correct inference (Katsikopoulos, 2011). In two of the four environments, the distribution of cue validities was linear (L), and in the other two they followed a J-shaped distribution. The two linear distributions differed with respect to their overall means (L-high versus L-low), and the two J-shaped distributions differed in their skewness, which mainly affected the validity of the most valid cues (J-flat versus J-steep; see Reimer & Hoffrage, 2006, for details).

In the next step, we selected from all the generated information environments those environments that contained a hidden profile—environments in which one choice alternative dominated the remaining alternatives by having the most positive and least negative attributes in the choice set but where information was distributed such that each individual group member's information favored another alternative. The simulations taught us several lessons. The simulated groups failed in more than 50 percent of the cases to solve the hidden-profile task when integrating individual preferences on the basis of a majority rule, irrespective of the strategy the individual members used. This result accords well with the common-knowledge effect (Gigone & Hastie, 1993): Hidden-profile tasks typically cannot be solved on the basis of a social combination rule that integrates individual preferences but require the exchange and integration of unshared information items that are known by different individual group members.

Unlike social combination rules, social communication rules integrate individual information items rather than individual choices or preferences. Similar to decision strategies for individual deciders, we implemented two types of communication-based strategies—strategies that process information *alternative-wise* and strategies that process information *attribute-wise*. The communication-based unit weight model described above is an example of a decision strategy that processes information alternative-wise: A group using this strategy discusses each choice alternative by exchanging all information on that alternative and forming an overall sum score. Once all the alternatives are discussed, the group will choose the alternative with the highest overall sum score. Conversely, the following strategy processes information attribute-wise: The strategy assumes that one group member draws the group's attention to one attribute on which this member has at least some knowledge. The group then compares the alternatives on this attribute by pooling all available values on this attribute. If the attribute discriminates among the alternatives such that one alternative has a positive characteristic that sets this alternative apart, group discussions and information processing stop, and the group will decide in favor of that alternative (see Reimer & Hoffrage, 2005, in which we also discussed variants where group members were not drawn randomly but according to their expertise). Both strategies are communication-based as they require group members to pool and share information. However, different from the alternative-based strategy, the attribute-based strategy has a stopping rule and is, thus, more frugal than the communication-based unit weight linear model. The simulations revealed that the described attribute-based strategy chose the hidden-profile alternative in a high percentage of cases, despite its frugality. As a general result, communication-based strategies led groups to choose the hidden-profile alternative much more often than combination rules. The described attribute-based strategy was particularly successful in identifying hidden profiles.

The simulation studies, thus, did not accord with the results of empirical research described in the literature. Whereas the vast majority of groups in empirical studies failed to connect the dots and choose hidden profiles in experiments, the groups in our simulations performed much better. Thus, the question arose: Why are interacting groups not able to detect hidden profiles if there are effective and efficient strategies? When we went through the literature, we discovered that all studies we could find used a peculiar information environment that might have hindered groups from using an attribute-based strategy: Groups were presented with unique attributes throughout that described only one of the choice alternatives.

Peculiar information environments trigger the use of sub-optimal strategies

The bounded rationality perspective suggests that not only characteristics of the task (e.g., Davis, 1982) but also characteristics of the information environment influence which decision strategies groups use. Research on hidden profiles provides a good example for this claim as studies on hidden profiles have used very peculiar information environments. We offer as an explanation for groups' failure to solve hidden-profile tasks that the specific information environments that have been used in the literature trigger decision strategies that are not adaptive nor goal-serving, as they do not enable groups to discover hidden profiles. Even though the sampling advantage for shared information and the hidden-profile effect have been evident in a variety of groups performing a variety of decision tasks, all of the studies held an important dimension of the information environment constant: Group members were provided with shared and unshared information for *unique attributes* that described only one of the alternatives (see Fraidin, 2004; Reimer et al., 2007). However, there is evidence from research relating to individuals that *attribute commonality* can affect which information a receiver samples and integrates into a decision.

The two dimensions of information sharedness and attribute commonality are orthogonal: The values of attributes can be shared or unshared, and attributes can be common or unique. *Sharedness of information* refers to whether an information item (i.e., an attribute value) is one that multiple group members know (shared information) or one that only one group member knows (unshared information). Conversely, *attribute commonality* refers to whether multiple (common attribute) or only one of the decision alternatives (unique attribute) has a known value for this particular attribute, irrespective of how many group members possess this knowledge (see Reimer et al., 2007). If multiple decision alternatives are described by this attribute, then this attribute is common; if only one alternative is described by this attribute, then the attribute is unique.

As in the information distribution among the members of Committee 1 (see Table 36.1), research on hidden profiles exclusively implemented unique attributes. Some of the information items on Peter and Steven are shared among group members and some information items are unshared. However, all information items refer to unique attributes. For each and every attribute, Committee 1 only has knowledge about one alternative. For example, Committee 1 knows that Peter is organized and that Steven is reliable and kind; however, the committee does not have any knowledge about whether or not Steven is organized and Peter is reliable and kind.

How does the exclusive use of unique attributes and lack of any common attributes affect the selection of strategies? Research on individuals suggests that the presentation of unique attributes triggers the use of *alternative-based* decision strategies (Burke, 1990, 1995; also see Payne, Bettman, & Johnson, 1988). Because the potential alternatives cannot be compared along the same attributes, deciders form a global impression of each alternative. Then, he or she chooses the alternative that creates the best overall impression, for example, the one with the most positive and least negative features. Conversely, the presentation of common attributes, for which *all* alternatives have a value, facilitates the implementation of *attribute-based* decision strategies—deciders compare alternatives on common attributes or features (Burke, 1990, 1995; Rieskamp & Hoffrage, 1999). Research on individuals suggests that attribute commonality can systematically influence which decision strategies are adopted at the individual level. We expected and observed that attribute commonality also has an effect on how *groups* form decisions and solve hidden-profile tasks.

To illustrate, a hidden profile within an information environment that contains common attributes is shown in the lower part of Table 36.1 (see Committee 2). As is indicated by the last row, which displays the information that is known to the group as a whole (*Group knowledge*), there are again three attributes in favor of Steven and six attributes in favor of Peter. However, in Committee 2, both candidates—Steven as well as Peter—can be described as being reliable and kind; and the group knows that both have a business degree. If group members mention Steven with respect to those three attributes during their discussion, they might also bring up what they know about Peter in regard to these attributes. This process should lead to several outcomes. First of all, the group members should realize that the attributes that support Steven do not discriminate between Steven and Peter. In other words, Steven does not possess any positive attribute that Peter would not have. Second, this process should prompt the discussion of unshared information. Imagine that Committee Member 1 tells the group that a plus for Steven is that he is kind. The other members of the group will agree because this is a shared piece of information that they all know. However, after Committee Member 1 mentions the attribute *kind*, Committee Member 2 may, in turn, mention that Peter has also been described as being kind, something the group does not already know.

As expected, we observed that providing common attributes facilitated the exchange of unshared pieces of information in group discussions (Reimer et al., 2007; Reimer et al., 2010). Note that the information environments in terms of the number of information items that are available to the individual group members as well as the candidates' sum scores are identical in the two examples displayed in Table 36.1. However, the information structure provided in the second example is decision-maker friendly insofar as a group will always detect the hidden profile if they process the available information in an attribute-wise fashion by looking for attributes that discriminate between the alternatives.

The concept of bounded rationality served as an eye-opener which enabled us to identify a major shortcoming in research on hidden profiles and to set up an experimental condition in which all groups were able to solve the hidden-profile task: In experiments systematically manipulating the attribute commonality (Reimer et al., 2007; Reimer et al., 2010), *none* of the studied groups selected the hidden-profile alternative when group members were given their information prior to group discussions, when they did not have access to their information during discussion, and when the information structure was exclusively composed of unique attributes (as in Committee 1 in Table 36.1). Conversely, *all* groups selected the hidden-profile alternative when group members were given their information about the alternatives at the onset of the group session, had access to their information sheets during group deliberation, and when information environments entailed common attributes (as in Committee 2 in Table 36.1). Distributing information at the beginning of group discussions prevented group members from forming strong individual preferences at the outset and, thus, prevented the common-knowledge effect (see Reimer et al., 2007; Reimer et al., 2010).

Bounded rationality as a research program and paradigm for group research

The study of the bounded rationality of groups and teams is in its infancy. Even though information-processing approaches in group research have a long tradition, and group research has acknowledged that group performance depends on the characteristics of the tasks that are studied (Davis, 1982; Kerr et al., 1996), only few studies have taken a bounded rationality perspective by looking at the match of decision strategies and characteristics of the information environment.

As the hidden-profile example illustrates, the concept of bounded rationality offers a new perspective to the study of groups and teams. In the remainder, we highlight two important quests for the study of group decision making from a bounded rationality perspective: (1) the focus on group adaptivity; and (2) the need to move beyond as-if models by providing process models of group decision making.

Group adaptivity

At the heart of the concept of bounded rationality is the idea of adaptive decision making. Group adaptivity refers to the match of decision strategies and the structure of information in the environment. Adaptivity can be achieved through the selection of decision strategies by groups as well as a change or even switch of the environment (e.g., as in the success story of the Beatles). As with individual decision making, there is no golden group decision strategy that fits all purposes and works well in all possible environments. Studying the bounded rationality of groups includes the methodological quest to describe not only possible decision strategies but also the information environments in which they are used, as specific strategies may yield better decisions in some environments than in others. Moreover, in group research, it is important also to consider characteristics of the social environments. For example, Luan, Katsikopoulos, and Reimer (2012) identified information environments, in which diversity in a group trumped individual accuracy and other environments in which individual accuracy trumped diversity. Specifically, individual accuracy was more important for the performance of a simulated group in task environments in which cues differed greatly in the quality of their information (as in environments with J-shaped validities as discussed above), and diversity mattered more when such differences were relatively small (as in environments with linear distributions of validities).

To the extent that groups encounter environments that demand different decision strategies and to the extent that groups encounter dynamic environments in which task demands change, it is important that groups are adaptive. It has been acknowledged in the team literature that adaptiveness is a vital competency and a component of effective teamwork (Kozlowski, 1998; Klein & Pierce, 2001). Team adaptation and the ability to select and change strategies based on information in the environment have been identified as a relevant skill in group decision making because group members must modify or replace routine performance strategies when they detect that the characteristics of the environment and task change (Salas, Sims, & Burke, 2005; Reimer, Opwis, & Bornstein, 2005; Burke, Stagl, Salas, Pierce, & Kandall, 2006). To be adaptive, teams have to be able to focus their attention on relevant information to accurately understand the situation and achieve a shared team situation model (Sonesh, Rico, & Salas, 2014). Some research suggests that groups are able to show some adaptivity in their strategy selection. Kaemmer, Gaissmaier, Reimer, and Schermuly (2014), for example, observed that groups could be best modeled by strategies that matched the predictive validity of a strategy in their groups (also see Reimer & Katsikopoulos, 2004). At the same time, groups often have difficulties in changing and adapting their behaviors in situations in which task dependencies and coordination requirements are high. This holds in particular for homogeneous groups in which group members have similar knowledge and apply the same decision or problem-solving strategies (Reimer et al., 2005). Organizations as well as teams within organizations often use routines to approach problems and form decisions (Reimer et al., 2017). Routines can have many advantages: As long as environments are stable, routines will allow teams to form decisions efficiently and reliably. Typically, members of teams who are in a routine mode have clear roles and do not have to negotiate and coordinate who is doing what. However, routine decision making is a burden in environments in which groups and teams have to make decisions under high uncertainty. In particular, if environments are dynamic and changing quickly, routines can hinder groups and teams from being adaptive. An important quest for boundedly rational groups consists in learning when to develop and apply routines and when to abandon routines or not to develop routines, to begin with. Likewise, more research is needed to better understand in which situations groups should actively alter or change their environment instead of changing the strategies and procedures that are used.

Despite the insight that the study of a group's information and social environments is necessary to understand and evaluate group decision making, only few studies have taken this quest seriously. Research on the Condorcet paradox provides an example of such an approach that can serve as a role model. The Condorcet paradox describes a situation in which plurality voting rules yield intransitive preferences. Specifically, plurality voting can yield a situation in which majorities prefer Candidate A over B, B over C, and yet C over A. However, empirical research suggests that the Condorcet paradox, even though it provides a theoretically fascinating challenge, practically hardly ever occurs (Regenwetter, 2009). Regenwetter (2009) developed a methodological framework for Behavioral Social Choice in which the mathematical properties of social choice procedures can be evaluated against empirical behavioral data. The application of this framework to large data sets revealed that the logically possible intransitivity is practically irrelevant as it does not occur in political elections (Regenwetter, 2009). The notion of bounded rationality comes with an invitation for group researchers to start systematically studying characteristics of information environments that groups and teams encounter.

By the same token, it would be worthwhile to understand how often groups face hidden-profile tasks. It is obvious that groups practically never encounter an environment in which they have only access to unique cues. We also know that the chance of the occurrence of a hidden profile depends on the distribution of cue validities in an environment (Reimer & Hoffrage, 2012). However, we do not have systematic data and insights about the prevalence and characteristics of hidden profiles that groups face outside of laboratories. These data would help understand whether hidden profiles are encountered by natural groups and how they could be solved.

As-if models vs. process models

The notion of bounded rationality focuses on the strategies that are used by deciders, on the adaptivity of their decision strategies, and the match between strategies and the structure of the information environment in which the strategies are used. This approach hinges on the appropriateness of the described decision strategies. Even though group research has a long tradition of formulating group decision strategies that integrate individual preferences or choices (such as the majority rule), the studied decision strategies have the character of as-if models. Different from actual process models, as-if models of decision making do not claim to provide a psychologically viable description of the actual decision process or mechanism but only provide a model that predicts the decision outcome (see Gigerenzer, Todd, & the ABC Research Group, 1999). Group research suggests that groups often behave *as if* they applied a majority rule; however, that does not mean that groups necessarily engage in voting, which would be an underlying process model.

The description of decision strategies has a long tradition in group research. Studies on social decision schemes, for example, have distinguished between majority/plurality rules, the truth-win principle, proportionality, and equiprobability as possible strategies to form a group decision. All of these strategies integrate individual opinions or preferences into a group decision (Davis, 1982). Empirical research across a variety of different groups, teams, tasks, and contexts revealed that the majority/plurality rule describes many group decisions well. If we predict that a group will go with the choice alternative that is preferred by most members at the outset, the prediction of the group choice will hold in many environments. Except for hidden-profile tasks, the majority rule is not only descriptive but also often prescriptive in that it yields good decisions in many situations (Hastie & Kameda, 2005).

The majority rule and other social decision schemes have typically been studied as *as-if models*, that is, groups behaved as if they integrated individual preferences in a certain way. However, there are many potential processes that would allow groups to implement a majority rule and alternative rules that yield the same decisions. One possible process model would be *voting*. However, groups only rarely engage in formal voting in empirical experiments unless they are explicitly asked to do so. Alternative process models to implement the majority rule include a process by which individual group members express their preference for a specific choice early in the group deliberation. Non-verbal signals such as nodding and the lack of disagreement can serve the function of communicating agreement. Another plausible mechanism consists in the imitation of group members. Future research may describe and test specific process models that are used by groups to form a joint group decision.

Conclusion

The concept of bounded rationality offers a new perspective on the study of groups and teams that moves beyond traditional group research. As a signature characteristic, group research that subscribes to the approach of bounded rationality focuses on the match between group strategies and characteristics of both the information and social environment. The history of group research using outcome and performance measures is, by and large, a history of demonstrating group failure. We illustrated how the concept of bounded rationality can broaden our view on process losses. It may well turn out that several process losses that are described in the literature reflect group behaviors that are functional in many environments.

It is the match in strategy and environment that leads to successful group outcomes. The presented research on hidden profiles provides evidence for that claim, and there is also anecdotal evidence that illustrates this principle. To return to the opening anecdote on The Beatles, "Those later world-changing Beatles ... [were the same] Beatles, just lesser-known, local not global" (Lewisohn, 2013, p. 3). The Beatles adapted to their initial British environment, as evidenced by a number of successful hits on the UK singles' charts prior to their American debut. However, it was the perfect match of group and the social environment of their audience that allowed them to truly shine. As Epstein put it: "One has thought about America in connection with the Beatles ... I always thought—I was always quite sure, really—that the Beatles would make it big over there" (Lewisohn, 2013, p. 506). More research is needed that enables us to understand to what extent groups and teams adapt to the information and social environments in which they make decisions.

References

Brodbeck, F. C., Kerschreiter, R., Mojzisch, A., Frey, D., & Schulz-Hardt, S. (2002). The dissemination of critical, unshared information in decision-making groups: The effects of prediscussion dissent. *European Journal of Social Psychology*, 32, 35–56.

Burke, C. S., Stagl, K. C., Salas, E., Pierce, L., & Kandall, D. L. (2006). Understanding team adaptation: A conceptual analysis and model. *Journal of Applied Psychology*, 91, 1189–1207.

Burke, S. J. (1990). The effects of missing information on decision strategy selection. *Advances in Consumer Research*, 17, 250–256.

Burke, S. J. (1995). The dimensional effects of missing information on choice processing. *Journal of Behavioral Decision Making*, 8, 223–244.

Chernyshenko, O. S., Miner, A. G., Baumann, M. R., & Sniezek J. A. (2003). The impact of information distribution, ownership, and discussion on group member judgment: The differential cue weighting model. *Organizational Behavior and Human Decision Processes*, 91, 12–25.

Davis, J. H. (1982). Social interaction as a combinatorial process in group decisions. In H. Brandstaetter, J. H. Davis, & G. Stocker-Kreichgauer (Eds.), *Group decision making* (pp. 27–58). London: Academic Press.

Fraidin, S. N. (2004). When is one head better than two? Interdependent information in group decision making. *Organizational Behavior and Human Decision Processes*, 93, 102–113.

Gigerenzer, G., & Gaissmaier, W. (2011). Heuristic decision making. *Annual Review of Psychology*, 62, 451–482.

Gigerenzer, G., & Selten, R. (Eds.) (2001). *Bounded rationality: The adaptive toolbox.* Cambridge. MA: MIT Press.

Gigerenzer, G., Todd, P. M., & the ABC Research Group (Eds.) (1999). *Simple heuristics that make us smart.* New York: Oxford University Press.

Gigone, D., & Hastie, R. (1993). The common knowledge effect: Information sampling and group judgment. *Journal of Personality and Social Psychology*, 65, 959–974.

Hastie, R., & Kameda, T. (2005). The robust beauty of majority rules in group decisions. *Psychological Review*, 112, 494–508.

Hinsz, V. B., Tindale, R. S., & Vollrath, D. A. (1997). The emerging conceptualization of groups as information processors. *Psychological Bulletin*, 121, 43–64.

Johnson, E. J., Payne, J. W., & Bettman, J. R. (1988). Information displays and preference reversals. *Organizational Behavior and Human Decision Processes*, 42, 1–21.

Kaemmer, J., Gaissmaier, W., Reimer, T., & Schermuly, C. C. (2014). The adaptive use of recognition in group decision making. *Cognitive Science*, 38, 911–942.

Katsikopoulos, K. V. (2011). Psychological heuristics for making inferences: Definition, performance, and the emerging theory and practice. *Decision Analysis*, 8, 10–29.

Kerr, N. L., MacCoun, R. J., & Kramer, G. P. (1996). Bias in judgment: Comparing individuals and groups. *Psychological Review*, 103, 687–719.

Kerr, N. L., & Seok, D.-H. (2011). "… with a little help from my friends": Friendship, effort norms, and group motivation gain. *Journal of Managerial Psychology*, 26, 205–218.

Klein, G. A., & Pierce, L. (2001). *Adaptive teams*. Paper presented at 6th International Command and Control Research and Technology Symposium, Annapolis, MD, June 19–21.

Kozlowski, S. W. (1998). Training and developing adaptive teams: Theory, principles, and research. In J. A. Cannon-Bowers & E. Salas (Eds.), *Decision making under stress: Implications for training and simulation* (pp. 115–153). Washington, DC: APA Books.

Luan, S., Katsikopoulos, K., & Reimer, T. (2012). When does diversity trump ability (and vice versa) in group decision making? A simulation study. *PLoS ONE*, 7, 1–9.

Lewisohn, M. (2013). *Tune in: The Beatles: all these years*. New York: Crown Archetype.

Payne, J. W., Bettman, J. R., & Johnson, E. J. (1988). Adaptive strategy selection in decision making. *Journal of Experimental Psychology: Learning, Memory, and Cognition*, 14, 534–552.

Regenwetter, M. (2009). Perspectives on preference aggregation. *Perspectives on Psychological Science*, 4, 403–407.

Reimer, T. (1999). Argumentieren und Problemlösen [Argumentation and problem solving]. Lengerich, Germany: Pabst Science Publishers.

Reimer, T., Bornstein, A.-L., & Opwis, K. (2005). Positive and negative transfer effects in groups. In T. Betsch & S. Haberstroh (Eds.), *The routine of decision making* (pp. 175–192). Mahwah, NJ: Lawrence Erlbaum Associates.

Reimer, T., & Hoffrage, U. (2005). Can simple group heuristics detect hidden profiles in randomly generated environments? *Swiss Journal of Psychology*, 64, 21–37.

Reimer, T., & Hoffrage, U. (2006). The ecological rationality of simple group heuristics: Effects of group member strategies on decision accuracy. *Theory and Decision*, 60, 403–438.

Reimer, T., & Hoffrage, U. (2012). Simple heuristics and information sharing in groups. In R. Hertwig, U. Hoffrage, & the ABC Research Group (Eds.), *Simple heuristics in a social world* (pp. 266–286). New York: Oxford University Press.

Reimer, T., & Katsikopoulos, K. (2004). The use of recognition in group decision-making. *Cognitive Science*, 28, 1009–1029.

Reimer, T., Kuendig, S., Hoffrage, U., Park, E., & Hinsz, V. (2007). Effects of the information environment on group discussions and decisions in the hidden-profile paradigm. *Communication Monographs*, 74, 1–28.

Reimer, T., Reimer, A., & Hinsz, V. (2010). Naïve groups can solve the hidden-profile problem. *Human Communication Research*, 36, 443–467.

Reimer, T., Roland, C., & Russell, T. (2017). Groups and teams. In L. Lewis & C. Scott (Eds.), *International encyclopedia of organizational communication* (pp. 1–21). Hoboken, NJ: Wiley-Blackwell.

Rieskamp, J., & Hoffrage, U. (1999). When do people use simple heuristics, and how can we tell? In G. Gigerenzer, P. M. Todd, & the ABC Research Group (Eds.), *Simple heuristics that make us smart* (pp. 141–167). New York: Oxford University Press.

Salas, E., Sims, D. E., & Burke, C. S. (2005). Is there a "big five" in teamwork? *Small Group Research*, 36, 555–599.

Sohrab, S. G., Waller, M. J., & Kaplan, S. (2015). Exploring the hidden-profile paradigm: A literature review and analysis. *Small Group Research*, 46, 489–535.

Sonesh, S., Rico, R., & Salas, E. (2014). Team decision making in naturalistic environments: A framework for and introduction to illusory shared cognition. In S. Highhouse, R. S. Dalal, & E. Salas (Eds.), *Judgment and decision making at work* (pp. 199–227). New York: Routledge.

Stasser, G. (1988). Computer simulation as a research tool: The DISCUSS model of group decision making. *Journal of Experimental Social Psychology*, 24, 393–422.

Stasser, G., & Abele, S. (2020). Collective choice, collaboration, and communication. *Annual Review of Psychology*, 71, 589–612.

Stasser, G., & Titus, W. (1985). Pooling of unshared information in group decision making: Biased information sampling during discussion. *Journal of Personality and Social Psychology*, 48, 1467–1478.

Wittenbaum, G. M., & Park, E. S. (2001). The collective preference for shared information. *Current Directions in Psychological Science*, 10, 70–73.

37

COGNITIVE BIASES AND DEBIASING IN INTELLIGENCE ANALYSIS

Ian K. Belton and Mandeep K. Dhami

Introduction

Simon (1947, p. 79) boldly asserted that "It is impossible for the behavior of a single, isolated individual to reach any high degree of rationality." He recognized that rationality is bounded by limitations of the unaided human mind and by the complexity and uncertainty of the task environment (Simon, 1957). Simon (1956, 1990) believed that organisms are adapted to the structure of their environments. "Human rational behavior ... is shaped by a scissors whose two blades are the structure of task environments and the computational capabilities of the actor" (Simon, 1990, p. 7). He believed that under such conditions people may opt to satisfice, i.e., settle on a "good enough" solution (Simon, 1956). Indeed, research has now identified a wide range of systematic deviations from normatively rational behavior, often referred to collectively as "cognitive biases" (for reviews, see Gilovich, Griffin, & Kahneman, 2002; Kahneman, 2011; Kahneman, Slovic, & Tversky, 1982).

However, as Katsikopoulos and Lan (2011) note, Simon also explored ways in which performance could be improved so that satisficing and boundedly rational behavior did not lead to poor outcomes. Similarly, in response to the findings regarding cognitive biases, researchers have begun to identify and test possible debiasing strategies (for reviews, see Arkes, 1991; Fischhoff, 1982; Larrick, 2004; Lilienfeld, Ammirati, & Landfield, 2009). Several classifications of cognitive bias have been proposed, and debiasing strategies may be informed by theories of how and why a bias may occur.

Fischhoff (1982) distinguishes between faulty decision makers, faulty tasks, and decision maker–task mismatches. Arkes (1991) focuses on the type of error made, distinguishing association-based errors (i.e., side-effects of the fact that triggering one concept in memory activates other, related concepts) from psychophysical errors based on risk aversion and our biased response to losses and gains, and strategy-based errors resulting from a person using a poor analytic strategy. Stanovich, Toplak, and West (2008) base their approach to bias on dual-process theories of cognition which distinguish System 1 thinking (i.e., fast, unconscious, automatic, associative, parallel processing, effortless, and intuitive) from System 2 thinking (i.e., slow, conscious, controlled, rule-based, sequential processing, effortful, and deliberative). Cognitive bias is considered to be the product of System 1, which can be mitigated when an individual uses System 2 to override a System 1 response. A successful override may fail to occur if, for example, there is a lack of effort/self-control ("override failures/cognitive miserliness"), a lack

DOI: 10.4324/9781315658353-43

of knowledge of the correct strategy to use ("mindware gaps"), or use of a flawed strategy ("contaminated mindware"; see also Stanovich & West, 2000). Similarly, Kahneman, Slovic, and Tversky (1982) distinguish between comprehension errors (i.e., mindware gaps) and application errors (i.e., override failures or cognitive miserliness).

Dual-process theories of mind have been criticized and alternative accounts exist. Viale (2018; 2019) argues that the dual-process account is undermined by recent psychological and neuroscientific evidence which suggests that the cognitive processes involved in creative incubation and mind wandering are both unconscious and analytical. Alternatively, Hammond's (1996, 2000) cognitive continuum theory proposes that there are many "quasi-rational" modes of cognition that lie in between the poles of intuitive and analytic thinking, and which comprise different combinations of intuition and analysis (see also Sloman's 1996 view that intuition and analysis are interactive). According to Hammond, the mode of cognition applied to a task is determined by task properties and/or the experience the individual has with the task. Success on a task inhibits movement along the cognitive continuum (or change in cognitive mode) while failure stimulates it.

When working in an organizational context, Simon (1947, p. 79) believed that organizations can place "members in a psychological environment that will ... provide them with the information needed to make decisions correctly." For instance, organizations can establish standard working practices, train individuals, and structure the work environment so that it encourages rational thinking and consistency or regularization of practice. In this chapter, we critically evaluate the solutions that intelligence analysis organizations have offered to combat cognitive bias in their intelligence analysts. We identify cognitive biases that may affect the practice of intelligence analysis and review debiasing strategies developed and tested by psychological research.

Intelligence analysis

The intelligence analyst must produce a coherent report that precisely communicates his/her conclusions about a current or future situation to a variety of consumers who may then make strategic and tactical decisions that affect national and international security. For example, what forces does North Korea have along the border with South Korea? What will be Russia's offensive cyber capability in 2025? Where are the headquarters of terror group X?

At its core, intelligence analysis is a cognitive task. Analysts must plan, search for, select, process, and interpret data in order to gain situational awareness and/or forecast an outcome of interest to customers. This is articulated in the generic analytic workflow (Dhami & Careless, 2015) which applies to different sorts of intelligence analysis (e.g., HUMINT, SIGNIT, as well as single and multi-source), conducted individually or in teams, for different purposes (e.g., strategic, tactical). The workflow is separated into six meaningfully different stages of activity that follow from one another, namely, capture requirements, plan analytic response, obtain data, process data, interpret outputs, and communicate conclusions.

The task of analysis is made difficult partly because the human mind is limited in terms of attention, perception, memory, and processing capacity, and partly because the task itself can be extremely constraining and demanding. Indeed, there may be not enough relevant data or there may be large volumes of data, the credibility of data sources may vary, the data may be formatted in different ways (e.g., structured/unstructured, textual/visual/audio), it may be ambiguous, unreliable, and sometimes intentionally misleading, and there may be time pressure and high stakes involved. This is further compounded by the lack of feedback which limits learning on how to perform analytic tasks.

It is no surprise, therefore, that critics have accused analysts of resorting to using simple heuristics which can lead to cognitive bias and error (Heuer, 1999). Some would even suggest that the only way to decide rationally is to use heuristics because no rules following normative canons of economic rationality may be applied (e.g., Gigerenzer, Todd, & the ABC Research Group, 1999). Nonetheless, heuristics can lead to systematic cognitive bias, and cognitive bias has been implicated in well-known intelligence failures such as the failure to find weapons of mass destruction in Iraq (Jervis, 2006). Although intelligence analysts are experts in their domain, this is unlikely to protect them from cognitive bias. Indeed, studies demonstrate that intelligence analysts are as susceptible to cognitive bias as anyone else (e.g., Cook & Smallman, 2008), and may be even more susceptible than non-experts (Reyna, Chick, Corbin, & Hsia, 2014). As we discuss in the next section, cognitive biases can manifest at each stage of the analytic workflow.

Cognitive biases in intelligence analysis

After a review of the extant literature on intelligence analysis and on cognitive biases, we identified at least 21 key biases that could affect individual analysis (rather than analysis conducted in groups/collaboratively). The biases can be assigned to stages of the analytic workflow based on an assessment of the cognitive tasks involved at each stage and how those might induce bias. Placing the biases along the workflow allows analysts, managers, and trainers to identify where issues may arise and can aid in tailoring debiasing support efforts.

For present purposes, we focus on eight biases that are particularly meaningful to one or more stages of the analytic workflow. These are described briefly below:

1   *Belief bias* (Evans, Barston, & Pollard, 1983) is the tendency to evaluate the logical strength of an argument based on the plausibility of its conclusion.
2   *Confirmation bias* can manifest in a variety of ways (see Klayman, 1995), i.e., remaining overconfident in an initial position, searching for evidence in a way that supports a favored viewpoint, interpreting evidence in a way that favors a preferred viewpoint, and resisting change or insufficiently adjusting confidence in a viewpoint in response to new conflicting evidence or when existing evidence is discredited.
3   *Explanation bias* (Ross, Lepper, Strack, & Steinmetz, 1977) refers to the idea that if you think about/imagine how or why an event may happen, you will then consider it more likely to happen than if you had not thought about it.
4   *Fluency effects* (Schwartz et al., 1991) refer to the idea that information which can be retrieved and/or processed fluently (e.g., because it is familiar) tends to be preferred and judged more likely and credible than less easily processed information (Reber & Schwarz, 1999; Tversky & Kahneman, 1973; Zajonc, 1968). When evaluating sources, this can lead to a preference for evidence received from an expert even if that expertise is irrelevant (also called expertise bias); overestimating the association between independent characteristics of a favored person or object (halo effect; Nisbett & Wilson, 1977); and evaluating people who share your characteristics more favorably than others who do not (similarity bias; Rand & Wexley, 1975). Some have suggested that fluency may sometimes be the most appropriate way to make decisions, at least where no other knowledge is available (Hertwig, Herzog, Schooler, & Reimer, 2008).
5   *The framing effect* has many facets (Tversky & Kahneman, 1981; see also Levin, Schneider, & Gaeth, 1998), i.e., the tendency for risk-aversion when a choice is framed as a gain (relative to the status quo), but risk-seeking when a choice is framed as a loss; making an evaluation

based on whether something is described as positive or negative; and choosing to engage in a behavior based on whether participation is described as advantageous or disadvantageous.

6   *Order effects* (see Hogarth & Einhorn, 1992) refer to the fact that the order in which information is presented affects the relative importance attached to it. Information presented first and last is particularly biasing.

7   *The planning fallacy* (Kahneman & Tversky, 1979) is the tendency to underestimate the time (and cost) required to complete a task by overlooking potential difficulties.

8   *Overconfidence* (Fischhoff, Slovic, & Lichtenstein, 1977) refers to when an individual's subjective confidence in the accuracy of his/her judgments is greater than the objective accuracy of those judgments.

These biases may manifest at various stages of the analytic workflow. At the *capture requirements* stage, analysts must understand the context for the intelligence question, including the customer's goal and how it will be achieved, and analysts should challenge this if necessary. Analytic performance at this stage can be affected by confirmation bias and framing. For instance, analysts might set out to look for evidence that confirms a customer's pre-existing assumptions or hypotheses rather than challenging these. In addition, the way an intelligence request is framed may bias the analysts' understanding of it (e.g., looking to determine how many casualties are likely to occur as a result of civil unrest rather than considering how many lives could be saved by one course of action or another).

In the *plan analytic response* stage, analysts must identify alternative methods that could be employed to answer the question, evaluate their potential effectiveness and efficiency, and prioritize how to proceed. Analytic performance may be affected by fluency effects and the planning fallacy. For instance, analysts may favor specific analytic lines to follow, consider particular information to be necessary to test hypotheses, and select methods for obtaining data that have been used recently or frequently in the past and therefore come to mind most easily. Analysts may also underestimate the time involved in completing the analytic task.

At the *obtain data* stage, analysts must select relevant data from the most appropriate sources in an efficient manner, as well as establish new sources of data if necessary. Performance at this stage may be affected by fluency effects, confirmation bias, and order effects. For instance, analysts' choice of data sources and search terms may be limited to those that come to mind most easily, partly because they have been used regularly or recently. In addition, analysts may be biased toward obtaining data from trusted experts (even if their expertise is inappropriate for the context in question), favored or familiar sources as well as sources that are similar to them (i.e., other intelligence organizations), believing them to be more credible. Analysts may search for new evidence in a way that favors their existing hypothesis (e.g., by avoiding sources likely to contradict the hypothesis). Data obtained first and last (e.g., in a list of search results) may be more likely to be filtered/selected even though these are not more reliable or valid.

At the *process data* stage, analysts must understand the 'raw' data, and this may involve collating, reformatting, and manipulating it using relevant tradecraft, tools, and technology. Here, analysts may suffer from fluency effects and confirmation bias. For instance, analysts may over-use analytic techniques that they are familiar with or use regularly. Data processing tasks such as identifying unexpected or anomalous results and generating visualizations may be biased toward favored analytic lines/hypotheses.

At the *interpret outputs* stage, analysts must evaluate alternative explanations for the (often incomplete) facts, and construct logical arguments to support conclusions as well as dismiss alternative ones, determine the degree of uncertainty in these conclusions, and identify any ambiguities. Here, analysts may be affected by belief bias, confirmation bias, and explanation bias. For instance, analysts may over-weight arguments that produce plausible conclusions rather than properly assess their logical strength. Analysts may be overconfident in an initial belief and so, even if they take an unbiased approach to new information, they will remain overconfident in their initial position. Analysts may reach conclusions about a hypothesis based on the presence of supporting rather than conflicting evidence. Analysts may interpret new evidence in a way that favors their existing hypothesis (e.g., by regarding supporting evidence as reliable and conflicting evidence as unreliable, or by interpreting ambiguous information in a way that supports a favored hypothesis). Analysts may be resistant to change so they insufficiently adjust their confidence in a hypothesis in response to new conflicting evidence or when existing evidence is discredited. By considering possible explanations for the data, analysts may conclude that those explanations are more likely than is really the case.

Finally, at the *communicate conclusions* stage, analysts must present the outcome of analysis in a clear and meaningful way; distinguishing fact from inference, highlighting the alternatives that were considered, and expressing uncertainty and confidence. Analytic performance at this stage may be affected by belief bias and overconfidence. For instance, where analysts have reached a plausible conclusion, they may overstate the strength of their supporting arguments or evidence. Analysts may not allow sufficiently for uncertainties and ambiguities in their reports.

Debiasing strategies

Intelligence organizations have made an attempt to help analysts overcome cognitive bias by investing in training analysts to use so-called structured analytic techniques (SATs) and in the development of specialized computer technologies to support and aid analysis. The intelligence community has largely eschewed psychologically informed and empirically tested cognitive debiasing interventions (Dhami, Mandel, Mellers, & Tetlock, 2015). Next, after a brief review of the intelligence community's preferred debiasing methods, we consider psychologically informed debiasing strategies relevant to the eight biases described above.

SATs (see Dhami, Belton, & Careless, 2016; Heuer & Pherson, 2014) are a collection of techniques designed to reduce cognitive bias. The primary rationale behind SATs is that externalizing and decomposing the cognitive process will result in bias mitigation. Some SATs, such as the Analysis of Competing Hypotheses (ACH), were developed specifically for use by intelligence analysts, while other SATs (e.g., the Delphi method) were originally used in other contexts but have since been applied in the intelligence analysis domain. However, to date, very few studies have tested whether SATs actually reduce bias. The research that does exist suggests that they may actually lead to errors such as base-rate neglect (e.g., Dhami, Belton, & Mandel, 2019; Mandel, Karvetski, & Dhami, 2018).

As Dhami et al. (2016) point out, SATs cannot guarantee accuracy. This is partly because they rely on the judgment skills of the analyst and his/her subjective input of the information and interpretation of the outputs. In addition, SATs may overcorrect one bias, potentially triggering an opposing bias, and the decomposition process can make judgments less reliable rather than more so (Chang, Berdini, Mandel, & Tetlock, 2017). Despite the limitations of SATs and the lack of evidence attesting to their efficacy, SATs often form part of the core skill set taught in analytic training programs (e.g., Marrin, 2008) and analysts are expected to apply them (e.g., UK MoD, 2013; US Government, 2009).

As mentioned, the intelligence community has also adopted different types of computer-based tools to support analysis (see Dhami, 2017). Indeed, there are currently a vast array of analytic tools available, and these can be used at different stages of the analytic workflow as they serve a variety of purposes. For instance, at the processing data stage, tools can be used to visualize data (e.g., Stasko, Gorg, Liu, & Singhal, 2007), perform network analysis and geospatial analysis, support argumentation (e.g., Kang & Stasko, 2011), and decision making (e.g., Svenson et al., 2010). In addition, some SATs, such as ACH, have been automated. Finally, "serious games" are video games that use technology and techniques from the entertainment sector to teach individuals to recognize and reduce cognitive biases. However, as with SATs, the ability of computer-based tools to reduce cognitive bias has generally not been empirically tested. A notable exception is serious games, which have been found to successfully reduce several biases, namely, confirmation bias, the fundamental attribution error, the bias blind spot, anchoring, the representativeness heuristic, and projection bias (e.g., Dunbar, Miller, et al., 2014; Morewedge et al., 2015; Mullinix et al., 2013; Shaw et al., 2016). These games involve interactive learning about biases and activities aimed at reducing them. The development of serious games has been informed by psychology.

The practical utility of computer-based tools may be limited because, as Dhami (2017) found in a recent survey of intelligence analysts, the lack of usability can be an important barrier to analysts' uptake of analytic tools. When there was a tradeoff between the usability and usefulness of a tool, analysts preferred usable tools over useful ones. In addition, like SATs, many computer-based tools rely on potentially biased subjective human inputs and interpretations of output (Büyükkurt & Büyükkurt, 1991; Montibeller & von Winterfeldt, 2015), which limits their ability to help analysts avoid bias and error. Despite this, the intelligence community considers analytic technology as potentially helpful, as illustrated by projects funded by the US Intelligence Advanced Research Projects Activity: (www.iarpa.gov/index.php/research-programs).

Psychologically informed interventions

Psychologists have investigated many different interventions for reducing cognitive bias. These are usually based on theories about the sources of bias, and empirically tested to examine their effectiveness in countering the bias. Table 37.1 provides a summary of the empirically tested debiasing strategies for the eight cognitive biases identified described earlier.

Psychologically informed and empirically tested debiasing interventions typically involve two elements. First, participants are given training or instructions that aim to increase understanding and awareness of cognitive biases. The goal here is to improve an individual's ability to identify tasks or situations where an intuitive response is likely to be biased, so that they can override their intuition with an appropriate deliberative strategy. Second, interventions aim to fill mindware gaps by teaching relevant rules (e.g., probability or logic), or specific strategies to use in a given task (e.g., consider the opposite of your original answer or unpack a task into component parts).

An alternative approach to debiasing involves restructuring the task environment to reduce biased behavior, either by encouraging more deliberative thinking or by inducing unbiased intuition. This kind of so-called "choice architecture" that "nudges" individuals towards better decisions (Thaler & Sunstein, 2008) has proved itself to be effective for promoting pro-social behaviors such as paying tax or becoming an organ donor and has become an increasingly popular policy-making tool (e.g., Hallsworth, Egan, Rutter & McCrae, 2018). In the public policy context, questions remain about whether some nudges may be unacceptably coercive (e.g., Viale, 2018, 2019). However, it is likely that there are many contexts within the intelligence community where choice architecture could usefully be employed to reduce biased thinking.

Table 37.1 Psychologically informed and empirically tested debiasing interventions

Cognitive bias	Psychological intervention
Belief bias	Evans, Newstead, Allen, and Pollard (1994) found that brief "instructional training in logical principles" reduced belief bias in basic logical reasoning tasks.
Confirmation bias	Several variations of the "consider-the-opposite" strategy have been found to reduce confirmation bias. For example, instructing individuals to imagine their response if given evidence pointed in the opposite direction reduced the tendency to discount conflicting evidence, and presenting conflicting evidence in advance of a search for information reduced the bias of that search towards supporting evidence (Lord, Lepper, & Preston, 1984). Similarly, instructions to consider multiple alternative hypotheses reduced subsequent belief perseverance (Lewandowsky et al., 2012). If too many alternatives are generated, this may undermine the mitigating effect of "consider-the-opposite" interventions because the difficulty of generating alternatives can undermine their perceived plausibility (Sanna, Schwartz, & Stocker, 2002). Fortunately, this "backfire" effect can be reduced by raising awareness of the difficulty of generating alternatives (Sanna & Schwartz, 2003). Actively searching for disconfirming evidence to falsify an initial hypothesis may also reduce confirmation bias (Lam, 2007).
Explanation bias	Considering multiple alternatives has been shown to reduce the explanation bias, as long as not too many alternatives are generated (Hirt & Markman, 1995; Sanna et al., 2002).
Fluency effects	"Consider-the-opposite" strategies of the kind successfully tested on confirmation bias and order effects may be effective here, since they aim to induce consideration of alternatives beyond those that spring to mind immediately. A simple, practical solution for biases relating to source evaluation is to get a second opinion from a colleague who is not familiar with the source and/or aggregate evidence from multiple sources wherever possible.
Framing effect	A range of strategies have been found to reduce the framing effect. These include: considering the opposite (Cheng, Wu & Lin, 2014); reframing the problem in an opposite way (Korobkin & Guthrie, 1998); listing advantages and disadvantages of two options before choosing between them (Almashat, Ayotte, Edelstein, & Margrett, 2008); giving reasons for the chosen option (Leboeuf & Shafir, 2003); presenting information in a frame-neutral way, for example, through graphical representations (Garcia-Retamero & Dhami, 2013); "causal cognitive mapping" or a node-link diagram of the variables used to make a decision and their cause-effect relationships (Hodgkinson, Bown, Maule, Glaister, & Pearman, 1999); scenario planning (Meissner & Wulf, 2013); and a strong warning message about the risk of the framing effect (Cheng & Wu, 2010)
Order effects	Mumma and Wilson (1995) found that considering the opposite of the first information item given and also sorting information based on diagnosticity removed the primacy effect, as did simply writing a list of the information items after viewing them on-screen. Ashton and Kennedy (2002) found that requiring individuals to rank information items by importance and then review them before making a judgment successfully removed the recency effect. Wickens, Ketels, Healy, Buck-Gengler, & Bourne (2010) found that instructing participants that newer data is likely to be more reliable increased the recency effect (when appropriate) but did not reduce the primacy effect. Logan and Fischman (2011) found that performing a simple manual task (i.e., rearranging a pair of water glasses) between viewing and recalling a list of words removed the recency effect, but not the primacy effect.

Table 37.1 Cont.

Cognitive bias	Psychological intervention
Overconfidence	Koriat, Lichtenstein, and Fischhoff (1980) found that overconfidence could be reduced using a form of the "consider-the-opposite" strategy, which involved listing counter-arguments to a preferred hypothesis or prediction. Multi-step strategies for eliciting forecasts in the form of confidence intervals have been found to reduce overconfidence (e.g., Speirs-Bridge et al., 2010). Simply instructing people on the risk of overconfidence when making judgments has also been found to have a debiasing effect (McGraw, Mellers, & Ritov, 2004).
Planning fallacy	Breaking down or "unpacking" the task into component parts and estimating the time needed for each can be an effective debiasing strategy, especially when the unpacking task is made relatively difficult, e.g., breaking the task into five rather than two steps (Kruger & Evans, 2004) and if individuals focus on obstacles to task completion (Peetz, Buehler, & Wilson, 2010). Thinking of multiple scenarios in which the task in question or similar tasks could take much more or less time has been found to reduce the planning fallacy in subsequent task time estimates (Newby-Clark, Ross, Buehler, Koehler, & Griffin, 2000). Taking an "outside view" of the task may also reduce the planning fallacy (Kahneman & Lovallo, 1993). Estimating the time another person would take to complete a task, based on that person's own estimate, improves estimation accuracy (Buehler, Griffin, & Ross, 1994). Estimates are somewhat more accurate when based on memories of the time taken to complete comparable tasks in the past (Buehler et al., 1994) and are likely to be even more accurate when benchmarked against the actual time taken to complete comparable tasks previously (Roy, Christenfeld, & McKenzie, 2005). Visualizing a third party completing the task can also mitigate bias (Buehler, Griffin, Lam, & Deslauriers, 2012). Backward planning, which involves working step-by-step back from the desired end goal, can also reduce the planning fallacy (Wiese, Buehler, & Griffin, 2016).

Conclusion

Intelligence analysts have been criticized for suffering from cognitive biases (Heuer, 1999), although there have been few empirical demonstrations of this. In this chapter, we identified eight biases applicable to the analytic workflow and we reviewed psychologically informed debiasing strategies that aim to counter those biases. The intelligence community's efforts to help their analysts become more rational thinkers may be inadequate because organizations rely on ad hoc SATs and a proliferation of computer-based tools that largely lack empirical evidence attesting to their efficacy. In addition, there seems to be little acknowledgment of the fact that SATs and computer-based tools may simply replace existing biases with new ones. In this sense, one could argue that intelligence organizations have failed to fulfill their function, as identified by Simon (1947), to provide analysts with an environment that encourages rational thinking.

The intelligence community has, to date, largely eschewed psychologically informed and empirically tested interventions. In essence, many of these interventions require the individual to stop and think before pursuing a course of action. As Simon (1947, p. 89) suggested, "If rationality is to be achieved, a period of hesitation must precede choice." Although further research is needed to confirm how well the effects of such interventions can be transferred to the intelligence analysis domain, this should not preclude their use in the meantime. Below, we conclude with a consideration of the potential challenges associated with debiasing people and the limitations of debiasing strategies, before highlighting the main barrier to debiasing in the intelligence analysis domain.

There are many challenges involved in successfully implementing any debiasing strategy. The first is the bias blind spot which is a meta-cognitive bias that refers to the tendency to believe that we are free of cognitive bias even though we recognize bias exists in others (Pronin, Lin, & Ross, 2002; West, Meserve, & Stanovich, 2012). This can make analysts resistant to training or instruction designed to mitigate cognitive biases since they will tend to think it does not apply to them. Second, individuals need to be convinced that debiasing is relevant to their work, and in order to reduce threats to self-esteem, they may need to be reassured that debiasing is about further enhancing their thinking rather than correcting cognitive faults. Indeed, it is often observed that analysts can be resistant to using debiasing techniques such as SATs or computer support tools (e.g., Trent, Voshell, & Patterson, 2007; Treverton & Gabbard, 2008). Third, the durability of the effects of most debiasing strategies is currently unknown (for exceptions, see the recent work on serious games which used follow-up periods between 8 and 12 weeks, e.g., Dunbar, Miller, et al., 2014; Morewedge et al., 2015; Mullinix et al., 2013; Shaw et al., 2016). Fourth, it is likely that individual differences such as personality, cognitive ability/style, and culture may affect how well people respond to debiasing strategies (Oreg & Bayazit, 2009; Stanovich & West, 2000), particularly as research suggests that individuals differ widely in their susceptibility to cognitive bias (e.g., Peters, 2012; Toplak, West, & Stanovich, 2011). Finally, some debiasing interventions may backfire, increasing rather than reducing the target bias (e.g., Sanna et al., 2002) or may even stimulate some other bias.

In addition, features of the intelligence analysis domain may make it difficult for intelligence organizations to build and maintain a psychological environment that is conducive to rational thinking. In particular, the intelligence community has traditionally held to the belief that intelligence analysis is a "tradecraft"—a skill that must be learnt "on-the-job" over a long period and which generates implicit knowledge handed down from one analyst to another. This hinders efforts to improve analysis through top-down approaches.

Despite the many challenges and barriers, there is scope for optimism. Simon (1947) observed that effective organizations enable individuals to think rationally. We suggest that by adopting an appropriately skeptical attitude to untested approaches such as SATs and some computer technologies, and by embracing a psychologically informed and empirically tested approach to reducing cognitive bias, intelligence organizations can assist their analysts to improve analytic performance.

Acknowledgments

The work presented in this chapter was supported by funding provided to Mandeep K. Dhami by HM Government. We would like to thank Kathryn Careless for providing us with feedback on the work.

References

Almashat, S., Ayotte, B., Edelstein, B., & Margrett, J. (2008). Framing effect debiasing in medical decision making. *Patient Education and Counselling*, 71(1), 102–107. doi:10.1016/j.pec.2007.11.004.

Arkes, H. (1991). Costs and benefits of judgment errors: Implications for debiasing. *Psychological Bulletin*, 110(3), 486–498. doi:10.1037/0033-2909.110.3.486.

Ashton, R. H., & Kennedy, J. (2002). Eliminating recency with self-review: The case of auditors' 'going concern' judgments. *Journal of Behavioral Decision Making*, 15(3), 221–231. doi:10.1002/bdm.412.

Buehler, R., Griffin, D., Lam, K. C. H., & Deslauriers, J. (2012). Perspectives on prediction: Does third-person imagery improve task completion estimates? *Organizational Behavior and Human Decision Processes*, 117(1), 138–149. doi:10.1016/j.obhdp.2011.09.001.

Buehler, R., Griffin, D., & Ross, M. (1994). Exploring the 'planning fallacy': Why people underestimate their task completion times. *Journal of Personality and Social Psychology*, 67(3), 366–381. doi:10.1037/0022-3514.67.3.366.

Büyükkurt, B. K., & Büyükkurt, M. D. (1991). An experimental study of the effectiveness of three debiasing techniques. *Decision Sciences*, 22(1), 60–73. doi:10.1111/j.1540-5915.1991.tb01262.x.

Chang, W., Berdini, E., Mandel, D. R., & Tetlock, P. E. (2017). Restructuring structured analytic techniques in intelligence. *Intelligence and National Security*, 33(3), 337–356. doi:10.1080/02684527.2017.1400230.

Cheng, F., & Wu, C. (2010). Debiasing the framing effect: The effect of warning and involvement. *Decision Support Systems*, 49(3), 328–334. doi:10.1016/j.dss.2010.04.002.

Cheng, F., Wu, C., & Lin, H. (2014). Reducing the influence of framing on internet consumers' decisions: The role of elaboration. *Computers in Human Behavior*, 37, 56–63. doi:10.1016/j.chb.2014.04.015.

Cook, M. B., & Smallman, H. S. (2008). Human factors of the confirmation bias in intelligence analysis: Decision support from graphical evidence landscapes. *Human Factors: The Journal of the Human Factors and Ergonomics Society*, 50(5), 745–754. doi:10.1518/001872008X354183.

Dhami, M. K. (2017). A survey of intelligence analysts' perceptions of analytic tools. Paper presented at 2017 European Intelligence and Security Informatics Conference. doi:10.1109/EISIC.2017.26.

Dhami, M. K., Belton, I. K., & Careless, K. E. (2016). Critical review of analytic techniques. Paper presented at 2016 European Intelligence and Security Informatics Conference. doi:10.1109/EISIC.2016.039.

Dhami, M. K., Belton, I. K., & Mandel D. R. (2019). The "analysis of competing hypotheses" in intelligence analysis. *Journal of Applied Cognitive Psychology*, 33(6), 1080–1090. doi: 10.1002/acp.3550.

Dhami, M. K., & Careless, K. E. (2015). Ordinal structure of the generic analytic workflow: A survey of intelligence analysts. Paper presented at 2015 European Intelligence and Security Informatics Conference. doi:10.1109/EISIC.2015.37.

Dhami, M. K., Mandel, D. R., Mellers, B. A., & Tetlock, P. E. (2015). Improving intelligence analysis with decision science. *Perspectives on Psychological Science*, 10(6), 753–757. doi:10.1177/1745691615598511.

Dunbar, N. E., Miller, C. H., Adame, B. J., Elizondo, J., Wilson, S. N., Lane, B. L., … Zhang, J. (2014). Implicit and explicit training in the mitigation of cognitive bias through the use of a serious game. *Computers in Human Behavior*, 37, 307–318. doi:10.1016/j.chb.2014.04.053.

Evans, J. St. B. T., Barston, J. L., & Pollard, P. (1983). On the conflict between logic and belief in syllogistic reasoning. *Memory & Cognition*, 11(3), 295–306. doi:10.3758/BF03196976.

Evans, J. St. B. T., Newstead, S. E., Allen, J. L., & Pollard, P. (1994). Debiasing by instruction: The case of belief bias. *Cognition*, 6(3), 263–285. doi:10.1080/09541449408520148.

Fischhoff, B. (1982). Debiasing. In D. Kahneman, P. Slovic, & A. Tversky (Eds.), *Judgement under uncertainty: Heuristics and biases* (pp. 422–444). New York: Cambridge University Press.

Fischhoff, B., Slovic, P., & Lichtenstein, S. (1977). Knowing with certainty: The appropriateness of extreme confidence. *Journal of Experimental Psychology: Human Perception and Performance*, 3(4), 552–564. doi:10.1037/0096-1523.3.4.552.

Garcia-Retamero, R., & Dhami, M. K. (2013). On avoiding framing effects in experienced decision makers. *Quarterly Journal of Experimental Psychology*, 66(4), 829–842. doi:10.1080/17470218.2012.727836.

Gigerenzer, G., Todd, P. M., & the ABC Research Group (Eds.) (1999). *Simple heuristics that make us smart*. New York: Oxford University Press.

Gilovich, T., Griffin, D., & Kahneman, D. (Eds.) (2002). *Heuristics and biases: The psychology of intuitive judgment*. Cambridge: Cambridge University Press.

Hallsworth, M., Egan, M., Rutter, J., & McCrae, J. (2018). Behavioural government: Using behavioural science to improve how governments make decisions. Retrieved from the Behavioural Insights Team at: www.bi.team/

Hammond, K. R. (1996). *Human judgment and social policy: Irreducible uncertainty, inevitable error, unavoidable injustice*. New York, NY: Oxford University Press.

Hammond, K. R. (2000). *Judgments under stress*. New York, NY: Oxford University Press.

Hertwig, R., Herzog, S. M., Schooler, L. J., & Reimer, T. (2008). Fluency heuristic: How the mind exploits a by-product of information retrieval. *Journal of Experimental Psychology: Learning, Memory, and Cognition*, 24(5), 1191–1206. doi: 10.1037/a0013025.

Heuer, R. J., Jr. (1999). *The psychology of intelligence analysis*. Washington, DC: CQ Press.

Heuer, R. J., Jr., & Pherson, R. H. (2014). *Structured analytic techniques for intelligence analysis*. Washington, DC: CQ Press.

Hirt, E. R., & Markman, K. D. (1995). Multiple explanation: A consider-an-alternative strategy for debiasing judgments. *Journal of Personality and Social Psychology*, 69(6), 1069–1086. doi:10.1037/0022-3514.69.6.1069.

Hodgkinson, G. P., Bown, N. J., Maule, A. J., Glaister, K. W., & Pearman, A. D. (1999). Breaking the frame: An analysis of strategic cognition and decision making under uncertainty. *Strategic Management Journal*, 20(10), 977–985.

Hogarth, R. M., & Einhorn, H. J. (1992). Order effect in belief updating: The belief-adjustment model. *Cognitive Psychology*, 24(1), 1–55. doi:10.1016/0010-0285(92)90002-J.

Jervis, R. J. (2006). Reports, politics, and intelligence failures: The case of Iraq. *Journal of Strategic Studies*, 29(1), 3–52. doi:10.1080/01402390600566282.

Kahneman, D. (2011). *Thinking, fast and slow*. London: Penguin Books.

Kahneman, D., & Lovallo, D. (1993). Timid choices and bold forecasts: A cognitive perspective on risk taking. *Management Science*, 39(1), 17–31. doi:10.1287/mnsc.39.1.17.

Kahneman, D., Slovic, P., & Tversky, A. (Eds.) (1982). *Judgement under uncertainty: Heuristics and biases*. Cambridge: Cambridge University Press.

Kahneman, D., & Tversky, A. (1979). Intuitive prediction: biases and corrective procedures. In S. Makridakis & S. C. Wheelright (Eds.), *Forecasting: TIMS studies in the management sciences*, vol. 12 (pp. 313–327). Amsterdam: North-Holland.

Kang, Y., & Stasko, J. (2011). Characterizing the intelligence analysis process: Informing visual analytics design through a longitudinal field study. In G. Santucci & M. Ward (Eds.), *Proceedings of IEEE Conference on Visual Analytics Science and Technology (VAST) 2011* (pp. 21–30). doi:10.1109/VAST.2011.6102438.

Katsikopolous, K. V., & Lan, C. (2011). Herbert Simon's spell on judgment and decision making. *Judgment and Decision Making*, 6(8), 722–732.

Klayman, J. (1995). Varieties of confirmation bias. In J. Busemeyer, R. Hastie, & D. L. Medin (Eds.), *Decision making from a cognitive perspective* (pp. 385–418). New York: Academic Press.

Koriat, A., Lichtenstein, S., & Fischhoff, B. (1980). Reasons for confidence. *Journal of Experimental Psychology: Human Learning and Memory*, 6(2), 107–118. doi:10.1037/0278-7393.6.2.107.

Korobkin, R., & Guthrie, G. (1998). Psychology, economics and settlement: A new look at the role of the lawyer. *Texas Law Review*, 76, 77–141.

Kruger, J., & Evans, M. (2004). If you don´t want to be late, enumerate: Unpacking reduces the planning fallacy. *Journal of Experimental Social Psychology*, 40(5), 586–598. doi:10.1016/j.jesp.2003.11.001.

Lam, C. (2007). Is Popper's falsificationist heuristic a helpful resource for developing critical thinking? *Educational Philosophy and Theory*, 39(4), 432–448. doi:10.1111/j.1469-5812.2007.00349.x.

Larrick, R. P. (2004). Debiasing. In D. J. Koehler & N. Harvey (Eds.), *Blackwell handbook of judgment and decision making* (pp. 316–337). Oxford: Blackwell.

Leboeuf, R. A., & Shafir, E. (2003). Deep thoughts and shallow frames: On the susceptibility to framing effects. *Journal of Behavioral Decision Making*, 16(2), 77–92. doi:10.1002/bdm.433.

Levin, I. P., Schneider, S. L., & Gaeth, G. J. (1998). All frames are not created equal: A typology and critical analysis of framing effects. *Organizational Behavior and Human Decision Processes*, 76(2), 149–188. doi:10.1006/obhd.1998.2804.

Lewandowsky, S., Ecker, U. K. H., Seifert, C. M., Schwarz, N., & Cook, J. (2012). Misinformation and its correction: Continued influence and successful debiasing. *Psychological Science in the Public Interest*, 13(3), 106–131. doi:10.1177/1529100612451018.

Lilienfeld, S. O., Ammirati, R., & Landfield, K. (2009). Giving debiasing away: Can psychological research on correcting cognitive errors promote human welfare? *Perspectives in Psychological Science*, 4(4), 390–398. doi:10.1111/j.1745-6924.2009.01144.x.

Logan, S. W., & Fischman, M. G. (2011). The relationship between end-state comfort effects and memory performance in serial and free recall. *Acta Psychologica*, 137(3), 292–299. doi:10.1016/j.actpsy.2011.03.009.

Lord, C. G., Lepper, M. R., & Preston, E. (1984). Considering the opposite: A corrective strategy for social judgment. *Journal of Personality and Social Psychology*, 47(6), 1231–1243. doi:10.1037/0022-3514.47.6.1231.

Mandel, D. R., Karvetski, C. W., & Dhami, M. K. (2018). Boosting intelligence analysts' judgment accuracy: What works, what fails? *Judgment and Decision Making*, 13(6), 607–621.

Marrin, S. (2008). Training and educating U.S. intelligence analysts. *International Journal of Intelligence and Counterintelligence*, 22(1), 131–146. doi:10.1080/08850600802486986.

McGraw, A. P., Mellers, B. A., & Ritov, I. (2004). The affective costs of overconfidence. *Journal of Behavioral Decision Making*, 17, 281–295. doi:10.1002/bdm.472.

Meissner, P., & Wulf, T. (2013). Cognitive benefits of scenario planning: Its impact on biases and decision quality. *Technological Forecasting & Social Change*, 80, 801–814. doi:10.1016/j.techfore.2012.09.011.

Montibeller, G., & von Winterfeldt, D. (2015). Cognitive and motivational biases in decision and risk analysis. *Risk Analysis*, 35(7), 1230–1251. doi:10.1111/risa.12360.

Morewedge, C. K., Yoon, H., Scopelliti, I., Symborski, C. W., Korris, J. H., & Kassam, K. S. (2015). Debiasing decisions: Improved decision making with a single training intervention. *Policy Insights from the Behavioral and Brain Sciences*, 2(1), 129–140. doi:10.1177/2372732215600886.

Mullinix, G. Gray, O., Colado, J., Veinott, E., Leonard, J., Papautsky, E. L, ... Flach, J. (2013). Heuristica: Designing a serious game for improving decision making. Paper presented at IEEE Games Innovation Conference, 23–25 September, Vancouver, BC. doi:10.1109/IGIC.2013.6659159.

Mumma, G. H., & Wilson, S. B. (1995). Procedural debiasing of primacy/anchoring effects in clinical-like judgments. *Journal of Clinical Psychology*, 51(6), 841–853.

Newby-Clark, I. R., Ross, M., Buehler, R., Koehler, D. J., & Griffin, D. (2000). People focus on optimistic scenarios and disregard pessimistic scenarios while predicting task completion times. *Journal of Experimental Psychology: Applied*, 6(3), 171–182. doi:10.1037//1076-898X.6.3.171.

Nisbett, R. E., & Wilson, T. D. (1977). The halo effect: Evidence for the unconscious alteration of judgments. *Journal of Personality and Social Psychology*, 35, 250–256. doi:10.1037/0022-3514.35.4.250.

Oreg, S., & Bayazit, M. (2009). Prone to bias: Development of a bias taxonomy from an individual differences perspective. *Review of General Psychology*, 13(3), 175–193. doi:10.1037/a0015656.

Peetz, J., Buehler, R., & Wilson, A. E. (2010). Planning for the near and distant future: How does temporal distance affect task completion predictions? *Journal of Experimental Social Psychology*, 46(5), 709–720. doi:10.1016/j.jesp.2010.03.008.

Peters, E. (2012). Beyond comprehension: The role of numeracy in judgments and decisions. *Current Directions in Psychological Science*, 21(1), 31–35. doi:10.1177/0963721411429960.

Pronin, E., Lin, D. Y., & Ross, L. (2002). The bias blind spot: Perceptions of bias in self versus others. *Personality and Social Psychology Bulletin*, 28(3), 369–381. doi:10.1177/0146167202286008.

Rand, T. M., & Wexley, K. N. (1975). Demonstration of the effect, 'similar to me', in simulated employment interviews. *Psychological Reports*, 36(2), 535–544. doi:10.2466/pr0.1975.36.2.535.

Reber, R., & Schwarz, N. (1999). Effects of perceptual fluency on judgments of truth. *Consciousness and Cognition*, 8(3), 338–342. doi:10.1006/ccog.1999.0386.

Reyna, V. F., Chick, C. F., Corbin, J. C., & Hsia, A. N. (2014). Developmental reversals in risky decision making: Intelligence agents show larger decision biases than college students. *Psychological Science*, 25(1), 76–84. doi:10.1177/0956797613497022.

Ross, L. D., Lepper, M. R., Strack, F., & Steinmetz, J. (1977). Social explanation and social expectation: Effects of real and hypothetical explanations on subjective likelihood. *Journal of Personality and Social Psychology*, 35(11), 817–829. doi:10.1037/0022-3514.35.11.817.

Roy, M. M., Christenfeld, N. J. S., & McKenzie, C. R. M. (2005). Underestimating the duration of future events: Memory incorrectly used or memory bias? *Psychological Bulletin*, 131(5), 738–756. doi:10.1037/0033-2909.131.5.738.

Sanna, L. J., & Schwarz, N. (2003). Debiasing the hindsight bias: The role of accessibility experiences and (mis)attributions. *Journal of Experimental Social Psychology*, 39, 287–295. doi:10.1016/S0022-1031(02)00528-0.

Sanna, L. J., Schwarz, N., & Stocker, S. L. (2002). When debiasing backfires: Accessible content and accessibility experiences in debiasing hindsight. *Journal of Experimental Psychology: Learning, Memory, and Cognition*, 28(3), 497–502. doi:10.1037/0278-7393.28.3.497.

Schwartz, N., Bless, H., Strack, F., Klumpp, G., Rittenauer-Schatka, H., & Simons, A. (1991). Ease of retrieval as information: Another look at the availability heuristic. *Journal of Personality and Social Psychology*, 61(2), 195–202. doi:10.1037/0022-3514.61.2.195.

Shaw, A., Kenski, K., Stromer-Galley, J., Martey, R. M., Clegg, B. A., ... Strzalkowski, T. (2016). Serious efforts at bias reduction: The effects of digital games and avatar customization on three cognitive biases. *Journal of Media Psychology*, 30(1), 16–28. doi:10.1027/1864-1105/a000174.

Simon, H. A. (1947). *Administrative behavior*. New York: Macmillan.

Simon, H. A. (1956). Rational choice and the structure of the environment. *Psychological Review*, 63(2), 129–138. doi:10.1037/h0042769.

Simon, H. A. (1957). *Models of man: Social and rational*. Oxford: Wiley.

Simon, H. A. (1990). Invariants of human behavior. *Annual Review of Psychology*, 41, 1–20. doi:10.1146/annurev.ps.41.020190.000245.

Sloman, S. (1996). "The empirical case for two systems of reasoning". *Psychological Bulletin*, 119, 3–22. doi: 10.1037/0033-2909.119.1.3.

Speirs-Bridge, A., Fidler, F., McBride, M., Flander, L., Cumming, G., & Burgman, M. (2010). Reducing overconfidence in the interval judgments of experts. *Risk Analysis*, 30(3), 512–523. doi:10.1111/j.1539-6924.2009.01337.x.

Stanovich, K. E., Toplak, M. E., & West, R. F. (2008). The development of rational thought: A taxonomy of heuristics and biases. *Advances in Child Development and Behavior*, 36, 251–285. doi:10.1016/S0065-2407(08)00006-2.

Stanovich, K. E., & West, R. F. (2000). Individual differences in reasoning: Implications for the rationality debate? *Behavioral and Brain Sciences*, 23(5), 645–726. doi:10.1017/S0140525X00003435.

Stasko, J., Görg, C., Liu, Z., & Singhal, K. (2007). Jigsaw: Supporting investigative analysis through interactive visualization. In W. Ribarsky & J. Dill (Eds.), *Proceedings of IEEE Symposium on Visual Analytics Science and Technology (VAST) 2007* (pp. 131–138). doi:10.1109/VAST.2007.4389006.

Svenson, P., Forsgren, R., Kylesten, B., Berggren, P., Fah, W. R. ... Hann, J. K. Y. (2010). Swedish-Singapore studies of Bayesian modelling techniques for tactical intelligence analysis. Paper presented at 13th Conference on Information Fusion (FUSION) 2010. Available at: http://ieeexplore.ieee.org/xpl/mostRecentIssue.jsp?punumber=5706806

Thaler, R., & Sunstein, C. R. (2008). *Nudge: Improving decisions about health, wealth, and happiness*. New Haven, CT: Yale University Press.

Toplak, M. E., West, R. F., & Stanovich, K. E. (2011). The cognitive reflection test as a predictor of performance on heuristics-and-biases tasks. *Memory and Cognition*, 39(7), 1275–1289. doi:10.3758/s13421-011-0104-1.

Trent, S., Voshell, M., & Patterson, E. (2007). Team cognition in intelligence analysis. Proceedings of the Human Factors and Ergonomics Society Annual Meeting, 51(4), 308–312.

Treverton, G. F., & Gabbard, C. B. (2008). Assessing the tradecraft of intelligence analysis. Technical report. Retrieved from the RAND Corporation at: www.rand.org/content/dam/rand/pubs/technical_reports/2008/RAND_TR293.pdf

Tversky, A., & Kahneman, D. (1973). Availability: A heuristic for judging frequency and probability. *Cognitive Psychology*, 5(1), 207–232. doi:10.1016/0010-0285(73)90033-9.

Tversky, A., & Kahneman, D. (1974). Judgment under uncertainty: Heuristics and biases. *Science*, 185(4157), 1124–1131. doi:10.1126/science.185.4157.1124.

Tversky, A., & Kahneman, D. (1981). The framing of decisions and the rationality of choice, *Science*, 211(4481), 453–458. doi:10.1126/science.7455683.

UK MoD (2013). Quick wins for busy analysts. London: Defence Intelligence, UK.

US Government (2009). A tradecraft primer: Structured analytic techniques for improving intelligence analysis. Retrieved from the CIA at: www.cia.gov/library/center-for-the-study-of-intelligence/csi-publications/books-and-monographs/Tradecraft%20Primer-apr09.pdf

Viale, R. (2018). The normative and descriptive weakness of behavioral economics-informed nudge: Depowered paternalism and unjustified libertarianism. *Mind & Society*, 17(1–2), 53–69.

Viale, R. (2019). Architecture of the mind and libertarian paternalism: Is the reversibility of System 1 nudges likely to happen? Thinking & Reasoning, (submitted).

West, R. F., Meserve, R. J., & Stanovich, K. E. (2012). Cognitive sophistication does not attenuate the bias blind spot. *Journal of Personality and Social Psychology*, 103(3), 506–519. doi:10.1037/a0028857.

Wickens, C., Ketels, S. L. Healy, A. F., Buck-Gengler, C. J., & Bourne, L. E., Jr. (2010). The anchoring heuristic in intelligence integration: A bias in need of de-biasing. *Proceedings of the Human Factors and Ergonomics Society Annual Meeting*, 54, 2324–2328. doi:10.1177/154193121005402722.

Wiese, J., Buehler, R., & Griffin, D. (2016). Backward planning: Effects of planning direction on predictions of task completion time. *Judgment and Decision Making*, 11(2), 147–167.

Zajonc, R. B. (1968). Attitudinal effects of mere exposure. *Journal of Personality and Social Psychology*, 9(2), 1–27. doi:10.1037/h0025848.

PART VII

Behavioral public policies
Nudging and boosting

38

"BETTER OFF, AS JUDGED BY THEMSELVES"

Bounded rationality and nudging

Cass R. Sunstein

Some nudges are designed to reduce externalities; consider fuel economy labels that draw attention to environmental consequences, or default rules that automatically enroll people in green energy (Reisch and Sunstein 2014). But many nudges are designed to increase the likelihood that people's choices will improve their own welfare. Richard Thaler and I argue that the central goal of such nudges is to "make choosers better off, *as judged by themselves*" (Thaler and Sunstein 2008, p. 5; italics in original; Thaler 2015). Social planners – or in our terminology, choice architects – might well have their own ideas about what would make choosers better off, but in our view, the lodestar is people's own judgments. To be a bit more specific: The lodestar is welfare, and people's own judgments are a good (if imperfect) way to test the question whether nudges are increasing their welfare.

The last sentence raises many questions, and it is certainly reasonable to wonder about potential ambiguities in the "as judged by themselves" (hereinafter AJBT) criterion. Should the focus be on choosers' judgments before the nudge, or instead after? What if the nudge alters people's preferences, so that they like the outcome produced by the nudge, when they would not have sought that outcome in advance? What if preferences are constructed by the relevant choice architecture (Lichtenstein and Slovic 2006)? Or what if people's ex ante judgments are wrong, in the sense that a nudge would improve their welfare, even though they do not think that it will (Dolan 2014)? Do we want to ask about choosers' actual, potentially uninformed or behaviorally biased judgments, or are we entitled to ask what choosers would think if they had all relevant information and were unaffected by relevant biases (Goldin 2015)?

My goal here is to explore the meaning of the AJBT criterion and to sort out some of the ambiguities. As we shall see, three categories of cases should be distinguished: (1) those in which choosers have clear antecedent preferences, and nudges help them to satisfy those preferences; (2) those in which choosers face a self-control problem, and nudges help them to overcome that problem; and (3) those in which choosers would be content with the outcomes produced by two or more nudges, or in which ex post preferences are endogenous to or constructed by nudges, so that the AJBT criterion leaves choice architects with several options, without specifying which one to choose. Cases that fall in category (1) plainly satisfy the AJBT criterion, and there are many such cases. From the standpoint of the AJBT criterion, cases that fall in category (2) are also unobjectionable, indeed they can be seen as a subset of category (1);

DOI: 10.4324/9781315658353-45

and they are plentiful. Cases that fall in category (3) create special challenges, which may lead us to make direct inquiries into people's welfare or to explore what informed, active choosers typically select.

An important question, pressed by Robert Sugden (Sugden 2016), is simple: "Do people really want to be nudged towards healthy lifestyles?" That is an empirical question, and we have a great deal of evidence about it. The answer is "yes," at least in the sense that in numerous nations – including the United States, the United Kingdom, Germany, France, Italy, and Australia – strong majorities endorse nudges toward healthy lifestyles (Jung and Mellers 2016; Reisch and Sunstein 2016; Sunstein 2016a, 2016b; Sunstein, Reisch, and Rauber 2017). One might object that general attitudes toward nudges do not specifically answer Sudgen's question, and that it is best not to ask people generally (1) whether they approve of nudges, but instead to ask more specifically (2) whether they themselves would like to be nudged (on potential differences between answers to the two questions, see Cornwell and Krantz 2014). But general approval of health-related nudges strongly suggests that the answer to (2) is probably "yes" as well, and in any case, the existing evidence suggests that the answer to (2), asked specifically, is also "yes" (Jung and Mellers 2016). To be sure, more remains to be learned on these issues.

These findings cannot speak to conceptual and normative questions. What does it even mean to say that people want to make the choices toward which they are being nudged? What is the relationship between people's preferences and imaginable nudges? In light of behavioral findings, how confidently can we speak of people's "preferences"? If people want to be nudged, why are they not already doing what they would be nudged to do? Those are important questions (and they do have empirical features).

Thaler and I are interested in "libertarian paternalism," in the form of approaches that preserve freedom of choice, but that steer people in a direction that will promote their welfare. Coercive paternalism is very different (Conly 2014). Reminders, warnings, information disclosure, invocations of social norms, and default rules are examples of what we have in mind (Sunstein 2016a, 2016b). Contrary to a common misconception, the AJBT criterion is not at all designed to counter the charge of paternalism. On the contrary, Thaler and I explicitly embrace (a mild form of) paternalism, and the purpose of the criterion is *to discipline the content of paternalistic interventions*. Consider, for example, a GPS device. It will identify the best route for you, given the direction that you identify; it makes you better off by your own lights. It increases *navigability*. At the same time, it is paternalistic in the sense that it purports to know, better than you do, how to get where you want to go. Its paternalism is one of means, not ends (Sunstein 2014). Means paternalism is unquestionably a form of paternalism, but it will typically satisfy the AJBT criterion, because it is respectful of people's ends. To be sure, we might find cases in which the distinction between means and ends is not straightforward (Sunstein 2014), but most cases are easy.

It is not possible to understand the operation of the AJBT criterion without reference to examples. In countless cases, we can fairly say that *given people's antecedent preferences*, a nudge will make choosers better off AJBT. For example:

1 Luke has heart disease, and he needs to take various medications. He wants to do so, but he is sometimes forgetful. His doctor sends him periodic text messages. As a result, he takes the medications. He is very glad to receive those messages.
2 Meredith has a mild weight problem. She is aware of that fact, and while she does not suffer serious issues of self-control, and does not want to stop eating the foods that she enjoys, she does seek to lose weight. Because of a new law, many restaurants in her city have clear

calorie labels, informing her of the caloric content of various options. As a result, she sometimes chooses low-calorie offerings – which she would not do if she were not informed. She is losing weight. She is very glad to see those calorie labels.

3   Edna is a professor at a large university, which has long offered its employees the option to sign up for a retirement plan. Edna believes that signing up would be a terrific idea, but she has not gotten around to it. She is somewhat embarrassed about that. Last year, the university switched to an automatic enrollment plan, by which employees are defaulted into the university's plan. They are allowed to opt out, but Edna does not. She is very glad that she has been automatically enrolled in the plan.

There is nothing unfamiliar about these cases. On the contrary, they capture a great deal of the real-world terrain of nudging, both by governments and by the private sector (Halpern 2015; Sunstein 2016a; 2016b). Choosers have a goal, or an assortment of goals, and the relevant choice architecture can make it easier or harder for them to achieve it or them. Insofar as we understand the AJBT criterion by reference to people's antecedent preferences, that criterion is met. Note that it would be easy to design variations on these cases in which nudges *failed* that criterion, because they would make people worse off by their own lights.

We could complicate the cases of Luke, Meredith, and Edna by assuming that they have clear antecedent preferences, that the nudge is inconsistent with those preferences, but that as a result of the nudge, their preferences are changed. For example:

> Jonathan likes talking on his cell phone while driving. He talks to friends on his commute to work, and he does business as well. As a result of a set of vivid warnings, he has stopped. He is glad. He cannot imagine why anyone would talk on a cell phone while driving. In his view, that is too dangerous.

After the nudge, Luke, Meredith, Edna, and Jonathan believe themselves to be better off. Cases of this kind raise the question whether the AJBT criterion requires reference to ex ante or ex post preferences. That is a good question, which might be answered by making direct inquiries into people's welfare; I will turn to that question below. My main point is that as originally given, the cases of Luke, Elizabeth, and Edna are straightforward. Such cases are common (Halpern 2015; Thaler 2015).

Some cases can be seen as different, because they raise questions about self-control (or akrasia):

1   Ted smokes cigarettes. He wishes that he had not started, but he has been unable to quit. His government has recently imposed a new requirement, which is that cigarette packages must be accompanied with graphic images, showing people with serious health problems, including lung cancer. Ted is deeply affected by those images; he cannot bear to see them. He quits, and he is glad.

2   Joan is a student at a large university. She drinks a lot of alcohol. She enjoys it, but not that much, and she is worried that her drinking is impairing her performance and her health. She says that she would like to scale back, but for reasons that she does not entirely understand, she has found it difficult to do so. Her university recently embarked on an educational campaign to reduce drinking on campus, in which it (accurately) notes that four out of five students drink only twice a month or less. Informed of the social norm, Joan finally resolves to cut back her drinking. She does, and she is glad.

In these cases, the chooser suffers from a self-control problem and is fully aware of that fact. Ted and Joan can be seen as both planners, with second-order preferences, and doers, with first-order preferences (Thaler and Sunstein 2008; Thaler 2015). A nudge helps to strengthen the hand of the planner. It is possible to raise interesting philosophical and economic questions about akrasia and planner-doer models (Stroud and Tappolet 2003), but insofar as Ted and Joan welcome the relevant nudges, and do so ex ante as well as ex post, the AJBT criterion is met. In a sense, self-control problems require their own GPS devices and so can be seen to involve navigability; but for choosers who face such problems, the underlying challenge is qualitatively distinctive, and they recognize that fact.

In such cases, the AJBT criterion is met. But do people acknowledge that they face a self-control problem? That is an empirical question, of course, and my own preliminary research suggests that the answer is "yes." On Amazon's Mechanical Turk, I asked about 200 people this question:

> Many people believe that they have an issue, whether large or small, of self-control. They may eat too much, they may smoke, they may drink too much, they may not save enough money. Do you believe that you have any issue of self-control?

A whopping 70 percent said that they did (55 percent said "somewhat agree," while 15 percent said "strongly agree"). Only 22 percent disagreed (8 percent were neutral).

This is a preliminary test, of course. Whatever majorities say, the cases of Ted and Joan capture a lot of the territory of human life, as reflected in the immense popularity of programs designed to help people to combat addiction to tobacco (Halpern et al. 2015) and alcohol. We should agree that nudges that do the work of such programs, or that are used in such programs (Halpern et al. 2015), are likely to satisfy the AJBT criterion.

There are harder cases. In some of them, it is not clear if people have antecedent preferences at all. In others – as in the case of Jonathan – their ex post preferences are an artifact of, or constructed by, the nudge. Sometimes these two factors are combined (as marketers are well aware). As Amos Tversky and Richard Thaler put it long ago, "values or preferences are commonly constructed in the process of elicitation" (Tversky and Thaler 1990). If so, how ought the AJBT criterion to be understood and applied?

For example:

1   George cares about the environment, but he also cares about money. He currently receives his electricity from coal; he knows that coal is not exactly good for the environment, but it is cheap, and he does not bother to switch to wind, which would be slightly more expensive. He is quite content with the current situation. Last month, his government imposed an automatic enrollment rule on electricity providers: People will receive energy from wind, and pay a slight premium, unless they choose to switch. George does not bother to switch. He says that he likes the current situation of automatic enrollment. He approves of the policy and he approves of his own enrollment.

2   Mary is automatically enrolled in a Bronze Health Care Plan – it is less expensive than Silver and Gold, but it is also less comprehensive in its coverage, and it has a higher deductible. Mary prefers Bronze and has no interest in switching. In a parallel world (a lot like ours, but not quite identical, Wolf 1990), Mary is automatically enrolled in a Gold Health Care Plan – it is more expensive than Silver and Bronze, but it is also more comprehensive in its coverage, and it has a lower deductible. Mary prefers Gold and has no interest in switching.

3   Thomas has a serious illness. The question is whether he should have an operation, which
is accompanied with potential benefits and potential risks. Reading about the operation
online, Thomas is not sure whether he should go ahead with it. Thomas's doctor advises
him to have the operation, emphasizing how much he has to lose if he does not. He decides
to follow the advice. In a parallel world (a lot like ours, but not quite identical), Thomas's
doctor advises him not to have the operation, emphasizing how much he has to lose if he
does. He decides to follow the advice.

In the latter two cases, Mary and Thomas appear to lack an antecedent preference; what they
prefer is an artifact of the default rule (in the case of Mary) or the framing (in the case of
Thomas). George's case is less clear, because he might be taken to have an antecedent preference
in favor of green energy, but we could easily understand the narrative to mean that his preference, like that of Mary and Thomas, is endogenous to the default rule.

These are the situations on which I am now focusing: People lack an antecedent preference,
and what they like is a product of the nudge. Their preference is constructed by it. After being
nudged, they will be happy and possibly grateful. We have also seen that even if people have
an antecedent preference, the nudge might change it, so that they will be happy and possibly
grateful even if they did not want to be nudged in advance.

In all of these cases, application of the AJBT criterion is less simple. Choice architects cannot
contend that they are merely vindicating choosers' ex ante preferences. If we look ex post,
people do think that they are better off, and in that sense the criterion is met. For use of the
AJBT criterion, the challenge is that *however Mary and Thomas are nudged, they will agree that they
are better off*. In my view, there is no escaping at least some kind of welfarist analysis in choosing
between the two worlds in the cases of Mary and Thomas. There is a large question about
which nudge to choose in such cases (for relevant discussion, see Dolan 2014). Nonetheless,
the AJBT criterion remains relevant in the sense that it constrains what choice architects can
do, even if it does not specify a unique outcome (as it does in cases in which people have clear
ex ante preferences and in which the nudge does not alter them).

Again: Thaler and I embrace paternalism, and so the AJBT criterion is emphatically not
designed to defeat a charge of paternalism. It is psychologically fine (often) to think that
choosers have antecedent preferences (whether or not "latent"), but that because of a lack of
information or a behavioral bias, their choices will not satisfy them. (Recall the cases of Luke,
Meredith, and Edna.) To be sure, it is imaginable that some forms of choice architecture will
affect people who have information or lack such biases; an error-free cafeteria visitor might
grab the first item she sees, because she is busy, and because it is not worth it to her to decide
which item to choose (Ullmann-Margalit 2017). Consider this case:

Gretchen enjoys her employer's cafeteria. She tends to eat high-calorie meals, but she
knows that, and she likes them a lot. Her employer recently redesigned the cafeteria
so that salads and fruits are the most visible and accessible. She now chooses salad and
fruit, and she likes them a lot.

By stipulation, Gretchen suffers from no behavioral bias, but she is affected by the nudge. But in
many (standard) cases, behaviorally biased or uninformed choosers will be affected by a nudge,
and less biased and informed choosers will not; a developing literature explores how to proceed in such cases, with careful reference to what seems to me a version of the AJBT criterion
(Goldin 2015; Goldin and Lawson 2016).

In Gretchen's case, and all those like it, the criterion does not leave choice architects at sea: If she did not like the salad, the criterion would be violated. From the normative standpoint, it may not be entirely comforting to say that nudges satisfy the AJBT criterion if choice architects succeed in altering the preferences of those whom they are targeting. (Is that a road to serfdom? Recall the chilling last lines of Orwell's *1984*: "He had won the victory over himself. He loved Big Brother" (cf. Elster 1983).) But insofar as we are concerned with subjective welfare, it is a highly relevant question whether choosers believe, ex post, that the nudge has produced an outcome of which they approve.

Countless nudges increase navigability, writ large, in the sense that they enable people to get where they want to go, and therefore enable them to satisfy their antecedent preferences. Many other nudges, helping to overcome self-control problems, are warmly welcomed by choosers, and so are consistent with the AJBT criterion. Numerous people acknowledge that they suffer from such problems. When people lack antecedent preferences or when those preferences are not firm, and when a nudge constructs or alters their preferences, the AJBT criterion is more difficult to operationalize, and it may not lead to a unique solution. But it restricts the universe of candidate solutions, and in that sense helps to orient choice architects.

Acknowledgments

The author is grateful to the Program on Behavioral Economics and Public Policy for support and to Lucia Reisch for valuable comments on a previous draft.

References

Conly, S. (2014). *Against Autonomy*. Oxford: Oxford University Press.

Cornwell, J. F., and Krantz, D. H. (2014). Public policy for thee, but not for me: Varying the grammatical person of public policy justifications influences their support. *Judgment and Decision Making, 5,* 433–444.

Dolan, P. (2014). *Happiness by Design*. London: Penguin.

Elster, J. (1983). *Sour Grapes*. Cambridge: Cambridge University Press.

Goldin, J. (2015). Which way to nudge? Uncovering preferences in the behavioral age. *Yale Law Journal,* 125, 226–271.

Goldin, J., and Lawson, N. (2016). Defaults, mandates, and taxes: Policy design with active and passive decision-makers. *American Journal of Law and Economics*, 18, 438–462.

Halpern, D. (2015). *Inside the Nudge Unit: How Small Changes Can Make a Big Difference*, London: W.H. Allen.

Halpern, S. D. et al. (2015). Randomized trial of four financial-incentive programs for smoking cessation. *The New England Journal of Medicine*, 372, 2108–2111.

Infante, G., Lecouteux, G., and Sugden, R. (2016). Preference purification and the inner rational agent: a critique of the conventional wisdom of behavioural welfare economics. *Journal of Economic Methodology*, 23, 1–25.

Jung, J. Y., and Mellers, B. A. (2016). American attitudes toward nudges. *Judgment and Decision Making*, 11(1), 62–74.

Lichtenstein, S., and Slovic, P. (2006). *The Construction of Preference*. Cambridge: Cambridge University Press.

Reisch, L., and Sunstein, C. R. (2016). Do Europeans like nudges? *Judgment and Decision Making*, 11, 310–325.

Sudgen, R. (2016). Do people really want to be nudged towards healthy lifestyles? *International Review of Economics*, 64, 113–123.

Stroud, S., and Tappolet, C. (Eds.) (2003). *Weakness of Will and Practical Irrationality*, Oxford: Clarendon Press.

Sunstein, C. R. (2014). *Why Nudge?* New Haven, CT: Yale University Press.

Sunstein, C. R. (2016a). The Council of Psychological Advisers. *Annual Review of Psychology*, 67, 713–737.

Sunstein, C. R. (2016b). *The Ethics of Influence*. Cambridge: Cambridge University Press.

Sunstein, C. R., Reich, L., and Rauber, J. (2017). Behavioral insights all over the world? Public attitudes toward nudging in a multi-country study, available at https://papers.ssrn.com/sol3/papers.cfm?abstract_id=2921217

Sunstein, C. R., and Reisch, L. A. (2014). Automatically green: Behavioral economics and environmental protection. *Harvard Environmental Law Review*, 38, 127–158.

Thaler, R. H. (2015). *Misbehaving*. New York: Norton.

Thaler, R. H., and Sunstein, C. R. (2008). *Nudge: Improving Decisions about Health, Wealth, and Happiness*. New Haven, CT: Yale University Press.

Tversky, A., and Thaler, R. H. (1990). Anomalies: Preference reversals. *Journal of Economic Perspectives*, 4, 201–211.

Ullmann-Margalit, E. (2017). *Normal Rationality*. Oxford: Oxford University Press.

Wolf, F. (1990). *Parallel Universes: The Search for Other Worlds*. New York: Simon & Schuster.

39

AN ALTERNATIVE BEHAVIOURAL PUBLIC POLICY

Adam Oliver

Introduction

The application of behavioural insights to public policy, defined here as behavioural public policy, is in any substantive sense, a relatively recent endeavour, although decades of social science research underpin the approach (see, for example, Oliver, 2017). Several conceptual frameworks have been developed within the field of behavioural public policy, but the dominant frameworks have thus far been forms of paternalism, with paternalistic approaches defined here as those that focus upon improving the position of those targeted by behaviour change initiatives, often (although not always) as judged deliberatively by those persons themselves. In other words, these approaches aim to improve internalities, rather than reduce negative externalities – i.e., harms – to third parties.

Moreover, the dominant behavioural public policy frameworks tend to retain the normative assumption of standard economic theory and rational choice theory that people ought to maximise utility (considered here to be synonymous with welfare and happiness). Yet they differ from standard theory by contending that, descriptively, people often fail to maximise utility due to being influenced by innate behavioural influences, such as present bias and loss aversion. As such, these frameworks can be defined as behavioural welfare economics and propose that policy makers ought to influence people's decisions such that they move to increase their utility.

In this chapter, I will contend that the focus on both internalities and utility is less than ideal for the future development of behavioural public policy. In its stead, I will propose a political economy of behavioural public policy that sits alongside the liberal economic tradition of John Stuart Mill, albeit with my approach being somewhat more interventionist than Mill would have allowed (and far more interventionist than followers of the Austrian School of Economics (e.g., von Mises, [1927] 2005)). But first let us unpick a little more some of the details introduced thus far.

Addressing internalities

Of the forms of paternalism, libertarian paternalism – policy applications of which are the fabled nudges (Thaler and Sunstein, 2003, 2008) – has thus far been the most prominent in the development of behavioural public policy. Like asymmetric paternalism (Camerer et al.,

DOI: 10.4324/9781315658353-46

2003), libertarian paternalism is a soft form of paternalism. In short, the approach seeks to guide people in particular directions so that they are more likely to make better (i.e. more welfare-enhancing) decisions for themselves but does not propose the use of force or mandates. People are free to continue with their existing behaviours if they wish, with Thaler and Sunstein (2008) contending that retaining the freedom to choose is the best safeguard against any misguided policy intervention.

Underpinning libertarian paternalism is the assumption that of the many decisions that each of us make quickly and automatically each day – decisions that are guided by simple rules of thumb (i.e., the heuristics famously associated with Herbert Simon (1956)) and influenced by various innate behavioural influences (e.g., present bias, loss aversion) – a few will lead us to act in ways that, if we deliberated a little more, we would prefer not to do (e.g., present bias might lead us to eat more doughnuts than we would ideally consume if we thought about our decisions a little more). It is noteworthy that these heuristics may have evolved because most of the time they guide us efficiently through our daily lives (e.g., Gigerenzer, 2015), but the basic idea in libertarian paternalism is that with knowledge of the behavioural influences, the 'choice architecture' (i.e., the context or environment) that people face can be redesigned, such that their automatic choices are even more likely to better align with their deliberative preferences.

Thus, to summarise, for an intervention to be a nudge, it has to target internalities, preserve liberty and be informed by behavioural science. Each of these three requirements is represented by an axis in Figure 39.1.

In Figure 39.1, moving towards the origin on the horizontal axis, the vertical axis and the diagonal axis respectively indicates that a policy is increasingly addressing internalities rather than externalities, is increasingly liberty-preserving rather than regulatory, and is increasingly informed by behavioural science rather than standard economic theory or rational choice theory. Consequently, a nudge in its purest form must lie at the point where the axes intersect. An oft-mentioned pure nudge, for instance, is the placing of apples at the front and cheesecake

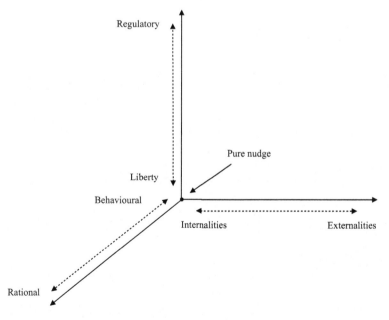

Figure 39.1   The requirements of libertarian paternalism

at the back of canteen shelves, to motivate those who would ideally like to eat more healthily to choose the healthier option (but people can still choose the cheesecake if they wish).

Some argue that by retaining the notion of liberty, soft forms of paternalism do not go far enough in that they will ultimately prove to be insufficiently effective at affecting behaviour change for those who threaten their own health and financial security (Conly, 2013). Those who adhere to this line of reasoning call instead for hard paternalism or coercive paternalism. They retain the notion that activities that they argue are not good for people – such as smoking and saving insufficiently for one's retirement – may be driven by behavioural influences such as present bias and the like. In short, whereas soft paternalists allow people to continue their pre-existing behaviours, coercive paternalists call for some activities, such as smoking, to be banned entirely.

By advocating behaviour change for some or all of those targeted for their own good, all forms of paternalism are, however, open to the criticism that they infantilise those whom they target, and that politicians and policy makers ought to have no role in influencing the behaviours of adults of sound mind if their activities impose no harms on others, a view consistent with Mill's harm principle (Mill, 1859/1972). The behavioural welfare economics counterargument is predicated on retaining the normative postulate of utility maximisation, i.e., libertarian paternalists (and, indeed, other types of paternalist) believe that due to the behavioural influences that contravene rational choice theory, people will sometimes fail to act and choose in their own best interests (i.e. to maximise utility) – and thus they contend that it is legitimate for policy makers to steer them (or, for coercive paternalists, to force them) in that normative direction. But is this assumption of legitimacy acceptable?

The view from nowhere

As aforementioned, behavioural welfare economics, like standard economic theory and rational choice theory, postulates that people ought to maximise utility (welfare or happiness). All of these approaches are thus underpinned by utilitarianism, the founding father of which was Jeremy Bentham. Bentham (1988 [1781]) believed that humans are governed by the two "sovereign masters" of pleasure and pain, and he viewed these as feelings that are experienced on a continuum and can thus be compared. He contended that they guide us on what we ought to do, and what we shall do.

By the beginning of the twentieth century, measures of Benthamite utility – i.e., numerical interpersonally comparable indicators of how much pain and pleasure individuals experience in the moment – were thought to be impossible to uncover, but modern neoclassical economic theory, which is based upon decisions over future experiences rather than experiences in the moment, retained the notion that people ought to, and will want to, maximise their utility. Therefore, other than making random mistakes, we can infer from this that the decisions that people make over future episodes, and their retrospective assessments of their previous courses of action, will be consistent with them wanting to maximise the amount of utility that they experience. There is now evidence to suggest that this inference is not always accurate.

Specifically, it has been demonstrated in experimental settings that when people are asked to offer retrospective preferences over different events, there is a tendency for their relative preferences to differ systematically from that which would be suggested by aggregating moment-to-moment instant utilities that they experienced as they lived through each event (similar observations have sometimes been observed with respect to prospective evaluations). The cause of these systematic discrepancies are salient features of events, known as the gestalt characteristics (Ariely and Carmon, 2000). The gestalt characteristics include the tendency for people, at least over relatively short events, to prefer worse outcomes to precede better outcomes rather than vice versa (Loewenstein and Prelic, 1993), an aversion to sudden, steep rates of change in outcomes (Hsee and Abelson, 1991), and the tendency for people to place a heavy emphasis on the peak and end moments of an episode (Fredrickson and Kahneman, 1993). This last gestalt characteristic, called peak-end evaluation, is the most studied, and can cause people to neglect the duration of the event (for a general review of the gestalts, see Kahneman et al., 1997).

Peak-end evaluation is nicely illustrated by a study by Redelmeier et al. (2003), who divided 682 sigmoidoscopy patients into two groups. For the patients in one of the groups, unbeknownst to them, the sigmoidoscopy tube was left inserted in their bodies for an additional short period at the end of the procedure for no clinical reason, which would have been uncomfortable but not as painful as when the tube was being moved around. The patients' discomfort was recorded every 60 seconds to measure their moments of instant disutility, and by aggregating these moments at the end of the procedures a measure of total experienced disutility of the procedure for each patient could be calculated. Following their procedures, the patients' retrospective evaluations of the total discomfort that they experienced was recorded on a ten-point scale. By comparing the retrospective evaluations to the moments of instant utility, Redelmeier et al. observed peak-end evaluation and a neglect of duration. They also reported that the group for whom the tube was left inserted tended to remember the procedure as less painful than those for whom it was removed as soon as the clinical procedure was over. That the former group must on average have experienced greater total experienced disutility as a consequence of having the procedure duration extended unnecessarily means that the authors recorded a violation of dominance. That is, in general, those who remembered the experience as less bad were exposed to an experience that in general caused greater aggregate pain.

Since the gestalt characteristics can cause people to choose options that conflict with the assumption of experienced utility maximisation, we must ask the question of whether they are causing people to make errors, or whether the gestalts are legitimate influences on preferences. Behavioural welfare economics would view preferences that are influenced as such as mistakes, which may sometimes be a fair conclusion to draw (after all, who, other than a masochist, would want to experience more pain?). But in many circumstances and for many people, it is legitimate to question whether a simple aggregation of moments of instant utility gives an accurate assessment of the underlying value of an experience. If the experience in question is a whole life, Daniel Hausman, for instance, has stated that

> a good life is not a sum of the net goodness of its moments ... The same sum of momentary experiences can add up to a wonderful life or an incoherent and mediocre one, depending on how the experiences are ordered and what overall narrative they sustain.
>
> *Hausman, 2015, p. 114*

When we look forward to an episode, or reflect back on it, the gestalts may often matter because they give meaning – a narrative – to the story. They may in part determine how fulfilling the event was to a person, and whether the person feels they had the opportunity, or will have the opportunity, to flourish.

Some economists might contend that the gestalts, and the concern with how the moments of an experience fit together, can be encapsulated by additional arguments in the utility function. Following this line of reasoning, although the gestalts may contrast with the assumptions of Benthamite utility maximisation, they might be consistent with a broader notion of utility maximisation. Placing anything in the utility function, however, presents the risk that utility maximisation can justify everything, but can really explain and specifically predict nothing. That is to say, if everything that a person does is attributed to her simply maximising her utility and we accept that this is what she ought to do, the theory is so general that it becomes empty and the person is allowed to do anything.

Rather than accept that the drive behind human behaviour and decision making is and ought to be the drive to increase utility/welfare/happiness, we might more modestly admit that we cannot know why people do the things they do. It may well be that people have various and varied legitimate reasons for their actions, both interpersonally and, across contexts, intrapersonally. To assume that utility (or welfare or happiness) maximisation is the universal normative condition is, as suggested by the economist, Robert Sugden (2018), the view from nowhere. On this basis, it is my contention that the role of policy makers should not be to seek to maximise utility, but rather to seek to improve the opportunities for people to flourish as they themselves see fit (which may for some be to seek to maximise utility, but that is their prerogative). Encouraging people to reciprocate with others, as opposed to acting upon their selfish egoistic instincts, is likely to facilitate the individuals that comprise a community in the pursuit of their own goals (for discussions of the benefits of reciprocity, see Bowles, 2016; Oliver, 2019; Sugden, 2018).

To reciprocate, to flourish

If the aim of policy makers is to help create the conditions for people to flourish as they themselves see fit, then, to reiterate, facilitating reciprocity, as an aspect of behavioural public policy, is potentially an important arm of this effort. Sugden suggests that since people are fundamentally reciprocators, then the tendency and scope for reciprocal actions can be aided simply by increasing the number of choices and opportunities that are available to them. However, although reciprocity is indeed a fundamental motivator of human actions, it can be crowded out by our baser motivations (namely, selfish egoism), and thus conditions need to be created in order to nurture reciprocity. Some suggestions for how policy makers might do this include emphasising the importance of this motivator of human behaviour in their rhetoric, decentralising public policy decision making to sub-national levels, and ensuring that income and wealth are not concentrated excessively in the hands of a small proportion of the population. Elaborations on these policy directions is beyond my scope here; more detailed discussions and references to support these propositions can be found in Oliver (2019).

The approach proposed here does not therefore aim to instil a view from nowhere onto targeted populations. Instead, it postulates that people in local communities organise themselves in any way they see fit to achieve the objectives that they wish to pursue in their private choices and actions, on the condition that they do not impose harms on others, although – consistent with Mill ([1859] 1972) – this does not preclude attempts at educating people openly about the possible self-harm inflicting consequences of some of their activities (and allows scope for "boosting", or, in other words, educating people openly in relation to how the heuristics and behavioural phenomena might influence their choices with a view to them making more informed decisions (Hertwig, 2017)). The members of the community need not share the same goals. They may reciprocate and collaborate in their pursuit of different personal conceptions of a flourishing life. If the conditions for mutually supportive efforts towards meeting personal goals are strengthened, then the suggestion here is that it is reasonable to expect that their goals will more likely be realised.

Allowing people great freedom to live their lives in the ways that they see fit is, however, not without risks, in that without interference, there will be much opportunity for selfish egoists to act upon their instincts. Mill's ([1859] 1972) harm principle, which allows the regulation of private actions that are imposing harms – or negative externalities – on others, of course recognises this danger. But Mill did not explicitly foresee that an actor or organisation could use the behavioural influences to impose harms on others. For more than a century the private marketing industry has used what are essentially behavioural insights to sometimes nefarious ends, activities that remain rife (Akerlof and Shiller, 2015). If providers of products and services implement measures that undermine the concept of a fair, reciprocal exchange, then policy action to regulate against these behaviourally-informed harms is justified.

Budging

An alternative (or, at the very least, a complement) to paternalistic interventions, budges are regulations against activities that rely on their effectiveness by being informed by behavioural insights, and where their effectiveness imposes harms on others (Oliver, 2013, 2015, 2017). For example, the marketing arms of confectionary companies know implicitly that salience and immediacy (i.e., factors associated with present bias) can have a large effect on consumer buying patterns, and this is why they have traditionally paid supermarkets substantial amounts of money so that their products are displayed close to checkout counters. If we were to conclude that consumers, as a consequence, are purchasing more confectionary than they otherwise would (i.e., more than in the absence of manipulation, which is particularly nefarious if the products or services in question impose harms on characteristics, such as health or finances, that might be considered important factors underlying a flourishing life, irrespective of what it means to flourish), then policy makers would have an intellectual justification to regulate against – to budge – this activity.

Budges can also be placed within a three-dimensional space, depicted as Figure 39.2. Compared to Figure 39.1, the horizontal and vertical axes have been inverted, such that a

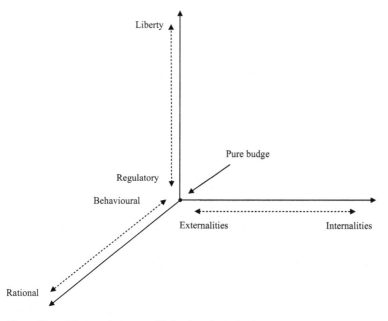

Figure 39.2 The requirements of behavioural regulation

policy placed at the origin would now be a regulation against a behaviourally-informed negative externality: a pure budge.

Conclusion

In this chapter, I have argued that the principal overarching political economy of behavioural public policy should not be to focus upon moving internalities towards some conception of utility (or welfare or happiness) maximisation, but ought to rather be focused on fostering reciprocity and cooperation so that people are better equipped to flourish and find fulfilment in their lives. This proposed approach is in the spirit of the liberal economic tradition (albeit recognising that the individual's conception of flourishing does not necessarily equate to consequentialist notions of utility, welfare or happiness), but goes somewhat further than that tradition specifies by recognising that giving people great freedom affords more opportunities for the egoistically inclined to use behavioural insights in order to manipulate people, and potentially impose harms on them. Thus, it is argued that when behavioural influences are being used by individuals or organisations towards self-serving and harmful ends, then there is a legitimate, intellectual justification for regulating against those activities. So, to sum up, the political economy of behavioural public policy proposed in this chapter has two arms: to nurture reciprocity so as improve the stock of human flourishing, and to regulate against harm-inducing egoism to protect the capacity of people to flourish as they themselves see fit.

References

Akerlof, G. A., and Shiller, R. J. 2015. *Phishing for Phools: The Economics of Manipulation and Deception.* Princeton, NJ: Princeton University Press.

Ariely, D., and Carmon, Z. 2000. Gestalt characteristics of experiences: The defining features of summarized events. *Journal of Behavioral Decision Making* 13: 191–201.

Bentham, J. [1781] 1988. *The Principles of Morals and Legislation.* New York: Prometheus Books.

Bowles, S. 2016. *The Moral Economy: Why Good Incentives Are No Substitute for Good Citizens.* New Haven, CT: Yale University Press.

Camerer, C., Issacharoff, S., Loewenstein, G., O'Donoghue, T., and Rabin, M. 2003. Regulation for conservatives: Behavioral economics and the case for 'asymmetric paternalism'. *University of Pennsylvania Law Review* 1151: 1211–1254.

Conly, S. 2013. *Against Autonomy: Justifying Coercive Paternalism.* Cambridge: Cambridge University Press.

Fredrickson, B. L., and Kahneman, D. 1993. Duration neglect in retrospective evaluations of affective episodes. *Journal of Personality and Social Psychology* 65: 44–55.

Gigerenzer, G. 2015. On the supposed evidence for libertarian paternalism. *Review of Philosophy and Psychology* 6: 361–383.

Hausman, D. M. 2015. *Valuing Health: Well-Being, Freedom and Suffering.* Oxford: Oxford University Press.

Hertwig, R. 2017. When to consider boosting: Some rules for policy-makers. *Behavioural Public Policy* 1: 143–161.

Hsee, C. K., and Abelson, R. P. 1991. Velocity relation: Satisfaction as a function of the first derivative of outcome over time. *Journal of Personality and Social Psychology* 60: 341–347.

Kahneman, D., Wakker, P. P., and Sarin, R. 1997. Back to Bentham? Explorations of expected utility. *The Quarterly Journal of Economics* 112: 375–405.

Loewenstein, G., and Prelec, D. 1993. Preferences for sequences of outcomes. *Psychological Review* 100: 91–98.

Mill, J. S. [1859] 1972. *On Liberty.* London: Dent.

Oliver, A. 2013. From nudging to budging: Using behavioural economics to inform public sector policy. *Journal of Social Policy* 42: 685–700.

Oliver, A. 2015. Nudging, shoving and budging: Behavioural economic-informed policy. *Public Administration* 93: 700–714.

Oliver, A. 2017. *The Origins of Behavioural Public Policy.* Cambridge: Cambridge University Press.

Oliver, A. 2019. *Reciprocity and the Art of Behavioural Public Policy*. Cambridge: Cambridge University Press.

Redelmeier, D., Katz, J., and Kahneman, D. 2003. Memories of colonoscopy: A randomized trial. *Pain* 104: 187–194.

Simon, H. A. 1956. Rational choice and the structure of the environment. *Psychological Review* 63: 129–138.

Sugden, R. 2018. *The Community of Advantage: A Behavioural Defence of the Liberal Tradition of Economics*. Oxford: Oxford University Press.

Thaler, R. H., and Sunstein, C. R. 2003. Libertarian paternalism. *The American Economic Review* 93: 175–179.

Thaler, R. H., and Sunstein, C. R. 2008. *Nudge: Improving Decisions about Health, Wealth and Happiness*. New Haven, CT: Yale University Press.

von Mises, L. [1927] 2005. *Liberalism*. Indianapolis: Liberty Fund.

40

AGAINST NUDGING

Simon-inspired behavioral law and economics founded on ecological rationality

Nathan Berg

Introduction

Paternalistic policy making in general—and Thaler and Sunstein's (2008) nudge program, in particular—assume that we have a reliable and relatively stable expert consensus regarding what we should eat, how much we should save for retirement, which types of securities should be held in our retirement portfolios, and how we ought to make sundry other decisions for which many lack conviction to take decisive action without a nudge (e.g., whether to become an organ donor). Critiques of the nudging program are many. Some of these critiques follow from: (1) debates over competing definitions of axiomatic rationality versus Simon-inspired bounded or ecological rationality (Gigerenzer and Selten, 2001; Berg, 2014a; Gigerenzer, 2016); (2) philosophical and methodological concerns over autonomy and the option to change one's mind raised by Sugden (2016, 2018) and Infante, Lecouteux, and Sugden (2016); (3) evidence regarding the stability of expert advice and social epistemologies on which appeals to authority rest discussed in Viale (2001, 2012, 2019, forthcoming); (4) and well-known incentive problems in the signaling literature that may impede the unbiased transmission of expert advice (Berg, 2018; Berg and Kim, 2019). A less frequently recognized implication of ecological rationality (in contrast to that of axiomatic rationality) is that *heterogeneity of beliefs and decision processes* is a beneficial social good responsible for numerous positive externalities (Berg and Watanabe, 2020).[1] How nudging risks reducing these important yet difficult-to-observe indirect benefits of heterogeneous beliefs and behavior is the focus of this chapter.

Heterogeneous beliefs and decisions can, of course, be costly. Not all behavioral deviations from what experts say we should do are good. Putting aside the uniformly distributed trembling hand (because that is not the kind of unsystematic deviation one often finds), many of the compelling behavioral findings in the last three decades reflect highly non-uniform *deliberate* deviations from normative decision theory—or *purposively systematic* deviations when they are unconscious or autonomomic (whether helpful or otherwise in the particular environment in which they are used, e.g., evolutionary mismatch). Although not yet mainstream (because it contradicts the Kahneman-inspired view among many behavioral economists that deviations from axiomatic rationality must somehow be costly and therefore pathological), there are, by now, abundant empirical evidence and numerous theoretical models demonstrating that some types of deviations, when well-matched to the environments in which they are used,

DOI: 10.4324/9781315658353-47

confer individual-level advantages or improved payoffs to deviators relative to non-deviators (Gigerenzer, Todd, and the ABC Research Group, 1999; Selten and Gigerenzer, 2001; Berg and Hoffrage, 2008; Berg, Biele, and Gigerenzer, 2016). My aim in this chapter is to focus instead on the less frequently considered *social* benefits of heterogeneity in beliefs and behavior. I argue that advocates of nudging policies—which risk jeopardizing both population- and individual-level benefits of behavioral diversity, in part, by inducing less resilient monocultures—would do well to incorporate these risks into their analysis.

Peter Kropotkin and Glen Shafer express the idea that heterogeneity among the decision processes that individuals employ—and heterogeneity among the metrics that individuals use to assess how well they perform—is broadly normative (Berg, 2003, 2018; Berg and Gigerenzer, 2010). In many real-world (and theoretical) decision-making environments, there is no one-size-fits-all "optimal" or "best" process that people would agree should be used to make decisions, form beliefs, or evaluate outcomes (Simon, 1957, 1979; Gigerenzer and Selten, 2001).[2] Social benefits from behavioral diversity include diversification of population-level risks, efficiencies from competition among differing views, ideas, and beliefs, and—less obviously—beneficial social coordination services achieved through voluntary choice in heterogeneous populations, which may be (inadvertently) blocked when paternalistic policies induce behavioral monocultures. For example, the social networks generated from voluntarily choosing to eat vegetarian or give money to charity may lose social significance once these behaviors become policy makers' desired outcomes. Just as financial incentives may crowd out cooperative or prosocial behavior (e.g., Eckel, Grossman, and Johnston, 2005; Mellström and Johannesson, 2008; Brown and Knowles, 2019), so, too, policy prescriptions may crowd out voluntary choice by individuals of the policy maker's preferred behavior. Policy prescriptions can be expected to alter coordination services, social meanings, and what can be inferred from voluntarily choosing behaviors that policy makers wish to induce with nudging. Another important aspect of social benefits of heterogeneity follow from the so-called triple-helix model in which nurturing distinct views and objectives that lead to complementary but distinct processes of innovation within a complex adaptive system raises special challenges for policy makers seeking to encourage innovation (Viale and Pozzali, 2010).

In addition to benefits, there are also costs of new complexities to consider when policy makers introduce framings and nudges. Nudges introduce strategic communication between experts and non-experts, which forces non-experts to filter information in new ways. Non-experts notice when experts shift from disseminating information *without paternalism* toward paternalism (even in the absence of coercion where the choice set is simply re-described but not materially altered, e.g., nudging).[3] Non-experts therefore cannot be sure of experts' objectives when disseminating information, which may reduce information flows, trust and social welfare (Berg, 2018; Berg and Kim, 2010).

There are additional informational benefits that heterogeneity may confer that are not mentioned above, which include discovery of hidden benefits from minority behaviors (e.g., therapeutic uses of tobacco in irritable bowel syndrome and Parkinson's and Alzheimer's Disease), innovation and welfare gains from competition and trade based on opposing beliefs, and subjective benefits from the option value and exercise of individual freedom (e.g., Sugden, 2018). In this context in which public health is used to justify restrictions on consumer choice (i.e., paternalism that goes beyond nudging), Popper's critiques of seemingly benign sympathy with totalitarian means to virtuous ends (among political philosophers' interpretations of Plato) as developed in *The Open Society and Its Enemies* are relevant. Similarly relevant is Hayek's discussion of world views about whether *order*,[4] as a foundational public good, should be understood as *cosmos* (endogenous or spontaneous order that arises through purposeful action in the face of "irremediable ignorance on everyone's part of most of the particular facts which determine the actions of all the several members of human society" (Hayek, 1973, p. 12)) or as if it were designed by policy makers, or choice architects, or some other unitary entity, as *taxis* (exogenously given or "made order" (Hayek, 1973, p. 36)).

Benefits of decentralization—once a foundational insight of welfare economics based in part on the First Fundamental Welfare Theorem—risk being mislaid (Berg, 2018). The possibility of social costs attributable to market failures are also underscored by the stringency of the Welfare Theorem's hypothesis, namely, the joint absence of market power, externalities, and information asymmetry. When failures of this hypothesis arise, as they often do, of course it is not automatic that intervention will satisfy the benefit-cost criterion and improve social welfare. And it would be naïve to fail to recognize numerous rent-seeking motives when political support for intervention forms.

As appealing and reasonable as it may sound to introduce nudges aimed at influencing individuals to make (what some experts claim would be) better choices as judged by themselves (about which many well-published experts would themselves disagree, e.g., fewer saturated fats; more cancer screenings; greater contributions to employer-sponsored retirement savings programs,[5] etc.), there *are* real risks of inadvertently hurting people who respond to nudges precisely in the way that those policies are intended to work.[6] If populations respond to nudges as they are designed to and bring the population's profile of beliefs and behaviors into closer conformity, then multiple beneficial streams of belief and behavioral heterogeneity also risk being reduced. This latter risk involves more subtle and indirect social benefits of heterogeneity forgone, which motivates its special consideration in evaluating the benefits and costs of nudging and paternalistic policies more broadly.

Expert advice and political uses of scientific claims

There is substantial disagreement in the nutrition and medical research literatures regarding macronutrient percentages (e.g., fat, protein, carbohydrate) in the diet and, specifically, whether polyunsaturated or saturated fats reduce or increase risk of chronic disease.[7] Policies concerning the screening of asymptomatic women and men for breast and prostate cancer, respectively, are another important area of contention among experts where proponents of nudging have nevertheless appeared and influenced governments.[8] Encouraging savers to accept more exposure to financial risk (which often means equities and high-yield bond funds) to earn higher rates of return is yet another case where behavioral economists have argued that influencing people to shift their behavior is obvious (e.g., Benartzi and Thaler, 1995) even though we know that large equity draw-downs, money-market-fund defaults, and severe liquidity crises are far from unlikely events that savers will face over their lifetimes.

Despite the standard advice from financial advisers to max out employer-matches in 401ks and the compounding tax benefits of individual retirement accounts, it should at least be acknowledged that this advice, when acted on, raises new risks of having one's wealth concentrated in brokerage accounts, Exchange Traded Funds, and asset classes with counterparty risk adverse liquidity events (e.g., New York money-market specialist, The Reserve, whose Primary Fund with exposure to Lehman-Brothers-issued commercial paper "broke the buck" on September 18, 2008). If a nudging program is "successful" by the narrow criterion of increasing savings rates and balances held in retirement accounts, the social-welfare consequences of homogenizing a population's otherwise more heterogeneous retirement savings decisions remain far from obvious.

Viale (2001) argues that expert knowledge could be reconfigured to strengthen the necessary appeals to authority in evaluating scientific claims. See Viale (2001, 2012) for more discussion of social epistemologies and the *methodological cognitivism* advocated in this context, which bear special relevance for evaluating prescriptive claims upon which nudging policies rest. It must be acknowledged, of course, how challenging it is to consistently apply any political principle (e.g., ranging from *laissez-faire* to totalitarian health dictatorship by public health experts), or a fixed set of normative principles, to guide policy makers' responses to serious problems such as insufficient retirement savings (Harrison and Ross, 2018), even when there is agreement that it is indeed a problem. Observers can agree on the population-level outcome they would like to see without finding common ground on the role of centralized power in bringing that outcome about. The question of "Should there be more or less government?" applied to such problems depends crucially on the counterfactuals considered. Part of the challenge involves how to appropriately circumscribe the answers we regard as admissible evidence when we ask "Without intervention, which harms would have occurred if not for the intervention?" versus the much subtler question of "Which socially beneficial behavioral innovations and new private organizations to address this problem would have appeared without the intervention?"

Given the available evidence regarding regulatory capture, falsehoods propagated by governments based on lobbying rather than scientific evidence (e.g., the "food pyramid"), regulatory failures to protect the public from dangerous drugs, and regulatory failures (of a distinct kind) that block research and availability of un-patentable approaches to treating disease and improving health—one would hope that advocates for more intervention would acknowledge that our answers to the question of whether more government regulation based on scientific expertise would improve social welfare are often ambiguous. Well-informed empiricists can, and do, frequently disagree. And transparent access to that disagreement is beneficial for those who want to make up their own minds. Disagreement is, once again, socially beneficial when it leads to collection and dissemination of new evidence. False harmonization of discordant expert views, as well as disparaging those who question evidence regarding what a political "consensus" claims to be "settled science," can do real harm.

Ecological rationality

Inspired by Herbert Simon,[9] the research program on *ecological rationality* (Gigerenzer and Selten, 2001; Smith, 2003; Berg and Gigerenzer, 2010; Berg, 2014a, 2015), focuses on a novel normative criterion that diverges from definitions of rationality used elsewhere in economics. Rather than rationality being an attribute solely of the decision maker—or the decision-making process a decision maker employs (as in axiomatic definitions of a preference ordering's rationality or the choice data it generates)—the definition of ecological rationality also depends on the external reward-generating environment in which the decision process is used.

Ecological rationality is a matching criterion. It requires that a decision process perform sufficiently well when measured by one or more performance metrics relevant to the environment in which it is used. There are virtually no decision processes that are universally ecologically rational. For any decision process (including constrained optimization), there exists some choice domains where it performs poorly according to one or more relevant performance metrics. Ecological rationality is therefore not an inherent attribute of a decision maker or a decision process. Decision processes can be ecologically rational in one set of environments (or decision domains) and ecologically *irrational* in others.

One theme in the ecological rationality research program is to clearly define domains of reward-generating environments and performance metrics with respect to which a given decision process performs well. Another theme relevant to Simon-inspired behavioral law and economics is how law and regulation—interaction with the population profile of decision processes actually in use—*jointly* construct the reward-generating environment. A heterogeneous ecology of decision rules employed by many different individuals and constrained by the institutional particulars of whichever laws and regulations are in effect at a particular time and place can perform well, by an appropriately specified aggregation rule or social welfare function. Epstein (1995), for example, argues that legal codes based on six simple rules could resolve many seemingly intractable complexities in contemporary societies arising from both technological innovation and timeless or nearly universal human moral principles.

As a normative criterion for evaluating the rationality of a decision process, ecological rationality is not domain-general, whereas axiomatic rationality is. Ecological rationality situates normative evaluations of rationality in a circumscribed set of environments or domains. The important role of the reward-generating environment and environment-specific metrics of performance make ecological rationality amenable to formal modeling. They also make ecological rationality *falsifiable* and, thus, not tautological. Such models describe rules of belief formation and behavior that do not necessarily arise as the solution to a constrained optimization problem.

Like axiomatic definitions of rationality, the possibility of *failing* to achieve ecological rationality is critical to its value as a normative concept. The possibility of failure gives meaning to statements or boundary conditions that circumscribe the set of environments in which a decision process performs well enough to achieve ecological rationality (given a threshold of performance in a particular class of environments). Clear partitioning of this set into disjoint sets of environments—one in which a decision process performs badly, and another in which it performs well enough—provides valuable information to the study of institutions, in general, and law and regulation in particular.

Having established that ecological rationality is distinct from axiomatic rationality,[10] it is also worthwhile to observe that both concepts of rationality support normative evaluations of a decision process that can be conceptually identified as characterizing *individual performance*. The criterion of ecological rationality requires *good-enough* performance in a particular environment. In contrast, axiomatic rationality requires that observed choice data conform to domain-general axioms (e.g., transitivity), which first came to prominence in economics as technical requirements for well-known utility representation theorems. These distinct concepts of rationality also map into distinct normative evaluations of public policies.

Public policy

Another relevant methodological observation when comparing the performance of public policies based on ecological versus axiomatic rationality is that they can lead to different rankings of policies based on policy makers' own objectives—apart from the social welfare effects they produce. For example, Berg and Gigerenzer (2007) show that a society of satisficers requires less paternalistic intervention from risk regulators than a society of risk-averse expected utility maximizers to achieve the policy makers' goal of limiting behavior they regard as dangerous.

In contrast, the nudging program assumes that *violations* of standard axiomatic definitions of rationality based on internal logical consistency (e.g., preference reversals, framing effects, transitivity violations, time inconsistency) are themselves pathological. The assumption that violations of logical invariance and axiomatic rationality must incur economically meaningful harms lacks much empirical evidence and is contradicted in many studies outside of Kahneman and Thaler's research program (only a small subset of which is cited in this chapter). Nevertheless, the de-biasing program proposes that violations of axiomatic rationality be "corrected" so that allegedly "biased" decision processes undergo paternalistic interventions to "de-bias" (e.g., Jolls, Sunstein, and Thaler, 1998). Paternalistic policy advice based on behavioral economics (e.g., Sunstein, 2014, 2016a, 2016b; Sunstein and Reisch, 2014; Sunstein, Reich, and Rauber, 2017)—and Sunstein and Thaler's nudge program, in particular—furthermore fail to explain why alleged biases that afflict people in general (not to mention rent-seeking motives) do not afflict paternalistic policy makers and choice architects.

Following Simon, March, Gigerenzer and others, one can point to compelling evidence that high-performing organisms, humans, and organizations (e.g., Alphabet, Amazon, or the New Zealand rugby team, the All Blacks) are not optimizers (e.g., Cyert and March, 1963; Gage, 2012). Instead, they perform to a high level (i.e., succeed in their respective endeavors) by using heuristics that are well-matched to the class of decisions and inference tasks in which they are used.[11] Note (once again) that ecological rationality measures "success"—of procedures for making decisions or inferences *and* the social institutions that influence those decisions and inferences—by domain-specific performance metrics (e.g., wealth, health, happiness, objective accuracy, etc.).

Heterogeneity of beliefs and behavior as a public good

Although one should be cautious about attributing specific policy views to Simon, my reading of him suggests a Simon-inspired approach to the design of institutions in general—and legal and regulatory frameworks in particular—which rests on the principle that *behavioral heterogeneity* is itself a public good that confers many important social benefits which are often difficult to observe directly. Based on this insight, one may consider heterogeneity itself to be a public good and that efforts to defend against policies that risk encroaching upon heterogeneity are worthwhile to consider in social-welfare analyses of nudging and other paternalistic policies. In contrast, the nudging program and related work in behavioral law and economics prescribe public policies aiming to induce greater conformity with "expert" views of what constitutes optimal behavior (based on the biases and heuristics program). In so doing, it tends to view behavioral heterogeneity as a *problem* requiring heterogeneity-reducing policy solutions.

By aiming to induce conformity with expert recommendations (e.g., Sunstein and Vermeule, 2008; Thaler and Sunstein, 2008), which are relatively static compared to the speed at which the adaptive dynamics of decentralized systems generate value from individual experimentation with non-orthodox behavior and beliefs, the nudging program risks reducing individual payoffs, as well as population-level robustness. The nudging program also risks blocking revelation of valuable information generated by heterogeneous individual approaches to decision making. In blocking the revelation of new information generated by heterogeneity, beneficial social equilibria based on voluntary choice instead of paternalistic intervention—or worse, authoritarian prescription and proscription—are disrupted. These social costs are separate from any direct consideration of individual autonomy as a weighted term in the social welfare function. Including autonomy or liberty as weighted terms in the social welfare function would only compound losses from nudging.

Viale (forthcoming) argues that the hypothesized "System 1," which uses fast, non-deliberative heuristic shortcuts, is one mechanism through which "choice architects" who advocate nudging policies such as defaults for organ donation believe that nudges affect decisions. Therefore, the claim that these nudges are "libertarian" is weakened because the vitally important preservation of a nudged decision maker's choice set and his or her capacity to choose to not take up the nudge (i.e., Rebonato's (2012) so-called "reversibility" criterion, required for the libertarian claim) is never engaged. (This is according to the choice architects' own theory of why the nudge will work.) The libertarian claim for nudging is therefore undermined and its coercive intent revealed. Nudges that are effective because of how System 1 reacts to choice architects' strategic framing stand in contrast to a second set of nudges (such as "cooling off" periods) that are designed to cue System 2 (i.e., more deliberation and analytic reflection of benefits and costs). Viale (2019) further analyses the implausibility of the dual theory of mind (i.e., Systems 1 and 2) upon which advocates of nudging rely.

Distinct normative interpretations of behavioral heterogeneity in Simon-inspired (as opposed to Kahneman-Thaler-inspired) schools of behavioral economics rest on opposing views about how stable the reward-generating environment is relative to the much slower speed at which institutions can change policies that seek to paternalistically influence people toward expert views of optimal behavior and belief. Is what we know about financial markets, human physiology and risk taking really stable enough to justify nudging individuals toward consensus views of optimal behavior in the current environment and given any currently available body of evidence, which nearly always include conflicting views and interpretations? Do institutions that provide expert advice and influence public policy (e.g., recommending that people invest more in the stock market, give more to charity, avoid sugar, and eat "healthy fats"—whichever those turn out to be) wind up processing new information fast enough, updating expert recommendations flexibly enough, and avoiding regulatory capture and the influence of lobbyists[12] reliably enough for us to have confidence that reducing heterogeneity by inducing conformity with expert recommendations is a good idea? These unsettled questions reveal how different assumptions regarding the stability of experts' partial knowledge about the reward-generating play an important and largely unrecognized role in driving these competing research programs within behavioral law and economics.

Heterogeneity forgone: costs and risks of nudging

In a world governed by a stable reward-generating environment that is simple enough to be described with a scalar-valued objective function, and exhaustively known (possibly vector-valued) constraint set which gives rise to a well-defined optimal choice (i.e., a "small world" (Savage, 1954; Shafer, 1986)), it is indisputable (within the confines of such a model) that deviations (i.e., suboptimal choices) are costly. Even in this case, however, where it *can* be calculated how much is lost by deviating from optimal choice (or, aggregating over individuals, lost social welfare), the *costs of nudging programs and paternalistic intervention* are not guaranteed to be fully offset by aggregate social welfare improvements achieved by nudging a non-optimizing population to optimize. Although gains are possible (as long as the payoff functions and contributions of heterogeneity to payoffs are correctly specified), new largely unforeseen risks emerge as a result of shifting the population profile of beliefs and actions toward greater homogeneity.

Advocates of nudging do not seem to take into account how changes in the *population* distribution of beliefs and behavior could adversely affect the social welfare function. Instead, they appear to rely on a *tacit* assumption of a Benthamite social welfare function under which payoff improvements at the individual level (predicated on their *explicitly* maintained assumption that individuals who respond to nudges will judge their own payoff to have improved as a result) cleanly aggregate into social welfare improvements.

Yet another problem when assessing possible payoff improvements achieved by paternalistic intervention—from the perspective of process-dependent (rather than consequentialist) preferences—concerns the loss of liberty and the subjective devaluation of payoffs associated with an outcome when that outcome is mandatory rather than voluntary (cf. Conly, 2014).

If the social welfare gains hypothesized by choice architects are the result of non-deliberative responses to nudges and fail the reversibility criterion emphasized by Rebonato (2012) and Viale (2019, forthcoming), then we should consider whether those subpopulations with process-dependent preferences that put positive weight on self-determination, autonomy, and liberty might evaluate the resulting population profiles of nudged beliefs and actions less favorably than if those same profiles were arrived at without nudging. Insofar as some members of society do put weight on self-determination, autonomy and liberty, even a utilitarian social welfare analysis should take these non-consequentialist aspects of preferences into account.

It is not difficult to imagine substantial violations of consequentialists' invariance-over-outcomes principle in subjective valuations attached to an outcome such as weight loss. The decision maker can lose weight by voluntarily paying to enter a "fat farm" where food choice is restricted. Or the decision maker could achieve an identical slimming outcome as the result of a legislative mandate, government control over the distribution of food, or active and successful nudging campaigns that change social norms and meanings associated with voluntarily preventing obesity. It does not seem far-fetched that many people would have strict preferences over an identical slimming outcome, ranking self-determined slimming ("I did it myself!") over market-assisted slimming ("I chose to go to the fat farm and achieved the desired result") over nudges ("I didn't notice that the desserts in the lunch room had been placed out of sight in the corner, and it seems they have caused me to lose weight") over coercive paternalism ("I stopped eating as much after sin taxes raised the prices of foods I like to eat"). A successful slimming nudge could reduce payoffs from the self-determined slimming outcome while achieving the same outcome by nudging. The social value associated with the slimming outcome for some likely depends on: (1) the population distribution of slimming outcomes, and (2) the process by which the outcome was brought about (e.g., slimming has greater subjective value when chosen autonomously rather than as the result of deception, coercion or command).

One could object to these points by recalling two justifications in Thaler and Sunstein (2008). First, proponents of "libertarian paternalism" argue that if all elements of the choice set remain available and a nudging policy only changes the default, or re-describes the choice set with a new framing, then "choice" is preserved. Although influenced by a centralized power, authority or government, Thaler and Sunstein claim that preservation of the availability of all elements in the choice set should make us regard nudging policies as libertarian. If the preserved items in the choice set are never considered or deliberated about (Rebonato, 2012; Viale, 2019, forthcoming), however, or if the social and individual values associated with those elements in the decision maker's choice set are materially altered (as I argue in this chapter), then the libertarian claim is unjustified.

A second justification put forward by Thaler and Sunstein, with which I agree, is that, in many cases, there is no neutral description of the choice set. For example, in arranging food items on a food buffet line, *some* item must be placed at the front. Similarly (their argument goes), regarding organ-donor status, the law must take a non-neutral stand on opt-in (as in Germany) versus opt-out (as in Austria). Granted that a non-neutral choice-influencing default must be selected, there is still a collision of conflicting principles. The libertarian principles of self-ownership and voluntarism clearly suggest that defaults should be set so that posthumous use of one's body reverts to the individual's estate in the absence of any directives "opting in" to organ-donor status. On the other hand, advocates of nudging claim that changing the default helps more individuals realize an otherwise unexpressed preference to be an organ donor. Social welfare analysis should at least acknowledge that there are conflicting normative principles and reasonable people can disagree about the appropriate weights to place on each principle and possible unintended consequences.

Another risk to consider more carefully before accepting the social welfare claims of those advocating for more nudging is that expert consensus is mistaken, or that no one-size-fits-all recommendation applies to everyone in the population. Expert recommendations are notorious for flip-flopping over time. Tragic episodes where regulators have recommended medicines that caused great harm (e.g., more than 10,000 disabled by thalidomide given to pregnant women for several years) are hardly unknown. When policy makers set out to influence individuals to make decisions with their money and health, risks of harm should be considered.

Honest errors and revision are to be expected as new medical, financial or behavioral research contravenes previous recommendations. Then there are more nefarious strategic distortions, such as the influence of lobbyists, rent seeking or deep capture. In my view, it makes little sense to exclude consideration of policy errors and unintended consequences from social welfare analysis of proposals to introduce nudges as public policy.

Beyond "as-if" to policy in a profoundly uncertain world

One of Gigerenzer's key arguments against modeling choice and inference *as if* it were the solution to a well-defined constrained optimization problem (Berg and Gigerenzer, 2010) is the instability of the reward-generating environment. What basis of evidence about behavioral "errors" could be relied upon for policy recommendations about savings, dietary choice, and charitable giving in such environments? Even with a well-defined and stable reward distribution, if that distribution is sufficiently fat-tailed so that the theoretical mean and conditional means do not exist (e.g., the Cauchy distribution), forming beliefs and basing actions on averages and correlations from the past would not provide a stable and informative set of mental processes to learn about the reward environment and make accurate predictions—let alone make public policies that prescribe optimal behavior from on high (i.e., nudging people to conform to expert recommendation).

This is not to say that public policy is impossible in such environments. Rather, Epstein (1995) argues, in effect, that the Simon-inspired behavioral and law economics founded on ecological rationality in *un-learnably unstable* and *unknowably complex* environments must rest on principles of liberty and voluntary choice, while mitigating the most harmful negative externalities (e.g., murder and theft) based on long-established legal principles that otherwise allow for wide-ranging preference and belief heterogeneity in decision making about money, health, and information (e.g., Epstein, 2003, 2018).

If behavioral heterogeneity consisted of random deviations from expert recommendations, then perhaps the lost payoffs from suboptimal decision making could be used as justification for nudging. Because real-world deviations are, by and large, non-random and constituted by purposeful (although oftentimes inconsistent) action, nudging programs that seek to limit or restrict those deviations lack both *normative* and *moral* authority (Epstein, 1995, 2011, 2018). Epstein's arguments in favor of long-established legal traditions and restraint against complexifying the legal environment with new policy objectives and their unintended consequences are largely compatible with Simon.[13]

Gigerenzer (2016, p. 364) argues for education, drawing motivation from Simon's (1985) assertion that "people are generally quite rational; that is, they usually have reasons for what they do:"

> the dismal picture of human nature painted by behavioral economists and libertarian paternalists is not justified by psychological research. Rather, it is largely the product of narrow logical norms of rationality and selective reporting of the psychological

literature. Most important for public policy, by comparing cognitive illusions with visual illusions, libertarian paternalists misleadingly suggest that attempts to liberate people from their biases through education are largely doomed to fail. However, as I will show, there is experimental evidence that even children can learn to deal with risk and uncertainty—if they are taught how. I will conclude that democratic governments should invest less in nudging and more in educating people to become risk savvy.

This basic normative question is raised too infrequently: Which normative principle is the basis for designing policies to "correct" alleged violations of rationality that are frequently often cited in the behavioral economics literature? Many arguments in favor of nudging begin by reciting extensive empirical evidence—which *is* indeed compelling and descriptively convincing that such empirical patterns exist. This evidence, by and large, reveals that axioms, which were originally used as technical criteria in representation theorems, are routinely violated. Observed violations of consistency axioms are not in doubt. Rather it is the *interpretation* of those important empirical findings that requires deeper investigation.

It may be the case that healthy and successful people do not typically have well-defined domain-general preferences (i.e., no single objective function explains the decisions they make). They may rather use a toolkit of simple action rules or heuristics. The use of a particular decision heuristic is thought to be applied when cued by context or situation. Without disputing the damning evidence against the descriptive realisms of stable and consistent preferences, the normative implications are, in contrast, far from straightforward.

Promoters of nudging argue that this evidence implies a need to roll out new policies to help people avoid "errors." This conclusion, however, reflects an odd normative interpretation given to the observation that most people's choice data do not conform to the strictures of perfect internal logical consistency. Their argument is that nudging policies that help restore behavioral consistency according to the neoclassical model of rationality will make people better off—or better off "as judged by themselves" as Sunstein writes.

The authoritarian turn

Economists undertaking normative analysis could, at this point, instead dispense with the assumption of stable internally consistent preferences which are required in both nudgers' and neoclassical revealed preference theorists' welfare claims based on the common premise of stable preferences represented by smooth utility functions that can be inferred or "recovered" based on observed choice data. They could circumscribe the universality of axiomatic definitions of rationality which, by their definitions, must hold across all choice domains. They could follow Simon and allow for contextually-cued piecewise-defined objective functions, which would mean applying distinct welfare criteria or multiple performance metrics depending on the choice domain.

For example, many of us behave as if we are free riders in some domains and, at the same time, inconsistently take the lead contributing to public goods in other domains (Kameda et al, 2011). Many of us are dogged own-payoff maximizers in some domains and generously prosocial in others. Sometimes we expend great effort to think analytically, and sometimes we use shortcuts, such as imitation, or follow intuition instead of cognitive analysis. Sometimes we exhibit such inconsistency with self-awareness and reflection. Yet sometimes our inconsistent behavior is autonomic or unconscious. Setting aside neoclassical definitions of rationality, an empiricist observing the regularity of inconsistent beliefs and behavior could more easily interpret them as descriptive of normal, healthy and productive decision making than pathological irrationality.

Behavioral economists could become more committed empiricists by observing the richly heterogeneous human population and seeking to describe the multiple decision processes and normative evaluations that people use to achieve success, thrive, and live "a life well-lived." Instead, the nudging program channels Orwellian visions of centralized control under guidance by experts. This unfortunate exclusion of the multiplicity of decision processes in use, and the multiplicity of relevant normative criteria, reveal an authoritarian turn in the intellectual history of behavioral economics. This authoritarian turn is based on inflexible and narrow norms.

Perhaps incidentally, the authoritarian turn also generates new demand for academics and "expert advice." Cynics could be forgiven for not writing it off as coincidence when they observe increased reports of "irrationality" in behavioral economists' academic findings and concurrent increases in public money and power over others allocated to them (as policy influencers, providers of research aimed at influencing policy, policy designers, choice architects, and program administrators).

Behavioral economists discovered that observed choice data fail to conform to axiomatic rationality. These axiomatic definitions of rationality require internal logical consistency above all else (even though the reward-generating process is dynamic and unstable). They were first used in utility representation theorems by Samuelson and von Neumann and Morgenstern, and later re-interpreted by Kahneman-inspired behavioral economists as a normative standard of rational or optimal behavior. There is little evidence that violations of axiomatic definitions of rationality in choice data lead to measurable economic harm, and some evidence that deviations from axiomatic rationality are positively associated with performance. Successful people (by many metrics of success) violate the axiomatic definitions of rationality as well as those less successful. Given that people's choice data generally fail to conform to that axiomatic standard, what should policy makers do about it? It would be surprising if many non-economists regarded this brief synopsis of the stylized facts surrounding the Kahneman-Thaler program as strong motivation for paternalistic intervention rather than revising the shortcomings of the narrow norms used and expanding the way rational behavior is defined.

A Simon-inspired alternative

Following Simon's notion of satisficing, ecological rationality requires that a behavioral rule or *heuristic*—a procedure for making a decision or inference—satisfies a threshold condition (i.e., is "good enough") when evaluated by a metric of performance that makes sense in the particular context in which it is used. This threshold requirement in ecological rationality provides an objective standard that usually (but not always) allows for more behavioral heterogeneity than in Kahneman-inspired models of rationality with prescriptive logical invariance. Although optimization problems may also have a large number of solutions and allow for an arbitrarily large degree of behavioral heterogeneity among optimizers, economic models used by those who advocate nudging programs typically have narrower views on what constitutes successful behavior—in decisions about retirement savings, diet, organ donation, charitable giving, etc. This narrowness gives substance to the critique of nudging as reducing heterogeneity of beliefs and behavior.

The standard of ecological rationality allows for multiple ways of being objectively successful. For example, if there is a threshold level of wealth that is required to be financially viable, then it follows that there is a plurality of purposeful decision processes that can achieve that criterion. The problem of designing an effective reward environment (in both private organizations and as public policy, e.g., legal institutions, restrictions on action in the legal code, fines, subsidies, and—perhaps—strategic framings used to induce law-abiding behavior) defines a naturally Simon-inspired approach to behavioral law and economics founded on the matching concept (between heuristics and reward environments) that underlies ecological rationality. Given the vast literature documenting legal institutions that fail to induce behavior consistent with policy makers' objectives (e.g., the War On Drugs aiming to reduce illicit drug use; Sarbanes-Oxley aiming to fix systematic risk caused by "too big to fail" financial institutions, which arguably led to increased market concentration in banking and finance since the Great Financial Crisis of 2008–2009; and immigration policies across most G30 countries that often bring results opposite to stated intentions), it would seem that more veridical study of decision processes—and the challenge of designing robust rules of the game that enable value generated by inter-action among the heterogeneous decision processes that individuals actually use—should be a research priority. Positive externalities from behavioral heterogeneity are missing in most social-welfare analyses of nudging. When policy is based on academic experts' views of optimal retirement savings behavior, optimal dietary choice, or optimal medical decision making, a number of social costs are incurred that rarely enter into benefit-cost analyses of such programs.

Insofar as nudging succeeds in concentrating more of a population's decisions on an allegedly optimal decision, population-level behavioral heterogeneity is reduced. The popula-tion loses portfolio diversification that would otherwise have been afforded by more heteroge-neous retirement savings decisions. Nudging workers of a certain age into similar retirement portfolios increases payoff variance in the event of a financial crisis. A generation of Japanese retirement savers would have been far worse off had they been nudged out of low-return "postal savings accounts" into professionally managed funds with greater exposure to equi-ties in the NIKKEI Index during the 1980s—which peaked in December 1989 and traded 80 percent lower more than 20 years later and currently, after a long bull market, trades at more than 40 percent below its peak. Japan's aggregate retirement savings would have endured greater volatility and sharply lower levels had Save More Tomorrow (as advocated by Thaler and Sunstein's (2008) nudging program) been used as a template for the design of Japan's retirement savings schemes.

One may argue that the importance of the Save More Tomorrow nudge was to increase the level of savings rather than shift the composition of retirement savings accounts (i.e., how retirement funds were invested). If the level of savings in retirement accounts is the sole nor-mative criterion used to evaluate the nudge, then we can regard it as successful. If we expand the normative criteria to include savers' subjective judgment of their own consumption-savings path, which includes the reduction in disposable income before retirement and related hardships that Zywicki (2018) reports—not to mention stress-testing its effects on wealth over time horizons that include a depression or 50 percent drawdown—then the question of whether the nudge is objectively beneficial to savers remains ambiguous. For more on species-, population- and individual-level benefits from heuristics that generate behavioral heterogeneity rather than uniformity (at an optimum at one particular time in one particular reward environment), see Bookstaber and Langsam (1985); Todd, Gigerenzer, and the ABC Research Group (2012); Hertwig, Hoffrage, and the ABC Research Group (2013); Mousavi and Kheirandish (2014).

As mentioned earlier, Zywicki (2018) reports evidence of individual-level harm inflicted by Save More Tomorrow nudging programs. Controlling for other differences, savers enrolled in Save More Tomorrow programs, on average, made larger contributions to their retire-ment savings accounts by direct debit each month but carried larger credit card balances and used other high-interest debt products such as payday lending at significantly higher rates than un-nudged workers. Thus, the seemingly worthy goal of encouraging workers to save more for retirement had unintended costs in the form of greater expenditures on interest and financing fees—and possibly greater stress and reduced financial flexibility with less disposable income.

Expert nutritional advice is famously contradictory, and perhaps justifiably so, given that contradictory information is frequently revealed by new studies, which includes randomized control trials, longitudinal population studies, and small-sample findings that bring new information to light despite lacking statistical precision or external validity (also potentially valuable in revealing previous mistakes and new breakthroughs). Optimal macronutrient composition (fats, carbs, protein), for example, remains unknown and likely varies across people and within person over time. More difficult questions would include: Which fats?, Which carbs?, Which proteins?

Well-informed scientists frequently disagree, sometimes reaching opposite conclusions based on the same available evidence. This disagreement, in turn, provides socially valuable informational benefits for those who have access to open debate rather than facing top-down, centralized one-size-fits-all food choice environments and incentive systems with sin taxes, agricultural subsidies, regulation of food imports, etc., based on a static conceptualization of "expert consensus." One thing that most nutrition researchers seem to agree on, however, is the inappropriateness and ineffectiveness of food pyramids promulgated by the U.S. and foreign governments. (e.g., the U.S. Department of Agriculture (USDA) introduced but then halted publication of its "Eating Right Pyramid" in 1991, which was followed by subsequent food pyramids, including "My Plate" (Rowland, 2016),[14] each eliciting controversial responses from nutrition experts and industry groups.) Nudging programs designed to influence what food people choose risks inflicting harm by influencing choices toward food choices that will subsequently be modified or contra-indicated. They also risk wasting information about discovery of the best practices in food choice, which may not follow any simple algorithm at the population level and, instead, require substantially different approaches to eating for different people.

Against nudging

Sunstein (Chapter 38 in this volume) acknowledges that the welfare implications of nudging are, in general, ambiguous. He asserts that there are three cases to consider. In the first case, there are stable preferences and nudging is unambiguously helpful as judged by the individual's own standard. The second case involves a self-control problem where it is argued there are multiple selves with different preferences. In this case, Sunstein claims that nudging is once again helpful by the individual's own standard, so long as the individual has a clear meta-preference (e.g., ranking the cool and sober self, who patiently deliberates about future-versus-future intertemporal trade-offs, over the impulsive and emotionally "hot" self, who prefers an immediate small payoff over a later larger payoff). In Sunstein's third case, preferences are endogenous to nudging, which therefore has ambiguous welfare implications. Sunstein claims that the first two cases comprise a "large" set of choice domains that gives ample justification (and enthusiasm) for nudging programs. In the third case with ambiguous welfare implications, he calls for case-by-case investigation into the welfare consequences, suggesting that they can be gleaned by "explor[ing] what informed, active choosers typically select."

Sunstein's list of three cases is incomplete, however. There are omitted cases that come up frequently: undefined preferences, undefined or dynamic discovery of new objectives, and multiple context-specific objectives across which there may be no one-size-fits-all nudging program whose social-welfare improvements exceed its expected costs from new risks imposed. The claim that the welfare implications in cases 1 and 2 are unambiguously positive can also be challenged, for example, with the example of Save More Tomorrow and the observation that its application in other places and times would not have led to social welfare improvements using an expanded set of reasonable performance metrics, such as net wealth at time of retirement. If applied decades prior to a 50 percent draw-down in stock market indexes and major dislocations in bond markets, as has occurred in multiple countries including the U.S. and Japan over the last 100 years, that nudge could have materially damaged savers' aggregate wealth and well-being, although it succeeded in its narrow objective of increasing retirement savings rates during most working years. Given the instability introduced by unconventional monetary policy since the GFC, who is to say whether increased savings into 401k retirement plans will prove to be an enabler or detriment to savers' well-being?[15] Serious risks of harming individual and aggregate well-being by introducing nudging programs as government policies should be considered with more attention to new costs and risks they introduce.

Controlling impulsiveness is widely acknowledged as a genuine behavioral challenge by people with a broad range of views on the advisability of nudging. It is instructive to recall here that, in addition to impulsive under-saving, Strotz (1955) also considered the problem of *excessive saving* among multiple time-inconsistent behavioral profiles in intertemporal choice domains. For many of us, introspection reveals important cases—perhaps just as many (as one wonders how these should be counted, weighted, or averaged)—in which excessive moderation, or too much emotional cool, can hurt us, too.[16] We sometimes regret staying cool and deliberative and wish we had been more strongly moved by emotion. Proponents of nudging and "System 1 versus System 2" dualism contend that System 2 is generally helpful and the true seat of rationality. But there are times when we *should* have made noise and we erred by *not* acting on emotion—*not* asking for a raise, *not* negotiating a better deal, or *not* giving into impulsively and asking someone who would have been a great life partner for a phone number for a first date.

Generalized prescriptions on the basis of behavioral economics at this early date, while we still lack conclusive evidence of economic harms attributable to violations of consistency axioms, would seem to reflect hubris on the part of behavioral economists. No doubt, many advocates of nudging are genuine, and their concern for helping others avoid mistakes is sincere. Given the risks of paternalistic policies uncovered already and lack of investigation into the unintended consequences of nudging and new paternalism, however, it would seem that recalling some of the fundamental observations by classical economists would be wise: social-welfare benefits from decentralization; heterogeneous endowments, preferences and beliefs as fundamental underpinnings of socially beneficial exchange; and the corrupting influence of power. These fundamentals generally encourage *caution* about introducing new policies. To these should be added the link between population heterogeneity, on one hand, and creativity and innovation on the other. Simon's corpus of work alerts us to many mechanisms by which successful adaptation can occur in the face of unstable reward environments. Its implication is a behavioral law and economics that depends beneficially on high-dimension heterogeneity of beliefs and behavior (e.g., Bennis et al., 2012; Berg, 2003, 2006, 2010, 2014b, 2017; Berg, Abramczuk, and Hoffrage, 2013; Berg, El-Komi and Kim, 2016; Berg and Gabel, 2015, 2017; Berg and Hoffrage, 2008; Berg, Hoffrage and Abramczuk, 2010; Berg and Kim, 2014, 2015, 2016, 2018a, 2018b, 2019; Berg and Maital, 2007; Berg and Murdoch, 2008; Dold and Schubert, 2018; Kameda et al., 2011; Rizzo and Whitman, 2018).

Notes

1 This chapter draws substantially on Berg and Watanabe's (2020) "Conservation of behavioral diversity: Nudging, paternalism-induced monoculture, and the social value of heterogeneous beliefs and behaviors."

2 According to Simon:

> The first consequence of the principle of bounded rationality is that the intended rationality of an actor requires him to construct a simplified model of the real situation in order to deal with it. He behaves rationally with respect to this model, and such behavior is not even approximately optimal with respect to the real world.
>
> *1957, p. 198*

Simon also states:

> The first is to retain optimization, but to simplify sufficiently so that the optimum (in the simplified world!) is computable. The second is to construct satisficing models that provide good enough decisions with reasonable costs of computation. By giving up optimization, a richer set of properties of the real world can be retained in the models.
>
> *1979, p. 498*

3 For example, we can expect some proportion of the population to formulate different beliefs and take different actions depending on whether expert advice is disseminated as "Consider this information and then you decide what is best'" as opposed to "This decision has been structured to influence you to choose what experts believe is best for you."

4 In *Law, Legislation and Liberty* (1973, p. 35), Hayek wrote: "Order is an indispensable concept for the discussion of all complex phenomena, in which it must largely play the role the concept of law plays in the analysis of simpler phenomena."

5 Zywicki (2018) reports that participants in the private nudging policy in the Save More Tomorrow Program succeeded at contributing more to tax-advantaged 401k retirement accounts. On average, those successfully nudged savers also wound up cash-strapped with significantly higher revolving balances on credit cards and other high-interest-rate credit products such as payday lending. In his evaluation, the evidence is far from clear that this nudge—when it worked as intended by inducing greater contributions to 401s—improved the targeted population's well-being. Of course, one can attribute the increased use of high-interest-rate financing as another behavioral mistake requiring further paternalistic regulation (and perhaps nudging) to discourage uptake. The observed pattern of one nudge leading to unintended secondary problems is unlikely to resolve disagreements about whether paternalism (or lack of more paternalism) is the root problem. The pattern does underscore, however, the conspicuous absence of serious consideration of unintended consequences from paternalistic interventions in the nudging literature that classical and neoclassical economists have identified.

6 These three allegedly "reasonable" behaviors are examples of decision domains where advocates of nudges have influenced real-world policy making despite remarkable disagreement among experts regarding what constitutes a reasonable inference based on available evidence and decisions.

7 Forouhi et al. (2018) report in the *British Medical Journal* that there is controversy rather than evidenced-based consensus regarding dietary recommendations on fat:

> The medical literature is still full of articles arguing opposing positions. For example, in 2017, after a review of the evidence, the American Heart Association Presidential Advisory strongly endorsed that "lowering intake of saturated fat and replacing it with unsaturated fats, especially polyunsaturated fats, will lower the incidence of CVD". Three months later, the 18-country observational Prospective Rural Urban Epidemiology (PURE) Study concluded much the opposite: "Total fat and types of fat were not associated with cardiovascular disease, myocardial infarction, or cardiovascular disease mortality". …
>
> In the absence of long term randomised controlled trials, the best available evidence on which to establish public health guidelines on diet often comes from the combination of relatively short term randomised trials with intermediate risk factors (such as blood lipids, blood pressure, or body weight) as outcomes and large observational cohort studies using reported intake or biomarkers of intake to establish associations between diet and disease. Although a controversial practice, many,

if not most, public health interventions and dietary guidelines have relied on a synthesis of such evidence ...

Although authorities still disagree, most consider that public health decisions should be made on the weight of the available evidence, acknowledging its limitations, and seeking to obtain further, better evidence when indicated. Equally important is to acknowledge when evidence is insufficient to formulate any guidance, in which case all the relevant options should be clearly outlined to enable informed choice.

8 In *JAMA*, Pace et al. (2014) report a newly updated (i.e., reversed) recommendation against default screening with mammography of asymptomatic women under 50, given the large numbers of false positives, biopsies with complications, anxiety, and overtreatment of cancers that would not have been lethal. Similarly, Tikkinen et al. (2018) report a revised recommendation against PSA screening of asymptomatic males for prostate cancer. In both cases, the revised guidelines suggest that the pros and cons should be presented to patients who should then make their own decisions based on personal weights applied to pros and cons of the test. Berg, Biele and Gigerenzer (2016) report on male economists' subjective beliefs about the PSA test.

9 According to Simon (1969, p. 53): "Human beings, viewed as behaving systems, are quite simple. The apparent complexity of our behavior over time is largely a reflection of the complexity of the environment in which we find ourselves." And Simon states (1990, p. 1): " Human rational behaviour is shaped by a scissors whose blades are the structure of task environments and the computational capabilities of the actor."

10 Behavioral economics often identifies rationality with the axioms of internal logical consistency used in neoclassical theory's utility representation theorems (e.g., Samuelson's use of transitivity; von Neumann and Morgenstern's use of the continuity and independence axioms; Kolmogorov axioms and Bayes rule as used in subjective probability theory). Identification of rationality with internal logical consistency underpins the *biases and heuristics research program* inspired largely by Kahneman, which focuses on deviations from neoclassical rationality axioms and its prescriptive program of inducing greater behavioral conformity with those consistency requirements (de-biasing as in Jolls, Sunstein, and Thaler (1998) or Thaler and Sunstein's (2008) *Nudge*; cf. Sheffrin, 2017).

11 See, for example, Gigerenzer and Selten (2001), Smith (2003), Berg and Gigerenzer (2010), Berg (2014a) and Mousavi and Kheirandish (2014) for definitions of *ecological rationality* and research programs based on Herbert Simon's seminal work on bounded rationality.

12 Hawkes (2018) reports allegations of influence from lobbyists representing pharmaceutical firms and complaints about removal of board members from Cochrane (a widely respected UK charity and Limited Liability Company). Many observers regard Cochrane as one of most influential and well-executed institutions designed to objectively evaluate drugs and medical procedures with evidence-based reasoning and sophisticated meta-analyses of the medical research literature. These allegations and recent controversy among former Board members of the Cochrane are just one example of how vulnerable attempts at evidenced-based medicine (and policy making) are to rent-seeking and non-transparent influence.

13 Of course, we cannot be sure that people's deviations are purposeful, given Hayek's "irremediable ignorance" about other people and the causal forces that structure various choice environments we encounter. Neither can advocates of nudging be sure that deviations are harmful or lack purpose and value.

14 The Chairman of Nutrition at the Harvard School of Public Health is quoted as saying: "Unfortunately, like the earlier U.S. Department of Agriculture pyramids, My Plate mixes science with the influence of powerful agricultural interests, which is not the recipe for healthy eating."

15 In financial crises, the correlation of most paper assets (e.g., bonds and stocks) approaches 1. In some instances, "safe" treasury bonds and "risky" stocks both decline, and the restricted universe of financial assets in many pension accounts may not provide an effective hedge against such risks. For those who assign greater probabilistic or subjective weight to wealth preservation in those states of the world, the nudge into greater exposure to the restricted asset classes offered in 401k accounts may hurt rather than help investors.

16 For example, Presidential Candidate Michael Dukakis' dispassionate response to journalist Bernard Shaw's question "about whether he would support the death penalty should his wife, Kitty, be raped and murdered" (Shepley, 2019) hurt Dukakis despite its logical consistency and valid evidence from his home State of Massachusetts about the death penalty's weak deterrent effect.

Nathan Berg

References

Benartzi, S. and Thaler, R. H. (1995). Myopic loss aversion and the equity premium puzzle. *Quarterly Journal of Economics* 110(1), 73–92.

Bennis, W., Katsikopolous, K., Goldstein, D., Dieckmann, A., and Berg, N. (2012). Designed to fit minds: Institutions and ecological rationality. In P. M. Todd, G. Gigerenzer, and the ABC Research Group (Eds.), *Ecological Rationality: Intelligence in the World* (pp. 409–427). New York: Oxford University Press.

Berg, N. (2003). Normative behavioral economics, *Journal of Socio-Economics* 32, 411–427.

Berg, N. (2006). A simple Bayesian procedure for sample size selection in an audit of property value appraisals, *Real Estate Economics* 34(1), 133–155.

Berg, N. (2010). Behavioral economics, In R. C. Free (Ed.), *21st Century Economics: A Reference Handbook*, (vol. 2., pp. 861–872). Los Angeles, CA: Sage.

Berg, N. (2014a). The consistency and ecological rationality schools of normative economics: Singular versus plural metrics for assessing bounded rationality, *Journal of Economic Methodology* 21(4), 375–395.

Berg, N. (2014b). Success from satisficing and imitation: Entrepreneurs' location choice and implications of heuristics for local economic development, *Journal of Business Research* 67(8), 1700–1709.

Berg, N. (2015). Gerd Gigerenzer. In M. Altman (Ed.), *Real World Decision Making: An Encyclopedia of Behavioral Economics*. Santa Barbara, CA: Praeger, ABC-CLIO.

Berg, N. (2017). Smart people's rational mistakes. In M. Altman (Ed.), *Handbook of Behavioral Economics and Smart Decision-Making: Rational Decision-Making Within the Bounds of Reason* (pp 43–67). Cheltenham: Edward Elgar Publishing.

Berg, N. (2018). Decentralization mislaid: On new paternalism and skepticism toward experts, *Review of Behavioral Economics* 5(3–4), 361–387. http://dx.doi.org/10.1561/105.00000099

Berg, N., Abramczuk, K., and Hoffrage, U. (2013). Schelling's neighborhood segregation model with FACE-Recognition. In R. Hertwig, U. Hoffrage, and The ABC Research Group (Eds.), *Simple Heuristics in a Social World* (pp. 225–257). New York: Oxford University Press.

Berg, N., Biele, G., and Gigerenzer, G. (2016). Consistent Bayesians are no more accurate than non-Bayesians: Economists surveyed about PSA. *Review of Behavioral Economics* (ROBE) 3(2), 189–219. http://dx.doi.org/10.1561/105.00000034

Berg, N., El-Komi, M., and Kim, J. Y. (2016). The puzzle of uniform standards and market segmentation among Islamic banks. *Journal of Economic Behavior and Organization* 132, 39–49.

Berg, N. and Gabel, T. (2015). Did Canadian welfare reform work? The effects of new reform strategies on Social Assistance participation, *Canadian Journal of Economics* 48(2), 494–528.

Berg, N. and Gabel, T. (2017). Did tax cuts on earned income reduce Social Assistance participation in Canada? *Australian Tax Forum* 32(1).

Berg, N., and Gigerenzer, G. (2007). Psychology implies paternalism?: Bounded rationality may reduce the rationale to regulate risk-taking, *Social Choice and Welfare* 28(2), 337–359.

Berg, N., and Gigerenzer, G. (2010). As-if behavioral economics: Neoclassical economics in disguise?, *History of Economic Ideas* 18(1), 133–166.

Berg, N., and Hoffrage, U. (2008). Rational ignoring with unbounded cognitive capacity, *Journal of Economic Psychology* 29, 792–809.

Berg, N., Hoffrage, U., and Abramczuk, K. (2010). Fast Acceptance by Common Experience: FACE-recognition in Schelling's model of neighborhood segregation, *Judgment and Decision Making* 5(5), 391–410.

Berg, N, and Kim, J. Y. (2014). Prohibition of Riba and Gharar: A signaling and screening explanation?, *Journal of Economic Behavior and Organization* 103, 146–159.

Berg, N, and Kim, J. Y. (2015). Quantity restrictions with imperfect enforcement in an over-used commons: Permissive regulation to reduce over-use?, *Journal of Institutional and Theoretical Economics* 171(2), 308–329.

Berg, N, and Kim, J. Y. (2016). Equilibrium national border and its stability, *Prague Economic Papers* 25(6), 637–654.

Berg, N., and Kim, J. Y. (2018a). Plea bargaining with multiple defendants and its deterrence effect. *International Review of Law and Economics* 55, 58–70.

Berg, N., and Kim, J. Y. (2018b). Free expression and defamation. *Law, Probability and Risk* 17(3), 201–223.

Berg, N., and Kim, J. Y. (2019). A good advisor. *Bulletin of Economic Research* 71(3), 558–572.

Berg, N., and Maital, S. (2007). Tailoring globalization to national needs and wellbeing: One size never fits all, *Global Business and Economics Review* 9(2/3), 319–334.

Berg, N., and Murdoch, J. (2008). Access to grocery stores in Dallas, *International Journal of Behavioural and Healthcare Research* 1(1), 22–37.

Berg, N. and Watanabe, Y. (2020). Conservation of behavioral diversity: Nudging, paternalism-induced monoculture, and the social value of heterogeneous beliefs and behaviors. *Mind and Society* 19, 103–120.

Bookstaber, R., and Langsam, J. (1995). On the optimality of coarse behavior rules. *Journal of Theoretical Biology* 116(2), 161–193.

Brown, P., and Knowles, S. (2019). Cash is not king in incentivising online surveys. Working Paper, University of Otago. Available at: www.otago.ac.nz/economics/otago707883.pdf

Conly, S. (2014). *Against Autonomy*. Oxford: Oxford University Press

Cyert, R., and March, J.G. (1992 [1963]). *A Behavioral Theory of the Firm* (2nd ed.). Oxford: Blackwell.

Dold, M. F., and Schubert, C. (2018). Toward a behavioral foundation of normative economics, *Review of Behavioral Economics* 5(3–4), 221–241. http://dx.doi.org/10.1561/105.00000097

Eckel, C., Grossman, P. J., and Johnston, R. M. (2005). An experimental test of the crowding out hypothesis. *Journal of Public Economics* 89(8) 1543–1560.

Epstein, R. A. (1995). *Simple Rules for a Complex World*. Cambridge, MA: Harvard University Press.

Epstein, R. A. (2003). *Skepticism and Freedom: A Modern Case for Classical Liberalism*. Chicago: University of Chicago Press.

Epstein, R. A. (2011). *Design for Liberty: Private Property, Public Administration, and the Rule of Law*. Cambridge, MA: Harvard University Press.

Epstein, R. A. (2018). The dangerous allure of libertarian paternalism, *Review of Behavioral Economics* 5(3–4), 389–416.

Forouhi, N. G., Krauss, R. M., Taubes, G., and Willet, W. (2018). Dietary fat and cardiometabolic health: Evidence, controversies, and consensus for guidance, *British Medical Journal* 361: k2139.

Gage, D. (2012). The venture capital secret: 3 out of 4 start-ups fail. Wall Street Journal February 18. Available at: www.wsj.com/articles/SB10000872396390044372020457800498047642919 0

Gigerenzer, G. (2016). On the supposed evidence for libertarian paternalism. *Review of Philosophy and Psychology* 6, 361–383.

Gigerenzer, G., and Selten, R. (2001). Rethinking rationality. In G. Gigerenzer and R. Selten (Eds.), *Bounded rationality: The adaptive toolbox* (pp. 1–12). Cambridge, MA: The MIT Press.

Gigerenzer, G., Todd, P. M., and the ABC Research Group (Eds.) (1999). *Simple Heuristics that Make Us Smart*. New York: Oxford University Press.

Harrison, G. W., and Ross, D. (2018). Varieties of paternalism and the heterogeneity of utility structures. *Journal of Economic Methodology* 25(1), 42–67.

Hawkes, N. (2018). Cochrane director's expulsion results in four board members resigning, *British Medical Journal* 362. https://doi.org/10.1136/bmj.k3945.

Hayek, F. A. (1973). *Law, Legislation and Liberty*. New York: Routledge. Available at: https://libsa.files.wordpress.com/2015/01/hayek-law-legislation-and-liberty.pdf

Hertwig, R., Hoffrage, U., and the ABC Research Group (Eds.) (2013). *Simple Heuristics in a Social World*. New York: Oxford University Press.

Infante, G., Lecouteux, G., and Sugden, R. (2016). Preference purification and the inner rational agent: a critique of the conventional wisdom of behavioural welfare economics. *Journal of Economic Methodology* 23(1), 1–25.

Jolls, C., Sunstein, C. R., and Thaler, R. (1998). A behavioral approach to law and economics. *Stanford Law Review* 50, 1471–1480.

Kameda, T., Tsukasaki, T., Hastie, R., and Berg, N. (2011). Democracy under uncertainty: The wisdom of crowds and the free-rider problem in group decision making, *Psychological Review* 118, 76–96.

Kropotkin, P. (1892). The Conquest of Bread. Chapter IV. Available at: http://dwardmac.pitzer.edu/anarchist_archives/kropotkin/conquest/ch9.html

Mellström, C., and Johannesson, M. (2008). Crowding out in blood donation: Was Titmuss right? *Journal of the European Economic Association* 6(4), 845–863, https://doi.org/10.1162/JEEA.2008.6.4.845

Mousavi, S., and Kheirandish, R. (2014). Behind and beyond a shared definition of ecological rationality: A functional view of heuristics. *Journal of Business Research* 67, 1780–1785.

Pace, L. E. et al. (2014). A systematic assessment of benefits and risks to guide breast cancer screening decisions. *JAMA* 311(13), 1327–1335.

Rebonato, R. (2012). *Taking Liberties*. New York: Palgrave Macmillan.

Rizzo, M. J., and Whitman, G. (2018). Rationality as a process, *Review of Behavioral Economics* 5(3–4), 201–219. http://dx.doi.org/10.1561/105.00000098

Rowland, M. P. (2016). The food pyramid of the future, Forbes, November 2. Available at: www.forbes.com/sites/michaelpellmanrowland/2016/11/02/the-food-pyramid-of-the-future/#50d3d2324da3

Savage, L. J. (1954). *The Foundations of Statistics*. New York: Wiley.

Shafer, G. (1986). Savage revisited, *Statistical Science* 1(4), 463–501.

Sheffrin, S. M. (2017). Behavioral law and economics is not just a refinement of law and economics, *Oeconomia* 7(3), 331–352.

Shepley, M. J. (2019). Dukakis' deadly response. Time. Available at: http://content.time.com/time/specials/packages/article/0,28804,1844704_1844706_1844712,00.html

Simon, H. A. (1957). *Models of Man*. Chichester: John Wiley.

Simon, H. A. (1969). *The Sciences of the Artificial*. Cambridge, MA: MIT Press.

Simon, H. A. (1979). Rational decision making in business organizations, Nobel Memorial Lecture 1978. *American Economic Review* 69(4), 493–513.

Simon, H. A. (1985). Human nature in politics: The dialogue of psychology with political science. *American Political Science Review* 79, 293–304.

Simon, H. A. (1990). Invariants of human behavior. *Annual Review of Psychology* 41, 1–19.

Smith, V. L. (2003). Constructivist and ecological rationality in economics. *American Economic Review* 93(3), 465–508.

Strotz, R. H. (1955). Myopia and inconsistency in dynamic utility maximization, *The Review of Economic Studies* 23(3), 165–180.

Sudgen, R. (2016). Do people really want to be nudged towards healthy lifestyles? *International Review of Economics*.

Sugden, R. (2018). Paternalism and entrepreneurship, *Review of Behavioral Economics* 5(3–4), 243–259. http://dx.doi.org/10.1561/105.00000089

Sunstein, C. R. (2014). *Why Nudge?* New Haven, CT: Yale University Press.

Sunstein, C. R. (2016a). The Council of Psychological Advisers. Annual Review of Psychology 67, 713–737.

Sunstein, C. R. (2016b). *The Ethics of Influence*. Cambridge: Cambridge University Press.

Sunstein, C. R., Reich, L., and Rauber, J. (2017). Behavioral insights all over the world? Public attitudes toward nudging in a multi-country study, available at https://papers.ssrn.com/sol3/papers.cfm?abstract_id=2921217

Sunstein, C. R., and Reisch, L.A . (2014). Automatically green: Behavioral economics and environmental protection. *Harvard Environmental Law Review* 38, 127–158.

Sunstein, C., and Vermeule, A. (2008). Conspiracy theories. Harvard Public Law Working Paper No. 08–03; U of Chicago, Public Law Working Paper No. 199; University of Chicago Law & Economics, Olin Working Paper No. 387.

Thaler, R. H., and Benartzi, S. (2004). Save More Tomorrow™: Using behavioral economics to increase employee saving, *Journal of Political Economy* 112, S164–S187.

Thaler, R. H., and Sunstein, C. R. (2008). *Nudge: Improving Decisions about Health, Wealth, and Happiness*. New Haven, CT: Yale University Press.

Tikkinen, K. A. O., et al. (2018). Prostate cancer screening with prostate-specific antigen (PSA) test: a clinical practice guideline. *British Medical Journal* 362: k3581.

Todd, P. M., Gigerenzer, G., and the ABC Research Group (Eds.) (2012). *Ecological Rationality: Intelligence in the World* (pp. 409–427). New York: Oxford University Press,

Viale, R. (Ed.) (2001). *Knowledge and Politics*. Berlin: Springer.

Viale, R. (Ed.) (2012). *Methodological Cognitivism*, vol. 1. Berlin: Springer.

Viale, R. (2019). Architecture of the mind and libertarian paternalism: Is the reversibility of System 1 nudges likely to happen? Herbert Simon Society Working Paper.

Viale, R. (forthcoming). The normative and descriptive weaknesses of behavioral economics-informed nudge: Depowered paternalism and unjustified libertarianism. *Mind and Society*.

Viale, R., and Pozzali, A. (2010). Complex adaptive systems and the evolutionary triple helix. *Critical Sociology* 36(4), 575–594. https://doi.org/10.1177/0896920510365923

Zywicki, T. J. (2018). The behavioral economics of behavioral law & economics, *Review of Behavioral Economics* 5(3–4), 439–471. http://dx.doi.org/10.1561/105.00000094

41
BOUNDED RATIONALITY IN POLITICAL SCIENCE

Zachary A. McGee, Brooke N. Shannon, and Bryan D. Jones

Bounded rationality's origins and principles

The father of bounded rationality, Nobel Prize-winner Herbert A. Simon was principally a political scientist with a special focus on public administration. Simon saw his scientific career as being motivated by the development of two big ideas, both originally developed in *Administrative Behavior*, bounded rationality and organizational identification[1] (Simon 1996). We will discuss each idea in turn and then show how it applies to different literatures in political and policy sciences. *Administrative Behavior*, a version of Simon's doctoral dissertation at the University of Chicago, argued that organizations need to be understood in terms of their decision-making processes (Simon 1945). Put another way, Simon thought the limits of cognitive processing must apply to individuals within organizations and those effects would carry over into how organizations operate. This book essentially combined bounded rationality and the study of organizations to explore the processes that determine outputs similar to the study of rational choices and decision-making processes at the individual level (Jones 1997; Ostrom 1998; Selten 2001).

Bounded rationality is, in part, based on the limitations that all actors have in cognitive processing. What does Simon mean when he refers to limitations of cognitive processing? A full exposition is beyond the scope of this chapter,[2] but central to his explanation are the failure to have perfect knowledge, imprecision in anticipation of consequences, and emotions related to imagined consequences, all of which contribute to our shortcomings as individual utility maximizers (Simon 1945). Limitations in cognitive processing explain the bounds of the individual's ability to process the overabundance of information, left to them to distill. Bounded rationality is the relationship between the individual's information processing ability, complicated by ever-present limitations and the complexity of the problems faced (Bendor 2003).

Complexity alone does not limit individual information processing in bounded rationality. The uncertainty of the decision-making environment plays an important role as well. Such uncertainty depends, in part, on whether decisions are being made in so-called "small world" or "large world" environments (Savage 1954). Consider a game of chess, the decision for which piece to move next and to where may be complex but have a finite and knowable number of variables. This describes a small world where choices may be risky (i.e., reliably assigned a probability) but not particularly uncertain (Knight 1921; Binmore 2006). The political world, and

DOI: 10.4324/9781315658353-48

the policy process, are large worlds. These so-called large worlds have significant uncertainty because many alternatives are unknowns and, in fact, unknowable. Therefore, decision making is not only a problem of computational difficulty and risk, as in a small-world chess game, but also has the added caveat that some outcomes will never be assessed. We will return to these principles shortly.

Bounded rationality challenges the central set of assumptions outlined by comprehensive rationality, also known as rational choice theory, which is the standard for formal models of politics. Rational choice hinges on behaviors of the individual, primarily focusing on vote choice in elections and legislatures. The behavioral theory of comprehensive rationality has a durable tradition in political science, conceptualizing individuals as rational, calculating actors who avail themselves of the entirety of available information regarding alternatives. Bounded rationality challenges these assumptions, fundamentally the infinite abilities of humans to recognize and process all information available in their environment.

Realistically, no human has the boundless ability to process information as a computer does. Human rationality is bounded both by limited cognitive abilities but also by the brain's limited size and speed, "but it can often function well by making coherence judgments rather than overextending itself by making too many deductions and calculations" (Thagard 2018, p. 8). Due to biological constraints as well as the complex environment humans make decisions in, humans can exclusively focus attention on only a small number of issues at once. For these reasons, decisions influenced by a complicated, or uncertain, environment are unable to meet the criteria for rationality under rational choice. The implication for political decisions is that an individual's ability to make rational responses to their environment can fail, particularly at critical moments and with complicated problems. This mismatch characterizes bounded rationality (Simon 1996; Jones 1999).

Bounded rationality's influence on political science

In political science, there are two main branches of research utilizing bounded rationality (Bendor 2003). We focus here on the first branch, which retains Simon's name and his core argument that cognitive limitations only show through in a person's decision making when the problem they are handling is sufficiently difficult.[3] That is, we can expect people to be able to solve simple problems in limited choice environments rationally, but beyond simple choice environments, our decision-making is impaired. The Simonian branch of bounded rationality is also heavily influenced by Charles Lindblom's "The Science of Muddling Through" (1959), imagining decision making as a set of successive limited approximations to problems rather than a comprehensive analysis of alternatives (Bendor 2015).

As time went on, bounded rationality gained acceptance in political science, especially as the discipline trended increasingly toward empirical work (Jones 1999). Lindblom (1959) builds on Simon's theory by characterizing decision making in policy formulation as a metaphorical tree's branches and roots. Comprehensive rationality takes a root approach; solving complex problems, formulating policy, or pulling a tree up from the root requires comprehensive action. The means to achieve any end must include all possible alternatives, isolating the means is necessary to make a rational decision toward an end. In this way, "analysis for the root method is comprehensive; every important relevant factor is taken into account" (Lindblom 1959). As one may imagine, creation or destruction by this method is drastic and not necessarily an incremental process.

Bounded rationality, on the other hand, assumes the branch method, for what Lindblom calls successive limited comparisons. Like a tree's branches building out from the center structure, branch analysis of policy formation improves the central problem in small steps, adding to an initial pre-existing foundation. As it relates to the policy process, rationality is bounded by a number of limitations, including cognitive processes and time constraints. For this reason, policy processes most often subscribe to the branch method, as policy making builds on itself in an endless cycle of formulating new policies and improving existing ones. As Simon famously argued, "it is impossible for the behavior of a single, isolated individual to reach any high degrees of rationality" (1997 [1945]], p. 92). Contrasted with comprehensive rationality as root analysis which relies heavily on its own theoretical framework and builds from the past only as embodied in the theory (Lindblom 1959), bounded rationality establishes new foundations for rationality by including institutional constraints, limited processing capability, and values. As Wildavsky (1964) showed, boundedly rational decision making led to incremental policy changes.

An institutional bridge between the individual and organizations

An institutional focus provides the link between Simon's emphasis on human nature and organization theory. The term "institution" refers to the rules that govern different kinds of organizations (and the norms that solidify them), as well as the legitimacy given to them. This legitimacy is invisible and tangible first through shared understanding and meaning, and more importantly through policy (Ostrom 1998; 2009). Political scientist Elinor Ostrom argued for a bounded rationality frame on institutional political science because it better reflects realistic politics. For example, in situations where an individual's preferences are not maximized but must nevertheless reach an outcome, rational choice predicts no action toward cooperation. Although action is not predicted, it regularly occurs; rational choice predictions fall flat here.

Institutions are able to bridge the divide between schools of thought in bounded rationality because they (exist) in the political environment and hold the norms and formal rules of action (Ostrom 2009). Bounded rationality adapts its rational choice predecessor to include the environment in which individuals make decisions, comprised of its institutions. Simon (1945) and Lindblom (1959) point to the relative success of the majority to handle simple tasks, and note that cognitive limitations show through for difficult situations. For simple problems, most make decisions rationally. Institutions support individuals' capacities to do better in terms of rational decision making, and minimize mistakes made with even simpler problems, and in this way bridge the two schools of thought in bounded rationality.

While much of the understanding of bounded rationality is rooted in individual decision-making processes, Simon's original target was organizational behavior. We argue for an understanding of institutions as a connection between the two schools of thought in bounded rationality because institutions moderate and inform individuals' behavior, to help them solve problems.

Understanding the institutional connection between the individual and organization helps to provide a more robust understanding of choice. Institutions exist to facilitate successes that would be impossible by individuals acting alone. In the more pessimistic view of bounded rationality, Tversky and Kahneman develop a view of actors that shows a dependence on mental shortcuts, or heuristics, that allow lower-information actors to behave like actors who have more knowledge of the process and alternatives. The role of heuristics in political decision making is to help citizens make up for a lack of information with mental shortcuts.

For the general public, heuristics help individuals make rational decisions in vote choice in elections. For policy makers, heuristics seek to benefit leaders in developing policy solutions to complex problems. Tversky and Kahneman (1974) point to the mistakes some make even in simple tasks and the prevalence of heuristics and bias in decision making for even highly knowledgeable individuals, and the universal dependence on mental shortcuts or heuristics, to help even low-information individuals make rational decisions (Gigerenzer et al. 1999; Boyd and Richerson 2001; Tversky and Kahneman 1974; Sniderman, Brody, and Tetlock 1991; Cherniak, Chapter 24 in this volume). We argue for a refocus on the role institutions play in political decision-making in part due to Simon's emphasis on one's environment during the decision-making process. This refocus further underlines the decision-making processes of both institutions and organizations in human nature.

Tversky and Kahneman show the disadvantages of bounded rationality. Heuristics are used by nearly everyone in their experiments, and their use is not restricted to low-information laymen (Tversky and Kahneman 1974, p. 1130). Intuitive thinking, a distinctive feature of bounded rationality, leads nearly all individuals to fail in rational decision making. These experiments conducted by Tversky and Kahneman are examples of risky environments and these same biases may become adaptive tools in uncertain, but more realistic, environments. Furthermore, when people can learn and have environmental feedbacks from their actions, they may also show unexpected convergent conformity. Even in uncertain environments, however, people will overestimate how much they know and rely again on heuristics and simple decision rules when making decisions.

Norms, "the result of shared notions of appropriate behavior and the willingness of individuals to reward appropriate behavior and punish inappropriate behavior" (Boyd & Richerson 2001; McAdams 1997), can also dictate behavior for individuals. Much of the extant literature on norms focuses on public goods and coordination dilemmas (March & Olsen 1984; Ostrom 1998, 2000). The institutional link with political heuristics is found in norms; the norm of utilizing heuristics is due to cost and risk. Simply put, it is easier to use shortcuts or copy others to determine the best behaviors, especially in complex environments and for individuals facing difficult decisions (Boyd & Richerson 2001). Instead of inventing a new behavior of each instance to test its utility, humans observe and imitate others (Boyd & Richerson 2001), akin to Lindblom's branch method of decision-making.

Institutions represent a link between the two schools of thought in bounded rationality. As Simon believed, in spite of cognitive limitations and attention constraints, some do very well and most do reasonably well in making rational decisions—even for very complex issues. Simon viewed organizations as adaptive, structuring choices made by individuals. Most importantly, hierarchies and specialization of labor allow for tasks to be accomplished that would be impossible for boundedly rational individuals. The institutions in government, with rules and processes for creating and passing policy, are based on rules and norms in the formal branches of government, interest groups, and bureaucracy (May 1991; Wagner 2010). Institutions allow individuals to participate, learn policy processes, and specialize attention to prioritize, which can serve to support and augment individuals' abilities to make rational political decisions with more information than would be available for individuals. Because cognitive limits show through in decision-making processes most when those processes are exceedingly complex, institutions are capable of easing the difficulty in specializing. When organizations specialize, full attention can be given to a specific problem within the noisy environment. Lindblom's branch method is assisted by institutions as well, as previous decisions constitute the base to which new decisions are added in incrementalism. The base is sustained by institutions, a key example being budgetary decisions, which will be considered in depth below.

Coming to prominence: bounded rationality and theories of the policy process

In the policy process literature, scholars took Simon's words to heart and began assuming that policy makers were boundedly rational actors, and like all individuals, the choices they made were rooted in a mixture of self-interest, budgetary constraints, and the demands of their constituency. The three considerations do not always mirror each other, and policy consideration typically reflects compromise. Because policy makers are rational but constrained by capacity, the institutions of government, and re-election, comprehensive rationality, as a model for policy makers, is too basic a theory to explain policy processes. Policy makers respond to both internal and external pressures when faced with policy considerations. The external environment puts pressure on actors and how one acts is a reflection on the environmental incentives, including institutional pressures from government actors and constituency, and internally, policy makers act based on preconceptions that make up preferences that may cause deviations from the external environment (Simon 1996; Jones 1999).

Bounded rationality is the microfoundation for agenda setting and policy processes literature because it expands the shared characteristics of individuals and institutions. Assuming at once that "actors are goal-oriented and takes into account the cognitive limitations of decision makers in attempting to achieve these goals" (Jones 1999), the theory of bounded rationality can easily be expanded to include institutions within the theoretical framework. Much like organizations described in *Administrative Behavior*, institutions are made up of individuals. This seems at once obvious but is fundamental to understanding actions in policy processes, because organizational studies rely on organizational behavior mimicking the behavior of individuals within the institutions (March 1994).

People in the policy process are boundedly rational goal-seeking actors who have limited cognitive abilities and capacities for processing information (Jones 2001). Critically important in policy process theories is attention allocation. Of course, if the environment is uncertain, it will not be an inability to allocate attention that limits decision making but instead the reality that some outcomes will never even be considered. The limited capacity of decision-makers to allocate attention in risky environments guarantees actors will miss issues they should pay attention to while building agendas to prioritize issues (Baumgartner and Jones 1993). Institutions like interest groups, political parties, and congressional committees expand the application of bounded rationality to the macro level of analysis. Bounded rationality is the microfoundation of policy processes because it maps individual theories of decision making, information processing, and agenda setting onto institutions and systems (Jones 2017; Jones and McGee 2018). The Lindblom-Wildavsky model of choice led to incremental policy change, but adding attention allocation, which must be disjoint and episodic, leads to punctuated equilibrium (Jones and Baumgartner 2005).

A definitive characteristic of American governmental decision making is its slow pace of change. Members of Congress are boundedly rational individuals, and they comprise the boundedly rational institution of Congress. If the status quo of the policy process is no change in policy, then taking action to incite is risky. Ostrom frames the policy process in government as a classic rational choice problem (Ostrom 1998). Collective actions arise when decisions are difficult; any option chosen will lead to short-term benefits for self-interests but ultimately leaves everyone worse off than before (Ostrom 1998). Due to the boundedly rationality and omnipresent self-interest of members of Congress, these social dilemmas occur in politics regularly, but theories of comprehensive rationality are unable to explain how decisions are made in them.

Bounded rationality is a more useful theory for explaining legislators' actions in social dilemmas; action is taken although the status quo is for no action to be taken and cooperation occurs that may not maximize the immediate self-interest of legislators in the short term. Legislators, as boundedly rational individuals, must make difficult decisions regularly and have a limited amount of time, cognitive processing ability, and attention to choose the best alternative, and often "satisfice," or choose an alternative that is both satisfactory and sufficient, the best option at the time (Simon 1945). With an institution that expects action and holds norms of cooperation (at the very least within the party), boundedly rational individuals will work within the expectations of the structure to make decisions and decide between alternatives. Members of Congress are influenced not only by their own self-interest, but their constituents, and the institutional structure of Congress itself. Assuming the boundedly rational character of individual decision makers, who inhabit a boundedly rational institution like government, cooperation and action are easier to understand. The decisions made in the policy process are likewise more easily understood, as they are created within a boundedly rational institutional framework.

One of the first sets of scholars to implement bounded rationality as a microfoundation were scholars studying public budgets. Budgetary considerations are suitable subjects for exploring institutional decision making, since there is a clear budgetary process, mimicking the policy process itself. The budgetary process begins with a proposal and ends with an output in measurable units. Objectives are also clearly stated in budgets; which objectives take priority reveal the values held internally by policy makers (Lindblom 1959). Budgets are also incremental actions that happen on a consistent basis from an existing base that methodically modify and build on the decisions made in previous years (Lindblom 1959; Davis, Dempster, and Wildavsky 1966). The incremental nature of budgets avoids mistakes by policy makers, because the decisions of individuals (including interest groups) "are powerful, persistent and strongly grounded in the expectations of others as well as in the internal requirements of the positions" (Davis, Dempster, and Wildavsky 1966).

Budgets prove to be branch processes as Lindblom posits, because models of the budgetary process borrow heavily from the existing base and are strategic in character. "For budgets, 'base' is previous appropriations for agency, similar to a bank of past decisions for individual decision makers" (Davis, Dempster, and Wildavsky 1966). Previous years' appropriations in the budgetary base are comprised of "sunk costs," commitments made by lawmakers in previous years. These commitments operate in a path-dependent relationship, as previous commitments can dictate what this year's lawmakers choose what to invest in and which organizational priorities to support. Sunk costs reinforce path dependence and the canalization of organizational practices (Pierson 1993; Jones and Baumgartner 2005, p. 57). In budgetary policy, sunk cost commitments provide the mechanism for understanding bounded rationality of institutional decision-making by demonstrating the direct link between current policy and previous decisions.

Sunk costs reflect the strength of the base in incremental budgets and how bounded rationality exists as a backdrop of the policy process. As a path-dependent continuation of previous years' budgets, sunk costs strengthen lawmakers' identification with the means. As a result of limited attention capacity and information processing ability, previous policy decisions become entrenched as foregone conclusions, and individuals come to identify emotionally and cognitively with these operating procedures. Identification with the means is a nonrational process motivated by bounded rationality, that exacerbates the additive and incremental branch-like nature of budgets, leading to inevitable trade-offs in decision-making, because the means become prioritized over the policy goal (Simon 1945; Jones 2003; Jones et al. 2014, p. 153).

Given the omnipresence of trade-offs in budgetary decisions, budgets are a consistent example of the trade-offs and outputs characteristic of bounded rationality and information processing abilities of individuals and institutions. They inherently hold prioritization of issues and values and reveal the capacity for attention in policy makers. The institutional constraint on policy makers in Washington for budgets is strong, as interest groups, rival parties, and a scarce amount of resources frame debate and compromise prior to policy output, two parameters for the budgetary process.

Using the budget process as an example, we can again consider that the political world is a large world. There are going to be budget alternatives that are never considered, but actors shaping budget policy fall back onto their decision rules and favor items that have been prioritized in the past despite this uncertainty (Jones 2001; Jones and Baumgartner 2005). While uncertainty, as opposed to risk, is a feature of the decision-making process for budgeting, the critical distinction is that attribute uncertainty (i.e., information about a policy problem or solution) and statistical uncertainty (i.e., being able to assign a probability to all possible outcomes or events) are distinct. Put another way, the policy problems being dealt with in major countries around the world are sufficiently multidimensional and complex that decision makers rely on attention to inform their preferences, despite the constant threat of not knowing all possible alternatives (Jones 1994). Relying on the policy problems plaguing the country or an identification with the means (whether that is to their district, state, party, congressional committee, or something else) legislators make decisions based on uncertainty surrounding attributes of policy problems or solutions when making budget decisions, even when operating in large world contexts (Simon 1996; Jones and Baumgartner 2005).

Following the budget scholars, Kingdon (1984) elaborated on the theory of bounded rationality. He expanded the policy process application by introducing policy streams. In the pre-decision-making phase, even preceding agenda setting, elites identify problems and then are able to offer solutions. When problems are identified, they are placed on the agenda, and then solutions can begin to be sought and offered.

Behavioral rationality still acknowledges the individuals and institutions have similar characteristics. While both individuals and institutions work towards fulfilling their agendas and are goal-oriented, their goals are impeded by a limited capacity for processing information. Since attention-space is limited, agendas must be set to change policy on the most pressing issues first in case time expires before reaching the end of the agenda. These shared characteristics make policy change not incrementally, but instead, in bursts.

Often, policy change does not occur in slow, incremental, steps but instead in great punctuations where there are many changes in a short period. Punctuated Equilibrium Theory (PET) (Baumgartner and Jones 1993), perceives policy change in this way. Like tectonic plates, policy change faces impassable friction most of the time. Policy processes are typically characterized as incremental, with slow, methodical, moving change through debate and grid-lock in Congress. However, for some policies like health care, criminal justice, and drug policy, change may not occur at a constant and slow pace, but in dramatic bursts following long periods of no change at all. Policy problems build up without policy solutions to alleviate them, and with them there is a creation of friction. Most of the time, problems in society continue to exist in this state, as problems without clear policy solutions. Once policies begin to be introduced to try to fix the problem, salience will increase and the problem is debated publicly by legislators. During punctuated periods, the system may overcorrect itself, and a dearth of solutions may be proposed, even passed into policy, for the same problem. In the time between punctuations, friction prevents policy change from getting through, then punctuations occur like earthquakes in stick-slip fashion.

Bounded rationality, the foundation for PET, hinges upon an actor's ability to process information in a complex environment. Both individuals and organizations process information, particularly applied to the policy process. The criteria for information processing are "collecting, assembling, interpreting, and prioritizing signals in the environment" (Jones & Baumgartner 2005, p. 7), which alludes to the inescapability of limited attention in bounded rationality due to the overabundance of information in one's environment. Boundedly rational individuals and organizations prioritize what they pay attention to, and for higher-order processing that require more conscious thinking or attract high levels of attention, processing is serial in nature (Bendor 2003; Jones & Baumgartner 2005; Workman et al. 2009). Information is processed serially when one issue at a time is processed and prioritized at the expense of others. Information is processed disproportionately due to attention limits, complex problems, and an overabundance of information in the environment.

For information to be processed serially, issues must be prioritized in comparison to others. Reasoning in prioritizing of information takes on a dual system framework. Characterizing mental processes that help to prioritize attention, System 1 is fast, automatic, and often unconscious reasoning. On the contrary, System 2 is deliberate, slow, and conscious (Kahneman 2011; Thagard, Chapter 25 in this volume). Applied to political decision-making, information processing of System 2 requires more time and attention than System 1 reasoning and will result in developing expertise through deliberate and reflective reasoning. Because individuals are boundedly rational, constrained by time and information processing capacity, and faced with trade-offs in attention allocation, System 2 reasoning occurs much less frequently than System 1 due to higher demands on finite attention.

For political organizations and systems, information processing is remedied by delegating processing of information to its subsystems. At the political system level, organizations specializing in a specific issue or policy area develop expertise and consequently are able to devote attention to this topic, informing policy makers and other organizations. The oversupply of information necessitates this delegation, called parallel processing. In the policy process, bounded rationality provides the theory of behavior connecting attention and information processing for individual policy makers, organizations involved, and the institutions that dictate the process via rules of the game.

Government systems are evaluated on their ability to solve social problems rather than from top-down democratic accountability of elections, which is an institutional metric for assessing government (Jones and Baumgartner 2005). Due to the uncertainty and complexity of the environment and the multidimensionality of issues in the complex problem environment, it is impossible to assume clear and static problems and preferences. Instead, government is boundedly rational as a system, its bureaucracy and organizations make decisions in the same complex environment and have limited attention to pay, therefore are also boundedly rational and must make calculated decisions for which issues to focus on at a time. In this way, government is a complex system that is constantly adapting to react to issues and problems becoming prominent and demanding attention. Policy makers, organizations, and government systems interact with the environment by processing information. Policy change is the result of information processing, which is often disproportionate due to environmental and cognitive constraints; moreover, attention and policy solutions are not often proportional to changes in the environment itself (Jones and Baumgartner 2005).

In an attempt to solve issues in the problem environment, the political system reacts by offering policy solutions. Low or high attention to an issue dictates whether policy reaction will be an under- or over-reaction. Over-reaction leads to policy punctuations, which are large changes in policy output representing drastic surges in attention to an issue. Disproportionate information processing provides the framework for policy reactions and punctuations, and a resulting effect is the inability for the policy response to be proportionate to the issue's severity (Jones et al. 2014). Responses to the overabundance of information and myriad issues in the environment are disproportionate, following familiar patterns of bounded rationality found in individuals. The inability of organizations to focus attention on numerous issues at once and differences in information processing mechanisms such as serial processing, determine imperfect reactions to issues in the environment.

The status quo for policy change is no change, or an under-reaction to problems in the environment. Policy over-reaction is more unusual because policy punctuations are rare due to the myriad of conditions necessary for a drastic change in output. First, attention to the issue must be exceedingly high. Second, institutional friction slows down policy change, often debilitating rapid action, assuring policy underreaction (Maor 2014). Institutional friction, often described as "gridlock," illustrates the preference for the status quo, found in policy making rules and procedures, governmental bodies, interest groups, and bureaucracy. Friction guarantees incremental policy change a majority of the time but is overcome from time to time to create a punctuation in policy change, or a burst in policy change. "Friction, in other words, is not an absolute barrier to action, but rather a major hindrance. As it operates, pressures can mount, making change, when it does occur, more profound" (Jones & Baumgartner 2005, p. 88).

Policy over-reaction attempts to address an issue, imposing "objective and/or social costs" without producing equal benefits (Maor 2012). A disproportionate reaction is a mismatch between issues and solutions, missing the mark. Likewise, a policy bubble becomes "wildly dissociated from its instrumental value in achieving a policy goal" (Jones et al. 2014, 147). Like asset bubbles in economics, which occur when an asset's price is substantially higher than its intrinsic value, policy bubbles are easily spotted in hindsight, but much more difficult to assess as they are happening.

Bubbles are often caused by imitation heuristics, such as when the actions of a single actor on a financial market trading floor, make an independent action that is seen and imitated by many others. This cascading effect, caused by many actors imitating the action of one, can lead to dramatic fluctuations or crashes, an effect that also characterizes asset bubbles in economics (Jones and Baumgartner 2005). Policy bubbles occur following a period of sustained overinvestment, demonstrating a mismatch between problems and policy action, and the accumulation of this mismatch leads to more severe shifts in policy action if and when the issue is addressed by policy. Policy overreaction that continues for a long period, even after attention has moved on to other problems, can lead to policy bubbles when policy "takes on a mind of its own," exacerbating the mismatch between policy and problem (Baumgartner and Jones 1993; Jones and Baumgartner 2005; Jones et al. 2014; Hallsworth et al. 2018).

Policy bubbles reflect an overinvestment in an issue beyond its initial value, which is extended for a long period of time (Jones et al. 2014; Maor 2014). Crime policy represents the clearest example of a policy bubble in twentieth-century American politics. In the early 1990s, as the national crime rate declined, policy output continued growing; as the problem indicator, crime rates decreased throughout the 1990s, and the policy instrument of incarceration increased (Jones et al. 2014). Ultimately, throughout the 1990s, the problem continued to decrease as prison populations remained static, which displays the mismatch between problem and policy response.

Bounded rationality serves as the foundational theory for other theories of social science, which offer theories inspired by bounded rationality that contribute to studies of public policy processes. Behavioral economic theories incorporate concepts familiar to bounded rationality, including attention allocation, heuristics, and framing, to explore how behavioral science affects governmental decision-making in creating policy (Amir et al. 2005; Shafir 2013; Hallsworth et al. 2018). Representative of behavioral economics is the concept of nudges, paternalistic intervention by government into decisions by individuals to make them better off, *as judged by themselves* (Thaler and Sunstein 2008; Sunstein, Chapter 38 in this volume).

Attention is a finite resource for everyone, and policy makers seek to nudge people in the direction they would have chosen had they not been subject to constraints and limitations of rationality. Key to the concept is the *liberty* in libertarian paternalism, that the government does not restrict information but frames it using heuristics to encourage people to make decisions in their best interest. Consider government as choice architects in healthy food and anti-smoking campaigns or encouraging sign-ups for health care plans through the Affordable Care Act. A nudge is a strategy to guide people to make decisions in their best interest, maintaining individual freedom of choice (including the choice to opt out), while "trying to influence people's behavior in order to make their lives longer, healthier, and better" (Thaler and Sunstein 2008, p. 7). These concepts show that the way policy is created and framed can enhance its effectiveness and is rooted in selective attention and heuristics, reflecting Simon's original work on bounded rationality (Jones 2017).

More directly, bounded rationality is the foundational theory for other theories of the policy process, including the Advocacy Coalition Framework (Sabatier 1986; Sabatier and Jenkins-Smith 1993; Jenkins-Smith et al. 2014), the Social Construction Framework (Schneider and Ingram 1993), the Multiple Streams Framework (Kingdon 1984), and even in some applications of diffusion (Boushey 2012) and the Institutional Analysis and Design Framework (Ostrom 2011). In the next section, we will discuss how bounded rationality has shaped contemporary political science research and speculate on future uses of the model.

The future of bounded rationality in political science: bridging organizational and individual choice

Bounded rationality allows for the connection of two disparate decision-making systems: the individual level and the systems level (Jones 2017). By connecting these two systems of decision making and applying an information-processing framework, bounded rationality will continue to be the micro-foundation of policy studies for decades to come. Since the publication of *Agendas and Instability in American Politics*, Baumgartner and Jones have generalized their theory of the public policy process to stress the importance of information processing and attention allocation for how lawmakers decide which problems to prioritize and act upon (Jones and Baumgartner 2005; Baumgartner and Jones 2015). Much like Simon did in *Administrative Behavior*, Baumgartner and Jones stress the decision-making process of elites as being a critical causal mechanism. This development provides a critical pathway for future work utilizing bounded rationality.

Attention allocation by organizations is inherently linked to attention allocation at the individual level (Jones 2017; Jones and McGee 2018). As we have already noted, attention allocation at the individual level is constrained; individuals can only focus on one thing at a time. While organizations expand individuals' abilities to process information (March and Simon 1958), organizations also tend to canalize the choices of individuals and lead to institutional attention being focused on the same recurring problems and/or solutions time and time again (Jones 2001). These canals can be difficult to escape and within organizations they can turn into bureaucratic decision-rules. Decision rules often lead to incrementalism (e.g., the early work on budgets) and in some cases can lead to policy bubbles (Jones et al. 2014). These policy bubbles are the result of overinvestment of attention in a given policy area and have been demonstrated to exist in many policy areas. The existence of policy bubbles demonstrates that canals in individuals have some sort of link to organizational attention allocation. Congressional committees provide another example. The issues committees pay attention to previously tend to get attention again; and, the solutions prescribed previously tend to be proposed again, sometimes in slightly different forms (Baumgartner and Jones 1993).

Information processing and a reintegration of institutions provide easy links between individual and organizational choice. Information processing, in the broadest sense, examines the supply and prioritization of information. Usually congressional committees will receive information and incrementally adjust the policies they deal with. Sometimes, however, new information or shifts in issue definitions might cause rapid changes in the problem and solution definitions. These changes can result in rapid changes in the proposed policy solutions. Taken together, these conditions are known as the *general punctuation thesis* (Jones and Baumgartner 2005). Information is not scarce within government; in fact, information is in oversupply. This oversupply of information leads actors to be overwhelmed by their choice environment. To deal with the oversupply, they must winnow out the information that is not useful; this winnowing process is boundedly rational. How actors search for and weight the information they receive (e.g., members in a committee hearing) is crucial to whether or not a policy problem is resolved, or a specific solution is chosen (Baumgartner and Jones 2015). Ultimately, the decisions made about what information is important are agenda-setting decisions. Therefore, to think about agenda setting, attention allocation, or information processing is to confront bounded rationality and its influence on the policy process literature (Jones and McGee 2018).

Scholars have already started utilizing the information-processing framework in examining political institutions, including Congress (Baumgartner and Jones 1993, 2015; Jones and Baumgartner 2005; Adler and Wilkerson 2012; Lewallen, Theriault, and Jones 2016), the bureaucracy (Workman 2015), and the media (Wolfe 2012; Boydstun 2013). It has been applied comparatively as well (Breunig 2006; Walgrave 2008; Green-Pedersen and Mortensen 2010; Bevan and Jennings 2014).

We are at a turning point in political science for modeling decision making. As Jones (2017) has stated, "few social scientists have any faith that the rational model can take us any further than it has. But we have not thought deeply enough about what elements are necessary and which are expendable." The information-processing perspective, rooted in Simon's model of bounded rationality, opens a new path for understanding choice in the study of politics. We are confident that this framework will continue to shed light on new phenomena in political science, and it would not have been possible with the foundation built by Herb Simon.

Notes

1 Sometimes known as "identification with the means."
2 See Jones (2001) for a comprehensive discussion and thoughtful extrapolation.
3 The second branch is the namesake of Tversky and Kahneman and is rooted in the idea that cognitive processes are limited in even the simplest of tasks. We will reference this school of thought, but see Bendor (2003) for a full explication of the differences between the two.

References

Adler, E. S., and Wilkerson, J. D. (2012). *Congress and the Politics of Problem Solving*, New York: Cambridge University Press.

Amir, O., Ariely, D., Cooke, A., Dunning, D., Epley, N. ... Silva, J. (2005). Behavioral economics, psychology, and public policy, *Marketing Letters* 16(3/4), 443–454.

Baumgartner, F. R., and Jones, B. D. (1993). *Agendas and Instability in American Politics*, Chicago: University of Chicago Press.

Baumgartner, F. R., and Jones, B. D. (2015). *The Politics of Information: Problem Definition and the Course of Public Policy in America*, Chicago: University of Chicago Press.

Bendor, J. (2003). HERBERT A. SIMON: Political scientist, *Annual Review of Political Science* 6(1), 433–471.

Bendor, J. (2015). Incrementalism: dead yet flourishing, *Public Administration Review* 75, 194–205.

Bevan, S., and Jennings, W. (2014). Representation, agendas and institutions, *European Journal of Political Research* 53(1), 37–56.

Binmore, K. (2006). Making decisions in large worlds. Paper presented at the ADRES Conference, Marseilles, France.

Boushey, G. (2012). Punctuated Equilibrium Theory and the diffusion of innovations, *The Policy Studies Journal* 40(1), 127–146.

Boyd, R., and Richerson, P. (2001). Norms and bounded rationality, in G. Gigerenzer and R. Selten (Eds.), *Bounded Rationality: The Adaptive Toolbox*, Cambridge, MA: MIT Press.

Boydstun, A. E. (2013). *Making the News: Politics, the Media, and Agenda Setting*, Chicago: University of Chicago Press.

Breunig, C. (2006). The more things change, the more things stay the same: A comparative analysis of budget punctuations, *Journal of European Public Policy* 13(7), 1069–1085.

Davis, O. A., Dempster, M. A. H., and Wildavsky, A. (1966). A theory of the budgetary process, *The American Political Science Review* 60(3), 529.

Gigerenzer, G., Todd, P., and the ABC Research Group (Eds.) (1999). *Simple Heuristics That Make Us Smart*, New York: Oxford University Press.

Green-Pedersen, C., and Moretensen, P. B. (2010). Who sets the agenda and who responds to it in the Danish parliament? A new model of issue competition and agenda-setting, *European Journal of Political Research* 49(2), 257–281.

Hallsworth, M., Egan, M., Rutter, J., and McCrae, J. (2018). *Behavioral Government: Using Behavioral Science to Improve how Governments Make Decisions*, London: The Behavioral Insights Team.

Jenkins-Smith, H. C., Nohrstedt, D., Weible, C. M., and Sabatier, P. A. (2014). The Advocacy Coalition Framework: Foundations, evolution, and ongoing research, in P. A. Sabatier and C. M. Weible (Eds.), *Theories of the Policy Process* (3rd edn, pp. 183–224). Boulder, CO: Westview Press.

Jones, B. D. 1994. A change of mind or a change of focus? A theory of choice reversals in politics. *Journal of Public Administration Research and Theory* 4(2), 141–177.

Jones, B. D. (1997). The rational decision-making model in politics, Technical report, University of Washington, Seattle.

Jones, B. D. (1999). Bounded rationality, *Annual Review of Political Science* 2, 297–321.

Jones, B. D. (2001). *Politics and the Architecture of Choice*, Chicago: University of Chicago Press.

Jones, B. D. (2003). Bounded rationality and political science: Lessons from public administration and public policy, *Journal of Public Administration Research and Theory* 13(4), 395–412.

Jones, B. D. (2017). Behavioral rationality as a foundation for public policy studies, *Journal of Cognitive Systems Research* 43, 63–75.

Jones, B. D., and Baumgartner, F. R. (2005). *The Politics of Attention*, Chicago: University of Chicago Press.

Jones, B. D., and McGee, Z. A. (2018). Agenda setting and bounded rationality, in A. Mintz and L. Terris (Eds.), *The Oxford Handbook of Behavioral Political Science*, Oxford: Oxford University Press.

Jones, B. D., Thomas, H. F., and Wolfe, M. (2014). Policy bubbles, *Policy Studies Journal* 42(1), 146–171.

Kahneman, D. (2011). Thinking, Fast and Slow, New York: Farrar, Straus and Giroux.

Kingdon, J. W. (1984). *Agendas, Alternatives, and Public Policies*, Boston: Little, Brown.

Knight, F. (1921). *Risk, Uncertainty, and Profit*, Boston: Houghton-Mifflin.

Lewallen, J., Theriault, S. M., and Jones, B. D. (2016). Congressional dysfunction: An information processing perspective, *Regulation and Governance* 10(2), 179–190.

Lindblom, C. (1959). The science of muddling through, *Public Administration Review* 19(2), 79–88.

Maor, M. (2012). Policy overreaction, *Journal of Public Policy* 32(3), 231–259.

Maor, M. (2014). Policy bubbles: Policy overreaction and positive feedback, *Governance* 27(3), 469–487.

March, J. G. (1994). *Primer on Decision Making: How Decisions Happen*, New York: Simon & Schuster.

March, J. G., and Olsen, J. P. (1984). The new institutionalism: Organizational factors in political life, *American Political Science Review* 77(2), 281–296.

March, J. G., and Simon, H. A. (1958). *Organizations* (2nd ed.), Oxford: Blackwell.

May, P. J. (1991). Reconsidering policy design: Policies and publics, *Journal of Public Policy* 11(2), 187–206.

McAdams, R. H. (1997). The origin, development, and regulation of norms, *Michigan Law Review* 96(2), 338–433.

Ostrom, E. (1998). A behavioral approach to the rational choice theory of collective action: Presidential Address, American Political Science Association, 1997, *The American Political Science Review* 92(1), 1.

Ostrom, E. (2000). Collective action and the evolution of social norms, *Journal of Economic Perspectives* 14(3), 137–158.

Ostrom, E. (2009). Institutional rational choice: An assessment of the institutional analysis and development framework, in *Theories of the Policy Process* (2nd ed.), Boulder, CO: Westview Press.

Ostrom, E. (2011). Background on the institutional analysis and development framework, *Policy Studies Journal* 39(1), 7–27.

Pierson, P. (1993). Review: When effect becomes cause: Policy feedback and political change, *World Politics* 45(04), 595–628.

Sabatier, P. A. (1986). Top-down and bottom-up approaches to implementation research: A critical analysis and suggested synthesis, *Journal of Public Policy* 6(01), 21.

Sabatier, P. A., and Jenkins-Smith, H. (1993). *Policy Change and Learning: An Advocacy Coalition Framework*, Boulder, CO: Westview Press.

Savage, L. J. (1954). *The Foundations of Statistics*, New York: John Wiley & Sons.

Schneider, A., and Ingram, H. (1993). Social construction of target populations: Implications for politics and policy, *American Political Science Review* 87(02), 334–347.

Selten, R. (2001). What is bounded rationality?, in G. Gigerenzer, and R. Selten (Eds.), *Bounded Rationality: The Adaptive Toolbox*, Cambridge, MA: MIT Press.

Shafir, E. (Ed.) (2013). *The Behavioral Foundations of Public Policy*, Princeton, NJ: Princeton University Press.

Simon, H. A. (1997 [1945]). *Administrative Behavior* (4th ed.), New York: Free Press.

Simon, H. A. (1996). *The Sciences of the Artificial*, Cambridge, MA: MIT Press.

Sniderman, P. M., Brody, R. A., and Tetlock, P. E. (1991). *Reasoning and Choice: Explorations in Political Psychology*, New York: Cambridge University Press,

Thaler, R. H., and Sunstein, C. R. (2008). *Nudge: Improving Decisions about Health, Wealth, and Happiness*, New Haven, CT: Yale University Press.

Tversky, A., and Kahneman, D. (1974). Judgment under uncertainty: Heuristics and biases, *Science* 185(4157), 1124–1131.

Wagner, W. E. (2010). Administrative law, filter failure, and information capture, *Duke Law Journal* 59, 1321–1432.

Walgrave, S. (2008). Again, the almighty mass media? The media's political agenda-setting power according to politicians and journalists in Belgium, *Political Communication* 25(4), 445–459.

Wildavsky, A. B. (1964). *Politics of the Budgetary Process*, Boston: Little, Brown.

Wolfe, M. (2012). Putting on the brakes or pressing on the gas? Media attention and the speed of policymaking, *Policy Studies Journal* 40(1), 109–126.

Workman, S. (2015). *The Dynamics of Bureaucracy in the US Government: How Congress and Federal Agencies Process Information and Solve Problems*, New York: Cambridge University Press,.

Workman, S., Jones, B. D., and Jochim, A. E. (2009). Information processing and policy dynamics, *Policy Studies Journal* 37(1), 75–92.

42

LAYERING, EXPANDING, AND VISUALIZING

Lessons learned from three "process boosts" in action

Valentina Ferretti

Introduction

Strategic decision making is a challenging process as the transformation of an undesirable state of things into a desirable one usually requires the identification of a set of often conflicting decision objectives, the careful consideration of multiple perspectives, the proper elicitation of value judgements and trade-offs, a creative effort in designing suitable solutions, as well as the consideration of high levels of uncertainty, to name just some of the relevant complexities involved in making important decisions (e.g., Keeney, 1982). Indeed, real-life problems and opportunities typically develop within a complex and uncertain environment, which leads to unclear consequences and difficulty in measuring probabilities and utilities (Viale, 2019). Within this context, human rationality is bounded because there are limits to our thinking capacity, to the available information regarding alternatives and their possible consequences, and to the time we can take to make the decision (Simon, 1955, 1982).

Since Tversky and Kahneman's seminal paper (1974), behavioural scientists have identified a large number of distortions in human judgement and decision-making which have now been studied in many different fields, ranging from economics (Camerer and Lowenstein, 2003), to finance (Bruce, 2010; Thaler, 1999), accounting (Birnberg et al., 2007), strategic management (Powell et al., 2011), operations management (Bendoly et al., 2015), Decision and Game Theory (Camerer 2003; von Winterfeldt and Edwards, 1986), multi-criteria decision analysis (Morton and Fasolo, 2009), risk analysis (Slovic, 1987), operational research (Franco and Hämäläinen, 2016), environmental economics (Shogren and Taylor, 2008) and environmental modelling (Hämäläinen, 2015). This multi-directional line of research is based on a concept of bounded rationality focused mainly on the study of the correspondence between judgement and decision-making performance in tests and laboratory simulations and canonical models of economic rationality, i.e., the maximization of subjective expected utility (Viale, 2019). Another perspective on bounded rationality is the one offered by Baumol and Quandt (1964), who provided an insight into how much information gathering, the amount of its retention, and reasoning in decision making is likely to be economically optimal, thus outlining a theory of optimally imperfect decisions.

DOI: 10.4324/9781315658353-49

The concept of bounded rationality underpinning the research presented in this chapter focuses instead on how the interactions between the mind and the uncertain and often constrained external environment bound human rationality as a form of ecological and adaptive rationality (Gigerenzer and Selten, 2002; Viale, 2012). These bounds on people's time, knowledge and computational powers do not necessarily prevent them from making good decisions, to the extent that they succeed in employing simple decisions strategies or techniques in the appropriate contexts, i.e., where there is a fit between cognition and environment (Gigerenzer et al., 2011). In this context, an emerging and promising approach is the one of boosts, i.e., interventions that target long-lasting competences (domain-specific or generalizable) rather than immediate behaviour and that foster these competences through changes in skills, knowledge, decision tools, or the external environment (Hertwig and Grune-Yanoff, 2017). As opposed to nudges (Thaler and Sunstein, 2008), boosts are necessarily transparent to the boosted individual and require cooperation. Indeed, people can then harness the new or boosted competence to make choices for themselves, thus benefitting from a capital stock that can be engaged at will and across situations (Hertwig and Grune-Yanoff, 2017). Boosts range from interventions that require little time and cognitive effort on the individuals' part to ones that require substantial amounts of training, effort and motivation. The boosting techniques that I propose in this chapter to improve strategic decision-making processes belong to the second category, as the intention is to effectively change the decision makers' repertoire of decision capabilities. In particular, what I propose is a multi-methodology (Myllyviita et al., 2014; Henao and Franco, 2016; Ferretti, 2016a) "process boost" aimed at improving both the decision-making process and its outcome.

Multi-methodology interventions are attracting increasing interest in both management and public contexts as they integrate qualitative and quantitative approaches to better support all stages of a decision-making process, from the initial divergent one to the final convergent one (Ferretti and Gandino, 2018). The multi-methodology process boosts presented in this chapter target the following two specific stages of the decision-making process: the framing stage, which requires a clear understanding of the problem or opportunity to be addressed as well as a clear understanding of what needs to be achieved (i.e., the decision objectives), and the preference elicitation stage, which requires sound reasoning about heterogeneous performances and value trade-offs.

Although there is a wide scholarly discussion on multi-methodology interventions, the assumed benefits of using mixed methods have not yet been systematically tested (Myllyviita et al., 2014; Henao and Franco, 2016). There is thus an evident need to pursue, and to better communicate, the benefits of mixing and the research presented in this chapter is an attempt to fill this gap. In particular, the aim of this chapter is twofold. First, to illustrate promising solutions to support human bounded rationality in the key steps of a decision-making process for both private organizations and public policy makers. Second, to discuss the lessons learned by implementing the proposed process boosts in three different interventions.

Following from these aims, the contributions of this research can be summarized as follows: (1) a new perspective that will feed the debate about multi-methodology interventions and their positive impacts from a bounded rationality point of view; and (2) real examples and guidelines on how to use the proposed solutions in other similar as well as different decision-making contexts.

The following sections report on the design and implementation of three interventions, carried out by the author, to provide support for complex decision-making problems in different settings, ranging from rural regeneration, to talent selection and territorial planning.

The three interventions are presented and discussed using the same lens, i.e., contextualization of the cognitive challenge with examples from real projects, proposed solutions, and observed results and impacts.

Framing the decision context: gaining focus for a rural regeneration project in a new World Heritage Site

The cognitive challenge and the context of the intervention

Decision framing is the critical first step in any decision-making process, as the decision frame helps us define the decision by answering the question "what problem or opportunity are we addressing?" (Tani and Parnell, 2012). Indeed, an appropriate frame, including a clear understanding of the problem and what needs to be achieved, is the first of the six requirements for Decision Quality (Spetzler et al., 2016). However, framing a decision in the appropriate way is a challenging task, as evidenced by the fact that inadequate or poor framing is an all-too-common cause of failure to achieve good decision making within an organisation (Tani and Parnell, 2012).

To give a few examples of common cognitive traps in the framing step, we can start by discussing the dangers of a too narrow frame. Indeed, a decision with a narrow frame has usually a very limited focus and may thus miss relevant objectives or solutions. On the other hand, also a too broad frame has drawbacks, as usually decisions with broad frames have long time horizons which result in higher uncertainty. They lead to more general objectives, which are difficult to measure, and they encompass many issues, which make it more difficult to disentangle the key decision that has to be made now. Another common tendency is to distort situations to fit our preconceptions. This is also known as comfort zone bias and consists in dragging a problem into our comfort zone and solving the problem we know how to solve rather than the problem than needs solving (Spetzler et al., 2016).

Finding the frame that is most appropriate for the situation is extremely important. If we get the frame wrong, we will be solving the wrong problem or addressing the opportunity in the wrong way (Spetzler et al., 2016).

Although narrow or broad representations may occur at the individual level for basic cognitive reasons (e.g., selective attention, anchoring, availability, confirmation, accessibility, satisficing tendencies), they are also often compounded by the social external environment in which we live and work (Larrick, 2009). Indeed, common training, common experiences, frequent interactions between people working within the same organization and group environments focusing on harmony or conformity to the boss's opinion, all have the effect of leading to shared and often incomplete views of the problem (Cronin and Weingart, 2007).

The following paragraphs provide an account of the framing challenge and a proposed solution tested within a rural regeneration project in the vineyard landscape of Langhe, Roero and Monferrato (Piedmont Region, Italy).[1] The region under analysis recently became a new UNESCO World Heritage Site as an exceptional living testimony of the historical tradition of grape growing and winemaking processes, of a social context, and a rural economy based on the culture of wine.

Gaining this important recognition means that conflicting needs coexist in the same area, i.e., conservation and protection needs as well as new development needs. The context under analysis represents thus a complex decision-making environment. As often happens in these environments, situations which are not acceptable to stakeholders may not yield at first glance a statement of a problem to be solved, or may yield multiple problems whose statements may be contradictory or messy (Johnson, 2012). Indeed, this project did not start with a clear statement of a problem to be solved but rather with a need expressed by the Tourism organization of Alba, Bra, Langhe and Roero to better know the territorial strengths and weaknesses of the region in order to properly support the planning of the future of an area considered of universal value (Ferretti and Gandino, 2018). We can consider this as a quite broad initial frame for the decision context, as "strengths" and "weaknesses" of a region can mean many different things.

Proposed solutions

To gain the knowledge needed to properly frame the decision context under analysis, we proposed the combined use of three complementary tools. More precisely, we integrated Strengths, Weaknesses, Opportunities and Threats (SWOT) analysis with Geographic Information Systems (GIS) and Multicriteria Decision Analysis (MCDA), all within a participative framework consisting of subsequent focus groups with the client organization (i.e., the Tourism organization of Alba, Bra, Langhe and Roero) and experts from the SiTI Research Institute (www.siti.polito.it/index.php?l=ENG), which was the leading actor involved in the UNESCO site candidacy preparation (SiTI, 2013). The rationale for the use and integration of these three tools can be summarized as follows: first, SWOT analysis is a powerful and commonly used tool to provide an overview of strengths and weaknesses of a concept/project/system as a basis for creating strategies. Second, given that the context under analysis is a territorial one, the spatial distribution of its characteristics (e.g., extension of the vineyards, proximity to negative aesthetic interferences to the landscape such as industrial buildings, etc.) plays a crucial role. To visualize the spatial distribution of each key element, we combined GIS and SWOT analysis by developing a geographical map for each indicator worth consideration in the analysis (e.g., Comino and Ferretti, 2016). Third, the indicators belonging to each of the four categories of the SWOT should be overlaid in order to obtain for each category an overview of the situation where hotspots requiring monitoring or mitigation measures can be identified. To do this, MCDA (Belton and Stewart, 2002) plays a crucial role as it compares heterogeneous information and properly assesses trade-offs among different performances.

We thus conducted a focus groups with experts who discussed, identified and agreed on the key indicators that better represented the Strengths, Weaknesses, Opportunities and Threats for the region under analysis (Table 42.1). We then studied the spatial distribution of each indicator with GIS and developed a map for each of them. Finally, we used MCDA to elicit the relative weight of each spatial indicator, taking into account its spread of values for each and used those weights to overlay the maps in each of the four categories. The reader interested in learning the details of the process can refer to Ferretti and Gandino (2018).

Results and impacts of the multi-methodology boost

The result of the framing stage in this project was the discovery that the network of abandoned historical rural buildings (one of the indicators spatially analysed in the SWOT analysis) represented both a weakness and an opportunity for the whole World Heritage Site. Indeed, this analysis initiated the creation of a geographical database with 292 abandoned rural historical buildings scattered across the World Heritage Site, which includes 101 municipalities. Fourteen of these buildings are concentrated in the Municipality of La Morra, making it the municipality with the highest concentration of abandoned rural buildings. These buildings represent a true landmark of the rural architectural and historical legacy and are usually located in beautiful

Table 42.1 SWOT indicators to be transformed into maps

Strengths	Weaknesses	Opportunities	Threats
Presence of the full wine production chain	Lack of public transportation	Network of cultural associations	Land use consumption
Wine biodiversity	Abandoned train stations	Future planned requalification projects	Ageing population
Historical continuity	Natural risks		Touristic pressure
Traditional festivals distribution	Presence of natural interferences with the landscape		Loss or increase of autochthonous vineyards
Landscape valuable elements	Abandoned architectural heritage		
Cultural and architectural heritage			
Presence of ongoing requalification projects			

surroundings. Their regeneration would thus create significant added value for the area, both from the residents' and from the tourists' points of view.

The key impacts observed after this transparent and transferable multi-methodology boost can be summarized as follows:

1   Actionable knowledge about the territory (online open spatial database).
2   New awareness of problem (i.e., density of abandoned buildings) and sense of urgency, which provided purpose for the organization.
3   Nudge to start a second phase of the project aimed at identifying the most strategic abandoned building to be regenerated first in the municipality of La Morra.
4   Transition from a very broad frame of the problem under analysis (i.e., need to improve the knowledge about the territory under analysis) to a more focused one (i.e., there is a problem with the density of abandoned buildings within the World Heritage site that can be turned into an opportunity for rural regeneration, but with which building is it more strategic to start the requalification process?). In particular, this multi-methodology intervention improved the frame by acting on all three components considered key to reach an appropriate frame, i.e., purpose, perspective and scope (Tani and Parnell, 2012). The integrated SWOT-GIS-MCDA approach developed through focus groups with experts allowed the team indeed: (a) to clarify why and when resources need to be allocated for the regeneration of abandoned buildings (i.e., purpose); (b) to highlight the advantage of including different perspectives in a focus group setting with both the client organization and external technical experts to avoid using the usual organizational frame even if the challenge is new (i.e., perspective), and (c) progressively to zoom in on the nature of alternative solutions, starting from the whole region under analysis, then zooming in to the municipal scale and finally focusing on the building scale (i.e., scope).

Expanding the set of relevant objectives: the case of an Educational Foundation for underprivileged children in Hungary

The cognitive challenge and the context of the intervention

The first of the six requirements for Decision Quality (Spetzler et al., 2016) mentioned in the contextualisation of the first intervention is an appropriate frame, which includes a clear understanding of the problem but also of what needs to be achieved, i.e., the fundamental objectives for the decision under analysis. Indeed, objectives should be the driving force in decision making as they represent what we care about, while alternatives are just means to achieve more fundamental values (Keeney, 1996).

Unfortunately, scientific research has demonstrated that the identification of the fundamental objectives associated with a decision is not an easy task from the cognitive point of view and that, without support, people are often aware of only half of the objectives that later turn out to be relevant to them (Bond et al., 2008). Moreover, and even more worrying, the objectives that are missed are not trivial, they are often as important as those identified at first (Bond et al., 2008). Two possible reasons may explain this impediment: not thinking broadly enough about the range of relevant objectives, and not thinking deeply enough to articulate every objective within the range that is considered (Bond et al., 2010). Moreover, research on time-relevant decisions and "temporal construal" shows that decision makers often focus only on either the near future or distant future, to the exclusion of the other (e.g., Trope and Liberman, 2000).

The following paragraphs provide an account of the objectives' generation challenge and a proposed solution tested within an intervention aimed to support the Csányi Educational Foundation for underprivileged children in Hungary.[2] To achieve its mission, the Foundation announces every year a tender for 15 applicants to enter the Foundation's Educational programme. Gifted children from underprivileged backgrounds who are completing their fourth year in primary school are eligible to apply to the programme.

As the Foundation spends approximately $4700/year/child (operating costs excluded), a crucial objective of the organization is to minimize dropout rates. However, mentors have highlighted that a large number of children who were admitted into the Foundation do not fit the profile and the focus of the programme for disparate reasons. Consequently, more than 25 per cent of the children quit the programme early.

After thoroughly examining these cases, the board of directors concluded that these problems are caused by the lack of an adequate selection process. The board also acknowledged that the selection criteria are not entirely reflective of the objectives of the Foundation and that the fundamental objectives have not been thoroughly discussed. The Foundation's board thus expressed the desire to improve the selection process for the admissions season in May 2017.

Proposed solutions

To address the objectives' generation challenge, we designed and deployed an intervention which integrated Value Focused Thinking (Keeney, 1996; see Table 42.2) and the specific Multicriteria Analysis technique called Multi Attribute Value Theory (Keeney & Raiffa, 1976).

The reason behind the integration of the two approaches is linked to the fact that MCDA supports the user in the prioritization of objectives, i.e., in understanding which trade-offs are more important in a complex decision-making problem, but without specific support during the objectives' identification phase. How then to be sure that the concerns we have in mind represent a comprehensive list of relevant objectives? The ten categories of specific questions illustrated in Table 42.2 have proved to be an effective solution to this challenge (e.g., Ferretti

Table 42.2 Value focused thinking techniques to be used for the identification of relevant objectives

Techniques	Key questions to be asked
A wish list	What do you want? What do you value? What should you want?
Alternatives	What is a perfect alternative, a terrible alternative, some reasonable alternative? What is good or bad about each?
Problems and shortcomings	What is wrong or right with your organization? What needs fixing?
Consequences	What has occurred that was good or bad? What might occur that you care about?
Goals, constraints, and guidelines	What are your aspirations? What limitations are place upon you?
Different perspectives	What would your competitor or your constituency be concerned about? At some time in the future, what would concern you?
Strategic objectives	What are your ultimate objectives? What are your values that are absolutely fundamental?
Generic objectives	What objectives do you have for your costumers, your employees, your shareholders, yourself? What environmental, social, economic or health and safety objectives are important?
Structuring objectives	Follow means–ends relationships: why is that objective important, how can you achieve it? Use specification: what do you mean by this objective?
Quantifying objectives	How would you measure achievement of this objective?

Source: Keeney (1996)

and Degioanni, 2017). We thus started the decision support process by organizing structured interviews with the President of the Foundation Advisory Board and with the Foundation Operational Director, in which we tested the list of questions from Table 42.2, adapted to fit the context under analysis, i.e., underprivileged children selection for educational programmes.

Table 42.3 represents the result of the Value Focused Thinking stage. While some key concerns and objectives were part of the initial mental model of the decision makers, those objectives highlighted in italics in Table 42.3 represent the new objectives that were identified after discussing the answers to the Value Focused Thinking questions. This now comprehensive set of objectives became the input to the MCDA model where, again in a focus group setting, we made the participants discuss the performance of the children under each objective and learn about the trade-offs between them (column "weight" in Table 42.3).

Results and impacts of the multi-methodology approach

As shown in Table 42.3, the solution proposed in this intervention generated 40 per cent more objectives with respect to the initial concerns that the decision makers had in mind.

Moreover, the newly identified objectives of "level of family support", "emotional steadiness", "character" and "open-mindedness" were recognized as the 4th, 6th, 7th and 8th respectively most important objectives among the 15 identified ones. These findings confirm that, when confronted with important decisions, we fail to think about nearly half of the relevant objectives that we later recognize as important and that the objectives that are missed are indeed important.

Table 42.3 Results of the combined value focused thinking and MCDA approach

	Key concerns	Fundamental objectives identified	Weight (%)
	Cognitive abilities	Mathematical abilities	14.04
		Reading comprehension	15.60
	Socio-economic background	Underprivileged background	17.33
		Support from the children's family	*13.86*
	Social competences	Communication skills	1.70
		Empathy	6.93
Identifying the most suitable candidates for the Foundation programme		Cooperative attitude	4.16
		Leadership ability	2.23
		Attention	0.90
		Creativity	2.77
	Personality	*Open-mindedness*	*4.85*
		Character	*5.40*
		Emotional steadiness	*6.07*
	Mentors' perception	*Mentors' approval*	*3.47*
		Mentors' enthusiasm	*0.70*

This intervention and its findings supported the selection process for the academic year 2016/2017, when the Foundation opened applications in two cities in Hungary for a total of 17 children. The feedback provided by the President of the Foundation Advisory Board and the Foundation Operational Director highlighted that the questions that were more effective in helping them to identify new objectives were the questions about alternatives, about problems and shortcomings and about goals, constraints and guidelines. This last category of questions in particular was the one that allowed them to identify the new objective about the level of family support, which emerged as a crucial indicator.

The key impacts observed after this multi-methodology boost can be summarized as follows:

1 *Learning effect*: the Foundation's members indeed discovered new important objectives for the programme, thanks to the combined value focused thinking and MCDA intervention.
2 *Consensus building*: the facilitated modelling approach employed in the intervention allowed the board members to adopt an inclusive perspective throughout the process and thus achieve consensus on both objectives to be achieved and the candidates to be selected.
3 *Innovation*: after the intervention, the Foundation board voted for the embedding of the new tool in all subsequent selection processes and unanimously approved it.
4 *Reduced drop-out rates*: after one year monitoring of the Foundation programme, no children have dropped-out for the academic year 2017–2018.

Visualizing preferences: how to support value functions' elicitation in decision making

The cognitive challenge and the context of the intervention

When decision makers have a clear set of objectives to achieve in a certain decision-making context, it is helpful to measure the performance of each alternative on these objectives and then aggregate performances and preferences into an overall score for each alternative. One of the most consolidated approaches to do so is Multi-Attribute Value Theory (Keeney & Raiffa,

1976), where the crucial step of preference elicitation revolves around the definition of the value functions and of the trade-offs coefficients.

Since people do not naturally express preferences and values using interval scales, value functions have to be estimated through a specially designed interviewing process in which the relevant judgements for the decision are organized and represented analytically.

Single-attribute value functions can be elicited with different methods (e.g., Von Winterfeldt and Edwards, 1986). A particularly promising one in the context of environmental decision making is the Mid-value Splitting Method (Bisection), which seems to lead to more reliable results than direct rating (Schuwirth et al., 2012). However, a disadvantage of the protocol consists in the generation of relatively abstract questions, which can dramatically increase the cognitive load on the interviewee and delay the elicitation process or even make it fail (e.g., Schuwirth et al., 2012; Ferretti, 2016b).

The following paragraphs provide an account of the preference elicitation challenge and a proposed solution tested within an abandoned railways requalification project in the Piedmont Region in Italy.[3] In 2012, in this region alone, 12 passenger railway lines, characterized by low patronage, have been replaced by bus services.

Among these lines, the Pinerolo-Torre Pellice, which stretches for 16.5 km between the city of Pinerolo and the Pellice Valley, crossing six municipalities, was selected as the most strategic one to be studied for requalification purposes. Thanks to the development of stakeholders' analysis, best practices' analysis and a value focused thinking approach, we were able to analyse the regeneration opportunity through nine objectives (i.e., maximizing the square metres of new green areas, maximizing the compatibility with the existing land use, minimizing the construction works' duration, minimizing the damage to the aesthetic impact on the landscape, minimizing costs, maximizing new job opportunities, maximizing the positive impacts on the touristic sector, maximizing the number of potential users, and maximizing the presence of local attractions) and five possible solutions (creation of a greenway, rail banking, extension of the urban railway service, old station recovery and "no action"). The reader interested in knowing more about the deployment of this intervention can refer to Ferretti and Degioanni (2017).

To allow for the aggregation of the alternatives' performances across objectives, we elicited value functions. Eliciting value functions means translating the performances of the alternatives into a value score, which represents the degree to which an objective is achieved. The value is a dimensionless score: 1 refers to a very good performance (i.e., full achievement of the objective), while 0 refers to a poor performance (i.e., low objective achievement). To elicit intermediate values in this intervention we used the mid-value splitting method and the interviewing process was organized as a series of two half-day meetings with an expert in the field of transportation planning and a consultant for different local authorities involved in transportation-related projects (see Ferretti and Degioanni, 2017, for more details). In this study two meetings were necessary for the value functions' elicitation task because during the elicitation of the value function for the attribute "new green areas" in the first meeting, the expert being interviewed highlighted some drawbacks of the elicitation protocol, which will be explained in the following paragraphs.

In particular, the elicitation protocol consists in interactively asking the interviewee to compare two intervals (e.g., from a to b and from b to c, where a is the worst performance value in the range and c is the best performance value in the range) in order to find the indifference point, i.e. the performance value for which the interviewee is indifferent between an improvement from a to b or from b to c.

In order to efficiently cope with time constraints inherently associated with real actors' participation, we elicited value functions by asking the expert for the mid-value of the intervals [v=0, v=1], [v=0, v=0.5], and [v=0.5, v=1]. The mid-value of the interval [v=0.25, v=0.75] was used as consistency check (see, e.g. Ferretti, 2016b, for a detailed explanation of the protocol). To provide an example, the expert was asked the following question with reference to the attribute "new green areas":

> Imagine two possible scenarios for this project: in the first scenario the square metres of new green areas increase from 0 to 80,000, while in the second scenario the square metres of new green areas increase from 80,000 to 160,000. Would you be equally satisfied in these two scenarios?

During the first meeting the involved expert stated that the mid-value splitting protocol was generating questions that were too abstract, making it difficult for him to provide a reliable answer.

Proposed solutions

To improve the operability of the protocol, we enhanced it with visualization analytics. In particular, each time we used a coordinate plane labelled with the attribute range and we interactively modified the extension of the two intervals considered in each question (Ferretti and Degioanni, 2017). Moreover, with reference to the attribute "new green areas", in order to make the questions more concrete and realistic, we linked each value of the subsequent intervals to physical pictures of urban parks that are well known to the inhabitants of the region under analysis. This helped the expert to clearly associate a quantity to the different extensions that were compared in each question and thus to better complete the elicitation task.

Figure 42.1 shows the first step of the combined use of interactive visual analytics and the mid-value splitting protocol that we experimented for the elicitation of the value function for

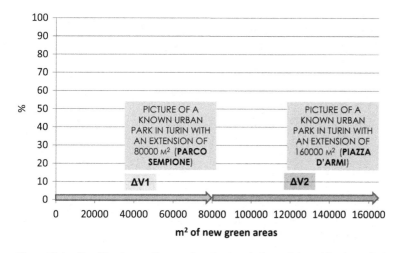

Figure 42.1 Combined use of interactive visual analytics and the mid-value splitting protocol for the attribute "m² of new green areas"

the attribute "m² of new green areas". Using this visual approach, the new question that we asked to the expert became:

> Imagine two possible scenarios for this project: in the first scenario the square metres of new green areas increase from nothing to something that is as big as Parco Sempione, while in the second scenario the square metres of new green areas increase from something that is as big as Parco Sempione to something that is as big as Piazza d'Armi. Would you be equally satisfied?

The expert was now able to relate to the question and provided coherent answers to all subsequent questions.

A similar procedure was repeated for the other similar attributes. The elicited midpoints were marked on the coordinate plane and were finally interpolated to a value function which was further discussed with the interviewee to stimulate the learning effect arising from graphical awareness and real-time visualization of results (Ferretti, 2016b).

Results and impacts of the multi-methodology boost

As a result, during the second workshop, the expert was able to understand the bisection questions and easily state his preference for some of the improvements proposed by the elicitation protocol. The combined use of visualization analytics and sound preference elicitation protocols thus reduced the scope insensitivity (e.g., Carson and Mitchell, 1993) linked to the quite abstract questions generated by the bisection elicitation protocol.

Figure 42.2 shows the elicited value function for the attribute "m² of new green areas". For example, the answer to the first question of the new type mentioned above was "I am not indifferent between these two scenarios, I actually prefer the first one." During the second iteration of the protocol we thus had to shorten the interval that satisfied most the expert being interviewed, i.e., the 0–80,000 one. The second question that we asked was then

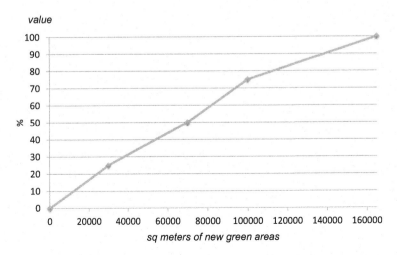

Figure 42.2   Final value function for the attribute "m² of new green areas"

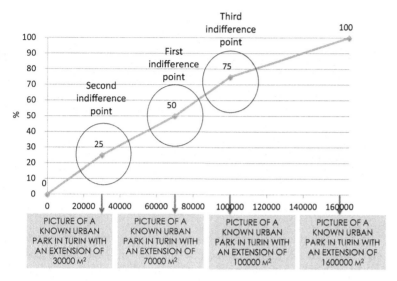

Figure 42.3 Visual supports used to interactively elicit three indifference points for the value function of the attribute "m² of new green areas"

Imagine two possible scenarios for this project: in the first scenario the square metres of new green areas increase from nothing to something that is as big as Parco della Tesoriera[4] while in the second scenario the square metres of new green areas increase from something that is as big as Parco della Tesoriera to something that is as big as Piazza d'Armi. Would you be equally satisfied with these two scenarios?

The answer was now yes and we were thus able to identify the first indifference point of the graph (Figure 42.3). We used the same approach to identify the other points of the function.

The key impacts observed after this multi-methodology intervention can be summarized as follows:

1 Enhanced operability of MCDA thanks to the combined use of visualization analytics and consolidated preference elicitation protocols. Such an integrated approach is expected to increase the use of MCDA in strategic decisions.
2 Development of an online software package which implements the integration of the proposed tools and approaches (Lopez, 2015), thus allowing for replicability of this framework in other decision contexts.[5]
3 Opening of a new research avenue on tools to mitigate scope insensitivity.

Conclusion

This chapter proposed three examples of multi-methodology boosts designed to support three key stages of the decision-making process, i.e., the framing of the problem/opportunity to be addressed, the expansion of the original decision makers' mental model about the objectives to be achieved and, finally, the elicitation of preferences about the worthiness of the alternatives' performances.

In the first intervention, the use of a spatially weighted SWOT analysis provided comprehensive support early in the life cycle of the project by highlighting the spatial density of some critical factors (e.g., abandoned farms in the World Heritage site) and thus significantly improving the components of purpose and scope of the decision frame.

In the second intervention, the combined use of value focused thinking and MCDA allowed the decision makers to update their initial mental models with new relevant objectives that promoted consensus, learning and greater commitment for the subsequent convergent phase of the decision-making process.

In the third intervention, the combination of the bisection elicitation protocol and visualization methods (i.e. a coordinate plane labelled with the attribute range where the extension of the two intervals is interactively modified and corresponding graphical pictures are associated to each quantity) led to a more user-friendly elicitation protocol for the construction of value functions within MCDA and to reduced scope insensitivity in the decision maker's judgements.

There are three common denominators to the behavioural decision analysis interventions discussed in this chapter. First, multi-methodology boosts require time and facilitators skilled in multiple methods. Second, a key advantage of the proposed boosts is their applicability to many different domains. Third, they stretch the bounds that the uncertain and often constrained external environment places on human rationality, thus mitigating some of the associated cognitive consequences such as poor framing of decisions, insufficient thinking about relevant objectives and scope insensitivity. In particular, the presence of limited information on alternatives and their consequences can be tackled through informed value judgements supported by the integration of sound preference elicitation protocols and visualization analytics, as well as through thought-provoking questions to expand the set of objectives and create better alternatives. To cope instead with the constraints on the time available to make the decision, it seems beneficial to use a structured approach like the one proposed in the three projects, as it has been shown to lead to decision quality in both the divergent and subsequent convergent phase of the strategic decision-making process, giving confidence in the decision and commitment for action, thus avoiding decision paralysis and decision postponing.

The techniques proposed in this chapter should thus be considered as "process boosts" and in particular as "framing boosts" and as "preference elicitation boosts", which could be added to first taxonomy of long-term boosts proposed by Hertwig and Grüne-Yanoff (2017), i.e., risk literacy boosts, uncertainty management boosts, and motivational boosts. A final highlight concerns the new competences developed or boosted by the proposed techniques, as summarized in Table 42.4. Current developments of this research are testing how long-lasting the developed competences are.

Table 42.4 New competences boosted by the proposed techniques

Stage of the decision-making process	Boosting techniques used	New or boosted competences
Framing the decision context	Spatial SWOT Analysis and MCDA	Boosted capacity to identify spatial correlations
Framing objectives	Value-focused thinking devices	Boosted capacity to think wider and deeper about objectives
Preference elicitation	Visual analytics and sound preference elicitation protocol	Boosted scope sensitivity

Notes

1 This project won the runner-up position in the INFORMS Decision Analysis Practice Award 2016.
2 This project won the INFORMS Decision Analysis Practice Award 2017.
3 This project was awarded the second position in the INFORMS 2017 Innovative Applications in Analytics Award.
4 The selected park covers a surface of 70000 m².
5 The work developed in this master's thesis won the title of Best Master Thesis 2015 for the IT4BI Master, Ecole Centrale, Paris).

References

Baumol, W. J., and Quandt, R. E. 1964. Rules of thumb and optimally imperfect decisions. *American Economic Review*, 54, 23–46.

Bazerman, M. 2008. *Judgment in managerial decision making*. Hoboken, NJ: John Wiley & Sons.

Belton V., and Stewart T. J. 2002. *Multiple criteria decision analysis: An integrated approach*. Boston: Kluwer Academic Publishers.

Bendoly, E., Van Wezel, W., and Bachrach, D. G. (Eds.) 2015. *The handbook of behavioural operations management: Social and psychological dynamics in production and service settings*. New York: Oxford University Press.

Birnberg, J. G., Luft, J., and Shields, M. D. 2007. Psychology theory in management accounting research. In C. S. Chapman and A.G. Hopwood (Eds.), *Handbook of management accounting research* (pp. 113–135). Oxford: Elsevier.

Bond, S., Carlson, K., and Keeney, R. 2008. Generating objectives: Can decision makers articulate what they want? *Management Science*, 54(1): 56–70.

Bond, S. D., Carlson, K. A., and Keeney, R. L. 2010. Improving the generation of decision objectives. *Decision Analysis*, 7(3): 238–255.

Bruce, B. (Ed.) 2010. *Handbook of behavioural finance*. Northampton: Edward Elgar Publishing.

Camerer, C. F. 2003. *Behavioral game theory: Experiments in strategic interaction*. Princeton, NJ: Princeton University Press.

Camerer, C. F., and Lowenstein, G. (Eds.) 2003. *Advances in behavioural economics*. Princeton, NJ: Princeton University Press.

Carson, R. T., and Mitchell, R. C. 1993. The issue of scope in contingent valuation studies. *American Journal of Agricultural Economics*, 75(5).

Comino, E., and Ferretti, V. 2016. Indicators-based spatial SWOT analysis: Supporting the strategic planning and management of complex territorial systems. *Ecological Indicators*, 60: 1104–1117.

Cronin, M.A., and Weingart, L.R. 2007. Representational gaps, information processing, and conflict in functionally diverse teams. *Academy of Management Review*, 32: 761–773.

Ferretti, V. 2016a. Exploring multi-methodology approaches for policy support: Case studies and lessons learned. OR58. Paper presented at The OR Society Annual Conference.

Ferretti, V. 2016b. From stakeholders analysis to cognitive mapping and Multi-Attribute Value Theory: An integrated approach for policy support. *European Journal of Operational Research*, 252(2): 524–541.

Ferretti, V., and Degioanni, A. 2017. How to support the design and evaluation of redevelopment projects for disused railways? A methodological proposal and key lessons learned. *Transportation Research Part D*, 52: 29–48.

Ferretti, V., and Gandino, E. 2018. Co-designing the solution space for rural regeneration in a new World Heritage site: A Choice Experiments approach. *European Journal of Operational Research*, 268(3): 1077–1091.

Franco, L. A., and Hämäläinen, R. P. 2016. Behavioural operational research: Returning to the roots of the OR profession. *European Journal of Operational Research*, 249: 791–795.

Galizzi, M. 2014. What is really behavioral in behavioral health policy? And does it work? *Applied Economic Perspective*, 36(1): 25–60.

Gigerenzer, G., and Selten, R. (Eds.) 2002. *Bounded rationality: The adaptive toolbox*. Cambridge, MA: MIT Press.

Gigerenzer, G., Hertwig, R., and Pachur, T. (Eds.). 2011. *Heuristics: The foundations of adaptive behaviour*. Oxford: Oxford University Press.

Hämäläinen, R. P. 2015. Behavioural issues in environmental modelling: The missing perspective. *Environmental Modelling & Software*, 73: 244–253.

Henao, F., and Franco, L. A. 2016. Unpacking multimethodology: Impacts of a community development intervention. *European Journal of Operational Research*, 253(3): 681–696.

Hertwig, R., and Grüne-Yanoff, T. 2017. Nudging and boosting: Steering or empowering good decisions. *Perspectives on Psychological Science*, 12(6): 973–986.

Johnson, M. 2012. Community-based operations research: Introduction, theory, and applications. In M. Johnson (Ed.), *Community-Based Operations Research: Decision Modeling for Local Impact and Diverse Populations* (pp. 3–36). Boston: Springer.

Keeney, R. L. 1982. Decision analysis: An overview. *Operations Research*, 30(5): 803–838.

Keeney, R. L. 1996. Value-focused thinking: Identifying decision opportunities and creating alternatives. *European Journal of Operational Research*, 92(3): 537–549.

Keeney, R. L., and Raiffa, H. 1976. *Decisions with multiple objectives: Preferences and value trade-offs.* New York: Wiley.

Larrick, R. P. 2009. Broaden the decision frame to make effective decisions. In E. A. Locke (Ed.), *Handbook of principles of organizational behavior* (2nd ed., pp. 461–480). Chichester: John Wiley & Sons, Ltd.

Lopez, A. M. 2015. ElectioVis. master's thesis. Ecole Centrale, Paris.

Morton, A., and Fasolo, B. 2009. Behavioural decision theory for multi-criteria decision analysis: A guided tour. *Journal of the Operational Research Society*, 60: 268–275.

Myllyviita, T., Hujala, T., Kangas, A., Eyvindson, K., Sironen, S., ... Kurttila, M. 2014. Mixing methods: Assessment of potential benefits for natural resources planning. *Scandinavian Journal of Forest Research*, 29(1): 20–29.

Powell, T. C., Lovallo, D., and Fox, C. R. 2011. Behavioural strategy. *Strategic Management Journal*, 32: 1369–1386.

Schuwirth, N., Reichert, P., and Lienert, J. 2012. Methodological aspects of multi-criteria decision analysis for policy support: A case study on pharmaceutical removal from hospital wastewater. *European Journal of Operational Research*, 220: 472–483.

Shogren, J. F., and Taylor, L. O. 2008. On behavioural environmental economics. *Review of Environmental Economics and Policy*, 2(1): 26–44.

Simon, H. A. 1955. A behavioral model of rational choice. *The Quarterly Journal of Economics*, 5: 99–118.

Simon, H. A. 1982. *Models of bounded rationality.* Cambridge, MA: MIT Press.

SiTI (Istituto Superiore sui Sistemi Territoriali per l'Innovazione) 2013. Dossier di Candidatura UNESCO per il sito piemontese I Paesaggi Vitivinicoli di Langhe-Roero e Monferrato, Turin.

Slovic, P. 1987. Perception of risk. *Science*, 236(4799): 280–285.

Spetzler, C., Winter, H., and Meyer, J. 2016. *Decision quality, value creation from better business decisions.* Hoboken, NJ: John Wiley and Sons.

Tani, S. N., and Parnell, G. S. 2012. Frame the decision opportunity. In G. S. Parnell, T. Bresnick, S. N. Tani, and E. R. Johnson (Eds.), *Handbook of decision analysis.* New York: Wiley.

Thaler, R. H. 1999. The end of behavioural finance. *Financial Analysts Journal*, 56(6): 12–17.

Thaler, R. H., and Sunstein, C. R. 2008. *Nudge: Improving decisions about health, wealth, and happiness.* New Haven, CT: Yale University Press.

Trope, Y., and Liberman, N. 2000. Temporal construal and time-dependent changes in preference. *Journal of Personality and Social Psychology*, 79(6): 876–889.

Tversky, A., and Kahneman, D. 1974. Judgment under uncertainty: Heuristics and biases. *Science*, 185(4157): 1124–1131.

Viale, R. 2012. *Methodological cognitivism.* Vol. I, *Mind, rationality and society.* Heidelberg: Springer.

Viale, R. 2019. The normative and descriptive weaknesses of behavioral economics–informed nudge: Depowered paternalism and unjustified libertarianism. *Mind & Society*, 17(1–2): 53–69.

Von Winterfeldt, D., and Edwards, W. 1986. *Decision analysis and behavioural research.* Cambridge: Cambridge University Press.

43

COGNITIVE AND AFFECTIVE CONSEQUENCES OF INFORMATION AND CHOICE OVERLOAD

Elena Reutskaja, Sheena Iyengar, Barbara Fasolo, and Raffaella Misuraca

Introduction

When interviewed in 1992 in Pittsburgh, Pennsylvania, the Nobel laureate Herbert Simon described a paradox at the heart of living in an economy that made every effort to design and produce ever more "choice alternatives" but that simultaneously allocated very little energy to encouraging people to devote the attention and time actually required to choose. He gave the example of a decision to buy a new house, commenting: "Before you even start the choice process, somebody has presented you with this, and this, and this house" (UBS, 1992).

The overabundance of alternatives was lamented by Simon in 1992, when computing power was slower. It is all the more alarming in the modern and constantly connected world, which now has the internet, smartphones, apps, and tablets—all used to make a plethora of decisions every day.

Nowadays, people receive information from ever-increasing and often simultaneous sources. The average US resident consumer views about 3,000 advertisements every day (Kardes, Cline, & Cronley, 2011) and while in the 1970s to the 1990s grocery stores in the United States carried around 7,000–8,000 items, the variety has increased to 40,000–50,000 items nowadays (Jacoby et al., 1974a; Malito, 2017), including around 285 varieties of cookies and 275 types of cereal (Schwartz & Ward, 2004). The explosion of choice is not limited to retail either and has begun to permeate even people's personal lives. A speed-dating event organized by China's Communist Youth League in 2017 was attended by about 5,000 young single people (Shim, 2017). And in a world where the internet increases an individual's access to information, it seems being surrounded by an overwhelming amount of information every day has become the new norm.

The aim of this chapter is to examine this state of affairs. What is information and choice overload, and what are the cognitive and emotional consequences of this overload?

Classical economics and psychology have argued that increased information and choice are often desirable and lead to better outcomes (Steiner, 1970; Zuckerman, Porac, Lathin & Deci, 1978; Walton & Berkowitz, 1979; Rolls et al., 1981; Deci & Ryan, 1985; Loewenstein, 1999; Ryan & Deci, 2000; Kahn & Wansink, 2004). However, theories of bounded and adaptive

DOI: 10.4324/9781315658353-50

rationality posit the opposite (Simon, 1957 1991;Gigerenzer & Selten, 2002) and have been supported by a large body of research. Extensive information and choice can be costly, demotivating, and unsatisfying (Miller, 1956; Newell & Simon, 1972; Jacoby, 1974; Malhotra, 1982; Iyengar & Lepper, 2000; Schwartz, 2004; Reutskaja & Hogarth, 2009; Grant & Schwartz, 2011; Reutskaja, Nagel, Camerer, Rangel, 2018). They can result in what Schwartz (2000) has called a "tyranny of freedom." However, using less information and making decisions based on less information can lead to higher-quality outcomes. (For a review, see Gigerenzer & Gaissmaier, 2011.)

Information and choice overload: a theoretical background
Definition of information and choice overload

Information load is closely connected to Herbert Simon's behavioral model of rational choice, or "a kind of rational behavior that is compatible with the access to information and the computational capacities that are actually possessed by organisms, including man, in the kinds of environments in which such organisms exist" (Simon, 1955, p. 99). In line with Simon, later research has sought to differentiate information "load" from "overload." The result has been a long-standing debate in the relevant literature about how "information load" and "information overload" can and should be measured. Jacoby (1977, p. 569) provides the following definitions:

> Information load refers to the variety of stimuli (in type and number) to which the receiver must attend. Information *overload* refers to the fact that there are finite limits to the ability of human beings to assimilate and process information during any given unit of time. Once these limits are surpassed, the system is said to be "overloaded" and human performance (including decision making) becomes confused, less accurate, and less effective.

Many researchers use these definitions and manipulate information load by varying both the number of items and the number of attributes describing those items (Jacoby, Speller & Berning, 1974; Jacoby, Speller & Kohn, 1974, Lee & Lee, 2004). Others argue that information load cannot be measured using the product of the number of items and number of attributes (Malhotra, Jain & Lagakos, 1982). As yet, there is no consensus on how to appropriately measure information load and, as a result, any effects driven by the number of choice alternatives and choice attributes remain controversial.

In addition to information overload, it is necessary to define a closely related concept, that of *choice overload*. Choice overload occurs when an increase in the number of options to choose from has detrimental consequences. For example, choice overload may manifest itself as lower intrinsic motivation to choose, decreased satisfaction with the option finally chosen, decreased satisfaction with the process of choosing, stress, anxiety and choice paralysis (Iyengar & Lepper, 2000; Schwartz, 2004; Shah & Wolford, 2007; Reutskaja & Hogarth, 2009; Grant & Schwartz, 2011; Chernev, Böckenholt, & Goodman, 2015; Nagar & Gandotra, 2016; Reutskaja et al., 2018).

Both information and choice overload can arise for both cognitive and affective reasons but they differ in one important way: choice overload occurs only when there is a need to choose an item from a set of alternatives. In contrast, information overload may occur regardless of whether there is a need to make a choice or not. In the latter case, information overload is driven not by choice per se but by the overwhelming amount of information to process.

Though it may be possible for choice overload to occur without information overload, the two often go hand in hand and, for this reason, this chapter will use the terms interchangeably. Despite the different approaches in methodology, most scholars do not dispute the premises of information or choice overload (with some exceptions, such as Scheibehenne, Greifeneder, & Todd, 2010).

Processes underlying the information-overload phenomenon

Next to be discussed are the underlying mechanisms of choice overload, which are connected to the benefits and costs of choice and information provision.

The benefits of increased access to information are nearly always self-evident. Generally, there is an increased likelihood that people's diverse needs and wants will be satisfied. Full and transparent information should also promote market competition by driving prices down and quality up (Loewenstein, 1999). Moreover, actual variety and perceived variety often have the potential to increase consumption (Kahn & Wansink, 2004; Rolls et al., 1981), while access to more choice offerings can improve consumers' welfare (Brynjolfsson, Hu, & Smith, 2003).

Full information and an abundance of choice can also be beneficial from a psychological point of view. As a thought experiment, contrast the emotional feelings experienced when entering a grocery store offering only a few options with what you might feel when entering a well-stocked competitor. In general, individuals are attracted to larger choice sets (see, for example, Iyengar & Lepper, 2000). This can be explained, at least in part, by research demonstrating the association between more choice alternatives and greater perceived decision freedom (Steiner, 1970; Reibstein, Youngblood, & Fromkin, 1975; Walton & Berkowitz, 1979).

On the other hand, information may also impose costs on an individual. Costs come in the form of extra time spent assimilating new information, the potential for error, the greater cognitive burden, and the potential to create an affectively taxing experience, such as feeling greater regret as the number of forgone options increases (Miller, 1956; Loewenstein, 1999; Botti & Iyengar, 2006; Reutskaja, 2008). Those are discussed in more detail below.

A theoretical model describing how the benefits and costs of choice can be integrated has been proposed in previous research (Reutskaja & Hogarth, 2009). This model suggests that, while choice implies both benefits ("goods") and costs ("bads"), which may both increase with the number of available alternatives (see also Coombs & Avrunin, 1977), the benefits increase more slowly than the costs. This proposition was also supported later by Grant and Schwartz (2011). As a result, their model's first implication is that an intermediate amount of choice leads almost always to a more optimal choice offering than a small or large number of choices. That is, the provision of choice is beneficial up to a certain point, after which it becomes detrimental and choice overload occurs. The net benefit to this outcome varies as a function of the number of alternatives, which can be graphed as an inverted U shape, as shown in Figure 43.1.

Another important consequence of this model is that changes in actual and perceived costs and benefits shift the location of the function's peak. For example, with benefits being held constant, lower costs will shift the peak to the right, allowing people to deal with more choice offerings. The costs and benefits of choice (and therefore, the location of the peak of the resulting function) can be moderated by several significant factors: features of information and the environment (such as perceptual attributes of information, organization of the information set, whether a decision is made with or without time pressure, the presence or absence of brand names) and individual differences between the decision makers (such as gender and age). A discussion of the moderators of choice overload is beyond the scope of this chapter but for

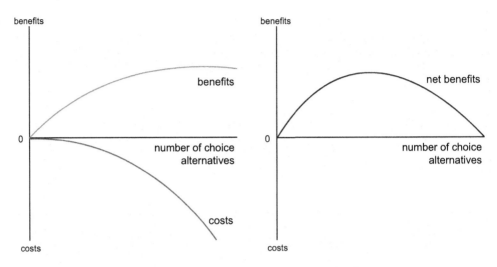

Figure 43.1 Satisfaction as a function of the number of alternatives in the choice set

Source: Adapted from similar figures originally published in Reutskaja and Hogarth (2009).

more on this subject, see Chapter 44 in this volume, "How much choice is 'good enough'? Moderators of information and choice overload."

Overall, the underlying mechanism described above can explain many findings from previous research. Empirical evidence indeed suggests that variables such as choice quality, motivation for choice and buying, and satisfaction with both process and outcome exhibit an inverted-U relationship with the number of choice alternatives and/or the complexity of each alternative.

Empirical evidence: effect of the provision of information and choice on the decision-making process and the outcomes

Next, this section considers empirical evidence of the effects of information and choice provision on the various steps of a decision-making process: information processing and usage, decision-making outcomes (quality and accuracy), motivation for choosing, consumption and buying, and subjective perceptions (individuals' subjective and emotional states).

Information processing and usage

The provision of information can impose cognitive costs on individual decision-makers. Cognitive costs include attention costs and the effort required to process information and make trade-offs. In his classic 1956 paper, "The magical number seven, plus or minus two" (Miller, 1956), George A. Miller argued that the amount of input information was not equal to the amount of information transmitted. This is due to a human's limited ability to receive, process, and remember information. In particular, Miller demonstrated that, as the quantity of input information increased, the amount of transmitted information would quickly plateau. The "channel capacity"—or the greatest amount of information that a human can process without error—was shown to be surprisingly low for unidimensional variables (around four for tastes, six for sounds or tones, and from 10 to 15 for visual positions). Miller suggested that the total "channel capacity" could be improved by increasing the number of dimensions in which given objects differed. However, the accuracy of judgment on each particular attribute would decline. Subsequently, Chase & Simon (1973) and Simon (1974) argued that the brain possessed a "chunk" capacity and that short-term memory was capable of retaining a range of five to seven pieces of information. It was shown that it took time to consciously identify an object—sometimes more than half a second. In addition, the amount of information that the brain can simultaneously maintain in its short-term memory is quite small: the brain is able to remember or monitor only about four objects at once, regardless of how many objects are shown to a person at a time (Marois & Ivanoff, 2005).

In addition, at any given time, the mind normally selects only a subset of relevant information from a scene to process in detail. When full attention is paid to a certain location or item, the attention given to other locations and objects is suppressed (Wedel & Pieters, 2007). This inattentional blindness has been well demonstrated in one of the most famous studies in psychology, known as the Invisible Gorilla Test (Simons & Chabris, 1999). In this experiment, participants were asked to watch a short video in which students, wearing either a black or a white T-shirt, passed a basketball between themselves. The participants' task was to count the number of times that players wearing a white T-shirt passed the ball. During the video a person in a gorilla suit walked through the center of the scene. However, about half of the participants did not actually see the gorilla, which suggests that the relationship between what is in our visual field and what we actually perceive is based mostly on attention.

Attention costs are important costs to consider when dealing with lots of choice or information because attention is limited and selective. However, it is hard to measure many covert processes behind the decisions. Therefore, recent research has used modern tools, including eye tracking and brain imaging to open the black box behind the phenomenon of choice overload. By tracking people's eye movements, previous research has found that attention costs increase when people make choices from large rather than small sets of alternatives under time pressure (Reutskaja et al., 2011). When the number of snacks that people were choosing from increased, the number of eye fixations[1] and the time spent on choosing a snack increased significantly. The increased number of eye fixations likely reflects higher attention and processing costs (or the time necessary to perceive and understand the information), which suggests that a higher number of alternatives in the set imposes higher processing and attention costs on decision makers.

The functional magnetic resonance imaging (fMRI) method, which tracks activity in the brain, was also used to examine the processes behind the choice-overload phenomenon and revealed that choices from large sets of alternatives were associated with a greater cognitive load. Subjects choosing from larger (rather than smaller) choice sets showed increased eye movement and stronger activity in visual and sensorimotor brain areas—areas previously associated with the planning and control of movement such as reaches and saccades, the processing of visual scenes or both (Andersen & Buneo, 2002; Grill-Spector & Malach, 2004; Orban, Van Essen, & Vanduffel, 2004).

The amount of processed information that people use for their decision making (information usage) is also constrained by bounded human processing abilities (Simon, 1976) and imposes cognitive and time costs on decision-makers. Empirical evidence suggests that information usage follows an inverted U-shaped curve with the increase in information load (Miller, 1956; Schroder, Driver & Streufert, 1967; Newell & Simon, 1972; Chewning & Harrell, 1990; Tuttle & Burton, 1999). Research has found that input-cue usage increases initially with the number of cues provided but does not show any further increase after a particular point (Chewning & Harrell, 1990; Stocks & Harrell, 1995). In addition, people consider and process smaller percentages of information when the number of options and amount of relevant information increase (Hauser & Wernerfelt, 1990). For example, a study tracking the eye movements of decision-makers has shown that, when participants chose a snack to consume out of different-sized sets, the average number of items seen in a larger set was greater compared to the smaller set but the percentage of items seen actually decreased with the set size (Reutskaja at al., 2011). So, when confronted with few items (two or three alternatives), people often process and use all the relevant information (Payne, Bettman, Coupey, & Johnson, 1992) but, in an environment with many alternatives, people shift to simpler choice strategies (Rolls et al., 1981). A more recent and large body of research found that the cognitive costs are not necessarily as high as the classical theory suggested. Research on adaptive decision-making (Payne, Bettman, & Johnson, 1993) and fast and frugal heuristics (such as Gigerenzer & Goldstein, 1996; Gigerenzer & Gaissmaier, 2011) established that humans could be good information processors when using simple heuristics. Simple heuristics use little of the large amounts of data available when the information is valid and the heuristic fits the choice environment well. Simple heuristics such as "take the best" (Gigerenzer & Goldstein, 1999) can also be used as techniques to simplify decisions, just like mnemonics and mnemotechnics can be used to overcome memory bottlenecks. To overcome overload, summaries, the prioritization of information, and mnemonics can be useful and have been used in medical education practice to help cope with feelings of information-caused stress (Smith, 2010).

Another cost of too much information and choice is the time cost. Over the decades, evidence has been accumulated that time is an increasing function of the amount of information and choice: There is a positive linear relationship between the total amount of information available and the time spent processing and evaluating information (Jacoby, 1974); people take longer to decide when confronted with larger as opposed to smaller choice sets (Iyengar & Lepper, 2000). Decision time rises over the entire range of task complexity as the number of alternatives in a choice set increases (Hogarth, 1975; Loewenstein, 2000).

However, there is some biological evidence (eye movements) showing that people can somewhat shorten processing times per item when the choice set increases (Reutskaja et al., 2011). Ironically, even if people actually take longer to choose from larger sets, the time that is *perceived* to pass often feels shorter (Fasolo, Carmeci, & Misuraca, 2009). This faulty perception can be harmful, leading to delays, further increases in time pressure, and time mismanagement. Indeed, many people tend to underestimate the time spent making a decision when facing an extensive array (say, 24 options) and, inversely, overestimate the time spent when facing a small choice set (say, only six options).

Motivation for choosing and consumption

Motivation to act refers to the intention to select one or more alternatives from a given set in order to then act upon them in one of many ways, including choosing, buying, or consuming them. More choice often means greater variety, and the provision of some variety has a positive effect on the motivation for choosing, purchasing and consumption. For example, in their study on food intake, Rolls et al. (1981) found that the participants consumed more yogurt when presented with three options—each differing in taste, color, and texture—compared to when just one yogurt flavor was offered. Interestingly, when the three yogurts were different flavors but visually indistinguishable, no increase in food consumption was observed. Moreover, consumption increases not only when the actual variety increases but also when the *perceived* variety increases (Kahn & Wansink, 2004).

However, too much information and choice may also lower the motivation to choose and cause people to defer choosing or simply to select a default option (Dhar, 1997; Shafir, Simonson, & Tversky, 1993). Probably the best-known evidence of choice overload is the "jam study" (Iyengar & Lepper, 2000), where a tasting booth offering either six or 24 different flavors of jam was set up in an "upscale grocery store" in California. Although more customers stopped at the larger booth (the one with 24 rather than six jam flavors), they purchased less when faced with the larger set of jam. A lab study carried out by the same authors (Iyengar & Lepper, 2000) found that participants who sampled from a limited rather than an extensive assortment of chocolate bars were more likely to choose chocolate instead of cash as compensation for participating. Large sets are more attractive at first sight but they are demotivating for decision makers.

So, is it better to have a larger or smaller choice set available when it comes to consumption, buying, or choosing? As this review has shown, research suggests that neither of these options is optimal, and it is best to offer a "golden mean" to decision makers. Purchasing behavior follows an inverted-U pattern according to the number of alternatives in the set, and the peak for buying is reached when people choose from sets of an intermediate size. In one experiment, people could purchase pens from sets of varying sizes. More people purchased pens from intermediate sets (10 alternatives) rather than from small sets or large sets (two or 20 alternatives). Intermediate sets were more "motivating" for people than larger or smaller sets (Shah & Wolford, 2007). There is also biological evidence of too little and too much choice being demotivating. A brain-imaging study in which participants had to choose images from different-sized sets demonstrated that the activity in several brain areas also follows an inverted-U pattern (Reutskaja et al., 2018). Activity in the striatum (the area that has been shown to reflect reward or value processing) and the anterior cingulate cortex (ACC, the area that integrates cost and benefits) was the highest when subjects actively chose from sets with an intermediate number of alternatives, which were considered to have the right number of alternatives. The fMRI activity in those areas was lower for sets that were considered by participants to be too small or too large. Reutskaja et al. (2018) suggested that the activity in those areas reflected a motivational signal that maintained cognitive and behavioral engagement in decision-making.

Additionally, when the choice set is large, people have a stronger preference for simple, easy-to-understand options (Iyengar & Kamenica, 2010). More importantly, when the choice becomes too difficult, people often defer that choice, even when it negatively affects their future well-being. Iyengar, Huberman, and Jiang (2004) studied the influence of "too much" choice on a life-changing decision: participation in the US 401(k) retirement plan. The plans offered anywhere from 2 to 59 investment options. For every 10-option increase, the predicted individual participation probabilities declined by 1.5–2 percent. If there were only two funds offered, participation rates peaked at 75 percent, while the participation rate dropped to 61 percent when the number of plans amounted to 59.

Decision accuracy and quality

Decision accuracy (defined as selecting the best item out of a set), like many of outcome variables discussed earlier, exhibits an inverted-U-shaped relationship with information load (Jacoby et al., 1974a). For example, in a laboratory experiment, subjects were asked to choose a detergent from among 4, 8, or 12 different brands, each of which was described using two, four or six items of information. As the information load increased, the decision accuracy initially increased but ultimately leveled off. The number of brands and the information available about each brand (which both constitute information load) had opposing effects on decision accuracy. The number of brands was negatively related to decision accuracy, while the information per brand had a positive effect on decision accuracy. The results were confirmed in the follow-up experiment by the same authors (Jacoby, Speller, & Berning, 1974), which used larger amounts of information. (See also Malhorta, 1982.)

However, an eye-tracking study demonstrated that people were able to make choices that were better than random from sets of all tested sizes (up to 16 alternatives) even under extreme time pressure of three seconds, although the probability of picking the best item from the set of seen alternatives decreased slightly when the choice set increased (Reutskaja et al., 2011).

Detrimental effects of extensive information load have been further confirmed in other disciplines and contexts. For example, one study on information overload in an online environment found that the probability of a correct choice decreased as the number of attributes where the products differed increased, although the number of alternatives had no effect on accuracy (Lee & Lee, 2004).

Feelings and subjective states

The provision of information and choice can also affect the subjective states of individuals. Having access to full information and choice can be beneficial from a psychological point of view, as people like to feel "informed" and defend their "right" to access relevant information (Jacoby, Speller, & Kohn, 1974). Research has also shown that the ability to make choices by themselves gives people a feeling of autonomy and self-control (Zuckerman et al., 1978; Deci & Ryan, 1985). For example, people in nursing homes feel happier and more satisfied when provided with choices, even when the decisions are relatively unimportant and inconsequential (Langer & Rodin, 1976). These positive psychological states have the potential to enhance life satisfaction, general well-being, and thus social welfare overall.

However, extensive information and choice offerings can impose high psychological costs on individuals. These costs may be emotional (rather than cognitive) and stem from discomfort caused by uncertainty about preferences, lack of expertise, concern or regret about making an incorrect decision, and the presence of trade-offs (see, for example, Loewenstein, 2000). The mere fact of making a decision naturally involves some degree of emotional conflict because the selection of one option always accompanies the rejection of other alternatives (Botti & Iyengar, 2006). Freedom to choose can thus turn into a "tyranny" (Schwartz, 2000). A choice offering may also induce attachment to the options in the choice set, and people can feel they have lost the items they have not chosen. In addition to this, as the choice increases and the number of forgone options increases, the nonchosen options appear more attractive and feelings of loss increase (Carmon, Wertenbroch, & Zeelenberg, 2003). As the amount of information increases, not only will more options necessarily be rejected but people's standards in relation to the outcomes will rise (Schwartz, 2000). If the result of the decision is unsatisfactory, people may feel personally responsible for choosing a "wrong" alternative. When people realize that their choices are not ideal, they fall prey to the "tyranny of freedom." This outcome may be exacerbated by a modern society that fosters high expectations of achieving perfection in every aspect of life.

Selection from larger choice sets is also associated with greater perceived decision difficulty (Iyengar & Lepper, 2000; Reutskaja & Hogarth, 2009), less desire to have additional information (Jacoby, Speller, & Kohn, 1974; Jacoby, Speller, & Berning, 1974), less confidence in one's choice, and greater confusion (Malhotra, 1982; Lee & Lee, 2004). Moreover, individuals experience less satisfaction with the task and choice when selecting from a large rather than a small sample of choices (Malhotra, 1982; Iyengar & Lepper, 2000). However, as with many other previously described variables, satisfaction with both the chosen item and the decision-making process itself are inverted U-shaped functions of the number of alternatives, with people being the most satisfied with intermediate rather than small or large sets of alternatives (Reutskaja & Hogarth, 2009). In addition, having many alternatives may lead to less satisfaction with decisions even when more choices yield better objective outcomes (Schwartz, 2000, 2004; Iyengar, Wells & Schwartz, 2006).

When the choice leads to painful ethical dilemmas, the emotional impact of having to choose is very strong, especially when the decision maker is personally responsible for making the choice. For instance, people who personally make psychologically painful decisions (e.g., ending a life-sustaining treatment) feel more intense negative emotions (such as anger, depression, guilt, and regret) compared to those who face the same outcome (e.g., the death of a loved one) as the result of a decision made by someone else. Personal responsibility adds to the feeling of loss (Botti, Orfali, & Iyengar, 2009).

The opportunity to choose, the amount of information, and the size of a choice set all influence not only actual post-choice feelings but also expectations about how one will feel about the choice, which can be quite different from the actual experience. For example, one study found that people anticipated experiencing greater satisfaction with their choice and with the selection process, as well as less regret over their choice, when choosing from a larger list of 20–50 potential dating candidates rather than from a smaller list of four. However, when participants actually chose a date from a mock website, they experienced greater memory confusion regarding their choices and showed no improvement in their affect when choosing from 20 rather than four profiles of potential partners. So, their expectation did not match their experience (Lenton, Fasolo, & Todd, 2008).

Overall, while the provision of information and choice can positively influence the feelings of individuals, extensive information and choice have a detrimental effect on the subjective states of decision makers, making intermediate sets the most satisfying. When the choice concerns painful outcomes, the mere act of choosing can trigger negative emotions.

Conclusion

This chapter has summarized evidence collected by researchers for more than half a century on the topic of information and choice overload, exploring how people deal with large amounts of information, how they make choices from sets with multiple alternatives, and what consequences choice provision has on decision-making process and choice outcomes. Traditionally, economics and psychology have emphasized the benefits of more information and more choice but a more recent body of research has demonstrated the negative consequences of too much choice. Too much information and choice hinder information processing and usage, the motivation, and the quality and accuracy of decisions, and detrimentally impact the affective states of decision-makers. All in all, empirical evidence suggests that both too little and too much choice and information are bad and there is a golden mean of how much choice is enough but not too much.

Note

1 A fixation occurs when a subject looks at an item for a continuous period of time: at least 100 ms, and usually for 200–400 ms (Salvucci & Goldberg, 2000).

References

Andersen, R. A., & Buneo, C. A. (2002). Intentional maps in posterior parietal cortex. *Annual Review of Neuroscience*, 25(1), 189–220.

Botti, S., & Iyengar, S. S. (2006). The dark side of choice: When choice impairs social welfare. *Journal of Public Policy & Marketing*, 25(1), 24–38.

Botti, S., Orfali, K., & Iyengar, S. S. (2009). Tragic choices: Autonomy and emotional responses to medical decisions. *Journal of Consumer Research*, 36(3), 337–352.

Brynjolfsson, E., Hu, Y., & Smith, M. D. (2003). Consumer surplus in the digital economy: Estimating the value of increased product variety at online booksellers. *Management Science*, 49(11), 1580–1596.

Carmon, Z., Wertenbroch, K., & Zeelenberg, M. (2003). Option attachment: When deliberating makes choosing feel like losing. *Journal of Consumer Research*, 30(1), 15–29.

Chase, W. G., & Simon, H. A. (1973). Perception in chess. *Cognitive Pscyhology*, 4, 55–81.

Chernev, A., Böckenholt, U., & Goodman, J. (2015). Choice overload: A conceptual review and meta-analysis. *Journal of Consumer Psychology*, 25(2), 333–358.

Chewning Jr, E. G., & Harrell, A. M. (1990). The effect of information load on decision makers' cue utilization levels and decision quality in a financial distress decision task. *Accounting, Organizations and Society*, 15(6), 527–542.

Coombs, C. H., & Avrunin, G. S. (1977). Single-peaked functions and the theory of preference. *Psychological Review*, 84(2), 216.

Deci, E. L., & Ryan, R. M. (1985). Cognitive evaluation theory. In E. L. Deci, & R. M. Ryan, *Intrinsic motivation and self-determination in human behavior* (pp. 43–85). Boston: Springer.

Dhar, R. (1997). Consumer preference for a no-choice option. *Journal of Consumer Research*, 24(2), 215–231.

Fasolo, B., Carmeci, F. A., & Misuraca, R. (2009). The effect of choice complexity on perception of time spent choosing: When choice takes longer but feels shorter. *Psychology & Marketing*, 26(3), 213–228.

Gigerenzer, G., & Gaissmaier, W. (2011). Heuristic decision making. *Annual Review of Psychology*, 62, 451–482.

Gigerenzer, G., & Goldstein, D. G. (1996). Reasoning the fast and frugal way: models of bounded rationality. *Psychological Review*, 103(4), 650.

Gigerenzer, G., & Goldstein, D. G. (1999). Betting on one good reason: The take the best heuristic. In G. Gigerenzer, P. M. Todd, & the ABC Research Group (Eds.), *Simple heuristics that make us smart* (pp. 75–95). New York: Oxford University Press.

Gigerenzer, G., & Selten, R. (Eds.) (2002). *Bounded rationality: The adaptive toolbox*. Cambridge, MA: MIT Press.

Grant, A. M., & Schwartz, B. (2011). Too much of a good thing: The challenge and opportunity of the inverted U. *Perspectives on Psychological Science*, 6(1), 61–76.

Grill-Spector, K., & Malach, R. (2004). The human visual cortex. *Annual Review Neuroscience*, 27, 649–677.

Hauser, J. R., & Wernerfelt, B. (1990). An evaluation cost model of consideration sets. *Journal of Consumer Research*, 16(4), 393–408.

Hogarth, R. M. (1975). Decision time as a function of task complexity. In D. Wendt, & C. A. Vliet (Eds.), *Utility, probability, and human decision making* (pp. 321–338). Dordrecht: Springer.

Iyengar, S. S., Huberman, G., & Jiang, W. (2004). How much choice is too much? Contributions to 401(k) retirement plans. In O. S. Mitchell & S. P. Utkus (Eds.), *Pension design and structure: New lessons from behavioral finance* (pp. 83–87). Oxford: Oxford University Press.

Iyengar, S. S., & Kamenica, E. (2010). Choice proliferation, simplicity seeking, and asset allocation. *Journal of Public Economics*, 94(7–8), 530–539.

Iyengar, S. S., & Lepper, M. R. (2000). When choice is demotivating: Can one desire too much of a good thing? *Journal of Personality and Social Psychology*, 79(6), 995.

Iyengar, S. S., Wells, R. E., & Schwartz, B. (2006). Doing better but feeling worse: Looking for the "best" job undermines satisfaction. *Psychological Science*, 17(2), 143–150.

Jacoby, J. (1974). Consumer reaction to information displays: Packaging and advertising. *Advertising and the Public Interest*, 11, 101–118.

Jacoby, J. (1977). Information load and decision quality: Some contested issues. *Journal of Marketing Research*, 14(4), 569–573.

Jacoby, J., Speller, D. E., & Berning, C. K. (1974). Brand choice behavior as a function of information load: Replication and extension. *Journal of Consumer Research*, 1(1), 33–42.

Jacoby, J., Speller, D. E., & Kohn, C. A. (1974). Brand choice behavior as a function of information load. *Journal of Marketing Research*, 11(1), 63–69.

Kahn, B. E., & Wansink, B. (2004). The influence of assortment structure on perceived variety and consumption quantities. *Journal of Consumer Research*, 30(4), 519–533.

Kardes, F. R., Cline, T. W., & Cronley, M. L. (2011). *Consumer behavior: Science and practice*. Boston: Cengage Learning, Incorporated.

Langer, E. J., & Rodin, J. (1976). The effects of choice and enhanced personal responsibility for the aged: A field experiment in an institutional setting. *Journal of Personality and Social Psychology*, 34(2), 191.

Lee, B. K., & Lee, W. N. (2004). The effect of information overload on consumer choice quality in an on-line environment. *Psychology & Marketing*, 21(3), 159–183.

Lenton, A. P., Fasolo, B., & Todd, P. M. (2008). "Shopping" for a mate: Expected versus experienced preferences in online mate choice. *IEEE Transactions on Professional Communication*, 51(2), 169–182.

Loewenstein, G. (1999). Is more choice always better? *Social Security Brief*, 7(1), 7.

Loewenstein, G. (2000). Emotions in economic theory and economic behavior. *American Economic Review*, 90(2), 426–432.

Malhotra, N. K. (1982). Information load and consumer decision making. *Journal of Consumer Research*, 8(4), 419–430.

Malhotra, N. K., Jain, A. K., & Lagakos, S. W. (1982). The information overload controversy: An alternative viewpoint. *Journal of Marketing*, 46(2), 27–37.

Malito, A. (2017). Grocery stores carry 40,000 more items than they did in the 1990s. Available at: www.marketwatch.com/story/grocery-stores-carry-40000-more-items-than-they-did-in-the-1990s-2017–06–07 (accessed July 31, 2019).

Marois, R., & Ivanoff, J. (2005). Capacity limits of information processing in the brain. *Trends in Cognitive Sciences*, 9(6), 296–305.

Miller, G. A. (1956). The magical number seven, plus or minus two: Some limits on our capacity for processing information. *Psychological Review*, 63(2), 81.

Nagar, K., & Gandotra, P. (2016). Exploring choice overload, internet shopping anxiety, variety seeking and online shopping adoption relationship: Evidence from online fashion stores. *Global Business Review*, 17(4), 851–869.

Newell, A., & Simon, H. A. (1972). *Human problem solving*. Englewood Cliffs, NJ: Prentice-Hall.

Orban, G. A., Van Essen, D., & Vanduffel, W. (2004). Comparative mapping of higher visual areas in monkeys and humans. *Trends in Cognitive Sciences*, 8(7), 315–324.

Payne, J. W., Bettman, J. R., Coupey, E., & Johnson, E. J. (1992). A constructive process view of decision making: Multiple strategies in judgment and choice. *Acta Psychologica*, 80(1–3), 107–141.

Payne, J. W., Bettman, J. R., & Johnson, E. J. (1993). *The adaptive decision maker*. Cambridge: Cambridge University Press.

Reibstein, D. J., Youngblood, S. A., & Fromkin, H. L. (1975). Number of choices and perceived decision freedom as a determinant of satisfaction and consumer behavior. *Journal of Applied Psychology*, 60(4), 434.

Reutskaja, E. (2008). Experiments on the role of the number of alternatives in choice. PhD thesis. Pompeu Fabra University.

Reutskaja, E., & Hogarth, R. M. (2009). Satisfaction in choice as a function of the number of alternatives: When "goods satiate." *Psychology & Marketing*, 26(3), 197–203.

Reutskaja, E., Lindner, A., Nagel, R., Andersen, R. A., & Camerer, C. F. (2018). Choice overload reduces neural signatures of choice set value in dorsal striatum and anterior cingulate cortex. *Nature Human Behaviour*, 2(12), 925.

Reutskaja, E., Nagel, R., Camerer, C. F., & Rangel, A. (2011). Search dynamics in consumer choice under time pressure: An eye-tracking study. *American Economic Review*, 101(2), 900–926.

Rolls, B. J., Rowe, E. A., Rolls, E. T., Kingston, B., Megson, A., & Gunary, R. (1981). Variety in a meal enhances food intake in man. *Physiology & Behavior*, 26(2), 215–221.

Ryan, R. M., & Deci, E. L. (2000). Self-determination theory and the facilitation of intrinsic motivation, social development, and well-being. *American Psychologist*, 55(1), 68.

Salvucci, D. D., & Goldberg, J. H. (2000). Identifying fixations and saccades in eye-tracking protocols. *Proceedings of the 2000 Symposium on Eye tracking Research & Applications*, November, 71–78.

Scheibehenne, B., Greifeneder, R., & Todd, P. M. (2010). Can there ever be too many options? A meta-analytic review of choice overload. *Journal of Consumer Research*, 37(3), 409–425.

Schroder, H. M., Driver, M. J., & Streufert, S. (1967). *Human information processing: Individuals and groups functioning in complex social situations*. New York: Holt, Rinehart and Winston.

Schwartz, B. (2000). Self-determination: The tyranny of freedom. *American Psychologist*, 55(1), 79.

Schwartz, B. (2004). *The paradox of choice: Why more is less*. New York: Ecco.

Schwartz, B., & Ward, A. (2004). Doing better but feeling worse: The paradox of choice. In P. A. Linley, & S. Joseph (Eds.), *Positive Psychology in Practice* (pp. 86–104). New York: John Wiley & Sons.

Shafir, E., Simonson, I., & Tversky, A. (1993). Reason-based choice. *Cognition*, 49(1–2), 11–36.

Shah, A. M., & Wolford, G. (2007). Buying behavior as a function of parametric variation of number of choices. *Psychological Science*, 18(5), 369.

Shim, E. (2017). China launches state-sponsored dating event. Available at: www.upi.com/China-launches-state-sponsored-dating-event/9821498584045/ (accessed July 31, 2019).

Simon, H. A. (1955). A behavioral model of rational choice. *The Quarterly Journal of Economics*, 69(1), 99–118.

Simon, H. A. (1957). *Models of man; social and rational*. Chichester: John Wiley & Sons, Ltd.

Simon, H. A. (1974). How big is a chunk? *Science*, 183(4124), 482–488.

Simon, H. A. (1976). From substantive to procedural rationality. In T. J. Kastelein, S. K. Kulpers, W. A. Nijenhuis, & G. R. Wagenaar (Eds.), *25 years of economic theory* (pp. 65–86.). Leiden: Martinus Nijhoff.

Simon, H. A. (1991). Bounded rationality and organizational learning. *Organization Science*, 2(1), 125–134.

Simons, D. J., & Chabris, C. F. (1999). Gorillas in our midst: Sustained inattentional blindness for dynamic events. *Perception*, 28(9), 1059–1074.

Smith, R. (2010). Dealing with the information overload: What about medical students? Available at: www.bmj.com/rapid-response/2011/11/03/dealing-information-overload-what-about-medical-students (accessed July 31, 2019).

Steiner, I. D. (1970). Perceived freedom. *Advances in Experimental Social Psychology*, 5, 187–248.

Stocks, M. H., & Harrell, A. (1995). The impact of an increase in accounting information level on the judgment quality of individuals and groups. *Accounting, Organizations and Society*, 20(7–8), 685–700.

Tuttle, B., & Burton, F. G. (1999). The effects of a modest incentive on information overload in an investment analysis task. *Accounting, Organizations and Society*, 24(8), 673–687.

UBS, 1992. Video recording. Available at: www.ubs.com/HerbertSimon

Walton, J. R., & Berkowitz, E. N. (1979). The effects of choice complexity and decision freedom on consumer choice behavior. *ACR North American Advances*, 6, 206–208.

Wedel, M., & Pieters, R. (Eds.) (2007). *Visual marketing: From attention to action*. Hove: Psychology Press.

Zuckerman, M., Porac, J., Lathin, D., & Deci, E. L. (1978). On the importance of self-determination for intrinsically-motivated behavior. *Personality and Social Psychology Bulletin*, 4(3), 443–446.

44

HOW MUCH CHOICE IS "GOOD ENOUGH"?

Moderators of information and choice overload

Raffaella Misuraca, Elena Reutskaja, Barbara Fasolo,
and Sheena Iyengar

Introduction

In today's world, people face an abundance of information and a great number of choices both in important domains, such as health care, retirement, and education, and in less important domains, such as the choice of breakfast cereal or chocolate. Choice overload and information overload have strong negative effects on many important decision-making aspects such as processing and using information, the motivation to act, the quality of choices, and post-choice feelings, which are discussed in Chapter 43 in this volume in more detail. However, small choice and information sets are not always optimal either. Several variables—such as information usage, decision accuracy, motivation to choose, and satisfaction with choice are "inverted-U" functions of the amount of information and the number of choice alternatives available. In other words, choosing from sets of an intermediate size usually brings more net benefits to the decision-maker than choosing from large or small choice sets (Grant & Schwartz, 2011; Reutskaja & Hogarth, 2009; Shah & Wolford, 2007). Indeed, in line with the assumptions of bounded rationality, intermediate sizes are preferable when they do not entail the same high, cognitively unmanageable load that large sets do, and simultaneously possess the benefits of variety that small sets lack. However, exactly how much choice is enough, or, as Herbert A. Simon would say, "good enough"? The size of the intermediate set is not always clear or universal, and is often influenced by a variety of factors. The aim of this chapter is to set out the factors which most affect and moderate the experience of too much choice, influencing feelings of how much is "enough." Broadly, there are two categories of moderators: one pertaining to the choice environment and one pertaining to the characteristics of the decision-making actor. This division is in line with Simon's scissors analogy (Simon, 1990), which views bounded rationality as the interplay between the two blades: the context or choice environment, on the one hand, and the capabilities and characteristics of decision-makers, on the other.

Context and choice environment

Within this first category, pertaining to the choice environment, we review the most critical moderators: perceptual attributes of the information, the complexity of the set of alternatives,

DOI: 10.4324/9781315658353-51

decision accountability, the physical arrangement of the options, and general contextual characteristics, such as the time and money involved.

Perceptual characteristics of the information presented

The first important moderator pertains to the perceptual nature of the choice presented, that is, the *perceptual attributes*. Miller (1956) suggests that the "channel capacity" for information processing is different for different stimuli: for tastes, it is four; for tones, it is six; and for visual stimuli, it reaches 10–15 items.

Visual presentation is one of the most important perceptual characteristics. Regardless of assortment size, consumers tend to prefer a visual rather than verbal representation of choice options (the "visual preference heuristic", Townsend & Kahn, 2013). Despite being preferred by consumers, visual depictions of large assortments lead to suboptimal decisions compared to verbal presentations, since visual presentation activates a less systematic approach. Visual depictions in large choice sets also result in greater perceptions of complexity and in a reduction of the likelihood to choose. With small assortments, however, visual representations of options seem to be preferable, as they increase consumers' perception of variety, improve the likelihood of making a choice, and speed up the time spent examining options.

Choice set complexity, decision accountability, and the presence of a brand

The notion of choice complexity directly pertains to choice overload. It comes from the important meta-analysis by Chernev, Böckenholt, and Goodman (2015) of choice overload studies and concerns all the aspects of a decision task that affect the *value* of the available choice options (Payne, Bettman, & Johnson, 1993). Choice set complexity, therefore, is not about the structural characteristics of the decision problem, such as the number of options, number of attributes of each option, or format in which the information is presented. Rather, choice complexity involves the following four factors:

1 the level of attractiveness of the options;
2 the presence or the absence of a dominant (or ideal) option;
3 the alignability of the options' attributes;
4 the complementarity of the choice options.

In terms of the first factor, choice-set complexity is higher when the assortment includes higher-quality, more attractive options (for example, an assortment of sandwiches made with premium, instead of average, ingredients; Chernev & Hamilton, 2009). Overall, when the variability in the relative attractiveness of the choice alternatives increases, the probability of a correct choice (if possible), the certainty about the choice, and the satisfaction with the task increase (Malhotra, 1982). More choice leads to a decline in consumer satisfaction if the number of attractive options is increased but it leads to an improvement in satisfaction if the number of unattractive options is increased. This effect occurs because more choice generally highlights the weaknesses of attractive choices and the strengths of unattractive choices (Chan, 2015).

In addition, when the attribute levels of a good are distributed unequally (i.e., the choice-set contains alternatives that are not equally attractive), the probability of choosing the correct option typically increases (Lee & Lee, 2004), whereas, people are less confident when attribute levels are distributed equally. Items with similar attractiveness may lead people to defer choice or simply choose a default option (Dhar, 1997).

Turning to the second factor of complexity, the presence of the ideal point simplifies large sets and therefore leads to a stronger preference for the chosen alternative. However, the presence of the ideal alternative in smaller sets leads to weaker preferences for the selected item (Chernev, 2003). Moreover, a brain-imaging experiment, where subjects chose from different-sized sets of landscape images, demonstrated that large sets were not always "bad" or "overwhelming" (Reutskaja, Lindner, Nagel, Andersen, & Camerer, 2018). Choosing from the sets containing an "ideal" item (e.g., those containing an image most preferred by participants) was associated with greater brain activity in the striatum and the anterior cingulate cortex (the areas involved in reward and value processing as well as in the integration of costs and benefits) compared to choosing from those sets with no item regarded as ideal. That is, the benefits of having an ideal item in the set might compensate for the costs of overwhelming set size in the bounded rational mind of humans.

The fact that large sets are not always more complex than small sets has been shown in other research. For example, Fasolo, Hertwig, Huber, and Ludwig (2009) measured the level of complexity due to the attractiveness of options in terms of assortment entropy, or the number of attribute levels and the distribution of products on the attribute levels within the assortment (Hoch, Bradlow, & Wansink, 2002; Lurie, 2004) and found that consumers considered it more difficult to choose from an assortment with higher entropy. For example, in an assortment of jams, for the same attribute (such as carb content), each jar can have different levels (such as 12 g, 15 g, or 7 g). Furthermore, in the same assortment, the distribution of jams on a given attribute level can be even or uneven. If the number of attribute levels is large and products are evenly distributed in attractiveness across the attribute levels, the assortment entropy is high. Entropy can be higher in a smaller set than in a larger set, which suggests that a small set can be more complex and difficult to choose from and can lead to poorer decisions than a large choice set.

Third, choice complexity is also a function of the alignability and complementarity of the attributes that differentiate the options available to the chooser (Chernev et al., 2015). Complexity and choice overload increase when the options have attributes that cannot be aligned (meaning that not all of options have attribute values for all attributes, as some options have unique attributes). For instance, a choice between a shirt that "keeps in heat" and a jacket that is "waterproof" might be said to contain non-aligned features. The shirt and jacket do different things in different ways and therefore a comparison of value becomes difficult (e.g., apples and oranges). Similarly, "complementary" (meaning that they have additive utility and need to be co-present to fully satisfy the consumer's need) can increase complexity. For example, gloves and scarves have complementary features, in that they provide warmth to different parts of the body.

Besides choice complexity, another important factor that affects the extent to which a wide choice causes overload is decision accountability, which can be defined as the requirement (often due to the context) for decision-makers to justify their choices. With greater account-ability, the preference for larger sets increases (Chernev et al., 2015).

Finally, the presence or absence of brand names in the choice sets can strongly influence the level of satisfaction with the chosen option. One study has shown that choice overload disappeared when the choice options contained brand names. Subjects showed the same level of satisfaction when choosing from small and large sets of branded cellphones. However, when the same cellphones were presented without brand names, a higher level of dissatisfaction was observed for larger sets compared to smaller sets (Misuraca, Ceresia, Teuscher, & Faraci, 2019).

Physical arrangement of assortment and option organization

The physical arrangement of information and the presentation format of options affect information perception, processing, and decision-making and are factors of choice difficulty, which is known to moderate the effect of choice overload (Chernev et al., 2015). The location of any alternatives in a space and the information structure embedded in their display allow people to retrieve additional information about the options, affecting choosers' abilities to distinguish among options, and helping in the evaluation of each option's attributes (see, for example, Chandon, Hutchinson, Bradlow, & Young, 2009). There is a vast amount of evidence that the order in which information is presented results in strong primacy and recency effects (Reutskaja, Nagel, Camerer, & Rangel, 2011). The order also affects the attention paid to the products in the store: products on the top and middle shelves attract more attention than those on lower shelves (Chandon et al., 2009). However, greater attention does not necessarily translate directly into more sales.

The order of attributes also affects the perception of choice overload by changing people's preferences about diverse goods (suits, cars, etc.). For example, when attributes are presented starting with the attribute for which there are the most options (such as 56 car interior colors) and ending with the one for which there are the least number of options (such as four gearshift knob styles), participants are more likely to accept default options and to be less satisfied with their final products than when participants face the opposite order of attributes (Levav, Heitmann, Herrmann, & Iyengar, 2010). Overall, the organization and presentation of information can be used as a tool to simplify information processing and therefore to let decision-makers deal with a greater information load without too much cost (see Anderson & Misuraca, 2017). For example, the organization of information into "chunks" or sequences facilitates information processing (Miller, 1956). In addition, the perceived variety is greater if the large sets are organized, and the smaller sets are disorganized (Kahn & Wansink, 2004). For highly varied sets, consumers are more satisfied (in terms of learning their own preferences), perceive less complexity, and are more willing to make choices when information about the product category is presented by attribute (e.g., consumers are asked how expensive or comfortable they want their sofa), compared to presentation by alternative (e.g., consumers are shown many sofas next to each other in a showroom) (Huffman & Kahn, 1998).

The alignment of the external organization of the information (the way the products are displayed by retailers) with decision-makers' internal schemes (that is, how decision-makers categorize those products in their mind) is extremely important for the perception of variety. In particular, for familiar product categories, consumers are likely to perceive more variety and be more satisfied when the external organization of an assortment matches their internal organizational schemas. However, for unfamiliar product categories, consumers feel more satisfied and perceive more variety if the assortment is arranged in a way that makes it easier to satisfy specific shopping goals (such as buying a backpack to carry a laptop) (Morales, Kahn, McAlister, & Broniarczyk, 2005).

Finally, presenting options either simultaneously (all at once) or sequentially (one at a time) strongly affects individuals' decisions and their subsequent satisfaction. Specifically, consumers are less satisfied with their choice when the options are presented sequentially rather than simultaneously (Mogilner, Shiv, & Iyengar, 2012). This happens because, in the simultaneous format, decision-makers tend to stay focused on the given set of options while, in the sequential format, decision-makers tend to evaluate each option by comparing it with an internal reference point, such as an imagined better option. This hope of finding the ideal option translates into a lower level of satisfaction with the chosen option.

Context specificity

Preferences are constructed by the context (Lichtenstein & Slovic, 2006; Payne et al., 1993; Tversky & Kahneman, 1974, 1981). The context, or domain, in which the decision is to be made plays an important role in the experience of choice overload. While people tend to like choice in a consumer context, they might not like choice in the context of making an unpleasant and stressful medical decision or choosing from a set of undesirable alternatives. In unpleasant choice domains, people often feel increased negative affect when they are personally responsible for the choice and decreased negative emotions when they are allowed to delegate the choice to someone else (Botti & Iyengar, 2006; Botti, Orfali, & Iyengar, 2009).

Whether the choice is presented online or offline is another important consideration. For instance, satisfaction with the choice of chocolate was not affected by the size of the assortment when the choice was presented online because e-commerce users expect larger choice sets compared to shoppers in physical retail spaces (Moser, Phelan, Resnick, Schoenebeck, & Reinecke, 2017).

Another important contextual factor is time pressure, which has been shown to affect the quality of decisions and the strategies people utilize when making decisions in two possible ways (Maule & Edland, 1997; Payne et al., 1993). First, people respond to time pressure by attempting to speed up processing and/or by eliminating breaks (Payne et al., 1993; Pieters & Warlop, 1999; Reutskaja et al., 2011). Second, decision-makers become more selective about the type of information they choose to process and use. This may be reflected in filtering (giving greater priority to the important information) or in omission (ignoring part of the information entirely and looking at lower proportion of the items in the choice set) (Payne et al., 1993; Reutskaja et al., 2011). People may also react to time pressure by choosing at random or avoiding making choices. One study found that people defer choices less often when high-conflict decisions were being made under time pressure, compared to the absence of time pressure. In low-conflict decisions, however, time pressure has no effect on choice deferral. Furthermore, under time pressure, people use more non-compensatory strategies, which partially mediate the influence of time pressure on choice deferral (Dhar & Nowlis, 1999).

Among the "negative" consequences of time stress that have been mentioned are forgetting important data, the neglect and denial of important data, and inaccurate judgments and evaluations (Zakay, 1993). However, time stress also has adaptive benefits (Gigerenzer & Garcia-Retamero, 2017). There is also an inverted-U relationship between information load and decision quality under conditions of time pressure, and no such relationship when the time pressure is removed (Hahn, Lawson, & Lee, 1992).

Monetary incentives have also been shown to affect the amount of information used and the response times. When the information load increases, individuals provided with monetary incentives use more information and take more time than those who are not offered such incentives. However, there is a limit to the amount of information that can be processed per time unit, and incentives do not affect information usage for decisions constrained by time (Tuttle & Burton, 1999).

Individual characteristics of the decision-maker

Within this second category pertaining to the decision-maker's characteristics, we review the most critical moderators: decision goal, knowledge and experience, preference uncertainty and mindset, affective state, decision style, and demographic variables such as age, gender, and culture.

Decision goal

The term "decision goal" refers to the extent to which a decision-maker seeks to minimize the amount of cognitive resources being spent on making a decision (Chernev et al., 2015). This has been operationalized in the form of decision intent—buying (or the goal of making a decision among the available options), versus browsing (or the goal of learning more about the options)—and decision focus (choosing an option from an assortment versus choosing an assortment). Concerning the decision intent, when consumers approach assortments with the goal of browsing, cognitive overload is less likely to occur than when consumers approach the assortments with the goal of buying. In the latter case, consumers need to make trade-offs among the pros and cons of the options, something that demands more cognitive resources. Accordingly, consumers whose goal is browsing, rather than buying, are less likely to experience cognitive overload when facing large assortments (Chernev & Hamilton, 2009).

The difference between browsing and choosing is also reflected in the brain activity of decision-makers who are choosing from different size of sets. When they were *choosing*, the activity in the striatum and the anterior cingulate cortex reflected the inverted-U-shaped function of the number of alternatives people chose from. This suggests that neither too much nor too little choice provides optimal cognitive net benefits. Whereas activity associated with *browsing* intent has been observed as an increasing function of the set size in those areas because the costs of choice were removed when subjects simply browse rather than when subjects were faced with the effort of choosing (Reutskaja et al., 2018).

With regard to the decision focus (Chernev et al., 2015), when consumers approach the assortments with the goal of choosing one of those assortments, rather than choosing an item from a given assortment, cognitive overload is less likely to occur because the task does not involve any process of evaluating the individual options or any trade-off among those options. As a consequence, consumers focusing their attention on choosing an assortment tend to prefer larger assortments, since they gain the benefit of variety without paying the cognitive costs associated with the difficult trade-offs involved in choosing an item. In contrast, consumers focusing their attention on choosing an option from one assortment experience greater decision difficulty and, as a consequence, tend to prefer smaller assortments (Chernev, 2006).

In addition, the order in which consumers decide whether to buy and which option to choose moderates the purchasing likelihood under choice overload (Scheibehenne, Greifeneder, & Todd, 2010). Large assortments are associated with a greater purchase likelihood when consumers first decide whether to buy from an assortment, rather than choosing an option from the set.

Knowledge and experience

Knowledge and experience play an important role when someone chooses from sets with multiple alternatives. For example, greater knowledge and experience are associated with increased brand processing (Bettman & Park, 1980), while moderate prior knowledge of a product is associated with processing more available information than either low or high levels of previous knowledge or experience of the subject. Low-knowledge individuals tend to give up when facing complex data, because it is hard for them to make sense of the data. People with high prior knowledge can process the information but have no motivation to do so, preferring to use the information they already possess. Moderate prior knowledge on the subject gives people both the ability and the motivation to engage in further information processing.

In addition, decision-makers with a greater need for cognition (Cacioppo & Petty, 1982) are less affected by choice overload and defer choice less than decision-makers with a lower need for cognition (Pilli & Mazzon, 2016). Consumers who are more cognitively complex (those who refer to a larger number of dimensions to interpret and evaluate the environment) also use more information. However, such consumers are significantly less likely to experience information overload with an optimizing goal than those who are more cognitively simple (Malhotra, 1982).

Preference uncertainty and assessment orientation

Bounded rationality can mean that individuals do not know what they prefer, before they choose, something Chernev et al. (2015) called "preference uncertainty." In these cases, articulating preferences and making trade-offs between alternatives before choosing can lead to stronger preferences when choosing from *large* sets but weaker preferences when choosing from small sets. Similarly, articulating one's ideal product can simplify the choice from large sets if the set contains this ideal product.

Assessment orientation or the motivation to evaluate and compare all the available options, in order to choose the one with the best attributes, is another factor that influences choice from large sets (Mathmann, Chylinski, de Ruyter, & Higgins, 2017). Customers with a high assessment orientation perceive greater value in products chosen from large assortments, compared to those who feel comfortable without many comparisons to make among the options.

Positive affect

Positive affect has a strong influence on consumer satisfaction when people are choosing from different sizes of sets. For example, one study discovered that individuals experiencing positive affect did not also experience dissatisfaction when choosing from larger choice sets (as though momentarily inoculating them), whereas individuals in neutral affect were more satisfied when choosing from a smaller choice set (Spassova & Isen, 2013). Positive affect, then, is likely to shift attention away from the difficulty of the task toward the quality of the assortment. The role of positive affect in choice satisfaction is in line with research on the affect heuristic, which is a mental shortcut that enables quick and efficient decisions, based on the immediate emotional response to a stimulus (Slovic, Finucane, Peters, & MacGregor, 2007).

Decision-making tendencies

Drawing on Simon's terminology, Schwartz et al. (2002) have argued that satisfaction with an extensive choice depends on whether one is a "maximizer," who actively seeks the best possible result, or a "satisficer," who is content with the first result that is "good enough." The authors observed that maximizers reported less satisfaction, happiness, and optimism with life in general, and, when facing choices, they engaged in more social comparisons, experienced more regret, and were less satisfied with their choices. Even while doing better (e.g., obtaining a higher salary for a job), maximizers may feel worse because of them "not always wanting what they get" (Iyengar, Wells, & Schwartz, 2006). However, it is important to note, that the literature on maximizing is controversial on account of the proliferation and use of several different maximization scales (e.g., Diab, Gillespie, & Highhouse, 2008; Misuraca Faraci, Gangemi, Carmeci, & Miceli, 2015; Turner, Rim, Betz, & Nygren, 2012), each of which is based on different definitions of the core maximizing construct (Misuraca & Fasolo, 2018).

Choosing for others versus oneself

The negative effects of choice overload are not replicated when individuals make choices for others rather than for themselves (Polman, 2012). Individuals making choices for others (about wines, ice-cream flavors, school courses, etc.) reported greater satisfaction when choosing from larger rather than smaller assortments. Conversely, when choosing for themselves, people reported higher satisfaction levels after choosing from smaller rather than larger assortments. This may occur because, when choosing for others, people are typically oriented toward positive outcomes and positive information whereas, when they are choosing for themselves, individuals' attention is directed to negative information and they are oriented away from negative outcomes (see regulatory focus theory for details, Higgins, 1997).

Gender

There are gender differences in reaction to choice overload, in part, because men and women may often employ different information-processing strategies. For example, one study has demonstrated that, while ad information is encoded and is equally available to both women and men, females are more likely to pay attention to the details, whereas males are less likely to access or use this information (Meyers-Levy & Maheswaran, 1991). Advertisements with many images are often more effective at targeting females, while male customers prefer simple images and information that will lead to quick decisions. However, gender differences in the desire for variety can depend on the type of choice. When choosing from different sizes of sets of gift boxes, women were shown to be more satisfied with their choices over the entire range of alternatives than men (Reutskaja, 2008). However, when choosing a potential mate from a set of online date options, women perceived 20 profiles as being close to the ideal set size, whereas men perceived this as being too limited (Lenton, Fasolo, & Todd, 2008). In addition, women were generally more selective than men when they searched for a potential mate during speed-dating events, which varied in size of potential mates (Fisman, Iyengar, Kamenica, & Simonson, 2006). The selectivity of males was similar between groups of different sizes, while women became much more selective when the speed-dating group size was increased to more than 15.

Age

The choice overload experience depends greatly on the age of the decision-maker. For example, when choosing from an extensive array of options, adolescents and adults suffer similar negative consequences (i.e., greater difficulty and dissatisfaction), while children and seniors suffer fewer negative consequences (i.e., less difficulty and dissatisfaction than adolescents and adults) (Misuraca, Teuscher, & Faraci, 2016). In domains where risk is not involved, adults and adolescents seem to adopt very similar decision-making processes (Furby & Beyth-Marom, 1992): a maximizing approach. This would explain their greater perceived difficulty and post-choice dissatisfaction when facing a high number of options (see Iyengar et al., 2006). Children, on the other hand, tend to approach decisions in a more intuitive manner and quickly develop strong preferences (Schlottmann & Wilkening, 2011). This mitigates the negative consequences of choice overload for this age group. Seniors tend to be overconfident in their judgments (Stankov & Crawford, 1996), demonstrating a pronounced focus on positive information (Mather & Carstensen, 2005), and they adopt a satisficing approach when making decisions (Tanius, Wood, Hanoch, & Rice, 2009). These tendencies would explain why the negative consequences of too many choices were milder among seniors.

Cultural background

People of different cultures have different preferences for variety (for further discussion, see Iyengar, 2010). For example, Anglo-Americans were shown to be more motivated by choice, especially by personal choice, and rated having choice as more important than Asian Americans did (Iyengar & Lepper, 1999). People from Eastern Europe were more satisfied with larger choice sets than their Western European counterparts, which could be explained by the fact that choice was limited in Eastern European countries for a long time (Reutskaja, 2008). Choice provision might have different effect on people from different cultures, because freedom and choice might not have the same meaning for Westerners and non-Westerners (Markus & Schwartz, 2010). In addition, Western and non-Western cultures seem to have different patterns of perception: while Asians tend to focus more on contextual information, Americans tend to focus on salient foreground objects (Miyamoto, Nisbett, & Masuda, 2006). This difference is due to the distinctive characteristics of each culture's perceptual environment, which afford distinctive ways to perceive information (see also Viale, 2012). Though there are cultural differences in choice perception, most of the research on choice overload to date has focused on university-educated samples from Western societies and should be taken with a grain of salt as freedom of choice may not be a universal aspiration.

Conclusion

In an interview in Pittsburgh, Herbert Simon was asked whether simple decision-making could be achieved by presenting a smaller number of alternatives. His response was: "Partly. I think the difficulty of decision-making centers very much around the degree of uncertainty and the gaps in our knowledge" (UBS, 1992). We agree with his statement: attempting to gird ourselves against the effects of choice overload, either by pursuing or presenting an "ideal" number of options, is an admirable goal but an incredibly challenging one. Previous research has shown that both too much and too little information and choice are bad. For more than half a century, researchers have tried to answer the question of how much information and choice are enough and what is the "ideal" number of alternatives to present to consumers and the public. As this chapter has demonstrated, the ideal number of choices depends greatly on many contextual and demographic factors, such as the availability of an ideal alternative in the choice set, the existence of time constraints, knowledge and expertise, and the gender, age, and culture of the decision-makers. Nevertheless, finding the ideal choice set may ultimately be worth the trouble when decisions are recurrent or strategic, such as pension schemes, health plans, or career options. This review has covered a substantial amount of research that can be utilized to mitigate these distinct challenges.

We believe that the most promising directions for offering long-lasting solutions against choice overload lie in understanding the roles of preference certainty, focused attention, and generated self-knowledge. As Simon (1971, p. 40) put it:

> In an information-rich world, the wealth of information means a dearth of something else: a scarcity of whatever it is that information consumes. What information consumes is rather obvious: it consumes the attention of its recipients. Hence a wealth of information creates a poverty of attention and a need to allocate that attention efficiently among the overabundance of information sources that might consume it.

Smart and ethical choice architecture should be designed based on goals, needs, and personal preferences by using apps, reminders, checklists, websites, buddy systems, and alerts (Johnson et al., 2012; Thaler & Sunstein, 2008) that direct and hold decision-makers' attention and respect decision-makers' freedom. How people's attention is managed in the ever more information-rich world will ultimately dictate their future.

References

Anderson, B. F., & Misuraca, R. (2017). Perceptual commensuration in decision tables. *Quarterly Journal of Experimental Psychology*, 70(3), 544-553.

Bettman, J. R., & Park, C. W. (1980). Effects of prior knowledge and experience and phase of the choice process on consumer decision processes: A protocol analysis. *Journal of Consumer Research*, 7(3), 234–248.

Botti, S., & Iyengar, S. S. (2006). The dark side of choice: When choice impairs social welfare. *Journal of Public Policy & Marketing*, 25(1), 24–38.

Botti, S., Orfali, K., & Iyengar, S. S. (2009). Tragic choices: Autonomy and emotional responses to medical decisions. *Journal of Consumer Research*, 36, 337–352.

Cacioppo, J. T., & Petty, R. E. (1982). The need for cognition. *Journal of Personality and Social Psychology*, 42(1), 116–131.

Chan, E. Y. (2015). Attractiveness of options moderates the effect of choice overload. *International Journal of Research in Marketing*, 32(4), 425–427.

Chandon, P., Hutchinson, J. W., Bradlow, E. T., & Young, S. H. (2009). Does in-store marketing work? Effects of the number and position of shelf facings on brand attention and evaluation at the point of purchase. *Journal of Marketing*, 73(6), 1–17.

Chernev, A. (2003). When more is less and less is more: The role of ideal point availability and assortment in consumer choice. *Journal of Consumer Research*, 30(2), 170–183.

Chernev, A. (2006). Decision focus and consumer choice among assortments. *Journal of Consumer Research*, 33(1), 50–59.

Chernev, A., Böckenholt, U., & Goodman, J. (2015). Choice overload: A conceptual review and meta-analysis. *Journal of Consumer Psychology*, 25(2), 333–358.

Chernev, A., & Hamilton, R. (2009). Assortment size and option attractiveness in consumer choice among retailers. *Journal of Marketing Research*, 46(3), 410–420.

Dhar, R. (1997). Consumer preference for a no-choice option. *Journal of Consumer Research*, 24(2), 215–231.

Dhar, R., & Nowlis, S. M. (1999). The effect of time pressure on consumer choice deferral. *Journal of Consumer Research*, 25(4), 369–384.

Diab, D. L., Gillespie, M. A., & Highhouse, S. E. (2008). Are maximizers really unhappy? The measurement of maximizing tendency. *Judgment and Decision Making*, 3(5), 364–370.

Fasolo, B., Hertwig, R., Huber, M., & Ludwig, M. (2009). Size, entropy, and density: What is the difference that makes the difference between small and large real world assortments? *Psychology & Marketing*, 26(3), 254–279.

Fisman, R., Iyengar, S. S., Kamenica, E., & Simonson, I. (2006). Gender differences in mate selection: Evidence from a speed dating experiment. *The Quarterly Journal of Economics*, 121(2), 673–697.

Furby, L., & Beyth-Marom, R. (1992). Risk taking in adolescence: A decision-making perspective. *Developmental Review*, 12(1), 1–44.

Gigerenzer, G., & García-Retamero, R. (2017). Cassandra's regret: The psychology of not wanting to know. *Psychological Review*, 124(2), 179–196.

Grant, A. M., & Schwartz, B. (2011). Too much of a good thing: The challenge and opportunity of the inverted U. *Perspectives on Psychological Science*, 6(1), 61–76.

Hahn, M., Lawson, R., & Lee, Y. G. (1992). The effects of time pressure and information load on decision quality. *Psychology & Marketing*, 9(5), 365–378.

Higgins, E. T. (1997). Beyond pleasure and pain. *American Psychologist*, 52(12), 1280–1300.

Hoch, S. J., Bradlow, E., & Wansink, B. (2002). Rejoinder to "The variety of an assortment: An extension to the attribute-based approach". *Marketing Science*, 21(3), 342–346.

Huffman, C., & Kahn, B. E. (1998). Variety for sale: Mass customization or mass confusion? *Journal of Retailing*, 74(4), 491–513.

Iyengar, S. S. (2010). *The art of choosing*. London: Little Brown.

Iyengar, S. S., & Lepper, M. R. (1999). Rethinking the value of choice: A cultural perspective on intrinsic motivation. *Journal of Personality and Social Psychology*, 76(3), 349–366.

Iyengar, S. S., Wells, R. E., & Schwartz, B. (2006). Doing better but feeling worse: Looking for the "best" job undermines satisfaction. *Psychological Science*, 17(2), 143–150.

Johnson, E. J., Shu, S. B., Dellaert, B. G. C., Fox, C., Goldstein, D., Häubl, G., ... Weber, E.U., 2012. Beyond nudges: Tools of a choice architecture. *Marketing Letters*, 23(2), 487–504.

Kahn, B. E., & Wansink, B. (2004). The influence of assortment structure on perceived variety and consumption quantities. *Journal of Consumer Research*, 30(4), 519–533.

Lee, B. K., & Lee, W. N. (2004). The effect of information overload on consumer choice quality in an on-line environment. *Psychology & Marketing*, 21(3), 159–183.

Lenton, A. P., Fasolo, B., & Todd, P. M. (2008). "Shopping" for a mate: Expected versus experienced preferences in online mate choice. *IEEE Transactions on Professional Communication*, 51(2), 169–182.

Levav, J., Heitmann, M., Herrmann, A., & Iyengar, S. S. (2010). Order in product customization decisions: Evidence from field experiments. *Journal of Political Economy*, 118(2), 274–299.

Lichtenstein, S., & Slovic, P. (Eds.) (2006). *The construction of preference*. New York: Cambridge University Press.

Lurie, N. H. (2004). Decision making in information-rich environments: The role of information structure. *Journal of Consumer Research*, 30(4), 473–486.

Malhotra, N. K. (1982). Information load and consumer decision-making. *Journal of Consumer Research*, 8(4), 419–430.

Markus, H. R., & Schwartz, B. (2010). Does choice mean freedom and well-being? *Journal of Consumer Research*, 37(2), 344–355.

Mather, M., & Carstensen, L. L. (2005). Aging and motivated cognition: The positivity effect in attention and memory. *Trends in Cognitive Sciences*, 9(10), 496–502.

Mathmann, F., Chylinski, M., de Ruyter, K., & Higgins, E. T. (2017). When plentiful platforms pay off: Assessment orientation moderates the effect of assortment size on choice engagement and product valuation. *Journal of Retailing*, 93(2), 212–227.

Maule, A. J., & Edland, A. C. (1997). The effects of time pressure on human judgment and decision making. In R. Ranyard, W. R. Crozier, & O. Svenson (Eds.), *Decision making: Cognitive models and explanations* (pp. 189–204). London: Routledge.

Meyers-Levy, J., & Maheswaran, D. (1991). Exploring differences in males' and females' processing strategies. *Journal of Consumer Research*, 18(1), 63–70.

Miller, G. A. (1956). The magical number seven, plus or minus two: Some limits on our capacity for processing information. *Psychological Review*, 63(2), 81–97.

Misuraca, R., Ceresia, F., Teuscher, U., & Faraci, P. (2019). The role of the brand on choice overload. *Mind & Society*, 18(1), 57–76

Misuraca, R., Faraci, P., Gangemi, A., Carmeci, F.A., & Miceli, S. (2015). The Decision Making Tendency Inventory: A new measure to assess maximizing, satisficing, and minimizing. *Personality and Individual Differences*, 85, 111–116.

Misuraca, R., & Fasolo, B. (2018). Maximizing versus satisficing in the digital age: disjoint scales and the case for "construct consensus". *Personality and Individual Differences*, 121, 152–160.

Misuraca, R., Teuscher, U., & Faraci, P. (2016). Is more choice always worse? Age differences in the overchoice effect. *Journal of Cognitive Psychology*, 28(2), 242–255.

Miyamoto, Y., Nisbett, R. E., & Masuda, T. (2006). Culture and the physical environment. Holistic versus analytic perceptual affordances. *Psychological Science*, 17(2), 113–119.

Mogilner, C., Shiv, B., & Iyengar, S. S. (2012). Eternal quest for the best: Sequential (vs. simultaneous) option presentation undermines choice commitment. *Journal of Consumer Research*, 39(6), 1300–1312.

Morales, A., Kahn, B. E., McAlister, L., & Broniarczyk, S. M. (2005). Perceptions of assortment variety: The effects of congruency between consumers' internal and retailers' external organization. *Journal of Retailing*, 81(2), 159–169.

Moser, C., Phelan, C., Resnick, P., Schoenebeck, S. Y., & Reinecke, K. (2017). No such thing as too much chocolate: Evidence against choice overload in e-commerce. In Proceedings of the 2017 CHI Conference on Human Factors in Computing Systems (pp. 4358–4369). ACM.

Payne, J. W., Bettman, J. R., & Johnson, E. J. (Eds.) (1993). *The adaptive decision-maker*. New York: Cambridge University Press.

Pieters, R., & Warlop, L. (1999). Visual attention during brand choice: The impact of time pressure and task motivation. *International Journal of Research in Marketing*, 16(1), 1–16.

Pilli, L. E., & Mazzon, J. A. (2016). Information overload, choice deferral, and moderating role of need for cognition. *Empirica: Revista de Administração*, 51(1), 36–55.

Polman, E. (2012). Self–other decision making and loss aversion. *Organizational Behavior and Human Decision Processes*, 119(2), 141–150.

Reutskaja, E. (2008). Experiments on the role of the number of alternatives in choice. thesis. Pompeu Fabra University, Spain.

Reutskaja, E., & Hogarth, R. M. (2009). Satisfaction in choice as a function of the number of alternatives: When "goods satiate". *Psychology & Marketing*, 26(3), 197–203.

Reutskaja, E., Lindner, A., Nagel, R., Andersen, R. A., & Camerer, C. F. (2018). Choice overload reduces neural signatures of choice set value in dorsal striatum and anterior cingulate cortex. *Nature Human Behaviour*, 2, 925–935.

Reutskaja, E., Nagel, R., Camerer, C. F., & Rangel, A. (2011). Search dynamics in consumer choice under time pressure: An eye-tracking study. *American Economic Review*, 101(2), 900–926.

Scheibehenne, B., Greifeneder, R., & Todd, P. M. (2010). Can there ever be too many options? A meta-analytic review of choice overload. *Journal of Consumer Research*, 37(3), 409–425.

Schlottmann, A., & Wilkening, F. (2011). Judgment and decision making in young children. In M. Dhami, A. Schlottmann, & M. Waldmann (Eds.), *Judgment and decision making as a skill* (pp. 55–83). New York: Cambridge University Press.

Schwartz, B., Ward, A., Monterosso, J., Lyubomirsky, S., White, K., & Lehman, D. R. (2002). Maximizing versus satisficing: Happiness is a matter of choice. *Journal of Personality and Social Psychology*, 83(5), 1178–1197.

Shah, A. M., & Wolford, G. (2007). Buying as a function of parametric variation of number of choices. *Psychological Science*, 18(5), 369–370.

Simon, H. A. (1971). Designing organizations for an information-rich world. In M. Greenberger (Ed.), *Computers, communication, and the public interest* (pp. 37–72). Baltimore: MD: Johns Hopkins University Press.

Simon, H. A. (1990). Invariants of human behavior. *Annual Review of Psychology*, 41, 1–19.

Slovic, P., Finucane, M. L., Peters, E., & MacGregor, D. G. (2007). The affect heuristic. *European Journal of Operational Research*, 177, 1333–1352.

Spassova, G., & Isen, A. M. (2013). Positive affect moderates the impact of assortment size on choice satisfaction. *Journal of Retailing*, 89(4), 397–408.

Stankov, L., & Crawford, J. D. (1996). Confidence judgments in studies of individual differences. *Personality and Individual Differences*, 21(6), 971–986.

Tanius, B. E., Wood, S., Hanoch, Y., & Rice, T. (2009). Aging and choice: Applications to Medicare Part 500. *Judgment and Decision Making*, 4(1), 92–101.

Thaler, R. H., & Sunstein, C. R. (2008). *Nudge: Improving decisions about health, wealth, and happiness*. New York: Penguin Books.

Townsend, C., & Kahn, B. E. (2013). The "visual preference heuristic": The influence of visual versus verbal depiction on assortment processing, perceived variety, and choice overload. *Journal of Consumer Research*, 40(5), 993–1015.

Turner, B. M., Rim, H. B., Betz, N. E., & Nygren, T. E. (2012). The maximization inventory. *Judgment and Decision Making*, 7(1), 48–60.

Tuttle, B, & Burton, F. G. (1999). The effects of a modest incentive on information overload in an investment analysis task. *Accounting, Organizations and Society*, 24(8), 673–687.

Tversky, A., & Kahneman, D. (1974). Judgment under uncertainty: Heuristics and biases. *Science*, 185(4157), 1124–1131.

Tversky, A., & Kahneman, D. (1981). The framing of decisions and the psychology of choice. *Science*, 211(4481), 453–458.

UBS (1992). Video recording. Available at: www.ubs.com/HerbertSimon

Viale, R. (2012). Cognitive diversity in Western and Eastern thinking. In R. Viale (Ed.), *Methodological Cognitivism*, vol. I: *Mind, Rationality and Society* (pp. 295–308). Berlin: Springer.

Zakay, D. (1993). The impact of time perception processes on decision making under time stress. In O. Svenson & A. J. Maule (Eds.), *Time pressure and stress in human judgment and decision making* (pp. 59–72). New York: Plenum Press.

INDEX

Printed in the United States
by Baker & Taylor Publisher Services